the future of lesbian travel

Sweet

Cruise, resort & adventure
vacations designed for lesbians

CALL 877 793 3830 DISCOVERSWEET.COM

CST# 2091755-40

frameline35

San Francisco International LGBT Film Festival

June 16-26, 2011   www.frameline.org

someone to spend your life with.

meet her **today.**

TRAVEL SMART

NEWS | ANALYSIS | COUNTRY INFORMATION

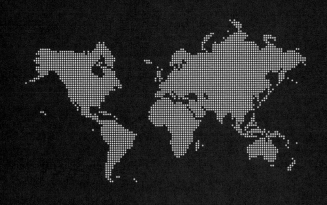

globalequality.org
globalequality.wordpress.com

The Council for
Global Equality

Advancing an American Foreign Policy
Inclusive of Sexual Orientation and Gender Identity

we
want
you
here

2011

Womenfest
Sept 6-11

THE ONLY TIME WE'LL TELL YOU TO GO STRAIGHT.

Getting to Key West couldn't be easier. Just take US1 straight through The Keys. Of course, when you get here, you can go any direction you want.

Key West rated "Favorite Gay Resort Town" - The Out Traveler

KEY LARGO
ISLAMORADA
MARATHON
BIG PINE KEY & THE LOWER KEYS
KEY WEST

Key West

Close To Perfect - Far From Normal

fla-keys.com/gaykeywest ~ 1-888-327-9831

**three
dollar bill
cinema**

There's more to see in Seattle than the sights.

Keeping audiences entertained since 1996, Three Dollar Bill Cinema promotes and produces LGBT film events throughout the year, including free outdoor movies every summer, our Spring Film Series of vintage queer classics, the Seattle Lesbian & Gay Film Festival in October, and other unique events every month!

Check out our website or find us on Facebook to see what's happening on your next visit to Seattle.

three
dollar bill
cinema

www.threedollarbillcinema.org

A place for remembrance and renewal

There is a NATIONAL memorial dedicated to all lives

touched by AIDS located in San Francisco's Golden Gate Park.

For more information, visit our website at

www.AIDSmemorial.org, or call 415 765-0497.

THE NATIONAL
AIDS MEMORIAL GROVE

ENSURING THAT THE GLOBAL TRAGEDY
OF AIDS WILL NEVER BE FORGOTTEN.

Traveller Codes

Most of the codes used in this book are self-explanatory. Here are the few, however, which aren't.

▶—This symbol marks an advertiser. Please look for their display ad near this listing, and be sure to tell them you saw their ad in the *Damron Women's Traveller*.

Popular—So we've heard from the business and/or a reader.

Mostly Women—80-90% lesbian crowd.

Mostly Gay Men—Women welcome.

Lesbians/Gay Men—Roughly 50/50 mix of lesbians and gay men.

LGBT—Lesbian, Gay, Bisexual, and Transgendered.

Gay/Straight—A little bit of everything.

Gay-Friendly—LGBT folk are definitely welcome but are rarely the ones hosting the party.

Neighborhood Bar—Regulars and a local flavor, often has a pool table.

Dancing/DJ—Usually has a DJ at least Fri and Sat nights.

Transgender-Friendly—Transsexuals, cross-dressers, and other transgendered people welcome.

Live Shows—From an open mic to live music.

Multiracial—A good mix of women of color and their friends.

Beer/Wine—Beer and/or wine. No hard liquor.

Nonsmoking—No smoking anywhere inside premises.

Private Club—Found mainly in the US South where it's the only way to keep a liquor license. Call the bar before you go out and tell them you're visiting. They will advise you of their policy regarding membership. Usually have set-ups so you can BYOB.

Wheelchair Access—Includes rest room.

WiFi—Wireless Internet access.

the Damron Women's Traveller®

Publisher	**Gina M. Gatta**
Editor-in-Chief	**Erika O'Connor**
Roving Editor	**Ian Philips**
Editorial Assistants	**Maggie Dolan**
	David Duckworth
	Biachi Notaro
Director of Art & Advertising	**Kathleen Pratt**
Cover Photo	**Mary Burroughs**
Cover Design	**Rick Avila**

Board of Directors

**Gina M. Gatta, Edward Gatta, Jr.,
Louise Mock**

How to Contact Us

Mail: PO Box 422458,
San Francisco, CA 94142-2458

Email: info@damron.com

Web: www.damron.com

Fax: 415/703-9049

Phone: 415/255-0404 & 800/462-6654

Table of Contents

United States

Table of Contents

ALABAMA

Statewide

PUBLICATIONS

Ambush Mag 504/522–8049 • LGBT newspaper for the Gulf South (TX through FL)

Birmingham

ACCOMMODATIONS

The Tutwiler Hotel 2021 Park Pl N (at 21st St N) **205/322–2100** • gay-friendly • also restaurant & lounge • WiFi • wheelchair access • $130+

BARS

The Garage Cafe 2304 10th Terrace S (at 23rd St S) **205/322–3220** • 11am-close, from 3pm Sun-Mon • gay-friendly • great sandwiches • live music

Our Place 2115 7th Ave S (at 22nd St) **205/715–0077** • 4pm-midnight, till 2am Fri-Sat • mostly gay men • neighborhood bar • videos • gay-owned

Wine Loft 2200 1st Ave N **205/323–8228** • gay-friendly • wine bar • light food served

NIGHTCLUBS

Pulse 2824 5th Ave S (at 29th St) • 6pm-close • lesbians/ gay men • dancing/DJ • drag shows • 18+

The Quest Club 416 24th St S (at 5th Ave S) **205/251–4313** • 24hrs • mostly gay men • dancing/DJ • 19+ Wed-Sun • drag shows • private club • patio • wheelchair access • cover charge

Steel Urban Lounge 2300 1st Ave N (at 23rd St) **205/324–0666** • 4pm-2am, clsd Sun • gay-friendly • upscale lounge • dancing/DJ

CAFES

Chez Lulu 1909 Cahaba Rd **205/870–7011** • lunch & dinner Tue-Sun, Sun brunch, clsd Mon • plenty veggie • also bakery • live shows

RESTAURANTS

Bottega Cafe & Restaurant 2240 Highland Ave S (btwn 22nd & 23rd) **205/939–1000** • 5:30pm-10pm, clsd Sun • some veggie • full bar • wheelchair access

The Bottletree 3719 3rd Ave S (at 37th St S) **205/533–6288** • 11am-9pm Tue-Sat • vegetarian/ vegan • also bar • also live music venue

Birmingham

LGBT PRIDE:
June. web: www.centralal-abamapride.org.

ANNUAL EVENTS:
March - Birmingham Shout: Gay & Lesbian Film Festival of Alabama 205/324-0888, web: www.bhamshout.com.
April/May - Birmingham International Festival 202/252-7652, web: www.birmingham-internationalcenter.org.
June - Alabama Shakespeare Festival 800/841-4273, web: www.asf.net.
June - City Stages 205/251-1272, web: www.citystages.org.

CITY INFO:
800/458–8085 or 205/458-8000, web: www.birminghamal.org.

BEST VIEW:
Overlook Park.

WEATHER:
Hot and humid in the 80°s and 90°s during the summer, mild in the 50°s to low 40°s during the winter.

TRANSIT:
Yellow Cab 205/328-4444.
Birmingham Transit Authority 205/521-0101, web: www.bjcta.org.

ATTRACTIONS:
Alabama Jazz Hall of Fame 205/254-2731, web: www.jazzhall.com.
Birmingham Zoo & Botanical Gardens 205/879-0409, web: www.birminghamzoo.com.
Civil Rights Museum 205/328-9696, web: www.bcri.org.
Sloss Furnaces Nat'l Historic Landmark 205/324-1911, web: www.slossfurnaces.com.
Vulcan Statue at 20th St S & Valley Ave, atop Red Mountain.

Highlands Bar & Grill 2011 11th Ave S (at 20th St) **205/939-1400** • 5:30pm-10pm, clsd Sun-Mon • wheelchair access

John's 112 21st St N (btwn 1st & 2nd Ave N) **205/322-6014** • lunch weekdays & dinner Mon-Sat, clsd Sun • seafood & steak • full bar • wheelchair access

Rojo 2921 Highland Ave S **205/328-4733** • 11am-10pm, clsd Mon, wknd brunch • Latin & American cuisine

Silvertron Cafe 3813 Clairmont Ave S (at 39th St S) **205/591-3707** • 7am-10pm, 11am-9pm Sun • also full bar • more gay Mon

Taj India 2226 Highland Ave S **205/939-3805** • lunch & dinner • Indian • plenty veggie

ENTERTAINMENT & RECREATION

Terrific New Theatre 2821 2nd Ave S (in Dr Pepper Design Complex) **205/328-0868**

Tragic City Rollers • Birmingham's female roller derby league • visit www.dixiederbygirls.com for events

EROTICA

Alabama Adult Books 801 3rd Ave N (at 8th) **205/322-7323** • 24hrs

Dothan

NIGHTCLUBS

Club Imagination 4129 Ross Clark Circle NW (off Hwy 431 N) **334/792-6555** • 6pm-4am, clsd Sun-Tue • lesbians/ gay men • dancing/DJ • transgender-friendly • karaoke • drag shows • 18+ • private club

Foley

NIGHTCLUBS

Club Evolution 8380 Hwy 59 **251/943-5557** • 9pm-close, from 6pm Fri-Sat, clsd Tue • lesbians/ gay men • dancing/DJ • karaoke • drag shows

Geneva

ACCOMMODATIONS

Spring Creek Campground & Resort 163 Campground Rd (at Hwy 52 & Country Rd 4) **334/684-3891** • mostly gay men • cabins • also tent & RV sites • BYOB • pool • nudity ok • some theme wknds w/ DJ • WiFi • gay-owned • $17-85

Huntsville

BARS

Club Ozz 1204 Posey (at Larkin) **256/534-5970** • 6pm-2am • lesbians/ gay men • neighborhood bar • DJ Th-Sun • drag shows Th-Sun • patio • wheelchair access

Partners 627 Meridian St (at Pratt Ave) **256/539-0975** • 5pm-2am, from 6pm wknds • lesbians/ gay men • dancing/DJ • food served • live entertainment • karaoke • wheelchair access • lesbian-owned

ENTERTAINMENT & RECREATION

Dixie Derby Girls • Huntsville's female roller derby league • visit www.dixiederbygirls.com for events

Mobile

see also Pensacola, Florida

INFO LINES & SERVICES

Pink Triangle AA Group 2201 Government St (at Cornerstone MCC) **251/479-9994 (AA#), 251/476-4621 (CHURCH)** • 7pm Tue, Th & Sat

ACCOMMODATIONS

Berney/ Fly B&B 1118 Government St **251/405-0949** • gay-friendly • full brkfst • pool • jacuzzi • nonsmoking • WiFi • wheelchair access • $50-139

BARS

Bacchus 54 S Conception St **251/445-4099** • 8pm-close Wed-Sat • lesbians/ gay men • neighborhood bar • non-smoking

Gabriel's Downtown 55 S Joachim St (off Government) **251/432-4900** • 7pm-close • lesbians/ gay men • videos • karaoke • patio • private club

Midtown Pub 153 S Florida St (at Emogene) **251/450-1555** • noon-2am • lesbians/ gay men • neighborhood bar • dancing/DJ • karaoke • food served

NIGHTCLUBS

B-Bob's Downtown 213 Conti St (at Joachim) **251/433-2262** • 6pm-close, from 7pm Sat • mostly men • dancing/DJ • also gift shop • wheelchair access

Saga 266 Dauphin St (at Jackson) **251/431-9002** • 4pm-close Tue-Sun • live shows • WiFi • wheelchair access

Montgomery

ACCOMMODATIONS

The Lattice Inn 1414 S Hull St (at Clanton) **334/262–3388** • mixed gay/ straight • pool • nonsmoking • WiFi • wheelchair access • $90-235

NIGHTCLUBS

Club 322 322 N Lawrence St **334/263–4322** • 5pm-close, from 9pm Fri-Sat, clsd Mon-Tue • lesbians/ gay men • dancing/DJ • drag shows

ALASKA

Statewide

ENTERTAINMENT & RECREATION

Out in Alaska PO Box 82096, Fairbanks 99708 **877/374–9958, 907/374–9958** • adventure travel throughout Alaska for LGBT travelers

Anchorage

INFO LINES & SERVICES

AA Gay/ Lesbian 336 E 5th Ave (at Community Center) **907/929–4528** • 6pm Mon

Anchorage

LGBT PRIDE:

June. web: www.anchoragepride.com.

ANNUAL EVENTS:

January - Anchorage Folk Festival, web: www.anchoragefolkfestival.org.

February - World Ice Art Championship 907/451-8250, web: www.icealaska.com.

March - Iditarod Sled Dog Race 907/376-5155, web: www.iditarod.com.

June - Mayor's Marathon 907/343-4562, web: www.mayors-marathon.com.

August - Alaska State Fair 907/745-4827, web: www.alaskastatefair.org.

October - Quyana Alaska (native dance celebration) 907/274-3611, web: www.nativefederation.org.

CITY INFO:

907/276-4118, web: www.anchorage.net.

BEST VIEW:

The 11-mile-long paved Tony Knowles Coastal Trail along Cook Inlet offers spectacular views of several mountains, including Denali (Mt McKinley).

WEATHER:

Anchorage's climate is milder than one might think, due to its coastal location. It is cold in the winter (but rarely below 0°F), and it warms up considerably in June, July, and August. Winter sets in around October. Expect more rain in late summer/ early fall.

TRANSIT:

Checker Cab 907/276-1234.
Alaska Shuttle 907/338-8888, 907/694-8888.
Rideline (bus) 907/343-6543, www.muni.org/transit1/rideline.cfm

ATTRACTIONS:

Alaska Museum of Natural History, 907/274-2400, web: www.alaskamuseum.org.
Alaska Native Heritage Center 907/330-8000, web: www.alaskanative.net.
Alaska Wildlife Conservation Center (in Portage) 907/783-2025, web: www.awcc.org.
Portage Glacier
Wolf Song of Alaska Museum 907/622-9653, web: www.wolf-songalaska.org.

Gay/ Lesbian Helpline 1300 East St
907/258-4777 • 6pm-11pm, ask about
women's events: usually every Sat except
summers when everyone's outdoors

Identity, Inc 336 E 5th Ave **907/929-4528** •
LGBT community center • newsletter

ACCOMMODATIONS

A Wildflower Inn B&B 1239 I St (at 13th)
907/274-1239, 877/693-1239 • gay/ straight •
close to hiking trails & scenic vistas • fun hosts
• nonsmoking • WiFi • gay-owned • $79-139

Alaska Bear Company B&B 535 E 6th Ave
(btwn Eagle & Fairbanks) **907/277-2327** •
gay/ straight • in downtown Anchorage •
nonsmoking • gay-owned • $49-85

Alaska Heavenly Lodge 34950 Blakely Rd
(at Mile 49 Sterling Hwy), Cooper Landing
907/595-2012, 866/595-2012 • gay-friendly •
hot tub • cedar sauna • nonsmoking • $450-
1,000

Alaska's North Country Castle B&B 14600
Joanne Ct **907/345-7296** • gay-friendly •
private decks • ocean & mtn views • full brkfst
• nonsmoking • $159-239

Anchorage Jewel Lake B&B 8125 Jewel
Lake Rd **907/245-7321, 877/245-7321** • gay/
straight • full brkfst • kids ok • WiFi •
nonsmoking • gay-owned • $145+

City Garden B&B 1352 W 10th Ave (at N St)
907/276-8686 • gay-straight • beautiful views
of Mt McKinley • 10-minute walk to downtown
area • nonsmoking • gay-owned • $100-150

Copper Whale Inn 440 L St **907/258-7999,
866/258-7999** • gay/ straight • located
downtown • WiFi • nonsmoking • gay-owned
• wheelchair access • $85-210

Earth B&B & Tours 1001 W 12th Ave
907/279-9907 • gay-friendly • close to
downtown • nonsmoking • WiFi • woman-
owned • $59-139

Gallery B&B 1229 G St (at 12th)
907/274-2567 • gay/ straight • kids/ pets ok •
wheelchair access • lesbian-owned • $35-85

Inlet Tower Hotel & Suites 1200 L St (at
12th) **907/276-0110, 800/544-0786** • gay/
straight • kids/ pets ok • WiFi • wheelchair
access • also bar & restaurant • $99-319

BARS

Kodiak Bar 225 E 5th Ave (btwn Cordova &
Barrow) **907/258-5233** • 3pm-2:30am, till
5am Fri-Sat • lesbians/ gay men • food served
• DJ wknds

Mad Myrna's 530 E 5th Ave (at Fairbanks)
907/276-9762 • 4pm-2:30am, till 3am Fri-Sat
• lesbians/ gay men • neighborhood bar •
dancing/DJ • karaoke • food served • drag
shows

Raven 708 E 4th Ave **907/276-9672** • 1pm-
2:30am, till 3am wknds • lesbians/ gay men •
neighborhood bar • wheelchair access

RESTAURANTS

China Lights 12110 Business Blvd, Eagle
River **907/694-8080** • 11:30am-10pm, till
10:30pm wknds

Club Paris 417 W 5th Ave **907/277-6332** •
11am-midnight, from 4pm Sun • perhaps the
finest restaurant in town

Garcia's 11901 Business Blvd #104 (next to
Safeway), Eagle River **907/694-8600** • 11am-
10:30pm, from noon wknds, till midnight Fri-
Sat • Mexican

Marx Brothers Cafe 627 W 3rd Ave
907/278-2133 • 5:30-10pm, clsd Sun-Mon •
great food and views

Simon & Seafort's 420 L St (btwn 4th & 5th)
907/274-3502 • lunch weekdays, dinner
nightly • seafood & prime rib • full bar 8 great
views

ENTERTAINMENT & RECREATION

Out North 3800 DeBarr Rd **907/279-3800,
907/279-8099** • community-based & visiting-
artist exhibits, screenings & performances

BOOKSTORES

Title Wave Books 1360 W Northern Lights
Blvd **907/278-9283** • 10am-8pm, till 9pm Fri-
Sat, 11am-7pm Sun • largest independent
bookstore in Alaska • also at 415 W 5th Ave,
907/258-9283

RETAIL SHOPS

The Sports Shop 570 E Benson Blvd
907/272-7755 • 10am-7pm, till 6pm Sat,
noon-5pm Sun • women's outdoor clothing,
adventure gear & equipment

PUBLICATIONS

Anchorage Press **907/561-7737** •
alternative paper • arts & entertainment
listings

EROTICA

Le Shop 305 W Diamond Blvd (at C St)
907/522-1987 • 8am-1am

Fairbanks

ACCOMMODATIONS

All Seasons B&B Inn 763 7th Ave (at Barnette St) **907/451-6649, 888/451-6649** • gay-friendly • full brkfst • nonsmoking • WiFi • wheelchair access • $99-215

Billie's Backpackers Hostel 2895 Mack Rd **907/479-2034** • gay-friendly • kids ok • food served • women-owned • $30-80

CAFES

Hot Licks Ice Cream 3453 College Rd **907/479-7813** • seasonal

Haines

ACCOMMODATIONS

The Guardhouse Boarding House 15 Fort Seward Dr **907/766-2566, 866/290-7445** • lesbians/ gay men • in former jail of Fort William H. Seward • great views of Lynn Canal • bald eagle-watching • nonsmoking • WiFi • lesbian-owned • $75-105

Homer

ACCOMMODATIONS

Sadie Cove Wilderness Lodge Kachemak Bay State Park **907/235-2350, 888/283-7234** • gay-friendly • 5 cabins • tree planted for every guest to offset carbon emissions • built from hand-milled driftwood • uses nonpolluting alternative energy • 3 full meals a day • nonsmoking • $400/ person

Spit Sister B&B Homer Spit Rd (at Harbor View Boardwalk #5, at Spit Sister Cafe) **907/235-4921 (SUMMER), 907/299-7748** • gay/ straight • full brkfst • kids/ 1 small pet ok • private deck overlooks Homer Harbor • nonsmoking • WiFi • cafe downstairs • women-owned • $85-120

CAFES

Spit Sister Cafe Homer Spit Rd (at Harbor View Boardwalk #5) **907/235-4921 (SUMMER), 907/299-6868/ 6767 (WINTER)** • 5am-4pm • gay/ straight • WiFi • also B&B • women-owned

ENTERTAINMENT & RECREATION

Alaska Fantastic Fishing Charters **800/478-7777** • deluxe cabin cruiser for big-game fishing (halibut)

Juneau

ACCOMMODATIONS

Pearson's Pond Luxury Suites & Adventure Spa 4541 Sawa Circle **907/789-3772, 888/658-6328** • gay-friendly • B&B resort & spa • hot tub • nonsmoking • $229+

The Silverbow 120 Second St **907/586-4146, 800/586-4146** • gay-friendly • ull brkfst • also restaurant & bakery • alternative cinema • gallery • kids ok • nonsmoking • WiFi • $89-218

RESTAURANTS

Hangar on the Wharf 2 Marine Way Ste 106 **907/586-5018** • lunch & dinner • full bar • great fish & chips

Ketchikan

ACCOMMODATIONS

Anchor Inn by the Sea 4672 S Tongass Hwy **907/247-7117, 800/928-3308** • gay-friendly • nonsmoking • WiFi • $105-160 (5-10–night minimum)

ENTERTAINMENT & RECREATION

Southeast Sea Kayak 1621 Tongass Ave, Ste 101B **907/225-1258, 800/287-1607** • trip planning • tours • wilderness kayaking

McCarthy

ACCOMMODATIONS

Ma Johnson's Hotel **907/554-4402** • gay-friendly • full brkfst also restaurant • kids ok • inside America's largest nat'l park, Wrangell St Elias • nonsmoking • $129-259

Palmer

ACCOMMODATIONS

Alaska Garden Gate B&B 950 S Trunk Rd **907/746-2333** • gay/ straight • full brkfst • hot tub • kids/ pets ok • WiFi • lesbian-owned • $75-159 (rooms), $135-250 (vacation home, 3-night minimum)

Seward

ENTERTAINMENT & RECREATION

Puffin Fishing Charters PO Box 606, 99664 **907/224-4653, 800/978-3346** • gay/ straight • day fishing trips

Sitka

CAFES

Backdoor Cafe 104 Barracks St (behind Old Harbor Books on Lincoln St, no street sign) **907/747–8856** • 6:30am-5pm, till 2pm Sat, clsd Sun • pleasant & funky hangout

ENTERTAINMENT & RECREATION

Esther G Sea Taxi 215 Shotgun Alley **907/738–6481** • marine wildlife tours

ARIZONA

Apache Junction

ACCOMMODATIONS

Susa's Serendipity Ranch 4375 E Superstition Blvd **480/288–9333** • women only • guesthouses on 15-acre ranch • 2 RV hookups • great views! • hot tub • nonsmoking • pets ok • lesbian-owned • $75-90/ night, $1,500/ month

Bisbee

ACCOMMODATIONS

Casa de San Pedro B&B 8933 S Yell Ln (at Hwy 92 & Palominas Rd), Hereford **520/366–1300, 888/257–2050** • gay-friendly • full brkfst • pool • hot tub • nonsmoking • WiFi • wheelchair access • gay-owned • $160+

Copper Queen Hotel 11 Howell Ave **520/432–2216** • gay-friendly • restored landmark hotel • kids ok • pool • nonsmoking • restaurant • wheelchair access • $89-197

David's Oasis Camping Resort 5311 W Double Adobe Rd, McNeal **520/979–6650** • lesbians/ gay men • 21+ • pool • also bar & internet cafe • WiFi • gay-owned • $12-20

Eldorado Suites 55 OK St **520/432–6679** • gay-friendly • on Nat'l Historic Register • territorial architecture • kitchens • nonsmoking • WiFi • $125+

Sleepy Dog Guest House 212A Opera Dr **520/432–3057, 520/234–8166 (CELL)** • gay-friendly • reclaimed miner's cabin • very quiet • patio • great views • very dog-friendly • lots of stairs • $115

BARS

Copper Rainbow Bistro 5311 W Double Adobe Rd, McNeal **520/979–6650** • 5pm-10pm Fri-Sat, 2pm-7pm Sun • lesbian/ gay men • beer/ wine only

St Elmo's 36 Brewery Ave **520/432–5578** • 10am-2am • gay-friendly • live bands Fri-Sat

Bullhead City

includes Laughlin, Nevada

BARS

The Lariat Saloon 1161 Hancock Rd (at 95) **928/704–1969** • 10am-2am • lesbians/ gay men • neighborhood bar • multiracial • patio • wheelchair access • woman-owned

Flagstaff

ACCOMMODATIONS

Abineau Lodge 10155 Mountainaire Rd **928/525–6212, 888/715–6386** • gay/ straight • B&B in Coconino Nat'l Forest • huskies on premises • cedar sauna • hot tub • full brkfst • nonsmoking • WiFi • gay-owned • $139-159

The Historic Hotel Monte Vista 100 N San Francisco St (at Aspen) **928/779–6971, 800/545–3068** • gay-friendly • historic lodging circa 1927 • some shared baths • full bar • nonsmoking • $65-175

Inn at 410 410 N Leroux St **928/774–0088, 800/774–2008** • gay-friendly• full brkfst • WiFi • wheelchair access • $150-200

Motel in the Pines 80 W Pinewood Blvd (exit 322), Pinewood **928/286–9699, 800/574–5080** • gay-friendly • 20 miles from Flagstaff • wheelchair access • $49-89

Starlight Pines B&B 3380 E Lockett Rd (at Fanning) **928/527–1912, 800/752–1912** • gay/ straight • full gourmet brkfst • kids ok (call for details) • nonsmoking • WiFi • gay-owned • $139-189

BARS

Charly's Pub & Grill 23 N Leroux (at Aspen, at Weatherford Hotel) **928/779–1919** • 8am-2am • gay-friendly • food served • some veggie • live shows nightly • patio • wheelchair access

Monte Vista Lounge 100 N San Francisco St (at Hotel Monte Vista) **928/774–2403** • noon-2am, from 11am Fri-Sun • gay-friendly • dancing/DJ • live bands • karaoke

CAFES

Macy's European Coffee House 14 S Beaver St **928/774–2243** • 6am-10pm • food served • vegetarian/ vegan

RESTAURANTS

Cafe Olé 119 S San Francisco (at Butler) **928/774–8272** • lunch & dinner, clsd Sun • Mexican • plenty veggie • beer/ wine • wheelchair access

Granny's Closet 218 S Milton Rd
928/774–8331 • lunch & dinner • also sports bar

Pasto 19 E Aspen (at San Francisco)
928/779–1937 • lunch & dinner, clsd Sun • Italian • beer/ wine • wheelchair access

RETAIL SHOPS

Crystal Magic 1 N San Francisco St
928/779–2528 • books, gifts & more

Golden Valley

EROTICA

Pleasure Palace Adult Bookstore 4150 US Hwy 68 **928/565–5600**

Jerome

ACCOMMODATIONS

The Cottage Inn Jerome **928/634–0701, 928/649–6759** • gay/ straight • full brkfst • kids/ pets ok • gay-owned • $75-95

Mile High Grill & Inn 309 Main St
928/634–5094 • gay-friendly • cool hotel • also daily restaurant (brkfst to burgers) • some veggie • lesbian-owned • $85-130

RESTAURANTS

Red Rooster Cafe 363 S Main St
928/634–7087 • 11am-3pm, till 4pm wknds • some veggie

Kingman

ACCOMMODATIONS

Kings Inn Best Western 2930 E Andy Devine Ave **928/753–6101, 800/750–6101** • gay-friendly • pool • nonsmoking rooms available • food served • kids/ pets ok • wheelchair access • $60-95

Lake Havasu City

INFO LINES & SERVICES

Lake Havasu City AA 877/652–9005

ACCOMMODATIONS

Nautical Inn 1000 McCulloch Blvd
928/855–2141, 800/892–2141 • gay-friendly • beachfront hotel • full restaurant & bar • private beach • WiFi • pool • $69-589

Lake Powell

ACCOMMODATIONS

Dreamkatchers of Lake Powell B&B
435/675–5828 • gay/ straight • spa on deck • full brkfst • gay-owned • $99-129

Mesa

ENTERTAINMENT & RECREATION

Broadway Palm Dinner Theatre 5247 E Brown Rd **480/325–6700** • a variety of musicals

EROTICA

Castle Megastore 8315 E Apache Trail E
480/986–6114 • 24hrs

Phoenix

see also Scottsdale & Tempe

INFO LINES & SERVICES

1N10 602/475–7456 • 7pm Th • youth age 14-22 only • HIV peer education • call for location

Phoenix Lambda Center 2622 N 16th St (at Virginia Ave) **602/635–2090** • space for many 12-step programs

ACCOMMODATIONS

Claremont House B&B 502 W Claremont Ave (btwn Maryland & Bethany Home, enter 7th Ave) **602/249–2974** • lesbians/ gay men • European-style B&B • full brkfst • pool • hot tub • nudity • nonsmoking • wheelchair access • gay-owned • $70-90

Clarendon Hotel & Suites 401 W Clarendon Ave (at 3rd Ave) **602/252–7363** • gay/ straight • modern boutique hotel in midtown • pool • WiFi • wheelchair access • gay-owned

Hotel San Carlos 202 N Central Ave
602/253–4121, 866/253–4121 • gay-friendly • boutique hotel • rooftop pool • restaurant • WiFi • $139

Inn at Eagle Mountain 9800 N Summer Hill Blvd, Fountain Hills **480/816–3000, 800/992–8083** • gay-friendly • on 18-hole championship golf course • 1/4 mile from Scottsdale • pool • nonsmoking • $119-295

Maricopa Manor B&B Inn 15 W Pasadena Ave **602/274–6302, 800/292–6403** • gay/ straight • in heart of N Central Phoenix • pool • hot tub • WiFi • wheelchair access • gay-owned • $189

Mondrian Hotel 7353 E Indian School Rd, Scottsdale **480/308–1100, 888/697–1791** • gay-friendly • hip boutique hotel • restaurant & bar • pool • hot tub • gym • nonsmoking • WiFi

Orange Blossom Hacienda 3914 E Sunnydale Dr, Gilbert **480/755–4346, 888/575–3484** • gay-friendly • pool • $95-135

Scottsdale Thunderbird Suites 7515 E Butherus Dr (at Scottsdale Rd), Scottsdale **480/951-4000, 800/951-1288** • gay-friendly • full brkfst • pool • hot tub • nonsmoking • WiFi • kids ok • also full bar • wheelchair access • $139

ZenYard 830 E Maryland Ave **623/252-1002, 866/594-0242** • gay/ straight • private suites w/ kitchens • saltwater pool • full brkfst • $60-115

BARS

Amsterdam 718 N Central Ave (btwn Roosevelt & Fillmore) **602/258-6122** • 4pm-2am, till 4am wknds • lesbians/ gay men • upscale bar • food served • karaoke • also Club Miami • dancing/DJ

Apollo's 5749 N 7th St (S of Bethany Home) **602/277-9373** • 8am-2am, till 2am wknds • mostly gay men • neighborhood bar • karaoke • male strippers • WiFi • patio

Bar 1 3702 N 16th St (at E Clarendon) **602/266-9001** • 10am-2am • mostly gay men • neighborhood bar • WiFi

Bar Smith 130 E Washington St **602/229-1265** • 11am-10pm, till 2am Fri-Sat, from 4pm Sat, clsd Sun • gay/straight • full menu

BS West 7125 E 5th Ave (in pedestrian mall), Scottsdale **480/945-9028** • 2pm-2am • lesbians/ gay men • dancing/DJ • videos • karaoke • wheelchair access

Phoenix

WHERE THE GIRLS ARE:
Everywhere. Phoenix doesn't have one section of town where lesbians hang out, but the area between 5th Ave & 32nd St, and Camelback & Thomas Streets does contain most of the women's bars.

LGBT PRIDE:
April. 602/277-7433, web: www.azpride.org.

ANNUAL EVENTS:
April - Phoenix Film Festival 602/955-6444, web: www.phoenixfilmfestival.com.
April - Phoenix Improv Festival 480/251-3697, web: www.phoeniximprovfestival.com.
October - Rainbows Festival 602/770-8241, web: www.rainbowsfestival.com.

CITY INFO:
Arizona Office of Tourism 602/364-3700 or 866/275-5816, web: www.arizonaguide.com.
Greater Phoenix Convention & Visitors Bureau 877/CALL-PHX, web: www.visitphoenix.com.

BEST VIEW:
South Mountain Park at sunset, watching the city lights come on.

WEATHER:
Beautifully mild and comfortable (60°s-80°s) October through March or April. Hot (90°s-100°s) in summer. August brings the rainy season (severe monsoon storms) with flash flooding.

TRANSIT:
Yellow Cab 602/252-5252.
Super Shuttle 602/244-9000.
Phoenix Transit 602/253-5000, www.valleymetro.org.

ATTRACTIONS:
Arizona Golf Association 602/944-3035, web: www.azgolf.org.
Castles & Coasters Park on Black Canyon Fwy & Peoria 602/997-7575, web: www.castlesncoasters.com.
Desert Botanical Garden in Papago Park 480/941-1225, web: www.dbg.org.
Heard Museum 602/252-8848, web: www.heard.org.
Hiking trails in Papago Park, Squaw Peak & Camelback Mtns.
Phoenix Zoo 602/273-1341, web: www.phoenixzoo.org.

Cash Inn Country 2140 E McDowell Rd (at 22nd St) **602/244-9943** • 2pm-close, from noon wknds • mostly women • dancing/DJ • country/ western • karaoke • wheelchair access

Cherry Bar 1028 E Indian School Rd (at N 10th Pl) **602/277-7729** • mostly gay men • neighborhood bar • bears • food served • karaoke • gay-owned

Cheuvront Wine Bar 1326 N Central Ave (at McDowell) **602/307-0022** • 11am-10pm, till midnight Fri-Sat, 4pm-9pm Sun • gay/ straight

Club Vibe 3031 E Indian School #7 (at 32nd St) **602/224-9977** • 8pm-2am, clsd Mon-Wed • mostly women • dancing/DJ • multiracial • drag shows • wheelchair access

Cruisin' 7th 3702 N 7th St (near Indian School) **602/212-9888** • 6am-2am, from 10am Sun • mostly gay men • transgender-friendly • drag shows • karaoke • wheelchair access

Ice Pics 3108 E McDowell Rd (at 32nd St) **602/267-8707** • 4pm-2am, from 2pm Sun • mostly men • video bar

Incognito Lounge 2424 E Thomas Rd (at 24th St) **602/955-9805** • 3pm-1am, till 3am Fri-Sat, clsd Mon-Wed • lesbians/ gay men • dancing/DJ • live shows • multiracial clientele • wheelchair access

Kobalt 3110 N Central Ave **602/264-5307** • noon-2am • lesbians/ gay men • live shows

Oz 1804 W Bethany Home Rd (at 19th) **602/242-5114** • noon-2am • lesbians/ gay men • neighborhood bar

Plazma 1560 E Osborn Rd (at N 16th St) **602/266-0477** • 4pm-close, from noon wknds • lesbians/ gay men • neighborhood bar • live shows • videos

The Rock/ La Roca 4129 N 7th Ave (at Indian School) **602/248-8559** • 9am-2am, from noon Sun • lesbians/ gay men • neighborhood bar • dancing/DJ • karaoke

Roscoe's on 7th 4531 N 7th St (at Minnezona) **602/285-0833** • 2pm-2am, from 10am wknds • lesbians/ gay men • sports bar • food served

Velocity 2303 E Indian School Rd **602/956-2885** • 1pm-2am • mostly gay men • dancing/DJ • leather • male revue

Z Girl Club 4301 N 7th Ave (at Indian School Rd) **602/265-3233** • 3pm-2am, from 10am Th-Sun • mostly women • dancing/DJ • multiracial • karaoke • live shows • wheelchair access • women-owned

NIGHTCLUBS

Forbidden 6820 E 5th Ave (at Indian Scool Rd), Scottsdale **480/994-5176** • 4pm-2am, clsd Mon • mostly gay men • dancing/DJ • theme nights

Hot Flash Phoenix 6820 E. 5th Ave (at Club Forbidden) • mostly women • dancing/DJ • 2nd Sat of the month

Karamba 1724 E McDowell (at 16th St) **602/254-0231** • 4pm-close, clsd Mon-Wed • mostly gay men • dancing/DJ • Latino/a • Latin wknds • wheelchair access

CAFES

Copper Star Coffee 4220 N 7th Ave (at Indian School) **602/266-2136** • 6am-close • coffee in a converted gas station • WiFi

RESTAURANTS

Alexi's 3550 N Central (at Osborn, in Valley Bank Bldg) **602/279-0982** • lunch Mon-Fri, dinner nightly, clsd Sun • full bar • patio • wheelchair access

AZ-88 7553 E Scottsdale Mall, Scottsdale **480/994-5576** • 11:30am-1am (food till 12:30am), from 5pm wknds • upscale American • some veggie

Barrio Cafe 2814 N 16th St **602/636-0240** • lunch Tue-Fri, dinner Tue-Sun, Sun brunch, clsd Mon • Mexican • live music • lesbian-owned

Coronado Cafe 2201 N 7th St **602/258-5149** • lunch Mon-Sat, dinner Tue-Sun, wknd brunch

Durant's 2611 N Central Ave **602/264-5967** • lunch Mon-Fri, dinner nightly • American

Fez 3815 N Central Ave (S of Clarendon) **602/287-8700** • 11am-midnight, from 8:30am wknds • Moroccan influence • full bar

Green 2240 N Scottsdale Rd #8, Tempe **480/941-9003** • 11am-9pm, clsd Sun • new American vegetarian/ vegan

Harley's Bistro 4221 N 7th Ave (N of Indian School) **602/234-0333** • lunch Tue-Fri, dinner nightly, clsd Mon • lesbians/ gay men • Italian

Los Dos Molinos 8684 S Central Ave **602/243-9113** • lunch & dinner, clsd Sun-Mon • Mexican homecooking

MacAlpines's Soda Fountain 2303 N 7th St **602/262-5545** • 11am-7pm, till 8pm Fri-Sat, great milkshakes

Malee's 7131 E Main, Scottsdale **480/947-6042** • lunch & dinner • Thai • plenty veggie • full bar

Mi Patio 3347 N 7th Ave **602/277-4831** • 10am-10pm • Mexican

My Florist Cafe 534 W McDowell Rd (at 7th Ave) **602/254-0333** • 7am-midnight • salads & sandwiches • full bar • piano

Persian Garden Cafe 1335 W Thomas Rd (at N 15th Ave) **602/263-1915** • lunch & dinner, lunch only Mon, clsd Sun • plenty veggie

Portland's 105 W Portland St (at Central Ave) **602/795-7480** • lunch Tue-Fri, dinner Mon-Sat, clsd Sun • also wine bar

Restaurant Mexico 423 S Mill Ave, Tempe **480/967-3280** • 11am-9pm, till 10pm Fri-Sat, clsd Sun

Rose & Crown 628 E Adams St **602/256-0223** • 11am-2am • British pub

Switch 2603 N Central Ave **602/264-2295** • 11am-midnight, from 10am wknds • full bar

Ticoz 5114 N 7th St (N of Camelback) **602/200-0160** • 11am-11pm, till midnight Fri-Sat • Latin cuisine • full bar • WiFi

Vincent on Camelback 3930 E Camelback Rd (at 40th St) **602/224-0225** • lunch Mon-Fri, dinner Mon-Sat, clsd Sun • Southwestern • wheelchair access

Wild Thaiger 2631 N Central Ave (S of Thomas Rd) **602/241-8995** • lunch & dinner, dinner only Sun • Thai

Z Pizza 53 W Thomas Rd **602/234-3289** • 11am-9pm, till 9:30pm Fri-Sat • healthy pizza

ENTERTAINMENT & RECREATION

Arizona Roller Derby • Arizona's female roller derby league • visit www.azrollerderby.com for events

Arizona Women in Tune 602/487-1940 • lesbian choral group

Arizona Women's Theater Company 480/422-5386 • an innovative forum for women's voices

Lesbian Social Network 480/946-5570 • 7:30pm-10pm Fri • popular informal social evenings of games, videos & discussions • smoke- & alcohol-free • call for location

Nearly Naked Theatre 100 E McDowell Rd (in the Little Theatre at Phoenix Theatre) **602/254-2151 (TICKETS), 602/274-2432 (OFFICE)** • for mature audiences

Phoenix Mercury 480/784-4444 (TICKETMASTER) • check out the Women's Nat'l Basketball Association while you're in Phoenix

Soul Invictus 1022 NW Grand Ave (near W Van Buren St) **480/371-5134** • queer-friendly art gallery & cabaret

Stray Cat Theatre 132 E 6th St, Tempe **480/820-8022** • provocative, off-the-beaten-path productions

BOOKSTORES

Changing Hands 6428 S McClintock Dr, Tempe **480/730-0205** • 10am-9pm, from 9am Sat, till 7pm Sun • new & used • LGBT section

RETAIL SHOPS

Exposed Studio & Gallery 4225 N 7th Ave (btwn N Indian School & Glenrosa) **602/248-8030** • noon-5pm, till 4pm Sat, clsd Sun • "new & established artists of all mediums" • wheelchair access • gay-owned

Off Chute Too 4115 N 7th Ave (at Indian School Rd) **602/274-1429** • 9am-9pm, till 10pm Fri-Sat, 10am-6pm Sun • LGBT gift shop in Melrose District

Root Seller Gallery 4015 N 16th St #H (at Indian School) **602/265-7668** • 10am-7pm, 11am-5pm Sun • LGBT books, music & gifts

PUBLICATIONS

Echo Magazine 602/266-0550, **888/324-6624** • bi-weekly LGBT newsmagazine

Ion Arizona Magazine 602/308-4662 x4 • entertainment guide

'N Touch Magazine 602/373-9390 • LGBT newsmagazine

Women's Community Connection 480/946-5570 • monthly newspaper w/ events listings, articles, personals & lesbian resources

GYMS & HEALTH CLUBS

Pulse Fitness 18221 N Pima Rd #130, Scottsdale **480/907-5900** • gay-friendly

EROTICA

Adult Shoppe 111 S 24th St (at Jefferson) **602/306-1130** • 24hrs • also 5021 W Indian School Rd (at 51st Ave), 623/245-3008 & 2345 W Holly St, 602/253-7126

Castle Megastore 300 E Camelback (at Central) **602/266-3348** • 24hrs • also 5501 E Washington, 602/231-9837; 8802 N Black Canyon Fwy, 602/995-1641; 8315 E Apache Tr, 480/986-6114

Fascinations 10242 N 19th Ave #1-7 **602/943-5859**

International Bookstore 3640 E Thomas Rd (at 36th St) **602/955-2000**

Modern World 1812 E Apache (at McClintock Dr), Tempe **480/967-9052** • 24hrs

Tuff Stuff 1716 E McDowell Rd (at 17th St) **602/254-9651, 877/875-4167** • 10am-6pm, till 5pm Sat, clsd Sun-Mon • custom leather shop

Zorba's Adult Book Shop 2924 N Scottsdale Rd (N of Thomas), Scottsdale **480/941–9891** • 24hrs • video rentals & arcade

Prescott

INFO LINES & SERVICES

Prescott Pride Center 111 Josephine St (at Gurley St) **928/445–8800** • call for open hours & calendar of events • wheelchair access

ACCOMMODATIONS

The Motor Lodge 503 S Montezuma St (at Leroux) **928/717–0157** • gay-friendly • nonsmoking • WiFi • gay-owned • $69-139

Sedona

ACCOMMODATIONS

A Woman's Way PO Box 127, 86339 **928/254–1897** • women only • "healing sanctuary" • retreats

A-Lodge at Sedona—A Luxury B&B Inn 125 Kallof Pl **928/204–1942, 800/619–4467** • gay/ straight • Mission-style B&B inn • Red Rock views • full gourmet brkfst • pool • nonsmoking • WiFi • wheelchair access • $189-349

Apple Orchard Inn 656 Jordan Rd **928/282–5328, 800/663–6968** • gay-friendly • full brkfst • hot tub • pool • hiking • scenic views • nonsmoking • wheelchair access • $150-205

Iris Garden Inn 390 Jordan Rd **928/282–2552, 800/321–8988** • gay/ straight • motel • jacuzzi • nonsmoking • WiFi • wheelchair access • gay-owned • $82-139

Sedona Rouge Hotel & Spa 2250 W Hwy 89-A **928/203–4111, 866/312–4111** • gay-friendly • pool • nonsmoking • WiFi • restaurant & bar • wheelchair access • $169-299

Southwest Inn at Sedona 3250 W Hwy 89-A **928/282–3344, 800/483–7422** • gay-friendly • pool • spa • workout room • WiFi • nonsmoking • $119-239

RESTAURANTS

Judi's 40 Soldiers Pass Rd **928/282–4449** • lunch & dinner, clsd Sun • some veggie • full bar

Piñon Bistro 1075 S State Rte 260 (Rte 89-A), Cottonwood **928/649–0234** • dinner Th-Sun only • upscale • wheelchair access • lesbian-owned

RETAIL SHOPS

Sedona Green Gallery & Gifts 273 N Hwy 89A #F (btwn Jordan & Mesquite) **928/239–5353** • 10-15% discount to self-identifying gay & lesbian customers

Tucson

INFO LINES & SERVICES

AA Gay/ Lesbian 3269 N Mountain Ave **520/624–4183** • 8pm Th

Wingspan, Southern Arizona's LGBT Community Center 425 E 7th St **520/624–1779, 800/553–9387** • 11am-2pm • resources • youth support (3pm-8pm Mon-Fri)

ACCOMMODATIONS

Armory Park Guesthouse 219 S 5th Ave **520/206–9252** • gay-friendly • renovated 1896 residence w/ 2 detached guest units • gay-owned • $60-110

Big Blue House 144 E. University Blvd **520/891–1827** • gay-friendly • all-suite B&B • food served • nonsmoking • WiFi • $90-190

Catalina Park Inn 309 E 1st St **520/792–4541, 800/792–4885** • gay/ straight • full brkfst • nonsmoking • kids 10+ ok • WiFi • gay-owned • $109-189

Desert Trails B&B 12851 E Speedway Blvd **520/885–7295, 877/758–3284** • gay-friendly • adobe hacienda on 3 acres bordering Saguaro Nat'l Park • far from the madding crowd • swimming • smoking outside only • $100-155 (rooms), $140-165 (guesthouse)

Hotel Congress 311 E Congress St **520/622–8848, 800/722–8848** • gay/ straight • historic hotel w/ vintage furnishings • WiFi • $69-119 • also Cup Cafe • plenty veggie • also full bar & club

La Casita Del Sol 407 N Meyer Ave (btwn Church Ave & Franklin Ave) **520/623–8882** • gay/ straight • 1880s adobe guesthouse • pets ok w/ permission • nonsmoking • WiFi • gay-owned • $100-115

Milagras Guesthouse 11185 W Calle Pima **520/578–8577** • gay/straight • natural adobe guesthouse • garden courtyard • private patio • hot tub • kitchen • nonsmoking • wheelchair access

Natural B&B & Retreat **520/881–4582, 888/295–8500** • gay/ straight • full brkfst • nonsmoking • nontoxic/ nonallergenic • some shared baths • kids ok • WiFi • massage available • gay-owned • $85-95

Royal Elizabeth B&B Inn 204 S Scott Ave (at Broadway) 520/670-9022, 877/670-9022 • gay/ straight • historic 1878 downtown mansion • full brkfst • pool • hot tub • kids ok • nonsmoking • WiFi • gay-owned • $219

Bars

Ain't Nobody's Bizness 2900 E Broadway #118 (at Country Club) 520/318-4838 • 5pm-2am, clsd Mon • mostly women • dancing/DJ • karaoke • Latin Night Sat • wheelchair access

Congress Tap Room 311 E Congress (at Hotel Congress) 520/622-8848 • 11am-2am • gay-friendly • neighborhood bar • dance club from 9pm • karaoke• live bands

Coyote Moon Pub 915 W Prince Rd 520/293-7339 • 3pm-1am, 11am-2am wknds • lesbians/ gay men • dancing/DJ • country/ western Fri • food served until 9pm • karaoke • WiFi

IBT's (It's About Time) 616 N 4th Ave (at University) 520/882-3053 • noon-2am • lesbians/ gay men • dancing/DJ • live shows • karaoke • wheelchair access

Woody's 3710 N Oracle Rd. (at W Thurber Rd) 520/292-6702 • 11am-2am • mostly gay men • karaoke • video/ sports bar • wheelchair access

Cafes

Revolutionary Grounds 606 N 4th Ave (at E 5th St) 520/620-1770 • 7am-7pm, till 11pm Fri-Sat, noon-7pm Sun • plenty veggie • WiFi • also leftist bookstore

Restaurants

Blue Willow 2616 N Campbell Ave (at Grant) 520/327-7577 • 7am-9pm, from 8am wknds • brkfst served all day

Cafe Poca Cosa 110 E Pennington St 520/622-6400 • 11am-9pm, till 10pm Fri-Sat, clsd Sun-Mon • Mexican-influenced bistro • patio

Colors Food & Spirits 5305 E Speedway 520/323-1840 • 4pm-10pm, till midnight Fri, 10am-10pm Sun • also bar from 4pm • lesbians/gay men • live shows

The Grill on Congress 100 E Congress St (at Scott) 520/623-7621 • 24hrs • plenty veggie • full bar

Tucson

LGBT Pride:
June & Oct 520/622-3200, web: www.tucsonpride.org.

Annual Events:
February - La Fiesta de los Vaqueros (rodeo & parade) 520/741-2233, web: www.tucsonrodeo.com.
April - Int'l Mariachi Music Conference 520/838-3908, web: www.tucsonmariachi.org.

City Info:
520/624-1817, web: www.visittucson.org.

Best View:
From a ski lift heading up to the top of Mount Lemmon.

Weather:
350 days of sunshine a year. Need we say more?

Attractions:
Arizona-Sonora Desert Museum 520/883-1380, web: www.desertmuseum.org.
Arizona State Museum 520/621-6302, web: www.statemuseum.arizona.edu.
Biosphere 2 520/838-6200, web: www.b2science.org.
Catalina State Park 520/628-5798.
Colossal Cave 520/647-7275, web: www.colossalcave.com.
Mission San Xavier del Bac, 520/294-2624, web: www.sanxaviermission.org.
Old Tucson.
Saguaro National Park 520/733-5153, web: www.nps.gov/sagu.

Transit:
Yellow Cab Tucson 520/624-6611.
Arizona Shuttle 520/795-6771 or 800/888-2749, web: www.arizonashuttle.com

ENTERTAINMENT & RECREATION

Tucson Roller Derby 520/390–1454 • Tucson's female roller derby league • visit tucsonrollerderby.com for events

BOOKSTORES

Antigone Books 411 N 4th Ave (at 7th St) **520/792–3715** • 10am-7pm, till 9pm Fri-Sat, noon-5pm Sun • LGBT/ feminist • gifts • wheelchair access

PUBLICATIONS

The Observer 520/622–7176

EROTICA

The Bookstore Southwest 5754 E Speedway Blvd **520/790–1550**

Caesar's Adult Shop 2540 N Oracle Rd (btwn Glen & Grant) **520/622–9479**

Hydra 145 E Congress (at 6th) **520/791–3711** • vinyl • leather • toys • shoes • lingerie

White Mountains

ACCOMMODATIONS

Arizona High Country Campground 5064 Sawmill Rd (1 mile off Hwy 260), Clay Springs **928/739–4383** • lesbians/ gay men • 10 campsites & RV hookups • WiFi • lesbian-owned • $30/ night, $2000/ season

Yuma

BARS

The Closet Lounge 3780 S 4th Ave **928/344–0969** • 10am-2am • lesbians/ gay men • dancing/DJ • live shows

EROTICA

Triple X Adult Super Store 3125 S Ave 3-E (at 32nd) **928/344–1799**

ARKANSAS

Statewide

PUBLICATIONS

Metro Star 918/835–7887 • monthly LGBT news publication serving AR, KS, MO & OK

Crossett

CAFES

Crosses Grocery & Cafe 4223 Hwy 16 (E of Elkins, outside Fayetteville) **479/643–3307** • 6am-8:30pm

Eureka Springs

ACCOMMODATIONS

A Byrds Eye View 36 N Main (at Douglas) **479/253–0200, 888/210–8401** • gay/ straight • in heart of downtown • porch • nonsmoking • WiFi • gay-owned • $99-129

Candlestick Cottage Inn 6 Douglas St (at N Main) **479/253–6813, 800/835–5184** • gay-friendly • private, romantic setting • full brkfst • nonsmoking • WiFi • lesbian-owned • $89-159

The Grand TreeHouse Resort 350 W Van Buren (at Pivot Rock Rd) **479/253–8733** • gay/ straight • outdoor showers up in trees • WiFi • gay-owned • $99-129

Heart of the Hills Inn 5 Summit St (on Historic Loop) **479/253–7468, 800/253–7468** • gay/ straight • historic inn near downtown • full brkfst • private decks • nonsmoking • gay-owned • $109-150

Lookout Lodge 3098 E Van Buren **479/253–9335, 877/253–9335** • gay-friendly • private entrances • pets/kids ok • WiFi • nonsmoking • $49-119

Mount Victoria 28 Fairmount St **479/253–7979, 888/408–7979** • gay-friendly • full brkfst & dinner • WiFi • $119-225

Out on Main 269 N Main St (at Magnetic Rd) **479/253–8449** • gay/ straight • 3-room cottage • full kitchen • nonsmoking • WiFi • gay-owned • $89-105

Palace Hotel & Bath House 135 Spring St **479/253–7474, 866/946–0572** • gay-friendly • historic bathhouse open to all • nonsmoking • WiFi • $168-198

Pond Mountain Lodge & Resort **479/253–5877, 800/583–8043** • gay/ straight • mountaintop inn on 150 acres • cabins • pool • nonsmoking • jacuzzis • wheelchair access • lesbian- & straight-owned • $90-155

Red Bud Manor Inn 7 Kingshighway **479/253–9649, 866/253–9649** • gay-friendly • full brkfst • WiFi • indoor hot tub • women-owned • $89-149

Roadrunner Inn 3034 Mundell Rd **479/253–8166, 888/253–8166** • gay-friendly • lake views • reservations advised • guestrooms & log cabins • $75-275

Texaco Bungalow 77 Mountain St **888/253–8093** • gay/ straight • art deco service station rentals • gay-owned • $79-139

The Woods Resort 50 Wall St (off Hwy 62) **479/253-8281** • lesbians/ gay men • cottages • some treehouse cottages • treehouse hot tub • jacuzzis • kitchens • nonsmoking • gay-owned • $139-175

BARS

Chelsea's Corner Cafe 10 Mountain St (at Center St) **479/253-6723** • 11am-2am, till 10pm Sun • gay-friendly • dancing/DJ • patio • also restaurant • live shows • WiFi • women-owned

Eureka Live 35 N Main **479/253-7020** • 4pm-1:30am, clsd Sun-Mon • gay/ straight • more gay Wed • dancing/DJ • food served • karaoke

Henri's 19 Spring St **479/253-5795** • noon-2am, cllsd Tue • gay/ straight • gay night Wed from 5pm • bar menu • live shows • WiFi

The Lumberyard Saloon & Steakhouse 105 E Van Buren **479/253-0400** • 3pm-2am, from noon wknds • gay/ straight • live shows • sports bar • karaoke • WiFi • lesbian-owned

Pied Piper Pub & Inn 82 Armstrong (at Main St) **479/363-9976, 866/363-9976** • noon-midnight • popular Reuben sandwich, fish & chips

Tiki Torch Club 75 S Main St **479/253-2305** • gay/ straight • also restaurant • live music • karaoke • big screen TV

CAFES

Mud Street Cafe 22G S Main St **479/253-6732** • 8am-3pm, clsd Wed

RESTAURANTS

Autumn Breeze 190 Huntsville Rd (1/2 mile off Hwy 62) **479/253-7734** • 5pm-9pm, clsd Sun, hrs vary in winter • cont'l • nonsmoking

Caribe Restaurant & Cantina 309 W Van Buren **479/253-8102** • 4pm-9pm, clsd Tue, from noon wknds • also bar

Cottage Inn 450 Hwy 62 W **479/253-5282** • 5pm-9pm, clsd Mon-Wed • Mediterranean • full bar

Ermilio's 26 White St **479/253-8806** • 5pm-9pm • Italian • plenty veggie • full bar

Gaskins Cabin Steak House 2883 Hwy 23 N (Hwy 187) **479/253-5466** • 5pm-9pm, till 8pm Sun, clsd Mon-Tue • full bar • reservations suggested

ENTERTAINMENT & RECREATION

Diversity Pride Events 479/253-2555 • produces events during Valentine's & Spring, Summer, Fall Diversity Wknds & more

PUBLICATIONS

Metro Star 918/835-7887 • monthly LGBT news publication serving AR, KS, MO & OK

Fayetteville

INFO LINES & SERVICES

AA Gay/ Lesbian 568 W Sycamore **479/443-6366 (AA#)** • 7pm Tue, 10am Sat

ACCOMMODATIONS

Hilton Garden Inn Bentonville 2204 SE Walton Blvd (Exit 85, off I-540), Bentonville **479/464-7300, 877/782-9444** • gay-friendly • pool • kids ok • WiFi • wheelchair access • $59-169

NIGHTCLUBS

Tangerine 21 N Block Ave **479/443-4600** • 9pm-2am, clsd Sun-Tue • lesbians/ gay men • dancing/DJ • karaoke • drag shows • 18+

CAFES

The Common Grounds 412 W Dickson St (at West) **479/442-3515** • 7am-midnight • full bar • also restaurant • lots of veggie

RESTAURANTS

Bordinos 310 W Dickson St. **479/527-6795** • dinner nightly, lunch Tue-Fri, clsd Sun • full bar

Hugo's 25 1/2 N Block Ave **479/521-7585** • 11am-10pm, clsd Sun

BOOKSTORES

Hastings Bookstore 2999 N College Ave (Fiesta Square Shopping Center) **479/521-0244** • 9am-11pm

Helena

ACCOMMODATIONS

The Edwardian Inn 317 Biscoe **870/338-9155, 800/598-4749** • gay-friendly • 60 miles from Memphis • full brkfst • nonsmoking • WiFi • $80-165

Hot Springs

ACCOMMODATIONS

Park Hotel of Hot Springs 211 Fountain St (at Central Ave) **501/624-5323, 800/895-7275** • gay/ straight • WiFi • $69-225

The Rose Cottage 218 Court St (at Exchange St) **501/623-6449** • gay-friendly • historic Victorian row house • kids/ pets ok • jacuzzi • $185

Little Rock

INFO LINES & SERVICES

Women's Project 2224 Main St (at 23rd) **501/372-5113** • 9am-5pm Mon-Fri • feminist resource • call for info

ACCOMMODATIONS

Legacy Hotel & Suites 625 W Capitol Ave (at Gaines) **501/374-0100, 888/456-3669** • gay-friendly • nat'l historic property in downtown area • kids ok • WiFi • wheelchair access • $79-1,299

BARS

Backstreet 1021 Jessie Rd (btwn Cantrell & Riverfront) **501/664-2744** • 9pm-5am Fri only • lesbians/ gay men • dancing/DJ • drag shows • male dancers • videos • 18+ • private club • wheelchair access

Discovery 1021 Jessie Rd (btwn Cantrell & Riverfront) **501/664-4784** • 9pm-5am Sat only • lesbians/ gay men • dancing/DJ • drag shows • male dancers • videos • 18+ • private club • wheelchair access

Off Center/ Pulse 307 W 7th St (at Center St) **501/372-3530** • 6pm-2am Tue-Sat • Pulse from 8pm • lesbians/ gay men • drag shows

Sidetracks 415 Main St, North Little Rock **501/244-0444** • 5pm-2am • mostly gay men • neighborhood bar • also restaurant • country/ western • bears • leather • older crowd • WiFi • wheelchair access

Star Bar 1900 W 3rd St **501/301-7827** • 4pm-close, from 6pm Sat • lounge • also tapas restaurant

Little Rock

WHERE THE GIRLS ARE:
Scattered. Popular hangouts are the Women's Project, local bookstores, and the monthly women's coffeehouse at Vino's Pizza.

LGBT PRIDE:
June, web: www.littlerockcapital-pride.org.

ANNUAL EVENTS:
October - State Fair 501/372-8341, web: www.arkansasstatefair.com.

CITY INFO:
Arkansas Dept of Tourism 800/NATURAL, web: www.arkansas.com.
Little Rock Convention & Visitors Bureau 800/844-4781, web: www.littlerock.com.

ATTRACTIONS:
(Check out Bill & Hillary's old digs at 18th & Center Sts.)
Arkansas Arts Center 501/372-4000, web: www.arkarts.com.
Central High Museum & Visitors Center 501/374-1957, web: www.nps.gov/chsc.
Clinton Presidential Library 501/374-4242, web: www.clin-tonlibrary.gov.
Historical Quapaw Quarter.

WEATHER:
When it comes to natural precipitation, Arkansas is far from being a dry state. Be prepared for the occasional severe thunderstorm or ice storm. Summers are hot and humid (mid 90°s). Winters can be cold (30°s) with some snow and ice. Spring and fall are the best times to come and be awed by Mother Nature.

TRANSIT:
Greater Little Rock Transportation 501/374-0333.
Central Arkansas Transit 501/375-6717, web: www.cat.org.

BEST VIEW:
Quapaw Quarter (in the heart of the city).

NIGHTCLUBS

UBU 824 W Capitol (at Izard) **501/375–8580** • 8pm-2am Fri, from 9pm Sat, clsd Sun-Th • lesbians/ gay men • dancing/DJ • multiracial • transgender-friendly • live shows • karaoke • drag shows • private club • wheelchair access • lesbian-owned

RESTAURANTS

Bossa Nova 2701 Kavanaugh Blvd (at Ash St) **501/614–6682** • lunch & dinner, Sun brunch, clsd Mon • Brazilian • plenty veggie

Juanita's 1300 S Main **501/372–1228** • 11am-close, clsd Sun • live music • reservations recommended

La Hacienda 3024 Cantrell Rd **501/661–0600** • Mexican

Lilly's Dim Sum, Then Some 11121 N Rodney Parham Rd **501/716–2700** • 11am-9pm, till 10pm Fri-Sat, noon-9pm Sun • contemporary Asian • plenty veggie • lesbian-owned

Vino's Pizza 923 W 7th St (at Chester) **501/375–8466** • 11am-close, from 11:30am Sat, from noon Sun • beer/ wine

ENTERTAINMENT & RECREATION

The Arts Scene 201 Maple St (at Broadway), North Little Rock **501/372–2130, 501/697–0196** • 10am-6pm Sat-Sun • gallery & art market • also Friday Night Art Party • 8pm-1am 2nd Fri • live music, performance & films

The Weekend Theater 1001 W 7th St (at Chester) **501/374–3761** • plays & musicals on wknds • gay-owned

BOOKSTORES

Wordsworth Books & Co 5920 R St **501/663–9198** • 9am-7pm, till 6pm Fri-Sat, noon-5pm Sun • independent

RETAIL SHOPS

A Twisted Gift Shop 1007 W 7th St (at Chester) **501/376–7723** • noon-midnight • gift shop

Mountain Home

ACCOMMODATIONS

Black Oak Resort PO Box 100, Oakland 72661 **870/431–8363** • gay/ straight • quiet mtn resort bordering Bull Shoals Lake • pool • kids/ pets ok • nonsmoking • $87-165

CALIFORNIA

Amador City

ACCOMMODATIONS

Imperial Hotel 14202 Hwy 49 (at Water St) **209/267–9172** • gay-friendly • B&B • brick Victorian hotel • nonsmoking • full brkfst • restaurant & bar (Tue-Sun) • $105-1205

Anaheim

see Orange County

Angels Camp

ACCOMMODATIONS

Cooper House B&B Inn 1184 Church St (at Raspberry Ln) **209/736–2145, 888/330–3764** • gay/ straight • full brkfst • WiFi • gay-owned • $109-239

Antelope Valley

see Lancaster

Arcata

see also Eureka

INFO LINES & SERVICES

Queer Humboldt PO Box 45, 95518-0045 **707/834–4839** • "Humboldt County's online resource for the LGBT community" • includes links & events calendar • check out www.queerhumboldt.org

BARS

The Alibi 744 9th St **707/822–3731** • lesbian/gay men• cocktail lounge w/ live music • neighborhood bar • also restaurant (8am-midnight) • young crowd

CAFES

Cafe Mokka 495 J St (at 5th) **707/822–2228** • from noon • coffee & soups (bread bowls) • live music • also Finnish sauna & hot tubs

North Coast Co-op 811 I St **707/822–5947** • 6am-9pm • co-op store w/ bakery, deli & espresso cafe • WiFi

RESTAURANTS

Wildflower Bakery & Cafe 1604 G St **707/822–0360** • 8am-8pm, till 9pm Th-Sat • popular • vegetarian • organic beer & wine

BOOKSTORES

Northtown Books 957 H St **707/822–2834** • 10am-7pm, till 9pm Fri-Sat, noon-5pm Sun • LGBT section • carries The L Word paper

Arnold

ACCOMMODATIONS

Dorrington Inn at Big Trees 3450 Hwy 4 (at Boards Crossing), Dorrington **209/795-2164, 877/795-2164** • gay/ straight • cottages & suites • gay-owned • $99-229

Bakersfield

INFO LINES & SERVICES

Gay AA 1001 34th St **661/322-4025 (AA#), 661/324-0371 (ALANO CLUB #)** • 7:30pm Mon

BARS

The Mint 1207 19th St (at M) **661/325-4048** • 6am-2am • gay/ straight • alternative • live music

NIGHTCLUBS

The Casablanca Club 1825 N St (at 19th St) **661/324-0661** • 8pm-2am, clsd Mon • gay/ straight • neighborhood bar • dancing/DJ • live entertainment • cabaret • drag shows • videos • wheelchair access

BOOKSTORES

Russo's Books 9000 Ming Ave #1-4 **661/665-4686** • 10am-8pm • independent

Benicia

see **Vallejo**

Berkeley

see **East Bay**

Big Bear Lake

ACCOMMODATIONS

Alpine Retreats 433 Edgemoor (at Big Bear Blvd) **909/725-4192, 909/878-4155 (RESERVATIONS)** • gay/ straight • 3 cottages • fireplaces • nonsmoking • kids ok • gay-owned • $95-225

Knickerbocker Mansion Country Inn 869 Knickerbocker Rd **909/878-9190, 877/423-1180** • gay/ straight • log mansion on lake • full brkfst • jacuzzi • hiking • nonsmoking • WiFi • wheelchair access • gay-owned • $125-240

Rainbow View Lodge 2726 View Dr (at Hilltop), Running Springs **909/867-1810, 888/868-1810** • gay/ straight • cottages w/ themed decor • kids ok • nonsmoking • women-owned • $69-149

Switzerland Haus 41829 Switzerland Dr **909/866-3729, 800/335-3729** • gay-friendly • $125-249

Big Sur

ACCOMMODATIONS

Eagle's Nest Pfeiffer Ridge #10 **831/667-2587, 888/742-9321** • gay-friendly • guesthouse on private road • wraparound deck w/ views of Pfeiffer Ridge & Pacific Ocean • full kitchen • WiFi • gay-owned • $250-350

Lucia Lodge 62400 Hwy 1 **831/668-4884, 866/424-4787** • gay-friendly • oceanview cabins • $150-275 • also restaurant & lounge • WiFi

Burlingame

see **San Francisco**

Cambria

ACCOMMODATIONS

Blue Dolphin Inn 6470 Moonstone Beach Dr **805/927-3300, 800/222-9157** • gay-friendly • inn on Cambria's Moonstone Beach • WiFi • wheelchair access • $89-319

The J Patrick House B&B 2990 Burton Dr (1/2 mile off Hwy 1) **805/927-3812, 800/341-5258** • gay-friendly • full brkfst • WiFi • fireplaces • nonsmoking • $165-215

Sea Otter Inn 6656 Moonstone Beach Dr **805/927-5888, 800/965-8347** • gay-friendly • pool • nonsmoking • WiFi • wheelchair access • $79-299

Capistrano Beach

ACCOMMODATIONS

Capistrano Seaside Inn 34862 Pacific Coast Hwy **949/496-1399, 800/252-3224 (RESERVATIONS ONLY)** • gay-friendly • outdoor jacuzzi • ocean views • kids/ pets ok • fireplaces • wheelchair access • packages available • $79-179

Carmel

see also **Monterey**

ACCOMMODATIONS

Best Western Carmel Mission Inn 3665 Rio Rd **831/624-1841, 800/348-9090** • gay-friendly • near Monterey Bay • pool • pets ok • also restaurant & lounge • nonsmoking

Carmel Resort Inn Carpenter Ave (btwn 1st & 2nd Ave) **831/624-3113, 800/454-3700** • gay-friendly • cottages • kids/ pets ok • WiFi • nonsmoking • $79-335

Carmel River Inn Hwy 1 at Carmel River Bridge 831/624-1575, 800/966-6490 • gay-friendly • kids/pets ok • pool • nonsmoking • $79-329

Cypress Inn Lincoln & 7th 831/624-3871, 800/443-7443 • gay-friendly • pets very welcome • owned by Doris Day • WiFi • $165-575

RESTAURANTS

Rio Grill 101 Crossroads Blvd 831/625-5436 • lunch & dinner daily, Sun brunch • "Creative American" • full bar

Chico

INFO LINES & SERVICES

Stonewall Alliance Center 2889 Cohasset Rd #5 (at Cameo Dr) 530/893-3336 • HIV testing & counseling • also recorded info • meetings • events

Chino

RESTAURANTS

Riverside Grill 5258 Riverside Dr (at Central) 909/627-4144 • 8am-9pm, till 3pm Sun-Tue

Clearlake

includes major towns of Lake County

ACCOMMODATIONS

Blue Fish Cove Resort 10573 E Hwy 20, Clearlake Oaks 707/998-1769 • gay-friendly • lakeside resort cottages • kitchens • kids ok • pets ok by arrangement • boat launch facilities & rentals • $75-140

Edgewater Resort 6420 Soda Bay Rd (at Hohape Rd), Kelseyville 707/279-0208, 800/396-6224 • "gay-owned, straight-friendly" • cabin • camping & RV hookups • lake access & pool • theme wknds • boat facilities • WiFi • kids/pets ok • lesbian-owned • $35-450

Gingerbread Cottages B&B 4057 E Hwy 20, Nice 707/274-0200, 888/880-5253 • gay/straight • lakefront w/ private beach • antiques & art • pool • nonsmoking • WiFi • $125-195

Sea Breeze Resort 9595 Harbor Dr, Glenhaven 707/998-3327 • gay/straight • lakefront cottages • swimming • nonsmoking • WiFi • wheelchair access • gay-owned • $95-155 (2-night minimum)

Cloverdale

see also Healdsburg

ACCOMMODATIONS

Vintage Towers B&B 302 N Main St (at 3rd) 707/894-4535, 888/886-9377 • gay-friendly • Queen Anne mansion • full brkfst • nonsmoking • $129-249

Concord

see East Bay

Costa Mesa

see Orange County

Cupertino

ACCOMMODATIONS

Cypress Hotel 10050 S De Anza Blvd 408/253-8900, 800/499-1408 • gay-friendly • pool • pets ok • WiFi • nonsmoking • also gym & restaurant

Dana Point

see Orange County

Danville

see East Bay

Davis

see also Sacramento

INFO LINES & SERVICES

LGBT Resource Center University House Annex 530/752-2452 • 9am-5pm, clsd wknds • info • referrals • meetings • library • WiFi • wheelchair access

CAFES

Mishka's Cafe 514B 2nd St 530/759-0811 • 7:30am-11pm

BOOKSTORES

The Avid Reader 617 2nd St 530/758-4040 • 10am-10pm • general independent • readings

Desert Hot Springs

see Palm Springs & Joshua Tree Nat'l Park

East Bay

includes major cities of Alameda and Contra Costa Counties: Alameda, Antioch, Berkeley, Concord, Danville, Fremont, Hayward, Lafayette, Newark, Oakland, Pleasant Hill, Richmond, San Leandro, Walnut Creek

INFO LINES & SERVICES

East Bay AA 510/839-8900 (AA#) • variety of LGBT-friendly mtgs

La Peña 3105 Shattuck Ave, Berkeley 510/849-2568 • multicultural center & cafe • hosts meetings, events, performance art • nonsmoking • wheelchair access

Lighthouse Community Center 1217 A St (near 2nd St), Hayward 510/881-8167 • LGBT support groups & social events

Pacific Center for Human Growth 2712 Telegraph Ave (at Derby), Berkeley 510/548-8283 • 4pm-10pm Mon-Fri • wheelchair access

Rainbow Community Center of Contra Costa County 3024 Willow Pass Rd #200 (btwn Parkside & Esperanza), Concord 925/692-0090 • 10am-5pm Mon-Fri

ACCOMMODATIONS

Hotel Durant 2600 Durant Ave, Berkeley 510/845-8981, 800/738-7477 • gay/ straight • nonsmoking • WiFi • restaurant on premises • $95-199

Washington Inn 495 10th St (at Broadway), Oakland 510/452-1776 • gay/ straight • historic boutique hotel • full brkfst • nonsmoking • also restaurant • wheelchair access • $99-200

Waterfront Hotel 10 Washington St, Oakland 510/836-3800, 888/842-5333 • gay-friendly • pool • bar & restaurant • WiFi • wheelchair access • $95-249

BARS

The Alley 3325 Grand Ave (btwn Lake Park & Elwood Aves), Oakland 510/444-8505 • 4pm-2am • gay/ straight • camptastic sing-along piano bar from 9pm • more gay Th • also restaurant

Bench & Bar 510 17th St, Oakland 510/444-2266 • 4pm-2am • popular • mostly gay men • dancing/DJ • drag shows • Latin nights Fri-Sat • wheelchair access

Butta Oakland 510/763-0404 • 3pm-8pm 3rd Sun • mostly women • BBQ & T-dance • dancing/DJ • multiracial • www.butterflyproductions.org for info

Cafe Van Kleef 1621 Telegraph Ave (at Broadway), Oakland 510/763-7711 • 4pm-2am, clsd Sun • gay-friendly • eclectic crowd & live-music scene—from cabaret to blue grass to jazz • cover

Club 21 2111 Franklin St (at 21st St), Oakland 510/268-9425 • mostly gay men • dancing/DJ • mostly Latino/a • theme nights • videos

Easy Lounge 3255 Lakeshore Ave, Oakland 510/338-4911 • 4:30pm-2am, from 2pm Sat-Sun • gay-friendly • cool lounge w/ theme nights

Rainbow Room 21859 Mission Blvd (at Sunset), Hayward 510/582-8078 • 2pm-2am, from 11am wknds • lesbians/ gay men • neighborhood bar • dancing/DJ Fri-Sat • wheelchair access • women-owned

White Horse 6551 Telegraph Ave (at 66th), Oakland 510/652-3820 • 1pm-2am, from 3pm Mon-Tue • popular wknds (also Sun beer bust) • lesbians/ gay men • dancing/DJ • karaoke Tue • wheelchair access

World Famous Turf Club 22519 Main St (at A St), Hayward 510/881-9877 • 2pm-2am, from noon Sat-Sun • lesbians/ gay men • dancing/DJ • drag shows • huge patio • wheelchair access

NIGHTCLUBS

Club 1220 1220 Pine St (at Civic Dr), Walnut Creek 925/938-4550 • 4pm-2am • lesbians/ gay men • dancing/DJ • karaoke • WiFi • wheelchair access

Honeydip 311 Broadway (at Aqua Lounge), Oakland • 2nd Sat only • women only • dancing/DJ • multiracial

CAFES

Au Coquelet Cafe 2000 University Ave, Berkeley 510/845-0433 • 6am-12am

Bittersweet 5427 College Ave (in Rockridge District), Oakland 510/654-7159 • 9am-7pm, till 9pm Fri-Sat

Caffe Strada 2300 College Ave (btw Way & Durant), Berkeley 510/843-5282 • 6:30am-midnight • students • great patio • wheelchair access

Raw Energy 2050 Addison St (btwn Shattuck & Milvia), Berkeley 510/665-9464 • 7:30am-7:30pm, 11am-4pm Sat, clsd Sun • organic juice cafe • gay-owned

World Ground Cafe 3726 MacArthur Blvd (btwn 35th & 38th Aves, in Laurel District), Oakland 510/482-2933 • 6:30am-6pm

Restaurants

Arizmendi Bakery & Pizzeria 3265 Lakeshore Ave, Oakland **510/268-8849** • 7am-7pm, till 3pm Mon, clsd Sun • excellent pastries, breads & pizzas

Cactus Taqueria 5642 College Ave (at Shafter, in Rockridge), Oakland **510/658-6180** • 11am-10pm, till 9pm Sun

César 1515 Shattuck Ave (in "Gourmet Ghetto," next door to Chez Panisse), Berkeley **510/883-0222** • noon-11pm • Spanish tapas • full bar • also 4039 Piedmont Ave, Oakland, 510/985-1200

Connie's Cantina 3340 Grand Ave (btwn Lake Park Ave & Mandana Blvd), Oakland **510/839-4986** • 10:30am-9pm, clsd Sun • popular • delicious homemade Mexican food • plenty veggie • patio • woman-owned

East Bay

WHERE THE GIRLS ARE:

Though there's no lesbian ghetto, you'll find more of us shacked up in North Oakland (Rockridge) and North Berkeley, Lake Merritt (Adams Point), around Grand Lake & Piedmont, along MacArthur (from Fruitvale Ave to High St—also known as The Fruit Hills), in the Solano/Albany area, or at a cafe along 4th St in Berkeley.

ANNUAL EVENTS:

October - Community Celebration for the Days of the Dead 510/238-2200, web: www.muse-umca.org.

CITY INFO:

Berkeley Convention & Visitors Bureau 800/847-4823, web: www.visitberkeley.com.
Oakland Convention & Visitors Bureau 510/839-9000, web: www.oaklandcvb.com.

ATTRACTIONS:

The Claremont Hotel & Restaurant, Berkeley 510/843-3000, web: www.claremontresort.com.
Emeryville Marina Public Market.
Jack London Square, Oakland, web: www.jacklondonsquare.com.
Oakland Museum of California 510/238-2200, web: www.museumca.org.
The Paramount Theater, Oakland 510/465-6400, web: www.para-mounttheatre.com.
UC Berkeley.

BEST VIEW:

Claremont Hotel, Tilden Park, various locations in the Berkeley and Oakland Hills. Or from the top of Sather Tower on the UC Berkeley campus.

WEATHER:

While San Francisco is fogged in during the summers, the East Bay remains sunny and warm. Some areas even get hot (90°s-100°s). As for the winter, the temperature drops along with rain (upper 30°s-40°s in the winter). Spring is the time to come – the usually brown hills explode with the colors of green grass and wildflowers.

TRANSIT:

Yellow Cab (Berkeley) 510/486-0404.
Veteran's Cab (Oakland) 510/533-1900.
Bayporter Express 877/467-1800, web: www.bayporter.com.
AC Transit 510/891-4700, web: www.actransit.org.
BART (subway) 510/465-2278, web: www.bart.gov.
Ferry, web: www.eastbayferry.com.

Dopo 4293 Piedmont Ave, Oakland **510/652-3676** • lunch & dinner, clsd Sun • Italian • worth the wait

Le Cheval 1007 Clay St, Oakland **510/763-8495** • 11am-9:30pm, from 5pm Sun • popular • Vietnamese • wheelchair access

Lois the Pie Queen 851 60th St (off Martin Luther King Jr Hwy), Oakland **510/658-5616** • 8am-2pm • popular • Southern homecooking & killer desserts

Mama's Royal Cafe 4012 Broadway (at 40th), Oakland **510/547-7600** • 7am-2:30pm, from 8am wknds • popular • come early for excellent wknd brunch • beer/ wine • wheelchair access

Rockridge Cafe 5492 College Ave (at Forest), Oakland **510/653-1567** • 7:30am-3pm • popular • great brkfsts • plenty veggie

Zachary's Chicago Pizza 5801 College Ave, Oakland **510/655-6385** • 11am-10pm • popular • pizza that is worth the crowds & the long wait!

ENTERTAINMENT & RECREATION

What's Up! Events Hotline for Sistahs **510/835-6126** • for lesbians of African descent

BOOKSTORES

Black Oak Books 2618 San Pablo Ave, Berkeley **510/486-0698** • 11am-7pm • independent • new & used

Diesel, A Bookstore 5433 College Avenue, Oakland **510/653-9965** • 10am-9pm, till 10pm Fri-Sat, till 6pm Sun • independent

Laurel Book Store 4100 MacArthur Blvd (2 blks from High St), Oakland **510/531-2073** • 10am-7pm, till 6pm Sat, 11am-5pm Sun • general • LGBT section • readings • wheelchair access • lesbian-owned

Pendragon Books 5560 College Ave (at Oceanview), Oakland **510/652-6259** • 9am-10pm, from 10am Sun • used books • magazines • great to browse while waiting for a table in Rockridge

RETAIL SHOPS

Ancient Ways 4075 Telegraph Ave (at 41st), Oakland **510/653-3244** • 11am-7pm • extensive occult supplies • classes • readings • woman-owned

See Jane Run Sports 5817 College Ave, Oakland **510/428-2681** • 11am-7pm, 10am-6pm Sat & Sun • women's athletic apparel

EROTICA

Good Vibrations 2504 San Pablo Ave (at Dwight Wy), Berkeley **510/841-8987** • 11am-8pm,10am-6pm Fri-Sat • clean, well-lighted sex toy store • workshops & events • also mail order • wheelchair access

Lingerie Etc 2298 Monument Blvd (at Buskirk), Pleasant Hill **925/676-2962** • 9am-midnight

Elk

RESTAURANTS

Queenie's Roadhouse Cafe 6061 S Hwy 1 **707/877-3285** • 8am-3pm, clsd Tue-Wed • fabulous all-day brkfsts • some veggie • lesbian-owned

Eureka

see also Arcata

ACCOMMODATIONS

Abigail's Elegant Victorian Mansion 1406 C St **707/444-3144** • gay-friendly • sauna • nonsmoking • $105-230

Carter House Victorians 301 L St **707/444-8062, 800/404-1390** • gay-friendly • enclave of 4 unique inns • full brkfst • nonsmoking • kids ok • restaurant • wine shop • wheelchair access • $155-595

Trinidad Bay B&B 560 Edwards St (at Trinity), Trinidad **707/677-0840** • gay-friendly • nonsmoking • WiFi • kids ok • full brkfst • gay- & straight-owned • $200-300

Trinidad Escape **707/677-3457** • lesbians/ gay men • WiFi • oceanfront house rental in Tinidad • $200-450 per night

BARS

Lost Coast Brewery 617 4th St (btwn G & H Sts) **707/445-4480** • 11am-1am • gay-friendly • food served till midnight • beer/ wine • WiFi • wheelchair access • women-owned

The Shanty 213 3rd St (at C St) **707/444-2053** • noon-2am • gay/ straight • neighborhood bar • lesbian-owned

NIGHTCLUBS

Aunty Mo's 535 5th St (btwn F & G Sts) **707/442-0772** • 6pm-close Th-Sat only • lesbians/ gay men • dancing/DJ • theme nights • WiFi

CAFES

North Coast Co-op 25 4th St (at B St) **707/443-6027** • 6am-9pm • co-op store w/ bakery, deli & espresso cafe

Ramone's Cafe & Bakery 209 E St (Old Town) 707/445–2923 • 7am-6pm

RESTAURANTS

Chalet House of Omelettes 1935 5th St (at U St) 707/442–0333 • 6am-3pm, brkfst & lunch • wheelchair access

Folie Deuce 1551 G St, Arcata 707/822–1042 • dinner Tue-Sat, clsd Sun-Mon • bistro • beer/ wine • reservations recommended • wheelchair access

Hurricane Kate's 511 2nd St (Old Town) 707/444–1405 • lunch & dinner, clsd Sun-Mon • World fusion • some veggie • wine

BOOKSTORES

Booklegger 402 2nd St (at E St) 707/445–1344 • 10am-5:30pm, 11am-4pm Sun • mostly used • wheelchair access • women-owned

PUBLICATIONS

The "L" Word PO Box 272, Bayside 95524 • lesbian newsletter for Humboldt County • available at Booklegger in Eureka & North Town Books in Arcata

EROTICA

Good Relations 223 2nd St 707/441–9570, 888/485–5063 • lingerie • toys • books • videos • wheelchair access • queer-owned/ run

Fairfield

see Vacaville

Fort Bragg

see also Mendocino

ACCOMMODATIONS

The Cleone Gardens Inn 24600 N Hwy 1 707/964–2788, 800/400–2189 (N CA ONLY) • gay-friendly • country garden retreat on 2.5 acres • hot tub • WiFi • nonsmoking • wheelchair access • $86-130

The Weller House Inn 524 Stewart St (at Pine) 707/964–4415, 877/893–5537 • gay-friendly • 1886 Victorian • full brkfst • jacuzzi • nonsmoking • WiFi • $135-210

RESTAURANTS

Cowlick's 250B N Main St 707/962–9271 • delicious homemade ice cream, including mushroom ice cream (in-season)—it's actually quite good!

Purple Rose 24300 N Hwy 1 707/964–6507 • 5pm-9pm, clsd Mon-Tue • Mexican • wheelchair access

ENTERTAINMENT & RECREATION

Skunk Train California Western foot of Laurel St 707/964–6371, 866/457–5865 • scenic train trips

BOOKSTORES

Windsong Books & Records 324 N Main St (at Redwood Ave) 707/964–2050 • 10am-5:30pm, till 4pm Sun • mostly used • large selection of women's/ lesbian titles

Fountain Valley

see Orange County

Fremont

see East Bay

Fresno

INFO LINES & SERVICES

Community Link 559/266–5465 • info • LGBT support, including LGBT youth group • also publishes Newslink

Fresno AA 559/221–6907 • call or check website (www.fresnoaa.org) for meetings

ACCOMMODATIONS

The San Joaquin Hotel 1309 W Shaw Ave (at Fruit) 559/225–1309, 800/775–1309 • gay-friendly • pool • WiFi • wheelchair access • $149-248

BARS

The Den 4538 E Belmont Ave (at Maple) 559/255–3213 • 5pm-2am • mostly gay men • country/ western • bears • leather • multiracial • videos • older crowd • popular beer busts • patio • gay-owned

Red Lantern 4618 E Belmont Ave (at Maple) 559/251–5898 • 2pm-2am • mostly gay men • neighborhood bar • country/ western • Latin night Sat very popular • food Sun • patio • WiFi • wheelchair access

NIGHTCLUBS

Express 708 N Blackstone (btwn Olive & Belmont, on Bremer) 559/445–0878 • 9pm-2am, clsd Mon-Tue • mostly gay men • dancing/DJ • theme nights • Latin night Th (drag shows) • videos • gay-owned • cover

RESTAURANTS

Cafe Rousseau 568 E Olive Ave (in Tower District) 559/445–1536 • lunch Tue-Fri, dinner from 5:30pm, clsd Sun-Mon • cont'l • also wine bar

Irene's Cafe 747 E Olive Ave (in Tower District) **559/237–9919** • 8am-9pm • some veggie • popular hamburgers • beer/ wine

Sequoia Brewing Company 777 E Olive Ave (in Tower District) **559/264–5521** • 11am-10pm, till midnight Fri-Sat, till 9pm Sun • microbrewery w/ restaurant • live music

Veni Vidi Vici 1116 N Fulton (S of Olive Ave, in Tower District) **559/266–5510** • California fine dining • nightclub later

EROTICA

Suzie's Adult Superstores 1267 N Blackstone Ave **559/497–9613** • 24hrs

Garden Grove

see Orange County

Graeagle

ACCOMMODATIONS

Molly's Bed & Breakfast 276 Lower Main St (Hwy 89), Clio **530/836–4436, 866/836–4730** • gay-friendly • near the Feather River • ful brkfst • kids/pets ok • women owned • $95-120

Grass Valley

see Nevada City

Gualala

ACCOMMODATIONS

Breakers Inn 39300 S Hwy 1 **707/884–3200, 800/273–2537** • gay/ straight • oceanfront • women-owned • $110-550

North Coast Country Inn 34591 S Hwy 1 **707/884–4537, 800/959–4537** • gay-friendly • B&B overlooking Mendocino coast • hot tub • nonsmoking • $195-225

RESTAURANTS

Redwood Grill 35517 Old Hwy 1 (at Ocean View Dr) **707/884–1639** • lunch & dinner, brkfst wknds, clsd Mon • beer/ wine • patio • wheelchair access • lesbian-owned

BOOKSTORES

The Four-Eyed Frog 39138 Ocean Dr (in Cypress Village) **707/884–1333** • 10am-6pm, till 5pm Sun • independent

Half Moon Bay

ACCOMMODATIONS

Mill Rose Inn 615 Mill St **650/726–8750, 800/900–7673** • gay-friendly • classic European elegance by the sea • full brkfst • hot tub • nonsmoking • WiFi • kids 10+ ok • $175-360

RESTAURANTS

Moss Beach Distillery 140 Beach Wy (at Ocean) **650/728–5595** • lunch & dinner, Sun brunch • popular • steak & seafood • some veggie • patio • even own ghost • wheelchair access

Pasta Moon 315 Main St (at Mill) **650/726–5125** • lunch & dinner • Italian • full bar • live shows • wheelchair access

Hayward

see East Bay

Healdsburg

see Russian River & Sonoma County

Huntington Beach

see Orange County

Idyllwild

ACCOMMODATIONS

Alderwood Cabins 25690 Alderwood St
951/659-3571 • gay-friendly • 1920s cabins
on 2 wooded acres • full kitchen • satellite TV

The Heritage House Inn 25880 Cedar St
951/659-5150, 877/659-4789 • gay-friendly •
inn & cabins • kids/ pets ok in cabins • $80-
130

Quiet Creek Inn & Vacation Rentals
26345 Delano Dr (at Toll Gate Rd)
951/659-6110, 800/450-6110 • gay-friendly •
vacation rentals • pets ok in certain cabins •
WiFi • nonsmoking • $117-500

The Rainbow Inn 54420 S Circle Dr
951/659-0111 • gay/ straight • full brkfst • kids
ok • nonsmoking • patio • fireplaces • WiFi •
also conference center • gay-owned • $105-
145+ tax

Strawberry Creek Inn B&B 26370 Hwy 243
(at S Cir Dr) 951/659-3202, 800/262-8969 •
gay-friendly • relaxing getaway w/ sundeck,
garden & hammocks • nonsmoking •
wheelchair access • gay-owned • $130-240

RESTAURANTS

Cafe Aroma 54750 North Circle
951/659-5212 • 7am-10pm • great ambience
& food • live music most nights

Irvine

see Orange County

Joshua Tree

ACCOMMODATIONS

Joshua Tree Highlands Houses
760/366-3636 • gay/ straight • private modern
desert vacation rentals • fully equipped • each
home on 5 acres • near Joshua Tree Nat'l Park
• nonsmoking • kids/ pets ok • WiFi •
wheelchair access • gay-owned • $175-300

Joshua Tree Nat'l Park

includes Twentynine Palms

ACCOMMODATIONS

The Desert Lily PO Box 139, 92252-0800
760/366-4676, 877/887-7370 • gay-friendly •
artist-owned adobe-style B&B on 5 acres •
also self-catering cabins • seasonal (clsd July-
Aug) • woman-owned • $140-155 (B&B) &
$275-525 (cabins)

Desert Wonderland & The Tile House
805/452-4898 • gay/ straight • in high desert
near Joshua Tree Nat'l Park • gay-owned • $95-
700

Moon Way Lodge 760/835-9369 • gay/
straight • WiFi • swimming • nonsmoking •
gay-owned • $120-165

Sacred Sands HC1 Box 1071 A, 63155 Quail
Springs Rd (at Desert Shadows), Joshua Tree
760/424-6407 • gay/ straight • private
outdoor living • spa • nonsmoking • WiFi •
gay-owned • $269-299

Spin & Margie's Desert Hideaway 64491
29 Palms Hwy 760/366-9124 • gay-friendly •
hacienda-style B&B • suites w/ private patios •
cool trading post on-site • $125-160

Starland Retreat Yucca Valley
760/364-2069 • mostly gay men & radical
faeries, but women very welcome •
membership-only rustic rural camp • hot tub •
nudity permitted

RESTAURANTS

The Crossroads Cafe & Tavern 61715 29
Palms Hwy 760/366-5414 • 7am-8pm, till
9pm Fri-Sat, clsd Wed

Kernville

ACCOMMODATIONS

River View Lodge 2 Sirretta St
760/376-6019 • gay/ straight • riverfront resort
• jacuzzi • kids/ pets ok • nonsmoking • gay-
owned • $79-199

La Mirada

RESTAURANTS

Mexico 1900 11531 La Mirada blvd
562/941-2016 • Mexican

Laguna Beach

see Orange County

Lake Tahoe

see also Lake Tahoe, Nevada

ACCOMMODATIONS

Alpine Inn & Spa 920 Stateline Ave (Lake
Ave/ Hwy 50), South Lake Tahoe
530/544-3340, 800/826-8885 • gay/ straight •
motel • just steps from casinos • swimming •
lesbian & gay & straight-owned • $30-45

Black Bear Inn 530/544-4451,
877/232-7466 • gay/ straight • full brkfst • hot
tub • fireplaces • nonsmoking • WiFi • gay-
owned • $200-600

The Cedar House Sport Hotel 10918 Brockway Rd, Truckee 530/582–5655, 866/582–5655 • gay-friendly • full bar • WiFi • kids/ pets ok • $150-295

➤Holly's Place 800/745–7041, 530/544–7040 • gay/ straight • cabins • kitchens • hot tubs • nonsmoking • kids/ dogs ok • WiFi • women-owned • $250-650

Spruce Grove Cabins 3599-3605 Spruce Ave, South Lake Tahoe 530/544–0549, 800/777–0914 • gay-friendly • full kitchens • near Heavenly Ski Resort • hot tub • dog-friendly • nonsmoking • $159-205

Tahoe Valley Lodge 2241 Lake Tahoe Blvd (at Tahoe Keys Blvd), South Lake Tahoe 530/541–0353, 800/669–7544 • gay-friendly • motel • pool • nonsmoking • WiFi • $125-295

RESTAURANTS

Driftwood Cafe 1001 Heavenly Vlg Way #1A 530/544–6545 • 7am-3pm • homecooking • some veggie • wheelchair access

Passaretti's 1181 Emerald Bay Rd/ Hwy 50, South Lake Tahoe 530/541–3433 • 11am-9pm • Italian • beer/ wine

Livermore

see East Bay

Long Beach

INFO LINES & SERVICES

AA Gay/ Lesbian 2017 E 4th St (at Cherry, at Gay & Lesbian Center) 562/434–4455 • 7pm Mon • lesbians/ gay men

The Gay & Lesbian Center of Greater Long Beach 2017 E 4th St (at Cherry) 562/434–4455 • 9am-9pm, by appt Sat • Lesbian Chat & Women of 40 Plus groups meet Tue • also newsletter

ACCOMMODATIONS

Beachrunners' Inn 231 Kennebec Ave (at Junipero & Broadway) 562/856–0202, 866/221–0001 • gay/ straight • B&B • near beach • hot tub • nonsmoking • $100-135

Dockside Boat & Bed Dock 5, Rainbow Harbor (at Pine Ave Pier) 562/436–3111 • gay-friendly • spend the night on a yacht • views of the Queen Mary • $210-325

Hotel Maya 700 Queensway Dr **562/435-7676** • gay/ straight • luxury boutique resort hotel w/ waterfront Fuego restaurant • pets ok • $139

Turret House B&B 556 Chestnut Ave (at Sixth St) **562/624-1991, 888/488-7738** • gay/ straight • restored Victorian • hot tub • pets ok • gay-owned • $109-135

The Varden Hotel 335 Pacific Ave (at 3rd St) **562/432-8950, 877/382-7336** • gay/ straight • urban boutique hotel • nonsmoking • WiFi • wheelchair access • $109-159

BARS

The Brit 1744 E Broadway (at Cherry) **562/432-9742** • 10am-2am • mostly gay men • neighborhood bar • patio • wheelchair access

The Broadway 1100 E Broadway (at Cerritos) **562/432-3646** • 10am-2am • lesbians/ gay men • neighborhood bar • karaoke Fri-Sat • wheelchair access

Club Broadway 3348 E Broadway (at Redondo) **562/438-7700** • 11am-2am • mostly women • neighborhood bar • videos • wheelchair access • women-owned

The Crest 5935 Cherry Ave (at South) **562/423-6650** • 2pm-2am • mostly gay men • leather

The Falcon 1435 E Broadway (at Falcon) **562/432-4146** • 7am-2am • mostly gay men but women very welcome • neighborhood bar • wheelchair access

Flux 17817 Lakewood Blvd (at Artesia), Bellflower **562/633-6394** • noon-2am • lesbians/ gay men • neighborhood bar • patio • theme nights

Liquid Lounge 3522 E Anaheim St **562/494-7564** • gay/ straight • neighborhood bar • food served • karaoke Fri-Sat • live music • patio • gay-owned

Long Beach

WHERE THE GIRLS ARE:
Schmoozing with the boys on Broadway between Atlantic and Cherry Avenues, or elsewhere between Pacific Coast Hwy and the beach. Or at home snuggling.

LGBT PRIDE:
3rd wknd in May. 562/987-9191, web: www.longbeachpride.com.

ANNUAL EVENTS:
June - AIDS Walk, web: www.aidswalklb.org.
Aug - Long Beach Jazz Festival, web: www.longbeachjazzfestival.com.
October - Out Loud LGBT art & film festival, web: www.centerlb.org.

CITY INFO:
800/452-7829, web: www.visitlong-beach.com.

WEATHER:
Quite temperate: highs in the mid-80°s July through September, and cooling down at night. In the winter, January to March, highs are in the upper 60°s, and lows in the upper 40°s.

TRANSIT:
Long Beach Taxi Co-op 562/435-6111.
Long Beach Transit & Runabout (free downtown shuttle) 562/591-2301. web: www.lbtransit.com.

ATTRACTIONS:
Belmont Shores area on 2nd St, south of Pacific Coast Highway— lots of restaurants & shopping, only blocks from the beach.
Long Beach Downtown Marketplace, 10am-4pm Fri.
The Queen Mary 562/435-3511, web: www.queenmary.com.
"Planet Ocean" mural at 300 E Ocean Blvd.

BEST VIEW:
On the deck of the Queen Mary, docked overlooking most of Long Beach. Or Signal Hill, off 405. Take the Cherry exit.

Mineshaft 1720 E Broadway (btwn Gaviota & Hermosa) **562/436-2433** • 10am-2am • popular • mostly gay men • bears

Paradise Piano Bar & Restaurant 1800 E Broadway Blvd (at Hermosa) **562/590-8773** • 3pm-1am, from 10am Sat-Sun • lesbians/ gay men • piano bar w/ restaurant

Pistons 2020 E Artesia (at Cherry) **562/422-1928** • 6pm-2am, till 3am Fri-Sat, from 3pm Sun, till midnight Mon • mostly gay men • bears • leather • patio

Que Será 1923 E 7th St (at Cherry) **562/599-6170** • 9pm-2am Tue, from 5pm Wed-Sat, from 3pm Sun, clsd Mon • gay/ straight • dancing/DJ • alternative • live music • cover after 9pm

Silver Fox 411 Redondo (at 4th) **562/439-6343** • 4pm-2am, from noon wknds • popular happy hour • mostly gay men • karaoke Wed & Sun • videos • wheelchair access

Sweetwater Saloon 1201 E Broadway (at Orange) **562/432-7044** • 6am-2am • popular days • mostly gay men • neighborhood bar • wheelchair access

NIGHTCLUBS

The Basement Lounge 149 Linden Ave (at E Broadway) **562/901-9090** • gay/ straight • dancing/DJ • live shows • also restaurant

Club Flaunt 3428 E Pacific Coast Hwy (at Redondo) **714/307-2643** • 8pm-2am 3rd Sat only • mostly women • dancing/DJ • live music

Club Ripples 5101 E Ocean (at Granada) **562/433-0357** • noon-2am • popular • mostly gay men • more women Fri for Debra's @ the Beach • dancing/DJ • theme nights • T-dance Sun • multiracial • food served • karaoke • videos • young crowd • patio

Debra's @ the Beach 5101 E Ocean (at Granada, at Ripples) **562/433-0357** • 7pm-2am Fri only • popular • mostly women • dancing/DJ • multiracial • food served • videos • live entertainment • karaoke • go-go girls • patio

Executive Suite 3428 E Pacific Coast Hwy (at Redondo) **562/597-3884, 310/547-4730** • 8pm-close Th-Sat • popular • lesbians/ gay men • dancing/DJ • Latin night Th • women's night Sat • 2 levels • wheelchair access

CAFES

Hot Java 2101 E Broadway Ave **562/433-0688** • 6am-11pm, till midnight Fri-Sat • also soups, sandwiches, salads • WiFi

iCandy Coffee 1708 E Broadway (at Gaviota) **562/437-3785** • 7am-10pm, till midnight wknds • mostly gay men • also sandwiches & desserts • WiFi

The Library 3418 E Broadway **562/433-2393** • 6am-midnight, till 1am Fri-Sat, from 7am wknds

RESTAURANTS

212 Degrees Bistro 2708 E 4th St **562/439-8822** • 8am-2pm Th-Sun only • Mexican-inspired

Cafe Sevilla 140 Pine St **562/495-1111** • dinner only, Sun brunch • Spanish • also music & dancing

Frenchy's Bistro 5137 E Anaheim St (at N Roswell Ave) **562/494-8787** • dinner nightly, lunch Fri only, clsd Mon

Hamburger Mary's 740 E Broadway (at Alamitos) **562/436-7900** • 11am-2am • lesbians/gay men • full bar • dancing/DJ • theme nights

Omelette Inn 318 Pine Ave **562/437-5625** • 7am-2:30pm

Open Sesame 5215 E 2nd St **562/621-1698** • lunch & dinner • Middle Eastern

Original Park Pantry 2104 E Broadway (at Junipero) **562/434-0451** • 6am-10pm, till 11pm Fri-Sat • int'l • some veggie • wheelchair access

The Raven's Nest 2941 E Broadway (btwn Temple & Redondo) **562/439-3672** • dinner only • Cuban • wheelchair access

Two Umbrellas Cafe 1538 E Broadway (at Gaviota Ave) **562/495-2323** • 8am-2pm • gay-owned

Utopia 445 E 1st St **562/432-6888** • dinner nightly, clsd Sun • seafood, California cuisine • plenty veggie

BOOKSTORES

Open 2226 E 4th St (btwn Cherry & Junipero, in heart of Retro Row) **562/499-6736** • 11am-7pm, till 8pm Sat, till 6pm Sun, clsd Mon • general • also films, art & events

RETAIL SHOPS

Hot Stuff 2121 E Broadway (at Junipero) **562/433-0692** • 11am-7pm, 10am-6pm Sat, noon-5pm Sun • cards • gifts • adult novelties • serving community since 1980 • gay- & lesbian-owned

So Cal Tattoo 339 W 6th St, San Pedro **310/519-8282** • woman-owned tattoo & piercing shop • reservations recommended

EROTICA

The Crypt on Broadway 1712 E Broadway (btwn Cherry & Falcon) 562/983–6560 • 10am-midnight • leather • toys

The RubberTree 5018 E 2nd St (at Granada) 562/434–0027 • 11am-9pm, till 10pm Fri-Sat, noon-7pm Sun • gifts for lovers • women-owned

LOS ANGELES

Los Angeles is divided into 8 geographical areas:
LA—Overview
LA—West Hollywood
LA—Hollywood
LA—West LA & Santa Monica
LA—Silverlake
LA—Midtown
LA—Valley
LA—East LA & South Central

LA—Overview

INFO LINES & SERVICES

Alcoholics Anonymous 323/936–4343 & 735–2089 (EN ESPAÑOL), 800/923–8722 • call or check web (www.lacoaa.org) for meetings

Crystal Meth Anonymous 213/488–4455 • call or check website (www.crystalmeth.org) for meetings in LA County

LA Gay & Lesbian Center 1625 N Schrader Blvd (McDonald/Wright Building) 323/993–7400 • 9am-9pm, till 1pm Sat, clsd Sun • wide variety of services

LA Gay & Lesbian Center's Village at Ed Gould Plaza 1125 N McCadden Pl (at Santa Monica) 323/860–7302 • 6pm-10pm, 9am-5pm Sat, clsd Sun • cybercenter • cafe • theaters

NIGHTCLUBS

Ladies Touch • mostly women • hip hop dance parties • mostly African American • check www.myspace.com/touchgirlent for info

ENTERTAINMENT & RECREATION

The Celebration Theatre 7051 Santa Monica Blvd (at La Brea) 323/957–1884 • LGBT theater • call for more info

The Ellen DeGeneres Show • you know you want to dance w/ Ellen! • check out ellen.warnerbros.com for tickets

The Gay Mafia Comedy Group • lesbians/ gay men • improv/ sketch comedy • gay-owned

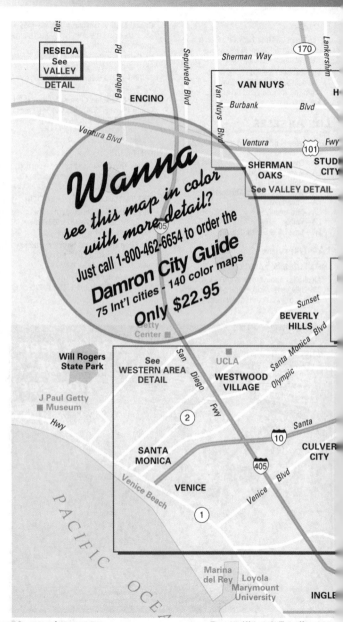

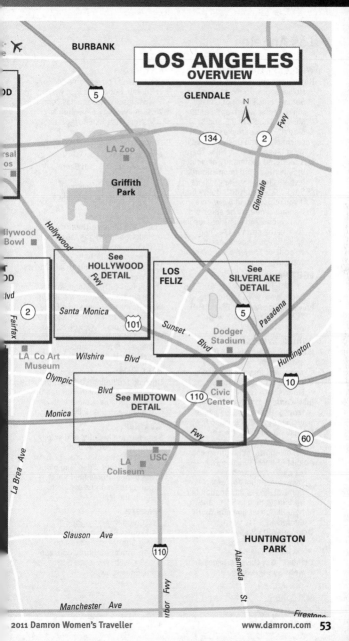

LOS ANGELES
OVERVIEW

BURBANK

GLENDALE

LA Zoo

Griffith Park

See HOLLYWOOD DETAIL

LOS FELIZ

See SILVERLAKE DETAIL

Dodger Stadium

Santa Monica

Sunset

Blvd

Pasadena

Huntington

Glendale Fwy

Hollywood Fwy

LA Co Art Museum

Wilshire Blvd

Olympic

Blvd

See MIDTOWN DETAIL

Civic Center

Monica

Fwy

LA Coliseum

USC

La Brea Ave

Fairfax

Slauson Ave

HUNTINGTON PARK

Manchester Ave

Alameda St

rbor Fwy

Firestone

Los Angeles

Where the Girls Are:

Hip dykes hang out in West Hollywood, with the boys along Santa Monica Blvd, or cruising funky Venice Beach and Santa Monica. The S&M ("Stand & Model") glamourdykes pose in chichi clubs and posh eateries in West LA and Beverly Hills. There's a scattered community of women in Silverlake. And more suburban lesbians frequent the gay bars in Studio City and North Hollywood. If you're used to makeup-free lesbians, you may be surprised that coiffed and lipsticked lesbian style is the norm in LA. Then again, if you've ever seen an episode of *The L Word*, how could you be?!

LGBT Pride:

June. Christopher St West 323/969-8302, web: www.lapride.org.
June-July. Los Angeles Black LGBT Pride 323/293-4285, web: www.atbla.com.

Annual Events:

June - AIDS LifeCycle 866/BIKE-4AIDS, web: www.aidslifecycle.org. AIDS benefit bike ride from San Francisco to LA.
July - Outfest 213/480-7088, web: www.outfest.org. Los Angeles' lesbian/ gay film & video festival.
August - Centre Court, web: www.lataweb.com. LA Tennis Association's int'l tournament.
August - Sunset Junction Fair 323/661-7771, web: www.sunsetjunction.org. Carnival, arts & information fair on Sunset Blvd in Silverlake to benefit Sunset Junction Youth Center.
October - AIDS Walk-a-thon 213/201-9255, web: www.aidswalk.net.
October - Gay Days at Disneyland, web: www.gayday2.com.

City Info:

Los Angeles Convention & Visitors Bureau, 800/228-2452, web: www.discoverlosangeles.com.
West Hollywood Convention & Visitors Bureau, 800/368-6020, web: www.visitwesthollywood.com.

Attractions:

3rd St outdoor mall in Santa Monica.
Chinatown, near downtown.
City Walk in Universal Studios.
The Getty Center 310/440-7300, web: www.getty.edu.
Grauman's Chinese Theatre on Hollywood Blvd 323/464-8111.
Griffith Observatory 213/473-0800, web: www.griffithobs.org.
Melrose Ave, hip commercial district in West Hollywood.
Theme Parks: Disneyland, Knotts Berry Farm, or Magic Mountain.
Watts Towers (Simon Rodia State Historical Park), 1765 E 107th St (not far from LAX), 213/847-4646.
Westwood Village premiere movie theaters & restaurants.
Venice Beach.

Best View:

Drive up Mulholland Drive, in the hills between Hollywood and the Valley, for a panoramic view of the city, and the Hollywood sign.

Weather:

Summers are hot, dry, and smoggy with temperatures in the 80°s-90°s. LA's weather is at its finest — sunny, blue skies, and moderate temperatures (mid 70°s) — during the months of March, April, and May.

Transit:

Taxi Co-op 877/733-3305.
LA Express 800/427-7483.
Super Shuttle 310/782-6600.
Metro Transit Authority 800/266-6883, web: www.mta.net. Includes subway.

The Getty Center 1200 Getty Center Dr, Brentwood 310/440-7300 • 10am-6pm, till 9pm Fri-Sat, clsd Mon • LA's shining city on a hill & world-class museum • of course, it's still in LA so you'll need to make reservations for parking (!)

Griffith Observatory enter on N Vermont St (in Griffith Park) 213/473-0800 • noon-10pm, from 10am wknds, clsd Mon

Highways 1651 18th St (at the 18th Street Arts Center), Santa Monica 310/315-1459 (RESERVATION LINE) • "full-service performance center"

IMRU Gay Radio KPFK LA 90.7 FM • 7pm Mon

LA Sparks 877/447-7275 (LA AREA ONLY), 310/426-6033 • check out the Women's Nat'l Basketball Association while you're in Los Angeles

Moonlight Rollerway Gay Skate 5110 San Fernando Rd (N of W Colorado St, near LA Zoo), Glendale 818/241-3630 • 8pm Wed only • lesbians/ gay men

Outfest 213/480-7088 • LGBT media arts foundation that sponsors the annual LGBT film festival each July • also screens LGBT films Wed at the Egyptian Theater in Hollywood • see listing in Film Festival Calendar

Purple Circuit Hotline 818/953-5072 • LGBT theater listings

Vox Femina 310/922-0025 • women's chorus

Women on a Roll 310/578-8888 • "largest lesbian organization in California" • offering sporting, cultural & social events, as well as worldwide travel, for women

PUBLICATIONS

Adelante Magazine 323/256-6639 • bilingual LGBT magazine

➤ Essential Gay & Lesbian Directory 310/841-2800, 866/718-GAYS • business directory serving the LGBT community

Frontiers Yellow Pages 323/930-3220 • annual survival guide to LGBT Southern CA & Bay Area

Gorgeous Magazine 323/436-7546 • bi-monthly

➤ Lesbian News (LN) 310/548-9888, 800/458-9888 • nat'l w/ strong coverage of Southern CA • see ad front color section

Odyssey Magazine 323/874-8788 • dish on LA's club scene

LA—West Hollywood

ACCOMMODATIONS

Chamberlain 1000 Westmount Dr (near Holloway) 310/657-7400, 800/201-9652 • gay/ straight • boutique hotel • fitness center • rooftop pool • bistro restaurant & lounge

The Elan Hotel Los Angeles 8435 Beverly Blvd (at Croft) 323/658-6663, 888/611-0398 • gay/ straight • hip & trendy • kids ok • wheelchair access • gay-owned • $185-325

The Grafton on Sunset 8462 W Sunset Blvd (at La Cienega) 323/654-4600, 800/821-3660 • gay/ straight • pool • sundeck • panoramic views • located in heart of Sunset Strip • wheelchair access

The Grove Guesthouse 323/876-7778, 888/524-7683 • lesbians/ gay men • 1-bdrm villa • hot tub • pool • kitchens • WiFi • pets ok by arrangement • gay-owned • $209+

Holloway Motel 8465 Santa Monica Blvd (at La Cienega) 323/654-2454, 888/654-6400 • gay/ straight • kitchens • nonsmoking • centrally located • $85-165

Hotel Le Petit 8822 Cynthia St (at Larrabee) 310/854-1114, 800/835-7997 • gay-friendly • all-suite hotel • hot tub • pool • kids ok • wheelchair access • $139-265

Hyatt West Hollywood 8401 Sunset Blvd (at Kings Rd) 323/656-1234, 800/233-1234 • gay/ straight • on the Sunset Strip • rooftop pool • nonsmoking • WiFi • wheelchair access • $99-299

Le Parc Suite Hotel 733 N West Knoll Dr (at Melrose) 310/855-8888, 800/578-4837 • popular • gay-friendly • deluxe-class all-suite hotel • pool • tennis courts • kids/ pets ok • also restaurant • wheelchair access • $300-400 (corp rates from $179)

The London West Hollywood 1020 N San Vicente Blvd 866/282-4560 • gay-friendly • luxury hotel • pool • WiFi • also Gordon Ramsay's restaurant

Mondrian 8440 Sunset Blvd 323/650-8999, 800/697-1791 • gay-friendly • home of trendy Skybar & Asia de Cuba restaurant • $185-425

Ramada Plaza Hotel—West Hollywood 8585 Santa Monica Blvd (at La Cienega) 310/652-6400, 800/845-8585 • gay-friendly • modern art deco hotel & suites • pool & poolside WiFi • kids ok • wheelchair access • $109-275

Sunset Marquis Hotel & Villas 1200 Alta Loma Rd (1/2 block S of Sunset Blvd) 310/657-1333, 800/858-9758 • gay/ straight • full brkfst • sauna • hot tub • pool • WiFi • kids ok • wheelchair access • $330-3,000

BARS

Comedy Store 8433 Sunset Blvd (at La Cienega) 323/650-6268 • 8pm-2am • gay-friendly • legendary stand-up club

East/ West Lounge 8851 Santa Monica Blvd (at San Vicente) 310/360-6186, 877/395-6864 • 4:30pm-2am • clsd Mon • popular • gay/ straight • très hip lounge that blends the best of both East & West Coasts • karaoke Tue

Fiesta Cantina 8865 Santa Monica Blvd (at San Vicente) 310/652-8865 • noon-2am • lesbians/ gay men • raucous Mexican restaurant & bar

Fuse 8811 Santa Monica (at Larrabee, at Eleven Nightcllub) • Th only • popular • mostly women • dancing/DJ • dress code • check fuse-events.com for other weekly events

Here Lounge 696 N Robertson Blvd (at Santa Monica) 310/360-8455 • 4pm-2am • lesbians/ gay men • more women Th for Fuse event & Fri for Truck Stop • swanky & stylish • DJ nightly

Improvisation 8162 Melrose Ave (at Crescent Heights) 323/651-2583 • gay-friendly • stand-up comedy • also restaurant

Micky's 8857 Santa Monica Blvd (at San Vicente) 310/657-1176 • noon-2am, after-hours wknds • mostly gay men • dancing/DJ • videos • younger crowd • food served • patio • gay-owned

The Palms on Las Olas 8572 Santa Monica Blvd (at La Cienega) 310/652-1595 • 8pm-2am, from 4pm wknds, after-hours Fri-Sat • popular • mostly women • multiracial • neighborhood bar • dancing/DJ • theme nights • karaoke Mon • alternative Tue • go-go dancers Wed & Fri-Sun • beer bust Sun • patio • wheelchair access • cover some nights

Platinum 8851 Santa Monica Blvd (at San Vicente, at East West) 310/360-6186, 877/395-6864 • 9pm Th only • mostly women • hip lounge

Viper Room 8852 Sunset Blvd (btwn San Vicente & Larrabee) 310/358-1881, 310/358-1881 (TICKETING) • doors open btwn 7pm-8pm nightly • gay-friendly • dancing/DJ • live bands • cover charge

NIGHTCLUBS

Area 643 N La Cienega Blvd 310/652-2012 • 10pm-2am Th-Sat • gay-friendly • dancing/DJ

Eleven Restaurant & Nightclub 8811 Santa Monica Blvd (at Larrabee St) 310/855-0800 • lunch & dinner • more gay for the bar atmosphere till 2am

The Factory 652 N La Peer Dr (at Santa Monica) 310/659-4551 • 9pm-2am Fri-Sat • mostly gay men • dancing/DJ • videos

Girl Bar 661 N Robertson Blvd (at Santa Monica, at Ultra Suede) 310/659-4551, 877/447-5252 • popular • 9pm-2:30am Fri only • women only • dancing/DJ

Jet Setter 7321 Santa Monica Blvd (at Fuller, at Crown Bar) • 9pm Th only • mostly women • dancing/DJ

Rage 8911 Santa Monica Blvd (at San Vicente) 310/652-7055 • noon-2am, lunch Tue-Sun, dinner nightly • popular • mostly gay men • dancing/DJ • live shows • videos • 18+ wknds • wheelchair access

The Ruby 7070 Hollywood Blvd (at Sycamore) 323/467-7070 • 10pm-3am • gay-friendly • dancing/DJ • theme nights: including '70s & '80s night, hip-hop, goth, electronica, house • 18+ • patio • cover charge

Ultra Suede 661 N Robertson Blvd (at Santa Monica) 310/659-4551 • 10pm-2am Wed-Sat • gay/ straight • dancing/DJ • theme nights • women only Fri for GirlBar

CAFES

Cafe Marco 1051 N Havenhurst Dr 323/650-7742 • 6:30am-10pm • coffeehouse • WiFi • occasional live music

Champagne French Bakery & Cafe 8917-9 Santa Monica Blvd 310/657-4051 • 6:30am-9pm, till 11pm Fri-Sat • coffees & pastries as well as brkfst, lunch & dinner • some outdoor seating

Mäni's Bakery 519 S Fairfax Ave (at Maryland Dr) 323/938-8800 • 7:30am-10pm, till 11pm Sat • plenty vegan & wheat-, sugar- & dairy-free • wheelchair access

Urth Caffe 8565 Melrose Ave (btwn Robertson & La Cienega) 310/659-0628 • 6:30am-midnight • organic coffees, teas & treats • food served • plenty veggie & vegan • patio

RESTAURANTS

The Abbey 692 N Robertson Blvd (at Santa Monica) 310/289-8410 • 8am-2am • lesbians/ gay men • popular • American/ cont'l • full bar • patio • wheelchair access

AOC 8022 W Third St (at Crescent Heights Blvd) 323/653-6359 • dinner nightly • wine bar • eclectic • upscale

Basix Cafe 8333 Santa Monica Blvd (at Flores) 323/848–2460 • 7am-11pm • outdoor seating

Bossa Nova 685 N Robertson Blvd (at Santa Monica) 310/657–5070 • 11am-midnight • Brazilian • beer/ wine • patio • wheelchair access

Cafe La Boheme 8400 Santa Monica Blvd (btwn Benecia Ave & Fox Hills Dr) 323/848–2360 • 5pm-10pm Fri-Sat, till 11pm Sun-Th • American eclectic/ California • full bar • patio w/ fireplace • wheelchair access

Canter's Deli 419 N Fairfax (btwn Melrose & Beverly) 323/651–2030 • 24hrs • hip after-hours • Jewish/ American • some veggie • full bar • wheelchair access

Eat-Well 8252 Santa Monica Blvd (at La Jolla) 323/656–1383 • 7am-9.30pm, 8am-3pm wknds • popular • comfort food diner

Falcon 7213 Sunset Blvd (btwn Poinsettia & Formosa) 323/850–5350 • dinner • gay/ straight • California/ cont'l fusion • full bar & lounge • hosts Rusty's Tue (lesbians/ gay men)

Fogo de Chao 133 N La Cienega Blvd, Beverly Hills 310/289–7755 • lunch Mon-Fri, dinner nightly • Brazilian churrascaria

Hamburger Mary's Bar & Grill 8288 Santa Monica Blvd 323/654–3800 • 11am-1am, till 2am Fri-Sat • lesbians/ gay men • full bar • transgender-friendly • ladies night Mon • theme nights • karaoke • drag shows

Hedley's 640 N Robertson Blvd 310/659–2009 • lunch & dinner, also wknd brunch, clsd Sun night & Mon

Il Piccolino Trattoria 350 N Robertson Blvd (btwn Melrose & Beverly) 310/659–2220 • lunch & dinner, clsd Sun • full bar • patio • wheelchair access

Joey's Cafe 8301 Santa Monica Blvd 323/822–0671 • 8am-10pm • a little bit coffeehouse, a little bit diner • popular at lunch

Kokomo Cafe 7385 Beverly Blvd (between La Brea Ave & Fairfax Ave) 323/933–0773 • 8am-4pm • diner • wheelchair access

Koo Koo Roo 8520 Santa Monica Blvd (at La Cienega Blvd) 310/657–3300 • 11am-11pm, till 10pm Sun • lots of healthy chicken dishes • plenty veggie • beer/ wine • wheelchair access

Lola's 945 N Fairfax Ave (at Santa Monica) 323/654–5652 • 5:30pm-2am

Louise's Trattoria 7505 Melrose Ave (at Gardner) 323/651–3880 • 11am-10pm • Italian • great foccacia bread • beer/ wine • patio

Lucques 8474 Melrose Ave (at La Cienega) 323/655–6277 • lunch Tue-Sat, dinner nightly • French • full bar • patio • wheelchair access

Marix Tex Mex 1108 N Flores (btwn La Cienega & Fairfax) 323/656–8800 • 11:30am-11pm, from 11am wknds • lesbians/ gay men • some veggie • great margaritas • patio • wheelchair access

Mexico Restaurant y Barra 8512 Santa Monica Blvd (at La Cienega) 310/289–0088 • 5pm-midnight, till 1:30am wknds, Mexican

Nyala 1076 S Fairfax (at Whitworth Dr) 323/936–5918 • many Ethiopian, Nigerian & other African restaurants to choose from on this block • Damron recommends Nyala, 1076 S Fairfax Ave, 323/936–5918

O-Bar 8279 Santa Monica Blvd (at Sweetzer) 323/822–3300 • 6pm-2am • gay/ straight • full bar

Real Food Daily 414 N La Cienega (btwn Beverly & Melrose) 310/289–9910 • 11:30am-10pm, till 11pm Fri-Sat, Sun brunch 10am-3pm • organic vegan • beer/ wine • patio • wheelchair access

Sante Libre 345 N La Brea (btwn Melrose & Beverly) 323/857–0412 • 9am-10pm • pastas, salads & wraps • plenty veggie & vegan • cheap

St Felix 8945 Santa Monica Blvd (at Hilldale) 310/275–4428 • 4pm-2am • small plates

Tango Grill 8807 Santa Monica Blvd (at San Vicente) 310/659–3663 • 11:30am-11:30pm • lesbians/ gay men • Argentinian • some veggie • beer/ wine • wheelchair access

Tart 115 S Fairfax Ave 323/556–2608, 800/334–1658 • 7am-midnight • Southern

Taste 8454 Melrose Ave (at La Cienega) 323/852–6888 • lunch & dinner, wknd brunch • upscale eclectic • full bar

BOOKSTORES

Book Soup 8818 W Sunset Blvd (at Larrabee) 310/659–3110, 800/764–2665 • 9am-10pm, till 7pm Sun • LGBT section

RETAIL SHOPS

665 Leather 8722 Santa Monica Blvd (at Huntley Dr) 310/854–7276 • noon-8pm, till 10pm Fri-Sat • custom leather & neoprene • also accessories & toys

Marginalized Tattoo 4228 Melrose Ave (at Vermont) **213/422-4801** • featuring Dave Davenport (aka "Dogspunk"), named best gay tattoo artist by *Frontiers* magazine

GYMS & HEALTH CLUBS

The Easton Gym 8053 Beverly Blvd (at Crescent Hts) **323/651-3636** • gay-friendly

The Fitness Factory 650 N La Peer Dr (at Santa Monica) **310/358-1838** • 6am-9pm, till 8pm Fri, 7am-5pm Sat, 8am-1pm Sun

EROTICA

Circus of Books 8230 Santa Monica Blvd (at La Jolla) **323/656-6533** • 6am-2am

Hustler Hollywood 8920 Sunset Blvd (at San Vicente) **310/860-9009** • 10am-2am • chic erotic department store • also cafe

Pleasure Chest 7733 Santa Monica Blvd (at Genesee), N Hollywood **323/650-1022** • 10am-midnight, till 1am Th-Sat

LA—Hollywood

ACCOMMODATIONS

Holiday Inn Hollywood 2005 N Highland (at Franklin) **323/876-8600, 866/696-3157** • gay-friendly • also restaurant & lounge • pool • jacuzzi • kids ok • WiFi • wheelchair access

Hollywood Hotel – The Hotel of Hollywood 1160 N Vermont Ave (at Santa Monica) **323/315-1800, 800/800-9733** • gay-friendly • full brkfst • pool • nonsmoking • WiFi • wheelchair access • $90-135

Hollywood Metropolitan Hotel 5825 Sunset Blvd (btwn Bronson & Van Ness) **323/962-5800, 800/962-5800** • gay-friendly • kids ok • nonsmoking • wheelchair access • also restaurant • $79-145

BARS

Boardner's 1652 N Cherokee Ave **323/462-9621** • 4pm-2am • gay/ straight • "a Hollywood legend & best-kept secret since 1942" • dancing/DJ • food served • karaoke

Faultline 4216 Melrose Ave (at Vermont) **323/660-0889** • 5pm-2am, from 2pm wknds, clsd Mon-Tue • popular • mostly gay men • cruisy • leather • bears • videos • patio

NIGHTCLUBS

Arena/ Circus Disco 6655 Santa Monica Blvd (at Seward, Circus behind Arena) **323/462-1291** • 9pm-2am Tue-Wed & Fri-Sat • popular • gay men • dancing/DJ • theme nights • multiracial • strippers

Avalon 1735 Vine St (at Hollywood Blvd) **323/462-8900** • gay/ straight • one of LA's best dance music clubs • call for events

Booby Trap 5100 Fountain (at Normandie, at Temporary Spaces) • 10pm Wed only • mostly women • cute girls • dive bar

Cinespace 6356 Hollywood Blvd (at Ivar Ave, 2nd flr) **323/817-3456** • 6pm-2am Th-Sat only • gay/ straight • theme nights • "Dinner & a Movie" 8pm Sat • reservations recommended

Dream 6608 Hollywood Blvd (at Whitley Ave, at Kress bar) • 4th Th only • monthly women's dance party

Miss Kitty's 6510 Santa Monica Blvd (at Wilcox, at Dragonfly) • monthly • gay/ straight • fetish/ goth/ rock 'n' roll dance club w/ electro cabaret • cover

Mr Black LA 1737 N Vine St (at Hollywood Blvd, at Bardot) **323/462-8900** • Tue only • lesbians/ gay men • dancing/DJ

Push Party 1006 Seward St (at Santa Monica, at Hollywood Canteen) • 9pm-2am every other Sat • mostly women • dancing/DJ • multiracial • hip hop, electro, reggae

TigerHeat 1735 Vine St (N of Hollywood Blvd, at Avalon nightclub) **323/462-1291** • 9:30pm-3am Th only • gay/ straight • dancing/DJ • transgender-friendly • live shows • videos • 18+ • cover charge

RESTAURANTS

Hollywood Canteen 1006 N Seward St (at Santa Monica) **323/465-0961** • 5pm-11pm, till 2am Th, 6pm-2am Fri-Sat, clsd Sun • popular • classic • full bar

La Poubelle 5907 Franklin Ave (at Bronson) **323/465-0807** • 5:30pm-midnight • French/ Italian • some veggie • full bar • wheelchair access

Lucy's Cafe El Adobe 5536 Melrose Ave (near Gower St) **323/462-9421** • 11:30am-11pm, clsd Sun • Mexican • patio

Musso & Frank Grill 6667 Hollywood Blvd (near Las Palmas) **323/467-5123** • 11am-11pm, clsd Sun-Mon • the grand-dame diner/ steak house of Hollywood • great pancakes, potpies & martinis!

Off Vine 6263 Leland Wy (at Vine) **323/962-1900** • lunch & dinner, wknd brunch • beer/ wine

Prado 244 N Larchmont Blvd (at Beverly) **323/467-3871** • lunch & dinner, dinner only Sun • Caribbean • some veggie • wheelchair access

Quality 8030 W 3rd St (at Laurel) **323/658–5959** • 8am-3:30pm • homestyle brkfst • some veggie • wheelchair access

Rockwell VT 1714 N Vermont Ave (at Prospect (enter in alley) **323/669–1550** • 5pm-2am, brunch wknds • gay night Fri

Roscoe's House of Chicken & Waffles 1514 N Gower (at Sunset) **323/466–7453** • 8:30am-midnight, till 4am Fri Sat

Sushi Hiroba 776 N Vine St **323/962–7237** • lunch Mon-Fri, dinner nightly

BOOKSTORES

Skylight Books 1818 N Vermont Ave (at Melbourne Ave) **323/660–1175** • 10am-10pm • way cool independent in Los Feliz • great fiction & alt-lit sections

RETAIL SHOPS

Panpipes Magickal Marketplace 1641 N Cahuenga Blvd **323/462–7078** • noon-7pm, till 9pm Wed & Sat, clsd Mon • "nation's oldest occult store" w/ custom spells & classes

Y-Que Trading Post 1770 N Vermont Ave **323/664–0021** • noon-8pm • kitsch boutique that's home to the "Free Wynona" & "Free Martha" T-shirts

GYMS & HEALTH CLUBS

Gold's Gym 1016 N Cole Ave (near Santa Monica & Vine) **323/462–7012** • 5am-midnight, 7am-9pm Sat-Sun • gay-friendly

LA—West LA & Santa Monica

ACCOMMODATIONS

Casa Malibu 22752 Pacific Coast Hwy, Malibu **310/456–2219** • gay-friendly • on the beach • WiFi • $179-529

The Georgian Hotel 1415 Ocean Ave (btwn Santa Monica & Broadway), Santa Monica **310/395–9945, 800/538–8147** • gay-friendly • food served • wheelchair access • $195+

Hotel Angeleno 170 N Church Ln (at Hwy 405) **310/476–6411, 866/264–3536** • gay/ straight • boutique hotel w/ landmark circular shape • pool • gym • nonsmoking • WiFi • $199+

Hotel Erwin 1697 Pacific Ave (at Venice Way), Venice Beach **310/452–1111, 800/786–7789** • gay/ straight • rooftop lounge and restaurant • gym • nonsmoking • WiFi • $169+

Hotel Palomar 10740 Wilshire Blvd (at Selby Ave) **310/475–8711, 800/475–8711** • gay/ straight • pool • wheelchair access • $259-2,500

The Inn at Venice Beach 327 Washington Blvd (at Via Dolce), Marina Del Rey **310/821–2557, 800/828–0688** • gay-friendly • 43-room European-style inn • kids ok • WiFi • wheelchair access • $99-159

The Linnington 310/422–8825 • lesbians/ gay men • B&B • jacuzzi • kids ok • lesbian-owned • $95

W Los Angeles 930 Hilgard Ave (at Le Conte) **310/208–8765, 800/421–2317** • gay-friendly • suites • also restaurant • gym • day spa • pool • $219-379

BARS

The Dolphin 1995 Artesia Blvd (at Green Ln), Redondo Beach **310/318–3339** • 7pm-2am, more women Mon • lesbians/ gay men • neighborhood bar • dancing/DJ Fri-Sat • karaoke Sun, Tue & Th • patio • wheelchair access

CAFES

The Novel Cafe 212 Pier Ave, Santa Monica **310/396–8566** • 7am-1am, from 8am Sat, 8am-midnight Sun • coffeehouse that doubles as used bookstore

RESTAURANTS

12 Washington 12 Washington Blvd (at Pacific), Marina Del Rey **310/822–5566** • 5pm-10pm, till 11pm Fri-Sun • cont'l

Axe 1009 Abbot Kinney, Venice **310/664–9787** • lunch & dinner, clsd Mon • healthy • plenty veggie

Baja Cantina 311 Washington Blvd (at Sanborn), Venice **310/821–2252** • 10:30am-1am, also brunch wknds • full bar

Border Grill 1445 4th St (at Broadway), Santa Monica **310/451–1655** • lunch & dinner from famous "Two Hot Tamales" chefs

Cantalini's Salerno Beach Restaurant 193 Culver Blvd (at Vista del Mar), Playa del Rey **310/821–0018** • lunch Mon-Fri, dinner nightly • Italian • homemade pastas • beer/ wine • live music Sun nights

Cora's Coffee Shop 1802 Ocean Ave (N of Pico Blvd), Santa Monica **310/451–9562** • 6:30am-3pm, from 7am wknds, clsd Mon • organic

Drago 2628 Wilshire Blvd (btwn 26th & Princeton), Santa Monica **310/828–1585** • lunch Mon-Sat, dinner nightly • Sicilian Italian • wheelchair access

Gjelina 1429 Abbot Kinney Blvd, Venice **310/450–1429** • pizzas & small plates • beer/ wine only

Golden Bull 170 W Channel Rd (at Pacific Coast Hwy), Santa Monica 310/230-0402 • gay/ straight • 4:30pm-10pm, till 11pm wknds, Sun brunch • American • full bar

Hamburger Habit 11223 National Blvd (at Sepulveda) 310/478-5000 • popular • 10am-11pm, till midnight Fri-Sat

Joe's 1023 Abbot Kinney Blvd, Venice 310/399-5811 • lunch Tue-Fri, dinner nightly, wknd brunch, clsd Mon • French/ Californian

Real Food Daily 514 Santa Monica Blvd (btwn 5th & 6th), Santa Monica 310/451-7544 • 11:30am-10pm • organic vegan • beer/ wine • wheelchair access

Wokcano 1413 5th St, Santa Monica 310/458-3080 • 11am-12:30am, till 1:30am Fri-Sat • sushi bar & Chinese cafe

ENTERTAINMENT & RECREATION

Will Rogers State Beach Pacific Coast Hwy (at Temescal Canyon Rd) • gay beach

BOOKSTORES

Diesel, A Bookstore 3890 Cross Creek Rd, Malibu 310/456-9961 • 10am-7pm, till 9pm Fri-Sat, till 6pm Sun • independent

EROTICA

The Love Boutique 2924 Wilshire Blvd (W of Bundy), Santa Monica 310/453-3459 • 11am-7pm, till 9pm Th, noon-6pm Sun • toys, books for women

Pleasure Island 18426 Hawthorne Blvd (btwn Artesia & 190th), Torrance 310/793-9477 • 11am-midnight, till 2am Fri-Sat

LA—Silverlake

ACCOMMODATIONS

Sanborn GuestHouse 1005 1/2 Sanborn Ave (near Sunset) 323/666-3947 • gay/ straight • private unit w/ kitchen • nonsmoking • WiFi • gay-owned • $59-109

Silver Lake Gardens 966 Manzanita St (at Delmar) 323/664-4987 • garden apt/studio • WiFi • gay-owned • $100-150

BARS

4100 Bar 4100 Sunset Blvd (at Manzanita) 323/666-4460 • 8pm-2am • gay/ straight • neighborhood bar

Cha Cha Lounge 2375 Glendale Blvd (at Silverlake) 323/660-7595 • 5pm-2am • gay-friendly • hipster lounge • gay-owned

Club Nur 2810 Hyperion Ave (at Rowena, at MJ's) 323/660-1503 • Th only • lesbians/ gay men • Middle Eastern night • dancing/DJ

Eagle LA 4219 Santa Monica Blvd (at Hoover) 323/669-9472 • 4pm-2am, from 2pm wknds • popular • mostly gay men • leather • wheelchair access

Good Luck Bar 1514 Hillhurst Ave (nr Hollywood Blvd) 323/666-3524 • 7pm-2am, from 8pm wknds • gay-friendly • stylish dive bar

Silverlake Lounge 2906 Sunset Blvd (at Silver Lake Blvd) 323/663-9636 • 3pm-2am • rock 'n' roll club (gay/ straight • live bands) till Fri-Sun when more gay (mostly gay men • Latino/a • drag shows)

NIGHTCLUBS

A Club Called Rhonda 4212 W Sunset Blvd (at Myra, at El Cid club) 213/995-3969 • gay/ straight • monthly party • "house, disco, and polysexual hard partying"

Club Cafe Con Leche 700 S Almansor St (at The Almansor Court), Alhambra 626/282-0330 (CLUB INFO) • 9pm-2am 2nd Fri only • mostly women • dancing/DJ • Latino/a • live bands

The Echo 1822 W Sunset Blvd (at Glendale Blvd) 213/413-8200 • gay/ straight • dancing/DJ • live shows

Full Frontal Disco 943 N Broadway (at W College St, at Grand Star club) 213/626-2285 • last Sat only • gay/ straight • dancing/DJ • transgender-friendy

CAFES

The Coffee Table 2930 Rowena Ave 323/644-8111 • 7am-11pm • patio • fab mosaic magic

RESTAURANTS

Casita Del Campo 1920 Hyperion Ave 323/662-4255 • 11am-midnight, till 2am Fri-Sat • popular • Mexican • patio

Cha Cha Cha 656 N Virgil Ave (at Melrose) 323/664-7723 • lunch & dinner • lesbians/ gay men • Caribbean • plenty veggie • wheelchair access

Cliff's Edge 3626 Sunset Blvd (at Griffith Park Blvd) 323/666-6116 • dinner only, wknd brunch • plenty veggie • romantic • outdoor seating

El Conquistador 3701 W Sunset Blvd (at Lucille) 323/666-5136 • lunch Tue-Sun, dinner nightly • Mexican • beer/ wine • patio

The Flying Leap Cafe 2538 Hyperion Ave (below The Other Side bar) 323/661-0618 • dinner Tue-Sun, Sun brunch • cont'l • full bar • also Mary's Metro Station

The Good Microbrew & Grill 3725 Sunset Blvd (at Lucille) **323/660–3645** • 11am-10pm, till 11pm Fri, 9am-10pm wknds • plenty veggie

Home 1760 Hillhurst Ave, Los Feliz **323/669–0211** • 9am-10pm, patio

The Kitchen 4348 Fountain Ave (at Sunset Blvd) **323/664–3663** • 5pm-1am, from 11am Sat, till 10pm Sun • neighborhood eatery • from veggie entrees to chicken & dumplings • gay-owned

Michelangelo Pizzeria Ristorante 2742 Rowena **323/660–4843** • lunch & dinner

SiLa Bistro 2630 Hyperion Ave (at Griffith Park Blvd) **323/664–7979** • lunch & dinner, clsd Mon • Sun brunch • beer/ wine • patio • gay-owned

Square One Dining 4854 Fountain Ave (at Vermont Ave) **323/661–1109** • 8am-3pm • great brkfst

Vermont Restaurant & Bar 1714 N Vermont Ave **323/661–6163** • lunch Mon- Fri, dnner nightly, clsd Sun • gay-owned

BOOKSTORES

Serifos 3814 W Sunset Blvd **323/660–7467** • independent

RETAIL SHOPS

Syren 2809 1/2 W Sunset Blvd **213/289–0334** • noon-10pm, clsd Mon • leather & latex

GYMS & HEALTH CLUBS

Body Builders 2516 Hyperion Ave (at Tracy) **323/668–0802** • gay-friendly

EROTICA

Romantix Adult Superstore 3147 N San Fernando Rd **323/258–2867** • 24hrs

LA—Midtown

BARS

Cafe Club Fais Do-Do 5257 W Adams Blvd (btwn Fairfax & La Brea) **323/931–4636** • 8pm-2am • gay-friendly • live music • also Cajun restaurant

NIGHTCLUBS

Bordello 901 E 1st St (at S Vignes St) **213/687–3766** • gay-friendly • burlesque shows • also restaurant

The Catwalk 801 W Temple St (at N Figueroa, at Vertigos bar) **213/977–0888** • 1st Fri only • mostly women • dancing/DJ

Coco Bongo 3311 S Main St **213/748-2682** • 9pm-2am, clsd Mon-Tue • lesbians/ gay men • dancing/DJ • Latino/a • drag shows • go-go dancers • 18+

Jewel's Catch One Disco 4067 W Pico Blvd (at Norton) **323/734–8849 (HOTLINE)**, **323/737–1159** • call for hours, clsd Wed-Th • gay/ straight • dancing/DJ • theme nights • wheelchair access

Mustache Mondays 336 S Hill St (at W 4th St, at La Cita bar) **213/687–7111** • 10pm Mon only • lesbians/ gay men • dancing/DJ • transgender-friendly • queer fashionistas

RESTAURANTS

Ciudad 445 S Figueroa St (at 5th St) **213/486–5171** • lunch & dinner & late night cocktails • wheelchair access • owned by celebrity chefs Mary Sue Milliken & Susan Feniger

Opus 3760 Wilshire Blvd (at S Western) **213/738–1600** • lunch & dinner • upscale contemporary • full bar

LA—Valley

includes San Fernando & San Gabriel Valleys

BARS

Cobra 10937 Burbank Blvd (1 block E of Vineland), North Hollywood **818/760–9798** • 4pm-9pm, till 2am Wed-Sun • popular • mostly gay men • dancing/DJ • country/ western (CW dance lessons Sun) • wheelchair access

MoonShadow 10437 Burbank Blvd (2 blocks E of Cahuenga), North Hollywood **818/508–7008** • 3pm-1:30am, from 1pm Fri-Sun • popular • mostly women • neighborhood bar • dancing/DJ • karaoke • live shows • wheelchair access

Oxwood Inn 13713 Oxnard (at Woodman), Van Nuys **818/997–9666 (PAY PHONE)** • 3pm-2am, from 2pm Sat, from 1pm Sun, from 5pm Mon-Tue • mostly women • neighborhood bar • dancing/DJ • karaoke • patio • one of the oldest lesbian bars in US • women-owned

Silver Rail 11518 Burbank Blvd (btwn Colfax & Lankershim) **818/980–8310** • 4pm-2am, from noon wknds • lesbians/ gay men • neighborhood bar

NIGHTCLUBS

C Frenz 7026 Reseda Blvd (at Sherman Way), Reseda **818/996–2976** • 3pm-2am, till 3am Sat • popular • lesbians/ gay men • neighborhood bar • dancing/DJ • multiracial • strippers Wed • karaoke Tue • patio • wheelchair access • gay-owned

CAFES

Aroma 4360 Tujunga Ave, Studio City
818/508–0677 • 6am-11pm, from 7am Sun •
coffeehouse w/ small bookstore

RESTAURANTS

Du-Par's 12036 Ventura Blvd (at Laurel
Canyon), Studio City **818/766–4437** • 24hrs •
plush diner schmoozing • also 75 W Thousand
Oaks Blvd, Thousand Oaks

Gourmet 88 230 N San Fernando Blvd,
Burbank **818/848–8688** • 11:30am-10pm, till
11pm Fri-Sat • Mandarin

GYMS & HEALTH CLUBS

Gold's Gym 6233 N Laurel Canyon Blvd (at
Oxnard), North Hollywood **818/506–4600**

EROTICA

The Love Boutique 18637 Ventura Blvd,
Tarzana **818/342–2400** • 11am-8pm, 10am-
9pm Fri-Sat, noon-6pm Sun • toys, books for
women

LA—East LA & South Central

BARS

Annex 835 S La Brea (at Arbor Vitae),
Inglewood **310/671–7323** • 6pm-2am, from
2pm Fri • mostly gay men • neighborhood bar
• mostly African American • karaoke Mon &
Sat-Sun • wheelchair access

Manhattan Beach

see also LA—West LA & Santa Monica

ACCOMMODATIONS

Sea View Inn at the Beach 3400 Highland
Ave **310/545–1504** • gay-friendly • ocean
views • pool • courtyard • nonsmoking • WiFi
• $130-270

RESTAURANTS

The Local Yolk 3414 Highland Ave (at
Rosecranz) **310/546–4407** • 6:30am-2:30pm •
WiFi • wheelchair access

Marin County

includes Corte Madera, Mill Valley, San
Anselmo, San Rafael, Sausalito, Tiburon

INFO LINES & SERVICES

AA Gay/ Lesbian 415/499-0400 • check
website (www.aasf.org) for meeting times

**Spectrum LGBT Center of the North
Bay** 30 N San Pedro Rd # 160, San Rafael
415/472–1945 • drop-in hours: 11am-5pm
Mon-Fri • wheelchair access

ACCOMMODATIONS

Acqua Hotel 555 Redwood Hwy, Mill Valley
415/380–0400, 888/662–9555 • gay-friendly •
nonsmoking • pets/ kids ok • WiFi •
wheelchair access • $129-199

Casa Madrona Hotel & Spa 801
Bridgeway, Sausalito **415/332–0502,
800/288–0502** • overlooks SF skyline

Larkspur Hotel 160 Shoreline Hwy, Mill
Valley **415/332–5700, 866/823–4669** • gay-
friendly • pool • nonsmoking • $219

The Lodge at Tiburon 1651 Tiburon Blvd,
Tiburon **415/435–3133, 866/823–4669** • gay-
friendly • pool • nonsmoking • kids/ pets ok •
WiFi • also restaurant & bar • $219+

Waters Edge Hotel 25 Main St, Tiburon
415/789–5999, 877/789–5999 • gay/ straight •
boutique hotel • kids ok • nonsmoking • WiFi
• wheelchair access • $169-439

RESTAURANTS

Guaymas 5 Main St (at ferry dock), Tiburon
415/435–6300 • gourmet Mexican • great
views of the Bay

BOOKSTORES

Book Passage 51 Tamal Vista Blvd, Corte
Madera **415/927–0960, 800/999–7909** • 9am-
9pm • beloved independent which draws the
biggest names to read • also cafe • WiFi

The Depot Bookshop & Cafe 87
Throckmorton, Mill Valley **415/383–2665** •
7am-7pm • independent • also cafe w/ patio

RETAIL SHOPS

Cowgirl Creamery 80 4th St (at Tomales
Bay Foods), Pt Reyes Station **415/663–9335** •
10am-6pm Wed-Sun • handmade cheeses •
picnic lunches to go • women-owned

Mendocino

see also Fort Bragg

ACCOMMODATIONS

Agate Cove Inn 11201 N Lansing St
707/937–0551, 800/527–3111 • gay-friendly •
full brkfst • fireplaces • nonsmoking • $179-
329

**The Alegria Quartet & Oceanfront Inn
Cottages** 44781 & 44800 Main St
707/937–5150, 800/780–7905 • gay-friendly •
located in the village • ocean views •
nonsmoking • WiFi • kids ok • $159-299

Blair House & Cottage 45110 Little Lake St (at Ford St) **707/937–1800, 800/699–9296** • gay-friendly • in former "home" of Jessica Fletcher of *Murder, She Wrote* • nonsmoking • $100-210

Brewery Gulch Inn 9401 N Hwy 1 **707/937–4752, 800/578–4454** • gay/ straight • oceanview B&B made of eco-salvaged redwood • full brkfst • jacuzzi • teens welcome • nonsmoking • WiFi • $210-465

Dennen's Victorian Farmhouse 7001 N Hwy 1 (at Hwy 128) **707/937–0697, 800/264–4723** • gay-friendly • nonsmoking • full brkfst • $135-265

Glendeven Inn 8205 N Hwy 1 (1.7 miles S of Mendocino), Little River **707/937–0083, 800/822–4536** • gay-friendly • charming farmhouse on the coast • full brkfst • nonsmoking • $155-305

Hill House Inn 10701 Palette Dr **707/937–0554, 800/422–0554** • gay/ straight • New England–style inn • also restaurant • $141-313

The Inn at Schoolhouse Creek 7051 N Hwy 1, Little River **707/937–5525, 800/731–5525** • gay/ straight • B&B w/ cottages & suites • full brkfst • hot tub • fireplaces • nonsmoking • WiFi • wheelchair access • $150-525

John Dougherty House 571 Ukiah St (at Kasten St) **707/937–5266, 800/486–2104** • gay-friendly • jacuzzi • gay-owned • $130-275

Little River Inn Resort & Spa 7901 N Hwy 1, Little River **707/937–5942, 888/466–5683** • gay-friendly • resort • ocean views, restaurant & bar • nonsmoking • WiFi • $130-365

MacCallum House Inn 45020 Albion St (at Lansing) **707/937–0289, 800/609–0492** • gay/ straight • nonsmoking • WiFi • wheelchair access • kids ok • also popular restaurant & full bar w/ cafe • $179-399

Orr Hot Springs 13201 Orr Springs Rd, Ukiah **707/462–6277** • gay-friendly • hostel-style cabins, private cottages & campsites • clothing-optional • kids ok • mineral hot springs • pool • guests must bring all own food • reservations required • $40 (camping), $185 (cottage)

Packard House 45170 Little Lake St (at Kasten St) **707/937–2677, 888/453–2677** • gay-friendly • full brkfst • jacuzzi • nonsmoking • WiFi • gay-owned • $190-275

Sallie & Eileen's Place **707/937–2028** • women only • cabin • hot tub • kitchens • fireplaces • kids/ pets ok • nonsmoking • lesbian-owned • $100-125, $25/ add'l person (2-night minimum stay)

Sea Gull Inn 44960 Albion St **707/937–5204, 888/937–5204** • gay-friendly • 9 units in the heart of historic Mendocino • nonsmoking • kids ok • WiFi • wheelchair access • $65-185

Stanford Inn by the Sea Coast Hwy 1 & Comptche-Ukiah Rd **707/937–5615, 800/331–8884** • gay-friendly • full brkfst • hot tub • pool • organic vegetarian restaurant • nonsmoking • WiFi • kids/ pets ok • wheelchair access • $195-785

Stevenswood Resort & Spa 8211 N Hwy 1 **707/937–2810, 800/421–2810** • gay/ straight • resort w/ forest spas & hot tubs • WiFi • wheelchair access • gay-owned • $225-895

RESTAURANTS

Cafe Beaujolais 961 Ukiah St **707/937–5614** • lunch& dinner • reservations recommended • some veggie • wheelchair access

BOOKSTORES

Gallery Bookshop Main & Kasten St S **707/937–2665** • 9:30am-6pm, till 9pm Fri-Sat • independent • also children's bookstore

Menlo Park

see Palo Alto

Mill Valley

see Marin County

Modesto

see also Stockton

ACCOMMODATIONS

Rodeway Inn 936 McHenry Ave (at Roseburg Ave) **209/523–7701** • gay-friendly • pool • WiFi

BARS

Brave Bull 701 S 9th St **209/529–6712** • 7pm-2am, clsd Mon • lesbians/ gay men • dancing/DJ • Latino/a (Latin Night Th w/ drag show & strippers) • drag shows Sun • karaoke Wed

Tiki Lounge 932 McHenry Ave (at Roseburg Ave) **209/577–9969** • 5:30pm-2am • gay-friendly • neighborhood bar • multiracial • transgender-friendly • karaoke

CAFES

Cafe Genowa 3025 McHenry Ave (at Rumble) **209/571–3337** • 8am-5pm

Deva Cafe 1202 J St **209/572–3382** • 7am-3pm, 8am-noon Sun • live music • patio • wheelchair access

RESTAURANTS

Minnie's Restaurant 107 McHenry Ave **209/524–4621** • lunch Tue-Fri, dinner Tue-Sun, clsd Mon • full bar

RETAIL SHOPS

Mystical Body 121 McHenry Ave **209/527–1163** • noon-8pm, clsd Sun-Mon • body piercing

EROTICA

Suzie's Adult Superstores 115 McHenry Ave (at Needham) **209/529–5546** • 8am-midnight

Monterey

ACCOMMODATIONS

Asilomar Conference Grounds 800 Asilomar Blvd, Pacific Grove **831/372–8016, 888/635–5310** • gay-friendly • Arts & Crafts–style buildings designed by Julia Morgan • pool • WiFi • $109+

Gosby House Inn 643 Lighthouse Ave (at 18th), Pacific Grove **831/375–1287, 800/527–8828** • gay-friendly • B&B • full brkfst • some shared baths • nonsmoking • kids ok • wheelchair access • $120-225

Monterey Fireside Lodge 1131 10th St **831/373–4172, 800/722–2624** • very gay-friendly • hot tub • fireplaces • nonsmoking rooms available • kids ok • WiFi • $59-399

The Monterey Hotel 406 Alvarado St **831/375–3184, 800/966–6490** • gay-friendly • turn-of-the-century boutique hotel • WiFi • $89-259

NIGHTCLUBS

Franco's Club 10639 Merritt St, Castroville **831/633–2090** • 10pm-2am Sat only, also Lush 2nd & 4th Th • lesbians/ gay men • dancing/DJ • Latino/a

RESTAURANTS

Old Fisherman's Grotto 39 Fisherman's Wharf #1 **831/375–4604** • 11am-10pm

Tarpy's Roadhouse 2999 Monterey Salinas Hwy (at Canyon Dr) **831/647–1444** • lunch & dinner, Sun brunch • patios & gardens • full bar

ENTERTAINMENT & RECREATION

Ag Venture Tours PO Box 2634, 93942 **831/761–8463** • customized wine-tasting, agriculture & sight-seeing tours of Monterey Bay area

Monterey Bay Aquarium 886 Cannery Row **831/648–4800** • come for the otters, stay for the day

Morro Bay

see San Luis Obispo

Mountain View

NIGHTCLUBS

King of Clubs Nightclub 893 Leong Dr (at Moffett Blvd) **650/968–6366** • 7pm-2am, clsd Wed • lesbians/ gay men • neighborhood bar • dancing/DJ • theme nights • karaoke • multiracial • transgender-friendly

Napa Valley

ACCOMMODATIONS

Beazley House B&B Inn 1910 First St, Napa **707/257–1649, 800/559–1649** • gay-friendly • historic inn • full brkfst • nonsmoking • very pet-friendly • WiFi • wheelchair access • $185-306

Brannan Cottage Inn 109 Wapoo Ave, Calistoga **707/942–4200** • gay-friendly • B&B in Victorian cottage • full brkfst • 1 block from downtown • nonsmoking • WiFi • $155-225

The Chablis Inn 3360 Solano Ave (Redwood Rd at Hwy 29), Napa **707/257–1944, 800/443–3490** • gay-friendly • motel • pool • hot tub • kids/ pets ok • nonsmoking • wheelchair access • $125-265

The Chanric Inn 1805 Foothill Blvd, Calistoga **707/942–4535, 877/281–3671** • gay/ straight • pool & spa • nonsmoking • WiFi • gay-owned • $209-329

Chateau de Vie 3250 Hwy 128, Calistoga **707/942–6446, 877/558–2513** • gay/ straight • chateau w/ gardens • full brkfst • pool • pets ok • WiFi • gay-owned • $229-429

Garnett Creek Inn 1139 Lincoln Ave, Calistoga **707/942–9797** • gay-friendly • on historic main street • nonsmoking • wheelchair access • $175-270

The Ink House B&B 1575 St Helena Hwy S, St Helena **707/963–3890** • gay-friendly • full brkfst • nonsmoking • WiFi • $179-299

The Inn on First 1938 1st St, Napa **707/253–1331, 866/253–1331** • gay/ straight • WiFi • pets ok • gay-owned • $205-375

Meadowlark Country House 601 Petrified Forest Rd, Calistoga **707/942–5651, 800/942–5651** • gay-friendly • full brkfst • clothing-optional mineral pool, sauna & hot tub • nonsmoking • WiFi • gay-owned • $195-450

Napa River Inn 500 Main St (at 5th), Napa **707/251–8500, 877/251–8500** • gay-friendly • luxury boutique hotel w/ spa • located in historic Napa Mill • WiFi • $169-499

Yountville Inn 6462 Washington St, Yountville **707/944–5600, 888/366–8166** • gay-friendly • alongside Hopper Creek • spa • nonsmoking • $175-375

RESTAURANTS

Brannan's 1374 Lincoln Ave (at Washington), Calistoga **707/942–2233** • lunch & dinner, brunch wknds • full bar • live jazz wknds • gay-owned

Flat Iron Grill 1440 Lincoln Ave (at Washington), Calistoga **707/942–1220** • dinner & seasonal wknd lunches • traditional American classics • gay-owned

Redd 6480 Washington St, Yountville **707/944–2222** • lunch Mon-Sat, dinner nightly, Sun brunch • American • reservations required

Tra Vigne 1050 Charter Oak Ave (Hwy 29), St Helena **707/963–4444** • 11:30am-10pm • Northern Italian • also wine bar • reservations recommended

ENTERTAINMENT & RECREATION

Harbin Hot Springs 18424 Harbin Springs Rd, Middletown **707/987–2477, 800/622–2477 (CA ONLY)** • gay-friendly • nonprofit retreat & workshop center • massage available • some sundecks clothing-optional

Lavender Hill Spa 1015 Foothill Blvd (at Lincoln Ave), Calistoga **707/942–4495, 800/528–4772** • 9am-9pm

BOOKSTORES

Copperfield's Books 1330 Lincoln Ave, Calistoga **707/942–1616** • 9am-7pm, till 9pm Fri-Sat, 10am-6pm Sun

Nevada City

ACCOMMODATIONS

The Flume's End B&B 317 S Pine St **530/265–9665** • gay/ straight • creekside Victorian • full brkfst • women-owned • $149-189

CAFES

Java John's 306 Broad St **530/265–3653** • 6:30am-5pm

RESTAURANTS

Friar Tuck's 111 N Pine St (at Commercial) **530/265–9093** • dinner from 5pm • American/ fondue • live shows • full bar • wheelchair access

Newport Beach

see Orange County

Oakland

see East Bay

Orange County

includes Anaheim, Costa Mesa, Garden Grove, Huntington Beach, Irvine, Laguna Beach, Newport Beach, Santa Ana

INFO LINES & SERVICES

AA Gay/ Lesbian Laguna Beach **714/556–4555 (AA#)** • call or visit www.oc-aa.org for meeting times

The Center Orange County 1605 N Spurgeon St, Santa Ana **714/953–5428** • 9am-5pm Mon-Fri or by appt or event

ACCOMMODATIONS

Best Western Laguna Brisas Spa Hotel 1600 S Coast Hwy (at Bluebird), Laguna Beach **949/497–7272, 888/296–6834** • gay/ straight • resort hotel • free brkfst • pool • in-room whirlpool spas • nonsmoking • WiFi • wheelchair access • $99-499

Best Western Raffles Inn & Suites 2040 S Harbor Blvd, Anaheim **714/750–6100, 800/308–5278** • gay-friendly • pool • WiFi • in walking distance of Disneyland

Casa Laguna Inn & Spa 2510 S Coast Hwy, Laguna Beach **949/494–2996, 800/233–0449** • gay-friendly • inn & cottages overlooking the Pacific • pool • kids/ pets ok • nonsmoking • WiFi • gay-owned • $139-599

Fairfield Inn Placentia 710 W Kimberly Ave, Placentia **714/996–4410, 800/308–5286** • gay-friendly • pool • WiFi • wheelchair access

Holiday Inn & Suites Anaheim 1240 S Walnut, Anaheim **714/535–0300, 800/308–5312** • gay-friendly • walking distance of Disneyland • pool • also restaurant • WiFi • wheelchair access

The Hotel Hanford 3131 S Bristol St (at Baker St), Costa Mesa **714/913–9055, 800/362–1655** • gay-friendly • pool • WiFi • wheelchair access • $129-189

Laguna Cliffs Inn 475 N Coast Hwy, Laguna Beach **949/497–6645, 800/297–0007** • gay-friendly • hot tub • pool • kids ok • easy beach access • WiFi • wheelchair access • $99-259

Laguna Cliffs Marriott Resort & Spa 25135 Park Lantern, Dana Point **949/661–5000, 800/533–9748** • gay-friendly • pool • restaurant • WiFi • wheelchair access • $129-438

St Regis Monarch Beach One Monarch Beach Resort, Dana Point 949/234-3200 • gay-friendly • restaurant • pool • nonsmoking • wheelchair access • $345-675

Surf & Sand Resort 1555 S Coast Hwy, Laguna Beach 949/497-4477, 888/869-7569 • gay-friendly • restaurant & spa • WiFi • wheelchair access

BARS

Club Bounce 1460 S Coast Hwy, Laguna Beach 949/494-0056 • 2pm-2am • lesbians/ gay men • dancing/DJ Fri-Sat • karaoke

Frat House 8112 Garden Grove Blvd (at Beach Blvd), Garden Grove 714/373-3728 • 3pm-2am • lesbians/ gay men • dancing/DJ • multiracial • drag shows & strippers • young crowd • wheelchair access

Metro Q Bar & Grill 19092 Beach Blvd (at Garfield Ave), Huntington Beach 714/968-6677 • 3:30pm-close, from 11:30am Sat & 10am Sun • lesbians/gay men • food served • WiFi

Tin Lizzie Saloon 752 St Clair (at Bristol), Costa Mesa 714/966-2029 • 11:30am-2am • mostly gay men • neighborhood bar • wheelchair access

NIGHTCLUBS

Bravo 1490 S Anaheim Blvd, Anaheim 714/533-2291 • more gay Th & Sat • gay/ straight • dancing/DJ • goth & electronica Sun • Latin music Wed & Fri-Sat

Club Lucky Presents 949/551-2998 • check www. clubluckypresents.com for weekly parties on OC

El Calor 2916 W Lincoln Ave (at E Beach Blvd), Anaheim 714/527-8873 • 8pm-2am • gay-friendly • dancing/DJ • mostly Latino/a • drag shows

Lions Den 719 W 19th St (at Pomona), Costa Mesa 949/645-3830 • 9pm-2am, clsd Mon • gay/ straight • only lesbian/ gay Fri for Fiesta Latina (Latino/a • drag shows) • dancing/DJ • karaoke Wed • size-acceptance club Sat (www.butterflylounge.com)

CAFES

Avanti Cafe 259 E 17th St (at Westminster), Costa Mesa 949/548-2224 • 11am-10pm, till 8pm Sun • brkfst, lunch & dinner • "hella fierce rockin' world food" • veggie & vegan • beer/ wine

The Koffee Klatch 1440 S Coast Hwy (btwn Mountain & Pacific Coast Hwy), Laguna Beach 949/376-6867 • 7am-11pm, till midnight Fri-Sat • brkfst & lunch • desserts • WiFi

Zinc Cafe 350 Ocean Ave (at Broadway), Laguna Beach 949/494-6302 • 7am-4pm, also market till 6pm • vegetarian • beer/ wine • patio • wheelchair access

RESTAURANTS

Cafe Zoolu 860 Glenneyre St, Laguna Beach 949/494-6825 • 5pm-10pm, clsd Mon • beer/ wine • wheelchair access

The Cottage 308 N Coast Hwy (at Aster), Laguna Beach 949/494-3023 • brkfst, lunch & dinner • homestyle cooking • some veggie

Dizz's As Is 2794 S Coast Hwy (at Nyes Pl), Laguna Beach 949/494-5250 • open 5:30pm, clsd Mon • full bar • patio

Madison Square & Garden Cafe 320 N Coast Hwy, Laguna Beach 949/494-0137 • 8am-3pm, clsd Tue • dog-friendly

Sorrento Grille 370 Glenneyre St, Laguna Beach 949/494-8686 • dinner only • upscale American bistro & martini bar

Sundried Tomato Cafe 361 Forest Ave #103, Laguna Beach 949/494-3312 • lunch & dinner • also full bar • gay-owned

ENTERTAINMENT & RECREATION

West St Beach Laguna Beach

PUBLICATIONS

Orange County/ Long Beach Blade 949/494-4898

EROTICA

Pink Kitty 17955 Sky Park Cir Ste A, Irvine 949/660-4990 • 10am-6pm • gay-owned

Oroville

CAFES

Mug Shots 2040 Montgomery St 530/538-8342 • 5:30am-6pm, 7am-3pm Sun • WiFi • gay-owned

Palm Springs

INFO LINES & SERVICES

AA Gay/ Lesbian 760/324-4880 (AA#) • call for meeting schedule

ACCOMMODATIONS

Caliente Tropics Resort 411 E Palm Canyon Dr 888/277-0999 • gay/ straight • hot tub • pool • nonsmoking resort • kids ok • very pet-friendly • wheelchair access • gay-owned • $69-295

Calla Lily Inn 350 S Belardo Rd (at Baristo) 760/323-3654, 888/888-5787 • gay-friendly • pool • "a tranquil oasis" • nonsmoking • WiFi • $129-398

Casitas Laquita 450 E Palm Canyon Dr (near Camino Real) **760/416–9999, 877/203–3410** • lesbian resort • pool • nonsmoking • small pets ok • WiFi • wheelchair access • lesbian-owned • $135-350

Desert Hearts Inn Avenida Olancha (across from Queen of Hearts) **760/322–5793, 888/275–9903** • women • pool • hot tub • full kitchens • small pets ok • lesbian-owned • $105-160

Desert Star Bungalows 1611 Calle Palo Fierro **760/778–1047, 800/399–1006** • gay-friendly • boutique hotel made up of bungalows w/ fully equipped kitchen • pool • WiFi • $130-406

The Horizon Hotel 1050 E Palm Canyon Dr **760/323–1858, 800/377–7855** • gay-friendly • pool • jacuzzi • WiFi

Hotel Zoso 150 S Indian Canyon Dr **760/325–9676** • gay-friendly • 4-acre resort • pool • WiFi • also bar & Nick & Stef's restaurant • also spa

Palm Springs

WHERE THE GIRLS ARE:

Vacationers will be staying on East Palm Canyon near Sunrise Way. Women do hang out at the boys' bars too. Try the bar at The Desert Palms Inn, or just about anywhere on Perez Rd.

LGBT PRIDE:

November, web: www.pspride.org.

ANNUAL EVENTS:

Spring - Kraft Nabisco Golf Tournament (aka "Dinah Shore") 760/324-4546, web: www.kncgolf.com. One of the biggest gatherings of lesbians on the continent. If you're more interested in the party than the golf, get the info at www.dinahshoreweekend.com.

Spring - White Party, web: www.jeffreysanker.com. Popular circuit party/fundraiser.

CITY INFO:

Palm Springs Visitors Bureau 760/778-8418 or 800/347-7746, web: www.palm-springs.org.

ATTRACTIONS:

Joshua Tree National Park, web: www.nps.gov/jotr.

Palm Springs Aerial Tramway to the top of Mt San Jacinto, on Tramway Rd, web: www.pstramway.com.

Palm Springs Art Museum 760/325-7186, web: www.psmuseum.org.

BEST VIEW:

Top of Mt San Jacinto. Driving through the surrounding desert, you can see great views of the mountains. Be careful in the summer—always carry water in your vehicle, and be sure to check all fluids in your car before you leave and frequently during your trip.

WEATHER:

Palm Springs is sunny and warm in the winter, with temperatures in the 70°s. Summers are scorching (100°+).

TRANSIT:

American Cab 760/416-2594.

Classic Cab 760/322-3111.

Desert Valley Shuttle 800/413-3999.

Sun Line Transit Agency 760/343-3451 or 800/347-8628, web: www.sunline.org.

Hyatt Regency Suites Palm Springs 285 N Palm Canyon Dr **760/322–9000, 800/554–9288** • gay-friendly • pool • WiFi • also restaurant & bar

Mojave 73721 Shadow Mountain Dr, Palm Desert **800/391–1104** • gay-friendly • boutique hotel • pool • hot tub • spa services • kids ok • nonsmoking • wheelchair access • $119-239

Queen of Hearts Resort 435 E Avenida Olancha **760/322–5793, 888/275–9903** • women • pool • full kitchens • WiFi • lesbian-owned • $105-160

Rendezvous 1420 N Indian Canyon Dr **760/320–1178, 800/485–2808** • gay-friendly • '50s chic • pool • WiFi • $160-240

Ruby Montana's Coral Sands Inn 210 W Stevens Rd (at N Palm Canyon) **760/325–4900, 866/820–8302** • gay/ straight • resort • pool • kitschy 1950s chic • kids/ pets ok • WiFi • wheelchair access • lesbian-owned • $139-189

Villa Mykonos 67–590 Jones Rd (at Cree), Cathedral City **800/471–4753** • lesbians/ gay men • timeshare condos & rental units • pool • WiFi • $150-275/ night (rentals) & $3,000-7,000/ week (condos)

Villa Royale 1620 Indian Trail **760/327–2314, 800/245–2314** • gay-friendly • pool • jacuzzi • also Europa Restaurant • "named one of the five best small inns in Southern California by *Sunset Magazine*" • $139-279

Bars

Azul 369 N Palm Canyon Dr **760/325–5533** • 11am-close, from 10am Sun • lesbians/ gay men • neighborhood bar • videos • also restaurant

Club Whatever 36–737 Cathedral Canyon Dr (at Commercial), Cathedral City **760/321–0031** • 2pm-2am • lesbians/ gay men • neighborhood bar • karaoke • drag shows & cabaret wknds • country/ western • patio

Georgie's Alibi 369 N Palm Canyon Dr **760/325–5533** • 11am-close, from 10am Sun • mostly gay men • neighborhood bar • food served • patio

Hunter's Video Bar 302 E Arenas Rd (at Calle Encilia) **760/323–0700** • 10am-2am • popular • mostly gay men • dancing/DJ • video bar • go-go boys Fri • theme nights

Pink 302 E Arenas Rd (at Calle Encilia, at Hunter's) **760/323–0700** • 7pm last Sat only • mostly women • dancing/DJ

Score 301 E Arenas Rd **760/327–0753** • 6am-2am • mostly gay men • neighborhood bar • game bar

Toucan's Tiki Lounge 2100 N Palm Canyon Dr (at Via Escuela) **760/416–7584** • noon-2am • lesbians/ gay men • dancing/DJ • live show Mon • drag shows Wed & Sun • male & female go-go dancers wknds

Cafes

Palm Springs Koffi 515 N Palm Canyon Dr (at Alejo) **760/416–2244** • 5:30am-8pm • WiFi

Restaurants

Amici 71380 Hwy 111, Rancho Mirage **760/341–0738** • lunch & dinner, Sun brunch • Italian patio • full bar

Bangkok Five 70-026 Hwy 111, Rancho Mirage **760/770–9508** • dinner nightly • Thai

Billy Reed's 1800 N Palm Canyon Dr (at Vista Chino) **760/325–1946** • 7am-9pm, till 10pm Fri-Sat • some veggie • full bar • also bakery • wheelchair access

Blame It on Midnight 777 E Tahquitz Canyon Wy, Stes 101-109 (at the Courtyard) **760/323–1200** • 5pm-10pm, till 11pm Fri-Sat • mostly gay men • live music Th-Sun • also full bar • patio • gay-owned

Blue Coyote Grill 445 N Palm Canyon Dr **760/327–1196** • 11am-10pm, till 11pm Fri-Sat • Southwestern

Blue Pear Texx Mexx 2249 N Palm Canyon Dr **760/778–5500** • lunch & dinner, Sun brunch from 10am • wheelchair access • gay-owned

Bongo Johnny's 214 E Arenas Rd **760/866–1905** • 8am-10pm, till 11pm Fri-Sat • burgers & sandwiches

Cafe Palette 315 E Arenas **760/322–9264** • 11am-10pm • also delivers

The Chop House 262 S Palm Canyon Dr **760/320–4500** • from 5pm • steak • reservations recommended

Copley's 621 N Palm Canyon Dr (btwn E Tamarisk Rd & E Granvia Valmonte) **760/327–9555** • 6pm-10pm • contemporary American • full bar

Davey's Hideaway 292 E Palm Canyon Dr **760/320–4480** • from 5pm • steak, seafood & pasta • piano • patio • full bar

Dink's Restaurant & Ultra Lounge 2080 Palm Canyon Dr **760/327–7676** • lunch & dinner • swank lounge

El Gallito 68820 Grove St (at Palm Canyon), Cathedral City **760/328–7794** • 10am-9pm • homemade Mexican • beer/ wine

Grill-A-Burger 166 N Palm Canyon Dr **760/327-8175** • 11am-9pm, till 4pm Tue-Wed & Sun, clsd Mon

Hamburger Mary's 415 N Palm Canyon Dr **760/778-6279** • 11am-close • full bar

Las Casuelas 368 N Palm Canyon Dr (btwn Amado & Alejo) **760/325-3213** • 11am-10pm • Mexican

Look 139 E Andreas Rd **760/778-3520** • 11am-10pm • patio bar till 2am

Matchbox 155 S Palm Canyon Dr (in Mercado Plaza, 2nd level) **760/778-6000** • 4pm-11pm, till 1am Fri-Sat • pizza

Ming's Chinese Cuisine 35300 Date Palm Dr, Cathedral City **760/770-3663** • 11:30am-9pm, clsd Sun

Nature's 555 S Sunrise Way #301 **760/323-9487** • 8am-7pm, 9am-5pm wknds • vegan/ vegetarian

Pomme Frite 256 S Palm Canyon Dr **760/778-3727** • dinner nightly, lunch wknds, clsd Tue • Belgian beer & French food

Red Tomato & House of Lamb 68-784 E Palm Canyon (btwn Date Palm & Cathedral Canyon), Cathedral City **760/328-7518** • 4pm-10pm, clsd Mon • Italian • beer/ wine • wheelchair access

Rick's Restaurant 1973 N Palm Canyon Dr **760/416-0090** • 6am-3pm • Cuban/ American

Rock Garden Cafe 777 S Palm Canyon Dr **760/327-8840** • 7am-9pm • Greek • patio

Shame on the Moon 69-950 Frank Sinatra Dr (at Hwy 111), Rancho Mirage **760/324-5515** • 5pm-9:30pm • cont'l • plenty veggie • full bar • patio • reservations recommended • wheelchair access

Sherman's Deli & Bakery 401 E Tahquitz Canyon Wy **760/325-1199** • 7am-9pm • kosher-style deli

Spencer's Restaurant 701 W Baristo Rd **760/327-3446** • 9am-2:30pm & 5pm-10pm • Sun brunch • upscale contemporary • reservations recommended

Tootie's Texas Barbeque 68-703 Perez Rd, Cathedral City **760/202-6963** • 11am-8pm, clsd Sun • the name says it all

Towne Center Cafe 44491 Town Center Wy, Palm Desert **760/346-2120** • 6am-8pm • Greek diner

Trio 707 N Palm Canyon Dr **760/864-8746** • dinner nightly • also lounge

Wang's in the Desert 424 S Indian Canyon Dr (at E Saturnino Rd) **760/325-9264** • from 5:30pm • Chinese • full bar

Zin American Bistro 198 S Palm Canyon (at Arenas) **760/322-6300** • lunch & dinner

ENTERTAINMENT & RECREATION

Desert Dyners PO Box 5072, 92263-5072 **760/202-6645** • lesbian social club • membership required • hosts mixers, dances, dinners & golf • singles & couples welcome

The Living Desert Zoo & Gardens 47-900 Portola Ave, Palm Desert **760/346-5694** • 9am-5pm (8am-1pm June-Aug) • zoo & endangered species conservation center

Ruddy's 1930s General Store Museum 221 S Palm Canyon Dr **760/327-2156** • 10am-4pm Th-Sun, clsd summers • "the most you can spend is 95¢"

BOOKSTORES

Q Trading Company 606 E Sunny Dunes Rd (at Indian Canyon) **760/416-7150, 800/756-2290** • 10am-6pm • LGBT • also cards, gifts, videos, etc

RETAIL SHOPS

GayMartUSA 305 E Arenas Rd (at Indian Canyon) **760/416-6436** • 10am-midnight

Mischief 210 E Arenas Rd (at Indian Canyon) **760/322-8555** • 11am-7pm, 10am-11pm Fri-Sat

PUBLICATIONS

The Bottom Line/ Pulp 760/323-0552 • the desert's LGBT bar guide & classifieds

Desert Daily Guide 760/320-3237 • LGBT weekly, travel, activity & lodging info for Palm Springs

Odyssey Magazine 323/874-8788 • dish on L.A. & Palm Springs' club scene

Talk Magazine 760/325-4848 • weekly LGBT publication

GYMS & HEALTH CLUBS

Gold's Gym 4070 Airport Center Dr (at Ramon) **760/322-4653** • gay-friendly

World Gym Palm Springs 1751 N Sunrise Way (at Vista Chino) **760/327-7100** • 5am-10pm, from 6am wknds • mostly gay men • day passes available • steam & sauna • club-quality sound system • wheelchair access • gay-owned

EROTICA

Gear Leather & Fetish 650 E Sunny Dunes #1 (at S Calle Palo Fierro) **760/322-3363** • noon-7pm, till midnight Fri-Sat • leather, fetish & piercing

Palo Alto

ACCOMMODATIONS

Creekside Inn 3400 El Camino Real (at Page Mill Rd) **650/493-2411, 800/492-7335** • gay/straight • pool • kids ok • WiFi • nonsmoking • restaurant & lounge • wheelchair access • $179-259

Hotel Avante 860 E El Camino Real, Mountain View **650/940-1000, 800/538-1600** • gay/ straight • in heart of Silicon Valley • pool • WiFi • $179-249

RESTAURANTS

Junnoon 150 University Ave **650/329-9644** • lunch Mon-Fri, dinner nightly • Indian • reservations recommended

BOOKSTORES

Books Inc 855 El Camino Real **650/321-0600** • 9am-8pm • LGBT section

Pasadena

BARS

The 35er 12 E Colorado Blvd (Old Town) **626/356-9315** • 3pm-1am, from 12:30pm Fri-Sun • gay/ straight • great neighborhood bar • food served

Boulevard/ Club S Karaoke 3199 E Foothill Blvd (at Sierra Madre Villa) **626/356-9304** • 4pm-2am, from 3pm Fri-Sun • mostly gay men • neighborhood bar • karaoke

RESTAURANTS

Chandra 400 S Arroyo Pkwy **626/577-6599** • 11am-10:30pm • Thai • full bar • wheelchair access

Paso Robles

ACCOMMODATIONS

Asuncion Ridge Vineyards & Inn **805/461-0675** • gay-friendly • WiFi • gay-owned • $249-349

ENTERTAINMENT & RECREATION

Cinema e Vino Paradiso 323/422-0987 • wine tasting, dinner & classic films under the stars at selected CA wineries • lesbian-run

Petaluma

RESTAURANTS

Brixx 16 Kentucky St (in Lanmart Bldg) **707/766-8162** • dinner from 5pm • popular • handmade pizzas & paninis • live bands Sat

BOOKSTORES

Copperfield's Books 140 Kentucky St (btwn Western & Washington, downtown) **707/762-0563** • 9am-9pm, 10am-6pm Sun

Placerville

ACCOMMODATIONS

Albert Shafsky House B&B 2942 Coloma St (at Spring St/ Hwy 49) **530/642-2776** • gay-friendly • full brkfst • nonsmoking • WiFi • kids ok • lesbian-owned • $135-185

Rancho Cicada Retreat 10001 Bell Rd, Plymouth **209/245-4841, 877/553-9481** • mostly gay men • secluded riverside retreat in the Sierra foothills w/ 2-person tents & cabin • swimming • nudity • gay-owned • $42-160

RETAIL SHOPS

Tony Matthews 447 Main St (at Bedford) **530/626-9161**

Pleasant Hill

see East Bay

Pomona

BARS

Alibi East 225 S San Antonio Ave (at 2nd) **909/623-9422** • noon-2am, till 3am Fri • mostly gay men • dancing/DJ • food • karaoke

The Hookup 1047 E 2nd St (at Pico) **909/620-2844** • noon-2am • lesbians/ gay men • neighborhood bar • food served • karaoke • beer bust Sun • wheelchair access • gay-owned

NIGHTCLUBS

The Brick Nightclub 340 S Thomas St **909/629-6333** • 9pm-4am, from 3pm Sun, clsd Mon-Tue • lesbian/gay men • more women Wed • dancing • drag shows • WiFi

Taste **909/657-8778** • check www.myspace.com/tastela page for events • mostly women • dancing/DJ • 18+

Redondo Beach

see also Los Angeles—West LA & Santa Monica

ACCOMMODATIONS

Best Western Sunrise Hotel 400 N Harbor Dr **310/376-0746, 800/334-7384** • gay-friendly • pool • hot tub • kids ok • WiFi • $119-169

Palos Verdes Inn 1700 S Pacific Coast Hwy **310/316-4211, 800/421-9241** • gay-friendly • jacuzzi • pool • food served • kids ok • WiFi • wheelchair access • $75-125

Riverside

see also San Bernardino

NIGHTCLUBS

El Destino 83085 Indio Blvd, Indio **760/775–0686** • 9pm-2am Wed-Sun • mostly gay men, Th ladies night • dancing/DJ • Latina clientele

Menagerie 3581 University Ave (at Orange) **951/788–8000** • 4pm-2am • lesbians/ gay men • dancing/DJ • karaoke • drag shows Th • wheelchair access

VIP Nightclub & Restaurant 3673 Merrill Ave (at Magnolia) **951/784–2370** • 5pm-2am • lesbians/ gay men • dancing/DJ • karaoke • drag shows Fri • food served • 18+

Russian River

includes Cazadero, Forestville, Guerneville & Monte Rio

INFO LINES & SERVICES

AA Meetings in Sonoma County **707/544–1300 (AA#)**, **800/224–1300** • call for meeting times

Russian River Chamber of Commerce & Visitors Center 16209 First St (on the plaza), Guerneville **707/869–9000**, **877/644–9001** • 10am-5pm, till 4pm Sun

Sonoma County Tourism Bureau **800/576–6662**

ACCOMMODATIONS

5 Seasons Resort & Spa 14880 River Rd, Guerneville **707/869–8139** • gay/ straight • cottages • pool • hot tub • kids/pets ok • nonsmoking • WiFi • wheelchair access • $90-195

Applewood Inn 13555 Hwy 116 (at Mays Canyon), Guerneville **707/869–9093**, **800/555–8509** • gay-friendly • full brkfst • pool • nonsmoking • WiFi • wheelchair access • also restaurant • gay-owned • $195-345

boon hotel & spa 14711 Armstrong Woods Rd, Guerneville **707/869–2721**, **877/668–8545** • gay/ straight • resort w/ full-service spa • kids/pets ok • pool • nonsmoking • jacuzzi • WiFi • gay-owned • $150-325

Fern Grove Cottages 16650 River Rd, Guerneville **707/869–8105** • gay-friendly • pool • kids/pets ok • nonsmoking • WiFi • $89-595

Guerneville Lodge 15905 River Rd (at Hwy 116), Guerneville **707/869–0102** • gay/straight • WiFi • nonsmoking • gay-owned • $35 (camping), $99-189 (inn)

Highland Dell Resort 21050 River Blvd (at Bohemian Hwy), Monte Rio **707/865–2300** • gay-friendly • WiFi • full bar & restaurant

➤ **Highlands Resort** 14000 Woodland Dr, Guerneville **707/869–0333** • lesbians/ gay men • country retreat on 4 wooded acres • hot tub • swimming • clothing-optional pool • $65-195; $20-25 rustic camping

Inn at Occidental 3657 Church St, Occidental **707/874–1047, 800/522–6324** • gay-friendly • full brkfst • wheelchair access • $199-379

New Dynamic Inn 14030 Mill St (at Main St), Guerneville **707/869–5082** • gay-friendly • kids/ pets ok • nonsmoking • WiFi • wheelchair access • $75-165

Rio Villa Beach Resort 20292 Hwy 116 (at Bohemian Hwy), Monte Rio **707/865–1143, 877/746–8455** • gay-friendly • kids ok • nonsmoking • WiFi • gay-owned • $99-279

Russian River Resort/ Triple R Resort 16390 4th St (at Mill), Guerneville **707/869–0691, 800/417–3767** • popular • lesbians/ gay men • hot tub • pool • nudity ok • also restaurant • full bar • wheelchair access • gay-owned • $85-200

Village Inn & Restaurant 20822 River Blvd, Monte Rio **707/865–2304, 800/303–2303** • gay/ straight • historic inn • nonsmoking • also restaurant & full bar • WiFi • wheelchair access • gay-owned • $105-205

Russian River

WHERE THE GIRLS ARE:
Guerneville is a small town, so you won't miss the scantily clad, vacationing women walking toward the bars downtown or the beach—especially during Women's Week. The rest of the year, look for gals in tie dye or flannel.

ANNUAL EVENTS:
May - Women's Weekend 877/644-9001 (chamber of commerce #), web: www.russianriverwom-ensweekend.org.
August - Sundance. Popular outdoor dance party, web: www.guspresents.com.
September - Jazz & Blues Festival, web: www.omegaevents.com/russian-riverfestivals.

CITY INFO:
Russian River Chamber of Commerce & Visitors Center 877/644-9001, web: www.russianriver.com.

BEST VIEW:
Anywhere in Armstrong Woods, the Napa Wine Country, and on the ride along the picture-postcard-perfect coast on Highway 1.

WEATHER:
Summer days are sunny and warm (80°s-90°s) but usually begin with a dense fog. Winter days have the same pattern but are a lot cooler and wetter. Winter nights can be very damp and chilly (low 40°s).

TRANSIT:
Bill's Taxi Service 707/869-2177. As far as public transit goes, this area is easiest to reach by car.

ATTRACTIONS:
Armstrong Redwood State Park.
Bodega Bay, web: www.bode-gabay.com.
Fort Ross.
Healdsburg.
Jenner & Goat Rock Beach.
Mudbaths of Calistoga.
Wineries of Napa and Sonoma Counties, web: www.napavalley.com & www.sonomacounty.com.

West Sonoma Inn & Spa 14100 Brookside Ln (at Main St), Guerneville **707/869-2470, 800/551-1881** • gay/straight • 6-acre resort a short walk from Johnson's Beach • pool • spa • some jacuzzis • nonsmoking • WiFi • wheelchair access • $99-299

Westside Lodge Westside Rd (at River Rd), Forestville **707/869-9030, 800/997-3312** • gay/straight • 1936 cabin-style home • sleeps 8 • nonsmoking • WiFi • lesbian-owned • $295 -394

The Woods Resort 16484 4th St (at Mill St), Guerneville **707/869-0600, 877/887-9218** • mostly gay men • swimming • WiFi • wheelchair access • gay-owned • $65-325

Bars

Mc T's Bullpen 16246 1st St (at Church), Guerneville **707/869-3377** • 10am-2am • gay/straight • patio • WiFi • wheelchair access

Rainbow Cattle Co 16220 Main St (at Armstrong Woods Rd), Guerneville **707/869-0206** • 6am-2am • gay/ straight • neighborhood bar • DJ Bruce Sat

Cafes

Coffee Bazaar 14045 Armstrong Woods Rd (at River Rd), Guerneville **707/869-9706** • 6am-8pm • cafe • soups • salads • sandwiches • WiFi

Coffee Catz 6761 Sebastopol Ave (at Hwy 116), Sebastopol **707/829-6600** • 7am-6pm, till 8pm Th, till 10pm Wed & Fri-Sat • live shows • WiFi • wheelchair access

Roasters Espresso Bar 6656 Front St (Hwy 116), Forestville **707/887-1632** • 6am-6pm, from 7am Sat-Sun • WiFi

Restaurants

Aioli 6536 Front St, Forestville **707/887-2476** • 8am-5pm, from 11am Sat, clsd Sun-Mon • gourmet deli • beer/ wine • outdoor seating

boon eat + drink 16248 Main St (at Hwy 116), Guerneville **707/869-0780** • lunch & dinner, clsd Tue-Wed • American

Cape Fear Cafe 25191 Main St, Duncans Mills **707/865-9246** • 9am-2:30pm & 5pm-9pm (clsd Wed & Th off season)

Chef Patrick 16236 Main St (at Hwy 116), Guerneville **707/869-9161** • dinner, clsd Tue-Wed

Farmhouse Inn Restaurant 7871 River Rd, Forestville **707/887-3300, 800/464-6642** • dinner, clsd Tue-Wed

Garden Grill 17132 Hwy 116, Guerneville **707/869-3922** • 8am-8pm, clsd Tue-Wed • great burgers & sandwiches • some veggie • patio

Main Street Station 16280 Main St (at Church St), Guerneville **707/869-0501** • 11am-7pm • Italian restaurant & pizzeria • cabaret dinner shows nightly

Mom's Apple Pie 4550 Gravenstein Hwy N, Sebastopol **707/823-8330** • 10am-6pm • pie worth stopping for on your way to & from Russian River!

Mosaic 6675 Front St (Hwy 116), Forestville **707/887-7503** • lunch, dinner, Sun brunch • wheelchair access • also wine lounge

River Inn Grill 16141 Main St, Guerneville **707/869-0481** • 8am-2pm • local favorite • wheelchair access

Tahoe Chinese Restaurant 6492 Mirabel Rd, Forestville **707/887-9772** • lunch & dinner Mon-Fri, dinner only Sat, clsd Sun • some veggie

Underwood Bar & Bistro 9113 Graton Rd, Graton **707/823-7023** • lunch & dinner, clsd Mon

Willow Wood Market Cafe 9020 Graton Rd, Graton **707/823-0233** • 8am-9pm, from 9am Sat, brunch 9am-3pm Sun

Entertainment & Recreation

Pegasus Theater Co **707/583-2343** • classic to contemporary plays

Bookstores

River Reader 16355 Main St (at Mill), Guerneville **707/869-2240** • 10am-6pm, till 5pm Fri (extended summer hours) • wheelchair access

Retail Shops

Et Cetera, Et Cetera 16270 Main St, Guerneville **707/869-5808**

Guerneville 5 & 10 16252 Main St, Guerneville **707/869-3404** • 10am-6pm • old-fashioned five & dime • lesbian-owned

Nexus 16218 Main St **707/869-3374** • home decor

Sonoma Nesting Company 16151 Main St, Guerneville **707/869-3434** • antiques & home decorating

Up the River 16212 Main St (at Armstrong Woods Rd), Guerneville **707/869-3167** • cards • gifts • T-shirts

Vine Life 16359 Main St (at Mill St), Guerneville **707/869-1234** • 11am-5pm • wine, cards & gifts

Sacramento

Info Lines & Services

Gay AA 916/454-1100

Sacramento Gay & Lesbian Center 1927 L St **916/442-0185** • noon-6pm Mon-Fri

Accommodations

Citizen Hotel 926 J Street **916/447-2700** • gay-friendly • bar & restaurant • wheelchair access • $149-249

Governors Inn 210 Richards Blvd (at I-5) **916/448-7224, 800/999-6689** • gay-friendly • pool • hot tub • nonsmoking • WiFi • $92-124

The Greens Hotel 1700 Del Paso Blvd (at Arden) **916/921-1736** • gay/ straight • pool •WiFi • wheelchair access • $119-199

Inn & Spa at Parkside 2116 6th St (at U St) **916/658-1818, 800/995-7275** • gay/ straight • full brkfst • jacuzzi • WiFi • also full-service spa • wheelchair access • gay-owned • $169-259

Bars

The Depot 2001 K St **916/441-6823** • 4pm-2am, till 4am Fri-Sat, from 2pm wknds • mostly gay men • neighborhood bar • transgender-friendly • live shows • • videos • wheelchair access

L Wine Lounge 1801 L St (at 19th St) **916/443-6970** • gay-friendly • upscale wine lounge • also restaurant

Nightclubs

Badlands 2003 K St **916/448-8790** • 6pm-2am • mostly gay men • dancing/DJ • wheelchair access

Club 21 1119 21st St (btwn K & L Sts) **916/443-1537** • Mexican restaurant during the day • gay/straight • dancing/DJ • women's night 2nd Sat • wheelchair access • cover • lesbian-owned

Faces 2000 K St (at 20th St) **916/448-7798** • 4pm-2am • popular • lesbians/ gay men • dancing/DJ • 3 bars w/ various theme nights • karaoke • videos • patio • wheelchair access • cover

Head Hunters Video Lounge & Grill 1930 K St (at 20th St) **916/492-2922** • dinner Tue-Sun, Sun brunch, bar open till 2am • lesbians/ gay men • various theme nights • more women Sun 2pm-9pm

Silk Bar & Cafe 1011 Del Paso Blvd (at Globe) **916/922-9994** • 10am-2am • cafe/restaurant by day, hip-hop/ dance music by night • cover

Cafes

Butch N Nellies Coffee Co. 1827 I St **916/443-6133** • 7am-7pm, from 8am Sun • Live music • WiFi

N Street Cafe 2022 N Street **916/491-4008** • 6:30am-6pm, 8am-3pm Sat-Sun • WiFi • wheelchair access

Restaurants

Chops 1117 11th St (at L St, across from State Capitol Building) **916/447-8900** • lunch Mon-Fri, dinner nightly • steak & seafood • full bar

Hamburger Patty's 1630 J St (at 17th) **916/441-4340** • 11am-10pm • full bar • karaoke • drag shows • wheelchair access

Hot Rod's Burgers 2007 K St **916/443-7637** • 11am-2am, till 3am Fri-Sat

Ink Eats & Drinks 2730 N St (at 28th) **916/456-2800** • lunch, dinner, late-night brkfst, wknd brunch • full bar • DJ wknds

Jack's Urban Eats 1230 20th St (at Capitol Ave) **916/444-0307** • 11am-8pm, from 5pm wknds • also 2535 Fair Oaks Blvd, 916/481-5225

Paesanos 1806 Capitol Ave (at 18th) **916/447-8646** • 11:30am-9:30pm, from noon wknds • Italian • funky artwork • patio • full bar • also 8519 Bond Rd, 916/690-8646

Paesanos Pronto 1501 16th St **916/444-5850** • from 11am • Italian paninis & salads • wheelchair access

Rick's Dessert Diner 2322 K St (btwn 23rd & 24th) **916/444-0969** • 10am-midnight, till 1am wknds, from noon Sun • coffee & dessert

Sofia Restaurant 815 11th St (at H St) **916/441-0030** • lunch & dinner Mon-Fri, dinner only Sat, clsd Sun • Italian • patio • full bar

Thai Palace 3262 J St (33rd St) **916/447-5353** • lunch & dinner

Zócalo 1801 Capitol Ave (at 18th St) **916/441-0303** • 11am-10pm • Mexican • full bar

Entertainment & Recreation

Lambda Players 1127 21st St. **916/444-8229** • LGBT theater company

Lavender Library, Archives & Cultural Exchange of Sacramento 1414 21st St **916/492-0558** • 4:30pm-8pm Th-Fri, noon-6pm wknds, clsd Mon-Wed

RETAIL SHOPS

Side Show Studios 5635 Freeport Blvd, Ste 6 (at Fruitridge) **916/391-6400** • 10am-10pm • tattoo studio • art gallery • reception w/ live music 2nd Sat • lesbian-owned

PUBLICATIONS

MGW (Mom Guess What) 916/441-6397

Outword Magazine 916/329-9280 • statewide LGBT newspaper w/ Northern & Southern CA editions

EROTICA

G Spot 2009 K St (at 20th) **916/441-3200** • 10am-midnight, till 2am Fri-Sat • gay-owned

Kiss-N-Tell 4201 Sunrise Blvd (at Fair Oaks) **916/966-5477** • clean, well-lighted erotica store • also 2401 Arden Wy, 916/920-5477

San Bernardino

see also Riverside

INFO LINES & SERVICES

AA Gay/ Lesbian 897 Via Lata, Colton **909/825-4700** • call or visit www.inlandempireaa.org for times

NIGHTCLUBS

The Lark 917 Inland Center Dr **909/884-8770** • 3pm-2am, from 7pm Mon, from 2pm Sat-Sun • lesbians/ gay men • DJ Fri-Sat • live & drag shows • karaoke • huge patio • WiFi • wheelchair access • lesbian-owned

EROTICA

Bearfacts Book Store 1434 E Baseline St **909/885-9176**

San Clemente

see Orange County

San Diego

INFO LINES & SERVICES

AA Gay/ Lesbian 1730 Monroe Ave (at The Live & Let Live Alano Club) **619/298-8008** • 10:30am-9pm, from 8:30am wknds • various LGBT meetings (see www.lllac.org)

San Diego LGBT Community Center 3909 Centre St (at University) **619/692-2077** • 9am-9pm, till 5pm Fri, clsd wknds

Women's Resource Center (WRC) 3909 Centre St (at University, in SD LGBT Community Center) **619/692-2077** • variety of resources • health care referrals • social services • community activities

ACCOMMODATIONS

Balboa Park Inn 3402 Park Blvd (at Upas) **619/298-0823, 800/938-8181** • gay-friendly • charming guesthouse in the heart of San Diego • theme rooms • nonsmoking • $99-249

Beach Area B&B/ Elsbree House 5054 Narragansett Ave (at Sunset Cliffs Blvd) **619/226-4133, 800/607-4133** • gay-friendly • near beach • nonsmoking • $150-250 (B&B) $350/ night, $1,800/ week (condo)

The Bristol Hotel 1055 First Ave **619/232-6141, 800/662-4477** • gay/ straight • hotel • kids ok • restaurant & bar • great collection of pop art • WiFi • wheelchair access • $119-289

Handlery Hotel & Resort 950 Hotel Circle N **619/298-0511, 800/676-6567** • gay-friendly • in Mission Valley, minutes from Hillcrest • pool • hot tub • nonsmoking • kids ok • WiFi • wheelchair access • $89-169

Keating House 2331 2nd Ave (at Juniper) **619/239-8585, 800/995-8644** • gay-friendly • graceful Victorian on Bankers Hill • full brkfst • nonsmoking • kids ok • WiFi • $115+

Kings Inn Hotel 1333 Hotel Circle S (Backman St) **619/297-2231, 800/785-4647** • gay/ straight • pool • WiFi • wheelchair access • $59-175

Lafayette Hotel & Suites 2223 El Cajon Blvd (btwn Louisiana & Mississippi) **619/296-2101, 877/343-4648** • gay-friendly • swimming • kids ok • also restaurant • internet access • nonsmoking • WiFi • wheelchair access • $99-159

Ocean Inn 1444 N Hwy 101, Encinitas **760/436-1988, 800/546-1598** • gay-friendly • 30 min from downtown San Diego • WiFi • wheelchair access • $59-189

Park Manor Suites 525 Spruce St (btwn 5th & 6th) **619/291-0999, 800/874-2649** • gay-friendly • 1926 hotel • kids ok • $99+

Sunburst Court Inn 4086 Alabama St (at Polk) **619/294-9665, 866/217-5490** • gay/ straight • all-suite inn • nonsmoking • WiFi • gay-owned • $99-309

W San Diego 421 W B St **619/398-3100, 888/625-5144** • gay-friendly • restaurant • rooftop bar • pool • WiFi • wheelchair access • $249-379

BARS

Bourbon Street 4612 Park Blvd (at Adams) **619/291-4043** • 4pm-2am • popular • mostly gay men • mostly women Sun • live shows & karaoke in front bar • lounge w/ DJ • patio

The Brass Rail 3796 5th Ave (at Robinson) **619/298-2233** • 7pm-2am, from 2pm Fri-Sun, clsd Tue • lesbians/gay men • dancing/DJ • Latin night Sat • wheelchair access

El Camino 2400 India St (at Kalmia, in Little Italy) **619/685-3881** • dinner nightly, Sun brunch • kitschy Mexican • live music • full bar

The Flame 3780 Park Blvd (at University) **619/795-8578** • popular • lesbians/gay men • dancing/DJ • theme nights • patio

Kickers 308 University Ave (at 3rd Ave) **619/491-0400** • Th & Sat only • lesbians/gay men • dancing/DJ • country/western • dance lessons • wheelchair access

Ladies Night at Bourbon Street 4612 Park Blvd (at Adams) **619/291-4043** • 8pm Sun • also TGIF ladies happy hour 7pm Fri • mostly women

San Diego

WHERE THE GIRLS ARE:
Lesbians tend to live near Normal Heights, in the northwest part of the city. But for partying, women go to the bars near I-5, or to Hillcrest to hang out with the boys.

LGBT PRIDE:
July. 619/297-7683, web: www.sdpride.org.

ANNUAL EVENTS:
February - Hillcrest Mardi Gras, web: www.hillcrestmardigras.org.
April - FilmOut San Diego, web: www.filmoutsandiego.com.
August - Hillcrest CityFest Street Fair, web: www.hillcrestassociation.com.
September - Street Scene, web: www.street-scene.com. Huge, outdoor music festival.

CITY INFO:
San Diego Convention & Visitors Bureau, web: www.sandiego.org.
SanDiego.com, web: www.sandiego.com.

BEST VIEW:
Cabrillo National Monument on Point Loma or from a harbor cruise.

WEATHER:
San Diego is sunny and warm (upper 60°s-70°s) year-round, with higher humidity in the summer.

ATTRACTIONS:
Coronado Island (& Hotel Del Coronado), web: www.coronado.ca.us.
Fleet Space Center 619/238-1233, web: www.rhfleet.org.
Hillcrest, web: www.hillquest.com.
Gaslamp Quarter, web: www.gaslamp.org.
Mingei Int'l Museum 619/239-0003, web: www.mingei.org.
La Jolla, web: www.lajollabythesea.com.
The Old Globe Theatre 619/234-5623 (box office), web: www.oldglobe.org.
San Diego Museum of Art 619/232-7931, web: www.sdmart.org.
San Diego Wild Animal Park 760/747-8702, web: www.sandiegozoo.org/wap.
San Diego Zoo 619/231-1515, web: www.sandiegozoo.org.
Sea World 800/257-4268, web: www.seaworld.com.

TRANSIT:
Yellow Cab 619/444-4444.
San Diego Cab 619/226-8294.
Silver Cab/Co-op 619/280-5555.
Super Shuttle 800/974-8885, web: www.supershuttle.com.
San Diego Transit System 619/238-0100, web: www.sdmts.com. San Diego Trolley (through downtown or to Tijuana).

someone to spend your life with.

meet her **today.**

curvepersonals.com

No 1 Fifth Ave (no sign) 3845 5th Ave (at University) **619/299–1911** • noon-2am • mostly gay men • neighborhood bar • videos nights • patio

Redwing Bar & Grill 4012 30th St (at Lincoln, North Park) **619/281–8700** • 11am-2am • mostly gay men • neighborhood bar • patio

SRO Lounge 1807 5th Ave (btwn Elm & Fir) **619/232–1886** • 10am-2am • mostly gay men • cocktail lounge • older, professional crowd • Ladies Night Out 1st & 3rd Sat • transgender-friendly

Nightclubs

Bacchus House 3054 University Ave (at 30th St) **619/299–2032** • 4pm-2am, clsd Mon • mostly gay men • dancing/DJ • theme nights • transgender-friendly • drag shows • videos • young crowd • wheelchair access • gay-owned

Repent 1051 University Ave (at Vermont, at Rich's) **619/295–2195 (CLUB #)** • 10pm Th only • mostly women • dancing/DJ

Rich's 1051 University Ave (at Vermont) **619/295–2195** • popular • open Wed-Sun • mostly gay men • ladies night Th • dancing/DJ • theme nights

Spin Saturdays 2028 Hancock St (at Noell St) **619/294–9590** • mostly men • dancing/DJ

Cafes

Babycakes 3766 5th Ave (at Robinson) **619/296–4173** • 9am-11pm, till midnight Fri-Sat • beer/ wine • patio

The Big Kitchen 3003 Grape St (at 30th) **619/234–5789** • 8am-2pm • wheelchair access • women-owned

Claire de Lune 2906 University Ave **619/688–9845** • 6am-10pm, till midnight Fri-Sat

Cream Coffee Bar 4496 Park Blvd (University Heights) **619/260–1917** • 7am-11pm • WiFi

Espresso Roma UCSD Price Center #76 (at Voight), La Jolla **858/450–2141** • 7am-10pm

Extraordinary Desserts 2929 5th Ave **619/294–2132** • also store in Little Italy: 1430 Union, 619/249-7001 • the name says it all

Gelato Vero Caffee 3753 India St **619/295–9269** • 7am-midnight • great desserts (yes, the gelato is truly delicious) as well as coffee

Twiggs 4590 Park Blvd (at Madison Ave, University Heights) **619/296–0616** • 7am-11pm

Urban Grind 3797 Park Blvd (at University) **619/299–4763** • 7am-10pm • popular • WiFi • gay-owned

Restaurants

Adams Avenue Grill 2201 Adams Ave (at Mississippi) **619/298–8440** • brkfst, lunch & dinner • bistro • plenty veggie • beer/ wine • wheelchair access • gay-owned

Arrivederci 3845 4th Ave **619/299–6282** • lunch & dinner

Bai Yook Thai 1260 University Ave **619/296–2700** • lunch & dinner, dinner only Sun

Baja Betty's 1421 University Ave (at Normal St) **619/269–8510** • 11am-midnight, till 1am Fri-Sat • popular • lesbians/ gay men • Mexican • some veggie • also tequila bar • patio • wheelchair access

Bamboo Lounge 1475 University Ave (at Herbert St) **619/291–8221** • 4pm-midnight, till 1am wknds • sushi

Brian's American Eatery 1451 Washington St **619/296–8268** • 6:30am-10pm, 24hrs Fri-Sat • beer/ wine

Cafe 222 222 Island Ave **619/236–9902** • 7am-2pm • great brkfst

California Cuisine 1027 University Ave (at 10th Ave) **619/543–0790** • 5pm-10pm • some veggie • also bar • wheelchair access • women-owned

Celadon 3671 5th Ave (at Pennsylvania) **619/297–8424** • lunch & dinner • upscale Thai

City Deli 535 University Ave (at 6th Ave) **619/295–2747** • 7am-midnight, till 2am wknds • NY deli • plenty veggie • full bar

Cody's La Jolla 8030 Girard Ave (at Coast Blvd S), La Jolla **858/459–0040** • brkfst & lunch daily, dinner Th-Sun • contemporary California cuisine • live music

The Cottage 7702 Fay (at Klein), La Jolla **858/454–8409** • 7:30am-3pm, dinner June-Sept

Crazee Burger 4201 30th St (at Howard) **619/282–6044** • 11am-9pm, till 11pm Fri-Sat • handcrafted burgers

Crest Cafe 425 Robinson (btwn 4th & 5th) **619/295–2510** • 7am-midnight • some veggie • wheelchair access

Gossip Grill 1440 University Ave (at Normal) **619/260–8023** • 2pm-close • also full bar • patio • wheelchair access • gay-owned

Gulf Coast Grill 4130 Park Blvd (at Normal) **619/295–2244** • lunch & dinner, also Sun brunch • New Orleans-inspired menu

Hash House A Go Go 3628 5th Ave **619/298-4646** • brkfst, lunch & dinner, clsd Mon • great brkfst

Inn at the Park 525 Spruce St (btwn 5th & 6th, at Park Manor Suites) **619/296-0057** • popular • dinner nightly • piano bar

Jimmy Carter's Mexican Cafe 3172 5th Ave (at Spruce) **619/295-2070** • 7am-9pm

Kemo Sabe 3958 5th Ave **619/220-6802** • 5:30pm-close, clsd Mon • int'l • lesbian celeb chef Deborah Scott • reservations required

Kous Kous 3940 4th Ave, Ste 110 (beneath Martinis on Fourth) **619/295-5560** • 5pm-11pm • Moroccan

Lei Lounge 4622 Park Blvd (at Madison Ave) **619/813-2272** • 5pm-2am, Sun brunch • also popular lounge • patio

Lips 3036 El Cajon Blvd **619/295-7900** • 5pm-close, Sun gospel brunch, clsd Mon • "the ultimate in drag dining" • Bitchy Bingo Wed • celeb impersonation Th • DJ wknds

Magnolias 342 Euclid Ave, Ste 403 **619/262-6005** • lunch & dinner • Southern • live jazz

Martinis Above Fourth 3940 4th Ave, Ste 200 (btwn Washington & University) **619/400-4500** • 5pm-11pm, 4pm-midnight Fri-Sat, clsd Sun-Mon • lesbians/ gay men • also cabaret lounge • outdoor bar • gay-owned

The Mission 3795 Mission Blvd (at San Jose), Mission Beach **858/488-9060** • 7am-3pm

Ono Sushi 1236 University Ave (at Richmond) **619/298-0616** • lunch wknds, dinner nightly

The Prado 1549 El Prado (in Balboa Park) **619/557-9441** • lunch & dinner • Latin/ Italian fusion

Roberto's 3202 Mission Blvd **858/488-1610** • open 24 hrs • the best rolled tacos & guacamole • multiple locations

Rudford's 2900 El Cajon Blvd (at Kansas St) **619/282-8423** • 24hrs • popular homestyle cooking

Saigon on Fifth 3900 5th Ave, Ste 120 **619/220-8828** • 11am-3am • Vietnamese

South Park Bar & Grill 1946 Fern St (at Grape St) **619/696-0096** • 5pm-9pm, till midnight Wed-Sat, bar till 2am

Taste of Szechuan 670 University Ave **619/291-1668** • 11:30am-11pm

Terra 3900 block of Vermont St (at 10th Ave) **619/293-7088** • lunch & dinner, clsd Mon for dinner

Urban Mo's 308 University Ave (at 3rd) **619/491-0400** • 9am-2am, 10am-midnight Sun • popular • lesbians/ gay men • some veggie • 3 full bars (Club Mo's) • patio • wheelchair access

Veg N Out 3442 30th St (North Park) **619/546-8411** • 11am-9pm, from noon Sun • vegetarian/ vegan

Waffle Spot 1333 Hotel Circle S (at King's Inn) **619/297-2231** • 7am-2pm

West Coast Tavern 2895 University Ave **619/295-1688** • lunch & dinner • upscale • also lounge

ENTERTAINMENT & RECREATION

Diversionary Theatre 4545 Park Blvd #101 (at Madison) **619/220-0097 (BOX OFFICE #), 619/220-6830** • LGBT theater

Ocean Beach I-8 West to Sunset Cliffs Blvd • very dog-friendly

BOOKSTORES

Traveler's Depot 1655 Garnet Ave (btwn Jewell & Ingraham) **858/483-1421** • 10am-6pm, 11am-5pm wknds • guides, maps & more

RETAIL SHOPS

Auntie Helen's 4028 30th St (at Lincoln) **619/584-8438** • 10am-4:30pm, clsd Sun-Mon • thrift shop benefits PWAs • wheelchair access

Babette Schwartz 421 University Ave (at 5th Ave) **619/220-7048** • 11am-9pm, till 5pm Sun • campy novelties & gifts • gay-owned

Flesh Skin Grafix 1155 Palm Ave, Imperial Beach **619/424-8983** • tattoos • piercing

Mankind 3425 5th Ave (at Upas St) **619/497-1970** • 11am-10pm, noon-6pm Sun • books, sex toys and videos

Obelisk the Bookstore 1029 University Ave (at 10th) **619/297-4171** • 10am-9pm, till 10pm wknds • LGBT • wheelchair access

PUBLICATIONS

The Bottomline 3314 4th Ave **619/291-6690** • bi-weekly • news, entertainment & listings • covers San Diego & Palm Springs

The Lavender Lens **619/342-6166** • Southern California's monthly lesbian magazine

San Diego PIX 1010 University Ave 877/727-5446

Gyms & Health Clubs

Frog's Athletic Club 901 Hotel Circle S (at Washington), Mission Valley 619/291-3500

The Gym at 734 734 University Ave #D (at 7th Ave) 619/296-7878

Erotica

The Crypt 3847 Park Blvd (at University) 619/692-9499

Pleasures & Treasures 2228 University Ave (at Texas St) 619/822-4280 • clsd Tue • gay-owned

Romantix Adult Superstore 1407 University Ave (at Richmond) 619/299-7186

The Rubber Rose 3812 Ray St (at N Park Way) 619/296-7673 • clsd Mon • women-owned sexuality shop

San Francisco

San Francisco is divided into 7 geographical areas:
SF—Overview
SF—Castro & Noe Valley
SF—South of Market
SF—Polk Street Area
SF—Downtown & North Beach
SF—Mission District
SF—Haight, Fillmore, Hayes Valley

SF—Overview

Info Lines & Services

AA Gay/ Lesbian 1821 Sacramento St 415/674-1821 • check www.aasf.org for meeting times

The Center for Sex & Culture 1519 Mission St 94103 415/255-1155 • very queer-friendly classes, workshops, gatherings, events, readings & more

Crystal Meth Anonymous 415/835-4747

GLBT Hotline of San Francisco 415/355-0999 • 5pm-9pm Mon-Fri • peer-counseling • info

LYRIC (Lavender Youth Recreation/ Information Center) 127 Collingwood (btwn 18th & 19th) 415/703-6150, 800/969-6884 (NATIONWIDE) & 246-7743 (CA ONLY) • Talkline 6:30pm-9:30pm Mon-Sat, peer-run support line for LGBT youth under 24, at 415/863-3636 (in SF) or 800/246-7743 (in CA) or 800/969-6884 (nationwide)

The San Francisco LGBT Community Center 1800 Market St (at Octavia) 415/865-5555 • noon-10pm, from 9am Sat, clsd Sun • cybercenter • cafe • classes • child care & more

Women's Building 3543 18th St (btwn Valencia & Guerrero) 415/431-1180 • 9am-5pm Mon-Fri, till 6pm Sat • social/ support groups • housing & job listings • beautiful murals

Bars

Thursday Ladies Night with "Betty's List" 415/777-1508 • Th only • mostly women • check bettyslist.com for location

Nightclubs

Trannyshack 415/863-6623 • occasional drag events, check trannyshack.com for info

Restaurants

Beach Chalet Brewery & Restaurant 1000 Great Hwy (at Fulton St) 415/386-8439

Entertainment & Recreation

Baker Beach Lincoln Blvd at Bowley, in the Presidio • popular nude beach

Bay Area Derby Girls • SF Bay Area's female roller derby league • visit www.bayareaderbygirls.com for events

Betty's List 415/503-1375 • online & email info service for LGBT community • events • check out www.bettyslist.com • lesbian-owned

Brava! 2781 24th St (btwn York & Hampshire) 415/641-7657, 415/647-2822 (BOX OFFICE) • theater w/ culturally diverse performances by women • wheelchair access

Castro Theatre 429 Castro (at Market) 415/621-6120 • art house cinema • many LGBT & cult classics • live organ evenings

Cruisin' the Castro Tours tour meets at the rainbow flag at Harvey Milk Plaza (corner of Castro & Market) 415/255-1821 • "The 'original' historical walking tour of the Castro, the world's largest gay mecca. Fun & easy!"

Femina Potens 2199 Market St (at Sanchez) 415/864-1558 • nonprofit art gallery & performance space promoting women & transfolk in the arts

➤**Frameline** 415/703-8650 • LGBT media arts foundation • sponsors annual SF Int'l LGBT Film Festival in June

The Intersection for the Arts 446 Valencia St (btwn 15th & 16th Sts) 415/626-2787, 415/626-3311 (BOX OFFICE) • San Francisco's oldest alternative arts space (since 1965!) w/ plays, art exhibitions, live jazz, literary series, performance art & much more

San Francisco

WHERE THE GIRLS ARE:

Younger, radical dykes call the Mission or the lower Haight home, while upwardly mobile couples stake out Bernal Heights and Noe Valley. Hip, moneyed dykes live in the Castro. The East Bay is home to lots of lesbian feminists, older lesbians, and lesbian moms (see East Bay listings).

ENTERTAINMENT:

Theatre Rhinoceros 415/861-5079, 2926 16th St.

LGBT PRIDE:

June. 415/864-3733, web: www.sfpride.org.

ANNUAL EVENTS:

June - San Francisco Int'l Lesbian/Gay Film Festival 415/703-8650, web: www.frameline.org.

July - Up Your Alley Fair 415/861-3247, web: folsomstreetevents.org. Local SM/leather street fair held in Dore Alley, South-of-Market.

September - Folsom Street Fair 415/861-3247, web: folsomstreetevents.org. Huge SM/leather street fair, topping a week of kinky events.

September - MadCat Women's Int'l Film Festival 415/436-9523, web: www.madcatfilmfestival.org.

October - Castro Street Fair 415/841-1824, web: www.castrostreetfair.org. Arts and community groups street fair.

CITY INFO:

San Francisco Convention & Visitors Bureau 415/391-2000, web: www.sfvisitor.org.

WEATHER:

A beautiful summer comes at the end of September and lasts through October. Much of the city is cold and fogged-in June through September, though the Castro and Mission are usually sunny. The cold in winter is damp, so bring lots of layers. When there isn't a drought, it also rains in the winter months of November through February.

ATTRACTIONS:

Alcatraz 415/981-7625, web: www.nps.gov/alcatraz.

Asian Art Museum 415/ 581-3500, www.asianart.org.

Cablecars.

California Academy of Sciences 415/ 379–8000, web: www.calacademy.org.

Chinatown.

Coit Tower.

Exploratorium 415/561-0360, web: www.exploratorium.edu.

Fisherman's Wharf & Pier 39 (take the F Car from the Castro down Market & along the Embarcadero to get there).

Golden Gate Park.

Haight & Ashbury Sts.

Japantown.

North Beach.

Mission San Francisco de Assisi.

SF Museum of Modern Art 415/357-4000, web: www.sfmoma.org.

Twin Peaks.

BEST VIEW:

After a great Italian meal in North Beach, go to the top floor of the North Beach parking garage on Vallejo near Stockton, next to the police station. If you're in the Castro or the Mission, head for Dolores Park, at Dolores and 20th St. Other good views: Golden Gate Bridge, Kirby Cove (a park area to the left, just past the Golden Gate Bridge in Marin), Coit Tower, Twin Peaks, Bernal Hill.

TRANSIT:

Yellow Cab 415/333-3333.

Luxor Cab 415/282-4141.

Quake City Shuttle 415/255-4899.

511, web: 511.org. Covers all Bay Area transit (also traffic).

Muni 415/673-6864, web: www.sfmuni.org.

Bay Area Rapid Transit (BART) 415/989-2278, subway, web: www.bart.gov.

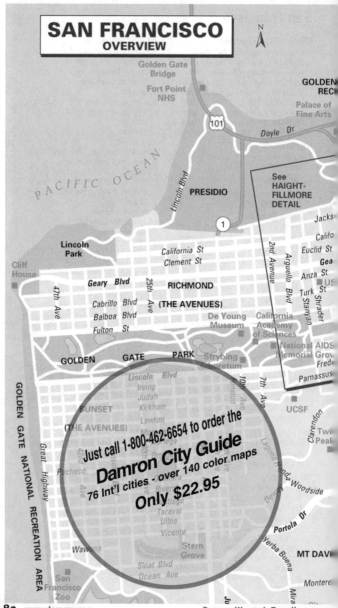

Local Tastes of the City Tours 415/665-0480, 888/358-8687 • explore the history & culture of local neighborhoods, including Chinatown & North Beach/ Little Italy • as "we eat our way through San Francisco"

The Marsh 1062 Valencia (at 22nd St) 415/826-5750 (EVENT INFO) & 641-0235 (OFFICE), 800/838-3006 (BOX OFFICE) • queer-positive theater

➤ **National AIDS Memorial Grove** Golden Gate Park (on corner of Middle Drive East & Bowling Green Dr) 415/765-0497, 888/294-7683 • located in a lush, historic dell in Golden Gate Park • guided tours available 9am-noon every 3rd Sat • wheelchair access

QComedy Gay Comedy Showcase 415/533-9133 • see website for locations • popular • lesbians/ gay men • cover charge (sliding scale) • see www.qcomedy.com for location

San Francisco Pride 1800 Market St, PMB #Q31 94102 415/864-3733 • one of the world's biggest

Sappho Sailors 415/345-1780 • sunset cruises, day adventures, sailing lessons & more

Steve Silver's Beach Blanket Babylon 678 Beach Blanket Babylon Ave (formerly Green St) (btwn Powell & Columbus, in Club Fugazi) 415/421-4222 • the USA's longest running musical revue & wigs that must be seen to be believed • very popular • 21+ except Sun

Thanks Babs, the Day Tripper 702/370-6961 • tours & getaways • full service concierge for San Francisco & Bay Area • it's like having a lesbian aunt in Northern California!

Theatre Rhinoceros 2926 16th St (at S Van Ness) 415/861-5079 (BOX OFFICE), 415/552-4100 • LGBT theater

Victorian Home Walks 415/252-9485 • custom-tailored walking tours w/ San Francisco resident • gay-owned

What's Up! Events Hotline for Sistahs 510/835-6126 • for lesbians of African descent

Yerba Buena Center for the Arts 701 Mission St (at 3rd St) 415/978-2787 (BOX OFFICE), 415/978-2700 (ADMINISTRATIVE) • annual season includes wide variety of contemporary dance, theater & music • also film theater & gallery

PUBLICATIONS

BAR (Bay Area Reporter) 415/861-5019 • the weekly LGBT newspaper

Bay Times 415/626-0260 • popular • good Bay Area resource listings

SF—Castro & Noe Valley

ACCOMMODATIONS

24 Henry & Village House 24 Henry St & 4080 18th St (btwn Sanchez & Noe) 415/864-5686, 800/900-5686 • B&B • mostly gay men • some shared baths • nonsmoking • WiFi • one-bdrm apt also available • gay-owned • $75-139

Andrew Whelan House 300 Castro St (at 16th St) 415/621-7736 • gay/ straight • Victorian home & garden • shared baths • nonsmoking • WiFi • gay-owned • $90-130

Beck's Motor Lodge 2222 Market St (at Sanchez) 415/621-8212, 800/955-2325 • gay-friendly • in the heart of the Castro • kids/ pets ok • wheelchair access • $93-151

➤ **Belvedere House** 598 Belvedere St (at 17th St) 415/731-6654, 877/226-3273 • popular • lesbians/ gay men • wall-to-wall books, art & style • WiFi • German spoken • nonsmoking • gay-owned • $115-159

Casa Buena Vista Corona Heights (near Market & Castro) 916/974-7409, 916/813-3119 (CELL) • gay-friendly • rental apts • nonsmoking • kids ok • WiFi • $225-250

Castro Suites 927 14th St (at Noe) 415/437-1783 • gay/ straight • furnished apts • kitchen • nonsmoking • WiFi • gay-owned • $200-220

Edwardian San Francisco 1668 Market St (btwn Franklin & Gough) 415/864-1271, 888/864-8070 • gay-friendly • hot tub • jacuzzi • some shared baths • nonsmoking • $119-249

Inn on Castro 321 Castro St (btwn 16th & 17th) 415/861-0321 • lesbians/ gay men • B&B known for its hospitality & friendly atmosphere • full brkfst • nonsmoking • WiFi • gay-owned • $100-250

Olive's Gate Guesthouse 3796 23rd St (at Church) 415/821-6039 • gay/ straight • studio apt • full kitchen • private entrance & garden • nonsmoking • WiFi • lesbian-owned • $115

The Parker Guest House 520 Church St (at 17th) 415/621-3222, 888/520-7275 • popular • mostly gay men • guesthouse complex w/ gardens • steam spa • nonsmoking • WiFi • gay-owned • $139-249

Travelodge Central 1707 Market St (at Valencia) 415/621-6775, 800/578-7878 (RESERVATIONS) • gay-friendly • nonsmoking rooms available • close to LGBT center • $99-179

➤**The Willows Inn** 710 14th St (at Church) 415/431–4770, 800/431–0277 • lesbians/gay men • "amenities, comfort, great location" • nonsmoking • WiFi • lesbian & gay-owned • $99-190

BARS

440 Castro 440 Castro St 415/621–8732 • noon-2am • popular • mostly gay men • neighborhood bar • leather • bears • women genuinely welcome

The Bar on Church 198 Church St (at Market) • 5pm-2am, from 3pm wknds • mostly gay men • more women Tues • neighborhood bar

Blackbird 2124 Market St 415/503–0630 • gay/straight • neighborhood bar • gay-owned

Buck Tavern 1655 Market St (at Gough) 415/874–9183 • 4:30pm-midnight, till 2:30am wknds, from noon Sun • gay/straight • neighborhood bar • food served

The Cafe 2369 Market St (at Castro) 415/861–3846 • 4pm-2am, from 3pm Sat, from 2pm Sun • popular • lesbians/gay men • dancing/DJ • young crowd • deck overlooking Castro & Market

Cafe du Nord 2170 Market St (at Sanchez) 415/861–5016 • gay-friendly • alternative • live music • theme nights • dinner some veggie

CAV Wine Bar & Kitchen 1666 Market St (at Gough) 415/437–1770 • 5:30pm-11pm, till midnight Fri-Sat, clsd Sun • gay/straight • also restaurant

Delicious 2369 Market St (at the Cafe) 408/792–3466 (INFO LINE) • 3:30pm-9pm 3rd Sat only • mostly women • T-dance • go-go girls • smoking patio

Harvey's 500 Castro St 415/431–4278 • 11am-11pm, 9am-2am wknds • popular • lesbians/gay men • neighborhood bar • occasional drag performers • also restaurant • wheelchair access

The Lookout 3600 16th St (at Market) 415/431–0306 • 11am-2am • mostly gay men • more women Th for Les Ladies

Martuni's 4 Valencia St (at Market) 415/241–0205 • 4pm-2am • gay/straight • piano bar & lounge • great martinis

The Mint 1942 Market St (at Buchanan) 415/626–4726 • noon-2am • lesbians/gay men • popular karaoke bar nights • also sushi restaurant • food served till 11pm (till midnight wknds)

The Mix 4086 18th St 415/431–8616 • 3pm-2am, from 8am wknds • mostly gay men • neighborhood bar • heated patio

Moby Dick 4049 18th St (at Hartford) • 2pm-2am, from noon wknds • mostly gay men • neighborhood bar • videos

Pan Dulce 2369 Market St (at the Cafe) 415/861–3846 • 9pm-2am Th only • lesbians/gay men • dancing/DJ • Latino/a • "The Castro's Biggest Latino Party!"

Pilsner Inn 225 Church St (at Market) 415/621–7058 • 10am-2am • popular • mostly gay men • neighborhood bar • great patio

Q Bar 456 Castro St 415/864–2877 • 4pm-2am, from 2pm wknds • popular • mostly gay men, more women Tue • neighborhood bar • dancing/DJ • sidewalk patio • wheelchair access

Swirl 572 Castro St (at 19th) 415/864–2262 • 1pm-8pm, till 9pm Fri-Sat • gay-friendly • wine bar & wine store

Tease 2344 Market St (at Castro, at Trigger) • 3pm-9pm 2nd Sat only • mostly women • dancing/DJ

Trigger 2344 Market St (at Castro) 415/551–2582 • 4pm-2am • mostly men • dancing/DJ

NIGHTCLUBS

Foreplay 2247 Market St (at Lime) • 6pm-10pm Tue only • mostly women • rotating female DJs • food served

CAFES

Cafe Flore 2298 Market St (at Noe) 415/621–8579 • 7am-2am • popular • lesbians/gay men • some veggie • full bar • great patio • WiFi

Caffe Trieste 1667 Market St (at Gough) 415/551–1000 • 6:30am-10pm, till 11pm Fri-Sat • popular • great coffee • live music

Duboce Park Cafe 2 Sanchez St (at Duboce) 415/621–1108 • 7am-8pm • outdoor seating

Jumpin' Java 139 Noe St (at 14th St) 415/431–5282 • 6:30am-7:30pm, 7am-8pm wknds • WiFi

Lovejoy's Tea Room 1351 Church St (at Clipper) 415/648–5895 • 11am-6pm, clsd Mon-Tue • popular • for a tea party fit for a queen

Orbit Room Cafe 1900 Market St (at Laguna) 415/252–9525 • 2pm-2am, till midnight Sun • also bar

Philz Coffee 4023 18th (at Noe) • 6am-8pm

Samovar Tea Lounge 498 Sanchez St (at 18th St) 415/626–4700 • 10am-10pm • tea culture from around the world

Sweet Inspiration 2239 Market St **415/621–8664** • 8am-11pm, 8am-12:30am Fri-Sat • popular wknd nights • food served • fabulous desserts

Restaurants

2223 Market 2223 Market St **415/431–0692** • dinner, Sun brunch • popular • contemporary American • full bar • wheelchair access

Anchor Oyster Bar 579 Castro St (at 19th) **415/431–3990** • 11:30am-10pm, from 4pm Sun • lesbians/ gay men • beer/ wine • women-owned

Bagdad Cafe 2295 Market St **415/621–4434** • open till midnight, 24hrs Th-Sat • lesbians/ gay men • diner • some veggie

Bisou 2367 Market St (at 17th) **415/556–6200** • dinner nightly, Sun brunch, clsd Mon • French

Blue 2337 Market St (btwn Castro & Noe) **415/863–2583** • 11:30am-11pm, wknd brunch from 10:30am • popular • homecooking served w/ style • some veggie • beer/ wine

Catch 2362 Market St **415/431–5000** • lunch & dinner, wknd brunch • seafood • live music

Chloe's 1399 Church St (at 26th St) **415/648–4116** • 8am-4pm • popular • come early for the excellent wknd brunch

Chow 215 Church St (at Market) **415/552–2469** • 8am-11pm, till midnight wknds • popular • patio

Cove Cafe 434 Castro St **415/626–0462** • 8am-9pm, till 10pm Fri-Sat • lesbians/ gay men • some veggie • wheelchair access

Eric's Chinese Restaurant 1500 Church St (at 27th St) **415/282–0919** • 11am-9pm • popular

Eureka Restaurant & Lounge 4063 18th St (at Hartford) **415/431–6000** • dinner nightly • lounge upstairs

Firewood Cafe 4248 18th St (at Diamond St) **415/252–0999** • 11am-11pm • rotisserie chicken, pastas, oven-fired pizzas, salads

Home 2100 Market St (at Church) **415/503–0333** • 11am-midnight, wknd brunch 10am-2pm • popular

Hot Cookie 407 Castro St **415/621–2350** • 6am-1am • hot cookies!

Ike's Place 3506 16th St (at Sanchez) **415/553–6888** • 10am-7pm • amazing sandwiches • plenty veggie/ vegan • long wait

It's Tops 1801 Market St (at Octavia) **415/431–6395** • 8am-3pm & 8pm-3am (Wed-Sat) • classic diner • great hotcakes

Kasa Indian Eatery 4001 18th St (at Noe) **415/621–6940** • 11am-10pm, till 11pm Fri-Sat • plenty veggie

La Méditerranée 288 Noe (at Market) **415/431–7210** • 11am-10pm, till 11pm Sat-Sun • beer/ wine

Leticia's 2200 Market St (at 15th) **415/864–5384** • lunch & dinner • Mexican

Nirvana Restaurant & Bar 544 Castro St (btwn 18th & 19th) **415/861–2226** • Southeast Asian • patio

Orphan Andy's 3991 17th St **415/864–9795** • 24hrs • diner • gay-owned

Poesia Osteria Italiana 4072 18th St (at Collingwood) **415/252–9325** • dinner nighly, great food & full bar

The Sausage Factory 517 Castro St **415/626–1250** • 11:30am-midnight • lesbians/ gay men • pizza & pasta • some veggie • beer/ wine

Sparky's 242 Church St (at Market) **415/626–8666** • 24hrs • popular late night • diner • some veggie

Squat & Gobble 3600 16th St **415/552–2125** • 8am-10pm • popular wknds for brkfst • outdoor seating

Sumi 4243 18th St (at Diamond) **415/626–7864** • 5pm-10pm • lesbians/ gay men • cont'l/ Japanese

Thailand Restaurant 438-A Castro St **415/863–6868** • 11am-10pm • plenty veggie

Triple Crown 1772 Market St (near Gough) **415/863–3516** • dinner nightly, Sun brunch • DJs by night • gay-owned

Woodhouse Fish Co 2073 Market St (at 14th) **415/437–2722** • noon-9:30pm • New England clam shack-style seafood

Zuni Cafe 1658 Market St (at Franklin) **415/552–2522** • lunch & dinner • clsd Mon • popular • upscale cont'l/ Mediterranean • full bar

Entertainment & Recreation

Castro Country Club 4058 18th St (at Hartford) **415/552–6102** • alcohol- & drug-free space

Pink Triangle Park near Market & Castro • "in remembrance of LGBT victims of the Nazi regime"

BOOKSTORES

A Different Light 489 Castro St
415/431-0891 • 10am-10pm, till 11pm Fri-Sat
• LGBT • readings

Aardvark Books 227 Church St
415/552-6733 • 10:30am-10:30pm • mostly
used • good LGBT section

Books, Inc 2275 Market St **415/864-6777** •
9:30am-11pm, till 10pm Sun • LGBT section •
readings • wheelchair access

Get Lost 1825 Market St (at Guerrero)
415/437-0529 • 10am-7pm, till 6pm Sat,
11am-5pm Sun • travel books • LGBT section

RETAIL SHOPS

Best in Show 545 Castro St (btwn 18th &
19th) **415/864-7387** • 11am-8pm, 11am-7pm
Sat, 11am-6pm Sun • pet boutique

Cold Steel America 2377 Market St (at 17th
St, 2nd flr) **415/621-7233** • noon-8pm •
piercing & tattoo studio • also 1783 Haight St,
415/933-7233

De La Sole Footwear 4126 18th St
415/255-3140 • 11am-7pm, till 8pm Sat

HRC Action Center & Store 600 Castro St
415/431-2200 • 10am-9pm, till 10pm wknds
• Human Rights Campaign merchandise &
info

Kenneth Wingard 2319 Market St (btwn
Castro & Noe) **415/431-6900**

Rolo 2351 Market St **415/431-4545** • 11am-
8pm, till 7pm Sun • designer labels

See Jane Run Sports 3910 24th St (at Noe)
415/401-8338 • 11am-7pm, 10am-6pm Sat,
till 5pm Sun • women's athletic apparel

Under One Roof 518 Castro **415/503-2300,
800/525-2125** • 10am-8pm, 11am-7pm Sun •
100% donated to AIDS relief • wheelchair
access

GYMS & HEALTH CLUBS

Gold's Gym Castro 2301 Market St
415/626-4488 • lesbians/ gay men • day
passes available

SF—South of Market

ACCOMMODATIONS

Americania Hotel 121 7th St (at Mission)
415/626-0200 • gay-friendly • pool • bar &
restaurant • wheelchair access • $149-249

Budget Hotel 1139 Market St **415/864-9343**
• gay-friendly • hostel • $66+

Holiday Inn Civic Center 50 8th St (at
Market) **415/626-6103, 800/972-3124** • gay-
friendly • pool • small pets ok • WiFi •
wheelchair access

Hotel Whitcomb 1231 Market St (btwn 8th
& 9th) **415/626-8000, 800/227-4747** • gay-
friendly • landmark hotel on Pride route • also
restaurant & Starbucks on-site • WiFi •
wheelchair access • $89+

The Mosser Hotel 54 4th St (btwn Market &
Mission) **415/986-4400, 800/227-3804** • gay/
straight • 1913 landmark hotel • some shared
baths • nonsmoking • kids ok • also
restaurant • SF cuisine • full bar • $79-319

Renoir Hotel 45 McAllister St (at Market St)
415/626-5200, 800/576-3388 • gay/ straight •
bar & restaurant • nonsmoking • WiFi •
wheelchair access • Damron discount • $89-
350

Vagabond Inn San Francisco 385 9th St
(at Harrison) **415/431-5131, 800/522-1555** •
gay/ straight • motel • close to SOMA bars •
limited parking • kids ok • WiFi • wheelchair
access • $69-139

W San Francisco 181 Third St
**415/777-5300, 877/WHOTELS (RESERVATIONS
ONLY)** • gay-friendly • pool • WiFi • wheelchair
access • also XYZ restaurant & bar • $229-429

The Westin San Francisco Market Street
50 3rd St **415/974-6400, 888/627-8561** • gay-
friendly • hip hotel w/ spectacular views •
sauna • kids ok • nonsmoking • $179-249

BARS

Chaps II 1225 Folsom St (at 8th)
415/255-2427 • 7pm-2am, from 3pm Fri-Sun
• mostly gay men

Dada SF Studio 86 2nd St (btwn Market &
Mission) **415/357-1367** • 4pm-midnight, till
2am Th-Sat, from 8pm Sat, clsd Sun • gay/
straight • art gallery • gay-owned

The Eagle Tavern 398 12th St (at Harrison)
415/626-0880 • noon-2am • mostly gay men
• popular • leather • occasional women's
leather events • live music • patio

Fem 46 Minna St (at 2nd, btwn Mission &
Howard, at Harlot) • 3pm-10pm 1st Sun only
• mostly women • dancing/DJ

Hole in the Wall Saloon 1369 Folsom
(btwn 9th & 10th) **415/431-4695** • noon-2am
• mostly gay men • neighborhood bar •
leather

NIGHTCLUBS

1015 Folsom 1015 Folsom St (at 6th) 415/431-1200 • 10pm-close Fri-Sat • gay/straight • popular • dancing/DJ • call for events • cover charge

Asia SF 201 9th St (at Howard) 415/255-2742 • 10pm-close Wed-Sat • popular • gay/straight • dancing/DJ • mostly Asian American • theme nights • go-go boys • cover charge • also Cal-Asian restaurant w/ en-drag dinner service

Bootie 375 11th St (at Harrison, at DNA Lounge) 415/626-1409 (DNA INFO LINE) • 9pm-close 2nd, 3rd & 4th Sat • gay-friendly • dancing/DJ • mashups, bootlegs, bastard pop • cover charge

Cat Club 1190 Folsom St (at 8th) 415/703-8965 • gay/straight • dancing/DJ • hosts many one-night clubs & events

The Crib SF 715 Harrison St (at 3rd) • 9:30pm-2am Th only • lesbians/gay men • dancing/DJ • "all-video pop club" • younger crowd • 18+ • cover

Eight 1151 Folsom St (btwn 7th & 8th St) 415/431-1151 • 9pm-3am • popular • gay/straight • dancing/DJ • theme nights • smoking patio

Endup 401 6th St (at Harrison) 415/646-0999 (INFO LINE), 415/357-0827 • gay/straight • dancing/DJ • multiracial • theme nights • popular Sun mornings

Flourish 1501 Folsom St (at 11th, at Paradise Lounge) • 9pm 3rd Fri only • mostly women • dancing/DJ • dress to impress!

Ghetto Disco 401 6th St (at Harrison, at Endup) • 11pm-11am Fri only • mostly gay men • dancing/DJ

Grind 316 11th St (at Folsom, at Mist) 415/552-6478 • 9pm Wed only • lesbians/gay men • dancing/DJ • multiracial • 18+ • hip hop

Les Ladies 1015 Folsom St 415/431-0306 • 2nd Sat only • mostly women

The Stud 399 9th St (at Harrison) 415/863-6623 • 5pm-2am • popular • lesbians/gay men • dancing/DJ • theme nights

Tool Box 93 9th St (at Jessie St, at Club 93) • 4th Th only • lesbians/gay men • drag • comedy • dancing/DJ

CAFES

Brain Wash 1122 Folsom St (at 7th St) 415/861-3663, 415/431-9274 • 7am-11pm, 8am-10pm Sun • popular • cafe & laundromat • beer/wine

RESTAURANTS

Ame 689 Mission St (at 3rd St, in St Regis Hotel) 415/284-4040 • lunch & dinner • full bar • reservations recommended

Ananda Fuara 1298 Market St (at 9th) 415/621-1994 • 8am-8pm, till 3pm Wed, clsd Sun • vegetarian

Anchor & Hope 83 Minna St (at 2nd St) 415/501-9100 • lunch Mon-Fri, dinner nightly • seafood

Bacar Restaurant & Wine Salon 448 Brannan St (btwn 3rd & 4th) 415/904-4100 • dinner nightly, Sun brunch • some veggie • live shows • reservations • wheelchair access

Butter 354 11th St (btwn Folsom & Harrison) 415/863-5964 • 6pm-2am, clsd Mon • "white trash bistro" • full bar • theme nights

Don Ramon's Mexican Restaurant 225 11th St (btwn Howard & Folsom) 415/864-2700 • lunch Tue-Fri, dinner nightly, clsd Mon • some veggie • full bar

Fringale 570 4th St (btwn Bryant & Brannan) 415/543-0573 • lunch Tue-Fri & dinner nightly • French bistro • wheelchair access

Heaven's Dog 1148 Mission St (at 7th) 415/863-6008 • 5pm-1am, till 9pm Sun • Chinese

Orson 508 4th St • 5pm-11pm, clsd Sun • lesbian-owned

Rocco's Cafe 1131 Folsom St (at 7th) 415/554-0522 • brkfst & lunch daily, dinner Wed-Sat only

The Slanted Door 1 Ferry Building #3 415/861-8032 • popular • Vietnamese • full bar • reservations recommended

Supperclub 657 Harrison St (btwn 2nd & 3rd) 415/348-0900 • 6:30pm-close • live performance art & acrobatics • also full bar & nightclub

Ted's 1530 Howard St (at 11th) 415/552-0309 • 6am-6pm, 8am-5pm wknds • excellent deli sandwiches

Tu Lan 8 6th St (at Market) 415/626-0927 • lunch & dinner, clsd Sun • Vietnamese • some veggie • dicey neighborhood but delicious (& cheap) food

Woodward's Garden 1700 Mission St (at Duboce) 415/621-7122 • dinner from 6pm, clsd Sun-Mon • wheelchair access

Yank Sing 101 Spear St (One Rincon Center, at Mission) 415/957-9300 • 11am-3pm Mon-Fri, 10am-4pm wknds • popular • dim-sum heaven! • also catering & delivery

ENTERTAINMENT & RECREATION

111 Minna Gallery 111 Minna St (at 2nd St) 415/974–1719 • gay/ straight • dancing/DJ Wed for Qool • call for events

RETAIL SHOPS

Dandelion 55 Potrero Ave (at Alameda St) 415/436–9500, 888/548–1968 • 10am-7pm, till 6pm Fri-Sat, noon-5pm Sun • gay-owned

Madame S 385 8th St (at Harrison) 415/863–9447 • 11am-7pm • women's bondage & fetish fashion & equipment

Mr S Leather & Fetters USA San Francisco 385 8th St (at Harrison) 415/863–7764, 800/746–7677 (ORDERS) • 11am-7pm • erotic goods • custom leather • latex

Off Ramp Leathers 342 9th St #205 415/255–8117 • custom motorcycle leathers

Stompers 323 10th St (at Folsom) 415/255–6422, 888/BOOTMAN • 11am-6pm, noon-4pm Sun, clsd Mon

Stormy Leather 1158 Howard St (btwn 7th & 8th) 415/626–1672, 800/486–9650 • noon-7pm • leather • latex • toys • magazines

GYMS & HEALTH CLUBS

Gold's Gym San Francisco 1001 Brannan St (at 9th) 415/552–4653 • popular • day passes available

SF—Polk Street Area

ACCOMMODATIONS

Broadway Manor Inn 2201 Van Ness Ave (at Broadway) 415/776–7900, 800/727–6239 • gay-friendly • motel • close to Fisherman's Wharf • kids ok • WiFi • wheelchair access • lesbian, gay & straight-owned • $54-119

Cathedral Hill Hotel 1101 Van Ness Ave 415/776–8200, 800/622–0855 • gay-friendly • pool • also restaurant & lounge

The Monarch Hotel 1015 Geary St (at Polk) 415/673–5232, 800/777–3210 • gay-friendly • Edwardian boutique-style hotel • kids ok • nonsmoking rooms available • $79+

Nob Hill Motor Inn 1630 Pacific Ave (at Van Ness Ave) 415/775–8160, 800/343–6900 • gay-friendly • hotel • kids ok • nonsmoking • WiFi • wheelchair access • $79-169

The Phoenix Hotel 601 Eddy St (at Larkin) 415/776–1380, 800/248–9466 • gay-friendly • 1950s-style motor lodge • popular • fave of celebrity rockers • pool • kids ok • WiFi • also Bambuddha lounge & restaurant • $139+

Radisson Hotel Fisherman's Wharf 250 Beach St (at Hyde) 415/392–6700, 800/333–3333 • gay-friendly • pool • WiFi • wheelchair access

San Francisco City Center Hostel 685 Ellis St (at Larkin) 415/474–5721, 888/464–4872 • gay-friendly • shared & private rooms available • free brkfst • kids ok • nonsmoking • WiFi • $23+ (dorm) & $82+ (private room)

BARS

The Cinch 1723 Polk St (at Clay) 415/776–4162 • 6am-2am • mostly gay men • neighborhood bar • patio • lots of pool tables & no attitude • DJ Th-Sat • drag shows Fri & Sun • WiFi • wheelchair access

Deco Lounge 510 Larkin (at Turk) 415/346–2025 • 10am-2am • mostly gay men • neighborhood bar • theme nights • drag shows

Edinburgh Castle 950 Geary St (at Polk) 415/885–4074 • 5pm-2am • mostly straight Scottish pub w/ single malts & authentic fish & chips • live bands

Gangway 841 Larkin St (btwn Geary & O'Farrell) 415/776–6828 • 8am-2am • mostly gay men • dive neighborhood bar

Kimo's 1351 Polk St (at Pine) 415/885–4535 • 8am-2am • mostly gay men • neighborhood bar • live bands upstairs • gay-owned

Lush Lounge 1092 Post (at Polk) 415/771–2022 • 3pm-2am, from noon wknds • popular • gay/ straight • wheelchair access

NIGHTCLUBS

Divas 1081 Post St (at Larkin) 415/474–3482 • 6am-2am • mostly gay men • neighborhood bar • dancing/DJ • multiracial • transsexuals, transvestites & their admirers • drag shows

CAFES

La Boulange de Polk 2310 Polk St (at Green St) 415/345–1107 • 7am-6:30pm, till 6pm Sun, clsd Mon • French bakery & cafe • outdoor seating • Parisian down to the attitude

Quetzal Internet Cafe 1234 Polk St (at Sutter) 415/673–4181, 888/673–4181 • 6:30am-10pm • popular • beer/ wine • live shows • videos • WiFi

RESTAURANTS

Antica Trattoria 2400 Polk St (at Union) 415/928–5797 • dinner, clsd Mon • Italian

Lemongrass 2348 Polk St (at Union) 415/929–1183, 415/346–1818 • 11am-10pm, till 10:30pm Fri-Sat • Thai • beer served

Rex Cafe 2323 Polk St **415/441–2244, 415/441–9244** • from 5pm, dinner, also brunch 10am-3pm Sat-Sun • American • full bar

Street 2141 Polk St (btwn Broadway & Vallejo) **415/775–1055** • dinner, clsd Mon • incredible hamburgers

BOOKSTORES

Books Inc Opera Plaza 601 Van Ness Ave (at Turk) **415/776–1111** • 8:30am-9:30pm • independent • LGBT section • many readings

EROTICA

Good Vibrations 1620 Polk St (btwn Sacramento & Clay) **415/345–0400** • 11am-7pm, till 8pm Th, till 9pm Fri-Sat • clean, well-lighted sex toy store • also mail order

SF—Downtown & North Beach

ACCOMMODATIONS

Adante Hotel 610 Geary St (at Jones) **415/673–9221, 888/423–0083** • gay/ straight • in Union Square/ Theater District • kids ok • nonsmoking • wheelchair access • $89-159

Andrews Hotel 624 Post St (btwn Taylor & Jones) **415/563–6877, 800/926–3739** • gay-friendly • Victorian hotel • also restaurant • Italian • nonsmoking • WiFi • $79-179

Argonaut Hotel 495 Jefferson St (at Hyde) **415/563–0800, 866/415–0704** • gay-friendly • boutique hotel in Fisherman's Wharf • pets ok • nonsmoking • wheelchair access • $129+

Dakota Hotel/ Hostel 606 Post St (at Taylor) **415/931–7475** • gay-friendly • near Union Square • kids ok • WiFi • $55+

Executive Hotel Vintage Court 650 Bush St (at Powell) **415/392–4666, 888/388–3932** • gay-friendly • nonsmoking • WiFi • also world-famous 5-star Masa's restaurant • French • wheelchair access • $109-239

Galleria Park Hotel 191 Sutter St (at Kearny) **415/781–3060, 800/792–9639** • gay/ straight • boutique hotel • kids ok • WiFi • nonsmoking • wheelchair access • $159-249

Grand Hyatt San Francisco 345 Stockton St (at Sutter) **415/398–1234, 800/233–1234** • gay-friendly • restaurant & lounge • gym • $165-345

Halcyon Hotel 649 Jones St (at Post) **415/929–8033, 800/627–2396** • gay-friendly • kids/ pets ok • nonsmoking • WiFi • gay & straight-owned/ run • $69-99/ night; $450/ week

Handlery Union Square Hotel 351 Geary St **415/781–7800, 800/995–4874** • gay-friendly • steps from Union Square • pool • WiFi • wheelchair access • $159-309

Harbor Court Hotel 165 Steuart St (btwn Howard & Mission) **415/882–1300, 866/792–6283** • gay-friendly • in the heart of the Financial District • gym • pool • pets ok • WiFi • wheelchair access • $139-249

Hotel Adagio 550 Geary St (at Shannon) **415/775–5000, 800/228–8830** • gay-friendly • hotel • kids ok • wheelchair access • $189+

Hotel Bijou 111 Mason St (at Eddy) **415/771–1200, 800/771–1022** • gay/ straight • nonsmoking • kids ok • WiFi • wheelchair access • $119-149

The Hotel California 580 Geary St (at Jones) **415/441–2700, 800/227–4223** • gay-friendly • also popular Millennium gourmet vegetarian restaurant & bar • nonsmoking • $149-219

Hotel Carlton 1075 Sutter (at Larkin) **415/673–0242, 800/922–7586** • gay-friendly • also Saha restaurant (Arabic-fusion) • $129+

Hotel Diva 440 Geary St (at Mason) **415/885–0200, 800/553–1900** • gay-friendly • hip hotel • also gym • nonsmoking • WiFi • $139-249

Hotel Fusion 140 Ellis St (at Powell St) **415/568–2525, 866/753–4244** • gay/ straight • nonsmoking • kids ok • WiFi • wheelchair access • $79-225

Hotel Griffon 155 Steuart St (at Mission) **415/495–2100, 800/321–2201** • gay/ straight • WiFi • also restaurant • bistro/ cont'l • wheelchair access • $139-599

Hotel Mark Twain 345 Taylor St (at Ellis) **415/673–2332, 877/854–4106** • gay-friendly • also Fish & Farm restaurant • wheelchair access • $89-250

Hotel Metropolis 25 Mason St (at Eddy) **800/553–1900** • gay-friendly • near Union Square shopping • WiFi

Hotel Monaco 501 Geary St (at Taylor) **415/292–0100, 866/622–5284** • gay-friendly • nonsmoking rooms available • pets ok • also Grand Cafe restaurant (French) • $229+

Hotel Nikko San Francisco 222 Mason St (at Ellis) **415/394–1111, 866/645–5673** • gay-friendly • pool • health club & spa • nonsmoking • also restaurant • wheelchair access • $200+

Hotel Palomar 12 4th St (at Market) **415/348–1111, 866/373–4941** • gay/ straight • boutique hotel • dogs ok • WiFi • $209-999

The Hotel Rex 562 Sutter St (at Powell) 415/433–4434, 800/433–4434 • gay-friendly • full bar • wheelchair access • $189+

Hotel Triton 342 Grant Ave (at Bush) 415/394–0500, 800/433–6611 • gay/ straight • designer theme rooms • kids/ pets ok • WiFi • wheelchair access • $149+

Hotel Union Square 114 Powell St (at Ellis) 800/553–1900 • gay-friendly • 1930s art deco lobby • original art by Gladys Perint Palmer in rooms • WiFi

Hotel Vitale 8 Mission St (at Steuart) 415/278–3700, 888/890–8688 • gay-friendly • 4-star, full-service waterfront luxury hotel • rooftop spa • restaurant & bar • nonsmoking • WiFi • wheelchair access • $199-399

Hyatt Regency San Francisco 5 Embarcadero Center (at California) 415/788–1234, 800/233–1234 • gay-friendly • luxury waterfront hotel • WiFi • $189-394

The Inn at Union Square 440 Post St (at Powell) 415/397–3510, 800/288–4346 • gay-friendly • steps from Union Square • nonsmoking • WiFi • $189-499

JW Marriott Hotel San Francisco 500 Post St (at Mason) 415/771–8600, 800/605–6568 • gay-friendly • hotel • kids ok • nonsmoking • WiFi • wheelchair access • $229-450

Kensington Park Hotel 450 Post St 800/553–1900 • gay-friendly • on Union Square • nonsmoking • WiFi • also Farallon Restaurant

King George Hotel 334 Mason St (at Geary) 415/781–5050, 800/288–6005 • gay/ straight • also The Windsor Tearoom • kids ok • WiFi • wheelchair access • $109-269

Larkspur Hotel 524 Sutter St (at Powell) 415/421–2865, 800/919–9779 • gay-friendly • B&B-inn on Union Square • afternoon tea & wine hour • WiFi • $89-219

Luz Hotel 725 Geary Blvd (at Leavenworth) 415/928–1917 • gay/ straight • clothing-optional jacuzzi • gay-owned • $65-85

The Maxwell/ Frank Hotel 386 Geary St (at Mason) 415/986–2000, 800/553–1900 • gay/ straight • newly restored 1908 art deco masterpiece • wheelchair access • $129+

Nob Hill Hotel 835 Hyde St (btwn Bush & Sutter) 415/885–2987, 877/662–4455 • gay/ straight • European-style hotel • jacuzzi • nonsmoking • kids ok • also restaurant • wheelchair access

Parkside SF 520 Grant Ave (at California St) 415/713–5476 • downtown apt • WiFi • lesbian-owned • $99-155

Petite Auberge 863 Bush St (at Taylor) 415/928–6000, 800/365–3004 • gay-friendly • B&B • kids ok • nonsmoking • $159+

Prescott Hotel 545 Post St (btwn Taylor & Mason) 415/563–0303, 866/271–3632 • gay-friendly • small luxury hotel • nonsmoking • WiFi • $199-340

San Francisco Downtown Hostel 312 Mason St (at O'Farrell) 415/788–5604, 800/909–4776 • gay/ straight • hostel • shared baths • kids ok • open kitchen • WiFi • wheelchair access • $23+ (dorm) & $60+ (private room)

Sir Francis Drake Hotel 450 Powell St (at Sutter) 415/392–7755, 800/795–7129 • gay-friendly • 1928 landmark • also restaurant & Starlight Room • WiFi

The Stratford Hotel 242 Powell St (at Geary) 415/397–7080, 877/922–5928 • gay-friendly • near Union Square • $69+

The Touchstone Hotel 480 Geary St (btwn Mason & Taylor) 415/771–1600, 800/620–5889 • gay-friendly • in Theater District • full brkfst • kids ok • wheelchair access • $79-169

Union Square Plaza Hotel 432 Geary St (at Mason) 415/776–7585, 800/841–3135 • gay-friendly • 1 block from Union Square • $69-109

Vertigo Hotel 940 Sutter St (at Leavenworth) 415/885–6800, 800/808–9675 • gay/ straight • boutique hotel • nonsmoking • WiFi • wheelchair access • $129+

BARS

Aunt Charlie's Lounge 133 Turk St (at Taylor) 415/441–2922 • 10am-midnight, till 2am Fri- Sat • mostly gay men • neighborhood bar • drag shows wknds

Bourbon & Branch 501 Jones St (at O'Farrell) • gay/ straight • in Prohibition-era speakeasy • drinks are worth the price • reservations required

CAFES

Caffe Trieste 601 Vallejo St 415/392–6739 • get a taste of the real North Beach (past & present)

Sugar Cafe 679 Sutter St (at Taylor) 415/441–5678 • 6am-2am • cafe by day, cocktails by night • WiFi

RESTAURANTS

Ar Roi 643 Post St (at Jones) 415/771–5146 • lunch Mon-Sat, dinner nightly • Thai

The Buena Vista 2765 Hyde St (at Beach) 415/474–5044 • 9am-2am, from 8am wknds • the restaurant that introduced Irish coffee to America

Cafe Claude 7 Claude Ln (near Bush & Kearny) **415/392-3515** • 11:30am-10:30pm, from 5:30pm Sun • live music Th-Sat • as close to Paris as you can get in SF • beer/ wine

Canteen 817 Sutter St **415/928-8870** • great brkfst

Le Colonial 20 Cosmo Pl (btwn Taylor & Jones) **415/931-3600** • dinner only • Vietnamese • full bar

Dottie's True Blue Cafe 522 Jones St (at Geary) **415/885-2767** • 7:30am-3pm, clsd Tue • plenty veggie • great brkfst • gay-owned

Golden Era 572 O'Farrell St **415/673-3136** • 11am-9pm, clsd Tue • vegetarian/ vegan

Mario's Bohemian Cigar Store Cafe 566 Columbus Ave (at Union) **415/362-0536** • 10am-close • great foccacia sandwiches • some veggie • beer/ wine • WiFi

Millennium 580 Geary St (at Jones) **415/345-3900** • dinner only • Euro-Mediterranean • upscale vegetarian

ENTERTAINMENT & RECREATION

Rrazz Room 222 Mason (at Nikko Hotel) **415/394-1189** • gay/ straight • cabaret w/ world-class performers • wheelchair access

Sunday's A Drag@The Starlight Room 450 Mason St (at Powell) **415/395-8595** • Sun brunch • noon & 2:30pm drag shows

BOOKSTORES

Book Passage 1 Ferry Bldg #42 **415/835-1020** • 10am-8pm, from 8am Sat, 10am-7pm Sun-Mon • independent

City Lights Bookstore 261 Columbus Ave (at Pacific) **415/362-8193** • 10am-midnight • historic beatnik bookstore • many progressive titles • LGBT section • whole floor for poetry

RETAIL SHOPS

Dragonfly Ink 760 Market St #854 (btw 3rd & 4th St) **415/550-1445** • tattoo studio • woman-owned

SF—Mission District

includes Bernal Heights

ACCOMMODATIONS

Bernal Heights Duplex, Carriage House 3 Porter St (at Crescent) **415/601-6460** • gay/ straight • 1-bdrm & studio apt vacation rentals • nonsmoking • WiFi • woman-owned • $700-850/ week

Elements 2516 Mission St (at 21st St) **415/647-4100, 866/327-8407** • gay/ straight • hostel w/ private or shared rooms • brkfst included • WiFi • also restaurant & cafe • $28

The Inn San Francisco 943 S Van Ness Ave (btwn 20th & 21st) **415/641-0188, 800/359-0913** • gay-friendly • Victorian mansion • hot tub • some shared baths • kitchens • fireplaces • patio • nonsmoking • WiFi • $125-335

Noe's Nest B&B 1257 Guerrero St (btwn 24th & 25th Sts) **415/821-0751** • gay-friendly • WiFi • nonsmoking • kids ok • $89-199

BARS

Argus Lounge 3187 Mission St, Bernal Heights (at Valencia) **415/824-1447** • 4pm-2am • gay/ straight • pool table

El Rio 3158 Mission St (at Cesar Chavez) **415/282-3325** • 5pm-close Mon-Th, from 3pm wknds • popular • gay/ straight • frequent women's events • neighborhood bar • multiracial • live shows • free oysters Fri • patio (check out the flyers to find out when the cool dyke musicians in town will be performing)

Esta Noche 3079 16th St (at Mission) **415/861-5757** • 1pm-2am • mostly gay men • dancing/DJ • mostly Latino/a • transgender-friendly • live shows • salsa & disco in a classic Tijuana dive

➤ **Lexington Club** 3464 19th St (btwn Mission & Valencia) **415/863-2052** • 5pm-2am, from 3pm Fri-Sun • popular • mostly women • neighborhood bar • hip young crowd • lesbian-owned

Lone Palm 3394 22nd St (at Guerrero) **415/648-0109** • 4pm-2am • gay/ straight • a bar for grown ups (we know you're out there)

Nihon 1779 Folsom St (at 14th St) **415/552-4400** • 6pm-close, clsd Sun • gay/ straight • whiskey lounge • dancing/DJ • also Japanese restaurant

Phone Booth 1398 S Van Ness Ave (at 25th) **415/648-4683** • noon-2am, from 1pm wknds • lesbians/ gay men • neighborhood bar

Pop's Bar 2800 24th St (btwn York & Bryant) **415/401-7677** • 1pm-2am • gay/ straight • neighborhood dive bar • photobooth • wheelchair access

Stray Bar 309 Cortland Ave, Bernal Heights (at Bocana) **415/821-9263** • 4pm-2am, from 2pm wknds • gay/ straight • women's night Wed • neighborhood bar • lesbian-owned

Truck Bar 1900 Folsom St (at 15th) **415/252-0306** • 11pm-2am, from 4pm Sat, from 2pm Sun • lesbians/ gay men • neighborhood bar • food served • gay-owned

Wild Side West 424 Cortland, Bernal Heights (at Wool) **415/647–3099** • 1pm-2am • gay/ straight • neighborhood bar • patio • magic garden • wheelchair access

Zeitgeist 199 Valencia St (at Duboce) **415/255–7505** • 9am-2am • divey biker bar & beer garden • food served

NIGHTCLUBS

Cream 550 Barneveld (at space550, 2 blocks off Bayshore Blvd at Industrial) **408/792–3466** • women's dance party • multiracial • check www.creamsf.com for dates

Hard French 3158 Mission (at El Rio) • 3pm-8pm 1st Sat only • lesbians/ gay men • soul dance party • food served

Heavy Rotation 3158 Mission St (at El Rio) **415/282–3325** • 10pm 2nd Fri • queer dance party, all sizes welcome!

The Make-Out Room 3225 22nd St (at Mission) • 6pm-2am • gay/ straight • dancing/DJ • popular Stay Gold party last Wed of month

Mango 3158 Mission (at El Rio) **415/339–8310** • 3pm-8:30pm 4th Sat March-Nov • women only • dancing/DJ • multiracial • food served • cover

Mighty 119 Utah St (at 15th St) **415/762–0151 (INFO LINE), 415/626–7001 (OFFICE)** • gay-friendly • dancing/DJ • call for events

Stay Gold 3225 22nd St (at Mission, at the Makeout Room) • 10:30pm last Wed only • lesbians/ gay men • dancing/DJ

Sundance Saloon 550 Barneveld Ave (at space550, 2 blocks off Bayshore Blvd at Industrial) **415/820–1403** • 5pm-10:30pm Sun (lessons at 5:30pm) & 6:30pm-10:30pm Th (lessons at 7pm) • mostly gay men • women welcome! • dancing/DJ • country/ western • gay-owned • cover

Thee Parkside 1600 17th St (at Wisconsin, Potrero Hill) **415/252–1330** • gay-friendly • live bands & events

CAFES

Dolores Park Cafe 501 Dolores St (at 18th St) **415/621–2936** • 7am-8pm • outdoor seating overlooking Dolores Park • live music Fri

Farleys 1315 18th St (at Texas St, Potrero Hill) **415/648–1545** • 6:30am-10pm, from 7:30am Sat & 8am Sun • coffeehouse • live music some nights

The Revolution Cafe 3248 22nd St (btwn Mission & Bartlett) **415/642–0474** • 9am-1am • live music

The **Lexington Club**

Your friendly neighborhood dyke bar!

Mon – Thur 5 PM to 2 AM
Fri – Sun 3 PM to 2 AM

3464 19th Street
San Francisco
www.lexingtonclub.com

Tartine Bakery 600 Guerrero St (at 18th St) **415/487–2600** • 8am-7pm, from 9am Sun • French bakery w/ a line out the door

RESTAURANTS

Aslam's Rasoi 1037 Valencia St (at 21st) **415/695–0599** • 5pm-11pm • Indian & Pakistani

Boogaloos 3296 22nd St (at Valencia) **415/824–4088** • 8am-3pm • worth the wait

Charanga 2351 Mission St (at 20th St) **415/282–1813** • 5:30pm-close, clsd Sun-Mon • Cuban-Caribbean tapas • beer/ wine/ sangria • plenty veggie • wheelchair access • women-owned

Circolo 500 Florida St (at Mariposa) **415/553–8560** • 5pm-close, clsd Mon • Latin-Asian fusion • full bar

Delfina 3621 18th St (at Dolores) **415/552–4055** • 5:30pm-10pm • popular • excellent Tuscan cuisine • full bar • reservations required • patio (summers)

El Farolito 2779 Mission St (at 24th) **415/824–7877** • popular • 10am-3am • delicious, cheap burritos & more

Farina 3560 18th St (at Guerrero) **415/565–0360** • dinner nightly, Sun brunch • Italian

Luna Park 694 Valencia St (at 18th) **415/553–8584**

Mabel's Just For You 722 22nd St (at 3rd St) **415/647–3033** • 7:30am-3pm • popular • lesbians/ gay men • Southern brkfst • some veggie • women-owned

Maverick 3316 17th St (btwn Mission & Valencia) **415/863–3061** • dinner nightly, also wknd brunch • upscale American • great wine selection

Medjool 2522 Mission St (at 21st St) **415/550–9055** • 5pm-10pm, till 11pm Fri-Sat, clsd Sun • tapas • plenty veggie • also cafe, lounge & rooftop bar • wheelchair access

Moki's Sushi & Pacific Grill 615 Cortland Ave (at Moultine) **415/970–9336** • dinner nightly

Pauline's Pizza Pie 260 Valencia St (btwn 14th & Duboce) **415/552–2050** • 5pm-10pm, clsd Sun-Mon • popular • lesbians/ gay men • gourmet pizza • beer/ wine

Picaro 3120 16th St (at Valencia) **415/431–4089** • 5pm-10pm, from 9:30am wknds • Spanish tapas bar • beer/ wine • wheelchair access

Pork Store Cafe 3122 16th St (at Valencia) **415/626–5523** • 8am-4pm daily & 7pm-3am Fri-Sat • popular • American/ diner food • great brkfsts • also 1451 Haight St, 415/864-6981

Range 842 Valencia St (btwn 19th & 20th Sts) **415/282–8283** • dinner nightly • popular • California contemporary • full bar

Slow Club 2501 Mariposa (at Hampshire) **415/241–9390** • lunch Mon-Fri, dinner Mon-Sat, wknd brunch • full bar • wheelchair access

ENTERTAINMENT & RECREATION

Dolores "Beach" Church & 19th St (at the top corner of Dolores Park) • popular "beach" in Dolores Park • crowded on sunny days

Metronome Ballroom 1830 17th St (at De Haro) **415/252–9000** • gay/ straight • dance lessons • salsa to swing • dance parties wknds • call for events • cover charge

Women's Building 3543 18th St (btwn Valencia & Guerrero) **415/431–1180** • check out some of the most beautiful murals in the Mission District

BOOKSTORES

Dog Eared Books 900 Valencia St (at 20th) **415/282–1901** • 10am-10pm, till 8pm Sun • new & used • good LGBT section

Modern Times Bookstore 888 Valencia St **415/282–9246** • 10am-9pm, 11am-6pm Sun • progressive • LGBT section • readings • wheelchair access

RETAIL SHOPS

Black & Blue Tattoo 381 Guerrero (at 16th St) **415/626–0770** • noon-7pm • mostly women • women-owned

Body Manipulations 3234 16th St (btwn Guerrero & Dolores) **415/621–0408** • noon-7pm, from 2pm Mon-Th • piercing (walk-in basis) • jewelry

The Scarlet Sage 1173 Valencia St (near 23rd St) **415/821–0997** • 11am-6pm • spiritual & metaphysical emporium • lesbian-owned

EROTICA

Good Vibrations 603 Valencia St (at 17th St) **415/522–5460, 800/289–8423** • 11am-7pm, till 8pm Th, till 9pm Fri-Sat • popular • clean, well-lighted sex toy store • wheelchair access • also mail order

SF—Haight, Fillmore, Hayes Valley

Accommodations

555 Haight Guesthouse 555 Haight St 415/551–2555, 800/785–5504 • gay/ straight • hostel • kids ok • nonsmoking • $22-44

The Chateau Tivoli 1057 Steiner St (at Golden Gate) 415/776–5462, 800/228–1647 • gay-friendly • historic San Francisco B&B • nonsmoking • WiFi • $130-290

Edward II Inn & Suites 3155 Scott St 415/922–3000, 800/473–2846 • gay-friendly • European-style B&B • own gym & pub • WiFi • $69-249

Francisco Bay Inn 1501 Lombard St (at Franklin) 415/474–3030, 800/410–7007 • gay-friendly • motel • kids ok • nonsmoking • WiFi • $75-169

Hayes Valley Inn 417 Gough St (at Hayes) 415/431–9131, 800/930–7999 • gay/ straight • European-style pension • shared baths • close to opera & symphony • nonsmoking • WiFi • $73-112

Heritage Marina Hotel 2550 Van Ness Ave 415/776–7500, 866/714–6835 • gay-friendly • vintage '50s hotel • located in the Marina District • pool • $72-169

Hotel Del Sol 3100 Webster St (at Greenwich) 415/921–5520, 877/433–5765 • popular • gay/ straight • pool • nonsmoking • wheelchair access • WiFi • $159+

Hotel Drisco 2901 Pacific Ave (at Broderick) 415/346–2880, 800/634–7277 • gay-friendly • 1903 hotel in Pacific Heights • kids ok • nonsmoking • $189+

Hotel Kabuki 1625 Post St (at Laguna) 415/922–3200, 800/333–3333 • gay-friendly • in the heart of Japantown • wheelchair access • $159+

Hotel Majestic 1500 Sutter St (at Gough) 415/441–1100, 800/869–8966 • gay-friendly • one of SF's earliest grand hotels • also restaurant • full bar • kids ok • WiFi • nonsmoking • wheelchair access • $125+

Hotel Tomo 1800 Sutter St (at Buchanan) 415/921–4000, 888/822–8666 • gay-friendly • in Japantown • restaurant & bar • nonsmoking • WiFi • $109+

Inn 1890 1890 Page St (near Stanyan) 415/386–0486, 888/INN-1890 • gay/ straight • Victorian near Golden Gate Park • kitchens • fireplaces • kids ok • nonsmoking • apt available • gay-owned • $99-169

Inn at the Opera 333 Fulton St (at Franklin) 415/863–8400, 800/325–2708 • gay-friendly • nonsmoking • wheelchair access • $145+

Jackson Court 2198 Jackson St (at Buchanan) 415/929–7670 • gay-friendly • 19th-c brownstone mansion • nonsmoking • kids ok • WiFi • $160+

The Laurel Inn 444 Presidio Ave (at Sacramento) 415/567–8467, 800/552–8735 • gay-friendly • hotel • in Pacific Heights • nonsmoking • kids/ pets ok • $139+

Metro Hotel 319 Divisadero St (at Haight) 415/861–5364 • gay-friendly • European-style pension • WiFi • $76-130

Queen Anne Hotel 1590 Sutter St (at Octavia) 415/441–2828, 800/227–3970 • gay-friendly • popular • 1890 landmark • wood-burning fireplaces • kids ok • nonsmoking • WiFi • gay-owned • $139-350 (mention Damron for discount)

San Francisco Fisherman's Wharf Hostel Fort Mason, Bldg 240 (at Franklin) 415/771–7277, 800/909–4776 • gay/ straight • hostel • shared baths • kids ok • cafe & kitchen • WiFi • nonsmoking • wheelchair access • $26+ (dorm) & $75+ (private room)

Shannon-Kavanaugh Guest House 722 Steiner St (at Hayes) 415/563–2727 • gay-friendly • 1-bdrm garden apt in SF's famous "Postcard Row" • kids/ pets ok • nonsmoking • wheelchair access • gay-owned • $150-300

Stanyan Park Hotel 750 Stanyan St (at Waller) 415/751–1000 • gay-friendly • restored Victorian hotel listed on the Nat'l Register of Historic Places • kids ok • completely nonsmoking • WiFi • wheelchair access • $139-350

Bars

Marlena's 488 Hayes St (at Octavia) 415/864–6672 • noon-2am • mostly gay men • neighborhood bar • drag shows Sat • also piano bar • Cheers for drag queens (a friendly oasis in hip & het Hayes Valley) • wheelchair access

Rickshaw Stop 155 Fell St (btwn Van Ness & Franklin) 415/861–2011 • Wed-Sat only, Rebel Girl 1st Sat • popular hipster bar, nightclub (live bands) • restaurant

Trax 1437 Haight St (at Masonic) 415/864–4213 • noon-2am • mostly gay men • neighborhood bar

Nightclubs

Cockblock 155 Fell St (at Rickshaw Shop) • 10pm-2am 2nd Sat • queer dance party for lezzies, the happy gays, you & your friends

Underground SF 424 Haight St (at Webster) **415/864-7386** • 5:30pm-2am, clsd Mon • gay/straight • dancing/DJ • alternative • theme nights • call for events • more gay Sat

CAFES

Blue Bottle Coffee Company 315 Linden St (at Gough St) **415/252-7535** • 7am-5pm, from 8am wknds • popular • organic coffee & treats from kiosk in front of artists' workshop—wonderful hidden treat

RESTAURANTS

Absinthe Brasserie & Bar 398 Hayes St (at Gough) **415/551-1590** • lunch & dinner, bar till 2am Fri-Sat, clsd Mon

Alamo Square Seafood Grill 803 Fillmore (at Grove) **415/440-2828** • dinner only

Burma Superstar 309 Clement St **415/387-2147** • lunch & dinner • Burmese food that will rock your world

Cheese Steak Shop 1716 Divisadero St (btwn Bush & Sutter) **415/346-3712** • 9am-10pm, from 11am Sun, from 10am Mon • best cheese steak outside Philly • also veggie versions

Citizen Cake 2125 Fillmore St (at California) • 8am-10pm Tue-Fri, from 10am Sat, 10am-5pm Sun, clsd Mon • popular • lesbian chef

Eliza's 2877 California (at Broderick) **415/621-4819** • lunch Mon-Wed, dinner nightly • excellent Chinese food & stylish decor

Ella's 500 Presidio Ave (at California) **415/441-5669** • brkfst & lunch Mon-Fri, dinner Wed-Sun • popular wknd brunch

Garibaldi's 347 Presidio Ave (at Sacramento) **415/563-8841** • open for lunch weekdays & dinner nightly • Mediterranean • full bar • wheelchair access • gay-owned

Greens Fort Mason, Bldg A (near Van Ness & Bay) **415/771-6222** • lunch Tue-Sat, dinner Mon-Sat, Sun brunch • gourmet vegetarian • spectacular view of the Golden Gate Bridge

Little Star Pizza 846 Divisadero St (btwn Fulton & McAllister Sts) **415/441-1118** • 5pm-10pm, till 11pm Fri-Sat, clsd Mon • Chicago-style deep dish pizza

Memphis Minnie's BBQ 576 Haight St **415/864-7675** • 11am-10pm, till 9pm Sun, clsd Mon

Nopa 560 Divisadero St (at Hayes) **415/864-8643** • dinner 6pm-1am, bar from 5pm • urban rustic

Park Chow 1238 9th Ave (btwn Irving & Lincoln) **415/665-9912** • 11am-10pm, brunch from 10am wknds • popular • eclectic & affordable

Patxi's Chicago Pizza 511 Hayes St (at Octavia St) **415/558-9991** • 11am-10pm, clsd Mon • Chicago-style deep dish pizza • also thin crust

Pluto's Fresh Food for a Hungry Universe 627 Irving St (btwn 7th & 8th Aves) **415/753-8867** • 11am-10pm • design your own sandwiches

Suppenküche 601 Hayes (at Laguna) **415/252-9289** • dinner, Sun brunch • German cuisine served at communal tables • beer/wine • gay-owned

Thep-Phanom 400 Waller St (at Fillmore) **415/431-2526** • 5:30pm-10:30pm • popular • excellent Thai food (worth the wait!) • beer/wine

BOOKSTORES

Bibliohead Bookstore 334 Gough St (at Hayes) **415/621-6772** • eclectic used books • queer section

The Booksmith 1644 Haight St **415/863-8688, 800/493-7323 (IN US)** • cool independent • big-name author readings

RETAIL SHOPS

Flight 001 525 Hayes St (btwn Octavia & Laguna) **415/487-1001, 877/354-4481** • 11am-7pm, till 6pm Sun • way cool travel gear

Timbuk 2 Store 506 Hayes St **415/252-9860**

GYMS & HEALTH CLUBS

Kabuki Springs & Spa 1750 Geary Blvd (at Fillmore) **415/922-6000** • 10am-9:45pm • traditional Japanese bath w/ extensive menu of spa sevices

San Jose

INFO LINES & SERVICES

AA Gay/ Lesbian 274 E Hamilton Ave, Ste D, Campbell **408/374-8511** • 24hr helpline • check www.aasanjose.org for meeting schedule

Billy DeFrank LGBT Community Center 938 The Alameda **408/293-3040** • 3pm-9pm, from 10am Wed, clsd Sat-Mon • wheelchair access

ACCOMMODATIONS

Hotel De Anza 233 W Santa Clara St **408/286-1000, 800/843-3700** • gay-friendly • art deco gem • nonsmoking • Italian restaurant • wheelchair access • $125-329

Moorpark Hotel 4241 Moorpark Ave **408/864-0300, 877/740-6622** • gay-friendly • hotel in heart of Silicon Valley • pool • also bar & restaurant • wheelchair access • $99-149

BARS

Brix 349 s 1st St (at San Salvadore) **408/947-1975** • 6pm-2am, from 4pm Sun • lesbians/ gay men • neighborhood bar • dancing/DJ • multiracial • transgender-friendly • karaoke • videos • wheelchair access

Mac's Club 39 Post St (btwn 1st & Market) **408/288-8221** • noon-2am • mostly men • neighborhood bar • patio

Renegades 501 W Taylor St (at Coleman Ave) **408/275-9902** • noon-2am • mostly gay men • neighborhood bar • leather • patio

NIGHTCLUBS

Afterglow 349 S 1st St (at Brix) • 5pm-10pm 3rd Sun only • mostly women • dancing/DJ

Octopussy 389 S 1st St (at Motif) **408/792-3466** • 2nd Fri only • mostly women • dancing/DJ • mostly Latina

Splash 65 Post St (at 1st) **916/441-6823 1** • 9pm-2am Th-Sat • mostly gay men • dancing/DJ • karaoke • videos • gay-owned

RESTAURANTS

Eulipia Restaurant & Bar 374 S 1st St (at San Carlos) **408/280-6161** • dinner only, clsd Mon • eclectic new American • full bar

Pasta Pomodoro 1205 The Alameda (at Race) **408/292-9929** • Italian

Vin Santo 1346 Lincoln Ave **408/920-2508** • lunch Wed-Fri, dinner nightly, clsd Mon • Northern Italian • wine bar

ENTERTAINMENT & RECREATION

Tech Museum of Innovation 201 S Market St (at Park Ave) **408/294-8324** • 10am-5pm • IMAX Dome Theater • a must-see for digital junkies

PUBLICATIONS

ON Magazine 1346 The Alameda 7-106 **408/287-7281** • LGBT newspaper

EROTICA

Leather Masters 969 Park Ave (at Race St) **408/293-7660** • noon-8pm, clsd Sun-Mon • handmade leather clothes • rubber/ fetishwear • electrical/ medical gear, etc

Pleasures from the Heart 1565 Winchester Blvd, Campbell **408/871-1826** • 11am-10pm, 1pm-7pm Sun • intimate apparel, toys & gifts • women-owned

San Luis Obispo

INFO LINES & SERVICES

GALA/ Gay and Lesbian Alliance of the Central Coast 1060 Palm St (at Santa Rosa St) **805/541-4252** • 9am-6pm, clsd wknds

Women's Community Center 4251 S Higuera St (SLO Business Ctr) **805/544-9313** • counseling • support • referrals

ACCOMMODATIONS

The Madonna Inn 100 Madonna Rd **805/543-3000, 800/543-9666** • gay-friendly • one-of-a-kind theme rooms • food served • pool • $168+

The Palomar Inn 1601 Shell Beach Rd, Shell Beach **805/773-4204, 888/384-4004** • gay/ straight • motel • non smoking • WiFi • $80-110

Sycamore Mineral Springs Resort 1215 Avila Beach Dr **805/595-7302, 800/234-5831** • gay-friendly • hot mineral spring spa • integrative retreat center • also award-winning restaurant

CAFES

Linnaea's Cafe 1110 Garden St (near Marsh) **805/541-5888** • 6:30am-11pm • plenty veggie • live entertainment

Outspoken Cafe 1422 Monterey St (at California) **805/788-0885** • 7am-5pm, 8am-4pm Sat, clsd Sun • cafe & juice bar • lesbian-owned

West End Espresso & Tea 670 Higuera St #A (at Nipomo) **805/543-4902, 805/544-3581** • 6am-7pm, till 9:30pm Th, till 8pm Fri-Sat • outdoor seating

RESTAURANTS

Big Sky Cafe 1121 Broad St (btwn Higuera & Marsh Sts) **805/545-5401** • 7am-10pm, 8am-9pm Sun-Th

Novo 726 Higuera St **805/543-3986** • lunch & dinner

BOOKSTORES

Coalesce Bookstore 845 Main St, Morro Bay **805/772-2880** • 10am-5:30pm, 11am-4pm Sun • LGBT section • women-owned

Volumes of Pleasure 1016 Los Osos Valley Rd, Los Osos **805/528-5565** • 10am-6pm, clsd Sun-Mon • wheelchair access • lesbian-owned

PUBLICATIONS

GALA News & Reviews **805/541-4252** • news & events for Central California coast

San Rafael

see Marin County

San Ramon

see East Bay

Santa Ana

see Orange County

Santa Barbara

see also Ventura

INFO LINES & SERVICES

Pacific Pride Foundation 126 E Haley St #A–11 **805/963-3636** • 9am-5pm Mon-Fri

ACCOMMODATIONS

Inn of the Spanish Garden 915 Garden St (at Carrillo) **805/564-4700, 866/564-4700** • gay/ straight • luxury hotel • pool • nonsmoking • kids ok • wheelchair access • $269-519

Old Yacht Club Inn 431 Corona Del Mar Dr **805/962-1277, 800/676-1676** • gay-friendly • only B&B on beach • full brkfst • nonsmoking • WiFi • $99-499

The Orchid Inn at Santa Barbara 420 W Montecito St **805/965-2333, 800/427-2156** • gay/ straight • 1900s Queen Anne Victorian • full brkfst • nonsmoking • WiFi • wheelchair access • gay-owned • $149-295

BARS

Reds Wine Bar 211 Helena Ave **805/966-5906** • 2pm-10pm, till 2am Th-Sat, clsd Mon • food served • live music • WiFi

NIGHTCLUBS

Flavor 15 W Ortega St (at Wildcat Lounge) **805/962-7970** • 9pm-2am Sun only • popular • lesbians/ gay men • dancing/DJ

CAFES

Our Daily Bread 831 Santa Barbara St **805/966-3894** • 6am-5:30pm, 7am-4pm Sat, clsd Sun • bakery/ cafe

RESTAURANTS

Joe's Cafe 536 State St **805/966-4638** • 7:30am-11pm

The Natural Cafe 508 State St **805/962-9494** • 11am-9pm

Opal Restaurant & Bar 1325 State St (at Sola St) **805/966-9676** • lunch (Mon-Sat) & dinner nightly • full bar

Sojourner Cafe 134 E Canon Perdido (at Santa Barbara) **805/965-7922** • 11am-11pm • plenty veggie • beer/ wine • wheelchair access

ENTERTAINMENT & RECREATION

Santa Barbara Mission 2201 Laguna St **805/682-4713** • the "queen of the missions" • take a self-guided tour btwn 9am-4:30pm daily & find out why

BOOKSTORES

Chaucer's Books 3321 State St (at Las Positas Rd, Loreto Plaza) **805/682-6787** • 9am-9pm, till 6pm Sun • popular •

EROTICA

The Riviera Adult Superstore 4135 State St (at Hwy 154 intersection) **805/967-8282** • 10am-midnight • pride items • community resources

Santa Clara

ACCOMMODATIONS

Avatar Hotel 4200 Great America Pkwy **408/235-8900, 800/586-5691** • gay/ straight • nonsmoking • WiFi • wheelchair access • $79-139

Biltmore Hotel & Suites 2151 Laurelwood Rd (at Montague Expwy) **408/988-8411, 866/469-9845** • gay-friendly • pool • also restaurant & gym • nonsmoking • WiFi • $89-359

NIGHTCLUBS

A Tinker's Damn (TD's) 46 N Saratoga Ave (at Stevens Creek) **408/243-4595** • 3pm-2am, from 1pm wknds • mostly gay men • dancing/DJ • drag shows

Santa Cruz

INFO LINES & SERVICES

AA Gay/ Lesbian 5732 Soquel Dr, Soquel **831/475-5782 (AA#)** • call or visit www.aasantacruz.org for meetings

The Diversity Center 1117 Soquel Ave **831/425-5422** • open daily • call for events • WiFi

ACCOMMODATIONS

Chaminade Resort & Spa 1 Chaminade Ln (at Soquel Ave) **831/475-5600, 800/283-6569** • gay-friendly • pool • nonsmoking • wheelchair access • $179-399

Dream Inn 175 W Cliff Dr **831/426-4330 , 866/774-7735** • gay/ straight • restaurant onsite • pool & hot tub • WiFi • wheelchair access • $150+

Pleasure Point Inn 23655 E Cliff Dr
831/475-4657 • gay-friendly • upscale
Mediterranean-style inn • overlooks Monterey
Bay • nonsmoking • WiFi • $225-295

BARS

Mad House 529 Seabright Ave (at Murray St)
831/425-2900 • 4pm-2am, clsd Mon • gay-
friendly • local bar • drag shows • gay-owned

NIGHTCLUBS

Blue Lagoon 923 Pacific Ave **831/423-7117**
• 3:30pm-2am • gay/ straight • dancing/DJ •
alternative • transgender-friendly • videos •
live bands some nights • wheelchair access

RESTAURANTS

Betty Burgers 505 Seabright Ave (at Murray)
831/423-8190 • 10am-10pm • retro burger
joint • outdoor seating • some veggie

Cafe Limelight 1016 Cedar St (at Locust St)
831/425-7873 • lunch & dinner, clsd Mon •
European • transgender-friendly • wheelchair
access • gay-owned

Cilantros Mexican Restaurant 1934 Main
St (in Town Center strip mall), Watsonville
831/761-2161 • lunch & dinner

Crêpe Place 1134 Soquel Ave (at Seabright,
across from Rio Theater) **831/429-6994** •
11am-midnight, from 9am Sat-Sun • live
music • full bar • garden patio • wheelchair
access

Saturn Cafe 145 Laurel St (at Pacific)
831/429-8505 • 10am-3am • light fare •
plenty veggie • lesbian-owned

Silver Spur 2650 Soquel Dr **831/475-2725** •
6am-3pm, clsd Sun

BOOKSTORES

Bookshop Santa Cruz 1520 Pacific Ave
831/423-0900 • 9am-10pm • cafe •
wheelchair access

GYMS & HEALTH CLUBS

Kiva Retreat House Spa 702 Water St (at
Ocean) **831/429-1142** • noon-11pm, till
midnight Fri-Sat • check for women-only &
men-only hours

EROTICA

Frenchy's Cruzin Books & Video 3960
Portola Dr (at 41st Ave) **831/475-9221** •
arcade, adult novelties, lingerie & DVDs

Santa Rosa

INFO LINES & SERVICES

AA Meetings in Sonoma County
707/544-1300 (AA#), 800/224-1300 • call or
visit www.sonomacountyaa.org for meeting
times

NIGHTCLUBS

The Vine 528 7th St **707/393-7104** •
4:30pm-2am Wed-Sat • gay-friendly •
dancing/DJ • theme nights • food served

CAFES

A' Roma Roasters 95 5th St (Railroad
Square) **707/576-7765** • 6am-close, from 7am
Sat-Sun • lesbians/ gay men • live music
wknds • wheelchair access • lesbian-owned

RESTAURANTS

Syrah 205 5th St (at Davis) **707/568-4002** •
lunch Tue-Sat & dinner nightly

EROTICA

Santa Rosa Adult Books 3301 Santa Rosa
Ave (at Todd) **707/542-8248**

Sausalito

see Marin County

Sebastopol

see Russian River & Sonoma County

Sonoma County

INFO LINES & SERVICES

AA Meetings in Sonoma County
707/544-1300 (AA#), 800/224-1300 • call or
check www.sonomacountyaa.org for meeting
times

Sonoma County Tourism Bureau
707/522-5800, 800/576-6662

ACCOMMODATIONS

Beltane Ranch 11775 Sonoma Hwy (Hwy
12), Glen Ellen **707/996-6501** • gay-friendly •
1892 New Orleans-style ranch house • $140-
220

Best Western Dry Creek Inn 198 Dry Creek
Rd, Healdsburg **707/433-0300, 800/222-5784**
• gay/ straight • near wineries • pool, gym
steam & sauna • pets ok • WiFi

Camellia Inn 211 North St, Healdsburg
707/433-8182, 800/727-8182 • gay-friendly •
Italianate Victorian • full brkfst • pool •
nonsmoking • WiFi • $189-259

The Gaige House 13540 Arnold Dr, Glen Ellen **707/935-0237, 800/935-0237** • gay-friendly • boutique hotel in the Wine Country • pool • WiFi • $225-695

Glenelly Inn & Cottages 5131 Warm Springs Rd, Glen Ellen **707/996-6720** • gay-friendly • B&B in 1916 inn • full brkfst • nonsmoking • WiFi • $119-299

Grape Leaf Inn 539 Johnson St, Healdsburg **707/433-8140, 866/433-8140** • gay-friendly • Queen Anne Victorian • full brkfst • WiFi • $200-395

Hyatt Vineyard Creek Hotel 170 Railroad St (at Third St), Santa Rosa **707/284-1234** • gay-friendly • resort • pool • kids/ pets ok • WiFi • seafood restaurant • wheelchair access • $149-249

Madrona Manor **707/433-4231, 800/258-4003** • gay-friendly • full brkfst • pool • nonsmoking • some rooms ok for kids • also restaurant • wheelchair access • $220-625

Magliulo's Rose Garden Inn 681 Broadway (at Andrieux), Sonoma **707/996-1031** • gay-friendly • WiFi • wheelchair access • $135-175

Midnight Sun Inn 428 Haydon St (at University), Healdsburg **707/433-1718** • gay-friendly • full brkfst • jacuzzi • nonsmoking • $145-165

Sonoma Chalet 18935 5th St W, Sonoma **707/938-3129, 800/938-3129** • gay-friendly • B&B inn & cottages • hot tub • $125-225

Thistle Dew Inn 171 W Spain St (at First St W), Sonoma **707/938-2909, 800/382-7895** • gay-friendly • located in Wine Country • whirlpool baths & fireplaces • free use of bikes • nonsmoking • WiFi • gay & straight-owned • $175-300

Vine Hill Inn B&B 3949 Vine Hill Rd, Sebastopol **707/823-8832** • gay-friendly • B&B in restored 1897 farmhouse • pool • $170

BARS

Black Cat Bar & Cafe 10056 Main St, Penngrove **707/793-9480** • 4pm-2am, 10am-11pm Sun, clsd Mon • mostly women • neighborhood bar • DJ Sat • also restaurant • live shows • lesbian-owned

CAFES

Coffee Catz 6761 Sebastopol Ave #300 (in Gravenstein Station), Sebastopol **707/829-6600** • 7am-6pm, till 10pm Wed (open mic), till 10pm Fri & Sat (live bands) • garden • WiFi

Screamin' Mimi's 6902 Sebastopol Ave (intersection of Hwy 12 & 116), Sebastopol **707/823-5902** • espresso drinks & homemade ice cream

RESTAURANTS

Estate 400 W Spain St, Sonoma **707/933-3663** • lunch & dinner, Sun brunch, clsd Mon • Italian

Mom's Apple Pie 4550 Gravenstein Hwy N, Sebastopol **707/823-8330** • pie worth stopping for on your way to & from Russian River!

Singletree Inn 165 Healdsburg Ave, Healdsburg **707/433-8263** • 7am-3pm • good brkfsts • famous BBQ sandwiches (including tofu) • some veggie • local wines • outdoor seating • lesbian-owned

Slice of Life 6970 McKinley St, Sebastopol **707/829-6627** • 11am-9pm, from 9am Sat-Sun, clsd Mon • vegan & vegetarian

ENTERTAINMENT & RECREATION

Out In The Vineyard **707/495-9732** • amazing tours of the wine country • gay owned

River's Edge Kayak & Canoe Company **707/433-7247** • river excursions • lesbian-owned

RETAIL SHOPS

Grower's Collective Tasting Room 452 First St E (at West Napa St), Sonoma **707/996-1364** • noon-5:30pm, clsd Tue-Th

Milk & Honey 123 N Main St, Sebastopol **707/824-1155** • 11am-7pm • transgender-friendly • goddess- & woman-oriented crafts • books • jewelry • cafe

EROTICA

The Sensuality Shoppe 2371-A Gravenstein Hwy S, Sebastopol **707/829-3999** • 11am-6pm • toys • books • videos • jewelry • woman-owned

Springville

ACCOMMODATIONS

Great Energy PO Box 473, 93265 **559/539-2382** • lesbians/ gay men • retreat in foothills of Sierra Nevada mtns • pool • hiking • kids ok • woman-owned • $85-125

Stockton

see also Modesto

NIGHTCLUBS

Paradise Club 10100 N Lower Sacramento Rd (near Grider) **209/477-4724** • 6pm-2am, from 3pm Sun • lesbians/ gay men • dancing/DJ • live shows • videos • young crowd

EROTICA

Suzie's Adult Superstores 3126 E Hammer Ln **209/952-6900** • 24hrs

Sunnyvale

see also San Jose

ACCOMMODATIONS

Wild Palms Hotel 910 E Fremont Ave (at Wolfe Ave) **408/738-0500, 800/538-1600** • gay-friendly • pool • hot tub • kids ok • WiFi • wheelchair access • $89+

Sutter Creek

ACCOMMODATIONS

The Foxes Inn of Sutter Creek 77 Main St (at Keys St) **209/267-5882, 800/987-3344** • gay-friendly • full brkfst • close to Shenandoah Valley wine region • nonsmoking • WiFi • gay-owned • $160-325

Temecula

NIGHTCLUBS

Club Escape 27497 Ynez Rd (at Aloha J's) **951/506-9889** • 9pm Wed only • lesbians/ gay men • dancing/DJ

Tiburon

see Marin County

Twentynine Palms

see Joshua Tree Nat'l Park

Ukiah

BARS

Perkins St Lounge 228 E Perkins St **707/462-0327** • 3pm-2am • gay-friendly • dancing/DJ • live shows • karaoke

Upland

NIGHTCLUBS

Oasis 1386 E Foothill Blvd #H (at Grove) **909/920-9590** • 6pm-2am Wed-Sat, from 8pm Sun • mostly gay men • dinner Wed-Sun • dancing/DJ • drag shows• wheelchair access

Vacaville

EROTICA

Sensations Love Boutique 1656 W Foothill Blvd (at Mountain) **909/985-1654**

INFO LINES & SERVICES

Solano Pride Center 1125 Missouri St #203-D, Fairfield **707/398-3463** • call for meeting times

Vallejo

includes Benicia

BARS

Town House Cocktail Lounge 401-A Georgia St (at Marin) **707/553-9109** • 1pm-midnight, from 10am Sat-Sun • gay-friendly • neighborhood bar • gay-owned

BOOKSTORES

Bookshop Benicia 856 Southampton Rd, Benicia **707/747-5155** • 10am-7pm, till 6pm wknds • wheelchair access

Ventura

see also Santa Barbara

INFO LINES & SERVICES

AA Gay/ Lesbian 805/389-1444 (AA#), 800/990-7750

Ventura County Rainbow Alliance 4567 Telephone Rd, Ste 100 **805/339-6340** • 9am-8pm • LGBT center

BARS

Paddy McDermott's 2 W Main St (at Ventura) **805/652-1071** • 2pm-2am • lesbians/ gay men • dancing/DJ • food served • live shows • karaoke • beer busts

EROTICA

Three Star Books 359 E Main St **805/653-9068** • 24hrs

Victorville

BARS

Ricky's 13728 Hesperia Rd #12 **760/951-5400** • 6pm-2am, clsd Mon • lesbians/ gay men, more women on Th • dancing/DJ • food served • karaoke

Westside 15 16868 Stoddard Wells Rd (off I-15) **760/243-9600** • 5pm-2am, from 4pm Sat, from 3pm Sun • lesbians/ gay men • neighborhood bar • ladies night Th • karaoke

Walnut Creek

see East Bay

Willits

Bookstores

Leaves of Grass 15 S Main St **707/459-3744**
• 10am-6pm, noon-5pm Sun

Yosemite Nat'l Park

Accommodations

The Ahwahnee Hotel Yosemite Valley Floor
559/252-4848, 866/875-8456 (reservations)
• gay-friendly • pool • non-smoking • also
restaurant • $408-984

Highland House B&B 3125 Wild Dove Ln
(at Jerseydale Rd), Mariposa **209/966-3737** •
gay-friendly • B&B near Yosemite & Sierra
Nat'l Forest • kids ok • $95-135

The Homestead 41110 Rd 600, Ahwahnee
559/683-0495, 800/483-0495 • gay-friendly •
cottages, suite & 2-bdrm house nestled under
the oaks on 160 acres • close to restaurants,
golf, hiking & biking • kitchens • fireplaces •
nonsmoking • kids ok • $110-374

June Lake Villager 2640 Hwy 158 (2.5 miles
W of Hwy 395), June Lake **760/648-7712,
800/655-6545** • gay-friendly • 20 minutes
from Yosemite • jacuzzi • nonsmoking • kids/
pets ok • women-owned • $65-300

Queen's Inn by the River 41139 Hwy 41,
Oakhurst **559/683-4354** • gay/ straight •
private patios & decks • some fireplaces •
garden w/ river view • nonsmoking • WiFi •
wheelchair access • lesbian-owned • $150-179

Rivendale Ranch 209/962-7425 • women
only • nonsmoking • also RV hookups •
women-owned • $110-150 ($25 RV)

Tenaya Lodge at Yosemite 1122 Hwy 41,
Fish Camp **559/683-6555, 888/514-2167** •
gay-friendly • resort w/ spa services •
restaurant • pets ok • pool

**The Yosemite Bug Rustic Mountain
Resort** 6979 Hwy 140, Midpines
209/966-6666, 866/826-7108 • gay-friendly •
hostel w/ dorms, cabins, private rooms & tents
• some shared baths • kids ok • nonsmoking •
WiFi • wheelchair access • $22-150

Yosemite View Lodge 11136 Hwy 140, El
Portal **209/379-2681, 888/742-4371** • gay-
friendly • 3 pools • lounge & 2 restaurants •
wheelchair access

Yosemite's Apple Blossom Inn B&B
559/642-2001, 888/687-4281 • gay-friendly
• B&B • 20 minutes from south entrance of
Yosemite Nat'l Park • hot tub • kids/ pets ok
nonsmoking • wheelchair access • $110-240

Colorado

Statewide

Publications

➤ **Out Front Colorado** 303/778-7900 •
statewide LGBT newspaper

Aspen

Accommodations

Aspen Mountain Lodge 311 W Main St
970/925-7650, 800/362-7736 • gay-friendly •
full brkfst • après-ski wine & cheese • kids/
pets ok • hot tub • pool • nonsmoking • $99-
379

Hotel Aspen 110 W Main St **970/925-3441,
800/527-7369** • gay-friendly • mountain brkfst
• après-ski wine & cheese • hot tub • pool •
nonsmoking • kids/ pets ok • $119+

Hotel Lenado 200 S Aspen St **970/925-6246,
800/321-3457** • gay-friendly • full brkfst • hot
tub • full bar • $145-335

St Moritz Lodge 334 W Hyman Ave
970/925-3220, 800/817-2069 • gay-friendly •
pool • hot tub/stream • nonsmoking • WiFi •
gay-owned • $20-298

Restaurants

Jimmy's 205 S Mill St (at Hopkins)
970/925-6020 • 5:30pm-11pm • also bar

Syzygy 308 E Hopkins Ave **970/925-3700** •
seasonal • 6pm-10:30pm, bar till 2am • some
veggie • live jazz • wheelchair access

Bookstores

Explore Booksellers & Bistro 221 E Main
(at Aspen) **970/925-5336, 800/562-7323** •
10am-10pm • also gourmet vegetarian
restaurant • WiFi • wheelchair access

Beaver Creek

Accommodations

Beaver Creek Lodge 26 Avondale Ln (at
Village Rd) **970/845-9800, 800/525-7280** •
gay-friendly • nonsmoking • also restaurant w/
mtn views & fire pits • pool • WiFi •
wheelchair access • $170-899

Boulder

Info Lines & Services

Boulder Pride 2132 14th St (at Pine)
303/499-5777 • LGBT resource center

ACCOMMODATIONS

The Briar Rose B&B 2151 Arapahoe Ave (at 22nd St) **303/442-3007, 888/786-8440** • gay-friendly • full organic brkfst • nonsmoking • WiFi • $139-204

CAFES

Walnut Cafe 3073 Walnut St (at 30th) **303/447-2315** • 7am-3pm • popular • plenty veggie • patio • wheelchair access • women-owned

ENTERTAINMENT & RECREATION

Boulder Area Bicycle Adventures **303/494-7062** • lesbian-owned

BOOKSTORES

Left Hand Books 1200 Pearl St #10 (E of Broadway) **303/443-8252** • 10am-9pm, noon-6pm Sun

RETAIL SHOPS

Enchanted Ink 1200 Pearl St #35 (at Broadway) **303/440-6611** • tattoos, piercing, henna • RN-owned • lesbian-owned

Breckenridge

ACCOMMODATIONS

Allaire Timbers Inn 9511 Hwy 9, S Main St **970/453-7530, 800/624-4904** • gay-friendly • full brkfst • hot tub • nonsmoking • WiFi • wheelchair access • $99-295

Valdoro Mountain Lodge 500 Village Rd **970/453-4880, 800/436-6780** • gay/ straight • condos w/ access to pool, massage facilities & outdoor hot tub • nonsmoking • wheelchair access

Colorado Springs

(includes Manitou Springs)

INFO LINES & SERVICES

Pikes Peak Gay/ Lesbian Community Center **719/471-4429** • 2pm-6pm • call for events

ACCOMMODATIONS

Blue Skies Inn B&B 402 Manitou Ave (at Mayfair), Manitou Springs **719/685-3899, 800/398-7949** • gay/ straight • Gothic Revival built by artist/ innkeeper • full brkfst • gazebo hot tub • WiFi • kids ok • nonsmoking • $145-240

Old Town Guesthouse 115 S 26th St **719/632-9194, 888/375-4210** • gay-friendly • full brkfst • 4 rooms w/ hot tub • nonsmoking • WiFi • wheelchair access • $99-237

Pikes Peak Paradise Woodland Park **719/687-6656, 800/728-8282** • gay-friendly • mansion w/ view of Pikes Peak • surrounded by nat'l forest • full brkfst • hot tub • fireplaces • nonsmoking • kids ok • WiFi • gay-owned • $160-250

Two Sisters Inn—A B&B 10 Otoe Pl, Manitou Springs **719/685-9684, 800/274-7466** • gay-friendly • kids over 10 years ok • full brkfst • women-owned • $69-145

BARS

Bijou Bar & Grill 2510 E Bijou **719/473-5718** • 4pm-2am, clsd Sun-Tue • lesbians/ gay men • dancing/ DJ • food served • karaoke • nonsmoking • patio

Club Q 3430 N Academy Blvd (at N Carefree) **719/570-1429** • 6pm-2am, till 4am Sat, clsd Mon • mostly men • ladies night Sun • neighborhood bar • dancing/DJ • karaoke • live entertainment • strippers • food served • 18+ • wheelchair access • gay-owned

CAFES

Spice of Life an Ingredients Emporium 727 Manitou Ave, Manitou Springs **719/685-5284** • 7am-6pm • WiFi

RESTAURANTS

Dale Street Cafe Bistro 115 E Dale (at Nevada) **719/578-9898** • lunch & dinner, brunch wknds • some veggie • full bar

ENTERTAINMENT & RECREATION

Out Loud **866/862-9382** • men's chorus

EROTICA

First Amendment Adult Bookstore 220 E Fillmore (at Nevada) **719/630-7676**

Denver

INFO LINES & SERVICES

Gay/ Lesbian AA **303/322-4440**

The GLBT Center of Colorado (The Center) 1050 Broadway **303/733-7743** • 10am-6pm Mon-Fri • extensive resources & support groups • wheelchair access

ACCOMMODATIONS

The Brown Palace 321 17th St (at N Broadway) **303/297-3111, 800/321-2599** • gay-friendly • stained glass canopy • sun in every room • WiFi • $149+

Capitol Hill Mansion B&B 1207 Pennsylvania (at 12th) **303/839-5221, 800/839-9329** • gay-friendly • B&B • full brkfst • hot tub • nonsmoking • kids ok • WiFi • $114-199

Castle Marne 1572 Race St **303/331–0621, 800/926–2763** • gay-friendly • 1889 mansion on Nat'l Register of Historic Places • some jacuzzis • WiFi • $120-270

The Curtis 1405 Curtis St **303/571–0300, 800/525–6651** • gay-friendly • hip hotel • pool • hot tub • WiFi

Elyria's Western Guest House 1655 E 47th Ave (near I–70 & Brighton, check in here) **303/291–0915** • lesbians/ gay men • Western ambiance in historic Denver neighborhood • shared baths • nonsmoking • gay-owned • $60+

The Gregory Inn, LoDo 2500 Arapahoe St (at 25th St) **303/295–6570, 800/925–6570** • gay-friendly • full brkfst • jacuzzis • fireplaces • nonsmoking • straight & gay-owned • $139-259

Hotel Monaco 1717 Champa St (at 17th) **303/296–1717, 800/990–1303** • gay-friendly • gym • spa • nonsmoking • WiFi • also Italian restaurant • pets ok • $125+

Lumber Baron Inn 2555 W 37th Ave (at Bryant) **303/477–8205** • gay-friendly • Victorian mansion furnished w/ antiques • full brkfst • hot tub • WiFi • $149+

Denver

WHERE THE GIRLS ARE:
Many lesbians reside in the Capitol Hill area, near the gay and mixed bars, but hang out in cafes and women's bars scattered around the city.

ENTERTAINMENT:
Denver Women's Chorus 303/274-4177.

LGBT PRIDE:
June. 303/733-7743, web: www.denverpridefest.org.

ANNUAL EVENTS:
July- 2nd weekend, Rocky Mountain Regional Rodeo (gay rodeo), web: cgra.us.
August/September - AIDS Walk, web: coloradoaidsproject.org.
September/October- Great American Beer Festival, web: www.gabf.org.

CITY INFO:
800/233-6837, web: www.denver.org.

BEST VIEW:
Lookout Mountain (at night especially) or from the top of the Capitol rotunda.

WEATHER:
Summer temperatures average in the 90ºs and winter ones in the 40ºs. The sun shines an average of 300 days a year with humidity in the single digits.

ATTRACTIONS:
16th Street Mall (pedestrian mall in Lower Downtown or LoDo).
Black American West Museum 303/482-2242, web: www.black-americanwestmuseum.com.
Cherry Creek Shopping Center 303/388-3900, web: www.shopcherrycreek.com.
Denver Art Museum 720/865–5000, web: denverartmuseum.org.
Denver Botanic Gardens 720/865-3500, web: www.botanicgardens.org.
Denver Center for the Performing Arts 303/893-4100, web: www.denvercenter.org.
Denver Zoo 303/376-4800, web: www.denverzoo.org.
Downtown Aquarium 303/561-4450.
Elitch Gardens 303/595-4386, web: www.elitchgardens.com.
LoDo (Lower Downtown).
Molly Brown House 303/832-4092, web: www.mollybrown.org.

TRANSIT:
Yellow Cab 303/777-7777.
Metro Taxi 303/333-3333.
Super Shuttle 303/370–1300 or 800/258-3826, web: www.super-shuttledenver.com.
RTD 303/628-9000 or 303/299-6000 & 800/366-7433 (infoline), web: www.rtd-denver.com.

OUT FRONT
Colorado

**Colorado's leading GLBT
publication – Since 1976**

**www.OutFrontColorado.com
303.778.7900**

The Oxford Hotel 1600 17th St
303/628-5400, 800/228-5838 • gay-friendly •
hotel • health club & spa • also 2 restaurants,
art deco lounge • WiFi • $169-369

BARS

Barker Lounge 255 S Broadway (at Byers)
303/778-0545 • noon-2am • mostly gay men
• neighborhood bar • patio w/ bar • dogs
welcome

Bender's Tavern 314 E 13th Ave (at Grant)
303/861-7070 • noon-2am • gay-friendly •
food served • live bands • karaoke Tue & Th

BJ's Carousel 1380 S Broadway (at Arkansas)
303/777-9880 • 4pm-2am, from 10am Sat-
Mon • popular • lesbians/ gay men •
neighborhood bar • karaoke Wed • drag
shows Fri-Sat • also restaurant, dinner Wed-
Sun • transgender-friendly • wheelchair access
• gay-owned

Broadways 1027 Broadway (at 11th Ave)
303/623-0700 • 2pm-2am, from noon Sat-
Sun • lesbians/ gay men • neighborhood bar •
cool mix of folk • karaoke Th • WiFi

Charlie's 900 E Colfax Ave (at Emerson)
303/839-8890 • 11am-2am • popular •
mostly gay men • 2 clubs • dancing/DJ •
country/ western • wheelchair access • also
restaurant

The Compound 145 Broadway (at 2nd Ave)
303/722-7977 • 7am-2am • popular • mostly
gay men • neighborhood bar • dancing/DJ Fri-
Sat • alternative

Dazzle 930 Lincoln St (btwn 9th & 10th Aves)
303/839-5100 • from 4pm Sun-Th, from 11am
Fri, also Sun brunch (9:30am-1pm) • gay-
friendly • jazz club & restaurant • live music

Denver Eagle 1475 36th St (at Blake)
303/291-0250 • mostly men • levi/ leather/
cruise bar • bears • never a cover charge •
wheelchair access • gay-owned

El Chapultepec 1962 Market St (at 20th)
303/295-9126 • 9am-2am • popular • gay-
friendly • live jazz & blues since 1951 • 1-drink
minimum per set • cover

El Potrero 320 S Birch St (at Leetsdale Dr),
Glendale 303/388-8889 • gay/ straight •
Mexican restaurant early • Latino gay bar late
(Wed, Sat-Sun)

Her Bar 629 E Colfax Ave 303/832-2687 •
4pm-1am, 2pm-2am Sat, 10am-10pm Sun,
clsd Mon-Tue • mostly women • Boyz night
Wed • dancing/DJ • karaoke • live music

JR's Bar 777 E 17th Ave (at Clarkson)
303/831-0459 • 3pm-2am • mostly gay men •
neighborhood bar • karaoke • drag shows •
videos • gay-owned

Lannie's Clocktower Cabaret 16th St Mall
at Arapahoe (in historic D&F Tower)
303/293-0075 • gay-friendly • upscale cabaret
w/ variety of acts weekly including drag &
burlesque

Mo's of Denver 1037 Broadway
720/235-8593 • 3pm-2am • lesbians/ gay
men • dancing/DJ Th • wheelchair access

Mozart Lounge 1417 Krameria (btwn 14th &
Colfax) 303/388-0701 • 4pm-2am • lesbians/
gay men • piano bar

R&R Denver 4958 E Colfax Ave (at Elm)
303/320-9337 • 3pm-2am, from 1pm Fri, from
11am wknds • lesbians/ gay men •
neighborhood bar

Rock Bar 3015 E Colfax 303/322-4444 •
5pm-2am • gay/ straight • dive bar • theme
nights

Swallows 3090 Downing St (at 31st Ave)
303/832-5482 • 4pm-11pm • lesbians/ gay
men • more women Fri • videos • food served

tHERe Coffee Bar & Lounge 1526 E Colfax
(btwn Humboldt & Franklin) 303/830-8437 •
10am-11pm, 10am-8pm Sun • mostly women
• transgendefr-friendly • live music • also cafe
• WiFi • lesbian-owned

NIGHTCLUBS

Beta Nighclub 1909 Blake St 303/383-1909
• gay/ straight, more gay Th & Sun •
dancing/DJ • cover charge

First Friday/ Babes Around Denver 3500
Walnut St (at 35th) 303/475-4620 • 6pm-
2am, 1st Fri only • mostly women • dancing/DJ

Hip Chicks Out • mostly women • roving
monthly • check www.hipchicksout.com

La Rumba 99 W 9th Ave (at Broadway)
303/572-8006 • gay-friendly • salsa dancing &
lessons Th & Sat • more gay for Lipgloss Fri
(Brit-pop & indie music) • cover

Tracks 3500 Walnut St (at 35th)
303/863-7326 • 9pm-2am • clsd Sun-Wed •
gay/ straight • women's night 1st Fri •
dancing/DJ

CAFES

City, O City 206 E 13th Ave (at Sherman)
303/832-7313 • 7am-2am, from 8am wknds,
vegetarian/ vegan • also bar

Common Grounds 3484 W 32nd Ave
(Howell) 303/458-5248 • 6:30am-10pm, till
11pm Fri-Sat • WiFi • also 1601 17th St,
303/296-9248 • WiFi

Dazbog 1201 E 9th Ave (at Downing)
303/837-1275 • 6am-10pm, from 7am Sun •
popular • gay/ straight • outdoor seating •
heated patio • WiFi

Geez Louise 4924 E Colfax Ave (E of Colorado Blvd) **303/322–3833** • 6am-6pm, from 8am wknds, till 2pm Mon • gay-owned

The Market at Larimer Square 1445 Larimer Sq **303/534–5140** • 6am-11pm, till midnight Fri-Sat, till 10pm Sun • food

Paris on the Platte 1553 Platte St (at 15th) **303/455–2451** • 7am-1am, till 3am Fri-Sat, from 8am wknds • soups, salads, sandwiches • WiFi • popular after-hours

RESTAURANTS

Annie's Cafe 4012 E 8th Ave **303/355–8197** • 7am-10pm, from 8am Sat • popular • diner • popular • some veggie

The Avenue Grill 630 E 17th Ave (at Washington) **303/861–2820** • 11:30am-11pm, till midnight Fri-Sat, 5pm-10pm Sun

Banzai Sushi 6655 Leetsdale Dr **303/329–3366** • lunch Mon-Fri, dinner nightly • sushi

Barracuda's 1076 Ogden St (at E 11th) **303/860–8353** • 10am-2am • also bar

Benny's Restaurante y Tequila Bar 301 E 7th Ave (at Grant St) **303/894–0788** • lunch & dinner • nonsmoking • patio

Devil's Food 1020 S Gaylord St (at E Tennessee) **303/733–7448** • 6am-4pm, 7am-3pm wknds • desserts & brkfst

Duo 2413 W 32nd Ave (at Zuni) **303/477–4141** • dinner nightly, wknd brunch • hip, organic, creative American • full bar

Fruition 1313 E 6th Ave **303/831–1962** • 5pm-10pm, till 8pm Sun • contemporary French • seasonal menu

Hamburger Mary's Bar & Grille 700 E 17th Ave (at Washington St, across from JR's bar) **303/832–1333** • 11am-2am, from 10am Sun • popular • gay/ straight • also Club M • dancing/DJ • karaoke

Il Vicino 550 Broadway **303/861–0801** • 11am-10pm • pizza • micro-brewed beer

Joseph's Southern Food, Carry Out & Drive In 2868 Fairfax St (at 29th) **303/333–5332** • 11am-8pm Tue-Sat • traditional Southern • also bakery, ice cream parlor, candy • gay-owned

Las Margaritas Uptown 1035 E 17th Ave (at Downing) **303/830–2199** • 11am-1am • popular • Mexican • some veggie • also bar • outdoor dining

Pete's Kitchen 1962 E Colfax Ave **303/321–3139** • 24hrs • diner • very popular after bars close

Racine's 650 Sherman St (at 6th Ave) **303/595–0418** • brkfst, lunch, dinner, late night & Sun brunch • some veggie • full bar

Sexy Pizza 1018 E 11th Ave **303/830–8111**

Steuben's 523 E 17th Ave **303/830–1001** • 11am-11pm, till midnight Fri, 10am-midnight Sat, till 11pm Sun • American comfort food served up hip • patio • full bar

Sunny Gardens 6460 E Yale Avenue **303/691–8830** • Chinese • plenty veggie/ vegan

Thai Pot Cafe 1550 S Colorado Blvd (at E Florida) **303/639–6200** • lunch & dinner • Thai

Tom's Home Cookin' 800 E 26th Ave (Clarkson St) **303/388–8035** • 11am-3pm, clsd Sat-Sun • Southern comfort food • gay-owned

Vesta Dipping Grill 1822 Blake St (near 18th St) **303/296–1970** • 5pm-10pm Sun-Th, till 11pm Fri-Sat • upscale

WaterCourse Foods 837 E 17th Ave (at Clarkston) **303/832–7313** • 7am-9pm, till 10pm Fri-Sat • vegetarian/ vegan

Wazee Supper Club 1600 15th St (at Wazee) **303/623–9518** • 11am-2am, noon-midnight Sun • classic comfort food • full bar

ENTERTAINMENT & RECREATION

Colorado OUT Spoken PBS KBDI, channel 12 **303/861–0829** • 10pm Sun • LGBT news & entertainment TV program

Denver Women's Chorus **303/274–4177**

Mercury Cafe 2199 California St **303/294–9281** • 5:30pm-close • swing, tango, salsa dancing • live shows • also restaurant • dinner only Tue-Sun, wknd brunch • nonsmoking

Pride Radio **303/631–2957** • gossip & music

Rocky Mountain Rainbeaus **303/863–7739** • all-inclusive, all-levels, high-energy square-dance club

Rocky Mountain Rollergirls **720/984–3132** • Denver's female roller derby league • visit www.rockymountainrollergirls.com for events

BOOKSTORES

Tattered Cover Book Store 2526 Colfax Ave (at Elizabeth) **303/322–7727, 800/833–9327** • 7am-9pm, from 9am Sat, 10am-6pm Sun • local independent • coffee shop • also 1628 16th St, 303/ 436–1070 • wheelchair access

RETAIL SHOPS

Arco Iris Design 82 S Broadway (Bayau Ave) **303/765-5116** • pride jewelry & design

Bound By Design 1332 E Colfax (at Humboldt) **303/830-7272, 303/832-TAT2** • 11am-11pm, noon-10pm Sun • piercing & tattoos

Heaven Sent Me 116 S Broadway (btwn Alameda & Virginia) **303/733-9000** • 11am-7pm • pride items, clothing, gifts • wheelchair access

Needz 135 Broadway (at 1st Ave) **303/722-0969** • 10am-10pm, noon-6pm Sun • LGBT • cards • gifts • toys • gay-owned

Rockmount Ranch Wear 1626 Wazee St **303/629-7777, 800/775-2566** • 7am-5pm, 11am-4pm wknds • makers of the shirts worn in *Brokeback Mountain*

PUBLICATIONS

Gayzette 720/435-8914 • LGBT monthly publication

➤ **Out Front Colorado** 303/778-7900 • statewide bi-weekly LGBT newspaper • since 1976

PINK Magazine 303/316-4688, 877/769-7465 • LGBT business directory & lifestyle magazine

GYMS & HEALTH CLUBS

Pura Vida Fitness & Spa 2955 E 1st Ave #200 303/321-7872

EROTICA

The Crypt on Broadway 8 Broadway (at Ellsworth) **303/733-3112** • 11am-11pm, till 8pm Sun • leather, clubwear & more

Smitten Kitten 70 Broadway **303/962-9520** • 11am-9pm, noon-7pm Sun • transgender-friendly • lesbian-owned • something for everyone!

Durango

ACCOMMODATIONS

Leland House B&B 721 E 2nd Ave **970/385-1920, 800/664-1920** • gay-friendly • full brkfst • nonsmoking • wheelchair access • $119-359

Mesa Verde Far View Lodge 1 Navajo Hill, Mesa Verde National Park **602/331-5210, 800/449-2288** • gay-friendly • hotel • camping • RV hookups • inside nat'l park at 8250' elevation • views of 4 states • full brkfst • nonsmoking • WiFi • $120-160

Rio Grande Southern B&B 101 S. 5th St (at Hwy 145), Dolores **970/882-2125** • gay-friendly • full brkfst • WiFi • kid/pets ok • $55-120

Rochester Hotel 721 E 2nd Ave **970/385-1920, 800/664-1920** • gay-friendly • popular • newly renovated 1892 house decorated in Old West motif • full brkfst • nonsmoking • kids/ pets ok • wheelchair access • $119-259

Estes Park

ACCOMMODATIONS

Mountain Sage Inn 553 W Elkhorn Ave **970/586-2833, 800/552-2833** • gay-friendly • pets ok • nonsmoking • $59-129

Stanley Hotel 333 Wonderview Ave **800/976-1377, 970/577-4000** • gay-friendly • pool • restaurant • WiFi • the inspiration for Stephen King's *The Shining*

Fort Collins

INFO LINES & SERVICES

The Lambda Community Center 212 South Mason St **970/221-3247** • 10am-3pm Mon-Fri • WiFi

Women's Resource Center 424 Pine St #201 **970/484-1902** • 9am-5pm Mon-Fri • "helping women lead healthy lives"

ACCOMMODATIONS

Archer's Poudre River Resort 33021 Poudre Canyon Hwy, Bellvue **970/881-2139, 888/822-0588** • gay-friendly • lesbian-owned • $85-420

BARS

Choice City Shots 124 LaPorte Ave (at College) **970/221-4333** • 6:30pm-midnight, till 1:30am Fri-Sat • lesbians/ gay men • neighborhood bar • karaoke Th • wheelchair access • lesbian- & gay-owned

Grand Junction

RESTAURANTS

Leon's Taqueria 505 30th Rd **970/242-1388** • 11am-9pm

Hotchkiss

ACCOMMODATIONS

Leroux Creek Inn & Vineyards 12388 3100 Rd **970/872-4746** • gay-friendly • Southwestern-style adobe on 54 acres • full brkfst • $175-195

RESTAURANTS

North Fork Valley Restaurant & Thirsty Parrot Pub 140 W Bridge St 970/872–4215 • 11am-9pm • American/ Mexican

Leadville

ACCOMMODATIONS

The Ice Palace Inn B&B 813 Spruce St 719/486–8272, 800/754–2840 • gay-friendly • historic Victorian • mtn views • fireplaces • hot tub • nonsmoking • lesbian-owned • $105-179

Pueblo

BARS

Pirate's Cove 105 Central Plaza (off 1st & Union) 719/543–2683 • 4pm-2am, 2pm-midnight Sun, clsd Mon • lesbians/ gay men • neighborhood bar • wheelchair access

Stratton

ACCOMMODATIONS

Claremont Inn 800 Claremont Dr (off exit 419, I-70) 888/291–8910 • gay/ straight • 2 hours from Denver • full brkfst • commitment ceremonies • gay-owned • $149-549

Vail

ACCOMMODATIONS

Antlers at Vail 680 W Lionshead Pl 970/476–2471, 888/268–5377 • gay-friendly • apts • kitchens • hot tub • pool • fireplace • balcony • kids ok • pets ok w/ prior approval • $204+

RESTAURANTS

Larkspur Restaurant & Market 458 Vail Valley Dr (in the Golden Peak Lodge) 970/754–8050 • lunch & dinner, seasonal hours • fine dining • also bar • patio • ski-in/ out • wheelchair access

Sweet Basil 193 E Gore Creek Dr 970/476–0125 • lunch & dinner • some veggie • full bar • wheelchair access

Winter Park

ACCOMMODATIONS

Bear Paw Inn 871 Bear Paw Dr 970/887–1351 • gay-friendly • massive log lodge on top of mtn w/ spectacular views of Rocky Mtn Nat'l Park • full brkfst • jacuzzi • nonsmoking • $180-235

CONNECTICUT

Statewide

PUBLICATIONS

Metroline 860/231–8334 • regional newspaper & entertainment guide • covers CT, RI & MA

Bethel

CAFES

Molten Java 102 Greenwood Ave 203/739–0313 • 6am-9pm, till 10pm Fri-Sat, 8am-8pm Sat-Sun • live entertainment • lesbian-owned

RESTAURANTS

Bethel Pizza House 206 Greenwood Ave 203/748–1427 • 11am-11pm, till midnight Fri-Sat

Bridgeport

RESTAURANTS

Bloodroot Restaurant & Bookstore 85 Ferris St (at Harbor Ave) 203/576–9168 • lunch Tue & Th-Sat, dinner Tue-Sat, brunch only Sun • clsd Mon • feminist vegetarian • patio • wheelchair access • women-owned

EROTICA

Romantix Adult Superstore 410 North Ave 203/332–7129

Bristol

EROTICA

Amazing Superstore 167 Farmington Ave 860/582–9000

Danbury

ACCOMMODATIONS

Maron Hotel & Suites 42 Lake Ave Extension (off I-84) 203/791–2200, 866/811–2582 • gay-friendly • kids/ pets ok • $70-199 • wheelchair access

BARS

Triangles Cafe 66 Sugar Hollow Rd, Rte 7 203/798–6996 • 5pm-1am, till 2am Fri-Sat • popular • lesbians/ gay men • dancing/DJ • live shows • karaoke • patio • gay-owned

RESTAURANTS

Goulash Place 42 Highland Ave 203/744–1971 • lunch & dinner, clsd Mon • Hungarian • beer/ wine

Sesame Seed 68 W Wooster St **203/743–9850** • lunch & dinner, clsd Sun, Mediterranean/ Italian • funky decor • plenty veggie

Thang Long 56 Padanaram Rd (near North Street Shopping Center) **203/743–6049** • lunch & dinner • Vietnamese • bring your own bottle

Enfield

EROTICA

Bookends 44 Enfield St/ Rte 5 **860/745–3988**

Hartford

INFO LINES & SERVICES

True Colors 576 Farmington Ave **860/649–7386, 888/565–5551** • support & mentoring for LGBT youth

ACCOMMODATIONS

Butternut Farm 1654 Main St, Glastonbury **860/633–7197** • gay/ straight • 18th-c house furnished w/ antiques • full brkfst • $99-125

Inn at Kent Falls 107 Kent Cornwall Rd, Kent **860/927–3197** • gay/ straight • 1 hr from Hartford • pool • kids ok • nonsmoking • WiFi • wheelchair access • gay-owned • $195-350

The Mansion Inn 139 Hartford Rd (at Main St), Manchester **860/646–0453** • gay-friendly • B&B • full brkfst • in-room fireplaces • $95-145

BARS

Chez Est 458 Wethersfield Ave (at Main St) **860/525–3243** • 3pm-1am, till 2am Fri-Sat • popular • lesbians/ gay men • dancing/DJ • food served • karaoke • drag shows • women's night 2nd Sat

Polo 678 Maple Ave (btwn Preston & Mapleton) **860/278–3333** • 9pm-1am, till 2am Fri-Sat, clsd Sun-Wed • lesbians/ gay men, Th ladies night • dancing/DJ • karaoke • drag shows

Women After Hours **860/930–8844** • bi-monthly dance/ social • call for schedule & location • cover

Hartford

LGBT PRIDE:
June, web:
www.connecticutpride.org.

ANNUAL EVENTS:
June - Conneticut Gay & Lesbian Film Festival, web:
www.outfilmct.org.

CITY INFO:
Greater Hartford Tourism District 800/446-7811, web: www.enjoy-hartford.com.

ATTRACTIONS:
Bushnell Park Carousel & Museum 860/232-6710, web: www.bush-nellpark.org.
Harriet Beecher Stowe Center 860/522-9258, web: www.harri-etbeecherstowecenter.org.
Mark Twain House 860/247-0998, web: www.marktwainhouse.org.
Real Art Ways 860/232-1006, web: www.realartways.org.
Wadsworth Atheneum Museum of Art 860/278-2670, web: www.wadsworthatheneum.org.

WEATHER:
Summer highs are in the low 80°s. But that 50%+ humidity will make it feel like more. Humidity all year round. Winter drops into the low 20°s. January is the cold-est and snowiest month. The full four seasons are in effect.

TRANSIT:
Yellow Cab 860/666-6666.
Primetime CT Airport Shuttle 866/284–3247, web: www.2theairport.com.
Connecticut Transit 860/525-9181, web: www.cttransit.com.

NIGHTCLUBS

Club Lucy 458 Wethersfield Ave (at Chez Est) 860/525-3243 • 2nd Sat only • monthly women's party

The Kitty Kat Party 960 Main St (at Room 960) 860/593-3093 • 1st Sat only • women • dancing/DJ

Krave 944 Cromwell Ave (at the Rock Cafe), Rocky Hill • 3rd Sat only • mostly women • dancing/DJ

CAFES

Tisane Tea & Coffee Bar 537 Farmington Ave (at Kenyon) 860/523-5417 • 7:30am-1am • food served • live entertainment • karaoke • WiFi • also bar • women's night 1st Sun

RESTAURANTS

Arugula 953 Farmington Ave, West Hartford 860/561-4888 • lunch and dinner, clsd Mon • Mediterranean • reservations recommended • wheelchair access

Peppercorns Grill 357 Main St 860/547-1714 • lunch Mon-Fri, dinner nightly, clsd Sun • Northern Italian

Pond House Cafe 1555 Asylum Ave 860/231-8823 • lunch & dinner Tue-Sat, wknd brunch • bring your own bottle • patio • wheelchair access

Trumbull Kitchen 150 Trumbull St (at Pearl St) 860/493-7417 • lunch Mon-Sat, dinner nightly • global cuisine/ tapas

ENTERTAINMENT & RECREATION

Real Art Ways 56 Arbor St 860/232-1006 • contemporary art • cinema • performance • also lounge • WiFi

RETAIL SHOPS

MetroStore 493 Farmington Ave (at Sisson Ave) 860/231-8845 • 8:30am-8pm, till 5:30pm Tue, Wed & Sat, clsd Sun • magazines • travel guides • DVD rentals • leather & more

PUBLICATIONS

Metroline 860/233-8334 • regional newspaper & entertainment guide • covers CT, RI & MA

EROTICA

Very Intimate Pleasures 100 Brainard Rd (exit 27, off I-91) 860/246-1875

Mystic

ACCOMMODATIONS

House of 1833 B&B Resort 72 N Stonington Rd 860/536-6325, 800/367-1833 • gay-friendly • full brkfst • pool • kids ok • nonsmoking • gay-owned • $139-179

The Mare's Inn B&B 333 Colonel Ledyard Hwy, Ledyard 860/572-7556 • gay-friendly • full brkfst • nonsmoking • wheelchair access • lesbian-owned • $125-220

Mermaid Inn of Mystic 2 Broadway 860/536-6223, 877/692-2632 • lesbians/ gay men (straight-friendly) • B&B w/ village location & river views • full brkfst • kids ok • nonsmoking • WiFi • lesbian-owned • $175-225

The Old Mystic Inn 52 Main St (at Rte 27), Old Mystic 860/572-9422 • gay-friendly • full brkfst • nonsmoking • WiFi • gay-owned • $1235-215

New Haven

INFO LINES & SERVICES

New Haven Pride Center 14 Gilbert St 203/387-2252 • events • meetings • resources • library • movies • call for info

ACCOMMODATIONS

Linden Point House 30 Linden Point Rd, Stony Creek 203/481-0472 • gay-friendly • WiFi • pets/kids ok • $200-375

Omni New Haven Hotel at Yale 155 Temple St (at Chapel) 203/772-6664, 800/843-6664 • gay-friendly • WiFi • wheelchair access • $129-439

BARS

168 York St Cafe 168 York St 203/789-1915 • 3pm-1am, till 2am Fri-Sat • lesbians/gay men • also restaurant • dinner Mon-Sat, Sun brunch • patio • gay-owned

The Bar 254 Crown St 203/495-8924 • 11:30am-1am, from 5pm Mon-Tu • gay/straight • more gay Tue • dancing/DJ • pizza • wheelchair access

Center Street Lounge 29 Center St (at Orange) 203/777-7264 • 8pm-close Th-Sun • gay/straight • gay night Fri, Hip Hop Sun • dancing/DJ • gay-owned

Partners 365 Crown St (at Park St) 203/776-1014 • 5pm-1am, till 2am Fri-Sat • lesbians/ gay men • dancing/DJ • karaoke • leather 1st & 3rd Sat • women's night 4th Sat

NIGHTCLUBS

Gotham Citi Cafe 130 Crown St (at Church) 203/498–2484 • 9pm-4am clsd Sun-Wed • gay/straight • more gay Sat • 18+ • dancing/DJ • drag shows • wheelchair access

Koji 182 Temple St 203/772–7900 • 9pm Tue only • lesbians/gay men • sushi restaurant other times

CAFES

Atticus Bookstore/ Cafe 1082 Chapel St (at York St) 203/776–4040 • 7am-9pm

RESTAURANTS

Beachhead 3 Cosey Beach Ave, East Haven 203/469–5450 • 4pm-close, from 1pm Sun • seafood • Italian • patio • live music

Claire's Corner Copia 1000 Chapel St (at College St) 203/562–3888 • 8am-9pm, till 10pm Fri-Sat • vegetarian • WiFi • wheelchair access

Soul de Cuba 238 Crown St 203/498–2822 • lunch & dinner • full bar

EROTICA

Very Intimate Pleasures 170 Boston Post Rd, Orange 203/799–7040

New London

BARS

Frank's Place 9 Tilley St (at Bank) 860/442–2782 • 4pm-1am, till 2am Fri-Sun • mostly gay men • dancing/DJ • live shows • food served • karaoke • patio • wheelchair access

O'Neill's Brass Rail 52 Bank St 860/443–6203 • 11am-1am, till 2am Fri-Sat • mostly gay men • karaoke • drag shows • WiFi

Norwalk

INFO LINES & SERVICES

Triangle Community Center 16 River St (Mechanic St entrance) 203/853–0600 • activities • newsletter • call for info

Ridgefield

RESTAURANTS

Caputo's East Ridge Cafe 5 Grove St 203/894–1940 • 11:30am-10pm • also mellow, upscale bar

Westport

ENTERTAINMENT & RECREATION

Sherwood Island State Park Beach left to gay area

DELAWARE

Rehoboth Beach

INFO LINES & SERVICES

Camp Rehoboth Community Center 37 Baltimore Ave 302/227–5620 • 9am-5:30pm Mon-Fri, 10am-4pm wknds • drop-in community center • support groups • magazine w/ extensive listings • HIV testing & counseling

Gay & Lesbian AA 302/856–6452 (SOUTHERN DELAWARE INTERGROUP #)

Narcotics Anonymous 37 Baltimore Ave (at Camp Rehoboth center) 302/227–5620 • 5:30pm Sun

ACCOMMODATIONS

An Inn by the Bay 205 Savannah Rd, Lewes 302/644–8878, 866/833–2565 • gay/straight • nonsmoking • hot tub • gay-owned • $100-299

At Melissa's B&B 36 Delaware Ave (btwn 1st & 2nd) 302/227–7504, 800/396–8090 • gay/straight • 1 block from beach • nonsmoking • WiFi • women-owned • $175-395

Bellmoor Inn 6 Christian St (at Delaware) 866/899–2779, 800/425–2355 • gay-friendly • upscale inn & spa • pool • $95-595

Breakers Hotel & Suites 105 2nd St (at Olive) 302/227–6688, 800/441–8009 • gay-friendly • pool & adjacent to Lake Gerar • kids pets ok • wheelchair access • $85-199

Cabana Gardens B&B 20 Lake Ave (at 3rd St) 302/227–5429 • gay/straight • lake & ocean views • deck • pool • nonsmoking • gay-owned • $75-250

Canalside Inn Canal at 6th 302/226–2006, 866/412–2625 • gay/straight • pool • hot tub • WiFi • nonsmoking • wheelchair access • gay-owned • $55-240

Delaware Inn B&B 55 Delaware Ave (at Bayard Ave) 302/227–6031, 800/246–5244 • gay-friendly • near beach • lesbian-owned • $200-250

The Homestead at Rehoboth B&B 35060 Warrington Rd (at John J Williams Hwy) 302/226–7625 • gay-friendly • small dogs ok • pool • nonsmoking • WiFi • wheelchair acces • lesbian-owned • $99-185

Lazy L at Willow Creek 16061 Willow Cree Rd (at Hwy 1), Lewes 302/644–7220 • gay/straight • full brkfst • pool • hot tub • very pe friendly • WiFi • lesbian-owned • $140-210

The Lighthouse Inn B&B 20 Delaware Ave (at 1st St) 302/226-0407 • seasonal • gay/ straight • also apt (weekly rental) • nonsmoking • kids/pets ok • gay-owned • $85-235

Rehoboth Guest House 40 Maryland Ave (btwn 1st & 2nd Sts) 302/227-4117, 800/564-0493 • lesbians/gay men • Victorian beach house • deck • near boardwalk & beach • nonsmoking • WiFi • gay-owned • $85-220

Sea Witch Manor Inn & Spa 71 Lake Ave (at Rehoboth Ave) 302/226-9482, 866/732-9482 • gay/straight • hot tub • nonsmoking • WiFi • wheelchair access • gay-owned • $79-530

Silver Lake Guest House 20388 Silver Lake Dr (at Robinson Dr) 302/226-2115, 800/842-2115 • lesbians/gay men • near Poodle Beach • nonsmoking • lakefront • ocean views • WiFi • gay-owned • $120-400

Rehoboth Beach

WHERE THE GIRLS ARE:

If it's summer, on the beach (the North Shores at S end of Cape Henlopen) with all the other women. If it's Sunday during the summer, hanging out at Frogg Pond. Every Fri-Sat all year, they're dancing at the Ladies Tea at Sky Bar.

LGBT PRIDE:

Every day, but Wilmington has their pride here in September.

ANNUAL EVENTS:

July - Fireworks 302/227-2772, web: www.rehomain.com/ fireworks.html.

October - Rehoboth Beach Autumn Jazz Festival, web: www.rehobothjazz.com.

October - Sea Witch Halloween Festival.

November - Rehoboth Beach Independent Film Festival 302/645-9095, web: www.rehobothfilm.com.

CITY INFO:

Rehoboth Beach-Dewey Beach Chamber of Commerce 302/227-2233 & 800/441-1329, web: www.beach-fun.com.

ATTRACTIONS:

Anna Hazzard Museum, 302/226-1119. Photos & memorabilia from when Rehoboth was a Christian resort.

DiscoverSea Shipwreck Museum, Fenwick Island, 302/539-9366, web: discoversea.com.

Dolphin- & whale-watching July-Oct. Boat tours leave from Fisherman's Wharf in Lewes, DE. 302/645-8862, web: www.fish-lewes.com/sightseeing.html.

Main Street 302/227-2772, web: www.rehomain.com.

Rehoboth Beach Boardwalk with 2 amusement parks (Funland, web: www.funlandRehoboth.com, & Playland).

Tanger Outlets, 302/226-9223, web: www.tangeroutlet.com. 130 designer stores with no sales tax.

BEST VIEW:

Watching the sun rise over the bay at Dewey Beach or eating a swanky sunset dinner at Victoria's (www.boardwalkplaza.com/resta urant.htm) on the Boardwalk.

WEATHER:

You're not far from DC, but you're on the coast. So, yes, it does get hot and muggy in the summers (90s for temps and humidity), but you can take a dip in the ocean. In the winter, a lot of businesses close as the temperatures drop along with the occasional snow flurries.

TRANSIT:

Seaport Taxi 302/645-6800.

Jolly Trolley 302/227-1197 (seasonal tour & shuttle), web: www.jollytrolley.com.

Summer Place Hotel 30 Olive Ave (at 1st) **302/226-0766, 800/815-3925** • gay/ straight • also apts • near beach • $39-175

BARS

The Blue Moon 35 Baltimore Ave (btwn 1st & 2nd) **302/227-6515** • 6pm-2am, clsd Jan • popular • lesbians/ gay men • live music • drag shows • also restaurant

Dogfish Head Brewings & Eats 320 Rehoboth Ave (at 4th) **302/226-2739** • gay-friendly • micro-brewery • wood-grilled food • live music wknds

Double L Bar 622 Rehoboth Ave (at Canal) **302/227-0818** • 4pm-2am • open year round • mostly gay men • leather • bears • patio

Finbar 316-318 Rehoboth Ave (at 4th) **302/227-1873** • from 3pm, from noon Sat-Sun, clsd Mon-Tue • gay-friendly • traditional pub • popular happy hour • also restaurant

Frogg Pond 3 S 1st St (near Rehoboth Ave) **302/227-2234** • 11am-1am gay-friendly • popular w/ women in summer • women's T-dance Sun • neighborhood bar • food served • karaoke • popular happy hour

Rigby's Bar & Grill 404 Rehoboth Ave (at State St) **302/227-6080** • 3pm-1am, from 10am Sun

NIGHTCLUBS

Ladies 2000 856/869-0193 • seasonal parties • call hotline for details

Sky Bar 234 Rehoboth Ave (at Cloud 9) **302/226-1999** • popular • Ladies Tea 5pm Fri-Sat • dancing/DJ • karaoke Mon & Th • wheelchair access

CAFES

The Coffee Mill 127B Rehoboth Ave **302/227-7530, 888/227-7530** • 7am-11pm, till 5pm (off-season) • WiFi • lesbian-owned

Lori's Cafe 39 Baltimore Ave (at 1st) **302/226-3066** • seasonal, call for hours • also sandwiches • courtyard • lesbian-owned

RESTAURANTS

Aqua Grill 57 Baltimore Ave **302/226-9001** • seasonal • deck • full bar

Back Porch Cafe 59 Rehoboth Ave **302/227-3674** • lunch & dinner • Sun brunch • seasonal • live shows • full bar • wheelchair access

Blue Plate Diner 329 Savannah Rd, Lewes **302/644-8400** • Fri-Mon (seasonal)

Buttery 102 2nd St, Lewes **302/645-7755** • lunch, dinner, Sun brunch • fine dining in elegant Victorian • reservations suggested

Cafe Sole 44 Baltimore Ave **302/227-7107** • lunch daily, dinner Wed-Sun • casual • patio • also full bar

Celsius 50 Wilmington Ave **302/227-5767** • dinner (clsd Th), Sun brunch • French-Mediterranean • some veggie • wheelchair access • $15-25

Cloud 9 234 Rehoboth Ave (at 2nd) **302/226-1999** • 4pm-2am • popular bar • fusion bistro • also Sky Bar • wheelchair access

The Cultured Pearl 301 Rehoboth Ave (2nd flr) **302/227-8493** • dinner, lunch Th-Mon • pan-Asian • cocktail lounge

Dos Locos 208 Rehoboth Ave (across from Fire Company) **302/227-3353** • 11:30am-10pm, till 11pm Fri-Sat • popular • Mexican • full bar

Eden 23 Baltimore Ave **302/227-3330** • dinner Tue-Sat • seasonal • wine list & martini bar • wheelchair access

Espuma 28 Wilmington Ave **302/227-4199** • 6pm-10pm, clsd Mon • modern Mediterranean • full bar from 5pm

Fins 243 Rehoboth Ave **302/226-3467** • dinner nightly, lunch Sat-Sun • fish house • raw bar

Go Fish! 24 Rehoboth Ave **302/226-1044** • 11:30am-9:30pm (in-season) • seafood & authentic British fish & chips

Hobo's Restaurant & Bar 56 Baltimore Ave **302/226-2226** • from 11am (in-season)

Iguana Grill 52 Baltimore Ave **302/227-0948** • lunch & dinner (summers) • Southwestern • full bar • patio

Jerry's Seafood 108 2nd St, Lewes **302/645-6611** • lunch & dinner daily • "home of the crab bomb"

Just in Thyme 31 Robinson Dr (at Rte 1) **302/227-3100** • seafood & steak by candlelight • also Sun brunch • local favorite

La La Land 22 Wilmington Ave **302/227-3887** • 6pm-1am (seasonal) • seafood & more • full bar • patio

Mariachi 14 Wilmington Ave **302/227-0115** • 11am-9pm, till 11pm Fri-Sat • Mexican-Latin American • nonsmoking • wheelchair access

Planet X Cafe 35 Wilmington Ave **302/226-1928** • seasonal, lunch, dinner, Sun brunch • organic global cuisine • some veggie • friendly service • kitschy decor housed in converted Victorian

Purple Parrot Grill 134 Rehoboth Ave **302/226–1139** • lunch & dinner daily, brunch Sun • karaoke & drag shows wknds • wheelchair access

Retro Cafe & Grille 10 Wilmington Ave (on the beach block, 1/2 block from boardwalk) **302/227–9752** • 8am-3pm • open daily during season, wknds-only off season

Seafood Shack 42 1/2 Baltimore Ave **302/227–5881** • patio seating • live music wknds

Seaside Thai 19 Rehoboth Ave **302/227–9525** • 1 block from beach

Tijuana Taxi 33401 Tenley Ct **302/644–8294** • lunch & dinner • full bar • wheelchair access

Venus on the Half Shell 136 Dagsworthy St, Dewey Beach **302/227–9292** • seasonal • waterside Asian-inspired restaurant w/ fun Morocco-Meets-the-Far-East setting

ENTERTAINMENT & RECREATION

Cape Henlopen State Park Beach 42 Cape Henlopen Dr, Lewes **302/645–8983** • 8am-sunset

Gordon Pond State Park/ North Shores S end of Cape Henlopen State Park (at jetty S of watch tower) • popular women's beach • 20-minute walk from boardwalk • by car follow the shoreline road to State Park entrance

Poodle Beach S of boardwalk at Queen St • popular gay beach

RETAIL SHOPS

Leather Central 36983 Rehoboth Ave **302/227–0700** • 10am-6pm, till 5pm Sun, clsd Tue-Wed • leather uniforms, toys, accessories

PUBLICATIONS

Letters from Camp Rehoboth **302/227–5620** • newsmagazine w/ events & entertainment listings

GYMS & HEALTH CLUBS

Body Shop 401 N Boardwalk (at Virginia) **302/226–0920** • 8am-7pm, till 6pm Sun • on the beach • $12 day pass

The Firm Fitness Center 803 Rehoboth Ave Ext **302/227–8363** • $10 day pass

Midway Fitness 34823 Derrickson Dr **302/645–0407** • $12 day pass

Wilmington

NIGHTCLUBS

Crimson Moon Tavern 1909 W 6th St (at Union St) **302/654–9099** • clsd Mon-Tue • mostly gay men • dancing/DJ • videos

RESTAURANTS

Eclipse 1020 Union St **302/658–1588** • lunch Mon-Fri, dinner nightly • upscale

The Green Room 11th & Market St (at Hotel Dupont) **302/594–3154** • brkfst, lunch & dinner, Sun brunch • full bar • live music

Mrs Robino's 520 N Union St. (at Pennsylvania) **302/652–9223** • 11am-9pm, till 10pm Fri-Sat, from Sat-Sun • family-style Italian • full bar • wheelchair access

DISTRICT OF COLUMBIA

Washington

INFO LINES & SERVICES

Triangle Club 2030 P St NW (at 21st St NW) **202/659–8641** • site for various 12-step groups • call for times

ACCOMMODATIONS

Artist Inn Residence B&B 1824 R St NW (at 19th) **202/667–6707** • gay/ straight • B&B & private art gallery • nonsmoking • WiFi • gay-owned • $239-325

Beacon Hotel & Corporate Quarters 1615 Rhode Island Ave NW (at 17th) **202/296–2100**

Bloomingdale Inn 2417 1st St NW (at Bryant) **202/319–0801** • gay-friendly • Victorian town house • $90-370

The Carlyle Suites Hotel 1731 New Hampshire Ave NW (btwn R & S Sts) **202/234–3200, 800/964–5377** • gay/ straight • art deco hotel • WiFi • gym • also restaurant & bar • popular gay Sun brunch • wheelchair access • $139-279

Chez Aimee **202/669–7708, 202/669–7708** (CELL) • gay-friendly • flat in 1910-era rowhouse in Adams Morgan district • nonsmoking • WiFi • $179-249

Comfort Inn Downtown DC—Convention Center 1201 13th St NW **202/682–5300, 877/424–6423** • gay/ straight • near Dupont Circle • kids ok • WiFi • wheelchair access • $99-279

Creekside B&B **301/261–9438** • mostly women • private home on the shore of the Chesapeake • 40 minutes from DC • hot tub • pool • nonsmoking • lesbian-owned • $100

DC GuestHouse 1337 10th St NW **202/332–2502** • gay/ straight • full brkfst • WiFi • gay-owned • $175-300

The District Hotel 1440 Rhode Island Ave NW (btwn 14th & 15th) **202/232–7800, 800/350–5759** • gay-friendly • conveniently located in Dupont/ Logan Circle Historic District • nonsmoking • kids ok • WiFi • $80+

Donovan House 1155 14th St NW (at Massachusetts Ave NW) **202/737–1200, 800/383–6900** • gay/ straight • stylish hotel • rooftop bar

Doubletree Hotel Washington 1515 Rhode Island Ave NW **202/232–7000** • gay-friendly • boutique hotel • WiFi • $166-399

Washington

WHERE THE GIRLS ARE:
Strolling around DuPont Circle or cruising a bar in the LGBT bar ghetto southeast of The Mall.

ENTERTAINMENT:
Gay Men's Chorus of Washington 202/338-7464, web: www.gmcw.org.

LGBT PRIDE:
June. 202/719-5304, web: www.capitalpride.org.
May. Black Lesbian/ Gay Pride, web: www.dcblackpride.org.

ANNUAL EVENTS:
March - Women's History Month at various Smithsonian Museums 202/633-5330, web: www.smith-sonianeducation.org.
October - Reel Affirmations Film Festival 202/986-1119, web: www.reelaffirmations.org.

CITY INFO:
DC Convention & Tourism Corporation. 800/422-8644, web: www.washington.org.

ATTRACTIONS:
Ford's Theatre 202/347-4833, web: www.fords.org.
Jefferson Memorial.
JFK Center for the Performing Arts 800/444-1324, web: www.kennedy-center.org.
Lincoln Memorial.
National Gallery 202/737-4215, web: www.nga.gov.

National Museum of Women in the Arts 202/783-5000, web: www.nmwa.org.
National Zoo 202/633-4800, web: natzoo.si.edu.
Smithsonian 202/633-5330, web: www.smithsonianeducation.org.
Vietnam Veteran's Memorial.
United States Holocaust Memorial Museum 202/488-0400, web: www.ushmm.org.

BEST VIEW:
From the top of the Washington Monument.

WEATHER:
Summers are hot (90°s) and MUGGY (the city was built on marshes). In the winter, temperatures drop to the 30°s and 40°s with rain and sometimes snow. Spring is the time of cherry blossoms.

TRANSIT:
Yellow Cab 202/544-1212.
Washington Flier 703/661-6655 (from Dulles or Ronald Reagan National).
Super Shuttle 800/258-3826.
Metro Transit Authority 202/637-7000, web: www.wmata.com.

The Embassy Inn 1627 16th St NW (at R St) 202/234-7800, 877/968-9111 • gay-friendly • small hotel w/ B&B atmosphere • WiFi • $79-179

Embassy Suites Alexandria 1900 Diagonal Rd, Alexandria, VA 703/684-5900, 800/362-2779 • gay/ straight • full brkfst • kids ok • pool • $119-450

Embassy Suites Hotel at the Chevy Chase Pavilion 4300 Military Rd NW (at Wisconsin) 202/362-9300, 800/362-2779 • gay-friendly • pool • gym • wheelchair access • $149-289

Embassy Suites Tysons Corner 8517 Leesburg Pike (at W Park), Vienna, VA 703/883-0707, 800/362-2779 • gay-friendly • full brkfst • kids ok • pool • wheelchair access • $109-329

Embassy Suites Washington, DC 1250 22nd St NW (btwn M & N) 202/857-3388, 800/362-2779 • gay-friendly • full brkfst • kids ok • pool • WiFi • $119-319

Hotel Helix 1430 Rhode Island Ave NW 202/462-9001, 800/706-1202 • gay-friendly • full-service boutique hotel • also Helix Lounge • nonsmoking • WiFi • wheelchair access • $129-359

Hotel Madera 1310 New Hampshire Ave NW (at N) 202/296-7600, 800/430-1202 • gay-friendly • boutique hotel • kids/ pets ok • Firefly bistro adjacent • WiFi • wheelchair access • $149-429

Hotel Monaco Washington DC 700 F St NW (at 7th) 202/628-7177, 800/649-1202 • gay-friendly • boutique hotel • kids/ pets ok • WiFi • wheelchair access • $129-350

Hotel Palomar 2121 P St NW (at 21st St) 202/448-1800, 866/866-3070 • gay-friendly • in Dupont Circle • gym • WiFi • pool • restaurant • wheelchair access • $175-440

Hotel Rouge 1315 16th St NW (at Rhode Island) 202/232-8000, 800/738-1202 • gay-friendly • ultra-hip, high-tech luxury hotel • kids/ pets ok • also restaurant & bar • WiFi • wheelchair access • $139-399

Kalorama Guest House at Kalorama Park 1854 Mintwood Pl NW (at Columbia Rd) 202/667-6369, 800/974-6450 • gay/ straight • Victorian town house near Dupont Circle • nonsmoking • WiFi • $50-120

Kalorama Guest House at Woodley Park 2700 Cathedral Ave NW (off Connecticut Ave) 202/328-0860, 800/974-9101 • gay/ straight • near Nat'l Zoo & Washington Cathedral • nonsmoking • WiFi • $55-105

Madison Hotel 1177 15th St NW (at M St NW) 202/862-1600, 800/424-8577 • gay-friendly • luxury hotel • WiFi • also Palette restaurant

Morrison-Clark Historic Hotel & Restaurant 1015 L St NW (at Massachusetts Ave NW) 202/898-1200, 800/322-7898 • gay-friendly • hotel in 2 Victorian town houses • very popular restaurant • WiFi • $155-325

Otis Place B&B 1003 Otis Place NW (at 10th St) 202/483-0241, 877/893-3233 • gay/ straight • 1910 Victorian town house • kids ok • WiFi • gay-owned • $75-145

The River Inn 924 25th St NW (at K St) 202/337-7600, 888/874-0100 • gay-friendly • suites w/ kitchen • gym • WiFi • also Dish + Drinks restaurant • wheelchair access • $99-299

Savoy Suites Hotel 2505 Wisconsin Ave NW (at Calvert, in Georgetown) 202/337-9700, 800/944-5377 • gay-friendly • also restaurant • Italian • WiFi • wheelchair access • $129-269

Swann House Historic B&B 1808 New Hampshire Ave NW (at Swann St) 202/265-4414 • gay/ straight • 1883 Victorian mansion in Dupont Circle • pool • roof deck • fireplaces • kids ok • WiFi • $150-365

Topaz Hotel 1733 N St NW (at Massachusetts Ave NW) 202/393-3000, 800/775-1202 • gay-friendly • boutique hotel • kids/ pets ok • also restaurant & bar • no smoking in rooms • WiFi • wheelchair access • $149-429

Toutorsky Mansion 1720 16th St NW (at Riggs) 202/302-1472 • gay-friendly • WiFi • six blocks from the White House • gay-owned • $145-185

Washington Plaza 10 Thomas Cir NW (at 14th & Massachusetts) 202/842-1300, 800/424-1140 • gay-friendly • full-service hotel • WiFi • pool • also restaurant • $99-299

The Windsor Inn 1842 16th St NW 202/667-0300, 800/423-9111 • gay-friendly • small hotel w/ B&B atmosphere • WiFi • $119-250

BARS

1409 Playbill Cafe 1409 14th St NW 202/265-3055 • 11am-2am, till 3am Fri-Sat • lesbians/ gay men • food served • also theater • wheelchair access

DC Eagle 639 New York Ave NW (btwn 6th & 7th) 202/347-6025 • 4pm-2am, 2pm-3am Fri-Sat • popular • mostly gay men • leather • wheelchair access

DIK Bar/ Windows 1637 17th St NW (at R St NW, upstairs) **202/328-0100** • 4pm-2am • mostly gay men • dancing/DJ • karaoke • older crowd

EFN Lounge 1318 9th St NW (at O St) **202/596-2336** • 5pm-2am, till 3am Fri-Sat • lesbians/ gay men • karaoke • shows • theme nights

The Fireplace 2161 P St NW (at 22nd St) **202/293-1293** • 1pm-2am, till 3am Fri-Sat • mostly gay men • neighborhood bar • multiracial • videos • wheelchair access

JR's 1519 17th St NW (at Church) **202/328-0090** • 2pm-2am, till 3am Fri, 1pm-3am Sat, 1pm-2am Sun • popular • mostly gay men • neighborhood bar • food served • videos • young crowd

Lace 2214 Rhode Island Ave NE **202/832-3888** • 6pm-3am Fri-Sat, till midnight Sun, clsd Mon-Th • upscale women's bar • mostly African American • also restaurant • lesbian-owned

Larry's Lounge 1840 18th St NW (at T St) **202/483-1483** • 4pm-1am, till 2am Fri-Sat • lesbians/ gay men • neighborhood bar • also Malaysian restaurant • wheelchair access • gay-owned

MOVA 1435 P St NW (at 15th St NW) **202/797-9730** • 5pm-close • lesbians/ gay men • neighborhood bar

Mr Henry's Capitol Hill 601 Pennsylvania Ave SE (at 6th St) **202/546-8412** • 11:30am-11:30pm • popular • gay-friendly • multiracial • live jazz Fri • also restaurant • nonsmoking • wheelchair access

Nellie's Sports Bar 900 U St NW (at 9th) **202/332-6355** • 5pm-midnight, 3pm-2am Fri, from 11am wknds • mostly gay men • gay sports bar

Phase One 525 8th St SE (btwn E & G Sts) **202/544-6831** • 7pm-2am, till 3am Fri-Sat (clsd Mon-Wed winter) • mostly women • oldest lesbian bar in the US! • neighborhood bar • dancing/DJ • karaoke • shows • multiracial • wheelchair access

POV Roof Terrace Bar 515 15th Street NW (at Alexander Hamilton Pl) **202/661-2400** • 11am-2am • gay-friendly • pricey cocktails • superior views of the White House & Lincoln Memorial • tapas served

Remington's 639 Pennsylvania Ave SE (btwn 6th & 7th) **202/543-3113** • 4pm-2am, till 3am Fri-Sat, 6pm-2am Sun • popular • mostly gay men • dancing/DJ • 2 flrs • country/ western • dance lessons Mon & Wed • karaoke Wed • T-dance Sun • videos

Tempting Tuesdays 1318 9th St NW (at O St, at EFN Lounge) **202/596-2336** • 6pm-mdnght Tue • women's night • dancing/DJ

Nightclubs

Apex 1415 22nd St NW (btwn O & P Sts) **202/296-0505** • 9pm-3am Th, till 4am Fri-Sat, clsd Sun-Wed • lesbians/ gay men • dancing/DJ • videos • young crowd • wheelchair access • cover

Bachelors Mill 1104 8th St SE (downstairs at Back Door Pub) **202/546-5979** • 5pm-2am, till 3am wknds • lesbians/ gay men • popular • dancing/DJ • 2 flrs • mostly African American • live shows • karaoke • wheelchair access

Bare 1639 R St NW (at 17th, at Cobalt) **202/232-4416** • 10pm 3rd Sat only • mostly women • dancing/DJ

Chief Ike's Mambo Room 1725 Columbia Rd NW (at Ontario Rd) **202/332-2211** • 4pm-2am, till 3am Fri, 6pm-3am Sat, clsd Sun • gay-friendly • dancing/DJ • also restaurant • American • wheelchair access

Club Fuego 1818 New York Ave NE (at Montana Ave, at Aqua) • 10:30pm-3am Fri only • lesbians/ gay men • dancing/DJ • multiracial • salsa, merengue, Latin pop

Cobalt/ 30 Degrees Lounge 1639 R St NW (at 17th) **202/232-4416** • 5pm-2am, till 3am Fri-Sat • mostly gay men • dancing/DJ • live shows • drag shows • videos

Delta Elite 3734 10th St NE (at Perry St NE, in Brookland) **202/529-0626** • midnight-4am Fri & Sat only • ladies night Fri • dancing/DJ • mostly African American

District Sundays 2473 18th St NW (at Columbia Rd, at District Lounge) • 9pm Sun • mostly women • dancing/DJ • multiracial

Elevate 2427 18th St NW (at Black Squirrel) **202/232-1011** • 9pm Fri only • mostly women • dancing/DJ

Fab Lounge 2022 Florida Ave NW (at Connecticut) **202/797-1122** • 5pm-close • lesbians/ gay men • dancing/DJ • multiracial

Jam 1435 P St NW (at Mova) **202/797-9730** • 9pm 1st Sat • mostly women • dancing/DJ • multiracial

Ladies First 2022 Florida Ave NW (at Connecticut, at Fab Lounge) • 6pm Wed • mostly women • dancing/DJ • multiracial

Mixtape • 3rd Sat only • alternative queer dance party • venue changes, check mixtapedc.com for info

Pink Sock 1101 Kenyon St NW (at 11th, at Wonderland Ballroom) 202/232–5263 • 9pm 3rd Wed only • lesbians/gay men • dancing/DJ • younger crowd

Town Danceboutique 2009 8th St NW (at U St NW) 202/234–8696 • 9pm-4am Fri-Sat • mostly gay men • dancing/DJ • drag shows • 18+ Fri

CAFES

Cosi 1647 20th St NW 202/332–6364 • 7am-11pm, till midnight Fri-Sat, 8am-10pm Sun • full bar from 4pm • popular • make your own s'mores • WiFi

Jolt 'n' Bolt 1918 18th St NW (at Florida) 202/232–0077 • 7am-11pm, till 8:30pm wknds • popular • patio

Soho Tea & Coffee 2150 P St NW (at 21st St) 202/463–7646 • 6:30am-1am, from 7:30am wknds • WiFi • food served • patio • wheelchair access

RESTAURANTS

18th & U Duplex Diner 2004 18th St NW (at Ave U) 202/265–7828 • 6pm-11pm, till 12:30am Tue-Wed, till 1:30am Fri-Sat • American comfort food • full bar

2 Amys Pizza 3715 Macomb St NW 202/885–5700 • lunch & dinner Tue-Sun, dinner only Mon • wheelchair access

Acadiana 901 New York Ave NW 202/408–8848 • lunch Mon-Fri, dinner nightly, brunch Sun • Cajun • great bourbon selection • reservations recommended

Annie's Paramount Steak House 1609 17th St NW (at Corcoran) 202/232–0395 • 10am-11:30pm, till 1am Th & Sun, 24hrs Fri-Sat • popular • full bar • wheelchair access

Armand's Chicago Pizza 4231 Wisconsin Ave NW (at Veazey) 202/363–5500 • 11am-10pm, till 11pm Fri-Sat, noon-10pm Sun • full bar • also 226 Massachusetts Ave NE, Capitol Hill, 202/547-6600

Asylum 2471 18th St NW 202/319–9353 • 5pm-2am, till 3am Fri, from 11am wknds • plenty veggie • also bar

Banana Cafe & Piano Bar 500 8th St SE (at E St) 202/543–5906 • 11am-10:30pm, till 11pm Fri-Sat, till 10pm Sun • Puerto Rican/Cuban food • some veggie • famous margaritas • piano bar • gay-owned

Bar Pilar 1833 14th St NW (at Swann St) 202/265–1751 • dinner nightly, Sun brunch • new American

Beacon Bar & Grill 1615 Rhode Island Ave NW (at 17th, at Beacon Hotel) 202/872–1126 • brkfst, lunch & dinner • popular Sun brunch • patio

Busboys & Poets 2021 14th St NW (at V St) 202/387–7638 • 8am-midnight, till 2am Fri-Sat, 10am-midnight Sun • also bookstore • live jazz & poetry • WiFi • wheelchair access

Cafe Green 1513 17th St NW 202/234–0505 • 11am-10pm, 10am-4pm Sun, clsd Mon • organic cafe • plenty veggie/vegan

Cafe Japoné 2032 P St NW (at 21st) 202/223–1573 • 6pm-1:30am, till 2:30am Fri-Sat • mostly Asian American • popular • Japanese food • full bar • live jazz Wed • karaoke

Cafe La Ruche 1039 31st St 202/965–2684 • dinner, Sun brunch • French • patio

Cafe Luna 1633 P St NW (at 17th) 202/387–4005 • 10am-11pm, till midnight wknds • popular • lesbians/gay men • healthy • plenty veggie

Cafe Saint Ex/ Gate 54 1847 14th St NW 202/265–7839 • lunch, dinner, Sun brunch • modern American • also Gate 54 club downstairs • popular Th dance party • gay-friendly

Chartwell Grill 1914 Connecticut Ave NW (in The Churchill Hotel) 202/797–2000 • 6:30am-10:30pm, also lounge till 12:30am, till 11pm Sun • cont'l • wheelchair access

Dupont Italian Kitchen & Bar 1637 17th St NW (at R St) 202/328–3222, 202/328–0100 • 11am-11pm, bar 4pm-2am • some veggie • wheelchair access

Firefly 1310 New Hampshire Ave NW 202/861–1310 • lunch & dinner, wknd brunch • plenty veggie

Floriana 1602 17th St NW (at Q St NW) 202/667–5937 • dinner nightly • Italian • full bar • patio • gay-owned

Food For Thought 1811 14th St NW (at the Black Cat) 202/667–4490 • 8pm-1am, 7pm-2am Fri-Sat • gay-friendly • mostly vegan/veggie • nonsmoking • also live music • readings • indie/ punk • young crowd • wheelchair access

Guapo's 4515 Wisconsin Ave NW (at Albemarle) 202/686–3588 • lunch & dinner • Mexican • some veggie • full bar • wheelchair access

Hello Cupcake 1361 Connecticut Avenue NW 202/861–2253 • 10am-7pm, till 9pm Fri-Sat, 11am-6pm Sun • cupcakes!

The Islander 1201 U St NW (at 12th) **202/234-4971** • lunch & dinner • Caribbean • some veggie • full bar • live music • karaoke

Jack's 1527 17th St NW **202/332-6767** • lunch Tue-Sun, dinner nightly, wknd brunch • also bar

Jaleo 480 7th St NW (at E St) **202/628-7949** • lunch & dinner • tapas • full bar • Sevillanas dancers Wed • wheelchair access

Java Green Eco Cafe 1020 19th St NW **202/775-8899** • 8am-8pm, 10am-6pm Sat, clsd Sun • organic cafe • plenty veggie/vegan

La Frontera Cantina 1633 17th St NW (btwn R & Q Sts) **202/232-0437** • 11am-11pm, till 1am Fri-Sat • Tex-Mex

Lauriol Plaza 1835 18th St NW (at S St) **202/387-0035** • 11:30am-11pm, till midnight Fri-Sat • Latin American • wheelchair access

Level One 1639 R St NW (at 17th) **202/745-0025** • dinner nightly, wknd brunch

Logan Tavern 1423 P St NW **202/332-3710** • lunch & dinner, wknd brunch • American comfort food • also gay-friendly neighborhood bar • gay-owned

Occidental Grill 1475 Pennsylvania Ave NW (btwn 14th & 15th) **202/783-1475** • lunch Mon-Sat, dinner nightly, clsd Sun • upscale • political player hangout

Perry's 1811 Columbia Rd NW (at 18th) **202/234-6218** • 5:30pm-10:30pm, till 11:30pm wknds, popular drag Sun brunch • contemporary American & sushi • full bar • roof deck

Pizza Paradiso 2003 P Street NW **202/223-1245** • 11am-11pm, till midnight wknds

Posto 1515 14th St NW **202/332-8613** • dinner nightly • terrific Italian

Rasika 633 D St NW **202/637-1222** • lunch Mon-Fri, dinner Mon-Sat, clsd Sun • Indian • wheelchair access

Rice 1608 14th St NW (at 'Q') **202/234-2400** • lunch & dinner • Thai

Rocklands 2418 Wisconsin Ave NW (at Calvert) **202/333-2558** • 11am-10pm, till 9pm Sun • BBQ & take-out

Sabores 3435 Connecticut Ave NW (btwn Porter & Ordway) **202/244-7196** • dinner nightly, Sun brunch • tapas • also lounge • live music

Sala Thai 1301 U St NW (at 13th) **202/462-1333** • lunch & dinner • some veggie

Skewers 1633 P St NW (at 17th) **202/387-7400** • 11am-11pm, noon-midnight wknds • popular • Middle-Eastern • belly dancing Sat • full bar

Soul Vegetarian Exodus 2606 Georgia Ave NW **202/328-7685** • 11am-9pm, till 3pm Sun (brunch) • all-vegan menu

Thaitanic 1326 14th St NW (at Rhode Island Ave) **202/588-1795** • lunch & dinner • Thai • plenty veggie

Trio 1537 17th St NW (at Q St NW) **202/232-6305** • 8am-midnight • American • some veggie • full bar • sidewalk cafe • wheelchair access

Twist Dupont 1731 New Hampshire (at 18th & R Sts, in the Carlyle Suites) **202/518-5011** • lunch & dinner • gay/ straight • also art deco bar • internet access • wheelchair access

Zaytinia 701 9th Street NW (at G St) **202/638-0800** • lunch & dinner • Greek/ Mediterranean • plenty veggie

ENTERTAINMENT & RECREATION

Anecdotal History Tours 301/294-9514 • gay-friendly • variety of guided tours

Bike & Roll Washington DC 1100 Pennsylvania Ave NW (off 12th St, at Old Post Office Pavilion) **202/842-2453** • 9am-6pm • tour the nation's capital on bike!

Hillwood Museum & Gardens 4155 Linnean Ave NW (at Tilden St NW) **202/686-5807, 877/445-5966** • 10am-5pm Tue-Sat • Fabergé, porcelain, furniture & more • reservations required

Lesbian & Gay Chorus of Washington, DC 202/546-1549

National Museum of Women in the Arts 1250 New York Ave **202/783-5000, 800/222-7270**

Phillips Collection 1600 21st St NW (at Q St) **202/387-2151** • clsd Mon • America's first museum of modern art • near Dupont Circle

Washington Mystics 202/266-2277, 877/324-6671 • check out the Women's Nat'l Basketball Association while you're in DC

BOOKSTORES

ADC Map & Travel Center 1636 I St NW (at 17th St) **202/628-2608, 800/544-2659** • 9am-6:30pm, till 5:30pm Fri, 11am-5pm Sat, clsd Sun • many maps & travel guides

G Books 1520 U St NW, BSMT (btwn 15th St & U St) **202/986-9697** • 4pm-10pm, till 11pm Fri-Sat, from noon wknds • new & used gay books • pride items • gay-owned

Kramerbooks & Afterwords Cafe & Grill 1517 Connecticut Ave NW (at Q St) **202/387–1400** • 7:30am-1am, 24hrs wknds • general • also cafe & bar • live music • wheelchair access

Retail Shops

HRC Action Center & Store 1633 Connecticut Avenue NW **202/232–8621** • 10am-9pm, till 10pm wknds • Human Rights Campaign merchandise & info

Leather Rack 1723 Connecticut Ave NW (btwn R & S Sts) **202/797–7401**

Pulp 1803 14th St NW **202/462–7857** • 11am-7pm, till 5pm Sun • cards • gifts • music

Universal Gear 1529 14th St NW (btwn P & Q) **202/319–0136** • 11am-10pm, till midnight Fri-Sat • casual, club, athletic & designer clothing

Publications

Metro Weekly **202/638–6830** • LGBT newsmagazine • extensive club listings

Washington Blade **202/797–7000** • huge LGBT newspaper • extensive resource listings

Gyms & Health Clubs

Results—The Gym 1612 U St NW (at 17th St) **202/234–5678** • gay-friendly • also women-only fitness area • also cafe

Washington Sports Club 1835 Connecticut Ave NW (at Columbia & Florida) **202/332–0100**

Erotica

Pleasure Place 1063 Wisconsin Ave NW, Georgetown (btwn M & K Sts) **800/386–2386** • 10am-10pm, till midnight Wed-Sat, noon-7pm Sun • erotica • clubwear • leather • adult toys • DVDs • clothing & more • wheelchair access

Pleasure Place 1710 Connecticut Ave NW (btwn Florida Ave & R St) **202/483–3297** • 10am-10pm, till midnight Wed-Sat, noon-7pm Sun • erotica • clubwear • leather • adult toys • DVDs • clothing & more

FLORIDA

Statewide

Publications

Ambush Mag **504/522–8049** • LGBT newspaper for the Gulf South (TX through FL)

HOTSPOTS! Magazine **954/928–1862** • "South Florida's largest gay publication"

She Magazine, "The Source for Women" **954/354–9751** • "The hippest & hottest source for women of the rainbow community"

Alligator Point

Accommodations

Mermaid's Tale **703/819–5243, 866/794–9640** • mostly women • elegant & private beach house on the Gulf of Mexico • kids ok, inquire about pets • nonsmoking • lesbian-owned • $875-1,275/ week

Amelia Island

Accommodations

The Hoyt House 804 Atlantic Ave **904/277–4300, 800/432–2085** • gay-friendly • full brkfst • pool • hot tub • nonsmoking • WiFi • wheelchair access • $190-229

Restaurants

Beech Street Grill 801 Beech St (at 8th St), Fernandina Beach **904/277–3662** • 6pm-9pm, also lunch Wed-Fri and Sun brunch • live music

Brett's Waterway Cafe 1 Front St **904/261–2660** • lunch & dinner • seafood

Auburndale

Nightclubs

Boots 340 Havendale Blvd **863/268–8294** • 2pm-2am, clsd Sun • lesbians/ gay men • neighborhood bar • dancing/DJ • karoake • wheelchair access

Boca Raton

Restaurants

Kyojin 21073 Powerline Rd **561/218–1708** • lunch & dinner • Japanese buffet

Boynton Beach

see West Palm Beach

Bradenton

see also Sarasota

ACCOMMODATIONS

Summer House 111 & 113 36th St, Holmes Beach **941/778-2333, 800/431-0278** • gay-friendly • cottage-style inn, includes 4-bdrm cottage • pool • nonsmoking • kids ok • $115-250 & $800-1,400/weekly

Clearwater

see also Dunedin, New Port Richey, Port Richey & St Petersburg

ACCOMMODATIONS

Holiday Inn Select 3535 Ulmerton Rd (Rte 688 W) **727/577-9100, 888/465-4329** • gay-friendly • pool • wheelchair access • close to airport & beach • WiFi • $98-169

BARS

Pro Shop Pub 840 Cleveland St (at Prospect) **727/447-4259** • 1pm-2am • popular • mostly gay men • neighborhood bar • bears • gay-owned

RETAIL SHOPS

Skinz 2027 Gulf to Bay Blvd (aka State Rd 60, at Hercules Rd) **727/441-8789** • 10am-6pm • men's & women's swimwear, gymwear & clubwear • also online store

Cocoa

BARS

The Ultra Lounge 407 Brevard Ave, Cocoa Village **321/690-0096** • 6pm-2am • mostly gay men • neighborhood bar

Cocoa Beach

ACCOMMODATIONS

Beach Place Guesthouses 1445 S Atlantic Ave **321/783-4045** • gay-friendly • on seashore • kids ok • nonsmoking • WiFi • gay-owned • $195-370

RESTAURANTS

Lobster Shanty 2200 S Orlando Ave **321/783-1350** • 11:30am-9pm, till 10pm Fri-Sat • full bar • wheelchair access

Daytona Beach

ACCOMMODATIONS

The August Seven Inn 1209 S Peninsula Dr (at Silver Beach) **386/248-8420, 877/797-3836** • gay-friendly • 1 block from ocean • full brkfst • WiFi • $125-185

Mayan Inn 103 S Ocean Ave **386/252-2378, 800/448-2286** • gay-friendly • some rooms w/ ocean views • pool • kids ok • wheelchair access

The Villa B&B 801 N Peninsula Dr **386/248-2020, 888/248-7060** • gay-friendly • hot tub • pool • nudity • nonsmoking • gay-owned • $95-300

BARS

Streamline Lounge 140 S Atlantic Ave (at Streamline Hotel) **386/258-6937** • 11am-3am (penthouse lounge) • gay-friendly • dancing/DJ • live entertainment • game room

NIGHTCLUBS

Savoy Daytona 546 Seabreeze Blvd (at Atlantic Ave) **386/226-5600** • 5pm-3am, from 3pm Sun • lesbians/gay men • neighborhood bar • dancing/DJ • videos • wheelchair access • gay-owned

CAFES

Java Joint & Eatery 2201 N A1A, Flagler Beach **386/439-1013** • 7am-4pm

RESTAURANTS

Anna's Trattoria 304 Seabreeze Blvd **386/239-9624** • 5pm-10pm, clsd Sun-Mon • Italian • beer/wine

Barnacles Restaurant & Lounge 869 S Atlantic Ave, Ormond Beach **386/673-1070** • 4pm-10pm

The Clubhouse 600 Wilder Blvd (at Daytona Beach Golf & Country Club) **386/257-0727** • 6am-7:30pm

Frappes North 123 W Granada Blvd (at S Yonge St), Ormond Beach **386/615-4888** • lunch Tue-Fri, dinner nightly, clsd Sun • "organically groovy" American • patio • full bar • wheelchair access

Sapporo 501 Seabreeze Ave **386/257-4477** • lunch Mon-Fri, dinner nightly • Japanese steak house & sushi bar • full bar

PUBLICATIONS

Watermark 407/481-2243 (ORLANDO OFFICE), 877/926-8118 • bi-weekly LGBT newspaper for Central FL

Delray Beach

ACCOMMODATIONS

Crane's BeachHouse 82 Gleason St (at Atlantic Ave) **561/278-1700, 866/372-7263** • gay-friendly • hotel • pool • kids/ pets ok • nonsmoking • $129-546

BOOKSTORES

Shining Through 426 E Atlantic Ave **561/276-8559** • metaphysical/ New Age • some LGBT titles • also incense, candles, crystals & gifts

Dunedin

see St Petersburg

Fort Lauderdale

INFO LINES & SERVICES

Lambda South Inc 1231-A E Las Olas Blvd (alley access only) **954/761-9072** • meeting space for LGBT in recovery • wheelchair access

The Pride Center at Equality Park 2040 N Dixie Hwy, Wilton Manors **954/463-9005** • 10am-10pm, noon-5pm wknds • outreach • wheelchair access

ACCOMMODATIONS

Alhambra Beach Resort 3021 Alhambra St **954/525-7601, 877/309-4014** • gay/ straight • motel • close to gay beach • pool • nonsmoking • WiFi • gay-owned • $99-269

Blue Lagoon Resort 3801 N Ocean Blvd **954/565-6666, 800/663-2985** • gay-friendly • pool • WiFi • gay-owned • $60-200

Fort Lauderdale

WHERE THE GIRLS ARE:
On the beach near the LGBT accommodations, just south of Birch State Recreation Area. Or at one of the cafes or bars in Wilton Manors or Oakland Park.

LGBT PRIDE:
March. 954/745-7070, web: www.pridesouthflorida.org. Also Stonewall Street Festival in June.

ANNUAL EVENTS:
March - AIDS Walk, web: www.floridaaidswalk.org.
March - GALLA gay/ lesbian arts festival, web: artsunitedonline.org.
April - Miami/Fort Lauderdale Gay & Lesbian Film Festival, web: www.mglff.com.
October-November - Int'l Film Fest 954/760-9898, web: www.fliff.com.

CITY INFO:
Greater Fort Lauderdale Convention & Visitors Bureau 954/765-4466 or 800/227-8669 (code 187), web: www.sunny.org.

WEATHER:
The average year-round temperature in this sub-tropical climate is 75-90°.

ATTRACTIONS:
Broward Center for the Performing Arts 954/462-0222, web: www.browardcenter.org.
Butterfly World 954/977-4400, web: www.butterflyworld.com.
Everglades.
Flamingo Gardens 954/473-2955, web: www.flamingogardens.org.
Museum of Art 954/525-5500, web: www.moafl.org.
Museum of Discovery & Science 954/467-6637, web: www.mods.org.
Sawgrass Mills, world's largest outlet mall 954/846-2300, web: www.sawgrassmillsmall.com.

TRANSIT:
Yellow Cab 954/777-7777.
Super Shuttle 954/764-1700.
Broward County Transit 954/357-8400, web: www.broward.org/bct.

The Deauville Hostel & Crewhouse 2916 N Ocean Blvd (Oakland Park Blvd & A1A) **954/568-5000** • gay-friendly • budget accommodations for backpackers, tourists, students • pool • wheelchair access • $25-225

Ed Lugo Resort 2404 NE 8th Ave (Wilton Manors) **954/275-8299** • gay-friendly • pool • WiFi • gay-owned • $50-200

Embassy Suites Hotel 1100 SE 17th St **954/527-2700, 800/362-2779** • gay-friendly • full brkfst • kids/ pets ok • WiFi • wheelchair access • $129-369

Fort Lauderdale Oceanfront Hotel 440 Seabreeze Blvd **954/524-8733, 866/273-9593** • gay-friendly • pool • sundeck bar • nonsmoking

Liberty Apartment & Garden Suites 1501 SW 2nd Ave (at Sheridan), Dania Beach **954/927-0090, 877/927-0090** • lesbians/ gay men • furnished apts • pool • WiFi • near beach • nonsmoking available • pets ok • wheelchair access • gay-owned • $79-199

Manhattan Tower 701 Bayshore Dr **754/224-7301** • gay-friendly • apt hotel • pets/kids ok • $120-275

Marriott Harbor Beach Resort 3030 Holiday Dr **954/525-4000, 800/222-6543** • gay-friendly • pool • also restaurant & spa • private beach access

The Royal Palms Resort 717 Breakers Ave (at Vistamar St) **954/564-6444, 800/237-7256** • mostly gay men • Fort Lauderdale's largest Gay resort and spa is located one block from the World famous Fort Lauderdale Beach. Luxurious modern accommodations, 3 swimming pools, jacuzzi, gym, spa, cafe and a bar. Recipient of many lodging awards, The Royal Palms is the place to stay • nonsmoking • WiFi • gay-owned • $89-369

Sandra Lee Inn 2307 NE 33rd Ave **954/249-0565** • "straight-friendly" • apts • pool • nonsmoking • gay-owned • $70-190

W Hotel Fort Lauderdale 401 N Fort Lauderdale Beach Blvd **954/414-8200** • gay/ straight • pool • kids ok • restaurant & lounge • WiFi • wheelchair access • $279-900

Westin Beach Resort 321 N Fort Lauderdale Beach Blvd (A1A) **954/467-1111, 888/627-7109** • gay-friendly • sports deck & gym • 2 pools • wheelchair access • $230+

Windamar Beach Club 533 Orton Ave **954/563-7062** • lesbians/ gay men • pool • WiFi • pets ok • $49-139

BARS

Beach Betty's 625 Dania Beach Blvd (at Fronton Blvd), Dania **954/921-9893** • noon-3am • mostly women • neighborhood bar • dancing/DJ • live music • karaoke • lesbian-owned

Bill's 2209 Wilton Dr (off NE 23rd St) **954/567-5978** • 2pm-2am, till 3am Fri-Sat, from noon Sat-Sun • neighborhood bar • karaoke • wheelchair access

Cloud 9 Lounge 7126 Stirling Rd, Davie **954/499-3525** • noon-4am • mostly women • multi-racial clienete • live shows • drag shows • live bands

Cozmos Lounge/ Club Oz 2674 E Oakland Park Blvd **954/616-8239** • 3pm-2am, Club Oz from 9pm Sat • mostly gay men • dancing/DJ • male strippers

The Depot 2935 N Federal Hwy **954/537-7076** • noon-2am, till 3am Fri-Sat • mostly gay men • neighborhood bar • karaoke

Exit 66 219 S Ft Lauderdale Beach Blvd **954/357-9981** • gay/ straight • dancing/DJ

Georgie's Alibi 2266 Wilton Dr (at NE 4th Ave) **954/565-2526** • 11am-2am, till 3am Fri-Sat • lesbians/ gay men • nonsmoking • food served • videos • WiFi • wheelchair access

Indulge Wednesdays at Whiskey Blue 401 N Fort Lauderdale Beach Blvd (at W Hotel) **954/414-8233** • gay night Wed only • lesbians/ gay men • indoor/ outdoor lounge

J's Bar 2780 Davie Blvd **954/581-8400** • 9am-2am, till 3am Fri-Sat, from noon Sun • lesbians/gay men • neighborhood bar • dancing/DJ

The Manor Complex 2345 Wilton Dr, Wilton Manors **954/626-0082** • 11am-11pm • lesbians/ gay men • also Epic nightclub & Ivy Lounge • live entertainment • also restaurant & cafe

Matty's on the Drive 2426 Wilton Dr, Wilton Manors **954/564-1799** • 11am-2am, till 3am Fri-Sat • mostly gay men • neighborhood bar • wheelchair access

Mona's 502 E Sunrise Blvd (at 5th Ave) **954/525-6662** • noon-2am, till 3am wknds • mostly gay men • neighborhood bar • karaoke

Monkey Business 2740 N Andrews Ave **954/565-3550** • 9am-2am, till 3am wknds • mostly gay men • neighborhood bar • theme nights • cabaret • drag shows

Naked Grape 2039 Wilton Dr (at NE 20th St), Wilton Manors **954/563-5631** • 4pm-midnight, from 2pm Fri-Sat, clsd Sun-Mon • gay-friendly • wine bar

New Moon 2440 Wilton Dr, Wilton Manors **954/563–7660** • 2pm-2am, from noon Fri, from11am Sat-Sun, from 4pm Mon • mostly women • karaoke Th • dancing/DJ Fri • live music Sat

Noche Latina Saturday 2345 Wilton Dr (at Manor Complex), Wilton Manors **954/626–0082** • 11pm Sat at Ivy nightclub • mostly gay men • dancing/DJ • multiracial

Ramrod 1508 NE 4th Ave (at 16th St) **954/763–8219** • 3pm-2am, till 3am wknds • popular • mostly gay men • leather/ levi cruise bar • patio • also LeatherWerks leather store

Scandals 3073 NE 6th Ave, Wilton Manors **954/567–2432** • noon-2am • mostly men • patio • dancing • country/ western • older crowd • wheelchair access

Sidelines Sports Bar 2031 Wilton Dr, Wilton Manors **954/563–8001** • 2pm-2am, from noon wknds • lesbians/ gay men

Smarty Pants 3038 N Federal Hwy (at Oakland Park Blvd) **954/561–1724** • 9am-2am, till 3am Sat, noon-2am Sun • popular • mostly gay men • neighborhood bar • live entertainment • karaoke • drag shows • wheelchair access

Nightclubs

Atomic Boom 2232 Wilton Dr, Wilton Manors **954/630–3556** • 4pm-2am, 2pm-3am wknds • popular • mostly gay men • dancing/DJ • live shows • karaoke • drag shows • T-dance Sun • gay-owned

Gloss at the Manor 2345 Wilton Dr, Wilton Manors • Th night women's party • check out www.pandoraevents.com

Living Room 300 SW 1st Ave (at Brickell) **888/992–7555** • gay Fri only • mostly men • dancing/DJ

➤**Pandora Events** 305/975–6933 • monthly women's parties • locations rotate so check website: www.pandoraevents.com • see ad in front color section

The Sea Monster 2 S New River Dr W (under the Andrews Drawbridge, across from Las Olas shopping center) **954/474–0183** • 9pm-3am, 4pm-2am Sun, clsd Mon-Th • lesbians/ gay men • more women Sat • dancing/DJ • transgender-friendly • wheelchair access • gay-owned

Torpedo 2829 W Broward Blvd (at 28th Ave) **954/587–2500** • 10pm-dawn • mostly men • dancing/DJ • strippers

Cafes

Cafe Emunah 3558 N Ocean Blvd **954/561–6411** • 11am-10pm, till 4pm Fri, sunset-1am Sat • kosher, kabbalistic cafe & teabar • food served

Fantasia's of Boston 1826 E Sunrise Blvd (next to Gateway Theater) **954/522–4886** • noon-9:30pm

Java Boys 2230 Wilton Dr, Wilton Manors **954/564–8828** • 8am-midnight • coffee, tea & desserts • WiFi

Jimmies Chocolates & Cafe 148 N Federal Hwy, Dania Beach **954/921–0688** • bistro w/ fresh fare & wine

The Storks 2505 NE 15th Ave (at NE 26th St, Wilton Manors) **954/567–3220** • 6:30am-midnight • patio • wheelchair access

Restaurants

Canyon 1818 E Sunrise Blvd **954/765–1950** • Southwestern • full bar

Diner 24 301 W Oakland Park Blvd, Wilton Manors **954/765–6349** • 7am-midnight, 24hrs Fri-Sat

The Floridian 1410 E Las Olas Blvd **954/463–4041** • 24hr diner

The Four Rivers 1201 N Federal Hwy #3-A **954/616–1112** • Thai lounge • full bar • DJ

Galanga 2389 Wilton Dr, Wilton Manors **954/202–0000** • dinner nightly, lunch weekdays • Thai • also sushi

Grandma's French Cafe 3354 N Ocean Blvd (N of Oakland Park Blvd) **954/564–3671** • clsd Mon • also ice cream parlor

Hi-Life Cafe 3000 N Federal Hwy (at Oakland Park Blvd, in the Plaza 3000) **954/563–1395** • dinner, clsd Mon • reservations recommended

Himmarshee Grille 210 SW 2nd St **954/524–1818** • lunch & dinner

Humpy's 2244 Wilton Dr, Wilton Manors **954/566–2722, 877/448–6797** • 11am-10pm, till 2am Th-Sat • pizza & panini

Kitchenetta 2850 N Federal Hwy **954/567–3333** • dinner nightly, clsd Mon

Kyojin 3485 N Federal Hwy **954/568–2208** • lunch & dinner • Japanese buffet

Lester's Diner 250 State Rd 84 **954/525–5641** • 24hrs • popular • more gay late nights

Lips 1421 E Oakland Park Blvd (at Dixie Hwy) **954/567–0987** • 6pm-close, Sun brunch, clsd Mon • "the ultimate in drag dining"

Maracas Mexican Gar & Grill 3001 N Federal Hwy 954/537-2002 • 11:30pm-10:30pm, till 11:30pm Fri-Sat • more gay Mon • patio

Rosie's Bar & Grill 2449 Wilton Dr, Wilton Manors 954/563-0123 • 11am-11pm • popular • full bar

Sebastian's Restaurant 17 S Fort Lauderdale Beach Blvd #228 (at Beach Place) 945/530-7433 • gay-friendly • beer & wine • wheelchair access • gay-owned

Simply Delish Cafe 2287 Wilton Dr, Wilton Manors 954/565-8646 • 8am-2pm, clsd Mon • reservations recommended

Sublime 1431 N Federal Hwy 954/539-9000 • 5:30pm-10pm, clsd Mon • vegan/ vegetarian

Tequila Sunrise Mexican Cafe 4711 N Dixie Hwy 954/938-4473 • 11:30am-10pm, till 11pm Th-Sat, 1pm-10pm Sun

Tropics Cabaret & Restaurant 2000 Wilton Dr (at 20th) 954/537-6000 • lunch & dinner, Sun brunch • new American • also piano bar, till 3am Sat • lesbians/ gay men • live shows • wheelchair access

Victoria Park Diner 1730 E Sunrise Blvd 954/759-0022 • 6:30am-10pm

The Wine Cellar 199 E Oakland Park Blvd 954/565-9021 • dinner, clsd Mon-Tue• Eastern European • gay-owned

ENTERTAINMENT & RECREATION

Gold Coast Roller Rink 2604 S Federal Hwy 954/547-3419 • 8pm-2am Tue • gay skate • lesbians/ gay men • transgender-friendly

Laffing Matterz 201 SW 5th Ave (at SW 2nd Ave, at Broward Center for Performing Arts) 954/642-0222 (BOX OFFICE) • gay-friendly • unique & surprising dinner fare followed by cutting-edge musical satire • wheelchair access

Sebastian Beach

BOOKSTORES

Pride Factory 850 NE 13th St 954/463-6600 • 10am-11pm, 11am-9pm Sun

RETAIL SHOPS

GayMartUSA 2240 Wilton Dr (at NE 6th Ave) 954/630-0360 • 10am-11pm

Out of the Closet 2097 Wilton Dr, Wilton Manors 954/358-5580 • 10am-7pm, till 6pm Sun

To The Moon 2205 Wilton Dr (at 6th Ave), Wilton Manors 954/564-2987 • 11am-midnight • pride gifts, cards & candy candy candy!

PUBLICATIONS

gir(L) Magazine 954/815-3220 • lesbian news & entertainment for south FL

GYMS & HEALTH CLUBS

Island City Health & Fitness 2270 Wilton Dr, Wilton Manors 954/318-3900 • 5am-11pm, 8am-8pm wknds

EROTICA

Fetish Factory 855 E Oakland Park Blvd 954/563-5777 • 11am-9pm, noon-6pm Sun

Hustler Hollywood 1500 Sunrise Blvd (at NE 15th Ave) 954/828-9769

Fort Myers

INFO LINES & SERVICES

Gay AA Lambda Drummers 3049 McGregor Blvd (at St John the Apostle MCC) 239/275-5111 (AA#) • 8pm Tue & Sat in social hall • wheelchair access

ACCOMMODATIONS

The Hibiscus House B&B 2135 McGregor Blvd 239/332-2651 • gay-friendly • nonsmoking • WiFi • wheelchair access

Lighthouse Resort Inn & Suites 1051 5th St, Fort Myers Beach 239/463-9392, 800/778-7748 • gay-friendly • pool • kids ok • nonsmoking • WiFi • wheelchair access

The Resort on Carefree Blvd 3000 Carefree Blvd (at Cleveland Ave) 239/731-6366 • mostly women • 1- & 2-bdrm homes & RV lots • pool • nature trails • tennis • gym • kids/ pets ok • older crowd • nonsmoking • woman-owned • $650-800/ week

BARS

Mardi Gras Nouveau 1341 SE 47th Terr, Cape Coral 239/541-8818 • 2pm-midnight, from 4pm Sat, from 11am Sun, till 2am Fri-Sat • lesbians/gay men • full menu • 18+ • wheelchair access

The Office Pub 3704 Cleveland Ave (at Grove) 239/936-3212 • noon-2am • mostly gay men • neighborhood bar • bears • theme nights

Tubby's 4350 Fowler St (off Colonial Blvd) 239/274-5001 • 2pm-2am • mostly gay men • karaoke • live shows • gay-owned

NIGHTCLUBS

The Bottom Line (TBL) 3090 Evans Ave (at Hanson) 239/337-7292, 800/839-6823 • 2pm-2am • lesbians/gay men • more women wknds • dancing/DJ • live shows • karaoke • videos • wheelchair access

RESTAURANTS

McGregor Food & Spirits Company
15675 McGregor Blvd, Ste 24 **239/437–3499** •
11am-2am, from 4pm Sun • pub fare • some
outdoor dining • also full bar • gay-owned

Oasis 2260 Martin Luther King Blvd (at
Hendry St) **239/334–1566** • breakfast, lunch &
dinner • beer/ wine • wheelchair access •
women-owned

Gainesville

INFO LINES & SERVICES

Free to Be AA 3131 NW 13th St (The Pride
Center) **352/372–8091 (AA#)** • 8pm Sun

Pride Community Center 3131 NW 13th St
352/377–8915 • 3pm-7pm, noon-4pm Sat,
clsd Sun • also switchboard

BARS

Spikes 4130 NW 6th St **352/376–3772** •
5pm-2am, till 11pm Sun • popular • lesbians/
gay men • neighborhood bar • wheelchair
access

The University Club 18 E University Ave
(enter rear) **352/378–6814** • 5pm-2am, from
9pm Sat, till 11pm Sun • lesbians/ gay men • 3
levels • young crowd • dancing/DJ • karaoke •
live shows • patio • wheelchair access

RESTAURANTS

Book Lovers Cafe 505 NW 13th St (at 5th
Ave, in Books Inc) **352/352–4241,
888/374–4241** • 10am-9pm • vegetarian cafe
& used bookstore

ENTERTAINMENT & RECREATION

Ponte Vedra LGBT Beach • Go N from
Gainesville on Waldo Rd to N 301, then E on I-
10. I-10 becomes 95. Go S on 95, then take a
left. Go E onto Butler Blvd, which ends at A1A.
Turn right onto A1A & then drive 5 to 7
minutes looking for Guana Boat Landing
parking lot on the right. Park in a parking lot or
get ticketed.

BOOKSTORES

Goerings Book Store 1717 NW 1st Ave
352/377–3703 • 10am-7pm, till 5pm Sat-Sun

Wild Iris Books 802 W University Ave (at 8th
St) **352/375–7477** • 11am-7pm, clsd Sun-Mon
• feminist/ LGBT

PUBLICATIONS

Kindred Sisters Magazine **352/502–4101**
• lesbian/ feminist monthly magazine for N
Central FL

Holiday

BARS

Frank & Tony's Pub 2419 Grand Blvd (near
Sunray Blvd) **727/942–9734** • 3pm-2am •
lesbians/ gay men • neighborhood bar •
karaoke • beer & wine • patio • gay-owned

Hollywood

BARS

Stonewall on the Beach 200 N Surf Rd
954/922–7993 • 10:30am-2am, from noon
Mon-Th • gay/ straight • food served • live
music • karaoke • wheelchair access

Trixie's Show Bar 600 S Dixie Hwy (S of
Hollywood Blvd) **954/923–9322** • 5pm-2am •
mostly gay men • neighborhood bar •
transgender-friendly (especially Th) • drag
shows

RESTAURANTS

Sushi Blues Cafe 2009 Harrison St
954/929–9560 • lunch Mon-Fri, dinner nightly
• sushi, burgers & steaks • live blues 8:30pm
Fri-Sat • also full bar

EROTICA

Pleasure Emporium 1321 S 30th Ave
954/927–8181

Islamorada

ACCOMMODATIONS

Casa Morada 136 Madeira Rd
305/664–0044, 888/881–3030 • gay-friendly •
luxury all-suite hotel w/ private island • pool •
pets ok • women-owned • $259-659

Lookout Lodge Resort 87770 Overseas
Hwy, mile marker 88 (at Plantation Blvd)
305/852–9915, 800/870–1772 • gay-friendly •
waterfront resort • kids/ pets ok • nonsmoking
• WiFi • $100-399

Jacksonville

INFO LINES & SERVICES

Free to Be LGBT AA 1562 LaSalle St
904/399–8535 (AA#) • 6:30pm Mon

Women's Center of Jacksonville 5644
Colcord **904/722–3000**

ACCOMMODATIONS

Comfort Inn Oceanfront 1515 N 1st St,
Jacksonville Beach **904/241–2311,
800/654–8776** • gay-friendly • oceanfront •
pool • fitness center • restaurant

Hilton Garden Inn Jacksonville JTB/ Deerwood Park 9745 Gate Pkwy (at Southside Blvd) 904/997-6600, 877/782-9444 • gay-friendly • 15 minutes to beach • pool • jacuzzi • kids ok • WiFi • wheelchair access • $89-169

Spring Hill Suites Jacksonville 4385 Southside Blvd (at J Turner Butler Blvd) 904/997-6650, 888/287-9400 • gay-friendly • pool • jacuzzi • kids ok • nonsmoking • $99-169

BARS

616 Bar 616 Park St (at I-95) 904/358-6969 • 4pm-2am • lesbians/ gay men • neighborhood bar • karaoke • patio

AJ's Bar & Grill 10244 Atlantic Blvd (in Regency Walk Shopping Center) 904/805-9060 • 4pm-2am • mostly women • dancing/DJ after 10pm • full menu • karaoke • wheelchair access • women-owned

Bo's Coral Reef 201 5th Ave N (at 2nd St), Jacksonville Beach 904/246-9874 • 2pm-2am • lesbians/ gay men • neighborhood bar • dancing/DJ • food served • live shows

Club Sappho 2929 Plum St (upstairs at Metro) 904/388-8719 • 4pm-2am, till 4am Fri-Sat • popular • mostly women • dancing/DJ • multiracial • also Lesbo-a-GoGo 1st Fri

InCahoots 711 Edison Ave (btwn Riverside & Park) 904/353-6316 • 8pm-2am, from 4pm Sun, clsd Mon-Tue • mostly gay men • 3 bars • dancing/DJ • multiracial • karaoke • drag shows • go-go girls 1st & 3rd Fri • wheelchair access

The Metro 2929 Plum St 904/388-8719 • 2pm-2am, till 4am Fri-Sat • popular • lesbians/ gay men • 6 bars • dancing/DJ • drag shows • nonsmoking • 18+ • wheelchair access

The New Boot Rack Saloon 4751 Lenox Ave (at Cassat Ave) 904/384-7090 • 3pm-2am • mostly gay men • country/ western • WiFi • beer/ wine • patio • wheelchair access

The Norm 2952 Roosevelt Blvd (at College) 904/384-9929 • 4pm-close • mostly women but everyone welcome • dancing/DJ • live shows • wheelchair access

Park Place Lounge 931 King St (at Post) 904/389-6616 • noon-2am • lesbians/ gay men • neighborhood bar • dancing/DJ • wheelchair access

NIGHTCLUBS

The Pearl 1101 Main St (E 1st St) 904/791-4499 • 9pm-2am, clsd Sun-Tue • gay/ straight • dancing/DJ • more women Wed • theme nights

RESTAURANTS

Al's Pizza 1620 Margaret St, Ste 201 904/388-8384 • 11am-10pm, till 11pm Fri-Sat, noon-9pm Sun • in Riverside/ Little 5 Points area

Biscotti's 3556 Saint Johns Ave (Talbot Ave) 904/387-2060 • 10:30am-10pm, till midnight Fri-Sat, from 8am Sat-Sun • popular • killer desserts • women owned

Bistro Aix 1440 San Marco Blvd 904/398-1949 • 11am-10pm, till 11pm Fri, 5pm-11pm Sat, 5pm-9pm Sun • upscale French bistro

Derby House 1068 Park St 904/356-0227 • 7am-2pm, till 9pm Fri-Sat • very popular wknds for brkfst

European Street Cafe 2753 Park St (at King) 904/384-9999 • 10am-10pm • salads • beer/ wine • patio • wheelchair access • gay-owned

The Grape Wine Bar & Bistro 10281 Midtown Pkwy #119 (at St Johns Town Center) 904/642-7111 • also retail shop & wine barp

Mossfire Grill 1537 Margaret St 904/355-4434 • lunch & dinner, clsd Sun • Southwestern • full bar

RETAIL SHOPS

Rainbows & Stars 1046 Park St (in historic 5 Points) 904/356-7702 • 10am-7pm Wed-Fri, noon-7pm Sat, noon-5pm Sun, clsd Mon-Tue • pride giftstore

Key West

INFO LINES & SERVICES

Gay/Lesbian Community Center 513 Truman Ave 305/292-3223 • many meetings & groups • call for info

Keep It Simple (Gay/ Lesbian AA) 305/296-8654 (AA #) • 8pm

➤ **Key West Business Guild** 305/294-4603, 800/535-7797

ACCOMMODATIONS

Alexander Palms Court 715 South St (at Vernon) 305/296-6413, 800/858-1943 • gay-friendly • pool • private patios • wheelchair access • gay-owned • $110-320

Alexander's Guest House 1118 Fleming St (at Frances) 305/294-9919, 800/654-9919 • lesbians/ gay men • pool • nudity • WiFi • wheelchair access • gay-owned • $125-410

Ambrosia House Tropical Lodging 615 & 618-622 Fleming St (at Simonton) **305/296–9838** • gay-friendly • pool • hot tub • $179-609

Andrews Inn Zero Whalton Ln (at Duval) **305/294–7730, 888/263–7393** • gay-friendly • pool • kids ok • nonsmoking • WiFi • $130-339

The Artist House 534 Eaton St (at Duval) **305/296–3977, 800/582–7882** • gay/ straight • nonsmoking • $99-245

Avalon B&B 1317 Duval St (at United) **305/294–8233, 800/848–1317** • gay-friendly • swimming • near beach • sundeck • WiFi • $89-329

Big Ruby's Guesthouse 409 Appelrouth Ln (at Duval & Whitehead) **305/296–2323, 800/477–7829** • mostly gay men • full brkfst • pool • nudity • nonsmoking • WiFi • wheelchair access • gay-owned • $125-629

Casa de Luces 422 Amelia St (at Whitehead) **305/294–5269, 800/833–0372** • gay-friendly • nonsmoking • WiFi • wheelchair access • $99-229

Cuban Club Suites 1102-1108 Duval St (at Virginia) **305/294–5269, 800/833–0372** • gay-friendly • suites w/ kitchens • kids/ dogs ok • $199-359

Key West

WHERE THE GIRLS ARE:

You can't miss 'em during WomenFest in September, but other times they're just off Duval St., somewhere between Eaton and South Streets. Or on the beach. Or in the water.

LGBT PRIDE:

June. 305/292–3223, web: www.pridefestkeywest.com.

ANNUAL EVENTS:

February - Kelly McGillis Classic Women's & Girls' Flag Football Tournament 888/464–9332, web: www.iwffa.com.

September - WomenFest, web: www.womenfest.com.

October - Fantasy Fest 305/296-1817, web: www.fantasyfest.net. Weeklong Halloween celebration with parties, masquerade balls & parades.

CITY INFO:

Key West Business Association 800/FLA-KEYS, web: www.fla-keys.com/keywest.

BEST VIEW:

Old Town Trolley Tour (1/2 hour) 305/296-6688, web: www.historictours.com/keywest.

ATTRACTIONS:

Audubon House and Gardens 305/294-2116, web: www.audubonhouse.com.
Dolphin Research Center 305/289–1121, web: www.dolphins.org.
Hemingway House, web: www.hemingwayhome.com.
Red Barn Theatre 305/296-9911, web: www.redbarntheatre.com.
Southernmost Point USA.
Sunset Celebration at Mallory Square.

WEATHER:

The average temperature year-round is 78°, and the sun shines nearly every day. Any time is the right time for a visit.

TRANSIT:

Friendly Cab 305/292-0000.
Key West Express 888/539–2628.
Key West Transit Authority 305/292-8160, web: www.kwtransit.com.

The Grand Guest House 1116 Grinnell St **305/294-0590, 888/947-2630** • lesbians/ gay men • in converted rooming house built in 1880s for cigar workers • nonsmoking • WiFi • gay-owned • $98-328

Heartbreak Hotel 716 Duval St (near Petronia) **305/296-5558** • lesbians/ gay men • kitchens • lesbian & gay-owned • $99-110

Heron House Court 412 Frances St (at Eaton) **800/932-9119** • gay-friendly • full brkfst • swimming • hot tub • sundeck • nonsmoking • wheelchair access • $119-359

Key West Harbor Inn B&B 219 Elizabeth St (at Greene) **305/296-2978, 800/608-6569** • lesbians/ gay men • pool • hot tub • nonsmoking • WiFi • $155-415

Knowles House B&B 1004 Eaton St (at Grinnell) **305/296-8132, 800/352-4414** • gay/ straight • restored 1880s Conch house • pool • nudity • nonsmoking • gay-owned • $109-229

La Te Da 1125 Duval St (at Catherine) **305/296-6706, 877/528-3320** • popular • lesbians/ gay men • full brkfst • nonsmoking • pool • restaurant & 3 bars • WiFi • gay-owned • $150-335

Marquesa Hotel 600 Fleming St (at Simonton) **305/292-1919, 800/869-4631** • gay-friendly • 2 pools • also restaurant • full bar • nonsmoking • WiFi • wheelchair access • $190-495

Marrero's Guest Mansion 410 Fleming St (btwn Duval & Whitehead) **305/294-6977, 800/459-6212** • gay-friendly • 1890 Victorian mansion • pool • nonsmoking • WiFi • $130-220

The Mermaid & the Alligator—A Key West B&B 729 Truman Ave (at Windsor Ln) **305/294-1894, 800/773-1894** • gay/ straight • full brkfst • pool • nonsmoking • WiFi • gay-owned • $168-338

Nassau House 1016 Fleming St (at Grinnell) **305/296-8513, 800/296-8513** • gay-friendly • pool • nonsmoking • sundeck • hot tub • WiFi • wheelchair access • $139-239

Old Town Manor 511 Eaton St (at Duval) **305/292-2170, 800/294-2170** • gay-friendly • nonsmoking • WiFi • $135-335

➤ **Pearl's Rainbow** 525 United St (at Duval) **305/292-1450, 800/749-6696** • popular • women only • hot tub • pool • sundeck • nudity • nonsmoking • WiFi • also bar & restaurant • wheelchair access • lesbian-owned • $89-379 • see inside front cover

Simonton Court Historic Inn & Cottages 320 Simonton St (at Caroline) **305/294-6386, 800/944-2687** • gay-friendly • built in 1880s • pool • nonsmoking • WiFi • $150-540

Tropical Inn 812 Duval St (at Petronia) **305/294-9977, 888/611-6510** • gay-friendly • also cottage suites • hot tub • pool • sundeck • WiFi • $134-398

BARS

The 801 Bourbon Bar 801 Duval St (at Petronia) **305/294-4737** • 10am-4am, from noon Sun • lesbians/ gay men • neighborhood bar • dancing/DJ • popular drag shows • Sun bingo

Bobby's Monkey Bar 900 Simonton St (at Olivia) **305/294-2655** • noon-4am • mostly gay men • neighborhood bar • wheelchair access

Bourbon Street Pub 724 Duval St (at Petronia) **305/294-4737** • 11am-4am, from noon Sun • mostly gay men • popular • garden bar w/ pool & hot tub • wheelchair access

Garden of Eden 224 Duval St **305/296-4565** • 10am-4am, from noon Sun • gay/straight • clothing optional sunbathing • danicng/DJ • live music

Hog's Breath Saloon 400 Front St **305/296-4222** • gay-friendly • food served • live music

La Te Da 1125 Duval St (at Catherine) **305/296-6706** • lesbians/ gay men • 3 bars (piano bar & cabaret) & restaurant • wheelchair access • gay-owned

➤ **Pearl's Patio** 525 United St (at Duval & Simonton, at Pearl's Rainbow) **305/292-1450, 800/749-6696** • noon-10pm, later on wknds • happy hour 5pm-7pm Mon-Sat • women only • sandwiches, burgers, salads & snacks • karaoke • special events

Virgilio's 524 Duval St (at Fleming in La Trattoria) **305/296-8118** • 7pm-4am • gay/ straight • martini bar • garden • food served • live music • late-night DJ

NIGHTCLUBS

Aqua 711 Duval St **305/294-0555** • 3pm-2am, till 4am Th-Sat, also Wet Bar, from 9pm Fri-Sat • lesbians/ gay men • dancing/DJ • drag shows • karaoke • wheelchair access

Bottle Cap Lounge 1128 Simonton St. **305/296-2807** • noon-4am • gay/ straight • dancing/ DJ • live music

CAFES

Croissants de France 816 Duval St
305/294-2624 • 7:30am-10pm, restaurant
open till 3pm • beer/ wine • patio

RESTAURANTS

Antonia's 615 Duval St (at Southard)
305/294-6565 • lunch & dinner • popular •
Italian • full bar

Bo's Fish Wagon 801 Caroline (at Williams)
305/294-9272 • lunch, dinner • popular •
"seafood & eat it"

Cafe Sole 1029 Southard St (at Frances)
305/294-0230 • dinner nightly, Sun brunch •
romantic • candlelit backyard

Camille's 1202 Simonton (at Catherine)
305/296-4811 • brkfst, lunch & dinner • bistro
• hearty brkfst

El Meson de Pepe 410 Wall St (in Mallory
Sq) **305/295-2620** • lunch & dinner, Cuban

The Flamingo Buoy Filet Co 1100 Packer
St **305/295-7970** • lunch & dinner

Flamingo's Cafe 503 Duval St **305/295-6411**
• 8:30am-3pm

Grand Cafe Key West 314 Duval St
305/292-4740 • lunch & dinner

Half Shell Raw Bar 231 Margaret St
305/294-7496 • 11am-10pm • waterfront •
full bar

Hurricane Hole 5130 Overseas Hwy
305/294-8025, 305/294-0200 • 10am-10pm •
dockside bar

Jack Flats 509 Duval St **305/294-7955** •
11am-2am

Kelly's Caribbean Bar Grill & Brewery
301 Whitehead St (at Caroline) **305/293-8484**
• lunch & dinner • full bar • owned by actress
Kelly McGillis

La Trattoria Venezia 524 Duval St (at
Fleming) **305/296-1075** • 5pm-10:30pm • full
bar

Lobos Mixed Grill 5 Key Lime Sq (south of
Southard St) **305/296-5303** • 11am-6pm •
sandwiches • plenty veggie • beer/ wine

Louie's Backyard 700 Waddell Ave (at
Vernon) **305/294-1061** • 11:30am-1am •
popular • fine cont'l dining

Mangia Mangia 900 Southard St (at
Margaret St) **305/294-2469** • dinner only •
fresh pasta • beer/ wine • patio

Mangoes 700 Duval St (at Angela)
305/292-4606 • lunch & dinner, bar till 1am •
"Floribbean" cuisine • full bar • patio •
wheelchair access

Michaels 532 Margaret St **305/295-1300** •
dinner only • steakhouse

New York Pizza Cafe 1075 Duval St (Duval
Square) **305/292-1991** • 11am-10pm

Nine One Five 915 Duval St **305/296-0669** •
dinner only • tapas & full bar

Pisces 1007 Simonton St (at Truman)
305/294-7100 • 6pm-11pm • French seafood
• full bar

Rooftop Cafe 308 Front St (at Fitzpatrick)
305/294-2042 • brkfst, lunch & dinner • best
Key Lime pie • some veggie

Salsa Loca 618 Duval St (in Cowboy Bills)
305/292-1865 • clsd Mon • gay-friendly •
tasty, inexpensive Mexican

Seven Fish 632 Olivia St (at Elizabeth)
305/296-2777 • 6pm-10pm, clsd Tue •
popular

Six Toed Cat 832 Whitehead St
305/294-3318 • brkfst & lunch

Square One 1075 Duval St (at Truman)
305/296-4300 • 6pm-10pm • full bar •
wheelchair access

Upper Crust 611 Duval St **305/293-8890** •
noon-11pm • excellent pizza

ENTERTAINMENT & RECREATION

Fort Zachary Taylor Beach • more gay to
the right

Gay & Lesbian Trolley Tour **305/294-4603**
• 10:50am Sat • check out all of the gay
hotspots & historical points • look for
rainbow-decorated trolley

Islescapes Gourmet Dinner Cruises
Schooner Wharf (at Pier 1) **305/923-3319** •
romantic setting w/ gorgeous sunsets

**The Key West Butterfly & Nature
Conservatory** 1316 Duval Street
305/296-2988, 800/839-4647 • gay-owned

Moped Hospital 601 Truman **866/296-1625**
• forget the car—mopeds are a must for
touring the island

**The Rude Awakening Radio
Extravaganza Ministry** 92.7 FM WEOW
305/296-7511 • 6am-10am Mon-Fri • a
"morning zoo" show w/ a lesbian twist • music
• Top 40 music • comedy • contests •
community info

Sebago Gay Cruises 201 William St (at
historic Key West Seaport) **305/292-4768,
800/507-9955** • gay/ straight • women's
sunset cruises Th • call for additional info

Experience the sea in the company of women

VENUS CHARTERS

Snorkeling & Dolphin Watching
Light Tackle Fishing
Sunsets
Unions @ Sea

Captain Karen Luknis
& Captain Debra Butler

305-304-1181

www.venuscharters.com

Lesbian Owned & Operated

P.O Box 4394 • Key West, FL 33041

➤ **Venus Charters** Garrison Bight Marina slip #10 **305/304–1181** • snorkeling • light-tackle fishing • dolphin-watching • personalized excursions • lesbian-owned

BOOKSTORES

Key West Island Books 513 Fleming St (at Duval) **305/294–2904** • 10am-9pm • new & used rare books • LGBT section

RETAIL SHOPS

Fast Buck Freddie's 500 Duval St (at Fleming) **305/294–2007** • 10am-6pm, till 8pm Th-Fri, till 10pm Sat • wheelchair access

Frank's In Touch 706-A Duval St (at Angela) **305/294–1995** • 9am-9pm • gay gifts

GYMS & HEALTH CLUBS

Body Zone South 2740 N Roosevelt Blvd **305/292–2930**

EROTICA

Fairvilla Megastore 520 Front St **305/292–0448** • 9am-midnight • clean, well-lighted adult store w/ emphasis on couples

Leather Master 418 Applerouth Ln (btwn Duval & Whitehead) **305/292–5051** • 11am-10pm, noon-8pm Sun • custom leather, toys & more

Lake Worth

see also West Palm Beach

INFO LINES & SERVICES

Compass LGBT Community Center 201 N Dixie Hwy **561/533–9699** • 9am-9pm, till 7pm Fri, 3pm-7pm Sat, clsd Sun • wheelchair access

BARS

The Bar 2211 N Dixie Hwy **561/370–3954** • 2pm-2am, noon-midnight Sun • lesbians/ gay men • neighborhood bar • dancing/DJ • karaoke • lesbian-owned

The Mad Hatter Bar & Grill 1532 N Dixie Hwy (16th Ave) **561/547–8860** • 1pm-2am, noon-midnight Sun • mostly men • neighborhood bar • karaoke • older crowd • gay-owned

NIGHTCLUBS

Mojitos 129 N Federal Hwy (btwn 1st & 2nd) **561/245–5216** • 8pm-2am, from 5pm Th clsd Sun-Wed • lesbians/gay men • dancing/DJ • more women Fri

CAFES

Mother Earth Coffee 410 Second Ave N
561/460-8647 • 8am-7pm, till 10pm Fri-Sat •
fair trade • organic beans

RESTAURANTS

The Cottage 522 Lucerne Ave **561/586-0080**
• dinner only • also bar

Lakeland

ACCOMMODATIONS

Swan Park Inn B&B 118 E Park St
863/248-2235, 888/211-1671 • gay/ straight •
full brkfst • pool • nudity at pool • wheelchair
access • gay-owned • $95-150

BARS

Pulse 1030 E Main St **863/683-6021** • 4pm-
2am, till midnight Sun, from 6pm Mon •
mostly gay men • dancing/DJ • transgender-
friendly • drag shows • strippers • wheelchair
access

Twisters 3770 Hwy 92 **863/226-2290** •
noon-2am, till midnight Sun • mostly gay men
• neighborhood bar • beer/ wine only • gay-
owned

Marathon

ACCOMMODATIONS

Tropical Cottages 243 61st St Gulf
305/743-6048 • gay-friendly • outdoor hot
tub • pets ok • nonsmoking • $69-150

ENTERTAINMENT & RECREATION

Bahia Honda State Park & Beach 12
miles S of Marathon

Melbourne

ACCOMMODATIONS

Beach Bungalow 312 Wavecrest Ave,
Indialantic by the Sea **321/594-4194,
888/414-5314** • gay-friendly • beachfront
town homes • private patios & spas •
nonsmoking • $1,400-2,000/wk

Crane Creek Inn B&B 907 E Melbourne
Ave **321/768-6416** • gay/ straight • full brkfst •
pool • hot tub • dogs ok • WiFi • $139-199

BARS

Cold Keg 4060 W New Haven Ave (1/2 mile
E of I-95) **321/724-1510** • 4pm-2am, clsd Sun
• popular • lesbians/ gay men • dancing/DJ •
drag shows • 18+ • wheelchair access

MIAMI

Miami is divided into 3 geographical areas:
  Miami—Overview
  Miami—Greater Miami
  Miami—Miami Beach/ South Beach

Miami—Overview

INFO LINES & SERVICES

Switchboard of Miami 305/358-4357
(HELPLINE #), 305/358-1640 (OFFICE #) • 24hrs •
gay-friendly info & referrals for Dade County

NIGHTCLUBS

Ladies Touch • mostly women • hip hop
dance parties • mostly African American •
check www.myspace.com/ladiestouchinmiami

ENTERTAINMENT & RECREATION

Sailboat Charters of Miami 3400 Pan
American Dr (at S Bayshore Dr) 305/772-4221
• lesbians/ gay men • private sailing charters
aboard all-teakwood 46-foot clipper to
Bahamas & the Keys

Miami—Greater Miami

NIGHTCLUBS

Club Sugar 2301 SW 32nd Ave (at Coral Wy)
305/443-7657 • 10:30pm-5am Th-Sat, 8pm-
3am Sun, clsd Mon-Wed

Discotekka 950 NE 2nd Ave (at Metropolis
Nightclub) 305/371-3773 • after hours Wed-
Sun • mostly gay men • dancing/DJ • 18+

JJ Waterfront 3615 NW South River Dr (at
NW 28th St) 786/277-4561 • open Th-Sat
only • lesbians/ gay men • women's night Th
• dancing/DJ • drag shows • mostly Latino/a •
18+

The L Night 3615 NW South River Dr (at NW
28th St, at JJ Waterfront) 786/277-4561 •
10pm Th • mostly women • dancing/DJ •
mostly Latina • 18+

Space Miami 34 NE 11th St (at NE 1st Ave)
305/375-0001 • gay-friendly • dancing/DJ •
popular club w/ int'l visiting DJs

Vlada Lounge 3215 NE 2nd Ave (at NE
32nd St) 305/381-5015 • mostly gay men •
dancing/DJ • drag shows

CAFES

Gourmet Station 7601 Biscayne Blvd (at NE
71st St) 305/762-7229 • 8am-9pm, till 8pm
Fri, Sat hrs vary, clsd Sun

RESTAURANTS

Area 31 270 Biscayne Blvd Way (at the Epic Hotel) **305/424-5234** • brkfst, lunch & dinner, open till 1am wknds • seafood • amazing view

Fratelli Milano 213 SE 1st St (at 2nd Ave) **305/373-2300** • 8am-10pm Mon-Fri, clsd Sat-Sun • homemade Italian

Habibi's Grill 93 SE 2nd St (at 1st Ave) **786/425-2699** • 11am-8pm, clsd Sun • Lebanese/ Mediterranean • plenty veggie

Jimmy's East Side Diner 7201 Biscayne Blvd **305/754-3692** • 7am-4pm

The Magnum Lounge & Restaurant 709 NE 79th St **305/757-3368** • 6pm-midnight, bar open 5pm-2am, clsd Mon • gay/ straight • neighborhood bar • live shows • piano bar • reservations recommended

Michy's 6927 Biscayne Blvd (at NE 69th) **305/759-2001** • dinner only • "luxurious comfort food"

Ortanique on the Mile 278 Miracle Mile (at Salzedo), Coral Gables **305/446-7710** • lunch Mon-Fri, dinner nightly • popular • Caribbean • full bar

Royal Bavarian Schnitzel Haus 1085 NE 79th St **305/754-8002** • 5pm-11pm

Soyka 5556 NE 4th Ct **305/759-3117** • lunch & dinner, wknd brunch • American • full bar

UVA 69 6900 Biscayne Blvd (at NE 69th St) **305/754-9022** • 11am-11pm, 8am-midnight wknds • European bistro & lounge • patio

BOOKSTORES

Lambda Passages Bookstore 7545 Biscayne Blvd (at 76th) **305/754-6900** • 11am-9pm, noon-6pm Sun • LGBT/ feminist

Miami—Miami Beach/ South Beach

ACCOMMODATIONS

Aqua Hotel & Lounge 1530 Collins Ave **305/538-4361** • gay/ straight • boutique hotel • $95-395

Beachcomber Hotel 1340 Collins Ave (at 13th St) **305/531-3755, 888/305-4683** • gay-friendly • nonsmoking • WiFi • $65-140

The Blue Moon Hotel 944 Collins Ave **305/673-2262, 800/553-7739** • gay-friendly • pool • also bar

Bresaro Suites at the Mantell 255 W 24th St **305/772-5665** • gay/ straight • pool • kitchens • gay-owned • $129-169

The Cardozo Hotel 1300 Ocean Dr **305/535-6500, 800/782-6500** • gay-friendly • restaurants • Gloria Estefan's plush hotel • kids ok • WiFi • wheelchair access • $170-505

The Century 140 Ocean Dr **305/674-8855, 888/982-3688** • gay-friendly • also Joia restaurant • nonsmoking • WiFi • wheelchair access • $115-200

Chesterfield Hotel, Suites & Day Spa 855 Collins Ave **305/531-5831, 877/762-3477** • gay/ straight • super stylish hotel • $99-450

Circa 39 Hotel 3900 Collins Ave (at 39th St) **305/538-4900, 877/824-7223** • gay-friendly • pool • lounge • WiFi • wheelchair access • $99-699

The Colony Hotel 736 Ocean Dr (at 7th St) **305/673-0088** • gay-friendly • bistro • oceanfront • WiFi • wheelchair access • $129-400

Delano Hotel 1685 Collins Ave **305/672-2000, 800/697-1791** • gay-friendly • food served • pool • kids ok • wheelchair access • $350-950

The European Guesthouse 721 Michigan Ave (btwn 7th & 8th) **305/673-6665** • lesbians/ gay men • B&B • full brkfst • hot tub • tropical garden w/ bar • WiFi • gay-owned • $99-199

The Hotel 801 Collins Ave **305/531-2222, 877/843-4683** • gay-friendly • interior design by Todd Oldham • Wish restaurant • also Spire bar • pool • nonsmoking • WiFi • wheelchair access • $255-525

Hotel Nash 1120 Collins Ave **305/674-7800, 800/403-6274** • gay-friendly • sleek & modern boutique hotel • spa • pool • kids ok • nonsmoking • wheelchair access • $155-1400

Hotel Ocean 1230-38 Ocean Dr **305/672-2579, 800/783-1725** • popular • gay/ straight • great location • pets ok • WiFi • wheelchair access • $199-950

The National Hotel 1677 Collins Ave **305/532-2311, 800/327-8370** • gay/ straight • pool • kids ok • restaurant & lounge • WiFi • wheelchair access • $400-799

Penguin Hotel 1418 Ocean Dr **305/534-9334, 800/235-3296** • lesbians/ gay men • full restaurant • kids ok • wheelchair access • $145-280

The Raleigh, Miami Beach 1775 Collins Ave (at Ocean Front) **305/534-6300, 800/848-1775** • gay-friendly • pool • restaurant & bars • kids/ pets ok • WiFi • wheelchair access • $225-550

The Savoy Hotel 425 Ocean Dr (at 5th St) **305/532-0200, 800/237-2869** • gay/ straight • 2 pools • kids ok • nonsmoking • WiFi • wheelchair access • $150-500

SoBeYou 1018 Jefferson Ave **305/534-5247, 877/599-5247** • gay/ straight • nonsmoking • WiFi • wheelchair access • lesbian-owned • $105-325

Something Special, A Lesbian Venture **305/696-8826** • women only • 1-bdrm apt on beach • also backyard camping & dining • $130

South Seas 1751 Collins Ave **305/538-1411, 800/345-2678** • gay-friendly • clean & basic • beach access • pool • WiFi • $349-439

The Strand Hotel 1052 Ocean Dr, Miami Beach **305/538-9830, 866/870-6044** • gay-friendly • pool • also restaurant

The Tides 1220 Ocean Dr **305/604-5070, 800/439-4095** • gay/ straight • private beach area • pool • WiFi • also La Marea restaurant • $350-5,000

Miami

WHERE THE GIRLS ARE:

In Miami proper, Coral Gables and the University district, as well as Biscayne Blvd. along the coast, are the lesbian hangouts of choice. You'll see women everywhere in South Beach, but especially along Ocean Dr., Washington, Collins and Lincoln Roads.

LGBT PRIDE:

April, web: www.miamibeach-gaypride.com.

ANNUAL EVENTS:

Feb/March - Winter Party 202/393-5177, web: www.winterparty.com. Beach dance party benefiting the National Gay & Lesbian Task Force.

April/May - Gay & Lesbian Film Festival 305/534-9924, web: www.mglff.com.

May - Aqua Girl 305/532-1997, web: www.aquagirl.org. A women's weekend.

November - White Party Vizcaya 305/576-1234, web: www.whiteparty.net. AIDS benefit.

CITY INFO:

Greater Miami Convention & Visitors Bureau 305/539-3000. 701 Brickell Ave, web: www.miamiandbeaches.com.

ATTRACTIONS:

Bayside Marketplace 305/577-3344, web: www.baysidemarket-place.com.

Miami Beach Botanical Garden 305/673-7256, web: www.mbgarden.org.

Miami Design Preservation League 305/672-2014. web: mdpl.org.

Miami Museum of Science & Planetarium 305/646-4200, web: www.miamisci.org.

Monkey Jungle 305/235-1611, web: www.monkeyjungle.com.

Museum of Contempory Art, N Miami 305/893-6211, web: www.mocanomi.org.

Parrot Jungle Island 305/258-6453, web: www.parrotjungle.com.

Sanford L Ziff Jewish Museum of Florida 305/672-5044, web: www.jewishmuseum.com.

BEST VIEW:

If you've got money to burn, a helicopter flight over Miami Beach is a great way to see the city. Otherwise, hit the beach.

WEATHER:

Warm all year. Temperatures stay in the 90°s during the summer and drop into the mid-60°s in the winter. Be prepared for sunshine!

TRANSIT:

Yellow Cab 305/266-7799.
Metro Taxi 305/888-8888.
A Plus 305/219-8219.
Metro Bus 305/770-3131.

The Winterhaven 1400 Ocean Dr 305/531-5571, 800/553-7739 • gay/ straight • ocean views • also bar • WiFi • wheelchair access • $109-339

BARS

Bar 721 721 N Lincoln Ln 305/532-1342 • 5pm-5am • gay-friendly • neighborhood bar • lounge

Buck15 Lounge 707 Lincoln Ln 305/538-3815 • 10pm-5am, clsd Mon • gay/ straight • more gay Th • gallery/ lounge

Creme Lounge 725 Lincoln Ln N (upstairs from Score) 305/535-1163 • open Tue & Th-Sat • lesbians/ gay men • Girl party Fri

Palace Bar & Grill 1200 Ocean Dr (at 12th St) 305/531-7234 • 10am-1am, till 2am Fri-Sat • lesbians/ gay men • also restaurant • drag shows

NIGHTCLUBS

Heathrow Lounge 681 Washington Ave 305/534-7583 • gay/straight, more gay Sun • dancing/DJ

La Descarga 501 Lincoln Rd (at Drexel Ave, at Yuca Lounge) • 10pm 1st Sat only • mostly women • Latin night • dancing/DJ • multiracial

Mova 1625 Michigan Ave 305/534-8181 • 3pm-3am, from noon Sun • lesbians/ gay men • lounge w/ DJ wknds

➤**Pandora Events** 305/975-6933 • monthly women's parties • locations rotate so check website: www.pandoraevents.com

Score 727 Lincoln Rd (at Meridian) 305/535-1111 • lounge opens 3pm, dance club 10pm-5am Tue & Th-Sat • popular • lesbians/ gay men • 4 bars • drag shows • karaoke • videos

Sweet 1625 Michigan Ave (at Mova) • 8pm Th only • mostly women • dancing/DJ

Twist 1057 Washington Ave (at 11th) 305/538-9478 • 1pm-5am • popular • mostly gay men • 7 bars • dancing/DJ • karaoke • drag shows • go-go boys • wheelchair access

CAFES

News Cafe 800 Ocean Dr (at 8th St) 305/538-6397 • 24hrs • popular • healthy sandwiches • some veggie • also bookstore & bar

RESTAURANTS

11th Street Diner 1065 Washington (at 11th) 305/534-6373 • 24hrs • full bar

8 Oz Burger Bar 1080 Alton Rd (at 11th St) 305/397-8246 • 11am-midnight, till 2am Th-Sat • also bar

A Fish Called Avalon 700 Ocean Dr (at Avalon Hotel) 305/532-1727 • 6pm-11pm • popular • seafood • some veggie • patio • full bar • wheelchair access

B&B: Burger & Beer Joint 1766 Bay Rd (at 18th St) 305/672-3287 • lunch & dinner • the name says it all

Balans 1022 Lincoln Rd (btwn Michigan & Lennox) 305/534-9191 • 8am-midnight

Big Pink 157 Collins (at 2nd St) 305/532-4700 • 8am-midnight, open late wknds • "real food for real people"

David's Cafe II 1654 Meridian Ave 305/672-8707 • 24hrs • Cuban

El Rancho Grande 1626 Pennsylvania Ave (S of Lincoln) 305/673-0480 • 11am-11pm • Mexican • 2nd location 72nd St (305/ 864-7404)

Juice & Java 1346 Washington Ave (at 14th St) 305/531-6675 • 9am-9pm, 11am-6pm Sun • healthy fast food • plenty veggie/vegan

Larios on the Beach 820 Ocean Dr (at 8th) 305/532-9577 • 11:30am-midnight • Cuban

Nexxt Cafe 700 Lincoln Rd (at Euclid Ave) 305/532-6643 • 11:30am-11pm, till midnight Fri-Sat • popular

Ruby J's Restaurant & Bar 239 Sunny Isles Blvd (at 163rd St & Collins Ave), Sunny Isles Beach 305/945-2040 • 6pm-close, clsd Sun-Mon • live music • drag shows • karaoke • Madame's cabaret Sat nights • wheelchair access

Something Special, a Lesbian Venture 305/696-8826 • women only • 6pm-10pm, clsd Mon-Tue • vegetarian • lesbian-owned

Spiga 1228 Collins Ave (at 12th St) 305/534-0079 • dinner only • tasty homemade pastas

Sushi Rock Cafe 1351 Collins Ave (at 14th) 305/532-2133 • noon-midnight • popular

Yuca 501 Lincoln Rd (at Drexel Ave) 305/532-9822 • noon-11:30pm • New Cuban cuisine • also nightclub

ENTERTAINMENT & RECREATION

Beach Scooter Rentals 1341 Washington Ave 305/538-7878

Fritz's Skate & Bike 730 Lincoln Rd (at Euclid & Meridian) 305/532-1954, 877/699-5252

The Gay Beach/ 12th St Beach 12th St & Ocean

Haulover Beach Park A1A S of Sunny Isle Blvd, North Miami Beach • popular nude beach

Lincoln Rd Lincoln Rd (btwn Bay Rd & Collins Aves) • pedestrian mall that embodies the rebirth of South Beach

South Beach Bike Tours 305/673-2002 • half-day bike tour of Art Deco district • gay-owned

RETAIL SHOPS

Pink Palm 723 Lincoln Rd (at Meridian Ave) • unique gifts

GYMS & HEALTH CLUBS

Crunch 1259 Washington Ave 305/674-8222

David Barton Gym 2323 Collins Ave 305/534-1660

EROTICA

Pleasure Emporium 1019 5th St 305/673-3311

Mt Dora

ACCOMMODATIONS

Adora Inn 352/735-3110 • gay/ straight • full brkfst • kids 6+ ok • nonsmoking • WiFi • gay-owned • $99-250

Naples

see also Fort Myers

ACCOMMODATIONS

Palm Tree Hideaway 239/348-1630 • mostly women • studio • pool • $75

BARS

Bambusa Bar & Grill 600 Goodlette Rd N (at 5th Ave N) 239/649-5657 • 4pm-midnight • gay-friendly • neighborhood bar • karaoke Sat • also restaurant • videos • gay-owned

Snappers Nightclub 2634 Tamiami Trail E (at Bay Shore Dr) 239/775-4114 • 3pm-2am, from 11am Wed-Sat, from noon Sun • lesbians/ gay men • neighborhood bar • dancing/DJ • transgender-friendly • karaoke • drag shows • wheelchair access

CAFES

Sunburst Cafe 2340 Pine Ridge Rd (at Airport Pulling Rd) 239/263-3123 • 7am-3pm • wheelchair access

RESTAURANTS

Caffe dell'Amore 1400 Gulf Shore Blvd N (at Banyan Blvd) 239/261-1389 • open Oct-May only • dinner • Italian • beer/ wine • wheelchair access

Patric's 1485 Pine Ridge Rd #3 239/248-0120 • 11am-9:30pm • gay/ straight • cont'l • eclectic shabby-chic • jazz piano

Ocala

BARS

Copa/ Tropix 2330 S Pine Ave 352/351-5721 • 2pm-2am • mostly gay men • dancing/DJ • drag shows • food served

BOOKSTORES

Barnes & Noble 4414 SW College Rd 352/237-1581 • 9am-10pm, till 11pm Fri-Sat • LGBT section

Orlando

INFO LINES & SERVICES

Gay, Lesbian & Bisexual Community Center of Central Florida 946 N Mills Ave 407/228-8272 • noon-9pm, till 5pm Fri-Sat, clsd Sun • full-service community center • helpline • extensive referrals

ACCOMMODATIONS

Clarion Hotel Universal 7299 Universal Blvd (at Carrier Dr) 407/351-5009, 800/445-7299 • gay-friendly • pool • sundeck • kids/pets ok • WiFi • wheelchair access • $100-150

EO Inn & Spa 227 N Eola Dr (at Robinson) 407/481-8485, 888/481-8488 • gay/ straight • boutique hotel • nonsmoking • sundeck • hot tub • WiFi • cafe on-site • $100-300

Four Points by Sheraton Studio City 5905 International Dr (at Kirkman) 407/351-2100, 866/716-8105 • gay-friendly • bar & restaurant • pool • WiFi • wheelchair access • $89-399

Grand Bohemian Hotel Orlando 325 S Orange Ave 407/313-9000, 866/663-0024 • gay-friendly • luxury hotel in downtown Orlando • pool • kids ok • nonsmoking • wheelchair access • $150-250

The Orlando-Mulford Retreat Mulford Ave (at East End Ave), Winter Park 407/898-4299 • gay/ straight • 1950s-era guest bungalow • gay-owned • $60-85

Parliament House Resort 410 N Orange Blossom Tr 407/425-7571 • lesbians/ gay men • pool • restaurant • wheelchair access • $64-104+tax • also 6 bars • multiracial • live shows • dancing/DJ • young crowd • gay-owned

South Beach Orlando Luxury Suites 4786 W Irlo Memorial Hwy (on Lake Cecile), Kissimmee 321/286-3888

The Veranda B&B 115 N Summerlin Ave (at Robinson) **407/849-0321, 800/420-6822** • gay-friendly • pool • hot tub • nonsmoking • wheelchair access • $99-189

The Winter Park Sweet Lodge 271 S Orlando Ave (at Fairbanks Ave), Winter Park **407/644-6099** • gay/ straight • motel • kids ok • gay-owned • $49-59

BARS

Copper Rocket 106 Lake Ave (at 17-92), Maitland **407/645-0069** • 11:30am-2am, from 4pm wknds, till midnight Sun • gay-friendly • also restaurant • wheelchair access

Hank's 5026 Edgewater Dr (at Lee Rd) **407/291-2399** • noon-2am • mostly gay men • neighborhood bar • beer/ wine • patio • wheelchair access

Jungle Sundays 26 Wall St Plaza (upstairs) **407/481-1199** • 4pm-2am Sun only • mostly gay men • dancing/DJ • drag shows

The New Phoenix 7124 Aloma Ave (at Forsythe), Winter Park **407/678-9070** • 6pm-2am, from 4pm Th-Sat • lesbians/ gay men • neighborhood bar • dancing/DJ • karaoke • live shows • drag shows

Paradise 1300 N Mills Ave (btwn Virginia & Colonial) **407/898-0090** • 4pm-2am, from noon wknds • mostly gay men • neighborhood bar • WiFi • gay-owned

The Peacock Room 1321 N Mills Ave (at Montana) **407/228-0048** • 4:30pm-2am, from 8pm wknds • gay-friendly • art shows

Sip 724 Virginia Dr (at Dauphin Ln) **407/894-4747** • gay/ straight • neighborhood bar • WiFi • theme nights

Stonewall Bar 741 W Church St (at Glenn Ln) **407/373-0888** • 5pm-2am • mostly gay men • wheelchair access • gay-owned

Western Bar 410 N Orange Blossom Tr (at Parliament House) **407/425-7571** • 6pm-2am, from noon wknds • mostly gay men • country/ western • levi/ leather • strippers • piano • also restaurant

Wylde's 3530 S Orange Ave (at Suddath Dr) **407/852-0612** • 5pm-2am • lesbians/ gay men • neighborhood bar • underwear Tue

NIGHTCLUBS

Legacy Club 3925 Clarcona Ocoee Rd (at Edgewater) **407/521-2007** • 4pm-close • mostly women • dancing/DJ • more mixed Sat night

Orlando

WHERE THE GIRLS ARE:
Women who live here hang out at Faces bar. Tourists are—where else?—at the tourist attractions, including Disney World.

LGBT PRIDE:
June.

ANNUAL EVENTS:
May-June - Gay Days at Disney World 407/896-8431, web: gaydays.com.
May-June - Orlando Fringe Festival, www.orlandofringe.org.

CITY INFO:
407/363-5872. 8723 International Dr, 8am-7pm, web: www.orlandoinfo.com.

WEATHER:
Mild winters, hot summers.

TRANSIT:
Yellow Cab 407/422-2222.
Kelley's Transportation 407/927-2500.
Lynx 407/841-5969, web: www.golynx.com.

ATTRACTIONS:
Gatorland 407/855-5496, web: www.gatorland.com.
Sea World 888/800-5447, web: www.seaworld.com.
Universal Studios 407/363-8000, web: themeparks.universalorlando.com.
Walt Disney World 407/824-4321, web: www.disneyworld.com.
Wet & Wild Waterpark 407/351-1800, web: www.wetnwildorlando.com.

Mr Sisters 5310 E Colonial Dr (at N Semoran Blvd, on Lake Barton) • 11am-2am • mostly gay men • dancing/DJ

Parliament House Resort 410 N Orange Blossom Tr (at South St) 407/425-7571 • 10:30am-3am • lesbians/ gay men • 6 bars • dancing/DJ • multiracial • live shows • videos • also restaurant • wheelchair access • gay-owned

Pulse Orlando 1912 S Orange Ave (at Kaley St) 407/649-3888 • 9pm-2am, clsd Sun • mostly gay men • dancing/DJ • theme nights • male dancers • 18+

Revolution 375 S Bumby Ave (at South St) 407/228-9900 • 4pm-close , from 10pm Sun • lesbians/ gay men • Sat Girl's night • dancing/DJ • multiracial • go-go dancers • videos • drag shows • 18+ • patio • wheelchair access

CAFES

Pom Pom's 67 N Bumby Ave 407/894-0865 • 11am-close, from noon wknds • tea & sandwiches

White Wolf Cafe & Antique Shop 1829 N Orange Ave (at Princeton) 407/895-9911 • 11am-10pm, till 9pm Mon, till 11pm Fri-Sat, clsd Sun • salads • sandwiches • beer/ wine • wheelchair access

RESTAURANTS

Brian's 1409 N Orange Ave (at Virginia) 407/896-9912 • 6am-4pm • popular Sun

Dandelion Communitea Cafe 618 N Thornton Ave (at Colonial) 407/362-1864 • 11am-10pm, till 3pm Mon, noon-5pm Sun • vegetarian/ vegan

Dexter's Thornton Park 808 E Washington St 407/648-2777 • lunch and dinner • also Winter Park & Lake Mary locations

Ethos Vegan Kitchen 1235 N Orange Ave (at Virginia Dr) 407/228-3898 • 11am-10pm Mon-Sat, brunch only Sun 10am-3pm

Funky Monkey Wine Company 912 N Mills Ave (at E Marks St) 407/427-1447 • 5pm-11pm • sushi • drag shows weekly

Garden Cafe 810 W Colonial Dr (at Westmoreland) 407/999-9799 • 11am-10pm, from noon wknds, clsd Mon • vegetarian Chinese

Hamburger Mary's Orlando 110 W Church St (at Garland) 321/319-0600 • 11am-11pm, till midnight Th-Sat • full bar • live shows • karaoke • wheelchair access • gay-owned

Houston's 215 South Orlando Ave, Winter Park 407/740-4005 • lunch & dinner • upscale American • wheelchair access

Hue 629 E Central Blvd (at N Summerlin Ave) 407/849-1800 • lunch & dinner, wknd brunch • new American • full bar

Lago 4979 New Broad St 407/331-5246 • dinner nightly, clsd Sun • upscale Italian

Loving Hut 2101 E Colonial Dr (at Palm Dr) 407/894-5673 • 11am-9pm, from 3pm Sun, clsd • vegetarian/ vegan

The Rainbow Cafe at Parliament House 407/425-7571 • 7am-11pm, till 3am Fri-Sun • lesbians/ gay men

ENTERTAINMENT & RECREATION

The Enzian Theater 1300 S Orlando Ave (at Magnolia), Maitland 407/629-1088 • Central FL's only art house cinema • cafe • beer & wine

Indian River Cruises Cocoa Beach 321/223-6825

Mad Cow Theatre 105 S Magnolia Ave 407/297-8788

BOOKSTORES

Mojo 930 N Mills Ave (at E Marks St) 407/896-0204 • 1pm-8pm, 3pm-6pm Sun • LGBT

RETAIL SHOPS

A Comic Shop 114 South Semoran Blvd, Winter Park 407/332-9636 • 11am-7pm, till 9pm Wed

Fun Factory 6203-A2 W Sand Lake Rd (at Universal Blvd) 407/826-1627 • gifts • adult toys • clothing

Harmony Designs 496 N Orange Blossom Tr 407/481-9850 • 3:30pm-10pm • pride store • wheelchair access • gay-owned

PUBLICATIONS

Hotspots 954/928-1862 • weekly entertainment guide

Watermark PO Box 533655, 32853 407/481-2243, 877/926-8118 • bi-weekly LGBT newspaper for Central FL

EROTICA

Fairvilla Megastore 1740 N Orange Blossom Tr 407/425-6005 • 9am-2am

Palm Beach

RESTAURANTS

Ta-boo 221 Worth Ave 561/835-3500 • 11:30am-10pm, till 11pm Fri-Sat • cont'l • wheelchair access

Panama City

ACCOMMODATIONS

Casa de Playa 20304 Front Beach Rd, Panama City Beach **850/236-8436** • lesbians/ gay men • guesthouse • steps from Gulf of Mexico • jacuzzi • heated pool • nonsmoking • patios • gay-owned • $150-175

Wisteria Inn 20404 Front Beach Rd, Panama City Beach **850/234-0557** • gay/ straight • tropical inn • hot tub • pool • nonsmoking • $69-179

BARS

La Royale Lounge & Liquor Store 100 Harrison (at Beach Dr) **850/763-1755** • 3pm-3am, till 4am Fri-Sat, from 7pm Sun • lesbians/ gay men • neighborhood bar • courtyard • wheelchair access

Splash Bar 6520 Thomas Dr, Panama City Beach **850/236-3450** • 6pm-2am, till 4am Th-Sat• mostly gay men • 18+ • also pride shop • wheelchair access • gay-owned

NIGHTCLUBS

Fiesta Room 110 Harrison Ave (at Beach Dr) **850/763-1755** • 3pm-3am • popular • lesbians/ gay men • dancing/DJ • drag shows • wheelchair access

Panama City Beach

EROTICA

Condom Knowledge 7510-A Thomas Dr **850/230-3961** • 10am-11pm • "The Funniest, Sexiest Novelty Shop on the Beach" • also 13208 Front Beach Rd

Pensacola

INFO LINES & SERVICES

Rainbow Group AA Gay/ Lesbian 461 Massachusetts (at W St) **850/433-4191 (AA#)** • 8pm Fri

ACCOMMODATIONS

Gulf-Front Villa Fort Morgan Rd, Gulf Shores, AL **865/522-8547** • gay-friendly • private condo • panoramic views • on golf course on the Gulf of Mexico • pool • nonsmoking • WiFi • wheelchair access • $795-1,295/ week

BARS

The Round-Up 560 E Heinberg **850/433-8482** • 2pm-3am • popular • mostly gay men • neighborhood bar • bear- & leather/ levi-friendly • videos • patio • wheelchair access

NIGHTCLUBS

Emerald City 406 E Wright St (at Alcaniz) **850/433-9491** • 3pm-3am (happy hour/ video bar), dance club from 9pm, clsd Tue • popular • lesbians/ gay men • dancing/DJ • live shows • 18+ • patio • wheelchair access

CAFES

End of the Line Cafe 610 E Wright St **850/429-0336** • 10am-10pm, 11am-5pm Sun, clsd Mon • vegetarian cafe • live bands

Pompano Beach

RESTAURANTS

J Marks Restaurant 1490 NE 23th St (at Federal Hwy/ US1) **954/782-7000** • 11am-10pm, till 11pm Fri-Sat • live music wknds • full bar • gay-owned

Port Richey

see also St Petersburg

BARS

Waterside Landing 7737 Grand Blvd (2 blocks off US 19) **727/841-7900** • 4pm-2am, from 6pm Sun • lesbians/ gay men • dancing/DJ • karaoke • strippers • drag shows • wheelchair access

Port St Lucie

NIGHTCLUBS

Rebar 8283 S Federal Hwy (at Fiesta Square) **772/340-7777** • 4pm-2am, till midnight Sun • lesbians/ gay men • neighborhood bar • dancing/DJ • videos • wheelchair access • gay-owned

Sarasota

INFO LINES & SERVICES

Gay AA 7225 N Lockwood Ridge Rd (in Pierce Hall, Church of the Trinity MCC) **941/355-0847 (CHURCH #)** • 7pm Sun & 7pm Th

ACCOMMODATIONS

The Cypress 621 Gulfstream Ave S **941/955-4683** • gay-friendly • B&B inn • overlooking Sarasota Bay • full gourmet brkfst • nonsmoking • WiFi • $150-289

Siesta Holidays 1011 Crescent St, Siesta Key **941/312-9882, 800/720-6885** • gay-friendly • condos near Crescent Beach • pool • nonsmoking • WiFi • $495-1,425/ wk

Turtle Beach Resort 9049 Midnight Pass Rd 941/349-4554 • gay-friendly • pool • nonsmoking • WiFi • wheelchair access • $150-500

RESTAURANTS

Caragiulos 69 S Palm Ave 941/951-0866 • lunch & dinner • Italian-American

PUBLICATIONS

Watermark 813/655-9890 (TAMPA OFFICE), 877/926-8118 • bi-weekly LGBT newspaper for Central FL

EROTICA

Tamiami Books 7338 S Tamiami Tr 941/923-7626

South Beach

see Miami Beach/ South Beach

St Augustine

see also Jacksonville

ACCOMMODATIONS

Alexander Homestead 14 Sevilla St 904/826-4147, 888/292-4147 • gay-friendly • Victorian inn • full brkfst • WiFi • $169-229

Casa Monica 95 Cordova St 904/827-1888, 888/213-8903 • gay-friendly • restaurant & piano bar • gym • pool • kids ok • wheelchair access • $150-1,500

The Inn at Camachee Harbor 201 Yacht Club Dr (at May St) 904/825-0003, 800/688-5379 • gay-friendly • WiFi • $119-179

Ocean View Lodge 2701 Anahma Dr (at Vilano Rd) 904/819-5555, 866/877-9297 • gay-friendly • pets ok in some rooms • wheelchair access • $119-159

Our House B&B 7 Cincinnati Ave 904/824-9204 • gay/ straight • full brkfst • WiFi • gay-owned • $169-230

Saragossa Inn B&B 34 Saragossa St (at Sevilla) 904/808-7384, 877/808-7384 • gay/ straight • full brkfst • kids 12 years & up ok • nonsmoking • $99-299

RESTAURANTS

Collage 60 Hypolita St 904/829-0055 • dinner nightly • "artful global dining" • reservations required

St Petersburg

see also Tampa

ACCOMMODATIONS

Bay Palm Resort 4237 Gulf Blvd, St Petersburg Beach 727/360-7642 • gay-friendly • pool • nonsmoking • WiFi • kids/ pets ok • mention Damron guide for 10% discount (restrictions apply) • $59-189

St Petersburg

LGBT PRIDE:
June.

ANNUAL EVENTS:
May - Tampa Bay Blues Festival 727/502-5000, web: www.tampabaybluesfest.com.

CITY INFO:
Chamber of Commerce 727/821-4069, 8am-5pm Mon-Fri, web: www.stpete.com.

ATTRACTIONS:
Great Explorations, interactive kids' museum, 727/821-8992, web: www.greatexplorations.org.
Salvador Dalí Museum 727/823-3767, web: www.salvadordalimuseum.org.

BEST VIEW:
Pass-A-Grille Beach in Tampa.

WEATHER:
Some say it's the Garden of Eden—winter temperatures occasionally dip into the 40°s, but for the rest of the year temperatures stay in the 70°-80°s.

TRANSIT:
Yellow Cab 727/799-2222, web: www.yellowcabfla.com.
727/572-1111.
727/540-1800, web: www.psta.net.

Boca Ciega B&B 727/381–2755 • women only • B&B in private home • pool • lesbian-owned • $40-50

Changing Tides Cottages 225 Boca Ciega Dr, Madeira Beach 727/397–7706 • lesbians/ gay men • fully furnished rental cottages on harbor • WiFi • lesbian-owned • $95-175

Dicken's House B&B 335 8th Ave NE 727/822-8622, 800/381–2022 • gay/ straight • pool • full brkfst • jacuzzi • WiFi • gay-owned • $109-235

Flamingo 4601 34th St South 727/321–5000 • lesbians/ gay men • pool • bar & restaurant • WiFi • wheelchair access • $60-100

The Pier Hotel 253 2nd Ave N (at 2nd St) 727/822–7500, 800/735–6607 • gay/ straight • kids ok • nightly cocktail hour • lesbian & gay-owned • $59-278

BARS

Christopher Street Bar 13344 66th St N (at Ulmerton Rd), Largo 727/538–0660, 727/520–4111 (INFO LINE) • 2pm-2am • mostly gay men • dancing/DJ • male dancers • WiFi

Club Nautico 4900 66th St N 727/546–7274 • 2pm-2am • lesbians/ gay men • dancing/DJ • karaoke • drag shows • 18+

Detour 2612 Central Ave (at 26th) 727/327–8204 • 2pm-2am • mostly gay men • neighborhood bar • dancing/ DJ • karaoke • patio • WiFi • wheelchair access

Gemini Lounge 2315 Central Ave (at 23rd St) 727/327–8600 • 4pm-2am • mostly women • neighborhood bar • karaoke • beer & wine only

The Hideaway 8302 4th St N (at 83rd) 727/570–9025 • 2pm-2am, from 4pm Mon • mostly women • neighborhood bar • live shows • karaoke • wheelchair access

Lucky Star Lounge 2760 Central Ave (28th St) 727/327–7359 • 2pm-2am • gay/ straight

Oar House 4807 22nd Ave S 727/327–1691 • 9am-2am, from 11am Sun • lesbians/ gay men • neighborhood bar • karaoke

Pepperz 4918 Gulfport Blvd S (at 49th), Gulfport 727/327–4897 • 2pm-2am • popular • lesbians/ gay men • dancing/DJ • shows • wheelchair access

A Taste for Wine 241 Central Ave (at 2nd St N) 727/895–1623 • 2pm-9pm, till midnight Fri-Sat, clsd Mon • occasional lesbian events • women-owned

NIGHTCLUBS

Georgie's Alibi 3100 3rd Ave N (at 31st St N) 727/321–2112 • 11am-2am • lesbians/ gay men • neighborhood bar • dancing/DJ • food served • drag shows • videos • WiFi • wheelchair access • patio • gay-owned

Glass 16 2nd St N (at Vintage Ultra Lounge) 727/898–2222 • 10pm Wed only • lesbians/ gay men • dancing/DJ • drag shows • transgender-friendly

RESTAURANTS

Central Avenue Oyster Bar 249 Central Ave 727/897–9728 • 11am-10pm, clsd Sun

Louis Pappas Market Cafe 1530 4th St N 727/822–0900 • 11am-9pm, till 7pm Sun • Greek specialties

Sea Porch Cafe 3400 Gulf Blvd (at Don Cesar Beach Resort) 727/360–1884 • beach views

Skyway Jack's 2795 34th St S 727/867–1907 • 5am-3pm • Southern cooking (diner-style)

ENTERTAINMENT & RECREATION

Bedrocks Beach/ Sunset Beach W Gulf Blvd (at S end of Treasure Island, Sunset Beach) • popular park

Fort DeSoto Park Pinellas Bayway S • beautiful gay beach

PUBLICATIONS

Watermark 813/655-9890 (TAMPA OFFICE), 877/926-8118 • bi-weekly LGBT newspaper for Central FL

Womyn's Words 727/323–5706 • monthly magazine

Tallahassee

INFO LINES & SERVICES

The Family Tree 5126C Woodside Cir 850/222-8555 • LGBT community center • call for hours

ACCOMMODATIONS

Hampton Inn Quincy 165 Spooner Rd (Pat Thomas Pkwy), Quincy 850/627–7555 • gay-friendly • full brkfst • swimming • WiFi • wheelchair access • $99-129

Tampa

see also St Petersburg

ACCOMMODATIONS

Don Vicente de Ybor Inn 1915 Republica de Cuba 813/241-4545, 866/206-4545 • historic boutique hotel

Gram's Place Hostel 3109 N Ola Ave 813/221-0596 • gay/ straight • nudity • kids ok • BYOB • nonsmoking • $25-68

Hampton Inn & Suites 1301 East 7th Ave 813/247-6700 • gay/straight • WiFi • wheelchair access

Hyatt Regency 211 N Tampa St 813/225-1234 • gay/straight • pool • WiFi • wheelchair access

Sawmill Camping Resort 21710 US Hwy 98, Dade City 352/583-0664 • popular • lesbians/ gay men • theme wknds w/ entertainment • RV hookups • cabins • tent spots • dancing • karaoke • pool • nudity • gay-owned • $17-120

Bars

2606 2606 N Armenia Ave (at St Conrad) 813/875-6993 • 2pm-3am • popular • mostly gay men • levi/ leather • strippers wknds • also leather shop from 9pm • wheelchair access • gay-owned

Baxter's 1519 S Dale Mabry (at W Neptune) 813/258-8830 • noon-3am • mostly gay men • neighborhood bar • karaoke • strippers • wheelchair access

Body Shop Bar 14905 N Nebraska 813/971-3576 • 3pm-3am • mostly gay men • neighborhood bar • karaoke Sat • gay-owned

Chelsea Lounge 1502 N Florida 813/228-0139 • 3pm-3am • mostly gay men • neighborhood bar • dancing/DJ • karaoke

City Side 3703 Henderson Blvd (at Dale Mabry) 813/350-0600 • 11am-3am • lesbians/ gay men • neighborhood bar • karaoke • WiFI patio

Dive Bar & Grill 3128 Beach Blvd S, Gulfport • mostly gay men • dancing/DJ • rooftop deck • also restaurant

Hamburger Mary's 1600 E 7th Ave (at N 16th St) 813/241-6279 • 11am-11pm, till 3am wknds • lesbians/ gay men • theme nights • also restaurant

Rainbow Room 421 S MacDill Ave (at Azeele St) 813/871-2265 • 3pm-close • mostly women • beer/ wine • live music Fri • karaoke Sat

Riverside Lounge 1807 N Tampa St 813/374-0196 • 2pm-3am • lesbians/ gay men • dancing/DJ • drag shows • 18+ • theme nights

Tampa

ENTERTAINMENT:

Tampa Bay Gay Men's Chorus 727/580–5517, web: www.tampabayarts.com.
Crescendo, Tampa Bay Womyn's Chorus 813/679-7585, web: www.crescendochorus.org.

LGBT PRIDE:

June. St Pete Pride.
July. Central Florida Black Pride, web: www.floridablackpride.org.

ANNUAL EVENTS:

October- Tampa International Gay & Lesbian Film Festival, web: www.tiglff.com.

CITY INFO:

Greater Tampa Chamber of Commerce 813/228-7777, web: www.tampachamber.com.

ATTRACTIONS:

Busch Gardens/Adventure Island 813/987-5082, web: www.4adventure.com.
Florida Aquarium 813/273-4000, web: www.flaquarium.com.
Harbour Island.
Museum of Science & Industry 813/987-6000, web: www.mosi.org.
Ybor Square.

TRANSIT:

Yellow Cab 813/251-5555, web: thecityoftampa.com/taxis.
Super Shuttle 727/572-1111.
Hartline Transit (bus) 813/254-4278, web: www.hartline.org.

Spurs 1701 E 8th Ave (at 17th St) **813/247-7877** • 8pm-1am Fri-Sat only • lesbians/ gay men • dancing/ DJ • country/ western • wheelchair access • gay owned

Streetcar Charlie's 1811 N 15th St (at 8th Ave) **813/248-1444** • 11am-3pm • lesbians/ gay men • theme nights • food served

NIGHTCLUBS

The Castle 2004 N 16th St **813/247-7547** • 10:30-3am clsd Mon-Tue • mixed gay/ straight • dancing/DJ

Crowbar 1812 N 17th St **813/241-8600** • 10pm-3am • mixed gay/ straight • dancing/DJ • live shows

G Bar 1401 E 7th Ave **813/247-1016** • 4pm-3am, clsd Sun-Mon, theme nights • lesbians/gay men • dancing/DJ • drag shows • videos • 18+ • more women Fri for Girl Butter

Girl Butter 1401 E 7th Ave (at G Bar) **813/247-1016** • 9pm Fri only • mostly women • dancing/DJ • videos • 18+

Metro Tampa 2606 N Armenia Ave (at St Conrad) **813/876-4650** • 3pm-3am, from 1pm Sun • mostly gay men • dancing/DJ

Steam Fridays 1507 E 7th Ave (at the Honey Pot) **813/247-4663** • 10pm Fri only • mostly gay men • dancing/DJ • 18+ • 3 flrs

Tease Saturdays 1507 E 7th Ave (at the Honey Pot) **813/247-4663** • 10pm Sat only • mostly women • dancing/DJ • 18+ • 3 flrs

Valentines Nightclub 7522 N Armenia Ave (btwn Sligh & Waters) **813/936-1999** • 3pm-3am • mostly gay men • dancing/DJ • drag shows • male dancers

W T-Dance 1801 E 7th Ave (at 18th) • 6pm-midnight Sun • mostly men • dancing/DJ

CAFES

Joffrey's Coffee 1600 E 8th Ave **813/247-4600** • 7am-10, till midnight wknds • WiFi

Sacred Grounds Coffeehouse 4819 E Busch Blvd **813/983-0837** • 6pm-midnight, till 2am Fri-Sat • lesbians/ gay men • live music • open mic Mon

Tre Amici 1907 19th St N **813/247-6964** • 8am-10pm, till 11pm wknds • cafe & wine bar

RESTAURANTS

Hamburger Mary's 1600 E 7th Ave (2nd flr), Ybor City **813/241-6279** • 11am-11pm • live music • karaoke • wheelchair acess • gay-owned

Bernini 1702 E 7th Ave **813/248-0099** • old school Italian

Buddha Lounge 1200 N Westshore Blvd **813/868-7600** • lunch & dinner, open late wknds, clsd Mon • plenty veggie/ vegan • full bar

Centro Cantina 1600 E 8th Ave **813/241-8588** • Tex Mex • great balcony

Columbia 2117 E 7th Ave **813/248-4961** • 11am-close, from noon Sun • Cuban & Spanish • historical restaurant

Crabby Bill's 401 Gulf Blvd, Indian Rocks Beach **727/595-4825** • inexpensive seafood joint

Fresh Mouth 1600 E 8th Ave (plaza level) **813/241-8845** • 11am-9pm, till 2am wknds

Gaspar's Grotto 1805 E 7th Ave **813/248-5900** • 11am-3am • patio

Jalapenos de Ybor 1604 N 17th St (at E 5th Ave) **813/241-8226** • 7am-2pm, till 3am wknds • traditional Mexican • patio

JJ's Cafe & Bar 1601 E 7th Ave (at N 16th St) **813/247-4125** • 11am-10pm, till 2:30am wknds

The Laughing Cat 1820 N 15th St **813/241-2998** • Italian

The Queen's Head 2501 Central Ave, St Petersburg **727/498-8584** • 3pm-2am, from noon wknds • European • full bar

Teatro on 7th 1600 E 8th Ave **813/248-9400** • upscale

ENTERTAINMENT & RECREATION

Picnic Island Picnic Island Blvd (across from the military base, on E side) • gay beach at end of park

RETAIL SHOPS

King Corona Cigars 1523 E 7th Ave **888/248-3812** • local, handmade cigars

The MC Film Festival 1901 N 15th St (at 8th Ave) **813/247-6233** • LGBT pride gift store

PUBLICATIONS

Watermark **813/655-9890, 877/926-8118** • bi-weekly LGBT newspaper for Central FL

Womyn's Words **727/323-5706** • monthly magazine

West Palm Beach

ACCOMMODATIONS

Grandview Gardens B&B 1608 Lake Ave (at Palm) **561/833-9023** • gay-friendly • pool • nonsmoking • WiFi • wheelchair access • gay-owned • $119-199

Hibiscus House B&B 501 30th St **561/863-5633, 800/203-4927** • gay/straight • full brkfst • pet-friendly • pool • nonsmoking • gay-owned • WiFi • $100-270

Scandia Lodge 625 S Federal Hwy (at 6th Ave), Lake Worth **561/586-3155** • gay/straight • pool • pets ok • nonsmoking • $65-95

BARS

Fort Dix 6205 Georgia Ave (at Colonial) **561/533-5355** • noon-3am, till 4am Fri-Sat • popular • mostly gay men • neighborhood dive bar • dancing/DJ wknds • patio • wheelchair access

HG Rooster's 823 Belvedere Rd (btwn Parker & Lake) **561/832-9119** • 3pm-3am, till 4am Fri-Sat • popular • mostly gay men • neighborhood bar • strippers • karaoke • food served • wheelchair access

NIGHTCLUBS

I Rock 2650 S Military Trail (at Dale Rd) **561/434-9917** • 8pm-5am • lesbians/gay men • dancing/DJ • shows • food served • theme nights • patio

The Lounge 517 Clematis St **561/655-9747** • 9pm-4am, clsd Sun-Mon • gay/straight • dancing/DJ • also sushi & sake bar

Monarchy 221 Clematis St **561/835-6661** • 10pm-3am, till 4am Fri-Sat, clsd Sun-Wed • gay/straight • dancing/DJ

Respectable Street 518 Clematis St **561/832-9999** • 9pm-3am, till 4am Fri-Sat, clsd Sun-Tue • gay-friendly • dancing/DJ • alternative • retro & new wave nights • live music

RESTAURANTS

Rhythm Cafe 3800-A S Dixie Hwy **561/833-3406** • 6pm-10pm, clsd Sun-Mon • some veggie • beer/wine

Thai Bay 1900 Okeechobee Blvd (in Palm Beach Market Pl) **561/640-0131** • lunch and dinner, clsd Sun

ENTERTAINMENT & RECREATION

MacArthur Beach Singer Island, N Palm Beach

BOOKSTORES

Changing Times Bookstore 911 Village Blvd #806 (at Palm Beach Lakes) **561/640-0496** • 10am-7pm, till 5pm Sat-Sun • community bulletin board • wheelchair access

RETAIL SHOPS

Eurotique 3111 45th St #16 (at Village Blvd) **561/684-2302, 800/486-9650** • 11am-7pm, noon-6pm Sat, clsd Sun • leather • books • videos

Studio 205 & Java Juice Bar 600 Lake Ave (at L St), Lake Worth **561/533-5272** • 10am-6pm, till 5pm Sun • gay pride items • books & home accessories

Wilton Manors

see Fort Lauderdale

Winter Haven

ACCOMMODATIONS

Ranch House Inn & Suites 1911 Cypress Gardens Blvd **863/324-5994, 800/366-5996** • gay-friendly • motel • pool • restaurant • kids/pets ok • WiFi • wheelchair access • $49-82

BARS

Old Man Frank's 1005 S Lake Howard Dr (at Central) **863/294-9179** • 11am-2am, from noon-midnight Sun • gay-friendly • on the lake • food served • smoking allowed • wheelchair access

GEORGIA

Athens

ACCOMMODATIONS

Ashford Manor B&B 5 Harden Hill Rd (at Main St), Watkinsville **706/769-2633** • gay-friendly • pool • nonsmoking • WiFi • gay-owned • $99-225

BARS

The Globe 199 N Lumpkin St (at Clayton) **706/353-4721** • 11am-2am, till midnight Sun • gay-friendly • 40 single-malt scotches • also restaurant

NIGHTCLUBS

Forty Watt Club 285 W Washington St (at Pulaski) **706/549-7871** • call for hours • gay-friendly • alternative • live music • wheelchair access

CAFES

Espresso Royale Cafe 297 E Broad St (at Jackson) **706/613-7449** • 7am-11pm, from 8am wknds • best coffee in Athens • gallery • wheelchair access

RESTAURANTS

The Grit 199 Prince Ave **706/543-6592** • 11am-10pm, great wknd brunch 10am-3pm • ethnic vegetarian • wheelchair access

Atlanta

INFO LINES & SERVICES

Galano Club 585 Dutch Valley Rd (at Monroe) **404/881-9188** • meetings throughout the day • LGBT recovery club • call for meeting times

ACCOMMODATIONS

The Gaslight Inn 1001 St Charles Ave NE **404/875-1001** • gay/ straight • 1913 craftsman-style B&B • nonsmoking • WiFi • gay-owned • $115-215

The Georgian Terrace Hotel 659 Peachtree St (at Ponce de Leon) **404/897-1991, 800/555-8000** • gay-friendly • "Atlanta's only historic luxury hotel" • hosted *Gone with the Wind* world-premier reception in 1939 • pool • kids ok • WiFi • wheelchair access • $119-299

Glenn Hotel 110 Marietta St NW (at Spring) **404/521-2250, 866/404-5366** • gay/ straight • boutique hotel • also restaurant & rooftop lounge

Hotel Indigo 683 Peachtree St NE (at 3rd) **404/874-9200** • cozy, stylish no-frills hotel • workout room • also restaurant • WiFi

Hotel Palomar Atlanta Midtown 866 W Peachtree St NW (at 7th St NE) **404/945-6285** • gay-friendly • hip boutique hotel in midtown

Microtel Inn & Suites 1840 Corporate Blvd (off Buford Hwy) **404/325-4446** • gay-friendly • WiFi • wheelchair access • $55-79

Midtown Carriage House **404/931-8791** • lesbians/ gay men • 2-story house • garden • patio • pool • nonsmoking • gay-owned • $175-250

Stonehurst Place Bed & Breakfast 923 Piedmont Ave NE (at 8th St) **404/881-0722, 877/285-2246** • gay/ straight • in 1896 shingle-style house furnished w/ antiques • full brkfst • nonsmoking • WiFi • lesbian-owned • $149 - $429

W Atlanta 111 Perimeter Center W (at Ashford Dunwoody Rd) **770/396-6800, 877/WHOTELS (RESERVATIONS ONLY)** • gay-friendly • pool • nonsmoking • WiFi • also restaurant • wheelchair access • $125-399

W Atlanta Midtown 188 14th St NE (at Juniper St NE) **404/892-6000** • gay/ straight • stylish hotel • convenient location

BARS

3-Legged Cowboy 931 Monroe Dr #B (at Midtown Promenade) **404/876-0001** • 6pm-2am, clsd Sun-Mon • popular • mostly gay men • more women Th • dancing/DJ • country/ western • live shows • wheelchair access

Amsterdam 502 Amsterdam Ave NE **404/892-2227** • 11:30am-close • mostly gay men • dancing/DJ • food served • video & sports bar

Atlanta Eagle 306 Ponce de Leon Ave NE (at Argonne) **404/873-2453** • 3pm-3am, clsd Sun • popular • mostly gay men • dancing/DJ • bears • leather • also leather store • gay-owned

BJ Roosters 2345 Cheshire Bridge Rd (at La Vista) **404/634-5895** • 2:30pm-3am • mostly gay men • neighborhood bar • karaoke • gospel drag show • gay-owned

Blake's on the Park 227 10th St (at Piedmont) **404/892-5786** • 11am-3am, till midnight Sun

Bulldogs 893 Peachtree St NE (btwn 7th & 8th) **404/872-3025** • 2pm-4am Sun-Fri, till 3am Sat

Burkhart's Pub 1492–F Piedmont Ave (at Monroe, in Ansley Square) **404/872–4403** • 4pm-2:30am, from 2pm wknds, till midnight Sun • lesbians/ gay men • neighborhood bar • food served • karaoke • live shows • patio • wheelchair access

Eastside Lounge 485-A Flat Shoals Ave (at Glenwood) **404/521–9666** • 9pm-2:30am, from 8pm Fri-Sat, clsd Sun • gay/ straight • dancing/DJ • multiracial • theme nights

Atlanta

WHERE THE GIRLS ARE:

Many lesbians live in DeKalb county, in the northeast part of the city of Decatur. For fun, women head for Midtown or Buckhead if they're professionals, Virginia-Highlands if they're funky or 30ish, Little Five Points if they're young and wild, and Castleberry Hill if they're artistic.

LGBT PRIDE:

October. 404/929-0071, web: atlantapride.org.

ANNUAL EVENTS:

July - National Black Arts Festival 404/730-7315, web: www.nbaf.org.
Labor Day weekend - Femmenomen-non (lesbian party), web: www.girlsinthenight.com.
November - Out on Film, lesbian/ gay film festival 404/352-4225, web: www.outonfilm.com.

CITY INFO:

404/521-6600 or 800/285-2682, web: www.atlanta.net.

BEST VIEW:

70th floor of the Peachtree Plaza, in the 3-story revolving Sun Dial restaurant (404/589-7506). Also from the top of Stone Mountain (only 20 feet taller).

WEATHER:

Summers are warm and humid (upper 80ºs to low 90ºs) with occasional thunderstorms. Winters are icy with occasional snow. Temperatures can drop into the low 30ºs. Spring and fall are temperate – spring brings blossoming dogwoods and magnolias, while fall festoons the trees with awesome fall colors.

ATTRACTIONS:

Atlanta Botanical Garden 404/876-5859, web: www.atlantabotanicalgarden.org.
Centennial Olympic Park.
CNN Center 404/827-2300, web: www.cnn.com/StudioTour.
Coca-Cola Museum 404/676-5151, web: www.woccatlanta.com.
Georgia Aquarium (largest aquarium in the US) 404/581-4000, web: www.georgiaaquarium.org.
High Museum of Art 404/733-4444, web: www.high.org.
Margaret Mitchell House 404/249-7015, web: www.gwtw.org.
Martin Luther King Jr. Memorial Center 404/526-8900, web: www.thekingcenter.org.
Piedmont Park.
Stone Mountain Park 770/498-5690, web: www.stonemountainpark.com.
Underground Atlanta 404/523-2311, web: underground-atlanta.com.

TRANSIT:

Yellow Cab 404/521-0200.
Superior Shuttle 770/457-4794.
Marta 404/848-5000, web: www.itsmarta.com.

Eddie's Attic 515–B N McDonough St (at Trinity Place), Decatur **404/377–4976** • 4:30pm-12:30am Mon-Th, till 2am Fri-Sat, open 1 hr before showtime Sun • gay/ straight • occasional lesbian hangout • live music • open mic & comedy • restaurant • rooftop deck

Felix's on the Square 1510-G Piedmont Ave NE (Ansley Square) **404/249–7899** • 2pm-3am, from 1pm Sat, 1pm-midnight Sun • mostly gay men • food served

Friends on Ponce 736 Ponce de Leon NE (at Ponce de Leon Pl) **404/817–3820** • 2pm-3am Mon-Fri, from noon Sat, till midnight Sun • rooftop patio

Halo Lounge 817 W Peachtree (6th St, btwn W Peachtree & Peachtree) **404/962–7333** • 4pm-3am, from 6pm Sat, clsd Sun • dinner • gay/ straight • DJ

Le Buzz 585 Franklin Rd A-10 (at S Marietta Pkwy, in Longhorn Plaza), Marietta **770/424–1337** • 7pm-3am, clsd Sun • lesbians/ gay men • neighborhood bar • dancing/DJ • drag shows • karaoke • also restaurant • patio • wheelchair access

Mary's 1287B Glenwood Ave (at Flat Shoals) **404/624–4411** • 5pm-3am, clsd Sun • lesbians/ gay men • friendly neighborhood • dancing/DJ • karaoke • videos

Mixx 1492–B Piedmont Ave (at Monroe, in Ansley Square) **404/228–4372** • 4pm-2am, till 3am Fri-Sat, clsd Mon • mostly gay men • neighborhood bar • dancing/DJ wknds

My Sister's Room 1271 Glenwood Ave **404/705–4585** • 6pm-close, from 7pm Sat, closed Sun-Mon • popular • mostly women • live music • karaoke • also restaurant • younger crowd • patio

Opus I 1086 Alco St NE (at Cheshire Bridge) **404/634–6478** • 11am-3am, from 9am Sat, 12:30pm-midnight Sun • mostly gay men • neighborhood bar • wheelchair access

Nightclubs

Bellissima 560-B Amsterdam Ave (at Monroe Dr) **404/917–0220** • 6pm-3am, clsd Mon-Tue • lesbians/ gay men • lounge • dancing/DJ • multiracial clientele • live entertainment • videos • food served • wheelchair access

Chaparral 2715 Buford Hwy (at Lenox Rd) **404/634–3737** • 10pm-4am • more gay Fri & Sun • dancing/DJ • Latino/a

Foreplay Fridays 1008 Brady Ave (at 11th St NW, at Compound) **404/367–8482** • 10pm Fri only • mostly women • dancing/DJ • multiracial

Girls in the Night • women's parties & events around Atlanta • check local listings or girlsinthenight.com

Masquerade 695 North Ave NE **404/577–8178, 404/577–2002** • hours vary • gay-friendly • dancing/DJ • live shows • call for events • food served • 18+ • private club • cover charge

Opera 1150 Peachtree St NE (at 14th St NE, enter on Crescent Ave) **404/874–3006** • gay/ straight • dancing/DJ

Phase One 4933 Memorial Dr (at Delano), Decatur **404/296–4895** • ladies night Wed, Fri & Sun • dancing/DJ • mostly African American

Traxx 1287 Columbia Dr, Decatur **866/602–5553** • Sat only • mostly gay men • dancing/DJ • mostly African American • live shows

Traxx Girls Night 3011 Buford Hwy (at Club Miami) **404/929–9991** • 10pm-close Fri only • mostly women • dancing/DJ • mostly African American

Traxx Girls Parties **678/368–6435** • weekly women's dance parties • check traxxgirls.com for info

Traxx Girls Sundays 50 Upper Alabama St (in Underground Atlanta, at Scores) **678/368–6435** • 11pm-close Sun only • mostly women • dancing/DJ • mostly African American

Who's Who? 79 Poplar St (at Fairlie St, at The Mark Ultralounge) **678/904–0050** • 10pm-3am Wed only • lesbians/ gay men • dancing/DJ • mostly African American

Wild Mustang/ Jungle 2115 Faulkner Rd NE (off Cheshire Bridge Rd NE) **404/844–8800** • 9pm-close, clsd Sun • lesbians/ gay men • dancing/DJ • also Stars of the Century (drag shows) Mon 11pm • cover charge

Cafes

Apache Cafe 64 3rd St NW **404/876–5436** • food served • poetry readings • events • gallery • multiracial

Australian Bakery Cafe 48 S Park Square **678/797–6222** • 7am-5:30pm, 8am-4pm wknds • also 463 Flat Shoals Rd, 404/653–0100

Intermezzo 1845 Peachtree Rd NE **404/355–0411** • 10:30am-3am • classy cafe • plenty veggie • full bar • great desserts • WiFi till 7pm

Urban Grounds 38 N Avondale Rd, Avondale Estates **404/499–2136** • 6:30am-9pm, till 10pm Fri, 7:30am-10pm Sat, 8am-4pm Sun

Restaurants

Amuse 560 Dutch Valley Rd **404/888-1890** • lunch & dinner, wknd brunch • full bar • int'l bistro

Apres Diem 931 Monroe Dr #C-103 **404/872-3333** • 11:30am-midnight, till 2am Fri-Sat, from 11am wknds, brunch Sat-Sun • French bistro • live jazz Wed • full bar

Aria 490 E Paces Ferry **404/262-5208** • dinner only, clsd Sun

Aurum 108 8th St **404/815-9426** • 8pm-3am, till 1am Wed • gay/ straight • lounge

Bacchanalia/ Star Provisions/ Quinones 1198 Howell Mill Rd NW **404/365-0410** • dinner Mon-Sat • upscale • American

Beleza 905 Juniper St (at 8th) **678/904-4582** • 5:30pm-1am, till 2am wknds, clsd Sun-Mon • Brazilian • also cocktails

Cafe Sunflower 2140 Peachtree Rd NW (at Bennett St NW) **404/352-8859** • lunch & dinner, clsd Sun • vegetarian

The Colonnade 1879 Cheshire Bridge Rd NE **404/874-5642** • lunch Wed-Sun, dinner nightly • traditional Southern

Cowtippers 1600 Piedmont Ave NE (at Monroe) **404/874-3751** • 11:30am-11pm, till midnight Fri-Sat • steak house • transgender-friendly • wheelchair access

Ecco 40 7th St **404/347-9555** • 5:30pm-10pm, till 11pm Fri-Sat, till 10pm Sun • Italian • reservations recommended

Einstein's 1077 Juniper (at 12th) **404/876-7925** • 11am-11pm, till midnight Fri-Sat, from 10am Sun, wknd brunch • popular • some veggie • full bar • patio • wheelchair access • reservations accepted

The Flying Biscuit Cafe 1655 McLendon Ave (at Clifton) **404/687-8888** • 7am-10pm, till 10:30pm Fri-Sat • popular • healthy brkfst all day • plenty veggie • beer/ wine • wheelchair access • multiple locations

Fresh To Order 860 Peachtree St (at 7th St NE) **404/593-2333** • 11am-10pm, brunch Sun from 10am • healthy fast food • patio

Frogs 931 Monroe Dr NE **404/607-9967** • 11am-10pm, till 11pm wknds • Mexican

Gilbert's Cafe & Bar 219 10th St NE (at Piedmont Ave) **404/872-8012** • lunch & dinner, wknd brunch, food till 2am, bar till 3am, till midnight Sun

Hobnob 1551 Piedmont Ave NE (at Monroe) **404/968-2288** • 11am-11pm, 10am-4pm Sun

Joe's On Juniper 1049 Juniper St **404/875-6634** • 11am-2am, till midnight Sun • American

Las Margaritas 1842 Cheshire Bridge Rd **404/873-4464** • lunch & dinner • Latin fusion

The Lobby at Twelve 361 17th St **404/961-7370** • brkfst, lunch & dinner • upscale American • reservations recommended

Majestic Diner 1031 Ponce de Leon (at Highland) **404/875-0276** • 24hrs • popular diner right from the '50s w/ cantankerous waitresses included • at your own risk • some veggie

Murphy's 997 Virginia Ave NE (at N Highland Ave) **404/872-0904** • 11am-10pm, till midnight Fri, from 8am wknds • popular • plenty veggie • wheelchair access

Nickiemoto's 990 Piedmont Ave NE **404/253-2010** • lunch & dinner • pan-Asian/ sushi • Drag-a-Magki drag show Mon

No Más! Cantina 180 Walker St **404/574-5678** • lunch & dinner daily, wknd brunch • Mexican • also huge furniture & gift store • gay-owned

Pastries A Go Go 235 Ponce De Leon Place, Decatur **404/373-3423** • 7:30am-4pm, clsd Tue • delicious baked goods

R Thomas Deluxe Grill 1812 Peachtree Rd NE (btwn 26th & 27th) **404/872-2942** • 24hrs • popular • beer/ wine • healthy Californian/ juice bar • plenty veggie • wheelchair access

Repast 620 N Glen Iris Dr **404/870-8707** • 5:30pm-10pm, till 10:30pm Fri-Sat, clsd Sun • upscale American • reservations recommended

Ria's Bluebird Cafe 421 Memorial Dr **404/521-3737** • 8am-3pm • very popular • gourmet brunch in quaint old diner in Grant Park • plenty veggie • everything made from scratch • wheelchair access • woman-owned

Roxx Tavern & Diner 1824 Cheshire Brg Rd NE (at Manchester) **404/892-4541** • lunch & dinner, Sun brunch • patio

➤ **Sauced** 753 Edgewood Ave (at Waddell St NE) **404/688-6554** • dinner nightly till 1am, clsd Mon • retro kitsch decor • Southern • plenty veggie • full bar

Slice 259 Peters St **404/588-1820** • 11am-midnight, till 3am Fri, noon-3am Sat, noon-midnight Sun • pizza & martinis • WiFi • gay-owned • second location 85 Poplar St, 404/ 917-1820

Swan Coach House 3130 Slaton Dr NW **404/261-0636** • 11am-2:30pm, clsd Sun • also gift shop & art gallery

Table 1280 1280 Peachtree St NE (at Woodruff Arts Center) **404/897-1280** • 11am-8pm Tue-Sat, till 6pm Sun, Sun brunch, clsd Mon • upscale American & tapas

Thumbs Up Diner 573 Edgewood Ave NE (at Bradley) • 7am-3pm, 8am-4pm wknds • brkfst all day

TWO urban licks 820 Ralph McGill Blvd **404/522-4622** • dinner nightly • great grill • full bar • live blues • reservations recommended

Veni Vidi Vici 41 14th St **404/875-8424** • lunch Mon-Fri, dinner nightly • upscale Italian • some veggie • WiFi

Wasabi 180 Walker St **404/574-5680** • lunch Th-Fri, dinner nightly, clsd Sun • sushi

Watershed 406 W Ponce de Leon Ave, Decatur **404/378-4900** • 11am-10pm, Sun brunch • wine bar • also gift shop • owned by Emily Saliers of the Indigo Girls

Entertainment & Recreation

AIDS Memorial Quilt/ NAMES Project 204 14th St **404/688-5500** • visit The Quilt at the foundation offices

Ansley Park Playhouse 1545 Peachtree St **404/875-1193** • some LGBT-themed productions

Atlanta Gay Men's Chorus 1379 Tullie Rd, Ste 200, 30329-2308 **404/320-1030**

Atlanta Rollergirls • Atlanta's female roller derby league • visit www.atlantarollergirls.com for events

Lambda Radio Report WRFG 89.3 FM **404/523-8989** • 6pm Tue • LGBT radio program

Little 5 Points, Moreland & Euclid Ave S of Ponce de Leon Ave • hip & funky area w/ too many restaurants & shops to list

Martin Luther King, Jr Center for Non–Violent Social Change 449 Auburn Ave NE **404/526-8900** • 9am-5pm daily • includes King's birth home, the church where he preached in the '60s & his gravesite

Bookstores

Brushstrokes/ Capulets 1510–J Piedmont Ave NE (near Monroe) **404/876-6567** • 10am-10pm, till 11pm Fri-Sat • LGBT variety store • gay-owned

Charis Books & More 1189 Euclid Ave NE (at Moreland) **404/524-0304** • 10:30am-6:30pm, till 8pm Wed, Fri-Sat, noon-6pm Sun • feminist • wheelchair access

Outwrite Bookstore & Coffeehouse 991 Piedmont Ave (at 10th) **404/607–0082** • 10am–11pm • popular • LGBT • music • videos • gifts • cafe • wheelchair access

RETAIL SHOPS

Atlanta Leather Company 2111 Faulkner Rd NE (at Chesire Bridge Rd) **404/320–8989** • 11am–8pm, noon–6pm Sun • leather • fetish

The Boy Next Door 1447 Piedmont Ave NE (btwn 14th & Monroe) **404/873–2664** • 10am–8pm, noon–6pm Sun • clothing

The Junkman's Daughter 464 Moreland Ave (at Euclid) **404/577–3188** • 11am–7pm, till 8pm Fri, till 9pm Sat, from noon Sun • hip stuff

Piercing Experience 1654 McLendon Ave NE (at Clifton) **404/378–9100, 800/646–0393** • noon–8pm, till 9pm Fri–Sat, till 6pm Sun

PUBLICATIONS

David Atlanta **404/876–1819** • gay entertainment magazine w/ extensive nightlife calendar, maps & directory

Labrys Magazine **404/223–6741** • monthly lesbian magazine

GYMS & HEALTH CLUBS

Gravity Fitness 2201 Faulkner Rd (off Cheshire Bridge Rd) **404/486–0506** • day passes available

Urban Body Fitness 742 Ponce de Leon Pl **404/885–1499**

EROTICA

Aphrodite's Toy Box 3040 N Decatur Rd (at Ponce De Leon), Scottdale **404/292–9700** • noon–8pm, till 9pm Fri–Sat, till 6pm Sun, clsd Tue • women-oriented erotic boutique • transgender-friendly • 18+ • also classes

Inserection 1739 Cheshire Bridge Rd **404/262–9113**

Lollipop Adult Treats 3165 Roswell Rd (at Peachtree St) **404/816–8299** • 24hrs

The Poster Hut, Inc 2175 Cheshire Bridge Rd (at Piedmont Rd) **404/633–7491** • 10am–9pm, till 11pm Fri–Sat, from 10pm–7:30pm Sun • clothing • toys • housewares • gifts

Southern Nights Videos 2205 Cheshire Br Rd (at Woodland Ave NE) **404/728–0701** • 24hrs

Starship 2275 Cheshire Bridge Rd **404/320–9101, 800/215–1053** • 24hrs • many locations in Atlanta

CRUISY AREAS

Publix on Ponce 1001 Ponce de Leon Ave • supermarket • dyke cruising territory

Augusta

see Aiken, South Carolina

Dahlonega

ACCOMMODATIONS

Mountain Laurel Creek 202 Talmer Grizzle Rd (at Hwy 19 & McDonald Rd) **706/867–8134** • gay-friendly • full brkfst • spa & pub • nonsmoking • gay-owned • $149-195

Swiftwaters Womanspace **706/864–3229, 706/429–6802** • women only • on scenic river • full brkfst • hot tub • seasonal • nonsmoking • deck • dogs ok • women-owned • $50-75 (indoors), $15 (camping)

RESTAURANTS

Smith House 84 S Chestatee St **706/867–7000, 800/852–9577** • lunch & dinner, clsd Mon • family-style Southern

Dalton

RESTAURANTS

Dalton Depot 110 Depot St **706/226–3150** • 11am–9pm, till 10pm Th–Sat, from 11:30am Sun

Decatur

see Atlanta

Dewy Rose

ACCOMMODATIONS

The River's Edge 2311 Pulliam Mill Rd **706/213–8081** • mostly gay men • cabins • camping • RV • live shows • pool • nudity • nonsmoking • wheelchair access • $16-100

Lake Lanier

ENTERTAINMENT & RECREATION

Gay Cove btwn Athens Park Rd & Frank Boyd Rd (Channel Marker 21) • a rainbow rendezvous for the pleasure-boating crowd— look for the rainbow flag

Macon

NIGHTCLUBS

Club Synergy 425 Cherry St (at MLK, Jr Blvd) **478/755–9383** • 9pm-close, clsd Sun-Tue • lesbians/ gay men • 4 bars • dancing/DJ • live shows • karaoke • wheelchair access

Marietta

see Atlanta

Savannah

INFO LINES & SERVICES

First City Network 307 E Harris St **912/236-2489** • complete info & events line • social group • also newsletter

ACCOMMODATIONS

912 Barnard Victorian B&B 912 Barnard St **912/234-9121** • lesbians/ gay men • fireplaces • nonsmoking • WiFi • gay-owned • $99+

The Azalea Inn & Gardens 217 E Huntingdon St (at Abercorn St) **912/236-2707, 800/582-3823** • gay-friendly • 19th-c Italianate • vintage gardens • pool • full Southern brkfst • nonsmoking • $199-300

Catherine Ward House Inn 118 E Waldburg St (at Abercorn) **912/234-8564, 800/327-4270** • gay/ straight • Victorian Italianate • full brkfst • WiFi • $149-249

Kehoe House 123 Habersham St **912/232-1020, 800/820-1020** • gay-friendly • full brkfst • WiFi

Mansion on Forsyth Park 700 Drayton St **912/238-5158, 888/711-5114** • gay-friendly • restored Victorian mansion in historic district • pool • nonsmoking • WiFi • wheelchair access • $156-600

Park Avenue Manor 107-109 W Park Ave **912/233-0352** • gay-friendly • full brkfst • nonsmoking • WiFi • $159

Statesboro Inn 106 S Main, Statesboro **912/489-8628, 800/846-9466** • gay-friendly • full brkfst • WiFi • $70-125

Thunderbird Inn 611 W Oglethorpe Ave (at MLK Blvd) **912/232-2661, 866/324-2661** • gay-friendly • motel • kids ok • nonsmoking • WiFi • gay-owned • $99-139

Tybee Vacation Rentals 1010 Hwy 80 E, Tybee Island **866/935-3861** • gay-friendly • rental homes, cottages & condos • pool • nonsmoking • WiFi • some gay-owned • $90-740

BARS

Chuck's Bar 305 W River St **912/232-1005** • 8pm-3am, from 7pm Th-Sat, clsd Sun • gay/ straight • neighborhood bar • young crowd • student & artist hangout

Rocks on the Roof 102 W Bay St (on the roof of The Bohemian Hotel) **912/721-3901** • 11am-midnight • fantastic views of Savannah River and the historic district

Venus Di Milo 38 MLK Jr Blvd **912/447-0901** • 5pm-3am, clsd Sun • gay-friendly

NIGHTCLUBS

Club One 1 Jefferson St (at Bay) **912/232-0200** • 5pm-3am, till 2am Sun • lesbians/ gay men • dancing/DJ • food served • live shows Th-Sun • karaoke • drag shows • dancers • videos

RESTAURANTS

B Matthews 325 E Bay St **912/234-6953** • 8am-10pm

Churchill's Pub 13 W Bay St **912/232-8501** • 5pm-1am

Clary's Cafe 404 Abercorn (at Jones) **912/233-0402** • 7am-4pm, from 8am Sat-Sun • country cookin' • also 4330 Habersham St, 912/351-0302, open till 9pm

The Distillery 416 W Liberty St **912/236-1772** • 11am-1am, till 3am Fri-Sat, noon-9pm Sun • wheelchair access

Fannie's on the Beach 1613 Strand Ave (at Silver Ave), Tybee Island **912/786-6109** • noon-11pm, till 2am wknds • dancing/DJ • live shows

Firefly Cafe 321 Habersham St **912/234-1971** • 10:30am-9pm, till 9:30pm Fri-Sat, 9am-3pm Sun • wheelchair access

Mellow Mushroom 11 W Liberty St **912/495-0705** • 11am-10pm • pizza & beer

Wright Square Cafe 21 W York St **912/238-1150** • 7:30am-5pm, from 9am Sat, clsd Sun • large chocolate selection • patio

ENTERTAINMENT & RECREATION

Savannah Walks, Inc **888/728-9255** • gay-friendly • walking tours of downtown Savannah

Unadilla

ACCOMMODATIONS

Lumberjack's Camping Resort 50 Hwy 230 (at Hwy 41) **478/783-2267, 877/888-1688** • mostly gay men • campsites & RV hookups • on 150 acres • pool • live shows • WiFi • pets ok • gay-owned • also restaurant • $39+

Washington

ACCOMMODATIONS

Holly Court Inn 301 S Alexander Ave (at Water St) **706/678-3982, 866/465-5928** • gay-friendly • 1 hour from Augusta & Athens • full brkfst • kids ok • dining & bar • WiFi • $90-175

HAWAII

Please note that cities are grouped by islands:
- Hawaii (Big Island)
- Kauai
- Maui
- Molokai
- Oahu (includes Honolulu)

STATEWIDE

Pacific Ocean Holidays Oahu
808/545-5252 • "Hawaii vacations for gay men & women"

ENTERTAINMENT & RECREATION

Hawaii Scuba Divers 866/926-3483 • "gay-friendly scuba diving lessons & tours in the state of Hawaii"

HAWAII (BIG ISLAND)

Captain Cook

ACCOMMODATIONS

Aloha Guest House 84-4780 Mamalahoa Hwy **808/328-8955, 800/897-3188** • gay/ straight • full organic brkfst • ocean views • nudity • nonsmoking • WiFi • wheelchair access • gay-owned • $160-280

Areca Palms Estate B&B **808/323-2276, 800/545-4390** • gay-friendly • full brkfst • gardens • jacuzzi • nonsmoking • $115-145

Horizon Guest House **808/328-2540, 888/328-8301** • gay/ straight • full brkfst • pool • nonsmoking • WiFi • wheelchair access • gay-owned • $250-350

Ka'awa Loa Plantation 82-5990 Napoopoo Rd 96704 **808/323-2686** • gay/ straight • plantation-style B&B on 5-acre start-up coffee farm & orchard near Kealakekua Bay • hot tub • nonsmoking • WiFi • wheelchair access • gay-owned • $125-195

Kealakekua Bay B&B **808/328-8150, 800/328-8150** • gay/ straight • Mediterranean-style villa • nonsmoking • kids ok • also 2-bdrm guesthouse • $140-300

Hilo

ACCOMMODATIONS

Aloha Healing Women **808/936-6067, 877/850-2250** • women only • all-inclusive holistic healing retreats • full brkfst • pool • accupuncture • guided tours • gourmet meals • women-owned

The Butterfly Inn for Women **808/966-7936, 800/546-2442** • women only • hot tub • kitchens • nonsmoking • women-owned • $55-85

Mele Kohola 15-991 Paradise Dr (Paradise Ala Kai) **808/965-0400** • vacation rental • bay views • seasonal whale watching • WiFi • $225-375

Seascape Gardens B&B 2107 A Kaiwiki Rd (at Wainaku) **808/961-3036** • women only • panoramic views • women-owned • $145+

CAFES

Kope-Kope Espresso 1261 Kilauea Ave #220 (in Hilo Shopping Center) **808/933-1221** • 6:30am-9pm, from 7:30am wknds, till 3pm Sun • WiFi

RESTAURANTS

Cafe Pesto 308 Kamehameha Ave **808/969-6640** • lunch & dinner • pizzas, salads, pastas • on the waterfront • also at Kawaihae Shopping Center 808/882-1071

ENTERTAINMENT & RECREATION

Richardson Beach at end of Kalanianaole Ave (Keaukaha)

Sun & Sea Hawaii 224 Kamehameha Ave (at Kalakaua Ave) **808/934-0902** • LGBT snorkel rental & tour company • women's party producers • lesbian-owned

RETAIL SHOPS

Pride Project 301 Keawe St **808/935-5566** • 10am-4pm, clsd Sun • LGBT community center & thrift store

Honaunau-Kona

ACCOMMODATIONS

Dragonfly Ranch Healing Arts Center 1 1/2 miles down City of Refuge Rd **808/328-2159** • gay/ straight • near ancient sanctuary w/ friendly dolphins • hot tub • nonsmoking • $100-300

Kailua-Kona

ACCOMMODATIONS

1st Class B&B Kona Hawaii 77-6504 Kilohana St **808/329-8778, 888/769-1110** • gay-friendly • private luxury suites • ocean views • full brkfst • nonsmoking • WiFi • $165-175

KonaLani Coffee Plantation Inn 76-5917H Mamalahoa Hwy **808/324-0793** • lesbians/ gay men • B&B inn • full brkfst • nonsmoking • gay-owned • $80-175

Royal Kona Resort 75–5852 Ali'i Dr **808/329–3111, 800/222–5642** • gay-friendly • overlooking Kailua Bay • pool • private beach • bar • live shows • WiFi • wheelchair access

Bars

The Mask-querade 75–5660 Kopiko St (at Cathedral Plaza) **808/329–8558** • 10am-2am • lesbians/ gay men • neighborhood bar • dancing/DJ • live shows • karaoke • Mon ladies night • gay-owned

Restaurants

Huggo's 75-5828 Kahakai Rd (on Kailua Bay) **808/329–1493** • dinner only • waterfront dining • also bar • live entertainment • patio

Gyms & Health Clubs

Hawaii Healing Ohana Spa 75-5799 Ali'i Dr A3 (Ali'i Sunset Plaza) **808/331–1050**

Kamuela

Accommodations

Waimea Views Guest House 65-1546 Kawaihae Rd (at Paki Pl) **808/885–8559** • gay/ straight • peaceful guesthouse on the slopes of Mauna Kea • kids ok • WiFi • wheelchair access • women-owned

Kehena

Accommodations

Kehena Beach Guesthouse 12-7114 Waioleka St **808/965–8625** • gay/ straight • non-smoking • gay-owned • $55

Na'alehu

Accommodations

Margo's Corner near South Point **808/929–9614** • cottage & 4 campsites • full brkfst & dinner • kids ok • sauna • WiFi • lesbian-owned • $90-130

Pahoa

Accommodations

Aloha Inn Hawaii **808/965–2211** • mostly women • ocean view • retreat on 4 acres • cooking & massage available • nonsmoking • wheelchair access • lesbian-owned • $60-120

Coconut Cottage B&B 13-1139 Leilani Ave (at Oneloa St) **808/965–0973, 866/204–7444** • gay/ straight • centrally located btwn Hilo & Volcanoes Nat'l Park • gay-owned • $110-140

Dakini Gardens & Retreat **808/965–9523** • gay/ straight • cottage • swimming at beach • hot tub • nonsmoking • women-owned • $120/ night & $660/ week (6 nights)

Green Fire Productions 14-4707 Ewa Ln (Kapoho Beach Estates) **808/965–1733** • women only • artesiian ocean pond • nonsmoking • lesbian-owned • commitment ceremonies and Hawaiian Blue Huna magic • $200

Hale 'Ae Kai Guesthouse 13-6768 Kapoho-Kalapana Beach Rd **808/936–8856** • gay/ straight • kids ok • nonsmoking • WiFi • lesbian-owned • $100 (double) & $25 each additional person

Hale 'Ohai 415/255–2497 (CA #) • gay/ straight • unique modern rental home amid giant monkeypod ('ohai) trees • 15-minute walk to clothing-optional beach • nonsmoking • gay-owned • $135-150

Kalani Oceanside Retreat **808/965–7828, 800/800–6886** • gay/ straight • coastal wellness retreat & spa • pool • nudity • nonsmoking • WiFi • food served • wheelchair access • $40 (camping), $110-265 (retreat)

Pamalu—Hawaiian Country House **808/965–0830** • gay/ straight • country retreat on 5 secluded acres • pool • near hiking • snorkeling • warm ponds • kids ok if family rents whole house • nonsmoking • WiFi • gay-owned • $85-150

➤ **Rainbow's Inn, Adventures & Retreat Center** **808/965–9011** • gay/ straight • B&B hideaway • large no-chemical pool • hot tub • kids/ pets ok • nonsmoking • wheelchair access • offers activity desk to plan your Hawaii experience • see also Rainbow Adventures • lesbian-owned • $85-135/ night, weekly & monthly rates available

Entertainment & Recreation

Kehena Beach off Hwy 137 (trailhead at 19-mile marker phone booth) • lava rock trail to clothing-optional black-sand beach

Rainbow Adventures **808/965–9011** • custom-made remote land & sea excursions • women's events • lesbian-owned

Volcano Village

Accommodations

The Chalet Kilauea Collection 19-4178 Wright Rd **808/967–7786, 800/937–7786** • gay-friendly • full brkfst • hot tub • nonsmoking • $60-735

Hale Ohia Cottages **808/967–7986, 800/455–3803** • gay/ straight • fireplaces • rainforest • WiFi • gay-owned • $109-189

Kulana: The Affordable Artists Sanctuary
808/985–9055 • mostly women • artist retreat
• camping, cabins & guest rooms available •
no smoking, drugs or alcohol • kids ok •
women-owned • $15 (camping), $18-40
(cabin); see website (www.discoverkulana.com)
for visitor-to-resident-transition guidelines

Volcano Artist Cottage 19-3834 Old
Volcano Rd (at Wright Rd) 808/985–8979 •
gay-friendly • kids/ pets ok • WiFi • $129-863

CAFES

Ono Cafe 19-3834 Old Volcano Rd (at Wright
Rd) 808/985–8979 • 10am-4pm

KAUAI

Anahola

ACCOMMODATIONS

Mahina Kai Ocean Villa 4933 Aliomanu Rd
808/822–9451, 800/337–1134 • gay/ straight •
pool • hot tub • nudity • nonsmoking • gay-
owned • $175-325

Hanalei

NIGHTCLUBS

Tahiti Nui 5–5134 Kuhio Hwy (near Hanalei
Center) 808/826–6277 • 11am-2am • gay-
friendly • dancing/DJ • live music most nights
• karaoke • also restaurant • Italian/ local •
wheelchair access

Kapaa

ACCOMMODATIONS

17 Palms Kauai 808/822–5659,
888/725–6799 • gay/ straight • 2 secluded
cottages 200 steps from beach • kids ok •
nonsmoking • wheelchair access • gay-owned
• $135-245

Fern Grotto Inn 4561 Kuamoo Rd (at Kuhio
Hwy) 808/821–9836 • gay/ straight • cottages
on the banks of the Wailua River • kids ok •
nonsmoking • $69-199

Mohala Ke Ola B&B Retreat 5663 Ohelo
Rd (at Kuamoo Rd/ Hwy 580) 808/823–6398,
888/465–2824 • gay-friendly • pool • jacuzzi •
nonsmoking • WiFi • gay-owned • $115-140

RESTAURANTS

Eggbert's 4–484 Kuhio Hwy (in Coconut
Plantation Marketplace) 808/822–4422 •
7am-2pm • also Hula Girl Bar & Grill for
dinner

Mema 4-369 Kuhio Hwy (in shopping
center) 808/823–0899 • lunch Mon-Fri, dinner
nightly • Thai & Chinese • BYOB

Kilauea

ACCOMMODATIONS

Kauai Vacation Hideaway North Shore
808/828–0228, 888/858–6562 • lesbians/ gay
men • 2 private homes on upscale 3-acres •
overlooking ocean • private path to secluded
beach • jacuzzi • kids ok • nonsmoking •
wheelchair access • $295-475

Lihue

ACCOMMODATIONS

Kauai Beach Resort 4331 Kauai Beach Dr
808/245–1955, 866/971–2782 • gay-friendly •
pool • waterslide • also restaurant/ bar • nonsmoking • WiFi

Poipu Beach

ACCOMMODATIONS

**Poipu Plantation B&B Inn & Vacation
Rental Suites** 1792 Pe'e Rd 808/742–6757,
800/634–0263 • gay/ straight • rooms &
cottages • full brkfst • hot tub • near beach •
kids ok • WiFi • gay-owned • $125-220

Princeville

ACCOMMODATIONS

Kauai Oceanfront Condo 5300 Ka Haku Rd
610/793–7539 • gay/ straight • pool •
nonsmoking • $1,390-1,575/ week

Puunene

RESTAURANTS

Roy's Poipu Bar & Grill 2360 Kiahuna
Plantation Dr 808/742–5000 • 5:30pm-
9:30pm • Hawaiian fusion

Wailua

RESTAURANTS

Caffe Coco 4–369 Kuhio Hwy 808/822–7990
• lunch Tue-Fri, dinner nightly, clsd Mon • art
gallery • live music nightly • patio • BYOB

Waimea

ACCOMMODATIONS

Aston Waimea Plantation Cottages
808/338–1625, 877/997–6667 • gay-friendly •
seaside cottages from restored plantation
homes • swimming • kids ok • WiFi • $198-
800

MAUI

INFO LINES & SERVICES

Both Sides Now • all-inclusive LGBT community organization • resources • events

Hana

ACCOMMODATIONS

The Guest Houses at Malanai Hana Hwy **808/248-8818** • gay-friendly • 2 guesthouses • nonsmoking • gay-owned • $225-275

Hana Accommodations 808/248-7868, 800/228-4262 • gay/ straight • studios & tropical cottages • kids ok • gay-owned • $68-170

Huelo

ACCOMMODATIONS

Cliff's Edge 808/268-4530, 866/262-6284 • gay-friendly • rental homes, suites & cottages • pool • WiFi • $185-350

Kaanapali

ACCOMMODATIONS

The Royal Lahaina Resort 2780 Kekaa Dr **808/661-3611, 800/214-5000** • gay-friendly • full-service resort • restaurants • pool • wheelchair access • $200+

Kihei

ACCOMMODATIONS

Anfora's Dreams 323/467-2991, 800/788-5046 • gay/ straight • rental condo near ocean • hot tub • pool • gay-owned • $89-135

Eva Villa 815 Kumulani Dr **808/874-6407, 800/884-1845** • gay-friendly • B&B • near Wailea beaches • hot tub • pool • WiFi • kids over 12 yrs ok • wheelchair access • $135-175

Koa Lagoon 800 S Kihei Rd **808/879-3002, 800/367-8030** • gay-friendly • oceanfront suites • pool • WiFi • wheelchair access • $140-200

➤ **Maui Sunseeker Resort** 551 S Kihei Rd (at Wailana Place) **808/879-1261, 800/532-6284** • lesbians/ gay men • ocean views • nudity allowed • nonsmoking • WiFi • gay-owned • $105-395

MAUI SUNSEEKER

Maui's Largest Lesbian and Gay Resort

mauisunseeker.com   800.532.6284

Two Mermaids on Maui B&B 2840 Umalu Pl **808/874-8687, 800/598-9550** • gay/straight • jacuzzi • pool • near beach • nonsmoking • lesbian-owned • $115-140

NIGHTCLUBS

Oceans Bar & Grill 1819 S Kihei Rd (in Kukui Mall) **808/891-2414** • 10pm-2am • gay-friendly • dancing/DJ • food served • live shows • karaoke

CAFES

Cafe at La Plage 2395 S Kihei Rd (at Kam Beach I) **808/875-7668** • 7am-5pm, till 3pm Sun

RESTAURANTS

Jawz Tacos 1279 S Kihei Rd **808/874-8226** • 11am-9pm • fresh fish tacos

Stella Blues 1279 S Kihei Rd (in Azeka II Shopping Center) **808/874-3779** • 7:30am-11pm • live music • wheelchair access

EROTICA

The Love Shack 1913 S Kihei Rd **808/875-0303** • intimate apparel • DVDs • gifts

Kula

ACCOMMODATIONS

The Upcountry B&B 4925 Lower Kula Rd (at Copp St) **808/878-8083** • gay-friendly • jacuzzi • pets ok • WiFi • wheelchair access • $150

Lahaina

RESTAURANTS

Betty's Beach Cafe 505 Front St **808/662-0300** • 8am-9pm • full bar

Lahaina Coolers 180 Dickenson St **808/661-7082** • 8am-1am • patio

RETAIL SHOPS

Skin Deep Tattoo 626 Front St (across from the Banyan Tree) **808/661-8531** • 10am-10pm, till 8pm Sun

Makawao

ACCOMMODATIONS

Hale Ho'okipa Inn B&B 32 Pakani Pl **808/572-6698, 877/572-6698** • gay-friendly • restored Hawaiian plantation home • nonsmoking • WiFi • wheelchair access • woman-owned • $125-170

RESTAURANTS

Casanova Restaurant & Deli 1188 Makawao Ave **808/572-0220** • lunch & dinner • Italian • full bar till 2am • gay-friendly • ladies night Wed • live music & shows Wed-Sat

Makena

ENTERTAINMENT & RECREATION

Little Beach at Makena • lesbians/gay men • Pilani Hwy S to Wailea, right at Wailea Ike Dr, left on Wailea Alanui Dr to public beach, then take trail up hill at right end of beach

Wailuku

ACCOMMODATIONS

Maalaea Kai Condo 70 Hauoli St (Maalaea Village) **562/301-3820** • gay-friendly • oceanfront 2-bdrm condo • WiFi • $130-210

MOLOKAI

Kaunakakai

RESTAURANTS

Kanemitsu Bakery & Coffee Shop 79 Ala Malama St **808/553-5855** • 5:30am-5pm, clsd Tue • great sweet bread

OAHU

PUBLICATIONS

Odyssey Magazine Hawaii **808/955-5959** • everything you need to know about gay Hawaii

Haleiwa

ACCOMMODATIONS

Kelea Surf Spa **949/492-7263** • women only • surf spa on Oahu's North Shore • open during spring only • 18+

Honolulu

INFO LINES & SERVICES

Gay/ Lesbian AA 310 Pa'okalani Ave, Room 203A **808/946-1438** • 8pm daily

ACCOMMODATIONS

Aqua Coconut Plaza 450 Lewers St (at Ala Wai Canal) **808/923-8828** • gay-friendly • boutique hotel in the heart of Waikiki • near the Kuhio (gay) District • pool • kitchenettes • wheelchair access

Aqua Palms & Spa 1850 Ala Moana Blvd (at Kalia & Ena) **808/947-7256, 866/406-2782** • gay-friendly • boutique hotel w/ retro-Hawaiian style • pool • kids ok • nonsmoking • full spa • wheelchair access • $129-210

Aston Waikiki Circle Hotel 2464 Kalakaua Ave (at Uluniu St, Waikiki) **808/923-1571, 877/997-6667** • gay-friendly • hotel overlooking Waikiki beach • kids welcome • nonsmoking • $180-220

Aston Waikiki Joy Hotel 320 Lewers St (at Kalakaua Ave, Waikiki) **808/923-2300, 877/997-6667** • gay-friendly • boutique hotel • pool • jacuzzis • near beach • nonsmoking • cafe • also bar • karaoke • wheelchair access • $180-315

The Cabana at Waikiki 2551 Cartwright Rd (off Kapahulu Ave) **808/926-5555, 877/902-2121** • popular • mostly gay men • 1-bdrm suites w/ kitchens & lanais • hot tub • gay-owned • $99-199

Hotel Renew 129 Paoakalani Ave (at Lemon Rd, Waikiki) **808/687-7700** • gay-friendly • WiFi • $175-235

Waikiki GLBT Vacation Rentals **808/922-1659** • gay-friendly • ask for Walt Flood • pool • nonsmoking • wheelchair access • $75-250

Waikiki Grand Hotel 134 Kapahulu Ave **808/923-1814, 808/923-1511** • gay/ straight rentals above Hula's Bar • near gay beach • Diamond Head views • nonsmoking • women-owned • $90-299

BARS

In Between 2155 Lau'ula St (off Lewers, across from Planet Hollywood, Waikiki) **808/926-7060** • 4pm-2am • mostly gay men • neighborhood bar • karaoke

Lo Jax 2256 Kuhio Ave, 2nd flr (at Seaside, Waikiki) **808/922-1422** • noon-2am • lesbians/ gay men • neighborhood bar • sports bar • food served • WiFi

Honolulu

WHERE THE GIRLS ARE:
Where else? On the beach. Or cruising Kuhio Ave.

LGBT PRIDE:
June, web: www.gayhawaii.com.

ANNUAL EVENTS:
April - Merrie Monarch Festival, hula competition in Hilo, web: www.kalena.com/merriemonarch.
April-May - Golden Week, celebration of Japanese culture.
May - Honolulu Rainbow Film Festival 808/675-8428, web: www.hglcf.org.
September - Aloha Festival, web: alohafestivals.com.

CITY INFO:
800/464-2924, web: www.gohawaii.com.
Also www.visit-oahu.com

BEST VIEW:
Helicopter tour.

WEATHER:
Usually paradise perfect, but humid. It rarely gets hotter than the upper 80ºs.

TRANSIT:
Charley's 808/947-0077.
The Bus 808/848-5555, web: www.thebus.org.

ATTRACTIONS:
Bishop Museum 808/847-3511, web: www.bishopmuseum.org.
Foster Botanical Gardens. 808/522-7066, web: www.hawaiimuseums.org/mc/isoahu_foster.htm.
Hanauma Bay.
Honolulu Academy of Arts 808/532-8700, web: www.honoluluacademy.org.
'Iolani Palace 808/522-0822, web: www.iolanipalace.org.
Polynesian Cultural Center 800/367-7060 or 808/293-3333, web: www.polynesia.com.
USS Arizona Memorial, 808/422-3200, web: www.nps.gov/valr.
Waimea Falls Park.

Tapa's Restaurant & Lanai Bar 407 Seaside, 2nd flr (at Kuhio Ave) **808/921–2288** • 9am-2am • gay/ straight • lanai bar • karaoke • also restaurant • East-West fusion • some veggie • gay-owned

Wang Chung's 2410 Koa Ave (at Kaiulani) **808/921–9176** • 2pm-2am • lesbians/ gay men • karaoke

NIGHTCLUBS

Bar 7 1344 Kona St (at Piikoi Rd) **808/955–2640** • 9pm-4am • gay/ straight • dancing/DJ • mostly Asian American • drag shows Sat

Chemisstry 197 Sand Island Rd (at Sand Island Sports Club) **808/847–5001** • 10:30pm-2am Fri only • mostly women • dancing/DJ

Downe Towne for Women 35 N Hotel St (at Bar 35) **808/537–3535** • 9pm-2am 1st Sat only • mostly women • dancing/DJ

Fusion Waikiki 2260 Kuhio Ave, 2nd flr (at Seaside) **808/924–2422** • 10pm-4am, from 8pm Fri-Sat • popular • mostly gay men • dancing/DJ • transgender-friendly • live shows • karaoke Mon-Tue • drag shows • videos

Hula's Bar & Lei Stand 134 Kapahulu Ave (2nd flr of Waikiki Grand Hotel) **808/923–0669** • 10am-2am • popular • mostly gay men • dancing/DJ • food served • live shows • videos • young crowd • weekly catamaran cruise • WiFi

CAFES

Cafe Hula Girl/Tapa's II 1888 Kalakaua Ave, C106 (in Waikiki Landmark Building) **808/979–2299** • 9am-10pm • full bar • patio • gay-owned

Leonard's Bakery 933 Kapahulu Ave **808/737–5591** • 5:30am-9pm, till 10pm Fri-Sat • irresistible malasadas & doughnuts

Mocha Java Cafe 1200 Ala Moana Blvd (in Ward Center) **808/591–9023** • 8am-9pm, till 6pm Sun • plenty veggie • outdoor seating

RESTAURANTS

Alan Wong's 1857 S King St (at Pumehana St) **808/949–2526** • dinner only • upscale, romantic Hawaiian dining

Arancino di Mare 2552 Kalakaua Ave (in Waikiki Beach Marriott) **808/931–6273**

Cafe Che Pasta 1001 Bishop St, Ste 108 (enter off Alakea St) **808/524–0004** • lunch & dinner, clsd Sat-Sun • full bar

Cafe Sistina 1314 S King St **808/596–0061** • lunch Mon-Fri, dinner nightly • northern Italian • some veggie • full bar • live music wknds • wheelchair access

Cha Cha Cha 342 Seaside Ave **808/923–7797** • 6am-midnight • Mexican • happy hour

Cheeseburger in Paradise 2500 Kalakaua Blvd **808/923–3731** • 7am-11pm • full bar

Eggs 'n' Things 343 Saratoga Rd **808/949–0820** • 6am-2pm, 5pm-10pm

House Without A Key 2199 Kalia Rd (at Lewers St, at Halekulani Hotel) **808/923–2311** • 7am-9pm • stunning sunset views • Hawaiian music nightly

Hula Grill 2335 Kalakaua Ave (in Outrigger Hotel) **808/923–4852**

Indigo 1121 Nu'uanu Ave **808/521–2900** • lunch Tue-Fri, dinner Tue-Sat • Eurasian • live music nightly

Keo's in Waikiki 2028 Kuhio Ave **808/951-9355** • 5pm-10pm • popular • reservations advised

La Cucaracha 2446 Koa Ave **808/924–3366** • noon-11pm • Mexican • full bar

Liliha Bakery 515 N Kuakini St (at Liliha St) **808/531–1651** • open 24hrs, clsd Mon • delicious diner fare & baked goods

Lulu's 2586 Kalakaua Ave **808/926–5222** • 7am-4am • full bar

Rock Island Cafe 131 Kaiulani Ave (off Kalakaua, in King's Village Waikiki) **808/923–8033** • old-fashioned soda fountain

Singha Thai 1910 Ala Moana Blvd **808/941–2898, 800/482–8424** • 4pm-10pm • Thai dancers

Tiki's Grill & Bar 2570 Kalakaua Ave (in ResortQuest Hotel) **808/923–8454**

ENTERTAINMENT & RECREATION

Diamond Head Beach Diamond Head Rd (at Beach Rd) • gay/ straight • take road from lighthouse to beach • some nude sunbathing

Dolphin Quest 5000 Kahala Ave (at Kahala Hotel & Resort) **808/739–8918, 800/248–3316** • variety of programs for all ages to interact one-on-one w/ dolphins

Girls Who Surf 2030 Auahi St, Bldg 4, Ste 4 (Ward Shopping Ctr) **808/772–4583** • surf lessons • beginners welcome

Honolulu Gay/ Lesbian Cultural Foundation 758 Kapahulu Ave #168 **808/728–3026** • last wknd of May annual Honolulu Rainbow Film Festival • art exhibits • concerts • plays • call for events

LikeHike 808/455–8193 • gay hiking tours every other Sun • also gay kayaking trips • call for info & locations

Rainbow Sailing Charters 808/347–0235 • lesbians/ gay men • day & overnight sailing adventures • whale-watching • snorkeling • sunset cocktail cruises • commitment ceremonies • lesbian-owned

RETAIL SHOPS

Eighty Percent Straight 134 Kapahulu Ave, Ste B (in Waikiki Grand Hotel) 808/923–9996 • 10am-11pm, till midnight Fri-Sat, noon-11pm Sun • LGBT clothing • books • videos • cards • toys

PUBLICATIONS

Expression 808/393–7994 • monthly glossy LGBT magazine

Odyssey Magazine Hawaii 808/955–5959 • everything you need to know about gay Hawaii

EROTICA

Suzie's Secrets 1370 Kapiolani Blvd 808/949–4383

Velvet Video 2155 Lau'ula St, 2nd flr (above In Between, Waikiki) 808/924–0868 • 24hrs • videos for sale & rent • preview booths • toys

Kaaawa

RESTAURANTS

Crouching Lion Inn Bar & Grill 51-666 Kamehameha Hwy 808/237–8981 • 11am-10pm • full bar • live shows • gay-owned

Windward Coast

ACCOMMODATIONS

Ali'i Bluffs Windward B&B 46–251 Ikiiki St, Kane'ohe 808/235–1124, 800/235–1151 • gay/ straight • pool • nonsmoking • gay-owned • $70-80

IDAHO

Statewide

PUBLICATIONS

Diversity Newsmagazine 208/336–3870 • statewide LGBT newspaper • monthly

Boise

INFO LINES & SERVICES

The Community Center 305 E 37th St, Garden City 208/336–3870 • volunteer staff

ACCOMMODATIONS

Courtyard Boise Downtown 222 S Broadway Ave 208/331–2700, 800/321–2211 • gay-friendly • nonsmoking • $149+

Hotel 43 981 Grove St 800/243–4622 • gay/straight • restaurant & bar • WiFi • $119+

BARS

The Lucky Dog 2223 W Fairview Ave (at 23rd) 208/333–0074 • 2pm-2am, from noon wknds • mostly gay men • neighborhood bar • patio • lounge • WiFi

Neurolux 111 N 11th St (at W Idaho) 208/343–0886 • 1pm-2am • gay-friendly • dancing/DJ • live music

Pitchers and Pints 1108 W Front St. • 5pm-2am • gay/ straight • neigborhood bar • scruffy outside but nice inside & nice patio • gay-owned

NIGHTCLUBS

The Balcony Club 150 N 8th St #226 (at Idaho) 208/336–1313 • 4pm-2am • lesbians/ gay men • popular • dancing/DJ • karaoke • theme nights • wheelchair access • gay-owned

CAFES

Big City Coffee 5517 W State St 208/853–9161 • 6am-6pm, till 4pm Sun

Flying M Coffeehouse 500 W Idaho St (at 5th St) 208/345–4320 • 6:30am-11pm, from 7:30am wknds • WiFi

Lucy's Coffee & Espresso 1079 Broadway Ave 208/344–5907 • 6am-10pm, 7am-8pm Sun • organic, fair trade coffee • gourmet pastries • WiFi

Tully's 794 Broad St 208/343–2953 • 7am-9pm, till 11pm Fri-Sat, 9am-8pm Sun • WiFi

RESTAURANTS

Lucky 13 Pizza 3662 S Eckert Rd 208/344–6967 • 11am-10pm

ENTERTAINMENT & RECREATION

The Flicks 646 Fulton St 208/342–4222 • opens 4pm, from noon Fri-Sun • 4 movie theaters • food served • beer/ wine • patio • wheelchair access

BOOKSTORES

Crone's Cupboard 712 N Orchard 208/333–0831 • 11am-8pm, clsd Sun-Mon • Wiccan • New Age • feminist/ lesbian books & art

RETAIL SHOPS

The Record Exchange 1105 W Idaho St (at 11th) 208/344–8010 • 9am-9pm, till 7pm Sun • gifts • music • also cafe

See Jane Run Sports 814 W Idaho St 208/338–5263 • 11am-7pm, noon-5pm Sun • women's athletic apparel

EROTICA

The O!Zone 1615 Broadway Ave
208/395-1977, 888/326-3713 • noon-7pm, till 5pm Sun

Pleasure Boutique 5022 Fairview Ave (at Orchard) **208/433-1161** • toys, videos

Coeur d'Alene

see also Spokane, Washington

ACCOMMODATIONS

The Clark House on Hayden Lake 5250 E Hayden Lake Rd, Hayden Lake **208/772-3470, 800/765-4593** • popular • gay-friendly • mansion on a wooded 12-acre estate • full brkfst • also fine dining • hot tub • nonsmoking • WiFi • gay-owned • $149-250

BARS

Mik-N-Mac's 406 N 4th St (at Wallace) **208/667-4858** • 4pm-2am, till 1am Mon • gay/ straight • neighborhood bar • dancing/DJ • karaoke • live shows

Lava Hot Springs

see also Pocatello

ACCOMMODATIONS

Lava Hot Springs Inn **208/776-5830, 800/527-5830** • gay-friendly • full brkfst • mineral hot pools • kids/ pets ok • nonsmoking • WiFi • $79-199

BOOKSTORES

Aura Soma Lava 196 E Main St **208/776-5800, 800/757-1233** • 7am-8pm • metaphysical & LGBT books

Moscow

INFO LINES & SERVICES

Inland Oasis LGBTA Center 412 E 3rd St (Friendship Hall, 1912 Bldg) • 7pm Sun • potluck • check inlandoasis.org for more info

BOOKSTORES

Bookpeople 521 S Main (btwn 5th & 6th) **208/882-7957** • 9am-8pm • general

Nampa

CAFES

Flying M Coffeegarage 1314 2nd St S **208/467-5533** • 6:30am-11pm, from 7:30am wknds • entertainment

Pocatello

NIGHTCLUBS

Club Charleys 331 E Center St **208/232-9606** • 5pm-2am, from 7pm Sun • lesbians/ gay men • dancing/DJ • live shows • karaoke • drag shows • wheelchair access

CAFES

Main St Coffee & News 234 N Main St (btwn Lander & Clark) **208/234-9834** • 6:30am-4pm, from 8am Sat, from 9am Sun

EROTICA

The Silver Fox 143 S 2nd St (at Center) **208/234-2477**

Twin Falls

CAFES

Annie's Lavender & Coffee Cafe 591 Addison Ave W (at 8th St) **208/736-2003** • 6am-6pm, till 4pm Sat, 8am-2pm Sun • food served • wheelchair access

RESTAURANTS

Pizza Planet 720 Main St (at 8th St), Buhl **208/543-8560** • 11am-9:30pm • also video/ DVD store

ILLINOIS

Alsip

see also Chicago

EROTICA

Slightly Sinful 12300 S Cicero (at 123rd) **708/388-6902**

Alton

see also St Louis, Missouri

NIGHTCLUBS

Bubby & Sissy's 602 Belle St (at 6th) **618/465-4773** • 3pm-2am, till 3am Fri-Sat, clsd Mon • lesbians/ gay men • dancing/DJ • drag shows • karaoke • wheelchair access

Arlington Heights

see Chicago

Aurora

see also Chicago

EROTICA

Denmark Book Store 1300 US Hwy 30 (2 miles S of Rte 34) **630/898-9838** • 24hrs

Belleville

see also St Louis, Missouri

Bloomington

INFO LINES & SERVICES

Connections Community Center 313 N Main St (at Monroe St) **309/827–2437, 866/694–5297** • call for hours & meeting times • extensive LGBT library • WiFi

BARS

Bistro 316 N Main St (at Jefferson) **309/829–2278** • 8pm-1am, from 4:30pm Fri, till 2am Fri-Sat • lesbians/ gay men • dancing/DJ Wed-Sat • WiFi • wheelchair access

CAFES

Coffee Hound 407 N Main St **309/827–7575** • 6:30am-6pm, 8am-5pm Sun • WiFi

Kelly's Bakery & Cafe 113 N Center St **309/820–1200** • 7am-6pm, till 2pm Sat, clsd Sun

Blue Island

see also Chicago

NIGHTCLUBS

Club Krave 13126 S Western (at Grove) **708/597–8379** • 8pm-2am, till 3am Fri-Sat, clsd Mon • lesbians/ gay men • neighborhood bar • dancing/DJ • transgender-friendly • karaoke • cabaret • drag shows • wheelchair access

Bradley

RESTAURANTS

La Villetta 801 W Broadway St **815/939–4960** • 11am-9pm, till 8pm Sun • Italian

EROTICA

Slightly Sinful 101 N Kinzie Ave (at Broadway), Alsip **815/937–5744**

Calumet City

see also Chicago & Hammond, Indiana

Carbondale

INFO LINES & SERVICES

AA Lesbian/ Gay 618/549-4633

NIGHTCLUBS

Club Traz 213 E Main St **618/549–4270** • 9pm-2am, clsd Mon-Tue & Th • gay-friendly • neighborhood bar • dancing/DJ • live shows • videos • gay-owned

Flirt 1215 E Walnut (at Sky Bar) • monthly party • check myspace.com/melissathebartender for dates • lesbians/ gay men • dancing/DJ • drag shows

Champaign/ Urbana

ACCOMMODATIONS

Sylvia's Irish Inn 312 W Green St, Urbana **217/384–4800** • gay-friendly • full brkfst • nonsmoking • WiFi • $85-200

BARS

Mike 'N Molly's 105 N Market St, Champaign **217/355–1236** • 4pm-2am • gay-friendly • live music • dancing/DJ • beer garden

NIGHTCLUBS

Chester Street 63 Chester St (at Water St), Champaign **217/356–5607** • 5pm-2am • lesbians/ gay men • dancing/DJ • drag show Sun • gay-owned • wheelchair access

CAFES

Aroma Cafe 118 N Neil St, Champaign **217/356–3200** • 7am-10pm, from 8am wknds • live music Th

Cafe Kopi 109 N Walnut, Champaign **217/359–4266** • 7am-midnight • full bar & menu • nonsmoking • WiFi

Espresso Royale 602 E Daniel (at 6th St), Champaign **217/328–1112** • 7am-midnight

Pekara Bakery & Bistro 116 N Neil St, Champaign **217/359–4500** • 7am-9pm, from 8am Sun

RESTAURANTS

Boltini Lounge 211 N Neil St, Champaign **217/378–8001** • 4pm-2am, clsd Sun • also full bar • upscale

Carmon's 415 N Neil St (at Washington), Champaign **217/352–5880** • 11am-10pm • full bar • wheelchair access • full bar

The Courier Cafe 111 N Race St, Urbana **217/328–1811** • 7am-11pm

Dos Reales 1407 N Prospect Ave, Champaign **217/351–6879** • 11am-10pm • Mexican

Farren's Pub & Eatery 308 N Randolph St, Champaign **217/359–6977** • 11am-9pm, till 10pm Fri, from noon wknds • American • full bar

Fiesta Cafe 216 S 1st St (at White, near U of IL campus), Champaign **217/352–5902** • 11am-11pm, bar till 1am • Mexican • gay-owned

The Great Impasta 156C Lincoln Sq, Urbana 217/359–7377 • 11am-9pm, till 10pm Fri, 5pm-10pm Sat, clsd Sun

Radio Maria 119 N Walnut St, Champaign 217/398–7729 • lunch Tue-Fri, dinner Tue-Sat, brunch Sun, clsd Mon • eclectic Mexican cuisine • also tapas bar till 2am

Silvercreek 402 N Race St, Urbana 217/328–3402 • lunch & dinner, brunch Sun

ENTERTAINMENT & RECREATION

Amasong PO Box 902, Urbana 61803 217/328–6828 • lesbian/ feminist chorus

BOOKSTORES

Jane Addams Book Shop 208 N Neil St (at University), Champaign 217/356–2555 • 10am-5pm, till 6pm Fri, from 1pm Sun • full-service antiquarian bookstore w/ children's room • LGBT & women's sections

RETAIL SHOPS

Dandelion 9 Taylor St, Champaign 217/355–9333 • 11am-6pm, noon-5pm Fri • vintage & used clothing

GYMS & HEALTH CLUBS

Refinery 2302 W John St, Champaign 217/355–4444 • gay-friendly

CHICAGO

Chicago is divided into 5 geographical areas:
Chicago—Overview
Chicago—North Side
Chicago—Boystown/ Lakeview
Chicago—Near North
Chicago—South Side

Chicago—Overview

includes some listings for Greater Chicagoland; please check individual cities like Oak Park as well

INFO LINES & SERVICES

AA/ Newtown Alano Club 909 W Belmont Ave, 2nd flr (btwn Clark & Sheffield) 773/529–0321 • 5pm-11pm, from 8:30am wknds • hosts a variety of recovery groups • wheelchair access

Affinity 5650 S Woodlawn Ave (at First Unitarian of Hyde Park) 773/324–0377 • nonprofit "serving Chicago's black lesbian & bisexual women's community" through "education, social & community collaborations"

The Center on Halsted 3656 N Halsted St (at Waveland) 773/472–6469, 773/472–1277 (TTY) • 8am-10pm • LGBT center • organic grocery store • cafe • theater • gym • technology center

Center on Halsted Info Line 773/929–4357, 773/871–2273 (LGBT VIOLENCE HOTLINE) • 8am-10pm • live counselors w/ info on wide variety of LGBT issues

ACCOMMODATIONS

Chicago Women's Residence 1957 S Spaulding Ave (at S 21st) 773/542–9126 • women only • furnished rooms in women's residence • WiFi • please call ahead • lesbian-owned • $35-55

NIGHTCLUBS

Doll House Entertainment • hot women's parties at clubs around the city • www.myspace.com/lezdollhouse

ENTERTAINMENT & RECREATION

About Face Theatre 773/784–8565 • roving LGBT theater company w/ popular Youth Theatre as well

Artemis Singers 773/764–4465 • lesbian feminist chorus

Bailiwick Arts Center 1229 W Belmont Ave 773/883–1090 (BOX OFFICE #) • many LGBT-themed productions w/ popular Pride Series & Lesbian Theater Initiative

Boi Toiz • Chicago's drag king troupe • check local listings for performances

Cafe Pride 716 W Addison St (at Broadway, at Lake View Presbyterian) 773/281–2655 (CHURCH #) • 8pm-midnight Fri • LGBT coffeehouse • for youth (17-24) only

Chicago Neighborhood Tours 77 E Randolph St (at Michigan Ave, at Chicago Cultural Center) 312/742–1190 • gay-friendly • the best way to make the Windy City your kind of town

Chicago Sky UIC Pavilion 877/329–9622 • check out the Women's Nat'l Basketball Association while you're in Chicago

GayCo 3656 N Halsted (at the Center) 312/458–9400, 773/478–6376 • sketch-comedy revues based on LGBT themes

The Hancock Observatory 875 N Michigan Ave (in John Hancock Center) 312/751–3681, 888/875–8439 • 9am-11pm, renovated 94th-flr observatory w/ outside Skywalk

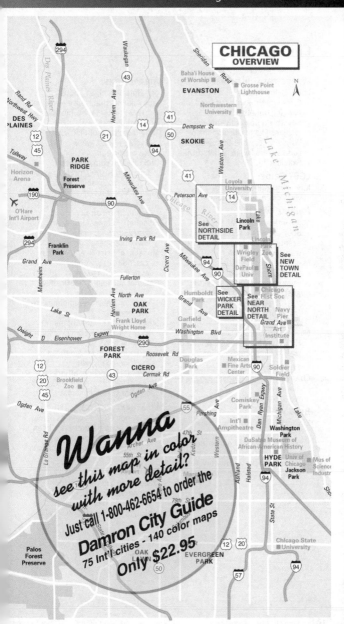

Chicago

WHERE THE GIRLS ARE:

In the Belmont area—on Halsted or Clark streets—with the boys, or hanging out elsewhere in Boystown. Upwardly-mobile lesbians live in Lincoln Park or Wrigleyville, while their working-class sisters live in Andersonville (way north).

LGBT PRIDE:

June. 773/348-8243, web: www.chicagopridecalendar.org.

ANNUAL EVENTS:

May - International Mr. Leather 800/545-6753. Weekend of events and contest on Sunday, web: www.imrl.com.

May-June- Chicago Blues Festival 312/744-3315, web: www.chicagobluesfestival.org.

August - Northalsted Market Days 773/883-0500, web: www.northalsted.com/ market_days.php.

November - Chicago Lesbian & Gay Film Festival 773/293-1447, web: www.reelingfilmfestival.org.

CITY INFO:

Chicago Office of Tourism 877/244-2246, web: www.explorechicago.org.

BEST VIEW:

Skydeck of the 110-story Sears Tower, web: www.theskydeck.com or the open-air observation deck at the John Hancock Observatory, web: www.hancockobservatory.com.

ATTRACTIONS:

900 North Michigan Shops.

Jane Addams Hull-House Museum 312/413-5353, www.hullhouse-museum.org.

The Art Institute of Chicago 312/443-3600, web: www.artic.edu.

DuSable Museum of African American History 773/947-0600, web: www.dusablemuseum.org.

Historic Water Tower.

LaSalle Bank Theatre (formerly Schubert Theatre).

Museum of Contemporary Art 312/280-2660, web: www.mcachicago.org.

Museum of Science and Industry 773/684-1414, web: www.msichicago.org.

National Museum of Mexican Art 312/738-1503, web: www.nationalmuseumofmexica-nart.org.

Steppenwolf Theatre Company, 312/335-1650, web: www.step-penwolf.org.

Terra Foundation for American Art, 312/664-3939, web: www.terraamericanart.org.

Wrigley Field, 773/404-CUBS, web: chicago.cubs.mlb.com.

WEATHER:

"The Windy City" earned its name. Winter temperatures have been known to be as low as -46°. Summers are humid, normally in the 80°s.

TRANSIT:

Yellow Cab 312/ 829-4222.

Continental Airport Express 888/284-3826.

Chicago Transit Authority 312/836-7000, web: www.transitchicago.com.

Metra Rail 312/322-6777, web: www.metrarail.com.

Heartland Cafe 7000 N Glenwood Ave (in Rogers Park) 773/465–8005 • cafe w/ full bar, theater, radio show • lots of live music including performers popular on women's music circuit

Leather Archives & Museum 6418 N Greenview Ave 773/761–9200 • noon-8pm Th-Fri, till 5pm Sat-Sun • membership required (purchase at door)

The Neo-Futurarium 5153 N Ashland Ave 773/275–5255 • alternative theater group

Second City 1616 N Wells St (at North) 312/337–3992, 877/778–4707 • gay-friendly • legendary comedy club • call for reservations

Willis/ Sears Tower Skydeck 233 S Wacker Dr (enter at Jackson Blvd) 312/875–9696 • see the city from the 99th & 103rd floors of North America's tallest building

Windy City Performing Arts 3656 N Halsted 773/404–9242 • includes Windy City Gay Chorus & Aria: Windy City Women's Ensemble

Windy City Rollers 1909 S Laramie (at Cicero Stadium), Cicero • Chicago's female roller derby league • visit www.windycityrollers.com for info

PUBLICATIONS

The Alternative Phone Book 619 W Stratford Pl 773/472–6319 • directory of local businesses

Gay Chicago 773/327–7271 • weekly • extensive resource listings

Identity 773/871–7610 • monthly news & features for LGBTs of color

Nightspots 773/871–7610 • weekly LGBT nightlife magazine

PINK Magazine 773/769–6328, 877/769–7465 • LGBT business directory & lifestyle magazine

Windy City Times 773/871–7610 • weekly LGBT newspaper & calendar guide

Chicago—North Side

ACCOMMODATIONS

House 5863 B&B 5863 N Glenwood (at Ardmore) 773/944–5555 • gay/ straight • nonsmoking • WiFi • gay-owned • $99-189

BARS

The Anvil 1137 W Granville (E of Broadway) 773/973–0006 • 9am-2am • mostly gay men • neighborhood bar • videos

Big Chicks 5024 N Sheridan (btwn Foster & Argyle) 773/728–5511 • 4pm-2am, from 3pm wknds • lesbians/ gay men • neighborhood bar • dancing/DJ • videos • patio • Sun BBQ • WiFi • wheelchair access

Cattle Call 1547 W Bryn Mawr (at Clark) • 4pm-2am • lesbians/ gay men • dancing/DJ • country/ western • drag shows

Crew 4804 N Broadway St (at Lawrence) 773/784–2739 • 11:30am-midnight, 11am-2am Fri-Sun • lesbians/ gay men • sports bar & grill • videos • patio

The Glenwood 6962 N Glenwood Ave (at Morse) 773/764–7363 • 3pm-2am, from noon Sun • lesbians/ gay men • neighborhood sports bar

Green Mill 4802 N Broadway St (at Lawrence) 773/878–5552 • noon-4am, till 5am Sat • gay/ straight • noted jazz venue • hosts the Uptown Poetry Slam

In Fine Spirits 5418 N Clark St (at Rascher Ave) 773/506–9463 • 4pm-midnight, till 2am wknds • wine bar • patio • food served • also wine store

Jackhammer 6406 N Clark St (at Devon) 773/743–5772 • 4pm-4am, till 5am Fri-Sat, from 2pm wknds • mostly gay men • 3 bars • videos • patio

Joie de Vine 1744 W Balmoral (at Paulina St) 773/989–6846 • 5pm-midnight, till 3am Sat • mostly women • wine bar • patio • WiFi • wheelchair access • lesbian-owned

Marty's 1511 W Balmoral Ave (at Clark) 773/561–6425 • 5pm-2am • gay-friendly • upscale wine & martini bar • food served

Scot's 1829 W Montrose (at Damen) 773/528–3253 • 3pm-2am, 11am-3am Sat, till 2am Sun • mostly gay men • neighborhood bar

Sofo 4923 N Clark St (at Argyle) 773/784–7636 • 5pm-2am, 3pm-3am Sat, till 2am Sun • mostly gay men • video bar • backyard beer garden

Spyner's Pub 4623 N Western Ave (at W Eastwood) 773/784–8719 • mostly women • neighborhood bar • karaoke

T's 5025 N Clark St (at Winnemac) 773/784–6000 • 5pm-2am, 11am-3am, till 2am Sun • mostly women • neighborhood bar • also restaurant

Touché 6412 N Clark St (at Devon) 773/465–7400 • 5pm-4am, 3pm-5am Sat, noon-4am Sun • popular • mostly gay men • leather

Wild Pug 4810 N Broadway St (at Lawrence) **773/784-4811** • 4pm-2am • mostly gay men • dancing/DJ

NIGHTCLUBS

Atmosphere 5355 N Clark St (at W Balmoral Ave) **773/784-1100** • 6pm-2am, till 3am Sat, 3pm-2am Sun • lesbians/ gay men • dancing/DJ • cabaret • male dancers Th-Sat • gay-owned

Planet Claire 4000 N Sheridan Rd (at Irving Park, at the Holiday Club) **773/348-9600** (HOLIDAY CLUB #) • 10pm-2am Fri only • gay/ straight • dancing/ DJ • videos • New Wave night

CAFES

Charmer's Cafe 1500 W Jarvis (at Greenview) **773/743-2233** • 6am-10pm, from 7am wknds • lesbians/ gay men • WiFi • wheelchair access

Coffee Chicago 5256 N Broadway St (btwn Berwyn & Foster) **773/784-1305** • 7am-9pm, till 9:30pm Fri, from 8am Sat, till 9pm Sun • soup, sandwiches, smoothies, ice cream • WiFi

KOPI: A Traveler's Cafe 5317 N Clark St (at Summerdale) **773/989-5674** • 8am-11pm, till midnight Fri-Sat, from 9am Sat, from 10am Sun • food served • also boutique & gallery

Metropolis Coffee 1039 W Granville Ave (at Kenmore) **773/764-0400** • 6:30am-8pm, from 7am Sat, from 7:30am Sun • popular • WiFi

RESTAURANTS

Andie's 5253 N Clark (btwn Berwyn & Farragut) **773/784-8616** • 10:30am-midnight, till 10:30pm Sun • eastern Mediterranean • plenty veggie • full bar • wheelchair access

Anteprima 5316 N Clark St (at Summerdale) **773/506-9990** • dinner nightly • Italian

Charlie's Ale House 5308 N Clark St (at Summerdale) **773/751-0140** • 11:30am-1am, 11am-2am Sat, 11am-midnight Sun, brunch Sun • American food • more lesbian wknds

Deluxe Diner/ Maria's 6349 N Clark St (at Devon) **773/743-8244** (DELUXE #), **773/743-9900** (MARIA'S #) • 24hr diner & pizza/ Italian restaurant till 11pm

Fat Cat 4840 N Broadway (at Lawrence Ave) **773/506-3100** • 4pm-2am, from 11am wknds • juicy burgers • full bar

Fireside 5739 N Ravenswood (at Rosehill) **773/561-7433, 877/878-7433** • 11am-4am, till 5am Sat, 10am-4am Sun • Cajun & pizza • patio • full bar

Hamburger Mary's/ Rec Room/ Attic 5400 N Clark St (at Balmoral) **773/784-6969** • opens 11am, from 10am Sun • lesbians/ gay men • also full bar • karaoke • drag shows

Hot Woks Cool Sushi 30 S Michigan Ave (at Madison) **312/345-1234** • 11:30am-8:30pm • sushi/ Thai • plenty veggie

Jin Ju 5203 N Clark St (at Summersdale) **773/334-6377** • dinner only • Korean • also bar

Pauline's 1754 W Balmoral (at Ravenswood) **773/561-8573** • 7am-3pm • hearty brkfsts • home of 5-egg omelette

Reza's Restaurant 5255 N Clark (btwn Berwyn & Farragut) **773/561-1898** • lunch, dinner & wknd brunch • Mediterranean/ Persian • plenty veggie • full bar • wheelchair access

Svea Restaurant 5236 N Clark (btwn Berwyn & Farragut) **773/275-7738** • 7am-2:30pm, till 3:30pm wknds • Swedish/ American comfort food • wheelchair access

Tedino's 5335 N Sheridan (at Broadway) **773/275-8100** • 11am-11pm, till midnight wknds • popular • pizza • full bar • wheelchair access

Thai Pastry & Restaurant 4925 N Broadway St, Unit E (at Argyle) **773/784-5399** • 11am-10pm, till 11pm Fri-Sat

Tweet 5020 N Sheridan Rd (at Argyle) **773/728-5576** • 9am-3pm, clsd Tue • brkfst & brunch • cash only • WiFi

ENTERTAINMENT & RECREATION

Hollywood Beach at Hollywood & Sheridan Sts • popular • "the" gay beach

BOOKSTORES

Women & Children First 5233 N Clark St (at Foster) **773/769-9299** • 11am-7pm, till 9pm Wed-Fri, 10am-7pm Sat, 11am-6pm Sun • popular • wheelchair access • women-owned

RETAIL SHOPS

Enjoy, An Urban General Store 4727 N Lincoln Ave (Lincoln Square) **773/334-8626** • from 11am, from 10am Sat-Sun • cards & gifts • pride items • lesbian-owned

Gaymart 3457 N Halsted St (at Cornelius) **773/929-4272** • 11am-7pm, noon-8pm Fri, till 6pm Sun • lots of kitsch & pride items

Leather 6410 6410 N Clark St (at Devon, btwn Jackhammer & Touché) **773/508-0900, 800/910-0666** • noon-midnight, till 4am Th, till 5am Fri, till 6am Sat, 4pm-midight Sun-Mon • gay-owned

Specialty Video Films 5307 N Clark St (at Berwin Ave) 773/878–3434 • 10am-11pm, till midnight Fri-Sat • foreign, cult, art house, LGBT & erotic videos • gay-owned

GYMS & HEALTH CLUBS

Cheetah Gym 5248 N Clark St (at Foster) 773/728–7777

EROTICA

Early to Bed 5232 N Sheridan Rd (at Foster) 773/271–1219, 866/585–2233 • clsd Mon • transgender-friendly • 18+ • lesbian-owned

Tulip Sex Toy Gallery 1480 W Berwyn (at Clark) 773/275–6110, 877/708–8547 • noon-10pm • sex toys for women • lesbian-owned

Chicago—Boystown/ Lakeview

ACCOMMODATIONS

Best Western Hawthorne Terrace 3434 N Broadway St (at Hawthorne Pl) 773/244–3434, 866/378–9790 • gay-friendly • in heart of Chicago's gay community • WiFi • wheelchair access • $139-299

City Suites Hotel 933 W Belmont Ave (btwn Clark & Sheffield) 773/404–3400, 800/248–9108 • gay-friendly • European style • nonsmoking rooms available • WiFi • $139-179

Majestic Hotel 528 W Brompton Ave (at Addison) 773/404–3499, 800/727–5108 • gay-friendly • romantic 19th-c atmosphere • nonsmoking • WiFi • $129-389

The Willows 555 W Surf St (at Broadway) 773/528–8400, 800/787–3108 • gay/ straight • 19th-c French flair • nonsmoking rooms available • WiFi • $109-379

BARS

3160 3160 N Clark St (at Belmont) 773/327–5969 • 3pm-2am, till 3am Sat • lesbians/ gay men • neighborhood bar • live shows • piano • cabaret • wheelchair access

Beat Kitchen 2100 W Belmont (btwn Hoyne & Damen) 773/281–4444 • 4pm-2am, from 11:30am Fri-Sun, till 3am Sat • gay-friendly • live bands • also grill • some veggie • wheelchair access

Blues 2519 N Halsted St (at Lill Ave) 773/528–1012, 773/549–9436 • 8pm-2am, till 3am Sat • gay-friendly • popular • classic Chicago blues spot • live shows

Bobby Love's 3729 N Halsted St (at Waveland) 773/525–1200 • 3pm-2am, from noon wknds, till 3am Sat • lesbians/ gay men • neighborhood bar • karaoke • wheelchair access

Buck's Saloon 3439 N Halsted St (btwn Cornelia & Newport) 773/525–1125 • noon-2am, till 3am Sat, 11am-2am Sun • mostly gay men • neighborhood bar • beer garden on the street

Cell Block 3702 N Halsted St (at Waveland) 773/665–8064 • 4pm-2am, from 2pm wknds • mostly gay men • dancing/DJ • leather • also Holding Cell from 10pm Fri-Sat w/ strict leather/ latex/ uniform code • wheelchair access

Charlie's Chicago 3726 N Broadway St (btwn Waveland & Grace) 773/871–8887 • 3pm-4am, till 5am Sat • mostly gay men • dancing/DJ • country/ western • karaoke • club music after 1am

The Closet 3325 N Broadway St (at Buckingham) 773/477–8533 • 2pm-4am, noon-5am Sat, till 4am Sun • popular • lesbians/ gay men • neighborhood video bar

Cocktail 3359 N Halsted St (at Roscoe) 773/477–1420 • 4pm-2am, from 2pm wknds, till 3am Sat • lesbians/ gay men • neighborhood bar • dancing/DJ • videos • go-go dancers Tue & Th • wheelchair access

Little Jim's 3501 N Halsted St (at Cornelia) 773/871–6116 • noon-4am, till 5am Sat • popular • mostly gay men • neighborhood bar

The Lucky Horseshoe Lounge 3169 N Halsted St (at Briar) 773/404–3169 • 3pm-2am, 2pm-3am Sat, till 2am Sun • mostly gay men • neighborhood bar • dancers nightly

Minibar 3341 N Halsted St (at Roscoe) 773/871–6227 • 5pm-2am, from 11am wknds • lesbians/ gay men • small lounge • specialty martinis • nonsmoking

The North End 3733 N Halsted St (at Grace) 773/477–7999 • 2pm-2am, from 11am wknds • mostly gay men • neighborhood sports bar • wheelchair access

Roscoe's 3354–56 N Halsted St (at W Roscoe) 773/281–3355 • 3pm-2am, 1pm-3am Sat, till 2am Sun • popular • lesbians/ gay men • neighborhood bar • dancing/DJ • live shows • videos • 6 bars • patio cafe in summer • food served

Scarlet 3320 N Halsted St (at Aldine) 773/348–1053 • 4pm-2am, till 3am Sat • mostly gay men • upscale piano bar • cabaret

Sidetrack 3349 N Halsted St (at Roscoe) **773/477–9189** • 3pm-2am, from 1pm wknds • popular • lesbians/ gay men • upscale video bar • wheelchair access

Stardust Thursdays 954 W Belmont (at Berlin) **312/523–9467** • 10pm-4am Th only • mostly women • dancing/DJ • food served

Winebar 3341 N Halsted St (at Roscoe) **773/871–6227** • dinner 5pm-11pm, bar till 3am • lesbians/ gay men

NIGHTCLUBS

Berlin 954 W Belmont (at Sheffield) **773/348–4975** • 5pm-4am, till 5am Sat, from 8pm Sun-Mon • popular • lesbians/ gay men • dancing/DJ • transgender-friendly • live shows • videos • wheelchair access

Boom Boom Room 2200 N Ashland (at Green Dolphin Street bar) **773/395–0066, 312/649–0101 (PROMOTER'S #)** • 11pm-4am Mon only • popular • gay/ straight • dancing/DJ • live shows • cover charge

Circuit 3641 N Halsted St (at Addison) **773/325–2233** • 9pm-4am, till 5am Sat, clsd Tue-Wed • mostly gay men • dancing/DJ • multiracial • theme nights • Latin nights Th & Sun (T-dance) • women's nights 1st-3rd Fri & 1st Sat

Girl Bar Chicago/ Circuit Girl 3641 N Halsted St (at Addison, at Circuit nightclub) **773/325–2233** • 9pm-4am Fri • mostly women • dancing/DJ • go-go dancers

Hydrate 3458 N Halsted St (at Cornelia) **773/975–9244** • 8pm-4am, till 5am Sat, opens earlier in summer • popular • gay/ straight • dancing/DJ • drag shows Wed • ladies night Sun

Planet Earth 2350 N Clark St (at Fullerton Pkwy, at Neo nightclub) **773/528–2622** • 10pm-4am Th • gay/ straight • dancing/DJ • New Wave

Smart Bar 3730 N Clark St (downstairs at the Metro) **773/549–0203** • 10pm-4am, till 5am Sat, clsd Mon-Tue • gay-friendly • dancing/DJ • popular • theme nights

Spin 800 W Belmont (enter on Halsted) **773/327–7711** • 4pm-2am, till 3am Sat, from noon wknds • lesbians/ gay men • dancing/DJ • live shows • videos • theme nights • 3 bars • lounge • young crowd

CAFES

Caribou Coffee 3300 N Broadway St (at Aldine) **773/477–3695** • from 5:30am, from 6:30am Sat, from 7am Sun • WiFi

The Coffee & Tea Exchange 3311 N Broadway St (at Roscoe) **773/528–2241** • 8am-8pm, till 7pm Fri, 9am-7pm Sat, 10am-6pm Sun • fair-trade coffee & tea

Starbucks 3358 N Broadway St (at Roscoe) **773/528–0343** • 5:30am-9pm • WiFi

RESTAURANTS

44th Ward Dinner Party 3542 N Halsted St **773/857–2911** • 5:30pm-midnight, till 2am wknds • grilled cheese sandwiches

Angelina Ristorante 3561 N Broadway St (at Addison) **773/935–5933** • 5:30pm-11pm, Sun brunch • Italian • full bar • wheelchair access

Ann Sather's 909 W Belmont Ave (at Sheffield) **773/348–2378** • 7am-3pm, till 4pm Sat-Sun • popular • Swedish diner & Boystown fixture

Arco de Cuchilleros 3445 N Halsted St (btwn Newport & Cornelia) **773/296–6046** • 5pm-11pm, till midnight Fri-Sat, 4pm-10pm Sun, clsd Mon • lesbians/ gay men • tapas • full bar • patio

Cesar's 2924 N Broadway (at Oakdale) **773/296–9097** • "home of the killer margaritas"

Chicago Diner 3411 N Halsted St (at Roscoe) **773/935–6696** • 11am-10pm, from 10am wknds, till 11pm Fri-Sat • hip & vegan • beer/ wine

Cornelia's/ Queens Tavern 750 W Cornelia Ave (at Halsted) **773/248–8333** • dinner only • some veggie • upscale Italian • full bar • live music nightly • wheelchair access

Firefly 3335 N Halsted St (at Roscoe) **773/525–2505** • 5pm-1:30am, till midnight Sun, clsd Tue • romantic French bistro

Halsted's Bar & Grill 3441 N Halsted St (btwn Newport & Cornelia) **773/348–9696** • dinner nightly, brunch wknds • neighborhood sports bar/ restaurant

Home Bistro 3404 N Halsted St (at Roscoe, btwn Addison & Belmont) **773/661–0299** • dinner only, clsd Mon-Tue • popular • upscale American • bring your own bottle

Horizon Cafe 3805 N Broadway St (corner w/ Halsted & Grace) **773/883–1565** • 7am-9pm, till 10pm Fri-Sat • diner • brkfst anytime

Istanbul Restaurant 3613 N Broadway (at Addison) **773/525–0500** • 9am-10am, from 8am wknds • Turkish/ Mediterranean • plenty veggie

Joy's Noodles & Rice 3257 N Broadway St (at Melrose) **773/327–8330** • 11am-10pm, till 11pm Fri-Sat • plenty veggie • patio

Kanok 3422 N Broadway St (at W Hawthorne Pl) **773/529–2525** • 4pm-10:30pm • sushi/Asian

Kit Kat Lounge & Supper Club 3700 N Halsted St (at W Waveland Ave) **773/525–1111** • 5:30pm-1am, brunch Sun (seasonal), clsd Mon • drag cabaret some nights • great martini menu • gay-owned

Kitsch'n On Roscoe 2005 W Roscoe (at Damen) **773/248–7372** • 9am-9pm, till 3pm Mon • brunch wknds • comfort food for hipsters • full bar

Las Mananitas 3523 N Halsted St (at Cornelia) **773/528–2109** • 11am-11pm, till midnight Fri-Sat • popular • gay/ straight • Mexican • full bar • strong margaritas

Mon Ami Gabi 2300 N Lincoln Park W (at Belden) **773/348–8886** • dinner only • French bistro

Nancy's Pizza 2930 N Broadway (at Oakdale) **773/883–1977** • deep-dish pizza

Nookie's Tree 3334 N Halsted St (at Roscoe) **773/248–9888** • 7am-midnight, 24hrs wknds • popular

Orange 3231 N Clark St **773/549–4400** • 8am-3pm • popular brunch spot

Panino's Pizzeria 3702 N Broadway (at Waveland) **773/472–6200** • 11:30am-11pm, from noon Sat, till 10pm Sun • Italian • full bar • wheelchair access

Pick Me Up Cafe & All Nite Express Lounge 3408 N Clark St (at Roscoe) **773/248–6613** • 11am-3am, 24hrs Fri-Sat • brkfst all day

Pie Hole Pizza 737 W Roscoe (at Halsted) **773/525–8888** • 5pm-3am, noon-5am wknds

Pingpong 3322 N Broadway St **773/281–7575** • 5pm-midnight • Asian fusion • patio

The Raw Bar & Grill 3720 N Clark St (at Waveland) **773/348–7291, 773/348–7961** • 11am-2am, till 3am Sat • seafood • lounge • live shows • wheelchair access

Sushisamba Rio 504 N Wells St (at W Illinois) **312/595–2300** • lunch & dinner, popular brunch • glitzy lounge atmosphere • theme nights

Tizi Melloul 531 N Wells St (at W Grand) **312/595–2300** • dinner nightly • Mediterranean

Yoshi's Cafe 3257 N Halsted St (at Melrose) **773/248–6160** • dinner Tue-Sun, also Sun brunch • Asian-inspired French

BOOKSTORES

Unabridged Books 3251 N Broadway St (at Aldine) **773/883–9119** • 10am-9pm, till 7pm wknds • popular • LGBT section

RETAIL SHOPS

Specialty Video Films 3221 N Broadway St (at Belmont) **773/248–3434** • 10am-11pm • foreign, cult, art house, LGBT & erotic videos • gay-owned

Uncle Fun 1338 W Belmont (at Racine) **773/477–8223** • heaven for kitsch lovers

Universal Gear 3153 N Broadway St (at Belmont) **773/296–1090** • 10am-9pm, till 10pm Fri-Sat, 11am-8pm Sun • casual, club, athletic & designer clothing

EROTICA

Batteries Not Included 3420 N Halsted St (at Newport) **773/935–9900** • 11am-midnight, till 1am Fri, 10am-2am Sat • also 1439 N Milwaukee Ave, 773/489–2200

The Pleasure Chest 3436 N Lincoln Ave (btwn Roscoe & Addison) **773/525–7152** • 10am-10pm, till midnight Fri-Sat

Tulip Sex Toy Gallery 3448 N Halsted St (btwn Newport & Cornelia) **773/975–1515, 877/708–8547** • noon-10pm, till midnight Fri-Sat • sex toys for women • lesbian-owned

Chicago—Near North

ACCOMMODATIONS

Allegro Chicago 171 W Randolph St (at LaSalle) **312/236–0123, 866/672–6143** • gay-friendly • Kimpton hotel • upscale lounge & restaurant • live shows • kids/ pets ok • WiFi • wheelchair access • $139-399

Chicago Getaway Hostel 616 W Arlington Pl (at Geneva Terr) **773/929–5380** • gay-friendly • in a trendy university area Lincoln Park • nonsmoking • WiFi • $25-108

Comfort Inn & Suites Downtown 15 E Ohio St (at State St) **312/894–0900, 888/775–9223** • gay-friendly • boutique hotel • gym • kids ok • WiFi • wheelchair access • $149-349

Dana Hotel & Spa 660 N State St (at Erie) **312/202–6000, 888/301–7946** • gay-friendly • rooftop lounge & Asian steakhouse • smoke free rooms • wheelchair access • $350-1,180

Flemish House of Chicago 68 E Cedar St (btwn Rush & Lake Shore Dr) **312/664–9981** • gay/ straight • B&B, studios & apts in greystone row house • nonsmoking • WiFi • gay-owned • $175-250

Gold Coast Guest House B&B 113 W Elm St (btwn Clark & LaSalle) **312/337–0361** • gay-friendly • 1873 town house • garden • nonsmoking • WiFi • women-owned • $129-229 • long-term rates available

The Hotel Burnham One W Washington St (at State) **312/782–1111, 877/294–9712** • gay-friendly • Chicago landmark • WiFi • wheelchair access • $149+

Hotel Cass—Holiday Inn Express 640 N Wabash Ave (btwn Ontario & Erie) **312/787–4030, 800/799–4030** • gay-friendly

Hotel Indigo Chicago 1244 N Dearborn Pkwy (btwn Goethe & Division) **312/787–4980, 800/972–2494** • gay-friendly • designer hotel • gym • WiFi • restaurant & lounge

Hotel Monaco 225 N Wabash (at S Water & Wacker Pl) **312/960–8500, 800/397–7661** • gay-friendly • 4-star luxury hotel • gym • restaurant • WiFi • $250+

Hyatt Regency Chicago 151 E Wacker Dr (at Michigan Ave) **312/565–1234, 800/233–1234** • gay-friendly • WiFi • fitness center • also restaurant, cafe & bar

Millennium Hotels & Resorts 163 E Walton Pl (Michigan Ave) **312/751–8100, 800/621–8140** • gay-friendly • restaurant • martini bar • gym • right off Magnificent Mile • wheelchair access • $129-269

Old Town Chicago Guest House 1442 N North Park Ave (at Wells) **312/440–9268** • gay/ straight • whole house or rent by room • nonsmoking • WiFi • $145-200; $500-800 whole house

Palmer House Hilton 17 E Monroe St (at State St) **312/726–7500** • gay-friendly • pool • fitness center • shopping arcade • business center

Parkview Hotel Chicago 1816 N Clark St (at Lincoln) **312/664–3040, 800/329–7466 (RESERVATIONS)** • gay-friendly • also restaurant & lounge • wheelchair access • $59-159

W Chicago—City Center 172 W Adams St (at LaSalle) **312/332–1200, 877/WHOTELS (RESERVATIONS ONLY)** • gay-friendly • in the Loop • nonsmoking • WiFi • also restaurant & bar • wheelchair access • $229-529

W Chicago—Lakeshore 644 N Lake Shore Dr (at Ontario) **312/943–9200, 877/WHOTELS (RESERVATIONS ONLY)** • gay-friendly • overlooking Lake Michigan • pool • nonsmoking • WiFi • also restaurant & bar • wheelchair access • $229-429

BARS

Club Foot 1824 W Augusta Blvd (in Wicker Park) **773/489–0379** • 8pm-2am, till 3am Sat • gay-friendly • neighborhood bar • dancing/DJ • kitschy • alternative

Davenport's 1383 N Milwaukee (in Wicker Park) **773/278–1830** • 7pm-midnight, till 2am Fri-Sat, till 11pm Sun, clsd Tue • cabaret • piano bar

NIGHTCLUBS

Baton Show Lounge 436 N Clark St (btwn Illinois & Hubbard) **312/644–5269** • showtimes at 8:30pm, 10:30pm, 12:30am, clsd Mon-Tue • lesbians/ gay men • drag shows • reservations recommended • wheelchair access • since 1969!

Chances Dances 2011 W North Ave (at Damen & Milwaukee, at Subterranean) • 9pm 3rd Mon only • lesbians/ gay men • dancing/DJ

Crobar 1543 N Kingsbury (at Sheffield) **312/266–1900** • 10pm-4am, clsd Mon-Th • popular • gay-friendly • dancing/DJ

The Rails/ The Prop House 1675 N Elston Ave (at North Ave, in Wicker Park) **773/486–2086 (PROP HOUSE #)** • 11pm-4am Fri only • popular • mostly gay men • dancing/DJ • live shows • mostly African American & Latino • cover charge

Underground Wonder Bar 10 E Walton St (at State St) **312/266–7761** • gay-friendly • live music • multi-racial cliente

CAFES

Earwax Cafe & Film 1561 N Milwaukee Ave (in Wicker Park) **773/772–4019** • 9am-10pm • food served (burgers, burritos, salads & vegan soups & stews) • also film section w/ 1,000 DVDs

RESTAURANTS

Blackbird 619 W Randolph St (at Des Plaines) **312/715–0708** • lunch Mon-Fri, dinner nightly, clsd Sun

Catch 35 35 W Wacker Dr (at Dearborn) **312/346–3500** • lunch Mon-Fri, dinner nightly • steak & seafood

Fireplace Inn 1448 N Wells St (at North Ave) **312/664–5264** • 4:30pm-1am, 11:30am-1am Fri-Sat • BBQ/ American • patio • full bar

Hot Chocolate 1747 N Damen Ave (in Wicker Park) 773/489–1747 • lunch, dinner & dessert, wknd brunch, clsd Mon • full bar • wheelchair access

Ina's 1235 W Randolph St (at Racine) 312/226–8227 • brkfst, lunch & dinner, full bar, free parking

Japonais 600 W Chicago Ave (at Larrabee) 312/822–9600 • lunch Mon-Fri, dinner nightly • upscale Japanese • lounge

Kiki's Bistro 900 N Franklin St (at Locust) 312/335–5454 • lunch Mon-Fri, dinner nightly, clsd Sun • French • full bar

Lou Mitchell's 565 W Jackson St (at Jefferson) 312/939–3111 • great brkfst

Manny's 1141 S Jefferson St (at Roosevelt) 312/939–2855 • 5am-8pm, clsd Sun • killer corned beef

Moonshine 1824 N Division St (at Honore, in Wicker Park) 773/862–8686 • lunch & dinner • American • also bar

Nacional 27 325 W Huron (at N Orleans) 312/664–2727 • 5:30pm-9:30pm, till 11pm Fri-Sat, clsd Sun • Nuevo Latino • live music Tue & Th • salsa dancing 11pm-2am Fri-Sat

Park Grill 11 N Michigan Ave (in Millennium Park) 312/521–7275 • 11am-10pm • classic American • seasonal outdoor dining

Parthenon Restaurant 314 S Halsted St (near W Jackson) 312/726–2407 • 11am-midnight • full bar • Greek • "best gyros in Chicago"

Shaw's Crab House 21 E Hubbard St (at State St) 312/527–2722 • lunch & dinner • full bar • wheelchair access

Topolobampo/ Frontera Grill 445 N Clark St (btwn Illinois & Hubbard) 312/661–1434 • lunch & dinner, Sat brunch (Frontera only), clsd Sun • Mexican

Vermilion 10 W Hubbard St (at State) 312/527–4060 • lunch Mon-Fri, dinner nightly • Latin-Indian fusion • full bar • patio upscale • wheelchair access

BOOKSTORES

After-Words New & Used Books 23 E Illinois (at State) 312/464–1110 • 10:30am-10pm, till 11pm Fri-Sat, noon-7pm Sun • internet access • cards • stationery • women-owned

Quimby's Bookstore 1854 W North Ave (at Wolcott, in Wicker Park) 773/342–0910 • noon-10pm, from 11am Sat, noon-6pm Sun • popular • alternative literature & comics • wheelchair access

RETAIL SHOPS

Flight 001 1133 N State St (at Division) 312/944–1001, 877/354–4481 • 11am-7pm, till 6pm Sun • way cool travel gear

GYMS & HEALTH CLUBS

Cheetah Gym 1934 W North Ave (at Damen, in Wicker Park) 773/394–5900

Thousand Waves Spa 1212 W Belmont Ave (at Racine) 773/549–0700 • noon-9pm, 10am-7pm wknds, clsd Mon • women only • health spa only • women-owned

Chicago — South Side

BARS

Club Escape 1530 E 75th St (at Stoney Island) 773/667–6454 • 4pm-2am, till 3am Sat • lesbians/ gay men • dancing/DJ • drag shows • mostly African American • food served • women's night Th

Inn Exile 5758 W 65th St (at Menard, near Midway Airport; 1 mile W of Midway hotel center at 65th & Cicero) 773/582–3510 • 8pm-2am, till 3am Sat • mostly gay men • dancing/DJ • videos • WiFi • wheelchair access

Jeffery Pub 7041 S Jeffery (at 71st) 773/363–8555 • 5pm-4am, from 1pm Fri, noon-5am Sat, noon-4am Sun, clsd Mon • popular • lesbians/ gay men • dancing/DJ • mostly African American • drag shows • wheelchair access

BOOKSTORES

57th St Books 1301 E 57th St, Hyde Park (at Kimbark St) 773/684–1300 • 10am-9pm, till 8pm Sat-Sun • LGBT section

Barbara's Bookstore 1218 S Halsted St (at W Roosevelt) 312/413–2665 • 9am-10pm, from 10am wknds, till 8pm Sun • popular • women's/ LGBT section • wheelchair access • other locations: at Macy's, 111 N State St, 312/781-3033; also 1100 Lake St, Oak Park, 708/848-9140

De Kalb

NIGHTCLUBS

Otto's 118 E Lincoln Hwy 815/758–2715 • 6:30pm-close • gay-friendly • live music venue

Decatur

BARS

The Flashback Lounge 2239 E Wood St (at 22nd) 217/422–3530 • 9am-2am • lesbians/ gay men • neighborhood bar • dancing/DJ • karaoke

RESTAURANTS

Robbies 122 Merchant St **217/423-0448** • 11am-9pm, till 2pm Sat, clsd Sun • American • full bar

EROTICA

Romantix Adult Superstore 2015 N 22nd St **217/362-0105**

Du Quoin

ACCOMMODATIONS

The Pit 7403 Persimmon Rd **618/542-9470** • lesbians/gay men • primitive camping • 18+ • nudity ok • swimming • gay-owned • free except $5 on holiday wknds

Elgin

see Chicago

Elk Grove Village

see also Chicago

NIGHTCLUBS

Hunter's Night Club 1932 E Higgins Rd (at Busse) **847/439-8840** • 4pm-2am, till 4am Th-Sat • popular • mostly gay men • dancing/DJ • transgender-friendly • live entertainment • karaoke • videos • patio • wheelchair access

Elkhart

CAFES

Bluestem Bake Shop 107 Governor Oglesby St **217/947-2222** • 9am-4pm, clsd Mon • soup • sandwiches • baked goods

Evanston

see Chicago

Forest Park

see also Chicago

NIGHTCLUBS

Hideaway 7301 W Roosevelt Rd (at Marengo) **708/771-4459** • 3pm-2am, till 3am Fri-Sat • mostly gay men • dancing/DJ • karaoke • drag shows • male dancers • videos

Forest View

BARS

Forest View Lounge 4519 S Harlem Ave • 11am-midnight, till 2am wknds, clsd Sun • mostly women • neighborhood bar

Franklin Park

NIGHTCLUBS

Moda VIP 2409 N Mannheim **312/480-7546**

Galesburg

ACCOMMODATIONS

The Fahnestock House 591 N Prairie St (at Losey) **309/344-0270** • gay/straight • full brkfst • Queen Anne Victorian • nonsmoking • pool • kids ok • clsd Nov-Jan • gay-owned • $150

EROTICA

Romantix Adult Superstore 595 N Henderson St (at Losey) **309/342-7019**

Granite City

see St Louis, Missouri

Joliet

INFO LINES & SERVICES

Community Alliance & Action Network 68 N Chicago St **815/726-7906, 815/382-2082** • by appointment • LGBT community center

Long Grove

RETAIL SHOPS

The Long Grove Popcorn Shoppe 318 Old McHenry Rd **847/821-9101** • 10am-5pm • try the "Pride Pop" • also gourmet coffee & doggie treats • lesbian-owned

Monticello

RESTAURANTS

The Brown Bag 212 W Washington St **217/762-9221** • 9am-7pm, till 8pm Tue & Fri, till 4pm Sat, clsd Sun

Normal

CAFES

Coffeehouse & Deli 114 E Beaufort **309/452-6774** • 7am-10pm • vegetarian/vegan

RESTAURANTS

Micheleo's Pizza 116 W North St **309/454-4444** • 11am-close

North Riverside

BARS

Rumors 2433 S Des Plaines Ave (at 22nd St) **708/443-1227** • 2pm-3am, from noon wknds • mostly gay men • neighborhood bar • karaoke • drag shows • gay-owned

O'Fallon

RESTAURANTS

Paulo's at the Mansion 1680 Mansion Wy (at Lakepointe Center Dr) **618/624-0629** • 4pm-10pm Tue-Sat • steakhouse • wheelchair access • gay-owned

Oak Park

see also Berwyn & Chicago

BARS

Velvet Rope 728 W Lake St **708/358-8840** • 5pm-1am, till 2am wknds, Sun brunch from 11am • lesbians/ gay men • entertainment • also restaurant

Ottawa

EROTICA

Brown Bag Video 3042 N Rte 71 (at I-80, exit 93) **815/434-0820** • 24hrs

Peoria

ACCOMMODATIONS

Hotel Pere Marquette 501 Main St **309/637-6500, 800/447-1676** • gay-friendly • buffet brkfst

BARS

Buddies On Adams 807 SW Adams St (at Oak St) **309/282-2125** • 6pm-1am, till 4am Fri-Sat, clsd Mon • lesbians/ gay men • neighborhood bar • karaoke • WiFi

CAFES

One World 1245 W Main St (at University) **309/672-1522** • 7am-11pm, from 8am wknds • nonsmoking • WiFi

RESTAURANTS

Two 25 225 NE Adams St (at Mark Twain Hotel) **309/282-7777** • lunch Mon-Fri, dinner nightly, clsd Sun

PUBLICATIONS

Out & About Illinois 4408 N Rockwood Rd #250 **309/699-6901**

EROTICA

Swingers World 335 SW Adams (at Harrison) **309/676-9275** • 24hrs

Quincy

NIGHTCLUBS

Irene's Cabaret 124 N 5th St (at Washington Park, enter rear) **217/222-6292** • 9pm-2:30am, from 7pm Fri-Sat, till 3:30am Sat, from 3pm Sun • lesbians/ gay men • dancing/DJ • multiracial • food served • karaoke • drag shows • wheelchair access • gay-owned

Rock Island

see also Davenport, Iowa

BARS

Augie's 313 20th St (at 3rd) **309/788-7389** • 3pm-3am • lesbians/ gay men • neighborhood bar • transgender-friendly • karaoke • wheelchair access

RESTAURANTS

Ragtime Grille and Supperclub 1524 4th Ave (at 17th St) **309/786-5030** • 11am-1am * full bar • wheelchair access • gay-owned

Rockford

NIGHTCLUBS

The Office Niteclub 513 E State St (btwn 2nd & 3rd) **815/965-0344** • 5pm-2am, noon-midnight Sun • popular • lesbians/ gay men • dancing/DJ • live shows • karaoke • drag shows • male & female strippers • videos

RESTAURANTS

Lucerne's Fondue & Spirits 845 N Church St (at Whitman) **815/968-2665** • 5pm-11pm, clsd Mon (also Sun summers) • fondue • full bar • wheelchair access

Maria's 828 Cunningham St (at Corbin) **815/968-6781** • 4:30pm-9pm, clsd Sun-Mon • Italian • full bar

Springfield

INFO LINES & SERVICES

The Phoenix Center 109 E Lawrence Ave **217/528-5253** • 8:30am-4:30pm, clsd wknds • Phoenix Cafe group from 6pm Tue & Fri

ACCOMMODATIONS

The State House Inn 101 E Adams St (at First St) **217/528-5100** • gay-friendly • hotel • full brkfst • kids/ pets ok • WiFi • wheelchair access • $89-159

BARS

Scandals 126 E Jefferson St **217/523-4500** • 11am-1am • mostly gay men • dancing/DJ • drag shows

RESTAURANTS

Caitie Girls 400 E Jefferson (in St Nicholas Hotel) **217/528–1294** • lunch Tue-Fri, dinner nightly, Sun brunch, clsd Mon

Country Cafe 3705 N Dirksen Pkwy (at North Grand Ave) **217/753–5537** • 6am-2pm, from 7am Sun • gay-owned

RETAIL SHOPS

New Age Tattoos & Body Piercings 2915 S MacArthur Blvd **217/546–5006** • 11am-8pm, till 6pm Sun

Utica

ACCOMMODATIONS

Landers House 115 E Church St **815/667–5170** • gay-friendly • full brkfst • WiFi • wheelchair access • $99-329

The Willows Hotel 325 Clark St **815/667–3400** • gay-friendly • full brkfst • WiFi • wheelchair access

INDIANA

Anderson

EROTICA

After Dark 2012 Mounds Rd **765/649–7597** • 10am-11pm, till midnight Fri-Sat, noon-10pm Sun • adult novelties, lingerie, videos, magazines

Bloomington

BARS

Uncle Elizabeth's 1614 W 3rd St **812/331–0060** • 4pm-3am, 7pm-midnight Sun • lesbians/ gay men • neighborhood bar • dance floor • drag shows • patio

CAFES

Soma Coffee House 322 E Kirkwood Ave (below Laughing Planet) **812/331–2770** • 7am-11pm, from 8am Sun • WiFi

RESTAURANTS

Laughing Planet Cafe 322 E Kirkwood Ave (enter on Grant) **812/323–2233** • 11am-9pm • outdoor seating

Village Deli 409 E Kirkwood **812/336–2303** • 7am-8pm, 8am-8pm wknds • lesbians/ gay men • some veggie

ENTERTAINMENT & RECREATION

BloomingOut WFHB 91.3 & 98.1 & 100.7 & 106.3FM **812/325–7870 & 323–1200** • 6pm Th • "your midwest queer connection"

RETAIL SHOPS

Athena Gallery 116 N Walnut **812/339–0734** • 10:30am-7pm, till 8:30pm Fri, noon-5pm Sun • clothing, drums, incense, gifts, etc • wheelchair access

Elkhart

see South Bend

Evansville

NIGHTCLUBS

Someplace Else 930 Main St (at Sycamore) **812/424–3202** • 4pm-3am, 4pm-midnight Sun • lesbians/ gay men • dancing/DJ • drag shows • karaoke • patio

EROTICA

Exotica 4605 Washington Ave **812/401–7399**

Fort Wayne

INFO LINES & SERVICES

Gay/ Lesbian AA 501 W Berry St (at Plymouth church) • 6:30pm Tue, 1pm Sun

NIGHTCLUBS

After Dark 1601 S Harrison St (at Grand St) **260/456–6235** • 6pm-3am, noon-3am Sun • mostly gay men • dancing/DJ • karaoke • drag shows • male strippers • wheelchair access • gay-owned

Babylon 112 Masterson St **260/247–5062** • 6pm-3am • lesbians/ gay men • dancing/DJ • also Lion's Den bar

CAFES

Firefly 3523 N Anthony Blvd **260/373–0505** • 6:30am-8pm, from 8am wknds • live entertainment • WiFi

RESTAURANTS

The Loving Cafe 7605 Coldwater Rd **260/489–8686** • 10am-8pm, clsd Sun • vegetarian/ vegan

RETAIL SHOPS

Boudoir Noir 512 W Superior St **260/420–0557** • 10am-midnight, noon-8pm Sun • gifts • sex toys • leather

PUBLICATIONS

Phoenix Magazine 260/409–2920 • LGBT publication

Gary

see also Chicago, Illinois

EROTICA

Romantix Adult Superstore 8801 W Melton Rd/ US 20 (at Ripley Rd) **219/938–2194** • 24hrs

Goshen

see also South Bend

CAFES

The Electric Brew 136 S Main St **574/533–5990** • 6am-10pm, clsd Sun • "Goshen's original coffeehouse" • live music

Hammond

BARS

Dick's R U Crazee? 1221 E 150th St **219/852–0222** • 7pm-3am, till midnight Sun • mostly gay men • neighborhood bar • karaoke • drag shows

Indiana Dunes

ACCOMMODATIONS

The Gray Goose Inn B&B 350 Indian Boundary Rd (at I-95), Chesterton **219/926–5781, 800/521–5127** • gay/ straight • full brkfst • WiFi • nonsmoking rooms available • $110-195

Indianapolis

INFO LINES & SERVICES

AA Gay/ Lesbian 317/632–7864, **317/631–5099 (EN ESPAÑOL)** • various LGBT meeting • check web (www.indyaa.org) for meeting times & locations

ACCOMMODATIONS

East Lake Retreat Home 335 W Lakeview Dr, Nineveh **812/376-0784** • furnished 2-bdrm on Prince's Lake • waterfall, lake access, boating, firepit • wheelchair access (main floor) • lesbian-owned • $200-300/wknd

Indianapolis

LGBT PRIDE:
June, web: www.indyprideinc.com.

ANNUAL EVENTS:
May - Broad Ripple Arts Fair, web: www.indplsartcenter.org.
Memorial Day Weekend - Indy 500 auto race, web: www.indycar.com.
July - Indianapolis International Film Festival, web: indyfilmfest.org.
Aug-Sept - Indianapolis Theatre Fringe Festival, web: www.indyfringe.org.

CITY INFO:
Indianapolis Convention & Visitors Association 317/639-4282, 800/323-INDY, web: www.indy.org.

TRANSIT:
Yellow Cab 317/487-7777.
IndyGo 317/635-3344, web: www.indygo.net.

WEATHER:
The spring weather is moderate (50°s-60°s) with occasional storms. The summers are typically midwestern: hot (mid-90°s) and humid. The autumns are mild and colorful in southeastern Indiana. As for winter, it's the wind chill that'll get to you.

ATTRACTIONS:
Benjamin Harrison Home, 317/631-1888, web: www.presidentbenjaminharrison.org.
Eiteljorg Museum of American Indians & Western Art, 317/636-9378, web: www.eiteljorg.org.
Indianapolis Museum of Art 317/923-1331 & 920-2660, web: www.ima-art.org.
Morris-Butler Home, 317/636-5409, web: www.historiclandmarks.org.
Speedway 500 317/481-8500, web: www.indianapolismotorspeedway.com.
Zoo 317/630-2001, web: www.indyzoo.com.

The Fort Harrison State Park Inn 5830 N Post Rd **317/638–6000** • gay-friendly • luxury inn in historic Fort Harrison in NE Indianapolis • nonsmoking • $120-220

Sycamore Knoll B&B 10777 Riverwood Ave, Noblesville **317/776–0570** • gay/ straight • fully restored 1886 estate near the White River • perennial gardens & apple orchard • quiet & casual • full brkfst • nonsmoking • WiFi • lesbian-owned • $110/ night

Wyndham Indianapolis West 2544 Executive Dr (off Airport Expy) **317/248–2481, 800/444–2326** • gay-friendly • seasonal pool • fitness center • WiFi in lobby, restaurant & lounge

Yellow Rose Inn 1441 N Delaware St **317/636–7673** • gay/ straight • B&B in restored Victorian • rooftop hot tub • $175-250

BARS

501 Eagle 501 N College (at Michigan St) **317/632–2100** • 5:30pm-3am, from 7:30pm Sat, 4pm-12:30am Sun • popular • mostly gay men • dancing/DJ • bears • leather

Downtown Olly's 822 N Illinois St (at St Clair) **317/636–5597** • 9am-3am Mon-Wed, 24hrs Th-Sun • mostly men • sports & video bar • brkfst, lunch, dinner

The Metro Nightclub & Restaurant 707 Massachusetts Ave (at College) **317/639–6022** • 4pm-3am, noon-12:30am Sun • popular • lesbians/ gay men • neighborhood bar • piano bar • karaoke • patio • also restaurant • giftshop • wheelchair access

Noah Grant's Grill House & Raw Bar 65 S 1st St (at W Oak St), Zionsville **317/732–2233** • 4pm-close, clsd Sun-Mon • gay-friendly • wine bar & bistro • full restaurant serving lunch & dinner, Sun brunch • patio

Varsity Lounge 1517 N Pennsylvania Ave (S of 16th) **317/635–9998** • 10am-3am, till midnight Sun • mostly gay men • neighborhood bar • food served • karaoke • WiFi

Zonie's Closet 1446 E Washington St (at Arsenal) **317/266–0535** • 8am-3am, noon-midnight Sun • gay/ straight • dancing/DJ • karaoke Th & Sat-Sun • drag shows Fri-Sat • wheelchair access

NIGHTCLUBS

Talbott Street 2145 N Talbott St (at 22nd St) **317/931–1343** • 9pm-3am, till 1am Sun, clsd Mon-Wed • gay/ straight • dancing/DJ • drag shows • theme nights

The Ten 1218 N Pennsylvania St (at 12th, enter rear) **317/638–5802** • 6pm-3am, till 1am Wed, till midnight Sun, clsd Mon-Tue • very popular w/ lesbians (gay men welcome) • dancing/DJ • live shows • drag shows • wheelchair access

The Unicorn Club 122 W 13th St (at Illinois) **317/262–9195** • 8pm-3am, till 12:30am Sun • popular • mostly gay men • dancing/DJ • male strippers nightly • private club

CAFES

Ah Barista Cafe 201 S Capitol Ave (btwn Maryland & South Sts) **317/638–2233** • 7am-3pm Mon-Fri • brkfst & lunch menu

Bjava 5510 Lafayette St **317/280–1236** • 6am-5pm, 7am-3pm Sat, clsd Sun

Cornerstone Coffeehouse 651 E 54th St (at N College Ave, Broad Ripple) **317/726–1360** • 6am-10pm, 7am-10pm Sat, 7am-9pm Sun • food served • WiFi

Earth House Collective 237 N East St **317/636–4060** • 11am-9pm, clsd Sun • coffeehouse • also art, music & classes

Henry's on E Street 627 N East St (next door to Out Word Bound Books) **317/951–0335** • 7am-7pm, till 9pm Fri, from 8am wknds • popular • gay-owned

Hubbard & Cravens 4930 N Pennsylvania St (in Broad Ripple) **317/251–5161** • 6am-7pm, 7am-3pm Sun

Monon Coffee Company 920 E Westfield Blvd (at Guilford) **317/255–0510** • 6:30am-8pm, till 10pm Fri, from 7am Sat, 8am-8pm Sun

RESTAURANTS

14 West 14 W Maryland St **317/636–1414** • lunch & dinner • seafood & steaks • patio

Adobo Grill 110 E Washington **317/822–9990** • lunch Fri-Sun, dinner nightly • Mexican • full bar • also Fiesta Fridays w/ salsa dancing • wheelchair access

Aesop's Tables 600 E Massachusetts Ave **317/631–0055** • lunch & dinner, clsd Sun • authentic Mediterranean • some veggie • beer/ wine • wheelchair access

Agio 635 Massachusetts Ave (at East) **317/488–0359** • dinner nightly • cont'l • nonsmoking

BARcelona 201 N Delaware St, Indiana **317/638–8272** • 11am-11pm • also full bar • tapas

Cafe Zuppa 320 N Meridian St **317/634–9877** • 7am-2:30pm, Sun brunch buffet

English Ivy's 944 S Alabama (at 10th) 317/822–5070 • lunch and dinner, till 3am Mon-Sat, 10am-1am Sun • eclectic • also full bar • WiFi • wheelchair access

Euphoria & Creation Cafe 337 W 11th St (in Buggs' Temple) **317/955–2389** • 8am-9pm, clsd Sun • outdoor seating

Hoaglin To Go 448 Massachusetts Ave **317/423–0300** • 8am-2:30pm, market till 6pm • wheelchair access

India Garden 830 Broad Ripple Ave (btwn Carrollton & Guilford) 317/253–6060 • lunch & dinner • Indian • also 207 N Delaware St, 317/634-6060 • lunch & dinner

Mama Carolla's 1031 E 54th St (at Winthrop) **317/259–9412** • dinner only • traditional Italian

Mikado 148 S Illinois St (at Georgia) **317/972–4180** • 11:30am-10:30pm, till 11:30pm Sat, till 10pm Sun • Japanese • enjoy the saketini

Naked Tchopstix 6253 N College Ave (in Broad Ripple) 317/252–5555 • lunch & dinner • popular • Korean, Japanese, Chinese cuisine • also sushi bar

Oakley's Bistro 1464 W 86th St (at Ditch Rd) **317/824–1231** • lunch & dinner, clsd Sun-Mon • popular • gourmet cont'l • reservations suggested

Pancho's Taqueria 7023 Michigan Rd (at Westlane) 317/202–9015 • 11am-9pm • popular • authentic Mexican • wheelchair access

Sawasdee 1222 W 86th St (at Ditch Rd) 317/844–9451 • lunch Mon-Sat, dinner nightly • Thai • some veggie • wheelchair access

Scholars Inn 725 Massachusetts Ave **317/536–0707** • dinner nightly, Sun brunch • also swank lounge • wheelchair access

Shanghai Lil 8505 Keystone Crossing (across from Keystone Mall) 317/205–9335 • lunch & dinner • upscale Chinese & Japanese • full bar • wheelchair access

Three Sisters Cafe 6360 N Guilford Ave (at Main St) 317/257–5556 • 8am-9pm, till 3pm Sun • plenty veggie & vegan • popular Sun brunch

Urban Element 901 N Pennsylvania St **317/423–2938** • 11am-3pm daily, also open 5pm-10pm Th-Sun • cafe & wine bar

Usual Suspects 6319 Guilford Ave (at Broad Ripple) 317/251–3138 • 5pm-10pm, till 11pm Fri-Sat, till 9pm Sun, clsd Mon • eclectic • full bar • patio

Yats 659 Massachusetts Ave (at Walnut) **317/686–6380** • 11am-9pm, till 10pm Fri-Sat, till 7pm Sun • Cajun • also 5363 N College Ave, 317/ 253-8817 • also 8352 E 96th St, 317/ 585-1792 • wheelchair access

ENTERTAINMENT & RECREATION

Indiana Fever 1 Conseco Ct (in Conseco Fieldhouse) **317/917–2500** • check out the Women's Nat'l Basketball Association while you're in Indianapolis

Indianapolis Women's Chorus PO Box 2919, 46206-2919 **317/931–9464** • various concerts throughout season

Indyindie 7780 Eagle Valley Pass **317/295–9302** • monthly women's music concert series • also events at Out Word Bound

Theatre on the Square 627 Massachusetts Ave (at East) **317/685–8687** • often presents gay-themed productions

BOOKSTORES

Big Hat Books 6510 Cornell Ave **317/202–0203** • 10am-6pm, noon-5pm Sun • general independent

Bookmamas 9 S Johnson Ave (at E Washington St, in Irvington) **317/375–3715** • open Wed-Sat • call for hours • used bookstore

RETAIL SHOPS

All My Relations 1008 Main St (at 10th), Speedway **317/227–3925** • noon-6pm, till 7pm Wed-Th, 10am-6pm Sat • New Age/ metaphysical store • also classes

The Magic Candle 204 S Audubon St (S of Washington) **317/357–8801** • 10am-7pm, clsd Sun • pagan supplies, books, gifts • also classes

Metamorphosis 828 Broad Ripple Ave (at Carrollton) **317/466–1666** • 1pm-9pm, till 5pm Sun • tattoo & piercing parlor

PUBLICATIONS

Nuvo **317/254–2400** • Indy's alternative weekly

The Word **317/725–8840** • LGBT newspaper

EROTICA

Southern Nights Videos 3760 Commercial Dr (at 38th St) **317/329–5505** • 10am-midnight, clsd Sun • videos • DVDs • toys, etc

Kokomo

BARS

Bar Blue 1400 W Markland Ave (at Park) **765/456-1400** • open Sat only • popular • lesbians/gay men • dancing/DJ • karaoke • drag shows • patio

Lafayette

INFO LINES & SERVICES

Pride Lafayette, Inc 640 Main St #218 **765/423-7579** • community center 6pm-8pm, 5pm-9pm wknds • support/social activities

NIGHTCLUBS

Zoolegers 644 Main St (at Columbia) **765/742-6321** • 8pm-3am, from 5pm Fri • lesbians/gay men • dancing/DJ

EROTICA

Fantasy East 2315 Concord Rd (at Teal) **765/474-2417** • open daily, books & videos

Lake Station

NIGHTCLUBS

Encompass Nightclub & Lounge 2415 Rush St (at I-80/94 & Ripley St) **219/962-4640** • 8pm-3am, 7pm-midnight Sun • popular • lesbians/gay men • dancing/DJ • cabaret • food served • wheelchair access

Marion

EROTICA

After Dark 1311 Johnson St **765/662-3688** • 10am-11pm, till midnight Fri-Sat, noon-10pm Sun • adult novelities, lingerie, videos, magazines

Michigan City

ACCOMMODATIONS

Duneland Beach Inn & Restaurant 3311 Pottawattomie Trail (at Duneland Beach Dr) **219/874-7729, 800/423-7729** • gay-friendly • B&B/restaurant/bar • 1 block away from Lake Michigan & private beach • 60 miles from Chicago • jacuzzi suites available • $99-239

Tryon Farm Guest House 1400 Tryon Rd (at Hwy 212) **219/879-3618** • gay-friendly • full brkfst • hot tub • kids/pets ok • nonsmoking • WiFi • women-owned • $108-228

Mishawaka

see also South Bend

ACCOMMODATIONS

The Beiger Mansion 317 Lincolnway E **574/255-6300, 800/437-0131** • gay-friendly • B&B in neo-classical mansion • pool • nonsmoking • WiFi • gay-owned • $140-225

Muncie

BARS

Mark III Tap Room 107 E Main St **765/282-1840** • 5pm-2am, till 3am wknds • lesbians/gay men • neighborhood bar • drag shows

CAFES

The MT Cup 1606 W University Ave (at N Dill St) **765/287-1995** • 7:30am-midnight • sandwiches • baked goods

New Albany

see Louisville, KY

Noblesville

see Indianapolis

South Bend

ACCOMMODATIONS

Innisfree B&B 702 W Colfax **574/283-0740** • gay-friendly • 1892 Queen Anne • full brkfst • nonsmoking • $85-175

BARS

Jeannie's Tavern 621 S Bendix (at Ford St) **574/288-2962** • 11am-2am • gay-friendly • neighborhood bar • transgender-friendly • gay-owned

Vickies Inc 112 W Monroe St (at S Michigan St) **574/232-4090** • 2pm-midnight Mon-Sat, open some Sundays • gay/straight • neighborhood bar • transgender-friendly • food served • football party every Sat in season • gay-owned

NIGHTCLUBS

Truman's Nightclub & Lounge/ Little T's 100 N Center St, Mishawaka **574/259-2282, 574/251-7507** • 8pm-3am, from 10pm Fri-Sat • popular • lesbians/gay men • dancing/DJ • drag shows • Little T's (sports bar, karaoke) open 8pm-2am Fri-Sat, till 12:30am Sun • also John's Grille • also gift shop

CAFES

Lula's Cafe 1631 Edison Rd **574/273-6216** • 7:30am-11pm, from 9am Sat, from 10am Sun • live entertainment

ENTERTAINMENT & RECREATION

GLBT Resource Center of Michiana
574/254-1411

EROTICA

Romantix Adult Superstore 2715 S Main
St (at Ewing) 574/291-1899

Terre Haute

NIGHTCLUBS

ZimMarss Nightclub 1500 Locust St (at
15th St) 812/232-3026 • 5pm-3am, 7pm-
12:30am Sun, clsd Mon • lesbians/ gay men •
dancing/DJ • transgender-friendly • also
restaurant • drag shows • strippers

Valparaiso

ACCOMMODATIONS

Inn at Aberdeen 3158 S State Rd 2
219/465-3753, 866/761-3753 • gay-friendly •
1880s Queen Anne • full brkfst • nonsmoking
• WiFi • wheelchair access • $106-201

Zionsville

see Indianapolis

IOWA

Statewide

PUBLICATIONS

Accessline 319/550-0957 • LGBT
newspaper

Ames

RESTAURANTS

Lucullan's Italian Grill 400 Main St (at
Burnett) 515/232-8484 • dinner Tue-Sun •
some veggie • full bar

EROTICA

Romantix Adult Superstore 117 Kellogg St.
(at Lincoln Wy) 515/232-7717 • 9am-3am

Burlington

ACCOMMODATIONS

Arrowhead Motel, Inc 2520 Mt Pleasant St
319/752-6353 • gay-friendly • kids/ pets ok •
WiFi • wheelchair access • gay-owned • $49-
129

RESTAURANTS

Steve's Place 852 Washington St (at Central
Ave) 319/754-5868 • 10am-2am, noon-6pm
Sun • also bar • wheelchair access

Cedar Falls

see Waterloo

Cedar Rapids

INFO LINES & SERVICES

Gay/ Lesbian Resource Center 6300
Rockwell Dr NE 319/366-2055 • support
groups • referrals

BARS

The Piano Lounge 208 2nd Ave SE, Cedar
Rapids 319/363-0606 • 4pm-2am, clsd Sun •
gay/ straight • live entertainment • game room

NIGHTCLUBS

Club Basix 3916 1st Ave NE (btwn 39th &
40th) 319/363-3194 • 5pm-2am, from noon
wknds • lesbians/ gay men • transgender-
friendly • dancing/DJ • drag shows • gay/
lesbian-owned

Karma 616 2nd Ave SE 319/362-3591 •
8pm-2am, Wed, Fri & Sat • gay/ straight •
dancing/DJ • drag shows • young crowd

CAFES

Blue Strawberry 118 2nd St SE
319/247-2583 • 7am-8pm, till 7pm Sat, 8am-
5pm Sun • live entertainment • nonsmoking

RESTAURANTS

Hamburger Mary's 222 Glenbrook Dr SE
319/378-4627 • 11am-midnight, till 2am Th-
Sat, till 10pm Sun • also full bar • lesbians/ gay
men • drag shows • entertainment

The Happy Chef 1906 Blairs Ferry Rd NE
319/395-7793 • 24hrs • all-American • salad
bar

ENTERTAINMENT & RECREATION

CSPS Arts Center 1103 3rd St SE
319/364-1580 • galleries • concerts • plays •
many LGBT events

Council Bluffs

see also Omaha, Nebraska

ACCOMMODATIONS

Historic Wickham B&B 616 S 7th Street
712/328-1872 • gay/ straight • full brkfst •
WiFi • gay-owned • $100

BARS

Broadway Joe's 3400 W Broadway
712/256-2243 • 4pm-2am • gay/straight •
neighborhood bar

EROTICA

Romantix Adult Superstore 3216 1st Ave
(at Broadway) 712/328-2673 • 24hrs

Davenport

see also Rock Island, Illinois

BARS

Mary's on 2nd 832 W 2nd St **563/884-8014** • 4pm-2am • lesbians/ gay men • neighborhood bar • dancing/DJ • occasional live shows • videos • patio • wheelchair access

NIGHTCLUBS

Club Fusion 813 W 2nd St (at Warren) **563/326-3452** • 4pm-2am • lesbians/ gay men • dancing/DJ • karaoke • drag shows • patio • deck • gay-owned

Connections 822 W 2nd St **563/322-1121** • 5pm-2am • lesbians/ gay men • dancing/ DJ • drag shows • karaoke

Des Moines

ACCOMMODATIONS

Hotel Fort Des Moines 1000 Walnut St (at 10th St) **515/243-1161, 800/532-1466** • gay-friendly • full brkfst • pool • hot tub • kids ok • gym • nonsmoking • WiFi • wheelchair access • $99-400

The Renaissance Savery Hotel 401 Locust St (at 4th) **515/244-2151, 800/514** • gay-friendly • pool • kids ok • restaurant • WiFi • wheelchair access • $109-600

BARS

The Blazing Saddle 416 E 5th St (btwn Grand & Locust) **515/246-1299** • 2pm-2am, from noon wknds • mostly gay men • dancing/DJ • leather • drag shows • WiFi • wheelchair access

Buddies Corral 418 E 5th St (btwn Grand & Locust) **515/244-7140** • noon-2am, from 10am Sat • gay-friendly • karaoke

NIGHTCLUBS

The Garden 112 SE 4th St **515/243-3965** • 8pm-2am, clsd Mon-Tue • lesbians/ gay men • more women Th • dancing/DJ • live shows • karaoke • videos • patio • young crowd • wheelchair access

CAFES

Baby Boomer's Cafe 303 5th St (at Walnut) **515/244-9107** • 6am-8pm, from 7am Sat, 8am-3pm Sun • great brkfst • gay-owned

Drake Diner 1111 25th St (btwn University & Cottage Grove) **515/277-1111** • 7am-10pm, from 10am Sun • try the cake shake • full bar • patio • wheelchair access

Java Joe's 214 4th St (at Court Ave) **515/288-5282** • 7am-11pm, till 12:30am Fri-Sat, till 10pm Sun • live shows • WiFi

Ritual Cafe 1301 E Locust St **515/288-4872** • 7am-7pm, till 11pm Fri-Sat, clsd Sun • live music

Zanzibar's Coffee Adventure 2723 Ingersoll Ave (at 28th St) **515/244-7694** • 6:30am-8pm, till 9pm Fri-Sat, 8am-6pm Sun

RESTAURANTS

Cafe di Scala 644 18th St (at Woodland) **515/244-1353** • dinner Th-Sat only • Italian • beer/ wine • wheelchair access

Chicago Dog & Deli 523 Euclid Ave (at 6th) **515/243-3085** • 8am-5pm, till 3pm Sat, clsd Sun • gay-owned

Kearney's Restaurant 60 School St (at 1st St), Carlisle **515/989-9080** • 5pm-10pm Fri-Sat only • full bar • wheelchair access • gay-owned

Paradise Pizza 2025 Grand Ave, West Des Moines **515/222-9959** • 11am-9pm, till 10pm Fri-Sat, clsd Mon

RETAIL SHOPS

Liberty Gifts 333 E Grand Ave, Ste 105 (entrance on E 4th St) **515/508-0825** • 11am-7pm, 10am-8pm Fri-Sat • pride store

EROTICA

Gallery Book Store 1000 Cherry St (at 10th) **515/244-2916** • 24hrs

Romantix Adult Superstore 2020 E Euclid Ave (at Delaware) **515/266-7992** • 24hrs

Dubuque

CAFES

Cafe Manna Java 269 Main St (at 4th St) **563/588-3105** • 7am-9pm • WiFi • lesbian-owned

Iowa City

INFO LINES & SERVICES

AA Gay/ Lesbian 500 N Clinton (at church) **319/338-9111 (AA#)** • 5pm Sun

Women's Resource & Action Center 130 N Madison St (at Market) **319/335-1486** • 9am-5pm, clsd wknds • community center • support groups • counseling • wheelchair access

BARS

Deadwood Tavern 6 S Dubuque St **319/351-9417** • 11am-2am • popular • gay-friendly • neighborhood bar • college crowd

Firewater 347 S Gilbert St **319/321-5895** • gay/straight • karaoke • 1st Wed drag king show • lesbian owned

The Piano Lounge 217 Iowa Ave, Iowa City **319/351–1797** • 7pm-2am, from 6pm Fri-Sat, clsd Sun-Tue • gay/ straight • live entertainment Wed

Studio 13 13 S Linn St (in the alley btwn Linn & Dubuque Sts) **319/338–7145** • 7pm-2am, clsd Mon lesbians/ gay men • dancing/DJ • drag shows Fri & Sun • 19+ • gay-owned

NIGHTCLUBS

J-Bar 18-20 S Clinton **319/351–0557** • 9pm-2am, from 7pm Th-Sat • gay/straight • dancing/DJ • drag shows

Studio 13 13 S Linn St (at Iowa Ave) **319/338–7145** • 7pm-2am, clsd Mon• gay/ straight • dancing/DJ • karaoke Tue • drag shows Wed, Fri-Sat • wheelchair access

RESTAURANTS

The Mill 120 E Burlington St **319/351–9529** • lunch & dinner, wknd brunch • popular Americana music venue

ENTERTAINMENT & RECREATION

Old Capitol City Roller Girls • Iowa City's own female roller derby league • www.myspace.com/oldcapitolcityrollergirls

BOOKSTORES

Prairie Lights Bookstore 15 S Dubuque St (at Washington) **319/337–2681** • 9am-9pm, till 6pm Sun • also cafe • wheelchair access

RETAIL SHOPS

New Pioneer Co-op & Bakehouse 22 S Van Buren **319/338–9441** • 7am-11pm • health food store & deli • also Coralville location at 1101 2nd St, 319/358-5513

EROTICA

Romantix Adult Superstore 315 Kirkwood Ave (at Gilbert) **319/351–9444** • 9am-3am

Marshalltown

EROTICA

Adult Odyssey 907 Iowa Ave E **641/752–6550** • videos • toys • leather

Okoboji

NIGHTCLUBS

Cocktails 575 Hwy 71 (in Fox Plaza), Arnolds Park **712/332–2032** • 4pm-2am • gay-friendly • neighborhood bar • food served • karaoke

Sioux City

NIGHTCLUBS

Jones Street Station 412 Jones St (at 5th St) **712/258–6338** • 7pm-2am, clsd Sun-Mon • gay/ straight • dancing/DJ• karaoke • wheelchair access • gay-owned

EROTICA

Romantix Adult Superstore 511 Pearl St **712/277–8566** • 9am-3am

Waterloo

ACCOMMODATIONS

Stella's Guesthouse 324 Summit Ave (at Chicago) **319/232–2122** • lesbians/ gay men • full brkfst • hot tub • clothing optional • shared baths • nonsmoking • gay-owned

NIGHTCLUBS

Kings & Queens Knight Club 304 W 4th St (at Jefferson) **319/232–3001** • 6pm-2am, clsd Mon• gay-friendly • dancing/DJ • transgender-friendly • drag shows • videos • young crowd • wheelchair access

KANSAS

Statewide

PUBLICATIONS

The Liberty Press **316/652–7737** • Kansas statewide LGBT newspaper

Junction City

NIGHTCLUBS

Xcalibur Club 384 Grant Ave **785/762–2050** • 6pm-2am, clsd Mon-Tue • gay/ straight • dancing/DJ • live shows • gay-owned

Kansas City

see also Kansas City, Missouri

ENTERTAINMENT & RECREATION

2nd Friday Art Walk downtown **913/371–0024** • 5pm-8pm 2nd Fri • art galleries & food

Lawrence

NIGHTCLUBS

Granada 1020 Massachusetts (at 11th) **785/842–1390** • hours vary, clsd Sun • gay/ straight • dancing/DJ • live bands • wheelchair access

Jazzhaus 926–1/2 Massachusetts St **785/749–3320, 785/749–1387** • 8pm-2am, clsd Sun • gay-friendly • live music • karaoke

Wilde's Chateau 2412 Iowa St **785/856–1514**
• 9pm-2am Wed, Fri & Sat only • gay/ straight
• dancing/DJ • theme nights

CAFES

Henry's 11 E 8th St (btwn Massachusetts St
& New Hampshire) **785/331–3511** • 8am-
2am • espresso & sandwiches • plenty veggie
• also full bar from 5pm upstairs

Java Break 17 E 7th St (at New Hampshire)
785/749–5282 • 24hrs • sandwiches •
desserts • gay-owned

RESTAURANTS

Teller's Restaurant & Bar 746
Massachusetts St (at 8th) **785/843–4111** •
11:30am-10pm, till 11pm Fri-Sat, from 10am
Sun • Italian • some veggie • wheelchair
access

BOOKSTORES

The Dusty Bookshelf 708 Massachusetts St
785/749–4643 • 10am-8pm, till 10pm Fri-Sat,
noon-6pm Sun • used books • feminist &
LGBT section • gay-owned

Manhattan

BOOKSTORES

The Dusty Bookshelf 700 N Manhattan Ave
785/539–2839 • 10am-8pm, till 6pm Sat,
noon-5pm Sun • used books • feminist &
LGBT section • live music • gay-owned

Overland Park

ACCOMMODATIONS

Holtze Executive Village 11400 College
Blvd **913/344–8100, 888/446–5893** • gay-
friendly • pool • jacuzzi • WiFi • wheelchair
access • $79-189

BARS

The Fox 7520 Shawnee Mission Pkwy (at
Metcalf) **913/384–0369** • 1pm-2am, from 6pm
Sat-Mon • mostly gay men • neighborhood
bar • dancing/DJ • transgender-friendly •
karaoke

Topeka

INFO LINES & SERVICES

Freedom Group AA 3916 SW 17th St
785/215–7436 • 8pm Fri

BARS

The Tool Shed Tap 921 S Kansas Ave (near
10th St) **785/234–0482** • 3pm-2am • mostly
gay men • neighborhood bar • dancing/DJ •
country/ western

BOOKSTORES

Barnes & Noble 6130 SW 17th St #101
785/273–9600 • 9am-11pm • LGBT section

Wichita

INFO LINES & SERVICES

Land of Awes Gay Info

One Day at a Time Gay AA 156 S Kansas
Ave (at MCC, enter on English) **316/522–7411,
316/522–2321** • 8pm Tue & Th

ACCOMMODATIONS

Hawthorn Suites 2405 N Ridge Rd
316/729–5700 • gay-friendly • kids/ small pets
ok • brkfst buffet • wheelchair access • $75-150

BARS

Club 1507 1507 E Pawnee (at Ellis St)
316/260–9070 • 2pm-2am • lesbians/ gay
men • dancing/DJ • wheelchair access • gay-
owned

J's Lounge 513 E Central (at Emporia)
316/262–1363 • 4pm-2am • lesbians/ gay
men • cabaret • live shows • karaoke • patio •
wheelchair access • "an upscale dive"

Side Street Retro Lounge 1106 S Pattie St
(near Lincoln & Hydraulic) **316/267–0324** •
2pm-2am • mostly gay men • dancing/DJ •
country/ western • wheelchair access

The Store 3210 E Osie (btw Harry &
Hillside) **316/683–9781** • 2pm-2am • mostly
women • men welcome • neighborhood bar

NIGHTCLUBS

Club XES 2828 E 31st South **316/871–1318**
• 8pm-2am, clsd Mon-Tue • lesbians/ gay men
• dancing/DJ • drag shows • karaoke

Fantasy Complex 3201 S Hillside (at 31st)
316/682–5494 • 8pm-2am Th-Sun • lesbians/
gay men • dancing/DJ • karaoke • drag shows
• also South Forty country/ western bar from
5pm Th-Fri, from 2pm Sun • wheelchair access

CAFES

Riverside Perk 1144 N Bitting Ave (at 11th)
316/264–6464 • 7am-10pm, till midnight Fri-
Sat, from 10am Sun • WiFi • also Lava Lounge
juice bar next door

The Vagabond 614 W Douglas Ave
316/303–1110 • 7am-2am • theme nights •
art gallery • also bar • WiFi

RESTAURANTS

Moe's Sub Shop 2815 S Hydraulic St (at
Wassall) **316/524–5511** • 11am-8pm, clsd Sun

Old Mill Tasty Shop 604 E Douglas Ave (at St Francis) 316/264-6500 • 11am-3pm, from 8am Sat, clsd Sun • old-fashioned soda fountain • some veggie

Rain Cafe & Lounge 518 E Douglas 316/261-9000 • 11am-2am, from 1pm Sun • full bar • DJ on the wknds

River City Brewing Company 150 N Mosley St 316/263-2739 • 11am-10pm, till 2am wknds • live music

Riverside Cafe 739 W 13th St (at Bitting) 316/262-6703 • 6am-8pm, till 2pm Sun

Uptown Bistro 301 N Mead (at 2nd) 316/262-3232 • lunch & dinner daily, noon-8pm Sun • Mediterranean

Zen Vegetarian 3101 N Rock Rd 316/425-7700 • 11am-10pm, till 9pm Sun, clsd Mon

ENTERTAINMENT & RECREATION

Cabaret Oldtown Theatre 412 1/2 E Douglas Ave (at Topeka) 316/265-4400 • edgy, kitschy productions

Mosley Street Melodrama 234 N Mosley St (btwn 1st & 2nd St) 316/263-0222 • melodrama, homestyle buffet & full bar!

Wichita Arts 334 N Mead 316/462-2787 • promotes visual & performing arts • ArtScene publication has extensive cultural calendar

RETAIL SHOPS

East & West Menswear 924 E Douglas 316/440-9210 • 11am-7pm, till 9pm Fri-Sat, clsd Mon

PUBLICATIONS

The Liberty Press 316/652-7737 • statewide LGBT newspaper

EROTICA

Adult Superstore 5858 S Broadway 316/522-9040

Circle Cinema/ Video 2570 S Seneca St (at Crawford St) 316/264-2245 • 24hrs

Fetish Lingerie 2150 S Broadway St (btwn E Clark & E Kinkaid Sts) 316/264-7800 • leather, toys, clubwear • all sizes available

Patricia's 6143 W Kellogg (at Dugan) 316/942-1244

Wichita

LGBT PRIDE:
June, web: www.wichitapride.org.

ANNUAL EVENTS:
May - River Festival, web: www.wichitariverfestival.org.
October - Tallgrass Film Festival 316/974-0089, web: www.tall-grassfilmfest.com. Gay-friendly independent film festival w/ some LGBT programming.

CITY INFO:
Kansas Travel & Tourism Dept 800/252-6727, web: www.trav-elks.com.

TRANSIT:
American Cab Co. 316/262-7511.
Emu Express 316/734-0100.
Metropolitan Transit Authority 316/265-7221.

ATTRACTIONS:
Botanica 316/264-0448, web: www.botanica.org.
Kansas African American Museum 316/262-7651.
Mid-America All-Indian Center 316/350-3340, web: www.thein-diancenter.org.
Old Cowtown Museum 316/219-1871, web: www.oldcowtown.org.
Oldtown.
Pyradomes.
Wichita Art Museum 316/268-4921, web: www.wichitaartmuseum.org.

KENTUCKY

Covington

see also Cincinnati, Ohio

BARS

701 Bar and Lounge 701 Bakewell St (at 7th St) **859/431–7011** • 5pm-1am • gay-friendly • neighborhood bar • dancing/DJ • live shows • karaoke • food served

Bar Monet 837 Willard St **859/491-2403** • 4pm-1am • lesbians/ gay men • bar food • dancing/DJ • karaoke • shows

Rosie's Tavern 643 Bakewell St (at 7th St) **859/291–9707** • 3pm-2:30am • gay/ straight • neighborhood bar • lesbian-owned

Yadda Club 404 Pike St (at Main St) **859/491–5600** • 8pm-2:30am Wed-Sat • lesbians/ gay men • neighborhood bar • dancing/DJ • T-dance Sun • multiracial • live shows • karaoke • food served • patio • wheelchair access • lesbian-owned

Lexington

INFO LINES & SERVICES

Gay/ Lesbian AA 472 Rose St (at St Augustine's Chapel) **859/225–1212 (AA#)** • 8pm Wed • also 7:30pm Fri at 205 E Short St (church)

GLSO Pride Center of the Bluegrass 389 Waller Ave #100 **859/253–3233** • 10am-3pm Mon-Fri

ACCOMMODATIONS

Ramada Limited 2261 Elkhorn Rd (off I-75) **859/294–7375, 800/272–6232** • gay-friendly • pool • WiFi • wheelchair access • $70-99

Weaver's Rest Cottage 106 Churchill Ct, Berea **859/582–3475** • rental home • WiFi • lesbian-owned • $75

BARS

The Bar Complex 224 E Main St (at Esplanade) **859/255–1551** • 4pm-2am, till 1am wknds • popular • lesbians/ gay men • dancing/DJ • drag shows • live shows • wheelchair access

Crossings 117 N Limestone St **859/233–7266** • 4pm-2am, clsd Sun • mostly gay men • neighborhood bar • live shows • karaoke • leather events • wheelchair access

Mia's 127 N Limestone **859/455–9903** • 4pm-2:30am, from 11am wknds for brunch • lesbians/ gay men • neighborhood bar • karaoke • kitchen open till 1am

RESTAURANTS

Alfalfa Restaurant 141 E Main St **859/253–0014** • lunch & dinner, brunch wknds • healthy multi-ethnic • plenty veggie • folk music wknds

Natasha's Bistro & Bar 112 Esplanade (at Main St) **859/259–2754, 888/901–8412 (SHOP #)** • lunch & dinner, clsd Sun • eclectic dining • plenty veggie • also live theater & music

BOOKSTORES

Joseph-Beth 161 Lexington Green Circle **859/273–2911, 800/248–6849** • 9am-10pm, till 11pm Fri-Sat, 11am-9pm Sun • also cafe • WiFi • wheelchair access

Sqecial Media 371 S Limestone St (at Euclid) **859/255–4316** • 10am-8pm, noon-6pm • also pride items

PUBLICATIONS

GLSO (Gay/ Lesbian) News **859/253–3233** • local news & calendar

EROTICA

Romantix Adult Superstore 933 Winchester Rd **859/252–0357** • 24hrs

Louisville

INFO LINES & SERVICES

Gay AA 1432 Highland Ave (at MCC) **502/587–6225** • 4:30pm & 6pm Sun, 7:30pm Tue, 6:30pm Wed, 7pm Fri

ACCOMMODATIONS

21c Museum Hotel 700 W Main **502/217–6300, 877/217–6400** • gay-friendly • boutique hotel w/ museum • also Proof on Main restaurant

The Brown Hotel 335 W Broadway (at 4th) **502/583–1234, 888/888–5252** • gay-friendly

Columbine B&B 1707 S 3rd St (near Lee St) **502/635–5000, 800/635–5010** • gay-friendly • 1896 Greek Revivial mansion • full brkfst • nonsmoking • WiFi • gay-owned • $119-165

Galt House Hotel & Suites 140 N 4th St (at W Main) **502/589–5200, 800/843–4258** • gay-friendly • waterfront hotel

Holiday Inn Southwest 4110 Dixie Hwy (at I-264) **502/448–2020** • gay-friendly • food served • swimming • lounge • wheelchair access

Hyatt Regency Louisville 320 W Jefferson St (at 3rd) **502/581–1234** • gay-friendly • pool • tennis • WiFi • wheelchair access

Inn at the Park 1332 S 4th St (at Park Ave) **502/638-0045** • gay-friendly • restored mansion • full brkfst • nonsmoking • WiFi • $129-229

BARS

Magnolia Bar 1398 S 2nd St (at Magnolia) **502/637-9052** • 4pm-4am • gay-friendly • neighborhood bar • young crowd

Teddy Bears Bar & Grill 1148 Garvin Pl (at St Catherine) **502/589-2619** • 11am-4am, from 1pm Sun • mostly gay men • neighborhood bar • wheelchair access

Tink's Pub 2235 S Preston St **502/634-8180** • 4pm-close, from 2pm Sun • lesbians/ gay men • neighborhood bar • drag shows • karaoke

Louisville

WHERE THE GIRLS ARE:
On Main or Market Streets near 1st, and generally in the north-central part of town, just west of I-65.

ENTERTAINMENT:
Community Chorus 502/327-4099.

LGBT PRIDE:
June. 502/649-4851, web: www.kentuckianapridefestival.com.

ANNUAL EVENTS:
May - Kentucky Derby, web: www.kentuckyderby.com.
June-July - Kentucky Shakespeare Festival 502/637-4933, web: www.kyshakes.org.
October - World's Largest Halloween Party, Louisville Zoo, web: www.louisvillezoo.org.
October - St James Court Art Show 502/ 635-1842, web: www.stjamescourtartshow.com.

CITY INFO:
Louisville Visitor Center 800/626-5646.
Convention & Visitors Bureau, web: www.gotolouisville.com.

BEST VIEW:
Aboard the *Belle of Louisville* steamboat at Waterfront Park.

WEATHER:
Mild winters and long, hot summers!

ATTRACTIONS:
Belle of Louisville steamboat 502/574-2992, web: www.belle-oflouisville.org.
Churchill Downs 502/636-4400, web: www.churchilldowns.com.
Farmington Historic Home 502/452-9920.
Hadley Pottery 866/584-2171, web: www.hadleypottery.com.
Kentucky Derby 502/584-6383.
Locust Grove Historic Farm 502/897-9845, web: www.locust-grove.org.
Louisville Slugger Tour 877/775-8443, web: www.sluggermu-seum.org.
St. James Court.
Waterfront Park, web: www.louisvillewaterfront.com.
West Main Street Historic District, web: www.mainstreetassocia-tion.com.

TRANSIT:
Yellow Taxi 502/636-5511.
Louisville Transportation Co 502/637-6511, web: www.loutrans.com.
TARC Bus System 502/585-1234, web: www.ridetarc.org.
Louisville Horse Trams 502/581-0100, web: www.louisvillehorse-trams.com.

Tryangles 209 S Preston St (at Market) **502/583–6395** • 4pm-4am, from 1pm Sun • mostly gay men • strippers • wheelchair access

NIGHTCLUBS

The Connection Complex 120 S Floyd St (at Market) **502/585–5752** • 7pm-4am, till 2am Mon-Tue • popular • lesbians/gay men • dancing/DJ • piano bar & cabaret • leather • videos • wheelchair access

Starbase Q 921 W Main St (at 9th St) • 8pm-close, from 4pm Wed, clsd Mon • mostly gay men • dancing/DJ • karaoke • industrial video bar

CAFES

Days Coffeehouse 1420 Bardstown Rd (at Edenside) **502/456–1170** • 6:30am-10pm, till 11pm Fri-Sat • lesbian-owned

RESTAURANTS

Cafe Mimosa 1543 Bardstown Rd **502/458–2233** • lunch & dinner • Vietnamese, Chinese & sushi

El Mundo 2345 Frankfort Ave **502/899–9930** • 11:30am-10pm, full bar till 2am Th-Sat, clsd Sun-Mon • popular • Mexican

Havana Rumba 4115 Oechsli Ave (off State Hwy 1447) **502/897–1959** • lunch & dinner • Cuban

Jack Fry's 1007 Bardstown Rd **502/452–9244** • lunch & dinner • steak/ southern • live jazz

Lynn's Paradise Cafe 984 Barret Ave (at Baxter) **502/583–3447** • 7am-10pm, from 8am wknds • popular • lesbians/gay men • colorful, funky decor • also bar • WiFi • lesbian-owned

Mayan Cafe 813 E Market St **502/566–0651** • lunch Mon-Fri, dinner nightly, clsd Sun • Mayan/ Mexican

Porcini 2370 Frankfort Ave **502/894–8686** • dinner nightly, clsd Sun • Italian

Proof on Main 702 W Main St (at 7th) **502/217–6360** • brkfst & lunch Mon-Fri, dinner nightly • upscale • modern American w/ Tuscan influence

Ramsi's Cafe on the World 1293 Bardstown Rd **502/451–0700** • 11am-1am, till 2am Fri-Sat, Sun brunch • eclectic menu

Rudyard Kipling 422 W Oak St **502/636–1311** • 6:30pm-close Fri-Sat • occasionally open for plays & special events

Third Avenue Cafe 1164 S 3rd St (at W Oak) **502/585–2233** • 11am-9pm, till 10pm Fri-Sat, clsd Sun • vegan/ vegetarian • patio

Vietnam Kitchen 5339 Mitscher Ave **502/363–5154** • Vietnamese • plenty veggie

Windy City Pizza 2622 S 4th St (at Winkler) **502/636–3708** • clsd Sun-Mon • gay-owned

Zen Garden 2240 Frankfort Ave **502/895–9114** • lunch & dinner, clsd Sun • Asian • vegetarian

ENTERTAINMENT & RECREATION

Pandora Productions PO Box 4185, 40204 • LGBT-themed productions

Voices of Kentuckiana **502/583–1013** • LGBT community chorus

BOOKSTORES

Borders 3024 Bardstown Rd (in Gardiner Lane Shopping Center) **502/456–6660, 800/844–7323** • 9am-9pm, 10am-6pm Sun • also 4600 Shelbyville Rd, Shelbyville Plaza, 502/893-0133

Carmichael's 1295 Bardstown Rd (at Longest Ave) **502/456–6950** • 8am-10pm, till 11pm Fri-Sat, from 10am Sun • large LGBT section

PUBLICATIONS

The Letter • LGBT newspaper

Midway

CAFES

Tavern 8:15 131 E Main St (inside Le Marché boutique mall) **859/846–4688** • 11am-3pm, till 4pm Sat • WiFi

Newport

see also Cincinnati, Ohio

BARS

The Crazy Fox Saloon 901 Washington Ave (at 9th) **859/261–2143** • 3pm-2:30am • gay/ straight • friendly neighborhood bar

Owensboro

BARS

Equals Bar 1006 E 4th St (at Hathaway) **270/313–0820** • 4:30-2am • lesbians/gay men • dancing/DJ • piano bar • karaoke • drag shows

Paducah

EROTICA

Romantix Adult Superstore 243 Brown (at Irvin Cobb Dr) **270/442–5584**

LOUISIANA

Statewide

PUBLICATIONS

Ambush Mag 504/522–8049 • oldest LGBT newspaper for the Gulf South (Texas through Florida)

Baton Rouge

INFO LINES & SERVICES

Freedom of Choice/ Gay AA 7747 Tom Dr (at MCC) **225/930–0026 (AA#)** • 8pm Th & 8pm Sat

BARS

George's Place 860 St Louis **225/387–9798** • 3pm-2am, from 5pm Sat, clsd Sun • popular • lesbians/ gay men • neighborhood bar • videos • karaoke • male strippers Fri • wheelchair access

Hound Dogs 668 Main St (at 7th) **225/344–0807** • 2pm-2am, from 4pm Mon-Tue, clsd Sun • lesbians/ gay men • neighborhood bar • wheelchair access

NIGHTCLUBS

Cajun Cove of Baton Rouge 4550 Concord Ave **225/246–8317** • 4pm-2am, from noon Sat, clsd Sun • lesbians/ gay men • neighborhood bar • dancing/DJ • karaoke • live shows • 18+ • wheelchair access

Splash 2183 Highland Rd **225/242–9491** • 9pm-2am, clsd Sun-Tue • popular • lesbians/ gay men • dancing/DJ • drag shows • 18+ • wheelchair access

RESTAURANTS

Dalton's 244 Lafayette St (at Florida Blvd) **225/387–5081** • 11am-2pm Mon-Fri, from 6pm Wed-Sat • full bar and live music

Drusilla Seafood 3482 Drusilla Ln (at Jefferson Hwy) **225/923–0896** • 11am-10pm

Ralph & Kacoo's 6110 Bluebonnet Blvd (off I-10 & Perkins) **225/766–2113** • 11am-9:30pm, till 10:30pm Fri-Sat • Cajun • full bar

PUBLICATIONS

Ambush Mag 504/522–8049 • LGBT newspaper for the Gulf South (TX through FL)

EROTICA

Grand Cinema Station 10732 Florida Blvd **225/272–2010**

Breaux Bridge

ACCOMMODATIONS

Maison des Amis 111 Washington St (at Bridge St) **337/507–3399** • gay-friendly • charming 1870 residence overlooking legendary Bayou Teche • full brkfst • WiFi • $100-250

Gretna

see New Orleans

Harvey

see New Orleans

Houma

NIGHTCLUBS

Pulse Video Lounge 6441 W Main St **985/876–7777** • 5pm-2am, from 7pm Sat, clsd Sun-Mon • gay-friendly • gay-owned

Lafayette

INFO LINES & SERVICES

AA Gay/ Lesbian 115 Leonie St **337/991–0830 (AA#)** • call for times & locations

BARS

Sadie's Niteclub 425 Jefferson St **337/267–7404** • 4pm-2am, 8pm-midnight Sun • dancing/DJ/ • bands • live shows •18+

Lake Charles

ACCOMMODATIONS

Aunt Ruby's B&B 504 Pujo St (at Hodges) **337/430–0603** • gay/ straight • full brkfst • WiFi • $85-150

NIGHTCLUBS

Crystal's 112 W Broad St **337/433–5457** • 9pm-2am, till 4am Fri • lesbians/ gay men • dancing/DJ • country/ western • drag shows • wheelchair access

RESTAURANTS

Pujo St Cafe 901 Ryan St (at Pujo) **337/439–2054** • 11am-9pm, till 10pm Fri-Sat, clsd Sun • full bar • gay-owned

Metairie

see New Orleans

Monroe

BARS

The Corner Bar 512 N 3rd St (at Pine) **318/329-0046** • 8pm-2am, 3pm-midnight Sun, clsd Mon & Wed, seasonal hrs • lesbians/ gay men • neighborhood bar • multiracial • live shows • karaoke • drag shows • 18+ • gay-owned

Natchitoches

ACCOMMODATIONS

Chez des Amis B&B 910 Washington St (btwn Texas & Pavie) **318/352-2647** • gay/ straight • full brkfst • nonsmoking • WiFi • gay-owned • $110-165

Judge Porter House B & B 321 Second St **318/527-1555, 800/441-8343** • gay/ straight • full brkfst • nonsmoking • WiFi • gay-owned • $145-175

New Orleans

INFO LINES & SERVICES

AA Lambda Center 638 Papworth Ave #101, Metairie **504/838-3399 (GENERAL AA OFFICE #)** • daily meetings • call for schedule

Lesbian/ Gay Community Center of New Orleans 2114 Decatur St (btwn Elysian Fields & Frenchmen) **504/945-1103** • 2pm-8pm, noon-6pm Fri-Sat, clsd Sun • call first • wheelchair access

ACCOMMODATIONS

1896 O'Malley House B&B 120 S Pierce St (at Canal St) **504/488-5896, 866/226-1896** • gay/ straight • jacuzzi • nonsmoking • kids ok • WiFi • gay-owned • $135-155

5 Continents B&B 1731 Esplanade Ave (at Claiborne) **504/324-8594, 800/997-4652** • gay/ straight • B&B • full brkfst • kids/ pets ok • WiFi • gay-owned • $100-300

Aaron Ingram Haus 1012 Elysian Fields Ave (btwn N Rampart & St Claude) **504/949-3110** • gay/ straight • guesthouse • apts • courtyard • WiFi • gay-owned • $68-175

American Creole House 1124 St Charles Ave (at Calliope) **504/522-7777, 800/999-7891** • gay/ straight • nonsmoking • WiFi • gay-owned • $79-329

Andrew Jackson Hotel 919 Royal St (btwn St Philip & Dumaine) **504/561-5881, 800/654-0224** • gay-friendly • historic inn • WiFi • $69-250

Antebellum Guest House 1333 Esplanade Ave (at Marais St) **504/943-1900** • gay/ straight • B&B in 1830s Grand Greek Revival • full brkfst • clothing-optional • nonsmoking • WiFi • gay-owned • $100-175

Ashton's B&B 2023 Esplanade Ave (at Galvez) **504/942-7048, 800/725-4131** • gay-friendly • quiet location • WiFi • $135-160

Auld Sweet Olive B&B 2460 N Rampart St (at Spain) **504/947-4332, 877/470-5323** • gay/ straight • popular • kids 13+ ok • nonsmoking • WiFi • $65-150

B&W Courtyards B&B 2425 Chartres St (btwn Mandeville & Spain) **504/945-9418, 800/585-5731** • gay-friendly • three 19th-c bldgs connected by courtyards • hot tub • nonsmoking • WiFi • gay-owned • $99+

Biscuit Palace Guest House 730 Dumaine (btwn Royal & Bourbon) **504/525-9949** • gay-friendly • 1820s Creole mansion • B&B & apts • in the French Quarter • kids ok • WiFi • wheelchair access • $105-150

Block-Keller House 3620 Canal St (at Telemachus) **504/483-3033, 877/588-3033** • gay/ straight • nonsmoking • WiFi • gay-owned • $125-165

Bon Maison Guest House 835 Bourbon St (btwn Lafitte's & Bourbon Pub) **504/561-8498** • gay/ straight • nonsmoking • gay-owned • $95-300

Bourbon Orleans Hotel 717 Orleans (at Bourbon St) **504/523-2222** • popular • gay-friendly • swimming • WiFi • Napoleon's Itch (popular lounge) • $99-189

The Burgundy B&B 2513 Burgundy St (at St Roch) **504/942-1463, 800/970-2153** • gay/ straight • near French Quarter • clothing-optional hot tub • nonsmoking • WiFi • gay-owned • $80-90

Bywater B&B 1026 Clouet St **504/944-8438** • gay-friendly • fireplace • nonsmoking • kids/ pets ok • WiFi • lesbian & gay-owned • $75-125

Chez Palmiers B&B 1744 N Rampart St **877/233-9449** • gay/ straight • pool • nonsmoking • kids 12+ ok • WiFi • gay-owned • $80-155

The Cornstalk Hotel 915 Royal St **504/523-1515, 800/759-6112** • gay-friendly • kids ok • WiFi • $95-210

The Degas House 2306 Esplanade Ave (at Tonti St) **504/821-5009, 800/755-6730** • gay-friendly • full brkfst • jacuzzi • WiFi • $149-175

Elysian Guest House 1008 Elysian Fields Ave (at Rampart St) 504/324-4311 • gay-friendly • hot tub • nonsmoking • WiFi • gay-owned • $85-135

Empress Hotel 1317 Ursulines Ave (btwn Treme & Marais) **504/529-4100, 888/524-9200** • gay-friendly • small Euro-style hotel • WiFi • kids/ pets ok • $35-75

The Frenchmen Hotel 417 Frenchmen St (where Esplanade, Decatur & Frenchmen intersect) **504/948-2166, 800/831-1781** • popular • gay/ straight • spa • pool • kids ok • nonsmoking • WiFi • wheelchair access • $89-299

New Orleans

WHERE THE GIRLS ARE:
Wandering the Quarter, or rebuilding the small artsy area known as Mid-City, north of the Quarter up Esplanade St.

ANNUAL EVENTS:
February - Mardi Gras 504/566-5011, web: www.mardigras.com. North America's rowdiest block party.

March - Tennesse Williams Festival, web: www.tennesseewilliams.net.

April - Gay Easter Parade 504/522-8049, web: www.gayeasterparade.com.

April - Gulf Coast Womyn's Sister Camp at Camp SisterSpirit (in Ovett, MS) 601/344-1411, web: www.campsisterspirit.com.

April/May - New Orleans Jazz & Heritage Festival, web: www.nojazzfest.com.

May - Saints & Sinners, LGBT writers' festival 504/581-1144, web: www.sasfest.org.

August - DecaFest, web: www.decafest.com. Celebration of LGBT culture during Labor Day.

August - Southern Decadence 504/522-8047, web: www.southerndecadence.com. Gay mini-Mardi Gras during Labor Day.

CITY INFO:
504/566-5011 or 800/672-6124, web: www.neworleanscvb.com.
Louisiana Office of Tourism 225/342-8100 or 800/677-4082, web: www.louisianatravel.com.

ATTRACTIONS:
Bourbon Street in the French Quarter.
Cabildo (to see the Louisiana Purchase) 504/568-6968.
Cafe du Monde for beignets 504/587-0835, web: www.cafe-dumonde.com.
Garden District.
Haunted History Tour 504/861-2727, web: www.hauntedhistory-tours.com.
Moon Walk.
New Orleans Museum of Art 504/488-2631, web: www.noma.org.
Pat O'Brien's for a hurricane 504/525-4823, web: www.pato-briens.com.
Preservation Hall 504/522-2841 or 888/946-5299, web: www.preservationhall.com.
Top of the Market.

WEATHER:
Summer temperatures hover in the 90°s with subtropical humidity. And on the heels of all that heat and humidity come hurricanes. Hurricane season stretches from June 1 to November 30. Winters can be rainy and chilly. The average temperature in February (Mardi Gras month) is 58°, while the average precipitation is 5.23".

TRANSIT:
United Cab 504/522-9771.
New Orleans Regional Transit Authority 504/248-3900, web: www.norta.com.

The Green House Inn 1212 Magazine St (at Erato) 504/525–1333, 800/966–1303 • lesbians/ gay men • 1840s guesthouse • gym • hot tub • pool • nonsmoking • pets ok • WiFi • gay-owned • $89-199

Hotel Maison de Ville 727 Rue Toulouse (btwn Bourbon & Royal Sts) 504/561–5858 • gay-friendly • upscale hotel • pool • WiFi • $199-699

Hotel Monteleone 214 Royal St (at Iberville) 504/523–3341, 800/535–9595 • gay-friendly • deluxe historic hotel • rumored to be haunted • $139-1,300

Inn The Quarter Reservation Service 888/523–5235 • gay-friendly • nonsmoking • gay & straight-owned • $79-600

Kerlerec House 928 Kerlerec St (at Dauphine St) 504/944–8544 • gay/ straight • 1 block from the French Quarter • hot tub • gardens • kids ok • nonsmoking • WiFi • gay-owned • $75-450

La Dauphine, Residence des Artistes 2316 Dauphine St (btwn Elysian Fields & Marigny) 504/948–2217 • gay/ straight • B&B • nonsmoking • WiFi • gay-owned • $85-185

La Maison Marigny B&B on Bourbon 1421 Bourbon St (at Esplanade) 504/948–3638, 800/570–2014 • gay-friendly • on the quiet end of Bourbon St • nonsmoking • WiFi • gay-owned • $129+

Lamothe House Hotel 621 Esplanade Ave (btwn Royal & Chartres) 504/947–1161, 800/367–5858 • gay/ straight • popular • jacuzzi • pool • kids ok • nonsmoking • WiFi • straight & gay-owned • $69-299

Le Papillon Guesthouse 2011 N Rampart St (at Touro St) 504/948–4993, 504/884–4008 (CELL) • gay/ straight • nonsmoking • pets ok • gay-owned • $95-135

Lions Inn 2517 Chartres St (btwn Spain & Franklin) 504/945–2339, 800/485–6846 • gay/ straight • handsome 1850s home • pool • hot tub • nudity ok • WiFi • nonsmoking • semi-tropical patio • gay-owned • $50-165

Maison Dupuy Hotel 1001 Toulouse St 504/586–8000, 800/535–9177 • gay-friendly • luxury boutique hotel • fine dining restaurant • swimming pool • hot tub • $99-489

Mentone B&B 1437 Pauger St (at Kerlerec) 504/943–3019 • gay-friendly • suite in Victorian in the Faubourg Marigny district • nonsmoking • WiFi • women-owned • $125-175

New Orleans Guest House 1118 Ursulines Ave (at N Rampart) 504/566–1177, 800/562–1177 • gay-friendly • Creole cottage dated back to 1848 • courtyard • nonsmoking • gay-owned • $79-199

The Olivier House 828 Toulouse 504/525–8456, 866/525–9748 • gay-friendly • pool • kids/ pets ok • WiFi • wheelchair access • $135-450

Pierre Coulon Guest House 504/943–6692, 866/328–1497 • gay-friendly • quiet apt patio • nonsmoking • $85-230

Royal Barracks Guest House 717 Barracks St (at Bourbon) 504/529–7269, 888/255–7269 • gay-friendly • hot tub • nonsmoking • WiFi • $89-159

Royal Street Courtyard 2438 Royal St (at Spain) 504/943–6818, 888/846–4004 • gay/ straight • suites in 1850s guesthouse • hot tub • pets ok • WiFi • gay-owned • $65-109

St Charles Guest House 1748 Prytania St (at Felicity) 504/523–6556 • gay-friendly • some shared baths • pool • patio • WiFi • $50-145

Ursuline Guest House 708 Ursuline Ave (btwn Royal & Bourbon) 504/525–8509, 800/654–2351 • gay/ straight • hot tub • nonsmoking • WiFi • wheelchair access • gay-owned • $75-145

W New Orleans—French Quarter 316 Chartres St 504/581–1200, 877/WHOTELS (RESERVATIONS ONLY) • gay-friendly • pool • WiFi • also restaurant • wheelchair access • $289-489

BARS

700 Club 700 Burgundy (at St Peter) 504/561–1095 • noon- 5am, til midnight Sun • lesbians/ gay men • videos

Big Daddy's 2513 Royal St (at Franklin) 504/948–6288 • 24hrs • lesbians/ gay men • neighborhood bar • occasional shows • wheelchair access

Bourbon Pub & Parade 801 Bourbon St (at St Ann) 504/529–2107 • 24hrs • popular • lesbians/ gay men • dancing/DJ • theme nights • Sun T-dance • drag shows/ strippers • videos • 18+ • WiFi

Cafe Lafitte in Exile/ The Balcony Bar 901 Bourbon St (at Dumaine) 504/522–8397 • 24hrs • popular • mostly gay men • dancing/DJ • live shows • videos • Balcony Bar upstairs w/ cyberbar

Club Tribute 3202 N Arnoult Rd (at 18th St), Metairie 504/455–1311 • 9pm-close Fri-Sat only • mostly women

Country Club 634 Louisa St (at Royal) **504/945–0742** • 11am-1am • popular • gay/straight • food served • cabaret • swimming • volleyball • nude sunbathing • not your father's country club!

Cutter's 706 Franklin Ave (at Royal) **504/948–4200** • 3pm-3am, from 11am wknds • lesbians/ gay men • neighborhood bar • WiFi • wheelchair access

The Double Play 439 Dauphine (at St Louis) **504/523–4517** • 24hrs • mostly gay men • neighborhood bar • transgender-friendly

The Four Seasons 3229 N Causeway Blvd (at 18th), Metairie **504/832–0659** • 3pm-close • popular • mostly gay men • neighborhood bar • live music & shows in summer • karaoke • patio • also the Out Back Bar summers • gay-owned

The Friendly Bar 2301 Chartres St (at Marigny) **504/943–8929** • 11am-close • popular • mostly gay men • neighborhood bar • wheelchair access • women-owned

Good Friends Bar 740 Dauphine (at St Ann) **504/566–7191** • popular • mostly gay men • neighborhood bar • professional crowd • karaoke Tue • wheelchair access • also Queens Head Pub upstairs Sun only • popular piano sing-along 4pm-8pm

Le Roundup 819 St Louis St (at Dauphine) **504/561–8340** • 24hrs • mostly gay men • neighborhood bar • very MTF-friendly crowd

Napoleon's Itch 734 Bourbon (at St Ann, in Bourbon Orleans Hotel) **504/371–5450** • noon-2am, till 4am Fri-Sat • popular • mostly gay men • wine & martini bar • nonsmoking

Rawhide 2010 740 Burgundy St (at St Ann) **504/525–8106** • 1pm-5am • popular • mostly gay men • neighborhood bar • dancing/DJ • alternative, underground sound • leather • videos

Rubyfruit Jungle 1135 Decatur St (at Governor Nicholls) **504/571–1863** • 5pm-close, from noon wknds • clsd Mon-Tue • mostly women • neighborhood bar • dancing/DJ • drag shows • transgender-friendly • videos • 18+

The Sanctuary 2301 N Causeway Blvd (at 34th), Metairie **504/834–7979** • 5pm-close • lesbians/ gay men • neighborhood bar • live shows • Sat • karaoke • monthly drag shows • wheelchair access

Spotted Cat 623 Frenchmen St **206/337–3273** • 4pm-2am • gay-friendly • excellent live jazz

Tubby's Golden Lantern 1239 Royal St (at Barracks) **504/529–2860** • noon-4am • mostly gay men • neighborhood bar • drag shows Fri-Sun

NIGHTCLUBS

Girl Bar New Orleans 801 Bourbon St (above the Bourbon Pub), Phoenix, AZ **504/529–2107** • 9pm-3am Tue only • mostly women • dancing/DJ • video • young crowd

Oz 800 Bourbon St (at St Ann) **504/593–9491** • 24hrs • popular • mostly gay men • dancing/DJ • drag shows • live shows • videos • young crowd • wheelchair access

Starlight by the Park 834 N Rampart (at Dumaine) **504/561–8939** • noon-2am, 24hrs Fri-Sun • lesbians/ gay men • neighborhood bar • drag shows • also courtyard bar • wheelchair access

CAFES

Cafe Rose Nicaud 632 Frenchmen St (btwn Royal & Chartres) **504/949–3300** • 7am-7pm • WiFi

CC's Coffee House 941 Royal St **504/581–6996** • 7am-7pm • WiFi

Croissants d'Or 617 Ursulines St **504/524–4663** • 7am-2pm, clsd Tue • delicious pastries

The Orange Couch 2339 Royal St **504/267–7327** • 7am-10pm • ultra mod cafe • food served

Royal Blend Coffee & Tea House 621 Royal St **504/523–2716** • 8am-5:30pm • on a quiet, hidden courtyard • also salads & sandwiches

Z'otz 8210 Oak St **504/861–2224** • 7am-2am • coffee shop & art space • live entertainment

RESTAURANTS

13 Monaghan's 517 Frenchmen St **504/942–1345** • 11am-4am • brkfst, lunch & dinner all the time • some veggie • full bar • wheelchair access

Angeli on Decatur 1141 Decatur St (at Gov Nicholls) **504/566–0077** • 11am-2am, till 4am Fri-Sat • pizza • WiFi

Bywater Bar-B-Que 3162 Dauphine St (at Louisa) **504/944–4445, 504/947–0000** • 11am-9pm, clsd Wed • also Lorenzo's Pizzeria • gay-owned

Cafe Amelie 912 Royal St (in Princess of Monaco Courtyard) **504/412–8965** • lunch & dinner, Sun brunch, clsd Mon-Tue • Creole

Cafe Bamboo 435 Esplanade Ave **504/940–5546** • lunch & dinner • vegetarian

Cafe Negril 606 Frenchman St (at Chartres St) 504/944-4744 • dinner, clsd Sun-Mon, Caribbean • live music • woman-owned

Casamento's 4330 Magazine St (at Napoleon Ave) 504/895-9761 • lunch, dinner Th-Sat, clsd Sun-Mon (also clsd June-Aug) • best oyster loaf in city

Clover Grill 900 Bourbon St (at Dumaine) 504/598-1010 • 24hrs • popular • diner fare

Commander's Palace 1403 Washington Ave (at Coliseum St, in Garden District) 504/899-8221 • lunch Mon-Fri, dinner nightly, jazz brunch wknds • popular • upscale Creole • dress code • reservations required

Coquette 2800 Magazine St 504/265-0421 • lunch Wed-Sat, dinner nightly, clsd Sun

The Court of Two Sisters 613 Royal St 504/522-7261 • daily jazz brunch buffet 9am-3pm, dinner nightly

Dante's Kitchen 736 Dante St 504/861-3121 • dinner nightly, wknd brunch, clsd Tue • cajun

EAT New Orleans 900 Dumaine St (at Dauphine) 504/522-7222 • lunch & dinner, wknd brunch, clsd Mon • Cajun/ Creole homecooking • some veggie

Elizabeth's 601 Gallier St 504/944-9272 • 11am-10pm, from 8am wknds, clsd Mon • cajun

Feelings Cafe 2600 Chartres St (at Franklin Ave) 504/945-2222 • dinner Th-Sun, also Sun brunch • Creole • piano bar • courtyard

Fiorella's Cafe 45 French Market Pl (at Gov Nicholls & Ursulines) 504/553-2155 • noon-midnight, till 2am Fri, 11:30am-2am Sat, 11:30am-midnight Sun • homecooking

Herbsaint 701 St Charles Ave 504/524-4114 • lunch & dinner, bistro menu afternoons, clsd Sun • French/ Southern

La Peniche 1940 Dauphine St (at Touro St) 504/943-1460 • 8am-9pm, clsd Tue-Wed • Southern comfort foods • popular for brkfst • some veggie

Marigny Brasserie 640 Frenchmen St 504/945-4472 • lunch Mon-Fri, dinner nightly, wknd brunch • French

Meauxbar Bistro 942 N Rampart St 504/569-9979 • 6pm-10pm, clsd Sun-Mon

Mike's On The Avenue 628 St Charles Ave (in the Lafayette Hotel) 504/523-7600 • lunch & dinner • great views of St Charles Ave

Mona Lisa 1212 Royal St (at Barracks) 504/522-6746 • 11am-10pm, from 5pm Tue-Wed • Italian • some veggie • beer/ wine • gay-owned

Mona's 504 Frenchmen St 504/949-4115 • 11am-10pm, till 11pm Fri-Sat, noon-9pm Sun • cheap Middle Eastern eats • some veggie

Moon Wok 800 Dauphine St 504/523-6910 • 11am-9pm, till 10pm Fri-Sat • Chinese

Napoleon House 500 Chartres St 504/524-9752 • lunch daily, dinner only Mon, clsd Sun • po' boys & muffulettas

Nola 534 St Louis St (btwn Chartres & Decatur) 504/522-6652 • lunch wknds, dinner nightly • fusion Creole from Emeril Lagasse • wheelchair access

Olivier's 204 Decatur St 504/525-7734 • 5pm-10pm • Creole • wheelchair access

Orleans Grapevine 718-720 Orleans Ave 504/523-1930 • 4pm-10:30pm, till 11:30pm Fri-Sat • wine bar & bistro

Phillips 733 Cherokee St (at Maple) 504/865-1155 • 4pm-2am • gay/ straight • also tapas restaurant • upscale • gay-owned

Praline Connection 542 Frenchmen St (at Chartres) 504/943-3934 • 11am-10pm • soul food

Quartermaster 1100 Bourbon St 504/529-1416 • 24hrs • "The Nellie Deli" • sandwiches & more

Restaurant August 301 Tchoupitoulas St (at Gravier St) 504/299-9777 • lunch Mon-Fri, dinner nightly • upscale French/ Mediterranean

Sammy's Seafood 627 Bourbon St (across from Pat O' Brien's) 504/525-8442 • 11am-11pm • Cajun/ Creole

Stanley 547 St Ann St (at Chartres) 504/593-0006 • 7am-7pm • upscale diner fare

Stella 1032 Chartres St (at Ursulines Ave) 504/587-0091 • dinner nightly • upscale global fusion cuisine

The Upperline Restaurant 1413 Upperline 504/891-9822 • dinner Wed-Sun • Creole • fine dining • full bar

ENTERTAINMENT & RECREATION

Big Easy Rollergirls • New Orleans' female roller derby league • visit www.bigeasyrollergirls.com for events

Cafe du Monde 800 Decatur St (at St Ann, corner of Jackson Square) 504/525-4544, 800/772-2927 • till you've had a beignet—fried dough, powdered w/ sugar, that melts in your mouth—you haven't been to New Orleans & this is "the" place to have them 24hrs a day

French Quarter Ceremonies
305/304-0806 • commitment ceremonies in the French Quarter • woman-owned

Gay Heritage Tour 909 Bourbon St
504/945-6789 • call for details • departs from Alternatives giftshop

Haunted History Tour 504/861-2727,
888/644-6787 • guided 2-1/2-hour tours of New Orleans' most famous haunts, including Anne Rice's former home

Mardi Gras World 1380 Port of New Orleans Pl 504/362-8211, 800/362-8213 • tour this year-round Mardi Gras float workshop

Pat O'Brien's 718 St Peter St (btwn Bourbon & Royal) 504/525-4823, 800/597-4823 • gay-friendly • more than just a bar—come for the Hurricane, stay for the kitsch

Preservation Hall 726 St Peter St
504/522-2841, 888/946-5299 • 8pm-midnight, set begins at 8:30pm • come & hear the music that started jazz: New Orleans-style jazz! • cover charge

St Charles Streetcar St Charles St (at Canal St) 504/248-3900 (RTA RIDELINE #) • it's not named Desire, but you should still ride it, Blanche, if you want to see the Garden District

BOOKSTORES

Barnes & Noble 1601 Westbank Expwy, Harvey 504/263-1146 • 9am-10pm, till 11pm Fri-Sat, 10am-9pm Sun • wheelchair access

FAB (Faubourg Marigny Art & Books) 600 Frenchmen St (at Chartres) 504/947-3700 • noon-10pm • LGBT

Garden District Book Shop 2727 Prytania St (at Washington) 504/895-2266 • 10am-6pm, till 4pm Sun • independent

Kitchen Witch Cook Books 631 Toulouse St (at Royal St) 504/528-8382 • 10am-7pm, clsd Tue • cook books from rare to campy

RETAIL SHOPS

Alternatives 909 Bourbon St (at Dumaine) 504/524-5222 • 11am-6pm • LGBT cards • gifts

Angela King Gallery 241 Royal St
504/524-8211, 504/566-1944 • lesbian-owned

Dress to Kill 227 Dauphine 504/587-7012 • 10am-10pm, till 11pm Wed-Sat • sexy footwear (up to size 14)

Hit Parade 741 Bourbon St 504/524-7700 • 3pm-11pm, 11am-2am Fri-Sat, 11am-midnight Sun • popular • LGBT books • designer circuit clothing & more

NOLA Tattoo 1820 Hampson St (Uptown, at Riverbend) 504/524-6147 • tattoos & piercing

Second Skin Leather 521 St Philip St (btwn Decatur & Chartres) 504/561-8167 • noon-8pm, till 10pm Fri-Sat

Wicked Orleans 1201 Decatur St (at Gov Nicholls) 504/529-4384, 866/297-9207 (OUTSIDE LA) • 11am-6pm • leather & goth clothes

PUBLICATIONS

Ambush Mag 504/522-8049 • LGBT newspaper for the Gulf South (TX through FL)

EROTICA

Bourbon-Strip Tease 205 Bourbon St
504/581-6633 • 10am-1am • erotic lingerie, dancewear, adult novelties

Panda Bear 415 Bourbon St (at St Louis)
504/529-8064 • leather • toys • wheelchair access

Paradise Adult Video 41 W 24th St (at Crestview), Kenner 504/461-0000 • arcade • wheelchair access

Shreveport

ACCOMMODATIONS

Twenty-Four Thirty-Nine Fairfield 2439 Fairfield Ave 318/424-2424, 877/251-2439 • gay-friendly • pets ok • $145-225

BARS

Korner Lounge II 800 Louisiana Ave (near Cotton) 318/222-9796 • 3pm-2am • mostly gay men • neighborhood bar • karaoke

NIGHTCLUBS

Central Station 1025 Marshall St (btwn Fairfield & Creswell) 318/222-2216 • 5pm-close, till 4am Fri-Sat • popular • lesbians/gay men • dancing/DJ • country/western wknds • drag shows Fri • transgender-friendly • wheelchair access

EROTICA

Fun Shop Too 9434 Mansfield Rd
318/688-2482 • clsd Sun • adult, novelty & gag gifts • toys

Slidell

see also New Orleans

BARS

Billy's 2600 Hwy 190 W 985/847-1921 • 5pm-2am • lesbians/gay men • neighborhood bar

MAINE

Aroostook County

ACCOMMODATIONS

Magic Pond Wildlife Sanctuary & Guest House Blaine 215/287-4174 • mostly women • artist-owned cottage • comfortable for women traveling alone • kitchen • nonsmoking • lesbian-owned • $600/week

Augusta

includes Hallowell

ACCOMMODATIONS

The Benjamin Wales House B&B 49 Middle St (at Chestnut St), Hallowell 207/512-2461, 877/323-4712 • gay/straight • 1820 house is listed on the Nat'l Register of Historic Places • full brkfst • WiFi • gay-owned • $99-169

Maple Hill Farm B&B Inn Hallowell 207/622-2708, 800/622-2708 • gay/straight • Victorian farmhouse on 130 acres • full brkfst • whirlpools • clothing-optional swimming pond • nonsmoking • WiFi • wheelchair access • gay-owned • $90-205

NIGHTCLUBS

PJ's (aka Papa Joe's) 80 Water St (btwn Laurel & Bridge) 207/623-4041 • 6pm-1am Wed-Sat • popular • lesbians/gay men • dancing/DJ • food served • piano bar • patio

RESTAURANTS

Slates 167 Water St (Franklin), Hallowell 207/622-9575, 207/622-4104 • lunch Tue-Fri, dinner Mon-Sat, brunch wknds • also bakery • live shows Mon

Bangor

BOOKSTORES

Pro Libris Bookshop 10 3rd St (at Union) 207/942-3019 • 10am-6pm, clsd Sun-Mon • new & used

Bar Harbor

ACCOMMODATIONS

Aysgarth Station 20 Roberts Ave 207/288-9655 • gay-friendly • 10-minute drive from Acadia • cats on premises • nonsmoking • WiFi • $70-145

The Colonial Inn 321 High St (at US1), Ellsworth 207/667-5548, 888/667-5548 • gay-friendly • pool • WiFi • also restaurant • woman-owned • $68-160

Manor House Inn 106 West St (near Bridge St) 207/288-3759, 800/437-0088 • open April-Oct • gay-friendly • 1887 Victorian mansion • full brkfst • some rooms w/ whirlpools • nonsmoking • WiFi • $83-250

RESTAURANTS

Mama DiMatteo's 34 Kennebec Pl (at Rodick St) 207/288-3666 • 4:30pm-10pm • upscale casual dining • full bar • gay-owned

ENTERTAINMENT & RECREATION

ImprovAcadia 15 Cottage St (2nd flr) 207/288-2503 • May-Oct • live improvised theater

Bath

ACCOMMODATIONS

The Galen C Moses House 1009 Washington St 207/442-8771, 888/442-8771 • gay/straight • 1874 Victorian • pets ok • full brkfst • nonsmoking • WiFi • gay-owned • $119-269

The Inn at Bath 969 Washington St 207/443-4294, 800/423-0964 • gay/straight • 1810 Greek Revival B&B • full brkfst • jacuzzi • nonsmoking • wheelchair access • $150-245

Boothbay Harbor

ACCOMMODATIONS

Hodgdon Island Inn PO Box 603, Boothbay 04571 207/633-7474, 800/314-5160 • gay/straight • 1810 sea captain's home • full brkfst • pool • nonsmoking • WiFi • $140-235

Sur La Mer Inn 18 Eames Rd, PO Box 663, 04538 207/633-7400, 800/791-2026 • gay-friendly • seasonal luxury oceanfront B&B • nonsmoking • kids ok • gay-owned • $145-295

Brunswick

BOOKSTORES

Gulf of Maine Books 134 Maine St (at Pleasant) 207/729-5083 • 9:30am-5:30pm, clsd Sun • alternative

Camden

ACCOMMODATIONS

Norumbega Inn 63 High St **207/236–4646, 877/363–4646** • gay-friendly • historic castle • nonsmoking • gay-owned • $225-600

Corea

ACCOMMODATIONS

The Black Duck Inn on Corea Harbor **207/963–2689** • gay/ straight • restored farmhouse • also cottages • full brkfst • nonsmoking • WiFi • gay-owned • $140-200

Deer Isle

RESTAURANTS

Fisherman's Friend 5 Atlantic Ave, Stonington **207/367–2442** • 11am-8pm, till 10pm Fri-Sat • open April-Dec

Dexter

ACCOMMODATIONS

Brewster Inn 37 Zion's Hill Rd **207/924–3130** • gay-friendly • historic mansion • full brkfst • kids ok • nonsmoking • WiFi • wheelchair access • $69-149+ tax

Farmington

BOOKSTORES

Devany, Doak & Garrett Booksellers 193 Broadway **207/778–3454** • 10am-5pm, till 5:30pm Th, till 6:30pm Fri, 9am-5pm Sat, noon-3pm Sun • LGBT section

Freeport

ACCOMMODATIONS

The Royalsborough Inn 1290 Royalsborough Rd, Durham **207/353–6372, 800/765–1772** • gay-friendly • full brkfst • spa services • massage • also alpaca farm • nonsmoking • kids ok • conference room for 20 • WiFi • $129-179

RESTAURANTS

Harraseeket Lunch & Lobster Co 36 Main St, S Freeport **207/865–4888, 207/865–3535** • lunch & dinner • open May-Oct

Hancock

RESTAURANTS

Le Domaine Restaurant & Inn **207/422–3395, 800/554–8498** • 6pm-9pm, Sun brunch, clsd Mon • open June-Oct

Kennebunkport

ACCOMMODATIONS

The Colony Hotel 140 Ocean Ave (at Kings Hwy) **207/967–3331, 800/552–2363** • May-Oct • gay-friendly • 1914 grand oceanfront property • private beach • pool • nonsmoking • WiFi • also rental cottages • lesbian-run • $99-625

White Barn Inn & Spa 37 Beach Ave **207/967–2321** • gay-friendly • pool • restaurant • nonsmoking • WiFi • $340-1,500

RESTAURANTS

Bartley's Dockside by the bridge **207/967–5050, 207/233–6037** • lunch & dinner • 11:30am-10pm • seafood • some veggie • full bar • wheelchair access

Kittery

see Portsmouth, New Hampshire

Lewiston

ACCOMMODATIONS

Ware Street Inn B&B 52 Ware St (at College St) **207/783–8171, 877/783–8171** • gay-friendly • elegant 1940s colonial • full brkfst • well-behaved kids ok • WiFi • nonsmoking • $110-210

NIGHTCLUBS

Lewiston Social Club Heaven & Hell 347 Lisbon St **207/312–5799** • 6pm-1am Wed-Sun • lesbians/ gay men • dancing/DJ • shows

EROTICA

Paris Adult Book Store 297 Lisbon St (at Chestnut) **207/783–6677, 800/581–6901**

Naples

ACCOMMODATIONS

Lambs Mill Inn **207/693–6253** • gay/ straight • 1890s farmhouse on 20 acres • full brkfst • hot tub • nonsmoking • WiFi • lesbian-owned • $100-170

RESTAURANTS

Sydney's 377 Roosevelt Tr/ Rte 302 **207/693–3333** • dinner April-Nov only • full bar

Newcastle

ACCOMMODATIONS

The Tipsy Butler B&B 11 High St
207/563-3394 • gay-friendly • on the
Damariscotta River • full brkfst • nonsmoking
• WiFi • $130-205

Ogunquit

ACCOMMODATIONS

Beauport Inn & Suites on Clay Hill 339
Agamenticus/ Clay Hill Rd **207/361-2400,
800/646-8681** • gay/ straight • English
country manor on 11 acres • full brkfst • pool •
jacuzzi • nonsmoking • wheelchair access •
$135-240

Beaver Dam Campground 551 School St,
Rte 9, Berwick **207/698-2267** • gay-friendly •
campground on 20-acre spring-fed pond •
pool • kids/pets ok • women-owned • $29-85

Belm House Vacation Units 207/641-2637
• lesbians/ gay men • private studio & 2-bdrm
apt rentals • hot tub • kids/ dogs ok • WiFi •
gay-owned • $700-1,300/ week

Black Boar Inn 277 Main St **207/646-2112**
• lesbians/ gay men • B&B built in 1674 • full
gourmet brkfst • afternoon tea • kids ok •
nonsmoking • also weekly cottages • gay-
owned • $165-185

Distant Sands B&B 207/646-8686 • gay/
straight • 18th-c farmhouse • full brkfst •
nonsmoking • overlooks Ogunquit River &
ocean • also cottage • gay-owned • $95-215

Leisure Inn 73 School St **207/646-2737** •
gay-friendly • B&B & apts • nonsmoking •
WiFi • seasonal • $99-249

Meadowmere Resort 74 S Main St (at Rte
1) **207/646-9661, 800/633-8718** • gay-friendly
• pool • health club & spa • kids ok •
nonsmoking • WiFi • wheelchair access • $64-
399

Moon Over Maine B&B Berwick Rd
207/646-6666, 800/851-6837 • lesbians/ gay
men • hot tub • nonsmoking • WiFi • gay-
owned • $70-150

Morning Dove 13 Bourne Ln **207/646-3891**
• lesbians/ gay men • nonsmoking • gay-
owned • $100-200

Ogunquit Beach Inn 67 School St
207/646-1112 • mostly men • guesthouse
B&B • also cottage • 5 minutes to beach •
some shared baths • WiFi • gay-owned • $89-
169

The Ogunquit Inn 17 Glen Ave
207/646-3633, 866/999-3633 • clsd Nov-April
• lesbians/ gay men • Victorian B&B •
nonsmoking • WiFi • gay-owned • $89-189

Ogunquit-by-the-Sea Lodging 44 School
St (at Main St) **207/646-4132** • mostly gay
men • charming 1- & 2-bdrm self-catering
vacation units rented weekly in Ogunquit
Village Center • rooms by the night • near
beach & nightlife • nonsmoking • WiFi • gay-
owned

OgunquitCottages.com 25 Mill St, N
Reading, MA 01864 **207/646-3840,
978/664-5813** • lesbians/ gay men • weekly
rentals • seasonal (June-Sept) • near bars &
beach • nonsmoking • pets/ kids ok • gay-
owned • $1,350-3,500/ week

Old Village Inn 250 Main St **207/646-7088**
• gay-friendly • 1880s B&B • ocean views •
kids/ pets ok • nonsmoking • WiFi • also
restaurant • seafood • upscale • $80-160

Rockmere Lodge B&B 150 Stearns Rd
207/646-2985 • gay/ straight • Maine shingle
cottage • near beach • nonsmoking • gay-
owned • $150-225

Two Village Square 14 Village Square Ln
207/646-5779, 412/683-0218 (WINTER #) •
open May-Oct • mostly gay men • Victorian w/
ocean views • heated pool • nonsmoking •
WiFi • gay-owned • $120-189

Yellow Monkey Guest Houses & Motel
280 Main St **207/646-9056** • gay/ straight •
seasonal • roof deck • ocean view • jacuzzi •
fitness room • kids/ pets ok • wheelchair
access • gay-owned • $90-200

BARS

Front Porch Cafe 9 Shore Rd (at Beach St)
207/646-4005 • lunch & dinner (seasonal) •
gay/ straight • piano bar upstairs • full menu

Vine Cafe 478 Main St **207/646-0288,
877/646-0288** • seasonal, 4pm-close • also
restaurant • good wine selection

NIGHTCLUBS

Maine Street 195 Main St/ US Rte 1
207/646-5101 • 5pm-1am, T-dance from 3pm
wknds • popular • lesbians/ gay men •
dancing/DJ • karaoke • cabaret • food served •
gay-owned

Women's T Dance 195 Main St/ US Rte 1 (at
Maine Street nightclub) **207/646-5101** •
monthly, call for dates • popular • mostly
women • dancing/DJ

CAFES

Bread & Roses 246 Main St 207/646-4227 • 7am-11pm, seasonal

Fancy That Cafe Main St (at Beach St & Rte 1) 207/646-4118 • 6:30am-11pm • open April-Oct • pastries • sandwiches

RESTAURANTS

Amore Breakfast 309 Shore Rd 207/646-6661, 866/641-6661 • brkfst only • seasonal

Angelina's Ristorante 655 Main St 207/646-0445 • dinner • Italian

Arrows 41 Berwick Rd (2 miles W of Rte 1), Cape Neddick 207/361-1100 • open April-Dec, 6pm-9pm, clsd Mon • popular • eclectic • some veggie • gardens • reservations recommended

Clay Hill Farm 220 Clay Hill Rd, Cape Neddick (York) 207/361-2272 • dinner only, clsd Tue • seafood • some veggie • also piano bar

Five-0 50 Shore Rd 207/646-5001 • popular • 5pm-midnight • martini bar & restaurant • full bar

Jonathan's 92 Bourne Ln 207/646-4777 • dinner nightly • steak/seafood • full bar • entertainment • wheelchair access

La Pizzeria 239 Main St 207/646-1143 • lunch & dinner • open April-Dec • some veggie • beer/wine • gay-owned

Wild Blueberry Cafe & Bistro 82 Shore Rd 207/646-0990 • brkfst, lunch & dinner, jazz brunch 10am-1pm Sun

ENTERTAINMENT & RECREATION

Ogunquit Playhouse US Route 1 207/646-5511 (BOX OFFICE), 207/646-2402 • summer theater • some LGBT-themed productions

Portland

ACCOMMODATIONS

Auberge by the Sea B&B 103 East Grand Ave, Old Orchard Beach 207/934-2355 • gay-friendly • private pathway to beach • nonsmoking • WiFi • $109-209

The Inn at St John 939 Congress St 207/773-6481, 800/636-9127 • gay/straight • unique historic inn • kids/pets ok • nonsmoking • WiFi • gay-owned • $50-190

The Inn by the Sea 40 Bowery Beach Rd, Cape Elizabeth 207/799-3134, 800/888-4287 • gay-friendly • condo-style suites w/ ocean views • pool • kids/pets ok • nonsmoking • wheelchair access • also restaurant • $179-709

The Percy Inn 15 Pine St (at Longfellow Square) 207/871-7638, 888/417-3729 • gay-friendly • B&B at Longfellow Square • nonsmoking • WiFi • $79-199

Portland

LGBT PRIDE:
June, web: www.southern-mainepride.org.

ANNUAL EVENTS:
August - Portland Chamber Music Festival 800/320-0257, web: www.pcmf.org.

CITY INFO:
207/772-5800, web: www.visitportland.com.

WEATHER:
Portland has a mild marine climate. Winter temperatures are in the 20°s-40°s, and summers are breezy and mild, with temperatures in the 60°s-80°s.

TRANSIT:
ASAP Taxi 207/791-2727, web: asaptaxi.net.
Metro (bus) 207/774-0351, web: www.gpmetrobus.com.

ATTRACTIONS:
Old Port.
Portland Head Light 207/799-2661, web: www.portlandheadlight.com.
Portland Museum of Art 207/775-6148, web: www.portlandmuseum.org.
Wadsworth-Longfellow House 207/774-1822, web: www.mainehistory.org/house_overview.shtml.

The Pomegranate Inn 49 Neal St **207/772–1006, 800/356–0408** • gay-friendly • upscale B&B • full brkfst • private garden • nonsmoking • WiFi • $150

Sea View Inn 65 W Grand Ave (at Atlantic Ave), Old Orchard Beach **207/934–4180, 800/541–8439** • gay/ straight • year-round oceanfront motel • pool • patio • kids/ pets ok • gift shop • WiFi • nonsmoking • wheelchair access • $55-320

West End Inn 146 Pine St **207/772–1377, 800/338–1377** • gay-friendly • 1870 town house • full brkfst • nonsmoking • WiFi • $120-225

Wild Iris Inn 273 State St **207/775–0224, 800/600–1557** • gay-friendly • B&B • conveniently located in downtown Portland • nonsmoking • kids ok • women-owned • $79-259

BARS

Blackstones 6 Pine St (off Longfellow Square) **207/775–2885** • 4pm-1am, from 3pm wknds • mostly gay men • neighborhood bar • leather 3rd Sat • theme nights • wheelchair access

The Wine Bar 38 Wharf St **207/772–6976** • 5pm-close • gay/ straight • food served

NIGHTCLUBS

Styxx 3 Spring St **207/828–0822** • 7pm-1am• popular • lesbians/ gay men • more women Th • dancing/DJ • live shows • theme nights • drag shows • gay-owned

CAFES

Coffee by Design 43 Washington Ave **207/879–2233** • 6:30am-5:30pm, from 7:30am Sat, clsd Sun

North Star Music Cafe 225 Congress St (at Washington Ave) **207/699–2994** • 7am-10pm, 10am-5pm Sun • entertainment • lesbian-owned

RESTAURANTS

Becky's 390 Commercial St **207/773–7070** • 4am-10pm • great brkfst & chowdah

Katahdin 27 Forest Ave **207/774–1740** • 5pm-11pm, clsd Sun-Mon • American menu • full bar

Street & Co 33 Wharf St (btwn Dana & Union) **207/775–0887** • 5:30pm-9:30pm, till 10pm Fri-Sat • popular • seafood • beer/ wine • wheelchair access

Walter's Cafe 2 Portland Sq (at Union) **207/871–9258** • lunch & dinner, dinner nightly • seafood/ pasta • some veggie

BOOKSTORES

Longfellow Books 1 Monument Way **207/772–4045** • 9am-7pm, till 6pm Sat, 9:30am-5pm Sun • LGBT section

RETAIL SHOPS

Communiques 3 Moulton St (at Commercial) **207/773–5181** • 10am-5pm • cards • gifts • clothing

The Corner General Store 154 Middle St **207/253–5280** • 8am-1am • great wine selection

Emerald City 611 Congress St (at High St) **207/774–8800** • 10am-6pm, First Friday Art Walk • gay owned

EROTICA

Condom Sense 424 Fore St (at Union) **207/871–0356, 877/871–0356** • 10am-8pm, till 9pm Th, till 10pm Fri-Sat, till 6pm Sun • condoms, lube, massage oils, novelties, etc

Richmond

ENTERTAINMENT & RECREATION

Kennebec Tidewater Charters Kennebec River & Casco Bay **207/650–3494, 207/737–4695** • guided fishing & kayak trips • scenic coastal tours • women-owned

Rockland

ACCOMMODATIONS

Captain Lindsey House Inn 5 Lindsey St **207/596–7950, 800/523–2145** • gay-friendly • 19th-c Maine sea captain's home • nonsmoking • WiFi • wheelchair access • $141-215

The Old Granite Inn 546 Main St **207/594–9036, 800/386–9036** • gay-friendly • stately 1880s stone guesthouse • full brkfst • harbor views • nonsmoking • WiFi • wheelchair access • $95-210

Rockport

RESTAURANTS

Chez Michel Rte 1, Lincolnville Beach **207/789–5600** • dinner, Sun brunch, clsd Mon • full bar • some veggie

Lobster Pound Rte 1, Lincolnville Beach **207/789–5550** • 11:30am-8pm • May-Oct • full bar • patio

Tenants Harbor

ACCOMMODATIONS

Eastwind Inn 207/372-6366, 800/241-8439 • clsd Dec-April • gay-friendly • rooms & apts • at water's edge • full brkfst • pets ok • $99-226 • also restaurant • old-fashioned New England fare

White Mtns

ACCOMMODATIONS

Mountain Village Farm B&B 164 Main St, Kingfield 04947 207/265-2030, 866/577-0741 • gay-friendly • rural & sophisticated B&B • full brkfst • nonsmoking • WiFi • $89-160

York Harbor

RESTAURANTS

York Harbor Inn Rte 1A 207/363-5119, 800/343-3869 • lunch Mon-Sat, dinner nightly, Sun brunch • also the Cellar Pub • also lodging

MARYLAND

Annapolis

INFO LINES & SERVICES

AA Gay/ Lesbian 199 Duke of Gloucester St (at St Anne's Parish) 410/268-5441 • 8pm Tue

ACCOMMODATIONS

Two-O-One B&B 201 Prince George St (at Maryland Ave) 410/268-8053 • gay/ straight • English country house • full brkfst • nonsmoking • WiFi • gay-owned • $180-240

William Page Inn B&B 8 Martin St 410/626-1506, 800/364-4160 • gay/ straight • elegantly renovated 1908 home • full brkfst • nonsmoking • WiFi • teens ok • gay-owned • $190-295

RESTAURANTS

Cafe Sado 205 Tackle Cir (at Castle Marina Rd), Chester 410/604-1688 • lunch & dinner • sushi/ Asian fusion

Baltimore

INFO LINES & SERVICES

AA Gay/ Lesbian 410/663-1922 • 6:30pm Sat • call for other mtg times

Gay, Lesbian, Bisexual & Transgender Community Center of Baltimore 241 W Chase St (at Read) 410/837-5445 • many groups & services

ACCOMMODATIONS

Abacrombie Fine Food & Accommodations 58 W Biddle St (at Cathedral) 410/244-7227, 888/922-3437 • gay/ straight • 1880s town house • nonsmoking • also restaurant • $98-195

Biltmore Suites 205 W Madison St (at Park) 410/728-6550, 800/868-5064 • gay-friendly • kids/ pets ok • nonsmoking • WiFi • $89

Harbor Magic 711 Eastern Ave (at President) 410/539-2000, 866/583-4162 • gay/ straight • full brkfst • restaurant • WiFi • wheelchair access • $219-1,495

BARS

Baltimore Eagle 2022 N Charles St (enter on 21st) 443/524-3333 • 4pm-2am • mostly gay men • also leather store • patio • wheelchair access

Blue Parrot 5860 Belair Rd 410/254-3785 • 4pm-10pm, noon-1am Fri-Sun • lesbians/ gay men • neighborhood bar • karaoke • food served • drag shows • patio

Club Bunns 608 W Lexington St (at Greene St) 410/234-2866 • 3pm-2am, till midnight Mon-Tue • lesbians/ gay men • dancing/DJ • multiracial • live shows • female strippers Sat

Club Gypsies 4020 E Lombard 410/522-1602 • 6pm-2am • lesbians/ gay men • neighborhood bar

Club Phoenix 1 W Biddle St 410/837-3906 • 4pm-2am, from noon-midnight Sun • lesbians/ gay men • dancing/DJ • multiracial • drag shows • talent shows • karaoke • videos • food served

The Gallery Bar & Studio Restaurant 1735 Maryland Ave (at Lafayette) 410/539-6965 • 2pm-1:30am • lesbians/ gay men • dinner Mon-Fri • wheelchair access

Grand Central 1001 N Charles St (at Eager) 410/752-7133 • 4pm-close • popular • lesbians/ gay men • Sapphos upstairs for women • also ladies night Sat • dancing/DJ • videos • karaoke • drag shows • 21+

Hippo 1 W Eager St (at Charles) 410/547-0069, 410/576-0018 • 4pm-2am • popular • lesbians/ gay men • more women 1st Sun for T-dance • dancing/DJ • transgender-friendly • karaoke • drag shows • piano bar • wheelchair access

Jay's on Read 225 W Read St 410/225-0188 • 4pm-1am • mostly gay men • piano bar

Leon's 870 Park Ave (at Chase) **410/539-4993** • 11am-2am • lesbians/ gay men • neighborhood bar • WiFi • wheelchair access • also Singer's restaurant

Mixers 6037 Belair Rd (at Glenarm Ave) **410/483-6011** • lesbians/ gay men • neighborhood bar • dancing/DJ • karaoke • live shows

Port In A Storm 4330 E Lombard St (at Kresson) **410/534-0014** • noon-2am, clsd Mon • mostly women

The Rowan Tree 1633 S Charles St (at E Heath) **410/468-0550** • noon-2am • gay/ straight • karaoke • "where diversity is our name"

Sapphos 1001 N Charles St (upstairs at Central Station) **410/752-7133** • 8pm-2am Fri-Sat only • mostly women • dancing/DJ

Waterstone Bar & Grille 311 W Madison (at Linden Ave) **410/383-6064** • 3pm-close, from noon Fri, clsd Mon • mostly women • dancing/DJ • food served • wheelchair access • lesbian-owned

Ziascoz 1313 E Pratt St (at Eden) **410/276-5790** • 5pm-2am • gay/ straight • neighborhood bar • karaoke • mostly African American

Nightclubs

Amnesia 2015 E Federal St (at Washington, at The Edge) **301/213-1179** • 9pm-2am Sat only • mostly women • dancing/DJ • mostly African American

Club 1722 1722 N Charles St (at Lafayette) **410/547-8423** • afterhours club • Fri & Sat only, 2am-close • gay/ straight • dancing/DJ • multiracial • 18+ • BYOB • dress code

Baltimore

Where the Girls Are:

The women's bars are in southeast Baltimore, near the intersection of Haven and Lombard. Of course, the boys' playground, downtown around Chase St. and Park Ave., is also a popular hang-out.

LGBT Pride:

June. 410/837-5445 x17 (GLCC #), web: www.baltimorepride.org.

City Info:

Maryland Office of Tourism 866/639-3526, web: www.visit-maryland.org.

Best View:

Top of the World Trade Center at the Inner Harbor. 401 E Pratt, 410/837-0845, web: www.view-baltimore.org.

Transit:

Yellow Cab 410/685-1212, web: yellowcabofbaltimore.com.
MTA Transit 410/539-5000, web: www.mtamaryland.com.

Attractions:

Baltimore Museum of Art 443/573-1700, web: www.artbma.org.
Fort McHenry 410/962-4290, web: www.nps.gov/fomc.
Harborplace 410/332-41941, web: www.harborplace.com.
Lexington Market 410/685-6169, web: www.lexingtonmarket.com.
National Aquarium 410/576-3800, web: www.aqua.org.
Poe House & Museum 410/396-7932, web: eapoe.org.
Walters Art Museum 410/547-9000, web: www.thewalters.org.

Weather:

A temperate and, at times, temperamental climate. Spring brings great temperatures (50°-70°s) and unpredictable rains and heavy winds. In summer, the weather can be hot (90°s) and sticky. Fall cools off with an occasional "Indian Summer" in October. Winter brings cool days and colder nights, along with snow and ice.

The Paradox 1310 Russell St (at Ostend) **410/837-9110** • 11pm-5am, midnight-6am Sat • popular • gay/ straight • more gay Sat • dancing/DJ • multiracial • food served • live shows • videos • wheelchair access

Rehab 1001 N Charles St (at Grand Central) **410/382-7252** • 9pm 2nd Sat only • mostly women • dancing/DJ • multiracial

CAFES

Donna's Coffee Bar 800 N Charles St **410/385-0180** • 7:30am-9pm, from 9am Sat-Sun, till 10pm Fri-Sat • beer/ wine

RESTAURANTS

Aldos 306 S High St **410/727-0700** • southern-influenced regional Italian

Alonso's 415 W Cold Spring Ln (at Keswick Rd) **410/235-3433** • 4pm-10:30pm, from11:30am Fri-Sat • pizza & burgers • full bar • wheelchair access

Cafe Hon 1002 W 36th St (at Roland) **410/243-1230** • 7am-9pm, 9am-close wknds • wheelchair access

The Dizz 300 W 30th St **443/869-5864** • 10am-2am, from 8am Fri-Sun • full bar

Golden West Cafe 1105 W 36th St **410/889-8891** • brkfst, lunch & dinner • New Mexican

Jerry D's Seafood 7804 Harford Rd, Parkville **410/668-1299**

Loco Hombre 413 W Cold Spring Ln (at Roland) **410/889-2233** • 4pm-10pm, till 11pm Fri-Sat, from 11:30am Fri-Sun

Mount Vernon Stable & Saloon 909 N Charles St (btwn Eager & Read) **410/685-7427** • 11:30am-midnight, from 10am-8pm Sun

Trinidad Gourmet 418 E 31st St **410/243-0072** • 7am-8:30pm, clsd Sun • Caribbean • delicious & inexpensive

Viccino 1317 N Charles St **410/347-0349** • 11am-11pm, till 9pm Sun • New American • full bar

Woodberry Kichen 2010 Clipper Park Rd #126 **410/464-8000** • organic meats and sustainable agriculture • full bar • wheelchair access

XS Baltimore 1307 N Charles St **410/468-0002** • 7am-midnight, till 2am Fri-Sat • sushi restaurant, cafe & lounge

ENTERTAINMENT & RECREATION

The Charm City Kitty Club 3134 Eastern Ave (at Creative Alliance) **410/276-1651** • performing arts cabaret for lesbian, dyke, bisexual, trans women & allies

Charm City Roller Girls 722 Dulaney Valley Rd #187, Towson • Baltimore's own female roller derby league • visit www.charmcityrollergirls.com for events

BOOKSTORES

Read Street Books 229 W Read St **410/669-4103** • 10am-6pm, will 8pm wknds • women's bookstore • also cafe

The Spiral Dance Womyn's Center & Bookstore 2505 E Oliver St **410/732-0451** • 9am-9pm Fri, till 5pm Sat only • bookstore • events & classes

PUBLICATIONS

Baltimore OUTloud **410/244-6780**

Gay Life **410/837-7748** • LGBT newspaper

EROTICA

Chained Desires 136 W Read St **410/528-8441, 888/886-8442** • 11am-8pm, till 9pm Fri-Sat, clsd Mon • custom leather crafts & apparel • adult toys

Sugar 927 W 36th St (at Roland) **410/467-2632** • 11am-close • lesbian-owned sex toy shop

Cumberland

ACCOMMODATIONS

Rocky Gap Lodge & Golf Resort 16701 Lakeview Rd NE, Flintstone **301/784-8400, 800/724-0828** • gay-friendly • expansive property w/ forests, lake & elegantly rustic lodge • pool • $120+

RESTAURANTS

Acropolis 47 E Main St, Frostburg **301/689-8277** • 4pm-10pm, clsd Sun-Mon • Greek & American • full bar

Au Petit Paris 86 E Main St, Frostburg **301/689-8946** • 6pm-9:30pm, clsd Sun-Mon • French • also lounge • reservations recommended • wheelchair access

Hagerstown

RETAIL SHOPS

Rainbow Connection LLC 14 1/2 E Washington St (at Potomac St) **301/739-6629** • 10am-7pm, till 6pm Sat, clsd Sun • pride gifts & more

Havre de Grace

ACCOMMODATIONS

La Cle D'Or 226 N Union Ave (at Chesapeake Bay) **410/939-6562, 888/484-4837** • gay/ straight • 1868 home of the Johns Hopkins family • full brkfst • teens ok (w/ prior approval) • gay-owned • $120-158

Laurel

BARS

PW's Sports Bar & Grill 9855 N Washington Blvd (at Whiskey Bottom Rd) **301/498-4840, 301/498-4841** • 5am-2am • lesbians/ gay men • sports bar • food served • drag shows • karaoke • WiFi • gay-owned

Princess Anne

ACCOMMODATIONS

The Alexander House Booklovers B&B 30535 Linden Ave (at corner of Beckford) **410/651-5195** • gay-friendly • literary-themed B&B • full brkfst • nonsmoking • $80-150

Rock Hall

ACCOMMODATIONS

Tallulah's on Main 5750 Main St (at Sharp St) **410/639-2596** • gay/ straight • small suite hotel • kids ok • nonsmoking • wheelchair access • gay-owned • $115-150

Rockville

RESTAURANTS

The Vegetable Garden 11618 Rockville Pk **301/468-9301** • lunch Mon-Fri, dinner nightly • vegetarian/ vegan

MASSACHUSETTS

Amherst

see also Northampton

BOOKSTORES

Amherst Books 8 Main St **413/256-1547, 800/503-5865** • 6:30am-9pm, till 5pm Sun • independent • LGBT section

Food For Thought 106 N Pleasant St (at Main) **413/253-5432** • 10am-6pm • progressive bookstore • wheelchair access • collectively run

Barre

ACCOMMODATIONS

Jenkins Inn & Restaurant 978/355-6444, **800/378-7373** • gay-friendly • full brkfst • restaurant • full bar • nonsmoking • English garden • WiFi • gay-owned • $170-195

Berkshires

ACCOMMODATIONS

The B&B at Howden Farm 303 Rannapo Rd, Sheffield **413/229-8481** • gay/ straight • 250-acre working farm • near river • full brkfst • nonsmoking • some shared baths • gay-owned • $69-179

Broken Hill Manor 771 West Rd (at Rte 23), Sheffield **413/528-6159, 877/535-6159** • gay-friendly • B&B • full brkfst • hot tub • kids 12+ ok • WiFi • gay-owned • $150-235

Cornell Inn 203 Main St, Lenox **413/637-4800, 800/375-9839** • gay-friendly • same-sex wedding ceremonies happily facilitated • full brkfst • jacuzzi • nonsmoking • WiFi • wheelchair access • $120-350

Gateways Inn 51 Walker St (at Church St), Lenox **413/637-2532, 888/492-9466** • gay-friendly • full brkfst • also bar & restaurant • nonsmoking • $120-515

Guest House at Field Farm 554 Sloan Rd, Williamstown **413/458-3135** • gay-friendly • transgender-friendly • nonsmoking • WiFi • $150-295

Hallig Hilltop House 68 West St, Mt Washington **413/644-0076** • gay-friendly • surrounded by State Park • near hiking & skiing • pool • nonsmoking • gay-owned • $75-250

Harrison House Lenox **413/637-1746** • gay-friendly • "eclectic upscale B&B" • fireplaces • gay-owned • $145-340

Mount Greylock Inn 6 East St, Adams **413/743-2665** • gay/ straight • some views of Mt Greylock • cat on premises • gay-owned • $84-154

River Bend Farm B&B 643 Simonds Rd, Williamstown **413/458-3121** • gay-friendly • restored 1770s home • shared baths • seasonal • well-behaved kids ok • nonsmoking • $120

The Rookwood Inn 11 Old Stockbridge Rd (at Walker St/ Rte 183), Lenox **413/637-9750, 800/223-9750** • gay/ straight • Victorian inn near Tanglewood & skiing • full brkfst • kids ok • nonsmoking • WiFi • women-owned • $175-450

The Thaddeus Clapp House 74 Wendell Ave, Pittsfield **413/499-6840, 888/499-6840** • gay-friendly • full brkfst • WiFi • nonsmoking • $125-295

Topia Inn 10 Pleasant St (at Rte 8), Adams **413/743-9605, 888/868-6742** • gay-straight • nonsmoking • WiFi • wheelchair access • eco-friendly B&B • organic gourmet brkfst • kids ok • lesbian-owned • $135-260

Windflower Inn 684 S Egremont Rd, Great Barrington **413/528-2720, 800/992-1993** • gay-friendly • gracious country inn • full brkfst • pool • nonsmoking • WiFi • kids ok • $100-225

Cafes

Stone Soup 27 Park St (at Rte 8), Adams **413/743-9600** • 7am-3pm, 10am-10pm Th-Fri, from 10am Sat, clsd Sun-Mon • beer/ wine • live music, theater, dance & poetry • WiFi • wheelchair access • lesbian-owned

Restaurants

Cafe Lucia 80 Church St, Lenox **413/637-2640** • dinner only, clsd Mon, seasonal

Church Street Cafe 65 Church St, Lenox **413/637-2745** • lunch & dinner, seasonal • American bistro • some veggie

Mezze Bistro & Bar 777 Cold Spring Rd, Williamstown **413/458-0123** • 5pm-9pm Sun-Mon, till 10pm Tue-Th, till 11pm Fri-Sat, bar open till 1am

Entertainment & Recreation

Tanglewood 197 Rte 183, Lenox **888/266-1200** • live music venue • summer home of the Boston Symphony/ Pops

Williamstown Theatre Festival just E of Rte 2 & Rte 7 junction, Williamstown **413/597-3400, 413/458-3200** • call for season calendar

Boston

Info Lines & Services

Gay AA 12 Channel St #604 **617/426-9444** (AA#)

GLBT Helpline **617/267-9001, 888/340-4528** • 6pm-11pm

Accommodations

463 Beacon St Guest House 463 Beacon St **617/536-1302** • gay-friendly • nonsmoking • WiFi • gay- & straight-owned • $79-169

Beacon Hill Hotel & Bistro 25 Charles St (at Chestnut St) **617/723-7575** • gay/ straight • food served • WiFi • $245-425

Carolyn's B&B 102 Holworthy St (at Huron Ave), Cambridge **617/864–7042** • gay-friendly • near Harvard Square • nonsmoking • women-owned • $115-150

➤**Chandler Inn** 26 Chandler St **617/482-3450, 800/842-3450** • gay-friendly • European-style hotel • centrally located • nonsmoking • WiFi • $100-180

The Charles Hotel 1 Bennett St, Cambridge **617/864-1200, 800/882-1818** • gay-friendly • in Harvard Square • also restaurants & bar

The Charles Street Inn 94 Charles St (at Mount Vernon, Beacon Hill) **617/314–8900, 877/772–8900** • gay/ straight • kids/ pets ok • nonsmoking • wheelchair access • lesbian-owned • $250-450

Clarendon Square Inn 198 W Brookline St (btwn Tremont & Columbus) **617/536–2229** • gay/ straight • restored Victorian town house • hot tub • kids ok • fireplaces • nonsmoking • WiFi • gay-owned • $155-495

Boston

WHERE THE GIRLS ARE:
Sipping coffee and reading somewhere in Cambridge or Harvard Square, strolling the South End near Columbus & Mass. Avenues, or hanging out in the Fenway or Jamaica Plain.

ENTERTAINMENT:
Gay Men's Chorus 617/542-7464, web: www.bgmc.org.
The Theatre Offensive 617/621-6090, web: www.thetheateroffensive.org.

LGBT PRIDE:
June. 617/262-9405, web: www.bostonpride.org.

ANNUAL EVENTS:
May - Gay & Lesbian Film/Video Festival 617/369-3300 (Museum of Fine Arts #).

CITY INFO:
Greater Boston Convention & Visitors Bureau 888/733-2678, web: www.bostonusa.com.

WEATHER:
Extreme—from freezing winters to boiling summers with a beautiful spring and fall.

TRANSIT:
Boston Cab 617/536-5010, web: www.bostoncab.us.
Metro Cab, web: www.bostoncab.com.
MBTA (the "T") 800/392-6100, web: www.mbta.com.

ATTRACTIONS:
Beacon Hill, web: www.beaconhillonline.com.
Black Heritage Trail, web: www.afroammuseum.org/trail.htm.
Boston Common.
Faneuil Hall, web: www.faneuilhall.com.
Freedom Trail 617/242-5642, web: www.thefreedomtrail.org.
Harvard University, web: www.harvard.edu.
Isabella Stewart Gardner Museum 617/566-1401, web: www.gardnermuseum.org.
Museum of African American History 617/725-0022, web: www.afroammuseum.org.
Museum of Fine Arts 617/267-9300, web: www.mfa.org.
Museum of Science 617/723-2500, web: www.mos.org.
New England Aquarium 617/973-5200, web: www.neaq.org.
Old North Church 617/523-6676, web: www.oldnorth.com.
Walden Pond, web: www.mass.gov/dcr/parks/northeast/wldn.htm.

The College Club 44 Commonwealth Ave (at Arlington St) **617/536–9510** • gay-friendly • B&B in Back Bay • some shared baths • kids ok • nonsmoking • WiFi • wheelchair access • $79-259

Encore B&B 116 W Newton St (at Tremont) **617/247–3425** • gay-friendly • 19th-c town house in Boston's historic South End • nonsmoking • gay-owned • $140-240

Fifteen Beacon Hotel 15 Beacon St **617/670–1500, 877/982–3226** • gay-friendly • in 1903 Beaux Arts bldg • pets/kids ok

Holiday Inn Express & Suites Boston Garden 280 Friend St (at Causeway) **617/720–5544** • gay-friendly • WiFi • nonsmoking • $109-359 • wheelchair access

Hotel 140 140 Clarendon St (at Stuart St) **617/585–5600** • gay/ straight • boutique hotel • near Copley Square • nonsmoking • wheelchair access • women-owned • $99-399

Hotel Onyx 155 Portland St **617/557–9955, 866/660–6699** • gay-friendly • kids/ pets ok • WiFi

The Liberty Hotel 215 Charles St (at Cambridge St) **617/224–4000, 866/507–5245** • gay-friendly • in the former Charles St Jail • full brkfst • nonsmoking • WiFi • wheelchair access • $295

Nine Zero Hotel 90 Tremont St (at Bosworth) **617/772–5800, 866/646–3937** • gay-friendly • luxury hotel • full brkfst • jacuzzi • kids/ pets ok • $249-3,000

➤ **Oasis Guest House** 22 Edgerly Rd **617/267–2262, 800/230-0105** • popular • gay/ straight • Back Bay location • some shared baths • nonsmoking • wheelchair access • gay-owned • $79-159

Victorian B&B **617/536–3285** • women only • full brkfst • nonsmoking • kids ok • WiFi • lesbian-owned • $95-105

Whitman House Inn 17 Worcester St (at Norfolk St), Cambridge **617/913–6189** • gay/straight • nonsmoking • WiFi • gay-owned • $99-119

Bars

Boston Ramrod 1254 Boylston St (at Ipswich, 1 block from Fenway Park) 617/266–2986 • noon-2am • popular • mostly gay men • bears • leather • dress code Fri-Sat • dancing/DJ • videos • game room • wheelchair access

▶**Club Cafe Bistro, Bar & Nightclub** 209 Columbus (at Berkeley) 617/536–0966 • 11:30am-2am, Sun brunch from 10:30am • popular • lesbians/ gay men • upscale • dancing/DJ • karaoke • piano bar • live shows • videos • 3 bars • wheelchair access

Dyke Night 284 Amory St (at Milky Way Lounge), Jamaica Plain 617/524–3740 • 4th Fri and also Sexy & Sophisticated 2nd Th • mostly women • dancing/DJ

Encore 275 Tremont St (at Stuart St, in hotel) 617/728–2162 • lounge & cabaret • gay/ straight • live entertainment

▶**Fritz** 26 Chandler St (in the Chandler Inn) 617/482–4428 • noon-2am, Sat-Sun brunch • mostly men • neighborhood sports bar

Jacque's 79 Broadway (at Stuart) 617/426–8902 • 11am-midnight, from noon Sun • mostly gay men • popular • drag cabaret • cover charge

Milky Way Lounge & Lanes 284 Amory St, Jamaica Plain 617/524–3740 • 6pm-1am • gay/ straight • food served • live music • poetry readings • karaoke • bowling • also restaurant

Rocca Kitchen & Bar 500 Harrison St 617/451–5151 • dinner & Sun brunch • gay TGIF parties in the summer

Ryles 212 Hampshire St (at Cambridge St, in Inman Square), Cambridge 617/876–9330 • gay/ straight • live shows • great wknd jazz brunch

Sister Sorel 647 Tremont 617/266–4600 • dinner only, wknd brunch • lesbians/gay men

Nightclubs

Blush Boston 105 Canal St (Hideaway at Anthony's), Malden 617/877–1808 • 7pm - 1:30am Sat only, from 8pm winter • mostly women • dancing/DJ • food served • live shows

dbar 1236 Dorchester Ave, Dorchester 617/265–4490 • 5pm-2am, from 11:30am Sun • gay/ straight • also restaurant • dinner nightly

Dyke Night Productions • special events in various locations • mostly women • dancing/DJ • live shows • younger crowd • wheelchair access • check www.dykenight.com for info

Epic Saturday 15 Landsdown St 617/338–7699 • 10:30pm Sat only • mostly gay men • dancing/DJ

The Estate 1 Boylston Pl 617/536–2100 • gay Th only • mostly gay men • dancing/DJ

The Glam Life 1 Boylston Pl (at Estate) 617/536–2100 • Th only • lesbians/ gay men • dancing/DJ • hip-hop • 19+ • cover charge

HBF Entertainment 617/792–3823 • Boston's LGBT drag queen events

Hot Mess Sundays 275 Tremont St (at Stuart St, at Underbar) 617/292–0080 • Sun only • mostly gay men • dancing/DJ

Machine 1256 Boylston St (below Boston Ramrod) 617/536–1950 • 10pm-2am • popular • mostly gay men • women's night 2nd Sat • dancing/DJ • go-go boys • wheelchair access

The Middle East 472 Massachusetts Ave (in Central Square), Cambridge 617/497–0576 • 11am-1am, till 2am wknds • gay-friendly • alternative • live music • young crowd • cover charge • also restaurant

Midway Cafe 3496 Washington St, Jamaica Plain 617/524–9038 • gay/ straight • mostly women Th • dancing/DJ • theme nights • karaoke • live shows

▶**Napoleon Cabaret** 209 Columbus (at Club Cafe) 617/536–0966 • 8pm-2am, Tue, Th-Sat • piano • older crowd • wheelchair access

Pure Fridays 75 Warrenton St (at Pearl nightclub) 617/542–4077 • 10pm Fri only • mostly women • dancing/DJ

Storm 665 Broadway, Rte 99 (at Rain Nightclub), Malden 781/547–1972 • Th gay night, club open nightly 8pm • mostly gay men • dancing /DJ

UpperEast 92 Winthrop St (at Om Restaurant), Cambridge 617/576–2800 • 10pm Th only • mostly women • dancing/DJ

Cafes

1369 Cafe 757 Massachusetts Ave (in Central Square), Cambridge 617/576–4600 • 7am-11pm • also 1369 Cambridge St (Inman Square), 617/576-1369

Berkeley Perk 69 Berkeley St (at Chandler) 617/426–7375 • 6:30am-5pm, clsd Sun • food served • gay-owned

Diesel Cafe 257 Elm St (in Davis Square), Somerville **617/629–8717** • 6am-11pm, from 7am wknds • pool tables • lesbian-owned

Fiore's Bakery 55 South St, Jamaica Plain **617/524–9200** • 7am-7pm, 8am-6pm wknds • some vegan • gay-owned

Francesca's 564 Tremont St (at Clarendon) **617/482–9026** • 8am-11pm • WiFi • wheelchair access

JP Licks 352 Newbury St **617/236–1666** • "homemade ice cream cafe"—& yes, they serve coffee too

June Bug Cafe 403A Centre St, Jamaica Plain **617/522–2393** • 8am-7pm, from 9am Sat-Sun • WiFi • also sandwiches • lesbian-owned

South End Buttery 314 Shawmut Ave (at Union Park St) **617/482–1015** • cupcakes! also brkfst, lunch & dinner

True Grounds 717 Broadway, Somerville **617/591–9559** • 7am-9pm, from 8am wknds • brkfst, lunch • live shows

Restaurants

28 Degrees 1 Appleton St (at Tremont St) **617/728–0728** • upscale restaurant & lounge

33 Restaurant & Lounge 33 Stanhope St **617/572–3311** • dinner nightly, Sun brunch • French/ Italian • patio

BarLola 160 Commonwealth Ave (at Dartmouth) **617/266–1122** • 4pm-2am, from 2pm wknds • tapas lounge • flamenco performed Sun • gay-owned

Boston Pita Pit 479 Harvard St (at Commonwealth), Brookline **617/738–7482** • 10:30am-midnight, till 2:30am wknds • lesbian-owned • wheelchair access

Casa Romero 30 Gloucester St **617/536–4341** • dinner • Mexican • also bar

Charlie's Sandwich Shoppe 429 Columbus Ave (at Pembroke St) **617/536–7669** • great brkfst, clsd Sun

City Girl Cafe 204 Hampshire St (at Prospect), Cambridge **617/864–2809** • 11am-10pm, from 10am Sat-Sun, clsd Mon • Italian • great sandwiches • lesbian-owned

➤**Club Cafe** 209 Columbus (adjacent to Club Cafe) **617/536–0966** • lunch, dinner & Sun brunch • popular • some veggie • also 3 bars • piano • videos • wheelchair access

the leader in boston nightlife

we offer

outdoor patio seating
casual to intimate dining
nightly entertainment

Napoleon Room

moonshine
dance club

CLUB CAFÉ

from dining to dancing

209 columbus ave | boston MA | (617) 536-0966

www.clubcafe.com

Geoffrey's Cafe 4257 Washington St, Roslindale **617/325–1000** • 4pm-1am, from 10am wknds, popular Disco brunch

Johnny D's Restaurant & Music Club 17 Holland St (in Davis Square), Somerville **617/776–2004** • 12:30pm-1am, from 9am wknds

Laurel 142 Berkeley St (at Columbus) **617/424–6711** • lunch weekdays & dinner nightly, Sun brunch

My Thai Cafe 3 Beach St, 2nd flr **617/451–2395** • 11am-10pm, till 11pm Fri-Sat • Asian • vegetarian/ vegan

Om 92 Winthrop, Cambridge **617/576–2800** • noon-3pm & 5pm-1am Mon-Fri, 5pm-2am only Th-Sat • American

Pho Republique 1415 Washington St (at Union Park St) **617/262–0005** • 5:30pm-1am • French-Vietnamese

Rabia's 73 Salem St (at Cross St) **617/227–6637** • 11am-10:30pm • fine Italian • wheelchair access

Ristorante Lucia 415 Hanover St **617/367–2353** • lunch & dinner • great North End pasta

Stella 1525 Washington St **617/247–7747** • dinner and Sun brunch, full bar till 2am

Stix 35 Stanhope St **617/456–7849** • dinner nightly, lounge till 2am, clsd Sun-Mon

Trattoria Pulcinella 147 Huron Ave (at Concord), Cambridge **617/491–6336** • 5pm-10pm • fine Italian

Veggie Planet 47 Palmer St (at Club Passim), Cambridge **617/661–1513** • 11:30am-10:30pm • live music venue nights

ENTERTAINMENT & RECREATION

Boston Derby Dames • Boston's female roller derby league • visit www.bostonderbydames.com for events

Center for New Words 7 Temple St **617/876–5310** • cultural & political events for women • multiracial

Freedom Trail **617/357–8300** • start at the Visitor Information Center in Boston Common (at Tremont & West Sts), the most famous cow pasture & oldest public park in the US, then follow the red line to some of Boston's most famous sites

Jamaica Pond • great girl-watching

New Repertory Theatre 321 Arsenal St, Watertown **617/923–8487** (**BOX OFFICE**), **617/923–7060**

Urban AdvenTours 103 Atlantic Ave (at Richmond St) **617/670–0637, 800/979–3370** • guided bike tours of Boston & bike rentals

BOOKSTORES

Calamus Bookstore 92-B South St **617/338–1931, 888/800–7300** • 9am-7pm, noon-6pm • complete GLBT bookstore

The Globe Corner Bookstore 90 Mt Auburn (Harvard Square), Cambridge **617/497–6277, 800/358–6013** • travel books & maps

Trident Booksellers & Cafe 338 Newbury St (off Mass Ave) **617/267–8688** • 8am-midnight • good magazine browsing • also restaurant • beer/ wine • WiFi • wheelchair access

PUBLICATIONS

Bay Windows 617/266–6670 • LGBT newspaper

Night Timez 398 Columbus Ave. #341 **617/438–4364**

GYMS & HEALTH CLUBS

Revolution Fitness 209 Columbus **617/536–3006**

EROTICA

Eros Boutique 581–A Tremont St, 2nd flr **617/425–0345** • 10am-10pm • fetishwear • toys

Good Vibrations 308 Harvard St, Brookline **617/264–4400** • noon-7pm, till 8pm Th-Sat • clean, well-lighted sex toy store • workshops & events • also mail order • wheelchair access

Hubba Hubba 534 Massachusetts Ave (at Brookline, in Central Square), Cambridge **617/492–9082** • fetish gear

Brookline

see Boston

Cambridge

see Boston

Cape Cod

see also Provincetown listings

INFO LINES & SERVICES

Gay/ Lesbian AA 1093 Country Rd (at Methodist Church), Hyannis **508/775–7060** • 7pm Tue

ACCOMMODATIONS

The Colonial House Inn & Restaurant 277 Main St, Rte 6A, Yarmouthport 508/362-4348, 800/999-3416 • gay-friendly • dinner & light brkfst included • pool • jacuzzi • also restaurant & lounge • nonsmoking • WiFi • $100-155

Josiah Sampson House 40 Old Kings Rd, Cotuit 508/428-8383 • gay-friendly • 1793 Federal-style house on Nat'l Register of Historic Places • some fireplaces • nonsmoking • WiFi • $129-199

Lamb & Lion Inn 2504 Main St (Rte 6A), Barnstable 508/362-6823, 800/909-6923 • gay-friendly • pool • pets ok • WiFi • $110-295

Night Heron Cottage B&B 35 Lucinda Ct, Eastham 508/255-7063, 845/797-1737 • gay-friendly • near birding, beaches, kayaking & canoeing • nonsmoking • WiFi • lesbian-owned • $130-240

White Swan B&B 146 Manomet Point Rd, 508/224-3759, 888/988-7666 • gay-friendly • in 200-year-old farmhouse • open year-round • at mouth of Cape Cod • nonsmoking • WiFi • $120-165

Woods Hole Passage 186 Woods Hole Rd, Falmouth 508/548-9575, 800/790-8976 • gay-friendly • full brkfst • non-smoking • WiFi • $100-195

NIGHTCLUBS

Club 477/ Mallory Dock 477 Yarmouth Rd, Hyannis 508/771-7511, 800/393-6161 • 6pm-1am, T-dance from 3pm (summer) • lesbians/ gay men • Cape Cod's largest gay complex • dancing/DJ Fri-Sat • patio • wheelchair access

Chelsea

see Boston

Greenfield

ACCOMMODATIONS

Brandt House 29 Highland Ave 413/774-3329, 800/235-3329 • gay-friendly • 16-rm estate on hill • full brkfst • kids ok • nonsmoking • WiFi • $95-295

The Charlemont Inn Rte 2, Mohawk Trail, Charlemont 413/339-5796 • gay-friendly • kids/pets ok • nonsmoking • $67-105 • also restaurant • full bar • live music Sat • lesbian-owned

RESTAURANTS

Hope & Olive 44 Hope St 413/774-3150 • lunch & dinner, clsd Mon

BOOKSTORES

World Eye Bookshop 156 Main St 413/772-2186 • 9:30am-6:30pm, 9am-5pm Sat, noon-5pm Sun • general • LGBT section • community bulletin board • women-owned

Haverhill

NIGHTCLUBS

Club Irge 717 S Main St

CAFES

Wicked Big Cafe 19 Essex St (at Wingate) 978/556-5656 • 7am-4pm, 8am-1pm Sat, clsd Sun • coffee house w/ excellent food • WiFi • wheelchair access • lesbian-owned

Lenox

see Berkshires

Lynn

BARS

Fran's Place 776 Washington (at Sagamore) 781/598-5618 • 3pm-1am • lesbians/gay men • dancing/DJ • karaoke • also sports bar • wheelchair access

The Pub at 47 Central 47 Central Ave 781/586-0551 • 2pm-1am • mostly gay men • neighborhood bar • dancing/DJ wknds • leather • karaoke • drag shows • videos • gay-owned

Martha's Vineyard

ACCOMMODATIONS

Arbor Inn 222 Upper Main St, Edgartown 508/627-8137, 888/748-4383 • gay-friendly • B&B • some shared baths • nonsmoking • $125-225

Martha's Vineyard Surfside Motel 7 Oak Bluffs Ave, Oak Bluffs 508/693-2500, 800/537-3007 • gay-friendly • non-smoking • jacuzzis some rooms • pets ok • WiFi • wheelchair access • $85-355

The Shiverick Inn 5 Pease's Pt Wy, Edgartown (at Pent Ln) 508/627-3797, 800/723-4292 • gay/ straight • full brkfst • nonsmoking • WiFi • gay-owned • $135-550

RESTAURANTS

The Black Dog Tavern Beach St Extension #21 508/693-9223 • brkfst, lunch & dinner, seasonal • wheelchair access

Le Grenier 96 Main St, Vineyard Haven 508/693-4906 • dinner • French • BYOB

BOOKSTORES

Bunch of Grapes 44 Main St, Vineyard Haven **508/693–2291, 800/693–0221** • 9am-6pm, till 9:30pm Fri & summers • some LGBT titles & magazines

New Bedford

BARS

Le Place 20 Kenyon St **508/990–1248** • 2pm-2am • popular • lesbians/ gay men • karaoke • dancing/DJ • women-owned

Newton

see Boston

North Adams

see Berkshires

Northampton

see also Amherst

ACCOMMODATIONS

Clarion Hotel & Conference Center 1 Atwood Dr **413/586–1211, 800/582–2929** • gay-friendly • pool • kids ok • nonsmoking • WiFi • also restaurants & bar • wheelchair access • $119+

Corner Porches 82 Baptist Corner Rd, Ashfield **413/628–4592** • gay/ straight • 1880s farmhouse • 30 minutes from Northampton • shared bath • pets on premises • full brkfst • kids ok • nonsmoking • woman-owned • $70-85

The Hotel Northampton 36 King St **413/584–3100, 800/547–3529** • gay-friendly • gym • cafe & historic tavern • nonsmoking • WiFi • wheelchair access • $180+

Northampton

WHERE THE GIRLS ARE:

Just off Main St., browsing in the small shops, strolling down an avenue, or sipping a beverage at one of the cafes.

LGBT PRIDE:

May. 413/586-5602, web: www.northamptonpride.org.

ANNUAL EVENTS:

October - Paradise City Arts Festival 800/511-9725, web: www.paradisecityarts.com.

CITY INFO:

413/584-1900, web: www.explorenorthampton.com.

BEST VIEW:

At the top of Skinner Mountain, up Route 47 by bus, car, or bike.

WEATHER:

Late summer/early fall is the best season, with warm, sunny days. Mid-summer gets to the low 90°s, while winter brings snow from November to March, with temperatures in the 20°s and 30°s.

ATTRACTIONS:

Academy of Music 413/584-9032, web: www.academyofmusicthe-atre.com.
The Berkshires.
Emily Dickinson Homestead, Amherst 413/542-8161, web: www.emilydickinsonmuseum.org.
Historic Northampton 413/584-6011, web: www.historic-northampton.org.
Northampton Center for the Arts 413/584-7327, web: www.nohoarts.org.

TRANSIT:

The Taxi 413/585-8259.
Peter Pan Shuttle 413/781-2900, 800/343-9999, web: www.peter-panbus.com.
Pioneer Valley Transit Authority (PVTA) 413/781-7882, web: www.pvta.com.

NIGHTCLUBS

Diva's 492 Pleasant St (at Conz St) **413/586-8161** • 9pm-2am, clsd Sun-Mon • lesbians/ gay men • dancing/DJ • live music • theme nights • 18+ Sun-Fri

Pearl Street 10 Pearl St **413/584-7771** • 7pm-1am • gay/ straight • dancing/DJ • live music • young crowd

CAFES

Haymarket Cafe 185 Main St **413/586-9969** • 7am-10pm, till 11pm Fri-Sat, from 8am Sun • popular • also restaurant

RESTAURANTS

Bela 68 Masonic St **413/586-8011** • noon-8:30pm, clsd Sun-Mon • vegetarian • wheelchair access • lesbian-owned

Bueno Y Sano 134 Main St **413/586-7311** • 11am-10pm, till 9pm Sun • Mexican

Paul & Elizabeth's 150 Main St (in Thorne's Marketplace) **413/584-4832** • lunch & dinner, Sun brunch • seafood • plenty veggie • beer/ wine • wheelchair access

Union Station 125A Pleasant St **413/586-5366** • dinner, clsd Mon • steak & seafood

ENTERTAINMENT & RECREATION

The Iron Horse 20 Center St **413/586-8686** • 7pm-close • restaurant & bar • live music • all ages • nonsmoking

RETAIL SHOPS

Oh My A Sensuality Shop 122 Main St **413/584-9669** • noon-7pm, till 8pm Fri-Sat, noon-5pm Sun • informative, helpful & intimate sex toy store

Pride & Joy 20A Crafts Ave **413/585-0683** • open 7 days • LGBT books & gifts • wheelchair access • gay-owned

PUBLICATIONS

Metroline 860/233-8334 • regional newspaper & entertainment guide • covers CT, RI & MA

The Rainbow Times 413/282-8881 • bi-weekly LGBT news magazine for MA, northern CT & southern VT

Plymouth

ACCOMMODATIONS

Symphony Hollow B&B at the Round House 82 Mayflower Rd, Plympton **781/640-6936** • gay/ straight • 1859 historic round house • full brkfst • gay-owned • $110-140

Provincetown

see also Cape Cod listings

INFO LINES & SERVICES

Provincetown Business Guild **508/487-2313, 800/637-8696**

ACCOMMODATIONS

Admiral's Landing Guest House 158 Bradford St (btwn Conwell & Pearl) **508/487-9665, 800/934-0925** • mostly gay men • 1840s Greek Revival home & studio efficiencies • WiFi • nonsmoking • gay-owned • $55-175

Aerie House & Beach Club 184 Bradford St (at Miller Hill) **508/487-1197, 800/487-1197** • lesbians/ gay men • hot tub • sundeck • WiFi • gay-owned • $40-310

Anchor Inn Beach House 175 Commercial St **508/487-0432, 800/858-2657** • gay/ straight • nonsmoking • private beach • wheelchair access • lesbian & straight-owned/ run • $125-400

Bayberry Accommodations 16 Winthrop St **508/487-4605, 800/422-4605** • lesbians/ gay men • hot tub • nonsmoking • WiFi • gay-owned • $75-255

Bayshore 493 Commercial St (at Howland) **508/487-9133** • gay/ straight • apts • private beach • kitchens • pets ok • WiFi • lesbian-owned • $95-210 ($1,350-3,295/ week in summer)

Beachfront Realty 139 Commercial St **508/487-1397** • vacation rentals

Beaconlight Guest House 12 Winthrop St **508/487-9603, 800/696-9603** • mostly gay men • WiFi • nonsmoking • parking • gay-owned • $85-365

Benchmark Inn & Central 6-8 Dyer St **508/487-7440, 888/487-7440** • lesbians/ gay men • hot tub • sauna • pool • nonsmoking • WiFi • wheelchair access • gay-owned • $165-460

The Black Pearl Inn 11 & 18 Pearl St **508/487-0302, 800/761-1016** • lesbians/ gay men • hot tub • pets ok • "friends of Bill welcome" • $69-250

Boatslip Resort 161 Commercial St **508/487-1669, 877/786-9662** • popular • mostly gay men • resort • pool • seasonal • also several bars • popular T-dance • gay-owned

The Bradford Carver House 70 Bradford St 508/487–0728, 800/826–9083 • lesbians/gay men • restored mid-19th-c home • centrally located • nonsmoking • gay-owned • $49-259

Bradford House & Motel 41 Bradford St 508/487–0173 • gay-friendly • near town center • 1 block from the beach • wheelchair access • women-owned • $85-245

Brass Key Guesthouse 67 Bradford St (at Carver) 508/487–9005, 800/842–9858 • popular • mostly gay men • hot tub • pool • nonsmoking • WiFi • wheelchair access • gay-owned • $120-695

Carpe Diem Guesthouse & Spa 12 Johnson St 508/487–4242, 800/487–0132 • lesbians/gay men • also cottage • full German brkfst • hot tub • nonsmoking • WiFi • gay-owned • $75-425

The Carriage House Guesthouse 7 Central St 508/487–8855, 800/309–0248 • gay/straight • hot tub • gay-owned • $135-345

Chicago House 6 Winslow St (at Bradford) 508/487–0537, 800/733–7869 • lesbians/gay men • rooms & apts • hot tub • some shared baths • nonsmoking • WiFi • gay-owned • $60-195

Christopher's by the Bay 8 Johnson St (at Bradford) 508/487–9263, 877/487–9263 • lesbians/gay men • Victorian guesthouse • full brkfst • some shared baths • patio • nonsmoking • gay-owned • $80-285

The Clarendon House 118 Bradford St (btwn Ryder & Alden) 508/487–1645, 800/669–8229 • gay/straight • hot tub • full brkfst • kids ok • nonsmoking • $85-209

Provincetown

WHERE THE GIRLS ARE:
In this small resort town, you can't miss 'em! At the beach, the girls gather on the left side at Herring Cove.

LGBT PRIDE:
August - Provincetown Carnival, web: ptown.org.

ANNUAL EVENTS:
August - Provincetown Carnival 800/637-8696.
October - Fantasia Fair - for trannies & their admirers, web: www.fantasiafair.org.
October - Women's Week 800/637-8696, web: www.womeninnkeepers.com. It's very popular, so make your reservations early!
December - Holly Folly, web: www.ptown.org. Gay & Lesbian Holiday Festival.

CITY INFO:
Provincetown Business Guild 508/487-2313, 800/637-8696, web: www.ptown.org.

BEST VIEW:
People-watching from an outdoor cafe or on the beach.

ATTRACTIONS:
The beach.
Galleries.
Herring Cove Beach.
Pilgrim Monument.
Provincetown Museum 508/487-1310, web: www.pilgrim-monument.org.
Whale-watching.

WEATHER:
New England weather is unpredictable. Be prepared for rain, snow, or extreme heat! Otherwise, the weather during the season consists of warm days and cooler nights.

TRANSIT:
Cape Cab 508/487-2222, web: capecabtaxi.com.
Ferry: Bay State Cruise Company (from Commonwealth/World Trade Center Pier in Boston, during summer) 877/783-3779, web: www.baystatecruisecompany.com.
Air: Cape Air 508/771-6944, 866/227-3247, web: www.flycapeair.com.

Crown & Anchor 247 Commercial St **508/487-1430** • lesbians/ gay men • pool • nonsmoking • WiFi • also bars • cabaret • gay-owned • $85-295

Crowne Pointe Historic Inn & Shui Spa 82 Bradford St **508/487-6767, 877/276-9631** • lesbians/gay men • full brkfst • heated pool• nonsmoking • WiFi • wheelchair access • gay-owned • $125-469

Designer's Dock 349 Commercial St **508/776-5746, 800/724-9888** • gay/ straight • weekly condos in town & on beach • June-Sept • kitchens • WiFi • gay-owned • $699-2,799/week

Dexter's Inn 6 Conwell St (at Railroad) **508/487-1911, 888/521-1999** • lesbians/gay men • B&B • nonsmoking • sundeck • gay-owned • $60-150

Enzo 186 Commercial St **508/487-7555, 888/873-5001** • gay/ straight • Italian restaurant & piano bar on premises • $75-225

➤ **Fairbanks Inn** 90 Bradford St **508/487-0386, 800/324-7265** • popular • lesbians/gay men • nonsmoking • WiFi • parking • fireplaces • lesbian-owned • $105-285 • see ad

Four Gables 15 Race Rd **866/487-2427** • gay/ straight • private cottages • kids/ pets ok • gay-owned • $1,250-1,850/ week in season

Gabriel's at The Ashbrooke Inn 102 Bradford St **508/487-3232** • popular • lesbians/ gay men • full brkfst • nonsmoking • sundecks • kids/pets ok • WiFi • lesbian & gay-owned • $125-380

Gifford House Inn 9 Carver St **508/487-0688, 800/434-0130** • lesbians/ gay men • seasonal • WiFi • also several bars • also 11 Carver restaurant • dinner only • seafood • gay-owned • $60-275

Grand View Inn 4 Conant St **508/487-9193, 888/268-9169** • lesbians/ gay men • nonsmoking • kids/ pets ok • gay-owned • $50-170

Harbor Hill at Provincetown 4 Harbor Hill Rd **508/487-0541** • gay-friendly • condo resort in West End • kids ok • gay-owned • $100-275

Heritage House 7 Center St **508/487-3692** • lesbians/ gay men • shared baths • WiFi • lesbian-owned • $100-150

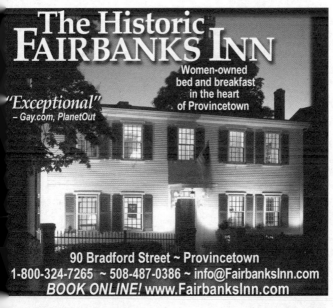

The Inn at Cook Street 7 Cook St 508/487-3894, 888/266-5655 • gay-friendly • nonsmoking • women-owned • $120-315

➤**Inn at the Moors** 59 Provincelands Rd 508/487-1342, 800/842-6379 • gay-friendly • motel • across from Nat'l Seashore Province Lands • seasonal • nonsmoking • WiFi • pool • lesbian-owned • $109-139

John Randall House 140 Bradford St (at Standish) 508/487-3533, 800/573-6700 • lesbians/gay men • kids ok • nonsmoking • WiFi • gay-owned • $69-199

Land's End Inn 22 Commercial St 508/487-0706, 800/276-7088 • seasonal • gay/ straight • nonsmoking • WiFi • gay-owned • $155-580

Lotus Guest House 296 Commercial St (at Standish) 508/487-4644, 888/508-4644 • lesbians/gay men • nonsmoking • decks • garden • teens ok • WiFi • lesbian & gay-owned • $45-260

Mayflower Apartments & Cottages 6 Bangs St (at Commercial St) 508/487-1916 • gay-friendly • kitchens • $160+ nightly (studio)/ $1,200+ weekly (cottages)

Moffett House 296-A Commercial St 508/487-6615, 800/990-8865 • lesbians/gay men • gay-owned • $55-170

The Oxford 8 Cottage St 508/487-9103, 888/456-9103 • lesbians/gay men • nonsmoking • WiFi • parking • gay-owned • $90-320

Pilgrim House Hotel 336 Commercial St 508/487-6424 • mostly women • seasonal • kids ok • also Vixen bar/ dance club • WiFi • wheelchair access • $99-150

Prince Albert Guest House 164-166 Commercial St 508/487-1850 • mostly gay men • Victorian • nonsmoking • WiFi • gay-owned • $80-325

Ravenwood Guest House 462 Commercial St (at Cook) 508/487-3203 • lesbians/gay men • also apts & cottage • nonsmoking • private beach • wheelchair accessible cottage • lesbian-owned • $85-175

The Red Inn 15 Commercial St (at Point) 508/487-7334, 866/473-3466 • gay-friendly • nonsmoking • wheelchair access • gay-owned • $135-525

Revere Guesthouse 14 Court St (btwn Commercial & Bradford) 508/487-2292, 800/487-2292 • lesbians/gay men • nonsmoking • gay-owned • $155-345

Rose Acre 5 Center St (at Commercial) 508/487-2347 • women only • suites • also apts & cottage • nonsmoking • decks • gardens • parking • always open • WiFi • women-owned • $125-250

Rose & Crown Guest House 158 Commercial St 508/487-3332 • gay/ straight • lesbian-owned • $30-210 (rooms)/ $160-230 (cottage)

Sandbars 570 Shore Rd, Beach Pt, North Truro 508/487-8700 • gay/ straight • private beach • $89-219

Seasons, An Inn for All 160 Bradford St (at Pearl) 508/487-2283, 800/563-0113 • lesbians/gay men • Victorian B&B • full brkfst • nonsmoking • WiFi • gay-owned • $80-159

The Secret Garden Inn 300-A Commercial St 508/487-9027, 866/786-9646 • lesbians/gay men • kids ok • nonsmoking • $60-170

Snug Cottage 178 Bradford St 508/487-1616, 800/432-2334 • gay/ straight • teens ok • nonsmoking • WiFi • gay-owned • $95-250

Somerset House 378 Commercial St (at Pearl) 508/487-0383, 800/575-1850 • lesbians/gay men • Victorian mansion • nonsmoking • WiFi • gay-owned • $75-295

Sunset Inn 142 Bradford St (at Center) 508/487-9810, 800/965-1801 • lesbians/gay men • some shared baths • seasonal • clothing-optional sundeck • nonsmoking • WiFi • gay-owned • $69-179

Surfside Hotel & Suites 543 Commercial (at Kendall Ln) 508/487-1726, 800/421-1726 • gay/ straight • waterfront hotel • lots of amenities • private beach • pool • nonsmoking • WiFi • kids/ pets ok • gay-owned • $139-329

The Tucker Inn 12 Center St 508/487-0381, 800/477-1867 • lesbians/gay men • full brkfst • WiFi • also cottage • nonsmoking • gay-owned • $125-245

Victoria House 5 Standish St 508/487-4455, 877/867-8696 • lesbians/gay men • gay-owned • $50-165

The Waterford 386 Commercial St (at Pearl) 508/487-7800, 800/487-0784 • gay/ straight • deck w/ full bar • also restaurant • $165-275

Watermark Inn 603 Commercial St 508/487-0165 • gay/ straight • kids ok • nonsmoking • WiFi • $140-450

Watership Inn 7 Winthrop St 508/487-0094, 800/330-9413 • mostly gay men • sundeck • WiFi • gay-owned • $55-278

White Wind Inn 174 Commercial St (at Winthrop) **508/487-1526, 888/449-9463** • lesbians/ gay men • WiFi • gay-owned • $95-275

➤**Women Innkeepers of Provincetown** PO Box 573, 02657 • women-owned accommodations in Provincetown

Bars

The Boatslip Resort 161 Commercial St **508/487-1669, 877/786-9662** • seasonal • popular • lesbians/ gay men • T-dance 4pm daily during season • young crowd • swimming • outdoor/ waterfront grill

Governor Bradford 312 Commercial St (at Standish) **508/487-2781** • 11am-1am, from noon Sun • gay-friendly • "drag karaoke" Sat (nightly in season) • also restaurant in summer

PiedBar 193-A Commercial St (at Court St) **508/487-1527** • seasonal May-Oct, noon-1am • popular • lesbians/ gay men • dancing/DJ • more women Fri-Sat • wheelchair access

Porchside Lounge 11 Carver St (in the Gifford House) **508/487-0688** • 5pm-1am • mostly gay men • neighborhood bar • also restaurant

Shipwreck Lounge 67 Bradford St (at Carver) **508/487-9005** • lesbians/ gay men • upscale lounge • outdoor seating w/ fire pit

Vixen/ Madeira Room 336 Commercial St (at Pilgrim House Inn) **508/487-6424** • noon-1am • mostly women • dancing/DJ • late night food • also wine bar • live shows • videos

Wave Video Bar 247 Commercial St (in the Crown & Anchor) **508/487-1430** • 6pm-1am, from noon in season • lesbians/ gay men • neighborhood bar • karaoke • T-dance Sun

Nightclubs

Atlantic House (The "A-House") 6 Masonic Pl **508/487-3169** • 10pm-1am • popular • mostly gay men • 3 bars • dancing/DJ • weekly theme parties • also The Little Bar from noon • neightborhood bar • Macho Bar upstairs • leather

Club Purgatory 9-11 Carver St (at Bradford St, in the Gifford House) **508/487-8442** • opens 7pm, from 9pm Sun (in season) • lesbians/ gay men • dancing/DJ

➤**Girl Power** 193-A Commercial St (at The PiedBar) **508/487-1527** • 9:30pm-close, Fri-Sat only, seasonal • mostly women • dancing/DJ • check www.girlpowerevents.com for events • see ad in front color section

Paramount in the Crown & Anchor **508/487-1430** • 10:30pm-1am (seasonal) • popular • lesbians/ gay men • dancing/DJ • live shows • drag shows • cabaret

Cafes

Post Office Cafe Cabaret 303 Commercial St (upstairs) **508/487-3892** • 8am-11pm, seasonal hours • lesbians/ gay men • some veggie

Restaurants

Bayside Betsy's 177 Commercial St **508/487-6566** • lunch & dinner, bar till 10pm • on waterfront • wheelchair access

Big Daddy's Burritos 205 Commercial St **508/487-4432** • 11am-10pm (May-Oct) • Tex-Mex, burritos, veggie wraps, salads & nachos

Bubala's by the Bay 183-185 Commercial **508/487-0773** • brunch & dinner • popular • seasonal • patio

Ciro & Sal's 4 Kiley Ct (btwn Bangs St & Lovett's Ct) **508/487-6444** • dinner from 5:30pm • Northern Italian • reservations recommended

Fanizzi's 539 Commercial St (at Kendall Lane) **508/487-1964** • popular • lunch & dinner • some veggie • full bar • on the water • wheelchair access

Front Street Restaurant 230 Commercial St **508/487-9715** • 6pm-10:30pm, bar till 1am • bistro beer/ wine • seasonal

Lobster Pot harborside (at 321 Commercial St) **508/487-0842** • 11:30am-10pm (April-Nov) • "a Provincetown tradition" • wheelchair access

Lorraine's 133 Commercial St **508/487–6074** • dinner, clsd Mon-Th off-season • popular • lesbians/ gay men • Mexican • some veggie • full bar • woman-owned

The Mews Restaurant & Cafe 429 Commercial St (btwn Lovett's & Kiley) **508/487–1500** • dinner • Sun brunch • popular • live shows • wheelchair access • waterfront dining

Napi's Restaurant 7 Freeman St **508/487–1145, 800/571–6274** • dinner • lunch Oct-April • int'l/ seafood • plenty veggie • wheelchair access

The Red Inn 15 Commercial St (at Point) **508/487–7334, 866/473–3466** • dinner nightly, brunch Th-Sun, clsd Jan-April • reservations a must • full bar

Relish 93 Commercial St **508/487–8077** • yummy baked goods • pick up a sandwich on the way to the beach!

Spiritus Pizza 190 Commercial St **508/487–2808** • noon-2am • popular • great espresso shakes & late-night hangout for a slice

ENTERTAINMENT & RECREATION

Art House Theatre 214 Commercial St **508/487–9222** • two theaters • also cafe

Art's Dune Tours 4 Standish St **508/487–1950, 800/894–1951** • day trips, sunset tours & charters through historic sand dunes & Nat'l Seashore Park • kids ok • gay-owned

Dolphin Fleet Whale Watch 305 Commercial St **508/240–3636, 800/826–9300** • gay-friendly • 3-hr day & evening cruises • full galley & bar on board • wheelchair access

Herring Cove Beach

Ptown Bikes 42 Bradford **508/487–8735** • 9am-6pm • rentals • gay-owned

Spaghetti Strip • nude beach • 1.5 miles south of Race Point Beach

Theatre Go Round **508/487–0931** • many LGBT-themed plays

BOOKSTORES

Now, Voyager Bookstore & Gallery 357 Commercial St **508/487–0848** • 10am-10pm (summers) • LGBT & general books • cards

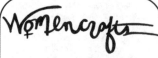

**376 Commercial St.
Provincetown, MA 02657
508 487-2501**

Here's a little bit about us.
Womencrafts is lesbian owned
and operated, and we are well into
our 3rd decade of celebrating women!

We represent over
50 women artists and artisans
from across the United States,
and offer a beautiful selection of
fine jewelry,
hand-thrown pottery,
porcelain,
sculpture,
photographs,
and
artwork.

In addition,
we carry over 700 lesbian and feminist
book titles, both fiction and non-fiction,
and a varied selection
of women's music and videos.

When you are visiting
Provincetown,
please stop in.

**Or look for us at
www.womencrafts.com**

RETAIL SHOPS

HRC Action Center & Store 209-211 Commercial St **508/487–7736** • 10am-9pm, till 10pm wknds • Human Rights Campaign merchandise & info

Piercings by the Bearded Lady 336 Commercial St #4 **508/487–7979** • noon-8pm • seasonal • lesbian-owned

Recovering Hearts 2–4 Standish St **508/487–4875** • 10am-11pm (in summer), call for off-season hours • recovery • LGBT & New Age books • wheelchair access

➤ **Womencrafts** 376 Commercial St (at Pearl St) **508/487–2501** • 11am-10pm (in summer), call for off-season hours • women-made jewelry, pottery, books, music, gifts, etc

PUBLICATIONS

Provincetown Banner 167 Commercial St **508/487–7400** • newspaper

Provincetown Magazine **508/487–1000** • seasonal • Provincetown's oldest weekly magazine

GYMS & HEALTH CLUBS

Mussel Beach Health Club 35 Bradford St (btwn Montello & Conant) **508/487–0001** • 6am-9pm, till 8pm in winter • lesbians/ gay men

Provincetown Gym 82 Shank Painter Rd (at Winthrop) **508/487–2776** • 6am-9pm, 7am-7pm wknds (till 9pm in season)

EROTICA

MG Leather Inc 338 Commercial St (at Standish St) **508/487–4036** • leather • fetish • toys • gifts • gay-owned

Wild Hearts 244 Commercial St **508/487–8933** • 11am-11pm (in summer), noon-5pm (off-season) • toys for women

Quincy

see also Boston

NIGHTCLUBS

My House 609 Washington St **617/302–4285** • 3pm-1am • lesbians/ gay men • dancing/DJ • food served • karaoke

Randolph

BARS

Randolph Country Club 44 Mazzeo Dr **781/961–2414** • 2pm-2am, from 10am summer • popular • lesbians/ gay men • dancing/DJ • food served • live shows • karaoke • male dancers • videos • volleyball court • pool • wheelchair access

Salisbury

BARS

Hobo's Club & Cafe 5 Broadway
978/465-4626 • lesbians/ gay men •
neighborhood bar • food seved • karaoke •
gay-owned

Shelburne Falls

RESTAURANTS

Cafe Martin 24 Bridge St (at Water St)
413/625-2795 • 11am-9pm, brunch Sun, clsd
Mon • full bar • wheelchair access • gay-
owned

Somerville

see Boston

Springfield

BARS

Pure 234 Chestnut St (E of Main)
413/205-1483 • noon-2am • mostly gay men
• neighborhood bar • food served •
wheelchair access

NIGHTCLUBS

Onyx 1150 W Columbus Ave **413/730-6699** •
10pm-2am Fri-Sat • gay/straight • dancing/DJ •
gay night Sat • restaurant open for dinner
nightly

Oz Nightclub 397 Dwight St (at Taylor)
413/732-4562 • 7pm-2am, clsd Sun-Mon •
neighborhood bar • dancing/DJ • karaoke

Xstatic 240 Chestnut St **413/736-2618,
800/710-2618** • 7pm-2am,rom 1pm wknds •
mostly gay men • dancing/DJ • strippers/ nude
dancers

Taunton

BARS

Bobby's Place 62 Weir St (at Route 44, 138
& 140, at Taunton Green) **508/824-9997** •
5pm-1am, till 2am Fri-Sat, from 2pm Sun •
lesbians/ gay men • dancing/DJ • food served •
karaoke • drag shows

Williamstown

see Berkshires

Worcester

INFO LINES & SERVICES

AA Gay/ Lesbian 100 Grove St #314 (St
Mark's Episcopal Church) **508/752-9000** •
7pm Sat • nonsmoking

BARS

MB Lounge 40 Grafton St (at Franklin)
508/799-4521 • 5pm-2am from 3pm Fri-Sun •
lesbians/ gay men • neighborhood bar • piano
bar • WiFi • wheelchair access

NIGHTCLUBS

Blu Ultralounge & Nightclub 105 Water St
508/756-2227 • 7:30pm-2am, from 9pm Sat,
clsd Mon-Tue • mostly men • dancing/DJ •
karaoke

RESTAURANTS

86 Winter Street 65 Water St **508/459-5400**
• lunch Wed-Fri, dinner Wed-Sun, clsd Mon •
gay-owned

RETAIL SHOPS

Glamour Boutique 850 Southbridge St,
Auburn **508/721-7800** • noon-8pm, 3pm-
6pm Sun • large-size dresses, wigs, etc

MICHIGAN

Statewide

PUBLICATIONS

What Helen Heard PO Box 811, East
Lansing 48826 **517/371-5257** • what's
happening for MI lesbians

Ann Arbor

INFO LINES & SERVICES

Lesbian/ Gay AA 734/482-5700

BARS

\aut\ Bar 315 Braun Ct (at Catherine)
734/994-3677 • 4pm-2am • popular •
lesbians/ gay men • also restaurant (dinner &
wknd brunch) • American/ Mexican • some
veggie • patio • wheelchair access

NIGHTCLUBS

The Necto 516 E Liberty **734/994-5436** •
9pm-2am • gay/ straight • dancing/DJ • videos
• young crowd • 18+ • theme nights • gay
night Fri

CAFES

Cafe Verde 214 N Fourth Ave **734/994-9174**
• 7am-9:30pm, 9am-8pm Sun • fair trade &
organic coffee & tea • also soups, sandwiches
& salads

RESTAURANTS

Dominick's 812 Monroe St (at Tappan Ave)
734/662-5414 • 10am-10pm, clsd Sun •
Italian • full bar • wheelchair access

The Earle 121 W Washington (at Ashley) 734/994-0211 • 5:30pm-10pm, till 11:30pm Fri-Sat, 5pm-9pm Sun • cont'l • some veggie • beer/ wine • wheelchair access

Seva 314 E Liberty 734/662-1111 • 11am-9pm, from 10am wknds • vegetarian • also cafe & wine bar

Zingerman's Delicatessen 422 Detroit St (at Kingsley) 734/663-3354 • 7am-10pm • also ship food worldwide

ENTERTAINMENT & RECREATION

The Ark 316 S Main St (btwn William & Liberty) 734/761-1818, 734/761-1800 • gay-friendly • concert house • women's music shows

BOOKSTORES

Common Language 317 Braun Ct 734/663-0036 • 11am-10pm, till midnight Fri-Sat, till 7pm Sun • LGBT • wheelchair access

Crazy Wisdom Books 114 S Main St (btwn Huron & Washington) 734/665-2757 • 10am-10pm, till 11pm Wed-Sat, 11am-6pm Sun • holistic & metaphysical

Nicola's Books 2513 Jackson Ave (at Maple, in Westgate) 734/662-0600 • 9am-9pm, till 6pm Sun

Battle Creek

NIGHTCLUBS

Partners 910 North Ave (at Morgan) 269/964-7276 • 7pm-2am, clsd Mon • lesbians/ gay men • dancing/DJ • karaoke • wheelchair access

EROTICA

Romantix Adult Superstore 690 W Michigan Ave (at Grand) 269/964-3070

Bellaire

ACCOMMODATIONS

Applesauce Inn B&B 7296 S M-88 231/533-6448 • gay-friendly • B&B in 100-year-old farmhouse • dog-friendly • WiFi • $90-135

Bellaire B&B 212 Park St (at Antrim) 231/533-6077, 800/545-0780 • gay/ straight • stately 1879 home • full brkfst • jacuzzi • nonsmoking • WiFi • gay-owned • $95-235

Big Bay

ACCOMMODATIONS

Big Bay Depot Motel 906/345-9350 • gay-friendly • overlooking Lake Independence • kids/ pets ok • lesbian-owned • $70

Coldwater

EROTICA

The Lion's Den Adult Superstore 570 Jonesville Rd (exit 16, off I-69) 517/278-9577 • 24hrs

Copemish

ACCOMMODATIONS

Jeralan's Farm B&B 18361 Viaduct Rd 231/378-2926, 866/250-8444 • gay-friendly • 1872 farmhouse on 80 acres of woods & ponds • full brkfst • nonsmoking • $110-160

Detroit

INFO LINES & SERVICES

Affirmations Lesbian/ Gay Community Center 290 W 9 Mile Rd (enter on Troy), Ferndale 248/398-7105, 800/398-4297 • 11am-close, 10am-10pm, clsd Sun • also cafe

Helpline 800/398-4297 • 4pm-9pm Tue-Sat • support & resources line

Together We Can (Gay/ Lesbian AA) P.O. Box 247 48068 313/831-5550 , 313/831-2555 • check website for meeting times

ACCOMMODATIONS

The Atheneum Suite Hotel 1000 Brush St (at Lafayette) 313/962-2323, 800/772-2323 • gay-friendly • restaurant & lounge • gym • wheelchair access

Detroit Marriott at the Renaissance Center Renaissance Center 313/568-8000, 800/228-9290 • gay-friendly • wheelchair access

Milner Hotel 1538 Centre St 313/963-3950, 877/645-6377 • gay-friendly • downtown

BARS

Centaur Bar 2233 Park Ave (at W Montcalm St) 313/963-4040 • 4pm-2am • gay/straight • sports bar • food served

Club Gold Coast 2971 E 7 Mile Rd (at Conant) 313/366-6135 • 7pm-2am • popular • mostly gay men • dancing/DJ • male dancers nightly • wheelchair access

Diamond Jim's Saloon 19650 Warren (1 block E of Evergreen) 313/336-8680 • noon-2am • mostly gay men • dancing/DJ • country western nights • multiracial • karaoke • also grill • WiFi • gay-owned

Gigi's 16920 W Warren (at Clayburn, enter rear) 313/584-6525 • noon-2am, from 2pm wknds • mostly gay men • dancing/DJ • transgender-friendly • male dancers Mon & Fri • drag shows • gay-owned

Menjo's 928 W McNichols Rd (at Hamilton) **313/863-3934** • 1pm-2am • popular happy hour • mostly gay men • dancing/DJ • karaoke • live shows • videos • young crowd

Pronto 608 S Washington (at 6th St), Royal Oak 248/544-7900 • 11am-2am Wed-Sat • popular • lesbians/gay men • patio • also restaurant

Soho 205 W 9 Mile (at Woodward), Ferndale **248/542-7646** • 4pm-close, from 6pm wknds • lesbians/gay men • karaoke • swank cocktail lounge

Stingers Lounge 19404 Sherwood (at 7 Mile) **313/892-1765** • 6pm-5am, from 8pm wknds • lesbians/gay men • neighborhood bar • drag shows • grill menu • gay-owned

Detroit

WHERE THE GIRLS ARE:
At the bars on 8-Mile Road between I-75 and Van Dyke Ave., with the boys in Highland Park or Dearborn, or shopping in Royal Oak.

LGBT PRIDE:
June. 313/537-3323 (Triangle Foundation #), web: www.pride-fest.net.

July. Hotter Than July 888/755-9165, web: www.hotterthanjuly.com. "The Midwest's oldest black lesbian, gay, bi-affectionate and transgender pride celebration."

ANNUAL EVENTS:
End of April/early May - London Lesbian Film Festival, web: www.llff.ca. Held in London, Ontario.

August - Detroit International Jazz Festival, web: www.detroitjaz-zfest.com.

Michigan Womyn's Music Festival 231/757-4766, web: www.mich-fest.com. One of the biggest annual gatherings of lesbians on the continent, in Walhalla, in Western Michigan.

CITY INFO:
313/202-1800 or 800/338-7648, web: www.visitdetroit.com.

BEST VIEW:
From the top of the 73-story Marriott Hotel at the Renaissance Center.

WEATHER:
Be prepared for hot, humid summers and cold, dry winters.

ATTRACTIONS:
Belle Isle Park

Detroit Institute of Arts 313/833-7900, web: www.dia.org.

Greektown.

Motown Historical Museum 313/875-2264, web: www.motownmuseum.com.

Museum of African American History 313/494-5800, web: www.maah-detroit.org.

North American Black Historical Museum in Windsor, Ontario, 800/713-6336, web: www.black-historicalmuseum.com.

Renaissance Center 313/568-5600, web: www.gmrencen.com.

TRANSIT:
Checker Cab 313/963-1000, 800/351-5466, web: www.check-ercab-det.com.

Detroit Cab 313/841-6000.

AA Airport Service 800/720-0797, web: www.metroairportservice.com.

DOT bus service 313/933-1300 & 888/336-8287 (outside 313 area code), web: www.detroittransit.org.

Detroit People Mover 313/224-2160, web: www.thepeoplemover.com.

The Woodward Bar & Grill 6426 Woodward Ave (at Milwaukee, rear entrance) **313/872-0166** • 2pm-2am • mostly gay men • DJ Th-Sun • karaoke • videos

NIGHTCLUBS

Backstreet 15606 Joy Rd (at Greenfield) **313/838-6699** • 9pm-2am Wed & Sat • popular • mostly gay men • dancing/DJ • 5 levels • 18+ • wheelchair access • cover charge

Eden 22061 Woodward Ave (at Hazelhurst), Ferndale **248/541-POSH** • 10pm-close Th-Sat • gay/ straight • dancing/DJ • cover charge

Leland City Club 400 Bagley St (at Leland Hotel) **313/962-2300** • 10pm-4:30am Fri-Sat • gay-friendly • dancing/DJ • goth/ alternative • 18+

Luna 1815 N Main St (at 12 Mile), Royal Oak **248/589-3344** • from 9pm, clsd Sun-Tue • gay-friendly • dancing/DJ • goth/ alternative • theme nights

Nine 141 W 9 Mile (at Woodward), Ferndale **248/582-7227** • lesbians/ gay men • ladies' night Sat • dancing/DJ • karaoke

Pandora's Box 6221 E Davison (at Mound) **313/892-8120** • 9pm-2am Th-Sat • popular • mostly women • more women Sat • dancing/DJ • mostly African American • karaoke • live shows • wheelchair access

Pink 19910 Hoover Rd • mostly women • dancing/DJ • live bands

The Rainbow Room 6640 E 8 Mile Rd (at Sherwood) **313/891-1020** • 7pm-2am Wed-Sun • lesbians/ gay men • dancing/DJ • drag shows • karaoke • 18+

Stiletto's 1641 Middlebelt Rd (btwn Michigan Ave & Cherry Hill Rd), Inkster **734/729-8980** • 8pm-2am Th-Sun • mostly women • dancing/DJ • live shows • karaoke

Temple 2906 Cass Ave (btwn Charlotte & Temple) **313/832-2822** • 11am-2am • mostly gay men • dancing/DJ • transgender-friendly • mostly African American • popular wknds • wheelchair access

CAFES

Avalon International Breads 422 W Willis (at Cass) **313/832-0008** • 6am-6pm, clsd Sun-Mon • lesbian-owned

Coffee Beanery Cafe 28557 S Woodward Ave (S of 12 Mile), Berkley **248/336-9930** • 7am-11pm • WiFi

Trixie's Cafe 25925 Gratiot Ave, Roseville • noon-1am, from 6pm Sun • live entertainment & open mics

RESTAURANTS

Amici's Living Room 3249 12 Mile Rd, Berkley **248/544-4100** • gourmet pizza & martinis

Atlas Global Bistro 3111 Woodward Ave **313/831-2241** • lunch & dinner • Sun brunch • American/ int'l • upscale

Cass Cafe 4620 Cass Ave (at Forest) **313/831-1400** • 11am-2am, 5pm-1am Sun • plenty veggie • full bar • WiFi

Coach Insignia 200 Renaissance Ctr, 71st Fl **313/567-2622** • dinner, clsd Sun • steakhouse

Como's 22812 Woodward (at 9 Mile), Ferndale **248/548-5005** • 11am-2am, till 3:30am Th-Sat • Italian • full bar • patio • wheelchair access

Elwood Bar & Grill 300 Adams (at Brush, by Comerica Park) **313/962-2337** • 11am-8pm, till 2pm Mon, clsd Sun (unless there's a Tiger's game) • Art Deco diner

Inn Season 500 E 4th St, Royal Oak **248/547-7916** • lunch & dinner • Sun brunch • clsd Mon • organic vegetarian

La Dolce Vita 17546 Woodward Ave (at McNichols) **313/865-0331** • lunch & dinner, Sun brunch, clsd Mon • lesbians/ gay men • Italian • plenty veggie • full bar • patio • wheelchair access

Laikon Cafe 569 Monroe St **313/963-7058** • 10am-11pm, till 1am Fri-Sat, clsd Tues • authentic Greek • full bar

Pete's Place Broadway Cafe 1225 Woodward Hts (at Hilton Rd), Ferndale **248/544-4215** • 10am-10pm, till midnight Fri-Sat • BYOB

Roast 1128 Washington Ave **313/961-2500** • dinner nightly • steakhouse

Sweet Lorraine's Cafe & Bar 29101 Greenfield Rd (at 12 Mile), Southfield **248/559-5985** • 11am-10pm, till midnight Fri-Sat • popular • modern American • some veggie • wheelchair access

Traffic Jam & Snug 511 W Canfield St (at SE corner of 2nd Ave) **313/831-9470** • 11am-10:30pm, till midnight Fri-Sat, from noon Sat, till 8pm Sun • eclectic • plenty veggie • also full bar, bakery, dairy & brewery

Via Nove 344 W 9 Mile Rd, Ferndale **248/336-9936** • Italian • also bar

Vivio's 2460 Market St (btwn Gratiot & Russell) **313/393-1711** • lunch & dinner, clsd Sun • Italian • full bar

Wolfgang Puck Grille 1777 3rd St (at the MGM Grand Hotel) **313/465–1648** • 5pm-10pm, 9am-2pm Sat-Sun, clsd Mon-Tue

ENTERTAINMENT & RECREATION

Charles H Wright Museum of African American History 315 E Warren Ave (at Brush) **313/494–5800**

Detroit Derby Girls 37637 Five Mile Rd #311, Livonia • visit www.detroitrollerderby.com for events

Motown Historical Museum 2648 W Grand Blvd **313/875–2264** • come see where the Motown Sound began • guided tours & gift shop

BOOKSTORES

Just 4 Us 211 W 9 Mile Rd (at Woodward), Ferndale **248/547–5878** • 11am-8pm, till 10pm Th-Fri, till 5pm Sun • also cafe • gay-owned

RETAIL SHOPS

Royal Oak Tattoo 820 S Washington Ave (at Lincoln), Royal Oak **248/398–0052** • noon-8pm, till 9pm Fri-Sat, clsd Sun • tattoo & piercing studio

PUBLICATIONS

Between the Lines **734/293–7200** • statewide LGBT weekly

Metra Magazine PO Box 71844, Madison Heights 48071 **248/543–3500** • covers IN, IL, MI, OH, PA, WI & Ontario, Canada

EROTICA

Noir Leather 124 W 4th St (at S Center St), Royal Oak **248/541–3979** • 11am-9pm, till 10pm Fri-Sat, noon-7pm Sun • wheelchair access

Douglas

see Saugatuck

Escanaba

EROTICA

Sensual Arts Adult Bookstore 615 N Lincoln Rd **906/786–9020** • gay-owned

Flint

BARS

MI 2406 N Franklin Ave (at Davison) **810/234–9481** • 3pm-2am • popular • lesbians/ gay men • dancing/DJ • multiracial

Pachyderm Pub G–1408 E Hemphill Rd (btwn I–475 & Saginaw St), Burton **810/744–4960** • 3pm-2am, from 5pm wknds • lesbians/ gay men • neighborhood bar & restaurant • dancing/DJ • videos • karaoke • male dancers • multiracial • transgender-friendly • patio • gay-owned

State Bar 2512 S Dort Hwy **810/767–7050** • 2pm-2am • popular • lesbians/ gay men • dancing/DJ • karaoke • wheelchair access

The Zoo 4511 S Saginaw St (at Bristol Rd) **810/249–0267** • 4pm-close Tue-Sun • lesbians/ gay men • dancing/DJ • food served • theme nights • gay-owned

NIGHTCLUBS

Club Triangle 2101 S Dort (at Lippincott) **810/767–7550** • 9pm-close Wed-Sun • popular • lesbians/ gay men • dancing/DJ • male dancers • 18+

Pride Night at Purple Moon 2525 S Dort Hwy **810/424–9579** • 9pm-2am 1st Mon only • lesbians/ gay men • dancing/DJ

CAFES

The Good Beans Cafe 328 N Grand Traverse (at 1st Ave) **810/237–4663** • 7:30am-4pm, till 9pm Th-Fri, open some wknds • espresso & pastries • live shows • gay-owned • wheelchair access

Frankfort

ACCOMMODATIONS

Wayfarer Lodgings 1912 S Scenic Hwy (M-22) **231/352–9264, 800/735–8564** • gay-friendly • cottages • near Frankfort, Lake Michigan & Betsie River • kids/ pets ok • nonsmoking • WiFi • $44/55 - 80/95

Glen Arbor

ACCOMMODATIONS

Duneswood at Sleeping Bear Dunes Nat'l Lakeshore **231/334–3346** • women only • located in northern MI • nonsmoking • lesbian-owned • $55-95

Grand Rapids

ACCOMMODATIONS

Radisson Riverfront Hotel 270 Ann St NW (at Turner Ave) **616/363–9001, 1–800/395–7046** • gay-friendly • nonsmoking • pool • wheelchair access • WiFi • $79-119

Bars

Apartment Lounge 33 Sheldon NE (at Library) 616/451-0815 • 1pm-2am, from noon wknds • mostly gay men • neighborhood bar • sandwiches served • wheelchair access

Diversions 10 Fountain St NW (at Division) 616/451-3800 • 8pm-2am • popular • lesbians/ gay men • dancing/DJ • karaoke • 18+ • videos • also cafe • wheelchair access

Pub 43 43 S Division St 616/458-2205 • 3pm-2am • lesbians/ gay men • neighborhood bar • food served

Nightclubs

Rumors Nightclub 69 S Division Ave (at Oakes St) 616/454-8720 • 4pm-2am • mostly gay men • women's night 1st & 3rd Fri • dancing/DJ • karaoke • male strippers • wheelchair access

Restaurants

Brandywine 1345 Lake Dr SE (in East Town) 616/774-8641 • 7am-9pm, 7:30am-9pm Sat, 8am-4pm Sun, 7am-8pm Mon

Cherie Inn 969 Cherry St SE (at Lake Dr) 616/458-0588 • 7am-2pm, till 3pm wknds, clsd Mon • some veggie • wheelchair access

Gaia Cafe 209 Diamond Ave SE (at Cherry St) 616/454-6233 • 8am-8pm, till 3pm wknds, clsd Mon • vegetarian

Entertainment & Recreation

Grand Raggidy Roller Girls 616/752-8475 • Grand Rapids' female roller derby league

Honor

Accommodations

Labrys Wilderness Resort 231/882-5994 • women only • cabins in Sleeping Bear Dunes Nat'l Lakeshore • lesbian-owned • $55-85

Kalamazoo

Info Lines & Services

Kalamazoo Gay/ Lesbian Resource Center 629 Pioneer St 269/349-4234 • educational/ support groups • youth group • hotline

Bars

Partners Kalamazoo 7638 S Westnedge, Portage 269/383-1814 • 5pm-2am, from 3pm Fri-Sat • lesbians/ gay men • neighborhood bar • dancing/DJ • theme nights

Lansing

Accommodations

The Leaven Center Lyons 989/855-2606 • gay/ straight • some events women only • spiritual retreat center • nonsmoking • also guesthouse available for individual use

Bars

Esquire 1250 Turner St (at Clinton) 517/487-5338 • 3pm-2am, from noon Wed & Sat • lesbians/ gay men • neighborhood bar • karaoke

Nightclubs

Spiral 1247 Center St (at Clinton) 517/371-3221 • 8pm-2am, clsd Mon-Tue • mostly gay men • women's night Wed • dancing/DJ • theme nights • shows • videos • 18+

X-cel 224 S Washington Square (at Washtenaw St) 517/484-2399, 517/281-9502 • 9pm-2am • popular • gay/ straight • gay Tue • dancing/DJ • live shows • young crowd • cover charge

Bookstores

Everybody Reads 2019 E Michigan Ave 517/346-9900 • 11am-7pm, 10am-4pm Sun • cool general bookstore • also coffeehouse

Retail Shops

Splash of Color 515 E Grand River Ave, Ste F, East Lansing 517/333-0990 • open daily • tattoo & piercing studio

Marquette

Accommodations

The Landmark Inn 230 N Front St 906/228-2580, 888/752-6362 • gay-friendly • historic boutique hotel overlooking Lake Superior • restaurant & bar • gym • nonsmoking • WiFi • kids ok • $124-269

Owendale

Accommodations

Windover Resort 3596 Blakely Rd 989/375-2586 • women only • seasonal private resort • campsites & RV hookups • pool • $25/ year membership fee • $21-76 camping fee

Petoskey

ACCOMMODATIONS

Coach House Inn 1011 N US 31 (at Mitchell) **231/347-8281, 877/347-8088** • gay-friendly • basic amenities • WiFi • gay-owned • $39-105

RESTAURANTS

220 Lake Street Food, Spirits & Nightclub 220 S Lake St (20 min form Petoskey), Boyne City **231/582-2272** • 11am-11pm • resort community • patio • wheelchair access • gay-owned

Pontiac

BARS

Tiki Bob's Cantina 25 S Saginaw **248/335-6100** • 9pm-2am, clsd Sun-Mon • gay/straight, more gay Th • dancing/DJ

Port Huron

NIGHTCLUBS

Seekers 3301 24th St (btwn Oak & Little) **810/985-9349** • 7pm-2am, from 4pm Fri-Sat, from 2pm Sun • lesbians/gay men • dancing/DJ • live shows

Saginaw

NIGHTCLUBS

The Mixx Nightclub 115 N Hamilton St (at Court St) **989/498-4022** • 5pm-close Wed-Sun • lesbians/gay men • dancing/DJ • food served • karaoke • videos • 18+ • wheelchair access

Saugatuck

ACCOMMODATIONS

Beechwood Manor Inn & Cottage 736 Pleasant St **269/857-1587, 877/857-1587** • gay/straight • full brkfst • nonsmoking • WiFi • gay-owned • $165-225

Bella Vita Spa & Suites 119 Butler St **269/857-8482** • gay-friendly • upscale, modern suites overlooking downtown Saugatuck • also day spa • WiFi

The Belvedere Inn & Restaurant 3656 63rd St **269/857-5777, 877/858-5777** • gay-friendly • full brkfrst • nonsmoking • gay-owned • $135-325

Bentley Waterfront Suites 326 Water St **269/857-5416, 877/858-5777** • gay-friendly • downtown & on water • nonsmoking • gay-owned • $150-325

Bird Center Resort 584-586 Lake St **269/857-1750** • gay-friendly • 3 cottages across from Sautatuck Harbor • 2 w/ hot tubs • WiFi

The Bunkhouse B&B at Campit **269/543-4335, 877/226-7481** • lesbians/gay men • cabins • private baths • access to Campit Resort amenities (see listing below) • pool • nonsmoking • WiFi $85-125

Campit Outdoor Resort 6635 118th Ave, Fennville **269/543-4335, 877/226-7481** • lesbians/gay men • campsites • RV hookups • separate women's area • pool • seasonal • pets ok • WiFi • membership required • lesbian & gay-owned • $20-65

Deerpath Lodge **269/857-3337, 888/333-8827** • women only • studios on 400 waterfront acres • heated pool • hot tub • swimming • kayaks & canoes

Douglas House B&B 41 Spring St, Douglas **269/857-1119, 248/478-9392 (WINTER)** • gay/straight • near gay beach • gay-owned • $125-145

The Dunes Resort 333 Blue Star Hwy, Douglas **269/857-1401** • lesbians/gay men • motel & cottages • transgender-friendly • pool • food served • women's wknds in April, June & Oct • dancing/DJ • live shows • pets ok • wheelchair access • gay-owned • $40-310

Hidden Garden Cottages & Suites 247 Butler St **269/857-8109, 888/857-8109** • gay-friendly • cottages & suites • nonsmoking • WiFi • $135-225

Hillby Thatch Cottages 1438-1440 71st St, Glenn **847/864-3553** • gay/straight • kitchens • fireplaces • kids ok • nonsmoking • woman-owned • $200-350/wknd & $400-550/week

The Hunter's Lodge 2790 Blue Star Hwy (at US 31), Douglas **269/857-5402** • gay/straight • motel in rustic lodge • kids ok • nonsmoking • $99-179

J Paules Fenn Inn 2254 S 58th St, Fennville **269/561-2836, 877/561-2836** • gay-friendly • B&B • full brkfst • kids/pets ok • nonsmoking • $110-465

The Kingsley House B&B 626 West Main St, Fennville **269/561-6425, 866/561-6425** • gay-friendly • full brkfst • nonsmoking • WiFi • gay-owned • $139-259

Kirby House 294 Center St (at Blue Star Hwy) **269/857-2904, 800/521-6473** • gay/straight • full brkfst • pool • nonsmoking • WiFi • gay-owned • $110-185

Lake Street Commons 790 Lake St **269/857–1680** • gay-friendly • suites w/ kitchen & private decks • WiFi • kids/ pets ok • gay-owned • $95-185

Lynn Dee Lea Boat & Breakfast, LLC 868 Holland St, Slip #1 **309/360–7498** • gay/ straight • B&B on houseboat • sleeps 6 • nonsmoking • $250

Maple Ridge Cottages 713-719 Maple **269/857–5211 (Pines #)** • gay/ straight • quaint 2-brdm & 1-bath cottages w/ private hot tubs • nonsmoking • gay-owned • $150-275/ night & $950-1,150/ week

The Newnham SunCatcher Inn 131 Griffith (at Mason) **269/857–4249, 800/587–4249** • gay-friendly • full brkfst • hot tub • pool • nonsmoking • WiFi • lesbian-owned • $90-160

The Park House Inn B&B 888 Holland St **269/857–4535, 866/321–4535** • gay-friendly • B&B in one of Saugatuck's oldest residences • full brkfst • nonsmoking • WiFi • also cottages • $115-205

The Pines Motor Lodge 56 Blue Star Hwy (at Center St), Douglas **269/857–5211** • gay/ straight • newly renovated boutique retro motel • nonsmoking • also retro gift gallery • gay-owned • $69-205

The Spruce Cutter's Cottage 6670 126th Ave (at Blue Star Hwy & M–89), Fennville **269/543–4285, 800/493–5888** • gay/ straight • full brkfst • gay-owned • $100-200

Timber Bluff 2731 Lakeshore Dr, Fennville **269/857–2586, 616/262–3974** • cottages on Lake Michigan • nonsmoking • kids ok • $195-275

The Timberline Motel 3353 Blue Star Hwy **269/857–2147, 800/257–2147** • gay-friendly • heated pool • WiFi

Bars

Dunes Disco 333 Blue Star Hwy (at the Dunes Resort) **269/857–1401** • 9am-2am • lesbians/ gay men • dancing/DJ • transgender-friendly • cabaret • patio • gay-owned

Saugatuck

Where the Girls Are:
Playing in the waves at Oval Beach.

Annual Events:
May - Tulip Time Festival, Holland 800/822–2770, web: www.tulip-time.com.

June - Waterfront Film Festival 269/857-8351, web: www.water-frontfilm.org.

August - Michigan Womyn's Music Festival 231/757-4766, web: www.michfest.com. One of the biggest annual gatherings of lesbians on the continent, in Walhalla.

August - Camp Trans, web: www.camp-trans.org.

City Info:
Saugatuck-Douglas Convention & Visitors Bureau 269/857-1701, web: www.saugatuck.com.

City of the Village of Douglas, web: www.douglasmichigan.com.

Holland Chamber of Commerce 616/392-2389, web: www.holland-chamber.org.

Attractions:
Fenn Valley Wineries 269/561-2396, web: www.fennvalley.com.

Galleries.

Historical Holland (home of the Wooden Shoe Factory), web: www.dutchvillage.com.

Mason Street Warehouse (theatre) 269/857-4898, web: www.masonstreetwarehouse.org.

Saugatuck Center for the Arts 269/857-2399, web: www.sc4a.org.

Saugatuck-Douglas Historical Society Museum 269/857–7900, web: www.sdhistory.com.

Saugatuck Dunes State Park.

Transit:
Saugatuck Douglas Taxi Service 269/857-1626, web: www.sa

CAFES

Uncommon Grounds 127 Hoffman (at Water) 269/857-3333 • 6:30am-10pm • coffee & juice bar

The Yum Yum Gourmet Cafe & Gelateria 98 Center St, lower level (at Union St), Douglas 269/857-4567 • gay/ straight • also paninis, soup, salad • gay-owned

RESTAURANTS

Back Alley Pizza Joint 22 Main St, Douglas 269/857-7277 • 11am-1-pm, till 11pm Fri-Sat • fresh grinder bread daily

Chequers 220 Culver St 269/857-1868 • 11:30am-9pm • seasonal • great fish & chips

Everyday People Cafe 11 Center St, Douglas 269/857-4240 • call for hours • live jazz

Kalico Kitchen Blue Star Hwy (Ferry St), Douglas 269/857-2678 • 7am-9pm winter, till 10pm summer

Marro's Italian 147 Water St 269/857-4248 • dinner only, clsd Mon-Tue • nightclub till 2am Fri-Sat

Monroe's Cafe-Grille 302 Culver St 269/857-1242 • 8am-9pm, clsd Nov-March • great brkfst

Phil's Bar & Grille 215 Butler St 269/857-1555 • 11:30am-10pm, till 11pm Fri-Sat • patio

Pumpernickel's 202 Butler St (at Mason) 269/857-1196 • 8am-4pm

Restaurant Toulouse 248 Griffith 269/857-1561 • dinner nightly, lunch wknds (seasonal) • full bar • reservations required • wheelchair access

Scooters 322 Culver St 269/857-1041 • 4pm-9pm, noon-10 wknds, clsd Tue • great pizza

The White House Bistro 149 Griffith (at Mason) 269/857-3240 • 4pm-10pm, 9am-midnight Sat, 9am-9pm Sun • live music

The Wicks Park 449 Water St 269/857-2888 • dinner nightly • live music wknds • wheelchair access

Wild Dog Grill 24 W Center St (at Spring), Douglas 269/857-2519 • dinner nightly, from noon wknds, clsd Mon-Tue

ENTERTAINMENT & RECREATION

Earl's Farm Market 1630 Blue Star Hwy, Fennville 269/227-2074 • 8am-9pm May-Oct only • pick your own berries! • gay-owned

Oval Beach consult local map for driving directions, Douglas • popular beach on Lake Michigan

Tulip Time Festival Holland 800/822-2770

RETAIL SHOPS

Amaru Leather 322 Griffith St 269/857-3745 • "original & custom creations in leather by two resident designers"

Groovy! Groovy! Retro Gift Gallery 56 Blue Star Hwy (at Center St), Douglas 269/857-2171 • seasonal hours • antiques, funky gifts & goods • gay-owned

Hoopdee Scootee 133 Mason (at Butler) 269/857-4141 • seasonal • clothing • gifts

Saugatuck Drug Store 201 Butler St 269/857-2300 • seasonal • old-fashioned corner drug store, including actual soda fountain!

GYMS & HEALTH CLUBS

Pump House Gym 6492 Blue Star Hwy 269/857-7867 • day passes

South Haven

ACCOMMODATIONS

Yelton Manor B&B 140 North Shore Dr (at Dyckman) 269/637-5220 • gay/ straight • full brkfst • jacuzzi • nonsmoking • WiFi • wheelchair access • $165-295

St Ignace

ACCOMMODATIONS

Budget Host Inn & Suites 700 N State St 906/643-9666, 800/872-7057 • gay-friendly • pool • facing harbor of Lake Huron & across from ferries to Mackinac Island • WiFi • kids/ pets ok • wheelchair access • $62-160

Traverse City

ACCOMMODATIONS

Neahtawanta Inn 1308 Neahtawanta Rd 231/223-7315, 800/220-1415 • gay-friendly • swimming • sauna • nonsmoking • WiFi • wheelchair access • $115-275

NIGHTCLUBS

Side Traxx 520 Franklin St 231/935-1666 • 5pm-2am • lesbians/ gay men • dancing/DJ • videos • gay-owned

BOOKSTORES

The Bookie Joint 124 S Union St (btwn State & Front) 231/946-8862 • 10am-6pm, till 5pm Sat, 1pm-4pm Sun • pride gifts • used books

Union Pier

ACCOMMODATIONS

Blue Fish Guest House & Cottage 10234 Community Hall Rd **269/469-0468 x112** • gay/ straight • cottages & guesthouses available • some shared baths • nonsmoking • kids/ pets ok • gay-owned

Fire Fly Resort 15657 Lakeshore Rd **269/469-0245** • gay/ straight • 1- & 2-bdrm units • kitchens • nonsmoking • gay-owned • $105-230 • also weekly/ monthly rates

Ypsilanti

see also Ann Arbor

NIGHTCLUBS

Club Divine 23 N Washington **734/485-4444** • gay/ straight • gay night Sun • dancing/DJ • theme nights

MINNESOTA

Statewide

PUBLICATIONS

Lavender Magazine 612/436-4660, **877/515-9969** • LGBT newsmagazine for IA, MN, ND, SD, WI

Duluth

see also Superior, Wisconsin

INFO LINES & SERVICES

Aurora: A Northland Lesbian Center 32 E 1st St #104 (at 1st Ave) **218/722-4903** • drop-in center • social events • library • newsletter

ACCOMMODATIONS

The Olcott House B&B Inn 2316 E 1st St (at 23rd Ave) **218/728-1339, 800/715-1339** • gay-friendly • Georgian colonial near Lake Superior • nonsmoking • WiFi • gay-owned • $145-215

CAFES

Amazing Grace Bakery & Cafe 394 Lake Ave S **218/723-0075** • 7am-10pm, till 11pm Fri-Sat • live shows • more women 2nd Sun for Chick Jam • WiFi

Jitters 102 W Superior St **218/720-6015** • 7am-7pm, clsd Sun • WiFi

BOOKSTORES

At Sara's Table Chester Creek Cafe 1902 E 8th (at 19th) **218/724-6811** • 7am-9pm • WiFi • wheelchair access • women-owned

Hastings

ACCOMMODATIONS

Classic Rosewood Inn & Spa 620 Ramsey St **651/437-3297** • gay-friendly • circa 1880 mansion • full brkfst • nonsmoking • WiFi • $97-277

Kenyon

ACCOMMODATIONS

Dancing Winds Farmstay Retreat 6863 County 12 Blvd **507/789-6606** • gay/ straight • farmstay on 20-acre working farm • work exchange available • nonsmoking • kids ok • lesbian-owned • $105-125

Lanesboro

ACCOMMODATIONS

Stone Mill Suites 100 E Beacon St (at Parkway Ave) **507/467-8663, 866/897-8663** • gay/ straight • WiFi • non-smoking • wheelchair access • gay-owned • $100-180

Mankato

CAFES

The Coffee Hag 329 N Riverfront Dr **507/387-5533** • 8am-11pm, till 10pm Sun • veggie menu • live shows • wheelchair access • women-owned

Minneapolis/ St Paul

INFO LINES & SERVICES

AA Intergroup 952/922-0880

OutFront Minnesota 310 38th St E #204, Minneapolis **612/822-0127, 800/800-0350** • info line w/ 24hr pre-recorded visitor info

Quatrefoil Library 1619 Dayton Ave #105, St Paul **651/641-0969** • 7pm-9pm, 10am-5pm Sat, 1pm-5pm Sun • LGBT library & resource center

ACCOMMODATIONS

The Chambers 901 Hennepin Ave, Minneapolis **612/767-6900** • gay-friendly • chic, art-filled hotel • also restaurant • WiFi • kids/ pets ok • wheelchair access • $239-500

Cover Park Manor 15330 58th St N (at Peller), Stillwater **651/430-9292, 877/430-9292** • gay-friendly • full brkfst • in-room jacuzzi & fireplace • nonsmoking • kids ok • $119-199

Graves 601 Hotel 601 1st Ave N (at 6th St NE), Minneapolis **612/677-1100, 866/523-1100** • gay-friendly • chic, upscale hotel

Millennium Hotel Minneapolis 1313 Nicollet Mall (btwn W Grant & 13th St), Minneapolis **612/332–6000, 866/866–8086** • gay-friendly • also restaurant & bar • pool • WiFi • wheelchair access • $99-289

BARS

19 Bar 19 W 15th St (at Nicollet Ave), Minneapolis **612/871–5553** • 3pm-2am, from 1pm wknds • mostly gay men • neighborhood bar • wheelchair access

Bev's Wine Bar 250 3rd Ave N (at Washington Ave), Minneapolis **612/337–0102** • 4:30pm-10pm, till 1am Fri-Sat, clsd Sun • gay-friendly • patio

Brass Rail 422 Hennepin Ave (at 4th), Minneapolis **612/332–7245** • noon-2am • popular • mostly gay men • live shows • karaoke • drag shows • videos • wheelchair access

Bryant Lake Bowl 810 W Lake St (near Bryant), Minneapolis **612/825–3737** • 8am-2am • gay-friendly • alternative • bowling alley • also theater • restaurant • plenty veggie/vegan • wheelchair access

Camp Bar 490 N Robert St (at 9th St), St Paul **651/292–1844** • 4pm-2am • mostly gay men • dancing/DJ • karaoke • male dancers • videos • also restaurant • wheelchair access

Minneapolis/St Paul

LGBT PRIDE:
June. 612/305-6900, web: www.tcpride.com.

ANNUAL EVENTS:
March - Diva (fashion show benefiting HIV/AIDS service organizations), web: www.divamn.org.
May - Minnesota AIDS Walk 612/341-2060, web: www.mnaidsproject.org.
August - Minnesota Fringe Festival 612/872-1212, web: www.fringefestival.org.
November - Flaming Film Festival, web: www.myspace.com/flamingfilmfest.

CITY INFO:
888/676–6757, web: www.minneapolis.org.

BEST VIEW:
Observation deck of the 32nd story of Foshay Tower, 821 Marquette Ave (closed in winter).

WEATHER:
Winters are harsh. If driving, carry extra blankets and supplies. The average temperature is 19°, and it can easily drop well below 0°, and then there's the wind chill! Summer temperatures are usually in the upper-80°s to mid-90°s and HUMID.

ATTRACTIONS:
American Swedish Institute 612/871–4907, web: www.americanswedishinst.org.
Collection of Questionable Medical Devices at The Science Museum of Minnesota 651/221-9444, web: www.smm.org.
Frederick R Weisman Art Museum 612/625-9494, web: www.weisman.umn.edu.
Mall of America (the largest mall in the US w/indoor theme park) 952/883-8800, web: www.mallofamerica.com.
Minneapolis American Indian Center 612/879–1700, web: www.maicnet.org.
Minneapolis Institute of Arts 888/642-2787, web: www.artsmia.org.
Walker Art Center/Minneapolis Sculpture Garden 612/375-7600, web: www.walkerart.org.

TRANSIT:
Yellow Cab (Minn) 612/824–4444.
Super Shuttle 612/827-7777.
MTC 612/373–3333, web: www.metrotransit.org.

Gladius Bar 1111 Hennepin Ave S (at 11th St), Minneapolis **612/332–9963** • 5pm-2am, from 3pm Fri-Sat • mostly gay men • lounge • dancing/DJ • karaoke

The Independent 3001 Hennepin Ave (in Calhoun Square, upstairs), Minneapolis **612/378–1905** • gay/ straight • 11am-2am • Sun brunch • great martini selection • also restaurant

Jetset 115 N First St (at 1st Ave N), Minneapolis **612/339–3933** • 5pm-close, from 6pm Sat, clsd Sun-Mon • lesbians/ gay men • cool space • nonsmoking

Lush Food Bar 990 Central Ave (at Spring St), Minneapolis • 4pm-2am, from 11am wknds, clsd Mon-Tue • lesbians/ gay men • dancing/DJ • cabaret • drag shows • food served • theme nights • brunch Sun

Tickles 420 S 4th St (at SE 4th Ave), Minneapolis **612/354–3846** • 11am-2am, from 10am wknds • lesbians/ gay men • sports bar • piano lounge • also restaurant • dinner & wknd brunch

The Town House 1415 University Ave W (at Elbert), St Paul **651/646–7087** • 2pm-2am, from noon wknds • popular • lesbians/ gay men • dancing/DJ • karaoke • drag shows • piano bar • open mic • women owned

Nightclubs

Coale's 719 N Dale St, St Paul **651/487–5829** • 11am-2am • gay/straight • dancing/DJ • food served • live shows • patio

Diva Riot Minneapolis • monthly women's dance parties • check www.divariot.com for details

Gay 90s 408 Hennepin Ave (at 4th St S), Minneapolis **612/333–7755** • 8am-2am (dinner Wed-Sun) • popular • mostly gay men • dancing/DJ • multiracial • karaoke • drag shows Wed-Sun • 18+ • wheelchair access

Ground Zero/ The Front 15 NE 4th St (at Hennepin), Minneapolis **612/378–5115** • 10pm-2am Th-Sat only • also The Front lounge from 4pm • gay/ straight • more gay Sat for Bondage-A-Go-Go • dancing/DJ • alternative • live shows • wheelchair access

Kitty Cat Klub 315 14th Ave SE (at SE University Ave), Minneapolis **612/331–9800** • gay-friendly • lounge w/ eclectic decor • live bands

Rumours/ Innuendo 213 E 4th St (at N Sibley St), St Paul **651/225–4528** • 4pm-3am • mostly gay men • dancing/DJ • karaoke • drag shows • theme nights

The Saloon 830 Hennepin Ave (at 9th), Minneapolis **612/332–0835** • noon-2am, from 11am Sun • popular • lesbians/ gay men • dancing/DJ • food served after 5pm • theme nights • go-go boys Fri • young crowd • 18+ Mon & Th • wheelchair access • gay-owned

Cafes

Anodyne at 43rd 4301 Nicollet Ave S (at 43rd), Minneapolis **612/824–4300** • 7am-10pm, till 8pm Sat • food served • open mic/ live music • wheelchair access

Black Dog Coffee & Wine Bar 308 Prince St (at Broadway), St Paul **651/228–9274** • 7am-10pm, till 9pm Sat, 8am-8pm Sun • food served

Blue Moon 3822 E Lake St, Minneapolis **612/721–9230** • 7am-11pm, from 8am wknds

Cahoots 1562 Selby Ave (at Snelling), St Paul **651/644–6778** • 6:30am-10:30pm, from 7am wknds • coffee bar

Moose & Sadie's 212 3rd Ave N (at 2nd St), Minneapolis **612/371–0464** • 7am-8pm, 9am-2pm wknds

Uncommon Grounds 2809 Hennepin Ave (at 28th Ave), Minneapolis **612/872–4811** • noon-midnight, till 1am Fri-Sat • gay/straight • outdoor seating

The Urban Bean 3255 Bryant Ave S (at 33rd), Minneapolis **612/824–6611** • 6:30am-11pm, from 7:30am Sun • patio • WiFi

Vera's Cafe 2901 Lyndale Ave S (at 29th St W), Minneapolis **612/822–3871** • 7am-11pm • cozy coffeehouse w/ baked goods & light meals • beer/ wine

White Rock Cafe 769 Cleveland, St Paul **651/699–5448** • 7am-9pm, till 6pm Sun • WiFi

Wilde Roast Cafe 518 Hennepin Ave E (at Central), Minneapolis **612/331–4544** • 7am-10pm • shares entrance w/ LGBT bookstore • beer/ wine • wheelchair access • gay-owned

Restaurants

Al's Breakfast 413 14th Ave SE (at 4th), Minneapolis **612/331–9991** • 6am-1pm, from 9am Sun • popular • great hash

Azia 2550 Nicollet Ave S, Minneapolis **612/813–1200** • 11am-2am, from 3pm Sun • Asian fusion • full bar

Birchwood Cafe 3311 E 25th St, Minneapolis **612/722–4474** • 7am-9pm, from 8am Sat, 9am-8pm Sun • organic • plenty veggie/vegan

Brasa Premium Rotisserie 600 E Hennepin, Minneapolis **612/379–3030** • 11am-9pm, till 10pm Fri-Sat

Cafe Barbette 1600 W Lake St (at Irving), Minneapolis **612/827–5710** • 8am-1am, till 2am Fri-Sat • lesbians/ gay men • French/ American • plenty veggie • beer/ wine • women-owned

French Meadow 2610 Lyndale Ave S, Minneapolis **612/870–7855** • 6:30am-10pm, till 11pm Fri-Sat • organic & local • plenty veggie/ vegan • beer/ wine

Fusion 2919 Hennepin Ave (at Lagoon Ave) **612/824–6300** • 4pm-11pm, till 2am wknds • restaurant & lounge • theme nights

Hard Times Cafe 1821 Riverside Ave, Minneapolis **612/341–9261** • 6am-4am • vegan/ vegetarian • punk rock ambiance • WiFi

Il Gatto 3001 Hennepin Ave S (in Calhoun Square Mall), Minneapolis **612/822–1688** • clsd Sun

Joe's Garage 1610 Harmon Pl, Minneapolis **612/904–1163** • lunch & dinner, full bar till 1am • rooftop seating

Lucia's Restaurant & Wine Bar 1432 W 31st St, Minneapolis **612/825–1572** • lunch & dinner, clsd Mon

Monte Carlo 219 3rd Ave N, Minneapolis **612/333–5900** • lunch & dinner, bar till 1am

Murray's 26 S 6th St (at Hennepin), Minneapolis **612/339–0909** • lunch Mon-Fri, dinner nightly • steak & seafood

Nye's Polonaise 112 E Hennepin Ave, Minneapolis **612/379–2021** • 11am-2am, clsd Sun • prime rib • piano bar • live polka & bands • full bar

Palomino Euro Bistro 825 Hennepin Ave (at 9th St), Minneapolis **612/339–3800** • lunch Mon-Sat, dinner nightly • Italian/ Mediterranean

Psycho Suzi's 2519 Marshall St NE, Minneapolis **612/788–9069** • 11am-2am • pu-pu's & pizza

Punch Neapolitan Pizza 704 Cleveland Ave S, St Paul **651/696–1066** • 11am-9:30pm, till 10pm Fri-Sat

Punch Pizza 210 E Hennepin Ave, Minneapolis **612/623–8114** • 11am-10pm • Neapolitan-style pizza

Red Stag Supperclub 509 1st Ave NE (at 5th St), Minneapolis **612/767–7766** • 11am-2am, from 9am Sat-Sun • live music • wheelchair access

Royal Orchid 2401 Fairview Ave N, St Paul **651/639–9999** • 11am-9pm, from noon Sat, clsd Sun • transgender-friendly • Thai

Rudolph's Bar-B-Que 1933 Lyndale (at Franklin), Minneapolis **612/871–8969** • 11am-2am, till 1am Sun • full bar • wheelchair access

Seward Cafe 2129 E Franklin Ave, Minneapolis **612/332–1011** • 7am-3pm, 8am-4pm wknds • vegetarian/vegan cafe

Toast Wine Bar & Cafe 415 N 1st St (in the Heritage Landing Bldg) **612/333–4305** • 5pm-11pm, till midnight Fri-Sat

Trattoria da Vinci 400 Sibley St, St Paul **651/222–4050** • 11am-9pm, 5pm-10pm Sat, clsd Sun-Mon

ENTERTAINMENT & RECREATION

Calhoun 32nd Beach 3300 E Calhoun Pkwy (33rd & Calhoun Blvd), Minneapolis **612/230–6400**

Fresh Fruit KFAI 90.3 FM, Minneapolis **612/341–0980** (ON-AIR STUDIO), **612/341–3144** (OFFICE) • 7:30pm-8:30pm Th • gay radio program • also a variety of LGBT programs 9pm-11pm Sun

Illusion Theater 528 Hennepin Ave (8th floor), Minneapolis **612/339–4944** • some LGBT-themed productions

Minnesota Lynx Target Center, Minneapolis **612/673–8400, 877/962–2849** • check out the Women's Nat'l Basketball Association while you're in Minneapolis

Minnesota RollerGirls **612/296–4743** • MN's female roller derby league • visit www.mnrollergirls.com for events

One Voice Mixed Chorus **651/298–1954** • LGBTA community chorus

Patrick's Cabaret 3010 Minnehaha Ave S, Minneapolis **612/724–6273, 612/721–3595** • gay/ straight • informal performance space w/ bi-weekly shows

Suburban World Theater 3022 Hennepin Ave S **612/822–9000** • historic theater • cinema, concerts, live performances • food served

BOOKSTORES

True Colors 4755 Chicago Ave S, Minneapolis **612/821–9630** • call for hours • feminist bookstore since 1970 • women-owned

RETAIL SHOPS

The Rainbow Road 109 W Grant (at LaSalle), Minneapolis **612/872-8448** • 10am-10pm • LGBT retail & video • wheelchair access

PUBLICATIONS

Lavender Magazine **612/436-4660, 877/515-9969** • LGBT newsmagazine for IA, MN, ND, SD, WI

Minnesota Women's Press 771 Raymond Ave, St Paul **651/646-3968** • newspaper

My Scene City **612/886-3151**

EROTICA

Fantasy Gifts 1437 University Ave, St Paul **651/256-7484** • 10am-10pm, noon-6pm Sun

The Smitten Kitten 3010 Lyndale Ave S, Minneapolis **612/721-6088, 888/751-0523** • 11am-9pm, noon-7pm Sun • transgender-friendly • lesbian-owned • something for everyone!

Moorhead

see also Fargo, North Dakota

INFO LINES & SERVICES

Pride Collective & Community Center 810 4th Ave #220 **218/287-8034** • 5:30-7:30 Tue & 3pm-5pm Sat

NIGHTCLUBS

The I-Beam 1021 Center Ave **218/233-7700** • 9pm-2am Fri-Sat only • lesbians/ gay men • dancing/DJ • drag shows

CAFES

Atomic Coffee 16 4th St S (at Main) **218/299-6161** • 6:30am-10pm, from 8am Sun • also gallery • live shows • gay-owned

Rochester

INFO LINES & SERVICES

Gay/ Lesbian Community Service • Wed at 7pm, contact www.glcsmn.org

Rushford

ACCOMMODATIONS

Windswept Inn 207 N Mill St **507/864-2545** • gay-friendly • gay-owned • $40-50

Statewide

PUBLICATIONS

Ambush Mag **504/522-8049** • LGBT newspaper for the Gulf South (TX through FL)

Bay Saint Louis

ACCOMMODATIONS

Nella's Park 16145 Hwy 603 (near I-10), Kiln **228/586-0053** • gay/ straight • camping • kids/pets ok • friendly & clean w/ fishing dock • casino nearby • close to New Orleans

Biloxi

BARS

Just Us Lounge 906 Division St (at Caillavet) **228/374-1007** • 24hrs • lesbians/ gay men • neighborhood bar • live shows • dancing/DJ • drag shows • go-go boys • karaoke

Gulfport

BARS

Salty Dawg Saloon 1105 Broad Ave (at Railroad) **228/864-0463** • 10am-2am • gay-friendly • neighborhood bar • dancing/DJ • karaoke • gay-owned

Jackson

INFO LINES & SERVICES

Gay/ Lesbian Community Info Line **601/371-3019, 601/346-4379** • 24hrs • switchboard for many organizations, including youth group • also HIV/AIDS hotline

Lambda AA 4866 N State St (at Unitarian Church) **601/856-5337** • 6:30pm Mon & Wed, 8pm Sat

BARS

Jack's Construction Site (JC's) 425 N Mart Plaza **601/362-3108** • 5pm-2am • clsd Mon • mostly gay men • more women Wed & Fri • neighborhood bar • BYOB • WiFi

NIGHTCLUBS

Dick & Jane's 206 W Capitol St • 9pm-close Th-Sun • lesbians/ gay men • dancing/DJ • drag shows • 18+ • young crowd

Natchez

ACCOMMODATIONS

The Antebellum Music Room B&B at the Stone House 804 Washington St 601/445-7466 • gay-friendly • antebellum Greek Revival on Nat'l Historic Register • gallery of rare antiques • full Southern brkfst • kids ok • WiFi • $110-125

Historic Oak Hill Inn B&B 409 S Rankin St (at Orleans St) 601/446-2500, 601/446-8641 • antebellum mansion near the Mississippi • nonsmoking • WiFi • gay-owned • $115-140

Mark Twain Guesthouse 25 Silver St 601/446-8023 • above Under the Hill Saloon • $65-110

BARS

King's Tavern Lounge 619 Jefferson St (at N. Rankin St) 601/446-8854 • 4pm-close • gay-friendly • neighborhood bar • food served • 18+

Under the Hill Saloon 25 Silver St 601/446-8023 • 10am-close • gay-friendly • neighborhood bar • live music • WiFi

MISSOURI

Statewide

PUBLICATIONS

Metro Star 918/835-7887 • monthly LGBT news publication serving AR, KS, MO & OK

Branson

see also Springfield & Eureka Springs, Arkansas

ACCOMMODATIONS

Branson Stagecoach RV Park 5751 State Hwy 165 417/335-8185, 800/446-7110 • gay-friendly • pull-thru & back-in RV sites • cabins • pool • WiFi • gay-owned • $90

Cape Girardeau

ACCOMMODATIONS

Rose Bed Inn 611 S Sprigg St 573/332-7673, 866/767-3233 • gay/ straight • B&B • full brkfst • hot tub • gourmet dining by reservation • nonsmoking • WiFi • wheelchair access • gay-owned • $85-200

NIGHTCLUBS

Independence Place 5 S Henderson St (at Independence, at Holiday Happenings) 573/334-2939 • 8:30pm-1:30am Mon-Th, from 7pm Fri-Sat, clsd Sun • lesbians/ gay men • dancing/DJ • transgender-friendly • drag shows

Columbia

BARS

SoCo Club 128 E Nifong Blvd #E (at Providence Rd) 573/499-9483 • 8pm-1:30am, clsd Sun-Mon • lesbians/ gay men • dancing/DJ • food served • karaoke Tue • drag shows • videos • patio • wheelchair access

CAFES

Ernie's Cafe 1005 E Walnut St (at 10th) 573/874-7804 • 6:30am-3pm

RagTag Cinema 10 Hitt St (Broadway) 573/443-4359, 573/441-8504 • 5pm-close, from 4pm Sat, from 1:30pm Sun • independent & alternative cinema • also theater, music & dance • food served • beer & wine

RESTAURANTS

Main Squeeze 28 S 9th St (at Cherry St) 573/817-5616 • 10am-8pm, till 5pm Sun • local organic ingredients • vegetarian • WiFi

BOOKSTORES

The Peace Nook 804 C East Broadway (btwn 8th & 9th) 573/875-0539 • 10am-9pm, noon-6pm Sun • LGBT section • books • pride products • women's music

EROTICA

Bocomo Bay 1122-A Wilkes Blvd 573/443-0873

Hannibal

ACCOMMODATIONS

Garden House B&B 301 N 5th St (at Bird) 573/221-7800, 866/423-7800 • gay-friendly • WiFi • nonsmoking • gay-owned • $90-139

Rockcliffe Mansion 1000 Bird St 573/221-4140, 877/423-4140 • gay-friendly • guilded-age Mansion built in 1898 on a limestone bluff • nonsmoking • WiFi • gay-owned • $129-179

RESTAURANTS

LaBinnah Bistro 207 N 5th St (at Center) 537/221-7800 • dinner only • in a Victorian home • beer/ wine • gay-owned

Hermann

ACCOMMODATIONS

Healing Stone Retreat & Spa
573/486-5000 • gay-friendly • full brkfst • nonsmoking • women-owned • $125-265

Joplin

INFO LINES & SERVICES

Gay Lesbian Family & Corporate Center
417/622-7821

BARS

Pla Mor Lounge 532 S Joplin Ave
417/624-2722 • 5pm-1am, clsd Sun-Mon • lesbians/ gay men • neighborhood bar • dancing/DJ • karaoke

PUBLICATIONS

Metro Star 918/835-7887 • monthly LGBT news publication serving AR, KS, MO & OK

Kansas City

see also Kansas City & Overland Park, Kansas

INFO LINES & SERVICES

Lesbian & Gay Community Center of Greater Kansas City 207 Westport Rd, Stes 212-218 816/931-4420 • 6pm-9pm Mon, Tue, Th-Fri • call for events

Live & Let Live AA 3901 Main St #211 (at 39th) 816/531-9668 • noon daily, 6pm Tue-Fri, 7pm Sat

ACCOMMODATIONS

Hotel Phillips 106 W 12th St (at Baltimore Ave) 816/221-7000, 800/433-1426 • gay-friendly • art deco landmark in downtown KC

The Porch Swing Inn 702 East St, Parkville 816/587-6282, 866/587-6282 • gay-friendly • B&B • full brkfst • kids ok • WiFi • lesbian-owned • $90-140

Q Hotel & Spa 560 Westport Rd (at Mill St) 816/931-0001, 800/942-4233 • gay-friendly • in Westport district • WiFi • wheelchair access • $99-189

The Raphael 325 Ward Pkwy (at Wornall Rd) 816/756-3800, 800/821-5343 • gay-friendly • WiFi • also restaurant • $139+

Southmoreland on the Plaza 116 E 46th St (at Main St) 816/531-7979 • gay-friendly • 1913 B&B • full brkfst • veranda • nonsmoking • $155-250

Su Casa B&B 9004 E 92nd St (off James A Reed Rd) 816/965-5647, 816/916-3444 (CELL) • gay-friendly • Southwest-style home • full brkfst wknds • kids/ dogs/ horses ok • jacuzzi • pool • nonsmoking • WiFi • woman-owned • $110-150

BARS

Balanca's 1809 Grand Blvd (at 18th) 816/474-6369 • 6pm-3am, from 2pm Sat, clsd Sun-Mon • gay/ straight • multiracial • very diverse crowd • dancing/DJ • food served

Danny's 3611 Broadway (at W 36th) 816/569-1878 • 11am-1:30am • mostly men • neighborhood bar

Flo's Cabaret 1911 Main St (at 19th) 816/283-3567 • 4pm-1:30am, clsd Sun • lesbians/ gay men • drag shows • cabaret • food served

Hamburger Mary's KC 101 Southwest Blvd (at Baltimore Ave) 816/842-1919 • 11am-1:30am, clsd Sun • lesbians/ gay men • theme nights • karaoke • live entertainment • food served • juicy burgers w/ a side of camp

Missie B's/ Bootleggers 805 W 39th St (at SW Trafficway) 816/561-0625 • noon-3am • lesbians/ gay men • neighborhood bar • dancing/DJ • transgender-friendly • 2 flrs • live shows • karaoke • drag shows

Outa Bounds 3601 Broadway St (W 36th) 816/756-2577 • 11am-1:30am, till midnight Sun • mostly gay men • neighborhood sports bar • food served

Sidekicks 3707 Main St (at 37th) 816/931-1430 • 2pm-3am, from 4pm Sun, clsd Mon • lesbians/ gay men • dancing/DJ • country/ western • drag shows • wheelchair access

Tootsie's New Place 1822 Main (at 18th) 816/471-7704 • 6pm-3am, clsd Mon • popular • mostly women • dancing/DJ • drag shows • grill menu • some veggie • wheelchair access

NIGHTCLUBS

Mint 334 E 31st St (at McGee St) 816/561-2640 • 9pm-3am • gay/ straight • more gay Th • swank dance club

NRG 220 Admiral Blvd (at Grand Blvd) 816/221-2674 • 9pm-3am Th-Sun only • gay-friendly • dancing/DJ • videos • rooftop deck • wheelchair access

CAFES

Broadway Cafe 4106 Broadway (at Westport) 816/531-2432 • 7am-9pm • food served • nonsmoking • also 301 Westport Rd, 816/931-9955

Restaurants

Bistro 303 303 Westport Rd **816/753–2303** • dinner nightly, brunch wknds • also martini bar

Blue Bird Bistro 1700 Summit **816/221–7559** • 7am-10pm, 10am-2pm Sun • oranic fare

Cafe Trio/ Starlet Lounge 4558 Main St **816/756–3227** • 5pm-11pm, clsd Sun • piano • gay-owned

Chubby's 3756 Broadway St (at 38th) **816/931–2482** • open 24 hrs • popular late nights • diner fare

Classic Cup Cafe 301 W 47th St (at Central) **816/753–1840** • brkfst, lunch, dinner, Sun brunch • great appetizers • wheelchair access

Grand Street Cafe 4740 Grand Ave (at @ 47th St) **816/561–8000** • lunch & dinner, Sun brunch • patio seating

Jardine's 4536 Main St **816/561–6480** • dinner nightly • steak/ sea food • live jazz

JP Wine Bar 1526 Walnut St (at 16th) **816/842–2660** • 4pm-1:30am, clsd Sun • wine & cheese flights • full dinner menu • patio seating

Le Fou Frog 400 E 5th St **816/474–6060** • dinner only, clsd Sun • French bistro

Mama's Diner 3906 Waddell St **816/531–6422** • 6:30am-10pm, till 3pm Sun-Tue • transgender-friendly

The Mixx 4855 Main St (at W 48th) **816/756–2300** • lunch & dinner • fast & healthy • huge selection of salads

One 80 435 Westport Rd (at Broadway) **816/389–4180** • 11am-3am, from 10am wknds • pizzas, pasta & more • also martini bar

Ortega's 2646 Belleview Ave **816/531–5415** • real deal Mexican food in the back of a Mom & Pop store

Sharp's 63rd St Grill 128 W 63rd St **816/333–4355** • 7am-10pm, from 8am wknds • full bar • wheelchair access

YJ's Snack Bar 128 W 18th St **816/472–5533** • 8am-10pm, 24hrs Th-Sat • inexpensive

Entertainment & Recreation

First Fridays Art Walk Crossroads District (Baltimore & 20th) **816/994–9325** • 5pm-10pm 1st Fri • art gallery walk • also live music & vendors

Kansas City

LGBT Pride:
June. web: www.gaypridekc.com.

Annual Events:
April - AIDS Walk 816/931-0959, web: www.aidswalkkansascity.org.

City Info:
Convention & Visitors Bureau 816/221-5242, web: www.visitkc.com.

Transit:
Yellow Cab 816/471-5000.
KCI Shuttle 816/ 243-5000.
Metro 816/221-0660, web: www.kcata.org

Attractions:
American Jazz Museum 816/474-8463, web: www.american-jazzmuseum.com.
Black Archives of Mid-America 816/701-3590, web: www.blackarchives.org.
Harry S Truman Nat'l Historical Site (in Independence, MO) 816/254-9929, web: www.nps.gov/hstr.
Historic 18th & Vine District (includes Kansas City Jazz Museum & the Negro Leagues Baseball Museum).
Nelson-Atkins Museum of Art 816/751-1278, web: www.nelson-atkins.org.
Thomas Hart Benton Home & Studio 816/931-5722, web: www.mostateparks.com/benton.htm.

Kansas City Roller Warriors 913/636–7894
• KC's female roller derby league • visit kcrollerwarriors.com for events

Nelson-Atkins Museum 4525 Oak St
816/751–1278 • Amercan Indian galleries

EROTICA

Erotic City 8401 E Truman Rd (at I–435)
816/252–3370

Hollywood at Home 9063 Metcalf (at 91st),
Overland Park, KS 913/649–9666 • 10am-11pm

Osage Beach

ACCOMMODATIONS

Utopian Inn 1962 Alcorn Hollow Rd, Roach
573/347–3605 • lesbians/ gay men • 3-bdrm rental on a lake • kids/ small pets ok • nonsmoking • gay-owned • $125-200

Overland

EROTICA

Patricia's 10210 Page Ave (E of Ashby)
314/423–8422

Springfield

INFO LINES & SERVICES

AA Gay/ Lesbian 518 E Commercial St
417/823–7125 (AA #) • 6pm Sat • nonsmoking

Gay & Lesbian Community Center of the Ozarks 518 E Commercial St 417/869–3978
• transgender support group 7pm Sun • youth group 4pm Tue • many other groups • newsletter • wheelchair access

BARS

The Edge 424 N Boonville 417/831–4700 •
4pm-1:30am, clsd Sun • lesbians/ gay men • dancing/DJ • karaoke • drag shows • wheelchair access • lesbian-owned

Martha's Vineyard 219 W Olive St
417/864–4572, 417/831–6144 • 5pm-1:30am, clsd Sun • lesbians/ gay men • neighborhood bar • dancing/DJ • drag shows • also martini lounge • patio • wheelchair access • cover charge wknds

BOOKSTORES

Renaissance Books & Gifts 1337 E
Montclair St 417/883–5161 • 10am-7pm, noon-5pm Sun • women's/ alternative • wheelchair access

EROTICA

Patricia's 1918 S Glenstone (at Sunshine)
417/881–8444

St Louis

ACCOMMODATIONS

A St Louis Guesthouse 1032 Allen Ave (at
Menard) 314/773–1016 • mostly gay men • located in historic Soulard district • hot tub (nudity ok) • nonsmoking • WiFi • gay-owned • $90-110

Brewers House B&B 1829 Lami St (at
Lemp) 314/771–1542, 888/767–4665 • lesbians/ gay men • 1860s home • jacuzzi • pets ok • nonsmoking • WiFi • gay-owned • $95

Dwell 912 B&B 912 Hickory St (at S 9th St)
314/599–3100 • gay-friendly • nonsmoking • WiFi • gay-owned • $150-175

Grand Center Inn 3716 Grandel Sq (at N
Grand Blvd) 314/533–0771 • gay/ straight • WiFi • gay-owned • $125-275

Millennium Hotel St Louis 200 S 4th St (at
Clark Ave) 314/241–9500, 866/866–8086 • gay-friendly • on Mississippi River • view of Gateway Arch • pool • wheelchair access

Napoleon's Retreat B&B 1815 Lafayette
Ave (at Mississippi) 314/772–6979, 800/700–9980 • gay/ straight • restored 1880s town house • full brkfst • nonsmoking • WiFi • gay-owned • $105-165

Park Avenue Mansion—A B&B
Guesthouse 2007 Park Ave (at Mississippi) 314/588–9004 • gay/ straight • B&B inn • full brkfst • jacuzzi • $89-225

BARS

Absolutli Goosed Martini Bar, Etc 3196 S
Grand (4 blocks S of Tower Grove Park) 314/771–9300 • 4pm-midnight, till 1am Fri-Sat, clsd Sun • lesbians/ gay men • neighborhood bar • also desserts • appetizers • patio • lesbian-owned

Bar 5 4237 Manchester (at S Boyle Ave)
314/652–3699 • open 6pm, clsd Mon • lesbians/gay men • homemade pizza • karaoke

Cicero's 6691 Delmar (at Kingsland Ave),
University City 314/862–0009 • 11am-1am, till midnight Sun • gay/ straight • Italian restaurant • tavern • live music venue

Clementine's 2001 Menard (at Allen)
314/664–7869 • 10am-1:30am, 11am-midnight Sun • popular • mostly gay men • neighborhood bar • leather • food served • patio • wheelchair access

Club Escapades 133 W Main St (at 2nd),
Belleville, IL 618/222–9597 • 6pm-2am • lesbians/ gay men • dancing/DJ • karaoke • live shows

Erney's 32 Degree 4200 Manchester Ave (at Boyle) 314/652-7195 • 8pm-3am, clsd Sun-Mon & Wed • lesbians/ gay men • swank neighborhood bar

Grey Fox Pub 3503 S Spring (at Potomac) 314/772-2150 • 2pm-1:30am, noon-midnight Sun • lesbians/ gay men • neighborhood bar • drag shows • transgender-friendly • patio

Hummel's Pub 7101S Broadway 314/353-5080 • 11am-1am • lesbians/gay men • neighborhood bar • full menu • karaoke • lesbian-owned

Just John 4112 Manchester Ave 314/371-1333 • 3pm-1:30am, from noon Sun • lesbians/ gay men • neighborhood bar • dancing/DJ Fri-Sat • drag shows • karaoke • videos

Korners Bar 7109 S Broadway (at Blow St) 314/352-3088 • 4pm-1:30am, clsd Sun-Mon • lesbians/ gay men • dancing/DJ • drag shows

Loading Zone 16 S Euclid (at Forest Park Pkwy) 314/361-4119 • 3:30pm-1:30am • popular • lesbians/ gay men • video bar • drag shows • wheelchair access • gay-owned

St Louis

WHERE THE GIRLS ARE:
Spread out, but somewhat concentrated in the Central West End near Forest Park. Younger, funkier crowds hang out in the Delmar Loop, west of the city limits, packed with ethnic restaurants.

LGBT PRIDE:
June. PrideFest 314/772-8888, web: www.pridestl.org.

ANNUAL EVENTS:
February - Soulard Mardi Gras 314/771-5110, web: www.mardigrasinc.com.
July - Fair St Louis & LIVE on the Levee 314/434-3434, web: www.celebratestlouis.org.
September - The Great Forest Park Balloon Race, web: www.greatforestparkballoonrace.com

CITY INFO:
314/421-1023 or 800/ 325-79621, web: www.explorestlouis.com.

BEST VIEW:
Where else? Top of the Gateway Arch in the Observation Room, web: www.gatewayarch.com.

WEATHER:
100% midwestern. Cold winters—little snow and the temperatures can drop below 0°. Hot, muggy summers raise temperatures back up into the 100°s. Spring and fall bring out the best in Mother Nature.

ATTRACTIONS:
Anheuser-Busch Brewery 800/342-5283 web: www.budweiser-tours.com.
Cathedral Basilica of St Louis (world's largest collection of mosaic art) 314/738-8200, web: www.cathedralstl.org.
Gateway Arch 877/982-1410, web: www.gatewayarch.com.
Grant's Farm 314/843-1700, web: www.grantsfarm.com.
Soulard, the "French Quarter of St Louis."
St Louis Art Museum 314/721-0072, web: www.slam.org.
Stone Hill Winery (in Hermann) 800/909-9463, web: www.stone-hillwinery.com.
The extremely quaint town of St Charles.

TRANSIT:
County Cab 314/993-8294, web: www.countycab.com.
TransExpress 314/428-7799, web: www.transexpress-stl.com.
MetroBus 314/231-2345, web: www.metrostlouis.org

Nancy's Place (NP) 4510 Manchester (at Taylor Ave) **314/533-3699** • open 5pm, clsd Sun-Mon • lesbians/gay men • martini bar

Novak's Bar & Grill 4121 Manchester (at Sarah) **314/531-3699** • noon-3am • mostly women • dancing/DJ Fri-Sat • live shows • karaoke • Trivia Tue • patio • wheelchair access

Premium Lounge 4199 Manchester **314/652-8585** • opens 4pm, clsd Sun • gay/straight

Rehab Lounge 4052 Chouteau (at Boyle) **314/652-3700** • 11:30am-1:30am • gay/straight • neighborhood bar • also restaurant

Soulard Bastille 1027 Russell (at Menard) **314/664-4408** • 11am-1:30am • mostly gay men • food served

NIGHTCLUBS

Atomic Cowboy 4140 Manchester (btwn Sarah & Boyle) **314/775-0775** • 11am-3am, from 5pm Sat-Sun, clsd Mon • gay/straight • dancing/DJ • live shows • burlesque • also Fresh-Mex Mayan grill • art lounge • WiFi • patio

Attitudes 4100 Manchester (at S Sarah) **314/534-0044** • 7pm-3am, clsd Sun-Mon • popular • lesbians/gay men • dancing/DJ • drag shows • karaoke

Bubby & Sissy's 602 Belle St (at 6th St), Alton, IL **618/465-4773** • 3pm-2am, till 3am Fri-Sat • lesbians/gay men • dancing/DJ • live shows • karaoke • drag shows • videos • wheelchair access

The Complex Nightclub & Restaurant 3515 Chouteau Ave (at Grand) **314/772-2645** • 9pm-3am • popular • lesbians/gay men • 5 bars • dancing/DJ • drag shows • videos • patio • food served • wheelchair access

Magnolia's 5 S Vandeventer Ave (at Laclede) **314/652-6500** • lesbians/gay men • dancing/DJ • mostly African American • hip hop/R&B club

CAFES

Coffee Cartel 2 Maryland Plaza (at Euclid) **314/454-0000** • 24hrs • popular • WiFi

MoKaBe's 3606 Arsenal (at S Grand) **314/865-2009** • 8am-midnight, from 9am Sun • popular • plenty veggie • occasional shows • wheelchair access

Soulard Coffee Garden Cafe 910 Geyer Ave (btwn 9th & 10th) **314/241-1464** • 6:30am-4pm, from 8am wknds • food served • WiFi

RESTAURANTS

Billie's Diner 1802 S Broadway **314/621-0848** • 5am-2:30pm, midnight-1:30pm wknds

Chez Leon 7927 Forsyth Blvd (at S Meramec Ave) **314/361-1589** • lunch Mon-Fri, dinner Tue-Sun • French bistro • full bar • gay-owned

City Diner 3139 S Grand **314/772-6100** • 7am-11pm, 24hrs Fri-Sat, till 10pm Sun

Dressel's 419 N Euclid (at McPherson) **314/361-1060** • 11am-1am, till midnight Sun • great Welsh pub food • full bar • live shows

Duff's 392 N Euclid Ave (at McPherson) **314/361-0522** • lunch & dinner, brunch wknds, clsd Mon • fine dining • some veggie • full bar • wheelchair access

Imperial Palace 2543 N Grand Blvd **314/531-1951** • lunch & dinner • soul food • full bar

Majestic Cafe 4900 Laclede (at Euclid) **314/361-2011** • 6am-9:30pm, bar till 11pm • Greek-American diner fare

Meskerem 3210 S Grand Blvd **314/772-4442** • lunch & dinner • Ethiopian • plenty veggie

Rue 13 1311 Washington **314/588-7070** • 5pm-3am, from 7pm wknds • sushi • full bar • dancing/DJ • burlesque

Ted Drewes Frozen Custard 6726 Chippewa (at Jameson) **314/481-2652, 314/481-2124** • 11am-10pm • seasonal • a St Louis landmark • also 4224 S Grand Blvd, 314/352-7376 • wheelchair access

Terrene 33 N Sarah **314/535-5100** • dinner nightly, clsd Mon • also bar • patio dining in season

Tony's 410 Market St (at Broadway) **314/231-7007** • dinner only, clsd Sun • Italian fine dining • reservations advised

Van Goghz 3200 Shenandoah **314/865-3345** • brkfst, lunch & dinner • also bar • WiFi

Vin de Set 2017 Chouteau **314/241-8989** • lunch & dinner, dinner only wknds, clsd Mon • rooftop bar & bistro

The Wild Flower Restaurant & Bar 4590 Laclede Ave (at Euclid) **314/367-9888** • lunch & dinner, bar till 1:30am, clsd Tue, Sun brunch

ENTERTAINMENT & RECREATION

Anheuser-Busch Brewery Tours/ Grant's Farm S 12th & Lynch **314/577-2626, 314/843-1700 (GRANT'S FARM)** • all-American kitsch: see the Clydesdales in their air-conditioned stables, or visit the Busch family estate that was once the home of Ulysses S Grant

Opera Theatre of Saint Louis 210 Hazel Ave (at Edgar & Big Bend) **314/961-0644 (BOX OFFICE)** • intimate theater w/ operas sung in English • wheelchair access

BOOKSTORES

Left Bank Books 399 N Euclid Ave (at McPherson) **314/367-6731** • 10am-10pm, 11am-6pm Sun • popular • feminist & LGBT titles • also at 321 N 10th St, 314/436-3049

RETAIL SHOPS

CheapTRX 3211 S Grand Blvd **314/664-4011** • alternative shopping • body piercing • tattoos

PUBLICATIONS

Vital Voice **314/256-1196** • bi-weekly news & features publication

Women's Yellow Pages of Greater St Louis **314/997-6262**

GYMS & HEALTH CLUBS

Marbles Yoga Studio 1905 Park Ave **314/621-4744** • 6:30am-8:30pm, drop-in yoga classes • gay-owned

EROTICA

Patricia's 3552 Gravois (at Grand) **314/664-4040** • 10am-10pm, 1pm-10pm Sun • fetish clothes • toys • videos • dating service

St Peters

EROTICA

Patricia's 1034 Venture Dr **636/928-2144**

MONTANA

Statewide

PUBLICATIONS

Out Words 127 N Higgins Ave #202, Missoula **406/543-2224** • Montana's LGBT publication

Billings

BARS

The Loft 1123 1st Ave N (at 12th) **406/259-9074** • 10am-2am • lesbians/gay men • dancing/DJ • karaoke • shows • wheelchair access

EROTICA

Big Sky Books 1203 1st Ave N (at 12th St) **406/259-0051**

The Victorian 2019 Minnesota Ave (at 21st) **406/245-4293** • noon-midnight, clsd Sun-Mon • fireplace & piano • HIV testing

Boulder

ACCOMMODATIONS

Boulder Hot Springs Inn & Retreat **406/225-4339** • gay-friendly • also B&B • massage • workshops • food served • pool • nudity ok in hot springs • nonsmoking • kids ok • wheelchair access • $99-139

Bozeman

ACCOMMODATIONS

Gallatin Gateway Inn 76405 Gallatin Rd/ Hwy 191 **406/763-4672, 800/676-3522** • gay-friendly • dinner nightly • hot tub • pool • nonsmoking rooms available • kids ok • wheelchair access • $89-245

Lehrkind Mansion B&B 719 N Wallace Ave **406/585-6932** • gay/ straight • full brkfst • hot tub • nonsmoking • WiFi • gay-owned • $119-229

CAFES

The Leaf & Bean 35 W Main St **406/587-1580** • 6am-9pm, till 10pm Fri-Sat • live shows • wheelchair access • women-owned • also 1500 N 19th Ave, 406/587-2132

The Nova Cafe 312 E Main St (at Rouse Ave) **406/587-3973** • 7am-2pm

RETAIL SHOPS

Jeannette Rankin Peace Center 519 S Higgins Ave **406/543-3955** • 10am-6pm, clsd Sun • fair trade gift store • peace resource center • events

EROTICA

Erotique 12 N Willson Ave (at Main) **406/586-7825**

Butte

RESTAURANTS

Matt's Place 2339 Placer St (btwn Montana & Rowe) **406/782-8049** • 11:30am-7pm, clsd Sun-Mon • classic soda-fountain diner

Pekin Noodle Parlor 117 S Main St, 2nd flr **406/782-2217** • 5pm-11pm, till midnight Fri-Sat, till 10:30pm Sun-Mon, clsd Tue • Chinese • some veggie

Pork Chop John's 2400 Harrison Ave **406/782-1783** • 10:30am-10:30pm, till 9:30pm Sun • also 8 W Mercury, 406/782-0812

Uptown Cafe 47 E Broadway **406/723-4735** • lunch weekdays & dinner nightly • bistro • full bar • wheelchair access

Great Falls

ACCOMMODATIONS

Graystone Inn 621 Central Ave (at 7th St) 406/452-1470, 877/452-1472 • gay/ straight • nonsmoking • WiFi • $44-74

RESTAURANTS

Black Diamond Bar & Supper Club 64 Castner St, Belt 406/277-4118 • 5pm-10pm, clsd Mon • steaks & seafood • 20 miles from Great Falls

Kalispell

INFO LINES & SERVICES

Flathead Valley Alliance 406/758-6707 • LGBT referral service

Livingston

ACCOMMODATIONS

Yellowstone River Inn Cabins 4950 Hwy 89 S 406/222-2429, 888/669-6993 • gay/ straight • cabins 40 ft from Yellowstone River • full brkfst • nonsmoking • $115-780

Missoula

INFO LINES & SERVICES

KISMIF Gay/ Lesbian AA 538 University Ave (at church) 406/543-0011 • 7pm Mon

Western Montana Gay/ Lesbian Community Center 127 N Higgins Ave #202 406/543-2224 • LGBT resource center • call for hours

ACCOMMODATIONS

Brooks St Motor Inn 3333 Brooks St (at MacDonald) 406/549-5115, 800/538-3260 • gay-friendly • motel • hot tub • nonsmoking rooms available • kids ok • wheelchair access • $60-125

BARS

The Oxford 337 N Higgins Ave (at Pine) 406/549-0117 • popular • gay-friendly • 8am-2am • 24hr cafe & casino

CAFES

The Catalyst 111 N Higgins 406/542-1337 • 7am-3pm

RESTAURANTS

Montana Club/ Red Baron Casino 2620 Brooks 406/543-3200 • 6am-10pm, till 11pm Fri-Sat, casino open till 2am • full bar • wheelchair access

BOOKSTORES

Fact & Fiction 220 N Higgins 406/721-2881 • 9am-6pm, 10am-5pm Sat, noon-4pm Sun • many LGBT titles • wheelchair access

University Center Bookstore 5 Campus Dr (at U of MT) 406/243-1234, 888/333-1995 • 8am-6pm, from 10am Sat, clsd Sun • gender studies section

PUBLICATIONS

Out Words 127 N Higgins Ave #202 406/543-2224 • Montana's LGBT publication

Ovando

ACCOMMODATIONS

Lake Upsata Guest Ranch 406/793-5890, 800/594-7687 • gay-friendly • cabins • hot tub • seasonal • wildlife programs & outings • meals provided • kids ok • nonsmoking • WiFi • $1,330-1,680/ wk

Swan Valley

ACCOMMODATIONS

Holland Lake Lodge 1947 Holland Lake Rd (at Hwy 83) 406/754-2282, 877/925-6343 • gay-friendly • resort w/ lakefront cabins • full brkfst • hot tub • kids ok • WiFi • restaurant & bar • wheelchair access • gay-owned • $145-290

NEBRASKA

Kearney

RETAIL SHOPS

Hastings Entertainment 9 W 39th St 308/234-1130 • 10am-10pm • some LGBT books • also adult section

Lincoln

INFO LINES & SERVICES

Rainbow Group Gay/ Lesbian AA 2325 S 24 St (at Sewell, at St Matthew's) 402/438-5214 • 7:30pm Mon & 7pm Fri

BARS

Panic 200 S 18th St (at N St) 402/435-8764 4pm-1am, from 1pm wknds • lesbians/ gay men • live shows • WiFi • patio • wheelchair access • gay-owned

NIGHTCLUBS

The Q 226 S 9th St (btwn M & N Sts) 402/475-2269 • 8pm-1am, clsd Mon • lesbians/ gay men • dancing/DJ • live shows • drag shows • weekly strip shows • bingo Tue (19+)

ENTERTAINMENT & RECREATION

No Coast Derby Girls • Lincoln's female roller derby league • visit www.nocoastderbygirls.com for events

BOOKSTORES

A Novel Idea Bookstore 118 N 14th **402/475-8663** • 10am-6pm, 1pm-5pm Sun • used, rare & out-of-print books

EROTICA

Romantix Adult Boutique 921 O St **402/435-9323** • 10am-2am

Omaha

INFO LINES & SERVICES

AA Gay/ Lesbian 851 N 74th St (at Presbyterian Church) **402/556-1880** • 8:15pm Fri

Rainbow Outreach Center 1719 Leavenworth St **402/341-0330** • 7:30pm-9pm Th, 6pm-11pm Fri, 3pm-6pm Sun

ACCOMMODATIONS

Castle Unicorn 57034 Deacon Rd (at Hwy 34 & I-29), Pacific Jct, IA **712/527-5930** • gay/ straight • medieval-style B&B • full brkfst • hot tub • WiFi • nonsmoking • patio • gay-owned • $169-219

The Cornerstone Mansion Inn 140 N 39th St (at Dodge) **402/558-7600, 888/883-7745** • gay-friendly • 1894 historic mansion • fireplaces • near downtown • brkfst served • nonsmoking • WiFi • commitment ceremonies • $85-150

BARS

Connections 1901 Leavenworth St (at 19th) **402/933-3033** • 4pm-1am, from 6pm Tue-Wed, clsd Mon • lesbians/ gay men • dancing/DJ • karaoke • wheelchair access • lesbian-owned

DC's Saloon 610 S 14th St (at Jackson) **402/344-3103** • 4pm-1am, from 2pm wknds • lesbians/ gay men • neighborhood bar • dancing/DJ • country/ western • live shows • wheelchair access

Myth 1105 Howard St (Old Market) **402/884-6985** • 7pm-1am, from 5pm Th-Sat, clsd Mon-Tue • gay/ straight • live music

NIGHTCLUBS

Flixx Lounge 1019 S 10th St **402/408-1020** • 5pm-1am • mostly men • dancing/DJ • cabaret • drag shows

The Max 1417 Jackson St (at 15th St) **402/346-4110** • 4pm-1am • popular • mostly gay men • 5 bars • dancing/DJ Wed-Sun • drag shows • strippers • videos • patio • wheelchair access • cover charge Fri-Sat

RESTAURANTS

The Boiler Room 1110 Jones St **402/916-9274** • dinner only, clsd Sun • full bar • wheelchair access

California Tacos & More 3235 California St **402/342-0212** • 11am-9pm, clsd Sun • beer/wine • wheelchair access

Dixie Quick's 1915 Leavenworth St **402/346-3549** • lunch & dinner, brunch from 9am wkds, clsd Mon • Southern • reservations recommended

The Flatiron Cafe 1722 St Marys Ave **402/345-7477** • dinner only, clsd Sun • full bar• wheelchair access

French Cafe 1017 Howard St (at 10th St) **402/341-3547** • dinner nightly, Sun brunch • full bar

M's Pub 422 S 11th St **402/342-2550** • 11am-1am, from 5pm Sun • full bar• wheelchair access

McFoster's Natural Kind Cafe 302 S 38th St **402/345-7477** • lunch & dinner • vegetarian • full bar• wheelchair access

ENTERTAINMENT & RECREATION

Omaha Rollergirls • Omaha's female roller derby league • visit www.myspace.com/omaharollergirls for events

BOOKSTORES

New Realities 1026 Howard St (in the Old Market) **402/342-1863** • 11am-9pm, noon-6pm Sun • progressive • wheelchair access

NEVADA

Baker

ACCOMMODATIONS

Silver Jack Inn 10 Main St **775/234-7323** • gay-friendly • motel & restaurant • WiFi • $49-75

Carson City

ACCOMMODATIONS

West Walker Motel 106833 Hwy 395, Walker, CA **530/495-2263** • gay-friendly • WiFi • kids/ pets ok • in Toiyabe Nat'l Forest near West Walker River • women-owned • $45-75

Gerlach

ACCOMMODATIONS

F Ranch 775/557–2804 • women only • B&B on remote NW Nevada working horse/ cattle ranch • April-Sept • bird-watching • kids ok • nonsmoking • $2,500-3,500 (per couple per week)

Lake Tahoe

see Lake Tahoe, California

Las Vegas

INFO LINES & SERVICES

Alcoholics Together 900 E Karen, 2nd flr #A-202 (at Sahara, in Commercial Center) 702/737–0035 • noon & 8pm daily • call for directions & other meeting times

Betty's Outrageous Adventures 702/991–9929 • Las Vegas' oldest & largest lesbian social organization • lesbian-owned

The Gay/ Lesbian Community Center of Southern Nevada 953 E Sahara Ave #B-31 702/733–9800 • 11am-7pm, clsd wknds

ACCOMMODATIONS

➤**Paris, Las Vegas Resort & Casino** 3655 Las Vegas Blvd S 702/946–7000, 800/630–7933 • gay-friendly • also restaurants, bars, spas • LGBT honeymoon packages • see ad in front color section

BARS

8 1/2 Ultra Lounge/ Piranha 4633 Paradise Rd (at Naples) 702/791–0100 • lesbians/ gay men • neighborhood bar • videos • dancing/DJ • wheelchair access

Backdoor Lounge 1415 E Charleston (near Maryland Pkwy) 702/385–2018 • 24hrs • mostly gay men • neighborhood bar • dancing/DJ • patio • Latino/a • wheelchair access

Badlands Saloon 953 E Sahara #22 (in Commercial Center) 702/792–9262 • 24hrs • mostly gay men • neighborhood bar • dancing/DJ • country/ western • wheelchair access • gay-owned

The Buffalo 4640 Paradise Rd #11 (at Naples) 702/733–8355 • 24hrs • popular • mostly gay men • leather • videos • wheelchair access

Charlie's Las Vegas 5012 S Arville St (at Tropicana) 702/876–1844 • popular • mostly gay men • dancing/DJ • country/ western • dance lessons 7pm-9pm Mon, Th-Sat • wheelchair access

Escape Lounge 4213 W Sahara Ave 702/364–1167 • 24hrs • lesbians/ gay men • neighborhood bar

Flex 4347 W Charleston (at Arville) 702/385–3539 • 24hrs • lesbians/ gay men • dancing/DJ • drag shows • strippers

Freezone 610 E Naples 702/794–2300 • 24hrs • lesbians/ gay men • women's night Tue • neighborhood bar • dancing/DJ • transgender-friendly • drag shows Fri-Sat • karaoke • young crowd • also restaurant • gay-owned

Goodtimes 1775 E Tropicana Ave (at Spencer, in Liberace Plaza) 702/736–9494 • 24hrs • mostly gay men • neighborhood bar • dancing/DJ Mon & after-hours Fri-Sat • wheelchair access

The Las Vegas Eagle 3430 E Tropicana (at Pecos) 702/458–8662 • 24hrs • mostly gay men • leather • DJ Wed, Fri-Sat

Las Vegas Lounge 900 E Karen Ave (at Maryland Pkwy) 702/737–9350 • 24hrs • gay-friendly • neighborhood bar • mostly transgender • drag shows

Lipstick 3430 E Tropicana (at Pecos) 702/456–5525 • 5pm-2am • mostly women • neighborhood bar • dancing/DJ

NIGHTCLUBS

Blush 3131 S Las Vegas Blvd (at Wynn) 702/770–3633 • 9pm-3am, clsd Sun-Mon • ultralounge • cover charge Wed, Fri-Sat

BootyBar 7700 S Las Vegas Blvd 702/518–4053 • hot monthly women's party • dancing

Dollhaus 3663 S Las Vegas Blvd (at Harmon St, next to Planet Hollywood, at Krave) 702/836–0830 • 9pm-3am Fri only • popular • mostly women • dancing/DJ • multiracial

The Gipsy 4605 S Paradise Rd (at Naples) 702/731–1919 • 9pm-close • mostly gay men • dancing/DJ • live shows

Girl Bar at Krave 3663 S Las Vegas Blvd (at Harmon St, next to Planet Hollywood, at Krave) 702/836–0830 • 9pm-3am Sat only • popular • mostly women • dancing/DJ • multiracial

Heaven at Bare 3400 S Las Vegas Blvd (at The Mirage) 702/693–8300 • 10pm Sat only • lesbians/ gay men • dancing/DJ • poolside party

Hot Flash Las Vegas • women's dance parties • check hotflashdances.com for upcoming dates

House of Blues 3950 Las Vegas Blvd S (at Hacienda Ave, in Mandalay Bay) **702/632–7600** • gay-friendly • dancing/DJ • also restaurant • live shows • cover charge

Krave 3663 S Las Vegas Blvd (at Harmon St, next to Planet Hollywood) **702/836–0830** • 11pm-close, clsd Mon • mostly gay men • dancing/DJ

Mix 3950 Las Vegas Blvd S (at Mandalay Bay) **702/632–9500** • gay-friendly • stylish lounge • DJ • cover charge wknds

Pure Nightclub 3570 S Las Vegas Blvd (at Caesar's Palace) **702/731–7873** • 10pm-4am, clsd Mon & Wed-Th • gay-friendly • upscale • top DJs • cover charge

RESTAURANTS

Bootlegger Bistro 7700 S Las Vegas Blvd **702/736–4939** • 24hrs • a Vegas classic • Italian • musical entertainment nightly

Border Grill 3950 Las Vegas Blvd S (at the Mandalay Bay Resort & Casino) **702/632–7403** • 11:30am-close • Mexican • full bar • patio

Carluccio's Tivoli Gardens 1775 E Tropicana **702/795–3236** • 4:30pm-10pm, clsd Mon • Italian • formerly owned by Liberace • check out the mirrored, autographed grand piano!

Las Vegas

LGBT PRIDE:
May. 866/930-3336, web: www.lasvegaspride.org.

ANNUAL EVENTS:
July - Gay Days & Nights Las Vegas 702/437–3800.
Sept - NGRA (Nevada Gay Rodeo Assn) Bighorn Rodeo, web: www.ngra.com.

CITY INFO:
Convention & Visitors Authority 877/847-4858, web: www.visit-lasvegas.com.

BEST VIEW:
Top of the Stratosphere, Top of the Fiffel Tower Experience, or hurtling through the loops of the rollercoaster atop the New York New York Hotel. (Note: Do not ride immediately after the buffet.)

WEATHER:
It's in the desert! Hotter by day, cooler by night.

ATTRACTIONS:
Bellagio Art Gallery 702/693-7871, web: www.bellagio.com.
Divas Las Vegas, web: www.frankmarinosdivas.com.
Fremont Street Experience, web: www.vegasexperience.com.
Hoover Dam & Museum, 866/730-9097, web: www.usbr.gov/lc/hooverdam.
Imperial Palace Auto Collection 702/794-3174, web: www.imperi-alpalace.com.
Las Vegas Art Museum 702/360-8000, web: www.lasvegasartmu-seum.com.
I iberace Museum 702/798-5595, web: www.liberace.org.
Museum of Natural History 702/384-3466, web: www.lvnhm.org.

TRANSIT:
Western Cab 702/382-7100.
Lucky Cab 702/477-7555.
Various resorts have their own shuttle service.
Las Vegas Monorail 866/466–6672, web: www.lvmonorail.com.
RTC (Regional Transportation Commission) 702/228-7433, web: www.rtcsouthernnevada.com.

Chicago Joe's 820 S 4th St **702/382-5637** • 11am-10pm, from 5pm Sat, clsd Sun-Mon • old-school Italian • in downtown arts district

Cupcakery 7175 W Lake Mead **702/835-0060**

The Egg & I 4533 W Sahara Ave (near Arville) **702/364-9686** • popular • 6am-3pm

Firefly 3900 Paradise Rd #A **702/369-3971** • 11am-2am • tapas • also bar

Go Raw 2381 Windmill Ln **702/450-9007** • 9am-9pm, 11am-6pm Sun • organic vegan • also juice bar • also at 2910 Lake East Dr, 702/254-5382

Guy Savoy 3570 Las Vegas Blvd (at Caesar's Palace) **877/346-4642** • 5pm-10:30pm, clsd Mon-Tue • French • reservations required

Joël Robuchon 3799 Las Vegas Blvd S (at MGM Grand Hotel) **702/891-7925** • 5:30pm-10pm, till 10:30pm Fri-Sat • French • reservations required

Lindo Michoacan 2655 E Desert Inn Rd (near Eastern) **702/735-6828** • 11am-11pm, till midnight wknds • popular • Mexican

Lotus of Siam 953 E Sahara Ave #A-5 (in Commercial Center) **702/735-3033** • lunch & dinner • Thai

Mon Ami Gabi 3655 Las Vegas Blvd S (at Paris Las Vegas) **702/944-4224** • outdoor seating

Mr Lucky's 4455 Paradise Rd (at Hard Rock Hotel) **702/693-5000** • 24hrs

Paymon's Mediterranean Cafe & Lounge 4147 S Maryland Pkwy (at E Flamingo Rd) **702/731-6000** • 11am-1am • plenty veggie • also at 8380 W Sahara Ave, 702/731-6030

Wichcraft at MGM Grand **702/891-1111** • 10am-5pm, till 8pm Fri-Sat • creative sandwiches • eat-in or take-out

ENTERTAINMENT & RECREATION

Cupid's Wedding Chapel 827 Las Vegas Blvd S (1 block N of Charleston) **702/598-4444, 800/543-2933** • commitment ceremonies • "Have the Vegas wedding you've always dreamed of!"

Erotic Heritage Museum 3275 Industrial Rd **702/369-6442** • 6pm-10pm Wed-Th, 3pm-midnight Fri, from noon wknds • clsd Mon-Tue

The Forum Shops at Caesars 3570 Las Vegas Blvd S (in Caesars Palace) • you saw it in *Showgirls* & many other movies, now come shop for yourself

Frank Marino's Divas Las Vegas 3535 Las Vegas Blvd S (at the Imperial Palace) **702/794-3261** • show at 7:30pm, clsd Tue • the biggest drag show in town: Frank Marino & friends impersonate the divas, from Joan Rivers to Tina Turner

Kà by Cirque du Soleil at MGM Grand **702/796-9999, 877/264-1844** • 6:30pm & 9:30pm Tue-Sat • martial arts, puppetry, interactive projections & pyrotechnics

Mystère by Cirque du Soleil at Treasure Island **702/796-9999, 800/963-9634** • 7:30pm & 10:30pm Wed-Sat, 4:30pm & 7:30pm Sun • high-energy acrobatics & vivid imagery

O by Cirque du Soleil at the Bellagio **702/796-9999, 800/963-9634** • 7:30pm & 10:30pm Wed-Sun • showstopper in a specially constructed aquatic theater

Red Rock Lanes 11011 W Charleston Blvd **702/797-7777** • 72 lanes • Cosmic Bowling wknds

Sin City Rollergirls • Vegas' female roller derby league • visit www.sincityrollergirls.com for events

Thanks Babs, the Day Tripper **702/370-6961** • tours, shows attractions & getaways • full service concierge for Las Vegas, state of NV, & the Southwest • it's like having a lesbian aunt in Las Vegas!

Viva Las Vegas Wedding Chapel 1205 Las Vegas Blvd **800/574-4450** • gay-owned

Zumanity at New York–New York Hotel & Casino **702/740-6815, 866/606-7111** • 7:30pm & 10:30pm Wed-Sun • explores human sexuality in an intimate, cabaret-style setting • 18+

BOOKSTORES

Borders 2323 S Decatur (at Sahara) **702/258-0999** • 9am-11pm, till 9pm Sun • LGBT section • cafe • wheelchair access

Get Booked 4640 S Paradise #15 (at Naples **702/737-7780** • 10am-midnight, till 2am Fri-Sat • LGBT

RETAIL SHOPS

Glamour Boutique II 714 E Sahara Ave #104 (at S 6th St) **702/697-1800, 866/692-1800** • clsd Sun, large-size dresses, wigs, etc

The Rack 953 E Sahara Ave, Ste 101, Bldg 1 (in Commercial Center) **702/732-7225** • leather • fetish

PUBLICATIONS

Las Vegas Night Beat 702/369-8441 • monthly news & entertainment paper

QVegas 702/650-0636 • monthly LGBT news & entertainment magazine

GYMS & HEALTH CLUBS

Hands On Therapeutic Massage 8335 S Las Vegas Blvd (at Cancun Resort) 702/458-8777 • licensed massage therapists visit home or hotel room • "open to all men & women" • mention Damron for discount

The Las Vegas Athletic Club 2655 S Maryland Pkwy 702/734-5822 • day passes

SEX CLUBS

Power Exchange 3610 S Highland Dr 702/255-4739 • play space open to hetero, gay, bi, trans, men & women • free for women & trans people

EROTICA

Bare Essentials Fantasy Fashions 4029 W Sahara Ave (near Valley View Blvd) 702/247-4711 • exotic/ intimate apparel • toys • gay-owned

Price Video 700 E Naples Dr #102 (at Swenson) 702/734-1342 • 10am-10pm

Rancho Adult Entertainment Center 4820 N Rancho #D (at Lone Mtn) 702/645-6104 • 24hrs

Romantix Adult Superstore 2923 S Industrial Rd (behind Circus Circus) 702/892-0699 • 24hrs

Sinderella's Adult Superstore 5570 S Valley View 702/736-9700

Laughlin

see Bullhead City, Arizona

Reno

ACCOMMODATIONS

Ramada Reno Hotel & Casino 1000 E 6th St (at Wells Ave) 775/786-5151 • gay-friendly • seasonal pool • kids/ pets ok • restaurant • WiFi • wheelchair access • $59-139

Terrible's Sands Regency Casino Hotel Downtown Reno 345 N Arlington Ave 775/348-2200, 866/386-7829 • gay-friendly • pool • live shows • also restaurants • $29-119

BARS

Cadillac Lounge 1114 E 4th St 775/324-7827 • noon-2am • lesbians/ gay men • neighborhood bar

Five Star Saloon 132 West St (at 1st) 775/329-2878 • 24hrs • gay/ straight • neighborhood bar • dancing/DJ • wheelchair access

The Patio 600 W 5th St (btwn Washington & Ralston) 775/323-6565 • 11am-2am • lesbians/ gay men • neighborhood bar • live shows • karaoke

Ten 99 Club 1099 S Virginia St (at Vassar) 775/329-1099 • 10am-2am, 24hrs Fri-Mon • popular • lesbians/ gay men • neighborhood bar • live shows • videos • patio • wheelchair access

NIGHTCLUBS

Neutron 340 Kietzke Ln (btwn Glendale & Mill) 775/786-2121 • 2pm-close • popular • gay/ straight • dancing/DJ • multi-racial • young crowd • patio

Tronix 303 Kietzke Ln (at E 2nd St) 775/333-9696 • 9am-3am, 24hrs wknds • lesbians/ gay men • more women Wed • dancing/DJ • multiracial • transgender-friendly • videos • young crowd • WiFi • wheelchair access • gay-owned

RESTAURANTS

Firehouse Grill & Deli 495 Morill Ave # 102 775/622-2797 • 8am-8pm

Pneumatic Diner 501 W 1st St (in Truckee River Apts, 2nd flr) 775/786-8888 x106 • 11am-10pm, from 8am Sun • vegetarian

ENTERTAINMENT & RECREATION

Brüka Theatre 99 N Virginia St 775/323-3221 • alternative theater & performance space

BOOKSTORES

Sundance Books 1155 W 4th St #106 (at Keystone) 775/786-1188 • 9am-9pm, 10am-6pm wknds • independent

PUBLICATIONS

Sierra Voice 775/322-7866 • monthly • bar & resource listings • community events • arts & entertainment

EROTICA

Suzie's 195 Kietzke Ln (at E 2nd St) 775/786-8557 • 24hrs

NEW HAMPSHIRE

Statewide

INFO LINES & SERVICES

Rainbow Resources of NH Inc
800/750-2524 • LGBT info for NH, VT, ME &
MA

Claremont

ACCOMMODATIONS

The Goddard Mansion B&B 25 Hillstead
Rd **603/543-0603, 800/736-0603** • gay-
friendly • mtn views • near skiing •
nonsmoking • WiFi • gay-owned • $95-150

Concord

ACCOMMODATIONS

Idleday Guest Rooms 180 W Parish Rd
603/520-6886, 603/753-6113 • women only
• secluded setting on river • nonsmoking

Dover

CAFES

Cafe on the Corner 478 Central Ave
603/749-4711 • 7am-9pm

Durham

ACCOMMODATIONS

Three Chimneys Inn 17 Newmarket Rd (Rte
108, off Rte 4) **603/868-7800, 888/399-9777** •
gay-friendly • elegant 1649 house on Oyster
River near Portsmouth • full brkfst • jacuzzi •
nonsmoking • kids 6+ ok • wheelchair access
• $139-219

Exeter

ACCOMMODATIONS

Inn by the Bandstand 6 Front St (at Water)
603/772-6352, 877/239-3837 • gay-friendly •
1809 historic home • full brkfst • WiFi • $139-
249

Keene

ACCOMMODATIONS

E F Lane Hotel 30 Main St **603/357-7070,
888/300-5056** • gay/ straight • rooms & suites
• internet access • also restaurant •
nonsmoking • wheelchair access • $139-300

Manchester

BARS

The Breezeway 14 Pearl St **603/621-9111** •
4pm-1am, from noon Sun • lesbians/ gay men
• neighborhood bar • dancing/DJ • theme
nights • cabaret • drag shows • gay-owned

Club 313 93 S Maple St (at S Willow)
603/628-6813 • 6pm-1am, from 7pm Sun •
popular • lesbians/ gay men • dancing/DJ •
food served • live entertainment • karaoke •
drag shows • videos • nonsmoking • WiFi •
wheelchair access

Element Lounge 1055 Elm St **603/627-2922**
• 3pm-1am • lesbians/ gay men • dancing/DJ •
food served • karaoke • drag shows

Nashua

NIGHTCLUBS

The Amber Room 53 High St **603/881-9060**
• 9pm-1:30am Th-Sun • gay/ straight • gay
night Fri

Newfound Lake

ACCOMMODATIONS

The Inn on Newfound Lake 1030 Mayhew
Tpke Rte 3-A, Bridgewater **603/744-9111,
800/745-7990** • gay/ straight • private beach
on cleanest lake in NH • also renowned
restaurant • full bar • nonsmoking • WiFi •
gay-owned • $105-295

Plaistow

BARS

David's Place 20 Plaistow Rd **603/819-4822**
• 7pm-1am • mostly gay men • live shows •
drag shows

Plymouth

ACCOMMODATIONS

Federal House Inn Historic B&B 27 Rte
25 (Rte 3 traffic circle) **603/536-4644,
866/536-4644** • gay/ straight • full brkfst • hot
tub • nonsmoking • WiFi • gay-owned • $135-
185

Portsmouth

ACCOMMODATIONS

Ale House Inn 121 Bow St (at Market St)
603/431-7760 • gay-friendly • WiFi • gay-
owned • $99-299

CAFES

Breaking New Grounds 14 Market Square
603/436–9555 • 6:30am-10pm • coffee • tea •
espresso shakes • WiFi

RESTAURANTS

The Mombo 66 Marcy St (at State St)
603/433–2340 • lunch & dinner, Sun brunch •
wheelchair access

EROTICA

Spaulding Book & Video 80 Spaulding
Tpke **603/430–9760** • gay-owned

Surry

ACCOMMODATIONS

The Surry House 50 Village Rd (at Crain Rd)
603/352–2268 • gay/ straight • B&B in private
home • full brkfst • pool • kids/pets ok •
nonsmoking • lesbian-owned • $85-150

White Mtns

ACCOMMODATIONS

Beal House 2 W Main St, Littleton
603/444–2661 • gay-friendly • French country
brkfst • WiFi • $119-269

Brookhill B&B Balcony Seat View, N
Conway **603/356–3061, 888/356–3061** • gay/
straight • 1- or 2-bdrm suite • full brkfst •
nonsmoking • WiFi • $199-398

Eagle Mountain House & Golf Club 179
Carter Notch Rd, Jackson **603/383–9111,
800/966–5779** • gay-friendly • full brkfst •
nonsmoking • WiFi • pool • indoor hot tub •
$69-249

➤**Highlands Inn** 240 Valley View Lane,
Bethlehem **603/869–3978, 877/LES–B–INN
(537–2466)** • Lesbian Paradise: legal marriage
in NH • 19 rms • full brkfst • outdoor & indoor
spas • pool • 100 mtn acres • special events •
concerts • kids/pets ok • non-smoking • WiFi
• wheelchair access • ignore No Vacancy sign
• lesbian-owned • $110-220 • see ad on page 1

The Horse & Hound Inn 205 Wells Rd,
Franconia **603/823–5501, 800/450–5501** •
clsd April & Nov • gay-friendly • 1830s
farmhouse • full brkfst • kids/pets ok •
nonsmoking • WiFi • also restaurant • gay-
owned • $90-165

The Inn at Bowman 1174 Rte 2
(Presidential Hwy), Randolph **603/466–5006**
• gay/ straight • B&B gracing the White Mtns •
swimming • hot tub • nonsmoking •
wheelchair access • gay-owned • $129-299

Inn at Crystal Lake 2356 Eaton Rd (at Rte
16), Eaton **603/447–2120, 800/343–7336** •
gay/ straight • full brkfst • also restaurant •
kids age 12+ ok • dogs ok • nonsmoking •
gay-owned • $109-239

Mulburn Inn at Bethlehem 2370 Main St/
Rte 302 (at Turner), Bethlehem **603/869–3389,
800/457–9440** • gay/ straight • Victorian B&B
• full brkfst • hot tub • nonsmoking • WiFi •
women-owned • $115-185

The Notchland Inn Rte 302, Hart's Location
603/374–6131, 800/866–6131 • gay/ straight •
full brkfst • other meals available •
nonsmoking • also cottages • gay-owned •
$199-380

Riverbend Inn B&B 273 Chocorua Mtn
Hwy (at Rte 113), Chocorua **603/323–7440,
800/628–6944** • gay/ straight • B&B • full
brkfst • located on the Chocorua River • WiFi •
nonsmoking • gay-owned • $110-250

Top Notch Vacations Rte 302, Glen
603/383–4133, 877/383–4111 • gay-friendly •
1- to 4-bdrm condos, cottages & chalets • mtn
views • nonsmoking

Wildcat Inn & Tavern Rte 16A, Jackson
Village **603/356–8700, 800/637–0087** • gay-
friendly • also cottage • full brkfst • also tavern
& dining room • nonsmoking • $99-329

Will's Inn Rte 302, Glen **603/383–6757,
800/233–6780** • gay-friendly • traditional New
England motor inn • 2-bdrm cottages
available • pool • also rental house, sleeps up
to 34, rent by floor or whole house • beach on
Saco River • nonsmoking • kids ok • $49-1,200

BARS

The Up Country Restaurant & Tavern Rte
16, North Conway **603/356–3336** • 11am-
1am, from 1pm wknds • more gay on wknds •
dancing/DJ • live shows • karaoke • video •
WiFi

RESTAURANTS

Polly's Pancake Parlor 672 Rte Sugar Hill
Rd (exit 38 off 93 N), Sugar Hill **603/823–5575**
• 7am-2pm, till 3pm wknds, clsd winters

The Red Parka Steakhouse & Pub Rte
302, Glen **603/383–4344** • open from 3pm,
also bar

ENTERTAINMENT & RECREATION

Reel North Fly Fishing **603/858–4103** •
casting lessons • half- & full-day river trips •
custom-tied flies • lesbian-owned

NEW JERSEY

Statewide

PUBLICATIONS

Out in Jersey 743 Hamilton Ave, Trenton 08629 **609/213-9310** • publication for all of New Jersey's LGBTI community

PM Entertainment Magazine **516/845-0759** • events, listings, classifieds & more for Long Island, NJ & NYC

Asbury Park

ACCOMMODATIONS

Empress Hotel 101 Asbury Ave **732/774-0100** • gay-friendly • swimming • also Empress Lobby Lounge on wknds

Sixth Avenue House 305 Sixth Ave (at Berg St) **732/361-6609** • gay/ straight • some shared baths • full brkfst • WiFi • gay-owned • $75-275

BARS

Georgie's 812 5th Ave (at Main) **732/988-1220** • 2pm-2am • lesbians/gay men • neighborhood bar • food served • karaoke • drag shows

NIGHTCLUBS

Ladies 2000 856/869-0193 • seasonal parties • call hotline for details

Paradise 101 Asbury Ave (at Ocean Ave) **732/988-6663** • 4pm-2am, from 2pm Sat, from noon Sun • lesbians/ gay men • dancing/DJ • 2 dance flrs • live shows • piano bar • tiki/ pool bar in summer

RESTAURANTS

Bistro Olé 230 Main St **732/897-0048** • lunch Tue-Sun, dinner nightly from 5pm • Spanish-Portuguese

The Harrison Restaurant 716 Cookman Ave **732/774-2200** • 4pm-close, Sun brunch, clsd Tue

Moonstruck 517 Lake Ave (at Grand) **732/988-0123** • dinner only, clsd Mon-Tue • also bar • live music wknds

Restaurant Plan B 705 Cookman Ave **732/807-4710** • dinner nightly, wknd brunch, clsd Mon • BYOB

Atlantic City

ACCOMMODATIONS

The Carisbrooke Inn 105 S Little Rock Ave, Ventnor **609/822-6392** • gay-friendly • on a beach block 1 mile from Atlantic City • nonsmoking • WiFi • $99-325

Tropicana Casino & Resort 2831 Boardwalk (at Brighton) **609/340-4000, 800/345-8767**

BARS

Westside Bar & Lounge 511 N Arkansas Ave (at Bacharach Blvd) **609/344-0883** • 6pm-4am • mostly men • dancing/DJ • multiracial clientele • transgender-friendly • karaoke • wheelchair access

RESTAURANTS

Dock's Oyster House 2405 Atlantic Ave **609/345-0092** • 5pm-10pm, till 11pm Fri-Sat • wheelchair access

White House Sub Shop 2301 Arctic Ave (at Mississippi) **609/345-1564** • 10am-10pm, till 11pm Fri-Sat, from 11am Sun

Boonton

NIGHTCLUBS

Switch 202 Myrtle Ave (off Washington) **973/263-4000** • 6pm-2am, from 4pm wknds • lesbians/ gay men • dancing/DJ • country/ western • food served • drag shows • 18+

Camden

see also Philadelphia, Pennsylvania

ENTERTAINMENT & RECREATION

The Walt Whitman House 30 Mickle Blvd (btwn S 3rd & S 4th Sts) **856/964-5383** • the last home of America's great & controversial poet

Cape May

ACCOMMODATIONS

Beauclaires B&B Inn 23 Ocean St (at Columbia Ave) **609/898-1222** • gay/ straight • full brkfst • 1/2 block from ocean • nonsmoking • $115-255

Cottage Beside the Point **609/204-0549, 609/898-0658** • gay/ straight • studio • kids ok • nonsmoking • lesbian-owned • $135-175

Highland House 131 N Broadway (at York) **609/898-1198** • gay-friendly • B&B • kids/ pets ok • gazebo • nonsmoking • gay & straight-owned • $120-165

The Virginia Hotel 25 Jackson St (btwn Beach Dr & Carpenter's Ln) **609/884–5700, 800/732–4236** • gay-friendly • WiFi • also The Ebbitt Room restaurant • seafood/cont'l • $100-495

BARS

The King Edward Room 301 Howard St (at The Chalfonte Hotel) **609/884–8409** • 5pm-1am summer only • mostly gay men

Cherry Hill

see Philadelphia, Pennsylvania

Hammonton

NIGHTCLUBS

Club In Or Out 19 N Egg Harbor Rd (at Orchard Ave) **609/561–2525** • lesbians/gay men • dancing/DJ • shows • kataoke • lesbian-owned

Highland Park

INFO LINES & SERVICES

Pride Center of New Jersey 85 Raritan Ave (at S 1st Ave) **732/846–2232** • info line • meeting space for various groups

Hoboken

BARS

The Cage 32 Newark St **201/216–1766** • 5pm-2am, till 3am Fri-Sat • lesbians/ gay men • neighborhood bar • dancing/DJ • karaoke • drag shows • theme nights

NIGHTCLUBS

Maxwell's 1039 Washington St **201/653–1703** • popular • gay-friendly • alternative • live music venue • food served

Jamesburg

RESTAURANTS

Fiddleheads 27 E Railroad Ave **732/521–0878** • lunch & dinner, Sun brunch, clsd Mon-Tue • upscale bistro • BYOB

Jersey City

INFO LINES & SERVICES

Hudson Pride Connections 32 Jones St **201/963–4779** • "serving the LGBT communities & all people living w/ HIV, since 1993"

ACCOMMODATIONS

Hyatt Regency Jersey City 2 Exchange Pl (on the Hudson) **201/469–1234** • gay-friendly • luxury waterfront hotel • short ride to NYC • pool • nonsmoking • WiFi • $199+

BARS

Lamp Post 382 2nd St **201/222–1331** • 11:30am-2am, till 3am Fri-Sat • gay/ straight • food served

LITM 140 Newark Ave (at Grove) **201/536–5557** • 5pm-1am, till 2am Fri-Sat, 11am-midnight Sun • gay/ straight • also restaurant & gallery

RESTAURANTS

Baja 117 Montgomery St **201/915–0062** • lunch & dinner • Mexican

Lambertville

see New Hope, Pennsylvania

Morristown

INFO LINES & SERVICES

GAAMC (Gay Activist Alliance in Morris County) 21 Normandy Hts Rd (at Unitarian Fellowship) **973/285–1595** • info line 7:30pm-9pm, also recorded info • also women's network

New Brunswick

BARS

The Den 700 Hamilton St (at Douglas), Somerset **732/545–7354** • 8pm-2am Wed-Sat only • popular • mostly gay men • more women last Sat • dancing/DJ wknds • theme nights • multiracial • live shows • also restaurant • wheelchair access

RESTAURANTS

The Frog & the Peach 29 Dennis St (at Hiram Square) **732/846–3216** • lunch Mon-Fri, dinner nightly • full bar • upscale • wheelchair access

Stage Left 5 Livingston Ave (at George) **732/828–4444** • popular • lesbians/ gay men • some veggie • full bar • patio • wheelchair access • expensive

Paterson

RESTAURANTS

E&V Ristorante 320 Chamberlain Ave **973/942–8080, 973/942–4664** • lunch & dinner nightly, clsd Mon • Italian • wheelchair access

Plainfield

ACCOMMODATIONS

The Pillars of Plainfield B&B 922 Central Ave (at 9th St) 908/753-0922, 888/745-5277 • gay/ straight • Georgian/ Victorian mansion • full brkfst • nonsmoking • kids/ dogs ok (call first) • WiFi • $125-250

Red Bank

BOOKSTORES

Earth Spirit 25 Monmouth St 732/842-3855 • 10am-10pm, till 11pm Fri-Sat, noon-5pm Sun • New Age center & bookstore • LGBT sections

River Edge

NIGHTCLUBS

Feathers 77 Kinderkamack Rd (at Grand) 201/342-6410 • 9pm-2am, till 3am Sat, from 7pm Sun • popular • mostly gay men • dancing/DJ • karaoke • live shows • videos • young crowd • wheelchair access

Rosemont

RESTAURANTS

The Cafe 88 Kingwood-Stockton Rd (intersection of CR 519 & 604) 609/397-4097 • lunch Tue-Fri, dinner Wed-Sun, wknd brunch, clsd Mon • BYOB

Sergeantsville

see New Hope, Pennsylvania

Stockton

ACCOMMODATIONS

Woolverton Inn 6 Woolverton Rd 609/397-0802, 888/264-6648 • gay-friendly • full brkfst • jacuzzi • WiFi • wheelchair access • $145-435

Trenton

BARS

The Mill Hill Saloon 300 S Broad (at Market) 609/394-7222 • 11:30am-2am, from 5pm Sat, clsd Sun, Brew Cellar from 10pm • gay-friendly • live bands from jazz to blues to rock to folk • also restaurant

CAFES

Cafe Ole 126 S Warren St 609/396-2233 • "alcohol-free, all-ages bistro w/ great food (some veggie dishes)" • hosts Trenton Q-Nite, queer coffeehouse, 6:30pm-9:30pm Fri

Union

RESTAURANTS

Rodizio 2185 Rte 22 West 908/206-0060 • 4pm-10pm, till 1pm Fri-Sat, noon-9pm Sun • Brazilian steakhouse

Westville

see Philadelphia, Pennsylvania

NEW MEXICO

Abiquiu

ACCOMMODATIONS

Casita de Chuparosa 505/685-0823 • gay-friendly • vacation rental in O'Keeffe country • huge views • 2 bdrms • fireplace • gourmet kitchen w/ full brkfst provisions • near hiking trails • nonsmoking • WiFi • $130+

Alamogordo

ACCOMMODATIONS

Best Western Desert Aire Motor Inn 1021 S White Sands Blvd 505/437-2110, 800/637-5956 • gay-friendly • pool • WiFi • wheelchair access • $68+

Albuquerque

includes Bernalillo, Corrales, Placitas & Rio Rancho

INFO LINES & SERVICES

AA Gay/ Lesbian 505/266-1900 (AA#) • 7pm Mon, Wed-Th

Common Bond Info Line 505/891-3647 • 24hrs • covers LGBT community

Steve Benoit, Associate Broker with Coldwell Banker Legacy Realtors 8200 Carmel NE # 103 505/292-8900, 800/658-6149 • New Mexico's community respected realtor • associate broker: buyer's agent, listing specialist, relocation manager

ACCOMMODATIONS

Adobe Nido 1124 Major Ave NW (at 12th St) 505/344-1310, 866/435-6436 • gay-friendly • B&B • also aviary • nonsmoking • WiFi • $119-234

Albuquerque Grand Hotel 2910 Yale Blvd SE (at Gibson) 505/843-7000, 800/227-1117 • gay-friendly • 4-star hotel • pool • also Rojo Grille restaurant • $99-209

Bottger Mansion of Old Town 110 San Felipe (at Central Ave) **505/243–3639, 800/758–3639** • gay-friendly • transgender-friendly • B&B • WiFi • $99-179

Brittania & W E Mauger Estate B&B 701 Roma Ave NW (at 7th) **505/242–8755, 800/719–9189** • gay-friendly • full brkfst • nonsmoking • WiFi • $99-204

Casa Manzano B&B 103 Forest Rd 321 (at State Rte 55), Tajique **505/384–9767** • gay/ straight • full brkfst • hot tub • nonsmoking • kids/pets ok • wheelchair access • $99-129

Casas de Suenos 310 Rio Grande SW **505/247–4560, 800/665–7002** • gay/straight • spacious casitas • patios & beautiful gardens • kids ok • nonsmoking • WiFi • $99-189

La Casita B&B 317 16th St NW (at Lomas Blvd) **505/242–0173** • gay-friendly • adobe guesthouse • nonsmoking • WiFi • $85-145

Golden Guesthouses 2645 Decker NW (at Glenwood) **505/344–9205, 888/513–GOLD** • lesbians/gay men • individual & shared units • nonsmoking • lesbian-owned • $125-145

Sandia Courtyard Hotel 10300 Hotel Ave (at Eubank) **505/296–4853, 800/877–4852** • gay-friendly • pool • pets/kids ok • WiFi • also restaurant • $80+

BARS

Albuquerque Social Club 4021 Central Ave NE (at Morningside, enter rear) **505/255–0887** • 3pm-midnight, till 2am Fri-Sat, noon-midnight Sun • popular • lesbians/gay men • dancing/DJ • private club

Exhale 6132 4th NW (near Osuna) **505/342–0049** • 6pm-close, from 4:30pm Sun, clsd Mon-Tue • mostly women • neighborhood bar • dancing/DJ wknds • food served • karaoke • dance lessons

Albuquerque

ENTERTAINMENT:
New Mexico Gay Rodeo Association www.nmgra.com.

LGBT PRIDE:
June. 505/873-8084, web: www.abqpride.com.

ANNUAL EVENTS:
September - Closet Cinema, LGBT film festival 505/243–1870, web: www.closetcinema.org.
October - Albuquerque Int'l Balloon Fiesta 505/821-1000 or 888/422-7277, web: www.balloonfiesta.com.

CITY INFO:
800/284–2282, web: www.itsatrip.org.

BEST VIEW:
Sandia Peak Tramway (505/856-7325) at sunset.

WEATHER:
Sunny and temperate. Warm days and cool nights in summer, with average temperatures from 65° to 95°. Winter is cooler, from 28° to 57°.

ATTRACTIONS:
Albuquerque Museum 505/842-0111, web: www.albuquerquemu-seum.com.
Indian Pueblo Cultural Center 505/843-7270 or 866/855-7902 (outside NM), web: www.indian-pueblo.org.
New Mexico Museum of Natural History & Science 505/841-2800, web: www.nmnaturalhistory.org.
Old Town.
Petroglyph National Monument 505/899-0205 x331, web: www.nps.gov/petr/.
Rattlesnake Museum 505/242-6569, web: www.rattlesnakes.com.
Sandia Peak Tramway 505/856-7325, web: www.sandiapeak.com.
Wildlife West Nature Park 505/281-7655, web: www.wildlifewest.org

Sidewinders Ranch 8900 Central SE (at Wyoming) **505/275-1616** • 2pm-2am, till midnight Sun-Mon • mostly gay men • dancing/DJ • country/western • leather • karaoke • wheelchair access

NIGHTCLUBS

Fire • monthly dance party • women only • check local listings for location

CAFES

Java Joe's 906 Park Ave SW **505/765-1514** • 6:30am-3:30pm • coffee & pastries • monthly art shows

RESTAURANTS

20 Carrots 2110 Central Ave SE (at Buena Vista Dr) **505/242-1320** • 10am-5pm, till 4pm Sat, clsd Sun • plenty vegetarian/vegan

Artichoke Cafe 424 Central Ave SE **505/243-0200** • lunch Mon-Fri, dinner nightly • bistro • plenty veggie

Cafe Cubano at Laru Ni Hati 3413 Central Ave NE **505/255-1575** • 9am-9pm, clsd Sun-Mon • cigars • cheap Cuban food • also unisex hair salon • gay-owned

Copper Lounge 1504 Central Ave SE (at Maple) **505/242-7490** • 11am-2am, clsd Sun • pizza, burgers • full bar

El Patio 142 Harvard St SE **505/268-4245** • 11am-9pm, from noon Sun • popular • young crowd • beer/wine • plenty veggie

El Pinto 10500 4th St NW (at Roy Ave) **505/898-1771** • lunch & dinner, Sun brunch • Mexican

Flying Star Cafe 3416 Central SE (2 blocks W of Carlisle) **505/255-6633** • 6am-11pm, till midnight Fri-Sat • plenty veggie • wheelchair access

Frontier 2400 Central SE (at Cornell) **505/266-0550** • 5am-1am • good brkfst burritos

The Original Garcia's Kitchen 1113 4th St NW **505/247-9149** • awesome little down home place

The Range Cafe 2200 Menaul NE (at University Blvd) **505/888-1660** • 7:30am-9pm • Southwestern

Romano's Macaroni Grill 2100 Louisiana NE (at Winrock Mall) **505/881-3400** • 11am-10pm • Italian

Sadie's Cocinita 6230 4th St NW (near Osuna) **505/345-5339** • 11am-10pm, 10am-9pm Sun • popular • New Mexican

Zinc Wine Bar & Bistro 3009 Central Ave NE **505/254-9462** • lunch & dinner, brunch wknds • live jazz Th & Sat-Sun till 1am • reservations recommended

ENTERTAINMENT & RECREATION

Duke City Derby • Albuquerque's female roller derby league • visit www.dukecityderby.com for events

Rio Grande Botanic Garden 2601 Central Ave NW (at New York Ave) **505/768-2000** • an oasis in the desert: native & exotic plants, butterflies

BOOKSTORES

Bird Song 1708 Central SE **505/268-7204** • 11am-7pm, clsd Mon • used • LGBT section

Page One 11018 Montgomery NE **505/294-2026, 800/521-4122** • 9am-9pm, till 7pm Sun • "New Mexico's largest independent bookstore"

RETAIL SHOPS

Newsland 2112 Central Ave SE (at Yale) **505/242-0694** • 8am-8pm, till 7pm Sun • some LGBT magazines

EROTICA

Castle Megastore 5110 Central Ave SE (at San Mateo) **505/262-2266**

Self Serve 3904B Central Ave SE (at Morningside) **505/265-5815** • erotica store & sexuality resource center • lesbian-owned

Chimayo

ACCOMMODATIONS

Casa Escondida B&B **505/351-4805, 800/643-7201** • gay-friendly • full brkfst • hot tub • kids/pets ok w/ approval • nonsmoking • WiFi • $99-155

Cloudcroft

RETAIL SHOPS

Off The Beaten Path 100 Glorietta Ave (at 1st) **575/682-7284** • eclectic gifts • original artwork • wheelchair access • lesbian-owned

Farmington

ACCOMMODATIONS

Quality Inn 1901 E Broadway **505/325-3700, 877/424-6423** • gay-friendly • kids/pets ok • WiFi • wheelchair access • $39-99

Las Cruces

RETAIL SHOPS

Spirit Winds Gifts & Cafe 2260 S Locust St **575/521-0222** • 7am-7pm, 9am-6pm Sun • live music some wknds • patio

Madrid

BARS

Mineshaft Tavern 2846 State Hwy 14 **505/473-0743** • 11am-close • gay-friendly • live shows • also restaurant • some veggie

CAFES

Java Junction 2855 State Hwy 14 **505/438-2772** • 7:15am-5pm, till 6pm wknds • WiFi • also B&B

Ojo Caliente

RESTAURANTS

Mesa Vista Cafe 35323 Hwy 285 **505/583-2245** • 8am-9pm

Ramah

ACCOMMODATIONS

El Morro RV Park, Cabins & Cafe 4018 Hwy 53 **505/783-4612** • gay/ straight • in Zuni Mtns • full brkfst • nonsmoking • WiFi • also cafe • lesbian-owned • $10-94

Ruidoso

RESTAURANTS

Mountain Annie's 2710 Sudderth (at Mechem) **575/257-7982** • 7pm-10pm Th-Sat • dinner theater • nonsmoking • patio • wheelchair access

Santa Fe

INFO LINES & SERVICES

AA Gay/ Lesbian 311 E Palace Ave **505/982-8932** • 7pm Th • also 6pm Mon at 1601 S St Francis Dr

ACCOMMODATIONS

Alexander's Inn 529 E Palace Ave (at Delgado) **505/986-1431, 888/321-5123** • gay/ straight • vacation rentals w/ kitchens • hot tub • kids/ pets ok • nonsmoking • WiFi • $185-260

Bishop's Lodge Resort & Spa 1297 Bishops Lodge Rd **505/983-6377, 800/419-0492** • gay-friendly • on 450 acres • kids/ pets ok • pool • hot tub • nonsmoking • wheelchair access • spa has indoor & outdoor treatment rooms • $149-459

Dragonfly Canyon Retreat Glorieta **505/757-2991** • gay/ straight • 3-bdrm casita • near Pecos Wilderness • nonsmoking • $150+ • also women's retreats • lesbian-owned

El Farolito B&B 514 Galisteo St (at Paseo de Peralta) **505/988-1631, 888/634-8782** • gay/ straight • adobe compound w/ romantic, private casitas • kids ok • nonsmoking • WiFi • gay-owned • $160-275

Four Kachinas Inn 512 Webber St **505/982-2550, 800/397-2564** • gay/ straight • courtyard • kids ok • nonsmoking • WiFi • wheelchair access • gay-owned • $150-240

Hacienda Las Barrancas 27 Country Rd 84-D (at Hwy 502) **505/455-2197, 866/455-2197** • gay-friendly • adobe hacienda located in scenic Pojoaque River Valley N of Santa Fe • full brkfst • hot tub • nonsmoking • WiFi • $116-182

Hacienda Nicholas 320 E Marcy St **505/986-1431, 888/284-3170** • gay/ straight • adobe home • full brkfst • teens/ pets ok • nonsmoking • WiFi • wheelchair access • $135-260

Inn of the Anasazi 113 Washington Ave **505/988-3030, 800/688-8100** • gay-friendly • luxury hotel 1/2 block from Plaza • kids ok • WiFi • nonsmoking • wheelchair access • also restaurant • $349-1,200

➤ **Inn of the Turquoise Bear B&B** 342 E Buena Vista St **505/983-0798, 800/396-4104** • lesbians/ gay men • B&B in historic Witter Bynner estate • nonsmoking • WiFi • gay-owned • $99-325

Inn on the Alameda 303 E Alameda **505/984-2121, 888/984-2121** • gay-friendly • afternoon wine reception • hot tubs • WiFi • wheelchair access • $125-390

Las Palomas 460 W San Francisco St **505/982-5560, 877/982-5560** • gay-friendly • luxury hotel 3 blocks from Plaza • kids ok • nonsmoking • WiFi • wheelchair access • $139-269

The Madeleine Inn 106 Faithway St **505/982-3465, 888/877-7622** • gay/ straight • Queen Anne Victorian • full brkfst • hot tub • kids ok • nonsmoking • WiFi • also spa • $120-265

Marriott Residence Inn 1698 Galisteo St (at St Michaels) **505/988-7300, 800/331-3131** • gay-friendly • hot tub • pool • nonsmoking • kids/ pets ok • WiFi • wheelchair access • $109-279

New Mexico Women's Guesthouse PO Box 130, Serafina 87569 **505/421–2533** • women only • 2 2-bdrm guesthouses on 1,000-acre wildlife refuge • also healing workshops • hot tub • nonsmoking • lesbian-owned • $60-140/ night, $375-740/ week

Tano Road Casita 15 Tano Pt Ln **505/989–7802, 505/989–7803** • gay/ straight • studio guesthouse • in quiet, residential area • nonsmoking • $90

The Triangle Inn—Santa Fe 14 Arroyo Cuyamungue (12 miles N of Santa Fe) **505/455–3375, 877/733–7689** • lesbians/ gay men • secluded rustic adobe compound • hot tub • nonsmoking casitas available • WiFi • kids/ pets ok • wheelchair access • lesbian-owned • $70-160

The Water Street Inn 427 W Water St **505/984–1193, 800/646–6752** • gay-friendly • historic adobe inn • jacuzzi • nonsmoking • kids/ pets ok • WiFi • wheelchair access • $170-270

Bars

SilverStarlight Lounge 500 Rodeo Rd **505/428–7781** • lesbians/ gay men • cabaret & lounge

Nightclubs

Fusion 135 W Palace Ave, 3rd flr (at Grant) **505/955–0400** • dinner Tue-Sat, lounge from 9pm Tue & Fri-Sat, clsd Sun-Mon • gay/ straight • dancing/DJ • tapas & sushi • gay-owned

Restaurants

Anasazi Restaurant 113 Washington Ave (at The Inn of the Anasazi) **505/988–3030** • brkfst, lunch, dinner & Sun brunch • wheelchair access

Cafe Pasqual's 121 Don Gaspar (at Water St) **505/983–9340, 800/722–7672** • brkfst, lunch, dinner & Sun brunch • popular • Southwestern • some veggie • beer/ wine

The Compound Restaurant 653 Canyon Rd **505/982–4353** • lunch Mon-Sat, dinner nightly • upscale • Southwestern • nonsmoking • patio • reservations recommended

Cowgirl BBQ 319 S Guadalupe St (btwn Aztec & Guadalupe) **505/982–2565** • 11am-2am • great margaritas • plenty veggie

Garbo's@RainbowVision 500 Rodeo Rd (ar Sawmill) **505/428–7781** • lunch & dinner, clsd Sun-Tue • full bar • wheelchair access

Geronimo's 724 Canyon Rd (at Camino del Monte Sol) **505/982-1500** • dinner nightly • eclectic gourmet • full bar 11am-11pm

Santacafe 231 Washington Ave **505/984-1788** • lunch & dinner • New American • some veggie • full bar • wheelchair access

Tune Up Cafe 1115 Hickox St (at Cortez) **505/983-7060** • 7am-10pm, from 8am wknds • New Mexican • some veggie • beer/ wine

Vanessie of Santa Fe 434 W San Francisco St (at Guadalupe) **505/982-9966** • 5:30pm-9pm (bar 4:30pm-midnight) • popular • lesbians/ gay men • steak house • piano bar

ENTERTAINMENT & RECREATION

Ten Thousand Waves 3451 Hyde Park Rd (4 miles out of town) **505/992-5025 (INFO), 505/982-9304 (RESERVATIONS)** • Japanese health spa & lodging • sit under the stars & look out at the mtns • clothing-optional in all tubs • kids ok • call for more info

Wise Fool New Mexico 2778 Agua Fria Unit D (at Siler Rd) **505/992-2588** • women & kids circus arts classes, workshops & performances • social justice theatre & puppetry • check local listings for upcoming events & info

BOOKSTORES

Downtown Subscription 376 Garcia St (at Acequia Madre) **505/983-3085** • 7am-6pm • newsstand • coffee shop

RETAIL SHOPS

The Ark 133 Romero St (at Agua Fria) **505/988-3709** • 9:30am-7pm, 10am-6pm Sat, 11am-5pm Sun • spiritual

Silver City

ACCOMMODATIONS

West Street Inn 575/534-2302 • guesthouse • kids/ pets ok (call for details) • $105-125

BARS

Isaac's Bar & Grill 200 N Bullard St **575/388-4090** • gay-friendly • 11am-midnight, till 2am Wed-Sat, noon-midnight Sun, wknd brunch • dancing/DJ • live shows

CAFES

Shevek & Co 602 N Bullard St (at 6th St) **575/534-9168** • dinner nightly, clsd Wed • Mediterranean cuisine • espresso • "the best service in town" • beer/ wine • patio • gay-owned

RESTAURANTS

Diane's Restaurant & Bakery 510 N Bullard **575/538-8722** • lunch daily, dinner Tue-Sat, wknd brunch, clsd Mon

Taos

ACCOMMODATIONS

Adobe & Stars B&B 584 State Hwy 150 (at Valdez Rim Rd) **575/776-2776, 800/211-7076** • gay/ straight • full brkfst • nonsmoking • WiFi • wheelchair access • woman-owned • $120-190

Casa Benavides B&B 137 Kit Carson Rd **575/758-1772, 800/552-1772** • fireplaces • hot tubs • extensive gardens • full brkfst • nonsmoking • kids ok • WiFi • wheelchair access • $105-325

Casa Europa Inn & Gallery 840 Upper Ranchitos Rd (at Ranchitos Rd) **575/758-9798, 888/758-9798** • gay/ straight • full brkfst • hot tub • sauna • nonsmoking • WiFi • $115-185

Casa Gallina 575/758-2306 • gay/ straight • charming guesthouse in quiet, pastoral setting • nonsmoking • wheelchair access • gay-owned • $160-200

Dobson House 484 Tune Dr 575/776-5738 • gay-friendly • luxury suites • N of Taos • full brkfst • solar-powered eco-resort • nonsmoking • $118-140

Dreamcatcher B&B 416 La Lomita Rd (at Valverde) **575/758-0613, 888/758-0613** • gay-friendly • near Taos Plaza • full brkfst • hot tub • nonsmoking • WiFi • wheelchair access • $115-175

The Historic Taos Inn 125 Paseo del Pueblo Norte **575/758-2233, 888/518-8267** • gay-friendly • several adobe houses date from the 1800s • pueblo-style fireplaces • also restaurant & bar • $75-275

Orinda B&B 461 Valverde St (on Valverde Park) **575/758-8581, 800/847-1837** • gay/ straight • full brkfst • nonsmoking • WiFi • $104-169

San Geronimo Lodge 1101 Witt Rd (off Kit Carson) **575/751-3776, 800/894-4119** • popular • gay/ straight • full brkfst • pool • hot tub • massage available • kids/ pets ok • nonsmoking • WiFi • wheelchair access • $95-160

RESTAURANTS

Sabroso 470 State Hwy 150, Arroyo Seco **575/776-3333** • 5pm-10pm • American & Mediterranean • also full bar • patio

ENTERTAINMENT & RECREATION

Llama Trekking Adventures
800/758–5262 • day hikes & multiday llama treks in Sangre de Cristo Mtns & Rio Grande Gorge

Truth or Consequences

ACCOMMODATIONS

The Belair Inn 705 N Date St (at 7th St) **505/740–4100** • gay/straight • "retro 1950s motel w/ 21st-century amenities" • nonsmoking • WiFi • gay-owned • $39-65

NEW YORK

Adirondack Mtns

ACCOMMODATIONS

The Cornerstone Victorian 3921 Main St (Rte 9), Warrensburg **518/623–3308** • gay-friendly • close to skiing, hiking, Saratoga & more • 5-course gourmet brkfst • beautiful gardens & wraparound porch • $98-194

Country Road Lodge B&B 115 Hickory Hill Rd (at State Rte 418), Warrensburg **518/623–2207** • gay-friendly • secluded riverside retreat at the end of a country road • full brkfst • nonsmoking • WiFi • $97-107

The Doctor's Inn 304 Trudeau Rd, Saranac Lake **518/891–3464, 888/518–3464** • gay-friendly • full brkfst • some shared baths • kids/pets ok (call first) • nonsmoking • $250-500

Falls Brook Yurts in Adirondacks John Brannon Rd, Minerva **518/761–6187** • gay-friendly • access to hiking, fishing & boating • kids/pets ok • $95

The Griffin House B&B 3 Hudson St (off Rte 9/ Main St), Warrensburg **518/623–2449, 888/664–4661** • gay-friendly • Victorian country inn • full brkfst • 5 miles from Lake George • nonsmoking • wheelchair access • women-owned • $95-145

Hudson River Beach House **518/361–2375** • lesbians/gay men • nonsmoking • 2-bdrm cottage w/ private beach on Upper Hudson River • women-owned • $120-190

Jake's Adirondack Place 609/354–2419 • gay/straight • 3-bdrm rental home • kids ok • nonsmoking • WiFi • lesbian-owned • $250+

King Hendrick Motel 1602 State Rte 9, Lake George **518/792–0418, 866/521–6883** • gay-friendly • swimming • nonsmoking • wheelchair access • $75-125

Tea Island Resort 3020 Lake Shore Dr, Lake George **518/668–2784** • gay-friendly • chalets, cottages & suites • $115-210

Albany

see Capital District

Binghamton

INFO LINES & SERVICES

AA Gay/ Lesbian 607/722–5983

ACCOMMODATIONS

Serenity Farms 386 Pollard Rd, Greene **607/656–4659** • gay/straight • B&B • full brkfst • camping on 100 secluded acres • pool • pets ok • gay-owned • $65-119

BARS

Merlin's 201 State St **607/722–1022** • 8pm-close, till 3am Fri-Sat • lesbians/gay men • neighborhood bar • dancing/DJ • live shows • karaoke • 18+ Wed-Fri & Sun

Squiggy's 34 Chenango St (at Court) **607/722–2299** • 6pm-1am, till 3am Fri-Sat, from 8pm Sat, clsd Sun • lesbians/gay men • neighborhood bar • dancing/DJ Fri-Sat • karaoke

NIGHTCLUBS

Zippers 165 Conklin Ave **607/437–9264** • 8pm-close Tue-Sat • lesbians/gay men • dancing/DJ • drag shows • 18+

CAFES

Lost Dog Cafe 222 Water St (at Henry) **607/771–6063** • 11:30am-10pm, till 11pm Fri-Sat, clsd Sun • popular • some veggie • beer/wine • live shows • wheelchair access

RESTAURANTS

The Whole in the Wall 43 S Washington St **607/722–5138** • 11:30am-9pm, clsd Sun-Mon

Buffalo

INFO LINES & SERVICES

Lesbian/ Gay AA 206 S Elmwood Ave, Elmwood **716/852–7743** • 8pm Mon, Wed & Fri

Pride Center of Western NY 206 S Elmwood Ave **716/852–7743** • 1pm-9pm Mon-Fri & 5pm-8pm Tue

ACCOMMODATIONS

Beau Fleuve B&B 242 Linwood Ave **716/882–6116, 800/278–0245** • gay-friendly • $115-160

The Mansion on Delaware 414 Delaware Ave 716/886-3300 • gay/straight • WiFi • wheelchair access • $195-375

BARS

Adonia's 20 Allen St 716/332-1205 • 3pm-2am, till 4am Fri-Sat, from noon Sun • lesbians/gay men • dancing/DJ • karaoke

Cathode Ray 26 Allen St (at N Pearl) 716/884-3615 • 1pm-4am, from 7am Sun • mostly gay men • neighborhood bar • wheelchair access

Fugazi 503 Franklin St (near Allen St) 716/881-3588 • 5pm-2am • gay/straight • intimate cocktail lounge • videos

K Gallagher's 73 Allen St 716/885-2244 • 5pm-10pm, till 11pm Fri-Sat • gay-friendly • neighborhood bar • multiracial clientele • comfort food served • wheelchair access

Q 44 Allen St 716/332-2223 • 3pm-4am, from noon wknds • lesbians/gay men • neighborhood bar

Roxy 884 Main St (at Carlton) 716/882-9293 • 8pm-4am Wed-Sat • mostly women • dancing/DJ • alternative • live shows • karaoke

The Underground 274 Delaware Ave (at Johnson) 716/853-0092 • noon-4am • mostly gay men • neighborhood bar • dancing/DJ • karaoke

NIGHTCLUBS

Club Marcella 622 Main St 716/847-6850 • 10pm-4am, clsd Mon-Wed • lesbians/gay men • dancing/DJ • drag shows • wheelchair access

CAFES

Allen Street Hardware Cafe 245 Allen St (at College) 716/882-8843 • 5pm daily • full bar

Cafe 59 59 Allen St (at Franklin) 716/883-1880 • 8am-6pm, 10am-5pm Sat, clsd Sun • WiFi

RESTAURANTS

Anchor Bar 1047 Main St 716/886-8920, 716/884-4083 • 11am-10pm, till midnight Fri-Sat

Mothers 33 Virginia Pl (at Virginia St) 716/882-2989 • 5pm-3am, 2pm-midnight Sun

Rue Franklin 341 Franklin St (at W Tupper) 716/852-4416 • 5:30pm-10pm, clsd Sun-Mon • upscale, contemporary French

Tempo 581 Delaware Ave (in Allentown) 716/885-1594 • upscale Italian/American

Towne Restaurant 186 Allen St 716/884-5128 • 7am-5am, clsd Sun, Greek

ENTERTAINMENT & RECREATION

Babeville 341 Delaware Ave (at W Tupper) 716/852-3835 • Ani Di Franco's rehabbed church performance space • also Hallwalls Arts Center

Buffalo United Artists 119 Chippewa (btwn Delaware & Elmwood) 716/886-9239 • theater company

BOOKSTORES

Talking Leaves 3158 Main St (btwn Winspear & Hertel Aves) 716/837-8554 • 10am-6pm, till 8pm Wed-Th, clsd Sun • also 951 Elmwood Ave, 716/884-9524

PUBLICATIONS

About Magazine PO Box 112, 14205 646/233-2153 • "the queer voice of western New York & southern Ontario"

Outcome Buffalo 495 Linwood Ave 716/883-2756, 716/228-8828 • monthly

EROTICA

Adult Mart 3102 Delaware Ave (at Sheridan), Kenmore 716/877-5027 • 24hrs • women receive 20% off Wed

Video Liquidators 1770 Elmwood Ave 716/874-7223

Canandaigua

ACCOMMODATIONS

Chalet of Canandaigua Bed & Breakfast 3770 State Rte 21 (at Nott Rd) 585/394-9080 • gay-friendly • rustic, elegant log cabin • perfect place for romantic getaways • WiFi • lesbian owned • $235-295

Capital District

includes Albany, Cohoes, Salem, Schenectady & Troy

INFO LINES & SERVICES

Capital District Lesbian/Gay Community Center 332 Hudson Ave, Albany 518/462-6138 • social & human service programs • also Rainbow Cafe 6pm-9pm, clsd Sat

Gay AA 332 Hudson Ave (at L/G Community Center), Albany 518/462-6138 • 7:30pm Sun

Women's Building 373 Central Ave, Albany 518/462-2871 • community center • call for hours

ACCOMMODATIONS

The Morgan State House 393 State St, Albany **518/427–6063, 888/427–6063** • gay-friendly • 1800s town house • nonsmoking • $135-260

BARS

Clinton Street Pub 159 Clinton St, Schenectady **518/377–8555** • 11am-close • lesbians/gay men • neighborhood bar • dancing/DJ • live shows • karaoke

George Bar 720 Central Ave, Albany **518/459–1596** • 4pm-2am • lesbians/gay men • Girlbar Th night • karaoke • WiFi • wheelchair access

Oh Bar 304 Lark St (at Madison), Albany **518/463–9004** • 2pm-4am • lesbians/gay men • neighborhood bar • multiracial • karaoke • videos • wheelchair access

Waterworks Pub 76 Central Ave (btwn Lexington & Northern), Albany **518/465–9079** • 1pm-4am • popular • mostly gay men • neighborhood bar • dancing/DJ wknds • garden bar • food served • karaoke • 18+ • wheelchair access

NIGHTCLUBS

Fuze Box 12 Central Ave, Albany **518/432–4472** • 2pm-4am, from 8pm Th-Sat • gay/straight • dancing/DJ • live shows • swing dancing • gay-owned

CAFES

Muddy Cup 1038 Madison Ave, Albany **518/458–6120** • 7am-midnight, 7am-2am wknds • WiFi • events • gay-owned

RESTAURANTS

Bob's Lunch & Dairy Bar 4139 Rte 22 (Junction Rtes 22 & 29), Salem **518/854–7505** • 11am-9pm April-Oct • great soft serve

Bomber's Burrito Bar 258 Lark St, Albany **518/463–9636** • 11am-2am, till 3am wknds • lots of veggie • gay-owned

Debbie's Kitchen 456 Madison Ave (btwn Lark St & Washington Park), Albany **518/463–3829** • 10am-7pm, 11am-6pm Sat, clsd Sun

El Loco Mexican Cafe 465 Madison Ave (btwn Lark & Willett), Albany **518/436–1855** • lunch Wed-Sat, dinner nightly, clsd Mon • healthy Tex-Mex • full bar

Yono's 25 Chapel St (at Sheridan), Albany **518/436–7747** • 5:30pm-10pm, clsd Sun-Mon • full bar • live music • wheelchair access

ENTERTAINMENT & RECREATION

Albany All Stars Albany • Albany's female roller derby league

RETAIL SHOPS

Romeo's Gifts 299 Lark St (at Madison), Albany **518/434–4014** • noon-9pm, till 5pm Sun

Catskill Mtns

INFO LINES & SERVICES

Sullivan County Visitors Association **800/882–2287** • LGBT info for the Catskills

Wise Woman Center **845/246–8081** • women only • workshops • correspondence courses • newsletter

ACCOMMODATIONS

Beds on Clouds 5320 Main St/ Rte 23 (at CR21), Windham **518/734–4692** • gay/straight • 1854 mansion features suites & famous artwork • woman-owned • $89-179

Bradstan Country Hotel 1561 Rte 17-B, White Lake **845/583–4114** • gay-friendly • also cottages • piano bar & cabaret from 9pm-1am Fri-Sat • $135-200

Cuomo's Cove 33 Cumo's Cove Rd (at South St), Windham **518/734–5903, 800/734–5903** • gay-friendly • nonsmoking • women-owned • $120-350

ECCE B&B 19 Silverfish Rd, Barryville **845/557–8562, 888/557–8562** • gay/ straight • B&B 300 ft above Upper Delaware River • full brkfst • WiFi • nonsmoking • gay-owned • $150-285

Inn at Stone Ridge Rte 209, Stone Ridge **845/687–0736** • gay-friendly • 1700s mansion • full brkfst • also fine dining • full bar • patio • $195-425

Kate's Lazy Meadow Motel 5191 Rte 28, Mt Tremper **845/688–7200** • gay-friendly • way-cool love shack owned by Kate Pierson of the B-52s • WiFi • nonsmoking • $230-280

Point Lookout Mountain Inn The Mohican Trail, Rte 23, East Windham **518/734–3381** • gay-friendly • near skiing • hot tub • nonsmoking • kids/ pets ok • also restaurant & cafe • wheelchair access • $90-200

The Roxbury, Contemporary Catskill Lodging 2258 County Hwy 41 (at Bridge St), Roxbury **607/326–7200** • gay/ straight • hip country motel • kids ok • nonsmoking • WiFi • wheelchair access • gay-owned • $90-350

Village Green 12 Tinker St, Woodstock **845/679–0313** • B&B • gay-owned • $115-150

BARS

Public Lounge 2318 City Hwy 41 (Bridge St), Roxbury 607/326-4026, 607/326-5056 • 5pm-9pm, till midnight Fri-Sat, clsd Mon-Tue • gay-friendly • tapas • gay-owned

RESTAURANTS

Catskill Rose 5355 Rte 212, Mt Tremper 845/688-7100 • 5pm-close Th-Sun • some veggie • full bar • patio • also lodging

ENTERTAINMENT & RECREATION

Frog Hollow Farm Old Post Rd, Esopus 845/384-6424 • riding school

BOOKSTORES

Golden Notebook 29 Tinker St, Woodstock 845/679-8000 • 10:30am-7pm, till 6pm Sun • LGBT section • wheelchair access

Cherry Creek

ACCOMMODATIONS

The Cherry Creek Inn 1022 West Rd (CR68) (at Center Rd) 716/296-5105 • gay-friendly • B&B • full brkfst • in wine & Amish country • kids ok • $85-150

Cooperstown

see Sharon Springs

Corning

ACCOMMODATIONS

Black Sheep Inn 8329 Pleasant Valley Rd (Rte 54), Hammondsport 607/569-3767, 877/274-6286 • gay/ straight • full brkfst • nonsmoking • WiFi • $139-259

Hillcrest Manor B&B 227 Cedar St (at Fourth St) 607/936-4548, 607/654-9136 • gay-friendly • elegant 1890 neo-classical mansion in quiet neighborhood • nonsmoking • WiFi • gay-owned • $155-185

Rufus Tanner House B&B 60 Sagetown Rd, Pine City 607/732-0213, 800/360-9259 • gay/ straight • full brkfst • hot tub • nonsmoking • WiFi • wheelchair access • $87-150

Croton-on-Hudson

ACCOMMODATIONS

Alexander Hamilton House 49 Van Wyck St 914/271-6737 • gay/ straight • full brkfst • pool • nonsmoking • kids ok • WiFi • $125-350

Elmira

BARS

Chill 200 W 5th 607/732-1414 • 6pm-1am, clsd Sun-Tue • lesbians/ gay men • neighborhood bar • dancing/DJ • karaoke • drag shows • gay-owned

Findley Lake

ACCOMMODATIONS

Blue Heron Inn 10412 Main St (at Shadyside Rd) 716/769-7852 • gay-friendly • B&B • full brkfst • kids ok • nonsmoking • $129-149

Fire Island

see also Long Island

INFO LINES & SERVICES

AA 631/669-1124 • call for meeting times

ACCOMMODATIONS

Dune Point Guesthouse 631/597-6261, 631/560-2200 (CELL) • lesbians/ gay men • hot tub • kids/ pets ok • nonsmoking • wheelchair access • lesbian & gay & straight-owned/ run • $75-525

GroveHotel Dock Walk, Cherry Grove 631/597-6600 • mostly gay men • pool • nudity • nonsmoking room available • wheelchair access • gay-owned • $50-550

Hotel Ciel Harbor Walk 631/597-6500 • mostly gay men • swimming • also restaurant • wheelchair access

The Madison Fire Island Pines 631/597-6061 • mostly gay men • guesthouse w/ full amenities • pool • nonsmoking • WiFi • gay-owned • $200-776

BARS

Blue Whale Harbor Walk, The Pines 631/597-6500 • seasonal • lesbians/ gay men • popular • dancing/DJ • popular Low Tea dance • also restaurant • wheelchair access

Cherry's On the Bay 158 Bayview Walk, Cherry Grove 631/597-7859 • seasonal • noon-4am • popular • lesbians/ gay men • dancing/DJ • piano bar • live shows • drag shows • also restaurant • patio

Pines Bistro & Martini Bar 36 Fire Island Blvd, The Pines 631/597-6862 • seasonal, opens 6pm

Sip n' Twirl 36 Fire Island Blvd, The Pines 631/597-3599 • seasonal • noon-4am • mostly gay men • dancing/DJ • also piano bar

NIGHTCLUBS

Ice Palace Bayview Walk, Cherry Grove **631/597-6600** • hours vary • popular • lesbians/gay men • dancing/DJ • drag shows • wheelchair access

The Pavilion Harbor Walk, The Pines **631/597-6500** • seasonal • noon-8am Fri-Sun only • lesbians/gay men • popular • dancing/DJ • popular High Tea dance • wheelchair access

CAFES

Canteen Harbor Walk, The Pines **631/597-6500** • coffee, smoothies, cocktails & food

RESTAURANTS

Cherry Grove Pizza Dock Walk (under the GroveHotel), Cherry Grove **631/597-6766** • seasonal • 11am-10pm

Jumpin' Jack's Seafood Shack Ocean Walk, Cherry Grove **631/597-4174** • seasonal • lunch & dinner • also piano bar

Marina Meat Market Harbor Walk, The Pines **631/597-6588** • great sandwiches, also sell Avon

Pines Pizza 36 Fire Island Blvd, The Pines **631/597-3597** • seasonal, 11am-11pm

ENTERTAINMENT & RECREATION

Cherry Grove Beach • lesbians/gay men • nude beach

Invasion of the Pines The Pines dock (July 4th wknd) • come & enjoy the annual fun as boatloads of drag queens from Cherry Grove arrive to terrorize the posh Pines

GYMS & HEALTH CLUBS

Deck Pool & Gym Harbor Walk, The Pines • 7am-6pm • day passes available

Fredonia

CAFES

Intermezzo Coffeehouse by Monika's Delites 12 Park Pl (on Barker Common) **716/672-6070** • 7am-5pm, 8am-4pm Sat, clsd Sun • gourmet soups, salads, sandwiches & desserts

Geneva

ACCOMMODATIONS

Belhurst 4069 Rte 14 S (near Snell Rd) **315/781-0201** • gay-friendly • in historic castle overlooking Seneca Lake • fireplaces • also restaurant • $65-365

Glens Falls

ACCOMMODATIONS

Glens Falls Inn 25 Sherman Ave **646/824-8379** • gay-friendly • B&B in Victorian • full brkfst • WiFi • woman-owned • $130-342

Hamptons

see Long Island—Suffolk/ Hamptons

Hudson Valley

Hudson Valley includes Catskill, High Falls, Highland, Hudson, Hyde Park, Kinderhook, Kingston, New Paltz, Poughkeepsie, Rhinebeck & Saugerties

ACCOMMODATIONS

Barclay Heights B&B 158 Burt St (at Trinity Place), Saugerties **845/246-3788** • gay-friendly • full brkfst • cozy Victorian cottage • nonsmoking • $175-245

The Country Squire B&B 251 Allen St (at 3rd), Hudson **518/822-9229** • gay/ straight • restored Queen Anne • kids ok • nonsmoking • WiFi • $135-195

Harmony House B& B 1659 Route 212, Saugertie **845/679-1277** • gay/straight • full brkfst • WiFi • gay-owned

Hudson City B&B 326 Allen St (at Rte 9-G/ 3rd St), Hudson **518/822-8044** • gay/ straight • 18th-c Victorian in antique district • hot tub • kids/ small pets ok • gay-owned • $100-199

Lefèvre House B&B 14 Southside Ave, New Paltz **845/255-4747** • gay/ straight • full brkfst • hot tub • kids ok • close to outdoor activities • WiFi • gay-owned • $185-265

Van Schaack House 20 Broad St (at Albany Rd), Kinderhook **518/758-6118** • gay-friendly • B&B • full brkfst • nonsmoking • gay-owned • $150-210

BARS

Congress 411 Main St (off Academy), Poughkeepsie **845/486-9068** • 3pm-4am, from 7pm Sat-Sun • lesbians/gay men • neighborhood bar • wheelchair access

NIGHTCLUBS

Primetime 3353 Rte 9 W, Highland **845/691-7878** • 9pm-4am Fri-Sat only • lesbians/gay men • dancing/DJ

CAFES

Mod Cafe 395 Main St, Catskill **518/943-0420** • 8am-3pm, from 5pm Th, clsd Sat-Sun • lesbian-owned

Muddy Cup 129 Main St, Beacon **845/440-8855** • 6am-10pm • WiFi • events • gay-owned

Muddy Cup 742 Warren St, Hudson **518/828-2210** • 7am-10pm, from 8am Sun • WiFi • events • gay-owned

RESTAURANTS

Armadillo Bar & Grill 97 Abeel St, Kingston **845/339-1550** • lunch wknds, dinner nightly, clsd Mon • full bar • patio

Barnbaby's Rte 32 N Chestnut (at Academy), New Paltz **845/255-2433** • 7 days a week, late night snacks

Locust Tree Restaurant 215 Hugenot St (behind conference center), New Paltz **845/255-7888** • 5pm-close, Sun brunch 11am-3pm, clsd Mon-Tue

Northern Spy Cafe Rte 213, High Falls **845/687-7298** • dinner only, clsd Mon • plenty veggie • full bar • wheelchair access

Quinn's Luncheonette 330 Main St, Beacon **845/831-8065** • 6am-1:30pm • great bread

Terrapin 6426 Montgomery St, Rhinebeck **845/876-3330** • lunch & dinner • bistro & bar • patio

The Would Restaurant 120 North Rd (off Rte 9 W), Highland **845/691-9883** • dinner nightly, clsd Sun • some veggie • full bar • patio • gay-owned

ENTERTAINMENT & RECREATION

Dia:Beacon Riggio Galleries 3 Beekman St (at Rte 9D), Beacon **845/440-0100** • modern art museum

Ithaca

INFO LINES & SERVICES

AA Gay/ Lesbian 607/273-1541

ACCOMMODATIONS

Frog Haven Women's B&B 578 W King Rd (off Rte 96B S) **607/272-3238** • women only • in contemporary log-sided home • swimmable pond • kids ok • nonsmoking • lesbian-owned • $80-90 + 11% tax

Juniper Hill B&B 16 Elm St (at Main St), Trumansburg **607/387-3044, 888/809-1367** • gay-friendly • full brkfst • nonsmoking • WiFi • gay-owned • $135+

Noble House Farm 215 Connecticut Hill Rd, Newfield **607/277-4798** • gay-friendly • near gorges & wine tours • kids/ pets ok • nonsmoking • wheelchair access • lesbian-owned • $100-135

William Henry Miller Inn 303 N Aurora St (at E Buffalo St) **607/256-4553, 877/256-4553** • gay-friendly • full brkfst • pets ok • kids over 12 ok • WiFi • nonsmoking • $165-250

BARS

Felicia's Atomic Lounge 508 W State St (Meadow St) **607/273-2219** • 4pm-1am • clsd Mon • gay-friendly • food served • live entertainment • piano bar • lesbian-owned

Oasis 1230 Danby Rd/ Rte 96-B (at Comfort) **607/273-1505** • 4pm-1am, clsd Mon • popular • lesbians/ gay men • dancing/DJ • multiracial • live music Fri • also restaurant • wheelchair access

CAFES

Sarah's Patisserie 200 Pleasant Grove Rd (at Hanshaw Rd) **607/257-4257** • 10am-6pm, clsd Sun-Mon • multiracial • transgender-friendly • lesbian-owned

ENTERTAINMENT & RECREATION

Out Loud Chorus 607/280-0374

BOOKSTORES

Colophon Books Inc 205 N Aurora St **607/277-5608** • 11am-7pm, clsd Sun-Mon • alternative independent • LGBT section • wheelchair access

Jamestown

ACCOMMODATIONS

Fairmount Motel 138 W Fairmount (Rte 394) **716/763-9550** • gay-friendly • near Chautauqua Institution • kids ok • WiFi • gay-owned • $45+

BARS

Sneakers 100 Harrison (at Institute) **716/484-8816** • 2pm-2am, clsd Tue • lesbians/ gay men • dancing/DJ Fri-Sat • wheelchair access

ENTERTAINMENT & RECREATION

The Lucille Ball Desi Arnaz Center 2 W 3rd St (at Main) **716/484-0800, 877/582-9326** • for those who love Lucy

Little Falls

CAFES

Piccolo Cafe 365 S Ann St **315/823-9856** • lunch Mon-Fri, dinner Wed-Sun

LONG ISLAND

Long Island is divided into 2 geographical areas:
Long Island—Nassau
Long Island—Suffolk/ Hamptons
see also Fire Island

Long Island—Nassau

INFO LINES & SERVICES

Gay/ Lesbian Switchboard of Long Island (GLSB of LI) 631/665-3700 • 7pm-10pm weekdays only

BARS

Kelli's Bar & Grill 2955 Merrick Rd, Bellmore 516/765-3893 • 5pm-4am, from noon Sun • lesbians/gay men • neighborhood bar • dancing/DJ • gay-owned

NIGHTCLUBS

Pure Silk 103 Post Ave (at Chi Lounge), Westbury 516/474-1707 • 4pm-9pm Sun only, no party June or July • mostly women • dancing/DJ

Shy Lounge 2686 Hempstead Tpke, Levittown 516/520-1332 • 10pm-4am Wed for Deluxe & Sat for Gation • lesbians/gay men • dancing/DJ

RESTAURANTS

RS Jones 153 Merrick Ave (off Sunrise), Merrick 516/378-7177 • dinner, clsd Mon • Tex-Mex • women-owned

ENTERTAINMENT & RECREATION

Pride for Youth Coffeehouse 2050 Bellmore Ave, Bellmore 516/679-9000 • 7:30pm-11:30pm Fri • ages 13-20 • live music

PUBLICATIONS

PM Entertainment Magazine 516/845-0759 • covers Long Island, NJ & NYC

Long Island—Suffolk/ Hamptons

ACCOMMODATIONS

East Hampton Village B&B 172 Newtown Ln (at McGuirk St), East Hampton 631/324-1858 • gay/ straight • lovely turn-of-the-century home • nonsmoking • WiFi • $179-499

EconoLodge—Bay Shore 501 E Main St (at Saxon Ave), Bay Shore 631/666-6000, 800/553-2666 • gay/ straight • close to beaches & ferries to Fire Island • kids ok • $79-179

Hampton Resorts & Hospitality 1655 Country Rd 39, Southampton 631/283-6100 • gay-friendly • pool • jacuzzi • kids/ pets ok • wheelchair access • $120-500

Mill House Inn 31 N Main St (at Newtown Lane), East Hampton 631/324-9766 • gay-friendly • B&B • full brkfst • nonsmoking • kids/ dogs ok • WiFi • wheelchair access • $225-1,950

Stirling House B&B 104 Bay Ave, Greenport 631/477-0654, 800/551-0654 • gay-friendly • full brkfst • jacuzzi • nonsmoking • WiFi • gay-owned • $150-295

Sunset Beach 35 Shore Rd, Shelter Island 631/749-2001 • gay-friendly • seasonal • food served • $245-635

NIGHTCLUBS

620 Lounge 620 Waverly Ave, Patchouge 631/291-9737 • 9pm-4am Tue & from 10pm Fri gay nights • dancing/DJ

Bunkhouse 192 N Main St/ Montauk Hwy (at Foster Ave), Sayville 631/319-6808 • 8pm-4am • mostly gay men • dancing/DJ • karaoke • live shows • wheelchair access • gay-owned

RESTAURANTS

Babette's 66 Newtown Ln, East Hampton 631/329-5377 • seasonal • brkfst, lunch & dinner • healthy • plenty veggie • woman-owned

ENTERTAINMENT & RECREATION

Fowler Beach Southampton

Middletown

ACCOMMODATIONS

Best Western Inn at Hunt's Landing 120 Rtes 6 & 209, Matamoras, PA 570/491-2400, 800/528-1234 • gay-friendly • pool • gym • restaurant & bar • WiFi

Montgomery

ACCOMMODATIONS

The Borland House B&B 130 Clinton St 845/457-1513 • gay-friendly • full brkfst • nonsmoking • WiFi • $120-185

Mt Morris

BARS

Fred's Tavern 36 Main St (at State) 585/658-3267 • noon-2am • gay/ straight • neighborhood bar

NEW YORK CITY

New York City is divided into 9
geographical areas:
NYC—Overview
NYC—Soho, Greenwich & Chelsea
NYC—Downtown
NYC—Midtown
NYC—Uptown
NYC—Brooklyn
NYC—Queens
NYC—Bronx
NYC—Staten Island

NYC—Overview

INFO LINES & SERVICES

AA Gay/ Lesbian Intergroup at Lesbian/
Gay Community Center **212/647–1680**

Lesbian Herstory Archives 718/768–3953
• exists to gather & preserve records of lesbian
lives & activities • located in Park Slope,
Brooklyn • wheelchair access

LGBT Community Center 208 W 13th (at
7th Ave) **212/620–7310** • 9am-11pm •
popular • many group meetings & resources •
museum • wheelchair access

ACCOMMODATIONS

Manhattan Getaways 212/956–2010 • gay/
straight • B&B rooms & private apts
throughout Manhattan • kids over 10 years old
ok • woman-owned

NIGHTCLUBS

Kurfew • teen/ twink/ 18+ parties around the
city

**Sholay Productions/ Desilicious
212/713–5111** • monthly party • lesbians/ gay
men • Bollywood, bhangra & house music •
multiracial • call for dates

ENTERTAINMENT & RECREATION

**Before Stonewall: A Lesbian & Gay
History Tour** meet: Washington Square Arch
(at Big Onion Walking Tours) **212/439–1090**

Gotham Girls Roller Derby 888/830–2253
• NYC's female roller derby league

New York Liberty Madison Square Garden
New York **212/465–6766** • check out the
Women's Nat'l Basketball Association while
you're in New York

PUBLICATIONS

Gay City News 646/229–1890 • LGBT
newspaper • weekly

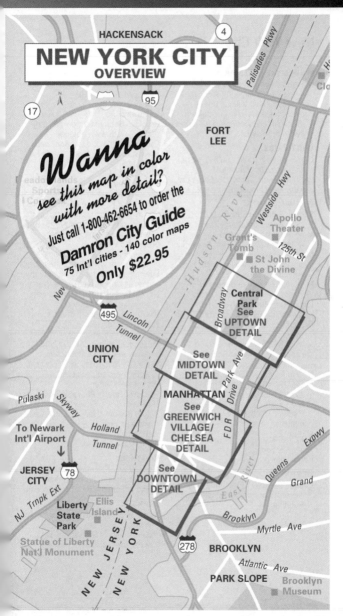

NEW YORK CITY
OVERVIEW

HACKENSACK · 4

17

95

FORT LEE

Wanna see this map in color with more detail?

Just call 1-800-462-6654 to order the

Damron City Guide

75 Int'l cities - 140 color maps

Only $22.95

Hudson River

Westside Hwy

Apollo Theater
125th St

Grant's Tomb
St John the Divine

Broadway

495 Lincoln Tunnel

UNION CITY

Central Park
See **UPTOWN DETAIL**

Park Ave

See **MIDTOWN DETAIL**

MANHATTAN

See **GREENWICH VILLAGE/ CHELSEA DETAIL**

FDR Drive

Pulaski Skyway

Holland Tunnel

To Newark Int'l Airport ↓

JERSEY CITY 78

NJ Trnpk Ext

Liberty State Park

Ellis Island

Statue of Liberty Nat'l Monument

See **DOWNTOWN DETAIL**

East River

Queens Expwy

Grand

Brooklyn

Myrtle Ave

278

BROOKLYN

Atlantic Ave

PARK SLOPE

Brooklyn Museum

NEW JERSEY · NEW YORK

New York City

WHERE THE GIRLS ARE:

Upwardly mobile literary types hang in the West Village, hipster dykes cruise the East Village, upper-crusty lesbians have cocktails in Midtown, and working-class dykes live in Brooklyn.

LGBT PRIDE:

Last Sunday in June. 212/807-7433, web: www.hopinc.org.

Brooklyn Pride - June. 718/670-3337, web: www.brooklynpride.org.

ANNUAL EVENTS:

March - Saint-at-Large Black Party, web: www.saintatlarge.com.

May - AIDS Walk 212/807-9255, web: www.aidswalk.net/newyork.

May/June - NewFest: NY LGBT Film Festival 212/571–2170, web: www.newfestival.org.

July - HOT Festival of queer performance, web: hotfestival.org.

July - Siren Music Festival, web: www.villagevoice.com/siren.

September - Howl Festival 212/243–3413, web: www.howlfestival.com. Poetry & cabaret in Tompkins Square Park in the East Village.

November - New York Lesbian/Gay Experimental Film/Video Fest 212/742–8880, web: www.mixnyc.org. Film, videos, installations & media performances.

CITY INFO:

212/484-1200. nycgo.com

BEST VIEW:

Coming over any of the bridges into New York or from the Empire State Building.

ATTRACTIONS:

American Museum of Natural History 212/769-5100, web: www.amnh.org.

Broadway.

Brooklyn Botanic Garden 718/623-7200, web: www.bbg.org.

Carnegie Hall 212/247-7800, web: www.carnegiehall.org.

Central Park.

Ellis Island, web: www.ellisisland.org.

Elizabeth A. Sackler Center for Feminist Art 718/638-5000, web: www.brooklynmuseum.org/eascfa.

Empire State Building 212/736-3100, web: www.esbnyc.com.

Greenwich Village.

Guggenheim Museum 212/423-3500, web: www.guggenheim.org.

International Center of Photography 212/857-0000, web: www.icp.org.

Lincoln Center 212/875-5000, web: www.lincolncenter.org.

Metropolitan Museum of Art 212/535-7710, web: www.metmuseum.org.

Museum of Modern Art 212/708-9400, web: www.moma.org.

Radio City Music Hall 212/307-7171, web: www.radiocity.com.

Rockefeller Center.

Statue of Liberty 866/782-8834.

Times Square.

United Nations 212/963-8687, web: www.un.org.

Wall Street.

World Trade Center Memorial.

WEATHER:

A spectrum of extremes with pleasant moments thrown in. Spring and fall are the best times to visit.

TRANSIT:

Wave an arm on any streetcorner for a taxi.

Public transit MTA 718/330-1234, web: www.mta.info

GO Magazine 888/466–9244 • the nation's most widely distributed, free, lesbian publication • "cultural road map for the city girl" • listings, features, entertainment, style, fitness & more

MetroSource 212/691–5127 • LGBT lifestyle magazine & resource directory

Next 212/627–0165 • entertainment & nightlife paper

PM Entertainment Magazine 516/845–0759 • events, listings, classifieds & more for Long Island, NJ & NYC

Velvetpark Magazine 347/881–1025, 888/616–1989 • quarterly lesbian/ feminist glossy w/ focus on the arts

Sex Clubs

Submit 718/789–4053 • monthly • women & trans play party • call for location

NYC—Soho, Greenwich & Chelsea

Accommodations

Abingdon Guesthouse 21 8th Ave (at W 12th St) 212/243–5384 • gay/ straight • quiet, mature clientele • nonsmoking • wheelchair access • $179-295

Ace Hotel 20 W 29th St (at Broadway) 212/679–2222 • gay-friendly • hip hotel near Flatiron District

Chelsea Inn 46 W 17th St (btwn 5th & 6th Aves) 212/645–8989, 800/640–6469 • gay/ straight • European-style inn • kids ok • $89-289

Chelsea Pines Inn 317 W 14th St (btwn 8th & 9th Aves) 212/929–1023, 888/546–2700 • gay/ straight • some shared baths • WiFi • gay-owned • $150-275

The Chelsea Savoy Hotel 204 W 23rd St (at 7th Ave) 212/929–9353, 866/929–9353 • gay/ straight • kids ok • WiFi • wheelchair access • $99-425

Chelsea Star Hotel 300 W 30th St (at 8th Ave) 212/ 244–7827, 877/ 827–6969 • gay/ straight • WiFi • $149-499

Crosby Street Hotel 79 Crosby St (at Spring) 212/226–6400 • gay-friendly • chic boutique hotel in Soho

Eventi 851 6th Ave (at 30th St) 212/564–4567, 866/996–8396 • gay-friendly • pets ok • $249+

➤ **The GEM Hotel Chelsea** 300 W 22nd St (at 8th Ave) 212/675–1911 • gay/ straight • WiFi • wheelchair access • see ad in front color section

➤ **The GEM Hotel SoHo** 135 E Houston St (btwn 1st & 2nd Aves) 212/358–8844 • gay/ straight • WiFi • wheelchair access • $149-499 • see ad in front color section

Gershwin Hotel 7 E 27th St (at 5th Ave) 212/545–8000 • gay-friendly • artsy, seedy hotel w/ model's floor dorms & rooms • art gallery • WiFi • $109+

Holiday Inn SOHO Downtown 138 Lafayette St (btwn Canal & Howard, in Chinatown) 212/966–8898 • gay-friendly • near SoHo, Chinatown & Little Italy • WiFi • $169-349

Hotel 17 225 E 17th St 212/475–2845 • gay-friendly • "East Village chic" budget hotel • shared baths • $100+

Incentra Village House 32 8th Ave (at W 12th St) 212/206–0007 • lesbians/ gay men • nonsmoking • WiFi • gay-owned • $169+

The Jane 113 Jane St (at Hudson River Pk) 212/924–6700 • gay/ straight • inspired by luxury train cabins • some shared baths • $69+

Mercer Hotel 147 Mercer St (at Prince St) 212/966–6060 • gay-friendly • food served • nonsmoking • WiFi • wheelchair access • $500+

Soho Grand Hotel 310 W Broadway (at Canal St) 212/965–3000, 800/965–3000 • gay-friendly • big, glossy, over-the-top hotel • WiFi • wheelchair access • $374+

The Standard Hotel 848 Washington St (at W 13th) 212/645–4646, 877/550–4646 • gay-friendly • ultra-modern, luxe hotel straddling the High Line

Tribeca Grand 2 Ave of the Americas 212/519–6600 • gay/ straight • WiFi • pets ok • $259+

W New York—Union Square 201 Park Ave S 212/253–9119 • gay/ straight • also restaurant & bar • WiFi • wheelchair access • $299-569

Washington Square Hotel 103 Waverly Pl (at MacDougal St) 212/777–9515, 800/222–0418 • gay-friendly • renovated 100-year-old hotel • also North Square restaurant & lounge • WiFi • $165+

Bars

Arrow Bar 85 Ave A (btwn 5th & 6th) 212/673–1775 • 4pm-close • gay/ straight • dancing/DJ • theme nights

Barracuda 275 W 22nd St (at 8th Ave) 212/645–8613 • 4pm-4am • popular • mostly gay men • live DJs • drag shows

Beauty Bar 213 E 14th St (at 3rd Ave) **212/539–1389** • 5pm-4am, from 7pm wknds • gay/ straight • dancing/DJ

The Boiler Room 86 E 4th St (at 2nd Ave) **212/254–7536** • 4pm-4am • popular • mostly gay men • neighborhood bar • WiFi

Boots and Saddle 76 Christopher St (at 7th Ave S) **212/633–1986** • noon-4am • mostly gay men • neighborhood bar • bears & leather crowd • multiracial clientele

Cake Shop 152 Ludlow St (btwn Stanton & Rivington) **212/253–0036** • 9am-2am, till 4am wknds • gay-friendly • vegan bakery by day, punk bands at night

Cubbyhole 281 W 12th St (at 4th St) **212/243–9041** • 4pm-4am, from 2pm wknds • lesbians/ gay men • neighborhood bar

Desire 45 W 8th St (btwn 5th & 6th Aves) **646/454–9950** • 3pm-close • mostly gay men • neighborhood bar • theme nights

Dusk 147 W 24th St (btwn 6th & 7th) **212/924–4490** • 5:30pm-close, from 7:30pm Sat, clsd Sun • gay/ straight • WiFi

Eastern Bloc 505 E 6th St (at Ave A) **212/777–2555** • 7pm-4am • popular • lesbians/ gay men • trendy lounge w/ DJ • go-go boys Th-Sat • wheelchair access

G Lounge 225 W 19th St (at 7th Ave) **212/929–1085** • 4pm-4am • popular • mostly gay men • lounge • live DJs • gay-owned

Gym Sports Bar 167 8th Ave (btwn 18th & 19th) **212/337–2439** • 4pm-close, from 1pm wknds • mostly gay men • neighborhood sports bar

Henrietta Hudson 438 Hudson (at Morton) **212/924–3347** • 4pm-4am, from 2pm wknds • mostly women • neighborhood bar • dancing/DJ • wheelchair access

Karma 51 1st Ave (btwn 3rd & 4th Sts) **212/677–3260** • 1pm-4am • gay/ straight • gay Tue night • hookah/ smoking bar

Marie's Crisis 59 Grove St (at 7th Ave) **212/243–9323** • 4pm-4am • lesbians/ gay men • piano bar from 9:30pm (from 5pm Fri-Sun)

The Monster 80 Grove St (at W 4th St, Sheridan Square) **212/924–3558** • 4pm-4am, from 2pm wknds • popular • mostly gay men • dancing/DJ • piano bar & cabaret • Sabor Latino Mon • disco Tue • T-dance Sun • wheelchair access

Mr Black 29 2nd Ave (at The Cock) • 11pm Fri only • mostly gay men • dancing/DJ

Nowhere 322 E 14th St (btwn 1st & 2nd) **212/477–4744** • 3pm-4am • lesbians/ gay men • transgender-friendly Th • neighborhood bar

Phoenix 447 E 13th (at Ave A) **212/477–9979** • 4pm-4am • lesbians/ gay men • neighborhood bar • patio

RF Lounge 531 Hudson St (at Charles St) **917/262–0836** • 4pm-2am, till 4am Th-Sat • mostly women

Stonewall Inn 53 Christopher St (at 7th Ave) **212/488–2705** • 1pm-4am • mostly gay men • neighborhood bar • dancing/DJ • drag shows

Vig 27 119 E 27th St (btwn Park & Lexington) **212/686–5500** • lesbians/ gay men • lounge • theme nights • food served

NIGHTCLUBS

Beige 40 E 4th St (at Bowery, at B-Bar) **212/475–2220** • 11pm Tue only • gay/ straight • swank lounge • garden

Big Apple Ranch 39 W 19th St, 5th flr (btwn 5th & 6th, at Dance Manhattan) **212/358–5752** • 8pm-1am Sat only • lesbians/ gay men • dancing/DJ • country/ western • two-step lessons • beer only • cover charge

The Box 189 Chrystie St (btwn Rivington & Stanton) **212/982–9301** • 11pm-close • gay/ straight • live shows • cabaret • transgender-friendly • cover charge

Creme de la Femme 30 E 16th St (at Union Square Lounge) • 8pm-3am Wed only, lounge around the eliptical stone fireplace at this upscale party for women

Happy Ending 302 Broome St (at Forsyth) **212/334–9676** • 7pm-4am, clsd Sun-Mon • gay/ straight • theme nights

Moments 116 MacDougal St (at Alibi, btwn 3rd & Bleecker) **917/608–5647** • 9pm-3am Mon only • mostly women • live entertainment • go-go dancers

Pyramid 101 Ave A (at 7th St) **212/228–4888** • lesbians/ gay men • 10pm-4am Fri for 1984 ('80s)

Rush 579 6th Ave (off 16th St) **212/243–6100** • open Wed-Sat • mostly gay men • young crowd • College Party Sat • dancing/DJ

Sea Tea leaves from Pier 40 (at Christopher St) **212/675–2971** • 6pm-10pm Sun (June-Oct) • mostly gay men • dancing/DJ • professional • multiracial • buffet • live shows • gay-owned • cover

Shescape • women only • dance parties held at various locations throughout NYC are • see www.shescape.com for info

Snapshot 35 E 35th St (at University Pl, at Bar 13) 212/254–9920 • Tue only • lesbians/gay men • dancing/DJ • younger crowd

Social Wednesdays 579 6th Ave (btwn 16th & 17th, at Club Rush) 718/832–1738 • 7pm-close Wed • mostly women • dancing/DJ • karaoke

Stiletto 363 W 16th St (at 9th Ave, at the Cabanas at Maritime Hotel) • 7pm-2am Sun only • mostly women • dancing/DJ • upscale party

Vandam 150 Varick St (btwn Spring & Vandam, at Greenhouse) 212/807–7000 • Sun only • mostly gay men • dancing/DJ • check out the club lighting

CAFES

Brown Cup Cafe 334 8th Ave (at 27th St) 212/675–7765 • 7am-7pm, 8am-6pm Sat, clsd Sun

RESTAURANTS

7A 109 Ave A (at 7th St) 212/673–6583 • 24hrs • popular • American

Agave 140 Seventh Ave (btwn 10th St & Charles) 212/989–2100 • noon-close • popular brunch • Southwestern

Angelica Kitchen 300 E 12th St (at 1st Ave) 212/228–2909 • 11:30am-10:30pm • vegetarian/vegan

Angon 320 E 6th (btwn 1st & 2nd Aves) 212/260–8229 • noon-11pm • Indian

Antica Venezia 396 West St (at W 10th St) 212/229–0606 • dinner nightly • Italian

ArtePasta 81 Greenwich Ave (at Bank St) 212/229–0234 • dinner nightly, Sun brunch • Italian

Awash 338 E 6th (btwn 1st & 2nd Aves) 212/982–9589 • 11am-11pm • Ethiopian

Bayard's Ale House 533 Hudson (at Charles) 212/989–0313 • lunch & dinner • Cajun • full bar

Benny's Burritos 93 Ave A (at 6th St) 212/254–2054 • 11am-midnight, till 1am Fri-Sat • cheap & huge • also 113 Greenwich (at Jane), 212/727-0584

Better Burger 178 Eighth Ave (at 19th St) 212/989–6688 • 11am-midnight • burgers, hot dogs, salads & more • plenty veggie

Blossom 187 9th Ave (at 21st) 212/627–1144 • lunch Fri-Sun, dinner nightly • gourmet vegan

Blue Ribbon 97 Sullivan St (at Spring St) 212/274–0404 • 4pm-4am • chef hangout • wheelchair access

Bone Lick Park 75 Greenwich Ave (at 7th Ave) 212/647–9600 • 11:30am-11pm • real pit BBQ • full bar • wheelchair access • gay-owned

Broadway East 171 E Broadway (btwn Rutgers & Jefferson) 212/228-3100 • mostly vegetarian • also wine bar & cafe • wheelchair access

Cola's 148 8th Ave (at 17th St) 212/633–8020 • lunch & dinner • popular • Italian • some veggie

Counter 105 1st Ave (at 7th St) 212/982–5870 • 4pm-midnight, 11am-1am wknds • vegan • '50s retro wine & martini bar • organic beer/wine • lesbian-owned

Cowgirl Hall of Fame 519 Hudson St (at W 10th) 212/633–1133 • lunch, dinner, wknd brunch

East of Eighth 254 W 23rd St (at 8th) 212/352–0075 • lunch & dinner, bar open late

Elmo 156 7th Ave (at 20th St) 212/337–8000 • lunch & dinner, also lounge

Empire Diner 210 10th Ave (at 22nd St) 212/243–2736 • 24hrs

Les Enfants Terribles 37 Canal St (at Ludlow) 212/777–7518 • 8am-4am • full bar • DJ • African/Moroccan, Brazilian, French

Garage 99 7th Ave S (at Grove St) 212/645–0600 • noon-3am • contemporary American • plenty veggie • live jazz

Gobo 401 Ave of the Americas (at W 8th) 212/255–3242 • 11:30am-11pm • vegetarian/vegan

Gonzo 140 W 13th St (btwn 6th & 7th Aves) 212/645–4606 • publisher's choice • 5pm-11pm, till midnight Fri-Sat, till 10:30pm Sun • great Tuscan menu • over 60 wines by the glass • full bar

I Coppi 432 E 9th St (at 1st Ave) 212/254–2263 • 5pm-11pm, 11am-3pm Sat-Sun

Intermezzo 202 8th Ave (at 21st St) 212/929–3433 • noon-midnight • Italian • great wknd brunch

Kate's Joint 58 Ave B (at 4th St) 212/777–7059 • 10am-11pm, till 1am Fri-Sat • vegetarian

LaVagna 545 E 5th St (btwn Aves A & B) 212/979–1005 • dinner only • Italian • some veggie

Life Cafe 343 E 10th St (at Ave B) 212/477–8791 • 10am-midnight, till 2am Fri-Sat • full bar • plenty veggie • artist hangout

Lips 2 Bank St (at Greenwich) **212/675-7710**
• 6pm-midnight, till 1:30am Fri-Sat, gospel
brunch noon-6pm Sun • "the Hard Rock Cafe
of drag" • Italian/American • served by queens

Lucky Cheng's 24 1st Ave (at 2nd St)
212/995-5500, 212/473-0516 • 5:30pm-
midnight • popular • Asian/fusion • full bar •
drag shows • karaoke

The Noho Star 330 Lafayette St (at
Bleecker) **212/925-0070** • 8am-midnight,
from 10:30am wknds • eclectic European &
Chinese

Omai 158 9th Ave (at 19th St) **212/633-0550**
• dinner nightly • Vietnamese

Philip Marie 569 Hudson St (at 11th St)
212/242-6200 • noon-11pm • New American
dining, outside seating

Sacred Chow 227 Sullivan St (btwn W 3rd St
& Bleecker) **212/337-0863** • 11am-10pm, till
11pm Fri-Sat • gourmet vegan • juice &
smoothie bar • baked goods • kosher •
wheelchair access

Sigiri 91 1st Ave (btwn 5th & 6th Sts)
212/614-9333 • lunch & dinner • Sri Lankan

Trattoria Pesce Pasta 262 Bleecker St (at
6th Ave) **212/645-2993** • noon-midnight

Tribeca Grill 375 Greenwich St (btwn N
Moore & Franklin) **212/941-3900** • popular •
lunch Sun-Fri, dinner nightly • chic
neighborhood restaurant co-owned by Robert
DeNiro • full bar • extensive wine list •
reservations recommended

Veselka 144 2nd Ave (at 9th St)
212/228-9682 • 24hrs • Ukrainian • great
pierogi

The Viceroy 160 8th Ave (at 18th St)
212/633-8484 • 11am-midnight, from 9am
wknds, till 1am Sat • popular • fusion • full bar

ENTERTAINMENT & RECREATION

Chelsea Classics 260 W 23rd St (btwn 7th &
8th, at Clearview Cinema) **212/691-5519** • Th
night only • drag diva Hedda Lettuce hosts
camp movies

Dixon Place 161 Chrystie St (at Delancey)
212/219-0736 • many gay-themed
productions • also HOT Festival of queer
performance in July

High Line enter on Gansevoort (at
Washington) **212/500-6035** • elevated train
track converted to beautiful urban park

La Mama 74 E 4th St **212/475-7710** •
experimental theater club

**Leslie/ Lohman Gay Art Foundation &
Gallery** 26 Wooster St **212/431-2609** • noon-
6pm, clsd Sun-Mon

PS 122 150 1st Ave (at E 9th St)
212/477-5829 • it's rough, it's raw, it's real
New York performance art

WOW Cafe Theatre 59-61 E 4th St, 4th flr
(btwn 2nd Ave & Bowery) **212/777-4280** •
open Th-Sat • women's theater

BOOKSTORES

Bluestockings Women's Bookstore 172
Allen St (btwn Stanton & Rivington)
212/777-6028 • 11am-11pm • also cafe •
nightly readings • performances • live music

RETAIL SHOPS

David Samuel Menkes Custom Leather
144 Fifth Ave #3 (at 19th St) **212/989-3706** •
custom leather • fetishwear

DeMask 144 Orchard St **212/466-0814** •
European fetish fashion

Flight 001 96 Greenwich Ave (btwn Jane &
12th) **212/989-0001, 877/354-4481** • 11am-
8pm, noon-6pm Sun • way cool travel gear

Rainbows & Triangles 192 8th Ave (at 19th
St) **212/627-2166** • 11am-10pm, noon-9pm
Sun • LGBT cards, books, gifts & more

Universal Gear 140 8th Ave (btwn 16th &
17th) **212/206-9119** • casual, club, athletic &
designer clothing

GYMS & HEALTH CLUBS

New York Sports Club 128 8th Ave (btwn
16th & 17th) **212/627-0065** • popular •
mostly gay men • day passes available

EROTICA

Babeland 43 Mercer St **212/966-2120** •
noon-10pm, till 11pm Wed-Sat

Babeland 94 Rivington (btwn Orchard &
Ludlow) **212/375-1701** • noon-10pm, till 6pm
Sun • owned by women

Pleasure Chest 156 7th Ave S (at Charles)
212/242-2158

NYC—Downtown

ACCOMMODATIONS

Best Western Seaport Inn 33 Peck Slip
(near Front St) **212/766-6600, 800/468-3569**
• gay-friendly • nonsmoking • WiFi •
wheelchair access • $250+

Embassy Suites Hotel New York City 102
North End Ave **212/945-0100, 877/692-4458**
• upscale all-suite hotel located on water in
downtown Manhattan • nonsmoking •
wheelchair access • $289+

Gild Hall Wall Street 15 Gold St (at Platt) **212/232–7700, 212/232–7800 (RESERVATIONS)** • gay/ straight • high-tech boutique hotel • also restaurant & lounge • wheelchair access • $199-469

Millenium Hilton 55 Church St **212/693–2001, 877/692–4458** • hotel close to all lower Manhattan's finest • pool • nonsmoking • wheelchair access • $189+

NIGHTCLUBS

Club Remix (LipStik Productions) Ladies Night 27 Park Pl (at Church & Broadway) **917/363–6907** • 10pm 1st Sat only • mostly women • dancing/DJ • multiracial • dress code

NYC—Midtown

ACCOMMODATIONS

Chambers Hotel 15 W 56th St (at 5th Ave) **212/974–5656, 866/204–5656** • gay-friendly • upscale boutique hotel • fabulous art collection

Distrikt Hotel 342 W 40th St (at 9th Ave) **646/831–6780** • gay-friendly • WiFi • upscale boutique hotel • $209+

Doubletree Guest Suites Times Square-New York City 1568 Broadway **212/719–1600, 877/692–4458** • all-suite hotel in heart of Times Square • nonsmoking • WiFi • wheelchair access • $265+

▶**The GEM Hotel Midtown West** 449 W 36th St (at 10th Ave) **212/967–7206** • gay/ straight • WiFi • wheelchair access • $149-499 • see ad in front color section

Hotel 57 130 E 57th St (at Lexington) **212/753–8841, 800/497–6028** • gay-friendly • upscale • nonsmoking • WiFi • wheelchair access • $295+

Hotel Grace 125 W 45th St (near Sixth Ave) **212/354–2323** • gay-friendly • swimming pool nonsmoking • WiFi • wheelchair access • $229-429

The Hotel Metro 45 W 35th St (at 5th Ave) **212/947–2500, 800/356–3870** • gay-friendly • art deco hotel • 1 block from Empire State Bldg • $175-550

Hudson Hotel 356 W 58th St (at 9th) **512/554–6000, 800/697–1791** • magical hotel w/ trendy bars

Ink48 653 11th Ave (at 48th St) • gay-friendly • WiFi • lux hotel in former printing house

Ivy Terrace 230 E 58th St **516/662–6862** • private studio rental • terrace • nonsmoking • women-owned • $245-300

The MAve 61 Madison Ave (at 27th St) **212/532-7373** • gay-friendly • $159+

The Pod Hotel 230 E 51st Street (near 2nd Ave) **212/355–0300, 800/742–5945** • gay-friendly • nonsmoking • WiFi • wheelchair access • compact rooms • rooftop lounge • $119+

The Strand 33 W 37th St **212/448–1024** • gay-friendly • WiFi • cont'l brkfst • $239+

Travel Inn 515 W 42nd St (at 10th Ave) **212/695–7171, 800/869–4630** • gay-friendly • outdoor pool • fitness center • wheelchair access • $125-200

W New York—The Tuscany 120 E 39th St **212/686–1600, 877/WHOTELS (RESERVATIONS ONLY)** • gay/ straight • WiFi • also Parisian-style cafe-bar • wheelchair access • $249-569

BARS

9th Avenue Saloon 656 9th Ave (at 46th St) **212/307–1503** • noon-4am • mostly gay men • neighborhood bar

Bar Centrale 324 W 46th St (at 8th Ave) **212/581–3130** • 5pm-close • gay/ straight • neighborhood bar • celebs a-plenty

Bar-tini Ultra Lounge 642 10th Ave (at 45th) **917/388–2897** • 4pm-4am • mostly gay men • theme nights

Don't Tell Mama 343 W 46th St (at 9th Ave) **212/757–0788** • 4pm-4am • popular • gay-friendly • young crowd • piano bar & cabaret • cover + 2 drink minimum for cabaret • call for shows

Evolve 221 E 58th St (at 2nd Ave) **212/355–3395** • 4pm-4am • mostly gay men • theme nights

HK Hell's Kitchen 523 9th Ave (at 39th St) **212/913–9092** • swank lounge • also restaurant • theme nights

The Ritz 369 W 46th St (btwn 8th & 9th Aves) **212/333–2554** • mostly gay men • dancing/DJ • great place for a drink pre- or post- theater

Therapy 348 W 52nd St (at 9th) **212/397–1700** • 5pm-4am • lesbians/ gay men • live shows • cabaret • food served

Uncle Charlie's 139 E 45th St (btwn 3rd & Lexington) **212/661–9097** • 4pm-4am • mostly gay men • mostly Asian • open mic Fri-Sun • karaoke • piano bar

Vlada 331 W 51st St **212/974–8030** • 4pm-3am, clsd Mon • mostly gay men • slick gay lounge

The Web 40 E 58th St (at Madison) 212/308–1546 • 4pm-close, from 8pm wknds • mostly gay men • dancing/DJ • mostly Asian American • go-go boys • theme nights

NIGHTCLUBS

Escuelita 301 W 39th St (at 8th Ave) 212/631–0588 • 10pm-5am Th-Sun • mostly gay men • more women Fri for Secret Fri • dancing/DJ • drag shows • Latino/a • cover • 18+

Girlnation 12 W 45th St (btwn 5th & 6th Ave) 212/391–8053 • 10pm Sat only • mostly women • popular lounge party • dancing/DJ • also restaurant

Jim Caruso's Cast Party 315 W 44th St (btwn 8th & 9th Aves, at Birdland) 212/581–3080 • 9:30pm-1am Mon only • popular • gay/ straight • live music • star-studded Broadway open mic & variety show

LoverGirl NYC 221 W 46th St (at 7th Ave) 212/252–3397 • 10:30pm-4am Sat • mostly women • dancing/DJ • multiracial • live shows • cover charge

RESTAURANTS

44 1/2 626 10th Ave (btwn 44 & 45) 212/399–4450 • 5:30pm-close, brunch wknds • wheelchair access • gay-owned

44 & X Hell's Kitchen 622 10th Ave (at 44th St) 212/977–1170 • lunch & dinner • American comfort food • wheelchair access • gay-owned

A Voce 41 Madison Ave (at 26th) 212/545–8555 • lunch Mon-Sat, dinner nightly • Sun brunch • Italian • reservations recommended

Bamboo 52 344 W 52nd St (btwn 8th & 9th Aves) 212/315–2777 • noon-4am, from 4pm Sun • sushi • also sake bar • garden

Bann 350 W 50th St (btwn 8th & 9th Aves) 212/582–4446 • lunch Mon-Fri, dinner nightly • Korean

Beacon 25 W 56th St (btwn 5th & 6th) 212/332–0500 • lunch & dinner, wknd brunch • open-fire cooking • also bar

Cafe Un Deux Trois 123 W 44th St (at Broadway) 212/354–4148 • noon-midnight, brunch wknds • popular • bistro

Country 90 Madison Ave (at 29th St) 212/889–7100 • brkfst, lunch & dinner • upscale American • reservations recommended

Market Cafe 496 9th Ave (at 38th St) 212/967–3892 • lunch & dinner, wknd brunch • great food • gay-owned

Rice 'N' Beans 744 9th Ave (at 50th St) 212/265–4444 • 11am-10pm, till 11pm Fri-Sat • Latin/ Brazilian • plenty veggie • beer/ wine

Vynl 754 9th Ave (at 51st St) 212/974–2003 • 11am-11pm, also bar

ENTERTAINMENT & RECREATION

Ars Nova 511 W 54th St (at 10th Ave) 212/977–1700 • many gay-themed productions

Empire State Building 350 5th Ave (btwn 33rd & 34th) • spectacular views of the city • visit day or night

Sex & the City Tour 5th Ave, in front of the Pulitzer Fountain (at 58th St) 212/209–3370 • 3 hours • reservations a must!

GYMS & HEALTH CLUBS

Club H Fitness 423 W 55th St (at 9th Ave) 212/245–5802

EROTICA

Come Again 353 E 53rd St (at 2nd Ave) 212/308–9394 • woman-owned erotica store

Eve's Garden 119 W 57th St #1201 (btwn 6th & 7th) 800/848–3837 • 11am-7pm, clsd Sun-Mon • women's sexuality boutique

NYC—Uptown

ACCOMMODATIONS

BB Lodges 1598 Lexington Ave (btwn 101st & 102nd) 917/345–7914 • gay/ straight • private rooms w/ private kitchens • nonsmoking • WiFi • gay-owned • $120-185

The Carlyle 35 E 76th St (at Madison Ave) 212/744–1600, 888/767–3966 • gay-friendly • on Madison Ave • full brkfst • sauna • massage • wheelchair access • $650-6,000

Country Inn the City W 77th St (at Broadway) 212/580–4183 • gay-friendly • studio apts in restored 1891 town house • nonsmoking • $210-375

The Harlem Flophouse 212/662–0678 • guesthouse • near Apollo Theatre • nonsmoking • kids ok • WiFi • $100-150

Harlem Renaissance House 212/226–1590 • gay/ straight • in heart of Harlem's Striver Row District • fully restored Stanford White town house • kids ok • nonsmoking • WiFi • gay-owned • $220+/ night, $1,250/ week

Hotel Newton 2528 Broadway 212/678–6500, 800/643–5553 • gay/ straight • hotel on Upper West Side • nearest to Columbia University • nonsmoking • kids ok • wheelchair access • $150-350

BARS

Brandy's Piano Bar 235 E 84th St (at 2nd Ave) 212/650-1944 • 4pm-4am • lesbians/ gay men • piano bar

Cava Wine Bar 185 W 80th St (at Amsterdam) 212/724-2282 • 5:30pm-2am, from 3:30pm Sun • gay-friendly • also tapas

Suite 992 Amsterdam (at 109th St) 212/222-4600 • 5pm-4am • mostly gay men • friendly neighborhood bar • karaoke • drag shows

RESTAURANTS

Billie's Black 271 W 119th St (btwn St Nicholas Ave & Frederick Douglass Blvd) 212/280-2248 • noon-midnight, till 4am Fri-Sat • soul food • also full bar • live music Th-Fri • karaoke • gay-owned

Orbit East Harlem 2257 1st Ave E (at E 116th St) 212/348-7818 • dinner nightly, Sun brunch • creative cuisine • full bar • live jazz & blues • karaoke • reservations recommended

NYC—Brooklyn

INFO LINES & SERVICES

Audre Lorde Project 85 S Oxford St 718/596-0342 • noon-6pm Mon & Fri, noon-9pm Tue-Th, 11:30pm-7pm Sat, clsd Sun • LGBT center for people of color • transgender welcoming • events • resources • HIV services

ACCOMMODATIONS

The Loralei B&B 667 Argyle Rd (at Foster Ave) 646/228-4656 • gay/ straight • 3-story Victorian • nonsmoking • WiFi • gay-owned • $125-165

South Slope Green B&B 452A 17th St (at 8th Ave) 347/721-6575 • gay/ straight • nonsmoking • WiFi • lesbian-owned • $140

BARS

The Abbey 536 Driggs Ave (btwn N 7th & 8th), Williamsburg 718/599-4400 • 3pm-4am • gay/ straight • neighborhood bar • dancing/DJ

Alligator Lounge 600 Metropolitan Ave (at Lorimer) 718/599-4440 • 3pm-4am • gay/ straight • free pizza from 6pm • karaoke Th

Bar 4 444 7th Ave (at 15th St, in Park Slope) 718/832-9800 • 6pm-4am • gay/ straight • neighborhood bar • DJ Fri-Sat • live music & performances

Belleville Bistro & Lounge 330 5th St (at 5th Ave) 718/832-9777 • lesbians/ gay men • lounge • theme nights • also restaurant • gay-owned

Blackout Bar 916 Manhattan Ave (at Kent St, Greenpoint) • gay/ straight • gay night Wed • hipster hangout • dancing/DJ

Excelsior 390 5th Ave (btwn 6th & 7th) 718/832-1599 • 6pm-4am, from 2pm wknds • lesbians/ gay men • patio

Ginger's Bar 363 5th Ave (btwn 5th & 6th Sts, in Park Slope) 718/788-0924 • 5pm-4am, from 2pm wknds • lesbians/ gay men • neighborhood bar • patio • occasional live shows

Kili 81 Hoyt St (btwn State & Atlantic) 718/855-5574 • 5pm-4am • popular • gay/ straight • neighborhood bar • live entertainment • funky local bar • acoustic music

Metropolitan 559 Lorimer St (at Metropolitan Ave), Williamsburg 718/599-4444 • 3pm-4am • lesbians/ gay men • comfy neighborhood bar w/ 2 fireplaces • more women Wed

R Bar 451 Meeker Ave (Graham Ave) 646/523-1813 • 5pm-close • gay-friendly • more gay Tue • neighborhood bar

Sugarland 221 N 9th St (at Driggs Ave) 718/599-4044 • 8pm-4am, from 4pm wknds • gay/ lesbian • dancing/DJ • live shows • karaoke

Superfine 126 Front St (at Pearl St) 718/243-9005 • 11:30am-4am, clsd Mon • gay/ straight • popular among hip lesbians • relaxed atmophere • live shows • also bar • lesbian-owned

NIGHTCLUBS

249 Bar & Lounge 249 4th Ave (btwn President & Carroll) 718/230-5740 • 6pm-2am Th, till 4am Fri-Sat, from 4pm Sun • lesbians/ gay men • dancing/DJ • multiracial • theme nights

Club Langston 1073 Atlantic Ave (btwn Franklin & Classon) 718/622-5183 • 4pm-4am • gay/ straight • theme nights

Glasslands Gallery 289 Kent Ave, Williamsburg (btwn S 1st & S 2nd) 718/599-1450 • performance, art & dance space

Gumbo 16 Main St (at Water St, at Galapagos Art Space) 718/222-8500 • 8pm 3rd Th only • lesbians/ gay men • dancing/DJ

Laid 125 5th Ave (btwn Sterling & St Johns, at Southpaw, in Brooklyn) 718/230-0236 • lesbians/ gay men • all-inclusive monthly queer dance party • transgender-friendly

Milk & Sugar 149 7th St (btwn 2nd & 3rd Aves, at Bell House) • 11pm 2nd Sat • lesbians/ gay men • dancing/DJ

Secret Faggot 289 Kent St (at the Glasslands, Williamsburg) • lesbians/ gay men • transgender-friendly • occasional freaky queer dance party

That's My Jam rotates btwn locations in Brooklyn • lesbians/ gay men • queer monthly dance party • check local listings for location

CAFES

Jacques Torres 66 Water St 718/875–9772 • 9am-7pm, 10am-6pm Sun • chocolatier

Outpost 1014 Fulton St (at Downing) 718/636–1260 • 8am-10:30pm, from 9am wknds • lesbians/ gay men • art gallery • young, artsy crowd • also beer/ wine • gay-owned

RESTAURANTS

Alma 187 Columbia St (at Degraw) 718/643–5400 • dinner nightly, wknd brunch • upscale Mexican • outdoor rooftop seating w/ view of Manhattan • also B61 Bar downstairs

Aunt Suzie 247 5th Ave (at Garfield Pl) 718/788–2868 • dinner only • Italian

Beast 638 Bergen St (at Vanderbilt Ave) 718/399–6855 • dinner nightly, wknd brunch, also bar from 5pm

Bogota Latin Bistro 141 5th Ave (at St John's Pl) 718/230–3805 • dinner nightly, wknd brunch, clsd Tue • live music • gay-owned

ChipShop/ The Curry Shop 383 5th Ave (at 6th St) 718/244–7746 • noon-10pm, till 11pm Th-Sat, from 11am wknds • English/ Indian • home of the famous fried Twinkie!

Faan 209 Smith St (at Baltic) 718/694–2277 • lunch & dinner • pan-Asian • also bar downstairs

Home Made 293 Van Brunt St (btwn Pioneer & King, at Home Made) 347/223–4135 • dinner & wknd brunch • women-owned

Johnny Mack's 1114 8th Ave (btwn 11th & 12th) 718/832–7961 • 4pm-11pm, till midnight Fri-Sat, Sun brunch

Melt 440 Bergen St (btwn 5th & Flatbush) 718/230-5925

Nita Nita 146 Wythe Ave (at N 8th) 718/388–5328 • 4pm-midnight, brunch wknds • also full bar • tapas

Santa Fe Grill 62 7th Ave (at Lincoln) 718/636–0279 • 5pm-close, from noon wknds • also bar

Tandem 236 Troutman St (btwn Wilson & Knickerbocker, in Bushwick) 718/386–2369 • 6pm-4am • also full bar • occasional gay parties

ENTERTAINMENT & RECREATION

The Elizabeth A Sackler Center for Feminist Art 200 Eastern Pkwy (at the Brooklyn Museum, at Washington Ave) 718/638–5000

EROTICA

Babeland 462 Bergen St (at 5th Ave) 718/638–3820

NYC—Queens

BARS

Albatross 36-19 24th Ave (at 37th), Astoria 718/204–9045 • 6pm-4am • gay/ straight • neighborhood bar • more gay wknds • gay-owned

Hell Gate Social 12-21 Astoria Blvd (at 14th St) 718/204–8313 • 7pm-4am • gay/ straight • dancing/DJ

Hombres Lounge 85-25 37th Ave #206, Jackson Heights 718/930–0886 • mostly gay men • neighborhood bar

Los Recuerdos 79-15 Roosevelt Ave (btwn 79th & 80th Sts, Jackson Hts) • 4pm-4am • mostly gay men • neighborhood bar • dancing/DJ • multiracial

Mix Cafe 40-17 30th Ave (at 41st St, Astoria) 347/642–4840 • 6pm-2am, noon-4am wknds • lesbians/ gay men • dancing/DJ • karaoke • theme nights • brunch wknds

Music Box 40–08 74th St (at Roosevelt Ave), Jackson Hts 718/424–8612 • 4pm-4am • mostly gay men • mostly Latino • drag shows • theme nights

NIGHTCLUBS

Bum Bum Bar 6314 Roosevelt Ave 718/651–4145 • 10pm-4am Th-Sun • mostly women • dancing/DJ • mostly Latina

Club Atlantis 76–19 Roosevelt Ave (at 77th St), Jackson Hts 718/457–3939 • 4pm-4am • lesbians/ gay men • dancing/DJ • mostly Latino/a • drag shows

Xcentric 34-01 36th Ave (at 34th St, Astoria) • 7pm-4am, clsd Mon • lesbians/ gay men • drag shows • theme nights

RESTAURANTS

Mezzo Mezzo 31-29 Ditmars Blvd **718/278-0444** • 11am-1am, till 2am Th-Sun • Greek

Mundo Cafe 31-18E Broadway (at 32nd St), Astoria **718/777-2829** • 5pm-11:30pm • Mediterranean/Turkish • plenty veggie

NYC—Bronx

BARS

Nina's Lounge 3159 Bruckner Blvd (at Waterbury) **646/201-1983** • 10pm-4am Th-Sun • mostly women • neighborhood bar • dancing/DJ • lesbian-owned

No Parking 4168 Broadway (at 177th St) **212/923-8700** • 6pm-3am, from 7pm Sat-Sun • lesbians/gay men • swank lounge

NIGHTCLUBS

Temptation Thursday 26 Bruckner Blvd (btwn Lincoln & Alexander, at The Gallery) **347/688-4251** • 9pm-4am Th only • mostly women • dancing/DJ • multiracial

NYC—Staten Island

NIGHTCLUBS

Q s.i.n.y. 632 Midland Ave • lesbians/gay men • dancing/DJ • also restaurant

Nyack

NIGHTCLUBS

Barz 327 Rte 9 W **845/353-4444** • 8pm-4am, from 3pm Sun, clsd Mon • lesbians/gay men • dancing/DJ • alternative • male dancers • karaoke

Orange County

RESTAURANTS

Gigi's Folderol 795 Rte 284, Westtown **845/726-3822** • 5pm-close, clsd Tue-Wed • French/farmhouse • some veggie • piano Fri-Sat • wheelchair access

EROTICA

Exotic Gifts & Videos 658 Rte 211 E (exit 120, off Rte 17), Middletown **845/692-6664**

Rochester

INFO LINES & SERVICES

Gay Alliance of the Genesee Valley (GAGV) 875 E Main St, 5th flr **585/244-8640** • events • education • youth services

ACCOMMODATIONS

Silver Waters Bed & Breakfast 8420 Bay St (at Lummis), Sodus Point **315/483-8098** • gay/straight • full brkfst • gay-owned • $75-125

BARS

140 Alex Bar & Grill 140 Alexander St (at Broadway) **585/256-1000** • 4pm-2am, from 2pm Sun • lesbians/gay men • neighborhood bar • also restaurant • dancing/DJ • live shows • karaoke • drag shows • gay-owned

Avenue Pub 522 Monroe Ave (at Goodman) **585/244-4960** • 4pm-2am • popular • mostly gay men • neighborhood bar • dancing/DJ • patio

NIGHTCLUBS

Tilt Nightclub 444 Central Ave **585/232-8440** • 10pm-2am Th & Sat only • lesbians/gay men • dancing/DJ • drag shows

Vertex 169 N Chestnut St **585/232-5498** • 10pm-2am Wed-Sat • gay/straight • dancing/DJ • goth club

CAFES

Little Theatre Cafe 240 East Ave **585/258-0412** • 5pm-10pm, till 11pm Fri-Sat, till 8pm Sun • popular • beer/wine • soups • salads • live jazz • wheelchair access • art gallery

RESTAURANTS

The Grill at Union Hill Country Store 1891 Ridge Rd, Webster **585/265-4443** • 6am-9pm, 7am-2pm Sun

RETAIL SHOPS

Equal Grounds 750 South Ave (at Caroline) **585/242-7840** • 7am-midnight, from 10am Sat-Sun • LGBT gifts & books • also coffeehouse

Outlandish 274 N Goodman St (in the Village Gate) **585/760-8383** • 11am-9pm, noon-5pm Sun • videos • pride items • books • toys • gay-owned

PUBLICATIONS

Empty Closet **585/244-8640** • LGBT newspaper • resource listings

Saratoga Springs

ACCOMMODATIONS

The Inn at Round Lake 14 Covel Ave (at Burlington), Round Lake **513/289-5018** • gay-friendly • Victorian B&B in quaint village btwn Albany & Saratoga Springs • pool • nonsmoking • WiFi • gay-owned • $129-359

The Mansion 801 Rte 29, Rock City Falls 518/885–1607, 888/996–9977 • gay-friendly • 1860 Victorian mansion • full brkfst • fireplaces • nonsmoking • wheelchair access • gay-owned • $129-450

Saratoga B&B/ Saratoga Motel 434 Church St 518/584–0920 • gay-friendly • B&B in 1850 farmhouse & motel • full brkfst • fireplaces • nonsmoking • gay-owned • $159-289

BARS

Desperate Annie's 12 Caroline St (off Broadway) 518/587–2455 • 4pm-close • gay-friendly • neighborhood bar

RESTAURANTS

Esperanto 6 1/2 Caroline St (off Broadway) 518/587–4236 • 11am-close • doughboys!

Little India 60 Court St 518/583–4151 • lunch & dinner • tasty & authentic Indian food • beer/ wine only

Seneca Falls

RETAIL SHOPS

WomanMade Products 91 Fall St 315/568–9364 • 10am-6pm, till 4pm wknds • lesbian & feminist T-shirts • crafts

Sharon Springs

ACCOMMODATIONS

American Hotel 192 Main St 518/284–2105 • gay/ straight • 1847 Nat'l Register hotel • kids ok • also restaurant & bar • WiFi • wheelchair access • gay-owned • $130-215

Cobblescote on the Lake 6515 State Hwy 80, Cooperstown 607/437–1146 • gay-friendly • spectacular views at this totally refurbished & impeccably manicured waterfront resort • food served • gay-owned • $155-245

Edgefield 153 Washington St 518/284–3339 • gay/ straight • full brkfst • nonsmoking • well-appointed English Country house • gay-owned • $135-205 (double)

The TurnAround Spa Lodge 105 Washington St 518/284–9708, 212/628–9008 • lesbians/ gay men • small hotel & health spa • full brkfst • hot tub • food served • nonsmoking • kids ok • clsd Nov-May • lesbian- & gay-owned • $45-85

RETAIL SHOPS

The Finishing Touch 197 Main St (Rte 10) 518/284–2884 • call for hours • gallery & gift shop

Syracuse

INFO LINES & SERVICES

AA Gay/ Lesbian 315/463–5011 (AA#) • call for meeting schedule

ACCOMMODATIONS

B&B Wellington 707 Danforth St (at Carbon) 315/474–3641, 800/724–5006 • gay-friendly • full brkfst wknds • kids ok • nonsmoking • WiFi • $115-160

Yellow Lantern Kampground 1770 Rte 13 N, Cortland 607/756–2959 • gay-friendly • kids/ pets ok • pool • short drive from Syracuse or Ithaca • 205 campsites & RV hookups • $23-28

BARS

Rain Lounge 218 N Franklin St (at Herald Pl) 315/474–3487 • 4pm-2am • mostly gay men • neighborhood bar • multiracial • transgender-friendly • videos • gay-owned

Sugarpearl Espresso Bar & Lounge 600 Burnet Ave (at N Crouse) 315/422–7427 • 7am-10pm • gay-friendly • food served • live shows • lesbian-owned

X Bar 205 N West St (at W Genessee) 315/471–9279 • 3pm-2am, 5pm-1am Mon-Tue • lesbians/ gay men • dancing/DJ wknds in summer • neighborhood bar • live shows

NIGHTCLUBS

The Mystic 1203 Milton Ave 315/218–5897 • 7pm-2am, clsd Mon • lesbians/gay men • also Mexican food

Trexx 319 N Clinton St (exit 18, off Rte 81) 315/474–6408 • 8pm-2am, till 4am Fri-Sat, clsd Sun-Wed • mostly gay men • dancing/DJ • drag shows Sun • videos • 18+ • wheelchair access

RESTAURANTS

Cafe Mira 14 Main St, Adams 315/232–4470 • open 5pm Wed-Sat • wheelchair access • lesbian-owned

BOOKSTORES

The Lavender Inkwell Bookshoppe 304 N McBride St 315/424–7191 • 11am-6pm, till 7pm Th-Sat, 11am-3pm Sun • LGBT

Utica

NIGHTCLUBS

That Place 216 Bleecker St (at Genesee) • 9pm-2am Wed-Sat • popular • mostly gay men • dancing/DJ • young crowd • wheelchair access

RESTAURANTS

The Hadley 2008 Genesee St (at Arnold Ave) 315/507–4265 • 11am-10pm, clsd Sun • also bar • pianist Fri-Sat • wheelchair access • gay-owned

Watertown

BARS

Clueless 545 Arsenal St 315/782–9006 • 8pm-2am Th-Sat • mostly gay men • neighborhood bar • dancing/DJ • videos

White Plains

INFO LINES & SERVICES

The LOFT 252 Bryant Ave 914/948–2932, 914/948–4922 (HELPLINE) • LGBT community center • call for hours • also newsletter

Westchester Lesbian Connection 914/517–5455, 914/949–3203

NORTH CAROLINA

Statewide

PUBLICATIONS

Q Notes 704/531–9988 • bi-weekly LGBT newspaper for the Carolinas

Asheville

includes Black Mountain

INFO LINES & SERVICES

Lambda AA 9 Swan St 828/254–8539 (AA#), 800/524–0465 • 7pm Mon

ACCOMMODATIONS

1889 WhiteGate Inn & Cottage 173 E Chestnut St 828/253–2553, 800/485–3045 • popular • gay/ straight • luxury, full-service B&B • 3-course brkfst • nonsmoking • WiFi • gay-owned • $219-279

27 Blake Street 27 Blake St 828/252–7390 • mostly women • romantic room w/ private entrance in Victorian home • gardens • Southern hospitality • nonsmoking • woman-owned • $80

A Bird's Nest Bed & Kitchen 41 Oak Park Rd 828/713–0141, 800/770-9055 • lesbians/ gay men • kids ok • nonsmoking • lesbian-owned • $135+

Biltmore Village Inn 119 Dodge St (at Irwin) 828/274-8707, 866/274-8779 • gay-friendly • luxury B&B near Biltmore Estate • mtn views • nonsmoking • WiFi • gay-owned • $220-325

Bittersweet Cottage 458 Elk Mountain Scenic Hwy (at Beaverdam Rd) 828/712–2414 • gay/ straight • 2 1-bdrm cottages • nonsmoking • WiFi • gay-owned • $195-295

Compassionate Expressions Mtn Inn & Healing Sanctuary 828/683–6633 • mostly women • cabins & rooms w/ a view of Blue Ridge Mtns • spa services • hot tub • on 40 acres • nonsmoking • wheelchair access • lesbian-owned • $90-120

Heron Cabin 828/216-4100 • gay/ straight • nonsmoking • lesbian-owned • $99 (3-night minimum)

Lofty Notions Campsite 828/287–0069 • lesbians/ gay men • 1 campsite overlooking waterfall • SE of Asheville • pool • kids ok • lesbian-owned • $200/ week

Mountain Laurel B&B 139 Lee Dotson Rd, Fairview 828/628–9903, 828/712–6289 (CELL) • lesbians/ gay men • 25 miles from Asheville • full brkfst • nonsmoking • kids ok • WiFi • lesbian-owned • $80-100

North Lodge on Oakland B& B 84 Oakland Rd (at Victoria Rd) 828/252–6433, 800/252–3602 • gay-friendly • nonsmoking • WiFi • gay-owned • $105-180

Rainbows End 23 Deaver St (at Reynolds) 253/732–0458 • mostly women • guest room in private home • shared baths • lesbian-owned • $45-55

The Tree House 190 Tessie Ln, Black Mountain 828/669–3889 • mostly women • transgender-friendly • guesthouse • fireplace • nonsmoking • lesbian/ trans-owned • $50-90

BARS

LaRue's Backdoor 237 Haywood St 828/252–1014 • 8pm-2am Wed-Sat only • lesbians/ gay men • neighborhood bar • drag shows • private club

O Henry's/ Straps 237 Haywood St 828/254–1891 • 2pm-2am • gay/ straight • neighborhood bar • also Straps leather bar Fri-Sat

Tressa's 28 Broadway 828/254–7072 • 4pm-2:30am, from 6pm Sat, clsd Sun-Mon • gay/ straight • jazz/ cigar bar • dancing/DJ • live shows

NIGHTCLUBS

Club Hairspray 38 N French Broad Ave (at Patton Ave) 828/258–2027 • 8pm-2am, clsd Sun • lesbians/ gay men • neighborhood bar • drag shows • game room • patio

Fred's Speakeasy 122 College St
828/281-0920 • 4:30pm-2am, till midnight
Tue, clsd Sun-Mon • gay-friendly • karaoke •
live music venue/ dive bar

Scandals 11 Grove St (at Patton)
828/252-2838 • 10pm-3am Th-Sun •
lesbians/ gay men • 4 bars • 3 dance floors •
dancing/DJ • drag shows • videos • 18+ •
private club • wheelchair access

CAFES

Laurey's 67 Biltmore Ave **828/252-1500** •
8am-6pm, till 4pm Sat, clsd Sun • popular •
bright cafe w/ "low-key" brkfst, delicious salads
& cookies • also dinners to go • lesbian-
owned • wheelchair access

RESTAURANTS

Barley's Taproom & Pizzeria 42 Biltmore
828/255-0504 • 11:30am-midnight, till 1am
Fri-Sat, noon-11pm Sun, bar open later • live
jazz, bluegrass & Americana

Charlotte Street Grill & Pub 157 Charlotte
St **828/253-5348, 828/252-2948** • lunch &
dinner Mon-Sat, full bar noon-2am daily •
some veggie • lesbian-owned

Early Girl Eatery 8 Wall St **828/259-9292** •
brkfst & lunch daily, dinner Tue-Sat, wknd
brunch • Southern • local ingredients

Firestorm Cafe & Books 48 Commerce St
828/255-8115 • 10am-11pm, clsd Sun •
vegetarian • also cafe & bookstore • WiFi •
events

Laughing Seed Cafe 40 Wall St (at
Haywood) **828/252-3445** • 11:30am-9pm, till
10pm Fri-Sat, Sun brunch from 10am, clsd Tue
• vegetarian/ vegan • beer/ wine • patio •
wheelchair access

Table 48 College St **828/254-8980,
828/254-8983** • 11am-2:30pm & 5:30pm-
11pm, Sun brunch, clsd Tue • moderately
priced New American

Tupelo Honey Cafe 12 College St
828/255-4404 • 9am-3pm daily & 5:30pm-
close Tue-Sun • "Southern homecookin' w/ an
uptown twist" • woman-owned

BOOKSTORES

Downtown Books & News 67 N Lexington
Ave (btwn Walnut & Hiawassee)
828/253-8654 • 8am-6pm, till 8pm Fri-Sat •
used books & new magazines • LGBT section

Malaprop's Bookstore/ Cafe 55 Haywood
St (at Walnut) **828/254-6734, 800/441-9829** •
9am-9pm, till 7pm Sun

Montford's Books 31 Montford Ave
828/285-8805 • 10am-7pm, till 8pm Fri-Sat,
noon-5pm Sun • used books

Asheville

ANNUAL EVENTS:
July - Folkmoot NC International
Festival (world cultural heritage
celebration) 828/452-2997 or
877/365-5872, web: www.folk-
mootusa.org.
July - Bele Chere (music & arts festival) 828/259-5800, web:
www.belecherefestival.com.

CITY INFO:
828/258-6101, web: www.ashevil-
lechamber.org.

ATTRACTIONS:
Biltmore Estate 800/624-1575,
web: www.biltmore.com.
Blue Ridge Parkway.
North Carolina Arboretum 828/665-
2492, web:
www.ncarboretum.org.

WEATHER:
Gorgeous: temperate summers and
mild winters, with a beautiful
spring and fall.

TRANSIT:
New Bluebird Taxi 828/258-8331.
Sky Shuttle 828/253-0006, web:
www.ashevillelimousine.com.
Asheville Transit System
828/253-5691, web:
www.ashevilletransit.com.

RETAIL SHOPS

Jewels That Dance: Jewelry Design 63 Haywood St **828/254–5088** • 10:30am-6pm, clsd Sun • gay-owned

PUBLICATIONS

Stereotypd **828/505–2870** • LGBT newspaper for NC & SC

EROTICA

BedTyme Stories 2334 Hendersonville Rd, Arden **828/684–8250**

Va Va Voom 36 Battery Park Ave **828/254–6329** • women's lingerie, toys, etc

Atlantic Beach

ACCOMMODATIONS

Palm Suites of Atlantic Beach 602 W Ft Macon Rd **252/247–6400, 800/972–3297** • gay-friendly • rental condos near beach • pool • nonsmoking • kids ok • wheelchair access • $95-199

Blowing Rock

ACCOMMODATIONS

Blowing Rock Victorian Inn 242 Ransom St (at US 321) **828/295–0034** • gay-friendly • B&B • full brkfst • jacuzzis • pets ok • nonsmoking • WiFi • gay-owned • $159-289

Maple Lodge 152 Sunset Dr **828/295–3331, 866/795–3331** • gay/ straight • WiFi • pets ok • nonsmoking • lesbian-owned

Boone

ACCOMMODATIONS

Beech Mountaintop Villa Beech Mtn Pkwy, Beech Mountain **865/522–8547** • gay-friendly • condo • highest resort east of the Rockies • panoramic views • pool • nonsmoking • WiFi • $695-995/ week

Brevard

ACCOMMODATIONS

Ash Grove Resort Cabins & Camping 749 E Fork Rd **828/885–7216** • gay/ straight • camping & cabins • on 14 wooded acres in Blue Ridge Mtns • hot tub • nonsmoking • WiFi • gay-owned • $100-145 (cabins), $22-45 (camping)

Burnsville

ACCOMMODATIONS

Cabin Branch **828/628–0005** • gay/ straight • nonsmoking • gay-owned • $100-125, $700/ wk

Chapel Hill

see Raleigh/Durham/Chapel Hill

Charlotte

INFO LINES & SERVICES

Acceptance Group Gay/ Lesbian AA 1991 Queens Rd (at church) **704/377–0244, 877/233–6853** • 8pm Fri

The Lesbian/ Gay Community Center 820 Hamilton St #B11 (at Seaboard St) **704/333–0144** • 5pm-8pm Tue-Th, 10am-1pm Fri-Sat, clsd Sun-Mon

ACCOMMODATIONS

Doubletree Guest Suites Charlotte/ South Park 6300 Morrison Blvd **704/364–2400, 800/222–8733** • gay-friendly • all-suite hotel • pool • fitness room • pets/ kids ok • $129-219

Four Points by Sheraton 315 E Woodlawn Rd (at Old Pineville Rd) **704/522–0852** • gay/ straight • fitness center • sundeck • outdoor pool • kids ok • WiFi • $129-229

The Morehead Inn 1122 E Morehead St (at Berkeley Ave) **704/376–3357, 888/667–3432** • gay-friendly • antique-filled suites in historic neighborhood • full brkfst • kids ok • WiFi • wheelchair access • $150-299

VanLandingham Estate 2010 The Plaza (at Belvedere) **704/334–8909, 888/524–2020** • gay-friendly • bungalow-style estate • on Nat'l Historic Register • full brkfst • nonsmoking • WiFi • gay-owned • $140-239

BARS

The Bar At 316 316 Rensselaer Ave (at South Blvd) **704/910–1478** • 5pm-2am, from 3pm Sun • popular • lesbians/ gay men • neighborhood bar • theme nights • 2 flrs • private club

Hartigan's Irish Pub 601 S Cedar St (at W Hill St) **704/347–1841** • 11am-10pm, till 2am wknds, from 6pm Sun • gay/ straight • neighborhood bar • dancing/DJ Fri-Sat • country-western • live shows • food served • popular lesbian hangout • gay-owned

Morehead Street Tavern 300 E Morehead St (btwn South Blvd & S Tryon) **704/334-2655** • 11:30am-2am, from 5pm Sun • gay-friendly • neighborhood bar • dancing/DJ Sat • live music • food served • 18+ Sat

Petra's Piano Bar 1917 Commonwealth Ave (at Thomas) **704/332-6608** • 7pm-2am, clsd Mon • gay/ straight • piano/ cabaret

Sidelines Sports Bar & Billiards 4544-C South Blvd (at Woodlawn) **704/525-2608** • 4pm-2am, from noon Sat-Sun • gay-friendly • neighborhood bar • food served • video • private club • wheelchair access • gay-owned

Wine Up 3306 N Davidson St (at E 36th St) **704/372-2633** • gay/ straight • neighborhood bar • poetry readings, open mic & live music • frequent LGBT events • multiracial

The Woodshed 4000 Queen City Dr (at Little Rock) **704/394-1712** • 5pm-2am, from 3pm Sun • mostly men • neighborhood bar • leather • private club • food served • wheelchair access

Nightclubs

The Closet 1202 Charlottetown Ave (at Park Dr) **704/375-1777** • 9pm-close Fri-Sat only • lesbians/ gay men • dancing/DJ • private club

Dammit Janet 3746 N Davidson St (btwn E Craighead & E Sugar) • gay/ straight • more gay Sun • dancing/DJ • 70's dance club

Halo 820 Hamilton St (at Seaboard St) **704/332-4256** • 10pm-2am Th-Sat • gay-friendly • dancing/DJ

The Nickel Bar 2817 Rozzelles Ferry Rd (at Judson Ave) **704/392-3225** • 9pm-2am, from 5pm Sun, clsd Mon-Wed • lesbians/ gay men • dancing/DJ • mostly African American

Scorpio's 2301 Freedom Dr (at Berryhill Rd) **704/373-9124** • 9pm-3am Wed & Fri-Sun • lesbians/ gay men • dancing/DJ • multiracial • videos • 18+ • private club • also Diva's show bar • wheelchair access

Tremont Music Hall 400 W Tremont Ave (at Tryon) **704/343-9494** • gay-friendly • live music venue

Cafes

Amelie's French Bakery 2424 N Davidson St **704/376-1781** • open 24 hrs • soup & sandwiches, and of course pastries!

Caribou Coffee 1531 East Blvd (near Scott) **704/334-3570** • 6am-11pm, till midnight Fri-Sat, from 7am Sat-Sun • popular gay hangout Wed nights • WiFi

Charlotte

LGBT Pride:
Fall. 704/333-0144, web: www.pridecharlotte.com.

Annual Events:
May - AIDS Walk 704/372-7246 x 161, web: www.aidswalkcharlotte.org.

City Info:
Visit Charlotte 704/334-2282 or 800/722-1994, web: www.charlottesgotalot.com.

Transit:
Yellow Cab 877/935-5692. Various hotels have their own shuttles.
Charlotte Transit 704/336-7433, web: charmeck.org

Attractions:
Blumenthal Performing Arts Center 704/372-1000, web: www.blumenthalcenter.org.
Charlotte Motor Speedway 800/455-3267, web: www.charlottemotorspeedway.com.
Daniel Stowe Botanical Gardens 704/825-4490, web: www.dsbg.org.
Discovery Place 704/372-6261, web: www.discoveryplace.org.
Mint Museum of Art 704/337-2000, web: www.mintmuseums.org.
Paramount's Carowinds Amusement Park
704/588-2600, web: www.carowinds.com.

Smelly Cat Coffee 514 E 36th St
704/374–9656 • 7am-7pm, till 11pm Fri

Tic Toc Coffeeshop 512 N Tryon St (btwn
8th & 9th) **704/375–5750** • 7am-3pm, clsd
wknds • plenty veggie

RESTAURANTS

300 East 300 East Blvd (at Cleveland)
704/332–6507 • 11am-10pm, till 11pm Fri-Sat,
Sun brunch • eclectic fusion • some veggie •
full bar • wheelchair access

Alexander Michael's 401 W 9th St (at Pine)
704/332–6789 • lunch & dinner, clsd Sun •
pub fare • full bar • wheelchair access

Cosmos Cafe 300 N College (at 6th)
704/372–3553 • 11am-2am, clsd Sun • gay-
friendly • eclectic cuisine • some veggie • also
martini lounge

Cuban Pete's 1308 The Plaza (at Central
Ave) **704/910–5233** • festive ambiance •
delish Cuban sandwich • full bar

Dish 1220 Thomas Ave (at Central)
704/344–0343 • 11am-10pm, till 11pm Fri-Sat,
clsd Sun • comfort food • outdoor seating

Lupie's Cafe 2718 Monroe Rd (near 5th St)
704/374–1232 • 11am-10pm, from noon Sat,
clsd Sun • homestyle cookin' • some veggie

Penguin Drive-In 1921 Commonwealth Ave
(at Thomas) **704/375–6959** • 11am-1am, till
2am wknds • diner extraordinaire • plenty
veggie • full bar

The Pewter Rose Bistro 1820 South Blvd
(near East Blvd) **704/332–8149** • lunch &
dinner • int'l/ American • live entertainment •
outdoor dining • also nightclub

ENTERTAINMENT & RECREATION

One Voice Chorus PO Box 9241, 28299 •
LGBT chorus

BOOKSTORES

Paper Skyscraper 330 East Blvd (at Euclid
Ave) **704/333–7130** • 10am-7pm, till 6pm Sat,
noon-5pm Sun • books • funky gifts •
wheelchair access

White Rabbit Books & Things 920 Central
Ave (at E 10th) **704/377–4067** • 10am-9pm,
noon-6pm Sun • LGBT • books • magazines •
T-shirts • gifts

PUBLICATIONS

Q Notes **704/531–9988** • bi-weekly LGBT
newspaper for the Carolinas

EROTICA

Carolina Video Source 8829 E Harris Blvd
(at Albemarle Rd) **704/566–9993**

Duck

ACCOMMODATIONS

Advice 5¢, a B&B 111 Scarborough Ln
252/255–1050, 800/238–4235 • gay-friendly •
welcoming seaside cottage Duck on North
Carolina's Outer Banks • nonsmoking •
women-owned • $155-265

Durham

see Raleigh/Durham/Chapel Hill

Fayetteville

NIGHTCLUBS

Alias 984 Old McPherson Church Rd (at
Raeford Rd) **910/484–7994** • 9pm-2:30am Fri-
Sat only • lesbians/ gay men • dancing/DJ •
multiracial • transgender-friendly • go-go
dancers • videos • 18+ • private club • gay-
owned

EROTICA

Cupid's Boutique 137 N Reilly Rd (at
Morganton) **910/860–7716** • gay-friendly •
DVDs • adult novelties

Fort Video & News 4431 Bragg Blvd (near
401 overpass) **910/868–9905** • 24hrs

Priscilla's 3800 Sycamore Dairy Rd (at Bragg
Blvd) **910/860–1776**

Franklin

ACCOMMODATIONS

Phoenix Nest 850/421–1984 • lesbians/ gay
men • mtn cabin • sleeps 4 • seasonal • kids
ok • nonsmoking • wheelchair access •
lesbian-owned • $85/ night, $385/ week

Rainbow Acres (Honey's) 850/997–8847 •
gay/ straight • mostly women • rental home •
nonsmoking • fireplace • some shared baths •
great views • women-owned • $750/ week

Gastonia

BARS

Night Owls 420 W Main Ave **704/866–7333** •
8pm-2:30am Th-Sun only • lesbians/ gay men
• dancing/DJ • cabaret • drag shows

Greensboro

INFO LINES & SERVICES

Live & Let Live AA 617 N Elm St (at
Presbyterian Church) **336/854–4278 (AA#)** •
8pm Tue • also Free Spirit, 8pm Sat, 2105 W
Market St (at Episcopal Church)

ACCOMMODATIONS

Biltmore Greensboro Hotel 111 W Washington St (at Elm St) **336/272–3474, 800/332–0303** • gay/ straight • fully restored historic hotel • gym • WiFi • kids/ pets ok • nonsmoking • gay-owned • $109-139

O Henry Hotel 624 Green Valley Rd (at Benjamin Pkwy) **336/854–2000, 800/965–8259** • gay-friendly • pool • full brkfst • afternoon tea • cloister garden • bar/ restaurant popular w/ local gay community • wheelchair access • $249-509

BARS

The Q 708 W Market St **336/272–2587** • 4pm-close, from 9pm Sat, from 7pm Sun • lesbians/ gay men • more women Sun • neighborhood bar • DJ • karaoke • 18+ • WiFi • patio

Time Out Saloon 330 Bellemeade St **336/272–8108** • 8:30pm-2:30am, clsd Sun-Mon • mostly women • neighborhood bar • dancing/DJ • karaoke • private club • lesbian-owned

NIGHTCLUBS

Aldo's After Party 1350 Polar Rd **336/340–5288** • 10pm-2:30am, clsd Sun-Mon • ladies night Tue • gay/ straight • gay wknds • dancing/DJ • drag shows • Latino

Warehouse 29 1011 Arnold St **336/333–9333** • 9:30pm-2:30am Th-Sun, add'l summer hours • mostly gay men • dancing/DJ • live shows • T-dance Sun (summers) • videos • patio bar • volleyball • 18+ • private club

RESTAURANTS

Much/ Level 2/ Heaven 113 Elm St **336/370–1311** • upscale restaurant & martini lounge • also nightclub

Greenville

NIGHTCLUBS

The Great American Mining Co of New Guinea, Inc 1008 B Dickinson Ave (at 10th St) **252/353–2623** • 10pm-3am • lesbians/ gay men • dancing/DJ • karaoke • drag shows • strippers • videos • private club • gay-owned

EROTICA

Late Show Video 1101 Charles Blvd (at 10th St) **252/758–5883** • adult DVDs • toys • gay-owned

Hickory

NIGHTCLUBS

Club Cabaret 101 N Center St (at 1st Ave) **828/322–8103** • 9pm-close, from 5pm Sun, clsd Mon-Wed • lesbians/ gay men • dancing/DJ • live shows • private club • wheelchair access

CAFES

Taste Full Beans 29 2nd St NW **828/325–0108** • 7am-5:30pm, till 3pm Sat, clsd Sun • art exhibits • gay-owned

Hot Springs

ACCOMMODATIONS

The Duckett House Inn **828/622–7621** • gay/ straight • Victorian farmhouse • full brkfst • shared baths • nonsmoking • WiFi • creek swimming • also vegetarian restaurant (reservations required) • gay-owned • $125-145

Jacksonville

CAFES

Monster's Pizza & Corner Cafe 1108 Henderson Dr **910/347–6100** • 11am-midnight or later • internet access • full bar • patio

EROTICA

Priscilla's 113–A Western Blvd **910/355–0765**

Madison

ACCOMMODATIONS

Hunter House B&B 216 W Hunter St **336/445–4730** • gay/ straight • patio • gardens • pool • pets on premises • nonsmoking • WiFi • gay-owned • $115-135

Mooresville

RESTAURANTS

Pomodoro's Italian American Cafe 168 Norman Station Blvd **704/663–6686** • 11am-10pm, till 7pm Sun • beer/ wine • wheelchair access • gay-owned

Mt Mitchell

ACCOMMODATIONS

Serendipity Cabin 2160 S Toe River Rd, Burnsville **800/379–0013** • gay/ straight • kids/ pets ok • nonsmoking • $100-130

New Bern

ACCOMMODATIONS

Harmony House Inn 215 Pollock St
252/636-3810, 800/636-3113 • gay-friendly •
1850 Greek Revival • full brkfst • kids ok •
nonsmoking • WiFi • $99-175

Raleigh/Durham/Chapel Hill

INFO LINES & SERVICES

Common Solutions Gay/ Lesbian AA 505
Alexander Ave (at Episcopal Student Center),
Durham **919/286-9499 (AA#)** • 6:30pm Mon

**The Gay/ Lesbian Helpline 919/747-4123,
919/256-3730** • 6:30pm-9:30pm Sun-Th

LGBT Center of Raleigh 316 W Cabarrus St
(at Dawson), Raleigh **919/710-9725** • social &
educational activities, services & groups

ACCOMMODATIONS

Carol's Garden Inn 2412 S Alston Ave (at
Riddle Rd), Durham **919/250-9336,
877/922-6777** • gay-friendly • on 3 acres •
whirlpools in 2 rms • nonsmoking • WiFi • $85-
100

Raleigh/Durham/Chapel Hill

LGBT PRIDE:
September, Durham. web:
www.ncpride.org.

ANNUAL EVENTS:
August - North Carolina Gay and
Lesbian Film Festival, web:
www.carolinatheatre.org/screen/
film-festivals.

CITY INFO:
919/834-5900 or 800/849-8499,
web: www.visitraleigh.com.
Chapel Hill/Orange County Visitors
Bureau 888/968-2060, web:
www.chocvb.org.

TRANSIT:
Regional Transit Information
919/485-7433, web: www.gotri-
angle.org.

ATTRACTIONS:
Ackland Art Museum, Chapel Hill
919/966-5736, web:
www.ackland.org.
African-American Dance Ensemble,
Durham 919/560-2729, web:
www.africanamerican-
danceensemble.org.
African-American Cultural Complex,
Raleigh 919/250-9336, web:
www.aaccmuseum.org.
City Market, Raleigh, web: citymar-
ketraleigh.com.
Duke University, Durham.
Exploris (interactive global learning
center), Raleigh 919/834-4040,
web:
www.marbleskidsmuseum.org.
Morehead Planetarium & Science
Center 919/962-1236, web:
www.moreheadplanetarium.org.
NC Botanical Garden, Chapel Hill
919/962-0522, web:
www.ncbg.unc.edu.
NC Museum of Art, Raleigh
919/839-6262, web: www.ncart-
museum.org.
NC Museum of Life & Science,
Durham 919/220-5429, web:
www.ncmls.org.
Oakwood Historic District, Raleigh.
University of North Carolina, Chapel
Hill.
W. Franklin St. in Chapel Hill, south
of UNC and into Carrboro—
charming and hip shopping area.

Fickle Creek Farm B&B 919/304-6287 •
gay/ straight • passive solar B&B on 61-acre
working farm • full brkfst • some shared baths
• kids ok • nonsmoking • gay-owned • $90+

Heartfriends Inn B&B 4389 Siler City/Snow
Camp Rd (at Ed Clapp Rd), Siler City
919/663-0407 • gay/ straight • WiFi • women-
owned • wheelchair access • $80-125

Morehead Manor B&B 914 Vickers Ave (at
Morehead), Durham 919/687-4366,
888/437-6333 • gay/ straight • splendid
colonial home • full brkfst • teens ok •
nonsmoking • WiFi • woman-owned • $145-
450

The Oakwood Inn B&B 411 N Bloodworth
St (at Oakwood), Raleigh 919/832-9712,
800/267-9712 • gay-friendly • Victorian in the
heart of Raleigh • full brkfst • kids ok •
nonsmoking • WiFi • $144-204

BARS

Hibernian Restaurant & Pub 311
Glenwood Ave (at W Lane St), Raleigh
919/833-2258 • 11am-2am daily • gay-
friendly • live music

NIGHTCLUBS

A Taste of Candy at Liquid 311 S
Harrington St (at W Martin), Raleigh
919/829-3676 • 9pm Th only • lesbians/ gay
men • dancing/DJ • 18+

The Capital Corral (CC) 313 W Hargett St
(at Harrington), Raleigh 919/755-9599 •
8pm-close, from 6pm Sun • mostly gay men •
dancing/DJ • more multiracial Th • live shows
• 18+ • also piano bar • private club •
wheelchair access

Cat's Cradle 300 E Main St, Carrboro
919/967-9053 • gay-friendly • live music
venue

Family Night 3201 New Bern Ave (at
Milburnie, at Envy), Raleigh 919/255-1314 •
gay Mon only • lesbians/ gay men •
dancing/DJ • theme nights • live shows • patio
• 18+ Wed • gay-owned

Icon Nightclub 320 E Durham Rd, Cary
919/460-4343 • lesbians/ gay men •
dancing/DJ • drag shows • karaoke • theme
nights • mostly African American

Legends/ View 330 W Hargett St (at S
Harrington St), Raleigh 919/831-8888 •
9:30pm-close, clsd Wed • theme nights • deck
• lesbians/ gay men • dancing/DJ • strippers •
drag shows • young crowd • private club •
wheelchair access

Steel Blue 1426 S Miami Blvd (at Sherron
Rd), Durham 919/596-5876 • 8pm-2am Fri,
9pm-3am Sat • mostly women • dancing/DJ •
live shows

Stir 201 E Franklin St (at East End Martini
Bar), Chapel Hill 919/929-0024 • 9pm Sun
only • mostly gay men • dancing/DJ

Tantra 310 S West St (at Martin), Raleigh
919/828-9994 • Fri-Sun only • gay-friendly •
dancing/DJ • 3 rooms • martini lounge •
young crowd • private club

CAFES

Bean Traders 105-249 W NC Hwy 54,
Durham 919/484-2499 • 6:30am-8pm, from
7:30am wknds

Cafe Helios 413 Glenwood Ave (at North St),
Raleigh 919/838-5177 • 7am-10pm, till
midnight wknds • in reclaimed Plumbing &
Heating Building • food served • also beer &
wine • patio

Caffe Driade 1215 E Franklin St #A (at
Elizabeth St), Chapel Hill 919/942-2333 • live
music • also beer & wine served

Caribou Coffee 110 West Franklin St (at N
Columbia St), Chapel Hill 919/933-5404 •
7am-11pm, till midnight Fri-Sat, from 8am Sun
• WiFi

Reverie: A Coffee Den 2522 Hillsborough
St (at Pogue), Raleigh 919/839-2233 • 7am-
6pm, 8am-4pm Sat • WiFi • patio

Third Place 1811 Glenwood Ave (at W
Whitaker Mill Rd), Raleigh 919/834-6566 •
8am-7pm, till 11pm wknds • also sandwiches
& salads • plenty veggie

RESTAURANTS

Blu Seafood & Bar 2002 Hillsborough Rd
(at 9th St), Durham 919/286-9777 • lunch &
dinner, clsd Sun

The Borough 317 W Morgan St, Raleigh
919/832-8433 • 4pm-2am • also bar • WiFi

Crooks Corner 610 Franklin St (at Merritt
Mill Rd), Chapel Hill 919/929-7643 • dinner
nightly, Sun brunch, clsd Mon • Southern •
some veggie • full bar • patio • wheelchair
access

Dain's Place 754 9th St (at Markham),
Durham • 11am-2am • great burgers & pub
food • also bar • WiFi

Elmo's Diner 776 9th St (in the Carr Mill
Mall), Durham 919/416-3823 • 6:30am-10pm,
till 11pm Fri-Sat • some veggie

Five Star 511 W Hargett St (at West St),
Raleigh 919/833-3311 • 5:30pm-2am, Asian-
fusion • sexy ambiance for cocktails & nibbles

Humble Pie 317 S Harrington St (at Martin), Raleigh **919/829–9222** • 5pm-11pm, till midnight Fri-Sat, bar open late, brunch only Sun • small plates

Irregardless Cafe 901 W Morgan St (at Hillsborough), Raleigh **919/833–8898** • lunch Tue-Fri, dinner Tue-Sat, Sun brunch, clsd Mon • plenty veggie • live music • dancing Sat

Lantern 423 W Franklin St, Chapel Hill **919/969–8846** • dinner nightly, clsd Sun • Asian • also cocktail lounge till 2am

The Mad Hatter's Bakeshop & Cafe 1802 W Main St (at Broad), Durham **919/286–1987** • brkfst, lunch & dinner • awesome cakes & baked goods

Magnolia Grill 1002 9th St (at Knox), Durham **919/286–3609** • dinner, clsd Sun-Mon • upscale Southern • full bar • wheelchair access

The Pit 328 W Davie St (at S Dawson), Raleigh **919/890–4500** • 11am-10pm, till 11pm wknds • upscale BBQ

Rue Cler 401 E Chapel Hill St (at Mangum St), Durham **919/682–8844** • lunch & dinner, wknd brunch • French

Solas 419 Glenwood Ave (at Tucker), Raleigh **919/755–0755** • dinner, Sun brunch • upscale dining • dress code • also rooftop lounge & nightclub

Spotted Dog 111 E Main St (at N Greensboro St), Carrboro **919/933–1117** • 11:30am-midnight, clsd Mon • full bar • plenty veggie

Sunrise Biscuit Kitchen 1305 E Franklin St, Chapel Hill **919/933–1324** • great brkfst • drive-thru only

Vivace 4209 Lassiter Mill Rd #115 (at Pamlico Dr), Raleigh **919/787–7747** • lunch & dinner, Sun brunch • Italian • patio seating • full bar

Weathervane Cafe 201 S Estes Dr (in the University Mall), Chapel Hill **919/929–9466** • 7am-9pm, till 10pm Fri-Sat, 10:30am-6pm Sun • plenty veggie • full bar • great brunch • live jazz • patio • wheelchair access

ENTERTAINMENT & RECREATION

Bull City HQ 723 N Magnum St, Durham • performance & musical events • gallery

Carolina Rollergirls • NC's female roller derby league • visit carolinarollergirls.com for events

Common Woman Chorus PO Box 51731, Durham 27717 • feminist chorus • visit www.commonwomanchorus.net for upcoming performances

BOOKSTORES

Internationalist Books & Community Center 405 W Franklin St (at Kenan St), Chapel Hill **919/942–1740** • 11am-8pm, noon-6pm Sun • progressive/ alternative • cooperatively run • nonprofit • literature readings & events

Quail Ridge Books 3522 Wade Ave (at Ridgewood Center), Raleigh **919/828–1588, 800/672–6789** • 9am-9pm • LGBT section

Reader's Corner 3201 Hillsborough St (at Rosemary), Raleigh **919/828–7024** • 10am-8pm, till 6pm Sat, noon-6pm Sun • used books

The Regulator Bookshop 720 9th St (btwn Hillsborough & Perry), Durham **919/286–2700** • 9am-9pm, 10am-6pm Sun

White Rabbit Raleigh 300 W Hargett St #56, Raleigh **919/856–1429** • 11am-9pm, noon-7pm Sun • LGBT • music • movies • cards • gifts • wheelchair access

EROTICA

Castle Video & News 1210 Capitol Blvd, Raleigh **919/836–9189** • 24hrs

Cherry Pie 1819 Fordham Blvd, Chapel Hill **919/928–0499** • 18+ • adult toys • gifts • drag bingo & other events

Frisky Business 1720 New Raleigh Hwy, Durham **919/957–4441** • adult toys • also classes

Rocky Mount

NIGHTCLUBS

Liquid Nightclub 313 Falls Rd **252/266–6464** • 8pm-close Wed, till 2am Fri, till 3am Sat only • mostly gay men • dancing/DJ • go-go dancers • mostly African American

Spruce Pine

ACCOMMODATIONS

The Lemon Tree Inn 872 Greenwood Rd **828/765–6161** • gay/ straight • central location for mtn attractions • gay-owned • $45-65

Shepherd's Ridge **828/765–7809, 828/713–0604** • open March-Nov • mostly women • cottage in the woods • nonsmoking • $70/ night, $350/ week • woman-owned

Washington

CAFES

Back Water Jack's Tiki Bar 1052 E Main St (at Havens St) **252/975-1090** • lunch & dinner, clsd Sun-Mon • also bar • wheelchair access

West Jefferson

ACCOMMODATIONS

Blue Ridge Hideaway 115 Arbor Pl (at Skyline) **615/360-7099, 615/484-7171** • gay-friendly • cozy log cabin • private river access • nonsmoking • WiFi • lesbian-owned

Wilmington

ACCOMMODATIONS

Best Western Coastline Inn 503 Nutt St **910/763-2800, 800/617-7732** • gay/ straight • kids ok • internet access • nonsmoking • wheelchair access • WiFi • gay-owned • $69-169

Blue Heaven B&B 517 Orange St **910/772-9929** • gay-friendly • 1800s historic home • full brkfst • nonsmoking • pets ok • WiFi • $100-150

Rosehill Inn B&B 114 S 3rd St (at Dock St) **910/815-0250, 800/815-0250** • gay-friendly • full brkfst • jacuzzi in 1 rm • nonsmoking • WiFi • $119-199

The Taylor House Inn 14 N 7th St **910/763-7581, 800/382-9982** • gay/ straight • romantic 1905 house • full brkfst • nonsmoking • kids ok • $140

BARS

Tool Box 2325 Burnett Blvd **910/343-6988** • 5pm-2am, from 3pm Sun • mostly gay men • neighborhood bar • dancing/DJ • karaoke • WiFi • gay-owned

NIGHTCLUBS

Ibiza 118 Market St (rear) **910/251-1301** • 8pm-3am Wed-Sun only • mostly gay men • dancing/DJ • more women Th • karaoke • drag shows • strippers • young crowd • private club • wheelchair access • gay-owned

RESTAURANTS

Caffe Phoenix 9 S Front St **910/343-1395** • 11:30am-10pm, Sun brunch • Mediterranean • some veggie • gay-owned

ENTERTAINMENT & RECREATION

Cinematique 310 Chestnut St (at Thalian Hall) **910/343-1640** • classic, foreign & notable films

Winston-Salem

NIGHTCLUBS

Club Odyssey 4019 Country Club Rd (at Hedgecock Ave) **336/774-7071** • 9pm-2:30am, till 3:30am Sat, clsd Mon • popular • lesbians/ gay men • dancing/DJ • live shows • cabaret • multiracial clientele • transgender-friendly • private club • 18+ • wheelchair access • cover charge • gay-owned

NORTH DAKOTA

Fargo

INFO LINES & SERVICES

Pride Collective & Community Center 116 12th St S (at Main Ave), Moorhead, MN **218/287-8034** • referrals • support • social groups • check www.pridecollective.com for events

NIGHTCLUBS

I-Beam 1021 Center Ave (at 11th), Moorhead, MN **218/233-7700** • 9pm-2am Fri-Sat only • lesbians/ gay men • dancing/DJ • drag shows

CAFES

Atomic Coffee 222 Broadway **701/478-6160** • 7am-11pm, till 9pm Sun, clsd Mon-Tue • WiFi

RESTAURANTS

Fargo's Fryn' Pan 300 Main St (at 4th) **701/293-9952** • 24hrs • popular • wheelchair access

RETAIL SHOPS

One World Imports 614 Main Ave (at Broadway) **701/297-8882** • 10am-7pm, till 6pm Fri-Sat, clsd Sun • gay-owned

Zandbroz Variety 420 N Broadway **701/239-4729** • 9am-8pm, noon-5pm Sun • books & gifts

EROTICA

Romantix Adult Superstore 417 N Pacific Ave **701/235-2640** • 24hrs

Grand Forks

EROTICA

Romantix Adult Superstore 102 S 3rd St (at Kittson) **701/772-9021** • 24hrs

Minot

EROTICA

Risque's 1514 S Broadway **701/838-2837**

OHIO

Statewide

NIGHTCLUBS

Femme Fatale Events • women's events across OH • dance parties • www.myspace.com/femmefataleevents

PUBLICATIONS

Gay People's Chronicle 216/916–9338 • Ohio's largest bi-weekly LGBT newspaper w/ extensive listings

Outlook Weekly 614/268–8525 • statewide LGBT newsweekly • good resource pages

Akron

INFO LINES & SERVICES

AA Intergroup 330/253–8181 (AA#)

Akron Pride Center 895 N Main St 330/785–0088 • call for meeting schedule

BARS

Adams Street Bar 77 N Adams St 330/434–9794 • 4:30pm-2:30am, from 9pm Sun • popular • mostly gay men • piano bar Wed • dancing/DJ Fri-Sat • strippers

Cocktails 1009 S Main St 330/376–2625 • 11am-2:30am, clsd Sun • mostly gay men • videos • drag king show Mon • Daddy's leather bar upstairs wknds

The Office 778 N Main St (at Cuyahoga Falls Ave) 330/376–9550 • 11am-2:30am • gay-friendly • bisexual friendly • neighborhood bistro & lounge • multiracial • piano bar • WiFi • wheelchair access

Roseto Club 627 S Arlington St 330/724–4228 • 6pm-2:30am, clsd Sun • mostly women • dancing/DJ • karaoke • wheelchair access

Tear-Ez 360 S Main St (near Exchange St) 330/376–0011 • 11am-2:30am, from noon Sun • lesbians/ gay men • neighborhood bar • drag shows Th & Sun • WiFi • wheelchair access

NIGHTCLUBS

Interbelt 70 N Howard St (near Perkins & Main) 330/253–5700 • 9pm-2:30am, from 10pm Th & Sun, clsd Tue • lesbians/ gay men • dancing/DJ • live shows • videos • patio

Square 820 W Market St (btwn Portage Pass & Rhodes Ave) 330/374–9661 • 5pm-2:30am, from 8pm Sat, from 7pm Sun • mostly gay men • dancing/DJ • karaoke • wheelchair access • gay-owned

CAFES

Angel Falls Coffee Company 792 W Market St (btwn S Highland & Grand) 330/376–5282, 877/218–6818 • lunch & desserts • patio • WiFi • wheelchair access • gay-owned

RESTAURANTS

Aladdin's Eatery 782 W Market St 330/535–0110 • 11am-10pm • Middle Eastern

Bricco 1 W Exchange St (at S Main St) 330/475–1600 • 11am-midnight, till 1am Fri-Sat, 4pm-9pm Sun • Italian • also bar • gay-owned

Bruegger's Bagels 1821 Merriman Rd 330/867–8394 • 6am-4pm

Athens

ACCOMMODATIONS

SuBAMUH (Susan B Anthony Memorial UnRest Home) Womyn's Land Trust PO Box 5853, 45701 740/448–6424, 740/448–7285 • women only • cabins & camping • summer workshops • swimming • hot tub • nonsmoking • lesbian-owned • $7 (tent), $12 (cabin) sliding scale • rates per person

Brunswick

see also Akron & Cleveland

RESTAURANTS

Pizza Marcello 67–A Pearl Rd (near Boston Rd) 330/225–1211 • 3pm-close, from noon wknds • Italian

Canton

NIGHTCLUBS

Crew 304 Cherry Ave NE 330/452–2739 • 6pm-2:30am, from 9pm Sat-Sun • lesbians/ gay men • dancing/DJ • karaoke • cabaret

Cincinnati

INFO LINES & SERVICES

AA Gay/ Lesbian 320 Resor Ave (in St John's Unitarian Church), Clifton 513/351–0422 (AA#) • 8pm Wed • call for locations of wknd meetings

Gay/ Lesbian Community Center of Greater Cincinnati 4119 Hamilton Ave (near Blue Rock) 513/591–0200 • 6pm-9pm, noon-4pm Sat, clsd Sun

ACCOMMODATIONS

Cincinnatian Hotel 601 Vine St (at 6th St) 513/381–3000, 800/942–9000 • gay-friendly • restaurant & lounge • kids ok • WiFi • wheelchair access • $158-1,500

Crowne Plaza 5901 Pfeiffer Rd (at I-71) 513/793–4500, 800/468–3597 • gay-friendly • pool • kids ok • WiFi •wheelchair access • $99-209

First Farm Inn 2510 Stevens Rd, Idlewild, KY 859/586–0199 • gay-friendly • 20 minutes from Cincinnati • full brkfst • WiFi • nonsmoking • wheelchair access • $99-154

Millennium Hotel Cincinnati 150 W 5th St 513/352–2100, 800/876–2100 • gay-friendly • city's only outdoor rooftop pool & sundeck • WiFi • wheelchair access • $89-199

Weller Haus B&B 319 Poplar St, Bellevue, KY 859/431–6829, 800/431–4287 • gay-friendly • jacuzzis • nonsmoking • WiFi • $109-199

BARS

Below Zero Lounge 1122 Walnut St (at E Central Pkwy) 513/421–9376 • 4pm-2:30am, clsd Mon-Tue • dancing/DJ • live music • karaoke • videos • food served

Club Nonta 4023 Hamilton Ave (at Blue Rock) 513/542–3400 • 7pm-2:30am, till 4am wknds • lesbians/ gay men • neighborhood bar • dancing/DJ • drag shows • karaoke

Golden Lion 340 Ludlow (at Telford), Clifton 513/281–4179 • 4pm-2:30am • mostly gay men • neighborhood bar • dancing/DJ • karaoke • dive bar

Hamburger Mary's 909 Vine St (at 9th St) 513/421–6279 • 11am-midnight, bar open till 2:30am • lesbians/ gay men • also Dirty Mary's • dancing/DJ Wed (girls night), Fri-Sat • drag shows • wheelchair access

Junkers Tavern 4158 Langland (at Pullan) 513/541–5470 • 8:30am-1am • gay-friendly • neighborhood bar

Little Bit Bar 2401 Vine St (at Hollister, Clifton Heights) 513/721–8484 • 7pm-2:30am, clsd Mon • lesbians/ gay men • ladies night Sat • neighborhood bar • dancing/DJ • karaoke • drag shows • wheelchair access

Milton's 301 Milton St (at Sycamore) 513/784–9938 • 4pm-2:30am • gay-friendly • neighborhood bar

Shooters 927 Race St (at Court) 513/381–9900 • 4pm-2:30am • mostly gay men • dancing/DJ • country/ western • more women Th • karaoke Wed

Simon Says 428 Walnut St (at 5th) 513/381–7577 • 11am-2:30am, from 1pm Sun • popular • mostly gay men • professional • neighborhood bar • wheelchair access

Cincinnati

LGBT PRIDE:
June. 513/591-0200, web: www.prideisalive.com.

ANNUAL EVENTS:
Oct - OUTReels LGBT film festival 513/591-0200.

CITY INFO:
513/621-2142 or 800/543–2613, web: www.cincyusa.com.

BEST VIEW:
Mt Adams & Eden Park.

TRANSIT:
Yellow Cab 513/821-8294, web: aaataxi.net.
SORTA 513/621-4455, web: www.sorta.com

ATTRACTIONS:
The Beach waterpark (in Mason) 513/398-7946, web: www.thebeachwaterpark.com.
Carew Tower 513/241-3888.
Cincinnati Art Museum 513/639-2995, web: www.cincinnatiartmuseum.org.
Fountain Square.
Krohn Conservatory 513/421-4086.
Museum Center at Union Terminal 513/287-7000, web: www.cincymuseum.org.
Paramount King's Island (24 miles N of Cincinnati) 513/754-5700, web: www.visitkingsisland.com.

NIGHTCLUBS

Adonis 4601 Kellogg Ave (at Stites Rd) 513/871–1542 • 9pm-3am Sat only • lesbians/ gay men • dancing/DJ • transgender-friendly • karaoke • drag shows

Bronz 4029 Hamilton Ave (at Blue Rock) 513/591–2100 • 8pm-2:30am, clsd Mon • lesbians/ gay men • dancing/DJ • live shows • karaoke • wheelchair access • patio • gay-owned

The Dock 603 W Pete Rose Wy (near Central) 513/241–5623 • 10pm-3am, till 4am Fri-Sat, clsd Mon-Wed • popular • lesbians/ gay men • dancing/DJ • drag shows • live shows • 19+ • volleyball court • wheelchair access

CAFES

College Hill Coffee Co 6128 Hamilton Ave 513/542–2739 • 6:30am-6:30pm, till 10pm Fri, 8:30am-10pm Sat, till 4pm Sun, clsd Mon • live music Sat • WiFi

Zen & Now 4453 Bridgetown Rd 513/598–8999 • 7am-9pm, till 11pmt Fri, 9am-1pm Sat, clsd Sun

RESTAURANTS

Boca 3200 Madison Rd, Oakley 513/542–2022 • dinner Tue-Sat, clsd Sun-Mon • full bar • patio • wheelchair access

Honey 4034 Hamilton Ave 513/541–4300 • dinner & Sun brunch, clsd Mon • casual fine dining

The Loving Cafe 6227 Montgomery Rd (at Woodmont) 513/731–2233 • 11am-7pm, clsd Sun-Mon • vegetarian/ vegan

Melt Eclectic Deli 4165 Hamilton Ave 513/681–6358 • 11am-9pm, till 10pm Fri-Sat, 10am-3pm Sun

Myra's Dionysus 121 Calhoun St 513/961–1578 • 11am-10pm, till 11pm Fri-Sat, from 5pm Sun • diverse menu • plenty veggie

Tinks Cafe 3410 Telford Ave 513/961–6500 • lunch & dinnner • live music • full bar

Tucker's 1637 Vine St 513/721–7123 • great brkfst hole in wall, vegan too

ENTERTAINMENT & RECREATION

Ensemble Theatre of Cincinnati 1127 Vine St 513/421–3555

Know Theatre 1120 Jackson St (at Central Pkwy) 513/300–5669 • contemporary multicultural theater

Ohio Lesbian Archives 3416 Clifton Ave (at Clifton United Methodist Church) 513/256–7695 • call first for appt

RETAIL SHOPS

Pink Pyramid 907 Race St (btwn 9th & Court) 513/621–7465 • noon-9pm, till 11pm Fri-Sat, 1pm-7pm Sun • pride items • also leather

PUBLICATIONS

Gay People's Chronicle 216/916–9338 • Ohio's largest bi-weekly LGBT newspaper

Cleveland

INFO LINES & SERVICES

AA Gay/ Lesbian 6600 Detroit Ave (at LGBT Center) 216/241–7387 • 7pm Fri women's meeting

Cleveland Lesbian/ Gay Community Center 6600 Detroit Ave 216/651–5428, 888/429–8761 • 1pm-8pm, clsd wknds • wheelchair access

ACCOMMODATIONS

Clifford House 1810 W 28th St (at Jay) 216/589–0121 • gay/ straight • 1868 historic brick home • near downtown • fireplaces • nonsmoking • WiFi • gay-owned • $95-135

Radisson Hotel Cleveland—Gateway 651 Huron Rd (at Prospect) 216/377–9000, 888/201–1718 • gay-friendly • also restaurant • kids ok • WiFi • wheelchair access • $94-149 + tax

Stone Gables B&B 3806 Franklin Blvd (at W 38th) 216/961–4654, 877/215–4326 • gay/ straight • full brkfst • jacuzzi • kids/ pets ok • WiFi • wheelchair access • gay-owned • $100-150

BARS

A Man's World 2909 Detroit Ave (at 29th St) 216/771–0369 • 7am-2:30am, from noon Sun-Mon • mostly gay men • more women Sun eve for line dancing • dancing/DJ wknds • patio

Club Argos 2032 W 25th St (at Lorain & 24th) 216/781–9191 • 3pm-close, from noon wknds • mostly gay men • more women Tue • alternative sports bar • dancing/DJ • bears • multiracial • young crowd

The Hawk 11217 Detroit Ave (at 112th St) 216/521–5443 • noon-2:30am, from 1pm Sun • lesbians/ gay men • neighborhood bar • wheelchair access

Mean Bull 1313 E 26th St (at St Clair) 216/812–3304 • 4pm-2am • mostly gay men • videos • piano bar

The Nickel/ Five Cent Decision 4365 State Rd (Rte 94, at Montclair) 216/661–1314 • 6pm-2am • mostly women • DJ • karaoke • live shows

Now That's Class 11213 Detroit Ave (at 112th St) 216/221-8576 • gay-friendly • punk & metal bands • food served • plenty veggie/ vegan

Paradise Inn 4488 State Rd (Rte 94, at Rte 480) 216/741–9819 • 11am-2:30am • lesbians/ gay men • neighborhood bar • lesbian-owned

Twist 11633 Clifton (at 117th St) 216/221–2333 • 11:30am-2:30am, from noon Sun • popular • lesbians/ gay men • neighborhood bar • dancing/DJ • professional crowd

Union Station Video Cafe 2814 Detroit Ave (at W 28th) 216/357–2997 • 5pm-2:30am • popular • lesbians/ gay men, more women Sat night • dancing/DJ • drag shows • videos • also Bounce nightclub Fri-Sat • also restaurant • gay-owned

View Ultra Lounge 618 Prospect Ave (at E 4th St) 216/664-1815 • gay/ straight • dancing/DJ • theme nights

NIGHTCLUBS

Bottoms Up 1572 W 117th (at Franklin), Lakewood 216/221–0065 • 4pm-close • lesbians/ gay men • dancing/DJ • food served • karaoke • drag shows • theme nights

CAFES

Gypsy Beans & Baking Co 6425 Detroit Ave (at W 65th St, next to Cleveland Public Theatre) 216/939–9009 • 7am-9pm, till 11pm Fri-Sat • popular • fresh-baked gourmet pastries, soups, sandwiches • WiFi

Lucky's Cafe 777 Starkweather Ave 216/622–7773 • 7am-8pm, 8am-5pm wknds • popular wknd brunch (9am-2am) • cafe & bakery • outdoor seating • woman-owned

Phoenix Coffee 2287 Lee Rd, Cleveland Heights 216/932–8227 • 6am-10pm, till 11pm Fri, from 7am Sat, 7am-7pm Sun • popular cafe w/ specialty beverages, pastries, great sandwiches • WiFi • outdoor seating

Truffles 11122 Clifton Blvd (btwn W 110th & 112th, in Edgewater) 216/961–0300 • 7am-10pm, till 11pm Fri-Sat • very gay-friendly • pastries • outdoor seating

Cleveland

WHERE THE GIRLS ARE:
Dancing downtown near Public Square, hanging out on State Rd below the intersection of Pearl and Broadview/ Memphis.

LGBT PRIDE:
June. 216/226-0004, web: www.clevelandpride.org.

ANNUAL EVENTS:
March - Cleveland International Film Festival 216/623-3456, web: www.clevelandfilm.org.
April - Tri-C JazzFest 216/987-4400, web: www.tricjazzfest.com.
June - Avon Heritage Duct Tape Festival 866/818-1116, web: www.avonducttapefestival.com.

CITY INFO:
216/621-4110 or 800/321–1004, web: www.positivelycleveland.com.

ATTRACTIONS:
Cleveland Metroparks Zoo 216/661-6500, web: www.clemetzoo.com.
Cleveland Museum of Art 216/421-7340, web: www.clemusart.com.
Coventry Road district.
Cuyahoga Valley National Recreation Area 216/524–1497, web: www.nps.gov/cuva.
The Flats.
Rock and Roll Hall of Fame 216/781-7625, web: www.rockhall.com.

TRANSIT:
Yellow Cab 216/623-1500.
AmeriCab 216/881-1111.
Regional Transit Authority (RTA) 216/566-5100, web: www.gcrta.org.
Lolly the Trolley 216/771-4484, web: www.lollytrolley.com.

RESTAURANTS

Ali Baba 12021 Lorain Ave (at W 120th St) **216/251–2040** • 4:30pm-10pm Th-Sat • popular • the best Middle Eastern food you'll have outside the Middle East • plenty veggie • BYOB • woman-owned

Bar Cento 1948 W 25th St (at Lorain Ave) **216/274–1010** • 4:30pm-2am, from noon Sat • great pizza • beer/ wine

Battiste & Dupree Cajun Grill & Bar 1992 Warrensville Ctr Rd **216/381–3341** • lunch & dinner, clsd Sun-Mon

Cafe Tandoor 2096 S Taylor Rd (at Cedar), Cleveland Heights **216/371–8500, 216/371–8569** • lunch & dinner, 3pm-9pm Sun • Indian • plenty veggie

The Coffee Pot 12415 Madison Ave, Lakewood **216/226–6443** • 6am-4pm, till 3pm Sat, till 2pm Sun, clsd Mon • diner • woman-owned

Crop Bistro 1400 W 6th St (at Frankfort) **216/696–2767** • lunch Tue-Fri, dinner nightly, clsd Mon • innovative American

Diner on Clifton 11637 Clifton Blvd (at W 117th St) **216/521–5003** • 7am-11pm

Flying Fig 2523 Market Ave (at W 25th St) **216/241–4243** • dinner only

Happy Dog 5801 Detroit Ave (at 58th St) **216/651–9474** • 4pm-2am, from 11am Fri • hot dogs w/ 50 toppings • veggie/ vegan choices • live bands • full bar

Hecks 2927 Bridge Ave (at W 30th) **216/861–5464, 800/677–8592** • lunch & dinner • popular • gourmet burgers • wheelchair access

The Inn on Coventry 2785 Euclid Heights Blvd (at Coventry), Cleveland Heights **216/371–1811** • 7am-8:30pm, from 8:30am Sat-Mon, till 3pm Sun-Mon • homestyle • popular Bloody Marys • some veggie • full bar • wheelchair access • women-owned

Jimmy O'Neill's Tavern 2195 Lee Rd, Cleveland Heights **216/321–1116** • 5pm-midnight, till 11pm Sun, bar till 2:30am

Johnny Mango World Cafe & Bar 3120 Bridge Ave (btwn Fulton & W 32nd, in Ohio City) **216/575–1919** • 11am-10pm, till 11pm Fri-Sat • healthy world food • juice bar • also full bar till 1am • nonsmoking • wheelchair access

Latitude 41N 5712 Detroit Ave (at W 58th St, Detroit Shoreway) **216/961–0000** • 8am-9pm, till 10pm Fri, till 3pm Sun • restaurant & cafe • lesbian-owned

Lolita 900 Literary Rd (at Professor Ave, in Tremont) **216/771–5652** • 5pm-11pm, till 1am Fri-Sat, 4pm-9pm Sun, clsd Mon • popular • upscale cont'l • full bar • also Lola's in Warehouse District downtown • both owned by Iron Chef Michael Symon

Luchita's 3456 W 117th St (at Governor) **216/252–1169** • lunch & dinner, clsd Mon • popular • Mexican • full bar

Luxe 6605 Detroit Ave (at W 65th St) **216/920–0600** • 5pm-midnight, lounge till 2am • gourmet comfort food • also lounge • directly across from LGBT Center

Momocho 1835 Fulton Rd **216/694–2122** • 5pm-close, from 4pm Sun • modern Mexican • also bar

My Friend's Deli & Restaurant 11616 Detroit Ave (at W 117th) **216/221–2575** • 24hrs • beer/ wine • WiFi

Pearl of the Orient 19300 Detroit Rd (in Beachcliff Market Sq), Rocky River **440/333–9902** • lunch & dinner • Chinese • some veggie • also restaurant on East Side

Tommy's 1824 Coventry Rd, Cleveland Heights **216/321–7757** • 9am-9pm, till 10pm Fri, 7:30am-10pm Sat • plenty veggie • great milkshakes • WiFi

ENTERTAINMENT & RECREATION

Rock & Roll Hall of Fame 1100 Rock & Roll Blvd (at E 9th & Lake Erie) **216/781–ROCK** • even if you don't like rock, stop by & check out IM Pei's architectural gift to Cleveland

BOOKSTORES

Borders Bookshop & Espresso Bar 2101 Richmond Rd (at Cedar, in LaPlace Mall), Beachwood **216/292–2660** • 10am-10pm, till 9pm Sun

Joseph-Beth Booksellers 24519 Cedar Rd (in Legacy Village shopping center), Lyndhurst **216/691–7000** • 9am-9pm, till 11pm Fri-Sat, till 7pm Sun • LGBT section • active reading series • also bistro

Loganberry Books 13015 Larchmere Blvd, Shaker Heights **216/795–9800** • 10am-6pm, till 8pm Th, clsd Sun • used & rare books • woman-owned

Mac's Backs 1820 Coventry Rd (next to Tommy's), Cleveland Heights **216/321–2665** • 10am-9pm, till 10pm Fri-Sat, 11am-8pm Sun • great new & used • 3 floors • reading series • some LGBT titles

RETAIL SHOPS

Big Fun 1814 Coventry Rd, Cleveland Heights **216/371-4386** • 11am-8pm, till 10pm Fri-Sat, till 6pm Sun • kitschy variety store

Dean Rufus House of Fun 1422 W 29th St (at Detroit) **216/348-1386** • 1pm-midnight, till 2:30am Fri-Sat, clsd Mon • clothing • DVDs

Goddess Blessed 15729 Madison Ave (at Hillard), Lakewood **216/221-8755** • 11am-7pm, clsd Sun-Mon • goddess-focused & occult gifts & supplies • tarot readings • events & classes

PUBLICATIONS

Erie Gay News 814/456-9833

Gay People's Chronicle 216/916-9338 • Ohio's largest bi-weekly LGBT newspaper w/ extensive listings

Columbus

INFO LINES & SERVICES

AA Gay/ Lesbian 614/253-8501, 800/870-3795 (IN OH)

Stonewall Columbus Community Center/ Hotline 1160 N High St (at E 4th Ave) 614/299-7764 • 9am-5pm, clsd wknds • wheelchair access

ACCOMMODATIONS

The Blackwell 2110 Tuttle Park Pl (at Lane Ave) **614/247-4000** • gay-friendly • on OSU campus • also restaurant

Garden Manor Bed & Breakfast 108 N 20th St (N of E Broad St) **866/925-4929** • gay-friendly • WiFi • wheelchair access • gay-owned • $119-169

Harrison House B&B 313 W 5th Ave (at Neil Ave) **614/421-2202, 800/827-4203** • gay-friendly • nonsmoking • WiFi • woman-owned • $129-169

The Lofts 55 E Nationwide Blvd **614/461-2663, 800/735-6387** • gay-friendly • boutique hotel

The Westin Columbus 310 S High St (at Main) **614/223-3800** • gay-friendly • beautiful old 100+ year old hotel, great location • also restaurant

BARS

Blazer's Pub 1205 N High St (at 5th) **614/299-1800** • 4pm-midnight, till 2am Th-Sat, clsd Sun • lesbians/ gay men • neighborhood bar • karaoke

Cavan Irish Pub 1409 S High St (at Jenkins) **614/725-5502** • 2pm-2:30am, from noon Sat • gay-friendly

Club Diversity 863 S High St (at Whittier) **614/224-4050** • 4pm-midnight, till 2:30am Fri, noon-2:30am Sat • lesbians/ gay men • piano bar Fri-Sat

Havana Video Lounge 862 N High (at 1st Ave) **614/421-9697** • 5pm-2:30am • popular • lesbians/ gay men • neighborhood bar • dancing/DJ • drag shows • martini lounge • food served

Inn Rehab 627 Greenlawn Ave (at Harmon) **614/754-7326** • 11am-2:30am • mostly gay men • food served • dancing/DJ • drag shows

Level Dining Lounge 700 N High St (at Lincoln) **614/754-7111** • 11am-2:30am • gay/ straight • restaurant with great bar

Score 145 N 5th St (at Spring) **614/849-0099** • 4pm-2:30am • lesbians/ gay men • gay sports bar • karaoke • drag bingo

Slammers 202 E Long St (at N 5th St) **614/221-8880** • 11am-12:30am, till 2:30am Fri-Sat, from 4pm wknds, clsd Mon • mostly women • dancing/DJ • food served • WiFi • wheelchair access

The South Bend Tavern 126 E Moler St (at 4th St) **614/444-3386** • noon-2:30am • lesbians/ gay men • neighborhood bar • drag shows Sat • wheelchair access

Trafik 205 N 5th St (at Spring) **614/222-2401** • 4pm-2am, from 1pm wknds • mostly gay men • dancing/DJ • transgender-friendly • karaoke • patio • gay-owned

Union Cafe 782 N High St (at Hubbard) **614/421-2233** • 11am-2:30am • popular • lesbians/ gay men • video bar • also restaurant • plenty veggie • WiFi • wheelchair access

NIGHTCLUBS

Axis 775 N High St (at Hubbard) **614/291-4008** • 10pm-2:30am Fri-Sat only • popular • mostly gay men • dancing/DJ • go-go boys • also Pump cabaret lounge • drag shows • 18+ • wheelchair access • gay-owned

Tradewinds II 117 E Chestnut (at 3rd St) **614/461-4110** • 4pm-2:30am, clsd Mon-Tue mostly gay men • dancing/DJ • also restaurant • wheelchair access

Wall Street 144 N Wall St (at Spring St) **614/464-2800** • 9pm-2:30am, from 10pm Wed, 8pm-midnight Th, clsd Mon-Tue • popular • lesbians/ gay men • more women Fri-Sat • dancing/DJ • country/ western Th • wheelchair access

CAFES

Cup-O-Joe Cafe 627 3rd St (at Sycamore) **614/221-1563** • 6am-10:30pm, till 11pm Fri-Sat, from 7am wknds, till 10pm Sun • food served

RESTAURANTS

Alana's Food & Wine 2333 N High St (at Patterson) **614/294-6783** • from 5pm, clsd Sun-Mon

Banana Leaf 816 Bethel Rd **614/459-4101** • 11:30am-9:30pm • vegetarian/vegan Indian

Betty's 680 N High St **614/228-6191** • 11am-2am • plenty veggie • also bar

Blue Nile 2361 N High St (at W Patterson) **614/421-2323** • lunch & dinner, clsd Mon • Ethopian

Cap City Diner 1299 Olentangy River Rd **614/291-3663** • 11am-10pm, till 11pm Fri-Sat, till 9pm Sun

Dragonfly 247 King Ave **614/298-9986** • 5pm-10pm Tue-Sat, Sat brunch, clsd Sun-Mon • upscale vegetarian • patio

L'Antibes 772 N High St #106 (at Warren) **614/291-1666** • dinner from 5pm, clsd Sun-Mon • full bar • wheelchair access • gay-owned

Lemongrass 641 N High (at Russell) **614/224-1414** • lunch & dinner, clsd Sun-Mon • popular • Asian cuisine • reservations advised

Northstar Cafe 951 N High St (at W 2nd Ave) **614/298-9999** • 9am-10pm • popular • plenty veggie

Surly Girl Saloon 1126 N High St **614/294-4900** • 11am-2am • plenty veggie • also bar • open mic comedy Wed & punk rock aerobics 6:30pm Tue

Tip Top Kitchen and Cocktails 73 E Gay St (at 3rd St) **614/221-8300** • 11am-2am

Columbus

WHERE THE GIRLS ARE:
Downtown with the boys, north near the University area, or somewhere in-between.

LGBT PRIDE:
June. 614/299-7764 (Stonewall #), web: www.columbuspride.org.

ANNUAL EVENTS:
June - Columbus Arts Festival 614/224-2606, web: www.gcac.org.
July/August - Ohio State Fair 888/646-3976, web: www.ohio-expocenter.com.
September - Ohio Lesbian Festival, web: www.ohiolba.org.

CITY INFO:
800/282-5393, web: www.ohio-tourism.com.

WEATHER:
Truly midwestern. Winters are cold, summers are hot.

ATTRACTIONS:
Brewery District.
Columbus Jazz Orchestra 614/294-5200, web: www.jazzartsgroup.org.
Columbus Museum of Modern Art 614/221-6801, web: www.columbusmuseum.org.
Columbus Zoo 800/666-5397 web: www.columbuszoo.org.
Franklin Park Conservatory 614/645-8733, web: www.fpconservatory.org.
German Village district.
The Short North neighborhood (popular "Gallery Hop" 1st Sat), 614/299-8050 web:www.shortnorth.org.
Wexner Center for the Arts 614/292-0330, web: www.wexarts.org.

TRANSIT:
Yellow Cab 614/444-4444.
Acme Taxi 614/777-7777.
Central Ohio Transit Authority (COTA) 614/228-1776, web: www.cota.com.

Whole World Bakery & Restaurant 3269 N High St **614/268-5751** • 11am-8pm, Sun brunch, clsd Mon • vegetarian/ vegan

ENTERTAINMENT & RECREATION

Ohio Roller Girls • Columbus' female roller derby league • visit www.ohiorollergirls.com for events

BOOKSTORES

The Book Loft of German Village 631 S 3rd St (at Sycamore) **614/464-1774** • 10am-11pm, till midnight Fri-Sat • LGBT section

RETAIL SHOPS

Hausfrau Haven 769 S 3rd St (at Columbus) **614/443-3680** • 10am-7pm, noon-5pm Sun • greeting cards • wine • gifts

Piercology 190 W 2nd Ave **614/297-4743** • noon-8pm, 1pm-7pm Sun • body-piercing studio • gay-owned

Schmidt's Fudge Haus 220 E Kossuth St (in Historic German Village) **614/444-2222** • noon-close • old-fashioned fudge & candy • gifts

Torso 772 N High St (at Warren) **614/421-7663** • 11am-10pm, till 5pm Sun-Mon • clothing

PUBLICATIONS

Gay People's Chronicle 216/916-9338

Outlook Weekly 614/268-8525 • statewide LGBT weekly • good resource pages

EROTICA

The Garden 1174 N High St (btwn 4th & 5th Ave) **614/294-2869** • 11am-3am, noon-midnight Sun • adult toys

Dayton

INFO LINES & SERVICES

AA Gay/ Lesbian 20 W 1st St (off Main, at Christ Episcopal Church) **937/222-2211** • 8pm Sat

Greater Dayton Lesbian/ Gay Center 117 E 3rd St **937/274-1776**

BARS

Argos Bar 301 Mabel Ave (near Linden & I-35) **937/252-2976** • 6pm-2:30am • men only • neighborhood bar • leather • gay-owned

MJ's Cafe 119 E 3rd St **937/223-3259** • 3pm-2:30am • mostly gay men • dancing/DJ • food served • karaoke • male strippes • deck

Stage Door 44 N Jefferson St (at 2nd) **937/223-7418** • noon-2:30am, from 2pm Wed & wknds • mostly gay men • leather • wheelchair access

NIGHTCLUBS

Aquarius 135 E 2nd **937/223-1723** • 8pm-2:30am • lesbians/ gay men • dancing/DJ • drag shows • wheelchair access

The Main Stop 1919 N Main St **937/278-3650** • 5pm-close, clsd Mon-Tue • mostly women • neighborhood bar • dancing/DJ • live shows • karaoke • wheelchair access • lesbian-owned

Masque 34 N Jefferson St (btwn 2nd & 3rd) **937/228-2582** • 7pm-2:30am, till 5am wknds • popular • mostly gay men • dancing/DJ • drag shows • strippers • 18+

CAFES

Signatures Gourmet Coffee 313 W Main St (Third St), Fairborn **937/878-1000** • 7am-9pm, 9am-2pm Sat, clsd Sun • live music Fri • gay-owned

RESTAURANTS

Cold Beer & Cheeseburgers 33 S Jefferson St (at 4th St) **937/222-2337** • 11am-close • grill • full bar • wheelchair access

The Spaghetti Warehouse 36 W 5th St (at Ludlow) **937/461-3913** • 11am-10pm, till 11pm Fri, noon-11pm Sat • more gay Tue w/ Friends of the Italian Opera

BOOKSTORES

Books & Co 350 E Stroop Rd (at Farhills) **937/298-6540** • 9am-11pm, till 8pm Sun

RETAIL SHOPS

Q Gift Shop 1904 N Main St (at Ridge Ave) **937/274-4400** • noon-7pm • LGBT gifts & movies

PUBLICATIONS

Gay Dayton 937/623-1590 • monthly LGBT publication

EROTICA

Deja Vu Love Boutique 1267 N Keowee St (off I-75) **937/222-1212** • 10am-3am, 24hrs Th-Sat • novelties, toys, DVDs, arcade

Kent

BARS

The Zephyr Pub 106 W Main St **330/678-4848** • 3pm-close • gay-friendly • live shows • wheelchair access

Lima

NIGHTCLUBS

Somewhere in Time 804 W North St
419/227-7288 • 7pm-2:30am, from 8pm
wknds • lesbians/ gay men • dancing/DJ • drag
shows • male & female strippers

Logan

ACCOMMODATIONS

Glenlaurel—A Scottish Country Inn 14940
Mt Olive Rd (off State Rte I-80), Rockbridge
740/385-4070, 800/809-7378 • gay/ straight •
full brkfst & dinner • hot tub • nonsmoking •
wheelchair access • $149-339

Inn & Spa at Cedar Falls 21190 State Rte
374 **740/385-7489, 800/653-2557** • gay/
straight • rooms, log cabins & cottages • fine
dining on-site • nonsmoking • WiFi • $125-289

Lazy Lane Cabins **740/385-3475,
877/225-6572** • gay-friendly • secluded
cabins sleep 2-8 • hot tubs • fireplaces •
satellite TV • nonsmoking • kids/ pets ok •
$119-229

Lorain

BARS

Tim's Place 2223 Broadway (btwn 22nd &
23rd) **440/218-2223** • 8pm-2:30am, clsd Mon
• lesbians/ gay men • neighborhood bar •
dancing/DJ • drag shows • patio • wheelchair
access

NIGHTCLUBS

La Sala 939 Broadway **440/242-2622** •
3:30pm-close, clsd Sun-Tue • gay/ straight •
bar menu • karaoke • Latin dancing Sat

Mansfield

BARS

The Gee Spot Dance Club 470 Newman
St **419/524-0007** • 6pm-close, from 4pm
Wed-Th • gay/ straight • dancing/DJ

Marietta

ACCOMMODATIONS

Fourth St B&B **614/638-1187** • gay/
straight • kids ok • nonsmoking • gay-owned •
$69-149

Monroe

BARS

Old Street Saloon 13 Old St **513/539-9183**
• 8pm-2am Th-Sat, till 1am Wed, clsd Sun-Tue
• lesbians/ gay men • neighborhood bar •
dancing/DJ • drag shows • karaoke

Oberlin

ACCOMMODATIONS

Hallauer House B&B 14945 Hallauer Rd
440/774-3400, 877/774-3406 • gay-friendly •
eco-friendly historic inn 3 miles S of Oberlin •
pool • nonsmoking • WiFi • $135-185

CAFES

Java Zone 5 W College St #A **440/774-5282**
• 8am-9pm, till 10pm Sat-Sun • also
sandwiches • WiFi

RESTAURANTS

The Feve 30 S Main St **440/774-1978** •
11am-midnight • popular wknd brunch
(9:30am-2:30pm) • plenty veggie • full bar
(5pm-2am)

Weia Teia 9 S Main St **440/774-8880** •
lunch & dinner • Thai/ Asian fusion • upscale •
beer/ wine • some veggie

BOOKSTORES

MindFair Books 13 W College St (shares
storefront w/ Ben Franklin) **440/774-6463** •
10am-6pm, till 8pm Fri, noon-5pm Sun

Pickerington

CAFES

Planet Coffee & Tea 1252 Hill Rd N
614/861-2040 • 6am-10pm, till 11pm Fri-Sat,
wknd hours vary

Sandusky

NIGHTCLUBS

Crowbar 206 W Market St (at Jackson St)
419/624-0109 • 4pm-2:30am • lesbians/ gay
men • ladies night Tue • dancing/DJ • karaoke
• gay-owned

Xcentricities 306 W Water St (at Jackson St)
419/624-8118 • 4pm-2:30am, from 2pm
wknds • lesbians/ gay men • dancing/DJ • drag
shows • male & female strippers • patio

RESTAURANTS

Mona Pizza Gourmet 135 Columbus Ave
(at Market St) **419/626-8166** • 11am-10pm,
till 3am wknds • multiracial • transgender-
friendly • gay-owned

Springfield

NIGHTCLUBS

Diesel 1912-14 Edwards Ave (at N Belmont Ave) **937/324-0383** • 8:30pm-2:30am, clsd Mon-Tue • gay-friendly • dancing/DJ • live shows • karaoke • patio

Why Not III 5 N Murray **937/324-9758** • 9:30pm-2:30am, till 1am Sun-Tue • lesbians/gay men • dancing/DJ

Why Not III 5 N Murray St **937/324-9758** • 9:30pm-2:30am, till 1am Sun-Tue • lesbians/gay men • dancing/DJ • karaoke • WiFi

Steubenville

BARS

PJ's 169 N 4th St **740/283-2747** • 11am-2:30am • lesbians/gay men • dancing/DJ Fri-Sat • food served • gay-owned

Toledo

INFO LINES & SERVICES

AA Gay/ Lesbian 2272 Collingwood Blvd (at St Mark's Episcopal Church) **419/380-9862** • 8pm Wed

ACCOMMODATIONS

Mansion View Inn 2035 Collingwood Blvd **419/244-5676** • gay-friendly • 1887 Victorian near downtown in Historic Old West End • nonsmoking • WiFi • $129-149

BARS

Outskirts 1515 W Laskey Rd (btwn Jackman & Lewis) **419/476-1577** • 3pm-2:30am, till 3:30am Fri-Sat, clsd Sun-Tue • mostly women • dancing/DJ • karaoke

R House 5534 Secor Rd (btwn Laskey & Alexis) **419/474-2929** • 4pm-2:30am • mostly gay men • dancing/DJ • patio

Rip Cord 115 N Erie St (btwn Jefferson & Monroe) **419/243-3412** • 9am-2:30am • mostly gay men • more women Mon • neighborhood bar • Sun brunch • karaoke • strippers • food served

NIGHTCLUBS

Bretz 2012 Adams St **419/243-1900** • 9pm-2:30am, till 4:30am Fri-Sat, clsd Mon-Tue • lesbians/gay men • dancing/DJ • karaoke • drag shows • strippers • 18+ • wheelchair access

BOOKSTORES

People Called Women 3153 W Central Ave (in Cricket West Center) **419/535-6455** • 11am-7pm, clsd Sun, clsd Mon • multicultural • feminist

Warren

NIGHTCLUBS

Club 441 441 E Market St (enter rear) **330/394-9483** • 4pm-2:30am, from 2pm wknds • lesbians/gay men • dancing/DJ • live shows • wheelchair access

The Funky Skunk 143 E Market St • 9pm-close • mostly gay men • ladies night Sun • dancing/DJ • drag shows • karaoke

West Lafayette

RESTAURANTS

Lava Rock Grill at Unusual Junction 56310 US Hwy 36 **740/545-9772** • '50s-style diner in restored railroad station • wheelchair access • gay-owned

Yellow Springs

RESTAURANTS

Winds Cafe & Bakery 215 Xenia Ave **937/767-1144** • lunch & dinner, Sun brunch, clsd Mon • plenty veggie • full bar • wheelchair access • women-owned

Youngstown

INFO LINES & SERVICES

The Mahoning Valley Pride Center 1523 Poland Ave (at Shirley Rd) • home to many of the local LGBT organizations including: Stonewall Democrats, PFLAG, All Families Matter, and Pride Youngstown

NIGHTCLUBS

Split Level 169 S Four Mile Run Rd (at S Mahoning Ave) **330/318-9830** • lesbians/gay men • dancing/DJ • drag shows • karaoke

Utopia Video Nightclub 876 E Midlothian Blvd **330/781-9000** • 5pm-close, clsd Mon • lesbians/gay men • dancing/DJ • drag shows

CAFES

The Lemon Grove Cafe 122 W Federal St (at Hazel St) **330/744-7683** • 7am-4am, from 11am wknds • food served • also bar • events, movies, art & more

ENTERTAINMENT & RECREATION

AnarKingz • Youngstown's drag king troupe, check www.myspace.com/theanarkingz for upcoming performances

OKLAHOMA

Statewide

PUBLICATIONS

Metro Star 918/835–7887 • monthly LGBT news publication serving AR, KS, MO & OK

Enid

EROTICA

Patricia's 4810-A W Garriott (at Garland) **580/233–5511** • toys • lingerie • books • videos

Grand Lake

ACCOMMODATIONS

Southern Oaks Resort & Spa 2 miles S of Hwy 28/82 Junction, Langley **918/782–9346, 866/452–5307** • gay-friendly • 19 cabins on 30 acres • pool • hot tub • nonsmoking • gay-owned • $49-289

RESTAURANTS

The Artichoke Restaurant & Bar 35896 S Hwy 82, Langley 918/782–9855, 866/682-9855 • 5pm-10pm, clsd Sun-Mon

Frosty & Edna's Cafe Highway 28, Langley 918/782–9123 • 6am-9:30pm

Lighthouse Supper Club Highway 85 & Main, Ketchum 918/782–3316 • from 5pm, clsd Sun-Tue

Lawton

BOOKSTORES

Ingrid's Books 1124 NW Cache Rd **580/353–1488** • 11am-8pm, clsd Sun • new & used books • magazines • also adult novelties

Norman

see also Oklahoma City

INFO LINES & SERVICES

GLBTF at University of Oklahoma 405/325–4452

RESTAURANTS

La Luna Mexican Cafe 529 Buchanan Ave (on historic Campus Corner) 405/329–9596 • 11am-9pm, 8am-9:30pm Th-Sat, clsd Sun-Mon • full cantina & bar

Oklahoma City

see also Edmond & Norman

INFO LINES & SERVICES

AA Live & Let Live 3405 N Villa 405/947–3834

Herland Sister Resources 2312 NW 39th St 405/521–9696 • 1pm-5pm Sat • women's resource center w/ books, crafts & lending library • also sponsors monthly events • wheelchair access

YGLA (Young Gay/ Lesbian Alliance) 2242 NW 39th (at Red Rock North) 405/ 525–5165, 405/524–6500 • drop-in testing 9am-5pm Mon-Th, till 4pm Fri • support group & more for LGBT youth (ages 13-20) 6pm-10pm Th

ACCOMMODATIONS

Days Inn Oklahoma City Northwest 2801 NW 39th St (at I-44 & May Ave, Exit 124) 405/946–0741 • gay-friendly • pool • WiFi

➤**Habana Inn** 2200 NW 39th St (at Youngs) 405/528–2221, 800/988–2221 (RESERVATIONS ONLY) • popular • lesbians/ gay men • resort • pool • nonsmoking • also 3 bars • restaurant • gift shop • wheelchair access • $40-108

Hawthorn Suites 1600 NW Expy (Richmond Square) 405/840–1440, 800/527–1133 (RESERVATIONS) • gay-friendly • full brkfst • pool

Waterford Marriott 6300 Waterford Blvd (at Pennsylvania) 405/848–4782, 800/228–9290 • gay-friendly • pool • fitness center • also bar & restaurant • nonsmoking • WiFi

BARS

Alibi's 1200 N Pennsylvania (at NW 11th) 405/605–3795 • 3pm-2am, from noon wknds • gay/ straight • neighborhood bar • transgender-friendly • karaoke • gay-owned

Bearz 3020 3020 N Pennsylvania (at NW 29th St) 405/524–9306 • 2pm-2am • gay/ straight • neighborhood bar • karaoke Th & Sun

The Boom 2218 NW 39th St (at Pennsylvania) 405/601–7200 • noon-2am, clsd Mon • lesbians/ gay men • neighborhood bar • karaoke Tue • drag shows • WiFi • patio • wheelchair access

Edna's 5137 N Classen Blvd (at NW 51st) 405/840–3339 • 10am-2am • gay/ straight • neighborhood dive bar • food served

➤**The Finishline** at Habana Inn 405/525–2900 • noon-2am • lesbians/ gay men • neighborhood bar • dancing/DJ • country/ western • poolside bar • wheelchair access

Hi-Lo Club 1221 NW 50th St (btwn Western & Classen) **405/843–1722** • noon-2am • lesbians/gay men • neighborhood bar • live bands weekly • drag shows

➤ **The Ledo** at Habana Inn **405/525-0730** • 4pm-10:30pm, till 2am Fri-Sat • lesbians/gay men • martini lounge • food served • karaoke • nonsmoking • wheelchair access

Partners 4 Club 2805 NW 36th St (at May Ave) **405/942–2199** • 5pm-close, from 7pm Fri-Sat, clsd Mon • popular • mostly women • neighborhood bar • dancing/DJ • karaoke • live shows • patio • wheelchair access

Oklahoma City

WHERE THE GIRLS ARE:
Scattered all over the largest (in square miles) city in the US. But Bricktown is a popular haunt for many of the city's residents with all its good eats and good bars.

LGBT PRIDE:
June, web: www.okcpride.com.

ANNUAL EVENTS:
May - Herland Spring Retreat 405/521-9696. Music, workshops, web: www.herlandsisters.org.
May - Paseo Arts Festival 405/525-2688, web: www.thepaseo.com.
October - Herland Fall Retreat.

CITY INFO:
405/297-8912 & 800/225-5652, web: www.okccvb.org.

BEST VIEW:
From a water taxi on the Bricktown Canal (www.brocktownwatertaxi.com). Or anywhere in Myriad Gardens.

WEATHER:
Spring brings out the best of Oklahoma—blue skies for miles and the dogwood, redbud, and azaleas in bloom. (It's also the start of tornado season.) Summer gets mighty hot (90°s-100°s), with thunderstorms thrown in for relief. Fall is the time to head east to the hills of "Green Country" and watch the leaves change. Winters bring cold temps (20°s-30°s), gray skies, a brown landscape, and the occasional dusting of snow and the even rarer but more serious ice storm.

ATTRACTIONS:
Bricktown—renovated nightlife district with canal.
Historic Paseo Arts District, web: www.thepaseo.com.
Myriad Gardens' Crystal Bridge 405/297-3995, web: www.myriadgardens.com.
National Cowboy and Western Heritage Museum 405/478-2250, web: www.nationalcowboymuseum.org.
National Softball Hall of Fame 405/424-5266, web: www.softball.org.
Oklahoma City Museum of Art 405/236-3100, web: www.okcmoa.com.
Oklahoma City National Memorial 405/235–3313, web: www.oklahomacitynationalmemorial.org.
Oklahoma City Zoo 405,424-3344, web: www.okczoo.com.
Science Museum Oklahoma 405/602-6664, web: www.sciencemuseumok.org.
State Capitol: only one in country with its own active oil well.
Sylvan Goldman monument (inventor of the shopping cart).
Will Rogers Park.

TRANSIT:
Yellow Cab 405/232-6161.
Airport Express 405/681-3311, web: www.airportexpressokc.com.
Metro Transit 405/235-7433, web: www.gometro.org.

Oklahoma City's
HABANA INN
The Southwest's Largest All Gay Resort

175 Guest Rooms ★ Two Swimming Pools
Poolside Rooms ★ Suites ★ Cable TV

Park Once And Party All Night!
Located In The Habana Inn Complex

THE COPA
HOTTEST CLUB IN TOWN

OKC's

Leader In Entertainment
We've Got It All

FINISHLINE
Open High Noon
7 Days a Week

OKC's
Only
Country
Club

Darts
Pool

Dancing
Fri & Sat
Nights

Pool Bar
In Season

Nik's Restaurant
Serving OKC's Finest Prime Rib

OPEN
Mon - Fri 11am /Sat & Sun 9am
SERVING UNTIL
Sun - Thurs 10:30pm / Fri & Sat 3:30am

The Ledo
Open 4pm Daily

Home of the
KING SIZE
Martini

DIVALICIOUS
The Hottest New
Variety Show In OKC
Every Saturday @ 10:00pm
Starring
Roxie Hart, Michael Evans,
Raven Delray

LIVE PIANO MUSIC
FRI & SAT

KRAZY KARAOKE
Thursday Nite
Beginning @ 9pm

2200 NW 39th Expressway, Oklahoma City, OK 73112

Call for rates and information
(405) 528-2221 Reservations only: 1-800-988-2221
Website: www.habanainn.com

Tramps 2201 NW 39th St (at Barnes) 405/521–9888 • noon-2am, from 10am wknds • popular • mostly gay men • dancing/DJ • drag shows • wheelchair access

NIGHTCLUBS

Angles 2117 NW 39th St (at Pennsylvania) 405/524–3431 • Fri-Sat only • lesbians/gay men • dancing/DJ

➤ **The Copa** at Habana Inn 405/525–0730 • 9pm-2am, clsd Mon • popular • lesbians/gay men • dancing/DJ • drag shows • karaoke • wheelchair access

The Park 2125 NW 39th St (at Pennsylvania) 405/528–4690 • 5pm-2am, from 3pm Sun (free buffet) • mostly gay men • dancing/DJ • patio • wheelchair access

Wreck Room 2127 NW 39th St (at Pennsylvania) 405/525–7610 • 10pm-close Fri-Sat only • popular • lesbians/gay men • dancing/DJ • live shows • drag shows • young crowd • 18+ after 1am

CAFES

The Red Cup 3122 N Classen Blvd (at NW 30th St) 405/525–3430 • 7am-5pm, till 10pm Th-Fri, 9am-10pm Sat • food served • nonsmoking • WiFi • live music

RESTAURANTS

Bricktown Brewery Restaurant 1 N Oklahoma Ave (at Sheridan) 405/232–2739 • 11am-10pm, till midnight Sat, from noon Sun • full bar

Cheever's Cafe 2409 N Hudson Ave (at NW 23rd) 405/525–7007 • 11am-9:30pm, 5pm-10:30pm Sat, brunch Sun • reservations recommended

Earl's Rib Palace 216 Johnny Bench Dr, Ste BBQ (in Bricktown) 405/272–9898 • 11am-9pm, till 10pm Fri-Sat, noon-8pm Sun

➤ **Gusher's** at Habana Inn 405/525–0730 • 11am-10:30pm, from 9am wknds, till 3:30am Fri-Sat for after-hours brkfst • wheelchair access

Iguana Bar & Grill 9 NW 9th St (at N Santa Fe Ave) 405/606–7172 • lunch & dinner • Mexican

Ingrid's Kitchen 3701 N Youngs (btwn Penn & May, on NW 36th) 405/946–8444 • 7am-8pm, 10am-2pm Sun • German/American bakery & deli

La Luna Mexican Cafe 409 W Reno Ave (at Walker) 405/235–9596 • full bar

Pops 660 W Hwy 66, Arcadia 405/928–7677 • brkfst, lunch & dinner • diner fare • look for the 66-foot tall soda bottle

Rococo Restaurant & Fine Wine 2824 N Pennsylvania (at NW 27th St) 405/528–2824 • lunch Mon-Fri, dinner nightly, Sun jazz brunch • full bar

Someplace Else Deli & Bakery 2310 N Western Ave 405/524–0887 • 7am-6:30pm, 9:30am-4pm Sat, clsd Sun • popular

Sushi Neko 4318 N Western (btwn 42nd & 43rd) 405/528–8862 • 11am-11pm, clsd Sun

Ted's Cafe Escondido 8324 S Western Ave (at 84th St) 405/635–8337 • lunch & dinner • popular • Tex-Mex

ENTERTAINMENT & RECREATION

Carpenter Square Theater 400 W Sheridan (at Stage Center) 405/232–6500 • occasional gay-themed material

First Friday Gallery Walk from 28th at N Walker to 30th at N Dewey 405/525–2688 • open tour of Paseo Arts District galleries • first Fri & Sat

BOOKSTORES

Full Circle Bookstore 50 Penn Pl, 1900 NW Expwy (in NE corner of 1st level) 405/842–2900, 800/683–7323 • 10am-9pm, noon-5pm Sun • also cafe & coffee bar

Nature's Treasures 6223 SE 15th St (btwn Sooner & Air Depot Blvd), Midwest City 405/741–4322 • 10am-7pm, from noon Sun • New Age books

RETAIL SHOPS

23rd St Body Piercing 411 NW 23rd St (btwn Hudson & Walker) 405/524–6824 • noon-9pm, 1pm-6pm Sun

➤ **Jungle Red** at Habana Inn 405/524–5733 • 1pm-close • novelties • leather • gifts • wheelchair access

PUBLICATIONS

The Herland Voice 405/521–9696 • monthly newsletter for OKC women's community

Oklahoma Gazette 405/528–6000 • "Metro OKC's independent weekly"

EROTICA

Christie's Toy Box 2904 S Perdue 877/684–2226 • multiple locations in OKC

Patricia's 615 E Memorial 405/755–8600

Tulsa

INFO LINES & SERVICES

Dennis R Neill Equality Center 621 E 4th St (at Kenosha) 918/743–4297 • 3pm-9pm, clsd Sun • many activities & Pride store • wheelchair access

Gay/ Lesbian AA 2545 S Yale Ave (at Community of Hope) **918/627-2224** • 7pm Mon, Wed & Fri, 5:30pm Sat

Openarms Youth Project 2015-B S Lakewood Ave **918/838-7104** • social events • support groups • HIV testing

Youth Services Tulsa 311 S Madison **918/582-0061** • 6pm-8pm Tue youth group meeting • activity center • coffeeshop • WiFi • gay/ straight shows Sat

ACCOMMODATIONS

Crowne Plaza 100 E Second St (at 2nd St) **918/582-9000, 800/980-6429** • gay-friendly • restaurant • pool • kids/ pets ok • wheelchair access • $189

Tulsa Select 5000 East Skelly Dr (at I-44 & Yale Ave) **918/622-7000, 800/836-9635** • gay-friendly • pool • kids/ pets ok • restaurant/lounge • WiFi • wheelchair access • $69-109

BARS

Bamboo Lounge 7204 E Pine **918/836-8700** • noon-2am • oldest gay bar in OK • mostly gay men • neighborhood bar • dancing/DJ • live shows • karaoke • patio • wheelchair access

Club 209 209 N Boulder Ave (at Brady) **918/584-9944** • 7pm-2am, till midnight Sun, clsd Mon-Wed • gay/ straight • karaoke • smokefree

New Age Renegade 1649 S Main St (at 17th) **918/585-3405** • 4pm-2am • lesbians/ gay men • neighborhood bar • live shows • karaoke • patio

TNT's 2114 S Memorial Dr **918/660-0856** • 6pm-2am, from 8pm Sat, clsd Sun-Tue • popular • mostly women • neighborhood bar • dancing/DJ • karaoke

The Yellow Brick Road 2630 E 15th St (at Harvard) **918/293-0304** • 1pm-2am • lesbians/ gay men • neighborhood bar • wheelchair access

NIGHTCLUBS

Club Majestic 124 N Boston (at Brady) **918/584-9494** • 9pm-2am Th-Sun • dancing/DJ • drag/live shows • transgender-friendly • young crowd • wheelchair access • gay-owned

Club Maverick 822 S Sheridan (at 9th) **918/835-3301** • 4pm-2am • lesbians/ gay men • dancing/DJ • country/ western • karaoke

CAFES

Gypsy's Coffee House 303 N Cincinnati Ave **918/295-2181** • 11am-midnight, till 3am Fri-Sat, noon-10pm Sun, clsd Mon • live shows • WiFi

RESTAURANTS

The Brasserie 3509 S Peoria **918/779-7070** • 4pm-10m, till 11pm Fri-Sat, 10am-9pm Sun

Eloté 514 S Boston Ave **918/582-1403** • 11am-10pm, till 2pm Mon, clsd Sun, fresh Mexican • full bar

James E McNellie's Public House 409 E 1st St **918/382-7468** • 10am-2am • great burgers • full bar • wheelchair access

White Lion Pub 6927 S Canton Ave (off 71st) **918/491-6533** • 4pm-10pm, clsd Sun-Mon • British-style pub

Wild Fork 1820 Utica Square **918/742-0712** • 7am-10pm, clsd Sun • full bar • wheelchair access • women-owned

ENTERTAINMENT & RECREATION

Gilcrease Museum 1400 N Gilcrease Museum Rd **918/596-2700, 888/655-2278** • one of the best collections of Native American & cowboy art in the US

Green Country Roller Girls 918/269-7228 • Oklahoma's female roller derby league • visit www.tulsarollerderby.com for events

Nightingale Theater 1416 E 4th St (at Quincy) **918/633-8666** • savvy, unconventional productions by the Midwestern Theater Troupe

Philbrook Museum of Art 2727 S Rockford Rd (1 block E of Peoria, at end of 27th St) **918/324-7941** • clsd Mon • Italian villa built in the '20s oil boom complete w/ kitschy lighted dance flr • the gardens are a must in spring & summer

RETAIL SHOPS

Brookside Piercing & Tattoo 3314 S Peoria Ave **918/712-1122** • noon-10pm, till midnight Fri-Sat

The Pride Store 621 E 4th St **918/743-4297** • 3pm-9pm, clsd Sun • LGBT products • wheelchair access

PUBLICATIONS

Urban Tulsa Weekly 918/592-5550 • "Tulsa Metro's only independent newsweekly"

OREGON

Statewide

PUBLICATIONS

Just Out 503/236–1252 • LGBT newspaper w/ extensive resource directory

Ashland

INFO LINES & SERVICES

Gay/ Lesbian AA 208 Oak St #112 (at Old Armory) 541/732–1850

ACCOMMODATIONS

The Arden Forest Inn 261 W Hersey St 541/488–1496, 800/460–3912 • gay/ straight • full brkfst • nonsmoking • pool • kids 10+ ok • wheelchair access • WiFi • gay-owned • $140–290

Ashland Creek Inn 70 Water St 541/482–3315 • gay-friendly • kitchens • full brkfst • nonsmoking • gay-owned • $110–425

Blue Moon B&B 312 Helman St (at Hersey) 541/482–9228, 800/460–5453 • gay-friendly • full brkfst • kids/ pets ok in cottage • nonsmoking • WiFi • gay-owned • $90–225

Country Willows B&B Inn 1313 Clay St 541/488–1590, 800/945–5697 • gay-friendly • full brkfst • pool • jacuzzi • nonsmoking • teens ok • WiFi • wheelchair access • gay-owned • $120–260

Lithia Springs resort 2165 W Jackson Rd 541/482–7128, 800/482–7128 • gay/ straight • full brkfst • natural hot-springs-fed whirlpools in rooms • nonsmoking • teens ok • WiFi • $179–359

RESTAURANTS

The Black Sheep 51 N Main St (on the Plaza) 541/482–6414 • 11:30am-1am • eclectic pub fare • WiFi • woman-owned

Geppetto's 345 E Main St 541/482–1138 • 11:30am-9:30pm • Italian • full bar • wheelchair access

Greenleaf Restaurant 49 N Main St (on The Plaza) 541/482–2808 • 8am-8pm • creekside dining • beer/ wine

BOOKSTORES

Bloomsbury Books 290 E Main St (btwn 1st & 2nd) 541/488–0029 • 8:30am-9pm, till 10pm Fri-Sat

RETAIL SHOPS

Travel Essentials 252 E Main St 541/482–7383, 800/258–0758 • 10am-5:30pm, 11am-5pm Sun • luggage • books • accessories

Bend

ACCOMMODATIONS

Dawson House Lodge 109455 Hwy 97 N, Chemult 541/365–2232, 888/281–8375 • gay-friendly • rustic inn w/ modern amenities • near Crater Lake • nonsmoking • kids/ pets ok • WiFi • gay-owned • $45-110

RESTAURANTS

Blacksmith Restaurant 211 NW Greenwood Ave 541/318–0588 • 4:30pm-close • new American • upscale

Corvallis

BOOKSTORES

Book Bin 215 SW 4th St 541/752–0040 • 8am-9pm, till 10pm Fri-Sat, 9am-7pm Sun

Grass Roots Bookstore 227 SW 2nd St (btwn Jefferson & Madison) 541/754–7668 • 9:30am-6pm, till 7pm Fri, 10am-5:30pm Sat, noon-5pm Sun • wheelchair access

Eugene

INFO LINES & SERVICES

Gay/ Lesbian AA 1414 Kincaid 541/342–4113 • 7pm Mon & Wed, 8pm Fri

ACCOMMODATIONS

C'est La Vie Inn 1006 Taylor St 541/302–3014, 866/302–3014 • gay-friendly • full brkfst • nonsmoking • WiFi • $110-250

BARS

Hot Flash Eugene 2222 MLK Jr Blvd (at Kow Loon's) • 7pm-11pm 2nd Sat • mostly women • dancing/DJ • "for seasoned lesbians 36+ (& the women who love us!)" • food served • cover charge

Sam's Place Tavern 825 Wilson St (at 11th St W) 541/484–4455 • 11am-2:30am, from 9am wknds, till midnight Sun • gay-friendly • neighborhood bar • dancing/DJ • live shows • karaoke • also restaurant

NIGHTCLUBS

Club Snafu 64 W 8th Alley 541/342–3272 • 9pm-2:30am Th-Sat only • lesbians/ gay men • dancing/DJ

Diablo's Downtown Lounge 959 Pearl St 541/343–2346 • gay-friendly • dancing/DJ • karaoke Sun • open mic Tue • theme nights • also restaurant

CAFES

Eugene Coffee Company 1840 Chambers St (at 18th) 541/344–0002 • 7am-6pm • lesbian-owned

RESTAURANTS

Glenwood Restaurant 1340 Alder St (at 13th St) 541/687-0355 • 7am-9pm

Keystone Cafe 395 W 5th Ave (at Lawrence) 541/342-2075 • 7am-3pm • popular brkfst • plenty veggie

RETAIL SHOPS

High Priestess Piercing 675 Lincoln St (at 7th St) 541/342-6585 • 11am-8pm, till 9pm Wed-Sat

EROTICA

Exclusively Adult 1166 South A St (at 10th St), Springfield 541/726-6969 • 24hrs

Grants Pass

ACCOMMODATIONS

Rainbow Flyfishers at Copperland 840 Copper Dr (at Gray's Creek Rd), Murphy 541/862-2086 • women's land on 40 acres • cabin, campsites, RV hookups • also guided flyfishing • nonsmoking • WiFi • lesbian-owned • $45-400

WomanShare 541/862-2807 • women only • cabins • shared kitchen • bathhouse • hot tub • girls/ pets ok • nonsmoking • lesbian-owned • $25-40

CAFES

Sunshine Natural Foods Cafe 128 SW H St (btwn 5th & 6th Sts) 541/474-5044 • 9am-6pm, 9:30am-5pm Sat, clsd Sun • vegetarian • also market • WiFi

Idleyld Park

ACCOMMODATIONS

Umpqua's Last Resort Wilderness RV Park & Campground 115 Elk Ridge Ln 541/498-2500 • gay/ straight • check calendar for LGBT events • WiFi • gay-owned

Jacksonville

ACCOMMODATIONS

The TouVelle House 455 N Oregon St (at E St) 541/899-8938, 800/846-8422 • gay-friendly • 1916 Craftsman on 1 1/2 acres • full brkfst • pool • WiFi • nonsmoking • $149-235

Klamath Falls

ACCOMMODATIONS

Crystal Wood Lodge 38625 Westside Road 541/381-2322, 866/381-2322 • gay-friendly • nonsmoking • WiFi • lesbian-owned

Lincoln City

ACCOMMODATIONS

Ashley Inn 3430 NE Hwy 101 541/996-7500, 888/427-4539 • gay-friendly • pool • non-smoking • WiFi • wheelchair access • $89-199

Surftides Inn 2945 NW Jetty Ave 800/452-2159 • gay/ straight • restaurant & bar • pool • WiFi • $209+

A Vista d' Mar 1421 NW Harbor 541/994-6300, 866/776-8659 • gay/ straight • kitchens • beach access • nonsmoking

RESTAURANTS

Dory Cove Restaurant 2981 SW Hwy 101 541/557-4000 • 11:30am-9pm • steak & seafood • beer/ wine

Mist Restaurant 2945 NW Jetty Ave (at Surftides Inn) 541/994-3877 • 8am-9pm • full bar open later

Newport

ACCOMMODATIONS

Cliff House B&B 541/563-2506 • gay-friendly • oceanfront • great view • full brkfst • hot tub • nonsmoking • WiFi • $125-225

RESTAURANTS

Mo's Annex 657 SW Bay Blvd 541/265-7512 • 11am-9pm • great chowder

Ontario

BOOKSTORES

Proud Mary's Salon 31 SW 3rd Ave 541/889-4711 • 10am-6pm, clsd Sun-Mon • LGBT books

Portland

see also Vancouver, Washington

INFO LINES & SERVICES

Live & Let Live Club 1210 SE 7th Ave 503/238-6091 • 12-step meetings • call for schedule

Q Center 4115 N Mississippi Ave 503/234-7837 • 4pm-8pm Mon-Wed, 1pm-5pm Sun • LGBTQ community center • WiFi

Sexual Minority Youth Resource Center (SMYRC) 3024 NE Martin Luther King, Jr Blvd 503/872-9664 • 4pm-9pm Wed, Fri-Sat • drop-in center for LGBTQ youth

ACCOMMODATIONS

The Ace Hotel 1022 SW Stark St (at 11th) 503/228-2277 • gay/ straight • hip hotel • nonsmoking • WiFi • kids/ pets ok • wheelchair access • $85-260

Forest Springs B&B 3680 SW Towle Ave, Gresham **503/674–8992, 877/674–9282** • gay/ straight • full brkfst • kids ok • nonsmoking • gay-owned • $80-175

Hotel deLuxe 729 SW 15th Ave **503/219–2094, 866/895–2094** • gay-friendly • 1940s Hollywood decor • $159-339

Hotel Monaco Portland 506 SW Washington (at 5th Ave) **503/222–0001, 866/861–9514** • gay-friendly • restaurant • gym • kids/pets ok • WiFi

Hotel Vintage Plaza 422 SW Broadway (at SW Washington) **503/228–1212, 800/263–2305** • popular • gay-friendly • upscale hotel • restaurant & lounge • WiFi • wheelchair access • $143-375

Inn at Northrup Station 2025 NW Northrup St **503/224–0543, 800/224–1180** • gay-friendly • cute, colorful boutique hotel

Jupiter Hotel 800 E Burnside **503/230–9200, 877/800–0004** • gay-friendly • boutique hotel • nonsmoking • restaurant & lounge • kids/ pets ok • WiFi • wheelchair access • $89-139

The Lion & the Rose 1810 NE 15th Ave **503/287–9245, 800/955–1647** • gay/ straight • in 1906 Queen Anne mansion • nonsmoking • WiFi • gay-owned • $134-224

The Mark Spencer Hotel 409 SW Eleventh Ave (near Stark) **503/224–3293, 800/548–3934** • gay-friendly • nonsmoking • kids/pets ok • WiFi • $99-209

Painted Lady Inn 1927 NE 16th Ave (at NE Hancock St) **503/335–0070** • gay/ straight • nonsmoking • full brkfst • $109-179

Portland's White House B&B 1914 NE 22nd Ave (at NE Hancock St) **503/287–7131, 800/272–7131** • gay/ straight • in 1911 Greek Revival mansion • nonsmoking • WiFi • gay-owned • $125-225

Portland

WHERE THE GIRLS ARE:
Try along SE Hawthorne & Belmont streets where some of the women's businesses are, or the NW section, 21st & 23rd Aves, for the more upscale lesbians.

LGBT PRIDE:
June. 503/295-9788, web: www.pridenw.org.

ANNUAL EVENTS:
May - QDoc Portland Queer Documentary Film Festival, web: www.queerdocfest.org.
May/June - Rose Festival, web: www.rosefestival.org.
August - Mount Hood Jazz Festival, web: www.mthoodjazz.com.
September - La Femme Magnifique International Pageant, web: www.darcellexv.com.
October - AIDS Walk 503/223-5907, web: www.cascadeaids.org.
October - Portland LGBT Film Festival, web: www.plgff.org.

CITY INFO:
503/275-9750, web: www.travel-portland.com.
Travel Oregon 800/962-3700.

ATTRACTIONS:
The Grotto 503/254-7371, web: www.thegrotto.org.
Microbreweries.
Old Town.
Pioneer Courthouse Square 503/223-1613, web: www.pioneercourthousesquare.org.
Portland Art Museum 503/226-2811, web: www.portlandartmuseum.org.
Washington Park.
World Forestry Center & Discovery Museum 503/228-1367, web: www.worldforestrycenter.org.

BEST VIEW:
International Rose Test Gardens at Washington Park.

WEATHER:
The wet and sometimes chilly winter rains give Portland a lush landscape that bursts into beautiful colors in the spring and fall. Summer brings sunnier days. (Temperatures can be in the 50°s one day and the 90°s the next.)

TRANSIT:
Radio Cab 503/227-1212.
Raz 503/684-3322.
Tri-Met System 503/238-7433,

BARS

Boxxes 1035 SW Stark (at SW 11th Ave) **503/226-4171** • 5pm-close • popular • mostly gay men • karaoke • videos • WiFi • wheelchair access • also Brig • lesbians/gay men • dancing/DJ • also Red Cap Garage

Candlelight Cafe & Bar 2032 SW 5th (at Lincoln St) **503/222-3378** • 3pm-2:30am • gay-friendly • live blues • food served • wheelchair access

CC Slaughter's 219 NW Davis (at 3rd) **503/248-9135, 888/348-9135** • 3pm-2am • popular • mostly gay men • dancing/DJ • karaoke • videos • also martini lounge • WiFi • wheelchair access

Chopsticks Express II 2651 E Burnside St (at SE 26th) **503/234-6171** • noon-2am • gay/straight • karaoke • young crowd • food served • wheelchair access

Crush 1400 SE Morrison (at SE 14th) **503/235-8150** • 4:30pm-2am, from 10am Sat, 9am-midnight Sun, clsd Mon • gay/straight • wine & martini bar • food • wheelchair access

Darcelle XV 208 NW 3rd Ave (at NW Davis St) **503/222-5338** • 6pm-11pm, till 2am Fri-Sat, clsd Sun-Tue • gay/straight • cabaret • strippers • drag shows • food served • wheelchair access

The Egyptian Club 3701 SE Division St (at SE 37th Ave) **503/236-8689** • 1pm-close, from 4pm wknds • popular • mostly women • dancing/DJ • karaoke • strippers • food served • transgender-friendly • wheelchair access • lesbian-owned

Fox & Hounds 217 NW 2nd Ave (btwn Everett & Davis) **503/243-5530** • 11am-2am • popular • mostly gay men • also restaurant • brunch wknds • wheelchair access

Hot Flash Portland 9 NW 2nd Ave (at Barracuda) **503/252-9333** • 5pm-9pm 4th Sat only • "for seasoned lesbians 36+ (& the women who love us!)" • dancing/DJ • cover charge

Invasion 412 SW 4th Ave **503/226-7777** • lesbians/gay men • theme nights

Moonstar 7410 NE Martin Luther King Jr Blvd (at NE Lombard St) **503/285-1230** • 11am-1:30am • gay/straight

Northbank 106 W 6th St (btwn Main & Washington), Vancouver, WA **360/695-3862** • 2pm-2am, clsd Mon • lesbians/gay men • dancing/DJ • food served • karaoke • drag shows • nonsmoking • wheelchair access

Rotture 315 SE 3rd Ave **503/234-5683** • 8pm-2:30am • gay-friendly • live music venue • also restaurant

Silverado 318 SW 3rd Ave (at SW Oak St) **503/224–4493** • 9am-2:30am • popular • mostly gay men • dancing/DJ • strippers • karaoke Mon • food served • wheelchair access • gay-owned

Starky's 2913 SE Stark St (at SE 29th Ave) **503/230–7980** • 11am-2am • popular • lesbians/ gay men • neighborhood bar • also restaurant • Sun brunch • some veggie • patio • wheelchair access

Vault Martini Bar 226 NW 12th Ave (btwn 12th & Davis Sts) **503/224–4909** • 4pm-1am, till 2am Th-Sat, 1pm-10pm Sun • gay/ straight • full menu • wheelchair access

Vino Vixens 2929 SE Powell Blvd **503/231–8466** • 1pm-9pm, till 11pm wknds, clsd Mon • gay/ straight • "Portland's first rock 'n' roll wine shop" • retail & lounge • nonsmoking • woman-owned

NIGHTCLUBS

Casey's 610 NW Couch (at 6th) **503/505–9468** • 7am-2:30am • lesbians/ gay men • dancing/DJ • go-go dancers

Embers 110 NW Broadway (at NW Couch St) **503/222–3082** • 9am-3am • popular • mostly gay men • dancing/DJ • drag shows • also restaurant • wheelchair access

Escape 333 SW Park (btwn SW Oak & SW Stark) **503/227–0830** • 10:30pm-close Fri-Sat only • Portland's only all-ages gay club • dancing/DJ • drag shows • videos

Holocene 1001 SE Morrison (at E 10th) **503/239–7639** • gay/ straight • popular dance club • many LGBT theme nights • live music • check local listings

Maricon at Matador 1967 W Burnside St (at Trinity) **503/222–5822** • 1st, 2nd & 3rd Sat only • lesbians/ gay men • dancing/DJ • drag shows

CAFES

Black Sheep Bakery 833 SE Main St **503/473–8534, 877/238–3426** • 8am-4pm, clsd Sat-Sun • vegan baked goods, brkfst & lunch sandwiches • bike-thru window & bake-at-home mixes • ship worldwide • lesbian-owned

Blend 2327 E Burnside St **503/234–8610** • 7am-6pm, from 8am Sun • WiFi

The Brews Brothers 445 NE 70th Ave **503/262–7613** • 7am-10pm, 8am-midnight wknds • outdoor garden • beer/ wine

Cup & Saucer Cafe 3566 SE Hawthorne Blvd (btwn 34th & 36th) **503/236–6001** • 7am-9pm • popular w/ lesbians • full menu • vegan-friendly • wheelchair access

Elephant's Delicatessan 115 NW 22nd Ave **503/299–6304** • 7am-7:30pm, 9:30am-6:30pm Sun • deli, desserts & coffee • wheelchair access

Half & Half 923 SW Oak St **503/222–4495** • 7:30am-6pm, from 8am wknds • wheelchair access

Haven Coffee 3551 SE Division St (at SE 35th Pl) **503/236–6890** • 7:30am-4pm • mostly women • live shows • WiFi • wheelchair access • lesbian-owned

Marco's Cafe & Espresso Bar 7910 SW 35th (at Multnomah Blvd), Multnomah **503/245–0199** • 7am-9pm, from 8am Sat, 8am-2pm Sun • food served • plenty veggie

The Pied Cow 3244 SE Belmont St (at 33rd Ave) **503/230–4866** • 4pm-midnight, till 1am Fri, noon-1am Sat, till midnight Sun • funky Victorian • great desserts • patio • WiFi • wheelchair access

Pix Pâtisserie 3402 SE Division St **503/232–4407** • 10am-midnight, till 2am Fri-Sat • dessert • wheelchair access

Three Friends Coffeehouse 201 SE 12th Ave (at Ash) **503/236–6411** • 7am-10pm, from 8am Sun • WiFi • wheelchair access

Voodoo Doughnut 22 SW 3rd Ave **503/241–4704** • 24hrs

RESTAURANTS

The Adobe Rose 1634 SE Bybee Blvd (at SE Milwaukee) **503/235–9114** • lunch & dinner, clsd Sun-Mon • New Mexican • some veggie • beer/ wine • wheelchair access

Andina 1314 NW Glisan St **503/228–9535** • lunch, dinner & tapas • Peruvian • full bar

Aura Restaurant & Lounge 1022 W Burnside St (btwn SW 10th & 11th) **503/597–2872** • 5pm-midnight, till 2:30am Fri-Sat, clsd Sun-Tue • also bar • wheelchair access

Bastas Trattoria 410 NW 21st (at Flanders) **503/274–1572** • dinner nightly • northern Italian • some veggie • full bar till late • wheelchair access

Belly 3500 NE Martin Luther King, Jr Blvd (at Fremont) **503/249–9764** • dinner Tue-Sat, Sun brunch, clsd Mon • local cuisine

Berbati's Pan 19 SW 2nd Ave (btwn Burnside & Ankeny) **503/226–2122** • 11am-2am, from 3pm Sun-Mon • Greek • full bar • live music venue • wheelchair access

Besaw's 2301 NW Savier (at NW 23rd) **503/228–2619** • 7am-10pm Tue-Fri, from 8am Sat, 8am-3pm Sun-Mon • American • wheelchair access

Bijou Cafe 132 SW 3rd Ave (at Pine St) **503/222–3187** • 7am-2pm, from 8am wknds • popular • plenty veggie • "farm-fresh brkfst" • wheelchair access

Bluehour 250 NW 13th Ave (at NW Everett St) **503/226–3394** • lunch Sun-Fri, dinner nightly, Sun brunch • extensive wine list • upscale • wheelchair access

Bread & Ink Cafe 3610 SE Hawthorne Blvd (at 36th) **503/239–4756** • brkfst, lunch & dinner, packed for brunch on Sun • popular • full bar • wheelchair access

Chameleon 2000 NE 40th Ave **503/460–2682** • 5:30pm-9:30pm, lounge open later Fri-Sat, clsd Sun-Mon • lesbians/gay men • Asian fusion • patio

Daily Cafe in the Pearl 902 NW 13th Ave (at Kearney St) **503/242–1916** • 7am-5pm, till 9pm Wed-Fri, 9am-9pm Sat, 9am-2pm Sun • Northwest cuisine • wheelchair access

Delta 4607 SE Woodstock (at 46th) **503/771–3101** • 5pm-midnight, wknd brunch, bar till 1am Fri-Sat • Southern • plenty veggie • wheelchair access

Dingo's Mexican Grill 4612 SE Hawthorne Blvd (at SE 39th) **503/233–3996** • noon-10pm, till 11pm Th, till 9pm Sun • popular Girls Night Out Th • wheelchair access • lesbian-owned

Dot's Cafe 2521 SE Clinton (at 26th) **503/235–0203** • noon-2am • popular • full bar • eclectic American • plenty veggie • wheelchair access

Equinox 830 N Shaver St **503/460–3333** • dinner, brunch wknds, clsd Mon • int'l • patio • wheelchair access

Esparza's Tex-Mex Cafe 2725 SE Ankeny St (at 28th) **503/234–7909** • 11:30am-10pm, clsd Sun • popular • funky • wheelchair access

Farm Cafe 10 SE 7th Ave (at E Burnside St) **503/736–3276** • 5pm-11pm • Northwest cuisine • wheelchair access

Fish Grotto 1035 SW Stark (at SW 11th Ave, at Boxxes) **503/226–4171** • 5pm-10pm, till 9pm Sun-Mon • popular • some veggie • full bar • live shows • wheelchair access

Genie's Cafe 1101 SE Division St **503/445–9777** • 8am-3pm • brunch • house-infused vodkas

Gypsy Restaurant & Lounge 625 NW 21st (btwn Hoyt & Irving) **503/796–1859** • 4pm-2:30am, clsd Sun-Mon, • some veggie • full bar • inexpensive • karaoke • wheelchair access

Hobo's 120 NW 3rd Ave (btwn Davis & Couch) **503/224–3285** • 4pm-2:30am • gay/straight • piano bar • also restaurant • some veggie • wheelchair access

Le Happy 1011 NW 16th Ave (btwn Lovejoy & Marshall) **503/226–1258** • 5pm-1am, till 2:30am Fri, 6pm-2:30am Sat, clsd Sun • crêpes • wheelchair access

Mama Mia Trattoria 439 W 2nd Ave **503/295–6464** • lunch & dinner • wheelchair access

Masu 406 SW 13th Ave **503/221–6278** • lunch Mon-Th, dinner nightly • sushi • WiFi • wheelchair access

Mayas Taqueria 1000 SW Morrison **503/226–1946** • 11am-10pm, till 8pm Sun • wheelchair access

Melt 716 NW 21st Ave (at Johnson) **503/295–4944** • 11am-10pm, clsd Sun • sandwiches & more

Mint 816 N Russell St **503/284–5518** • 4pm-10pm, till 11pm Fri-Sat • fusion food • also 820 Lounge • wheelchair access

Montage 301 SE Morrison **503/234–1324** • lunch Tue-Fri, dinner till 2am, till 4am Fri-Sat • popular • Louisiana-style cookin' • full bar • wheelchair access

Mother's Bistro & Bar 212 SW Stark St (at 2nd Ave) **503/464–1122** • brkfst, lunch & dinner, clsd Mon • American • wheelchair access

Nicholas' 318 SE Grand **503/235–5123** • 11am-9pm, from noon Sun • Middle Eastern • wheelchair access

Noble Rot 1111 E Burnside St **503/233–1999** • 5pm-midnight, clsd Sun • small plates • also wine bar • wheelchair access

Nostrana 1401 SE Morrison **503/234–2427** • lunch Mon-Fri, dinner nightly • fresh, local, wood-fired Italian

Old Town Pizza 226 NW Davis **503/222–9999** • 11:30am-11pm, till midnight Fri-Sat, clsd Sun • above Shanghai Tunnels • supposedly home to 100-year-old ghost • wheelchair access

Old Wives Tales 1300 E Burnside St (at 13th) **503/238–0470** • 8am-9pm, till 10pm Fri-Sat • multi-ethnic vegetarian • beer/wine • popular • wheelchair access

The Original Pancake House 8601 SW 24th Ave **503/246–9007** • 7am-3pm, clsd Mon-Tue • crowded on wknds • wheelchair access

Paley's Place 1204 NW 21st Ave (at NW Northrup St) **503/243–2403** • dinner nightly • Northwest cuisine

Papa Haydn 701 NW 23rd Ave (at NW Irving) **503/228–7317** • 11am-9:30pm, till midnight Fri-Sat, 10am-10pm Sun • bistro • some veggie • full bar • reservations recommended • wheelchair access • also at 5829 SE Milwaukee, 503/232-9440

Paradox Cafe 3439 SE Belmont **503/232–7508** • brkfst, lunch & dinner • popular • vegetarian diner • killer Reuben • wheelchair access

Pizzacato 505 NW 23rd (at Glisan) **503/242–0023** • 11:30am-9pm, till 10pm Fri-Sat • popular • plenty veggie • beer/ wine • many locations

Pour 2755 NE Broadway **503/288–7687** • 4:30pm-11pm, till close Fri-Sat, clsd Sun • wine bar & bistro • wheelchair access

The Roxy 1121 SW Stark St (btwn 11th & 12th) **503/223–9160** • noon-midnight, from 8am Tue, clsd Mon • popular • lesbians/ gay men • retro American diner • wheelchair access

Santa Fe Taqueria 831 NW 23rd (at Kearney) **503/220–0406** • 11am-midnight • live entertainment • wheelchair access

Saucebox 214 SW Broadway (at Burnside) **503/241–3393** • 5pm-close • lesbians/ gay men • pan-Asian • plenty veggie • full bar • DJ • wheelchair access • gay-owned

Under Wonder Lounge 128 NE Russell **503/284–8686** • 5pm-midnight, open show nights only • full bar • transgender-friendly • nonsmoking • gay-owned

Vino Paradiso Wine Bar & Bistro 417 NW 10th Ave (btwn NW Glisan & Flanders) **503/295–9536** • 4pm-11pm, 3pm-9pm Sun, clsd Mon • nonsmoking • gay-owned by Timothy Nishimoto of Pink Martini • wheelchair access

Vista Spring Cafe 2440 SW Vista (at Spring) **503/222–2811** • 11am-9:30pm, from noon wknds, till 9pm Sun • pasta & pizza • beer/ wine • wheelchair access

Vita Cafe 3023 NE Alberta St (btwn 30th & 31st) **503/335–8233** • brkfst, lunch & dinner • mostly vegetarian • some free-range meat

West Cafe 1201 SW Jefferson St (12th Ave) **503/227–8189** • lunch Mon-Fri, dinner nightly, Sun brunch • "comfort food w/ a twist" • live entertainment • wheelchair access

Wildwood 1221 NW 21st Ave (at Overton) **503/248–9663** • lunch Mon-Fri, dinner nightly • full bar • upscale • wheelchair access

Yakuza Lounge 5411 NE 30th Ave (at Killingsworth) **503/450–0893** • 5pm-close, clsd Mon-Tue • Japanese • full bar

ENTERTAINMENT & RECREATION

Brian Marki Fine Art 2236 NE Broadway **503/249–5659** • gallery • gay-owned

Froelick Gallery 714 NW Davis St **503/222–1142** • gay-owned art gallery

Gay Skate 1 SE Spokane St (at Oaks Park Way, at Oaks Rink) • 7pm-9pm 3rd Mon only • lesbians/ gay men

Onda Gallery 2215 NE Alberta St **503/493–1909** • Latin American arts & crafts gallery

Out Dancing 975 SE Sandy Blvd (at SE Ankeny St & SE 9th Ave) **503/236–5129** • LGBT dance lessons

Portland Shockwave 2205 NE 138th Ave (at McKenzie Stadium), Vancouver, WA • of the Independent Women's Football League • see www.portlandshockwave.com for info

Rose City Rollers • Portland's female roller derby league • visit www.rosecityrollers.com for events

Rose City Softball Association 503/552–4769 • LGBT softball league

Sauvie's Island Beach 25 miles NW (off US 30) • follow Reeder Rd to the Collins beach area, park at the farthest end of the road, then follow path to beach

Wonder Ballroom 128 NE Russell St **503/284–8686** • live music venue

BOOKSTORES

CounterMedia 927 SW Oak (btwn 9th & 10th) **503/226–8141** • 11am-7pm, noon-6pm Sun • alternative comics • vintage gay books/ periodicals/ erotica

In Other Words 8 NE Killingsworth St (at Williams) **503/232–6003** • 10am-9pm, noon-6pm Sat, clsd Sun • women's books • music • resource center • wheelchair access

Laughing Horse Bookstore 12 NE 10th St (near Burnside) **503/236–2893** • 11am-7pm, clsd Sun • alternative/ progressive • wheelchair access

Looking Glass Bookstore 7983 SE 13th Ave (in Stellwood) **503/227–4760** • 9am-6pm, 10am-5pm Sun, clsd Mon • general • some LGBT titles

Powell's Books 1005 W Burnside St (at 10th) **503/228–4651, 800/878–7323** • 9am-11pm • popular • largest new & used bookstore in the world • cafe • readings • wheelchair access

Reading Frenzy 921 SW Oak St (at 9th) **503/274–1449** • noon-6pm • zines • comics • LGBT selection • wheelchair access

RETAIL SHOPS

Fat Fancy 1013 SW Morrison (btwn 10th & 11th) • plus-size clothing boutique

Hip Chicks Do Wine 4510 SE 23rd Ave (SE Holgate & 26th) **503/234–3790** • 11am-6pm

The Jellybean 721 SW 10th Ave (at Morrison) **503/222–5888** • 10am-6pm, noon-5pm Sun • cards • T-shirts • gifts • wheelchair access

Presents of Mind 3633 SE Hawthorne (at 37th Ave) **503/230–7740** • 10am-7pm • jewelry • clothing • unique gifts • wheelchair access

Robot Piercing & Tattoo 2330 NW Westover Rd **503/224–9916**

PUBLICATIONS

Just Out **503/236–1252** • LGBT newspaper w/ extensive resource directory

GYMS & HEALTH CLUBS

Inner City Hot Tubs at Common Ground Wellness Center 5010 NE 33rd Ave (at Alberta St) **503/238–1065** • 10am-11pm • gay-friendly • wellness center • reservations required

EROTICA

Fantasy for Adults 1512 W Burnside (near 15th) **503/295–6969** • 24hrs

It's My Pleasure 3106 NE 64th Ave (at Sandy Blvd) **503/280–8080** • noon-7pm, till 6pm Sun • books • erotica • toys • gifts • workshops

Spartacus Leathers 300 SW 12th Ave (at Burnside) **503/224–2604**

Salem

ACCOMMODATIONS

Eagle Crest B&B 4401 Eagle Crest Rd NW **503/588–8315** • gay-friendly (mostly women) • full brkfst • nonsmoking • $100-130

NIGHTCLUBS

Southside Speakeasy 3529 Fairview Industrial Dr SE (at Madrona) **503/362–1139** • 11am-2am, from 3:30pm wknds • gay/ straight • neighborhood bar • dancing/DJ • food served • karaoke • drag shows• WiFi • gay-owned

RESTAURANTS

Davinci's 180 High St SE **504/399–1413** • dinner only, clsd Sun • full bar

Off Center Cafe 1741 Center St NE (at 17th) **503/581–6418** • brkfst & lunch Tue-Fri, brunch wknds, clsd Mon • some veggie • wheelchair access

Word Of Mouth 140 NE 17th St **503/930–4285** • 7am-3pm

Silverton

ACCOMMODATIONS

The Oregon Garden Resort 895 W Main St **800/966–6490** • gay-friendly • restaurant & lounge • pool • WiFi • $89-199

Yachats

ACCOMMODATIONS

See Vue Motel 95590 Hwy 101 **541/547–3227, 866/547–3237** • gay/ straight • ocean view • kids/ pets ok • nonsmoking • WiFi • lesbian-owned • $90-170

PENNSYLVANIA

Abington

BARS

Kitchen Bar 1482 Old York Rd **215/576–9766** • 7am-2am • gay-friendly • dancing/DJ • food served • live entertainment

RESTAURANTS

Vintage Bar & Restaurant 1116 Old York Rd **215/887–8500** • 11am-2am

Allentown

see also Bethlehem

BARS

Candida's 247 N 12th St (at Chew) **610/434–3071** • 4pm-2am, from 2pm Fri-Sun • lesbians/ gay men • neighborhood bar • food served • karaoke

Stonewall, Moose Lounge Bar & Grille 28 N 10th St (at Hamilton) **610/432–0215** • 7pm-2am, clsd Mon • popular • mostly gay men • dancing/DJ • food served • live shows • karaoke • drag shows • male dancers • videos • 18+ Th

Bethlehem

NIGHTCLUBS

Diamonz 1913 W Broad St (at Pennsylvania Ave) **610/865–1028** • 4pm-2am, from 8pm Mon-Tue, from 6pm Sun • mostly women • dancing/DJ • live shows • karaoke • also restaurant • some veggie • wheelchair access

Bristol

EROTICA

Bristol News World 576 Bristol Pike/ Rte 13 N **215/785–4770**

Butler

NIGHTCLUBS

Vertigo 564 W Cunningham St • 6pm Wed & Sun, from 9pm Fri-Sat • lesbians/ gay men • dancing/DJ •BYOB •

Erie

ACCOMMODATIONS

The Boothby Inn 311 W 6th St **814/456–1888, 866/266–8429** • gay-friendly • full brkfst • $130-170

NIGHTCLUBS

Craze 1607 Raspberry St **814/456–3027** • 9pm-2am, from 5pm Wed, clsd Tue• gay/ straight • dancing/DJ • karaoke • drag shows • 18+ Mon • patio

The Zone 133 W 18th St (at Peach) **814/452–0125** • 8pm-2am, rom 4pm Wed • lesbians/ gay men • dancing/DJ • food served

RESTAURANTS

La Bella 802 W 18th St **814/456–2244**

Matthew's Trattoria & Martini Lounge 153 E 13th St (btwn French & Holland) **814/459–6458** • dinner, clsd Sun-Mon • martini lounge • courtyard

Pie in the Sky Cafe 463 W 8th St (at Walnut) **814/459–8638** • lunch & dinner, clsd Sun-Mon • BYOB • reservations recommended • wheelchair access

RETAIL SHOPS

Ink Assassins Tattoos & Piercings 2601 Peach St **814/455–6752** • noon-10pm, till 6pm Sun

PUBLICATIONS

Erie Gay News **814/456–9833** • covers news & events in the Erie, Cleveland, Pittsburgh, Buffalo & Chautauqua County (NY) region

Gay People's Chronicle **216/916–9338** • Ohio's largest bi-weekly LGBT newspaper w/ extensive listings

Gettysburg

ACCOMMODATIONS

Battlefield B&B 2264 Emmitsburg Rd (at Ridge Rd) **717/334–8804, 888/766–3897** • gay/ straight • full brkfst • Civil War home • kids ok • WiFi • lesbian-owned • wheelchair access • $175-249

The Beechmont Inn B & B 315 Broadway, Hanover **717/632–3013, 800/553–7009** • gay-friendly • WiFi • wheelchair access

Sheppard Mansion B&B 117 Frederick St (at High St), Hanover **717/633–8075, 877/762–6746** • gay/ straight • full brkfst • kids 12 years & up ok • nonsmoking • WiFi • also restaurant & bar • $140-250

Greensburg

NIGHTCLUBS

Longbada Lounge 108 W Pittsburgh St (at Pennsylvania Ave) **724/837–6614** • 9pm-2am, clsd Sun-Mon • popular • lesbians/ gay men • dancing/DJ • karaoke • drag shows • patio • wheelchair access

Harrisburg

INFO LINES & SERVICES

LGBT Community Center Coalition of Central PA 221 N Front St, 3rd flr **717/920–9534** • www.centralpalgbtcenter.org

BARS

Bar 704 704 N 3rd St **717/234–4226** • 4pm-2am • mostly gay men • neighborhood bar • older crowd • wheelchair access

The Brownstone Lounge 412 Forster St (btwn 3rd & 6th) **717/234–7009** • 11am-2am, from 5pm wknds • lesbians/gay men • neighborhood bar • karaoke • wheelchair access

The Liquid 891 891 Eisenhower Blvd (near exit 19) **717/939–3590** • 8pm-2am, till 11pm Th, clsd Sun-Wed • lesbians/ gay men • popular • transgender-friendly • dancing/DJ • food served • live shows • drag shows • video

Neptune's Lounge 268 North St (at 3rd) **717/233–0581** • 4pm-2am, from 2pm Sun • lesbians/ gay men • neighborhood bar • dancing/DJ • young crowd

NIGHTCLUBS

Stallions 706 N 3rd St (enter rear) 717/232–3060 • 7pm-2am • popular • mostly gay men • dancing/DJ • live shows • karaoke • drag shows • strippers • Sun 18+ • wheelchair access

Irwin

NIGHTCLUBS

The Link 91 Wendel Rd, Herminie 724/446–7717 • 7pm-2am • lesbians/gay men • dancing/DJ • live shows • drag shows • male dancers • food served

Johnstown

NIGHTCLUBS

Lucille's 520 Washington St (near Central Park) 814/539–4448 • 6pm-2am, clsd Sun-Mon • lesbians/gay men • dancing/DJ • drag shows • strippers • karaoke

Kutztown

ACCOMMODATIONS

Grim's Manor B&B 10 Kern Rd 610/683–7089 • lesbians/gay men • 200-yr-old stone farmhouse on 5 acres • full brkfst • nonsmoking • gay-owned • $80

Lancaster

ACCOMMODATIONS

Cameron Estate Inn 1855 Mansion Ln (at Donegal Springs Rd), Mount Joy 717/492–0111, 888/422–6376 • gay/ straight • B&B inn • full brkfst • jacuzzi • nonsmoking • restaurant • wheelchair access • gay-owned • $129-299

Candlelight Inn B&B 2574 Lincoln Hwy E (at Rte 896/ Hartman Bridge Rd), Ronks 717/299–6005, 800/772–2635 • gay-friendly • full brkfst • $89-179

The Railroad House B&B, Restaurant & Tavern 280 W Front St (at S Perry St), Marietta 717/426–4141 • gay/ straight • full brkfst • nonsmoking • WiFi • wheelchair access • $119-189

BARS

Dad's Pub 168 S Main St, Manheim 717/665–1960 • 4pm-2am, from 11am Fri & ga/straight • food served • karaoke • Dawg Haus & Club 168 7pm Fri-Sat • dancing/DJ

Tally Ho 201 W Orange St (at Water) 717/299–0661 • 8pm-2am • popular • lesbians/ gay men • dancing/DJ • karaoke • drag shows • young crowd

RESTAURANTS

The Loft above Tally Ho bar 717/299–0661 • lunch Mon-Fri, dinner Mon-Sat • contemporary American/ French

Meadville

RESTAURANTS

Peppercorn & Vine 994 Market St 814/337–0005 • steak & seafood • also lounge • 18+ • gay-owned

Milford

ACCOMMODATIONS

Hotel Fauchere 401 Broad St (at Catharine St) 570/409–1212 • gay-friendly • historic boutique hotel • Hudson River School paintings throughout • full brkfst • also restaurant & bar • nonsmoking • kids/ pets ok • wheelchair access • $170-350

Mt Haven Resort RD 1 Log Tavern Rd 570/296–7262, 800/553–1530 • gay-friendly • in Poconos • kids/ pets ok • pool • WiFi • $75-1,000 • also Italian restaurant

New Hope

see also Lambertville & Sergeantsville, New Jersey

ACCOMMODATIONS

Ash Mill Farm B&B 5358 York Rd (at Rte 202), Holicong 215/794–5373 • gay-friendly • full brkfst • nonsmoking • WiFi • gay-owned • $130-295

Fox & Hound B&B 246 West Bridge St 215/862–5082 • gay-friendly • 1840s stone manor • full brkfst • nonsmoking • WiFi • $105-195

The Lexington House 6171 Upper York Rd 215/794–0811 • gay/ straight • 1749 country home • pool • nonsmoking • gay-owned • $175-205

The Mansion Inn 9 S Main St (at Bridge St) 215/862–1231 • lesbians/ gay men • pool • nonsmoking • restaurant • gay-owned • $155-275

The Nevermore 6426 Lower York Rd/ Rte 202 215/862–5221, 800/467–3202 • gay-friendly • pool • also restaurant & lounge • kids/ pets ok • wheelchair access

Silver Maple Organic Farm & B&B 483 Sergeantsville Rd (Rte 523), Flemington, NJ **908/237-2192** • gay/ straight • full brkfst • hot tub • pool • nonsmoking • kids/ pets ok • WiFi • wheelchair access • gay-owned • $99-175

The Wishing Well Guesthouse 144 Old York Rd **215/862-8819** • gay/ straight • B&B • nonsmoking • kids ok • gay-owned • $99-150

York Street House B&B 42 York St, Lambertville, NJ **609/397-3007, 888/398-3199** • gay-friendly •1909 Manor house • nonsmoking • $125-250

Bars

Harlans 6426 Lower York Rd (at the Nevermore Hotel) **215/862-5225** • gay/ straight • cabaret • dinner served • also hotel

Restaurants

Eagle Diner 6522 Lower York Rd **215/862-5575** • 24hrs • wheelchair access

Havana 105 S Main St **215/862-9897** • noon-midnight, from 11am wknds, bar till 2am • some veggie • live music • karaoke

Karla's 5 W Mechanic St (at Main) **215/862-2612** • noon-11pm, till midnight Fri-Sat, from 10am Sun • some veggie • full bar

Mother's 34 N Main St **215/862-5857** • 11am-9pm, till 10pm Fri-Sat • some veggie

Wildflowers 8 W Mechanic St **215/862-2241** • seasonal, noon-9pm • full bar • outdoor dining

Erotica

Grownups 2 E Mechanic St (at Main) **215/862-9304** • toys etc • gay-owned

Le Chateau Exotique 27 W Mechanic St **215/862-3810** • fetishwear

New Milford

Accommodations

Oneida Campground & Lodge **570/465-7011** • mostly gay men • seasonal • dedicated to the gay community • RV hookups • 1 guest cottage • pool • nudity • WiFi • gay-owned • $30-85

Norristown

Bars

Beagle Tavern 1003 E Main St **610/272-3133** • 11am-2am • gay/ straight, more gay Wed & Fri • DJ/dancing • lunch & dinner served • karaoke

Philadelphia

Info Lines & Services

William Way LGBT Community Center 1315 Spruce St (at Juniper) **215/732-2220** • 10am-9pm, from noon Sat, till 7pm Sun

Accommodations

Alexander Inn Spruce (at 12th St) **215/923-3535, 877/253-9466** • gay/ straight • restored hotel • gym • nonsmoking • WiFi • gay-owned • $119-159

Antique Row B&B 341 S 12th St (at Pine) **215/592-7802** • gay-friendly • 1820s town house in heart of gay community • full brkfst • $65-110

The Conwell Inn 1331 Polett Walk (at Montgomery Ave) **215/235-6200, 888/379-9737** • gay-straight • B&B on Temple University campus • pool • nonsmoking • kids/ pets ok • WiFi • wheelchair access • $109-229

Embassy Suites Center City 1776 Ben Franklin Pkwy (at 18th) **215/561-1776, 800/362-2779** • gay-friendly • $179-299

The Gables B&B 4520 Chester Ave **215/662-1918** • gay/ straight • in Victorian home • garden • nonsmoking • WiFi • gay-owned • $115-185

Hampton Inn Center City Philadelphia 1301 Race St (13th St) **215/665-9100, 800/426-7866** • gay/ straight • hotel • brkfst included • pool • jacuzzi • WiFi • wheelchair access • $105-209

The Independent Hotel 1234 Locust St (at 13th) **215/772-1440** • gay/ straight • boutique hotel • WiFi • wheelchair access

The Inn at Chester Springs 815 N Pottstown Pike (Exit 312), Exton **610/363-1100, 888/253-6119** • gay-friendly • full-service hotel • pool • kids/ pets ok • WiFi • $89-149

Latham Hotel 135 S 17th St (at Walnut) **215/563-7474, 877/528-4261** • gay-friendly • WiFi • wheelchair access

Morris House Hotel 225 S 8th St **215/922-2446** • gay-friendly • nonsmoking • WiFi • also M Restaurant • $179+

Rittenhouse Hotel 210 W Rittenhouse Square (at 19th) **215/546-9000, 800/635-1042** • gay-friendly • also restaurants & bar • nonsmoking • kids/ pets ok • WiFi

Bars

L' Etage 624 S 6th St (at Bainbridge) **215/592-0656** • 7:30pm-1am, till 2am Fri-Sat, clsd Mon • gay/ straight • dancing/DJ • food served • cabaret 1st Th • also restaurant downstairs • noon-11pm, from 10am wknds • crêperie

JR's Lounge 1305 Locust St (at S 13th) • mostly gay men • neighborhood bar • food served

The Khyber 56 S 2nd St (btwn Market & Chestnut) **215/238-5888** • noon-2am, from 4pm Sat • gay-friendly • live bands • wheelchair access

North Third 801 N 3rd (at Brown) **215/413-3666** • 5pm-midnight, till 2am wknds, wknd brunch • gay/ straight • also restaurant

Q Lounge 1234 Locust St (at 13th) **215/732-1800** • 5pm-2am • lesbians/ gay men • also restaurant • Sun brunch from 11am • dancing/DJ • "Austin-Powers chic"

Stir Lounge 1705 Chancellor St (at Rittenhouse Sq btwn Walnut & Spruce) **215/732-2700** • 4pm-2am • lesbians/ gay men • neighborhood bar • dancing/DJ • videos

Philadelphia

Where the Girls Are:
Partying downtown near 12th St., south of Market.

LGBT Pride:
June. 215/875-9288, web: www.phillypride.org.

Annual Events:
April/May - Equality Forum 215/732-3378, web: www.equalityforum.com. Weekend of LGBT film, performances, literature, sports, seminars, parties & more.

June - Womongathering 856/694-2037, web: www.womongathering.com. Women's spirituality fest.

July - QFest Int'l Gay & Lesbian Film Festival 267/765-9800 x701, web: www.qfest.com.

October - OutFest 215/875-9288, web: www.phillypride.org.

City Info:
Philadelphia Convention & Visitors Bureau 215/636-3300, web: www.pcvb.org.

Best View:
Top of Center Square, 16th & Market.

Weather:
Winter temperatures hover in the 20ºs. Summers are humid with temperatures in the 80ºs and 90ºs.

Attractions:
Academy of Natural Sciences 215/299-1000, web: www.acnatsci.org.

African American Museum 215/574-0380, web: www.aampmuseum.org.

Betsy Ross House 215/686-1252, web: www.betsyrosshouse.org.

Independence Hall 215/965-2305, web: www.nps.gov/inde.

Liberty Bell Pavilion.

National Museum Of American Jewish History 215/923-3811, web: www.nmajh.org.

Philadelphia Museum of Art 215/763-8100, web: www.philamuseum.org.

Reading Terminal Market, web: www.readingterminalmarket.org.

Rodin Museum 215/568-6026, web: www.rodinmuseum.org.

Transit:
Quaker City Cab 215/728-8000.

Transit Authority (SEPTA) 215/580-7800, web: www.septa.org.

Tavern on Camac 243 S Camac St (at Spruce) **215/545-0900** • 4pm-3am, 11:30am-3:30pm Sun brunch • lesbians/ gay men • dancing/DJ • piano bar • food served

Venture Inn 255 S Camac (at Spruce) **215/545-8731** • 11am-2am, from noon Sat • lesbians/ gay men • neighborhood bar • food served

The Westbury 261 S 13th (at Spruce) **215/546-5170** • 11am-2am, dinner till 10pm (till 11pm wknds) • lesbians/ gay men • neighborhood bar • wheelchair access • gay-owned

Woody's 202 S 13th St (at Walnut) **215/545-1893** • 11am-2am • popular • mostly gay men • dancing/DJ • country/ western • dance lessons • videos • full restaurant • karaoke Mon • Latin Th • strippers • young crowd • 18+ Wed • wheelchair access

NIGHTCLUBS

Bike Stop 204-206 S Quince St (btwn 11th & 12th, Walnut & Locust) **215/627-1662** • 4pm-2am, from 2pm wknds • popular • mostly gay men • 4 flrs • DJ • leather (very leather-women-friendly) • karaoke 5pm Sun

Bob & Barbara's Lounge 1509 South St **215/545-4511** • 3pm-2am, from 5pm Sun • gay/ straight • drag shows Th • live jazz Fri-Sat

Fluid 613 S 4th St (at Kater) **215/629-3686** • 9pm-2am • gay-friendly • more gay wknds • dancing/DJ • drag shows • theme nights • cover charge

FUSE South St (btwn 15th & Broad, at XO Lounge) **215/546-4195** • 10pm-3am 3rd Sat only • mostly women • dancing/DJ • drag shows • transgender-friendly • gay-owned

Ladies 2000 856/869-0193 • seasonal parties • call hotline for details

Lounge 125 125 S 2nd St (at Chestnut) **215/351-9026** • midnight-3:30am, from 11pm Wed-Sat • gay/ straight • dancing/DJ • live shows • food served • private club

The Scene • 4th Sat only • lesbians/ gay men • dancing/DJ • check www.myspace.com/thescenephilly for location

Shampoo 417 N 8th St (at Willow) **215/922-7500** • 9pm-2am, clsd Mon-Tue & Th • gay/ straight • more gay Fri • dancing/DJ

Sisters 1320 Chancellor St (at Juniper) **215/735-0735** • 5pm-2am, from noon Sun, from 8pm Mon • mostly women • dancing/DJ • live shows • karaoke • also restaurant • lesbians/ gay men • dinner Wed-Sat, Sun brunch • wheelchair access

Voyeur 1221 St James St (off 13th & Locust) **215/735-5772** • 1am-3am, from 9pm wknds • mostly gay men • dancing/DJ • piano bar • karaoke • cabaret • private club

CAFES

10th Street Pour House 262 S 10th St (at Spruce) **215/922-5626** • 7:30am-3pm, from 8:30am wknds, popular brunch wknds • wheelchair access

Brew HaHa! 212 S 12th (btwn Locust & Walnut) **215/893-5680** • 7am-9pm • WiFi • also newsstand

Cosi 1128 Walnut St **215/413-1608** • 6:30am-midnight, from 7am wknds

Green Line Cafe 4239 Baltimore Ave **215/222-3431** • 7am-11pm, 8am-8pm Sun • live shows • food served

Joe Coffee Bar 1100 Walnut St (at 11th St) **215/592-7384** • 6:30am-8pm, till 6:30pm Mon, from 8am Sat, clsd Sun • WiFi

RESTAURANTS

13th Street Pizza 209 S 13th St (at Chancellor St) **215/546-4453** • 11am-4am • popular late night

The Adobe Cafe 4550 Mitchell St (at Greenleaf), Roxborough **215/483-3947** • lunch Th-Sun & dinner nightly • plenty veggie • live shows

Alfa 1709 Walnut St (at 17th) **215/751-0201** • 4:30pm-2am • also Walnut Room lounge

Bar Ferdinand 1030 N 2nd St • great tapas and wine

The Caboose Grille 2 W Broad St, Souderton **215/721-1001** • lunch & dinner Tue-Sat, brkfst wknds, clsd Mon

The Continental 138 Market St (at 2nd) **215/923-6069** • lunch, dinner, wknd brunch • also bar until 2am • eclectic • some veggie

Figs 2501 Meredith St **215/978-8440** • lunch Tue-Fri, dinner nightly • wknd brunch • clsd Mon • eclectic Mediterranean • BYOB • wheelchair access

A Full Plate Cafe 1009 Bodine St (at George St) **215/627-4068** • 11am-9pm, till 10pm Fri, 10am-10pm Sat, till 3pm Sun • multiracial • transgender-friendly • BYOB • patio • lesbian-owned

The Gold Standard Cafe 4800 Baltimore Ave 215/727-8247 • brkfst, lunch & dinner

The Happy Rooster 118 S 16th St (at Sansom St) 215/963-9311 • 11:30am-1pm, from 3pm Sat • cont'l • upscale • karaoke • entertainment • full bar till 1am

Hinge Cafe 2652 E Somerset St 215/425-6614 • 8am-10pm, till 4pm Mon-Tue

Honey's 800 N 4th St 215/925-1150

Knock 226 S 12th St 215/925-1166 • lunch & dinner, Sun brunch • American • also bar

L2 2201 South St (at 22nd) 215/732-7878 • dinner nightly, clsd Mon • Asian/fusion • also bar

Liberties 705 N 2nd St (at Fairmount) 215/238-0660 • lunch & dinner • full bar till 2am

Little Pete's 219 S 17th St (at Locust) 215/545-5508 • 24hrs • diner

Lolita 106 S 13th St (at Sansom) 215/546-7100 • 5pm-10pm • upscale Mexican • BYOB

Mercato 1216 Spruce St 215/985-2962 • dinner • Italian • BYOB

Midtown II 122 S 11th St 215/627-6452 • 24 hrs • diner • popular late night • transgender-friendly

Mixto 1141-43 Pine St 215/592-0363 • lunch & dinner, brkfst wknds • Latin American

More Than Just Ice Cream 1119 Locust St (at 12th) 215/574-0586 • 11am-11pm • American

My Thai 2200 South St (at 22nd) 215/985-1878 • 5pm-10pm, till 11pm Fri-Sat • full bar

New Harmony 135 N 9th St (at Cherry) 215/627-4520 • 11am-11pm • vegan

The Plough & the Stars 123 Chestnut St (at 2nd) 215/733-0300 • lunch & dinner, popular wknd brunch • Irish pub fare • full bar • live music Sun

Sabrina's 910 Christian St 215/574-1599 • 8am-10pm, till 4pm Sun-Mon

Valanni 1229 Spruce St 215/790-9494 • dinner nightly, Sun brunch • Mediterranean/Latin • full bar

White Dog Cafe 3420 Sansom St (at Walnut) 215/386-9224 • lunch & dinner, brunch Sun • full bar • cool Mon reading & Sun film series

Zócalo 3600 Lancaster Ave (at 36th) 215/895-0139 • lunch Mon-Fri, dinner nightly • Mexican/New Southwestern

ENTERTAINMENT & RECREATION

Anna Crusis 215/864-5991 • women's choir

Mauckingbird Theatre Co 215/923-8909 • gay-themed plays

Philly Roller Girls • Philly's female roller derby league • visit www.phillyrollergirls.com for events

The Walt Whitman House 328 Mickle Blvd (btwn S 3rd & S 4th Sts), Camden, NJ 856/964-5383 • the last home of America's great & controversial poet, just across the Delaware River

BOOKSTORES

Giovanni's Room 345 S 12th St (at Pine) 215/923-2960 • 11:30am-7pm, from 1pm Sun • popular • legendary LGBT bookstore

Robin's Bookstore 108 S 13th St 215/735-9600 • 11am-7pm, noon-5pm Sun • oldest independent bookstore in Philly

RETAIL SHOPS

Infinite Body Piercing 626 S 4th St (at South) 215/923-7335 • noon-10pm, till 8pm Sun

PHAG/ Philadelphia Home Art Garden 1225 Walnut St 215/627-0461 • 11am-8pm, noon-6pm Sun • boutique

TLA Video 1520 Locust St (btwn 15th & 16th) 215/735-7887 • 10am-midnight, extensive LGBT titles

TLA Video 517 S 4th St (btwn 4th & Lombard) 215/735-7887 • 11am-midnight , from 10am Fri-Sun • extensive LGBT titles

TLA Video 7630 Germantown Ave 215/248-4448 • 10am-11pm • extensive LGBT titles

PUBLICATIONS

PGN (Philadelphia Gay News) 215/625-8501 • LGBT newspaper w/ extensive listings

Women's Yellow Pages of Greater Philadelphia 610/446-4747

GYMS & HEALTH CLUBS

12th St Gym 204 S 12th St (btwn Locust & Walnut) 215/985-4092 • pool • day passes

EROTICA

The Mood 531 South St 215/413-1930

Passional Boutique 704 S 5th St (at Bainbridge) 215/829-4986, 877/826-7738 • noon-10pm • corsets • fetish wear • toys • woman-owned

Passional Toys 620 S 5th St 215/923-1398 • noon-10pm • workshops • gallery

Pittsburgh

Info Lines & Services

AA Gay/ Lesbian 412/471–7472 • call for times & location

Gay/ Lesbian Community Center 210 Grant St 412/422–0114 • 6pm-9pm Tue, Wed & Th, noon-9pm Sat, noon-6pm Sun, clsd Mon

Accommodations

Camp Davis 311 Red Brush Rd, Boyers 724/637–2402 • April-Oct • lesbians/ gay men • cabins, trailer, & campsites • pool • adults 21+ only • 1 hour from Pittsburgh • $17 (tent sites), $25 (cabins), $30 (trailer) • rates per person

The Inn on Negley 703 S Negley Ave (at Elmer St) 412/661–0631 • gay-friendly • full brkfst • nonsmoking • WiFi • wheelchair access • women-owned • $180-240

The Inn on the Mexican War Streets 604 W North Ave 412/231–6544 • lesbians/ gay men • nonsmoking • also restaurant & bar • WiFi • gay-owned • $119-189

Morning Glory Inn B&B 2119 Sarah St 412/431–1707 • gay-friendly • in 1862 Italianate-style Victorian townhouse • WiFi • woman-owned • $145-450

The Parador Inn 939 Western Ave 412/231–4800, 888/540–1443 • gay-friendly • Caribbean-style B&B • fireplaces • gardens • WiFi • gay-owned • $150

The Priory 614 Pressley St (near Cedar Ave) 412/231–3338, 866/377–4679 • gay-friendly • 24-room Victorian • renovated 1888 monastery • fitness center • nonsmoking • kids ok • WiFi • wheelchair access • $99-230

Bars

5801 5801 Ellsworth Ave (at Maryland) 412/661–5600 • 4pm-2am • popular • lesbians/ gay men • also restaurant Th-Sun only • some veggie • deck • wheelchair access

Blue Moon Bar & Lounge 5115 Butler St (at Stanton) 412/781–1119 • 4pm-2am, till midnight Mon • mostly gay men • neighborhood bar • transgender-friendly • go-go dancers

Pittsburgh

LGBT Pride:

June. 412/422-0114 (GLCC #), web: www.glccpgh.org.

Annual Events:

June - Three Rivers Arts Festival 412/471–6070, web: www.arts-festival.net.

October - Pittsburgh International Lesbian & Gay Film Festival 412/422-6776, web: www.plgfs.org.

City Info:

800/359-0758, web: www.visitpitts-burgh.com.

Transit:

Yellow Cab 412/665-8100. 888/258-3826.
Port Authority Transit (PAT) 412/442-2000, web: www.portau-thority.org.

Attractions:

Andy Warhol Museum 412/237-8300, web: www.warhol.org.
Carnegie Museums of Pittsburgh 412/622-3131, web: www.carnegiemuseums.org.
Fallingwater (in Mill Run) 724/329-8501, web: www.paconserve.org.
Frick Art & Historical Center 412/371-0600, web: www.frickart.org.
Golden Triangle District.
Shopping & dining in the Strip District.
National Aviary 412/323-7235, web: www.aviary.org.
Phipps Conservatory 412/622-6914, web: www.phipps.conservatory.org.
Rachel Carson Homestead (in Springdale) 724/274-5459, web: www.rachelcarsonhomestead.or
Station Square.

Brewer's Tavern 3315 Liberty Ave (at Herron Ave) 412/681–7991 • 10am-2am, from 11am Sun • gay-friendly

Cattivo 146 44th St 412/687–2157 • 4pm-2am Wed-Sun, clsd Mon-Tue • mostly women • dancing/DJ • karaoke • drag shows • food served

Images 965 Liberty Ave (at 10th St) 412/391–9990 • 2pm-2am • mostly gay men • karaoke • videos

Pittsburgh Eagle 1740 Eckert St (off Chateau) 412/766–7222 • 9pm-2am Fri-Sat only • popular • mostly gay men • dancing/DJ • leather • wheelchair access

PTown 4740 Baum Blvd 412/621–0111 • 5pm-2am • lesbians/gay men • dancing/DJ

Real Luck Cafe 1519 Penn Ave (at 16th) 412/566–8988 • 4pm-2am • lesbians/gay men • neighborhood bar • go-go dancers • food served • some veggie • wheelchair access

Remedy 5121 Butler St, Lawrenceville 412/781–6771 • 3pm-2am, from 5pm Sun • gay/straight • multiracial • neighborhood bar • dancing/DJ • also restaurant upstairs

Spin Bartini/Ultra Lounge 5744 Ellsworth Ave, Shadyside 412/362–7746 • 4pm-2am • gay/straight • bartini lounge • live Jazz Tue • wheelchair access

There Ultra Lounge 931 Liberty Ave (at Smithfield) 412/642–4435 • 5:30pm-2am, from 8pm Sat-Sun • lesbians/gay men • wheelchair access

NIGHTCLUBS

1226 on Herron 1226 Herron Ave (at Liberty) 412/682–6839 • 6pm-2am, clsd Mon-Tue • mostly men • dancing Fri-Sat from 9pm

941 Saloon 941 Liberty Ave (at Smithfield St, 2nd flr) 412/281–5222 • 2pm-2am • popular • lesbians/gay men • dancing/DJ • karaoke

Club 818 818 Liberty 412/281–2131 • 10pm-2am, clsd Mon-Tue • popular • lesbians/gay men • dancing/DJ • young crowd

Heat 108 19th St (at Middle St) 917/519–3575 • 9pm-2am Wed-Sat • lesbians/gay men • dancing/DJ • drag shows • theme nights • 18+

House of Tilden 941 Liberty Ave (at Smithfield St, upstairs) 412/391–0804 • mostly gay men • dancing/DJ • after hrs on wknds only • membership required

Pegasus 1740 Eckert St (off Chateau) 412/281–2131 • 10pm-2am, clsd Mon-Tue • popular • lesbians/gay men • dancing/DJ • young crowd

Sugar 7 E Carson St (at Whim nightclub) 412/281–9888 • 9pm Th only • lesbians/gay men • dancing/DJ • 18+

CAFES

Hoi Polloi Vegetarian Cafe 1100 Galveston Ave (at W North Ave) 412/586–4567 • 7am-5pm

Square Cafe 1137 S Braddock Ave 412/244–8002 • 7am-3pm, from 8am Sun • live shows monthly • lesbian-owned

RESTAURANTS

Abay 130 S Highland Ave (at Baum Blvd) 412/661–9736 • lunch & dinner, clsd Mon • Ethiopian • plenty veggie

Capri 6001 Penn Ave (at Highland Ave) 412/661–0495 • 6pm-2am Th-Sat • pizza

Dish 128 S 17th St (at Sarah) 412/390–2012 • 5pm-2am, clsd Sun • Italian • also bar

Double Wide Grill 2339 E Carson St (at S 24th St) 412/390–1111 • lunch & dinner, wknd brunch • BBQ • plenty veggie/vegan

Eleven 1150 Smallman St (at 11th) 412/201–5656 • lunch Mon-Fri, dinner nightly, Sun brunch • American • upscale

Harris Grill 5747 Ellsworth Ave 412/362–5273 • dinner nightly, wknd brunch • full bar

Kaya 2000 Smallman St (at 20th) 412/261–6565 • lunch & dinner • Latin/Caribbean • plenty veggie

OTB Bicycle Cafe 2518 East Carson St (at S 26th) 412/381-3698 • noon-10pm • burgers • plenty veggie • also bar • occasional events

Point Brugge Cafe 401 Hastings (at Reynolds) 412/441–3334 • lunch & dinner, Sun brunch, clsd Mon • Belgian/European

Quiet Storm 5430 Penn Ave (at Graham St) 412/661–9355 • 8am-7pm, till 10pm Fri-Sat, till 4pm Sun • vegetarian/vegan • WiFi • wheelchair access

Red Oak Cafe 3610 Forbes Ave (at Lothrop) 412/621–2221 • 7am-7pm, till 5pm Fri, till 3pm wknds • salads & sandwiches • plenty veggie/vegan

Serendipity 422 Foreland St (at James) 412/918–1496 • lunch & dinner, clsd Sun-Mon • hip American bistro

Zenith 86 S 26th St 412/481–4833 • 11am-9pm, Sun brunch, clsd Mon-Wed • vegetarian/vegan • also antiques store • wheelchair access

ENTERTAINMENT & RECREATION

Andy Warhol Museum 117 Sandusky St (at General Robinson) 412/237-8300 • 10am-5pm, till 10pm Fri, clsd Mon • is it soup or is it art? see for yourself

RETAIL SHOPS

Slacker 1321 E Carson St (btwn 13th & 14th) 412/381-3911 • 11am-9pm, till 11pm Fri-Sat, 11am-6pm Sun • magazines • clothing • leather • piercing • wheelchair access

PUBLICATIONS

Cue Pittsburgh • monthly LGBT glossy

Erie Gay News 814/456-9833 • covers news & events in the Erie, Cleveland, Pittsburgh, Buffalo & Chautauqua County, NY region

Out 412/381-3350 • LGBT newspaper

EROTICA

Monroeville News - Adult Mart 2735 Stroschein Rd (off Rte 22), Monroeville 412/372-5477 • 24hrs, 13 miles from Pittsburgh

Poconos

ACCOMMODATIONS

The Arrowheart Inn 3021 Valley View Dr (at Fox Gap Rd), Bangor 610/588-0241 • gay/ straight • B&B • full brkfst • hot tub • nonsmoking • WiFi • kids ok • gay-owned • $110-189

Blueberry/Stoney Ridge 570/629-5036 • women only • hot tub • nonsmoking • secluded log home • pets OK • lesbian-owned • $125-175

Frog Hollow 570/595-2814 • lesbians/ gay men • secluded 1920s cottage • deck • fireplace • kids/ pets ok • lesbian-owned • $100-150

Rainbow Mountain Resort 570/223-8484 • lesbians/ gay men • transgender-friendly • resort w/ suites • cabins (seasonal) • swimming • hot tub • WiFi • gay-owned • $46-248 • also restaurant & full bar • dancing/DJ Fri-Sat • piano bar • karaoke

The Woods Campground 845 Vaughn Acres Ln, Lehighton 610/377-9577 • lesbians/ gay men • 84 campsites • RV spots • also cabins • swimming • 18+ • WiFi • $22-63

Reading

BARS

The Peanut Bar & Restaurant 332 Penn St 610/376-8500, 800/515-8500 • 11am-11pm, till midnight Fri-Sat, clsd Sun • a Reading landmark! • non-smoking • WiFi

The Red Star 11 S 10th St (at Penn St) 610/375-4116 • 9pm-2am, clsd Sun-Tue • popular • mostly gay men • neighborhood bar • dancing/DJ • leather • multiracial • transgender-friendly • older crowd • gay-owned

RESTAURANTS

Judy's On Cherry 332 Cherry St 610/374-8511 • lunch Tue-Fri, dinner Tue-Sat, clsd Sun-Mon • Mediterranean

The Ugly Oyster 21 S 5th St (at Cherry) 610/373-6791 • 11:30am-10pm, from noon Sat, clsd Sun • traditional Irish pub (bar open till 2am) • live shows

GYMS & HEALTH CLUBS

Gold's Gym 1119 Bern Rd, Wyomissing 610/372-9131 • gay-friendly

Scranton

BARS

Twelve Penny Saloon 3501 Birney Ave, Moosic 570/941-0444 • 6pm-2pm, from 3pm wknds • lesbians/ gay men • neighborhood bar • dancing/DJ • transgender-friendly • food served • karaoke • drag shows • wheelchair access • gay-owned

GYMS & HEALTH CLUBS

FitnessQUEST 6270 Rte 502 (at Rte 435), Moscow 570/842-2000

State College

INFO LINES & SERVICES

Women's Resource Center 140 W Nittany Ave (at Frasier) 877/234-5050 (24HR HOTLINE), 814/234-5050 • 9am-7pm, clsd wknds

ACCOMMODATIONS

The Atherton Hotel 125 S Atherton St (at College Ave) 814/231-2100, 800/832-132 • gay-friendly • nonsmoking • WiFi • also restaurant & bar • wheelchair access • $95-310

BARS

Chumley's 108 W College 814/238-4446 • 5pm-2am, from 6pm Sun • popular • lesbians/ gay men • neighborhood bar • wheelchair access

NIGHTCLUBS

Indigo 112 W College Ave **814/234–1031** • 9pm-2am, clsd Mon-Wed • gay/ straight • "Alternative" night Sun • dancing/DJ • videos • young crowd

Sunbury

BARS

CC's 555 Klinger Rd **570/286–6022** • 7pm-2am Th-Sat, from 5pm Sun • lesbians/ gay men • karaoke • drag shows

Uniontown

BARS

Eddie's Tavern 200 Francis St **724/438–9563** • 11am-midnight • gay-friendly • karaoke • try the wings

NIGHTCLUBS

Club 231 231 Pittsburgh St/ Rte 51 (at Fulton) **724/430–1477** • 8pm-close • mostly men • neighborhood bar • dancing/DJ • transgender-friendly • food • karaoke • drag shows • gay-owned

Wilkes-Barre

INFO LINES & SERVICES

NEPA Rainbow Alliance Resource Center 512 Northampton St #218, Edwardsville **570/763–9877** • coalition of NE PA's LGBT organizations & businesses • WiFi

NIGHTCLUBS

Twist 1170 Hwy 315 (in Fox Ridge Plaza) **570/825–7300** • 8pm-2am, from 6pm Sun • mostly gay men • dancing/DJ • patio • drag shows • wheelchair access

Williamsport

NIGHTCLUBS

Club Z 321 Pine St **570/322–6900** • 5pm-2am, clsd Sun-Mon • lesbians/ gay men • dancing/DJ wknds • karaoke

York

NIGHTCLUBS

Altland's Ranch 8505 Orchard Rd, Spring Grove **717/225–4479** • 8pm-2am Fri-Sat only • lesbians/ gay men • dancing/DJ • country western 3rd Fri • karaoke

Club XS 36 W 11th Ave (at Hwy 30 & N George St) **717/846–6969** • 4pm-2am • lesbians/ gay men • dancing/DJ • drag shows • cabaret • also Underground Lounge

EROTICA

Cupid's Connection Adult Boutique 244 N George St (at North) **717/846–5029**

RHODE ISLAND

Narragansett

ACCOMMODATIONS

Blueberry Cove Inn 75 Kingstown Rd **401/792–9865, 800/478–1426** • gay/straight • 3 blks from beach • full brkfst • nonsmoking • WiFi • $150-300

RESTAURANTS

Crazy Burger 144 Boon St **401/783–1810** • 8am-9pm • great brkfst

Newport

INFO LINES & SERVICES

Sobriety First 135 Pelham St (at Channing Memorial Church) **401/438–8860** • 8pm Fri

ACCOMMODATIONS

Architect's Inn 2 Sunnyside Pl **401/845–2547, 877/466–2547** • gay-friendly • fireplaces • near beach, shops & restaurants • WiFi • gay-owned • $49-420

Brinley Victorian Inn 23 Brinley St **401/848–6242, 800/718–1446** • gay-friendly • jacuzzis in some rooms • nonsmoking • WiFi • $129-229

Francis Malbone House Inn 392 Thames St (at Memorial Blvd) **401/846–0392, 800/846–0392** • gay-friendly • nonsmoking • WiFi • wheelchair access • $175-475

Hilltop Inn 2 Kay St **800/846–0392** • gay-friendly • craftsman-style inn • jacuzzis • full brkfst • nonsmoking • WiFi • gay-owned • $245-425

Hydrangea House Inn 16 Bellevue Ave **401/846–4435, 800/945–4667** • popular • gay/ straight • full brkfst • near beach • nonsmoking • WiFi • gay-owned • $225-475

Inn Bliss B&B 10 Bliss Rd (at Broadway) **401/845–2547, 877/466–2547** • gay/ straight • Victorian B&B • walk to beaches, mansions & downtown area • hot tub • nonsmoking • WiFi • gay-owned • $99-339

The Spring Seasons Inn 86 Spring St (btwn Mary St & Touro) **401/849–0004, 877/294–0004** • gay-friendly • full brkfst • jacuzzi baths • nonsmoking • $125-275

RESTAURANTS

Restaurant Bouchard 505 Thames St **401/846–0123** • dinner, clsd Tue

Whitehorse Tavern 26 Marlborough St (at Farewell) **401/849-3600** • lunch & dinner, Sun brunch • upscale dining • nonsmoking • patio

Pawtucket

Info Lines & Services

Gay & Lesbian AA 71 Park Place (at Park Place Congregational Church) **401/438-8860** • 7:30pm Tue

Providence

Accommodations

Courtyard by Marriott 32 Exchange Terr (at Memorial Blvd) **401/272-1191, 888/887-7955** • gay-friendly • nonsmoking

Edgewood Manor 232 Norwood Ave (at Broad) **401/781-0099** • gay-friendly • 1905 Greek Revival mansion • some fireplaces & whirlpools • nonsmoking • WiFi • $129-299

Hotel Dolce Villa 63 De Pasquale Square (at Atwells) **401/383-7031** • gay/ straight • boutique hotel • nonsmoking • $179-499

The Hotel Providence 311 Westminister St (at Mathewson) **401/861-8000, 800/861-8990** • gay/ straight • Aspire rerstaurant on-site • WiFi • nonsmoking • $179-709

Providence Biltmore Hotel 11 Dorrance St (at Washington) **401/421-0700, 800/294-7709** • gay-friendly • WiFi • pets ok • historic hotel

Renaissance Providence Hotel 5 Avenue of the Arts (at Francis) **401/919-5000, 800/468-3571** • gay/ straight • restaurant & bar • WiFi • nonsmoking • $229-499

Bars

Alleycat 17 Snow St (at Washington) **401/272-6369** • 3pm-1am, till 2am Fri-Sat • lesbians/ gay men • neighborhood bar • videos • gay-owned

Club Gallery 150 Point St (at Parsonage) **401/751-7166** • noon-1am, till 2am Fri-Sat, from 4pm Sun • popular • lesbians/ gay men • mostly women Sat • fetish night Fri • neighborhood bar • dancing/DJ Th-Sat • wheelchair access

GLO Bar 93 Clemence St (at Weybosset) **401/421-4744** • gay/ straight • dancing/DJ

The Providence Eagle 198 Union St (at Westminster) **401/421-1447** • 3pm-1am, till 2am Fri, from noon wknds

The Stable 125 Washington (at Mathewson) **401/272-6950** • 2pm-1am, till 2am Fri-Sat, from noon Sat-Sun • lesbians/ gay men • neighborhood bar • videos • wheelchair access

Sunset Bar & Grille 888 Charles St (at Admiral) **401/726-8889** • 6pm-1am Fri-Sat • lesbians/ gay men • women's night Fri • dancing/DJ • food served • live music • karaoke

Nightclubs

Gay Latin Night 44 Hospital St (at Lot 401) **401/640-7688** • 9pm Sun only • lesbians/ gay men • dancing/DJ • Latino/a

Girl Spot 150 Point St (at Club Gallery) **401/751-7166** • Sat only • mostly women • dancing/DJ • live music • 18+ • cover charge

Providence

LGBT Pride:
June. 401/467-2130, web: www.prideri.com.

Annual Events:
Aug - Rhode Island Int'l Film Festival 401/861-4445, web: www.film-festival.org.

City Info:
401/456-0200 or 800/233-1636, web: www.goprovidence.com.

Attractions:
Newport.
RISD Museum 401/454-6500, web: www.risd.edu.
Waterfire 401/273-1155, web: www.waterfire.com.

Transit:
Yellow Cab 401/941-1122.
RIPTA Bus Service 401/781-9400, web: www.ripta.com.

Mirabar 35 Richmond St (at Weybosset) **401/331-6761** • 3pm-1am, till 2am Fri-Sat • mostly gay men • dancing/DJ • live shows • male dancers • wheelchair access

Platforms Dance Club 165 Poe St **401/781-3121** • gay/straight • dancing/DJ • gay night Sat, Salsa Sun

State Ultra Lounge 1 Throop Alley (at Canal St) **401/854-6464** • gay/ straight • gay night Sun only • live piano • food served • tapas

Therapy 7 Dike St (at Troy) **401/490-7202** • 9pm-2am, till 4am Fri-Sat, clsd Sun-Mon • gay-friendly • also gallery & cafe from 10am • young crowd • wheelchair access

CAFES

Coffee Exchange 207 Wickenden St **401/273-1198** • 6:30am-11pm • deck

Nicks on Broadway 500 Broadway **401/421-0286** • lunch & dinner Wed-Sat, Sun brunch, clsd Mon-Tue

Pastiche Fine Desserts 92 Spruce St **401/861-5190** • 8:30am-11pm, 10am-10pm Sun

White Electric Coffee 711 Westminster **401/453-3007** • 7am-6:30pm

RESTAURANTS

Al Forno 577 S Main St **401/273-9760** • dinner only, clsd Sun-Mon

Blaze Restaurant 776 Hope St **401/277-2529** • lunch & dinner, clsd Mon • lesbian-owned

Bravo Brasserie 123 Empire St **401/490-5112** • lunch Tue-Sat, dinner nightly, Sun brunch

Caffe Dolce Vita 59 DePasquale Plaza (at Spruce St) **401/331-8240** • 8am-1am, till 2am wknds, wknd brunch • authentic Italian cafe • patio

Camille's 71 Bradford St (at Atwell's Ave) **401/751-4812** • lunch & dinner, clsd Sun • full bar

CAV 14 Imperial Pl **401/751-9164** • 11am-10pm, till 1am Fri, wknd brunch • eclectic menu & decor

DownCity 50 Weybosset St **401/331-9217** • lunch weekdays, dinner nightly • wknd brunch • full bar • wheelchair access

Fellini Pizzeria 166 Wickenden St **401/751-6737** • open late • free delivery • lesbian-owned

Haven Brothers Diner 72 Spruce St (in a truck outside City Hall) **401/861-7777** • 5pm-3am • since the 1930s

Julian's 318 Broadway (at Vinton) **401/861-1770** • lunch & dinner • beer/wine only

Local 121 121 Washington St (at Matthewson St) **401/274-2121** • lunch Tue-Sat, dinner nightly

Lot 401 44 Hospital St **401/490-3980** • dinner, clsd Sun-Mon • also club

Rue de l'Espoir 99 Hope St (at John) **401/751-8890** • brkfst & lunch daily, dinner Fri-Sun, Sun brunch • full bar • wheelchair access • women-owned

ENTERTAINMENT & RECREATION

AS220 115 Empire St (at Washington) **401/831-9327** • non-profit community arts space; performance, poetry, open mics, also classes; also bar & restaurant

Cable Car Cinema & Cafe 204 S Main St **401/272-3970** • art-house flicks & free popcorn refills

Perishable Theatre 95 Empire St **401/331-2695** • plays • also late-night comedy

Providence Roller Derby • Providence's female roller derby league • visit www.providencerollerderby.com for events

WaterFire Waterplace Park **401/272-3111** • May-Oct only • bonfire installations along the Providence River at sunset • check local listings for dates

BOOKSTORES

Books on the Square 471 Angell St (at Wayland) **401/331-9097, 888/669-9660** • 9am-9pm, 10am-6pm Sun • some LGBT

PUBLICATIONS

Metroline 860/231-8845, 800/233-8334 • regional newspaper & entertainment guide • covers CT, RI & MA

Options 401/724-5428 • LGBT community magazine

EROTICA

Mister Sister 268 Wickenden St **401/421-6969** • women-oriented • fetishwear • sex toys • classes

SOUTH CAROLINA

Statewide

PUBLICATIONS

Q Notes 704/531–9988 • bi-weekly LGBT newspaper for the Carolinas

Stereotypd 828/505–2870 • LGBT newspaper for NC & SC

Aiken

see also Augusta, Georgia

NIGHTCLUBS

Marlboro Station 141 Marlboro St 803/644–6485 • 10pm-close Fri-Sun • lesbians/gay men • dancing /DJ • live shows

Beaufort

RESTAURANTS

Old House Restaurant Hwy 462 (at Hwy 336), Ridgeland 843/258–4444 • 5pm-9pm, till 10pm Fri-Sat • wheelchair access • gay-owned

Blacksburg

EROTICA

BedTyme Stories 145 Simper Rd (I-85, exit 100) 864/839–0007, 828/650–3001

Charleston

INFO LINES & SERVICES

Acceptance Group (Gay AA) 67 Anson St (btwn Society & George, at St Stephen's Episcopal) 843/723–9633 (AA#) • 8pm Tue, 6:30pm Sat-Sun

ACCOMMODATIONS

A B&B @ 4 Unity Alley 4 Unity Alley 843/577–6660 • gay/ straight • 18th-c warehouse • full brkfst • nonsmoking • parking inside • $175-275

Alice's Carriage House B&B 22 New St (at Tradd St) 843/973–3458 • gay-friendly • pool • hot tub • nonsmoking • WiFi • $165-195

Folly Flamingo 116 E Ashley Ave (at Center St), Folly Beach 843/276–7779 • gay-friendly • rental home • nonsmoking • kids over 10 yrs ok • $125-175

Phoebe Pember House 26 Society St (at East Bay) 843/722–4186 • gay-friendly • also yoga classes • $140-250

Wentworth Mansion 149 Wentworth St 843/853–1886, 888/466–1886 • gay-friendly • nonsmoking • kids ok • also restaurant • $269+

NIGHTCLUBS

Club Pantheon 28 Ann St (at King) 843/577–2582 • 10pm-2am Fri-Sun only • mostly gay men • dancing • multiracial • live shows • drag shows • cabaret • 18+ • gay-owned

Club Patrick's 1377 Ashley River Rd/ Hwy 61 843/571–3435 • 6pm-2am • lesbians/ gay men • transgender-friendly • DJ Fri-Sat • karaoke Th • live shows & music • wheelchair access

Deja Vu II 4628 Spruill Ave 843/554–5959 • 5pm-close Th, from 10pm Fri-Sat • mostly women • dancing/DJ • live shows • food served • karaoke • private club • wheelchair access • lesbian-owned

CAFES

Bear E Patch 1980A Ashley River Rd 843/766–6490 • 7am-9pm, 8am-8pm Sat, clsd Sun • wheelchair access

RESTAURANTS

82 Queen 82 Queen St 843/723–7591, 800/849–0082 • lunch & dinner, Sun brunch • Lowcountry cuisine

Blossom Cafe 171 E Bay St 843/722–9200 • 11:30am-10pm, till 11pm wknds • Sun brunch • seafood • courtyard • wheelchair access

Fat Hen 3140 Maybank Hwy, St Johns Island 843/559–9090 • dinner nightly, Sun brunch • French bistro • seafood

Fig 232 Meeting St (near Hasell) 843/805–5900 • 5:30pm-10:30pm, till 11pm Fri-Sat, clsd Sun • local ingredients • full bar • wheelchair access

High Cotton 199 E Bay St 843/724–3815 • dinner nightly, lunch Sat, Sun brunch • Southern cuisine • full bar

Hominy Grill 207 Rutledge Ave (at Cannon) 843/937–0930 • brkfst, lunch & dinner, wknd brunch

Jim 'N Nick's Bar-B-Q 288 King St 843/577–0406 • 10:30am-9pm, till 10pm Fri-Sat

Joe Pasta 428 King St (at John) 843/965–5252 • 11:30am-11pm, till midnight Fri-Sat • also full bar

Magnolias 185 E Bay St #200 843/577–7771 • lunch & dinner, brunch Sun • Southern

Melvin's Legendary Bar-B-Que 538 Folly Rd 843/762–0511 • 10:45am-9:30pm, clsd Sun • "the #1 cheeseburger in America"

ENTERTAINMENT & RECREATION

Historic Charleston Foundation 40 E Bay St 843/723–1623 • call for info on city walking tours (March-April only)

Spoleto Festival USA 843/722–2764 • 2-week avant-garde performing art festival in late May–early June

PUBLICATIONS

Q Notes 704/531–9988 • bi-weekly LGBT newspaper for the Carolinas

Columbia

INFO LINES & SERVICES

The Harriet Hancock Center for Gay & Lesbian SC 1108 Woodrow St 803/771–7713 • 5:30pm-9pm, 1pm-3pm wknds, clsd Mon & Fri

Primary Purpose Gay/ Lesbian AA 5220 Clemson (in the house behind St Martin's Church) 803/254–5301(AA#) • 7pm Sun

BARS

Art Bar 1211 Park St 803/929–0198 • 8pm-2am • gay/ straight • dancing/DJ • karaoke

Capital Club 1002 Gervais St 803/256–6464 • 5pm-2am • mostly gay men • neighborhood bar • professional crowd • private club • wheelchair access

NIGHTCLUBS

The "L" Word 625 Frink St (at State St), Cayce 803/794–2111 • 5pm-close • mostly women • dancing/DJ • live shows • karaoke • wheelchair access

PTS 1109 1109 Assembly St (at Gervais St) 803/253–8900 • 5pm-2am, till 6am Fri, till 3am Sat-Sun • lesbians/ gay men • dancing/DJ • live shows • WiFi • multiracial • transgender-friendly • private club • gay-owned

ENTERTAINMENT & RECREATION

Rainbow Radio 803/771–7713 • 10am Sun • weekly LGBT radio program

RETAIL SHOPS

Papa Jazz Record Shoppe 2014 Greene St 803/256–0095 • 10am-7pm, 1pm-6pm Sun

Greenville

ACCOMMODATIONS

Walnut Lane Inn 110 Ridge Rd (at Groce Rd), Lyman 864/949–7230, 800/949–4686 • gay-friendly • B&B • full brkfst • kids ok • WiFi • gay-owned • $129-139

BARS

Sugar Shack 424 Laurens Rd 864/242–0294 • 7pm-close Th-Sun • lesbians/ gay men • dancing/DJ • live music • drag shows • private club

NIGHTCLUBS

The Castle 8-B Legrande Blvd 864/235–9949 • 9:30pm-3am Wed-Sun • popular • lesbians/ gay men • dancing/DJ • drag shows • videos • young crowd • private club • wheelchair access

BOOKSTORES

Out of Bounds 21 S Pleasantburg Dr 864/239–0106 • 2pm- 8pm, till 6pm Sun, from 11am Fri-Sat • community pride store

Hilton Head

BARS

Twist/ Two Dollar Bill's 32 Palmetto Bay Rd #D-2 (at Sea Pines Cir) 843/341–6933 • 4pm-3am, from 8pm Sat, clsd Sun • lesbians/ gay men • neighborhood bar • transgender-friendly • food served

Lake Wylie

NIGHTCLUBS

The Rainbow In 4376 Charlotte Hwy 803/831–0093 • 8pm-2am, from 6pm Sun, clsd Mon-Wed • lesbians/ gay men • dancing/ DJ • drag shows • private club

Myrtle Beach

INFO LINES & SERVICES

The Center Project 307 Hwy 15 (at 3rd Ave S) 843/626–4953 • 2pm-9pm, till 6pm Sat-Mon • LGBT community center

ACCOMMODATIONS

Aquarius Motel 301 12th Ave N 843/448–7596, 800/244–4386 • gay/ straight • pool • pets/kids ok • WiFi • $55-200

Bars

Time Out 520 8th Ave N (at Oak) 843/448–1180 • 5pm-close, till 2am Sat • popular • mostly gay men • neighborhood bar • dancing/DJ • karaoke • drag shows • live shows • patio bar • private club • wheelchair access

Nightclubs

Rainbow House 815 N Kings Hwy 843/626–7298 • 11am-5am, till 2am wknds • lesbians/gay men • dancing/DJ • drag shows • patio • wheelchair access

Restaurants

Cedar Hill Landing Seafood & Oyster Roast 5225 Hwy 17 (at Business), Murrells Inlet 843/651–8706 • 10am-10pm • live shows • wheelchair access • full bar

Retail Shops

Kilgor Trouts Music & More 512 8th Ave N 843/445–2800

Rock Hill

Info Lines & Services

Catawba Care Coalition 1151 Camden Ave 803/909–6363 • HIV/AIDS support & services • free testing • free condoms

Bars

Hideaway 405 Baskins Rd 803/328–6630 • 9pm-close Th-Sat • lesbians/gay men • neighborhood bar • drag shows • karaoke • private club

SOUTH DAKOTA

Statewide

Publications

Lavender Magazine 612/436–4660, 877/515–9969 • LGBT newsmagazine for IA, MN, ND, SD, WI

Murdo

Accommodations

Iversen Inn 108 E 5th St (on I-90 Business Loop) 605/669–2452 • gay-friendly • kids/pets ok • WiFi • gay-owned

Rapid City

Info Lines & Services

The Black Hills Center For Equality 1102 West Rapid St (at Omaha St) 605/348–3244 • 11am-5pm, till 6pm sat, clsd Sun, LGBT resource center

Unified Live & Let Live AA 522 7th St #218 605/209–9225 • 8pm Fri

Salem

Accommodations

Camp America 25495 US 81 605/425–9085 • gay-friendly • 35 miles west of Sioux Falls • camping • RV hookups • pool • kids/pets ok • nonsmoking • WiFi • lesbian-owned • $18-31

Sioux Falls

Info Lines & Services

The Center 3600 S Minnesota Ave #5 605/331–1153 • support groups • counseling • library & more

Bars

Toppers 1213 N Cliff Ave 605/339–7686 • 3pm-close, till 2am Th-Sat, clsd Sun • lesbians/gay men • more women Wed • karaoke

Nightclubs

Club David 214 W 10th St (btwn Main & Dakota) 605/274–0700 • 4:30pm-2am • lesbians/gay men • dancing/DJ • karaoke • drag shows • also restaurant

Erotica

Romantix Adult Superstore 311 N Dakota Ave (btwn 6th & 7th) 605/332–9316 • 24hrs

Spearfish

Cafes

The Bay Leaf Cafe 126 W Hudson St 605/642–5462 • lunch & dinner • plenty veggie • espresso bar

TENNESSEE

Chattanooga

Bars

Chuck's II 27–1/2 W Main St (at Market) 423/265–5405 • 6pm-1am, till 3am Fri-Sat • lesbians/gay men • neighborhood bar • dancing/DJ • patio

Nightclubs

Alan Gold's 1100 McCallie Ave (at Central) 423/629–8080 • 4:30pm-3am • popular • lesbians/gay men • dancing/DJ • drag shows • strippers • food served • young crowd • wheelchair access

Images 6005 Lee Hwy 423/855-8210 • 5pm-3am Th-Sun • lesbians/ gay men • dancing/DJ • drag shows • also restaurant • wheelchair access

Gatlinburg

ACCOMMODATIONS

Big Creek Stables & Big Creek Outpost 5019 Rag Mtn Rd, Hartford 423/487-5742, 423/487-3490 • gay/ straight • cabins • camping • horseback riding • kids ok • wheelchair access • $25-150

Christopher Place, An Intimate Resort 1500 Pinnacles Wy, Newport 423/623-6555, 800/595-9441 • gay/ straight • full brkfst • pool • nonsmoking • wheelchair access • $165-330

English Mountaintop Villa Cove Rd, Sevierville 865/522-8547 • gay-friendly • private condo in Great Smoky Mtns Nat'l Park • panoramic views • pool • nonsmoking • WiFi • wheelchair access • $695-995/ week

Four Seasons Getaways 3588 Four Seasons Ln (at Little Cove Rd), Sevierville 386/837-1458 • lesbians/ gay men • private home in Wears Valley • sleeps 5 • near Smoky Mtns • great views • hot tub • nonsmoking • gay-owned • $110-175

Mountain Vista Cabins 1805 Shady Grove Rd (at Old Birds Creek Rd), Sevierville 865/712-9897 • lesbians/ gay men • hot tub • well-behaved kids/ pets welcome • nonsmoking • WiFi • woman-owned • $120-140

Stonecreek Cabins 865/429-0400 • lesbians/ gay men • 23-acre paradise in Smoky Mtns • hot tub • nonsmoking • lesbian-owned • $135-185

Johnson City

ACCOMMODATIONS

Safehaven Farm 336 Stanley Hollow Rd, Roan Mountain 423/725-4262 • gay-friendly • cabins • creekside privacy • fireplace & wraparound porch • kids/ pets ok • $90/ night, $450/ week

NIGHTCLUBS

Fuzzy Holes 1410 E Main St (at S Broadway St) 423/929-9800 • 8pm-close • transgender-friendly • sex-positive strip club • food served • 18+ • wheelchair access • lesbian-owned

New Beginnings 2910 N Bristol Hwy 423/282-4446 • 9pm-2am, from 8pm Fri-Sat, clsd Sun-Mon • popular • mostly gay men • dancing/DJ • drag shows • also restaurant • wheelchair access

RETAIL SHOPS

My Secret Closet 2910 N Bristol Hwy (inside New Beginnings) 423/282-4446 • 10pm-3am Fri-Sat only • pride gifts

Knoxville

INFO LINES & SERVICES

AA Gay/ Lesbian 2931 Kingston Pike (at Unitarian Church) 865/522-9667 (AA#) • 8pm Fri

Lesbian Social Group 865/531-7788 • meet 7pm Wed • call for info

BARS

Chrome Pony Saloon 2909 Alcoa Hwy 865/680-1899 • 4pm-3am, clsd Mon-Tue • lesbians/gay men • neighborhood bar • drag shows • great pizza • karaoke

NIGHTCLUBS

Club XYZ 1215 N Central 865/637-4999 • 5:30pm-3am, from 9pm Sat, from 7pm Sun • lesbians/ gay men • dancing/DJ • drag shows • karaoke

GyrlGroove 865/356-7671 • bi monthly womens dance parties • check gyrlgroove.com for location

The New Rainbow Club West 7211 Kingston Pike SW 865/588-8030 • 5pm-3am • lesbians/ gay men • dancing/DJ • food served • karaoke • drag shows • wheelchair access

Memphis

INFO LINES & SERVICES

AA Intergroup 1835 Union Ave #302 901/726-6750 • call for times & locations

Memphis Gay/ Lesbian Community Center 892 S Cooper (at Nelson) 901/278-6422, 901/278-4297 (HOTLINE) • 24-hour recorded info • groups

ACCOMMODATIONS

Shellcrest Guesthouse 671 Jefferson Ave (at N Orleans St) 901/277-0223 • gay/ straight • suites in downtown Victorian • pool • nonsmoking • WiFi • gay-owned • $170-250

Talbot Heirs Guesthouse 99 S 2nd St (btwn Union & Peabody Pl) 901/527-9772, 800/955-3956 • gay-friendly • suites w/ kitchens • funky decor • nonsmoking • kids ok • $135-275

Bars

Dru's Place 1474 Madison (at McNeil) **901/275-8082** • 11am-midnight, till 3am Fri-Sat, from noon Sun • mostly women • neighborhood bar • beer & set-ups only

Lorenz/ Aftershock 1528 Madison Ave (at Avalon) **901/274-8272** • 11am-3am • lesbians/ gay men • neighborhood bar • dancing/DJ • drag shows • mutl-racial clientele

The Metro 1349 Autumn St (at Cleveland) **901/274-8010** • 4pm-3am • lesbians/gay men • dancing/DJ • karaoke • food served • patio • wheelchair access

Mollie Fontaine Lounge 679 Adams Ave (at Orleans) **901/524-1886** • 5pm-2am, clsd Sun-Tue • gay/ straight • food served

RP Billiards 525 S Highland St (at Southern Ave) **901/452-6583** • 5pm-3am • gay-friendly

The Vault 529 S Highland St (at Southern Ave) **901/452-6583** • 5pm-3am • gay/ straight • dancing/DJ • karaoke • live jazz Wed

Nightclubs

901 Complex 136 Webster Ave (at S 2nd St) **901/522-8459** • from 10pm Fri-Sat only • lesbians/ gay men • ladies night Fri • mostly African American • dancing/DJ • drag shows • BYOB

Backstreet 2018 Court Ave (at Morrison) **901/276-5522** • 8pm-6am Wed-Sun only • lesbians/ gay men • dancing/DJ • karaoke • cabaret • 18+ • wheelchair access • beer & set-ups only

Crossroads 1278 Jefferson (at Claybrook) **901/272-8801** • 4pm-midnight, 3pm-3am Fri-Sun • lesbians/ gay men • neighborhood bar • drag shows Fri-Sat • karaoke

Mary's 405 N Cleveland (at Autumn Ave) **901/725-7334** • lesbians/ gay men • dancing/DJ • WiFi

Senses 2866 Poplar Ave (at Walnut Grove Rd) **901/454-4081** • gay/ straight • dancing/DJ • multiracial • theme nights

Memphis

Where the Girls Are:
On Madison Ave., of course, just east of US-240.

LGBT Pride:
June. Mid-South Pride 901/382-6349, web: www.midsouth-pride.org.

Annual Events:
September - OutFlix International GLBT Film Festival 901/283-5935, web: www.outflixfestival.org.

September - The Cooper-Young Festival (arts, crafts & music) 901/276-7222.

City Info:
901/543-5300, web: www.memphistravel.com.

Best View:
A cruise on any of the boats that ply the river.

Weather:
Suth'n. H-O-T and humid in the summer, cold (30°s-40°s) in the winter, and a relatively nice (but still humid) spring and fall.

Attractions:
Beale Street.
Graceland 800/238-2000, web: www.elvis.com/graceland.
Mud Island 800/507-6507, web: www.mudisland.com.
Nat'l Civil Rights Museum 901/521-9699, web: www.civil-rightsmuseum.org.
Rock N Soul Museum 901/205-2533, web: www.memphisrocknsoul.org.
Overton Square.
Stax Museum 901/946-2535, web: www.staxmuseum.com.
Sun Studio 800/441-6249, web: www.sunstudio.com.

Transit:
Yellow Cab 901/577-7777. 877/300-4VAN.
MATA 901/274-6282, web: www.matatransit.com.

CAFES

Java Cabana 2170 Young Ave (at Cooper) **901/272–7210** • 6:30am-10pm, 9am-midnight Fri-Sat, noon-10pm Sun, clsd Mon • poetry readings & live shows • also art gallery

Otherlands Coffee Bar 641 S Cooper (at Central) **901/278–4994** • 7am-8pm • live music till 11pm Fri-Sat • plenty veggie • WiFi • also gift shop

P&H Cafe 1532 Madison (at Adeline) **901/726–0906** • 3pm-3am, from 5pm Sat, clsd Sun • beer/ wine • food served • live shows • wheelchair access

RESTAURANTS

Automatic Slim's Tonga Club 83 S 2nd St (at Union) **901/525–7948** • lunch & dinner, Sun brunch • Caribbean & Southwestern • plenty veggie • full bar • wheelchair access

Cafe Eclectic 603 N McLean Blvd (at Faxon Ave) **901/725–1718** • 6am-10pm, 9am-3pm Sun

Cafe Society 212 N Evergreen Ave (btwn McLean & Belvedere) **901/722–2177** • lunch Mon-Fri, dinner nightly • full bar • wheelchair access

Circa 119 S Main St #100 (at Peabody Pl) **901/522–1488** • dinner nightly • American

India Palace 1720 Poplar Ave **901/278–1199**

Leonard's Pit Barbecue 5465 Fox Plaza Dr **901/360–1963** • 11am-9pm • Elvis ordered the pork sandwich at the original Leonard's (now closed), but the food is just as good here!

Molly Gonzales' La Casita 2006 Madison Ave (at Rembert) **901/726–1873** • Mexican • also bar

Molly's La Casita 2006 Madison Ave (at N Morrison St) **901/726–1873** • lunch & dinner • Mexican

Quetzal 668 Union Ave **901/521–8388** • cafe & restaurant • gay events during the evening

Restaurant Iris 2146 Monroe Ave **901/590–2828** • dinner Tue-Sat, Sun brunch, clsd Mon • French • upscale

RP Tracks 3547 Walker Ave (at Brister) **901/327–1471** • lunch & dinner, open till 3am • burgers • some veggie

Saigon Le 51 N Cleveland **901/276–5326** • 11am-9pm, clsd Sun • Chinese/ Vietnamese/ Thai

Tsunami 928 S Cooper **901/274–2556** • dinner only • Pacific rim cuisine

ENTERTAINMENT & RECREATION

Center for Southern Folklore 119 S Main St (at Peabody Pl) **901/525–3655** • 11am-6pm, clsd Sun, open later for shows • live music • gallery • cybercafe • food served

Graceland 3734 Elvis Presley Blvd **901/332–3322, 800/238–2000** • no visit to Memphis would be complete w/out a trip to see The King

Memphis Rock 'N Roll Tours **901/359–3102** • historical tour of Memphis music scene

BOOKSTORES

Davis-Kidd Booksellers 387 Perkins Rd Ext (at Poplar & Walnut Grove) **901/683–9801** • 9am-9pm, till 8pm Sun • general • some LGBT titles • also cafe

RETAIL SHOPS

Inz & Outz 553 S Cooper (at Peabody) **901/728–6535** • 10am-8pm, noon-6pm Sun • pride items • books • gifts • wheelchair access

PUBLICATIONS

Triangle Journal News **901/857–8523** • LGBT newspaper • extensive resource listings

EROTICA

Cherokee Books 2947 Lamar **901/744–7494**

Romantix Adult Superstore 1617 Getwell Rd **901/744–4513**

Romantix Adult Superstore 2220 E Brooks Rd **901/396–9050**

Romantix Adult Superstore 5939 Summer Ave **901/373–5760**

Nashville

INFO LINES & SERVICES

AA Gay/ Lesbian **615/831–1050** • call for info

ACCOMMODATIONS

The Big Bungalow B&B 618 Fatherland St **615/256–8375** • gay-friendly • full brkfst • live music • massage available • nonsmoking • woman-owned • $125-185

Doubletree Nashville 315 4th Ave N **615/244–8200** • gay-friendly • also restaurant & lounge • fitness center • WiFi

Hutton Hotel 1808 West End Ave **615/340–9333** • gay-friendly • also restaurant • WiFi • fitness center • WiFi • $199+

Top O' Woodland Historic B&B Inn 1603 Woodland St (at 16th) **615/228–3868, 888/228–3868** • gay-friendly • full brkfst • also wedding chapel • nonsmoking • WiFi • woman-owned • $160

BARS

McFadden's 134 2nd Ave N (at Commerce) **615/256–9140** • gay Mon only • also restaurant

Purple Heys 1401 4th Ave S (btwn Lafayette & Chestnut) **615/244–4433** • 11am-3am • lesbians/gay men • neighborhood bar • food served • wheelchair access

Stirrup Nashville 1529 4th Ave S (at Mallory Ave) **615/782–0043** • noon-3am • mostly gay men • multiracial • transgender-friendly • neighborhood bar • food served • patio • wheelchair access

Trax 1501 2nd Ave S (at Carney) **615/742–8856** • noon-3am • mostly gay men • neighborhood bar • karaoke • WiFi

Tribe/ Suzy Wong's House of Yum 1517 Church St (at 15th Ave S) **615/329–2912** • 4pm-midnight, till 2am wknds • lesbians/gay men • live entertainment • videos • upscale • full restaurant • wheelchair access • gay-owned

Nashville

WHERE THE GIRLS ARE:
Just north of I-65/40 along 2nd Ave. S. or Hermitage Ave.

LGBT PRIDE:
June. 615/650-6736, web: www.nashvillepride.org.
October. Black Pride 800/845-4266 x 269, web: www.brother-sunited.com.

ANNUAL EVENTS:
September - Nashville Film Festival (some gay films), web: nashville-filmfestival.org.
September - AIDS Walk 615/259-4866, web: www.nashvillecares.org.
November - Artrageous 615/259-4866, web: www.nashvillecares.org.

CITY INFO:
800/657-6910, web: www.nashvil-lecvb.com.

BEST VIEW:
Try a walking tour of the city.

WEATHER:
See Memphis.

TRANSIT:
Yellow Cab 615/256-0101.
Gray Line Airport Shuttle 615/275-1180.
MTA 615/862-5969, web: www.nashvillemta.org

ATTRACTIONS:
Country Music Hall of Fame 615/416-2001, web: www.coun-trymusichalloffame.com.
Grand Ole Opry & Opryland USA 615/871-OPRY, web: www.opry.com.
Jack Daniel's Distillery 615/279-4100, web: www.jackdaniels.com.
The Parthenon 615/862-8431, web: www.parthenon.org.
Ryman Auditorium 615/889-3060, web: www.ryman.com.
Tennessee Antebellum Trail 888/852-1860, web: www.ante-bellum.com.

Vibe 1713 Church St (at 17th & 18th) **615/329–3838** • 9pm Sat only • lesbians/ gay men • dancing/DJ • drag shows • patio

NIGHTCLUBS

508 508 Lea Ave (at 6th) **615/259–3223** • midnight-7am Fri-Sat night only • gay/ straight • dancing/DJ

Bluebird Cafe 4104 Hillsboro Pike (nr Warfield Dr) **615/383–1461** • live country music venue

Lipstick Lounge 1400 Woodland St (at 14th) **615/226–6343** • 4pm-close, from 7pm Fri, from 6pm wknds • mostly women • dancing/DJ • karaoke • live music

Play Dance Bar 1519 Church St **615/322–9627** • 9pm-3am Wed-Sun • mostly gay men • dancing/DJ • multiracial • transgender-friendly • drag shows • 18+ • wheelchair access

CAFES

Bongo Java 2007 Belmont Blvd **615/385–5282** • 7am-11pm, from 8am wknds • coffeehouse • deck • also serves brkfst, lunch & dinner

Fido 1812 21st Ave S **615/777–3436** • 7am-11pm, till midnight Fri-Sat, from 8am wknds • also full menu

RESTAURANTS

Battered & Fried 1008 Woodland St **615/226–9283** • lunch & dinner • seafood • full bar • also Wave sushi bar

Beyond the Edge 112 S 11th St **615/226–3343** • 11am-2am • pizza & sandwiches • full bar

Cafe Coco 210 Louise Ave **615/321–2626** • 24hrs • live music • beer/ wine • patio

Calypso Cafe 2424 Elliston Pl **615/321–3878** • 11am-9pm, 11:30am-8:30pm wknds • Caribbean

International Market 2010 Belmont Blvd (at International) **615/297–4453** • 10:30am-9pm • Thai/ Chinese • plenty veggie

Mad Donna's 1313 Woodland St (at 14th) **615/226–1617** • 11am-10pm, till 11pm Sat, clsd Mon • also lounge • drag bingo Tue

The Mad Platter 1239 6th Ave N (at Monroe) **615/242–2563** • lunch Mon-Fri, dinner Wed-Sun • Californian • some veggie • wheelchair access

Nuvo Burrito 1000 Main St (at Woodland) **615/866–9713** • 11:30am-9pm • eclectic burrito menu • also bar • theme nights

Pancake Pantry 1796 21st Ave S (at Wedgewood Ave) **615/383–9333** • 6am-3pm, till 4pm wknds • popular for brkfst

Rumba 3009 W End Ave **615/321–1350** • 4pm-close, from 5pm Sun • Latin/ Asian • exotic drinks

Rumours Wine & Art Bar 2304 12th Ave S **615/292–9400** • 5pm-midnight, clsd Sun

Sky Blue Coffeehouse & Bistro 700 Fatherland St (at S 7th St) **615/770–7097** • brkfst & lunch

Sole Mio 311 3rd Ave S **615/256–4013** • 11am-10pm, till midnight Fri-Sat, clsd Mon • Italian

The Standard at the Smith House 167 8th Ave N (btwn Church & Commerce) **615/254–1277** • dinner Tue-Sat, clsd Sun-Mon

Watermark 507 12th Ave S (at Division) **615/254–2000** • dinner nightly, clsd Sun • seafood & more • great wine list

Yellow Porch 734 Thompson Ln (at Bransford Ave) **615/386–0260** • lunch & dinner, clsd Sun • fresh southern cuisine

ENTERTAINMENT & RECREATION

NashTrash Tours tours leave from the Farmers Market (900 8th Ave N) **615/226–7300, 800/342–2132** • campy tours of Nashville w/ the Jugg Sisters • ages 13+ • reservations required

Tennessee Repertory Theater 505 Deaderick St (at the Tennessee Performing Arts Center) **615/244–4878**

BOOKSTORES

Davis-Kidd Booksellers 2121 Green Hills Village Dr **615/385–2645** • 9am-9pm, till 10pm Fri-Sat, 10am-7pm Sun • LGBT section

Outloud Books & Gifts 1703 Church St (btwn 17th & 18th Ave) **615/340–0034** • 11am-8pm, till 10pm Fri-Sat • LGBT • also cafe • gay-owned

PUBLICATIONS

Inside Out Nashville **615/831–1806** • LGBT newspaper & bar guide

Out & About Newspaper **615/596–6210** • LGBT newspaper for Nashville, Knoxville, Chattanooga & Atlanta area • monthly

Pigeon Forge

ENTERTAINMENT & RECREATION

Dollywood 1020 Dollywood Ln **800/365–5996** • Dolly Parton's "wholesome Smoky Mountain theme park" • 35 miles SE of Knoxville

TEXAS

Statewide

PUBLICATIONS

Ambush Mag 504/522-8049 • LGBT newspaper for the Gulf South (TX through FL)

Amarillo

INFO LINES & SERVICES

OUTstanding Amarillo 616 S Harrison (at 7th) **806/337-1688** • 7pm-10pm Fri • LGBT community center

BARS

212 Club 212 W 6th St (at Harrison) **806/372-7997** • 2pm-2am • lesbians/ gay men • neighborhood bar • dancing/DJ • drag shows • wheelchair access

Kick Back 521 E 10th St (at Lincoln) **806/371-3535** • 3pm-2am, clsd Sun • lesbians/ gay men • neighborhood bar • karaoke • lesbian-owned

R&R 701 S Georgia St **806/342-9000** • 4pm-2am • gay-friendly • neighborhood bar • gay-owned

Sassy's 309 W 6th St **806/374-3029** • 3pm-2am Wed, 6pm-3am Fri-Sat • lesbians/ gay men • dancing/DJ • karaoke • drag shows

Whiskers 1219 W 10th Ave **806/371-8482** • 5pm-2am • lesbians/ gay men • neighborhood bar

RESTAURANTS

Furrbie's 210 W 6th Ave **806/220-0841** • clsd Mon, 11am-4pm, 11am-7:30pm Sat • gay-owned

EROTICA

Fantasy Gifts & Video 440 N Lakeside **806/372-6500**

Arlington

see also Dallas & Fort Worth

INFO LINES & SERVICES

Tarrant County Lesbian/ Gay Alliance 817/877-5544 • info line• meetings

NIGHTCLUBS

The 1851 Club 1851 W Division (at Fielder) **817/801-9303** • 3pm-2am • lesbians/ gay men • dancing/DJ • drag shows • karaoke • videos • wheelchair access

ENTERTAINMENT & RECREATION

Int'l Bowling Museum & Hall of Fame 621 Six Flags Dr **817/649-5105** • 9:30am-5pm, clsd Sun-Mon • 5,000 years of bowling history (!) & 4 free frames

Austin

INFO LINES & SERVICES

Lambda AA (Live & Let Live) 7801 N Lamar Blvd (at W Anderson Ln) **512/444-0071, 512/832-6767 (EN ESPAÑOL)** • 8pm daily, also 6:30pm Mon-Tue & Th-Fri, 10am Sat, 11am Sun

ACCOMMODATIONS

Austin Folk House 506 W 22nd St (at Nueces) **512/472-6700, 866/472-6700** • gay/ straight • B&B in restored 1880 house • kids/ pets ok • nonsmoking • wheelchair access • $95-225

Brava House 1108 Blanco St (at W 11th) **512/478-5034, 866/892-5726** • gay-friendly • 1880s Victorian close to downtown & 6th Street • nonsmoking • WiFi • lesbian-owned • $139-199

Days Inn North 820 E Anderson Ln/ Hwy 183 (at I-35) **512/835-4311, 866/835-4311** • gay-friendly • pool • kids/ pets ok • wheelchair access • $79-89

Driskill Hotel 604 Brazos St (at 6th) **512/474-5911, 800/252-9367** • gay-friendly • full restaurant • gym • wheelchair access • $230-599

Hotel Saint Cecilia 112 Academy Dr **512/852-2400** • gay-friendly • swimming • wheelchair access • $350+

Hotel San Jose 1316 S Congress Ave **512/444-7322, 800/574-8897** • gay/ straight • popular • small boutique hotel • pool • nonsmoking • kids/ pets ok • wheelchair access • $95-375

Kimber Modern 110 The Circle **512/912-1046** • gay/ straight • WiFi • women owned • $250-320

Mi Yard B&B 2307 Riverside Farms Rd (of I-35) **512/789-3486** • gay-friendly • minutes from downtown Austin • hot tub • nonsmoking • WiFi

Mt Gainor Inn B&B 2390 Prochnow Rd (at Mt Gainor Rd), Dripping Springs **512/858-0982, 888/644-0982** • gay/ straight • nonsmoking • hot tub • WiFi • $125-150

Omni Austin Hotel Downtown 700 San Jacinto (at 8th) 512/476-3700, 800/843-6664 • gay-friendly • 4-diamond hotel • rooftop pool • health club • WiFi • wheelchair access • $179-409

Park Lane Guest House 221 Park Ln (at Drake) 512/447-7460, 800/492-8827 • gay/ straight • full brkfst • pool • also cottage • wheelchair access • lesbian-owned • $148-244

riverbarnsuites 30 minutes from Austin airport, Kingsbury 512/488-2175 • women only • river resort w/ lots of outdoor activities • swimming • lesbian-owned • $125

Robin's Nest 1007 Stewart Cove 512/266-3413 • gay-friendly • B&B in 3 homes on Lake Travis • $135-375

Star of Texas Inn 611 W 22nd St (at Rio Grande) 512/472-6700, 866/472-6700 • gay-friendly • neo-classical Victorian • full brkfst • nonsmoking • kids/ pets ok • $99-225

BARS

'Bout Time 9601 N Ih 35 (at Rundberg) 512/832-5339 • 2pm-2am • popular • lesbians/ gay men • neighborhood bar • transgender-friendly • drag shows • karaoke • volleyball court • WiFi • wheelchair access

Austin

WHERE THE GIRLS ARE:
Downtown along Red River St., or 4th/5th St. near Lavaca, or at the music clubs and cafes downtown and around the University.

LGBT PRIDE:
June. www.aglcc.org.

ANNUAL EVENTS:
March - South by Southwest Music Festival, web: www.sxsw.com.
May & Labor Day - Splash Days. Weekend of parties in clothing-optional Hippie Hollow, web: www.houstonsplash.com.
September/October - Austin G/L Int'l Film Festival 512/302-9889, web: www.agliff.org.

CITY INFO:
Austin Convention & Visitors Bureau 800/926-2282, web: www.austintexas.org.
Greater Austin Chamber of Commerce 512/478-9383, web: www.austin-chamber.org.

BEST VIEW:
Texas State Capitol or the University of Texas Tower, web: www.utexas.edu/tower.

WEATHER:
Summers are real scorchers (high 90°s–low 100°s) and last forever. Spring, fall, and winter are welcome reliefs.

ATTRACTIONS:
Aqua Festival.
Austin Museum of Art at Laguna Gloria 512/458-8191, web: www.amoa.org.
Elisabet Ney Museum 512/458-2255, web: www.ci.austin.tx.us/elisabetney.
George Washington Carver Museum 512/974-4926, web: www.ci.austin.tx.us/carver.
Hamilton Pool 512/264-2740, web: www.texasoutside.com/hamilton-pool.htm.
LBJ Library & Museum 512/721-0200, web: www.lbjlib.utexas.edu.
McKinney Falls State Park 512/243-1643, web: www.tpwd.state.tx.us/park/mckinney.
Mount Bonnell.
Museo del Barrio de Austin 1402 E 1st St.
Zilker Park/Barton Springs, web: www.ci.austin.tx.us/zilker.

TRANSIT:
Yellow Cab 512/452-9999.
Various hotels have their own shuttles.
Capital Metro 512/474-1200, web: www.capmetro.org.

Casino El Camino 517 E 6th St (at Red River) **512/469-9330** • 4pm-2am • gay-friendly • neighborhood bar • psychedelic punk jazz lounge • great burgers • WiFi • wheelchair access

Rusty Spurs 405 E 7th Street (E of Trinity) **512/482-9002** • 4pm-2am, till midnight Sun, clsd Mon • lesbians/gay men • Th ladies night • dancing/DJ • country western & hip hop nights on patio

NIGHTCLUBS

Elysium 705 Red River (7th St) **512/478-2979** • 9:30pm-2am • Tue 90's night • Sun 80's night • dancing/DJ • rest of the week goth, industrial & electronica club

Kiss & Fly 404 Colorado **512/476-7799** • 9pm-close Wed-Sat, from 5pm Sun • mostly gay men • dancing/DJ

Rain 217-B W 4th St (at Colorado St) **512/494-1150** • 4pm-close, from 3pm Fri-Sun • mostly gay men • dancing/DJ • upscale gay lounge

CAFES

Austin Java Cafe & Coffeehouse 1608 Barton Springs Rd (at Kinney Ave) **512/482-9450** • 7am-11pm, till midnight Fri, from 8am Saturday, till 11pm Sun • also 1206 Parkway (at 12th & Lamar), 512/476-1829 & 300 W 2nd St, Ste 100, 512/481-9400

Bouldin Creek Coffeehouse 1501 S 1st St (at Elizabeth) **512/416-1601** • 7am-midnight, from 9am wknds • completely vegetarian menu (brkfst all day) • occasional live music

Joe's Bakery & Coffee Shop 2305 E 7th St (at Morelos & Northwestern) **512/472-0017** • 6am-3pm, clsd Mon • Tex-Mex

Little City Espresso Bar & Cafe 916 Congress Ave (at E 11th St) **512/476-2489** • 8am-midnight, from 9am wknds, till 10pm Sun • popular gay hangout • food served • beer/wine • WiFi • wheelchair access

Spider House Patio Bar & Cafe 2908 Fruth St (at West Dr) **512/480-9562** • 7am-2am • food served • plenty veggie • beer/wine • art & performance • patio

RESTAURANTS

The Belmont 305 W 6th St **512/457-0300** • 11:30am-2am, from 5pm wknds • swank midcentury modern eatery & lounge

Chez Nous 510 Neches St **512/473-2413** • lunch Tue-Fri, dinner nightly, clsd Mon • French

Chuy's 1728 Barton Springs Rd **512/474-4452** • 11am-10pm, till 11pm Fri-Sat • Tex-Mex • full bar

Corazon at Castle Hill 1101 W 5th St (at Baylor) **512/476-0728** • lunch weekdays & dinner nightly, clsd Sun • inspired cuisine • some veggie • wheelchair access

Eastside Cafe 2113 Manor Rd (at Coleto, by bright yellow gas station) **512/476-5858** • 11:30am-9:30pm, 10am-10pm wknds • some veggie • beer/wine • wheelchair access

El Sol y La Luna 600 E 6th St (at Red River) **512/444-7770** • 7am-11pm, till 2pm Fri-Sat, 9am-4pm Sun • popular • Latin American • great brkfst • live music Fri-Sat • wheelchair access • lesbian-owned

Fonda San Miguel 2330 W North Loop (at Hancock Rd) **512/459-4121** • dinner only Mon-Sat, popular Sun brunch • Mexican • full bar

Galaxy 1000 W Lynn **512/478-3434** • 7am-10pm • quick, stylish & tast

Guero's 1412 S Congress (at Elizabeth) **512/447-7688** • 11am-11pm, from 8am wknds • great Mexican & people-watching • outdoor seating • live music outdoors on wknds

Imperia 310 Colorado St **512/472-6770** • dinner only • upscale Asian • full bar

Jo's Hot Coffee & Good Food 1300 S Congress Ave (at James) **512/444-3800** • 7am-9pm, till 10pm Sat • "best lazy day outdoor dining scene" • wheelchair access • also 242 W 2nd St, 512/469-9003 • lesbian-owned

Katz's 618 W 6th St (at Rio Grande) **512/472-2037** • 24hrs • NY-style deli • full bar • wheelchair access

Kenichi 419 Colorado St **512/320-8883** • dinner nightly • Asian/sushi

The Kitchen Door 3742 Far West Blvd (at Hart Ln) **512/794-1100** • 7am-7pm, clsd Sun • also at 221 W 6th St, 512/476-1000 • gay-owned

Mother's Cafe & Garden 4215 Duval St (at 43rd) **512/451-3994** • 11:15am-10pm, from 10am wknds • vegetarian • popular

Nueva Onda 2218 College Ave (off S Congress & Oltorf) **512/447-5063** • 7:30am-3pm, from 8am Sun • Mexican • some veggie • patio • lesbian-owned

The Phoenix 409 Colorado St **512/472-8882** • 9pm-2am Th-Sat • ultra lounge

Polvos 2004 S 1st St (at Johanna)
512/441–5446 • 7am-11pm • Mexican •
outdoor seating

Restaurant Jezebel 914 Congress Ave
512/499–3999 • dinner nightly • French/
American

Santa Rita 1206 W 38th St **512/419–7482** •
lunch & dinner, wknd brunch • Tex Mex

Threadgill's 6416 N Lamar (at Koenig)
512/451–5440 • 10am-10pm, till 9pm Sun •
great chicken-fried steak • live music Wed •
also 301 W Riverside Dr, 512/472-9304 • beer
garden • live music

Wink 1014 N Lamar Blvd **512/482–8868** •
dinner nightly, clsd Sun • upscale • also wine
bar

ENTERTAINMENT & RECREATION

Austin Cabaret Theatre 701 W Riverside
Drive (at the Long Center) **512/453–2287**

Barton Springs Barton Springs Rd (in Zilker
Park) • natural swimming hole

Bat Colony Congress Ave Bridge (at Barton
Springs Dr) • everything's bigger in Texas—
including the colony of bats that flies out from
under this bridge every evening March-Oct

Capital City Men's Chorus 512/477–7464 •
call for events

Historic Austin Tours 209 E 6th St (in the
Visitor Information Center, open 9am-5pm,
till 6pm Sat-Sun) **512/478–0098,
866/468–8784** • free guided & self-guided
tours of the Capitol, Congress Ave & 6th St,
Texas State Cemetery, Hyde Park

Kings N Things • "Austin's premier drag
king troupe" • check web
(www.kingsnthings.org) for events

Queer Radio on KOOP 91.7 FM
512/472–1369 • "Outcast" 6pm-6:30pm Tue •
queer culture

Texas Rollergirls • Austin's female roller
derby league • visit txrollergirls.com for events

Zachary Scott Theatre Center 1510
Toomey Rd (off S Lamar Blvd) **512/476–0541**
• diverse theater

BOOKSTORES

Bookpeople 603 N Lamar Blvd (at 6th)
512/472–5050, 800/853–9757 • 9am-11pm,
clsd Thanksgiving Day • independent •
readings

BookWoman 5501 N Lamar Blvd (at Nelray)
512/472–2785 • 10am-8pm, clsd Sun • books
• cards • jewelry • music • DVDs • posters • T-
shirts • stickers • wheelchair access • woman-
owned

Resistencia Bookstore 1801-A S 1st St (at
W Annie) **512/416–8885** • emphasis on
Chicana/o, Latino/a & Native American titles •
also some LGBT of color titles • readings

RETAIL SHOPS

Tapelenders 1114 W 5th St (at Baylor)
512/472–0844 • 10am-10pm, till midnight Fri-
Sat, noon-10pm Sun • LGBT videos •
novelties • gay-owned

PUBLICATIONS

Ambush Mag 504/522–8049 • LGBT
newspaper for the Gulf South (TX through FL)

Austin Chronicle 512/454–5766 • Austin's
alternative paper • weekly • has extensive
online gay guide as well as events calendar
(check out www.austinchronicle.com)

L Style G Style 512/443–6677 • glossy mag

GYMS & HEALTH CLUBS

Hyde Park Gym 4125 Guadalupe (at 42nd
St) **512/459–9174** • 5am-10pm, 7am-7pm Sat,
8am-7pm Sun • gay-friendly • day passes

EROTICA

Forbidden Fruit 512 Neches (btwn 5th &
6th) **512/478–8358** • woman-owned &
operated

Beaumont

INFO LINES & SERVICES

Lambda AA 1385 Calder Ave **409/832–1107**
• 8pm Wed & Sat

BARS

Orleans Street Pub & Patio 650 Orleans St
409/835–4243 • 7pm-2am, clsd Mon-Tue •
lesbians/ gay men • neighborhood bar •
dancing/DJ • karaoke • drag shows

NIGHTCLUBS

Copa 304 Orleans St (at Liberty)
409/832–4206 • 9pm-2am Wed-Sun • popular
• lesbians/ gay men • dancing/DJ • drag shows
• wheelchair access

Brownsville

NIGHTCLUBS

Karma 1655 Ruben Torres Blvd # 212
866/552–5720 • 9pm-2am, Th gay night, clsd
Sun-Wed • dancing/DJ

Bryan

BARS

Revolution Cafe & Bar 211 B S Main St (btwn 26th & 28th) **979/823-4044** • 4pm-2am, from 8pm Sun-Mon, from 6pm Sat, • gay-friendly • neighborhood bar • food served • live music • WiFi • wheelchair access

NIGHTCLUBS

Halo Bar 121 N Main St (at William J Bryan Pkwy) **979/823-6174** • 9:30pm-2am Th-Sat • lesbians/ gay men • dancing/DJ • drag shows • Karaoke • wheelchair access

Corpus Christi

INFO LINES & SERVICES

Clean & Serene AA 1315 Craig (at church) **361/992-8911, 866/672-7029** • 8pm Fri

ACCOMMODATIONS

Anthony's By The Sea 732 S Pearl St, Rockport **361/729-6100, 800/460-2557** • gay/ straight • quiet retreat 4 blocks from water • full brkfst • pool • wheelchair access • lesbian-owned • $105-125

Port Aransas Inn 1500 11th St (at Ave G), Port Aransas **361/749-5937** • gay/ straight • near beach & restaurants • pool • hot tub • WiFi • wheelchair access • $39-338

BARS

Get Happy 526 S Staples St (at Park St) **361/881-8910** • noon-2am • lesbians/ gay men • neighborhood bar • dancing/DJ • food served • gay-owned

The Hidden Door 802 S Staples St (at Coleman) **361/882-5002** • noon-2am • lesbians/ gay men • neighborhood bar • dancing/DJ • patio • wheelchair access

The Rose 213 S Staples **361/881-8181** • 7pm-2am, from 3pm Sun, clsd Mon • mostly women • neighborhood bar • karaoke

NIGHTCLUBS

Sixx 1212 Leopard St • 9pm-2am Wed & Sun, till 4am Fri-Sat • mostly men • live shows • drag shows • strippers • 18+

ENTERTAINMENT & RECREATION

Robert James Provisioners 837 Redmond **361/937-4880** • 8am-10pm • gay-friendly • sailboat charters • classes • transgender-friendly • gay-owned

Dallas

see also Arlington, Fort Worth

INFO LINES & SERVICES

Gay/ Lesbian Switchboard 214/528-0022 • 9am-9pm, 10am-5pm Sat, noon-5pm Sun

John Thomas Gay/ Lesbian Community Center 2701 Reagan St (at Brown) **214/528-0144, 214/528-0022** • 9am-9pm, 10am-6pm Sat, noon-5pm Sun • wheelchair access

Lambda AA 2438 Butler #106 **214/267-0222, 214/887-6699 (CENTRAL OFFICE #)** • call for meeting details

ACCOMMODATIONS

Bailey's Uptown Inn 2505 Worthington St (at Hibernia) **214/720-2258** • gay-friendly • elegant B&B • nonsmoking • WiFi • $199-259

Daisy Polk Inn 2917 Reagan St (at Dickason Ave) **214/522-4692** • gay-friendly • B&B in 1909 Arts & Crafts home • nonsmoking • WiFi • $139-169

Holiday Inn Select Dallas Central 10650 N Central Expwy (at Meadow) **214/373-6000, 888/477-STAY** • gay/ straight • pool • WiFi • wheelchair access • $99+

Hotel Zaza 2332 Leonard St (at State) **214/468-8399, 800/597-8399** • gay-friendly • full spa & restaurant • $249-450

Melrose Hotel 3015 Oak Lawn Ave (at Cedar Springs) **214/521-5151, 800/635-7673** • gay-friendly • nonsmoking rooms available • also piano bar & lounge • also 4 1/2-star restaurant • wheelchair access • $225-350

Quality Inn Market Center 1955 Market Center Blvd (at Turtle Creek Blvd) **800/250-1978** • gay-friendly • swimming • WiFi • wheelchair access • $80-130

The Stoneleigh Hotel 2927 Maple Ave (at Randall St) **214/871-7111** • gay-friendly • landmark hotel • gym • also restaurant • $199+

BARS

Barbara's Pavillion 325 Centre St (1blk W o Zang) **214/941-2145** • 4pm-2am, from 6pm Sat • mostly gay men • neighborhood bar • bi-weekly karaoke • patio • wheelchair access

Grapevine 3902 Maple Ave (at Shelby) **214/522-8466** • 3pm-2am • gay/ straight • classic dive bar

The Hidden Door 5025 Bowser Ave (at Mahanna) **214/526-0620** • 7am-2am, from noon Sun • mostly gay men • neighborhood bar • leather • patio • wheelchair access

Illusions 4100 Maple Ave (at Throckmorton) **214/252–0552** • 4pm-2am, from noon wknds • lesbians/ gay men • neighborhood bar • drag shows • potlucks Sun

Jack's Backyard 2303 Pittman St (at W Commerce St) **214/741–3131** • 11am-2am • gay/ straight • also bar

JR's Bar & Grill 3923 Cedar Springs Rd (at Throckmorton) **214/528–1004** • 11am-2am, from noon Sun • upscale • popular • lesbians/ gay men • grill till 4pm • live shows Sun • videos • young crowd • WiFi • wheelchair access

Dallas

WHERE THE GIRLS ARE:
Oak Lawn in central Dallas is the gay and lesbian stomping grounds, mostly on Cedar Springs Ave.

LGBT PRIDE:
September. www.dallastavern-guild.org.

ANNUAL EVENTS:
March-April - AFI Dallas Int'l Film Festival, web: dallasfilm.org.

March-April - Dallas Blooms at Dallas Arboretum & Botancial Garden with over 400,000 spring-blooming bulbs.

April – Deep Ellum Arts Festival, web: www.deepellumartsfesti-val.com.

September-October - Texas State Fair, web: www.bigtex.com. Largest in the country.

October - Out Takes Dallas 972/988-6333, web: www.outtakesdallas.org. LGBT film festival.

CITY INFO:
214/571–1000, web: www.visitdal-las.com.

BEST VIEW:
Hyatt Regency Tower.

WEATHER:
Can be unpredictable. Hot summers (90°s – 100°s) with possible severe rain storms. Winter temperatures hover in the 20°s through 40°s range.

TRANSIT:
Yellow Cab 214/426-6262. Dallas Area Rapid Transit (DART) 214/979-1111, web: www.dart.org.

ATTRACTIONS:
African American Museum 214/565-9026, web: www.aamdallas.org.

Crow Collection of Asian Art 214/979-6430, web: www.crow-collection.com.

Dallas Arboretum & Botanical Garden 214/515–6500, web www.dallasarboretum.org.

Dallas Museum of Art 214/922-1200, web: www.dallasmuseum-ofart.org.

Dallas Theater Center/ Frank Lloyd Wright 214/522–8499, web: www.dallastheatercenter.org.

Dallas World Aquarium 214/720-2224, web: www.dwazoo.com.

Deep Ellum district.

Fair Park, web: www.fairpark.org. 277-acre park since 1880, home to Cotton Bowl, many museums, and Texas State Fair.

Meadows Museum at SMU 214/768-2516, web: smu.edu/meadows/museum/index.htm.

Modern Art Museum, Fort Worth 817/738-9215, web: www.themodern.org.

Nasher Sculpture Center 214/242-5100, web: www.nashersculp-turecenter.org.

Sixth Floor Museum 214/747-6660, web: www.jfk.org.

Texas State Fair & State Fair Park 214/565-9931, web: www.bigtex.com.

The Women's Museum 214/915–0860, web: www.thewomensmuseum.org.

Pekers 2615 Oak Lawn Ave, Ste 101 (btwn Fairmount & Brown) **214/528–3333** • 10am-2am • lesbians/ gay men • neighborhood bar • live music • karaoke • wheelchair access

Sisters Club 4025 Maple Ave (at Throckmorton) **214/559–2511** • 5pm-2am, from 2pm wknds • mostly women • dancing/DJ • karaoke • drag shows

Sue Ellen's 3014 Throckmorton (at Cedar Springs) **214/559–0707** • 5pm-2am, 2pm-close wknds • popular • mostly women • dancing/DJ • live shows/ bands • Sun BBQ (summers) • patio • wheelchair access

Tin Room 2514 Hudnall St (at Maple Ave) **214/526–6365** • 10am-2am, from noon Sun • mostly gay men • neighborhood bar

Woody's 4011 Cedar Springs Rd (btwn Douglas & Throckmorton) **214/520–6629** • 2pm-2am • lesbians/ gay men • live shows • sports bar • videos • nonsmoking upstairs • karaoke • patio • wheelchair access

NIGHTCLUBS

Alexandre's 4026 Cedar Springs Rd (at Knight St) **214/559–0720** • 9am-2pm, from 2pm Sun-Mon • gay/ straight • live music

Between Us 2208 Main St (at Bacy's) • 10pm 1st Sat only • lesbians/ gay men • dancing/DJ • mostly African American

The Brick 2525 Wycliff Ave (btwn Maple & Tollway) **214/521–2024, 214/521–3154** • 10pm-4am Fri-Sun • lesbians/ gay men • dancing/DJ • multiracial

Elm and Pearl 2204 Elm St (at S Pearl) **214/741–0000** • mostly men Fri • mostly women Sat • dancing/DJ • drag shows Sun • mostly African American

Havana Bar & Grill 4006 Cedar Springs Rd (at Throckmorton) **214/526–9494** • grill 5pm-10pm Wed-Sun, lounge from 10pm • gay/ straight • dancing/DJ

Joe's Dallas 4125 Maple Ave (at Throckmorton) **214/521–2024** • noon-2am • mostly gay men • more women Wed & Fri • neighborhood bar • dancing/DJ • karaoke • food seved • live shows • patio • cover charge • wheelchair access

Kaliente 4350 Maple Ave (at Hondo) **214/520–6676** • 9pm-2am, clsd Tue • mostly gay men • mostly Latino • dancing/DJ • salsa & Tejano • karaoke • drag shows

Klub Hot 4207 Maple Ave (at Knight St) **469/556–1395** • 9pm-close Th-Sun • lesbians/ gay men • dancing/DJ • drag shows • mostly Latino/a

Once in a Blue Moon 10675 E Northwest Hwy, Ste 2600B (at DanceMasters Ballroom) **972/264–3381** • 7pm-midnight 2nd Sat • monthly women's dance • dancing/DJ • nonsmoking • BYOB

Round-Up Saloon 3912 Cedar Springs Rd (at Throckmorton) **214/522–9611** • 3pm-2am, from noon wknds • popular • mostly gay men • dancing/DJ • country/ western • karaoke • dance lessons • 6 bars • patio • wheelchair access

Station 4 3911 Cedar Springs Rd (at Throckmorton) **214/526–7171** • 9pm-4am Wed-Sun • popular • lesbians/ gay men • dancing/DJ • drag shows • videos • also Rose Room cabaret • 18+

CAFES

Buli 3908 Cedar Springs Rd **214/528–5410** • 7am-midnight • WiFi

Opening Bell Coffee 1409 S Lamar St, Ste 012 **214/565–0383** • 7am-10pm, till midnight wknds, clsd Sun • beer/ wine • live music

RESTAURANTS

Ali Baba Cafe 1901 Abrams Rd (near La Vista Dr) **214/823–8235** • lunch & dinner, clsd Sun • Middle Eastern

Bangkok Orchid 331 W Airport Fwy (N Beltline), Irving **972/252–7770** • lunch & dinner, clsd Mon • ask for Danny • BYOB • wheelchair access • gay-owned

Black-Eyed Pea 3857 Cedar Springs Rd (at Reagan) **214/521–4580** • 11am-10pm • Southern homecookin' • some veggie • wheelchair access

Blue Mesa Grill 5100 Beltline Rd (at Tollway), Addison **972/934–0165** • 11am-10pm, till 10:30pm Fri-Sat, 10am-9pm Sun • great fajitas • full bar

Bread Winners 3301 McKinney Ave **214/754–4940** • brkfst & lunch daily, dinner Tue-Sun, Sun brunch • gay/ straight • int'l • some veggie • full bar • wheelchair access

The Bronx Restaurant & Bar 3835 Cedar Springs Rd (at Oak Lawn) **214/521–5821** • lunch & dinner, Sun brunch, clsd Mon • some veggie • wheelchair access • gay-owned

Cafe Brazil 3847 Cedar Springs Rd **214/461–8762** • open 24 hrs

Cosmic Cafe 2912 Oak Lawn Ave **214/521–6157** • 11am-10:30pm, till 11pm Fri-Sat, noon-10pm Sun • vegetarian food served • also yoga & meditation • live events

Cremona Bistro & Cafe 2704 Worthington St (at Howell) 214/871–1115 • lunch weekdays & dinner nightly • Italian • full bar • patio • live music Fri-Sat

Dish 4123 Cedar Springs Rd #110 214/522–3474 • lunch & dinner, wknd brunch • full bar • patio

Dream Cafe 2800 Routh St (in the Quadrangle) 214/954–0486 • 7am-9pm, till 8pm Fri-Sat, brkfst served till 5pm • plenty veggie • beer/ wine • WiFi • wheelchair access

Excuses Art Bar & Cafe 3025 Main St (in Deep Ellum) 214/741–1111 • 3pm-2am, clsd Sun-Tue

Fitness Essentials 3878 Oak Lawn, Ste 100E (near Avondale) 214/528–5535 • 9am-7pm, till 6pm Sat, clsd Sun • organic • plenty veggie • wheelchair access • gay-owned

Hattie's 418 N Bishop Ave 214/942–7400 • lunch daily, dinner Tue-Sun • Southern

Hibiscus 2927 N Henderson Ave 214/827–2927 • dinner only, clsd Sun • steak & seafood

Hung Dinger 4000-E Cedar Springs Rd (at Throckmorton) 214/522–4864 • 11am-midnight, clsd Mon-Tue, wknd brunch • kitschy Italian supperclub • drag shows • cabaret • transgender-friendly

Hunky's 4000 Cedar Springs Rd (at Throckmorton) 214/522–1212 • 11am-10pm, till 11pm Fri-Sat, from noon Sun • popular • burgers & salads • beer/ wine • patio • wheelchair access • gay-owned

Lucky's Cafe 3531 Oak Lawn 214/522–3500 • 7am-10pm • classic comfort food • great brkfst

McCormick & Schmick's Seafood Restaurant 307 NorthPark Center (at W Northwest Hwy) 214/891–0100, 888/226–6212 • 11am-10pm, till 9pm Sun • fresh seafood • full bar

Monica Aca y Alla 2914 Main St (at Malcolm X) 214/748–7140 • lunch Mon-Fri, dinner Tue-Sun, brunch wknds • popular • trendy • contemporary Mexican • full bar • live music wknds • Latin jazz/ salsa • transgender-friendly • wheelchair access

Rocco's 2916 McKinney Ave 214/871–9207, 214/871–9208 • lunch & dinner • pizza & pasta • WiFi

Stephan Pyles 1807 Ross Ave, Ste 200 214/580–7000 • lunch Mon-Fri, dinner Mon-Sat, clsd Sun • Southwestern cuisine

Thai Soon 101 S Coit, Ste 401 (at Beltline) 972/234–6111 • lunch & dinner

Vitto 316 W 7th St (at Bishop) 214/946–1212 • lunch Mon-Sat, dinner nightly • Italian • beer/ wine • wheelchair access • gay-owned

Ziziki's 4514 Travis St, #122 (in Travis Walk) 214/521–2233 • 11am-10pm, Sun brunch • Greek • full bar • wheelchair access

ENTERTAINMENT & RECREATION

Assassination City Derby 400 S Buckner Blvd (at What's Hot Fun World) • Dallas' female roller derby league • visit www.acderby.com for events

Lambda Weekly KNON 89.3 FM 972/263–5305 • noon Sun • LGBT radio show for northern TX

Uptown Players 214/219–2718 • many gay-themed productions

The Women's Chorus of Dallas (TWCD) 3630 Harry Hines Blvd (at Sammons Center for the Arts) 214/520–7828 • several subscription & benefit concerts throughout year & nine CDs

The Women's Museum 3800 Parry Ave 214/915–0860, 888/337–1167 • noon-5pm, clsd Mon

RETAIL SHOPS

Obscurities 4000-B Cedar Springs 214/559–3706 • 11am-9pm, 2pm-8pm Sun, clsd Mon • tattoo & piercing

Tapelenders 3926 Cedar Springs Rd (at Throckmorton) 214/528–6344 • 9am-midnight • LGBT gifts • video rental • gay-owned

PUBLICATIONS

Dallas Voice 214/754–8710 • LGBT newspaper w/ extensive resource listings

EROTICA

Alternatives 1720 W Mockingbird Ln (at Hawes) 214/630–7071 • 24hrs

Leather Masters, Dallas 3000 Main St 214/528–3865 • noon-10pm, clsd Sun-Mon • handmade leather clothes • rubber/ fetishwear • electrical/ medical gear & more

Denison

BARS

Good Time Lounge 2520 Hwy 91 N 903/463–6086 • 7pm-2am Wed-Sun • lesbians/ gay men • karaoke Th & Sun • drag shows • private club

Denton

CAFES

Cupboard Natural Foods 200 W Congress St (at Elm) 940/387–5386 • 8am-9pm, 10am-8pm Sun • health food store & cafe

El Paso

see also Ciudad Juárez, Mexico

BARS

Briar Patch 508 N Stanton St (at Missouri) 915/577–9555 • noon-2am • lesbians/ gay men • neighborhood bar • karaoke • patio

Chiquita's Bar 310 E Missouri Ave (at Stanton) 915/351–0095 • 2pm-2am • lesbians/ gay men • neighborhood bar • mostly Latino/a • wheelchair access

The Whatever Lounge 701 E Paisano Dr (at Ochoa) 915/533–0215 • 2pm-2am • lesbians/ gay men • dancing/DJ • karaoke • mostly Latino/a • wheelchair access

NIGHTCLUBS

The New Old Plantation 301 S Ochoa St (at Paisano) 915/533–6055 • 9pm-2am, till 4am Fri-Sat • popular • lesbians/ gay men • dancing/DJ • drag shows Sun • videos • wheelchair access • also Generation Q II pride store upstairs

San Antonio Mining Co 800 E San Antonio Ave (at Ochoa) 915/533–9516 • 3pm-2am • popular • lesbians/ gay men • dancing/DJ • drag shows • videos • patio • wheelchair access

RESTAURANTS

The Little Diner 7209 7th St, Canutillo 915/877–2176 • 11am-8pm, clsd Wed • true Texas fare

Fort Worth

see also Arlington & Dallas

INFO LINES & SERVICES

Tarrant County Lesbian/ Gay Alliance 817/877–5544 • info line • newsletter

ACCOMMODATIONS

Hotel Trinity InnSuites Hotel 2000 Beach St 817/534–4801, 800/989–3556 • gay-friendly • pool • nonsmoking • kids/ pets ok • WiFi • wheelchair access • $80-159

BARS

Best Friends Club 2620 E Lancaster Ave 817/534–2280 • 3pm-2am, clsd Mon • lesbians/ gay men • neighborhood bar • dancing/DJ • food served • karaoke

Crossroads 515 S Jennings Ave (at Pennsylvania) 817/332–0071 • 11am-2am, from noon Sun • mostly gay men • neighborhood bar

NIGHTCLUBS

Rainbow Lounge 651 S Jennings Ave (at Pennsylvania) 817/819–5277 • 9am-2am • mostly gay men • dancing/DJ • drag shows • theme nights • wheelchair access

PUBLICATIONS

Dallas Voice 214/754–8710 • LGBT newspaper w/ extensive resource listings

Galveston

ACCOMMODATIONS

Cottage by the Gulf 810 Ave L (at Seawall & 8th) 409/770–9332 • gay-friendly • 6 private rental homes • patio • pets ok • wheelchair access • gay-owned • $90-170+

Hotel Galvez 2024 Seawall Blvd 409/765–7721, 877/999–3223 • gay-friendly • nonsmoking • WiFi • kids ok • wheelchair access • $120-300

Lost Bayou Guesthouse B&B 1607 Ave L (at 16th) 409/770–0688 • gay/ straight • 1890 Victorian home survived hurricane of 1900 • nonsmoking • kids ok • WiFi • gay-owned • $125-195

Oasis Beach Cottage 713/256–3000 • gay-friendly • on the Gulf of Mexico • kids ok • nonsmoking • gay-owned • $125-175 & $750-950/ week

BARS

3rd Coast Beach Bar 2416 Post Office St 409/765–6911 • 4pm-2am, from 2pm wknds • mostly gay men • drag shows • male dancers • deck

Pink Dolphin 1828 Strand 409/621–1808 • noon-2am • mostly gay men • drag shows • karaoke

Robert's Lafitte 2501 Q Ave (at 25th St) 409/765–9092 • 7am-2am, from 10am Sun • mostly gay men • drag shows wknds • patio • wheelchair access

Stars Beach Club 3102 Seawall Blvd 409/497–4113 • noon-2am • lesbians/gay men, more women Th • dancing/DJ • karaoke • drag shows

CAFES

Mod Coffee & Tea House 2126 Post Office St (at 22nd) 409/765–5659 • 7am-10pm • live shows • also art gallery • WiFi

Restaurants

Eat Cetera 408 25th St **409/762-0803** • 11am-7pm, clsd Sun

Luigi's 2328 The Strand (at Tremont) **409/763-6500** • lunch & dinner, clsd Sun • Italian

Mosquito Cafe 628 14th St (at Winnie) **409/763-1010** • 11am-9pm, 8am-9pm Sat, till 3pm Sun, clsd Mon • some veggie

The Spot 3204 Seawall Blvd (at 32nd St) **409/621-5237** • good burgers, great view • also Tiki Bar

Star Drug Store 510 23rd St **409/766-7719** • 9am-4pm • old-fashioned drug store & soda fountain

Groesbeck

Accommodations

Rainbow Ranch Campground 1662 LCR 800 **254/729-8484, 888/875-7596** • lesbians/ gay men • open all year • on Lake Limestone • pool • campsites • cabins • house rental • nonsmoking • gay-owned • $20-200

Gun Barrel City

Bars

Friends 410 S Gun Barrel/ Hwy 198 **903/887-2061** • 4pm-midnight, from 3pm wknds, till 1am Sat • lesbians/ gay men • neighborhood bar • food served • private club • wheelchair access

Houston

Info Lines & Services

Gay & Lesbian Switchboard Houston **713/529-3211** • 24hr crisis hotline

Houston GLBT Community Center 3400 Montrose # 207 (at Hawthorne) **713/524-3818** • noon-9pm

Lambda AA Center 1201 W Clay (btwn Montrose & Waugh) **713/521-1243** • wheelchair access

Accommodations

Alden Hotel 1117 Prairie St (at Fannin) **832/200-8800, 877/348-8800** • gay-friendly • boutique hotel • dogs ok • also restaurant

Hotel Derek 2525 W Loop S (at Westheimer) **713/961-3000** • gay-friendly • modern, chic hotel

Hotel Sorella 800 W Sam Houston Pkwy N **713/973-1600** • gay-friendly • $109+

The Houstonian 111 N Post Oak Ln (near Woodway Dr) **713/680-2626, 800/231-2759** • gay-friendly • urban resort

The Lovett Inn 501 Lovett Blvd, Montrose (at Whitney) **713/522-5224, 800/779-5224** • popular • gay/ straight • pool • nonsmoking • WiFi • gay-owned • $115-250

Robin's Nest B&B Inn 4104 Greeley St **713/528-5821, 800/622-8343** • gay-friendly • Victorian & Craftsman in Montrose Museum District • WiFi • $99-240

Sycamore Heights B&B 245 W 18th St **713/861-4117** • gay-friendly • circa 1905 • garden • nonsmoking • WiFi • gay-owned

Bars

Bayou City Bar & Grill 2409 Grant St (at Hyde Park Blvd) **713/522-2867** • 4pm-2am, clsd Mon • lesbians/ gay men • theme nights • food served • more women Tue

Beer Island 2631 White Oak Dr (at Studewood) **713/862-4670** • 3pm-2am • gay-friendly • dog-friendly • gay-owned

Blur 710 Pacific St (at Crocker) **713/529-3447** • 10pm-2am, clsd Mon-Tue • lesbians/ gay men • dancing/DJ • 18+

Boom Boom Room 2518 Yale St **713/868-3740** • 4pm-2am, from 10am wknds, clsd Mon • gay-friendly • wine & panini bar

Brazos River Bottom (BRB) 2400 Brazos (btwn Hadley & McIlhenny) **713/528-9192** • noon-2am • popular • mostly gay men • dancing/DJ • country/ western

Chances 1100 Westheimer (at Montrose) **713/523-7217** • 2pm-2am • mostly women • dancing/DJ • live shows • wheelchair access

Club 2020 2020 Leeland **713/227-9667** • lesbians/ gay men • dancing/DJ • 2 floors • mostly African American • hip hop • 18+

Club Adam/ Eden 522 W Nasa Pkwy, Webster **281/554-3336** • 7pm-2am • lesbians/ gay men • dancing/DJ • country/ western Sat

Crocker 2312 Crocker St **713/529-3355** • 11am-2am • mostly gay men • neighborhood bar • theme nights • WiFi

Decades 1205 Richmond (btwn Mandel & Montrose) **713/521-2224** • 11am-2am, from noon Sun • lesbians/ gay men • neighborhood bar • women-owned

Guava Lamp 570 Waugh **713/524-3359** • 4pm-2am, from 2pm Sun • lesbians/ gay men • swanky lounge w/ martinis & more • karaoke • video lounge • wheelchair access

In & Out 1537 N Shepherd (at 16th St) **713/589–9780** • 4pm-2am • lesbians/gay men

JR's 808 Pacific (at Grant) **713/521–2519** • noon-2am • popular • mostly gay men • karaoke • drag shows • videos • patio • wheelchair access

Meteor 2306 Genesee (at Fairview) **713/521–0123** • 4pm-2am • mostly gay men • cocktail lounge • professional crowd • videos • gay-owned

Michael's Outpost 1419 Richmond (at Mandell) **713/520–8446** • 3pm-2am, from noon wknds • mostly gay men • neighborhood bar • piano • live entertainment • older crowd

The New Barn Saloon 1100 Westheimer (at Montrose) **713/523–7217** • Fri-Sat only • mostly women • dancing/DJ • country/western

TC's 817 Fairview (at Converse) **713/526–2625** • 8am-2am, from noon Sun • lesbians/gay men • neighborhood bar • drag shows • transgender-friendly

Tony's Corner Pocket 817 W Dallas (btwn Arthur & Crosby) **713/571–7870** • noon-2am • lesbians/gay men • neighborhood bar • karaoke • male dancers • large 2-level deck • WiFi

The Usual Pub 5519 Allen St **281/501–1478** • 4pm-2am, from 2pm wknds, from 6pm Mon-Tue • gay/straight • neighborhood bar • karaoke • more women Wed • lesbian-owned

Houston

WHERE THE GIRLS ARE:
Strolling the Montrose district near the intersection of Montrose and Westheimer or out on Buffalo Speedway at the Plaza.

LGBT PRIDE:
June. 713/529-6979, web: www.pridehouston.org.

ANNUAL EVENTS:
March - AIDS Walk 713/403-9255, web: www.aidswalkhouston.org.
Easter weekend - Jungle, web: www.junglehouston.com. Dance party benefiting HIV/AIDS education, research & care.
Sept - Q Fest LGBT Film Festival, web: www.q-fest.org.

CITY INFO:
713/437-5200, web: www.visithoustontexas.com.

BEST VIEW:
JP Morgan Chase Tower, web: www.chasetower.com.

WEATHER:
Humid all year round—you're not that far from the Gulf. Mild winters, although there are a few days when the temperatures drop into the 30°s. Winter also brings occasional rainy days. Summers are very hot.

TRANSIT:
Yellow Cab 713/236-1111.
Metropolitan Transit Authority 713/635-4000, web: www.ridemetro.org

ATTRACTIONS:
Contemporary Arts Museum 713/284-8250, web: www.camh.org.
The Galleria, 713/622–0663, web: www.galleriahouston.com.
The Menil Collection 713/525-9400, web: www.menil.org.
Museum of Fine Arts 713/639-7300, web: www.mfah.org.
Rothko Chapel 713/524-9839, web: www.rothkochapel.org.
San Jacinto Monument 281/479–2421, web: www.sanjacinto-museum.org.
SplashTown 281/355–3300, web: www.splashtownpark.com.

Whispers 226 1st St E (off I-59), Humble 281/359-2900 • 4pm-midnight, till 2am Th-Sat • lesbians/gay men • dancing/DJ • karaoke

NIGHTCLUBS

Crystal 6684 Southwest Fwy (at Colorado) 713/278-2582 • mostly gay men • dancing/DJ • Latino club • drag shows • theme nights

G Spot 1100 Westheimer (at Montrose, at Chances) 713/523-7217 • 8pm-2am Fri-Sat • mostly women • dancing/DJ • wheelchair access

Girls Night Out 1312 W Alabama (at Bocado's) 713/523-5230 • 2nd Wed only • mostly women • dancing/DJ • also Mexican restaurant

Numbers 300 Westheimer (at Taft) 713/526-6551 • gay-friendly • dancing/DJ • 80's Fri • also live music venue • video • young crowd

Ranch Hill Saloon 24704 I-45 N, Spring 281/298-9035 • 1pm-2am • lesbians/gay men • neighborhood bar • dancing/DJ • country/western • professional crowd • karaoke • wheelchair access • lesbian-owned

Throb • roving women's dance parties • check www.throbparties.info for details • mostly women • dancing/DJ • live shows

CAFES

Dirk's Coffee 4005 Montrose (btwn Richmond & W Alabama) 713/526-1319 • 6am-11pm, till midnight Fri-Sat, 7am-10pm Sun

Empire Cafe 1732 Westheimer Rd 713/528-5282 • 7:30am-10pm, till 11pm Fri-Sat

Java Java Cafe 911 W 11th (at Shepherd) 713/880-5282 • 7:30am-3pm, from 8:30am wknds • popular

The Path of Tea 2340 W Alabama St 713/252-4473 • 10am-9pm, till 11pm Fri-Sat, 1pm-6pm Sun • tea house

RESTAURANTS

Aka 2390 W Alabama St 713/807-7875 • noon-11pm • sushi

Argentina Cafe 3055 Sage Rd (at Hidalgo St) 713/622-8877 • 9am-9pm, till 7pm Sun • Argentinian

Baba Yega's 2607 Grant (at Pacific) 713/522-0042 • 11am-10pm, till 11pm Fri-Sat, from 10am Sun • popular • plenty veggie • full bar • patio • wheelchair access

Barnaby's Cafe 604 Fairview (btwn Stanford & Hopkins St) 713/522-0106 • 11am-10pm, till 11pm Fri-Sat • popular • beer/wine • wheelchair access • also 1701 S Shepherd, 713/520-5131

Beaver's 2310 Decatur (at Sawyer) 713/864-2328 • 11am-10pm, till midnight Fri-Sat, clsd Mon • BBQ

Block 7 Wine Company 720 Shepard Dr 713/572-2565 • 11am-11pm, from 3pm Sun

Bocado's 1312 W Alabama 713/523-5230 • lunch & dinner, clsd Sun-Mon • Mexican • gay/straight • full bar • more women Wed for dancing/DJ

Brasil 2604 Dunlavy (at Westheimer) 713/528-1993 • 7:30am-1am • bistro • plenty veggie • beer/wine

Captain Benny's Half Shell 8506 S Main 713/666-5469 • 11am-10pm • beer/wine

Chapultepec 813 Richmond (btwn Montrose & Main) 713/522-2365 • 24hrs • Mexican • some veggie • beer/wine

El Tiempo Cantina 1308 Montrose Blvd 713/807-8996 • 11am-9pm, till 10pm Wed-Th, till 11pm Fri-Sat • Mexican seafood

House of Pies 3112 Kirby Dr (btwn Richmond & Alabama) 713/528-3816 • 24hrs • popular • wheelchair access

Hugo's 1602 Westheimer Rd (at Mandell) 713/524-7744 • lunch & dinner • Mexican • popular brunch

Julia's Bistro 3722 Main St (at W Alabama) 713/807-0090 • lunch Mon-Fri, dinner Mon-Sat, clsd Sun • Mexican

Kelley's Country Cookin' 8015 Park Pl (at Gulf Fwy) 713/645-6428 • 6am-10pm, till 11pm wknds • great brkfst

Magnolia Bar & Grill 6000 Richmond Ave (at Fountainview Dr) 713/781-6207 • 11am-10pm, till 11pm Fri-Sat, from 10:30am Sun • Cajun • full bar • wheelchair access

Mark's American Cuisine 1658 Westheimer Rd 713/523-3800 • lunch Mon-Fri, dinner nightly • located in renovated 1920s church

Mo Mong 1201 Westheimer #B (at Montrose) 713/524-5664 • 11am-10pm, clsd Sun • Vietnamese • full bar

Ninfa's 2704 Navigation Blvd 713/228-1175 • 11am-11pm • popular • Mexican • some veggie • full bar

Ninos 2817 W Dallas (btwn Montrose & Waugh Dr) 713/522-5120 • lunch Mon-Fri, dinner Mon-Sat, clsd Sun • Italian • some veggie • full bar

Spanish Flowers 4701 N Main (at Airline) **713/869-1706** • 24hrs, till 10pm Tue, from 9am Wed • Mexican • beer/ wine

Tafia 3701 Travis St **713/524-6922** • dinner Tue-Sat • Mediterranean • also bar • patio • lesbian-owned

ENTERTAINMENT & RECREATION

After Hours KPFT 90.1 FM (also 89.5 Galveston) **713/526-4000, 713/526-5738** (**REQUEST LINE**) • 1am-4am Sat • LGBT radio

Beer Can House 222 Malone St **713/926-6368** • noon-5pm Sat-Sun only • 50,000+ beer cans cover the building!

DiverseWorks Art Space 1117 East Fwy (I-10 at N Main) **713/223-8346, 713/335-3443** • gallery noon-6pm Wed-Sat • call for events • some LGBT-themed art & performance

Dominic Walsh Dance Theater 2311 Dunlavy St, Ste 210 **713/652-3938** • contemporary dance theater • annual Illumination Project benefits Baylor Int'l Pediatric AIDS Initiative • call for events

Houston Roller Derby • Houston's female roller derby league • visit ww.houstonrollerderby.com for events

Orange Show Center for Visionary Art 2402 Munger St **713/926-6368** • performance, music, public art • produces annual Art Car Parade

Queer Voices • 9pm Mon

Unhinged Productions 832/250-7786 • LGBT theater company • see www.u-p.org for events

RETAIL SHOPS

The Chocolate Bar 1835 W Alabama St **713/520-8599** • chocolate gifts & yummy desserts

Hollywood Super Center 2409 Grant St (at Crocker St) **713/527-8510** • 10am-1am, till 3am wknds • gifts • T-shirts • novelties

Lucia's Garden 2216 Portsmouth (at Greenbriar) **713/523-6494** • 10am-6pm, till 7pm Tue & Th, clsd Sun • spiritual herb center

PUBLICATIONS

abOUT Magazine PO Box 130948, **713/492-0485**

OutSmart **713/520-7237** • free monthly LGBT newsmagazine

GYMS & HEALTH CLUBS

Houston Gym 1501 Durham Rd (at Washington & Eigel) **713/880-9191** • 5am-10pm, 8am-8pm wknds • gay-owned

YMCA Downtown 1600 Louisiana St (btwn Pease & Bell) **713/659-8501** • 5am-10pm • gay-friendly • pool

EROTICA

Dare Ware 6363 Westheimer **713/953-9393** • sinful clothing & shoes

Eros 1207 1207 Spencer Hwy (at Allen Genoa) **713/910-0220** • gay-owned

Loveworks 25170 I-45 N, Spring **281/292-0070**

Lockhart

ACCOMMODATIONS

Lazy J Paradise Campground & Park 270 Hidden Path (CR 303 and FM 2001) **210/863-9314** • campground with RV area catering to the GLBT community • pool • WiFi • $7-35

Longview

BARS

Decisions 2103 E Marshall (2 blocks E of Eastman Rd) **903/757-4884** • 5pm-2am • lesbians/ gay men • dancing/DJ • country/ western • karaoke • drag shows • wheelchair access

Lubbock

INFO LINES & SERVICES

AA Lambda 4501 University Ave (at MCC) **806/792-5562** • 8pm Fri

ACCOMMODATIONS

LaQuinta Inns & Suites North 5006 Auburn St (at Winston) **806/749-1600** • gay-friendly • indoor hot tub • pool • pets ok • laundry • gym • nonsmoking • WiFi • wheelchair access • gay-owned

NIGHTCLUBS

Club Luxor 2211 4th St **806/744-3744** • 9pm-2am Fri-Sun • gay/ straight, more gay Fri & Sun • dancing/DJ • karaoke Wed • drag shows Sun

Heaven Nightclub 1928 Buddy Holly Ave (at I-27) **806/762-4466** • Th-Sun • gay-friendly • dancing/DJ • multiracial • drag shows • 18+ • young crowd

Marfa

ACCOMMODATIONS

El Cosmico Hwy 67 **432/729-1950, 877/822-1950** • gay/ straight • vintage trailer, yurt & teepee hotel & campground • WiFi • lesbian-owned • $20-128

McAllen

see Rio Grande Valley

Plano

see Dallas

Rio Grande Valley

includes McAllen

BARS

PBD's 2908 N Ware Rd (at Daffodil), McAllen **956/682–8019** • 8pm-2am, clsd Mon • mostly gay men • dancing/DJ Th-Sat • drag shows • wheelchair access

Trade Bar 2010 Nolana (at Bicentennial), McAllen **956/630–6304** • 10pm-3am Tue & Th-Sat • lesbians/gay men • dancing/DJ • strippers • 18+ • young crowd • gay-owned

NIGHTCLUBS

Club 33 3300 N McColl Rd, McAllen **956/627–3312** • 9pm-2am, clsd Sun-Tue • lesbians/gay men • dancing/DJ • drag shows

San Antonio

INFO LINES & SERVICES

Lambda AA 319 Camden Rm #4 (Madison Square Presbyterian Church) **210/979–5939** • 8:15pm daily

ACCOMMODATIONS

1908 Ayres Inn 124 W Woodlawn Ave (at N Main) **210/736–4232** • gay/ straight • Nat'l Historic Place in historic Monte Vista neighborhood • built by architect Atlee B. Ayres • eclectic mix of chic furnishings & luxurious surroundings • nonsmoking • WiFi • wheelchair access • gay-owned • $109+

Alamo Lodge 1126 E Elmira (at Wilmington) **210/222–9463, 210/222–9820** • gay-friendly • pool • kids/ pets ok • wheelchair access • $49+

Arbor House Suites B&B 109 Arciniega (btwn S Alamo & S St Mary's) **210/472–2005, 888/272–6700** • gay/ straight • kids/ pets ok • hot tub • nonsmoking • wheelchair access • gay-owned • $100-200

Beauregard House B&B 215 Beauregard St (at King William St) **210/222–1198, 888/667–0555** • gay-friendly • Victorian in historic district • nonsmoking • WiFi • $129-179

San Antonio

WHERE THE GIRLS ARE:
Coupled up in the suburbs or carousing downtown.

LGBT PRIDE:
June. web: www.alamopridefest.org.

ANNUAL EVENTS:
Late April - Fiesta San Antonio 877/723–4378, web: www.fiesta-sa.org.

CITY INFO:
800/447-3372, web: www.visit-sanantonio.com.

BEST VIEW:
High in the Sky Lounge in the Tower of the Americas.

WEATHER:
60°s-90°s in the summer, 40°s-60°s in the winter.

ATTRACTIONS:
The Alamo 210/225-1391, web: www.thealamo.org.
El Mercado.
Hemisfair Park.
The Majestic Theatre 210/226-5700, web: www.majesticempire.com.
McNay Art Museum 210/824-5368, web: www.mcnayart.org.
Plaza de Armas.
River Walk.
San Antonio Museum of Art 210/978-8100, web: www.samuseum.org.

TRANSIT:
Yellow-Checker 210/222-2222.
Via Info 210/362-2020, web: www.viainfo.net.

Beckman Inn 222 E Guenther St (at King William St) 210/229-1449, 800/945-1449 • gay-friendly • B&B in King William historic district • nonsmoking

Brackenridge House 230 Madison (at Beauregard) 210/271-3442, 800/221-1412 • gay-friendly • B&B in historic King William district • pool • hot tub • WiFi • $130+

Desert Hearts Cowgirl Club Bandera 830/796-7001 • women only • 1-room cabin on 30-acre ranch • swimming • horseback riding • nonsmoking • lesbian-owned • $75

Emily Morgan Hotel 705 E Houston St (at Ave E) 210/225-5100 • gay-friendly • gym • pets ok

The Painted Lady Inn on Broadway 620 Broadway (at 6th) 210/220-1092 • lesbians/ gay men • full brkfst • kids/pets ok • rooftop deck & spa • nonsmoking • WiFi • wheelchair access • lesbian- & gay-owned • $109-229

BARS

2015 Place 2015 San Pedro (at Woodlawn) 210/733-3365 • 4pm-2am • mostly gay men • neighborhood bar • karaoke Wed

The Annex 330 San Pedro Ave (at Euclid) 210/223-6957 • 2pm-2am • mostly gay men • neighborhood bar • wheelchair access

Bermuda Triangle 10127 Coachlight Dr (at San Pedro) 210/342-2276 • 8pm-3am Wed-Sat • mostly women • neighborhood bar • dancing/DJ wknds • live shows • karaoke • wheelchair access

Club Unity 1210 E Elmira (at Myrtle) 210/320-3787 • noon-2am • lesbians/gay men • neighborhood bar

Cobalt Club 2022 McCullough (at Ashby) 210/734-2244 • 7am-2am, from 10:30am Sun • lesbians/gay men • neighborhood bar • live shows • wheelchair access

Electric Company 820 San Pedro Ave (at W Laurel) 210/212-6635 • 9pm-3am Wed-Sun • lesbians/gay men • more women Wed & Sun • dancing/DJ • live shows • 18+

Essence 1010 N Main Ave (at E Euclid) 210/223-5418 • 2pm-2am • mostly gay men • neighborhood bar

The Flying Saucer 11255 Huebner Rd #212 (at I-10) 210/647-7468 • 11am-1am, till 2am Th-Sat, noon-midnight Sun • gay-friendly • large beer selection

Lava Lounge 2702 N St Mary's St (at French Pl) 210/320-1740 • open Wed-Sun • gay/ straight • dancing/DJ • mostly Latino/a

One-Oh-Six Off Broadway 106 Pershing St (at Broadway) 210/820-0906 • noon-2am • lesbians/gay men • neighborhood bar

Silver Dollar Saloon 1818 N Main Ave (at Dewey) 210/227-2623 • 4pm-2am • lesbians/ gay men • dancing/DJ • country/western • karaoke

Sparks 8011 Webbles 210/599-3225 • 5pm-2am • mostly gay men • live shows • strippers

Sparky's Pub 1416 N Main Ave (at Evergreen) 210/320-5111 • 3pm-2am • pub atmosphere

NIGHTCLUBS

The Bonham Exchange 411 Bonham St (at 3rd/Houston) 210/271-3811, 210/271-9219 • 4pm-2am, 9pm-4am Fri-Sat • popular • in 111-year-old mansion • lesbians/gay men • dancing/DJ • videos • 18+ • gay-owned

Club Venom 2407 N St Mary's St (at Ashby) 210/738-8080 • mostly gay men • dancing/DJ • drag shows • karaoke

The Industry 8021 Pinebrook Dr (at Callaghan) 210/584-0103 • 9pm-2am Th-Sat • gay/straight • dancing/DJ

SA Hot Lezbian 210/777-8127 • mostly women • dancing/DJ • hot lesbian events around town

The Saint 1430 N Main (at Evergreen) 210/225-7330 • 4pm-2am • mostly gay men • dancing/DJ • drag shows • 18+

CAFES

Candlelight Coffeehouse & Wine Bar 3011 N St Mary's (at Rte 281) 210/738-0099 • 4pm-midnight, Sun brunch 10am-2pm, clsd Mon • WiFi

Timo's Coffee House 2021 San Pedro 210/733-8049 • 8am-8pm, 10am-4pm Sat, clsd Sun

RESTAURANTS

Casbeers 1150 S Alamo (at E Johnson St) 210/271-7791 • 11am-11pm, till midnight wknds, Gospel brunch only Sun, lunch only Mon • burgers • live music

Chacho's 7870 Callaghan Rd (at I-10) 210/366-2023 • 24hrs • Mexican • live bands • karaoke

Cool Cafe 123 Auditorium Circle 210/224-2665 • brkfst, lunch & dinner • Mediterranean • great river views

Giovanni's Pizza & Italian Restaurant 913 S Brazos (at Guadalupe) 210/212-6626 • 11am-7pm • some veggie

Guenther House 129 E Guenther (at S Alamo St) 210/227–1061 • 7am-3pm • located in restored Pioneer Flour Mills founding family home

Lulu's Bakery & Cafe 918 N Main (at W Elmira) 210/222–9422 • 24hrs • Tex-Mex • wheelchair access

Luther's Cafe 1425 N Main Ave 210/223–7727 • 11am-3am • great burgers • gay-owned

Madhatter's Tea 320 Beauregard 210/212–4832 • 9am-9pm, till 3pm Sun-Mon • BYOB • patio • wheelchair access

El Mirador 722 S St Mary's St (at Durango St) 210/225–9444 • 6:30am-9pm, till 2pm Sun • Tex-Mex • plenty veggie • beer/ wine • patio • wheelchair access

Taco Taco Cafe 145 E Hildebrand 210/822–9533 • 7am-2pm

WD Deli 3123 Broadway St 210/828–2322 • 10:30am-5pm, till 4pm Sat, clsd Sun

ENTERTAINMENT & RECREATION

Alamo City Rollergirls 223 Recoleta Rd (at the Rollercade) • San Antonio's female flat track roller derby league • visit www.alamocityrollergirls.com for events

First Friday Art Walk S Alamo St (at S St Mary's St) • 6pm-10pm 1st Fri only • stroll the Southtown arts district

San Antonio Silver Stars One AT&T Center 210/444–5090 • check out the Women's Nat'l Basketball Association while you're in San Antonio

RETAIL SHOPS

On Main/ Off Main 120 W Mistletoe Ave 210/737–2323 • 10am-6pm, till 5pm Sat, clsd Sun • gifts • cards • T-shirts

ZEBRAZ.com 1608 N Main Ave (at E Park Ave) 210/472–2800, 800/788–4729 • 9am-midnight, till 10pm Sun-Tue • LGBT dept store • also online version

PUBLICATIONS

Ignite SA • LGBT publication for San Antonio

EROTICA

Dreamers Apollo 2376 Austin Hwy (at Walzem) 210/653–3538 • 24hrs

Tyler

ACCOMMODATIONS

Cross Timber Ranch B&B 6271 FM 858 (at Hwy 64), Ben Wheeler 903/833–9000, 877/833–9002 • gay/ straight • resort-style pool & hot tub • full brkfst • nonsmoking • WiFi • gay-owned • $95-155

Waco

NIGHTCLUBS

Club Trix 110 S 6th St 254/714–0767 • 10pm-2am Wed-Th, 8pm-2am Fri-Sat • lesbians/ gay men • dancing/DJ • videos

Wichita Falls

BARS

Odds 1205 Lamar St (at 12th) 940/322–2996 • 4pm-2am, from 3pm Sun • lesbians/gay men • more women Th • neighborhood bar • dancing/DJ • karaoke Th • drag shows • 18+ • beer/ wine

Wimberley

ACCOMMODATIONS

Bella Vista 2121 Hilltop 512/847–6425 • gay/ straight • pool • nonsmoking • gay-owned • $95-125

UTAH

Bryce Canyon

ACCOMMODATIONS

Hatch Station 177 S Main, Hatch 435/735–4015 • gay-friendly • also steak house & diner, laundry facility & a convenience store • "We are a safe oasis for LGBT travelers in Southern Utah" • WiFi • wheelchair access • $54-73

The Red Brick Inn of Panguitch B&B 161 N 100 West (at 200 North), Panguitch 435/676–2141, 866/733–2745 • gay-friendly • full brkfst • kids ok • $99-199

Holladay

RESTAURANTS

Loco Lizard Cantina 1612 Ute Blvd (in Kimball Jct Shopping Ctr) 435/645–7000 • 11am-10pm, till 11pm Fri-Sat, brunch wknds • Mexican • full bar • transgender-friendly • wheelchair access

Moab

ACCOMMODATIONS

Los Vados Canyon House 801/532-2651 • gay/ straight • retreat house in a red rock canyon • pool • kids 10 & over ok • nonsmoking • $250 • also tent cabin $25/ night when cabin is rented

Mayor's House B&B 505 Rose Tree Ln (at 400 E) 435/259-6015, 888/791-2345 • gay-friendly • full brkfst • pool • hot tub • kids ok • nonsmoking • gay-owned • $100-200

Mt Peale Resort Inn, Lodge & Cabins 1415 E Hwy 46 (at mile marker 14), Old La Sal 435/686-2284, 888/687-3253 • gay/ straight • B&B & cabins • full brkfst • hot tub • hiking • nonsmoking • kids/ pets ok • lesbian-owned • $99-199

Red Cliffs Lodge Hwy 128 (at mile marker 14) 435/259-2002, 866/812-2002 • gay-friendly • resort • on Colorado River • pool • hot tub • kids ok • nonsmoking • wheelchair access • $139-320

Park City

ACCOMMODATIONS

Resort Quest Park City 435/649-6606, 800/401-9913 • gay-friendly • vacation rentals

Salt Lake City

INFO LINES & SERVICES

Utah Pride Center 361 N 300 W, 1st flr 801/539-8800, 888/874-2743 • info • resource center • meetings • coffee shop • programs • youth activity center • much more

ACCOMMODATIONS

Anniversary Inn 460 S 1000 E (at 400) 801/363-4900, 800/324-4152 • gay-friendly • elaborate, kitschy theme rms • $139-319

Anton Boxrud B&B 57 S 600 E (at S Temple) 801/363-8035, 800/524-5511 • gay-friendly • full brkfst • hot tub • some shared baths • kids ok • nonsmoking • WiFi • $75-170

High Aves Modern 625 Northcrest Dr (at N 1st St) 801/355-3521 • gay/ straight • B&B in private home • pool • nonsmoking • WiFi • $50-75

Hotel Monaco Salt Lake City 15 W 200 S (at S Main) 801/595-0000, 877/294-9710 • gay-friendly • restaurant & bar • gym • kids/ pets ok • wheelchair access • $119-279

Parrish Place 720 E Ashton Ave (at 700 E) 801/832-0970, 888/832-0869 • gay/ straight • Victorian mansion • hot tub • nonsmoking • full brkfst • WiFi • $89-129

Peery Hotel 110 W 300 S 801/521-4300, 800/331-0073 • popular • gay-friendly • full brkfst • kids ok • $20/ day for pets • also 2 restaurants • full bar • nonsmoking • WiFi • wheelchair access • $90-190

Under the Lindens 128 S 1000 E (downtown) 801/355-9808 • mostly gay men • studios • hot tub • nonsmoking • WiFi • commitment ceremonies • mention Damron for discount • gay-owned • $125-160

BARS

Jam 751 North 300 West (at Reed Ave) 801/891-1162 • 5pm-2am, clsd Sun-Mon • lesbians/ gay men • neighborhood bar • dancing/DJ • karaoke • beer only

Paper Moon 3737 S State St (at E 3750 S) 801/713-0678 • 3pm-1am, clsd Mon • mostly women • dancing/DJ • karaoke • live music • private club • food served • wheelchair access

Speakeasy 63 West 100 South (at Temple) 801/521-7000 • gay-friendly • live jazz & blues • some gay theme nights

The Tavernacle Social Club 201 E 300 South (at 200 E) 801/519-8900 • 5pm-close, from 8pm Sun-Mon • gay-friendly • food • karaoke • "Duelin' Pianos" • nonsmoking • private club

The Trapp 102 S 600 W (at 100 S) 801/531-8727 • 11am-2am • lesbians/ gay men • dancing/DJ • country/ western • food Sun • private club • wheelchair access

W Lounge 358 SW Temple 801/359-0637 • 8pm-2am • gay/ straight • dancing/DJ • nonsmoking • private club

NIGHTCLUBS

Area 51 451 South 400 West (at 400 S) 801/534-0819 • gay/ straight • dancing/DJ • 80s & goth theme nights Tue, Th & Sat

Club Manhattan 5 E 400 S (at Main) 801/364-7651 • 9pm-2am • dancing/DJ • more gay Sat for Latin salsa

Gossip 579 W 200 S (at 600 W, at Club Sound) 801/328-0255 • 10pm-2am Fri only • mostly gay men • dancing/DJ • live bands rest of the week

Pachanga 1051 East 2100 South (at Karamba) 801/637-9197 • 9pm Sun only • mostly gay men • gay Latin night • dancing/DJ

CAFES

Coffee Garden 878 E 900 S **801/355-3425** • 6am-11pm, till midnight Fri-Sat, 7am-11pm Sun • light fare • wheelchair access

RESTAURANTS

Bambara 202 S Main St **801/363-5454** • lunch Mon-Fri, brkfst & dinner daily • upscale American

Blue Plate Diner 2041 S 2100 E **801/463-1151** • 7am-9pm, till 10pm Fri-Sat

Cafe Med 420 E 3300 South **801/493-0100** • lunch & dinner • Mediterranean

Cafe Trio Downtown 680 S 900 E **801/533-8746** • 11am-10pm, Italian

Cedars of Lebanon 152 E 200 South (at State St) **801/364-4096** • lunch & dinner • Lebanese • veggie/ vegan-friendly • belly dancers wknds • WiFi

Citris Grill 2991 E 3300 South **801/466-1202** • 11am-10pm, from 8am wknds

Finn's 1624 S 1100 East (at Logan) **801/467-4000** • 7:30am-2:30pm

Fresco Italian Cafe 1513 S 1500 East **801/486-1300** • dinner nightly

Lamb's Grill Cafe 169 S Main St **801/364-7166** • 7am-9pm, from 8am Sat, clsd Sun • wheelchair access • live jazz wknds • "oldest restaurant in Utah"

Market St Grill 48 W Market St **801/322-4668** • brkfst & lunch Mon-Sat, dinner nightly, Sun brunch • seafood & steak • full bar • wheelchair access •

The Metropolitan 173 W Broadway **801/364-3472** • lunch Mon-Fri, dinner nightly, clsd Sun • upscale New American • reservations recommended

The New Yorker 60 W Market St **801/363-0166** • lunch Mon-Fri, dinner nightly, clsd Sun • fine dining • steak

Nick-N-Willy's Pizza 4536 S Highland Dr **801/273-8282** • 11am-8pm, till 9pm wknds

Off Trax 259 W 900 S **801/364-4307** • 7am-7pm, till 3pm Fri, brunch Sun, also from 1am-3am Fri-Sat nights • lesbians/ gay men • WiFi • gay-owned

Omar's Rawtopia 2148 Highland Dr **801/486-0332** • noon-8pm, till 9pm Fri-Sat, clsd Sun • raw food

Red Iguana 736 W North Temple **801/322-1489** • popular • lunch & dinner • Mexican

Salt Lake City

LGBT PRIDE:
June. 801/539-8800, web: www.utahpride.org.

ANNUAL EVENTS:
Jan-Feb - Gay/ Lesbian Ski Week 877/429-6368, web: www.gayski-ing.org.

CITY INFO:
801/534-4900, web: www.visitsalt-lake.com.

WEATHER:
Home of "The Greatest Snow on Earth," the Wasatch Mtns get an average of 535 inches of powder, while the valley averages 59 inches. Spring is mild with an average of 62°, while summer temps average 88°, topping out at an average of 92° in July.

ATTRACTIONS:
Family History Library, one of the largest genealogical research databases in the country 801/240-2584, web: www.family-search.org.
Great Salt Lake.
Mormon Tabernacle Choir 801/240-4150, web: www.mormontabernaclechoir.org.
Skiing!
Temple Square.
Trolley Square.

TRANSIT:
Yellow Cab 801/521-2100.
Utah Transit Authority (UTA) 801/743-3882, web: www.utabus.com.

Rio Grande Cafe 270 S Rio Grande St
801/364–3302 • lunch Mon-Sat & dinner
nightly • popular • Mexican • some veggie •
full bar • wheelchair access

Sage's Cafe 473 E 300 S **801/322–3790** •
lunch & dinner, brkfst wknds • vegan/
vegetarian

Stoneground 249 E 400 South
801/364–1368 • 11am-11pm, 5pm-9pm Sun •
pizza & more

Vertical Diner 2280 S West Temple
801/484–8378 • 10am-9pm • vegetarian diner
• wheelchair access

ENTERTAINMENT & RECREATION

Lambda Hiking Club • hiking & other
activities

Plan B Theatre Company 138 West 300
South (at Rose Wagner Performing Arts
Center, btwn W Temple & 200 West)
801/355–2787 • at least one LGBT-themed
production each season

**Pygmalion Productions Theatre
Company** 138 W Broadway (at Rose Wagner
Performing Arts Center) **801/355–2787,
888/451–2787** • a "feminine perspective" on
theatre

Tower Theatre 876 E 900 South
801/321–0310 • alternative films • many
LGBT movies

BOOKSTORES

Golden Braid Books 151 S 500 E
801/322–1162, 801/322–0404 (CAFE) • 10am-
9pm, till 6pm Sun • also Oasis Cafe, 8am-9pm,
till 10pm wknds • gay/ straight

Sam Weller's 254 S Main St **801/328–2586,
800/333–7269** • 10am-7pm Mon-Sat

RETAIL SHOPS

Cahoots 878 E 900 S (at 900 E) **801/538–0606**
• 10am-9pm • unique gift shop • wheelchair
access • gay-owned

Gypsy Moon Emporium 1011 E 900 S
801/521–9100 • call for hours • Celtic &
goddess-oriented gifts

PUBLICATIONS

Q Salt Lake **801/649–6663, 800/806–7357** •
bi-weekly LGBT newspaper

EROTICA

All For Love 3072 S Main St (at 33rd St S)
801/487–8358 • clsd Sun • lingerie & S/M
boutique • transgender-friendly • wheelchair
access

Blue Boutique Sugarhouse 1383 E 2100
South **801/485–2072** • also piercing

Mischievous 559 S 300 W (at 6th St S)
801/530–3100 • clsd Sun

Torrey

ACCOMMODATIONS

Capitol Reef Inn & Cafe 360 W Main St
435/425–3271 • gay-friendly • seasonal • hot
tub • gift shop • $48-61 • also restaurant •
plenty veggie • beer/ wine

SkyRidge Inn B&B **435/425–3222,
877/824–1508** • gay-friendly • full brkfst • hot
tubs • near Capitol Reef Nat'l Park •
nonsmoking • WiFi • $119-142

Zion Nat'l Park

ACCOMMODATIONS

Canyon Vista B&B 2175 Zion Park Blvd (at
Hwy 9), Springdale **435/772–3801** • gay-
friendly • nonsmoking • $110-160

Red Rock Inn 998 Zion Park Blvd,
Springdale **435/772–3139** • gay/ straight •
cottages w/ canyon views • full brkfst • hot tub
• 1 mile to Zion Nat'l Park • nonsmoking •
wheelchair access • lesbian-owned • $122-192

CAFES

Cafe Soleil 205 Zion Nat'l Park Blvd
435/772–0505 • 6am-8pm seasonal • lesbian-
owned

VERMONT

Statewide

INFO LINES & SERVICES

Vermont Gay Tourism Association •
Vermont's official organization to promote gay
& lesbian travel throughout the state • see
www.vermontgaytourism.com

Arlington

ACCOMMODATIONS

Arlington Inn 3904 Rte 7-A **802/375–6532,
800/443–9442** • country inn • kids ok • WiFi •
$99-319 • also restaurant & tavern • dinner
from 5:30pm, clsd Sun-Mon • cont'l

Brattleboro

RESTAURANTS

Peter Havens 32 Elliot St (at Main)
802/257–3333, 802/257–3000 • 6pm-10pm,
clsd Sun-Mon • cont'l • gay-owned

BOOKSTORES

Everyone's Books 25 Elliot St **802/254–8160** • 9:30am-6pm, till 5:30pm Mon, till 8pm Fri, till 7pm Sat, 11am-5pm Sun • wheelchair access

Bridgewater Corners

RESTAURANTS

Blanche & Bill's Pancake House 586 US Rte 4 **802/422–3816** • 7am-2pm Th-Sun • great flapjacks & maple syrup

Brookfield

RESTAURANTS

Ariel's Restaurant & Pond Village Pub 29 Stone Rd (at Rte 65) **802/276–3939** • dinner, clsd Sun-Tue • eclectic • overlooking Sunset Lake

Burlington

INFO LINES & SERVICES

R.U.1.2? Community Center 34 Elmwood Ave (across from Burlington post office) **802/860–RU12 (7812)** • drop-in & cybercenter • advocacy & support • events

ACCOMMODATIONS

The Black Bear Inn 4010 Bolton Access Rd, Bolton Valley **802/434–2126, 800/395–6335** • gay/ straight • mtn-top inn on 6,000 acres • full brkfst • hot tub • pool • kids/ pets ok • nonsmoking • WiFi • $89-355

Hartwell House B&B Gallery 170 Ferguson Ave **802/658–9242, 888/658–9242** • gay-friendly • pool • shared bath • nonsmoking • woman-owned • $70-90

The Inn at Essex 70 Essex Way, Essex **802/878–1100, 800/727–4295** • gay-friendly • pool • kids/ pets ok • WiFi • wheelchair access • $159-499

One of a Kind B&B 53 Lakeview Terrace **802/862–5576, 877/479–2736** • nonsmoking • WiFi • woman-owned • $95-135

NIGHTCLUBS

Metronome/ Nectar's 188 Main St **802/865–4563, 802/658–4771** • clsd Mon-Tue • gay-friendly • popular 80's night Sat • live bands • also restaurant

CAFES

Muddy Waters 184 Main St **802/658–0466** • 7:30am-11pm, till midnight Fri-Sat, till 10pm Sun • coffeehouse • also beer • try the white hot chocolate

Radio Bean Coffeehouse 8 N Winooski Ave (at Pearl) **802/660–9346** • 8am-midnight, till 2am Th-Sat, 10am-11pm Sun • cool bohemian coffeehouse • live bands & open mic nights

RESTAURANTS

Bluebird Tavern 317 Riverside Ave **802/540–1786** • 4pm-10pm Th-Sat, 5pm-9pm Tue-Wed, clsd Sun-Mon • locally grown • beer/wine • lesbian-owned

Daily Planet 15 Center St (at College) **802/862–9647** • 4pm-close, also bar till 2am • plenty veggie

Loretta's 44 Park St (near 5 Corners), Essex Junction **802/879–7777** • lunch weekdays, dinner nightly, clsd Sun-Mon • Italian • plenty veggie • lesbian-owned

Parima Thai 185 Pearl St (btwn Winooski & Church) **802/864–7917** • lunch & dinner • courtyard garden • entertainment • WiFi

Shanty on the Shore 181 Battery St **802/864–0238** • 11am-10pm • seafood • views of Lake Champlain

Silver Palace 1216 Williston Rd **802/864–0125** • 11:30am-9pm, till 10pm Fri-Sat, 3pm-9pm Sun • Chinese • some veggie • full bar

RETAIL SHOPS

Peace & Justice Store 60 Lake St (at College St) **802/863–2345** • 9am-7pm, limited hrs in winter • fair trade retail store

Chester

ACCOMMODATIONS

Chester House Inn 266 Main St **802/875–2205, 888/875–2205** • gay/ straight • full brkfst • nonsmoking • kids ok • WiFi • wheelchair access • gay-owned • $125-209 • also restaurant • beer/ wine

Craftsbury Common

ACCOMMODATIONS

Greenhope Farm 2478 Wylie Hill Rd **802/586–7577** • gay/ straight • nonsmoking • kids ok • WiFi • lesbian-owned • $75-150

Greensboro

ACCOMMODATIONS

Highland Lodge 1608 Craftsbry Rd **802/533–2647** • gay-friendly • open May-Oct & Dec-March • includes brkfst & dinner • nonsmoking • WiFi • wheelchair access • $138-550

Jay Peak

ACCOMMODATIONS

Four Seasons Apartments 2 10 Elm St (at Main St), North Troy **802/578-7103** • gay/straight • kids ok • nonsmoking • WiFi • $85-225

Grey Gables Mansion 122 River St, Richford **802/848-3625, 800/299-2117** • gay-friendly • circa 1888 B&B inn • full brkfst • kids ok • nonsmoking • WiFi • $99-139

Phineas Swann B&B 802/326-4306 • gay/straight • restored Victorian on Trout River • full brkfst • nonsmoking • WiFi • gay-owned • $99-289

Jeffersonville

ACCOMMODATIONS

Donomar Inn 916 Rte 108 S **802/644-2937** • gay/straight • full brkfst • hot tub • WiFi • gay-owned • $75-175

Killington

ACCOMMODATIONS

Salt Ash Inn 4758 Rte 100A (at Rte 100), Plymouth **802/672-3224** • gay/straight • 1830s country inn • full brkfst • hot tub • food served • pub • near skiing • kids/ small pets ok • WiFi • wheelchair access • $109-289

RESTAURANTS

Grist Mill 200 Killington Rd (on Summit Pond) **802/422-3970** • lunch & dinner • New England fare • entertainment

Ludlow

ACCOMMODATIONS

Happy Trails Motel 321 Rte 103 S **802/228-8888, 800/228-9984** • gay-friendly • rooms, suites & cottage • seasonal hot tub • near skiing • nonsmoking • WiFi • $65-425

RESTAURANTS

Cappuccino's Restaurant 41 Depot St **802/228-7566** • dinner, clsd Mon-Tue • meat, pasta & seafood

Lyndonville

RESTAURANTS

Miss Lyndonville Diner 686 Broad **802/626-9890** • 6am-3pm, till 9pm Fri-Sat

Manchester

ACCOMMODATIONS

Hill Farm Inn 458 Hill Farm Rd (at Historic Rte 7-A), Arlington **802/375-2269, 800/882-2545** • gay-friendly • full brkfst • nonsmoking • WiFi • $130-235

CAFES

Little Rooster Cafe Rte 7-A (at Hillvale Dr), Manchester Center **802/362-3496** • 7am-2:30pm, clsd Wed (winters)

RESTAURANTS

Bistro Henry 1942 Depot St (.5 mile E of Rte 7), Manchester Center **802/362-4982** • dinner only, clsd Mon • Mediterranean • also bar • reservations advised

Chantecleer Rte 7-A N, E Dorset **802/362-1616** • call for hours • seasonal

BOOKSTORES

Northshire Bookstore 4869 Main St, Manchester Center **802/362-2200, 800/437-3700** • 10am-7pm, till 9pm Th-Sat

Marshfield

ACCOMMODATIONS

Marshfield Inn & Motel 5630 US Rte 2 **802/426-3383** • gay-friendly • full brkfst • WiFi • lesbian-owned • $68-108

Montgomery Center

CAFES

Tosca's at Trout River Traders 91 Main St (at Rte 242) **802/326-3058** • 9am-5pm, tapas & dinner till 9pm Fri-Sat, Sun brunch • gay-friendly • food served • also gift shop • WiFi • gay-owned

Montpelier

RESTAURANTS

Julio's 54 State **802/229-9348** • 11:30am-11pm, till midnight Wed & Fri-Sat • Mexican

Sarducci's 3 Main St **802/223-0229** • 11:30am-9:30pm, from 4:30pm Sun • Italian • some veggie • full bar • wheelchair access

Wayside Restaurant 1873 Rte 302 **802/223-6611** • 6:30am-9:30pm • wheelchair access

Plainfield

ACCOMMODATIONS

Comstock House 1620 Middle Rd
802/272-2693 • gay-friendly • 1891 house on
former dairy farm overlooking Winooski River
Valley • full brkfst • WiFi • gay-owned • $115-
135

Richmond

RESTAURANTS

The Kitchen Table Bistro 1840 W Main St
802/434-8686 • 5pm-9pm, clsd Sun-Mon •
seasonal menu • local food

Rutland

ACCOMMODATIONS

The Inn of the Six Mountains 2617
Killington Rd, Killington **802/422-4302,
800/228-4676** • gay-friendly • hotel • pool •
jacuzzi • WiFi • kids ok • wheelchair access •
$89-249

Lilac Inn 53 Park St, Brandon **802/247-5463,
800/221-0720** • full brkfst • teens/pets ok •
wheelchair access • $135-255

Maplewood Inn 1108 S Main St (Rte 22-A),
Fair Haven **802/265-8039, 800/253-7729** •
gay/straight • romantic, historic-register 1843
Greek Revival • full brkfst • beautiful antiques
• centrally located • nonsmoking • $109-199

Saxtons River

ACCOMMODATIONS

The Saxtons River Inn 27 Main St (at
Academy Ave) **802/869-2110** • gay-friendly •
historic Victorian inn w/ charming pub &
restaurant • located in quaint New England
village • nonsmoking • WiFi • pets ok • $99-
179

Shelburne

RESTAURANTS

Bistro Sauce 97 Falls Rd (at Shelburne
Shopping Park) **802/985-2830** • lunch &
dinner, Sun brunch • local food

St Albans

RESTAURANTS

Jeff's Maine Seafood 65 N Main St
802/524-6135 • lunch daily, dinner Tue-Sat,
clsd Sun • full bar

St Johnsbury

ACCOMMODATIONS

Comfort Inn & Suites 703 US Rte 5 S (at I-
91) **802/748-1500, 800/424-6423** • gay-
friendly • hotel • pool • hot tub • kids ok •
WiFi • wheelchair access • $119-359

➤ **Highlands Inn** Bethlehem, NH
603/869-3978, 877/LES-B-INN (537-2466) • a
lesbian paradise • "one of the most romantic
lesbian destinations on the planet" (*Planet
Out*) • 19 antique-filled rooms • full brkfst •
outdoor & indoor spas • pool • 100 mtn acres
• special events • concerts • VT civil union
honeymoons • kids/pets ok • non-smoking •
WiFi • wheelchair access • ignore No Vacancy
sign • lesbian-owned • $110-220 • see ad on
page 1

RESTAURANTS

Elements 98 Mill St **802/748-8400** • dinner,
clsd Sun-Mon • local food

Stowe

ACCOMMODATIONS

Arbor Inn 3214 Mountain Rd **802/253-4772,
800/543-1293** • gay/straight • full brkfst • hot
tub • pool • nonsmoking • WiFi • $75-220

Fitch Hill Inn 258 Fitch Hill Rd, Hyde Park
802/888-3834, 800/639-2903 • gay/straight •
full brkfst • hot tub • older kids ok • WiFi •
$99-149

The Green Mountain Inn 18 Main St
802/253-7301, 800/253-7302 • gay-friendly •
kids ok • heated pool • hot tub • nonsmoking
• WiFi • wheelchair access • 2 restaurants •
$119-849

Northern Lights Lodge 4441 Mountain Rd
802/253-8541, 800/448-4554 • gay-friendly •
full brkfst • hot tub • pool • sauna • kids/pets
ok • WiFi • gay-owned • $79-154

The Old Stagecoach Inn 18 N Main St (at
Stowe St), Waterbury **802/244-5056,
800/262-2206** • gay-friendly • historic village
inn • full brkfst • kids/pets ok • also full bar •
nonsmoking • $80-190

Timberholm Inn 452 Cottage Club Rd
802/253-7603, 800/753-7603 • gay/straight •
B&B • full brkfst • hot tub • nonsmoking •
$90-225

**Winding Brook, A Classic Mountain
Lodge** 199 Edson Hill Rd **802/253-7354,
800/426-6697** • gay/straight • rustic mtn
retreat • full brkfst • pool • nonsmoking • kids
ok • gay-owned

Townshend

ACCOMMODATIONS

Townshend State Park 2755 State Forest Rd 802/365-7500, 888/409-7579 • gay-friendly • campground • great hiking • open Memorial Day wknd to Labor Day wknd

Vergennes

RESTAURANTS

Basin Harbor Club 4800 Basin Harbor Rd 802/475-2311, 800/622-4000 • brkfst & dinner, Sun jazz brunch (seasonal) • eclectic New England fare • upscale

Waterbury

ACCOMMODATIONS

The Belding House B&B 746 Rte 100 (at VT Rte 100B), Moretown 802/496-7420 • gay/straight • full brkfst • nonsmoking • gay-owned • $149-175

Grünberg Haus B&B & Cabins 94 Pine St, Rte 100 S 802/244-7726, 800/800-7760 • gay/straight • Austrian chalet • also cabins May-Oct • full brkfst • fireplace • nonsmoking • WiFi • $90-180

Moose Meadow Lodge 607 Crossett Hill 802/244-5378 • gay/straight • full brkfst • nonsmoking • WiFi • gay-owned • $189-229

RESTAURANTS

Cider House BBQ & Pub 1675 US Rte 2 802/244-8400 • lunch Fri-Sat, dinner nightly, clsd Mon • full bar • patio • gay-owned

West Dover

ACCOMMODATIONS

Deerhill Inn 14 Valley View Rd 802/464-3100, 800/993-3379 • gay/straight • inn • pool • teenagers ok • nonsmoking • WiFi • also restaurant • $143-355

Inn at Mount Snow 401 Rte 100 802/464-8388, 866/587-7669 • gay-friendly • at foot of Mt Snow • near skiing • kids ok • nonsmoking • WiFi • gay-owned • $59-309

The Inn at Sawmill Farm 7 Crosstown Rd (at Rte 100) 802/464-8131, 800/493-1133 • gay-friendly • full brkfst • kids/pets ok • nonsmoking • WiFi • wheelchair access • $185-345

Red Oak Inn 45 Rte 100 (at Rte 9) 802/464-8817, 866/573-3625 • gay-friendly • pool • kids/pets ok • also tavern & gameroom • nonsmoking • $95-269

Wilmington

ACCOMMODATIONS

Nordic Hills Lodge 34 Look Rd (at Route 101) 802/464-5130, 800/326-5130 • pool • WiFi • fireplace • game room • exercise room • nonsmoking • kids/pets ok • full restaurant & bar • WiFi • $90-275

Windham

ACCOMMODATIONS

A Stone Wall Inn 578 Hitchcock Hill Rd 802/875-4238 • gay/straight • hot tub • nonsmoking • gay-owned • $125-175

Woodstock

ACCOMMODATIONS

The Ardmore Inn 23 Pleasant St 802/457-3887, 800/497-9652 • gay-friendly • 1880s Greek Revival • full brkfst • jacuzzi • nonsmoking • WiFi • $120-225

Cabin in the Woods 1944 Chateauguay Rd, Bridgewater Corners 802/672-5141 • gay-friendly • hot tub • swimming hole • fireplace • smoking outdoors only • seasonal May-Oct • pets ok • transgender-owned/run • $225

Deer Brook Inn 535 Woodstock Rd 802/672-3713 • gay-friendly • B&B • full brkfst • kids ok • WiFi • gay-owned • $120-185

Village Inn of Woodstock 41 Pleasant St 802/457-1255, 800/722-4571 • gay-friendly • restored Victorian Inn • full brkfst • WiFi • nonsmoking • WiFi • $165-350

VIRGINIA

Alexandria

see also **Washington, District of Columbia**

ACCOMMODATIONS

Hotel Monaco Alexandria 480 King St 703/549-6080, 800/368-5047 • gay-friendly • restaurant on-site • kids/pets ok • wheelchair access • $220-679

Arlington

see also **Washington, District of Columbia**

INFO LINES & SERVICES

Arlington Gay/Lesbian Alliance • monthly meetings • outreach events • check website for schedule: www.agla.org

Bars

Freddie's Beach Bar & Restaurant 555 S 23rd St **703/685-0555** • 11am-2am, from 4pm Mon, wknd brunch • lesbians/gay men • karaoke • drag show • patio • live bands • food served • wheelchair access

Cafes

Java Shack 2507 N Franklin Rd (at Wilson Blvd & N Barton) **703/527-9556** • 7am-8pm, till 10pm Fri-Sat • lesbians/gay men

Bowling Green

Accommodations

Column Wood B&B 233 N Main St (at Broaddus Ave) **804/633-5606, 866/633-9314** • gay-friendly • full brkfst • nonsmoking • WiFi • gay-owned • $99-169

Cape Charles

see also Norfolk & Virginia Beach

Accommodations

Cape Charles House B&B 645 Tazewell Ave (at Fig) **757/331-4920** • gay-friendly • 1912 colonial revival home filled w/ antiques • nonsmoking • $140-200

Sea Gate B&B 9 Tazewell Ave **757/331-2206** • gay-friendly • full brkfst • afternoon tea • near beach on quiet, tree-lined street • WiFi • gay-owned • $120-130

Sterling House B& B 9 Randolph Ave (at Harbor Ave) **757/331-2483** • gay/ straight • WiFi • gay-owned

Restaurants

The Chesapeake Restaurant & Nightclub 307 Mason Ave **757/331-3123** • lunch & dinner, clsd Mon-Tue • live music

Charlottesville

Accommodations

The Barboursville Inn 12421 Albano Rd, Barboursville **540/832-0550** • gay/ straight • full brkfst • kids/pets ok • gay-owned • $100-125

CampOut **804/301-3553, 888/357-6697** • women only • 100-acre rustic campground w/ 50 campsites • nonsmoking • wheelchair access • women-owned • $20-60 membership fee

The Inn at Court Square 410 E Jefferson St **434/295-2800, 866/466-2877** • gay-friendly • restored house w/ period antiques • jacuzzi • lunch served Mon-Fri • kids ok • nonsmoking • women-owned • $99-329

Nightclubs

Club 216 216 W Water St (enter on South St) **434/296-8783** • 10pm-5am Fri-Sat, some Sun events popular • lesbians/gay men • dancing/DJ • live shows • private club • wheelchair access

Restaurants

Escafe 227 W Main St (next to the Omni Hotel) **434/295-8668** • 5:30pm-11pm, 4:30pm-9:30pm Sun, clsd Mon • Asian/ American fusion • full bar • live music • gay-owned

Entertainment & Recreation

The Eclectic Woman WTJU 91.1 FM **434/924-3418** • 7pm Th • women's music show

Erotica

Pamela's Secrets 3051 S Main St, Harrisonburg **540/432-6403** • sex toys & videos

Sneak Reviews Video 2244 Ivy Rd **434/979-4420**

Chincoteague Island

Accommodations

1848 Island Manor House 4160 Main St (at Smith St) **757/336-5436, 800/852-1505** • gay/ straight • B&B • full brkfst • nonsmoking • WiFi • gay-owned • $125-250

Hampton

see also Newport News

Cafes

The Java Junkies 768 Settlers Landing Rd **757/722-6300** • 7am-7pm, from 8am wknds, till 3pm Sun • food served

Harrisonburg

Cafes

Artful Dodger Coffeehouse 47 W Court Square **540/432-1179** • 8am-2am, noon-midnight Sun • DJ • entertainment • also bar • wheelchair access

Luray

see Shenandoah Valley

Newport News

see also Norfolk & Virginia Beach

BARS

Corner Pocket 6157 Jefferson Ave (at Mercury) **757/825–0440** • 5pm-2am • lesbians/ gay men • neighborhood bar • shows • food till midnight • wheelchair access

Norfolk

see also Virginia Beach

INFO LINES & SERVICES

Hampton Roads Outreach Center

Saturday Night Live Gay/ Lesbian AA 1301 Colley Ave (at First Lutheran Church) **757/625–1953 (CHURCH #)** • 8pm Sat

ACCOMMODATIONS

B&B @ Historic Page House Inn 323 Fairfax Ave **757/625–5033, 800/599–7659** • gay-friendly • B&B in 1899 mansion • nonsmoking • WiFi • $145-230

Tazewell Hotel & Suites 245 Granby St (at Tazewell St) **757/623–6200** • gay-friendly • kids ok • WiFi • wheelchair access • $95+

BARS

The Garage 731 Granby St (at Brambleton) **757/623–0303** • 9am-2am, from 11am Sat, from noon Sun • popular • mostly gay men • neighborhood bar • food served • karaoke • wheelchair access

Hershee Bar 6117 Sewells Pt Rd (at Norview) **757/853–9842** • 4pm-2am • mostly women • dancing/DJ • live shows • food served • some veggie • Sun buffet • wheelchair access • woman-owned

Nutty Buddy's 143 E Little Creek Rd **757/588–6474** • 4pm-2am Wed-Sun • mostly gay men • more women Wed • dancing/DJ • multiracial • drag shows • also restaurant • some veggie • wheelchair access

The Wave 4107 Colley Ave (at 41st St) **757/440–5911** • 4pm-2am, from 5pm Sat, clsd Sun • lesbians/ gay men • dancing/DJ • live shows • also restaurant • dinner only • wheelchair access

CAFES

Oasis Cafe 142 W York St #101A (in York Center bldg) **757/627–6161** • 7:30am-3pm Mon-Fri • gay-owned

Norfolk

TRANSIT:

Checker Cab 757/855-3333, web: www.norfolkcheckertaxi.com.
Norfolk Airport Shuttle 877/455-7462, web: www.norfolkairport-express.com.
Hampton Roads Transit 757/222-6100, web: www.hrtransit.org.

LGBT PRIDE:

September. 757/624-6886, web: www.hamptonroadspride.com.

CITY INFO:

757/441-1852 or 800/368-3097, web: www.norfolkcvb.com.

ATTRACTIONS:

Busch Gardens (in Williamsburg) 800/343-7946, web: www.buschgardens.com.
The Chrysler Museum of Art 757/664-6200, web: www.chrysler.org.
Douglas Macarthur Memorial 757/441-2965, web: www.macarthurmemorial.org.
The Ghent historic district.
Hermitage Foundation Museum 757/423-2052, web: www.hermitagefoundation.org.
Historic Williamsburg.
Norfolk Naval Base 757/322–2337, web: www.cnic.navy.mil/norfolk-sta/index.htm.
St Paul's Episcopal Church 757/627-4353, web: www.saint-paulsnorfolk.org.
Waterside Festival Marketplace 757/627-3300, web: www.water-sidemarketplace.com.

RESTAURANTS

Charlie's Cafe 1800 Granby St (at 18th) 757/625–0824 • 7am-2pm • some veggie • beer/ wine

Enrico's Ristorante 4012 Colley Ave 757/423–2700 • 11am-10pm, till 11pm Fri, 5pm-11pm Sat, clsd Sun • Greek & Italian • wheelchair access

Tortilla West 508 Oropax St 757/440–3777 • dinner only, open till 1am • Mexican • plenty veggie/ vegan

RETAIL SHOPS

Kindred Spirit 7510-C Granby St (at Wards Corner) 757/480–0424 • 10am-7pm, till 5pm Sat, from noon Sun • gifts • books • massage • readings & more

EROTICA

Leather & Lace 149 E Little Creek Rd (at Granby) 757/583–4334

Petersburg

ACCOMMODATIONS

Walker House B&B 3280 S Crater Rd (at Wagner) 804/861–5822 • gay-friendly • antebellum farmhouse • full brkfst • nonsmoking • WiFi • kids ok • gay-owned • $98-120

Richmond

INFO LINES & SERVICES

AA Gay/ Lesbian 1205 W Franklin (at St James Episcopal Church) 804/355–1212

ACCOMMODATIONS

Omni Richmond Hotel 100 S 12th St (at Cary St) 804/344–7000, 800/843–6664 • gay-friendly • pool • views of city & James River • WiFi • wheelchair access • $159-269

BARS

Babes of Carytown 3166 W Cary St (at Auburn) 804/355–9330 • 11am-2am, from noon Sat, from 9am Sun • lesbians/ gay men • dancing/DJ • country/ western • karaoke • drag shows • live music • food served • wheelchair access • women-owned

Barcode 6 E Grace St (btwn 1st & Foushee Sts) 804/648–2040 • 11am-2am, from 3pm wknds • mostly gay men • neighborhood bar • karaoke • videos • food served • some veggie • wheelchair access

Godfrey's 308 E Grace St (btwn 3rd & 4th) 804/648–3957 • lunch Tue-Fri, dinner Wed-Sun, clsd Mon, brunch Sun • lesbians/ gay men • dancing/DJ • karaoke • drag shows • also restaurant

NIGHTCLUBS

Club Colours 536 N Harrison St (at Broad) 804/353–9776 • 9pm-3am Sat • lesbians/ gay men • dancing/DJ • multiracial • food served • live shows • wheelchair access

RESTAURANTS

Galaxy Diner 3109 W Cary St 804/213–0510 • 11am-midnight, till 2am wknds • some veggie • full bar

The Village 1001 W Grace 804/353–8204 • 8am-2am • American • plenty veggie

ENTERTAINMENT & RECREATION

Richmond Triangle Players 2033 W Broad St (at Fieldens Cabaret Theater) 804/346–8113 • alternative theater group

Venture Richmond 804/788–6466 • tour the James River • lots of shops, restaurants, etc

BOOKSTORES

Carytown Books 4021 MacArthur 804/261–7710 • 10am-7pm, till 5pm Sun • LGBT section • wheelchair access

Phoenix Rising 19 N Belmont Ave 804/355–7939, 800/719–1690 • 11am-7pm, clsd Tue • LGBT • wheelchair access

Roanoke

BARS

Backstreet Cafe 356 Salem Ave (off Jefferson) 540/345–1542 • 7pm-2am, clsd Sun-Mon • lesbians/ gay men • neighborhood bar • food served

Cuba Pete's 120 Church Ave SW (at First St SW, inside Macado's) 540/342–7231 • 11am-2am • gay-friendly • more gay wknds • also Macado's restaurant • karaoke • wheelchair access

NIGHTCLUBS

The Park 615 Salem Ave 540/342–0946 • 9pm-close Fri-Sun • popular • lesbians/ gay men • dancing/DJ • drag shows Sun • videos • young crowd • wheelchair access

Shenandoah Valley

INFO LINES & SERVICES

SVGLA (Shenandoah Valley Gay/ Lesbian Assoc) 540/574-4636 • 24-hr touchtone info • weekly meetings • also dances & potlucks

ACCOMMODATIONS

Frog Hollow B&B 492 Greenhouse Rd (at Rte 11), Lexington 540/463-5444 • gay/ straight • full brkfst • hot tub • also cottage • gay-owned • $115-155

Mayneview B&B 439 Mechanic St, Luray 540/743-7921 • gay-friendly • full brkfst • Victorian w/ mountain views • near Luray Caverns, wineries & hiking • nonsmoking • $111-150

The Olde Staunton Inn 260 N Lewis St, Staunton 540/886-0193, 866/653-3786 • gay/ straight • B&B • hot tub • WiFi • nonsmoking • $60-135

Piney Hill B&B 1048 Piney Hill Rd (at Mill Creek Crossroads), Luray 540/778-5261, 800/644-5261 • gay/ straight • 1750s farmhouse in Shenandoah Valley • full brkfst • hot tub • gay-owned • $150-195

White Fence B&B 275 Chapel Rd, Stanley 540/778-4680, 800/211-9885 • gay-friendly • 1890 Victorian w/ cottages • full brkfst • jacuzzi • nonsmoking • kids ok • $150+

Urbanna

ACCOMMODATIONS

Inn at Urbanna Creek 804/758-4661 • gay-friendly • 1870s home 2 hours from DC • full brkfst • jacuzzi • nonsmoking • $95-160

Virginia Beach

see also Norfolk

ACCOMMODATIONS

Capes Ocean Resort Hotel 2001 Atlantic Ave (at 20th St) 757/428-5421, 800/456-5421 • gay-friendly • oceanfront rooms • private balconies • some jacuzzis • pool • nonsmoking • WiFi • kids ok • wheelchair access • $75-259

BARS

In Between 5266 Princess Anne Rd (btwn Witchduck & Newton Rds) 757/490-9498 • 4pm-2am, from 5pm Sat • lesbians/ gay men • male dancers • also restaurant • Sun brunch • gay-owned

Klub Ambush 475 S Lynnhaven Rd (at Lynnhaven Pkwy) 757/498-4301 • 5pm-2am • lesbians/ gay men • neighborhood bar • dancing/DJ • food served • shows • karaoke • gay-owned

Rainbow Cactus 3472 Holland Rd (at Diana Lee) 757/368-0441 • 7pm-2am, clsd Mon-Tue • mostly gay men • dancing/DJ • country/ western • drag shows • food served • wheelchair access

PUBLICATIONS

Lambda Directory 757/486-3546

EROTICA

Nancy's Nook 1301 Oceana Blvd 757/428-1498 • 24hrs

Washington

ACCOMMODATIONS

Gay Street Inn 160 Gay St 540/675-3288 • gay-friendly • nonsmoking • WiFi • gay-owned • $165-255

Windsor

ACCOMMODATIONS

Blackwater Campground 7651 Whispering Pines Trail 757/357-7211 • gay-friendly • RV hookups & primitive camping • pool • pagan, medieval & gay events on wknds • kids/ pets ok • $25+

WASHINGTON

Bainbridge Island

BOOKSTORES

Eagle Harbor Book Co 157 Winslow Wy E 206/842-5332 • 9am-7pm, till 9pm Th, till 6pm Sat, 10am-6pm Sun

Bellevue

see also Seattle

Bellingham

BARS

Rumors 1119 Railroad Ave (at Chestnut) 360/671-1849 • 4pm-2am • lesbians/ gay men • dancing/DJ • multiracial • also restaurant • wheelchair access

CAFES

Tony's Cafe 1101 Harris Ave (at 11th), Fairhaven 360/738-4710 • 7am-6pm • plenty veggie • patio • wheelchair access

RESTAURANTS

Bobbylees Pub & Eatery 108 W Main St (Washington Ave), Everson 360/966-8838 • 11am-2am • gay-friendly • gay-owned • wheelchair access

Skylark's Hidden Cafe 1308-B 11th St (at McKenzie) **360/715-3642** • 7am-midnight • great soups • full bar • outdoor seating • live jazz wknds

BOOKSTORES

Village Books 1200 11th St (at Harris) **360/671-2626** • 10am-7:30pm, till 7pm Sun • new & used

EROTICA

Great Northern Bookstore 1308 Railroad Ave (at Holly) 360/733-1650

Bender Creek

ACCOMMODATIONS

Triangle Recreation Camp PO Box 1226, Granite Falls 98252 • lesbians/gay men • members-only camping on 80-acre nature conservancy • (see www.camptrc.org) • $15/ night or $150/ year

Bremerton

INFO LINES & SERVICES

AA Gay/ Lesbian 700 Callahan Dr (at St Paul's Episcopal) **360/475-0775, 800/562-7455** • 7:30pm Tue

BARS

Brewski's 2810 Kitsap Wy (enter off Wycuff St) **360/479-9100** • 11am-2am, from 10am wknds • gay-friendly • neighborhood bar • food served • wheelchair access

Everett

INFO LINES & SERVICES

AA Gay/ Lesbian 2624 Rockefeller 425/252-2525 • 7pm Sun

NIGHTCLUBS

Twisted 1212 California St (enter in the alley) **425/438-4111** • 6pm-2am, till midnight Sun • lesbians/gay men • dancing/DJ • karaoke Wed • food served • wheelchair access

Glacier

ACCOMMODATIONS

Mt Baker B&B & Cabins 9434 Cornell Creek Rd **360/599-2299** • gay/ straight • modern chalet • full brkfst • hot tub • kids ok • some shared baths • nonsmoking • $149-369

Kent

BARS

Swank 24437 Russell Rd 253/854-2110 • 3pm-2am, from noon wknds • lesbians/gay men • dancing/DJ • patio

Vibe 226 1st Ave S (btwn Meeker & Gowe) **253/852-0815** • noon-2am, till midnight Sun-Mon • lesbians/gay men • dancing/DJ • karaoke

EROTICA

The Voyeur 604 Central Ave S 253/850-8428 • videos • toys • clothing

La Conner

ACCOMMODATIONS

The Wild Iris 121 Maple Ave 360/466-1400, 800/477-1400 • gay-friendly • inn • nonsmoking • full brkfst • kids ok • wheelchair access • gay-owned • $119-199

Long Beach Peninsula

ACCOMMODATIONS

Anthony's Home Court 1310 Pacific Hwy N, Long Beach 360/642-2802, 888/787-2754 • gay/ straight • cabins & RV hookups • nonsmoking • WiFi • gay-owned • $100-175

The Historic Sou'wester Lodge, Cabins & RV Park Beach Access Rd (38th Pl), Seaview 360/642-2542 • gay-friendly • inexpensive suites • cabins w/ kitchens • vintage trailers • RV hookups • pets ok in cabins & trailers • nonsmoking

Senator TC Bloomer's Mansion 1004 41st Pl (at Oceanfront), Seaview 360/642-8598, 800/747-2096 • gay-friendly • rental home • hot tub • kids ok • lesbian & gay-owned • $575+

Shakti Cove Cottages 360/665-4000 • lesbians/gay men • cabins on the peninsula • pets ok • nonsmoking • lesbian-owned • $80-120

Lynnwood

RETAIL SHOPS

Colorbomb Tattoo 15315 Hwy 99, #7 (at 153rd) 425/742-8467 • 11am-9pm, noon-11pm Fri-Sat

Mt Vernon

RESTAURANTS

Deli Next Door 202 S 1st St (at Memorial Hwy) **360/336–3886** • 8am-9pm, 9pm-8pm Sun • healthy American • plenty veggie • wheelchair access

Olympia

INFO LINES & SERVICES

Free at Last AA 11th & Washington #106 (at United Church) **360/352–7344** • call for info

ACCOMMODATIONS

Swantown Inn B&B 1431 11th Ave SE (at Central St) **360/753–9123, 877/753–9123** • gay-friendly • nonsmoking • full brkfst • WiFi • $99-179

BARS

Hannah's 123 5th Ave W (at Columbia) **360/357–9890** • 11am-2am, till midnight Sun-Mon • gay/ straight • neighborhood bar • food served

NIGHTCLUBS

Jakes on 4th 311 E 4th **360/956–3247** • 4pm-2am • lesbians/ gay men • dancing/DJ • karaoke

CAFES

Darby's Cafe 211 SE 5th Ave (at Washington) **360/357–6229** • 7am-2pm, 8am-2pm wknds, clsd Mon-Tue • gay/ straight • gay-owned

RESTAURANTS

Saigon Rendez-Vous 117 5th Ave SW (btwn Columbia & Capitol Wy) **360/352–1989** • lunch & dinner • Vietnamese • plenty veggie

Urban Onion 116 Legion Wy SE (at Capitol) **360/943–9242** • 7am-9pm, till 10pm Fri, 8am-10pm Sat, till 9pm Sun • plenty veggie • wheelchair access

RETAIL SHOPS

Dumpster Values 302 4th (at Franklin) **360/705–3772** • 10am-8pm, noon-6pm Sun • new & used clothing • zines • records • toys • women-owned

EROTICA

Desire Video 3200 Pacific Ave SE (off I-5, at exit 107) **360/352–0820** • 24hrs • videos • toys • 100-channel video arcade • extensive LGBT section

Pasco

NIGHTCLUBS

Out & About Restaurant & Lounge 327 W Lewis **509/543–3796, 877/388–3796** • 6pm-2am, clsd Sun-Mon • dancing/DJ wknds • karaoke • drag shows • cabaret • 18+ Fri • also restaurant • wheelchair access

Port Townsend

ACCOMMODATIONS

Aunt Jenny's Guest House 1705 Monroe **360/385–2899** • gay/ straight • quiet cottage • kids ok • nonsmoking • wheelchair access • woman-owned • $95-135

The James House 1238 Washington St **800/385–1238, 360/385–1238** • gay-friendly • Victorian B&B • full brkfst • nonsmoking • WiFi • gardens • $125-250

Ravenscroft Inn 533 Quincy St (at Clay St) **360/385–2784, 800/782–2691** • gay-friendly • seaport inn w/ views of Puget Sound • gourmet brkfst • hot tub • nonsmoking • $100-210

Quinault

ACCOMMODATIONS

Lake Quinault Lodge South Shore Rd (off US 101) **360/288–2900, 800/562–6672** • gay-friendly • $105-195

San Juan Islands

ACCOMMODATIONS

Inn on Orcas Island **360/376–5227, 888/886–1661** • gay-friendly • luxury • full brkfst • nonsmoking • wheelchair access • gay-owned • $145-285

Lopez Farm Cottages & Tent Camping 555 Fisherman Bay Rd, Lopez Island **360/468–3555, 800/440–3556** • gay/ straight • on 30-acre farm • hot tub • nonsmoking • $40 (camping), $170-205 (cottages)

Spring Bay Inn on Orcas Island Orcas Island **360/376–5531** • gay/ straight • full brkfst • hot tub • kayak tour included in price • nonsmoking • WiFi • $220-260

ENTERTAINMENT & RECREATION

Western Prince Whale & Wildlife Tours 2 Spring St (at Front), Friday Harbor **360/378–5315, 800/757–6722** • whale-watching & wildlife tours April-Oct

Seattle

INFO LINES & SERVICES

Capitol Hill Alano 1900 E Madison St **206/860-9560** (CLUB), **206/587-2838** (AA#) • 12-step meetings daily

Seattle LGBT Community Center 1122 E Pike St (btwn 11th & 12th Aves) **206/323-5428** • 10am-9pm, 11am-8pm Sun • wheelchair access

ACCOMMODATIONS

11th Avenue Inn 121 11th Ave E (at Boren) **206/720-7161, 800/720-7161** • gay-friendly • nonsmoking • WiFi • kids 12+ ok • full brkfst • $79-179

The Ace Hotel 2423 1st Ave (at Wall St) **206/448-4721** • gay/ straight • kids/ pets ok • nonsmoking • WiFi • restaurant & bar • $75-195

Alexis Hotel 1007 1st Ave (at Madison) **206/624-4844, 800/426-7033** • gay-friendly • luxury hotel w/ Aveda spa • kids/ pets ok • WiFi • wheelchair access • $299-595

Artist's Studio Loft B&B 16529 91st Ave SW, Vashon Island **206/463-2583** • gay-friendly • on 5 acres • garden • hot tub • nonsmoking • $131-195

Bacon Mansion 959 Broadway E (at E Prospect) **206/329-1864, 800/240-1864** • gay/ straight • Edwardian-style Tudor • nonsmoking • WiFi • wheelchair access • $94-234

Barclay Court East 1206 E Barclay Ct (at 12th Ave) **206/329-3914** • gay/ straight • nonsmoking • WiFi • gay-owned • $148

Bed & Breakfast on Broadway 722 Broadway Ave E (at Aloha) **206/329-8933** • gay/straight • nonsmoking • WiFi • $125-175

Gaslight Inn 1727 15th Ave (at E Howell St) **206/325-3654** • popular • gay/ straight • B&B in Arts & Crafts home • pool • nonsmoking • gay-owned • $98-158

Hotel 1000 1000 First Ave **206/957-1000** • gay-friendly • WiFi • wheelchair access • $189-450

MarQueen Hotel 600 Queen Anne Ave N (btwn Roy & Mercer) **206/282-7407, 888/445-3076** • gay/ straight • in Theater District • wheelchair access • $125-325

Seahurst Garden Studio 13713 16th Ave SW (at Ambaum Ave), Burien **206/551-7721** • women only • nonsmoking • WiFi • wheelchair access • lesbian-owned • $55-100

Sleeping Bulldog Bed & Breakfast 816 19th Ave S (at S Dearborn St) **206/601-9274** • gay/ straight • nonsmoking • WiFi • gay owned • $106-206

Warwick Seattle Hotel 401 Lenora St (at 4th) **206/443-4300** • gay/ straight • full brkfst • pool • kids ok • wheelchair access • $119-290

Wild Lily Cabins B&B 25 miles W of Stevens Pass, Index **360/793-2103** • gay/ straight • cabins on Skykomish River • 1 hour from Seattle • cedar sauna • hot tub • camping available • nonsmoking • gay-owned • $118-175

BARS

The Baltic Room 1207 Pine St (at Melrose) **206/625-4444** • 9pm-2am, clsd Wed & Sun • gay/ straight • live music

Bar Myx 2810 Western Ave (at Clay) **206/588-1834** • 11am-11pm, till 2am Fri-Sat • gay/straight • food served • video bar

Beacon Pub 3057 Beacon Ave S (at Hanford) **206/726-0238** • 2pm-2am, from noon wknds • gay/ straight • neighborhood bar • karaoke

The Bottleneck Lounge 2328 Madison St (at John St) **206/323-1098** • 4pm-midnight, till 2am Th-Sat • gay/ straight • lesbian-owned

Cafe Metropolitain 1701 E Olive Way (at Boylston) **206/324-0771** • gay/ straight • Vegas-style decor • food served

The Can Can 94 Pike St (in the Pike Place Market) **206/652-0832** • 4:30pm-2am • gay/ straight • food served • cabaret

Canterbury Ale and Eats 534 15th Ave E (at Mercer) **206/322-3130** • 11am-2am • gay-friendly • neighborhood bar • food served • dogs welcome

CC Attle's 1501 E Madison (at 15th Ave) **206/323-4017** • noon-2am • popular • mostly gay men • neighborhood bar • videos • also restaurant • wheelchair access

Cha Cha Lounge & Bimbo's Cantina 1013 E Pike St (at 11th Ave) **206/322-0703** • 5pm-2am • gay-friendly • hipster lounge & big burritos • gay-owned

Changes 2103 N 45th St (at Meridian) **206/545-8363** • noon-2am • mostly gay men • neighborhood bar • food served • karaoke • videos • wheelchair access

Chapel 1600 Melrose Ave (at E Pine) **206/447-4180** • 5pm-1am, till 2am Fri-Sat • gay/ straight • DJ • food served

The Crescent Lounge 1413 E Olive Wy (at Bellevue) • noon-2am • gay/straight • neighborhood bar • karaoke nightly • wheelchair access

The Cuff 1533 13th Ave (at Pine) **206/323-1525** • 2pm-2am, after-hours wknds, T-dance Sun • popular • mostly gay men • dancing/DJ • country/ western • levi crowd • patio • wheelchair access

Double Header 407 2nd Ave S Extension (at Washington) **206/464-9918** • 10am-11pm, till 1am Fri-Sat • gay/straight • neighborhood bar

Elite Tavern 1520 E Olive Way (at Denny Way) **206/860-0999** • noon-2am • lesbians/ gay men • neighborhood bar

Hot Flash Seattle 1509 Broadway (at Neighbors) **206/324-5358** • T-dance 5pm-9pm 1st Sat only • "for seasoned lesbians 36+ (& the women who love us!)" • cover charge

Seattle

WHERE THE GIRLS ARE:
Living in the Capitol Hill District, south of Lake Union, and working in the Broadway Market, Pike Place Market, or somewhere in between.

ENTERTAINMENT:
Team Seattle 206/322-7769, web: www.teamseattle.org, a 35-team gay network.

LGBT PRIDE:
Last Sunday in June. 206/322-9561, web: www.seattlepride.org.

ANNUAL EVENTS:
September - Bumbershoot music & arts festival 206/281-7788, web: www.bumbershoot.org.

September - AIDS Walk 206/329-6923.

October - Seattle Gay & Lesbian Film Festival 206/323-4274, web: www.seattlequeerfilm.com.

CITY INFO:
206/461-5800, web: www.seattle.com.

BEST VIEW:
Top of the Space Needle, or from Admiral Way Park in West Seattle.

WEATHER:
Winter's average temperature is 50° while summer temperatures can climb up into the 90°s. Be prepared for rain at any time during the year.

ATTRACTIONS:
Experience Music Project 206/367-5483, web: www.empsfm.org.

Fremont, web: www.fremontseattle.com.

International District.

Museum of Flight 206/764-5720, web: www.museumofflight.org.

Pike Place Market, web: www.pikemarketplace.org.

Pioneer Square, web: www.pioneersquaredistrict.org.

Seattle Art Museum 206/654-3100, web: www.seattleartmuseum.org.

Seattle Aquarium 206/386-4300, web: www.seattleaquarium.org.

Seattle Center Monorail 206/905-2620, web: www.seattlemonorail.com

Seattle Underground 206/682-4646, web: www.undergroundtour.com.

Space Needle 206/905-2100, web: www.spaceneedle.com.

Woodland Park Zoo 206/684-4800, web: www.zoo.org.

TRANSIT:
Farwest 206/622-1717.

Yellow Gray Top 206/282-8222.

Airport Shuttle Express 206/622-1424.

Metropolitan Transit 206/553-3000, web: www.metrokc.gov/tran.htm.

Hula Hula 106 1st Ave N (at Denny) **206/284–5003** • 4pm-close • gay-friendly • tiki bar • karaoke

The Lobby Bar 916 E Pike St (at Broadway) **206/328–6703** • 3pm-midnight, till 2am Th-Sat • mostly gay men • bar food • live shows

Poco Wine Room 1408 E Pine St (at 14th Ave) **206/322–9463** • 5pm-close • gay/ straight • food served

R Place 619 E Pine St (at Boylston) **206/322–8828** • 4pm-2am, from 2pm wknds • mostly gay men • neighborhood bar • dancing/DJ • food served • karaoke • videos • WiFi • wheelchair access

Rendezvous 2322 2nd Ave (at Battery) **206/441–5823** • 4pm-2am • gay/ straight • live bands • cabaret • theater • also restaurant

The Seattle Eagle 314 E Pike St (at Bellevue) **206/621–7591** • 2pm-2am • mostly gay men • Vibrator every 3rd Tue for "a club for dykes & their friends" • leather • rock 'n' roll • patio • wheelchair access

Temple Billiards 126 S Jackson **206/682–3242** • 11am-2am, from 3pm wknds • gay-friendly • more women Wed • food served

Wildrose Bar & Restaurant 1021 E Pike St (at 11th) **206/324–9210** • 3pm-2am, till 1am Sun & Mon • mostly women • neighborhood bar • dancing/DJ • karaoke • live shows • food served • wheelchair access

NIGHTCLUBS

Club Heaven 172 S Washington St (at 2nd) **206/622–1863** • 6pm-2am • gay/ straight • call for events • also restaurant • cover

Contour 807 1st Ave (at Columbia) **206/447–7704** • 11:30am-2am, till 4:30am Th, till 6am Fri, 2pm-6am Sat, till 2am Sun, 3pm-2am Mon • fire performances • gay-friendly • dancing/DJ • also bar & restaurant

Dimitriou's Jazz Alley 2033 6th Ave (at Lenora) **206/441–9729** • gay-friendly • call for events & reservations • live music • nonsmoking • cover charge • also restaurant

Girl4Girl Productions • 2nd Sat only • mostly women • dancing/DJ • live shows • go-go dancers • check girl4girlseattle.com for info

Neighbours Dance Club 1509 Broadway (at Pike & Pine) **206/324–5358** • 9pm-2am, till 3am Th, till 4am Fri-Sat • popular • lesbians/ gay men • dancing/DJ • 2 flrs • also 18+ room Th-Sat • young crowd • wheelchair access

Purr 1518 11th Ave (at Pike St) **206/325–3112** • 3pm-2am, till midnight Sun • mostly gay men • karaoke • food served

Re-bar 1114 Howell (at Boren Ave) **206/233–9873** • 10pm-2am, clsd Mon • popular • gay/ straight • more women Sat • dancing/DJ Wed-Sun • cabaret/ theater

Showbox 1426 1st Ave (at Pike) **206/628–3151** • gay-friendly • live music venue • no cover charge in Green Room

CAFES

The Allegro 4214 University Wy NE (at NE 42nd St) **206/633–3030** • 7am-10:30pm • WiFi

Cafe Besalu 5909 24th Ave NW **206/789–1463** • 7am-3pm, clsd Mon-Tue • great pastries

Espresso Vivace 532 Broadway Ave **206/860–2722** • 6:30am-11pm • popular

Fuel Coffee 610 19th Ave E **206/329–4700** • 6am-9pm • WiFi

Insomniax Coffee & Juice 102 15th Ave E **206/322–6477** • 7am-5pm, clsd wknds • WiFi

Kaladi Brothers Coffee 511 E Pike St (at Summit) **206/388–1700** • 6am-9pm, from 8am wknds

Louisa's 2379 Eastlake Ave E **206/325–0081** • 7am-7pm, 8am-2pm Sun

RESTAURANTS

Al Boccalino 1 Yesler Wy (at Alaskan) **206/622–7688** • lunch Tue-Fri, dinner nightly • classy southern Italian

Bamboo Garden 364 Roy St (at Mercer St) **206/282–6616** • 11am-10pm • Chinese vegetarian & kosher

The Broadway Grill 314 Broadway E (at E Harrison) **206/328–7000** • 11am-11pm, from 8am wknds • popular • full bar

Cafe Flora 2901 E Madison St **206/325–9100** • lunch, dinner, wknd brunch • vegetarian • beer/ wine • nonsmoking • wheelchair accessible

Canlis 2576 Aurora Ave N **206/283–3313** • dinner only, fancy seafood

Capitol Club 414 E Pine St **206/325–2149** • tapas • live entertainment

Dahlia Lounge 2001 4th Ave (at Virginia) **206/682–4142** • lunch Mon-Fri, dinner nightly, wknd brunch • some veggie • full bar

Dick's Drive In 115 Broadway E (at Denny) **206/302–1300** • 10:30am-2am • excellent fries & shakes

Flying Fish 2234 1st Ave (at Bell) **206/728–8595** • 5pm-midnight, bar till 2am • lesbian chef

Fresh Bistro 4725 42nd Ave SW (btwn Alaska St & Edmunds) **206/935–3733** • 11am-11pm

Galerias 611 E Broadway (at Mercer) **206/322–5757** • 11am-10pm, brunch wknds • traditional Mexican

Glo's 1621 E Olive Wy (at Summit Ave E) **206/324–2577** • 7am-3pm, till 4pm wknds • brkfst only • popular

Julia's 300 Broadway E (at Thomas) **206/860–1818** • 8am-11pm, till midnight Fri-Sat • full bar • drag shows Sat

Kabul 2301 N 45th St **206/545–9000** • 5pm-9:30pm, till 10pm Fri-Sat • Afghan • some veggie

Kurrent 600 E Pine **206/323–1923** • 4pm-1am, till 2am Th -Sat, full bar

Lola 2000 4th Ave (at Virginia) **206/441–1430** • 6am-midnight, till 2am wknds • popular brunch

Mae's Phinney Ridge Cafe 6412 Phinney Ridge N (at 65th) **206/782–1222** • 8am-2pm, till 3pm wknds • popular • brkfst menu • some veggie • wheelchair access

Mama's Mexican Kitchen 2234 2nd Ave (in Belltown) **206/728–6262** • lunch & dinner • cheap & funky

Paseo 4225 Fremont Ave N (at N 43rd St) **206/545–7440** • 11:30am-9pm, clsd Sun-Mon • Cuban

Queen City Grill 2201 1st Ave (at Blanchard) **206/443–0975** • dinner only • popular • fresh seafood • some veggie • full bar • wheelchair access

Restaurant Zoe 2137 2nd Ave **206/256–2060** • dinner only

Snappy Dragon 8917 Roosevelt Wy NE **206/528–5575** • 11am-9:30pm, 4pm-9pm Sun • Chinese

Sunlight Cafe 6403 Roosevelt Wy NE (at 64th) **206/522–9060** • 8am-9pm • vegetarian • beer/ wine • wheelchair access

Szmania's 3321 W McGraw St (in Magnolia Bluff) **206/284–7305** • lunch Tue-Fri, dinner nightly, clsd Mon • full bar

Tamarind Tree 1036 S Jackson St **206/860–1404** • 10am-10pm, till midnight Fri-Sat • Vietnamese

Teapot Vegetarian House 345 15th Ave E **206/325–1010** • 11am-10pm • vegan

Thaiger Room 4228 University Wy NE **206/632–9299** • 11am-10pm, from noon wknds • Thai

Tidbit Bistro 2359 10th Ave E (at E Miller) **206/323–0840** • dinner nightly • tapas • full bar • patio

Verve Wine Bar & Cellar 3820 S Ferdinand St **206/760–0977** • 5pm-10pm, till 11pm Fri-Sat, Sun brunch • women-owned

Wild Ginger Asian Restaurant & Triple Bar 1401 3rd Ave (at Union) **206/623–4450** • lunch Mon-Sat, dinner nightly • popular • bar till 1am

Wild Mountain 1408 NW 85th St **206/297–9453** • 8:30am-9:30pm, clsd Tue • woman-owned

ENTERTAINMENT & RECREATION

Alki Beach Park 1702 Alki Ave SW, West Seattle • popular on warm days

Century Ballroom 915 E Pine, 2nd flr (at Broadway) **206/324–7263** • Outdancing 9pm 3rd & 4th Fri, lessons at 8:30pm • lesbians/ gay men • dancing/DJ • also restaurant

Garage 1130 Broadway **206/322–2296** • 3pm-2am • popular • way-cool pool hall • food served • full bar • ladies 1/2 price Sun • also bowling alley • 21+

Gay Bingo 155 N 35th St (at Phinney, at Fremont Studios) **206/323–0069, 206/328–8979** • 2nd Sat only, Jan-June

Northwest Lesbian & Gay History Museum Project **206/903–9517** • exhibits & publication

Rat City Roller Girls • Seattle's female roller derby league • visit www.ratcityrollergirls.com for events

Richard Hugo House 1634 11th Ave **206/322–7030** • noon-6pm, till 5pm Sat, clsd Sun • houses the Zine Archive & Publishing Project • open later for events • also cafe & cabaret

Tacky Tourist Clubs • fabulous social events

The Vera Project corner of Warren Ave N & Republican St (in Seattle Center) **206/956–8372** • gay-friendly • all-ages music arts center

BOOKSTORES

Elliott Bay Book Company 1521 10th Ave N **206/624–6600, 800/962–5311** • 9:30am-10pm, 11am-7pm Sun

Fremont Place Book Company 621 N 35th (at Fremont Ave N) **206/547–5970** • 10am-8pm, noon-6pm Sun

Left Bank Books 92 Pike St (at 1st Ave)
206/622-0195 • 10am-7pm, 11am-6pm Sun •
worker-owned collective

RETAIL SHOPS

Broadway Market 401 Broadway E (at
Harrison & Republican) • popular mall full of
funky, hip stores

Lifelong Thrift Store 1017 E Union St
206/328-8979 • all proceeds to AIDS
organization

Metropolis 7220 Greenwood Ave N (at 73rd)
206/782-7002 • 10am-7pm, till 6pm Sat,
noon-5pm Sun • cards & gifts

PUBLICATIONS

'Mo Seattle 410 Broadway Ave E
206/235-3320 • monthly LGBT mag

SGN (Seattle Gay News) 206/324-4297 •
weekly LGBT newspaper

The Stranger 206/323-7101 • queer-
positive alternative weekly

GYMS & HEALTH CLUBS

Hothouse Spa & Sauna 1019 E Pike St (at
11th, 2 blocks E of Broadway) **206/568-3240**
• noon-midnight, clsd Tue • women only •
baths • hot tub • massage

EROTICA

Babeland 707 E Pike (btwn Harvard &
Boylston) **206/328-2914** • 11am-10pm, noon-
7pm Sun • wheelchair access • lesbian-owned

The Crypt Off Broadway 1516 11th Ave (at
E Pine) **206/325-3882**

Hollywood Erotic Boutique 12706 Lake
City Wy NE **206/363-0056** • 24hrs • toys •
lingerie

Sequim

ACCOMMODATIONS

Sunset Marine Resort 40 Buzzard Ridge Rd
360/681-4166 • gay-friendly • waterfront
cabins • nonsmoking • kids ok • lesbian-
owned • $150-250

Spokane

INFO LINES & SERVICES

AA Gay/ Lesbian 1614 W Riverside
509/624-1442 • call for meeting times

Inland Northwest LGBT Center 508 W 2nd
Ave **509/489-1914** • support groups • events
• also art gallery

ACCOMMODATIONS

Montvale Hotel 1005 W First Ave (at
Monroe) **509/747-1919, 866/668-8253** • gay-
friendly • luxury, boutique hotel • transgender-
friendly • also bars & restaurant • kids ok •
nonsmoking • WiFi • gay-owned • $179+

NIGHTCLUBS

Dempsey's Brass Rail 909 W 1st St (btwn
Lincoln & Monroe) **509/747-5362** • 3pm-
2am, till midnight Sun • popular • lesbians/
gay men • dancing/DJ Th-Sat • drag shows Fri-
Sat • also restaurant • wheelchair access

RESTAURANTS

Mizuna 214 N Howard **509/747-2004** •
lunch Mon-Fri, dinner nightly • seasonal menu
• plenty veggie • full bar

BOOKSTORES

Auntie's Bookstore & Cafe 402 W Main St
(at Washington) **509/838-0206** • 9am-9pm,
11am-6pm Sun • wheelchair access

Suquamish

INFO LINES & SERVICES

Kitsap Lesbian/ Gay AA 18732 Division Ave
NE (at Congregational Church of Christ)
360/475-0775, 800/562-7455 • 7:30pm Sun

Tacoma

INFO LINES & SERVICES

AA Gay/ Lesbian 3640 S Cedar #5
253/474-8897 • 7:30pm Fri

Rainbow Center 741 St Helens Ave
253/383-2318 • 1pm-5pm Mon-Fri •
community center • call for meetings & events

Tacoma Lesbian Concern 253/476-9540 •
social events • resource list • newsletter

ACCOMMODATIONS

**Chinaberry Hill—An 1889 Grand
Victorian Inn** 302 Tacoma Ave N
253/272-1282 • gay-friendly • 1889 Victorian
inn • also cottage • very romantic • full brkfst •
jacuzzis • bay views • fireplaces • kids ok •
nonsmoking • WiFi • $149-245

Hotel Murano 1320 Broadway Plaza (at S
15th) **253/572-3200, 888/862-3255** • gay-
friendly • restaurants & bars • WiFi
• wheelchair access

BARS

Airport Bar & Grill 5406 S Tacoma Wy (at
54th) **253/475-9730** • 2pm-2am • lesbians/
gay men • neighborhood bar

Nightclubs

Club Silverstone 739 1/2 St Helens Ave (at 9th) 253/404-0273 • 11am-2am • lesbians/ gay men • neighboorhood bar • dancing/DJ • karaoke

Cafes

Shakabrah Java Cafe 2618 6th Ave 253/572-2787 • 7am-4pm, clsd Sun • live entertainment • wheelchair access

Erotica

Castle Superstore 6015 Tacoma Mall Blvd 253/471-0391

Vancouver

see also Portland, Oregon

Bars

Northbank 106 W 6th St (at Main) 360/695-3862 • 2pm-2am • lesbians/ gay men • more women Th • dancing/DJ • food served • karaoke • drag shows • nonsmoking • wheelchair access

Walla Walla

Accommodations

The Boyer House 741 Boyer Ave 509/200-9931 • gay-straight • pool • nonsmoking • full brkfst • gay-owned • $115-180

Wenatchee

Cafes

The Cellar Cafe 249 N Mission St (at 5th) 509/662-1722 • 9am-5pm, 10am-4pm Sat, clsd Sun • some veggie • beer/ wine • patio • lesbian-owned • $5-$9

Whidbey Island

Accommodations

Whidwood Inn 360/720-6228 • gay/ straight • near historic Coupeville • nonsmoking • hot tub • gay-owned • $85-125

Winthrop

Accommodations

Chewuch Inn 223 White Ave 509/996-3107, 800/747-3107 • gay-friendly • inn & cabins • E of N Cascades Mtns • hot tub • kids ok • nonsmoking • WiFi • wheelchair access • $85-200

WEST VIRGINIA

Statewide

Publications

Graffiti 304/485-1891 • alternative entertainment guide

Berkeley Springs

Accommodations

The Lodge 304/258-9454 • mostly gay men • in Sleepy Creek Mtns • shared bath • also bar • gay-owned • $225-325

Charleston

Nightclubs

Broadway 210 Leon Sullivan Wy (at Lee) 304/343-2162 • 4pm-3am, from 1pm Sat-Mon • mostly gay men • dancing/DJ • live shows

Entertainment & Recreation

Living AIDS Memorial Garden corner of Washington St E (at Sidney Ave) 304/346-0246

Bookstores

Taylor Books 226 Capitol St 304/342-1461 • 7:30am-8pm, till 10pm Fri, 9am-10pm Sat, till 5pm Sun • WiFi • also cafe, art gallery & boutique

Follansbee

Bars

Wild Coyote Saloon 869 Main St 304/527-7191 • 6pm-close • lesbians/ gay men • dancing/ DJ Fri-Sat • drag shows

Harpers Ferry

Accommodations

Laurel Lodge 844 Ridge St 304/535-2886 • gay-friendly • rustic stone bungalow overlooking scenic Potomac River gorge • full brkfst • nonsmoking • WiFi • gay-owned • $95-150

Huntington

Accommodations

Pullman Plaza Hotel 1001 3rd Ave (at 10th St) 304/525-1001, 866/613-3611 • gay-friendly • downtown • full brkfst • pool • nonsmoking • WiFi • wheelchair access

BARS

Jackhammer 2127 Manchester Ave (at 22nd St & 3rd Ave) **304/781–2520** • 5pm-2am • mostly gay men • neighborhood bar • bears • leather • karaoke • shows • multiracial clientele • wheelchair access • gay-owned

Polo Club 1037 7th Ave (at 11th St) **304/522–3146** • 5pm-2am, from 2pm wknds • mostly gay men • dancing/DJ Th-Sun • live shows • private club • wheelchair access

The Stonewall 820 7th Ave (enter in alley) **304/523–2242** • 8pm-3am, clsd Mon • popular • lesbians/ gay men • dancing/DJ • karaoke • live shows • wheelchair access • gay-owned

RESTAURANTS

Sharkey's 410 10th St **304/523–3200** • 4pm-2:30am, clsd Sun • full bar

Lewisburg

ACCOMMODATIONS

Lee Street Inn B&B 200 N Lee St **304/647–5599, 888/228–7000** • gay-friendly • grand 1876 house • jacuzzi • WiFi • teens ok • gay-owned • $75-135

Lost River

ACCOMMODATIONS

Guest House at Lost River 288 Settlers Valley Wy (at Mill Gap Rd) **304/897–5707** • lesbians/ gay men • full brkfst • also fine-dining restaurant • full bar • pool • hot tub • gym • nonsmoking • WiFi • gay-owned • $145-200

RESTAURANTS

Lost River Grill & Motel St Rd 259 **304/897–6482** • 11:45am-9pm, 8am-10pm Sat, till 9pm Sun, 4pm-9pm Mon • full bar • also motel & cabins

Martinsburg

EROTICA

Variety Books & Video 255 N Queen St (at Race) **304/263–4334** • 24hrs

Morgantown

NIGHTCLUBS

Vice Versa 335 High St (enter rear) **304/292–2010** • 8pm-3am Th-Sun • lesbians/ gay men • dancing/DJ • karaoke • live shows • private club • 18+ • wheelchair access

Weezie's Pub & Club 3438 University Ave **304/292–3939** • 8pm-close, clsd Sun • lesbians/ gay men • dancing/DJ • live music

Parkersburg

NIGHTCLUBS

Woodstarr 322 5th St **304/422–3711** • clsd Sun-Tue • lesbians/ gay men • dancing/DJ • karaoke • drag shows

Shepherdstown

ACCOMMODATIONS

Thomas Shepherd Inn 300 W German St (at Duke St) **304/876–3715, 888/889–8952** • gay-friendly • B&B • full brkfst • nonsmoking • WiFi • $125-195

Sissonville

RESTAURANTS

Topspot Country Cookin' 7139 Sissonville Rd **304/984–2816** • 7am-8pm, till 7pm Sun, clsd Mon

Wheeling

EROTICA

Market St News 1437 Market St (at 14th St) **304/232–2414** • 24hrs, till midnight Sun-Mon

WISCONSIN

Algoma

RETAIL SHOPS

The Flying Pig N6975 Hwy 42 (at Tenth) **920/487–9902** • 9am-6pm May-Oct, 10am-5pm Fri-Sun only off-season • art gallery & coffee bar • lesbian-owned

Appleton

BARS

Rascals Bar & Grill 702 E Wisconsin Ave (at Lawe) **920/954–9262** • 5pm-2am, from noon Sun • lesbians/ gay men • fish-fry Fri • patio

Ravens 215 E College Ave **920/364–9559** • 8pm-2am, clsd Sun-Mon • mostly gay men, Th ladies night • dancing/DJ • karaoke • drag shows

CAFES

Harmony Cafe 233 E College Ave **920/734–2233** • 7am-9pm, 9am-9pm Sat, clsd Sun • live entertainment • also educational & support groups

EROTICA

Eldorado's 2545 S Memorial Dr (at Hwys 47 & 441) 920/830-0042

Beloit

BARS

Club Impulse 132 W Grand Ave 608/361-0000 • 4pm-2am, till 2:30am Fri-Sat, from 7pm Sat, from 3pm Sun • lesbians/gay men • dancing/DJ

Eagle River

ACCOMMODATIONS

The Edgewater Inn & Cottages 5054 St Hwy 70 W 715/479-4011, 888/334-3987 • gay/straight • also waterfront cottages • nonsmoking • WiFi • $65-175

Eau Claire

INFO LINES & SERVICES

LGBT Community Center of the Chippewa Valley 510 S Farwell St 715/552-5428 • drop-in 7pm-10pm Fri, call for other hours • library & variety of events

ACCOMMODATIONS

Fireside Lake Lodge W 12745 Fireside Lake Rd, New Auburn 715/868-1172 • gay-friendly • WiFi • gay-owned • $45-95

NIGHTCLUBS

Scooters 411 Galloway (at Farwell) 715/835-9959 • 3pm-2am • lesbians/gay men • dancing/DJ • karaoke • drag shows • wheelchair access

Green Bay

INFO LINES & SERVICES

Gay AA 920/469-9999 • call for times & locations

BARS

Ape Hangers 301 S Broadway 920/455-1005 • 10am-close • gay-friendly • karaoke

Napalese Lounge 1351 Cedar St 920/432-9646 • 11am-close • mostly gay men • neighborhood bar • DJ Fri-Sat • food served • drag shows • wheelchair access

Sass 840 S Broadway 920/437-7277 • 6pm-2am Tue, Fri & Sat • lesbians/gay men • dancing/DJ wknds • karaoke

NIGHTCLUBS

The Shelter 730 N Quincy St (at 54302) 920/432-2662 • lesbians/gay men • dancing/DJ • country/western • transgender-friendly • food served • karaoke • drag shows • gay-owned

CAFES

Harmony Cafe 1660 W Mason St 920/569-1593 • 7am-9pm, 10am-6pm Sun • live entertainment

PUBLICATIONS

Outbound/ Quest 920/655-0611, 800/578-3785 • news & arts reviews for WI's LGBT community

EROTICA

Lion's Den Adult Superstore 836 S Broadway (at 5th) 920/433-9640

Hayward

ACCOMMODATIONS

The Lake House 5793 Division, Stone Lake 715/865-6803 • lesbians/gay men • full brkfst • swimming • nonsmoking • kids ok by arrangement • WiFi • wheelchair access • lesbian-owned • $90-160

Hurley

ACCOMMODATIONS

Anton-Walsh House 202 Copper St (at US Hwy 51) 715/561-2065 • gay-friendly • historic B&B • full brkfst • WiFi • $89-129

Kenosha

see also Racine

BARS

Club Icon 6305 120th Ave (on E frontage road of 94) 262/857-3240 • 7pm-2am, from 3pm Sun, clsd Mon • lesbians/gay men • dancing/DJ • drag shows

La Crosse

ACCOMMODATIONS

Rainbow Ridge Farms B&B N 5732 Hauser Rd (at County S), Onalaska 608/783-8181, 888/347-2594 • gay-friendly • working hobby farm on 35 acres • WiFi • nonsmoking • $89-150

BARS

Chances R 417 Jay St (at 4th) 608/782-5105 • 3pm-close, from noon wknds • lesbians/gay men • neighborhood bar

My Place 3201 South Ave (at East Ave) **608/788-9073** • 3pm-close, from noon wknds • lesbians/ gay men • friendly neighborhood bar • games • gay-owned

Players 300 S 4th St (at Jay St) **608/784-4200** • 5pm-2am, from 3pm Fri-Sun, till 2:30am Fri-Sat • popular • lesbians/ gay men • dancing/DJ • transgender-friendly • wheelchair access • gay-owned

EROTICA

Pleasures 405 S 3rd **608/784-6350** • DVDs • toys • magazines • lingerie

Madison

INFO LINES & SERVICES

OutReach, Inc 600 Williamson St #P-1 **608/255-8582** • 9am-9pm, noon-3pm Sat, clsd Sun • drop-in center

ACCOMMODATIONS

Hawks Nest Log Home Rentals 2455 Fairview (at Door Creek Rd), Stoughton **608/445-7468** • lesbians/ gay men • log homes on Lake Kegonsa • 20 minutes from Madison • nonsmoking • lesbian-owned • $150-240 (for 2)

BARS

Club 5 5 Applegate Ct (btwn Fish Hatchery Rd & W Beltline Hwy) **608/277-9700, 877/648-9700** • 4pm-2am • popular • lesbians/ gay men • dancing/DJ • karaoke • live shows • also G Bar women's bar & Planet Q video bar • 18+ Tue

Green Bush 914 Regent St (at Park) **608/257-2874** • 4pm-midnight, clsd Sun • gay-friendly • also restaurant

OUT Restaurant and Nightclub 1262 John Q Hammons Dr **608/203-8338** • 11am-9pm, later Th-Sat, clsd Sun • lesbians/gay men • danicng/DJ • live shows • whelchair access

Shamrock 117 W Main St (at Fairchild) **608/255-5029** • 11am-close, brunch wknds • popular • lesbians/ gay men • also grill

Woof's 114 King St **608/204-6222** • 4pm-2am, from noon Sun • lesbians/ gay men • neighborhood bar • dancing/DJ

NIGHTCLUBS

Cardinal 418 E Wilson St (at S Franklin) **608/257-2473** • 7pm-2am, from 4pm Fri, clsd Tue • gay-friendly • call for gay nights• dancing/DJ • live shows

IQ/ IndieQueer • weekly & monthly queer parties in Madison, check local listings for dates & info

CAFES

Java Cat 3918 Monona Dr (at Cottage Grove Rd) **608/223-5553** • 5:30am-8pm, till 9pm Fri-Sat, 7am-7pm Sun • light food served • WiFi

RESTAURANTS

Fromagination 12 S Carroll (on Capital Sq) **608/255-2430** • 9:30am-6pm, 8am-4:30pm Sat, clsd Sun

La Hacienda 515 S Park St **608/255-8227** • 9am-3am • popular • Mexican • post-Club 5 spot

Monty's Blue Plate Diner 2089 Atwood Ave (at Winnebago) **608/244-8505** • 7am-9pm • some veggie • beer/ wine • wheelchair access

BOOKSTORES

A Room of One's Own Feminist Books & Gifts 307 W Johnson St **608/257-7888** • 10am-8pm, till 6pm Sat, noon-5pm Sun • wheelchair access

PUBLICATIONS

Our Lives • LGBT publication • www.ourlivesmadison.com

EROTICA

A Woman's Touch 600 Williamson (at Gateway Mall) **608/250-1928, 888/621-8880** • 11am-6pm, till 8pm Wed-Th, clsd Sun • wheelchair access

Red Letter News 2528 E Washington (btwn North & Milwaukee) **608/241-9958**

Milwaukee

INFO LINES & SERVICES

AA Galano Club 315 W Court #201 (in LGBT Community Center) **414/276-6936**

Gay People's Union Hotline 414/645-0585

Milwaukee LGBT Community Center 315 W Court St #101 (btwn W Cherry & Galena) **414/271-2656** • 10am-10pm, from 6pm Sat, till 5pm Mon, clsd Sun

ACCOMMODATIONS

Acanthus Inn B&B 3009 W Highland Blvd (at N 29th) **414/342-9788, 800/361-3698** • gay-friendly • in 1897 mansion • some shared baths • nonsmoking • $105-235

Ambassador Hotel 2308 W Wisconsin Ave (at N 24th) **414/345-5000, 888/322-3326** • gay/ straight • nonsmoking • WiFi • wheelchair access • $129-249

The Brumder Mansion 3046 W Wisconsin Ave (at N 31st) **414/342–9767, 866/793–3676** • gay-friendly • nonsmoking • WiFi •$99

Comfort Inn & Suites 916 E State St (at Marshall) **414/276–8800, 800/328–7275** • gay-friendly • also restaurant • WiFi • wheelchair access •$90-200

Hotel of the Arts/ Days Inn 1840 N 6th St (at Reservoir Ave) **414/265–5629** • gay-friendly • nonsmoking

The Iron Horse Hotel 500 W Florida St (at S 5th St) **888/543–4766** • gay-friendly hotel geared toward motorcycle enthusiasts

The Milwaukee Hilton 509 W Wisconsin Ave (at 5th St) **414/271–7250, 800/445–8667** • gay-friendly • also restaurant & pub • pool

BARS

Art Bar 722 E Burleigh St (at Fratney) **414/372–7880** • 4pm-1am, till 2:30am Fri-Sat • gay/ straight • live entertainment • also gallery • gay-owned

Boom/ The Room 625 S 2nd (at W Bruce) **414/277–5040** • 5pm-2am, from 2pm Sat & 11am Sun • lesbians/ gay men • neighborhood bar • food served • videos • patio • also martini bar

City Lights Chill & Grill 111 W Howard Ave (at S Howell Ave) **414/481–1441** • 4pm-2am • lesbians/ gay men • neighboorhood bar • food served

Fluid 819 S 2nd St (at W National) **414/643–5843** • 5pm-close, from 2pm wknds • mostly gay men • neighborhood bar

Hybrid Lounge 707 E Brady (at Van Buren) **414/810–1809** • 4pm-close, from 10am Sat & Sun • mostly gay men

Milwaukee

WHERE THE GIRLS ARE:
In East Milwaukee south of downtown, spread out from Lake Michigan to S Layton Blvd.

LGBT PRIDE:
June. 414/272-3378, web: www.pridefest.com.

ANNUAL EVENTS:
June-July - Summerfest, web: www.summerfest.com.
August - Wisconsin State Fair 414/266-7000, 800/884-3247 web: wistatefair.com
September - AIDS Walk 800/348–WALK, web: www.aidswalkwis.org.

CITY INFO:
414/273-7222 or 800/554-1448, web: www.visitmilwaukee.org.

WEATHER:
Summer temperatures can get up into 90°s. Spring and fall are pleasantly moderate but too short. Winter brings snow, cold temperatures, and even colder wind chills.

ATTRACTIONS:
Annunciation Greek Orthodox Church 414/461–9400, web: www.annunciationwi.com.
Breweries.
Grand Avenue.
Harley-Davidson Museum, web: www.hdmuseum.com.
Milwaukee Art Museum, web: www.mam.org.
Mitchell Park Horticultural Conservatory, 414/649-9830.
Pabst Theatre 414/286-3663, web: www.pabsttheater.org.

TRANSIT:
Yellow Cab 414/271-1800.
Milwaukee Transit 414/344-6711, web: www.ridemcts.com.

The Nomad 1401 E Brady St (at Warren) 414/224–8111 • 2pm-close, from noon wknds • gay-friendly • soccer pub

Nut Hut 1500 W Scott St (at 15th St) 414/647–2673 • 2pm-2am, from noon Fri-Sun • mostly women • neighborhood bar

Redroom Cocktail Lounge 1875 N Humboldt (at Kane) 414/224–7666 • 5pm-close, from 8pm wknds • gay/ straight • DJ Fri-Sat • coffee bar • patio • wheelchair access

Taylor's 795 N Jefferson St (at Wells) 414/271–2855 • 4pm-close, from 5pm wknds • gay/ straight • neighborhood bar • patio • wheelchair access • gay-owned

Two 718 E Burleigh St (at Fratney) 414/372–7880 • Th-Sat 7pm-close • gay/ straight • romantic hideaway

Walker's Pint 818 S 2nd St (at National Ave) 414/643–7468 • 4:30pm-2am, till 2:30am Fri-Sat, from noon Sun • mostly women • neighborhood bar • dancing/DJ • live shows • karaoke • patio • lesbian-owned

Woody's 1579 S 2nd St (at Lapham St) 414/672–0806 • 4pm-close, from 2pm wknds • mostly men • neighborhood sports bar

NIGHTCLUBS

La Cage/ Montage Lounge 801 S 2nd St (at National) 414/383–8330 • 10pm-close Fri-Sat • 6pm-close nightly • mostly gay men • dancing/DJ • live shows • videos • wheelchair access

Mad Planet 533 E Center St (at N Holton) 414/263–4555 • gay-friendly • retro dance Fri • dancing/DJ • live shows • live rock/ alternative shows

MONA'S 1407 S 1st St (at Greenfield) 414/643–0377 • 4pm-close, from 6pm Sat-Mon • lesbians/ gay men • also restaurant • lesbian-owned

Pump 1905 E North Ave (at Cramer, at Decibel nightclub) • 9pm Sun only • also Tues at Crisp • lesbians/ gay men • dancing/DJ

Tempt 324 E Mason (at N Milwaukee) 414/221–0228 • 4pm- close • lesbians/gay men • dancing/DJ

Tropical Ultra Lounge 626 S 5th St (at Bruce) • lesbians/ gay men • dancing/DJ • mostly Latino/a

CAFES

Alterra Coffee Roasters 2211 N Prospect Ave (at North) 414/273–3753 • 7am-6pm

Bella Caffe 189 N Milwaukee St 414/273–5620 • 6:30am-9pm, till 11pm Fri-Sat, 8am-6pm Sun

Fuel Cafe 818 E Center St 414/374–3835 • 7am-10pm • WiFi • wheelchair access

RESTAURANTS

Beans & Barley 1901 E North Ave (at Oakland Ave) 414/278–7878 • 8am-9pm • vegetarian cafe & deli

Cafe Vecchio Mondo 1137 N Old World 3rd St (at Juneau) 414/273–5700 • dinner, Sun brunch • full bar

Coquette Cafe 316 N Milwaukee St (btwn Buffalo & St Paul) 414/291–2655 • 11am-10pm, 5pm-11pm Sat, clsd Sun • bistro fare

Crisp Pizza Bar & Lounge 1323 E Brady St 414/727–4217 • 11am-2am • pizza • also full bar

Harvey's 1340 W Towne Sq Rd, Mequon 262/241–9589 • dinner nightly • cont'l

Honeypie Cafe 2643 S Kinnickinnic Ave (at Potter) 414/489–7437 • 10am-midnight, 9am-9pm wknds • homemade midwestern classics

The Knick 1030 E Juneau Ave (at Waverly) 414/272–0011 • 11am-midnight, from 9am wknds • popular • some veggie • full bar • wheelchair access

La Perla 734 S 5th St (at National) 414/645–9888 • 11am-10pm, till 11:30pm Fri-Sat • Mexican • also bar

Lulu 2261 & 2265 S Howell Ave 414/294–5858 • 11am-2am • also bar till late • live music wknds

Meritage 5921 W Vliet St 414/479–0620 • 5pm-10pm, till 11pm Fri-Sat, clsd Sun-Mon • American

Range Line Inn 2635 W Mequon Rd, Mequon 262/242–0530 • 4:30pm-10pm, clsd Sun-Mon • reservations recommended

Sanford Restaurant 1547 N Jackson St 414/276–9608 • dinner only, clsd Sun • Milwaukee fine dining Euro-style

ENTERTAINMENT & RECREATION

Boerner Botanical Gardens 9400 Boerner Dr (in Whitnall Park), Hales Corners 414/525–5650 • 8am-dusk • 40-acre garden & arboretum, garden clsd in winter

Harley-Davidson Museum 400 Canal St (at N 6th St) 877/436–8738

Milwaukee Gay Arts Center 703 S 2nd St 414/383–3727 • performance, classes & more

Mitchell Park Domes 524 S Layton Blvd (27th St, at Pierce) 414/649–9830 • 9am-5pm • botanical gardens

Rosebud Cinema 6823 W North Ave, Wauwatosa 414/607–9446 • mainstream & art house films • food served • full bar

BOOKSTORES

OutWords Books, Gifts & Coffee 2710 N Murray Ave (at Park Pl) 414/963–9089 • 11am-7pm, till 8pm Fri-Sat, noon-6pm Sun • LGBT • pride items • DVDs, CDs, cards, etc • wheelchair access

Peoples' Books 2122 E Locust St (at Maryland) 414/962–0575 • 10am-6pm, clsd Sun

Woodland Pattern 720 E Locust St 414/263–5001 • 11am-8pm, noon-5pm wknds, clsd Mon

RETAIL SHOPS

Adambomb Gallerie 2028 N Dr Martin Luther King Dr 414/276–2662 • 11am-8pm, from noon Sun, clsd Mon • tattoo studio

Miss Groove 1225 E Brady St (btwn Arlington & Franklin) 414/298–9185 • 11am-7pm, 10am-6pm Sat, noon-5pm Sun • accessories & apparel

Yellow Jacket 1237 E Brady (at North Ave) 414/372–4744 • noon-7pm, till 5pm Sun • vintage clothes

PUBLICATIONS

Outbound/ Quest 920/655–0611, 800/578–3785 • news & arts reviews for WI's LGBT community

EROTICA

Booked Solid 7035 Greenfield Ave (at 70th), West Allis 414/774–7210

Norwalk

ACCOMMODATIONS

Daughters of the Earth 18134 Index Ave 608/269–5301 • women only • women's land • camping • retreat space • lesbian-owned • $9 (camping), $15 (guest rooms)

Oshkosh

BARS

Deb's Spare Time 1303 Harrison St (btw main & New York) 920/235–6577 • 11am-2am, from 9am wknds • lesbians/gay men • neighborhood bar • food served • live shows • 18+ • gay-owned

EROTICA

Pure Pleasure 1212 Oshkosh Ave (off Hwy 21) 920/235–9727

Racine

NIGHTCLUBS

JoDee's International 2139 Racine St/ S Hwy 32 (at 22nd) 262/634–9804 • 7pm-close • lesbians/ gay men • dancing/DJ • live shows • karaoke • drag shows • courtyard • park in rear

Rhinelander

ACCOMMODATIONS

Musky Bay Resort 3724 N Limberlost Rd (at County Hwy C) 262/554–6763, 866/855–9971 • gay-friendly • nonsmoking • 3 cabins on the Moens Chain of Lakes • kids ok • lesbian-owned • $130-145/ night & $625-725/ week

Woodwind Health Spa & Resort 3033 Woodwind Wy (at S River Rd & Hwy 8) 715/362–8902 • gay/ straight • full brkfst • pool • nonsmoking • wheelchair access • lesbian-owned • $85-110

Sheboygan

BARS

The Blue Lite 1029 N 8th St (off Rte 143) 920/457–1636 • 7pm-close, from 3pm Sun • lesbians/ gay men • neighborhood bar • dancing/DJ Fri-Sat

Somerset

BARS

Bootleggers Bar & Grill 235 Main St 715/247–2668 • 11am-2am, from 7am wknds • gay/straight • live shows

Stevens Point

BARS

Club Night Out 2533 County Rd M (4 miles W of town) 715/342–5830 • 8pm-close, clsd Mon-Tue • mostly men • neighborhood bar • dancing/DJ

EROTICA

Eldorado's 3219 Church St (at Business 51 S) 715/343–9877

Stoughton

RETAIL SHOPS

Look At That Leather 2459 Fairview 608/877–1558 • 11am-7pm, till 8pm Fri-Sat, clsd Sun-Mon • biker leather • fetish • pride items • toys • lesbian-owned

Sturgeon Bay

ACCOMMODATIONS

The Chadwick Inn 25 N 8th Ave **920/743–2771** • gay-friendly • 1890 Queen Anne • nonsmoking • lesbian-owned • $100-135

The Chanticleer Guest House 4072 Cherry Rd **920/746–0334, 866/682–0384** • popular • gay-friendly • on 70 acres • pool • hot tub • nonsmoking • wheelchair access • gay-owned • $120-350

Superior

BARS

The Flame 1612 Tower Ave **715/395–0101** • 3pm-2:30am • lesbians/ gay men • dancing/DJ • live entertainment • karaoke

JT's Bar & Grill 1506 N 3rd St (at Blatnik Bridge) **715/394–2580** • 11am-2am, from 1pm Sat-Sun • lesbians/ gay men • neighborhood bar • dancing/DJ • food served • karaoke • drag shows • patio • wheelchair access

The Main Club 1217 Tower Ave (at 12th) **715/392–1756** • 3pm-2am • mostly gay men • dancing/DJ • live shows • country/ western • WiFi • wheelchair access

Wausau

NIGHTCLUBS

Oz 320 Washington **715/842–3225** • 7pm-close • mostly gay men • dancing/DJ • karaoke • drag shows • videos

Wisconsin Dells

BARS

Captain Dix 4124 River Rd (at Rainbow Valley Resort) **608/253–1818, 866/553–1818** • 4pm-close, from 11am wknds, from 6pm Mon-Tue • lesbians/ gay men • karaoke • theme nights

WYOMING

Alpine

ACCOMMODATIONS

The Nordic Inn/ Brenthoven's Restaurant 1 Colonial Ln (1 mile E of junction Hwys 89 & 26) **307/654–7556** • gay-friendly • inn & cottages • open June-Oct • also 4-star restaurant • $90+

Cheyenne

see also Fort Collins, Colorado

INFO LINES & SERVICES

Wyoming Equality/ United Gays & Lesbians of Wyoming **307/778–7645** • 10am-2pm Mon-Fri • info • referrals • newsletter • social activities • also youth services

BARS

Choice City Shots 124 LaPorte Ave (at College), Fort Collins, CO **970/221–4333** • 5pm-midnight, till 2am wknds • lesbians/ gay men • "womyn's night" Tue • neighborhood bar • dancing/DJ Fri-Sat • karaoke • live shows wknds • wheelchair access • lesbian/ gay-owned

Etna

RETAIL SHOPS

Blue Fox Studio & Gallery 107452 N US Hwy 89 **307/883–3310** • open 7 days • hours vary • pottery, jewelry & mask studio • local travel info

Evanston

EROTICA

Romantix Adult Superstore 1939 Harrison Dr **307/789–0800** • 6am-2am

Jackson

ACCOMMODATIONS

Spring Creek Ranch 1800 Spirit Dance Rd **307/733–8833, 800/443–6139** • popular • gay-friendly • food served • pool • nonsmoking rooms available • also condos & mtn homes • wheelchair access • $170-1,400

ENTERTAINMENT & RECREATION

Mighty Reel South Fork of the Snake River **208/847–5262** • guided flyfishing trips on the south fork of the Snake River • lesbian-owned

Laramie

INFO LINES & SERVICES

Rainbow Resource Center Knight Hall, Rm 112, 1000 E University Ave (at University of Wyoming) **307/766–3478** • 8am-5pm, clsd wknds • safe & supportive place for LGBT & questioning individuals & allies • wheelchair access

ACCOMMODATIONS

Cowgirl Horse Hotel 32 Black Elk Trail **307/745–8794 OR 399–2502** • specializing in women travelers & their horses • men welcome • $85

BOOKSTORES

The Second Story 105 Ivinson Ave **307/745–4423** • 10am-6pm, clsd Sun • independent

Riverton

RESTAURANTS

Country Cove 301 E Main (at First) **307/856–9813** • 7am-3pm, till noon Sat, clsd Sun • plenty veggie • wheelchair access • women-owned

Thermopolis

BOOKSTORES

Storyteller 528 Broadway **307/864–3272** • 8am-5pm • independent

Note: In most countries other than the USA and Canada, listings are alphabetical by city rather than by state, province, or region.

Canada

ALBERTA

Provincewide

PUBLICATIONS

Perceptions 306/244-1930 • covers the Canadian prairies

Banff

see also Lake Louise

ACCOMMODATIONS

Fairmont Banff Springs 405 Spray Ave **403/762-2211** • gay-friendly • in Canadian Rockies • also Willow Stream Spa

Simpson's Num-Ti-Jah Lodge 403/522-2167 • gay-friendly • overlooks Bow Lake & Canadian Rockies • 40km N of Lake Louise

Spruce Grove Inn 545 Banff Ave **403/762-3301, 800/879-1991** • gay-friendly • nonsmoking • wheelchair access • Can$95-275

Calgary

INFO LINES & SERVICES

Calgary Outlink: Centre for Gender & Sexual Diversity #4, 1230-A 17th Ave SW **403/234-8973, 877/688-4765 (24HR CRISIS & SUPPORT LINE)** • 11am-5pm Mon & Wed, 1pm-7pm Tue & Th, by appt Fri, clsd wknds • many groups

Front Runners AA 1227 Kensington Close NW (at Hillhurst United Church) **403/777-1212** • 8:30pm Tue, Th & Sat

Inside Out #4, 1230-A 17th Ave SW **403/234-8973** • 7pm Mon • support group for LGBTQ ages 15-25

ACCOMMODATIONS

11th Street Lodging 403/209-1800 • gay/ straight • kids 10+ ok • "no shoe" policy inside • nonsmoking • gay-owned • Can$65-220

Calgary Westways Guest House 216 25th Ave SW **403/229-1758, 866/846-7038** • gay/ straight • full brkfst • hot tub • nonsmoking • pets ok • WiFi • gay-owned • Can$79-199

Executive Royal Inn North Calgary 2828 23rd St NE **403/291-2003, 888/388-3932** • gay-friendly • jacuzzi • pets ok • also restaurant

The Westin Calgary 320 4th Ave SW **403/266-1611** • gay-friendly • downtown 4-diamond hotel • pool • nonsmoking • also restaurant • wheelchair access

BARS

The Back Lot 209 10th Ave SW (at 1st St SW) **403/265-5211** • 2pm-2am • mostly gay men • martini lounge • patio • wheelchair access

Fab Bar 1742 10th Ave SW (near 14th St) **403/263-7411** • 4pm-11pm Tue-Th, 11am-2am wknds, clsd Mon • lesbians/ gay men • neighborhood bar • food served • karaoke • rooftop patio • wheelchair access

Ming 520 17th Ave SW **403/229-1986** • 4pm-2am • gay-friendly • martini lounge • food served

NIGHTCLUBS

Girls Groove • women's dance parties • check local listings for upcoming events

The Twisted Element 1006 11th Ave SW **403/802-0230** • 9pm-close, clsd Mon • mostly men • dancing/DJ • karaoke • drag shows • strippers • WiFi

The Warehouse 731 10th Ave SW (alley entrance) **403/264-0535** • 9pm-8am Fri-Sat only • gay-friendly • dancing/DJ • live music • young crowd • private club • guests welcome

CAFES

Cafe Beano 1613 9th St SW (at 17th Ave) **403/229-1232** • 6am-midnight, from 7am wknds • some veggie • wheelchair access

RESTAURANTS

Halo 13226 Macleod Trail SE **403/271-4111** • lunch & dinner • steak, seafood & wine bar

Melrose Cafe & Bar 730 17th Ave SW (at 7th St) **403/228-3566** • 11am-2am, from 10am wknds • full bar till 2am • patio

Thai Sa-On 351 10th Ave SW (at 4th) **403/264-3526** • lunch & dinner, clsd Sun • Thai

Wicked Wedge Pizza 618 17th Ave SW (at 6th St) **403/228-1024** • 11am-close, noon-10pm Sun

ENTERTAINMENT & RECREATION

Calgary Men's Chorus PO Box 23217, Connaught RPO T2S 3B1

BOOKSTORES

Daily Globe News Shop 1004 17th Ave SW (at 10th St) **403/244-2060** • 9am-10pm • periodicals

Self Connection Books 4004 19th St NW
403/284–1486, 866/735–3457 • 10am-6pm, till
8pm Th, till 5pm Sun • also 10816
Macleod Trail SE, 403/225-8887

RETAIL SHOPS

Priape 1322 17th Ave SW (enter on 16th)
403/215–1800, 800/461–6969 #25 • noon-
9pm, till 6pm Sun • clubwear • leather • books
• toys & more

PUBLICATIONS

Gay Calgary & Edmonton Magazine
888/543–6960 • monthly LGBT publication

Edmonton

INFO LINES & SERVICES

AA Gay/ Lesbian 11355 Jasper Ave (at
church) **780/424–5900** • 7:30pm Mon; also
8pm Fri at 10804 119th St

Pride Centre of Edmonton 9540 - 111 Ave
780/488–3234 • 10am-10pm Tue-Fri, 2pm-
6pm Sat, clsd Sun-Mon• youth group 7pm
Sat

Womonspace 9540 111 Ave (Pride Centre of
Edmonton) **780/482–1794** • social &
recreational society • dances & other events •
bi-monthly newsletter

ACCOMMODATIONS

Labyrinth Lake Lodge **780/878–3301** •
gay/ straight • lodge on private lake • hot tubs
• kids/ pets ok • nonsmoking • Can$200-250

McCracken Country Inn & Tea House 146
Brookhart St, Hinton **780/865–5662,
888/865–5662** • gay-friendly • $99-149

Northern Lights B&B **780/483–1572** •
lesbians/ gay men • full brkfst • pool •
nonsmoking • gay-owned • Can$60-70

BARS

Boots 10242 106th St **780/423–5014** • 4pm-
close • lesbians/ gay men • dancing/DJ • live
music • drag shows • private club

Prism Bar & Grill 10524 101 St (enter rear)
780/990–0038 • 4pm-2am, from 7pm Sat, clsd
Sun • mostly women • neighborhood bar •
dancing/DJ • also restaurant • karaoke Tue •
wheelchair access

Woody's Pub & Cafe 11723 A Jasper (above
Buddy's) **780/488–6557** • 3pm-midnight, till
3am wknds • lesbians/ gay men •
neighborhood bar • food served • karaoke

NIGHTCLUBS

Buddy's Nite Club 11725-B Jasper
780/488–6636 • 9pm-3am, from 8pm Fri •
lesbians/ gay men • dancing/DJ • drag shows

Play 10320 102nd Ave NW (at 3rd St)
780/497–7529 • open Th-Sun • lesbians/ gay
men • dancing/DJ • theme nights

RESTAURANTS

Cafe de Ville 10137 124th St (side entrance)
780/488–9188 • 11:30am-10pm, till midnight
Fri-Sat, 9:30am-2:30pm & 5pm-10pm Sun •
nonsmoking • reservations recommended

Garage Burger Bar & Grill 10242 106th St
(at 103rd Ave) **780/423–5014** • 11am-8pm

ENTERTAINMENT & RECREATION

Edmonton Vocal Minority **780/479–2038** •
LGBT chorus

Gaywire CJSR FM 88.5 **780/492–2577** •
6pm-7pm Th • LGBT radio

BOOKSTORES

Audrey's Books 10702 Jasper Ave (at 107th
St) **780/423–3487** • 9am-9pm, 9:30am-
5:30pm Sun, noon-5pm Sun • large LGBT
section • wheelchair access

Greenwood's Bookshoppe 7925 104th St
(at 80th) **780/439–2005, 800/661–2078** • 9am-
9pm, 9:30am-5:30pm Sat, noon-5pm Sun

RETAIL SHOPS

Divine Decadence 10441 82nd Ave (at
105th) **780/702–1982** • hip fashions •
accessories

PUBLICATIONS

Gay Calgary & Edmonton Magazine
Calgary **888/543–6960** • monthly LGBT
publication

Lake Louise

see also Banff

ACCOMMODATIONS

Lake Louise Inn 210 Village Dr
403/522–3791, 800/661–9237 • gay-friendly •
mtn resort near Pipestone River • pool

Lethbridge

INFO LINES & SERVICES

**GALA/LA (Gay/ Lesbian Alliance of
Lethbridge & Area)** 403/308–2893 • call
for events

Westrose

ACCOMMODATIONS

Pine Trails Getaway RR1 **780/586–0002** •
gay campground

BRITISH COLUMBIA

Birken

ACCOMMODATIONS

Birken Lakeside Resort 9179 Portage Rd **604/452–3255** • gay-friendly • cabins • campsites • hot tub • swimming • pets ok • lesbian-owned • Can$80-212

Chilliwack

RESTAURANTS

Bravo Restaurant & Lounge 46224 Yale Rd (at Nowell St) **604/792–7721** • 5pm-close, clsd Sun-Mon • also available for private functions • martinis • wheelchair access • gay-owned

Courtenay

ACCOMMODATIONS

Moonlight Inn Guest House **250/334–0085** • lesbian guesthouse, w/ wedding package in a gay-supportive community midway up the east coast of Vancouver Island • Can$1,200/ wk

Gulf Islands

INFO LINES & SERVICES

Gays & Lesbians of Salt Spring Island (GLOSSI) PO Box 644, Salt Spring Island V8K 2W2 **250/537–7773** • social events • newsletter • support • info line

ACCOMMODATIONS

Anne's Oceanfront Hideaway B&B 168 Simson Rd, Salt Spring Island **250/537–0851, 888/474–2663** • gay-friendly • full brkfst • ocean views • nonsmoking • WiFi • wheelchair access • Can$195-285

Bellhouse Inn 29 Farmhouse Rd, Galiano Island **250/539–5667, 800/970–7464** • gay/ straight • historic waterfront inn • full brkfst • nonsmoking • Can$85-195

Birdsong B&B 153 Rourke Rd, Salt Spring Island **250/537–4608** • gay/ straight • ocean & harbor views • Can$115-155

Blue Ewe Cottage in the Woods 1207 Beddis Rd, Salt Spring Island **250/537–5827** • lesbians/ gay men • hot tub w/ ocean view • nonsmoking • gay-owned • Can$150-235

Fulford Dunderry Guest House 2900 Fulford-Ganges Rd, Salt Spring Island **250/653–4860** • gay-friendly • oceanfront guesthouse • nonsmoking • WiFi • gay-owned • Can$100-185

Hummingbird Lodge B&B 1597 Starbuck Ln (at Whalebone Dr), Gabriola **250/247–9300, 877/551–9383** • gay-friendly • close to beaches & kayaking • Can$99-129

Island Farmhouse B&B 185 Horel Rd W, Salt Spring Island **250/653–9898, 877/537–5912** • gay/ straight • kids/ pets ok • nonsmoking • lesbian-owned • Can$70-155

Salt Spring Inn & Restaurant 132 Lower Ganges Rd (at Hereford Ave), Salt Spring Island **250/537–9339, 877/537–9339** • gay-friendly • full brkfst • $75-160

Sun Raven Lodge 1356 MacKinnon Rd (at Ferry Terminal), North Pender Island **250/629–6216** • mostly women • rental cottage • sauna • pool • nonsmoking • lesbian-owned • Can$95-125

Kamloops

ACCOMMODATIONS

Mystic Mountain Acres B&B 1030 Bo Hill Pl, Blue River **250/674–2700** • gay- friendly • private home • full brkfst

Watauga Village B&B 734 Clearwater Village Rd, Blue River **250/674–0085** • gay-friendly • cabins w/ kitchenettes • Mei Mei's Art Cafe

Okanagan Lake

includes Kaleden, Kelowna, Oliver, Penticton & Vernon

ACCOMMODATIONS

Creek View B&B 1520 Pasadena Rd, Kelowna **250/862–3653** • gay/ straight • swimming • lesbian-owned • $70-90

Eagles Nest B&B 15620 Commonage Rd (at Carrs Landing Rd), Kelowna **250/766–9350, 866/766–9350** • mostly men • overlooking Lake Okanagan • full brkfst • hot tub • nonsmoking • WiFi • gay-owned • Can$80-150

Grapeseed Guesthouse & Gardens 607 Munson Mountain Rd, Penticton **250/809–9998** • lesbians/gay men • lesbian-owned

Morningside B&B 1645 Carmi Ave (at Government St), Penticton **250/492–5874** • gay/ straight • full brkfst • shared baths • nonsmoking • Can$65-85

CAFES

Bean Scene 274 Bernard Ave, Kelowna **250/763–1814** • 7am-10pm, till 11pm Fri-Sat patio • wheelchair access

RESTAURANTS

Greek House 3159 Woodsdale Rd, Kelowna 250/766-0090 • 4pm-9pm • cont'l

Okanagan Valley

INFO LINES & SERVICES

Okanagan Rainbow Coalition 1476 Water St, Kelowna 250/860-8555, 866/844-3444 • 24-hr recorded info • support groups • social events • dances

ACCOMMODATIONS

A Kelowna Getaway 2188 Bennett Rd (at McKinley Rd), Kelowna 250/860-5245 • gay/straight • kids ok • WiFi • Can$110-135

Powell River

ACCOMMODATIONS

Beacon B&B & Spa 3750 Marine Ave 604/485-5563, 877/485-5563 • gay-friendly • full brkfst • hot tub • massage • nonsmoking • wheelchair access • Can$99-129

Prince George

INFO LINES & SERVICES

GALA North 250/614-1661 • 24-hr recorded info • social group • call for drop-in hours & location

EROTICA

XXXtreme Adult 1412 Patricia Blvd 250/614-1411

Qualicum Beach

ACCOMMODATIONS

Bahari Oceanside Inn 5101 Island Hwy W 877/752-9278 • gay-friendly • full brkfst • hot tub • apt rental • nonsmoking • kids ok • WiFi • Can$125-235

Tofino

ACCOMMODATIONS

Beachwood 1368 Chesterman Beach Rd 250/725-4250 • gay-friendly • private apt • steps to the beach • gay-owned • $135-225

BriMar B&B 1375 Thornberg Crescent 250/725-3410, 800/714-9373 • gay/ straight • on the beach • full brkfst • teens ok • Can$110-200

Eagle Nook Wilderness Resort & Spa Barkley Sound 800/760-2777 • gay-friendly • private log cabins • gourmet meals • "all the comforts of a four-star resort" • adventure tours include kayaking, fishing & heli-venturing • health spa

RESTAURANTS

Blue Heron 634 Campbell St 250/725-4266 • 5am-10pm • full bar • wheelchair access

Vancouver

INFO LINES & SERVICES

AA Gay/ Lesbian 604/434-3933

The Greater Vancouver Pride Line 604/684-6869 x290, 800/566-1170 • 7pm-10pm • info & support

Vancouver Gay/ Lesbian Centre 1170 Bute St (btwn Davie & Pendrell Sts) 604/684-5307, 800/566-1170 • also Out on the Shelves LGBT lending library

ACCOMMODATIONS

Arbutus Guest House 1904 Arbutus St (at W Third Ave) 604/325-3013 • gay-friendly • lesbian-owned • Can$125-300

Barclay House B&B 1351 Barclay St (at Jervis) 604/605-1351, 800/971-1351 • gay/ straight • restored Victorian • full brkfst • nonsmoking • gay-owned • Can$155-295

The Buchan Hotel 1906 Haro St (btwn Denman & Gilford) 604/685-5354, 800/668-6654 • gay-friendly • built in 1926 • some shared baths • nonsmoking • kids ok • Can$78-138

Granville B&B 5050 Granville St (at 34th Ave) 604/307-2300, 866/739-9002 • gay-friendly • B&B in Tudor Revival • nonsmoking • Can$100-200

Hostelling International—Vancouver Central 1025 Granville St (at Nelson) 604/685-5335, 888/203-8333 • gay/ straight • hostel right on Granville St • kids ok • WiFi • also bar • wheelchair access • Can$26-34 (dorms)/ Can$62-99 (privates)

Hostelling International—Vancouver Jericho Beach 1515 Discovery St 604/224-3208, 888/203-4303 • gay/ straight • summer only • beachfront • kids ok • WiFi • wheelchair access • Can$20-28 (dorms)/ Can$60-80 (privates)

L' Hermitage Hotel 788 Richards St (at Robson) 778/327-4100 • gay/ straight • pool • nonsmoking • WiFi • wheelchair access

The Langtry 968 Nicola St (at Barclay) **604/687–7892, 800/699–7892** • gay/ straight • B&B apts in West End • nonsmoking • gay-owned • Can$85-300

Moda Hotel 900 Seymour St (at Smithe) **604/683–4251, 877/683–5522** • gay/ straight • restaurant • kids ok • Can$109-119 • also 3 bars

Vancouver

WHERE THE GIRLS ARE:
Cruising Commercial Drive, mixing w/ the boys on Davie St, or shopping in Gastown.

ENTERTAINMENT:
Wreck Beach (great gay beach).

LGBT PRIDE:
August. 604/687-0955, web: www.vancouverpride.ca.

ANNUAL EVENTS:
January-February - Gay & Lesbian Ski Week, web: www.gaywhistler.com.

May - Vancouver International Marathon 604/872-2928, web: www.bmovanmarathon.ca.

June - Dragon Boat Festival 604/688-2382, web: www.dragonboatbc.ca.

June-July - Vancouver Int'l Jazz Festival 604/872-5200, web: www.coastaljazz.ca.

July - Folk Music Festival 604/602-9798, web: www.thefestival.bc.ca.

August - Queer Film & Video Festival 604/844-1615, web: www.outonscreen.com.

September - BOLD Fest (Bold, Older Lesbians & Dykes), web: www.soundsandfuries.com/BOLD.html.

September/October - International Film Festival 604/685-0260, web: www.viff.org.

CITY INFO:
604/683-2000, web: www.tourismvancouver.com.

BEST VIEW:
Biking in Stanley Park, or on a ferry between peninsulas and islands. Atop one of the surrounding mountains.

ATTRACTIONS:
Capilano Suspension Bridge, web: www.capbridge.com.

Chinatown.

Dr Sun Yat-Sen Chinese Garden 604/662–3207, web: vancouverchinesegarden.com

Gastown.

Granville Island, web: www.granvilleisland.com.

Grouse Mountain, web: www.grousemountain.com.

Museum of Anthropology 604/822–5087, web: www.moa.ubc.ca.

Science World 604/443-7443, web: www.scienceworld.ca.

Stanley Park.

Vancouver Aquarium 604/659–3474, web: www.vanaqua.org.

Vancouver Lookout 604/689–0421, web: www.vancouverlookout.com.

Vancouver Museum 604/736–4431 web: www.museumofvancouver.ca.

Van Dusen Botanical Gardens 604/878-9274, web: www.vandusengarden.org.

WEATHER:
It's cold and wet in the winter (32-45°F), but it's absolutely gorgeous in the summer (52-75°F)!

TRANSIT:
Yellow Cab 604/681-1111, web: www.yellowcabonline.com.

TransLink 604/953-3333, web: www.translink.bc.ca.

A Visitors' Map of all bus lines is available through the tourist office.

Nelson House B&B 977 Broughton St (btwn Nelson & Barclay) **604/684–9793, 866/684–9793** • lesbians/gay men • Edwardian mansion • full brkfst • jacuzzi in suite • sundeck • WiFi • lesbian- & gay-owned • Can$108-198

"O Canada" House B&B 1114 Barclay St (at Thurlow) **604/688–0555, 877/688–1114** • gay/straight • restored 1897 Victorian home • full brkfst • WiFi • gay-owned • Can$135-285

Opus Hotel 322 Davie St (at Hamilton, Yaletown) **604/642–6787, 866/642–6787** • gay-friendly • hip luxury boutique hotel • also bar & Elixer French brasserie • wheelchair access • Can$299+

Plaza 500 Hotel 500 W 12th Ave (at Cambie St) **604/873–1811, 800/473–1811** • gay-friendly • full brkfst • kids ok • gym •WiFi • Can$165+

Rosedale on Robson 838 Hamilton St (at Robson) **604/689–8033, 800/661–8870** • gay-friendly • all-suite w/ kitchenette • pool • kids/pets ok • WiFi • Can$125-250

Sandman Suites on Davie 1160 Davie St (at Thurlow St) **604/681–7263, 800/726–3626** • gay/straight • West End suites • pool • nonsmoking • wheelchair access • Can$119+

The Sutton Place Hotel 845 Burrard St (at Smithe) **604/682–5511, 866/378–8866** • gay-friendly • luxurious boutique hotel

The West End Guest House 1362 Haro St (at Broughton) **604/681–2889, 888/546–3327** • gay/straight • full brkfst • nonsmoking • gay-owned • Can$95-275

BARS

1181 1181 Davie St (at Bute) **604/687–3991** • 4pm-close • mostly gay men • upscale cocktail lounge

Avanti's Pub 1601 Commercial Dr (at 1st Ave) **604/254–5466** • 11am-midnight, till 1am Fri-Sat • gay-friendly • sports bar • popular w/ local lesbian ball teams

The Fountainhead Pub 1025 Davie St (at Burrard) **604/687–2222** • 11am-midnight, till 2am Fri-Sat • wknd brunch • lesbians/gay men • neighborhood bar • transgender-friendly • patio

Gerard Lounge 845 Burrard St (in Sutton Place Hotel) **604/682–5511** • 11:30am-1am, 4:30pm-midnight Sun • gay-friendly • food served • great martinis

Lotus Lounge/ Honey 455 Abbott St (at Keefer, in The Lotus Hotel) **604/685–7777 (HOTEL #)** • clsd Sun • gay/straight • dancing/DJ • live bands • food served

The Oasis 1240 Thurlow (at Davie) **604/685–1724** • 5pm-close Wed-Sat • gay/straight • martini bar • live shows • piano • tapas

NIGHTCLUBS

816 Granville/ The World 816 Granville • midnight-6am Fri-Sun • mostly gay men • dancing/DJ

The Black Parade Kings • mostly women • drag shows • check local listings for info

Celebrities 1022 Davie St (at Burrard St) **604/681–6180** • mostly gay men • dancing/DJ

Club 23 West 23 W Cordova (at Carrall) **604/662–3277** • 10pm-4am Fri-Sat • gay/straight • dancing/DJ

Five Sixty 560 Seymour St (at Pender) **604/678–6322** • gay/straight • dancing/DJ • live bands • art gallery

Flygirl 1795 Beach Ave (at The Boathouse) **604/839–9819** • 2nd & 4th Sat • mostly women • dancing/DJ

Hershe Bar 604/839–9819 • long wknds only • mega lesbian dance party • check local listings for info

The Junction Public House 1138 Davie St **604/669–2013** • 11am-2am, till 3am Fri-Sat • mostly gay men • dancing/DJ • sports bar • patio

Lick/ The Mix 455 Abbott St (at Keefer, in The Lotus Hotel) **604/685–7777 (HOTEL #)** • mostly women

The Odyssey 1251 Howe St (at Drake) **604/689–5256** • 9pm-2am, till 3am Fri-Sat • popular • mostly gay men • dancing/DJ • drag shows • young crowd • theme nights • patio

Shine 364 Water St (at Richards) **604/408–4321** • gay-friendly • dancing/DJ

CAFES

Coffee A Go-Go 829 Davie St **604/687–2909** • 7am-9pm, 9am-6pm wknds • WiFi • local art • food served

Coming Home 753 6th St (at 8th Ave), New Westminster **604/288–9850** • 8am-8pm, till 3pm Mon & Tue, from 10am Sun • gay-owned

Delaney's 1105 Denman St **604/662–3344** • 6am-11pm, from 6:30am wknds • coffee shop

JJ Bean 2206 Commercial Dr **604/254–3723**

Rhizome Cafe 317 E Broadway **604/872–3166** • 11am-10pm, till midnight Fri-Sat, 9pm-10pm Sun, clsd Mon • plenty veggie/vegan • local artists • workshops

Sweet Revenge 4160 Main St (at 26th) **604/879-7933** • 7pm-midnight, till 1am Fri-Sat • patisserie • gay-owned

Turk's Coffee Exchange 1276 Commercial Dr **604/255-5805** • 6:30am-11pm

RESTAURANTS

Accents Restaurant 1967 W Broadway (at Arbutus) **604/734-6660** • lunch Tue-Fri, dinner Tue-Sun, clsd Mon • European/ int'l fine-dining • gay-owned

Bin 941 941 Davie St **604/683-1246** • 5pm-2am, till midnight Sun • tiny tapas parlor • popular • also 1521 W Broadway, 604/734-9421

Brioche 401 W Cordova (at Homer, in Gastown) **604/682-4037** • 7am-7pm, 9am-6pm wknds • Italian restaurant & bakery

Cafe Deux Soleils 2096 Commercial Dr **604/254-1195** • 8am-midnight, till 5pm Sun • lesbians/ gay men • vegetarian • live shows

Cafe Luxy 1235 Davie St (btwn Bute & Jervis) **604/669-5899** • 11am-10:30pm, wknd brunch 9am-3pm • some veggie • full bar • wheelchair access • live jazz

Cascade Room 2616 Main St (at 10th) **604/709-8650** • 4pm-midnight, from noon wknds

Chill Winston 3 Alexander St **604/288-9575** • 11am-1am • humble smaill restaurant lounge in Gastown

Cincin 1154 Robson St (off Bute) **604/688-7338** • dinner nightly • Italian/ Mediterranean • full bar

Delilah's 1789 Comox St (at Denman) **604/687-3424** • 5:30pm-11pm • prix-fixe menu • full bar • extensive martini menu • wheelchair access

The Dish 1068 Davie St **604/689-0208** • 7am-10pm, 9am-9pm Sun • veggie fast food • gay-owned

Elbow Room Cafe 560 Davie St (at Seymour) **604/685-3628** • 8am-4pm, till 5pm wknds • great brkfst

Foundation Lounge 2301 Main St **604/708-0881** • noon-1am, till 2am wknds • vegetarian

Glowbal Grill & Satay Bar 1079 Mainland St (Yaletown) **604/602-0835** • lunch, dinner, brunch wknds • also check out Afterglow next door, nightly 6pm-late

Hamburger Mary's 1202 Davie St (at Bute) **604/687-1293** • 8am-3am, till 4am Fri-Sat, till 2am Sun • some veggie • full bar

Havana 1212 Commercial Dr **604/253-9119** • 11am-11pm, from 10am wknds • popular • Cuban fusion • full bar • patio • also gallery & theater

India Gate 616 Robson St (at Granville) **604/684-4617** • lunch Mon-Sat, dinner nightly

J Lounge 1216 Bute St (at Davie St) **604/609-6665** • 5pm-1am, from 11am Sun • live entertainment • DJs • cocktails

Lickerish 903 Davie St (at Hornby) **604/696-0725** • 5:30pm-midnight, till 1am Th-Sun • global cuisine • cocktail lounge

Lift Bar & Grill 333 Menchions Mews **604/689-5438** • 11:30am-midnight

Lolita's 1326 Davie St (at Jervis) **604/696-9996** • 4:30pm till late, wknd brunch • innovative Mexican • tiny space but worth the wait

Maenam 1938 W 4th Ave **604/730-5579** • lunch Tue-Sat, dinner 5pm-midnight

Martini's Whole Wheat Pizza 151 W Broadway (btwn Cambie & Main) **604/873-0021** • 11am-2am, from 2pm Sat, till 1am Sun • great pizza • full bar

Naam 2724 W 4th St (at MacDonald) **604/738-7151** • 24hrs • vegetarian • live music • wheelchair access

Score 1262 Davie St (at Jervis St) **604/632-1646** • 10am-late • lesbians/ gay men • sports bar • also popular restaurant

Seasons in the Park Cambie St & W 33rd Ave **604/874-8008** • from 11:30am, from 10:30am Sun

Tanpopo Sushi 1122 Denman (at Pendrell) **604/681-7777** • lunch & dinner • excellent, affordable sushi

ENTERTAINMENT & RECREATION

Capilano Suspension Bridge 3735 Capilano Rd, N Vancouver **604/985-7474**

Cruisey T leaves from N foot of Denman St (at Harbor Cruises) **604/551-2628** • Sun (seasonal) • 4-hour party cruise around Vancouver Harbour • lesbians/ gay men • dancing/DJ • live shows • food served

Girl Gig Productions • women's performance promoters • popular "Chicks With Picks" series • check girlgigs.com for info

Rockwood Adventures 839 W 1st St #C, North Vancouver **604/741-0802, 888/236-6606** • rain forest walks & city tours for all levels w/ free hotel pickup

Sunset Beach Beach Ave, right in the West End (near Burrard St Bridge) • home of Vancouver AIDS memorial

Timberline Dance Society 1130 Jervis St

Vancouver Nature Adventures 1251 Cardero St #2005 **604/684-4922, 800/528-3531** • orca-watching safari • guided kayaking day trip & beach BBQ • no experience required • free hotel pickup

Wreck Beach below UBC

BOOKSTORES

Little Sister's 1238 Davie St (btwn Bute & Jervis) **604/669-1753, 800/567-1662 (IN CANADA ONLY)** • 10am-11pm • popular • LGBT • wheelchair access

People's Co-op Bookstore 1391 Commercial Dr (btwn Kitchener & Charles) **604/253-6442, 888/511-5556** • LGBT section

RETAIL SHOPS

Cupcakes 1116 Denman St (at Pendrell) **604/974-1300** • 10am-9pm, till 10pm Fri-Sat • women-owned cupcake shop • also at 2887 W Broadway

Liquid Amber Tattoo 1252 Burrard St #100 (at Burnaby) **604/738-3667**

Mintage 1714 Commercial Dr **604/871-0022** • vintage & future fashions • woman-owned • also Gastown location

Next Body Piercing 1068 Granville St (at Nelson) **604/684-6398** • noon-6pm, 11am-7pm Fri-Sat • also tattooing

Priape 1148 Davie St (btwn Bute & Thurlow) **604/630-2330** • clubwear • leather • books • toys & more

PUBLICATIONS

Xtra! West **604/684-9696** • LGBT newspaper

GYMS & HEALTH CLUBS

Fitness World 1214 Howe St (at Davie) **604/681-3232** • gay-friendly • day passes

Spartacus Athletic Club 1522 Commercial Dr **604/254-6267**

EROTICA

Love's Touch 1069 Davie St **604/681-7024**

Womyn's Ware 896 Commercial Dr (at Venables) **604/254-2543, 888/WYM-WARE (ORDERS ONLY)** • 11am-6pm, till 7pm Th-Fri, till 5:30pm Sun • toys • fetishwear • lesbian-owned

Victoria

ACCOMMODATIONS

Ambrosia Historic B&B 522 Quadra (at Humboldt) **250/380-7705, 877/262-7672** • gay/ straight • 5-star B&B 3 blocks from Victoria's inner harbor • full brkfst • jacuzzi • nonsmoking • Can$145-295

The Fairmont Empress 721 Government St **250/384-8111, 800/257-7544** • gay-friendly • Victoria landmark • pool • spa • afternoon tea • kids/ small pets ok • nonsmoking • wheelchair access • Can$159-479

Hostelling International—Victoria 516 Yates St **250/385-4511, 888/883-0099** • gay/ straight • hostel in heritage bldg downtown • kids ok • WiFi • wheelchair access • Can$20-68

Howard Johnson Hotel & Suites Victoria 4670 Elk Lake Dr **250/704-4656, 866/300-4656** • gay-friendly • pool • hot tub • kids ok • restaurant & lounge • wheelchair access • Can$109-369

Ifanwen B&B 44 Simcoe St **250/384-3717** • lesbians/ gay men • full brkfst • gardens • sundeck • gay-owned • Can$65-105

Inn at Laurel Point 680 Montreal St (at Quebec St) **250/386-8721, 800/663-7667** • gay-friendly • restaurant • pool • WiFi • nonsmoking • kids/pets ok • wheelchair access

Oak Bay Guest House 1052 Newport Ave **250/598-3812, 800/575-3812** • gay-friendly • 1912 Tudor-style house in quiet garden setting • full brkfst • near beaches • kids 10+ ok • nonsmoking • Can$99-205

Prior House 620 St Charles (at Rockland Ave) **250/592-8847, 877/924-3300** • gay-friendly • 5-star inn in historic 1912 manor home • full brkfst • nonsmoking • Can$185-310

Ryan's B&B at Albion Manor 224 Superior St **250/389-0012, 877/389-0012** • gay/ straight • full brkfst • jacuzzi • nonsmoking • WiFi • wheelchair access • gay-owned • Can$109-239

Sandman Hotel Victoria 1852 Douglas St **250/388-0788, 888/388-0787** • gay-friendly • pool • Can$69-169

BARS

Paparazzi 642 Johnson St (enter on Broad St) **250/388-0505** • 3pm-2am, from 1pm wknds • lesbians/ gay men • dancing/DJ • karaoke • drag shows • videos • wheelchair access

NIGHTCLUBS

Hush 1325 Government St (in basement) **250/385-0566** • 9pm-2am, clsd Sun-Tue • gay/ straight • dancing/DJ

RESTAURANTS

Green Cuisine 560 Johnson St #5 (in Market Square) **250/385-1809** • 10am-8pm • vegan • also juice bar & bakery

Rosie's Diner 253 Cook St **250/384-6090** • 8am-9pm • '50s & '60s music & videos • wheelchair access • gay-owned

Santiago's Cafe 660 Oswego St **250/388-7376** • 11am-9pm • tapas bar • patio • gay-owned

ENTERTAINMENT & RECREATION

Butchart Gardens 800 Benvenuto Ave, Brentwood Bay **250/652-5256, 866/652-4422**

BOOKSTORES

Bolen Books 1644 Hillside Ave #111 (in shopping center) **250/595-4232** • 8:30am-10pm • LGBT section

RETAIL SHOPS

Oceanside Gifts 812 Wharf St, Ste 102 (across from Empress Hotel on the lower causeway) **250/380-1777** • 10am-10pm • gifts from across Canada • wheelchair access

EROTICA

Kiss & Tell 531 Herald St **250/380-6995**

Whistler

ACCOMMODATIONS

Alpine Vacation Accommodation **604/938-0707, 888/938-0707** • gay-friendly • ski-in/ ski-out luxury townhouses • nonsmoking • $360

Best Western Listel Whistler Hotel 4121 Village Green (at Whistler Way) **604/932-1133, 800/663-5472** • gay-friendly • pool • hot tub • wheelchair access • Can$249-799

Coast Blackcomb Suites at Whistler 4899 Painted Cliff Rd **604/905-3400, 800/716-6199** • gay-friendly • full-service resort hotel • full bar & restaurant • hot tub • pool • nonsmoking • wheelchair access • Can$120+

Fairmont Chateau Whistler 4599 Chateau Blvd **604/938-8000, 800/606-8244** • gay-friendly • pool • ski-in/ ski-out hotel & spa • nonsmoking • wheelchair access

Four Seasons Resort Whistler 4591 Blackcomb Wy **604/935-3400, 800/268-6282** • gay-friendly • luxury resort & spa • pool • nonsmoking • wheelchair access

Hostelling International—Whistler 1035 Legacy Way **604/962-0025, 866/762-4122** • gay/ straight • facility was built for 2010 Olympics • nonsmoking • WiFi • Can$28-32 (dorms)/ Can$71-79 (privates)

Westin Whistler 4090 Whistler Wy **604/905-5000, 800/937-8461** • gay-friendly • full-service resort hotel • full bar & restaurant • spa • hot tub • pool • nonsmoking • WiFi • wheelchair access

RESTAURANTS

Araxi 4222 Village Square **604/932-4540** • lunch & dinner • local ingredients • also seafood bar & lounge

The Bearfoot Bistro 4121 Village Green **604/932-3433** • 6pm-midnight • excellent wine cellar • reservations recommended

Boston Pizza 2011 Innsbruck Dr **604/932-7070** • 11am-11pm, till midnight wknds • full bar

La Rua 4557 Blackcomb Blvd **604/932-5011** • 6pm-close, clsd Tue • Italian/ cont'l

Monks Grill 4555 Blackcomb Wy **604/932-9677** • 11:30am-10pm • grill menu • full bar

Quattro 4319 Main St **604/905-4844** • dinner nightly • Italian

Sachi Sushi 106-4359 Main St **604/935-5649** • lunch & dinner

Southside Diner 2102 Lake Placid Rd (off Hwy 99) **604/966-0668** • 7am-midnight • hosts monthly Gay Social

Trattoria di Umberto 4417 Sundial Crescent **604/932-5858** • lunch & dinner • reservations recommended

ENTERTAINMENT & RECREATION

ZipTrek EcoTours PO Box 734, V0N 1B0 **604/935-0001, 866/935-0001** • ziplines crisscross the Fitzsimmons Creek btwn Whistler & Blackcomb

GYMS & HEALTH CLUBS

Solarice 202-4230 Gateway Dr (above Visitor Info Centre) **604/935-1222, 888/935-1222** • spa & wellness center • yoga studio • lesbian-owned

EROTICA

The Love Nest #102-4338 Main St **604/932-6906**

MANITOBA

Provincewide

PUBLICATIONS

Perceptions 306/244–1930 • covers the
Canadian prairies

Winnipeg

INFO LINES & SERVICES

Rainbow Resource Centre 170 Scott St (at
Wardlaw) 204/474–0212, 204/284–5208 •
1pm-4:30pm Wed-Fri, 7:30pm-10pm Mon-Fri,
clsd wknds • also info line • many social/
support groups

BARS

Club 200 190 Garry St (at St Mary Ave)
204/943–6045 • 4pm-2am, 6pm-midnight
Sun • lesbians/ gay men • dancing/DJ •
karaoke • drag shows • go-go dancers •
wheelchair access

NIGHTCLUBS

The Estate 441 Main St 204/956–5544,
/943–2623 • 9pm-2am Fri, 9pm-4am Sat •
gay-friendly • dancing/DJ • karaoke • multi-
level • theme nights

Gio's Club & Bar 155 Smith St (at York St)
204/786–1236 • 4pm-11pm, till 2am Wed-Sat,
till midnight Sun • lesbians/ gay men •
dancing/DJ • live shows • drag shows •
screened patio

RESTAURANTS

Buccacino's Cucina Italiana 155 Osborne
St 204/452–8251 • 11am-11pm, till 1am Fri,
till midnight Sat, 10am-10:30pm Sun • live
music • full bar • patio

Pizza Place 2140 McPhillips 204/940–6720 •
3pm-10pm, till midnight Fri-Sat

Right There! 472 Stradbrook Ave (at
Osborne) 204/775–5353 • noon-11pm, from
1pm wknds, till 10pm Sun, from 4pm Mon-Tue
• Korean

Step'N Out 157 Provencher Blvd
204/956–7837 • lunch Mon-Fri, dinner Mon-
Sat, clsd Sun • fresh dynamic entrees •
wheelchair access

ENTERTAINMENT & RECREATION

Queer in Your Ear CKUW 95.9 FM
204/786–9782 • 9pm Mon

BOOKSTORES

McNally Robinson 1120 Grant Ave #4000 (in
the mall) 204/475–0483, 800/561–1833 •
9am-10pm, till 11pm Fri-Sat, noon-6pm Sun •
some gay titles • wheelchair access

PUBLICATIONS

Outwords 204/942–4599 • LGBT newspaper

EROTICA

Discreet Boutique 340 Donald (at Ellice)
204/947–1307, 800/247–0454 • also Discreet
Video next door

Dominion News 262 Portage Ave (btwn
Garry & Smith) 204/942–6563 • 8am-9pm,
from 9am Sat, noon-6pm Sun • some gay
periodicals

Love Nest 172 St Anne's Rd 204/254–0422 •
also 1341 Main St, 204/589–4141 • also
Portage & Westwood, 204/ 837–6475

NEW BRUNSWICK

Fredericton

ACCOMMODATIONS

River's Edge Campground 19 Cottage Ln,
Durham Bridge 506/458–1049, 800/370–1644
• lesbians/ gay men • pool • outdoor activities
• gay-owned • camping/ RV hookups • WiFi •
Can$25-32

NIGHTCLUBS

boom! 474 Queen St 506/463–2666 • 8pm-
2am, 4pm-7pm Sun, clsd Mon-Wed • lesbians/
gay men • dancing/DJ

RESTAURANTS

Molly's Cafe 554 Queen St 506/457–9305 •
9:30am-11pm, noon-close Fri-Sun • full bar •
garden patio • some veggie

EROTICA

X-Citement 558 Queen St 506/458–2048 •
videos • magazines • adult novelties

Lower Sackville

EROTICA

X-Citement 295 Sackville Dr 902/864–4159 •
videos • magazines • adult novelties

Moncton

ACCOMMODATIONS

Auberge Au Bois Dormant Inn 67 rue John
(at Birch) 506/855–6767, 866/855–6767 • gay-
friendly • affordable luxury inn • full brkfst •
nonsmoking • WiFi • gay-owned • Can$95-120

NIGHTCLUBS

Triangles 234 St George St (at Archibald) **506/857-8779** • 8pm-2am • lesbians/ gay men • neighborhood bar • dancing/DJ • karaoke Th

RESTAURANTS

Calactus Cafe 125 Church (at St George) **506/388-4833** • 11am-10pm • vegetarian

EROTICA

X-Citement 651 Mountain Rd **506/388-2226** • videos, magazines, adult novelties

Petit-Rocher

NIGHTCLUBS

Club GNG 702 rue Principle, Bloc C **506/783-3277** • 10pm-2am Sat, call for info • lesbians/ gay men • dancing/DJ • 19+

St Andrews

ACCOMMODATIONS

Fairmont Algonquin 184 Adolphus St **506/529-8823, 800/441-1414** • gay-friendly • swimming • kids/ pets ok • $129-499

St John

ACCOMMODATIONS

Mahogany Manor 220 Germain St **506/636-8000, 800/796-7755** • gay/ straight • full brkfst • nonsmoking • kids ok • wheelchair access • gay-owned • Can$100-124

BARS

A Khord 30 Water St **506/657-8474** • 7pm-2am, clsd Sun-Mon • gay-friendly • bar, cafe & gallery • WiFi

NIGHTCLUBS

Happinez Wine Bar 42 Princess St **506/634-7340** • 4pm-midnight, till 2am Fri-Sat • gay-friendly

RESTAURANTS

Opera Bistro 60 Prince William St **506/642-2822** • lunch & dinner

NEWFOUNDLAND

Dildo

ACCOMMODATIONS

George House Heritage B&B 80 Front St **709/582-3170, 888/339-7829** • gay-friendly • full brkfst • nonsmoking • WiFi • Can$129-189

Inn by the Bay 78 Front St **709/582-3170, 888/339-7829** • gay-friendly • full brkfst • nonsmoking • WiFi • Can$99-199

L'Anse aux Meadows

RESTAURANTS

The Norseman Harbour Front **709/623-2018, 877/623-2018** • 9am-10pm seasonally

St George's

ACCOMMODATIONS

The Palace Inn 2 School Rd (at Main St) **709/647-1377, 877/999-1377** • gay-friendly • 19th-c B&B • bay views • $95-135

St John's

ACCOMMODATIONS

Abba Inn B&B 36 Queen's Rd (at Prescott St) **709/754-0058, 800/563-3959** • gay/ straight • full brkfst • fireplaces • nonsmoking • pets ok • Can$75-185

Banberry House 116 Military Rd (at Rawlins Cross) **709/579-8006, 877/579-8226** • gay/ straight • full brkfst • kids/ small pets ok • nonsmoking • $99-169

Bluestone Inn 34 Queen's Rd (at Water St) **709/754-7544, 877/754-9876** • gay-friendly • full brkfst • jacuzzi • gay-owned • also studio apts • Can$89-169

Gower House B&B 180 Gower St (at Prescott St) **709/754-0058, 800/563-3959** • gay/ straight • full brkfst • in downtown • some shared baths • nonsmoking • $75-225

NaGeira House 7 Musgrave St (at Water St) Carbonear **709/596-1888, 800/600-7757** • gay-friendly • B&B • full brkfst • jacuzzi • nonsmoking • kids ok • Can $99-149

NIGHTCLUBS

Zone 216 216 Water St **709/754-2492** • 9pm-close Fri-Sat • lesbians/ gay men • dancing/DJ

RESTAURANTS

Oliver's 160 Water St **709/754-6444** • 11am-10pm, till 11pm Fri, 10am-11pm Sat • building was home to early suffragist Ladies' Reading Room

Zapatas 10 Bates Hill (off Queens Rd) **709/576-6399** • lunch & dinner • full bar • Mexican • some veggie

NOVA SCOTIA

Annapolis

ACCOMMODATIONS

By the Dock of the Bay Cottages 28 Haddock Alley (at Lower Road), Margaretsville **416/588-1500, 800/407-2856** • gay-friendly • lesbian-owned • Can$110-250

Annapolis Royal

ACCOMMODATIONS

Bailey House B&B 150 St George St (at Drury Ln) **902/532-1285, 877/532-1285** • gay/straight • circa 1770 historic waterfront home • full brkfst • nonsmoking • WiFi • Can$100-200

King George Inn **902/532-5286, 888/799-5464** • lesbians/ gay men • full brkfst • jacuzzi • nonsmoking • seasonal • Can$89-299

Antigonish

INFO LINES & SERVICES

Antigonish Women's Resource Centre 219 Main St, Ste 204 (Kirk Place) **902/863-6221** • 9am-4:30pm Mon-Fri • info • support services & programs

Baddeck

ACCOMMODATIONS

The Dunlop Inn **902/295-1100, 888/263-9840** • gay-friendly • waterfront B&B inn • nonsmoking • WiFi • Can$99-160

Cape Breton

ENTERTAINMENT & RECREATION

Rising Tide Expeditions Gabarus Hwy, Gabarus **902/884-2884, 877/844-2884** • Sea kayaking tours

Chester

ACCOMMODATIONS

The Mecklenburgh Inn 78 Queen St **902/275-4638** • gay-friendly • century-old inn constructed by shipwrights • full brkfst • cat on premises • WiFi

ENTERTAINMENT & RECREATION

The Chester Playhouse 22 Pleasant St **902/275-3933, 800/363-7529** • eclectic programming March-Dec

Digby

ACCOMMODATIONS

Harbourview Inn 25 Harbourview Rd (at Hwy 1), Smith's Cove **902/245-5686, 877/449-0705** • gay-friendly • century-old country inn • full brkfst • pool • kids ok • nonsmoking • WiFi • wheelchair access • gay-owned • Can$109-149

Seawinds Motel 90 Montague Row **902/245-2573, 877/245-2570** • gay-friendly • views of Annapolis Basin & Digby Harbour • kids/ pets ok • nonsmoking • gay-owned • Can$114-134

Thistle Down Country Inn 98 Montague Row (at Warwick) **902/245-4490, 800/565-8081** • April-Nov • gay-friendly • full brkfst • kids/pets ok • nonsmoking • gay-owned • Can$105-130

Guysborough

ACCOMMODATIONS

Barrens at Bay Coastal Cottages 6870 Hwy 16 (at Halfway Cove) **902/358-2157** • gay/ straight • jacuzzi • kids/ pets ok • nonsmoking • wheelchair access • gay-owned • Can$150-275

DesBarres Manor Inn 90 Church St **902/533-2099** • gay-friendly • nonsmoking • kids ok • WiFi • Can$149-259

Halifax

ACCOMMODATIONS

Forevergreen House B&B 5560 Hwy 1, St Croix **902/792-1692** • gay-friendly • Victorian farmhouse • full brkfst • nonsmoking • women-owned • $65-85

Fresh Start B&B 2720 Gottingen St (at Black) **902/453-6616, 888/453-6616** • gay-friendly • Victorian mansion • some shared baths • nonsmoking • kids/ pets ok • women-owned • Can$85-120

BARS

Reflections Cabaret 5184 Sackville St (at Barrington) **902/422–2957, 877/422–2957** • 10pm-4am, clsd Tue-Wed • lesbians/ gay men • dancing/DJ • live shows • cabaret • drag shows • wheelchair access

CAFES

Coburg Coffee House 6085 Coburg Rd **902/429–2326** • 7am-9pm

The Daily Grind 5686 Spring Garden Rd (near South Park) **902/429–6397** • 7am-9pm, till 10pm Th-Sat, 8am-6pm Sun • also newsstand

The Second Cup 5425 Spring Garden Rd **902/429–0883** • 7am-11pm, till midnight Th-Sat • internet access

Uncommon Grounds 1030 S Park St **902/431–3101** • 7am-10pm • gay-friendly • WiFi

RESTAURANTS

Chives Canadian Bistro 1537 Barrington St **902/420–9626** • 5pm-9:30pm

Heartwood 6250 Quinpool Rd **902/425–2808** • 11am-8pm, clsd Sun • vegetarian

Jane's on the Common 2394 Robie St **902/431–5683** • lunch Tue-Sat, dinner nightly, Sun brunch, clsd Mon

Satisfaction Feast 3559 Robie (N of Lady Hammond Rd) **902/422–3540** • 10am-9pm • vegetarian • patio

Trinity Restaurant 1333 S Park (near Spring Garden Rd) **902/423–8428** • 11am-9pm • full bar • wheelchair access

ENTERTAINMENT & RECREATION

The Khyber 1588 Barrington St **902/422–9668** • noon-5pm, clsd Sun-Mon • visual & performing arts center

BOOKSTORES

Atlantic News 5560 Morris St (at Queen) **902/429–5468** • 8am-10pm, from 9am Sun • periodicals

Schooner Used Books 5378 Inglis St (at Victoria Rd) **902/423–8419** • 9:30am-5:30pm, till 6pm Fri, clsd Sun • rare & out-of-print books

Smithbooks 5201 Duke St (in Scotia Square) **902/423–6438** • 9:30pm-6pm, till 8pm Th-Fri, clsd Sun

Trident Booksellers & Cafe 1256 Hollis St (at Morris St) **902/423–7100** • 8am-5:30pm, 8:30am-5pm Sat, 11am-5pm Sun • used • popular cafe • WiFi

RETAIL SHOPS

Venus Envy 1598 Barrington St **902/422–0004, 877/370–9288** • 10am-6pm, till 7pm Th-Fri, noon-5pm Sun • "a store for women & the people who love them" • books • sex toys • alternative health products

PUBLICATIONS

Wayves PO Box 34090 Scotia Square B3J 3S1 **902/889–2229** • monthly magazine "for the rainbow community of Atlantic Canada"

EROTICA

Night Magic Fashions 5268 Sackville St **902/420–9309** • clsd Sun • lingerie, toys, videos

X-Citement 6260 Quinpool Rd **902/492–0026** • videos • magazines • adult novelties

Kemptville

ACCOMMODATIONS

Trout Point Lodge 189 Trout Point Rd (off East Branch Rd & Hwy 203) **902/761–2142, 902/761–2142** • gay-friendly • near Tusket River & Tobeatic Wilderness Area • gourmet meal plans • wheelchair access • clsd winter • Can$165-450

Lunenburg

ACCOMMODATIONS

1880 Kaulbach House Historic Inn 75 Pelham St **902/634–8818, 800/568–8818** • gay-friendly • full brkfst • nonsmoking • WiFi • gay-owned • Can$99-169

Atlantic Sojourn B&B 56 Victoria Rd **902/634–3151, 800/550–4824** • gay-friendly • teddy bear museum in lower level • also beautiful garden w/ fish pond • WiFi • women-owned • Can$80-105

New Glasgow

INFO LINES & SERVICES

Pictou County Women's Centre 503 S Frederick St **902/755–4647** • 9am-4:30pm Mon-Fri • support, advocacy & information

North Sydney

ACCOMMODATIONS

Chambers Guest House 64 King St **902/794–7301, 866/496–9453** • gay/ straight • full brkfst • kids/pets ok • nonsmoking • Can$70-100

Scotsburn

ACCOMMODATIONS

The Mermaid & the Cow West Branch
902/351–2714 • lesbians/ gay men • cabin &
20 campsites • dogs ok on leash • pool •
lesbian-owned • $150 (cabin) & $25 (camping)

Tangier

ACCOMMODATIONS

Spry Bay Campground & Cabins 19867
Highway #7 **902/772–2554, 866/229–8014** •
gay/straight • also cafe & convenience store •
lesbian-owned

Windsor

BOOKSTORES

Readers' Haven 40 Water St **902/798–0133**
• 9am-5pm, till 3pm Sat, clsd Sun

Wolfville

RESTAURANTS

Tempest 117 Front St **902/542–0588,
866/542–0588** • lunch wknds, dinner nightly,
clsd Mon • world cuisine

Yarmouth

ACCOMMODATIONS

MacKinnon-Cann Historic Inn 27 Willow St
(at Collins St) **902/742–9900, 866/698–3142** •
gay-friendly • nonsmoking • wheelchair access
• gay-owned • Can$128-195

Murray Manor B&B 225 Main St (at Forest
St) **902/742–9625, 877/742–9629** • gay-
friendly • full brkfst • shared baths • kids ok •
Can$85-139

ONTARIO

Brighton

ACCOMMODATIONS

Apple Manor 96 Main St, Box 11
613/475–0351 • gay-friendly • 150-year-old
Victorian • full brkfst • shared baths •
nonsmoking • $65-85

Burken Cottage 14257 County Rd # 2
613/475–5267 • gay-friendly • nonsmoking •
WiFi • gay-owned • Can$65-75

BOOKSTORES

Lighthouse Books 65 Main St **613/475–1269**
• 9:30am-5:30pm, clsd Sun-Mon

Cobourg

ACCOMMODATIONS

Victoria View B&B Retreat 198 Bagot St
(at Albert) **905/377–0620** • gay/ straight •
1874 heritage home • "an elegant & peaceful
retreat destination" • gay-owned • $130-160

Elora

ACCOMMODATIONS

Log Cabin Heaven 7384 Middlebrook Rd
(at Wellington Rd) **519/846–9439** • gay/
straight • pool • jacuzzi • nonsmoking •
women-owned • Can$195

Gananoque

ACCOMMODATIONS

**Boathouse Country Inn & Heritage Boat
Tours** 17–19 Front St, 1000 Islands, Rockport
613/659–2348, 800/584–2592 • gay/ straight •
full brkfst • nonsmoking • also tavern •
wheelchair access • $75-200

Trinity House Inn 90 Stone St S, 1000
Islands **613/382–8383, 800/265–4871** • gay-
friendly • historic country inn • fine dining
restaurant • nonsmoking • kids ok; call ahead
• sailing charters • gay-owned • Can$99-262

Grand Valley

ACCOMMODATIONS

Rainbow Ridge Resort Country Rd 109 (at
Hwy 25 S) **519/928–3262** • lesbians/ gay men
• trailers & tents • located on 72 acres on
Grand River • pool • restaurant • dance hall •
day visitors welcome • seasonal • pets ok •
gay-owned • Can$15+/ person

Hamilton

ACCOMMODATIONS

BurrBrookHaven 336 8th Concession Rd E
(Centre Rd), Carlisle **905/689–7550** • women
only • country home, single or groups 8-10 •
lesbian-owned • Can$90-120

Cedars Campground 1039 5th Concession
W Rd, Millgrove **905/659–3655, 905/659–7342**
• lesbians/ gay men • private campground •
pool • also bar • dancing/DJ • restaurant
wknds • some veggie • Can$65-95 (cabins),
Can$16 (camping)

Bars

The Embassy Club 54 King St E (at Houston) **905/522-1100** • noon-3am, nightclub from 8pm wknds • lesbians/ gay men • dancing/DJ • transgender-friendly • karaoke • drag shows • videos

The Werx 121 Hughson St N (at Canon) **905/972-9379, 866/796-0701** • 11am-3am • lesbians/ gay men • 3 levels • neighborhood bar • dancing/DJ • karaoke • gay-owned

Erotica

Stag Shop 58 Centennial Pkwy N **905/573-4242** • also 980 Upper James St, 905/385-3300

Kitchener

Nightclubs

Club Renaissance 24 Charles St W **519/570-2406, 877/635-2352** • 9pm-3am, clsd Sun-Tue • lesbians/ gay men • dancing/DJ • food served • drag shows • also billiards lounge

Erotica

Stag Shop 10 Manitou Dr **519/895-1228** • also 30 King St E

London

Bars

Buck Wild Bar 722 York St (at Central Spa) **519/438-2625** • 8pm-close Th-Sat • gay/ lesbian • dancing/DJ • drag shows • karaoke • gay-owned

Nightclubs

Club Lavish 238 Dundas St **519/667-1222** • 9pm-2am clsd Sun-Wed •gay/straight • dancing/DJ • karaoke

Restaurants

Blackfriars Cafe 46 Blackfriars (2 blocks S of Oxford) **519/667-4930** • lunch & dinner, Sun brunch • popular • plenty veggie • full bar

Veranda 546 Dundas St (at William St) **519/434-6790** • dinner nightly, clsd Sun-Mon • gay-owned

Erotica

Stag Shop 1548 Dundas St E **519/453-7676** • also 371 Wellington Rd S, 519/668-3334

Niagara Falls

see also Niagara Falls & Buffalo, New York, USA

Accommodations

Absolute Elegance B&B 6023 Culp St (at River Rd) **905/353-8522, 877/353-8522** • gay/ straight • full brkfst • kids ok • nonsmoking • gay-owned • $100-170

Angels Hideaway 4360 Simcoe St (at River Rd) **905/354-1119** • gay-friendly • full brkfst • jacuzzi • nonsmoking • Can$65-125

Britaly B&B 57 The Promenade (at Charlotte & John), Niagara-on-the-Lake **905/468-8778** • gay-friendly • full brkfst • gay-owned • Can$95-120

Kia-Ora B&B 127 Mary St (at Hwy 55/ Mississauga St), Niagara-on-the-Lake **905/468-1328, 888/208-2340** • gay-friendly • 1843 home • full brkfst • garden • courtesy bikes • nonsmoking • Can$140+

Niagara Inn B&B 4300 Simcoe St (at River Rd) **905/353-8522, 877/353-8522** • gay-friendly • full brkfst • kids ok • nonsmoking • WiFi • gay-owned • $50-105

Stone Boutique Suites 5225 River Rd (at Otter St) **905/357-4366** • gay-friendly • 2 self-contained cottage suites • 10 minutes to falls • nonsmoking • Can$125-135

Oshawa

Nightclubs

Club 717 717 Wilson Rd S #7 **905/434-4297** • 9pm-midnight, till 2am Fri-Sat, clsd Mon-Wed • lesbians/ gay men • dancing • drag shows • also referral service

Erotica

Forbidden Pleasures 1268 Simcoe St N **905/728-0834**

Ottawa

see also Hull, Province of Québec

Info Lines & Services

Pink Triangle Services 251 Bank St #301 **613/563-4818** • many groups & services • library • call for times

Accommodations

Ambiance B&B 330 Nepean St **613/563-0421, 888/366-8772** • gay/ straight • full brkfst • some shared baths • kids ok • nonsmoking • WiFi • lesbian-owned • Can$85-160

Fairmont Château Laurier 1 Rideau St **613/241-1414, 800/441-1414** • gay-friendly • also restaurants • nonsmoking • wheelchair access • Can$189-319

Home Sweetland Home B&B 62 Sweetland Ave (at Laurier Ave) **613/234-1871** • gay/ straight • full brkfst • kids ok • close to tourist attractions • nonsmoking • WiFi • gay-owned • Can$72-125

Inn on Somerset 282 Somerset St W (at Elgin) **613/236-9309, 800/658-3564** • gay/ straight • full brkfst • some shared baths • kids ok • nonsmoking • gay-owned • Can$75-140

Rideau Inn 177 Frank St **613/688-2753, 877/580-5015** • gay-friendly • some shared baths • nonsmoking • gay-owned • Can$70-110

BARS

Centretown Pub 340 Somerset St W (at Bank) **613/594-0233** • 2pm-3am • lesbians/ gay men • dancing/DJ • videos • leather bar upstairs • Silhouette Lounge piano bar Fri-Sat

Collection/ Bar 56 56 Byward Market **613/562-1120** • gay/ straight • popular martini lounge

The Edge 212 Sparks (at Bank) • 10pm-2am • mostly gay men • dancing/DJ • drag shows • young crowd

The Lookout 41 York, 2nd flr (in Byward Market) **613/789-1624** • noon-2am • lesbians/ gay men • more women Fri • food served • wheelchair access • lesbian-owned

Swizzles 246 Queen St **613/232-4200** • 11am-2am • lesbians/ gay men • karaoke • drag shows

NIGHTCLUBS

Mercury Lounge 56 Byward Market Sq (side door upstairs) **613/789-5324** • 8pm-3am, clsd Sun-Tue • popular Wed Hump night party • gay/ straight • dancing/DJ

Zaphod Beeblebrox 27 York **613/562-1010** • 4pm-2am • gay/ straight • neighborhood bar • dancing/DJ • live music

CAFES

Bridgehead Coffee 366 Bank St (at Gilmour) **613/569-5600** • 7am-9pm • gay-owned

RESTAURANTS

Ahora Mexican Cuisine 307 Dalhousie St (below Sweet Art) **613/562-2081** • gay-owned

The Buzz 374 Bank St **613/565-9595** • dinner nightly, Sun brunch • also bar

Elgin Street Freehouse 296 Elgin St **613/233-5525** • lunch Wed-Fri, dinner nightly • full bar • patio

Kinki 41 York St **613/789-7559** • lunch & dinner • Asian fusion • full bar • DJ • live entertainment • patio

Savana Cafe 431 Gilmour St (at Bank) **613/233-9159** • lunch wkdays, dinner nightly • Caribbean • popular patio in summer

Shanghai Restaurant 651 Somerset St W (at Bronson Ave) **613/233-4001** • lunch Tue-Fri, dinner nightly, clsd Mon • also bar • DJ • karaoke

BOOKSTORES

After Stonewall 370 Bank St (near Gilmour) **613/567-2221** • 10am-6pm, till 5pm wknds • LGBT

Mags & Fags 254 Elgin St (btwn Somerset & Cooper) **613/233-9651** • till 10pm • gay magazines

mother tongue books/ femmes de parole 1067 Bank St (at Sunnyside Ave) **613/730-2346, 800/366-0514 (CANADA ONLY)** • 10am-6pm, till 8pm Fri (clsd Sun summer)

RETAIL SHOPS

Venus Envy 320 Lisgar (at Bank St) **613/789-4646** • 11am-6pm, till 8pm Fri, till 7pm in winter, noon-5pm Sun • "a store for women & the people who love them" • books • sex toys • workshops

Wilde's 367 Bank St (at Gilmour) **613/234-5512** • 11am-9pm, noon-6pm Sun • pride items • wheelchair access

PUBLICATIONS

Capital Xtra! **613/237-7133** • LGBT newspaper

To Be Publications **613/236-8888** • LGBT magazine covering Ottawa & Montréal

SEX CLUBS

Breathless 318 Lisgar St (at Bank St, above Venus Envy) • gay/ straight • sexual community center for alternative lifestyles

EROTICA

Wicked Wanda's 382 Bank St **613/820-6032**

Perth

ACCOMMODATIONS

Perth Manor Boutique Hotel 23 Drummond St W (at D'Arcy & Boulton) **613/264-0050** • gay/ straight • boutique hotel • kids/ pets ok • English gardens • nonsmoking • WiFi • gay-owned • Can$145-155

Stratford

ACCOMMODATIONS

A Hundred Church Street 100 Church St **519/272-8845** • gay/ straight • full brkfst • hot tub • some shared baths • nonsmoking • kids 10+ ok • WiFi • gay-owned • Can$90-120

The Maples of Stratford 220 Church St **519/273-0810** • gay-friendly • nonsmoking • some shared baths • woman-owned • Can$65-120

Rundles-Morris House 7-9 Cobourg St **519/271-6442** • lesbians/ gay • full brkfst • WiFi • house rental • gay-owned • Can$595

RESTAURANTS

Down the Street 30 Ontario St **519/273-5886** • 11am-midnight, clsd Mon • popular • int'l • full bar till 2am

Rundles 9 Cobourg St **519/271-6442** • dinner Tue-Sun, lunch wknds • BYOB • wheelchair access • gay-owned

Sudbury

NIGHTCLUBS

Zig's 54 Elgin St (at Elm St) **705/673-3873** • 8pm-close, clsd Mon-Tue • lesbians/ gay men • neighborhood bar • dancing/DJ • transgender-friendly • karaoke • drag shows

Toronto

INFO LINES & SERVICES

519 Church St Community Centre 519 Church St (on Cawthra Park) **416/392-6874** • 9am-10pm, till 5pm wknds • numerous events • LGBT info center • cafe open 10am-3pm Mon-Fri • wheelchair access

AA Gay/ Lesbian **416/487-5591**

Canadian Lesbian/ Gay Archives 34 Isabella **416/777-2755** • 7:30pm-10pm Tue-Th & by appt

ACCOMMODATIONS

1871 Historic House B&B 65 Huntley St (at Selby) **416/923-6950** • gay-friendly • 1871 historic house • full brkfst • nonsmoking • Can$95-145

213 Carlton Street—Toronto Townhouse B&B **416/323-8898, 877/500-0466** • gay/ straight • upscale town house • full brkfst • some shared baths • nonsmoking • WiFi • gay-owned • Can$119-169

312 Seaton 312 Seaton (at Gerrard) **416/968-0775, 866/968-0775** • gay/ straight • B&B • also rental apt • dog on premises • nonsmoking • gay-owned • $95-185

Allenby B&B 351 Wolverleigh (near Danforth & Woodbine) **416/461-7095** • gay-friendly • nonsmoking • shared bath • Can$65+

Banting House Inn 73 Homewood Ave (at Maitland) **416/924-1458, 800/823-8856** • lesbians/ gay men • • nonsmoking • WiFi • gay-owned • Can$85-125

Bonnevue Manor B&B 33 Beaty Ave (at Queen St & Roncesvalles) **416/536-1455** • gay/ straight • B&B • full brkfst • kids ok • nonsmoking • WiFi • Can$99+

Corner Cafe 1150 Queen St W (at Beaconsfield, Drake Hotel) **416/531-5042** • 8am-11pm, till midnight wknds • popular brkfst spot

Drake Hotel 1150 Queen St W (at Beaconsfield) **416/531-5042, 866/372-5386** • gay-friendly • boutique hotel • nonsmoking • Can$189-299

Dundonald House 35 Dundonald St (at Church) **416/961-9888, 800/260-7227** • mostly gay men • full brkfst • hot tub • sauna • gym • bicycles • nonsmoking • gay-owned • Can$80-185

The Gladstone Hotel 1214 Queen St W (at Gladstone Ave) **416/531-4635** • gay/ straight • artistic • nonsmoking • WiFi • Can$185-475 • also Melody bar & cafe

The Grange Hotel 165 Grange Ave (at Queen) **416/603-7700, 888/232-0002** • gay-friendly • kitchenettes • kids ok • Can$95+

Hazelton Hotel 118 Yorkville Ave (at Avenue Rd) **416/963-6300, 866/473-6301** • gay-friendly • luxury property • nonsmoking • Can$395

Hotel Le Germain 30 Mercer St (at Peter St) **416/345-9500, 866/345-9501** • gay-friendly • kids/ pets ok • also restaurant & bar • wheelchair access

House on McGill 110 McGill St (at Church & Carlton) **416/351-1503, 877/580-5015** • gay/ straight • shared baths • nonsmoking • WiFi • gay-owned • Can$55-110

Pimblett's Rest B&B 242 Gerrard St E (at Ontario St) **416/929-9525, 416/921-6896** • Victorian • gay/ straight • full brkfst • hot tub • theme rooms • nonsmoking • gay-owned • Can$85-125

BARS

Andy Poolhall 489 College St (at Markham) **416/923-5300** • 7pm-2am, clsd Sun • gay/ straight • Pop Art pool hall

Baby Huey 70 Ossington Ave (at Humbert St) **416/992-5462** • 7pm-2am • gay/ straight

Beaver Cafe 1192 Queen St W (at Northcote Ave) **416/537-2768** • 10am-2am • lesbians/gay men • DJs • food served • patio • gay-owned

Bistro 422 422 College St (at Bathurst St) **416/963-9416** • 4pm-2am • gay/staright • food served

Toronto

WHERE THE GIRLS ARE:

In "The Ghetto"—south of Bloor St., between Yonge and Parliament. The Cabbagetown area (Parliament St.) is more laid-back, while the intersection of Church & Wellesley is queer ground zero. The West Village draws a younger, mixed crowd.

LGBT PRIDE:

June. 416/927-7433, web: www.pridetoronto.com.

ANNUAL EVENTS:

April - International Gay & Lesbian Comedy & Music Festival 416/907-9099, web: www.were-funnythatway.com.

May - Inside Out: Lesbian & Gay Film & Video Festival 416/977-6847, web: insideout.on.ca.

June - Downtown Jazz Festival 416/928-2033, web: www.toron-tojazz.com.

June - International Dragon Boat Race Festival 416/595-1739, web: www.dragonboats.com.

June - Queer West Arts Festival 416/879-7954, web: www.queer-west.org.

September - International Film Festival 416/968-3456, web: www.tiff.net.

November - Mr Leatherman Toronto Competition, web: www.mrlt.com.

CITY INFO:

800/499-2514, web: www.seetorontonow.com.

BEST VIEW:

The top of one of the world's tallest buildings, of course: the CN Tower. Or try a sight-seeing air tour or a three-masted sailing ship tour.

ATTRACTIONS:

Art Gallery of Ontario 416/979-6648, web: www.ago.net.

Bata Shoe Museum 416/979-7799, web: www.batashoemuseum.ca.

CN Tower 416/868-6937, web: www.cntower.ca.

Dr Flea's International Flea Market 416/745-3532, web: www.drfleas.com.

Gardiner Museum of Ceramic Art, 416/586-8080, web: www.gardinermuseum.on.ca.

Harbourfront Centre 416/973-4000, web: www.harbourfrontcentre.com.

Hockey Hall of Fame 416/360-7765, web: www.hhof.com.

Kensington Market, web: www.kensington-market.ca.

Ontario Place 416/314-9900, web: www.ontarioplace.com.

Rogers Centre 416/341-1707, web: www.rogerscentre.com.

Royal Ontario Museum 416/586-8000, web: www.rom.on.ca.

St Lawrence Market, web: www.stlawrencemarket.com.

Underground City.

WEATHER:

Summers are hot (upper 80°s—90°s) and humid. Spring is gorgeous. Fall brings cool, crisp days. Winters are cold and snowy, just as you'd imagined they would be in Canada!

TRANSIT:

Co-op Taxi 416/504-2667, web: co-opcabs.com.

TTC 416/393-4636, web: www.3ttc.ca.

The Cameron House 408 Queen St W (at Cameron St) 416/703-0811 • 4pm-close • gay/ straight • live music • also theater

The Churchmouse & Firkin 475 Church St (at Maitland) 416/927-1735 • 11am-2am • lesbians/ gay men • English pub • neighborhood bar • leather brunch 3rd Sun

Dakota Tavern 249 Ossington Ave (at Dundas) 416/850-4579 • 5pm-3am • gay-friendly • live country music • bluegrass brunch Sun

George's Play 504 Church St (at Alexander) 416/963-8251 • 11am-2pm • mostly men • drag shows • bingo daily

The Hair of the Dog 425 Church St (at Wood) 416/964-2708 • 11am-2am • gay/ straight • neighborhood pub & restaurant • patio

The House on Parliament Pub 456 Parliament St (at Carlton) 416/925-4074 • 11:30am-2am • gay/ straight • neighborhood bar • food served • patio

LeVack Block 88 Ossington Ave (at Humbert) 416/916-0571 • 5pm-close, from 11am wknds, clsd Mon • gay/ straight • dancing/DJ • also restaurant

Lo'la 7 Maitland (at Yonge) 416/920-0946 • 4pm-2am, from 11am Fri-Sun, clsd Mon-Tue • mostly gay men • dancing/DJ • martini lounge

Melody Bar 1214 Queen St W (at Gladstone Hotel) 416/531-4635 • clsd Mon, more gay Wed • gay/ straight • karaoke • live music

O'Grady's 518 Church St (at Maitland) 416/323-2822 • 11am-2am, till 3am Fri-Sat • gay/ straight • casual dining • huge patio • also lounge upstairs

Pegasus 489-B Church St (at Wellesley, upstairs) 416/927-8832 • 11am-2am • lesbians/ gay men • neighborhood bar

The Raq 739 Queen St W, 2nd flr (at Palmerston) 416/504-9120 • 5pm-1am, from 4pm Th-Sun, clsd Mon • gay/ straight • DJs • upscale pool hall

Slack's Restaurant & Bar 562 Church St (at Wellesley) 416/928-2151 • 4pm-2am, clsd Mon • popular • mostly lesbian • dancing/DJ Fri-Sat • also restaurant • lesbian-owned

Smiling Buddha 961 College St (at Dovercourt) 416/516-2531 • 4pm-2am • gay/ straight • food served • karaoke • cabaret • younger crowd

Snatch 582 Church St (at Dundonald, at Voglie) 416/929-9108 • Sat only • mostly women • dancing/DJ • martini bar • also restaurant • patio

Sneaky Dee's 431 College St (at Bathurst) 416/603-3090 • 11am-3am, from 9am Sun • gay-friendly • live bands • kitchen open late • Tex/Mex

Voglie 582 Church St (at Dundonald) 416/929-9108 • 5pm-close, from 11am Sun, clsd Mon • lesbians/ gay men • women's night Sat • dancing/DJ • martini bar • also restaurant • patio

Woody's/ Sailor 465-467 Church St (at Maitland) 416/972-0887 • 1pm-2am • popular • mostly gay men • neighborhood bar • live shows • drag shows • theme nights • 18+ • wheelchair access

NIGHTCLUBS

The Annex Wreck Room 794 Bathurst St (at Bloor) 416/536-0346 • 10pm-close Fri-Sat only • gay/ straight • dancing/DJ • alternative music venue

Big Primpin' 1279 Queen St W (at Wrongbar) • 10pm 1st Fri • lesbians/ gay men • monthly hip-hop, dancehall, R&B club • check local listings

Cherry Bomb 489 College St (at Andy Poolhall) 416/923-5300 (CLUB#) • 9pm 3rd Fri • mostly women • transgender-friendly • dancing/DJ

The Comfort Zone 480 Spadina Ave (N of College) 416/763-9139 • after-hours wknds only • gay/ straight • dancing/DJ

El Convento Rico 750 College St (at Crawford) 416/588-7800 • 9pm-4am, 7pm-3am Sun, clsd Mon-Th • gay/ straight • dancing/DJ • Latin/ salsa music • mostly Latino • transgender-friendly • drag shows

Fly Nightclub 8 Gloucester St (2 streets N of Yonge & Wellesley) 416/410-5426, 416/925-6222 • open Fri-Sat only • popular • mostly gay men • dancing/DJ • cover charge

Guvernment 132 Queens Quay E (at Lower Jarvis) 416/866-0045 • gay-friendly • dancing/DJ • visiting big-name DJs

Henhouse 1525 Dundas St W (at Dufferin) 416/534-5939 • 6pm-2am, wknd brunch from 10am • gay/ straight • neighborhood bar • food served • lesbian-owned

Lee's Palace/ Dance Cave 529 Bloor St (at Albany) 416/532-1598 • gay/ straight • live bands • dance cave Mon, Th & Sat

The Mod Club 722 College (at Crawford) 416/588-7625 • 9pm Sat • gay/ straight • dancing/DJ

Pacha Lounge 1305 Dundas St W (at Coolmine Rd) 416/530-4781 • check for gay events • gay/straight • dancing/DJ

Pink Mafia • alternative queer & straight events in hip locations • check www.pinkmafia.ca

Straight 553 Church St (at Dundonald) **416/926-2501** • lesbians/gay men • dancing/DJ • sophisticated lounge & dance club

Swagger Productions • parties & events for women of color • check lovinyourswagger.com for details

Tattoo Rock Parlour 567 Queen St W (at Denison) **416/703-5488** • gay/straight • more gay Th for motown, funk & soul

Wrongbar 1279 Queen St W (at Brock) **415/516-8677** • gay/ straight • dancing/DJ • Big Primpin 1st Fri • check listing for other queer events

CAFES

Alternative Grounds 333 Roncesvalles Ave **416/534-5543** • 7am-7pm

Cafe Diplomatico 594 College (at Clinton, in Little Italy) **416/534-4637** • 8am-2am, clsd Mon • Italian

JetFuel 519 Parliament St **416/968-9882** • 7am-8pm

Timothy's 500 Church St (at Alexander) **416/925-8550** • lesbians/gay men • 7am-midnight, till 3:30am wknds

RESTAURANTS

Allen's Restaurant 143 Danforth Ave (at Broadview) **416/463-3086** • lunch & dinner • great scotch selection • Irish music/ dancing • patio

Big Mammas Boy 554 Parliament St **416/927-1593/7777** • 4:30pm-1am, 11am-midnight Sun • organic & gluten free menu • occasional women's dance parties

Black Hoof 938 Dundas St W **416/551-8854** • 6pm-midnight • charcuterie & cheese • not for vegetarians!

Byzantium 499 Church St (S of Wellesley) **416/922-3859** • 5:30pm-11pm, Sun brunch 11am-3pm • mostly gay men • dancing/DJ • patio • gay-owned

Cafe 668 885 Dundas St W **416/703-0668** • lunch & dinner • vegetarian

Commensal 655 Bay St (enter on Elm St) **416/596-9364** • brkfst, lunch & dinner • vegetarian

Easy Restaurant 1645 Queen St W **416/537-4893** • 9am-5pm

Fire on the East Side 6 Gloucester St (at Yonge) **416/960-3473** • noon-1am, 10am-midnight wknds • Southern comfort food • patio

Flo's Diner 70 Yorkville Ave (near Bay St) **416/961-4333** • 7:30am-8pm, till 10pm Th-Sat, from 8am-8pm wknds • gay-owned

Fresh 147 Spadina (at Queen St W) **416/599-4442** • lunch & dinner • vegetarian • patio • also at 894 Queen St W, 416/ 913-2720

Fressen 478 Queen St W (at Denison) **416/504-5127** • dinner nightly, wknd brunch • upscale vegan

Fuzion 580 Church St **416/944-9888** • 5pm-2am, clsd Sun-Mon • also martini bar

Golden Thai 105 Church St (at Richmond) **416/868-6668** • 11:30am-9pm, from 5pm wknds

Il Fornello 1560 Yonge St (1 block N of St Clair) **416/920-7347** • lunch Mon-Fri, dinner nightly, Sun brunch • Italian • plenty veggie • also 214 King W (at Simcoe), 416/977-2855 • also 576 Danforth Ave (at Carlaw), 416/466-2931

Joy Bistro 884 Queen St E **416/465-8855** • 11am-10pm, 8am-4pm wknds • nonsmoking • patio • also Over Joy lounge upstairs 6pm-2am Th-Sat

Kalendar 546 College St **416/923-4138** • 11am-midnight, till 2am Fri-Sat, wknd brunch from 10:30am • eclectic • patio

La Hacienda 640 Queen St W (near Bathurst) **416/703-3377** • noon-1am, from 11am wknds

Mitzi's Cafe 100 Sorauren Ave (at Pearson) **416/532-2570** • 7:30am-4pm, popular wknd brunch from 9am • gay-owned

Mitzi's Sister 1554 Queen St W **416/532-2570** • 4pm-2am, popular wknd brunch from 10am • upscale pub eats • full bar • live music • gay-owned

Naco Gallery Cafe 1665 Dundas St W (at Margueretta St) **647/347-6499** • 8am-2am, from 9am wknds • Mexican-inspired • also gallery & nightclub

Nota Bene 180 Queen St W • lunch Mon-Fri, dinner nightly, clsd Sun • Mediterranean

OddFellows 936 Queen St W **416/534-5244** • 7pm-11pm, brunch wknds 10am-3pm, bar till 2am Fri-Sat

River 413 Roncesvalles Ave **416/535-3422** • dinner Tue-Sun, also lounge till 2am • supports homeless & at-risk youth

Saving Grace 907 Dundas St W (at Bellwoods) **416/703–7368** • brkfst & lunch

Splendido 88 Harbord St (at Spadina) **416/929–7788** • 5pm-10pm, clsd Sun • great decor & gnocchi • full bar • wheelchair access

The Superior Restaurant 253 Yonge St (across from Eaton Centre) **416/214–0416** • 11:30am-11pm, till 9pm Mon, clsd Sun • oysters • full bar • wheelchair access

Supermarket 268 Augusta Ave (at College) **416/840–0501** • dinner only • Thai • also bar w/ DJs

Urban Herbivore 64 Oxford St (at Augusta) **416/927–1231** • 9am-7pm • vegetarian/vegan

The Village Rainbow 477 Church St (at Maitland) **416/961–0616** • 8am-midnight • full bar • WiFi • big patio • wheelchair acccess

Wine Bar 9 Church St **416/504–9463** • 11am-11pm • tapas-style dishes

Xyclo Lounge 459 Church St **416/923–2695** • Vietnamese • also bar • DJs

Zelda's Living Well 692 Yonge **416/922–2526** • noon-10pm, till 1am Fri-Sat from 11am Sat-Sun • popular • lesbians/ gay men • drag shows • full bar • patio

ENTERTAINMENT & RECREATION

AIDS Memorial in Cawthra Park

The Bata Shoe Museum 327 Bloor St W **416/979–7799** • 10,000 shoes from over 4,500 years—including the platforms of Elton John & the pumps of Marilyn Monroe

Buddies in Bad Times Theatre 12 Alexander St (at Yonge) **416/975–8555** • LGBT theater • also Tallulah's cabaret Fri-Sat w/ DJ/dancing

Hanlan's Pt Beach Toronto Islands • nude beach • 10 minutes from downtown

Queer West **416/879–7954** • arts collective • produces annual Queer West Festival

BOOKSTORES

Glad Day Bookshop 598–A Yonge St (at Wellesley) **416/961–4161, 877/783–3725** • 10am-6:30pm, till 9pm Th-Fri, noon-7pm Sat, noon-6pm Sun • LGBT books, mags & videos

This Ain't The Rosedale Library 86 Nassau (at Bellevue) **416/929–9912** • 11am-8pm, till 10pm Fri-Sat, 10am-6pm Sun • LGBT books & magazines

Toronto Women's Bookstore 73 Harbord St (at Spadina) **416/922–8744, 800/861–8233** • 10:30am-6pm, clsd Sun

RETAIL SHOPS

Flatirons 449 Church St (at Alexander) **416/968–9274** • wonderful kitsch & gay gifts

Out on the Street 551 Church St **416/967–2759, 800/263–5747** • 10am-6pm, till 8pm Th-Fri, 11am-6pm Sun • LGBT

Passage Tattoo 473 Church St, 2nd flr **416/929–7330** • noon-7pm, clsd Sun-Mon

Secrets From Your Sister 560 Bloor St W **416/538–1234, 888/868–8007** • 11am-7pm• "beautiful lingerie in realistic sizes for the modern woman" • wheelchair access

Take a Walk on the Wild Side 161 Gerrard St E (at Jarvis) **416/921–6112, 800/260–0102** • "hotel, boutique & club for crossdressers, transvestites, transexuals & other persons of gender"

PUBLICATIONS

The Pink Pages **416/926–9588** • annual LGBT directory

Xtra! **416/925–6665, 800/268–9872** • LGBT newspaper

SEX CLUBS

Pussy Palace Toronto 231 Mutual St (at Carlton, at Club Toronto) **416/925–9872x2115** • occasional women- & trans-only sex club • call for dates & info

EROTICA

Come As You Are 701 Queen St W (at Bathurst) **416/504–7934** • 11am-7pm, till 9pm Th-Fri, noon-5pm Sun • co-op–owned sex store

Good For Her 175 Harbord St (near Bathurst) **416/588–0900, 877/588–0900** • 11am-7pm • women & trans-only hours: noon-5pm Sun • women's sexuality products • wheelchair access

Lovecraft 27 Yorkville Ave (btwn Bay & Yonge) **416/923–7331**

North Bound Leather 586 Yonge (W of Wellesley St) **416/972–1037** • toys and clothing • wheelchair access

Priape 501 Church St () **416/586–9914, 800/461–6969** • popular • clubwear • leather • books • toys & more

Seduction 577 Yonge St **416/966–6969**

Stag Shop 239 Yonge St **416/368–3507** • also 449 Church St, 416/323-0772

Turkey Point

ACCOMMODATIONS

The Point Tent & Trailer Resort 918 Charlotteville Rd #2, RR 1, Vittoria **519/426-7275** • mostly gay men • nudity ok • pool on 50 acres • gay-owned • Can$18-65

Waterloo

ACCOMMODATIONS

Colonial Creekside 485 Bridge St W (at Lexingron) **519/886-2726** • gay/ straight • pool • WiFi • gay-owned • $115-145

RESTAURANTS

Ethel's Lounge 114 King St N (at Spring) **519/725-2361** • 11:30am-2am • full bar • patio

EROTICA

Stag Shop 7 King St N **519/886-4500**

Windsor

see also Detroit, Michigan

ACCOMMODATIONS

University Place Accommodations 3140 Peter St (btwn Sandwich & Mill) **519/254-1112, 866/618-1112** • gay/ straight • nonsmoking • WiFi • wheelchair access • Can$199-399/ week

Windsor Inn on the River 3857 Riverside Dr E (at George Ave) **519/945-2110, 866/635-0055** • gay-friendly • jacuzzi • full brkfst • kids ok • nonsmoking • Can$79-179

BARS

Club 783 783 Wyandotte St E **519/973-4916** • 5pm-2am • lesbians/ gay men • neighborhood bar • karaoke

The Honest Lawyer 300 Ouellette Ave **519/977-0599** • 11am-2am, from 4pm Sun • gay-friendly • food served

Phog 157 University Ave W (at Church St) **519/253-1605** • gay-friendly • food served • art & events

Vermouth 333 Ouellette **519/977-6102** • 4pm-2am, from 6pm Sat, clsd Sun • gay-friendly • popular martini lounge

NIGHTCLUBS

The Loop 156 Chatham St W (at Ferry St) **519/256-9844** • 9pm-2am • gay-friendly • dancing/DJ • alternative • live shows • theme nights • young crowd

Rise 800 Wellington **519/258-7473** • 9:30pm-2:30am Fri-Sat only • lesbians/ gay men • neighborhood bar • dancing/DJ

CAFES

The Coffee Exchange 266 Ouellette **519/971-7424** • 7am-11pm, 8am midnight wknds • WiFi

EROTICA

Stag Shop 2950 Dougall Ave **519/967-8798**

PRINCE EDWARD ISLAND

Albany

ACCOMMODATIONS

Evening Primrose 114 Lord's Pond Rd **902/437-3134** • gay-friendly • full brkfst • nonsmoking • kids/ pets ok • cottage wheelchair access • seasonal • WiFi • lesbian-owned • Can$70/ night (B&B)/ $600/ week (cottage)

Brackley Beach

RESTAURANTS

The Dunes RR #9 **902/672-2586** • 11:30am-10pm • also gallery & art studio

Charlottetown

INFO LINES & SERVICES

Abegweit Rainbow Collective 144 Prince St (in AIDS PEI bldg) **902/894-5776, 877/380-5776** • 24-hour info line, drop-in hrs 6:30pm-7:30pm Mon • monthly dances & other social activities

ACCOMMODATIONS

Blooming Breezes Executive Cottage 108 Lowe Ln, Blooming Point **902/626-4475** • gay/ straight • cottage • close to beach • kids ok • gay-owned • Can$140-250/ night (weekly rates available)

Delta Prince Edward 18 Queen St **902/566-2222, 888/890-3222** • gay-friendly • in heart of Olde Charlottetown • kids/ pets ok • pool • also restaurant

Dunescape Cottages 629 Queen St C1A 9C8 **902/368-3603, 800/719-3603** • gay-friendly • nonsmoking • kids ok • waterfront properties near golf • Can$1,050-2,500/ week

The Great George 58 Great George **902/892-0606, 800/361-1118** • gay-friendly • kids ok • nonsmoking • wheelchair access • gay-owned • Can$155-399

Rainbow Lodge 902/651–2202, 800/268–7005 • lesbians/ gay men • full brkfst • 15 minutes outside of town • nonsmoking • gay-owned • Can$70-90

Rodd Charlottetown Hotel 75 Kent St (at Pownall) 902/894–7371, 800/565–7633 • gay-friendly • pool • sauna • hot tub • kids/ pets ok • WiFi • also restaurant • cont'l/ seafood • lounge clsd Sun

Shipwright Inn Heritage B&B 51 Fitzroy St 902/368–1905, 888/306–9966 • gay-friendly • award-winning inn • central location • full brkfst • nonsmoking • Can$99-299

BARS

Baba's Lounge 81 University Ave 902/892–7377 • noon-2am, 5pm-midnight Sun • gay-friendly • live bands • also Cedars restaurant • Canadian/ Lebanese • some veggie

RESTAURANTS

Off Broadway Restaurant 125 Sydney St (at Queen St) 902/566–4620 • 11am-10pm, till 11pm Fri-Sat • also 42nd Street Lounge

ENTERTAINMENT & RECREATION

Blooming Point Blooming Point • nude beach

BOOKSTORES

Book Mark 172 Queen St (in mall) 902/566–4888 • 9am-8pm, till 9pm Th-Fri, till 5:30pm Sat, noon-5pm Sun • will order lesbian titles

Souris

ACCOMMODATIONS

Johnson Shore Inn RR #3 Rte16 902/687–1340, 877/510–9669 • gay/ straight • country inn on 50 acres • full brkfst • kids 10+ ok • wheelchair access • lesbian-owned • Can$175-350

York

ACCOMMODATIONS

Little York B&B 775 Rte 25 902/569–0271, 800/953–6755 • gay-friendly • 1840 B&B • near beaches & Confederation trail • full brkfst • cats on premises • WiFi • gay-owned • Can$95

Stanhope Beach Resort 3445 Bayshore Rd 902/672–2701, 866/672–2701 • gay-friendly • ocean views • golf • tennis • pool • WiFi • gay-owned

PROVINCE OF QUÉBEC

Bromont

ACCOMMODATIONS

Auberge-Spa Le Madrigal 46 boul Bromont 450/534–3588, 877/534–3588 • gay-friendly • variety of spa treatments available • full brkfst • nonsmoking • Can$130

Drummondville

ACCOMMODATIONS

Motel Alouette 1975 boul Mercure 819/478–4166, 866/478–4166 • gay/ straight • 3-star motel • sauna • hot tub • gay-owned • $80-140

Havre-Aubert

CAFES

Cafe de la Grave 969 ch de la Grave 418/937–5765 • 9am-3pm, from 10am Sun • local LGBT hang-out

Hull

see also Ottawa, Ontario

RESTAURANTS

Le Twist 88 Montcalm St, Gatineau 819/777-8886 • opens 11am daily, full bar

Îles de la Madeleine

ACCOMMODATIONS

La Butte Ronde 70 chemin des Buttes, Havre-aux-Maisons 418/969–2047, 866/969–2047 • gay-friendly • converted country school • near beach • Can$100-140

Joliette

ACCOMMODATIONS

L' Oasis des Pins 381 boul Brassard, St-Paul-de-Joliette 450/754–3819 • lesbians/ gay men • pool • camping May-Sept • restaurant open year-round

La Malbaie

ACCOMMODATIONS

Auberge au Petit Berger 20 rue Desbiens 800/314–4428 • gay-friendly • tennis court • pool • near casino • Can$34-169

Laurentides (Laurentian Mtns)

ACCOMMODATIONS

Auberge de la Gare 1694 chemin Pierre-Peladeau, Ste-Adèle **450/228-3140, 888/825-4273 (IN QUÉBEC ONLY)** • lesbians/gay men • B&B • superb ancestral home • near slopes • pool • Can$60-80

Havre du Parc Auberge 2788 Rte 125 N, St-Donat **819/424-7686** • gay/ straight • quiet lakeside inn for nature lovers • full brkfst • gay-owned • Can$130-150

Le Septentrion B&B 901 chemin St-Adolphe, Morin-Heights/ St-Sauveur **450/226-2665, 866/355-2665** • lesbians/gay men • Victorian • full brkfst • pool • hot tub • sauna • nonsmoking • gay-owned • Can$120-250

Le Bic

ACCOMMODATIONS

Auberge du Mange Grenouille 148 rue Ste-Cecile **418/736-5656** • gay-friendly • May-Oct only • nonsmoking • also restaurant • Can$79-179

Gîte de la Baie Hâtée 2271 Rte 132 E **418/736-5668** • gay-friendly • circa 1820 home decorated w/ antiques • shared baths • Can$65-80

Les Eboulements

RESTAURANTS

Les Saveurs Oubliées 350 rang St-Godefroy (route 362) **418/635-9888** • dinner • specializes in lamb • BYOB • reservations required

Magdalen Islands

ACCOMMODATIONS

Les Réfugiés L'Etang du Nord **418/986-4192** • gay-friendly • B&B • full brkfst • nonsmoking • gay-owned • Can$60-80

Magog

see also Sherbrooke

ACCOMMODATIONS

À Tout Venant 624 rue Bellevue **819/868-0419, 888/611-5577** • gay-friendly • massage • full brkfst • on cycling path "La Route Verte" • near beach & skiing • WiFi • Can$95-130

Au Gîte du Cerf Argenté 2984 chemin Georgeville Rd (off Hwy 10) **819/847-4264** • gay/ straight • B&B in century-old farmhouse • 4 beaches nearby • kids ok • nonsmoking • gay-owned • Can$115-135

Auberge aux Deux Pères 680 chemin des Pères **819/769-3115, 514/616-3114** • gay-friendly • near golf, biking & other outdoor activities • pool • Can$75-130

La Maison Ô Quatre Pattes 30 chemin Gendron **819/847-4195** • gay-friendly • very pet-friendly • shared baths • nonsmoking

Montréal

Note: M°=Metro station

INFO LINES & SERVICES

AA Gay/ Lesbian 514/376-9230 • call for meeting times & locations (in French or English)

Gay/ Lesbian Community Centre of Montréal 2075 rue Plessis, Ste110 (at Ontario) **514/528-8424** • 10am-noon & 1pm-5pm, till 8pm Wed & Fri, clsd wknds • library

Gay Line/ Gai Ecoute 514/866-0103 **(ENGLISH), 888/505-1010 (IN CANADA ONLY)** • 7pm-11pm

The Village Tourism Information Center/ Gay Chamber of Commerce 249 rue St-Jacques #302 **514/522-1885, 888/595-8110** • 10am-6pm, clsd wknds

ACCOMMODATIONS

Abri du Voyageur Hotel 9 rue Ste-Catherine Ouest (at St-Laurent) **514/849-2922, 866/302-2922** • gay-friendly • charming, good-value hotel in downtown Montréal • 15-minute walk to the Village • Can$48+

Absolument Montréal B&B 1790 Amherst (at rue Robin) **514/223-0017, 866/360-1351** • gay/ straight • full brkfst • hot tub • nonsmoking • WiFi • gay-owned • Can $119-259

Alexandre Logan 1631 rue Alexandre DeSève (at Logan) **514/598-0555, 866/895-0555** • gay-friendly • WiFi • Can$99-185

Alexandrie-Montréal 1750 Amherst (at Robin) **514/525–9420** • gay-friendly • also bistro • kids/pets ok • nonsmoking • WiFi • gay-owned • Can$50-200

Angelica Blue B&B 1213 Ste-Elisabeth (at Ste-Catherine) **514/844–5048, 800/878–5048** • gay/straight • full brkfst • some shared baths • nonsmoking • WiFi • Can$75-155

Montréal

WHERE THE GIRLS ARE:
In the popular Plateau Mont-Royal neighborhood or in the bohemian area on Ste-Catherine est.

ENTERTAINMENT:
Info Gay Events Hotline 514/252-4429.
Tourisme Québec www.bonjourquebec.com/gay.

LGBT PRIDE:
July/August. 514/285-4011, web: www.diverscite.org.

ANNUAL EVENTS:
February/March - Festival Montréal en Lumière (Montréal High Lights Festival) 514/288-9955, web: www.montrealenlumiere.com.
June/July - L'International des Feux Loto-Québec (fireworks competition) 514/397-2000, web: www.internationaldesfeux.com.
June - Festival International de Jazz de Montréal 514/871–1881, 888/515-0515, www.montrealjazzfest.com.
July - Festival International Montréal en Arts 514/522-4646, web: www.festivaldesarts.org.
July - Just For Laughs Comedy Festival 888/244-3155, web: www.hahaha.com.
August/September - Montréal World Film Festival 514/848-3883, web: www.ffm-montreal.org.
October - Black & Blue Party 514/875-7026, web: www.bbcm.org. AIDS benefit dance & circuit party.
November - International Gay/Lesbian Film Festival, web: www.image-nation.org.

Harvest Theatre Festival: A cornucopia of diversity in the performance arts, web: www.villagescene.com.

CITY INFO:
514/844–5400, web: www.tourism-montreal.org.

ATTRACTIONS:
Bonsecours Market 514/872-7730, web: www.marchebonsecours.qc.ca.
Latin Quarter.
Montréal Biodome 514/868–3000, web: www2.ville.montreal.qc.ca/biodome.
Montréal Botanical Garden & Insectarium 514/872-1400, web: www2.ville.montreal.qc.ca/jardin.
Montréal Museum of Fine Arts 514/285-2000, web: www.mmfa.qc.ca.
Old Montréal & Old Port.
Olympic Park.
Underground City.

BEST VIEW:
From a caleche ride (horse-drawn carriage) or from the top of the Montréal Tower or from the patio of the old hunting lodge atop Mont Royal.

WEATHER:
It's north of New England so winters are for real. Beautiful spring and fall colors. Summers get hot and humid.

TRANSIT:
Diamond Cab 514/273-6331.
Montréal Urban Transit 514/786–4636, web: www.stcum.qc.ca.

Auberge de la Fontaine 1301 rue Rachel Est (at Chambord) **514/597-0166, 800/597-0597** • gay/ straight • kids ok • WiFi • wheelchair access • Can$119-360

Auberge La Raveaudiere B&B 11 Chemin Hatley Center, North Hatley **819/842-2554, 866/272-2554** • gay/ straight • 19th-c country inn • food seved • 1.5 hours from Montréal • gay-owned • Can$115-160

Auberge le Pomerol 819 boul de Maisonneuve E (at St-Christophe) **514/526-5511, 800/361-6896** • gay-friendly • also restaurant • nonsmoking • WiFi • Can$105-195

B&B Le Cartier 1219 rue Cartier (at Ste-Catherine Est) **514/917-1829, 877/524-0495** • gay/ straight • B&B • newly renovated 100-year-old stone house in Gay Village • WiFi • gay-owned • Can$60-90

B&B Le Terra Nostra 277 rue Beatty (at Lasalle) **514/762-1223, 866/550-5235** • gay-friendly • full brkfst • nonsmoking • WiFi • woman-owned • Can$124-169

Belles Vues B&B 1407 rue Pânet #2 **514/521-9998** • gay-friendly • located in the center of Village • WiFi • Can$80-300

Les Bons Matins 1401 Argyle Ave **514/931-9167, 800/588-5280** • lesbians/ gay men • apt rental • nonsmoking • WiFi • Can$119-399

Brigadoon B&B 29 Main Rd, Hudson **450/458-0233** • gay-friendly • 1 hour from Montréal • full brkfst • nonsmoking • Can$110-125

Le Chasseur B&B 1567 rue St-André (at Maisonneuve) **514/521-2238, 800/451-2238** • gay/ straight • Victorian row house • summer terrace • gay-owned • Can$39-149

Delta Montréal 475 Ave President Kennedy (at City Councilor) **514/286-1986, 877/286-1986** • gay-friendly • hotel • hot tub • pool • kids/ pets ok • restaurant • bar • garden terrace • wheelchair access • Can$165-255

Hôtel Dorion 1477 rue Dorion (at Maisonneuve) **514/523-2427, 877/523-5908** • gay/ straight • in the Gay Village • Can$55-85

Hotel du Fort 1390 rue du Fort (at Ste-Catherine) **514/938-8333, 800/565-6333** • gay/ straight • wheelchair access • Can$135-275

Hotel Dynastie 1723 St-Hubert (at Ontario) **514/529-5210, 877/529-5210** • gay/ straight • nonsmoking • WiFi • gay-owned • Can$68-98

Hôtel Gouverneur Montréal Place Dupuis 1415 rue St-Hubert (at Maisonneuve) **888/910-1111** • gay-friendly • pool • also restaurant & bar • WiFi

Hotel L' St-André 1285 rue St-André (at Ste-Catherine) **514/849-7070, 800/265-7071** • gay/ straight • B&B inn • on edge of Gay Village • kids ok • WiFi • Can$78-148

Hotel La Tour Centre Ville 400 René-Lévesque Blvd Ouest (at Bleurry) **514/866-8861, 800/361-2790** • gay-friendly • pool • non-smoking • Can$70-140

Hotel Lord Berri 1199 rue Berri (at Ste-Catherine) **514/845-9236, 888/363-0363** • gay-friendly • nonsmoking rooms available • also Italian resto-bar • wheelchair access • $99-170

Hotel Manoir des Alpes 1245 rue St-André (at Ste-Catherine) **514/845-9803, 800/465-2929** • gay-friendly • 3-star hotel • WiFi • kids ok • Can$70-100+

Hotel XIXe Siècle 262 rue St-Jacques W (at St Nicolas) **514/985-0019, 877/553-0019** • gay-friendly • also bar and lounge • WiFi • Can$145-325

Jade Blue B&B 1225 Bullion St (at Ste-Catherine) **514/878-9843, 800/878-5048** • gay/ straight • theme rooms • full brkfst • nonsmoking • WiFi • Can$75-155

Lindsey's B&B for Women 3974 Laval Ave (near Duluth) **514/843-4869, 888/655-8655** • popular • women only • charming town house near Square St-Louis & rue Prince Arthur • full brkfst • nonsmoking • WiFi • lesbian-owned • Can$85-155

Loews Hotel Vogue 1425 rue de la Montagne (near Ste-Catherine) **514/285-5555, 800/465-6654** • gay-friendly • full-service 5-star hotel • kids/ pets ok • wheelchair access • Can$169+

La Loggia Art & Breakfast 1637 rue Amherst (at Maisonneuve) **514/524-2493, 866/520-2493** • gay/ straight • nonsmoking • in Gay Village • WiFi • gay-owned • Can$80-195

Montréal Boutique Suite Guesthouse 1269 rue de Champlain (at Ste-Catherine) **514/521-9436, 514/521-3523** • lesbians/ gay men • nonsmoking • WiFi • gay-owned • Can$145-160

Ruta Bagage 1345 rue Ste-Rose (at Panêt) **514/598-1586** • gay/ straight • Victorian B&B • full brkfst • shared baths • Can$70-125

Turquoise B&B 1576 rue Alexandre DeSève (at Maisonneuve) **514/523–9943, 877/707–1576** • mostly gay men • Victorian B&B • shared baths • gay-owned • Can$70-90

BARS

Bar Le Cocktail 1669 Ste-Catherine Est (at Champlain) **514/597–0814** • 11am-3am • lesbians/ gay men • neighborhood bar • karaoke

Bar Rocky 1673 rue Ste-Catherine Est (at Papineau) **514/521–7865** • 10am-close • mostly gay men • videos • older crowd • live shows wknds

Cabaret Mado 1115 rue Ste-Catherine Est (at Amherst, below Le Campus) **514/525–7566** • 11am-3am • popular • lesbians/ gay men • theme nights • dancing/DJ • karaoke • cabaret • drag shows • owned by the fabulous Mado! • wheelchair access

Citibar 1603 Ontario Est (at Champlain) **514/525–4251** • 11am-3am • gay/ straight • neighborhood bar • live shows

Club Bolo 2093 rue de la Visitation (at Association Sportive) **514/849–4777** • 9:30pm-12:30am Fri, special events Sat, T-dance from 3:30pm Sun • lesbians/ gay men • dancing/DJ • country/ western • also lessons • cover charge

Club Date Piano Bar 1218 rue Ste-Catherine Est (at Beaudry) **514/521–1242** • 8am-3am • lesbians/ gay men • neighborhood bar • karaoke nightly • piano

Le Drugstore 1366 rue Ste-Catherine Est (at Panêt) **514/524–1960** • 10am-3am • popular • lesbians/ gay men • 8-bar complex w/ boutiques, restaurants, even travel agency • food served

Foufounes Electriques 87 Ste-Catherine Est (at St-Laurent) **514/844–5539** • 4pm-3am • gay-friendly • dancing/DJ • live bands • patio

Fun Spot 1151 rue Ontario Est (at Wolfe) **514/522–0416** • 11am-3am • lesbians/ gay men • neighborhood bar • dancing/DJ • transgender-friendly • food served • drag shows • karaoke

La Relaxe 1309 rue Ste-Catherine Est, 2nd flr (at Visitation) **514/523–0578** • noon-3am • mostly gay men • neighborhood bar • open to the street • as the name implies, a good place to relax & people-watch

St-Sulpice 1680 rue St-Denis (at Ontario) **514/844–9458** • 11am-3am, till midnight Sun • gay/ straight • 3 flrs • large terrace

NIGHTCLUBS

Beat Me Up 3699 St-Laurent (at Ave des Pins, at Club Saphir) **514/284–5093** • Th only • gay/ straight • popular electronica dance party

Cherry 417 St-Pierre (in Old Montréal) **514/841–9669** • gay/straight • house music party marches into the late, late hours

Circus After Hours 915 rue Ste-Catherine Est **514/844–3626** • 2am-10am Th-Sat only • gay/ straight • dancing/DJ

Cirque du Boudoir **514/789–9068** • quarterly • gay/ straight • opulent theme parties • dancing/DJ • performance

Complexe Sky 1474 rue Ste-Catherine Est (Alexandre de séve) **514/529-6969, 514/529–8989** • 11am-3am • lesbians/ gay men • 3 levels • cabaret & dance club Fri-Sat • T-dance Sun

Faggity Ass Fridays 5656 Ave du Parc (at The Playhouse) • last Fri only • lesbians/ gay men • dancing/DJ • performance • benefits Head & Hands sex ed organization

Meow Mix 4848 Boul St-Laurent (at Sala Rossa) • monthly Sat dance party • mostly women • check listings for dates

Parking Night Club 1296 rue Amherst (at Ste-Catherine) **514/282–1199** • 10am-3am, clsd Tue-Wed • popular • mostly gay men • more women Th • dancing/DJ

Pink 28 • monthly events for professional gay women • check www.pink28montreal.com for details

Red Lite (After Hours) 1755 de Lierre, Laval **450/967–3057** • Fri-Sun only 2am-10am • popular • gay-friendly

Stéréo 858 rue Ste-Catherine Est (at St-Andre) **514/286–0325** • after-hours Fri-Sun only • gay/ straight • cover • popular

Unity II 1171 rue Ste-Catherine Est (at Montcalm) **514/523–2777** • 9pm-close Fri-Sat only • lesbians/ gay men • dancing/DJ • 4 flrs & great rooftoop terrace • live shows • young crowd

CAFES

Cafe Titanic 445 St-Pierre (in Old Montréal) **514/849–0894** • 8am-4:30pm, clsd wknds • popular • salad & soup • WiFi

Kilo 6744 rue Hutchison **514/270–3024, 877/270–3024** • 9am-5pm, clsd wknds • cakes, coffee & light meals

Restaurants

L' Anecdote 801 rue Rachel Est (at St-Hubert) **514/526-7967** • 7:30am-10pm, from 9am wknds • lesbians/ gay men • burgers • plenty veggie

Après le Jour 901 rue Rachel Est (at St-Andre) **514/527-4141** • 5pm-9pm, till 9:30pm wknds • lesbians/ gay men • Italian/ French • seafood • BYOB • wheelchair access

Au Pain Perdu 4489 rue de la Roche **514/527-2900** • 7am-3pm • charming brunch spot in renovated garage

Bato Thai 1310 rue Ste-Catherine Est **514/524-6705** • lunch weekdays & dinner nightly • lesbians/ gay men • beer/ wine

Beauty's 93 Mont-Royal Ouest **514/849-8883** • 7am-4pm, till 5pm wknds • diner/ Jewish deli • worth the wait

La Binerie 367 Mt-Royal **514/285-9078** • brkfst, lunch & dinner • Québecois

Le Cagibi 5490 boul St-Laurent **514/509-1199** • 9am-1am, from 10:30am wknds, 6pm-midnight Mon • vegetarian • also live music & events

Chu Chai 4088 rue St-Denis (at Rachel) **514/843-4194** • lunch & dinner • vegetarian Thai • full bar • wheelchair access

Cluny Art Bar 257 rue Prince (at rue William) **514/866-1213** • 8am-5pm Mon-Fri • Mediterranean

La Colombe 554 Duluth Est **514/849-8844** • 5:30pm-midnight, clsd Sun-Mon • BYOB • French

Commensal 1720 rue St-Denis (at Ontario) **514/845-2627** • 11am-10:30pm, till 11pm Fri-Sat • vegetarian • beer/ wine • wheelchair access

Ella Grill 1237 Amherst **514/523-5553** • upscale Mediterranean/Greek • lesbian-owned

L' Exception 1200 rue St-Hubert (at Réné-Lévèsque) **514/282-1282** • 11am-9pm, clsd wknds • burgers & sandwiches • plenty veggie • terrace

L' Express 3927 rue St-Denis (at Duluth) **514/845-5333** • 8am-3am, from 10am Sat-Sun • popular • French bistro • full bar • great pâté • reservations recommended • wheelchair access

Fantasie 1355 rue Ste-Catherine Est **514/523-3466** • lunch & dinner • sushi • gay-owned

La Strega 1477 rue Ste-Catherine Est **514/523-6000** • 10am-midnight, from 4:30pm wknds • inexpensive Italian • some veggie • wheelchair access

La Paryse 302 rue Ontario Est (near Sanguinet) **514/842-2040** • lunch & dinner, clsd Mon • lesbians/ gay men • '50s-style diner • lesbian-owned

Piccolo Diavolo 1336 rue Ste-Catherine Est (at Panêt) **514/526-1336** • dinner nightly • popular • Italian • wheelchair access

Le Planète 1451 rue Ste-Catherine Est (at Plessis) **514/528-6953** • lunch weekdays & dinner nightly, brunch only Sun • global cuisine • young crowd • beer/ wine

Resto du Village 1310 rue Wolfe **514/524-5404** • 24hrs • "cuisine canadienne"

Saloon Cafe 1333 rue Ste-Catherine Est (at Panêt) **514/522-1333** • dinner nightly, lunch wknds only • plenty veggie • big dishes & even bigger drinks

Santropol 3900 St-Urbain (at Duluth) **514/842-3110** • 11:30am-10pm • unique sandwiches • wheelchair access

Schwartz's Deli 3895 boul St-Laurent **514/842-4813** • 8am-12:30am, till 1:30am Fri, till 2:30am Sat

Thai Grill 5101 boul St-Laurent (at Laurier) **514/270-5566** • lunch Mon-Fri, dinner nightly • one of Montréal's best Thai eateries

Entertainment & Recreation

Ça Roule 27 rue de la Commune Est **514/866-0633, 877/866-0633** • join the beautiful people skating up & down Ste-Catherine

Cinéma du Parc 3575 Av du Parc (btwn Milton & Prince Arthur) **514/281-1900** • repertory film theater

Prince Arthur Est at boul St-Laurent, not far from Sherbrooke Métro station • closed-off street w/ many outdoor restaurants & cafés • touristy but oh-so-European

Retail Shops

Cuir Mont-Royal 826-A Mont Royal Est (at St-Hubert) **514/527-0238, 888/338-8283** • leather • fetish

Priape 1311 Ste-Catherine Est (at Visitation) **514 /521-8451, 800/461-6969** • 10am-9pm, noon-9pm Sun • clubwear • leather • books • toys & more

Screaming Eagle 1424 boul St-Laurent **514/849-2843** • leather shop

PUBLICATIONS

2B • English-language LGBT publication covering Québec

Fugues 514/848–1854, 888/848–1854 • glossy LGBT bar/ entertainment guide

The Mirror 514/393–1010 • free queer-positive weekly • reviews, event listings & more in English

EROTICA

Il Bolero 6846 St-Hubert (btwn St-Zotique & Bélanger) **514/270–6065** • fetish & clubwear emporium • ask about monthly fetish party

North Hatley

see Sherbrooke

Orford

ACCOMMODATIONS

Au Chant du Coq 2387 Chemin du Parc **819/843–2247** • gay-friendly • near cycling, hiking, skiing & other outdoor activities • Can$75-115

Provincewide

INFO LINES & SERVICES

Gay Line/ Gai Ecoute 888/505–1010, 514/866–5090 • 7pm-11pm • transgender-friendly

Québec City

ACCOMMODATIONS

ALT Hotel Québec 1200 av Germain des Prés (at Laurier Blvd), Sainte-Foy **418/658–1224, 800/463–5253** • gay-friendly • hotel • modern & elegant • kids ok • restaurant • wheelchair access • women-owned • Can$129-169

L' Auberge du Quartier 170 Grande Allée Ouest (at av Cartier) **418/525–9726, 800/782–9441** • gay/ straight • kids ok • nonsmoking • Can$89-175

Auberge Place D'Armes 24 rue Ste-Anne (at St-Louis) **418/694–9485, 866/333–9485** • gay-friendly • nonsmoking • WiFi • Can$90-324

Le Château du Faubourg 429A rue St-Jean (at Claire Fontaine) **418/524–2902** • gay-friendly • B&B in château • nonsmoking • also beauty salon • also rental cottage 50 minutes from the city • gay-owned

Le Coureur des Bois Guest House 15 rue Ste-Ursule (at St-Jean, in Old Québec) **418/692–1117, 800/269–6414** • lesbians/ gay men • also apts • shared baths • nonsmoking • gay-owned

Dans les Bras de Morphée 225 chemin Royal, St-Jean-De-L'Ile d'Orléans **418/829–3792, 866/220–4061** • gay/ straight • full brkfst • near beach • pool • kids ok • WiFi • Can$125-158

Gîte aux Deux Lions 25 boul René-Lévesque Est (at Ave Salaberry) **418/780–8100, 877/777–9444** • gay-friendly • cozy B&B in refined 1909 home • WiFi • Can$149-209

Hôtel Dominion 1912 126 rue St-Pierre (at Marché Finlay) **418/692–2224, 888/833–5253** • gay-friendly • boutique hotel in city's 1st skyscraper • pets ok • wheelchair access

Hotel Le Clos Saint-Louis 69 St-Louis (at St-Ursule) **418/694–1311, 800/461–1311** • gay/ straight • small Victorian-style boutique hotel located in historic district near shops & restaurants • nonsmoking • WiFi • Can$175-305

Hôtel-Motel Le Voyageur 2250 boul Ste-Anne (at Estimauville) **418/661–7701, 800/463–5568** • gay/ straight • pool • kids ok • restaurant & bar • WiFi • Can$79-120

Loews Le Concorde 1225 cours du Général De Montcalm (at Grande Allée E) **418/647–2222, 800/463–5256** • gay-friendly • located on Grand Allée • pool • kids/ pets ok • revolving restaurant • WiFi • wheelchair access • Can$119-334

Maison du Cocher 31 rue Dauphine (at Ste-Ursule) **418/261–6610, 888/694–1388** • gay-friendly • historic-style apts & coach house • WiFi • Can$140

Le Moulin de St-Laurent Chalets 754 chemin Royal, St Laurent, Ile d' Orleans **418/829–3888, 888/629–3888** • gay/ straight • cottages • pool • kids/ pets ok • also restaurant • nonsmoking • Can$110-270

BARS

889/ Bar St Matthew's 889 côte Ste-Geneviève (at St-Gabriel) **418/524–5000** • 11am-3am • lesbians/ gay men • neighborhood bar • patio

L' Alterno 1018 rue St-Jean (at Ste-Ursule)

Bar Le Drague 815 rue St-Augustin (at St-Jean) 418/649–7212 • 10am-3am • popular • mostly gay men • neighborhood bar • dancing/DJ Thu-Sun • food served • karaoke • cabaret • drag shows • terrace • wheelchair access

RESTAURANTS

Le Commensal 860 rue St-Jean 418/647–3733 • 11am-9pm, till 10pm Th-Sat • vegetarian/ vegan

Le Hobbit 700 rue St-Jean (at Ste-Geneviève) 418/647–2677 • 9am-10pm • some veggie

Le Moulin de St-Laurent Restaurant 754 chemin Royal, St Laurent, Ile d' Orleans 418/829–3888 • lunch & dinner, May-Oct only • live music Sun

La Piazzetta 707 rue St-Jean 418/529–7489 • 11am-10:30pm, till 11pmFri-Sat

Le Poisson d'Avril 115 quai St-André (at St-Thomas) 418/692–1010, 877/692–1010 • 5pm-close • name is French for "April Fools"

Vertige 540 Ave Duluth E 514/842–4443 • 5pm-10pm, till 11pm Fri-Sat, clsd Sun

ENTERTAINMENT & RECREATION

Fairmont Le Château Frontenac 1 rue des Carrières 418/692–3861, 800/257–7544 • this hotel disguised as a castle remains the symbol of Québec—even if you can't afford the princess' ransom to stay the night, come & enjoy the view from outside

Ice Hotel /Hôtel de Glace 75, Montée de l'Auberge, Pavillon Ukiuk, Sainte-Catherine-de-la-Jacques-Cartier 418/875–4522, 877/505–0423 • sometimes getting put on ice isn't a bad thing—check this gay-friendly hotel out before it melts away, 9 km E of Québec City in Montmorency Falls Park (Jan-March only)

PUBLICATIONS

2B • English-language LGBT publication covering Québec

EROTICA

Importation André Dubois 46 côte de la Montagne (at Frontenac Castle) 418/692–0264 • transgender-friendly • wheelchair access

Québec City

ENTERTAINMENT:
Tourisme Québec web: www.bonjourquebec.com/gay.

LGBT PRIDE:
September. 418/809–3383.

ANNUAL EVENTS:
January/February - Carnaval (Winter Celebration) 866/422-7628, web: www.carnaval.qc.ca.
July - Summer Festival 888/992–5200, web: www.infofestival.com.

CITY INFO:
877/266–5687 and 514/873–2015, web: www.bonjourquebec.com.

ATTRACTIONS:
Change of Guards at the Citadel.
Château Frontenac 418/692-3861, web: www.fairmont.com/frontenac.
Grand Allée.
Hôtel du Parlement.
Musée de la Civilisation 418/643-2158, web: www.mcq.org.
Notre-Dame-de-Québec Basilica.
Old Québec.
Quartier du Petit-Champlain 418/692-2613, web: www.quartierpetitchamplain.com

TRANSIT:
Taxi Québec 418/525-8123.
Autobus La Quebecoise 888/872-5525, web: www.autobus.qc.ca
RTC (bus service) 418/627-2511, web: www.rtcquebec.ca.

Sherbrooke

NIGHTCLUBS

Complex 13–17 13–15–17 Bowen Sud (at rue King) **819/569–5580 (SAUNA), 819/562–2628 (CLUB)** • 11am–3am • lesbians/ gay men • dancing/DJ • pub & dance club • strippers Fri-Sun • lesbian bar downstairs • also sauna

St-Ferréol-les-Neiges

ENTERTAINMENT & RECREATION

Les Sept Chutes 4520 Ave Royale **877/725–8837, 418/826–3139** • historical village w/ hiking trails

St-Georges-de-Beauce

BARS

Bar L'Envol 11270 1ère Ave, 5th flr, St-Georges **418/227–5550** • 5pm–3am Wed-Sat, 3pm-midnight Sun • lesbians/ gay men • dancing/DJ • drag shows

St-Hyacinthe

BARS

Bar L'Illusion 460 ave Mondor **450/252–4011** • 4pm–3am Wed-Sun • dancing/DJ • patio (summer)

St-Joachim

ENTERTAINMENT & RECREATION

Cap Tourmente 570 chemin du Cap-Tourmente **418/827–4591** • nat'l wildlife area

Ste-Anne-de-la-Pérade

ACCOMMODATIONS

Auberge à l'Arrêt du Temps 965 boul de Lanaudière **418/325–3590, 877/325–3590** • gay-straight • 18th-c mansion • nonsmoking • gay-owned • also restaurant • Can$75-150

Trois Rivières

ACCOMMODATIONS

Le Gîte du Huard 42 rue St-Louis **819/375–8771** • gay-friendly • B&B • Can$65-132

SASKATCHEWAN

Provincewide

PUBLICATIONS

Perceptions 306/244–1930 • covers the Canadian prairies

Ravenscrag

ACCOMMODATIONS

Spring Valley Guest Ranch 306/295–4124 • popular • gay/ straight • 1913 character home • also cabin • full brkfst • kids/ pets ok • nonsmoking • also restaurant • country-style • gay-owned • Can$55-75

Regina

INFO LINES & SERVICES

The Gay & Lesbian Community of Regina 2070 Broad St (at Victoria) **306/569–1995, 306/522–7343** • 4pm-2am

NIGHTCLUBS

The OUTside 2070 Broad St (at Victoria, at Gay Center) **306/569–1995** • 5pm–3am, from 8pm Sun-Wed • lesbians/ gay men • dancing/DJ

RESTAURANTS

Abstractions Cafe 2161 Rose St **306/352–5374** • 9am-6pm, from 11am Sat, clsd Sun • some veggie

The Creek in Cathedral Bistro 3414 13th Ave **306/352–4448** • lunch & dinner, clsd Sun • contemporary

Pacific Fresh Fish 3005 13th Ave (at Robinson) **306/525–9147**

Saskatoon

INFO LINES & SERVICES

Avenue Community Centre 201-320 21st S W **306/665–1224, 800/358–1833** • 10am-5pm, till 9pm Wed-Fri, clsd wknds • library • many social/ support groups • queer gift store

Circle of Choice Gay/ Lesbian AA 505 10t St E (at Grace Westminster United Church) **306/665–5626** • 8pm Wed

NIGHTCLUBS

Diva's 220 3rd Ave S #110 (alley entrance) **306/665–0100** • 8pm-2am, till 3am wknds, clsd Mon-Tue • lesbians/ gay men • dancing/DJ • drag shows • private club (guest welcome)

RESTAURANTS

2nd Ave Grill 10-123 2nd Ave **306/244-9899** • 11am-11pm, 5pm-9pm Sun

The Berry Barn 830 Valley Rd **306/978-9797** • open daily • seasonal • home-style eatery w/ views of river

The Ivy Dining & Lounge 24th St E & Ontario St **306/384-4444** • lunch & dinner Mon-Fri, dinner only Sat-Sun

Prairie Ink 3130 8th St E **306/955-3579** • 9am-10pm, till 11pm Fri-Sat, 10am-9pm Sun • also bookstore & cafe

Seasons Cafe & Eatery 102 Cardinal Crescent (at Heritage Inn) **306/665-8121, 888/888-4374** • 6:30am-10pm, 6am-11pm Fri-Sat, 7am-9pm Sun • fresh soups & salad bar

ENTERTAINMENT & RECREATION

AKA Gallery 424 20th St W **306/652-0044** • noon-6pm, clsd Sun-Mon • contemporary art & performance

Bridge City Chorus • LGBT chorus

Rainbow Radio **306/664-6678** • 9:30pm Sun

BOOKSTORES

Turning the Tide 525 11th St E **306/955-3070** • noon-8pm, till 10pm Th-Sat, till 5pm Sun • Saskatoon's alternative bookstore

RETAIL SHOPS

The Trading Post 226 2nd Ave S **306/653-1769** • 10am-5:30pm, clsd Sun • clothing

YUKON

Whitehorse

INFO LINES & SERVICES

Victoria Faulkner Women's Centre 503 Hanson St **867/667-2693** • drop-in centre • 11am-3pm, 3pm-9pm Th, clsd wknds • wheelchair access

ACCOMMODATIONS

Inn on the Lake **867/660-5253** • gay-friendly • luxury lakefront log inn • Canada Select rated 4.5 stars • nonsmoking • WiFi • pets ok • Can$135-290

BAHAMAS

Nassau

NIGHTCLUBS

Club Waterloo E Bay St (1/2 mile E of Paradise Island Bridge) 242/393-7324 • 4pm-close • gay-friendly • more women Th • indoor/outdoor complex w/ 5 bars • dancing/DJ • live music • restaurant • swimming

BARBADOS

Bridgetown

RESTAURANTS

The Waterfront Cafe The Careenage 246/427-0093 • 10am-midnight, clsd Sun • trendy • also bar • live music • outdoor seating

BRITISH VIRGIN ISLANDS

see also US Virgin Islands

Tortola

ACCOMMODATIONS

Fort Recovery Villa Beach Resort Road Town, Tortola 284/495-4467, 800/367-8455 (WAIT FOR RING) • gay-friendly • grand home on beach & private beachfront villas • pool • kids ok • wheelchair access • women-owned • $185-950

DOMINICAN REPUBLIC

Boca Chica

ACCOMMODATIONS

Costalunga 3 Av del Sur 809/523-6883 • gay-friendly • closest beach to Santo Domingo

Puerto Plata

ACCOMMODATIONS

Casa de la Luna La Catalina Cabrera (at Calle 5) 809/589-7711 • gay/straight • villa rental close to La Playa Grande Beach • $550-1100 per week

Tropix Hotel 809/571-2291 • gay-friendly • full brkfst • garden setting near center of town & beach • pool • kids/pets ok • lesbian & gay-owned • $55-70

Santo Domingo

ACCOMMODATIONS

Camilo House Apartments Calle Padre Billini 455, Zona Colonial (btwn Palo Hincado & Pina) 809/221-1842, 809/768-5461 • apts w/in walking distance of historical architecture, gay nightlife, restaurants & the seaside boulevard • $70

Caribe Colonial Hotel Isabel Catolica 159 809/688-7799 • gay-friendly • boutique hotel

Foreigners Club Hotel 102 Calle Canela (at Estrelleta) 809/689-3017 • lesbians/gay men • nonsmoking • WiFi • wheelchair access • gay-owned • $50-60

Hotel Aida Calle El Conde 464 809/685-7692 • gay-friendly

Hotel Venezia Av Independencia 45 (Gazcue) 809/682-5108 • gay-friendly

BARS

Esedeku 341 Mercedes (at Santome) 809/869-6322 • 8pm-close, from 5pm Sun, clsd Mon • lesbians/gay men • food served

Jay Dee's Jose Reyes 10, Zona Colonial 809/335-5905 • 9pm-4am • mostly gay men • neighborhood bar • strippers • videos

Parios Bar 51 Arzobispo Nouel (at Jose Reyes) 809/803-5100 • mostly men • multiracial • neighborhood bar

NIGHTCLUBS

Cha Av George Washington 165 (btwn Lincoln & Maximo Gomez) • Fri-Sun only • mostly men • dancing/DJ • drag shows • performance • opened by local gay celebrity Chachita Rubio

Gazela Club Av Bolivar 72 (at Dr Delgado)

RESTAURANTS

El Conuco 152 Casimiro de Moya (behind Jaragua Hotel) 809/686-0129 • touristy local landmark

DUTCH & FRENCH WEST INDIES

Aruba

BARS

Jimmy's Place Kruisweg 15 (at Digicel), Oranjestad 297/582-2550 • 5pm-2am, till 4am Fri-Sat, from 8pm Sun, clsd Mon • neighborhood bar • dancing/DJ • food served

The Paddock LG Smith Blvd #13, Oranjestad 297/583-2334, 297/583-2606 • 10am-2am • gay/straight • neighborhood bar • food served

RESTAURANTS

Cafe the Plaza Seaport Marketplace, Oranjestad **297/583–8826** • 10am-2am • lunch & dinner

Barbados

ACCOMMODATIONS

Gemini House B&B 70 Plover Court, Inch Marlow, Christ Church **246/428–7221** • gay-friendly • WiFi • $65-85

Inchcape Seaside Villas Silver Sands **246/428–7006** • private villa rentals • WiFi • $95-500

Bonaire

ACCOMMODATIONS

Coco Palm Garden/ Casa Oleander Kaya Statius van Eps 9 **599/717–2108** • gay/ straight • studios, apts & houses • pool • wheelchair access • $66-86

Ocean View Villas Kaya Statius van Eps 6 **599/717–6105** • gay/ straight • luxury apts w/ secluded patios & outdoor showers • WiFi • gay-owned • $80-140

Curaçao

ACCOMMODATIONS

The Avila Beach Hotel 130 Penstraat, Willemstad **800/747–8162 (FROM US & CANADA)** • gay-friendly • $170-275

Floris Suite Hotel Piscadera Bay **800/781–1011 (IN US & CANADA), 5999/462–6111** • gay-friendly • $160-285

Kura Hulanda Langestraat 8, Willemstad **888/264–3106 (FROM US & CANADA), 5999/434–7700** • gay-friendly • also Jacob's Bar • $210-1,000

Lodge Kura Hulanda & Beach Club Langestraat 8 (Willemstad) **5999/434–7700, 877/264–3106** • gay-friendly • pool • diving lessons

Papagayo Beach Resort Willemstad **800/652–2962 (FROM US), 5999/747–4333** • gay-friendly

BARS

Cafe De Heeren Zuikertuintjeweg 1 **599/736–0491** • 9am-1am, till 2:30 Th-Fri, clsd Sun • gay/straight • live shows • also restaurant

NIGHTCLUBS

Cabana Beach at Seaquarium Beach **599/946–5158** • open Wed-Sat • gay/straight • dancing/DJ • also restaurant

Tu Tu Tango Plasa Mundo Merced, Punda **5999/465–4633** • 11pm-4am • more gay Fri • also restaurant

RESTAURANTS

Mambo Beach Bapor Kibra, Seaquarium Beach **5999/461–8999** • 9am-midnight, till 4am Sat • full bar • more gay Sat

ENTERTAINMENT & RECREATION

Cas Abao Beach • gay-friendly • popular local beach

Dolphin Academy at Curaçao Aquarium, Bapor Kibra z/n (east of Willemstad, at Sea Aquarium Park) **5999/465–8900, 5999/465–8300** • swim w/ dolphins!

Jan Thiel Beach • good people-watching

Museum Kura Hulanda Klipstraat 9, Willemstad **5999/434–7765** • African history & culture • Antillean art

Saba

ACCOMMODATIONS

Juliana's Hotel Windwardside **599/416–2269, 888/289–5708** • gay/ straight • pool • hot tub • full brkfst • ocean & garden views • also Saban-style cottages • kids ok • WiFi • $85-255

Shearwater Resort Cliff Side (Booby Hill) **589/416–2498** • gay-friendly • full brkfst • pool • nonsmoking • WiFi • also restaurant • gay-owned • $195-345

RESTAURANTS

Rainforest Restaurant Windwardside **599/416–3888, 599/416–5507** • brkfst, lunch & dinner • full bar

Restaurant Eden The Road (Windwardside), Windwardside **599/416–2539** • 5:30pm-9:30pm, clsd Tue

St Barthélemy

ACCOMMODATIONS

Hotel le Village St-Jean St-Jean Hill **590–590/27–61–39, 800/651–8366** • gay-friendly • hotel & cottages • pool • € 110-190 (rooms), € 145-570 (cottages), € 570-850 (villas)

Hotel Normandie Quartier Lorient **590–590/27–61–66** • gay-friendly • $125-175

Hotel St-Barth Isle De France Plage des Flamands **508/528–7727, 800/421–3396** • gay-friendly • ultraluxe hotel • € 495-2450

NIGHTCLUBS

Le Sélect Gustavia **590–590/27–86–87** • gay-friendly • more gay after 11pm

RESTAURANTS

Le Grain de Sel Grand Saline Beach **590/524–605** • lunch & dinner, clsd Mon • relaxing & open setting • ideal before & after sunbathing

ENTERTAINMENT & RECREATION

Anse Gouverneur St-Jean Beach • nudity

Anse Grande Saline Beach • nudity • gay section on the left side of Saline

Orient Beach • gay beach

St Maarten

See also St Martin

ACCOMMODATIONS

Blue Ocean Villas 352/505–2805 • private villa rentals • $2,000-3,000

Holland House 43 Front St, Philipsburg **599/542–2572** • gay-friendly • on the beach • restaurant • bar • $109-365

RESTAURANTS

Cheri's Cafe Rhine Rd #45 (Maho Reef) **599/54–53–361** • 11am-1:30am, clsd Tue • full bar • dancing • live music • touristy • wheelchair access

St Martin

see also St Maarten

ACCOMMODATIONS

Orient Bay Hotel & Jardins de Chevrise Mont Vernon 1 **59-0590/87–31–10** • gay-friendly • studios • 1- & 2-bdrm villas • pool • steps from St-Martin's most beautiful clothing-optional beach • $115-395

BARS

Tantra Rhine Road, Maho Bay, Marigot (at the Marina Royale) **599/545–2861** • 6pm-close • lesbians/ gay men

RESTAURANTS

L' Escapade 94 Blvd de Grand Case **590–590/87–75–04** • French • some veggie • reservations recommended

Le Pressoir 30 Blvd de Grand Case **590–590/87–76–62** • dinner nightly, clsd Sun • French

JAMAICA

Montego Bay

ACCOMMODATIONS

Half Moon Golf, Tennis & Beach Club **876/953–2211, 866/648–6951** • gay-friendly • upscale resort • $205-1520

Negril

ACCOMMODATIONS

Seagrape Villas The Cliffs, West End Rd **831/625–1255 (US#)** • gay/ straight • 3 seafront villas • excellent sunsets • teens ok • $120-275

Ocho Rios

ACCOMMODATIONS

Golden Clouds Villa North Coast Rd, Oracabessa **941/922–9191, 888/625–6007** • gay-friendly • private estate • full brkfst • fully staffed • jacuzzi • pool • kids ok • wheelchair access • gay-owned • $9,200-16,000/ week

Port Antonio

ACCOMMODATIONS

Hotel Mocking Bird Hill **876/993–7267, 876/993–7134** • gay-friendly • eco-friendly inn • fresh local food served • pool • massage • kids ok • wheelchair access • lesbian-owned • $135-260

Westmoreland

ACCOMMODATIONS

Moun Tambrin Retreat set in the mtns 28 miles from Montego Bay **876/437–4353, 876/357–6363** • gay/ straight • art deco estate • food served • pool • $100-150 per person

PUERTO RICO

Please Note: For those with rusty or no Spanish, "carretera" means "highway" and "calle" means "street."

Aguada

BARS

Franky's Bar Carr 115 en el Bo Asomante • lesbians/ gay men • dancing/DJ • drag shows

Baja Sucia

ENTERTAINMENT & RECREATION

Playa Sucia S of Cabo Rojo Nat'l Wildlife Refuge, Guanica • beautiful, secluded beach

Boqueron

BARS

El Schamar Bar at corner of Muñoz Rivera & Jose de Diego **787/851-0542** • mostly gay men • drag shows • also hotel • gay-owned

Sunset Sunrise Cabo Rojo **787/255-1478** • 10am-close • gay/straight

Cabo Rojo

ENTERTAINMENT & RECREATION

Gay Pride • 2nd wknd in June

Camuy

BARS

Distortion Carr 119 Norte, KM 7.6 (Barrio Membrio) **787/614-3404** • 10pm Sat only • lesbians/gay men • dancing/DJ • swimming

Ceiba

ACCOMMODATIONS

Ceiba Country Inn Carretera 977 **787/885-0471, 888/560-2816** • gay-friendly • dramatic ocean views • also bar • 15 minutes to Vieques/Culebra ferry • WiFi • gay-owned • $85

Guanica

ENTERTAINMENT & RECREATION

Gilligan's Island take Rd 333 to Copamarina Resort, then take ferry to island • beautiful beach located in a biosphere on Southern coast of PR

Guaynabo

NIGHTCLUBS

Pride Night at Club Eggo Carazo 53 **787/708-4982** • gay/straight • gay night Wed only

Mayaguez

BARS

Cafe Nova Ley Calle Munoz Rivera 15 • gay/straight • dancing/DJ • drag shows • live music • karaoke • art gallery

Rincon

ACCOMMODATIONS

Bunger's Bon-Accord Barrio Buntas Carr 413, km 3.3 Int, Sector Sandy Beach **787/823-2525, 866/461-8936** • gay/straight • pool • jacuzzi • also restaurant • near beach • wheelchair access • $110-200

Horned Dorset Primavera Hotel Apartado 1132 **800/633-1857** • gay/straight • swimming pool • kids welcome over age 12

Lemontree Oceanfront Cottages Carr 429, km 4.1 (at Carr 115) **787/823-6452, 888/418-8733** • gay/straight • kids ok • nonsmoking • WiFi • wheelchair access • $100-250

San Juan

ACCOMMODATIONS

Acacia Seaside Inn 8 Taft St (at McLeary) **787/727-0668, 800/946-3244** • gay-friendly • hotel • kids ok • pool • WiFi • $80-210

At Wind Chimes Inn 1750 McLeary Ave, Condado (at Taft) **787/727-4153, 800/946-3244** • gay-friendly • restored Spanish villa • pool • kids/pets ok • nonsmoking • WiFi • wheelchair access • $65-185

Caribe Mountain Villas Carr 857, km 6.0, Carolina **787/769-0860** • gay-friendly • resort in rain forest (25 miles from San Juan) • pool • gay-owned • $100-225

Casa del Caribe Guest House Calle Caribe 57, Condado (at Magdalena) **787/722-7139, 877/722-7139** • gay-friendly • B&B in heart of Condado • kids ok • nonsmoking • WiFi • $50-125

La Concha 1077 Ashford Ave, Condado **787/721-7500** • gay/straight • retro urban showcase & architectural landmark • restaurants & bar

Condado Inn Av Condado 6 (at Av Ashford) **787/724-7145** • mostly men • near beach • also bar • gay-owned • $59-79

Coqui del Mar 2218 Calle General del Valle (at General Patton, Ocean Park) **727/220-4204** • gay-friendly • full kitchens • gay-owned • $65-

Hotel El Convento Calle Cristo 100, Old San Juan (btwn Caleta de las Monjas & Calle Sol) **787/723-9020, 800/468-2779** • popular • gay-friendly • 17th-c former Carmelite convent • pool • WiFi • gym • $265+

Miramar Hotel 606 Ave Ponce de Leon (at Miramar) 787/977–1000 • gay-friendly • WiFi • also restaurant & bar • $109-195

Normandie Hotel 199 W Muñoz Rivera Ave 787/729–2929 • gay-friendly • art deco hotel • also restaurant & lounge • WiFi

Numero Uno on the Beach Calle Santa Ana 1, Ocean Park (near Calle Italia) 787/726–5010, 866/726–5010 • gay/ straight • pool • kids ok • also Pamela's • full bar & grill • wheelchair access • $89-279

Ocean Hostal Playero 1853 McLeary Ave, Condado (at Calle Atlantic Pl) 787/728–8119 • gay/ straight • budget accommodations • great beach location • nonsmoking • vegetarian restaurant

The San Juan Water & Beach Club Hotel 2 Tartak St (Isla Verde), Carolina 787/728–3666, 888/265–6699 • gay-friendly • boutique hotel on the beach • restaurant & lounge • kids ok • rooftop pool • nonsmoking • WiFi • wheelchair access • $139-599

Studio by the Sea 1123 Calle Seaview 2B (at Ashford) 787/525–9398 • gay/ straight • full kitchens •WiFi • gay-owned • $90/ night, $600/ week

Bars

Angelu's Cafe Calle Eleanor Roosevelt 239, Hato Rey • clsd Sun-Mon • mostly women • neighborhood bar

Cafe Bohemio Calle Cristo 100, Old San Juan (in Gran Hotel El Convento) 787/723–9202 • 11am-2am, clsd Wed • gay-friendly • professional crowd • more gay Tue • live music Th-Sat • also restaurant • food served till 11pm

Cups Bar & Lounge Calle San Mateo 1708 (btwn Calles Barbe & San Jorge), Santurce 787/594–2317, 787/513–5672 • 7pm-close, from 8pm Sat, clsd Sun-Tue • popular • mostly women • dancing/DJ • live music • karaoke

Esechys 478 Calle Jose Canals (near Calle Rodrigo de Triana, Placita Roosevelt), Hato Rey 787/636–7268 • open Tue-Sun • mostly women • live music Fri

Rabanal Petit Club 1700 Ave Ponce de Leon (at Hotel San Jorge), Santurce 787/390–0336 • 6pm-close Tue-Sun • mostly gay men • neighborhood bar

Starz/ Fice Bar 365 Ave Jose de Diego (at Ponce de Leon), Santurce 787/531–1818, 787/593–3645 • lesbians/ gay men • dancing/DJ • transgender-friendly • drag shows • strippers • also Fice bar on 3rd floor terrace level

Tia Maria's 326 Ave Jose de Diego, Parada 22 (at Ponce de León), Santurce 787/724–4011 • 11am-midnight, till 2am Fri-Sat • popular • lesbians/ gay men • neighborhood bar • also liquor shop

Nightclubs

Circo Bar Calle Condado 650, Parada 18, Santurce 787/725–9676 • 9pm-5am • mostly men • dancing/DJ • karaoke • theme nights

Club Lazer Calle Cruz 251, Old San Juan 787/725–7581, 787/721–4479 • 8pm-close • popular w/ gay cruises

Junior's Calle Condado 613 (btwn Calle del Carmen & Av Ponce de León), Santurce 787/723–9477 • 8pm-close • lesbians/ gay men • neighborhood bar • drag & strip shows • transgender-friendly • local crowd

Kali 1407 Ashford Ave, Condado 787/721–5104 • gay-friendly • popular after hrs club • dress code • also lounge & sushi restaurant

Krash Klub Av Ponce de León 1257 (btwn Calles Villamil & Labra), Santurce 787/722–1131 • 10pm-4am, clsd Sun-Mon • popular • lesbians/ gay men • dancing/DJ • drag shows • gay-owned

Metro Lounge Av Roosevelt 1367 (Hato Rey) 787/447–5253 • Th-Sun • lesbians/gay men, more women on Fri • dancing/DJ

S Lounge Av Roosevelt 1109 787/783–8332 • Th-Sat only • lesbians/ gay men • more women Sat • dancing/DJ • drag shows

Cafes

Cafe Berlin Calle San Francisco 407, Plaza Colón, Old San Juan (btwn Calles Norzagary & O'Donnel) 787/722–5205 • 11am-11pm • popular • espresso bar • plenty veggie

Kasalta Bakery 1966 McLeary Ave (at Teniente Matta) 787/727–7340 • 6am-10pm • bakery & deli

Restaurants

Aguaviva 364 Calle La Fortaleza, Old San Juan 787/722–0665 • dinner nightly • fresh seafood & ceviche • wheelchair access

Ajili Mojili 1052 Ashford Ave, Condado (at Aguadilla) 787/725–9195 • local specialties • live music • great ambiance

Al Dente 309 Calle Recinto S, Old San Juan **787/723–7303** • lunch & dinner, clsd Sun • Italian • also wine bar

Bebo's Cafe 1600 Calle Loiza (at Del Parque) **787/268–5087** • cheap & delicious • cafeteria-style Puerto Rican favorites

La Bombonera Calle San Francisco 259, Old San Juan **787/722–0658** • 7:30am-8pm • popular • come for the strong coffee & pastries • wheelchair access

El Buren 103 Calle Christo, Old San Juan (at Sol) **787/977–5023** • Italian/ Puerto Rican • outdoor seating

Cafe Puerto Rico 208 O'Donnell, Old San Juan **787/724–2281** • noon-11pm • great mofongo, outdoor seating

La Casita Blanca 351 Calle Tapia (off Ave Eduardo Conde, near Laguna Los Corozas) **787/726–5501** • 11am-4pm, till 6pm Th, till 9pm Fri-Sat • amazing local cuisine • best reached by car • no English spoken • beware of neighborhood

San Juan

LGBT Pride:
June.

Annual Events:
January - San Sebastian Street Festival 787/724-4788.

February - Ponce Carnival.

February/ March - Festival Casals, web: www.festcasalspr.gobierno.pr.

May - Heineken Jazz Fest 787/272–8877, web: www.prheinekenjazz.com.

June - San Juan Bautista Day. San Juan celebrates Puerto Rico's own saint w/ week-long music, dance, religious processions, parties. On midnight of the eve before June 24th (the official saint's day), revelers walk/jump backwards into the sea 3 to 7 times to ward off evil spirits & renew good luck for the coming year.

City Info:
Puerto Rico Tourism Company, 800/866-7827, web: www.gotopuertorico.com.

Best View:
From El Morro or alternatively, one of the harbor cruises that depart from Pier 2 in Old San Juan.

Weather:
Tropical sunshine year-round, with temperatures that average in the mid-80°s from November to May. Expect more rain on the northern coast.

Attractions:
Cathedral de San Juan 787/722–0861, web: www.catedralsanjuan.com.

Condado Beach.

La Fortaleza 787/ 721–7000, web: www.fortaleza.gobierno.pr.

Historic Old San Juan.

El Morro Fortress & Fort San Cristobal (San Juan National Historic Site) 787/729-6777, web: www.nps.gov/saju.

La Casita weekly festival 787/721–2891.

Pablo Casals Museum 787/723-9185.

Paseo de la Princesa.

Quincentennial Plaza.

San José Church.

San Juan Museum of Art & History 787/724-1875.

Santurce Marketplace.

Transit:
TaxiVan, 787/645-8294, web: www.taxivansanjuan.com.

American Taxi, 787/982-2222, web: www.americantaxipr.com.

Santana Taxi Service, 787/547-1926.

Metropolitan Bus Authority (AMA, its Spanish initials, and Metrobus) 787/294-0500, web: www.dtop.gov.pr/ama/ama.htm.

Also look for the free trolley that winds through Old Town.

Colombo 1024 Ashford Ave (at Aguadilla St) 787/725–1212 • 8am-1am, till 3am wknds • American • also bar • WiFi

Dragonfly 364 S Fortaleza St, Old San Juan (across from Parrot Club) 787/977–3886 • opens 5:30 daily • full bar • Latin/ Asian fusion

Fleria 1754 Calle Loiza, Santurce 787/268–0010 • lunch & dinner, clsd Sun-Mon • Greek • some veggie

El Jibarito Calle Sol 280 787/725–8375 • Puerto Rican/ criolla • also bar

The Parrot Club Calle Fortaleza 363, Old San Juan (btwn Plaza Colón & Callejón de la Capilla) 787/725–7370 • lunch & dinner • chic Nuevo Latino bistro & bar • live music

Perla 1077 Ashford Ave, at La Concha Resort, Condado 787/721–7500 • enjoy an upscale dining experience inside a gigantic conch shell • swank!

Pura Vida 1853 McLeary Ave, Condado (at Calle Atlantic Pl) 787/728–8119 • noon-10pm • vegetarian • WiFi

Vidy's Cafe Ave Universidad 104 (Rio Piedras) 787/767–3062 • 10am-1am • plenty veggie • karaoke

ENTERTAINMENT & RECREATION

Atlantic Beach in front of Atlantic Beach Hotel • very gay-friendly beach

Nuyorican Cafe San Francisco 312 (by El Callejon) 787/977–1276, 787/366–5074 • live music & arts venue

Ocean Park Beach E of Condado • gay/ straight beach • adult-oriented (less kids)

La Placita/ Plaza del Mercado Santurce • open-air market by day, street-party by night • lots of bars & restaurants

BOOKSTORES

Bookworm Av Ashford 1129, Condado (at Calle Vendig) 787/722–3344 • 10am-9pm, from 1pm Sun

RETAIL SHOPS

The Rainbow Shop Av Ponce de León 1418 #202 (upstairs), Santurce 787/724–9093 • 9am-5pm • gay items

PUBLICATIONS

Conexion G 787/607–3939 • LGBT paper, in Spanish

GYMS & HEALTH CLUBS

International Fitness Av Ashford 1131, Condado (btwn Avs Cervantes & Caribe) 787/721–0717 • 5am-10pm, till 9pm Fri • gay/ straight

Vieques Island

ACCOMMODATIONS

Bravo! North Shore Rd (at Lighthouse) 787/741–1128 • gay/ straight • pool • gay-owned • $175-475

Casa de Amistad 27 Benitez Castano 787/741–3758 • gay/ straight • guesthouse in heart of Isabel Segunda • WiFi • gay-owned • $70-90

Crow's Nest Inn 787/741–0033, 877/276–9763 • gay-friendly • small inn • pool • nonsmoking • restaurant • $124-245

Inn on the Blue Horizon 787/741–3318 • gay-friendly • country inn & cottages • pool • beach access • restaurant • nonsmoking • WiFi • $125-400

TRINIDAD & TOBAGO

Tobago

ACCOMMODATIONS

Grafton Beach Resort 868/639–0191, 888/790–5264 • gay-friendly • pool • food served • $200-344

Kariwak Village Hotel & Holistic Haven Store Bay Local Rd, Crown Point 868/639–8442, 868/639–8545 • gay-friendly • 1-room cabañas • kids ok • pool • outdoor jacuzzi w/ waterfall • restaurant • wheelchair access • $108-150

VIRGIN ISLANDS
see also British Virgin Islands

St Croix

ACCOMMODATIONS

King Christian Hotel 59 Kings Wharf, Christiansted 340/773–6330, 800/524–2012 • gay-friendly • pool • also restaurant • $105-145

The Palms at Pelican Cove 4126 La Grande Princesse 340/778–8920, 888/790–5264 • lesbians/ gay men • beachfront resort • food served • pool • gay-owned • $110-265

➤ **Sand Castle on the Beach** 127 Smithfield, Frederiksted 340/772–1205, 800/524–2018 • lesbian, gay & straight-friendly • hotel • pool • WiFi • also restaurant & bar • $89-399+tax • lesbian & gay-owned

MEXICO

Please Note: Mexican cities are often divided into districts or "Colonias," which we abbreviate as "Col." Please use these when giving addresses for directions.

Acapulco

ACCOMMODATIONS

Casa Condesa Bella Vista 125 **52–744/484–1616, 800/816–4817 (US & CANADA)** • mostly gay men • full brkfst • near beach • pool • $75-150

Hotel Boca Chica Punta Caletilla (Fraccionamiento las Playas) **800/337–4685** • gay-friendly • pool • also restaurant

Hotel Encanto Jacques Cousteau 51 (Fraccionamiento Brisas Marques) **52–744/446–7101** • gay-friendly • pool • WiFi • also restaurant

Las Brisas Carretera Escenica 5255 **52–744/469–6900, 866/221–2961** • popular • gay-friendly • luxury resort • private pools • kids ok • wheelchair access • $330+

Sunscape Acapulco Calle Caracol 70 (Fracc. Amiento Farallón) **52–744/484–3707** • gay-friendly • pool • food served • $59-125

BARS

Parranderías Av Cuauhtémoc (Col. Progresso, around corner from Hotel Palacio) • 11pm-close • lesbians/ gay men • dancing • strippers

NIGHTCLUBS

Baby 'O Costera Miguel Alemán 22 **52–744/484–7474** • 10:30pm-5am, till midnight Sun • gay/ straight • classic disco for over 30 years

Cabaré-Tito Beach Privada de Piedra Picuda 17 PA (nr Torres Gemelas) **52–744/484–7146** • 9pm-close, clsd Sun-Tue • lesbians/ gay men • dancing/DJ

Prince Calle Juan de la Cosa 12 (across from Hotel Continental) **52–744/484–7601** • after-hours • mostly men • popular • dancing/DJ

Relax Calle Lomas de Mar 4 (Zona Dorada) **52–744/482–0421** • 10pm-late, clsd Mon-Wed • popular • lesbians/ gay men • dancing/DJ • drag & strip shows wknds • videos • young crowd

RESTAURANTS

100% Natural Av Costera Miguel Alemán 200 (near Acapulco Plaza) **52–744/485–3982** • 24hrs • fast (healthy) food • plenty veggie

Becco al Mare Ave Escénica 14 **52–744/446–7402** • lunch & dinner • Italian • nice views

Beto's Restaurant Av Costera Miguel Alemán 99 (at Condesa Beach) **52–744/484–0473** • 11am-midnight • lesbians/ gay men • full bar • seafood • palapas

El Cabrito Av Costera Miguel Alemán 1480 (near Convention Center) **52–744/484–7711** • 2pm-midnight, till 11pm Sun • local favorite • you must try the roasted goat

Carlos & Charlie's Blvd de las Naciones #1813 (in La Isla Shopping Village) **52–744/462–2104** • lunch & dinner • entertainment • int'l

Le Jardin des Artistes Vincente Yanez Pinzón 11 (in front of Hotel Continental Plaza) **52–74/84–8344, 52–74/84–3422** • 7pm-close • French • reservations required

Kookaburra 3 Fracc (at Marina Las Brisas) **52–744/446–6039** • lunch & dinner • int'l • expensive

La Cabaña de Caleta Playa Caleta Lado Oriente s/n (Fracc. las Playas) **52–744/469–8553, 52–744/469–7919** • 9am-9pm • seafood • right on Playa Caleta • great magaritas

La Tortuga Calle Lomas del Mar 5 **52–744/484–6985** • noon-midnight, clsd Mon • full bar • good Mexican • seafood • patio • gay-owned

Pampano Carretera Escénica 33-B (past La Vista shopping center) **52–744/446–5636** • 7pm-11pm, bar till 1am • incredible view • reservations recommended

Shu Blvd de las Naciones 1813 (Centro Comercial La Isla) **52–744/462–2001** • Japanese

Su Casa Angel and Shelly Av Anahuac 110 **52–744/484–1261, 52–744/484–4350** • seafood • tasty margaritas • great views

Suntory de Acapulco Costera Miguel Alemán 36 **52–744/484–8088** • 2pm-midnight • Japanese • gardens

El Zorrito's Av Costera Miguel Alemán (at Anton de Alaminos) **52–744/485–3735** • traditional Mexican • several locations along Costera • some all night

Aguascalientes

NIGHTCLUBS

Mandiles Av Lopez Mateos Poniente 730 W (btwn Agucate & Chabacano) 52-449/153-281 • 10pm-3am Fri-Sat only • lesbians/gay men • dancing/DJ

Cabo San Lucas

ACCOMMODATIONS

Cabo Villas Beach Resort Callejon del Pescador s/n (Col. El Medano) 52-624/143-9199 • gay-friendly • resort on Medano Beach • pool • $180-450

Posada Chabela Calle Tropico y Arcoiris 310/492-5629 • gay/straight • private hideaway • pool • women-owned • $110-145

Solmar Suites Av Solmar 1 800/344-3349, 310/459-9861 (US#) • gay-friendly • oceanfront suites at southernmost tip • 2 pools • hot tub • $155-285

The Todos Santos Inn Calle Legaspi #33 (Topete), Todos Santos 52-612/145-0040 • gay/straight • colonial inn in Todos Santos' historic district • pool • nonsmoking • also bar • gay-owned • $125-225

NIGHTCLUBS

Las Varitas Calle Vallentin Gomez Farias (at Camino Viejo a San Jose) 52-624/143-9999 • 9pm-3am, clsd Mon • gay-friendly • dancing/DJ • live shows • rock 'n' roll bar • Ladies Night Fri

RESTAURANTS

Mi Casa Av Cabo San Lucas (at Lazarus Cardenas) 52-624/143-1933 • clsd Sun • lunch & dinner • great chicken mole • reservations recommended

Cancún

see also Cozumel & Playa del Carmen

ACCOMMODATIONS

Rancho Sak Ol Puerto Morelos 52-998/871-0181 • gay-friendly • beachfront palapa-style B&B • 30 minutes from Cancún • $55-130

BARS

Cappucino Cafe Calle Magaritas (at Calle Azecenas) • early evening gay hangout

Picante Bar Av Tulúm 20, Centro (E of Av Uxmal, next to Plaza Galerías) • 9pm-5am • popular • mostly gay men • dancing/DJ • young crowd • drag shows & strippers Wed-Sat

NIGHTCLUBS

Glow 30 Avenida Tulum (Tulipanes, around the corner from Karamba) 52-998/898-4552 • 11pm-6:30am, clsd Sun-Mon • popular • lesbians/gay men • women's night every other Fri • dancing/DJ (huge dance flr) • drag shows • strippers • rooftop terrace lounge

Karamba Av Tulúm 9 (Azucenas 2nd flr, SM 22) 52-998/884-0032 • 10:30pm-close, clsd Mon • popular • lesbians/gay men • dancing/DJ • karaoke • drag shows • go-go boys Fri

RESTAURANTS

100% Natural Sunyaxchen 62 52-998/884-3617 • healthy fast food

Cafe D'Pa Ave Alcatraces (at corner of Las Palapas Park) 52-998/884-7615 • opens afternoons • streetfront French restaurant • popular crêpes • also bar • gay-owned

Casa Angelus Av Sayil 10 (Smza 4 Lote 72 y 73 Mza 12) 52-998/887-9444 • upscale int'l • full bar

Modern Art Cafe Kukulcán Blvd, km 12.5 (at La Isla Shopping Center) 52-998/883-4511 • 5pm-3am • full bar • gallery

Perico's Av Yaxhilan 61 52-998/884-3152 • noon-1am • traditional Mexican served up w/ huge theatrical flare

ENTERTAINMENT & RECREATION

Chichén Itza • the must-see Mayan ruin 125 miles from Cancún

Playa Delfines in the Hotel Zone (next to Hilton's beach) • gay beach

Chihuahua

ACCOMMODATIONS

Hacienda Huiyochi Copper Canyon 52-614/195-3240 • first & only hotel in Copper Canyon that caters to the LGBT community • full brkfst • kids/pets ok

Ciudad Juárez

see also El Paso, Texas, USA

BARS

Club La Escondida Calle Ignacio de la Peña 366 W • gay/straight • neighborhood bar

Cordoba

BARS

Salon Bar El Metro Av 7 no. 117–C (btwn Calles 1 & 3) • lesbians/gay men • dancing

Cozumel

see Cancún & Playa del Carmen

Cuernavaca

ACCOMMODATIONS

Casa del Angel Calle Clavel 18, Col. Satelite (at Begonia) **52-777/512-6775** • gay/ straight • contemporary guesthouse on hill overlooking Cuernavaca • hot tub • nonsmoking • full brkfst • gay-owned • $65

Las Mañanitas Ricardo Linares 107 **52-777/312-8982 & 314-1466, 888/413-9199 (US ONLY)** • gay-friendly • gardens • pool • restaurant • peacocks! • $215-482

La Nuestra Calle Mesalina 18 (at Calle Neptuno) **52-777/315-2272, 404/806-9694** • gay/ straight • B&B • full brkfst • pool • kids ok • WiFi • lesbian-owned • $65-75

BARS

Barecito Comonfort 17 (at Morrow) **52-777/314-1425** • 10am-1am, clsd Sun-Mon • lesbians/ gay men • food served • lesbian-owned

NIGHTCLUBS

Oxygen Av Vincente Guerrero 1303 (near Sam's Club) **52-777/317-2714** • 10pm-close, Fri-Sat only • mostly gay men • dancing/DJ • food served • live shows • drag shows • videos • 18+ • young crowd

RESTAURANTS

La India Bonita Dwight Morrow 15 (btwn Morelos & Matamoros) **52-777/312-5021** • 9am-9pm, till 5pm Sun-Mon

La Maga Calle Morrow #9 Altos **52-777/310-0432** • clsd Sun, popular lunch buffet • plenty veggie • live music

Marco Polo Calle Hidalgo 30 (in front of cathedral, 2nd flr) **52-777/312-3484, 52-777/318-4032** • 1pm-close • Italian (pasta & pizza) • overlooking cathedral

ENTERTAINMENT & RECREATION

Diego Rivera Murals Plaza de Museo (in Cuauhnáhuac Regional Museum)

Ensenada

NIGHTCLUBS

Sublime Plaza Blanca , 3rd Fl **52-646/128-8798** • 9pm-close • mostly gay men • dancing/DJ

RESTAURANTS

Casamar Blvd Costero 987 **52-646/174-0417** • 8am-10:30pm • popular • seafood • also bar • Ensenada landmark for 30 years

Guadalajara

ACCOMMODATIONS

Casa de las Flores B&B Santos Degollado 175, Tlaquepaque **52-33/3659-3186, 888/5828/30/20104896** • gay-friendly • 15 minutes from Guadalajara • great brkfsts & margaritas • $95-105

Casa Venezuela Calle Venezuela 459 (at Col. Americana) **52-33/3826-6590** • gay/ straight • B&B in 100-year-old colonial house • full brkfst • nonsmoking • WiFi • gay-owned • $115-145

Hotel Calinda Roma Av Juárez 170 (Sector Juárez) **52-33/3614-8650** • gay-friendly • also rooftop restaurant

Hotel Casa Campos B&B Francisco de Miranda 30-A (Col. Centro), Tlaquepaque **52-33/3838-5296, 52-33/3838-5297** • gay-friendly • hotel 15 minutes SE of Guadalajara • WiFi • also bar & restaurant • $80-140

Hotel Puerta del Sol Av López Mateos Sur 4205 (Col. Loma Bonita), Zapopan **52-33/3133-0808, 52-33/3133-0852 & 0862** • gay-friendly • hotel • pool • bar & restaurant • 450-790 pesos

Hotel San Francisco Degollado 267 **52-33/3613-3256** • gay-friendly • hotel w/ Old World charm • close to gay bars • also restaurant • $45-82

Old Guadalajara B&B Belén 236 (Centro Histórico) **52-33/3613-9958** • gay/ straight • nonsmoking • gay-owned • $95

La Perla B&B Prado 128, Col. Americana (Vallarta y Lopez Cotilla) **52-33/3825-1948** • gay/ straight • full brkfst • nonsmoking • WiFi • gay-owned • $100-200

La Villa del Ensueño Florida St 305, Tlaquepaque **52-33/3635-8792** • gay/ straight • full brkfst • $95-125

BARS

El Botanero Calle Javier Mina 1348 (at Calle 54, Sector Libertad) **52-33/3643-0545** • 6pm-3am, till 1am Sun, clsd Mon-Tue • mostly gay men, dancing/DJ • food served • karaoke • drag shows • T-dance Sun • cover charge

Cactus Beer Bar Galeana 279 (btwn Priscilliano Sanchez & Miguel Blanco) • 5pm-1am • gay/ straight • wide selection of int'l beers • food served • western theme

Cafe Bar Butterfly Hidalgo 907 (at Col. Americana) 52–33/3826–0107

Castro Street Av Vallarta 1840 • lesbians/ gay men • also cafe/ restaurant

Caudillos Bar Calle Prisciliano Sánchez 305, Centro (at Ocampo) 52–33/3613–5445 • 5pm-3am • popular • mostly gay men • dancing from 9pm • friendly bar • also restaurant

Chueca López Cotilla 1988 (Zona Centro Magno) 52–33/3615–5940 • from 6pm, clsd Sun • mostly gay men • lounge • tapas menu

Club YeYe Prisciliano Sánchez 395 (Zona Centro) 52–33/1337–5253 • 5pm-3am • lesbians/ gay men • chic video lounge • food served

Equilibrio Restaurant & Bar Ocampo 293 (at Miguel Blanco)

Luminare Hospital 882 (btwn Puebla & Federalismo) 52–33/3825–2085 • 6:30pm-12:30am, clsd Sun • lesbians/ gay men • lounge • terrace • also cafe & gallery

Maskaras Calle Maestranza 238 (at Prisciliano Sánchez) 52–33/3614–8103 • 9pm-3am • lesbians/ gay men • neighborhood bar • colorful atmosphere • live music • food served

Mundo Cool Prisciliano Sánchez 410 (Zona Centro) 52–33/3614–7481 • 6pm-3am Wed-Sun • lesbians/ gay men • karaoke

Pink Pavo 114 (btwn Lopez Cotilla & Juarez Ave) 52–33/3613–0299 • lesbians/ gay men • dancing/DJ • drag shows

La Prisciliana Prisciliano Sánchez 395 (Zona Centro) 52–33/3562–0725 • 5pm-3am • gay friendly • young crowd • mellow vibe

Rendibu Bar & Deli 8 de Julio #5 (at Morelos, Zona Centro) 52–333/613–1521 • 5:30pm-2am, clsd Sun-Mon • movie night Wed • mostly men • food • art & culture

Sexy Bar Degollado 273 (Zona Centro) 52–33/3658–2838 • 6pm-3am • lesbians/ gay men • dancing/DJ • shows

Sunrise López Cotilla 497 (at Donata Guerra) • 6pm-3am, clsd Mon • mostly gay men • laid back lounge

NIGHTCLUBS

7 Sins Pedro Moreno 532 (at Donato Guerra, Zona Centro) 52–33/3658–0713 • mostly gay men • dancing/DJ

Angels López Cotilla 1495-B, Col. Americana (btwn Av Chapultepec & Marsella, Zona Rosa) 52–33/3630–5478 • 10pm-4am Fri-Sat, till 3am Wed, after-party Sun 6am-10am • mostly gay men • dancing/DJ • videos • cover charge • restaurant

Azul Disco Ocampo 341 (Centro Historico) • 8pm-4am, clsd Mon-Tue • lesbians/ gay men • dancing/DJ • karaoke

Babylon Disco Bar Morelos #84 (Plaza Tapatia) 52–33/1287–9628 • lesbians/ gay men • women's night Wed • drag shows • strippers

Black Cherry Grand Popocatepetl 40 (at Adolfo Lopez Mateos Sur) 52–33/3647–9024 • 10pm-5am Sat only • mostly gay men • dancing/DJ

Circus Galeana 277 (at Prisciliano Sánchez, Centro Histórico) 52–33/3613–0299 • 9pm-5am • popular • lesbians/ gay men • dancing • live shows

Enigma Galeana 378 (at 9 Las Esquinas) • 9pm-5am • gay-friendly • dancing/DJ • cabaret • drag shows • videos • 18+ • young crowd • gay-owned

Freedom Diversity Club López Mateos Sur 1495 52–33/3121–7726 • open Fri-Sun only • mostly gay men • dancing/DJ

Light Kiss Club Av Hidalgo 838 (Zona Centro) 52–33/3563–4332 • 8pm-4am, clsd Mon • lesbians/ gay men • dancing/DJ • transgender-friendly • drag shows • strippers

Mayday Av Revolucion 173 52–33/3618–3195 • mostly gay men • dancing/DJ

Mónica's Av Álvaro Obregón 1713 (btwn Calles 68 & 70, Sector Libertad; no sign, look for canopy under a big palm tree) 52–33/3643–9544 • 9pm-5am, clsd Mon-Tue • popular after midnight • mostly gay men • dancing/DJ • drag & strip shows wknds • young crowd • cover charge • take a taxi to & from

SOS Club Av La Paz 1413 (Sector Hidalgo, Zona Centro) 52–33/1201–0892 • 9pm-3am, till 5am wknds, clsd Mon • lesbians/ gay men • dancing/DJ • drag shows • strippers Fri-Sat (men only) & Sun (women only) • patio • cover charge

Velvet Lope de Vega 325 (corner of Agustin Yanez) 52–33/3830–4165 • 9pm-5am • lesbians/ gay men • dancing/DJ

CAFES

Efebo Av Chapultepec 29-2 (btwn Pedro Moreno & Morelos) **52–33/3827–5133, 52–33/1380–9236** • cybercafe

Queer Nation López Cotilla 611 • 5pm-midnight, clsd Sun • souvenirs

RESTAURANTS

Sanborns Av 16 de Septiembre 127 **52–33/3613–6264** • many locations • WiFi

PUBLICATIONS

GAYGDL • online magazine at www.gaygdl.com

Revista Estilo Libre **52–33/1410–3806** • LGBT lifestyle magazine

Urbana Revista • gay lifestyle magazine w/ bars & clubs for Guadalajara & Puerto Vallarta

Isla Mujeres

ACCOMMODATIONS

Casa de los Amigos Col. La Gloria **52–998/877–1169** • gay/ straight • rental villa on Mayan Riviera • WiFi • gay-owned • $330-390/ week

Casa Sirena on Isla Mujeres 52-**998/161–2424**

Jalapa

NIGHTCLUBS

La Mansión take a cab toward Banderillas (20 minutes NW of town, turn right at sign for El Paraíso Campestre & go past RR tracks) • 9pm-4am Fri-Sat only • lesbians/ gay men • dancing/DJ • live shows • cover charge

La Paz

ACCOMMODATIONS

La Casa Mexicana Inn Calle Nicolas Bravo 106 (btwn Madero & Mutualismo) **52–612/125–2748** • open Nov-June • gay/ straight • Spanish/ Moorish retreat • 1 block from La Paz Bay • nonsmoking • WiFi • wheelchair access • woman-owned • $65-95

Hotel La Casa Jalisco 480 Jalisco (at Ignacio Ramierez) **52–612/128–4311** • gay/ straight • WiFi • nonsmoking • swimming • close to downtown • $69-99

Hotel Mediterrane Allende 36 (at Malecón) **52–612/125–1195** • gay/ straight • WiFi • nonsmoking • bar & restaurant • sun terrace • gay-owned • $65-95

BARS

Cafe La Pazta Allende 36 (at Hotel Mediterrane) **52–612/125–1195** • 7am-11pm • gay/ straight • neighborhood bar • also restaurant • young crowd • gay-owned

NIGHTCLUBS

Las Varitas Calle Independencia 111 (at Malecón) **52–612/123–1590** • 9pm-3am, clsd Mon • gay-friendly • dancing/DJ • live shows • rock 'n' roll bar • Ladies Night Fri

León

BARS

G*bar Madero 226 (at Gante, Centro Histórico) **52–477/740–8863** • 6pm-2am • café-bar w/ terrace • young crowd

NIGHTCLUBS

La Madame Blvd A López Mateos 1709 Oriente (in front of Torre Banamex) **52–477/763–3086** • 10pm-3am, clsd Mon-Wed • mostly gay men • dancing/DJ • drag shows • go-go boys

Nation Francisco Villa (nr Blvd Mariano Escobedo) **52–477/716–3695** • gay/straight • dancing/DJ

Manzanillo

ACCOMMODATIONS

Las Hadas Av Vista Hermosa s/n (Fracc. Península de Santiago) **52–314/331–0101, 888/559–4329** • gay-friendly • great resort & location • $180+

Mexico's Villa Montaña Adventure Outpost 46 Los Angeles Locos, La Manzanilla **206/937–3882** • gay-friendly • 2-bdrm hilltop villa • ocean views • 1/2 hour N of Manzanillo • kids/ pets ok • nonsmoking • wheelchair access • $65-139

Red Tree Melaque Inn Primaveras 32 (30 miles N of Manzanillo), Melaque-Villa Obregon **52–315/355–8917** • gay-friendly • bungalows • near ocean • pool • kids/ pets ok • nonsmoking • gay-owned • $35-50

BARS

OK Independencia 42 (Centro) • Th-Sun only • mostly gay men • dancing/DJ • drag shows • cover charge

Mazatlán

ACCOMMODATIONS

El Cid Resort **866/306–6113, 52–669/913–3333** • gay-friendly • $79-729

Hotel Los Sábalos Av Playa Gaviotas 100 (Zona Dorada) **52–669/983–5333, 800/528–8760 (US#)** • gay-friendly • upscale resort • swimming • beach • health club • also popular Joe's Oyster Bar

Old Mazatlan Inn 18 Pedergoso (Angel Flores/Compania) **52–520/366–8487, 866/385–2945** • gay-friendly • swimming • WiFi • gay-owned • $40–115

The Pueblo Bonito Emerald Bay Ave Ernesto Coppel Compaña 201 **52–669/989–0525, 800/990–8250** • gay-friendly • resort on 20 acres • jacuzzi • pool • restaurant • piano bar • gym • $145–370

Bars

La Alemana Calle Zaragoza 16 (at Benito Juarez & Serdan) • gay/ straight • sports bar

Pepe Toro Av de las Garzas 18 (1 block W of Av Camarón Sábalo, Zona Dorada) **52–669/914–4176** • 9:30pm-4am, clsd Mon-Th • popular • mostly gay men • dancing/DJ • drag & strip shows

Vitrolas Bar Heriberto Frías 1608 (in Centro Historico) **52–669/985–2221** • 6pm-2am, clsd Mon • lesbians/ gay men • lunch menu • karaoke • drag shows & strippers Sun

Restaurants

Panamá Restaurant & Pastelería at Avs de las Garzas & Camarón Sábalo (Zona Dorada) **52–669/913–6977**

Roca Mar Av del Mar (at Calle Isla de Lobos, Zona Costera) **52–669/981–6008** • till 2am • popular • seafood • full bar • lesbian-owned

Mérida

Accommodations

Angeles de Mérida Calle 74-A, #494-A (at Calle 57 & Calle 59) **52–999/923–8163** • gay-friendly • B&B in 18th-c home on quietest streets of Mérida • full brkfst • nonsmoking • pool • spa services available • gay-owned • $85–130

Los Arcos B&B Calle 66 **52–999/928–0214** • gay-friendly • pool • gay-owned • $75–95

Casa Ana B&B Calle 52 #469 (btwn 51 & 53) **52–999/924–0005** • gay-friendly • pool • nonsmoking • women-owned • $30–45

La Casa Lorenzo Calle 41 #516 A (btwn 62 & 64) **52–999/139–0423 , 866/515–4105** • gay-friendly • pool • nonsmoking • WiFi • gay-owned • $49–60

Casa San Juan B&B 545-A Calle 62 (btwn Calle 69 & Calle 71) **52–999/986–2937, 866/979–6753** • gay/ straight • nonsmoking • kids ok • wheelchair access • gay-owned • $35–55

Casa Santiago B&B Calle 63 #562 (btwn Calles 70 & 72) **52–999/928–9375** • gay/ straight • colonial restored house • pool • nonsmoking • WiFi • wheelchair access • gay-owned • $59-79

Gran Hotel Calle 60 #496 (nr Parque Cepeda Peraza) **52–999/924–7730 & 923–6963** • gay-friendly • historic turn-of-the-century hotel • pets ok • also restaurant

Las Arecas Guesthouse Calle 59 #541 (btwn Calle 66 & Calle 68) **52–999/928–3626** • gay-friendly • guesthouse • garden • gay-owned • $31-46

Posada Santiago Guesthouse Calle 57 No 552 (between Calle 66 & 68, Centro Historico) **52–999/928–4258** • gay/ straight • pool • nonsmoking • WiFi • wheelchair access • gay-owned • $65-75

Bars

El Establo Calle 60 #482 (btwn Calle 56 & 58) **52–999/924–2289** • gay-friendly • dancing/DJ • food served • popular w/ tourists & locals

Nightclubs

Kabuki's Jacinto Canek 381

Pancho's Bar Avenida Juarez 33

Pride Disco Campeche A (200 meters del Puente de Ulman), Anillo Periferico **52–999/946–4401** • mostly gay men • dancing/DJ • strippers • south of town, all taxi drivers know where it is located

Restaurants

Cafe La Habana Calle 59 #511-A (at Calle 62) **52–999/928–6502** • 24hrs • also bar & café

Cafe Pop Calle 57 (btwn Calle 60 & 62) **52–999/928–6163** • brkfst, lunch & "light dinner" • beer & wine

La Bella Época Calle 60 #447 (upstairs in the Hotel del Parque) **52–99/928–1928** • 4pm-1am • Yucatécan cuisine • try to get one of the balcony tables

Villa Maria Hotel & Restaurant Calle 59 No. 553 x 68 **52–999/923–3357**

Mexicali

BARS

El Rey de Copas Av Baja California (at Av Tuxtla Gutierrez, Pueblo Nuevo) • open till 3am • lesbians/ gay men • neighborhood bar

El Taurino Av Juan de Zuazua 480 (near Jose Morelos) • 1pm-2am, clsd Mon • popular • lesbians/ gay men • dancing/DJ

NIGHTCLUBS

Mirage Disco Av Lerdo #430 (Zona Centro) 52–686/214–1285 • 6pm-2am Wed-Sun • popular • dancing/DJ

Mexico City

Note: M°=Metro station

Note: Mexico City is divided into "Zonas" (ie, Zona Rosa) & "Colonias" (abbreviated here as "Col."). Remember to use these when giving addresses to taxi drivers.

INFO LINES & SERVICES

Cálamo (LGBT AA) Av de Chapultepec 465, desd 202 (Col. Juárez) 52–55/5574–1210 • 8pm Mon-Fri, 7pm Sat, 6pm Sun • LGBT AA group

Centro Cultural de la Diversidad Sexual Colima 267 (Col. Roma Norte) 52–55/5514–2565, 52–55/1450–9511 • Mexico City's LGBT center • also cafe

Jovenes La Villa Calle 521 #248 (nr Ave 510) 52–55/2603–7696

ACCOMMODATIONS

Best Western Majestic Hotel Ave Madero 73, Col. Centro 52–55/5521–8600, 800/528–1234 • gay-friendly • 4-star hotel on the Zócalo Plaza • rooftop restaurant • wheelchair access • $115+

Condesa Haus Cuernavaca 142 (at Campeche) 52–55/5256–2494 • gay-friendly • WiFi • full brkfst • $85-100 • gay-owned

Hotel Casa Blanca Lafragua 7 (Col. Tabacalera) 52–55/5096–4500, 800/905–2905 (US & CANADA #) • gay-friendly • 5-star hotel • pool • restaurant & bar • $116-445

Hotel Gillow Isabel la Católica 17 (Col. Centro) 52–55/5518–1440, 52–55/5510–2636 • gay-friendly • also restaurant & bar • $42-90

Hotel Polanco Edgar Allan Poe 8 (Col. Polanco) 52–55/5280–8082, 800/221–9044 • gay-friendly • steps from Paseo de la Reforma • 1,395-2,620 pesos

Marco Polo Amberes 27, Col. Juárez (Zona Rosa) 52–55/5080–4500, 800/448–8355 (US#) • gay-friendly • small boutique hotel • $80-248

W Mexico City Campos Eliseos 252 52–55/9138–1800 • gay-friendly • in trendy Polanco • 2 restaurants & bar • WiFi • $199+

BARS

Amsterdam 219 Amesterdam 219 (in Condesa) 52–55/5564–3034 • gay/ straight

Black Out Amberes 11 (Zona Rosa) • gay/ straight • upscale lounge • also restaurant

Cafeína Nuevo Leon 73 (in Condesa) 52–55/5212–0090 • 7pm-4am, 6pm-10pm Sun • gay-friendly • dancing/DJ • co-owned by Diego Luna of Y Tu Mama También fame

Enigma Calle Morelia 111, Col. Roma (4 blocks from M° Niños Héroes, Zona Rosa) 52–55/5207–7367 • 9pm-3:30am, 6pm-2am Sun, clsd Mon • lesbians/ gay men • dancing/DJ • shows for women Th • live shows • cover charge

La Gayta Freezing Bar Amberes 18 (Zona Rosa) 52–551/055–5873 • lesbians/ gay men • neighborhood bar • young crowd

Lipstick Amberes 1 (at Paseo de la Reforma, Zona Rosa) 52–55/5514–4920 • clsd Sun • gay/ straight • more lesbian Th • lounge • videos • live shows

Tom's Leather Bar Av Insurgentes 357 (Col. Condesa) 55–84/5564–0728 • 9pm-4am, clsd Mon

NIGHTCLUBS

Butterflies/ Buttergold Calle Izazaga 9 (at Av Lazaro Cárdenas S, Centro Historico) 52–55/5761–1351 & 1861 • 9pm-3am, till 4:30am Fri-Sat, clsd Mon • popular • lesbians/ gay men • dancing/DJ • 2 flrs • lavish drag shows Fri-Sat • cover charge

Cabaré-Tito Fusion Londres 77 (Zona Rosa) 52–55/5511–1613 • open 4pm, clsd Mon-Tue • lesbians/ gay men • drag shows Th • 18+

Cabaré-Tito Neón Calle Londres 161, Local 20-A, Plaza del Angel (Zona Rosa) 52–55/5514–9455 • 6pm-close • mostly gay men • dancing/DJ • go-go dancers

Exacto/ The Doors Calle Monterrey 47, Col. Roma (Zona Rosa) 52–55/5533–1691 • 9pm-4am • popular • lesbians/ gay men • 3 flrs • The Doors, 1st floor, is a mixed restaurant/ bar • Exacto, 2nd floor, is for women • food served • live shows • cover charge

Hibrido Calle Londres 161, Plaza del Angel, 2nd flr (Zona Rosa) 52-55/5511-1197 • Th-Sun • lesbians/ gay men • dancing/DJ

Liverpool 100 Liverpool 100 (Col. Juarez) 52-55/5208-4507 • 9pm-close Wed, Fri & Sat only • mostly gay men • dancing/DJ

Living Bucareli 144 55-55/5512-7281 • 10pm-close Fri-Sat only • popular • mostly men • popular • theme nights

RESTAURANTS

La Antigua Cortesana Chiapas 173-A (Col. Roma) • 1pm-11pm, till midnight Fri-Sat, till 7pm Sun • popular Mexican cuisine • also bar

El Cardenal Calle de Palma 23 52-55/5521-8815 • incredible pastries

Casa Merlos Victoriano Zepeda 80 (at Observatoria) 52-55/5277-4360 • traditional poblano food • definitely try the molé

Fonda San Ángel Plaza San Jacinto 3, Col. San Ángel (across from Bazar San Ángel) 52-55/5550-1641 & 1942 • popular after 7pm Fri-Sat • classic Mexican dishes

La Flores del Mar Alvaro Obregon 99, Roma 52-55/525-0678 • hip Mexican-fusion in old mansion • patio

Ligaya Nuevo Leon 68 (in Condesa) 52-55/5286-6268 • nouvelle Mexican • dinner nightly • outdoor seating

La Nueva Opera Ave Cinco de Mayo 10 (Centro Historico) 52-55/5512-8959 • 1pm-midnight, clsd Sun • legendary cantina since Pancho Villa fired a bullet into the ceiling

Punto y Aparte Amberes 62 (btwn Calles Londres & Liverpool, Zona Rosa) 52-55/5533-5442

Xel-Ha Parral 78 Bis (in Col. Condesa) 52-55/5553-5968 • traditional cuisine of the Yucatan

Mexico City

CITY INFO:
Mexican Tourism 800-44-MEXICO (US #), web: www.visitmexico.com.

ATTRACTIONS:
Ballet Folklorico, web: www.balleta-malia.com.
Frida Kahlo House.
Metropolitan Cathedral.
Diego Rivera Web Museum, web: www.diegorivera.com.
Museo Dolores Olmedo (largest collection of Kahlo's works) 52-55/5555-1016, web: www.museodoloresolmedo.org.mx.
Museum of Anthropology 52-55/5286-2923, web: www.mna.inah.gob.mx.
Museum of the Palace of Fine Arts 52-555/512-2593, web: www.bellasartes.gob.mx.
Museum of Modern Art 52-55/5553-6233, web: www.conaculta.gob.mx/mam.
Shrine to Our Lady of Guadalupe.
Teotihuacan Pyramids.

WEATHER:
Temperate and dry most of the year, with most of the annual rainfall coming in May-Oct. When the smog gets unbearable, head for a museum or other indoor activity.

TRANSIT:
Official Radio Taxis 52-55/5271-9146 or 52-55/5271-9058, web: www.taxi-mexico.com.
Don't hail a taxi on the street. It costs more to call an official taxi, but it's worth it.
Metro & microbuses

ENTERTAINMENT & RECREATION

El Hábito Madrid 13 (Coyacán District) **52–55/5659–1139** • avant-garde theater & bar

Museo de Arte Carrillo Gil Av Revolución 1608 (Col San Angel) **52–55/5550–6260, 52–55/5550–3983** • 10am-6pm, clsd Mon • contemporary art

Museo de Frida Kahlo Calle Londres 247 (Coyacán) **52–55/5554–5999** • 10am-5:45pm, clsd Mon • original paintings, furniture, letters & Frida's dresses • also garden & café

Museo Templo Mayor Calle Seminario 8 (at República de Guatemala, enter on plaza, near Cathedral) **52–55/5542–4943** • 9am-5pm, clsd Mon • artifacts from the central Aztec temple at Tenochtitlán

BOOKSTORES

El Armario Abierto Agustín Melgar 25 (Col. Condesa) **52–55/5286–0895** • Mexico's only bookstore specializing in sexuality • some LGBT titles

PUBLICATIONS

Homópolis **52–55/2616–0456, 52–55/2616–0457** • twice-weekly LGBT magazine & guide

LeS VOZ Magazine AP 33-091, 15900 **52–55/5535–0456** • "The magazine of Mexico's lesbian feminist culture, by & for women."

Rola Gay • nat'l monthly LGBT newspaper • see www.rolaclub.org.mx

Ser Gay **52–55/1450–9511** • quarterly magazine • covers all Mexico nightlife

Monterrey

ACCOMMODATIONS

Holiday Inn Monterrey Centro Av Padre Mier 194 N (at Garibaldi, Centro) **52–81/8228–6000** • gay-friendly • near Zona Rosa • pool • also restaurant • $50-135

BARS

Akbal Abasolo 870B, 2nd Flr, Casa del Maíz **52–81/1257–2986** • 9pm-2am, clsd Mon • gay/straight • more gay Sun

Casa de Lola Padre Mier 867 (btwn Porfirio Diaz & Vallarta) **52–81/8343–6210** • Th-Sat only • mostly gay men • dancing/DJ • karaoke

NIGHTCLUBS

Baby Shower Ocampo 433 Puente (btwn Rayon & Aldama Centro) **52–81/8881–5632** • 9pm-close, clsd Mon-Tue • lesbians/ gay men • dancing/DJ • strippers • videos

Parking Allende 120 Ote (btwn Juarez & Guerrero) **52–81/8343–2624** • 10pm-close Wed-Sat • mostly gay men • dancing/DJ

Venneno Club Av de los Héroes 47 (at Av Francisco I Madero) **52–81/8244–5499** • 9pm-close, clsd Mon-Tue • lesbians/ gay men • dancing/DJ • drag shows • strippers

Morelia

ACCOMMODATIONS

Casa Camelinas B&B Jacarandas 172 (Col. Nueva Jacarandas) **707/942–4822 (US#)** • gay-friendly • mostly women • 3 1/2 hours from Mexico City • nonsmoking • also Spanish classes • $75

BARS

Amnesia Happy Bar Gertrudis Bocanegra 905 (Col Ventura Puente) **52–443/312–1578** • 5pm-2am, clsd Sun • lesbians/ gay men • lounge w/ DJ

NIGHTCLUBS

Con la Rojas Calle Aldama 343 (Centro) **52–443/312–1578** • 10pm-2:30am, clsd Sun-Wed • mostly gay men • dancing/DJ • cover charge

RESTAURANTS

La Capilla Ignacio Zaragoza 90 (at Posada de la Soledad Hotel) **52–443/312–1888** • in charming old hotel in converted convent

Fonda Las Mercedes Calle Leon Guzmán 47 **52–443/312–6113 & 313–3222** • popular • inside beautiful colonial home

Oaxaca

ACCOMMODATIONS

El Camino Real Oaxaca Calle 5 de Mayo 300 **52–951/501–6100, 800/722–6466** • gay-friendly • 5-star hotel in restored 16th-c convent • frescoes & courtyards abound • restaurant • swimming • $242-430

Casa Adobe B&B Independencia 11, Tlalixtac de Cabrera **52–951/517–7268** • gay/ straight • 15 minutes from center of Oaxaca • WiFi • gay-owned • $37-65

La Casa de Don Pablo Hostel Melchor Ocampo 412, Centro (at Rayon St) **52–951/516–8384** • gay/ straight • nonsmoking • 80 pesos

Casa Machaya B&B Sierra Nevada 164, Col. Loma Linda **52/951–1328203** • gay-friendly • kids ok • private level w/ patio & valley views • $50-75

Casa Sagrada Murguia 403 **310/929–7099** • gay/straight • 30 minutes from Oaxaca • full brkfst • kids ok • nonsmoking • wheelchair access • $85-145

Posada Arigalan Mazunte, San Agustinillo **52-958/111–5801** • gay/straight • hotel sits above the pacific ocean and set of stairs leads to the beach • women-run • $80-100

NIGHTCLUBS

Club Privado 502 (aka El Número) Calle Porfirio Díaz 502 (Centro, ring to enter) • 10pm-close, clsd Sun-Tue • gay/straight • dancing/DJ (wknds) • cover charge

Gavana Dance Club Calzada Porfirio Diaz #216 (Col. Reforma) • 9pm-close Th-Sat • gay/straight

RESTAURANTS

El Asador Vasco Portal de Flores 10-A (Centro) **52-951/514–4755** • popular • great views • authentic Oaxacan cuisine (can you say ¡mole!)

Sonadores Dreamers 1301 Gardenia (at Palma Real), Huatulco **52-958/105–1592** • 6pm-11pm, till midnight Fri-Sat, clsd Mon • dancing/DJ • live shows • gay-owned

Playa del Carmen

see also Cancún & Cozumel

ACCOMMODATIONS

Acanto Hotel & Suites 16th St N (btwn 5th Ave & the beach) **631/882–1986** • gay-friendly • pool • nonsmoking • WiFi • $155-265

Aventura Mexicana Hotel Av 10 (at Calle 24) **52-984/873–1876, 800/455–3417** • gay-friendly • pool • also restaurant & bar • $50-225

Hotel Copa Cabana 5ta Av Norte (btw 10 & 12) **52-984/873–0218** • gay-friendly • WiFi • wheelchair access • $40-100

Hotel Playa del Carmen & OM Lounge Calle 12 Norte con 1.ra privada, n.195 **52-984/147–0949** • gay/straight • WiFi • gay-owned • $20-75

Luna Blue Hotel & Bar Calle 26 (at 5th Av) **415/839–8541**

NIGHTCLUBS

Playa 69 Av 5 (btwn Calle 4 & Calle 6, ground flr) • wknds 9pm-4am • mostly gay men • dancing/DJ • gay-owned

RESTAURANTS

100% Natural Av 5 (btwn 10th & 12th) **52-984/73–2242** • vegetarian

La Kalaka Calle 4 N (btwn 15th & 20th Ave) **52-984/135–4822** • noon-11pm • full bar • WiFi • lesbian-owned

Puebla

BARS

La Cigarra Ave 5 Poniente 538 (at Calle 7, Centro) **52-222/246-6356** • 6pm-3am • mostly gay men • beer bar • videos

NIGHTCLUBS

Garotos 22 Orient E 602 (close to Blvd 5 de Mayo, Xenenetla) **52-222/242-4232** • 9pm-3am Fri-Sat only • gay-friendly • dancing/DJ • cover charge

Puerto Vallarta

ACCOMMODATIONS

Blue Seas Malecon 1 Esq Abedul Col Emiliano Zapata **813/855–0190** • gay/straight • all suites • pool

Boana Torre Malibu Condo Hotel Calle Amapas 325 **52-322/222–0999, 52-322/222–6695** • gay/straight • food served • pool • poolside bar • gay-owned • $40-360

Bugambilia Blanca Condos Carretera Barra de Navidad 602, Col. Emiliano Zapata (Off Hwy 200) **52-322/222–1152** • gay/straight • 6-minute walk to gay beach • kids ok • gay-owned • $80-385

Casa Cúpula Callejon de la Igualdad 129, Col. Amapas **52-322/223–2484, 866/352–2511** • lesbians/gay men • swimming • nonsmoking • WiFi • wheelchair access • gay-owned • $145-355

Casa dos Comales Calle Aldama 274 **52-322/223–2042** • gay-friendly • guesthouse & apts near Old Town • pool • gay-owned • $65-125

Casa Fantasía Pinot Suarez 203, Col. Emiliano Zapata (near the Rio Cuale) **52-322/223–2444** • gay/straight • B&B made up of 3 traditional haciendas • full brkfst • terrace • pool • nonsmoking • wheelchair access • gay-owned • $70-150

Casa Tranquila Morelos #7-A, Bucerias, Nayarit **52-329/298–1767, 322/728–7519** • gay/straight • apts • near beach • WiFi • lesbian-owned • 550-700 pesos

Los Cuatro Vientos Matamoros 520 **52-322/222–0161** • gay-friendly • hotel that's home to El Nido rooftop bar & restaurant & sponsors annual week-long Women's Getaway • pool • WiFi

➤**Hotel Mercurio** 52-322/222-4793, 866/388-2689 • popular • lesbians/ gay men • traditional & alternative families welcome • 1 1/2 blocks from beach • pool • WiFi • gay-owned • $65-125

Hotelito Desconocido Playon de Mismaloya, La Cruz de Loreto, Tomatlán 52-322/281-4010, 800/851-1143 • gay/ straight • eco-resort on the beach • 60 miles S of Puerto Vallarta • pool • sauna • $302-697

El Panorama Oceano Atlantico 82, La Penita 52-327/274-3499, 888/246-1369 • gay/ straight • pool • WiFi • nonsmoking • gay-owned • $79-99

Quinta Maria Cortez Calle Sagitario 132, Playa Conchas Chinas 888/640-8100 • gay/ straight • pool • $85-1,500 + tax

The San Franciscan Resort & Gym Calle Pilitas #213 (at Playa Los Muertos) 52-322/222-6473 x0 • gay/ straight • pool • WiFi • $98-450

Villa Safari Condo Francisca Rodriguez 203 269/469-0468 (US #) • gay/ straight • hillside 2-bdrm condo • 2 blocks from Los Muertos beach • pool • nonsmoking • gay-owned • $125-200

Yelapa Casa/ Casa Pericos 51 El Camino Huachanango, Yelapa 52-322/417-4367 • gay/ straight • full brkfst • gay-owned • $110-1,000

BARS

Los Amigos Bar Calle Venustiano Carranza 237 (upstairs, next to Paco's Ranch) 52-322/222-7802 • 6pm-4am • lesbians/ gay men • Mexican cantina • patio

Apaches Olas Altas 439 (at Rodriguez) 52-322/222-4004 • 5pm-2am, till 1am Sun-Mon • gay/ straight • classy martini bar • tapas • lesbian-owned

Blue Sunset Rooftop Bar Los Muertos Beach (at Blue Chairs Resort) • 10am-midnight • mostly gay men • karaoke • drag shows • food served

Encuentros Lazaro Cardenas 312 (Col Emiliano Zapata) 52-322/222-0643 • 6pm-2am • lesbians/ gay men • great pizza

Frida 301-A Insurgentes (at Venustiano Carranza) 52-322/222-3668 • 1pm-2am, from 7pm Mon-Tue • gay/ straight • Mexican cantina • bears • more gay later in evening • food served • gay-owned

Garbo Pulpito 142 (at Olas Altas) 52-322/223-5753 • 6pm-2am • gay/ straight • upscale martini lounge • live jazz Fri-Sat • piano Wed-Th • gay-owned • 18+

Kit Kat Bar Pulpito 120 (next door to Chiles restaurant) 52-322/223-0093 • 5pm-1:30am • lesbians/ gay men • swanky New York–style cocktail lounge • drag shows • also restaurant (pricey but fun) • gay-owned

La Noche Lázaro Cárdenas 257 (Zona Romantica) 52-322/222-3364 • 7pm-2am • lesbians/ gay men • cocktail lounge

Sama Olas Altas 510 (at Rodolfo Gomez) 52-322/223-3182 • 5pm-2am • lesbians/ gay men • small martini bar w/ sidewalk seating

Vanilla & Kinky 200-A Basilio Badillo, upstairs (Col Emiliano Zapata) 52-322/223-1797 • 5pm-2am • gay/ straight

NIGHTCLUBS

Cheeky Monkey Paseo Diaz Ordaz 556 (at Corona) 52-322/222-8938 • noon-2am • gay-friendly • food served

Club Manana Venustiano Carranza #290 (at Col Emiliano Zapata) 52-322/222-7779, 323/230-9876 (US) • 10pm-6am, till 8am Fri-Sun, clsd Mon • popular • lesbians/ gay men • dancing/DJ • drag shows • strippers • swimming

Paco's Ranch 237 Ignacio Vallarta 52-322/222-1899 • 9pm-6am • popular • lesbians/ gay men • dancing/DJ • also rooftop terrace • drag shows • cover charge • gay-owned

Stereo Lazaro Cardenas 267 (Emiliano Zapata Centro) 52-322/1114-243, 52-322/1238-030 • 9pm-4am • lesbians/ gay men • dancing • small hip dance bar

CAFES

A Page in the Sun Olas Altas 299 52-322/222-3608 • 8am-11pm coffee shop & English bookstore

Cafe San Angel Olas Altas 449 (at Francisco Rodreguez) 52-322/223-1273 • 7am-1am • sidewalk café

ChocoBanana Calle Amapas 147 (at Calle Pulpito) 52-322/222-2114 • 8am-10pm, clsd Sun • contemporary Mexican cuisine

The Coffee Cup Rodolfo Gómez 146-A (at Olas Altas) 52-322/222-8584 • 7am-10pm, clsd Sun in summer • gay-owned

CyberSmoothie Rodolfo Gómez 111 52-322/223-4784 • 9am-9:30pm • WiFi

Dee's Coffee Company Rodolfo Gomez 120 (in Zona Romantica) 52–322/222–1197 • 7am-10pm • homemade pastries

Este Cafe Libertad 336, Centro (around corner from flea market) 52–322/222–4261 • 8am-10pm, clsd Sun • popular • espresso & juice bar • desserts • gay-owned

Uncommon Grounds Buddha Lounge Lazaro Cardenas 625 52–322/223–3834 • 5pm-close, clsd Mon-Tue • also aromatherapy & gifts

RESTAURANTS

El Arrayan Allende #344 (at El Centro) 52–322/222–7195 • 6pm-11pm, clsd Tue • lesbian-owned

Banana Cantina Calle Amapas 147 (at Calle Pulpito) 52–322/222–2114 • 4pm-11pm, clsd Mon • Mexican

Blue Shrimp Morelos #779 (Col. Centro) 52–322/222–4246 • 11am-midnight

El Brujo Venustiano Carranza 510 (at Naranjo) 52–322/223–3026 • 1pm-9:30pm, clsd Mon • Mexican/seafood • expect a wait

Cafe Bohemio Rodolfo Gómez 127 (at Olas Altas) 44–322/134–2436 • 5pm-2am, clsd Sun • lesbians/ gay men • open-air café • late-evening happy hour • gay-owned

Cafe des Artistes Calle Guadalupe Sánchez 740 (at Leona Vicario) 52–322/222–3228 • 6pm-11:30pm • popular • upscale French w/ a Mexican twist • reservations required

Chez Elena Matamoros 520, Centro (at Los Quatro Vientos Hotel) 52–322/222–0161 • 6pm-11pm • seasonal • garden restaurant • also rooftop bar • woman-owned

Cilantros Abasolo 169 (at Morelos) 52–322/222–7147 • 5:30pm-1am, clsd Sun • Mexican/fusion • rooftop deck • also bar

Daiquiri Dick's Olas Altas 314 (on Playa Los Muertos) 310/697-3799 • 8:30am-1:30pm & 5:30pm-11pm, clsd Tue & clsd Sept

De Santos 771 Morelos 52–322/223–3052 • 5pm-4am • chic Mediterranean • also dance club

Le Bistro Jazz Cafe Isla Rio Cuale 16–A (on the island, at the East Bridge) 52–322/222–0283 • 9am-midnight, clsd Sun • popular • PV's classiest • gay-owned

Memo's Casa de los Hotcakes Calle Basilio Badillo 289 **52-322/222-6272** • 8am-2pm • popular • long lines for cheap & good brkfst • indoor patio

Mesa 61 Ignacio L Vallarta 264 **52-322/223-2175** • brkfst served • popular lounge upstairs

Mezzogiorno Ristorante Italiano Avenida del Pacifico 33 (North Beach Bucerias Nayarit) **52-329/298-0350** • 6pm-11pm (clsd Mon off-season)

La Palapa Pulpito 103, Col Emiliano Zapata **52-322/222-5225** • brkfst, lunch & dinner, beachside dining

La Piazzetta Rodolfo Gomez #143 (at Olas Atlas, Romantic Zone) **52-322/222-0650** • 4pm-11pm

Planeta Vegetariano Iturbide 270 (Centro) **52-322/222-3073** • 8am-10pm, clsd Sun • buffet-style

Red Cabbage Calle Rivera del Rio 204-A (at Basilio Badillo) **52-322/223-0411** • 5pm-11pm, clsd Sun (Apr-Oct) • on Rio Cuale w/ great kitschy decor • lesbian-owned

Trio Guerrero 264 (Centro) **52-322/222-2196** • 6pm-midnight, clsd Sun • Mediterranean/ Mexican • patio • live music • reservations advised

ENTERTAINMENT & RECREATION

Boana Tours Calle Amapas 325 (at Casa Boana Torre Malibu) **52-322/222-0999, 52-322/222-6695** • horseback tours daily

Diana's Cruise the Bay Tour meet at Los Muertos pier **52-322/222-1510** • 9:30am-5pm Th • lesbians/ gay men • cruise on 33-ft trimaran • snorkeling equipment • food served • open bar • $75

Ocean Friendly Paseo del Marlin 510-103, Col. Aralias **52-322/225-3774, 044-322/294-0385 (CELL)** • whale-watching tours • Dec 15-March 31

Playa Los Muertos/ Playa del Sol S of Rio Cuale • popular • the gay beach • now spans "Blue Chairs" & "Green Chairs"

RETAIL SHOPS

La Rosa de Cristal Insurgentes 272 (at Cardenas) **52-322/222-5698** • 10am-8pm • local handicrafts & beautiful blown-glass items • gay-owned

Liquid Men Ignacio L Vallarta 245 (Old Town) **52-322/223-3165** • 10am-10pm, men's clothes & accessories • also tickets to gay events like Latin Fever

PUBLICATIONS

Revista Estilo Libre **52-322/1379-4486** • LGBT lifestyle magazine

Urbana Revista **52-333/844-6471** • gay lifestyle magazine

GYMS & HEALTH CLUBS

Acqua Day Spa & Gym Calle Constitución 450 (F Rodriguez) **52-322/223-5270** • 7am-9pm, till 5pm Sat, clsd Sun • spa services • also small gym

Gold's Gym Calle Pablo Picasso s/n (Zona Hotelera Las Glorias) **52-322/225-6671** • 6am-10pm, 7am-7pm Sat, 9am-3pm Sun

Total Fitness Gym Calle Timon 1 (Marina Vallarta) **52-322/221-0770** • 6:30am-9:30pm, Sat 8am-2pm, clsd Sun • women only • offers wide variety of classes: yoga, aerobics, pilates, spinning & more

Querétaro

NIGHTCLUBS

Con la Rojas Ave Constituyents Pte 42A (Centro) **52-442/212-4795** • 10pm-2:30am, clsd Sun-Wed • mostly gay men • dancing/DJ • cover charge

San Jose del Cabo

ACCOMMODATIONS

El Encanto Inn 133 Calle Morelos **210/858-6649, 52-614/142-0388** • gay-friendly • spa and restaurant • swimming • $95-240

One & Only Palmilla Apartado Postal 52, 23400 **52-624/146-7000, 866/829-2977 (US#)** • gay-friendly • upscale resort w/ golf course • swimming • $450-3,000

RESTAURANTS

Voila Bistro & Catering 1705 Comonfort (Plaza Paulina) **52-624/130-7569** • noon-10pm, from 4pm Sun • popular • Mexican w/ French twist • full bar • patio

San Miguel de Allende

ACCOMMODATIONS

Casa de Sierra Nevada Calle Hospicio 42 (Centro) **52-415/152-7040, 800/701-1561** • gay-friendly • horseback riding • also spa • swimming • patios • 2,880-4,250 pesos

Casa Schuck Boutique B&B Garita 3, Centro **52-415/152-6618, 937/684-4092** • gay-friendly • boutique hotel w/ private garden & rooftop deck • full brkfst • pool • $157-226

Dos Casas Calle Quebrada 101 (Guanajuato) **52–415/154–4073** • gay-friendly • full brkfst • $280-480

Las Terrazas San Miguel Santo Domingo 3 **52–415/152–5028, 707/534–1833 (US#)** • gay/ straight • 4 rental homes • nonsmoking • WiFi • gay-owned • $770-1,225/ week

Tijuana

BARS

Arco Iris Taberna Av Pacifico 395 **52–664/631–8290** • gay/straight • food served • beach bar a with great deck overlooking the new Malacon • gay-owned

Noa Noa Av D 150/ Miguel F Martínez (at Calle 1) • 5pm-3am, till 4am Fri, till 5am Sat • lesbians/ gay men • dancing/DJ • drag shows • young crowd

NIGHTCLUBS

Los Equipales Calle 7/ Galeana 2024 (at Av Revolución) **52–664/688–3006** • 9pm-3am, clsd Mon-Tue • popular • lesbians/ gay men • dancing/DJ • drag shows • young crowd

Extasis Larroque 213 (in Plaza Viva Tijuana, next to the border) **52–664/682–8339** • 8pm-late, clsd Mon-Wed • popular • mostly gay men • women's night Th • dancing/DJ • strippers • cover charge

Mike's Disco Av Revolución 1220 (at Calle 6A) **52–664/685–3534** • 8pm-5am, till 3am Th, clsd Wed • popular • lesbians/ gay men • dancing/DJ • drag shows • videos

Terraza 9 Calle 5a (at Av Revolución) **52–664/685–3534** • 5pm-2am, till 5am Fri-Sat, clsd Mon • gay-friendly • dancing/DJ

Tulúm

ACCOMMODATIONS

EcoTulum Resorts & Spa Carretera Tulum Ruinas Km 5 **54–115/5918–6400, 877/301–4666** • gay-friendly • WiFi

Om Tulum Caraterra Ruinas Punta -Allen Km 9.5 **521–98/4114–0538** • gay-friendly • WiFi

Posada Luna del Sur Calle Luna Sur 5 **52–984/871–2984** • gay-friendly • $70-95

Veracruz

ACCOMMODATIONS

Casa de la Luz Tropical Guest House Tlacotalpan **52–288/884–2331** • gay-friendly • charming studio apt • $45-75

Hotel Villa del Mar Blvd Miguel Ávila Camacho 2431 (across street from Playa del Mar beach) **52–229/989–6500** • gay-friendly • hotel w/ separate motel & bungalows • near aquarium • 1,150-2,340 pesos

ENTERTAINMENT & RECREATION

San Juan de Ulua Fortress • 9am-4:30pm, clsd Mon • impressive early colonial-era floating fortress

Veracruz Aquarium Blvd Avila Camacho (at Xicolencat) **52–229/932–7984** • 10am-7pm • one of the largest & best in the world • don't miss it!

Zacatecas

ACCOMMODATIONS

Quinta Real Zacatecas Av Ignacio Rayón 434 (Col. Centro) **52–492/1105–0 00, 866/621–9288** • gay-friendly • 5-star hotel built into grandstand of bullfighting ring

Zihuatanejo

ACCOMMODATIONS

Casa Bulmaro Calle Adelita 52- **755/112–1295, 908/497–7939** • gay/ straight • WiFi • wheelchair access • gay-owned

Hotel Las Palmas Calle de Aeropuerto (at lot 5) **52–755/557–0634, 888/527–7256** • gay-friendly • full brkfst • pool • $225

NIGHTCLUBS

Tequila Town Cuauhtemoc 3 (Col Centro) **52–755/553–8587** • 8pm-4am • gay-friendly • more gay after 11pm • karaoke • videos

Wilde's Calle La Laja s/n (Col. Centro) **52–755/557–1042** • 8pm-4am • lesbians/ gay men • dancing/DJ • drag shows & strippers Fri-Sun

COSTA RICA

Alajuela

see San José

Arenal

ENTERTAINMENT & RECREATION

The Arenal Volcano • hourly eruptions

Escaleras

ACCOMMODATIONS

Paradise Costa Rica 800/708–4552 • gay/straight • vacation villas • pools • nonsmoking • gay-owned • $375-750

Guanacaste

ACCOMMODATIONS

Villa Decary Nuevo Arenal, 5717 Tilaran **506–2/383–3012, 506–2/694–4330** • gay-owned • former coffee farm overlooking Lake Arenal • gay-friendly • $75-139

Malpais

ACCOMMODATIONS

Kelea Surf Spa 949/492–7263 • women-only • surf spa • $1,745-1,975

Manuel Antonio, Quepos

ACCOMMODATIONS

Casa Antonio Enter at Arboleda Hotel **506-2/777–5174** • lesbians/ gay men • luxury rental house in the jungle • nonsmoking • gay-owned • $2,000-4,000

Casa Bumerango 213/330–0231 • gay/straight • kids ok • wheelchair access • gay-owned • $95-125

Casa de Frutas 506–2/825–3257 (CELL), 800/936–9622 • gay/ straight • luxury villa in Tulemar Gardens • $4,500-11,000/ week

Casa Romano 404/290–6919 • gay/ straight • pool • near gay beach • WiFi • wheelchair access • gay-owned • $250-700

Casitas Eclipse KM 5 Manuel Antonio Rd **506–2/777–0408** • gay/ straight • detached casitas • $86-172

Costa Verde 506–2/777–0584, 866/854–7958 (FROM US & CANADA) • gay/ straight • bungalows, studios & apts • pool • gay-owned • $127-300 + tax

Gaia Hotel & Reserve km 2.7 Carretera Quepos a Manuel Antonio **506–2/777–9797, 800/226–2515** • gay-friendly • boutique hotel • surrounded by wildlife refuge • full brkfst • pool • WiFi • gay-owned • $275-970

Géminis del Pacifico in the hills **506–2/777–5029** • gay-friendly • luxurious vacation home • pool • near beaches & bars • kids ok • nonsmoking • WiFi • gay-owned • $2,500-3,500/ wk

Hotel Casa Blanca 506–2/777–0253, 506–2/777–1790 • lesbians/ gay men • short hike to gay beach • pool • kids ok • wheelchair access • lesbian & gay-owned • $60-190

Hotel Parador 506–2/777–1414, 877/506-1414 • gay-friendly • large luxury resort w/ mini golf course & health club • swimming • also gourmet restaurant • WiFi • $145-950

Hotel Villa Roca 506–2/777–1349 • mostly gay men • great ocean views • near beaches • pool • nonsmoking • wheelchair access • gay-owned • $180-400

La Mansion Inn 506–2/777–3489, 800/360–2071 • gay/ straight • luxury hotel • pool • also restaurant • bar • ocean views • gay-owned • $125-1,600

La Posada 506–2/777–1446 • gay-friendly • 4 bungalows & 2 guest rooms • pool • full brkfst • gay-owned • $90-225

Si Como No 506–2/777–0777, 800/282–0488 x300 • gay-friendly • 30-acre wildlife refuge w/ butterfly garden across from hotel • also spa • pool • wheelchair access • $165-310

BARS

Tutu/ Gato Negro KM 5 Manuel Antonio Rd (at Casitas Eclipse) **506–2/777–0408** • 4pm-close • popular • gay/ straight • also restaurant • great view

RESTAURANTS

El Barba Roja Carretera al Parque Nacional **506–2/777–0331** • 7am-10pm, from 4pm Mon • American • popular • great sunset location

El Gran Escape & Fish Head Bar Quepos Centro **506–2/777–0395** • brkfst, lunch, dinner, clsd Tue • seafood • full bar

La Hacienda Restaurante Plaza Yara **506–2/777–3473** • 5pm-11pm, clsd Sun • live shows

The Plinio at the Hotel Plinio **506–2/777–0055** • int'l • full bar • Asian • some veggie

Rico Tico in Hotel Si Como No • lunch & dinner • Tex/Mex • includes use of pool bar • popular • live shows • also Claro Que Sí (seafood restaurant)

Osa Peninsula

ACCOMMODATIONS

Blue Osa Yoga Sanctuary and Spa Playa Tamales, Puerto Jimenez 506/8398-8905 • gay/ straight • all meals included • kids/ ok • nonsmoking • WiFi • gay-owned

Playa Sámara

ACCOMMODATIONS

Casitas LazDívaz 506/2656-0295 • gay/straight • full brkfst • wheelchair access • lesbian diva-owned • $75-95

San José

ACCOMMODATIONS

Colours Oasis Resort El Triangulo Noroeste, Blvd Rohrmoser (200 meters before end of blvd) 506/2-296-1880, 866/517-4390 • mostly gay men • pool • also bar & restaurant • gay-owned • $59-169

Hotel Kekoldi Av 9 (btwn Calles 5 & 7, Barrio Amón) 506/2-248-0804, 786/221-9011 (FROM US) • gay/ straight • in art deco bldg in downtown • secluded garden • WiFi • gay-owned • $49-95

Secret Garden B&B 506/2-224-1837 • gay/ straight • in historic Rohrmoser district • private courtyard • WiFi • gay-owned • $35-50

BARS

Bar Al Despiste in front of Mudanzas Mundiales (W of Universal Zapote) 506/2-234-5956 • 6pm-2am, 5pm-10pm Sun, clsd Mon • gay/ straight • theme nights • karaoke

Buenas Vibraciones Paseo de los Estudiantes 506/2-223-4573 • lesbians/ gay men

CeroEsTres Bar nr the Int'l Airport in Alajuela (from the Fiesta Casino continue the old road into town) • traditional local bar • lesbians/gay men

Marguiss in the suburbs of Alajuela • traditional local bar • gay/ straight

WERD Bar & Lounge 100 Metres Oeste de la Musmanni, Santa Ana 506/2-203-3624 • 5pm-2:30am • gay-friendly • food served • live shows • 18+ • wheelchair access • gay-owned

NIGHTCLUBS

La Avispa 834 Calle 1 (pink house btwn Avs 8 & 10) 506/2-223-5343 • 8pm-2am, popular T-dance from 5pm Sun, clsd Mon-Wed • lesbians/ gay men • mostly women last Wed • dancing/DJ

El Bochinche Calle 11 (btwn Avs 10 & 12, Paseo de los Etudiantes), San Pedro 506/2-221-0500 • 7pm-2am, till 5pm Fri-Sat, clsd Sun-Tue • also full restaurant • Mexican • dancing/DJ after 10pm • videos

Club Oh! Calle 2 (btwn Avs 14 & 16) 506/22-221-9341 • 9pm-close Wed, Fri-Sat • gay/ straight • more gay wknds • dancing/DJ • 2 dance flrs • take taxi to avoid bad area

Puchos Calle 11 & Av 8 (knock to enter) 506/2-256-1147, 506/2-222-7967 • 8pm-2:30am, from 4pm Sun • mostly gay men • also restaurant • drag shows

CAFES

Cafeteria 1830 Ave 2 (at the Gran Hotel Costa Rica)) 506/2-221-4011 • great people watching at Plaza de la Cultura

RESTAURANTS

Ankara San José de la Montaña (Heredia, San Antonio de Belén, S of church) 506/2-266-0303, 506/2-293-0089

Cafe Mundo Av 9 & Calle 15 (200 meters E of parking lot for INS, Barrio Amón) 506/2-222-6190 • 11am-11pm, 5pm-midnight Sat, clsd Sun • Italian • garden seating • also cafe/ bar • gay-owned

La Cocina de Leña in El Pueblo complex 506/2-255-1360, 506/2-256-5353 • 11am-11pm • 5 minutes from downtown • reservations recommended

Machu Piccu Calle 32 (btwn Aves 1 & 3) 506/2-222-7384 • Peruvian

Mirador Ram Luna Del centro de Aserrí, cuatro kilómetros sobre la carretera a Tabarca., Aserri 506/2-230-3060 • dinner nightly, lunch & dinner wknds, clsd Mon • hillside restaurant w/ amazing views • special buffet Wed

Olio Escalante, Bario California (N of Baselman's, San Pedro/ Los Yoses) 506/2-281-0541 • lunch & dinner, clsd Sun • Spanish • also full bar

Vishnu Vegetarian Restaurant Av 1 (btwn Calles 3 & 1) 506/2-256-6063 • 8am-9:30pm

ENTERTAINMENT & RECREATION

Gay Tours Costa Rica 506/2-305-8044 • daily events & excursions • Nov-April

Mercado Central/ Central Market Central Avenida (btwn Calles 6 & 8) • bustling market selling food, clothing, souvenirs & more

San Ramon

ACCOMMODATIONS

Angel Valley Farm B&B 200m N & 300m E of Iglesia de Los Angeles (at Autopista to Arenal Volcano) **506-2/456-4084, 506-2/350-7647 (CELL)** • gay/ straight • full brkfst • kids over 5 & small pets ok • nonsmoking • WiFi • wheelchair access • $35-65

Inn at Coyote Mountain Calle San Francisco 3 **506-2/383-0544, 902/482-8360** • gay/ straight • eco-lodge • full brkfst • pool • gay-owned • $139-450

Santa Clara

ACCOMMODATIONS

Tree Houses Hotel Costa Rica **506-2/475-6507** • gay/ straight • private treehouses in canopy of trees on wildlife refuge • full brkfst • nonsmoking • lesbian-owned • kids/ pets ok • $75-85

Tamarindo

ACCOMMODATIONS

Cala Luna Hotel & Villas Playa Langosta (at Playa Tamarindo) **506-2/653-0214, 800/503-5202** • gay-friendly • pools • kids ok • $183-640

Hotel Sueño del Mar Playa Langosta **506-2/653-0284** • gay-friendly • private hacienda on the beach • full brkfst • pool • nonsmoking • WiFi • $145-325

ARGENTINA

Buenos Aires

INFO LINES & SERVICES

La Casa del Encuentro/ Lesbian Feminist Cultural Center Rivadavia 3917 **54-1/4982-2550**

Comunidad Homosexual Argentina Tomas Liberti 1080 **54-11/4361-6382**

La Fulana Callao 339, 5th Fl **54-1/4383-7413**

ACCOMMODATIONS

1555 Malabia House Malabia 1555, Palermo Viejo (at Honduras) **54-11/4832-3345** • gay-friendly • pets ok • WiFi • $140+

The Cocker Av Juan de Garay 458 (at Defensa) **54-11/1436-28451** • WiFi • full breakfast • pets ok • gay-owned • $90-130

Don Sancho Youth Hostel Constitucion 4062 (at Boedo) **54-11/4923-1422** • gay/ straight • hostel • full brkfst • some shared baths • hot tub • kids ok • WiFi • $7-15

Faena Hotel & Universe 445 Martha Salotti St **54-11/4010-9000** • gay/ straight • luxury hotel • WiFi • live shows at The Universe

Home Hotel Honduras 5860 **54-11/4778-1008** • gay-friendly boutique hotel • pool • loft apts available • WiFi

Hotel Axel Venezuela 649 **54-11/4136-9393** • lesbians/ gay men • luxury gay hotel • WiFi • also restaurant • $173-385

Hotel Intercontinental Buenos Aires Moreno 809 **888/424-6835 (US#)**, **54-11/4340-7100** • gay-friendly • near commercial/ financial district • WiFi • fitness center • bar • restaurants

Hotel Vitrum 5641 Gorriti **866/986-5844** • gay-friendly • stylish boutique hotel

Palermo Viejo B&B Niceto Vega 4629 (at Av Scalabrini Ortiz) **54-11/4773-6092** • gay/ straight • nonsmoking • WiFi • near shopping & gay nightlife • gay-owned • $75-115

Solar Soler B&B Soler 5676 (at Bonpland) **54-11/4776-3065** • gay-friendly • kids ok • nonsmoking • $50-96

Telmho Hotel Boutique 1086 Defensa St (at Humberto Primo) **54-11/4116-5467** • gay-friendly • WiFi • $95+

BARS

Bach Bar Antonio Cabrera 4390 **54-11/5184-0137** • 11pm-close, clsd Mon • lesbians/ gay men • live shows Th-Fri • karaoke • videos

Bulnes Class Bulnes 1250 (Palermo) **54-11/4861-7492** • from 7pm Th & 11pm Fri-Sat • lesbians/ gay men • dancing/DJ

Cero Consecuencia Cabrera 3769 • 2pm-close, clsd Mon • lesbians/ gay men

La Cigale 25 May 597 **54-11/4893-2332** • 6pm-close, from 10pm Sat • gay/ straight • DJs • also restaurant

Flux Bar Marcelo T de Alvear 980 (at 9 de Julio) **54-11/5252-0258** • 7pm-close, from 8pm wknds, clsd Sun • lesbians/ gay men • dancing/DJ • art • English, Portuguese, & Russian spoken

Inside Bartolomé Mitre 1571 **54-11/4372-5439** • 6pm-close • mostly men • also restaurant • live shows • older crowd

Kim Y Novak Guemes 4900 **54-11/4773-7521** • lesbians/ gay men • kitschy cocktail lounge • transgender-friendly

KM Zero Av Santa Fe 2516 **54-11/4822-7530** • 7pm-close, clsd Sun • also restaurant • lesbians/ gay men • dancing/DJ • drag shows • strippers • videos

Mundo Bizarro 1222 Serrano **54-11/4773-1967** • gay-friendly • 1950s American-style cocktail lounge • food served

Sitges Córdoba 4119 **54-11/4861-3763** • 10:30pm-4am, till 6am Fri-Sat, clsd Mon-Tue • lesbians/ gay men • women go earlier

NIGHTCLUBS

Alsina Alsina 940 (near Plaza de Mayo) **54-11/4334-0097, 54-11/4334-0098** • 2am Fri & 10pm Sun only • lesbians/ gay men

Ambar La Fox Av Federico Lacroze 3455 (at Alvarez Thomas, at El Teatro) • Sat only • lesbians/ gay men • dancing/ DJ • young, alternative mixed crowd

Amerik Gascón 1040 (at Cordoba) **54-11/4865-4416** • open late • mostly gay men • dancing/DJ • cruisy

Angel's Viamonte 2168 • midnight-7am Th-Sat • lesbians/ gay men • dancing/DJ

Bahrein Lavalle 345 • 6pm-7am Wed & Fri, from 10pm Sat, from midnight Tue • gay/ straight • dancing/DJ • also restaurant

Club 69 Niceto Vega 5510 (btwn Humboldt & Fitzroy, Palermo) 54-1/4779-9396 • 11:30pm Th only • gay/ straight • dancing/DJ • drag shows • performance • over-the-top theme parties

Cocoliche Rivadavia 878 • gay/ straight • dancing/DJ

Fiesta Eyeliner Campichuelo 472 • monthly queer/ alternative dance party • check www.fiestaeyeliner.tk for dates

Glam Cabrera 3046 54-11/4963-2521 • midnight-close wknds • mostly gay men • popular • dancing/DJ

Juana 775 Av 44 54-1/557-6807 • from 11:30pm Fri-Sat only • lesbians/ gay men • dancing/DJ

Pacha Av Costanera y Pampa 54-11/4788-4280 • popular dance club • gay-friendly

CAFES

Gout Cafe Juncal 2124 54-11/4825-8330 • sandwiches, pastries • gay-owned

Pride Cafe Balcarce 869 (in San Telmo) 54-11/4300-6435 • 10am-10pm • live show Th night

Pure Vida Reconquista 516 (btwn Tucuman & Lavalle) 54-11/4393-0093 • 8:30am-7pm, 10am-5:30pm Sat, clsd Sun • juice bar • food served • plenty veggie

RESTAURANTS

10 Mil y Pico Cabrera 4799 54-11/4833-2385 • Mediterranean

Arevalito Arevalo 1478 54-11/4776-4252 • 9am-midnight • vegetarian

Bio Humbolt 2199 (Palermo Viejo) 54-11/4774-3880 • lunch & dinner • vegetarian • organic market

La Cabana Rodriguez Peña 1967 (at Posadas) 54-11/4814-0001 • brkfst, lunch & dinner • popular • upscale 2-flr steak house

Casa Cruz 1658 Uriarte 54-11/4833-1112 • 8:30pm-3am, later Fri-Sat • upscale, trendy restaurant • also bar

Cumana Rodriguez Pena 1149 (at Arenales) 54-11/4813-9207 • popular • regional cuisine

El Palacio de la Papa Frita Lavalle 735 (at Maipu) 54-11/4393-5849 • popular • hearty traditional meals • also Av Corrientes 1612, 11/4374-8063

Empire Tres Sargentos 427 54-11/4312-5706 • noon-midnight, 7pm-1am Sat • popular • Thai food, tapas • American bar

Filo San Martin 975 54-11/4311-0312, 54-11/4311-1871 • 8pm-close • Italian • trendy • also art gallery

Lobby Nicaragua 5944 54-11/4770-9335

Mark's Deli & Coffeehouse El Salvador 4107 (in Palermo) 54-11/4832-6244 • 11am-8pm, till 9pm Sun, clsd Mon • popular

Milion Parana 1048 54-11/4815-9925 • popular • swank lounge/ restaurant spread over 3-flr mansion • garden

Naturaleza Sabia Balcarce 958 (at Carlos Calvo) 54-11/4300-6454 • clsd Mon • vegetarian

Rave Gorriti 5092 54-11/4833-7832 • lunch Tue-Sun & dinner nightly • popular

Sucre Sucre 676 54-11/4782-9082 • upscale contemporary

Verde Llama Jorge Newbery 3623 54-11/4554-7467 • 11am-6pm, till midnight Th-Sat • organic vegetarian cafe

ENTERTAINMENT & RECREATION

Casa Brandon Luis Maria Drago 236 (at Lavalleja) 54-11/4858-0610 • events, dance parties, poetry readings, art & more • also bar/ restaurant

Espanol al Sur Pichincha 1031 #2 (at Carlos Calvo) 54-11/4942-9582, 54-11/6449-5447 • gay-friendly • Spanish language & tango classes • lesbian-owned

La Marshall Maipu 444 54-11/4912-9043 • 8:30pm Wed • exclusively gay tango lessons

Museo Evita Peron Lafinur 2988 (in Palermo) 54-11/4807-9433 • 2pm-7:30pm, clsd Mon

Out And About Pub Crawl • make new friends on a tour of the local gay bars

RETAIL SHOPS

Gay Wine Store Viamonte 579 54-11/4313-2909, 54-11/4313-2896 • lesbians/ gay men

PUBLICATIONS

AG Magazine 54-11/4304-6357

G-Maps Buenos Aires Franklin 1463, Florida Oeste 54-11/4730-0729 • free pocket-size gay map of Buenos Aires

La Otra Guía Apartado 78 (Suc Olivos) • free gay monthly guide

BRAZIL

Rio de Janeiro

Note: M°=Metro station

INFO LINES & SERVICES

Grupo Arco-Iris Rio de Janeiro Rua Monte Alegre 167, Santa Teresa **55–21/2215–0844** • 1pm-7pm, till 11pm Sat, clsd Sun • LGBT community center

Rainbow Kiosk Atlantic Av (in front of Copacabana Palace Hotel) **55–21/2275–1641** • popular • 24hrs • lesbians/ gay men • tourist info • drag shows

ACCOMMODATIONS

Ananab Guesthouse Rio Rua Alice (Laranjeiras) **55–21/2557–6789** • gay/ straight • guesthouse • also apt rental • full brkfst • WiFi • gay-owned • $45-125

Casa Dois Gatos Rua Rosalina Terra 6, Cabo Frio **561/282–0023, 55–22/2645–5806** • mostly gay men • free transportation from Rio airport • pool • WiFi • gay-owned • $1,095/ week

Copacabana Panorama 3806 Av Atlantica (at Souza Lima) **617/803–9164** • oceanfront condo w/ gorgeous view of Copacabana Beach • short walk to gay night life • $70-125

Ipanema Plaza Rua Farme Amoedo (at Rua Prudente de Morais) **55–21/3687–2000** • gay/ straight • near gay beach • rooftop pool • also restaurant • $150-265

MyRioCondo.com 3150 Avenida Atlantica, Apt 901 (Copacabana) **808/536–4263 (US#), 888/236–0799** • gay/ straight • WiFi • kids ok • gay-owned • $180-375

Rio Penthouse **55–21/2541–3882** • gay-friendly • beachfront apts & penthouse suites

BARS

Casa da Lua Rua Barao da Torre 240 **55–21/3813–3972** • 11am-2am, clsd Mon • mostly women • cozy neighborhood bar • food served • occasional live music

Melt Rua Rita Ludolf 47 **55–21/2249–9309** • gay-friendly • lounge • also restaurant

Star's Club (Buraco da Lacraia) Rua André Cavalcante 58 (Centro) **55–21/2242–0446, 55–21/2224–8880** • popular • gay/ straight • dancing/DJ • drag shows • transgender-friendly

NIGHTCLUBS

Boite 1140 1140 Rua Capitao Menezes **55–21/7830–8867** • 11pm-5am Th-Sun • lesbians/ gay men • dancing/DJ • drag shows

Casa da Matriz Rua Henrique de Novaes 107 **54–11/2226–9691, 54–11/2266–1014** • 11pm-close, clsd Tue • gay/ straight • dancing/DJ • 18+

Dama de Ferro Rua Vinicius de Moraes 288 (Ipanema) **55–21/2247–2330** • lesbians/ gay men • dancing/DJ

Fosfobox Rua Siqueira Campos 143 **55–21/2548–7498** • open Th-Sun • gay/ straight • underground techno

Galeria Cafe Rua Teixeira de Melo 31 (Ipanema) **55–21/2523–8250** • 10:30pm-close, clsd Sun-Tue • gay/ straight • dancing/DJ • also gallery

La Girl Club Rua Raul Pompeia 102 (Copacabana) **55–21/2247–8342** • 9pm-3am, clsd Mon-Wed • popular • mostly women • dancing/DJ • strippers • young crowd

Ideal Party Rua da Carioca 64 **55–21/2252–3460** • gay/ straight • dancing/DJ • huge club w/ visting big-name DJs

Papa G 42 Almerinda Freitas **55–21/2450–1253** • lesbians/ gay men • dancing/DJ • drag shows • theme nights

Up Turn 2000 Av das Americas **55–21/3387–7957** • lesbians/ gay men • dancing/DJ • food served • outdoor seating

The Week 154 Rua Sacadura Cabral **55–21/2253–1020** • gay-friendly dance club

CAFES

Copa Cafe Av Atlantica 3056 **55–21/2235–2947**

Expresso Carioca Rua Farme de Amoedo 76 **55–21/2267–8604**

RESTAURANTS

Bar d'Hotel Av Delfim Moreira 696 (2nd Flr, inside Marina All Suites Hotel, Leblon) **55–21/2172–1100** • food served all day, bar till late • Mediterranean • see & be seen

Caroline Cafe 10 Rua JJ Seabra **55–21/2540–0705** • sushi • full bar

Pizzaria Guanabara 1228 Ave Ataulfo de Paiva, Leblon **55–21/2294–0797**

Tamino Rua Arnaldo Quintela 26 **55–21/2295–1849** • 7pm-4am, clsd Mon-Wed • club by night (lesbians/ gay men) • women's night Fri

To Nem Ai Rua Farme de Amoedo 57 **55–21/2513–3775** • lesbians/ gay men • popular bar with outdoor seating

Via Sete Rua Garcia D'Avila 125 (in Ipanema) **55–21/2512–8100** • noon-midnight • plenty veggie

Zero Zero Av Padre Leonel Franca 240 (inside planetarium) **55–21/2540-8041** • gay/ straight • more gay Sun • dancing/DJ • upscale restaurant • nightclub

ENTERTAINMENT & RECREATION

Copacabana Beach at Rua Rodolfo Dantas • gay across from Copacabana Palace Hotel

Farme de Amoedo/ Farme Gay Beach across from Rua Farme de Amoedo • see & be seen at this popular gay beach

Ipanema Beach • gay E of Rua Farme Amoedo

PUBLICATIONS

Rio For Partiers **55–21/2523–9857** • great guide book

CHILE

Santiago

Note: M°=Metro station

ACCOMMODATIONS

B&B Santiago Corte Suprema 177 (Departamento B) **56–2/696-9499** • lesbians/ gay men • full brkfst • gay-owned • $70-100

Hotel Castillo Pio Nono 420 (Bellavista) **56–2/735-0243** • lesbians/ gay men • 1920s building w/ ornate interior decor • includes brkfst • $35-71

BARS

Amor del Bueno Ernesto Pinto Lagarrigue 106 **56–2/737-2790** • 5pm-1am, till 4am Fri-Sat • clsd Sun • mostly women • also restaurant • lesbian-owned

Bar 105 Bombero Nuñez 105 • 9pm-late Th-Sat • lesbians/ gay men

Bar de Willy Av 11 de Septiembre 2214 (Común Providencia) **56–2/381-1806** • 10pm-4am, till 5am wknds • lesbians/ gay men • live shows

El Closet Santa Filomena 138 (at Bombero Nuñez) • lesbians/ gay men • karaoke

Dionisio Bombero Nuñez 111 (at Dardinac) **56–2/737-6065** • 9pm-close, clsd Sun-Mon • lesbians/ gay men • food served • live shows

Farinelli Bombero Nuñez 68 (Recoleta) **56–2/732-8966** • 5pm-2am • internet access • food served • live shows • drag shows • strippers

Pub Friend's Bombero Nuñez 365 (at Dominica, barrio Bellavista) **56–2/777-3979** • 9:30pm-4am, till 5am Fri-Sat • lesbians/ gay men • drag shows

Vox Populi Ernesto Pinto Lagarrigue 364 (Bellavista) **56–2/671-1267** • 9:30pm-3am, clsd Sun-Mon • mostly gay men • also restaurant • garden patio

NIGHTCLUBS

Blondie Alameda 2879, loc 104 **56–2/681–7793** • gay/ straight • alternative • dancing/DJ • theme nights

Bokhara Discoteque Pio Nono 430 (at Constitución, barrio Bellavista) **56–2/732–1050, 56–2/735–1271** • 10pm-6am, till 7am wknds • popular • mostly gay men • dancing/DJ • food served • strippers • drag shows

Bunker Bombero Nuñez 159 (Bellavista) **56–2/738-2301, 56–2/738-2314** • 11pm-close Fri-Sat • lesbians/ gay men • dancing/DJ • food served • live shows

Club Principe Pio Nono 398 **56–2/777-6381** • mostly gay men • dancing/DJ • drag shows • strippers

Mascara Purísima 129 (Bellavista) **56–2/737-4123** • mostly women • dancing/DJ

Nueva Cero Euclides 1204 par 2 Gran Avenida • mostly gay men • dancing/DJ • drag shows

CAFES

Mitos Diagonal Paraguay 477 (at Alameda) **56–2/632-7163** • 10am-3am, 11am-5am Fri-Sat, 2pm-1am Sun • internet cafe

Tavelli Andrés de Fuenzalida 34 (Providencia) **56–2/231-9862** • 8:30am-10pm, from 9:30am Sat • popular

RESTAURANTS

Ali Baba 102 Santa Filomena (Barrio Bellavista, Recoleta) **56–2/732-7036** • Middle Eastern

Capricho Español Purisima 65 (barrio Bellavista) **56–2/777-7674** • dinner only • Spanish • full bar

La Pizza Nostra Av Providencia 1975 & Pedro de Valdivia **56–2/231-8941** • Italian

Santo Remedio 152 Roman Diaz, Providencia **56–2/235-0984** • 6:30pm-close, from 10:30pm wknds • global cuisine • full bar • live DJs

El Toro Loreto 33 **56–2/737-5937** • noon-midnight

Austria

Vienna

Info Lines & Services

Gay & Lesbian AA 43–1/799–5599, 43–665/490–5603 **(English)** • call for info

Hosi Zentrum Heumuhlgasse 14 43–1/216–6604 • many groups & events • also quarterly news magazine

Rosa-Lila-Villa Linke Wienzeile 102 (near Hofmühlgasse, U4-Pilgramgasse) 43–1/586–8150 **(WOMEN)**, 43–1/585–4343 **(MEN)** • LGBT center • staffed 5pm-8pm Mon, Wed, Fri • info • gay city maps • also meeting place for various groups • also cafe-bar

Accommodations

Arcotel Wimberger Neubaugürtel 34–36 (at Goldschlagstr) 43–1/521–650 • gay-friendly • restaurant & bar on premises • also fitness club

Designapartment Vienna Glockengasse 25/9 43–650/592–8941 • gay-friendly • full kitchen • terrace • WiFi • gay-owned • €100-130

Golden Tulip Art Hotel Vienna Brandmayergasse 7-9 43–1/5445–108 • gay-friendly • stylish hotel • central location • €81-112

Hotel Urania Obere Weißgerberstr 7 (U-Schwedenplatz) 43–1/713–1711 • gay-friendly • centrally located & inexpensive art hotel • wheelchair access • gay-owned •€48-140

Le Méridien Wien Opernring 13-15 43–1/588–900, 800/543–4300 • gay-friendly • pool • sauna • hot tub • also restaurant & bar

Pension Wild Lange Gasse 10 (off Lerchenfelder Str) 43–1/406–5174 • mostly gay men • rooms & apts • also restaurant • gay sauna & bar in basement • gay-owned • €48-114

Das Tyrol Mariahilfer Str 15 43–1/587–5415 • gay-friendly • small luxury hotel • € 109-259

Bars

Cafe Cheri Franzensg 2 43–650/208–1471 • 10pm-4am • mostly gay men • also cafe

Cafe Savoy Linke Wienzeile 36 (at Köstlergasse) 43–1/586–7348 • 8am-2am • popular • lesbians/ gay men • upscale cafe-bar

Felixx Gumpendorferstr 5 43–1/920–4714 • 7pm-3am, from 10am Sat, 7pm-1am Sun • lesbians/ gay men • food • WiFi

Frauenzentrum Bar Währingerstr 59 (enter on Prechtlgasse) 43–1/402–8754 • 7pm-midnight Th-Sat • women • dancing/DJ

Marea Alta Gumpendorferstr 28 43–699/1159–7131 • 7pm-2am, till 4am Fri-Sat, clsd Sun-Mon • mostly women • young crowd

Peter's Operncafé Hartauer Riemergasse 9 (at Singer) 43–1/512–8981 • 6pm-2am, clsd Sun-Mon • gay/ straight • food served • terrace

Studio 67 Gumpendorferstr 67 43–1/966–7182 • 10am-4am Th-Sat • gay/ straight • dancing/DJ • also upscale lounge

Das Versteck Nikolaigasse 1 (at Grünangergasse, U1-Stephansplatz) 43–1/513–4053 • 6pm-midnight, from 7pm Sat, clsd Sun • gay/ straight • young crowd

Village Bar Stiegengasse 8 (near Naschmarkt) 43–1/676–3848977 • 8pm-3am • mostly men • young crowd

Wiener Freiheit Schönbrunner Str 25 (U4-Kettenbrückengasse) 43–1/931–9111 • 8pm-midnight, till 4am Fri-Sat, clsd Sun-Mon • lesbians/ gay men • transgender-friendly • 3 flrs • disco 10pm-4am Fri-Sat • also cafe

Nightclubs

g.spot Neubaugasse 2 (at Camera Club) 43–1/523–3063 • 9pm 1st Fri • mostly women • dancing/DJ • monthly parties • call for info

Heaven Gay Night 43–1/523–3063 • 10pm-6am Sat • mostly men • dancing/DJ • transgender-friendly • strippers • young crowd

Las Chicas Lerchenfelderstr 35 (at Phoenix Supperclub) • 4th Sat only • women only • dancing/DJ

Queer Beat Landstr Hauptstr 38 (at the Viper Room) • 2nd & 4th Sat only • mostly gay men • dancing/DJ

Up! Mariahilfer Str 3 (at Lutz Club) • 2nd Fri only • mostly gay men • uplifting house music

Why Not? Tiefer Graben 22 (at Wipplinger, U-Schottentor) 43–1/925–3024 • 10pm-close Fri-Sat & before public holidays • mostly gay men • dancing/DJ • live shows • videos

Cafes

Bakul Margaretenstr 58 • 9am-2am • also guesthouse

Cafe Berg Berggasse 8 (at Wasagasse, U2-Schottentor) 43–1/319–5720 • 10am-1am • popular • lesbians/ gay men • cafe-bar

Cafe Central Herrengasse 14 (at Strauchgasse) **43–1/533–3763** • 7:30am-10pm, from 10am Sun & public holidays • "world's most famous coffeehouse"

Cafe Standard Margaretenstr 63 **43–1/581–0586** • 8am-midnight, from 11am wknds

Cafe Stein Währinger Str 6–8 (near U-Schottentor) **43–1/319–7241** • 7am-1am, from 9am Sun • gay-friendly • cafe-bar • internet access • terrace

Das Möbel Burggasse 10 (Spittelberg) **43–1/524–9497** • 10am-1am • trendy • also art gallery • WiFi

Point of Sale Schleifmuhlgasse 12 **43–1/941–6397** • 7am-1am • cafe & deli • also vegan items • WiFi • also bar

Vienna

LGBT PRIDE:

Rainbow Parade in July, web: www.regenbogenparade.at.

ANNUAL EVENTS:

January - Regenbogenball (Rainbow Ball), web: www.hosiwien.at/ball.

January - Resonanzen (classical music festival), web: www.konzerthaus.at.

March/ April - OsterKlang (classical music festival), web: www.theater-wien.at.

May - Life Ball (AIDS benefit), web: www.lifeball.org.

May - Vienna Festival, web: www.festwochen.at.

June - Queer Film Festival 43-1/524.62.74, web: www.identities.at.

June/ July - Jazz Fest Wien, web: www.viennajazz.org.

July/ August - ImPulsTanz (dance festival), web: www.impulstanz.com.

October - Viennale Film Festival 43-1/526-5947, web: www.viennale.at.

October - Vienna In Black.

October - Wien Modern (contemporary music festival) 43-1/242-00, web: www.wienmodern.at.

CITY INFO:

43–1/24–555, web: www.info.wien.at.

BEST VIEW:

Overlooking the city from the top of the Giant Ferris Wheel.

ATTRACTIONS:

Art Nouveau buildings.

Belvedere Palace/Austrian Gallery 43–1/795–57–0, web: www.belvedere.at.

Sigmund Freud Museum 43–1/319–1596, web: www.freud-museum.at.

House of Music 43-1/51–648, web: www.hdm.at.

Imperial Palace, web: www.hofburg-wien.at.

Jewish Museum 43–1/535–0431, web: www.jmw.at.

Museum of Fine Arts 43–1/525–24–0, web: www.khm.at.

Schönbrunn Palace 43–1/811–13-239, web: www.schoenbrunn.at.

St Stephen's Cathedral 43-1/515–52–3767, web: www.stephansdom.at.

State Opera House 43–1/514–44–2250, web: www.staatsoper.at.

Vienna Boys' Choir, web: www.wsk.at.

WEATHER:

Mild, rainy summers and chilly winters. September is a good time to visit.

TRANSIT:

43–1/60-160, web: www.taxi60160.at.

Vienna Airport Lines, web: postbus.at.

Schik Schikanedergasse 5 • 7pm-2am, till 4am Fri-Sat, clsd Sun • lesbians/ gay men • WiFi • also bar

Smart Cafe Kostlergasse 9 43–1/585–7165 • 6pm-2am, Fri-Sat till 4am, clsd Sun-Mon • gay/ straight • S/M & fetish cafe

Restaurants

Andino Münzwardeingasse 2 (U4-Pilgramgasse) 43–1/587–6125 • 11am-2am, from 10am Sat, 11am-midnight Sun • Latin American • live music • also full bar

Aux Gazelles Rahlgasse 5 43–1/585–6645 • French/ Moroccan restaurant 6pm-midnight • Arabian-style lounge, cafe & deli 11am-2am • also Turkish steam baths noon-10pm

Bin Im Leo Servitengasse 14 43–1/391–7763 • 4pm-midnight, from noon wknds • beer/ wine • plenty veggie

Cafe-Restaurant Willendorf Linke Wienzeile 102 (near Hofmuhlgasse, U4-Pilgramgasse) 43–1/587–1789 • 6pm-2am, food served till midnight • lesbians/ gay men • plenty veggie • full bar • terrace

Gina's Weibar Marchettigasse 11 0699/1507–1507 • 6pm-1am, 11am-10pm Sun • mostly women • Italian • patio

Halle Museumsquartier 1 43–1/523–7001 • 10am-2am, modern bistro • artsy crowd

Kantine Porzellangasse 19 43–1/319–5918 • 6pm-2am • Thai

Motto Schönbrunner Str 30 (enter on Rüdigergasse) 43–1/587–0672 • 6pm-2am, till 4am Fri-Sat • popular • trendy • also bar • patio • reservations recommended

Santo Spirito Kumpfgasse 7 43–1/512–9998 • 6pm-11pm, bar till 2am • classical music

Schon Schön Lindengasse 53 (Ecke Andreagasse) • lunch & dinner • fashionable restaurant • also bar • also clothing & hair salon

Stöger Ramperstorffergasse 63 43–1/544–7596 • 11am-midnight, clsd Sun • Viennese

Zum Roten Elefanten Gumpendorferstrasse 3 43–1/966–8008 • lunch & dinner, open late Fri-Sat, clsd Sun

Entertainment & Recreation

Haus der Musik/ House of Music Seilerstätte 30 43–1/516–4810 • 10am-10pm • interactive museum of sound • also cafe

Kunsthistorisches Museum Maria Theresien-Platz (enter Heldenplatz) 43–1/525–240 • 10am-6pm, till 9pm Th, clsd Mon • not to be missed • works from Ancient Egypt to the Renaissance to Klimt

Resis.Danse Novarragasse 40 (at Hosi Gay & Lesbian Center) 43–1/216–6604 • 7pm-midnight Fri • women only • ballroom dancing • dance classes • contact for dates & location

Bookstores

American Discount Rechte Wienzeile 5 (at Paniglgasse) 43–1/587–5772 • 9:30am-6:30pm, till 5pm Sat, clsd Sun • int'l magazines & books • also Neubaugasse 39, 43–1/523–37–07

Löwenherz Berggasse 8 (next to Cafe Berg, enter on Wasagasse, U2-Schottentor) 43–1/317–2982 • 10am-7pm, till 8pm Fri, till 6pm Sat, clsd Sun • LGBT • large selection of English titles

Publications

Vienna Gay Guide 43–1/789–1000 • city map & guide

Erotica

Art-X Percostr 3 43–1/25804–4413 • 10am-8pm, till 9pm Th, till 6pm Sat, clsd Sun • leather, latex, rubber • toys • music • videos • magazines

Tiberius Lindengasse 2 (at Stiftgasse, U3-Neubaugasse) 43–1/522–0474 • clsd Sun • wheelchair access • leather, rubber & toys

CZECH REPUBLIC

Prague (Praha)

Note: M°=Metro station

Prague is divided into 10 city districts: Praha—1, Praha—2, etc.

Praha—Overview

INFO LINES & SERVICES

➤ **GayGuide.net Prague** • gay tourist info

Prague Gay Guided Tours • tour Prague by foot or car

ACCOMMODATIONS

Apartments in Prague 420/251–512–502, 303/800-0858 • gay/straight • WiFi • kids/ pets ok • €65-160

Praha—1

ACCOMMODATIONS

The Castle Steps Nerudova 7 (at Malostranske Namesti) 420/257–216–337, 800/860-0571 • gay/straight • located in city center • WiFi • €47-173

Hotel Metropol Narodni 33 (at Na Perstyne) 420/246–022–100 • gay/ straight • design hotel • all-glass facade • €89-220

The ICON Boutique Hotel V Jame 6 (at Vodickova) 420/221–634–100 • gay/straight • full brkfst • WiFi • wheelchair access

Old Town Apartments • mostly gay men • in city center

Prague Center Guest Residence Stepanska Street (at Zitna) • lesbians/ gay men • near Wenceslas Square & river • kids ok • gay-owned • €58-178

Prague (Praha)

ANNUAL EVENTS:

May/June - Prague Spring International Music Festival, web: www.festival.cz.

October - Mezipatra, Czech Gay & Lesbian Film Festival, web: www.mezipatra.cz.

CITY INFO:

Tourist Info Center Mostecka 4, web: www.prague-information.eu.

ATTRACTIONS:

Charles Bridge.

Jewish Museum 420/221-711-511, web: www.jewishmuseum.cz.

Museum of Fine Arts 420/222–220–218, web: www.cmvu.cz.

Old Jewish Quarter.

Prague Castle 420/224-373-368, web: www.hrad.cz/en/prazsky_hrad/n avsteva_hradu.shtml.

Wenceslas Square.

BEST VIEW:

For a great view of the whole of Prague, head for the Observation Tower (a mini version of the Eiffel Tower) on Petrin Hill. The Old Town Bridge Tower affords a fabulous view of Old Town, the Charles Bridge, and the Vltava River.

WEATHER:

Continental climate. Late spring or early fall are the best times to visit, especially in June before the tourist season is in full swing. Winters can get very cold with average daytime highs of 34° F.

TRANSIT:

Taxi AAA 420/222-333-222, web: www.radiotaxiaaa.cz.

Profi Taxi 420/261-314-151.

CSA shuttle.

There are 6 Transportation Info Centers throughout city with info on metro, trams, buses & funicular, Ruzyne Airport

BARS

Friends Bar Bartolomejská 11 **420/226–211–920** • 6pm-4am • popular • mostly men • dancing/DJ • neighborhood bar • DJ Wed-Sat • videos • WiFi

K.U. Bar Rytirská 13 (at Perlová, near Oldtown Square) **420/221–181–081** • 7pm-4am • gay/ straight • upscale & trendy

Silwer Cafe and Bar Jungmannova Namesti 21 (at Vaclavske) **420/222–212–702** • 10am-2am • gay/straight • WIFi

Tingl Tangl Karolíny Svetlé 12 (at Konviktska) **420/224–238–278** • 11am-10pm • lesbians/ gay men • dancing/DJ • cabaret 9pm-5am Wed & Fri-Sat • drag shows • full restaurant

CAFES

Cafe Cafe Rytirská 10 (at Perlová, near Oldtown Square) **420/224–210–597** • 10am-11pm

Cafe Erra Konviktská 11 **420/222–220–568** • 10am-midnight • gay/ straight • salads, sandwiches & entrées

Cafe Louvre Národni 22 (Mº Narodni Trida) **420/224–930–949** • 8am-11:30pm, from 9am wknds • gay/ straight • food served • billiard tables • nonsmoking

Vertigo Havelská 4 (at Perlová) **420/744–744–356** • cafe & restaurant • also nightclub • gay-friendly • theme nights • DJs

RESTAURANTS

Casa Andina Dusni 15 **420/224–815–996** • lunch & dinner • Peruvian/ Latin American

Petrinské Terasy Seminarská Zahrada 13, Petrin **420/257–320–688, 420/602–224–096** • noon-11pm • in a former monastery • great view • gay-owned

ENTERTAINMENT & RECREATION

Sex Machines Museum Melantrichova 18 **420/ 227–186–260** • 10am-11pm

BOOKSTORES

Globe Patrossova 6 **420/224–934–203** • English-language bookstore • also cafe

Praha—2

ACCOMMODATIONS

Balbin Penzion Balbinova 26 (near Wenceslas Square) **420/222–250–660** • gay/straight • located in city center • full brkfst • WiFi • €44-207

Prague Saints Polska 32 (office location) (at Trebizkeho, at Saints Bar) **420/775–152–041, 420/775–152–042** • lesbians/ gay men • apts in gay Vinohrady district • gay-owned • €60-120

BARS

Charmisma Cafe Anglicka 1 (at Legeerova) **420/773–973–812** • 5pm-2am, clsd Sun • lesbians/gay men

Fan Fan Club Dittrichova 5 (at Trojanova) **420/776–360–698** • 5pm-2am • mostly gay men • karaoke

JampaDampa V Tunich 10 (at Zitna) **420/737–105–193, 420/739–592–099** • 2pm-2am, 4pm-6am Fri-Sat, clsd Sun • popular • mostly women • dancing/DJ • karaoke

Klub 21 Rimska 21 (at Balbinova) **420/603–539–475** • 6pm-close, clsd Sun • lesbians/ gay men • cellar bar/ gallery • food • young crowd • mostly Czechs

Klub Strelec Zitna 51 (at Legerova) **420/224–941–446** • 5pm-2am, till midnight Sun • gay-friendly • beer & wine

Saints Polska 32 (at Trebizkeho) **420/222–250–326** • 7pm-4am • lesbians/ gay men

NIGHTCLUBS

Termix Trebizkeho 4 (at Vinohradska) **420/222–710–462** • 8pm-5am, clsd Mon-Tue • popular • lesbians/ gay men • dancing/DJ

Valentino Vinohradska 40 (at Blanicka) **420/222–513–491, 420/776–360–698 (CELL)** • 2pm-5am • lesbians/ gay men • dancing/DJ • video • 3 levels • darkroom

CAFES

Angels Cafe Vinohradská 30 • 6pm-midnight, from 2pm Sat, 11am-10pm Sun • cafe & lounge • stylish interior

RESTAURANTS

Bejkarna Slezka 19 **420/222–524–663** • 11am-midnight, till 1am Fri-Sat • also bar • WiFi

Celebrity Cafe Vinohradska 40 (in Vinohrady) **420/222–511–343** • 8am-2am, noon-3am Sat, noon-midnight Sun • gay/ straight • also bar

Radost FX Belehradska 120, Vinohrady **420/224–254–776, 420/603–193–711** • fabulous wknd brunch • vegetarian cafe • also straight nightclub w/ popular monthly gay party

Sahara Cafe Namesti Miru 6 **420/222–514–987** • lunch & dinner • salad, pasta & meat

Praha—3

BARS

Gulliver Milicova 6 (at Siefertova) **420/721-031-965** • noon-10pm, from 5pm Sat, clsd Sun • lesbians/ gay men • wine bar • lesbian-owned

Latimerie Club Cafe Slezska 74 (at Nitranska) **420/224-252-049** • 4pm-close • lesbians/ gay men

Piano Bar Milesovská 10 (at Ondrickova) **420/775-727-796** • 7pm-close • lesbians/ gay men • mostly Czech older crowd • food served

ENTERTAINMENT & RECREATION

TV Tower Mahlerovy sady 1 **420/242-418-778, 420/242-418-766** • get a bird's-eye view of the city from the top of this tower • also restaurant 10am-11pm

Praha—4

GYMS & HEALTH CLUBS

Plavecky Stadion Podoli Podolská 74 **420/241-433-952** • 6am-9:45 pm • gay/ straight • public baths • restaurants • women's sauna Th-Fri & Sun

Praha—5

ACCOMMODATIONS

Andel's Hotel Stroupeznickeho 21 (at Pizenska) **420/296-889-688** • gay/straight

Praha—7

CAFES

Duhova Cajovna Milada Horáková 73 (at Ovenecka) **420/775-269-699** • 3pm-midnight • "Rainbow Tearoom" • food served

Praha—8

ACCOMMODATIONS

Hotel Villa Mansland Prague Stepnicná 9, Liben (at Na Malem Klinu) **420/286-884-405, 420/777-839-733** • mostly gay men • pool • restaurant • WiFi • gay-owned • CZK1.350-3.000

Praha—10

ACCOMMODATIONS

Ron's Rainbow Guest House Bulharska 4 (at Finská) **420/271-725-664, 420/731-165-022 (CELL)** • gay/ straight • quiet & friendly atmosphere • near city center • gay-owned • €70-336

DENMARK

Copenhagen

INFO LINES & SERVICES

Kafe Knud Skindergade 21 **45/3332-5861** • 4pm-10pm Tue & Th only • HIV resource center • cafe open Tue & Th only

Wonderful Copenhagen Convention & Visitors Bureau Vesterbrogade 4A **45/7022-2442 (TOURIST INFO)**

ACCOMMODATIONS

Carstens Guesthouse Christians Brygge 28, 5th flr **45/3314-9107, 45/4050-9107 (CELL)** • lesbians/ gay men • B&B, hostel & apts • shared baths • kids/ pets ok • WiFi • 5 minutes from gay area • DKK180-1,185

First Hotel Skt. Petri Krystalgade 22 **45/3345-9100** • hotel embodying the ultra-coolest of Scandinavian design • great bar • WiFi • wheelchair access

Hotel Fox Jarmers Plads 3 **45/3395-7755, 45/3313-3000** • gay/ straight • nonsmoking • artistic rooms • central location • roof terrace • also lounge & restaurant • DKK945-1,620

Hotel Windsor Frederiksborggade 30, 1360 **45/3311-0830** • mostly gay men • near gay scene • shared baths • gay-owned • €66-76

BARS

Cafe Intime Allegade 25, Frederiksberg **45/3834-1958** • 6pm-2am • gay-friendly • cafe-bar • piano bar

Can-Can Mikkel Bryggers Gade 11 **45/3311-5010** • 2pm-2am, till 5am Fri-Sat • mostly gay men • friendly neighborhood bar

Centralhjørnet Kattesundet 18 **45/3311-8549** • noon-2am • mostly gay men • WiFi

Chaca Studiestraede 39 **45/5039-1797** • 7pm-5am Wed-Sat • mostly women

Dunkel Bar Vester Voldgade 10 • 6pm-5am, clsd Sun-Mon • gay/ straight • dancing/DJ

Gimmick Istedgade 24 **45/2646-4678** • 4pm-close, clsd Sun • lesbians/ gay men • WiFi • lesbian-owned

Masken Studiestræde 33 **45/3391-0937** • 2pm-3am, till 5am Fri-Sat • popular • lesbians/ gay men • cafe-bar • WiFi

Never Mind Nørre Voldgade 2 **45/3311-8886** • 10pm-6am • mostly gay men

Oscar Bar Cafe Radhuspladsen 77 **45/3312-0999** • noon-2am • mostly men • lesbians welcome • food served • great happy hour

Vela Viktoriagade 2-4 45/3331-3419 • 8pm-
midnight Wed, till 2am Th, till 5am Fri-Sat, clsd
Sun-Tue • mostly women • neighborhood bar

Restaurants

Jailhouse Restaurant & Bar Studiestraede
12 45/3315-2255 • 3pm-2am, till 5am Fri-Sat
• popular

Entertainment & Recreation

Amager Strandpark • beach 5 km from
city center

Bellevue Beach • mostly gay beach, left
end is nude

BLUS (Bøsse/ Lesbiske Studerende)
Købmagergade 52 (at Studenterhuset) •
7pm-midnight Tue • lesbians/ gay men •
student-run GayDay cafe

Erotica

Lust Mikkel Bryggersgade 3A 45/3333-0110 •
erotica for women

Copenhagen

Where the Girls Are:
Strolling Studiestraede with the
boys, or enjoying a beverage at
Cafe Ziraf.

LGBT Pride:
August. www.copenhagenpride.dk

Annual Events:
October - Gay & Lesbian Film
Festival 45/3313-0766, web:
www.cglff.dk.

City Info:
Copenhagen Visitors Bureau
45/7022-2442, web: www.visit-
copenhagen.com.

Best View:
From the dome of Marble Church, or
from the spiral tower of Our
Savior's Church.

Weather:
Winters are cold & wet, with
temperatures in the upper 30ºs.
Early summer is the best time to
visit, when locals enjoy long days
and temperatures around 70º.

Transit:
Kobenhavns Taxa 3535-3535, web:
www.4x35.dk.
Metro 45/3311-1700, www.m.dk.
Ask about the Copenhagen Card,
which offers bargains on museums and public transportation.
Bycyklen 45/3616-4233, web:
www.bycyklen.dk. 110 racks
around the city center offering
free bicycle rental!

Attractions:
Botanisk Have (Botanical Garden)
45/3532-2222, web:
www.botanik.snm.ku.dk.
Dansk Design Center
45/3369-3369, web:
www.ddc.dk.
Latin Quarter.
The Little Mermaid.
Marmorkirken (Marble Church)
45/3315-0144, web:
www.marmorkirken.dk.
Nationalmuseet (National Museum)
45/3313-4411, web:
www.natmus.dk.
Statens Museum for Kunst (Royal
Museum of Fine Arts)
45/3374-8494, web:
www.smk.dk.
Strøget shopping district.
Tivoli 45/3515-1001, web:
www.tivoli.dk.
Vor Frelsers Kirke (Our Savior's
Church), web:
www.vorfrelserkirke.dk.

ENGLAND

London

London is divided into 6 regions:
London—Overview
London—Central
London—West
London—North
London—East
London—South

London—Overview

INFO LINES & SERVICES

London Lesbian/ Gay Switchboard
44–(0)20/7837-7324 • 10am-11pm

NIGHTCLUBS

Stiletto • sexy monthly women's party • check www.stilettoparty.co.ukfor details

Torture Garden 44–020/7613-4733 • the worlds largest fetish / body art club • check www.torturegarden.com for venue locations

ENTERTAINMENT & RECREATION

London Gay Symphony Orchestra
44–(0)79/6385-3099

The Women's Library, London Metropolitan University Old Castle St 44–(0)20/7320-2222 • clsd Sun • also cafe • museum • cultural center • call for events • nonsmoking

PUBLICATIONS

Diva 44–(0)20/7424-7400 • glorious glossy magazine for lesbians & bisexual women

g3 44–(0)20/7272-0093 • free monthly lesbian glossy

The Pink Paper 44–(0)20/7424-7414 • free LGBT newspaper

London—Central

London—Central includes Soho, Covent Garden, Bloomsbury, Mayfair, Westminster, Pimlico & Belgravia

ACCOMMODATIONS

Dover Hotel 42/44 Belgrave Rd 44–(0)20/7821-9085 • gay-friendly • WiFi • £70-140

Fitz B&B Colville Place (btwn Charlotte St & Whitfield St) 44–(0)78/3437-2866 • lesbians/ gay men • 18th-c townhouse • nonsmoking • WiFi • gay-owned • £50-75

George Hotel 58–60 Cartwright Gardens (N of Russell Square) 44–(0)20/7387-8777 • gay-friendly • full brkfst • some shared baths • kids ok • £45-99

Hazlitt's 6 Frith St (Soho Sq) 44–(0)20/7434-1771 • gay-friendly • WiFi • £175-395

Lincoln House 33 Gloucester Pl, Marble Arch (at Baker St) 44–20/7486-7630 • gay/ straight • B&B • full brkfst • WiFi • wheelchair access • £63-139

Manors & Co 1 Baker St (at Fitzhardinge) 44–(0)20/430-2006, 800/454-4385 • gay-friendly • luxury apts • wheelchair access

Waverley House Hotel 130-134 Southampton Row (Bloomsbury) 44–(0)20/7833-3691, 44–(0)20/7833-2579 • gay-friendly • full brkfst • WiFi • also restaurant & bar

BARS

Note: "Pub hours" usually means 11am-11pm Mon-Sat and noon-3pm & 7pm-10:30pm Sun

The Admiral Duncan 54 Old Compton St (Soho) 44–(0)20/7437-5300 • pub hours • popular • lesbians/ gay men • neighborhood bar • transgender-friendly

Bar Soho 23-25 Old Compton St (at Frith St) 44–(0)20/7439-0439 • noon-1am, till 3am Fri-Sat, from 4pm Sun

The Candy Bar 4 Carlisle St, S (at Dean) 44–(0)20/7494-4041 • 5pm-11:30pm, till 2am Fri-Sat • women only (men welcome as guests) • dancing/DJ • food served • karaoke • strippers • also a location in Brighton

Compton's of Soho 51-53 Old Compton St (at Dean St) 44–(0)20/7479-7961 • noon-11pm, till 10:30pm Sun • popular • mostly gay men • leather • food served Sun • wheelchair access

Dog and Duck 18 Bateman St (at Frith St) 44–020/7494-0697 • 10am-11:30pm • gay/ straight • neighborhood bar • food served

Duke of Wellington 77 Wardour (Soho) 44–(0)20/7439-1274 • pub hours • lesbians/ gay men • snacks

The Edge 11 Soho Square (at Oxford St) 44–(0)20/7439-1313 • noon-1am, till 10:30pm Sun • popular • dancing/DJ • live music • good food • outdoor seating • wheelchair access

The Escape 10-A Brewer St (at Rupert) 44–(0)20/7734-2626 • 5pm-3am, clsd Sun-Mon • popular • mostly gay men • dancing/DJ • videos

Freedom Bar 66 Wardour St (off Old Compton St) **44-(0)20/7437-3490** • 5pm-3am, from 2pm Fri-Sat, 2pm-11:30pm Sun • lesbians/gay men • dancing/DJ • food served • young crowd

Friendly Society 79 Wardour St (the basement at Old Compton, enter Tisbury Ct) **44-(0)20/7434-3805** • 4pm-11pm, till 10:30pm Sun • lesbians/gay men • young crowd

The G.A.Y Bar 30 Old Compton St (at Frith) **44-(0)20/7494-2756** • noon-midnight • lesbians/gay men • basement women's bar • 3 floors • videos

G Spot 10 Adelaide St, at Kudos (off the Strand, Charing Cross) **44-(0)20/7379-4573** • 5pm-midnight Th-Sat • mostly women • professional crowd • trendy cafe-bar • multiracial • wheelchair access • gay-owned

Geisha 75 Charing Cross Rd (at Litchfield) **44-(0)20/7734-6887** • 4pm-11:30pm, from 1pm Fri-Sat, clsd Sun • lesbians/gay men

Girl Friday 52 St Giles High St (btwn Charing Cross & Shaftesbury, at First Out) **44-(0)20/7240-8042** • 7pm-11pm Fri • mostly women

Green Carnation 4-5 Greek St (Soho Sq) **44-(0)20/7434-3323** • 4pm-2am • inspired by the time and life of Oscar Wilde

London

LGBT Pride:
June-July. www.pridelondon.org.

Annual Events:
March-April - Lesbian & Gay Film Festival 44-(0)20/7928-3232, web: www.llgff.org.uk.
June-July - Pride Festival Fortnight 44-(0)20-7164-2182, web: www.pridelondon.org.
August - Mr Gay UK Contest, web: www.mrgayuk.co.uk.

City Info:
44-(0)20/7292-2333, web: www.visitlondon.com, www.londoninformation.org.

Best View:
London Eye, 44-(0)87/0990-8883, web: www.londoneye.com

Weather:
London is warmer and less rainy than you may have heard. Summer temperatures reach the 70⁰s and the average annual rainfall is about half of that of Atlanta, GA or Hartford, CT.

Transit:
Freedom Cars 44-(0)20-7734-1313.
Ladycabs 44-(0)20/7254-3501.
London Travel Information (Tube & buses) 44-(0)20/7222-1234, 24hr info, web: www.tfl.gov.uk.

Attractions:
British Museum 44-(0)20/7323-8299, web: www.britishmuseum.org.
Buckingham Palace 44-(0)20/7766-7300, web: www.royal.gov.uk.
Globe Theatre 44-(0)20/7902-1400, web: www.shakespeares-globe.org.
Kensington Palace 44-(0)87/0751-5170.
Madame Tussaud's 44-(0)87/0999-0046, web: www.madame-tussauds.co.uk.
National Gallery 44-(0)20/7747-2885, web: www.national-gallery.org.uk.
Oscar Wilde's house (34 Tite Street).
St Paul's Cathedral 44-(0)20/7236-4128, www.stpauls.co.uk.
Tate Gallery 44-(0)20/7887-8008, web: www.tate.org.uk.
Tower of London 44-(0)87/0756-6060.
Westminster Abbey 44-(0)20/7654-4900, www.westminster-abbey.org.

Ku Bar/ Ku Klub 30 Lisle St (Leicester Sq) 44-(0)20/7437-4303 • 12:30pm-2am • lesbians/ gay men • karaoke • young crowd • WiFi • also Soho bar at 25 Frith St

Kudos 10 Adelaide St (off the Strand) 44-(0)20/7379-4573 • noon-midnight, till 11pm Sun • lesbians/ gay men • professional crowd • trendy cafe-bar • multiracial • wheelchair access • gay-owned

Madam JoJo's 8-10 Brewer St (at Rupert) • mostly gay men • live shows • Tranny Shack Wed

Profile 56 Frith St (at Bateman) 44-(0)20/7734-8300 • 4pm-close, from noon wknds • lesbians/ gay men • dancing/DJ • Sun T-dance & late night parties Fri-Sat

The Retro Bar 2 George Ct (at Strand) 44-(0)20/7321-2811 • pub hours • lesbians/ gay men • neighborhood bar • dancing/DJ • alternative/ indie music • karaoke

Ruby Tuesday 30 Lisle St (at Ku Bar, Leicester Sq) 44-(0)20/7437-4303 • 2nd Tue only • mostly women • dancing/DJ • entertainment

Rupert Street 50 Rupert St (off Brewer) 44-(0)20/7292-7141 • pub hours • popular • lesbians/ gay men • upscale "fashiony-types" • food served • wheelchair access

Star at Night 22 Great Chapel St (at Hollen St) 44-(0)20/7494-2488 • 6pm -11.30pm clsd Sun-Mon • lesbians/ gay men • dancing/DJ • relaxed cafe/ bar • live shows

The Village Soho 81 Wardour St (at Old Compton) 44-(0)20/7434-2124 • 3pm-1am, till 11:30pm Sun • popular • mostly gay men • videos • young crowd • wheelchair access

The Yard 57 Rupert St (off Brewer) 44-(0)20/7437-2652, 871/426-2243 • pub hours • popular • lesbians/ gay men • 2 levels • young crowd • food served • wheelchair access

Nightclubs

Club Wotever 12 Denman St (at Masters Club) 44-(0)20/7734-4243 • 9pm-3am • mostly women • dancing/DJ • genderqueers & their admirers

Code 25-27 Brewer St (at The Enclave, Soho) • 1st & 3rd Fri only • mostly women • dancing

The Den & Centro 18 W Central St (at New Oxford St) 44-(0)20/7240-1083 • popular • 10pm-4am Fri • gay/ straight • dancing/DJ • cover charge • theme nights, popular Popstarz party Fri

The Enclave 25-27 Brewer St (Soho) 44-(0)20/7434-2911 • mostly gay men • dancing/DJ • theme nights • food served

G.A.Y. 157 Charing Cross Rd (at Oxford St, in London Astoria theatre complex) 44-(0)20/7734-6963 • 11pm-3am • popular • mostly gay men • dancing/DJ • live shows • young crowd • Camp Attack Fri • cover charge

Heaven 9 The Arches (off Villiers St) 44-(0)20/7930-2020 • the mother of all London gay clubs • call for hours/ events • mostly gay men • dancing/DJ

KU Bar Frith St 25 Frith St (at Old Compton St, Soho) 44-(0)20/7437-4303 • noon-11pm, till midnight wknds • lesbians/ gay men • dancing/DJ

Lounge 1 Leicester Sq (at Vertigo) 44-020/7734-0900 • 9pm-3am 2nd Th & last Fri • women only • call for schedule • men welcome as guests

Popstarz 18 W Central St (at New Oxford St) 44-(0)20/7240-1900 • popular • 10pm-4am Fri • lesbians/ gay men • dancing/DJ • cover charge

Profile/ Lo Profile 84-86 Wardour St (at Peter St) 44-(0)20/7734-1053 • mostly gay men • bar/ restaurant upstairs • hip basement club downstairs wknds • dancing/DJ

Salvation 37 Southampton Row (Bloomsbury Ballrooms, Bloomsbury Sq) 44-(0)20/7287-3834 (venue), 44-(0)87/1474-6002 (tickets) • 1st Sun • gay/ straight • cover charge

The Shadow Lounge 5 Brewer St (Soho) 44-(0)20/7287-7988 • 10pm-3am, from 9pm Th-Sat, clsd Sun • lesbians/ gay men • dancing/DJ • swanky late night club

T Tease 93 Dean St (at the Black Gardenia) • Fri only • lesbians/ gay men • transgender-friendly

Cafes

Balans Cafe 34 Old Compton St 44-(0)20/7439-3309 • 8am-5am, till 2am Sun • popular • lesbians/ gay men • all-day brkfst • terrace

Caffe Nero 43 Frith St

First Out 52 St Giles High St (btwn Charing Cross & Shaftesbury) 44-(0)20/7240-8042 • 10am-11pm • popular • gay cafe • full bar • nonsmoking upstairs

Flat White 17 Berwick St 44-(0)20/7734-0370 • 8am-7pm, 9am-6pm wknds • Australian-style cafe

LJ Coffee House 3 Winnett St (at Rupert) 44-020/7434-1174 • 7am-7pm, 10am-8pm Sat, from 1pm Sun • cozy cafe • street views

RESTAURANTS

Asia de Cuba 45 St Martin's Ln (near Leicester Square) 44-(0)20/7300-5588 • 7am-midnight • reservations required • chic scene

Bar Bruno 101 Wardour St 44-(0)20/7734-3750 • Italian cafe • hearty dishes

Cha Cha Moon 15-21 Ganton St 44-(0)20/7297-9800 • noon-11pm, till 10pm Sun • inexpensive Chinese

Food for Thought 31 Neal St, downstairs (Covent Garden) 44-0871/332-8808 • 9:30am-8:30pm, noon-5pm Sun • vegetarian • inexpensive hole-in-the-wall • BYOB

The Gay Hussar 2 Greek St (on Soho Square) 44-(0)20/7437-0973 • lunch & dinner, clsd Sun • Hungarian • wheelchair access

Just Falafs 155 Wardour St 44-(0)20/7734-1914 • 9am-6pm, clsd Sun • organic falafel

Mildred's 45 Lexington 44-(0)20/7494-1634 • noon-11pm, clsd Sun • popular • vegetarian • plenty vegan

Nusa Dua 11-12 Dean St (Oxford Circus) 44-(0)20/7437-3559, 44-(0)87/1332-7468 • Indonesian

Randall & Aubin 16 Brewer St (at Walkers Court) 44-(0)20/7287-4447 • noon-11pm • casual French • good people-watching

Satsuma 56 Wardour St 44-(0)20/7437-8338 • popular • Japanese

Wagamama Noodle Bar 10-A Lexington St 44-(0)20/7292-0990 • noon-11pm • Japanese • nonsmoking • chain w/ locations throughout city

ENTERTAINMENT & RECREATION

Comedy Camp 3-4 Archer St (at Barcode, btwn Windmill & Rupert, off Shaftesbury, Soho) 44-(0)20/7483-2960, 08-700/600-100 (TICKETWEB) • 8:30pm Tue • gay/ straight • amateur & established comedy acts

Drill Hall 16 Chenies St (btwn Alfred Pl & Ridgmount, Bloomsbury) 44-(0)20/7307-5060 (BOX OFFICE), 44-(0)20/7307-5061 (ADMIN) • gay/ straight • theatre company • many lesbian-themed performances • nonsmoking • wheelchair access

Prince Charles Cinema 7 Leicester Pl (off Leicester Square) 44-020/7222-1234 • sing-alongs • often show LGBT & alternative films

BOOKSTORES

Gay's the Word 66 Marchmont St (near Russell Square) 44-(0)20/7278-7654 • 10am-6:30pm, 2pm-6pm Sun • LGBT • magazines

RETAIL SHOPS

Prowler Soho 5-7 Brewer St (behind Village Soho bar) 44-(0)20/7734-4031 • 11am-10pm, noon-8pm Sun • popular • large gay department store

London—West

London—West includes Earl's Court, Kensington, Chelsea & Bayswater

ACCOMMODATIONS

Cardiff Hotel 5, 7, 9 Norfolk Sq (Hyde Park) 44-(0)20/7723-3513, 44-(0)20/7723-9068 • gay-friendly • B&B hotel in 3 Victorian townhouses • some shared baths • WiFi • £45-120

Millennium Bailey's Hotel 140 Gloucester Rd (at Old Brompton Rd, Kensington) 44-(0)20/7373-6000, 44-(0)20/7331-6331 • gay-friendly 4-star hotel • located in the heart of Kensington • also Olives restaurant & bar • Mediterranean

Parkwood Hotel 4 Stanhope Pl (Marble Arch) 44-(0)20/7402-2241 • gay-friendly • full brkfst • nonsmoking • £50-115

BARS

Catch 22 1a Wellington Ter, 679 Green Lanes (at Falkland Rd, Harringay) 44-(0)20/8881-1900 • 4pm-12:30am, till 1am Th, till 3am Fri-Sat • lesbians/ gay men • neighborhood bar • karaoke

The Culvert 54 Cowley Mill Rd (Uxbridge) 44-(0)70/9042-1416 • 4pm-close • mostly gay men • neighborhood bar • food served • cabaret • drag shows

The Hope & Anchor 20 Macbeth St (at King St, Hammersmith) 44-020/8748-8256 • gay/ straight • neighborhood bar

Richmond Arms 20 The Square (at Princes, Richmond) 44-(0)20/8940-2118 • pub hours • lesbians/ gay men • dancing/DJ • professional crowd • karaoke • drag shows • cabaret

West Five (W5) 5 Popes Ln (South Ealing) 44-(0)20/0871-971-4569 • 6pm-midnight ,open later Th-Sat • lesbians/ gay men • cabaret • lounge • piano bar • garden

NIGHTCLUBS

Lush 280 High St (at Hillingdon Rd), Uxbridge 44-01895/252 2282 • 9pm-2am, from 8pm Sun • lesbians/ gay men • dancing/DJ • WiFi

RESTAURANTS

The Churchill Arms 119 Kensington Church St 44-(0)20/7727-4242 • inexpensive, fantastic Thai • also pub

The Gate 51 Queen Caroline St, Hammersmith • lunch & dinner, clsd Sun, vegetarian

Star of India 154 Old Brompton Rd 44-(0)20/737-2901 • lunch & dinner • upscale

Thai Princess 30-31 Philbeach Gardens 44-(0)20/7373-1244 • 6pm-11:30pm • lesbians/ gay men • transgender-friendly • wheelchair access

ENTERTAINMENT & RECREATION

Walking Tour of Gay SOHO 56 Old Compton St (at Admiral Duncan Pub) 44-(0)20/7437-6063 • 2pm Sun • world-famous historical walking tour covering over 600 years of gay history in London's "square mile of sin"

London—North

London—North includes Paddington, Regents Park, Camden, St Pancras & Islington

ACCOMMODATIONS

Ambassadors Bloomsbury 12 Upper Woburn Pl (at Euston Rd, Bloomsbury) 44-0207/693-5400 • gay-friendly • near Kings Cross St Pancras & Euston Stations • good Italian restaurant onsite • nonsmoking • £00-200

Ossian Guesthouse 20 Ossian Rd (at Mt Pleasant Villas, Crouch Hill) 44-(0)20/8340-4331 • Victorian house on quiet street in quiet suburb • gay-friendly • £75-90

BARS

Blush 8 Cazenove Rd (Stoke Newington) 44-(0)20/7923-9202 • 5pm-midnight, 1pm-midnight Sun, clsd Mon • mostly women • friendly cafe-bar • beer garden • live music Sun • karaoke Fri • lesbian-owned

Erin's Hope 189 Edgware Rd (Colindale) 44-020/8205 8594 • sports pub

The George Music Bar 114 Twickenham Rd (Isleworth) 44-(0)20/8560-1456 • 5pm-close, from noon wknds • transgender-friendly • George Cabaret every Fri-Sat & every other Sun • gay-owned

The Green 74 Upper St (Angel tube) 44-(0)871/971-4097 • 4pm-midnight, till 2am Fri-Sat, from11am-Sat-Sun • lesbians/ gay men • full menu

King Edward VI/ Sunroom Cafe 25 Bromfield St (at Parkfield St, Islington) 44-(0)20/7704-0745 • noon-midnight • popular • mostly gay men • neighborhood cafe-bar • beer garden • wheelchair access

King William IV (KW) 77 Hampstead High St (Hampstead) 44-(0)20/7435-5747 • pub hours • lesbians/ gay men • food served • beer garden

Klub Fukk 37 Wharfdale Rd (at Central Station, King's Cross) 44-(0)20/7278-3294 • 7pm-midnight 2nd Sat only • lesbians/ gay men • transgender-friendly • queer sex play space

The Oak Bar 79 Green Lanes (Stoke Newington) 44-(0)20/7354-2791 • 5pm-midnight, till 2am Fri-Sat, from 1pm Sun • mostly women • Lower the Tone last Fri • dancing/DJ • food served • karaoke • dancers • theme nights • women-owned

Wotever World 37 Wharfdale Rd (at Central Station, King's Cross) 44-(0)20/7278-3294 • 6pm-midnight Tue (Bar Wotever) & Wed (Film Wotever) • dancing/DJ • genderqueers & their admirers

NIGHTCLUBS

Club Kali 1 Dartmouth Park Hill (at The Dome) 44-(0)20/7272-8153 (DOME #) • 10pm-3am 3rd Fri • popular • lesbians/ gay men • dancing/DJ • mostly Asian • transgender-friendly • South Asian music • cover charge

Club Motherfu*ker 38-44 Stoke Newington Rd (at Bardens Boudoir) 44-(0)20/7249-9557 • 8pm-2am 2nd Sat • lesbians/ gay men • dancing/DJ • live music

Dream Bags Jaquar Shoes 34-36 Kingsland Rd 44-020/7729-4192 • 5pm-1am • jam-packed club in a former shoe shop • also art exhibts

Egg 200 York Way (Kings Cross) 44-(0)20/7609-8364 • 10pm Fri-10am Sat, 10pm Sat until late afternoon Sun • gay/ straight • dancing/DJ

Electrogogo 184 Camden High St (at Electric Ballroom, in Camden) **44–(0)7963–145138** • 8pm-3am 1st Th • gay/ straight • live music

Festival of Sins 65 Crowndale Rd (at the Purple Turtle, Camden) • bi-monthly polysexual bash • lesbians/ gay men • burlesque • fetish

RESTAURANTS

Manna 4 Erskine Rd (at Ainger Rd, Camden) **44–(0)20/7722–8028** • lunch Tue-Sun, dinner nightly • vegetarian • reservations recommended

Providores/ Tapa Room 109 Marylebone High St (at New Cavendish St) **44–(0)20/7935–6175** • lunch & dinner • Asian fusion

ENTERTAINMENT & RECREATION

Rosemary Branch Theatre 2 Shepperton Rd **44–020/7704–2730 (BAR)**, **44–020/7704–6665 (THEATRE)** • gay/ straight • also restaurant & bar • many gay-themed plays

RETAIL SHOPS

Fettered Pleasures 90 Holloway Rd **44–(0)20/7619–9333** • 11pm-7pm, clsd Sun

London—East

London—East includes City, Tower, Clerkenwell & Shoreditch

ACCOMMODATIONS

The Hoxton 81 Great Eastern St **44–020/7550–1000** • gay-friendly • also restaurant • nonsmoking • WiFi • occasional £1 room deals • usually £119+

BARS

The Angel 21 Church St (at W Ham Ln, Stratford) **44–020/8555–1148** • mostly gay men • dance bar • cabaret

Bar Music Hall 134 Curtain Rd (Shoreditch) **44–(0)20/7613–5951, 44–(0)20/7729–7216** • 11am-midnight, till 2am Fri-Sat • gay-friendly • great wknd brunch • dancing/DJ • live shows

Bethnal Green Working Men's Club 42-44 Pollard Row (at Squirries St, Bethnal Green) **44–020/7739–7170** • lesbians/ gay men • performance art • cabaret • drag shows • transgender-friendly

Charlie's Bar 124 Globe Rd (Stepney) **44–(0)20/7790–1007** • pub hours • lesbians/ gay men • neighborhood pub

Dalston Superstore 117 Kingsland High St (at Sandringham Rd) **44–020/7254 2273** • noon-2am • gay/straight • neighborhood bar • food served • WiFi

The George & Dragon 151 Cleveland St **44–(0)20/7387–1492** • pub hours • gay-friendly • bohemian/ retro • neighborhood bar

The Macbeth 70 Hoxton St (at Crondall St, Old St) **44–020/ 7749–0600** • 9pm-2am • mostly gay men • live shows • terrace

The Old Ship 17 Barnes St (Stepney) **44–(0)20/7790–4082** • 4pm-11pm, from 7pm Tue-Th & Sat, from 5:30pm Sun • lesbians/ gay men • neighborhood bar • cabaret • wheelchair access

Royal Oak 73 Columbia Rd (at Hackney Rd, Old St) **44–020/7729–2220** • 6pm-11pm, from noon Sat-Sun • mostly gay men • popular Sun for the Columbia Rd Flower market

NIGHTCLUBS

Kaos at Stunners 566 Cable St (at Butcher Row, Cable St Studios, Limehouse) **44–(0)77/1022–2549** • monthy parties check www.kaoslondon.com • transgender • dancing/DJ • private club

Rhythm Factory 16-18 White Chapel Rd **44–020/7375–3774** • check www.rhythmfactory.co.uk for Queen of the Night party

Rumours 64-73 Minories (at The Minories) **44–(0)79/4947–7804** • last Sat • popular • women only • dancing/DJ

Trailer Trash 25 Kingsland Rd (at On the Rocks) • steamy Fri night party • popular • lesbians/ gay men • dancing/DJ

Unskinny Bop 359 Bethnal Green Rd (btwn Cambridge Heath Rd & Squirries St, at The Star) **44–(0)77/1466–0977** • 9pm 3rd Sat only • mostly women • dancing/DJ • live music

Urban Desi 61 Turnmill St (at Anexo Club, Farmington) **44–(0)79/5568–3144, 44–(0)79/5568–3134** • 11pm-5am 2nd Sat • lesbians/ gay men • dancing/DJ • mostly South Asian

Way Out Club 9 Crosswall (at Charlie's) **44–(0)77/7815–7290** • 9pm-4am Sat only • transsexuals & their friends • dancing/DJ • live shows • private club • cover charge

Wish 60-62 Commercial St (at Gramophone) • 9pm-4am 1st Sat only • lesbians/ gay men • dancing/DJ • fashion fashion fashion!

RESTAURANTS

Bistrotheque 23-27 Waderson St **44-(0)20/8983-7300** • expensive & glamorous • also cabaret shows after dinner

Bonds Restaurant & Bar 5 Threadneedle St **44-(0)20/7657-8088** • hours vary, clsd wknds • formerly a bank lobby • tapas served

Cafe Spice Namaste 16 Prescott St **44-(0)20/7488-9242** • lunch Mon-Fri, dinner nightly, clsd Sun • Indian

Cantaloupe 35-42 Charlotte Rd (Shoreditch) **44-(0)20/7729-5566** • 11am-midnight • popular • also bar

Canteen 2 Crispin Pl (Spitalfield) **44-(0)84/5686-1122** • place to be for brkfst

Hoxton Square Bar & Kitchen 2 Hoxton Square **44-(0)87/1971-3196** • great dark spot for brkfst • also popular gay scene Sun night

Les Trois Garçons 1 Club Row (at Bethnal, Shoreditch) **44-(0)20/7613-1924** • 7pm-midnight, clsd Sun • eclectic decor • reservations recommended

Lounge Lover 1 Club Row (Old Street) **44-020/7012-1234** • fancy Japanese cuisine in a posh lounge • reservations required • wheelchair access

Rootmaster Old Truman Brewery, in Elys Yard, off Brick Ln (Algate East tube) **44-(0)79/1238-9314** • vegetarian restaurant in refurbished double-decker bus

Saf 152-154 Curtain Rd, Shoreditch **44-(0)20/7613-0007** • lunch & dinner, also bar till midnight • upscale vegan/ raw food

SoSho 2 Tabernacle St **44-(0)20/7920-0701** • lounge & bar hours

EROTICA

Expectations 75 Great Eastern St (Shoreditch) **44-(0)20/7424-7493** • 11am-7pm, till 8pm Sat, noon-5pm Sun • leather/ rubber store • also mail order

Sh! Women's Erotic Emporium 57 Hoxton Sq (off Old St, Shoreditch) **44-(0)20/7613-5458** • noon-8pm • men very welcome when accompanied by a woman

London—South

London—South includes Southwark, Lambeth, Kennington, Vauxhall, Battersea, Lewisham & Greenwich

ACCOMMODATIONS

Griffin House 22 Stockwell Green **44-(0)20/7096-3332** • lesbians/ gay men • 2 rental apts near Vauxhall Gay Village & West End • kitchens • WiFi • gay-owned • £90-110

BARS

Battersea Barge Riverside Walk Nine Elms Ln (Vauxhall) **44-(0)20/7498-0004** • 11:30am-late, clsd Mon • gay-friendly • cabaret • comedy • food served • some veggie • gay-owned

The Bird in Hand 291 Sydenham Rd, Croydon **44-020/8683-3104** • 4pm-midnight • lesbians/ gay men • neighborhood bar

Escape Bar & Art 214-216 Railton Rd (Herne Hill) **44-(0)20/7737-0333** • 10am-midnight • gay-friendly • dancing/DJ • features local & int'l artists

George & Dragon 2 Blackheath Hill (Greenwich) **44-(0)20/8691-3764** • 6pm-2am, till 4am Fri-Sat • mostly gay men • karaoke Th • cabaret

Kazbar 50 Clapham High St (Clapham) **44-(0)20/7622-0070** • 4pm-midnight, till 1am Fri-Sat, from 1pm Sun • lesbians/ gay men

The Little Apple 98 Kennington Ln **44-(0)20/7582-7911** • noon-midnight, till 3am Sat • lesbians/ gay men • dancing/DJ • transgender-friendly • food served • terrace • wheelchair access

Rose & Crown 1 Crooms Hill (at Gloucester Circus, Greenwich) **44-020/8293-1898** • pub hrs • lesbians/ gay men • 'straight-friendly' pub • sing-alongs • 'Glee' nights

The Two Brewers 114 Clapham High St (Clapham) **44-(0)20/7498-4971** • 5pm-2am, till 3am Fri-Sat, 2pm-12:30am Sun • lesbians/ gay men • dancing/DJ • karaoke • cabaret • videos

Two8Six 286 Lewisham High St **44-020/8690-5758** • 11am-late, 7pm-1am Sun • lesbians/ gay men • dancing/DJ

NIGHTCLUBS

Area/ Embankment Bar 67-68 Albert Embankment (Vauxhall) **44-020/7091-0173** • mostly gay men • dancing/DJ • Th-Sat night

Black Sheep Bar 68 High St (at S Norwood Hill, Croydon) **44-(0)20/8680-2233**

Bootylicious 1 Nine Elms (at Club Colosseum) • 11pm 4th Sat • popular black gay club

Ego 82 Norwood High St (at Ernest Ave, Lambeth) 44–(0)28/971–4567 • from 8pm doors close at 11pm, ring bell for assistance • dancing/DJ • karaoke • cabaret

Escape 184 London Rd (Kingston) 44–(0)20/8549–9911 • 7pm-midnight , till 3am Fri-Sat , clsd Mon-Tue • mostly gay men • dancing/DJ

Exilio St Thomas St (at Guy's Bar) 44–(0)79/3137–4391 • 10pm-3am Fri • lesbians/ gay men • dancing/DJ • Latino/a

Fire 47B S Lambeth Rd (Vauxhall) 44–(0)79/0503–5682 • after-hours, Th-Mon nights & Sun afternoons • dancing/DJ • cover charge

The Fridge 1 Town Hall Parade (Brixton Hill) 44–(0)20/7326–5100 • 9pm-3am Th, 10pm-6pm Fri-Sat • popular • gay/ straight • dancing/DJ • dancing/DJ • call for current events

Hard On at Hidden 100 Tinworth St (at Hidden, in Vauxhall) 44–020/7820–1702 (HIDDEN) • 4th Sat only • monthly pansexual fetish dance party • strict dress code • private club

Royal Vauxhall Tavern 372 Kennington Ln (Vauxhall) 44–(0)20/7820–1222 • 8pm-late, 9pm-3am Fri-Sat, 2pm-midnight Sun • mostly gay men • popular wknds • more women Sat for Duckie • neighborhood bar • dancing/DJ • transgender-friendly • food served • wheelchair access

CAFES

Glow Lounge 6 Cavendish Parade (Clapham Common S Side) 44–(0)77/3179–9530 • cafe by day, mellow club by night

ENTERTAINMENT & RECREATION

Gay City Rollers at Renaissance Rooms Off Miles Street, opposite Arch #8 (Vauxhall) 44–020/7720–9140 • 7pm-midnight, 1st Wed of the month

Oval Theatre Cafe Bar 52-54 Kennington Oval 44–(0)20/7582–0080 • 6pm-11pm Tue-Sat (cafe) • inquire about current theatre & art

RETAIL SHOPS

The Host 44a Parry St 44–(0)20/7793–1551 • by appt only • rubber & fetish gear

FRANCE

Paris

Note: M°=Métro station

Paris is divided by arrondissements (city districts); 01=1st arrondissement, 02=2nd arrondissement, etc

Paris—Overview

Note: When phoning Paris from the US, dial the country code + the city code + the local phone number

INFO LINES & SERVICES

Centre Gai et Lesbien 63 rue Beaubourg 33–1/4357–2147 • drop-in evenings • call for other events/ groups

Gay AA 7 rue August Vacquerie (at St George's Anglican) 33–1/4634–5965 • 7:30pm Tue

ACCOMMODATIONS

Gay Accommodation Paris 271, rue du Faubourg Saint Antoine 33–1/4348–1382 • studios for rent in central Paris • gay-owned

Marais Flats/ Studios 20 rue Pierre Lescot 33–6/3256–5727 (EUROPEAN DAYTIME ONLY) • apt rentals in different Paris locations • gay-owned • €850/1,290/ week

NIGHTCLUBS

Eve'nt • bi-monthly women's party on a boat • check web for details

Pinky Boat • huge women's party for gay pride • other lesbian events • pinkyboat.com

Womexx • mostly women • dancing/DJ • lesbian parties in cool spaces • www.womexx.fr

PUBLICATIONS

PREF Mag 33–1/4087–1070 • bimonthly magazine

Têtu 33–1/5680–2080 • stylish & intelligent LGBT monthly (en français)

Paris—01

ACCOMMODATIONS

Hotel Louvre Richelieu 51 rue de Richelieu (M° Palais-Royal) 33–1/4297–4620 • gay/ straight • nonsmoking • WiFi •€76-168

Hotel Louvre Saint-Honoré 141 rue Saint-Honoré (at rue du Louvre) 33–1/4296–2323 • gay/ straight • modern 3-star hotel • full brkfst • kids ok • WiFi • wheelchair access • €135-150

Bars

Le Banana Cafe 13–15 rue de la Ferronnerie (near rue St-Denis, M° Châtelet) **33–1/4233-3531** • 6pm-dawn • trendy • lesbians/gay men • dancing/DJ • tropical decor • theme nights • piano bar • live shows • young crowd • wheelchair access • terrace

Bar du Kent'z 2-4 rue Vauvilliers (M° Chatelet-Les Halles) **33–1/4221-0116** • mostly gay men • 1920s style cocktail lounge

Le Tropic Cafe 66 rue des Lombards (M° Châtelet) **33–1/4013-9262** • 4pm-5am • lesbians/gay men • dancing/DJ Fri-Sat • transgender-friendly • kitschy, fun bar • tapas served • terrace • young crowd • wheelchair access

Le Vagabond 14 rue Thérèse (at av de l'Opera, M° Pyramides) **33–1/4296-2723** • 6pm-close, clsd Mon • oldest gay bar & restaurant in Paris • older crowd

Nightclubs

Afrodisiack/ Lick'n Licious 14 rue St-Denis (at rue des Lombards, at Le Club, M° Châtelet) **33–1/4508-9625** • Sat only • mostly women • dancing/DJ • multiracial • cover charge

Le Klub 14 rue St-Denis (at rue des Lombards, M° Châtelet) **33–1/4508-9625** • midnight-close Fri-Sat only • lesbians/gay men • dancing/DJ • multiracial • theme nights • private club • cover charge

Paris

LGBT Pride:
June. web: www.gaypride.fr.

Annual Events:
May-June - French Open tennis championship, web: french.open-tennis.com.
July 14 - Bastille Day.
July - Tour de France, web: www.letour.fr.
November-December - Paris Gay & Lesbian Film Festival, web: www.ffglp.net.

City Info:
Pyramides Welcome Center 3308/9268-3000, 25 rue des Pyramides, web: en.parisinfo.com. Also www.paris-visit.info.

Best View:
Eiffel Tower (but of course!) and Sacre Coeur.

Weather:
Paris really *is* beautiful in the springtime. Chilly in the winter, the temperatures reach the 70°s during the summer.

Transit:
Alpha Taxi 33–1/4585-8585, web: www.alphataxis.fr.
Taxi Bleu 33–8/9170-1010, web: www.taxis-bleus.com.
RATP (bus and Métro) web: www.ratp.fr.

Attractions:
Arc de Triomphe 33-1/5537-7377, web: www.monuments-nationaux.fr.
Eiffel Tower (up in lights for 10 minutes each hour from sunset till past midnight!) 33–1/4411-2323, web: www.tour-eiffel.fr.
Louvre 33–1/4020-5760, web: www.louvre.fr.
Musée d'Orsay 33–1/4049-4814, web: www.musee-orsay.fr.
Notre Dame Cathedral 33–8/9270-1239.
Picasso Museum 33–1/4271-2521, web: www.musee-picasso.fr.
Rodin Musuem 33–1/4418-6110, web: www.musee-rodin.fr.
Sacre-Coeur Basilica 33–1/5341-8900, web: www.sacre-coeur-montmartre.com.
Sainte-Chapelle 33–1/5340-6096, web: www.monuments-nationaux.fr.

Rexy Club 9 rue de la Grande Truanderie (M°
Etienne Marcel) **33–1/4026–5105** • gay-
friendly • dancing/DJ

RESTAURANTS

L' Amazonial 3 rue Ste-Opportune (at rue
Ferronnerie, M° Châtelet) **33–1/4233–5313** •
lunch & dinner, brunch wknds • lesbians/gay
men • Brazilian/int'l • cabaret • drag shows •
heated terrace • wheelchair access

Au Diable des Lombards 64 rue des
Lombards (at rue St-Denis, M° Châtelet)
33–1/4233–8184 • 8am-1am • American • full
bar • terrace

Au Rendez-Vous des Camionneurs 72
quai des Orfèvres (M° Pont Neuf)
33–1/4354–8874 • noon-2:30pm & 7pm-
11:30pm, noon-11:30pm Sun • mostly gay
men • traditional French bistro

Chez Max 47 rue Saint Honoré (M° Louvre)
33–1/4508–8013 • lunch & dinner • traditional
French

Jet Lag 2-4 rue Montmartre (M° Etienne
Marcel) **33–1/4488–2230** • 9am-2am • 2
patios

Marc Mitonne 60 rue de l'Arbre-Sec (M° Les
Halles) **33–1/4261–5316** • 6pm-2am, clsd
Sun-Mon • live shows • cabaret • theme
nights

La Poule au Pot 9 rue Vauvilliers (M° Les
Halles) **33–1/4236–3296** • 7pm-5am, clsd
Mon • clsd Aug • bistro • traditional French

Velvet Room 43 rue Saint Honore • lounge
& Thai restaurant

ENTERTAINMENT & RECREATION

Forum des Halles 101 Porte Berger (M°
Châtelet-Les Halles) **33–1/4476–9656** •
underground sports/entertainment complex
w/museums, theater, shops, clubs, cafes &
more

GYMS & HEALTH CLUBS

Club Med Gym 147 rue St–Honoré (M°
Louvre) **33–1/4020–0303** • gay/straight • day
passes available • many locations throughout
the city

Paris—02

BARS

La Champmeslé 4 rue Chabanais (at rue
des Petits Champs, M° Pyramides)
33–1/4296–8520 • 4pm-3am, till 7am Fri-Sat,
clsd Sun • popular • mostly women • cabaret
Th • theme nights • older crowd • WiFi •
wheelchair access • a lesbian landmark, in
business for over 20 years

NIGHTCLUBS

Rex Club 5 blvd Poissonière (M° Bonne
Nouvelle) **33–1/4236–1096** • gay-friendly •
call for events • clsd August • cover

CAFES

Stuart Friendly 16 rue Marie Stuart • noon-
11pm, till midnight Fri-Sat, till 5:30pm Sun •
"straight-friendly" cafe • food served

RESTAURANTS

Aux Trois Petits Cochons 31 rue
Tiquetonne (at rue St-Denis, M° Etienne-
Marcel) **33–1/4233–3969** • 8pm-1am •
popular • lesbians/gay men • gourmet French
made w/fresh seasonal produce • menu
changes daily • reservations recommended •
gay-owned

Le César 4 rue Chabanais (M° Pyramides)
33–1/4296–8113 • 6:30pm-5am • lesbians/
gay men • also bar

Le Dénicheur 4 rue Tiquetonne (M°
Etienne-Marcel) **33–1/4221–3101** • noon-
midnight, clsd Mon • sandwiches, quiche,
salads • kitschy decor

Le Loup Blanc 42 rue Tiquetonne (M°
Etienne-Marcel) **33–1/4013–0835** • 7:30pm-
midnight, till 1am Sat, also brunch 11am-
4:30pm Sun • popular • lesbians/gay men •
French/int'l

Paris—03

ACCOMMODATIONS

Absolu Living 236 rue St Martin
33–1/4454–9700 • lesbians/gay men • fully
furnished apts in central Paris • short & long-
term stays • gay-owned • €65-259

Adorable Apartment in Paris (M°
Rambuteau) **415/397–6454 (US#)** • gay-
friendly • 2-bdrm flat in heart of Marais •
nonsmoking • lesbian & gay-owned • $2,100/
week

Hôtel du Vieux Saule 6 rue de Picardie
33–1/4272–0114 • gay-friendly • €75-250

BARS

Le Duplex 25 rue Michel-Le-Comte (at rue
Beaubourg, M° Rambuteau) **33–1/4272–8086**
• 8pm-2am, till 4am Fri-Sat • lesbians/gay
men • neighborhood bar • bohemian types •
live shows • internet access

Le Tango/ La Boite à Frissons 13 rue au
Maire (M° Arts-et-Métiers) **33–1/4272–1778** •
10:30pm-5am, clsd Mon • lesbians/gay men •
T-dance Sun • food served

Unity Bar 176–178 rue St-Martin (near rue Réaumur, M° Rambuteau) **33–1/4272–7059** • 4pm-2am • mostly women • men welcome as guests • neighborhood bar • young crowd

NIGHTCLUBS

Escualita 7 rue Bourg L'Abbe • midnight Sun only • mostly men • transgender-friendly • fab tranny dance party • all are welcome

RESTAURANTS

La Fontaine Gourmande 11 rue Charlot **33–1/4278–7240** • noon-2pm Tue-Fri & 7:30pm-close Tue-Sun, clsd Mon • French

ENTERTAINMENT & RECREATION

Musée Picasso 5 rue de Thorigny (in the Hôtel Salé, M° St-Paul) **33–1/4271–2521** • 9:30am-5:30pm, clsd Tue • wheelchair access

EROTICA

Rex 42 rue de Poitou (at rue Charlot, M° St-Sébastien-Froissard) **33–1/4277–5857** • 1pm-8pm, clsd Sun • new, custom & secondhand leather & S/M accessories

Paris — 04

ACCOMMODATIONS

Chambres D'Hôte Rivoli **33–06/1991–5828** • lesbians/ gay men • B&B • WiFi • gay-owned • €75-90

Hôtel Beaubourg 11 rue Simon le Franc (btwn rue Beaubourg & rue du Temple, M° Hôtel-de-Ville) **33–1/4274–3424** • gay/ straight • next to Centre Pompidou • WiFi • €120-136

Hôtel de la Bretonnerie 22 rue Ste-Croix-de-la-Bretonnerie (M° Hôtel-de-Ville) **33–1/4887–7763** • gay-friendly • 17th-c hotel w/ Louis XIII decor • €135-215

Hôtel du Vieux Marais 8 rue du Plâtre (M° Hôtel-de-Ville) **33–1/4278–4722** • gay-friendly • centrally located • WiFi • €92-140

Paris-Apart 14 rue François Miron • gay/ straight • loft in old Le Marais • kids ok • WiFi • gay-owned • €875/ week • monthly rental available

BARS

3W Kafe 8 rue des Ecouffes (M° St Paul) **33–1/4887–3926** • 5pm-2am, till 4am Fri-Sat • mostly women • dancing/DJ • live shows • videos

L' Amnésia Café 42 rue Vieille du Temple (at rue des Blancs-Manteaux, M° Hôtel-de-Ville) **33–1/4272–1694** • 11am-close • popular • lesbians/ gay men • dancing • food served

Au Mange Disque 15 rue de la Reynie (at Boule de Sebastopol) **33–1/4804–7817** • 11am-2am, from 5pm Sun-Mon • mostly gay men • theme nights • colorful, modern decor

Le Bar du Palmier 16 rue des Lombards (at bd de Sébastopol, M° Châtelet) **33–1/4278–5353** • 2pm-6am • lesbians/ gay men • food served • terrace

Le Carrefour 8 rue des Archives (at rue de la Verrerie) **33–1/4029–9005** • mostly gay men • neighborhood bar

L' Enchanteur 15 rue Michel Lecomte (M° Rambuteau) **33–1/4804–0238** • 11am-2am • lesbians/ gay men • piano bar

Les Filles de Paris 57 rue Quincampoix **33–1/4271–7220** • 10pm-5am Wed-Sat, also restaurant from 7pm, clsd Sun-Mon • gay/ straight • dancing/DJ • drag shows, burlesque & cabaret

Free DJ 35 rue Ste-Croix-de-la-Bretonnerie (at rue du Temple, M° Hôtel-de-Ville) **33–1/4029–4440** • 5pm-2am, till 4am Th-Sun • lesbians/ gay men

L' Imprevu Cafe 9 rue Quincampoix **33–1/4278–2350** • 3pm-2am, from 1pm Sun • mostly gay men • low key neighborhood cafe/ bar • food served

Les Jacasses 5 rue des Ecouffes (M° St Paul) **33–1/4271–1551** • 5pm-2am • mostly women • men welcome

Le Mixer Bar 23 rue Ste-Croix-de-la-Bretonnerie (at rue des Archives, M° Hôtel-de-Ville) **33–1/4887–5544** • 4pm-2am • popular • lesbians/ gay men • dancing/DJ • 3-flr techno/ house bar • theme nights • young crowd

L' Oiseau Bariolé 16 rue Saint-Croix-de-la-Bretonnerie (M° Hotel de Ville) **33–1/4272–3712** • lesbians/ gay-men • 5pm-close • quiet

Okawa 40 rue Vieille du Temple (at rue Ste-Croix-de-la-Bretonnerie, M° Hôtel-de-Ville) **33–1/4804–3069** • 10am-2am, till 4am Fri-Sat • gay/ straight • trendy cafe-bar in 12th- & 13th-c caves • cabaret • piano bar Tue-Wed • also restaurant from 7pm

L' Open Cafe 17 rue des Archives (at rue Ste-Croix-de-la-Bretonnerie, M° Hôtel-de-Ville) **33–1/4887–8025** • 11am-2am, till 4am Fri-Sat • popular • lesbians/ gay men • sidewalk cafe-bar

Le Raidd 23 rue du Temple (M° Hotel de ville) **33–1/4277–0488** • 5pm-5am • mostly men • dancing/ DJ • go-go boys

So What 30 rue du Roi de Sicile (M° Hôtel-de-Ville) • 5pm-2am • lesbians/ gay men • stylish new bar • dancing/DJ • lesbian-owned

Les Souffleurs 7 rue de la Verrerie (M° Hôtel-de-Ville) **33-1/4478-0492** • lesbians/ gay men • artsy younger crowd • events in the basement • monthly dyke party Butch is Beautiful

Le Troisieme Lieu 62 rue Quincampoix **33-1/4804-8564** • 6pm-2am, clsd Sun • mostly women • also restaurant & nightclub

Le Voulez-Vous 18 rue du Temple (M° Hôtel-de-Ville) **33-1/4459-3857** • 11am-2am • lesbians/ gay men • lounge & restaurant • terrace

Yono 37 rue Vieille du Temple **33-1/4274-3165** • 6pm-2am Tue-Sat, 4:30-11pm Sun • lesbians/ gay men • dancing/DJ, cozy basement bar • Mustache monthy party • also restaurant

Ze Baar 41 rue des Blancs Manteaux (at rue du Temple) **33-1/4271-7508** • 5pm-2am • mostly gay men • neighborhood bar • also restaurant

NIGHTCLUBS

Le Scarron 3 rue Geoffroy l'Angevin **33-1/4277-4405** • clsd Sun-Mon • lesbians/ gay men • cozy dance club & piano bar

CAFES

Le Kofi du Marais 54 rue Ste-Croix-de-la-Bretonnerie (M° Hôtel de Ville) **33-1/4887-4871** • 6pm-midnight, clsd Sun • lesbians/ gay men • coffee & light meals

RESTAURANTS

Auberge de la Reine Blanche 30 rue St Louis en l'Ile **33-1/4633-0787** • romantic bistro

Le Chant des Voyelles 3 rue des Lombards (M° Châtelet) **33-1/4277-7707** • 11:30am-3pm & 6:30pm-midnight, open all day in summer • traditional French • terrace

Curieux Spaghetti Bar 14 rue Saint Merri (M° Rambuteau) **33-1/4272-7597** • noon-2am, till 4am Th-Sat, brunch wknds • home of scented vodka "Chup" shots

Equinox 33 rue des Rosiers (M° St-Paul) **33-1/4271-9241** • 7pm-midnight • Québecois/ French • full bar • piano bar • drag shows

Etamine Cafe 13 rue des Ecouffes (at rue des Rosiers, M° Hotel de Ville) **33-1/4478-0962** • 11am-midnight, clsd Mon • also bar

Le Gai Moulin 10 rue St-Merri (at du Temple, M° Hôtel-de-Ville) **33-1/4887-0600** • noon-midnight • lesbians/ gay men • French/ int'l

La Pas-Sage-Oblige 29 rue du Bourg-Tibourg (M° Hôtel-de-Ville) **33-1/4041-9503** • lunch & dinner • vegetarian

Le Petit Picard 42 rue Ste-Croix-de-la-Bretonnerie (M° Hôtel-de-Ville) **33-1/4278-5403** • lunch & dinner, clsd Mon • lesbians/ gay men • reservations recommended

Les Piétons 8 rue des Lombards (M° Châtelet) **33-1/4887-8287** • noon-2am • gay/ straight • Spanish/ tapas • also bar • dancing/DJ from 8pm Wed

BOOKSTORES

Les Mots à la Bouche 6 rue Ste-Croix-de-la-Bretonnerie (near rue du Vieille du Temple, M° Hôtel-de-Ville) **33-1/4278-8830** • 11am-11pm, 1pm-9pm Sun • LGBT • English titles

RETAIL SHOPS

Abraxas 9 rue St-Merri **33-1/4804-3355** • tattoos • piercing • large selection of body jewelry

EROTICA

Dollhouse 24 rue du Roi de Sicile (at Ferdinand Duval) **33-1/4027-0921** • women's erotica store

Paris—05

ACCOMMODATIONS

Historic Rentals 3415 W Cypress St, Tampa, FL 33607 **800/537-5408 (US#)** • gay-friendly • 1-bdrm apts • full kitchen • steps to Notre Dame & Luxembourg Gardens • nonsmoking • WiFi • $850-1,400/ week

RESTAURANTS

L' AOC 14 Rue des Fossés St Bernard **33-1/4354-2252** • lunch & dinner, clsd Sun • upscale favorite for fancy lesbians

Le Petit Prince 12 rue de Lanneau (M° Maubert-Mutualité) **33-1/4354-7726** • 7:30pm-midnight • popular • French

ENTERTAINMENT & RECREATION

Friday Night Fever 16 Bol Saint Germain • 10pm-1am Fri (weather-permitting), meet 9:30pm • rollerblade through the city • gay/ straight

Open-Air Sculpture Museum Quai Saint-Bernard • along the Seine btwn the Jardin des Plantes & the Institut du Monde Arabe

GYMS & HEALTH CLUBS

Hammam de la Mosque de Paris 39 rue Geoffroy St-Hilaire **33–1/4331–3820** • traditional Turkish baths • women welcome Mon & Wed-Sat • men welcome Tue & Sun

Paris—06

BARS

La Venus Noire 25 rue de l'Hirondelle (M° St-Michel) • 6pm-1am, till 2am Fri-Sat, clsd Sun • mostly women • neighborhood bar • live music

NIGHTCLUBS

Le Rive Gauche 1 rue du Sabot (M° St-Sulpice) **33–1/4020–4323** • 11pm-dawn Fri-Sat only • mostly women • dancing/DJ • cover charge

BOOKSTORES

The Village Voice 6 rue Princesse (M° Mabillon) **33–1/4633–3647** • 10am-7:30pm, from 2pm Mon, noon-6pm Sun • English-language bookshop

Paris—08

ACCOMMODATIONS

François 1er 7 rue Magellan **33–1/4723–4404** • gay-friendly • boutique hotel near the Champs-Elysées • also bar • WiFi • €350-1000

BARS

Le Day Off 10 rue de l'Isly (M° Gare-St-Lazare) **33–1/4522–8790** • 5pm-3am Mon-Fri only • heavy drinking enjoyed by work-weary lesbians, crowded in the early evening • food served • woman-owned

NIGHTCLUBS

Le Queen 102 av des Champs-Élysées (btwn rue Washington & rue de Berri, M° Georges-V) **33-8/5389-0890** • midnight-dawn • popular • gay/ straight • more women Wed • dancing/DJ • theme nights • drag shows • young crowd • selective door • cover charge

Paris—09

ACCOMMODATIONS

The Grand 2 rue Scribe **33–1/4007–3232, 888/424-6835** • gay-friendly • ultraluxe art deco hotel • WiFi

NIGHTCLUBS

Folies Pigalle 11 place Pigalle (M° Pigalle) **33–1/4878-5525, 33–1/4280–1203 (BBB INFO LINE)** • midnight-dawn • gay/ straight • dancing/DJ • theme nights • transgender-friendly • multiracial • cover charge

Paris—10

BARS

Baxo 21 rue Juliette Dodu (M° Colonel Fabien) **33–1/4202–9971** • 9am-2am, from noon Sun • gay/ straight • dancing/DJ • trendy bar/ restaurant • patio

L' Okubi 219 rue St-Maur (M° Goncourt) **33–1/4201–3508** • 6pm-2am, clsd Sun • mostly women • dancing/DJ

Paris—11

ACCOMMODATIONS

Hôtel Beaumarchais 3 rue Oberkampf (btwn bd Beaumarchais & bd Voltaire, M° Filles-du-Calvaire) **33–1/5336-8686** • gay/ straight • beautiful hotel • WiFi • €75-190

BARS

Le Bataclan 50 blvd Voltaire (at Bataclan club, M° Saint Ambroise) **33–1/4314-0030** • gay-friendly • live music venue • more gay for the Follivores & Crazyvores • call for events

L' Escalme 140 Blvd Richard Lenoir **33–1/4805-2955** • 9am-2am • mostly men • also restaurant

Follivores/ Crazyvores 50 blvd Voltaire (M° Saint Ambroise) **33–1/4314-0030** • lesbians/ gay men • monthly sing-along dance parties • Follivores is 1960s-1990s French pop • Crazyvores is English-speaking • kitsch factor very high!

Interface 34 rue Keller (rue de La Roquette) **33–1/4700-6715** • 3pm-2am, till 4am wknds • mostly gay men • art exhibitions

NIGHTCLUBS

Les Disquaires 6 rue des Taillandiers (M° Bastille) **33–1/4021–9460** • gay/ straight • dance bar • live bands

La Scène Bastille 2 bis rue des Taillandiers (M° Bastille) **33–1/4806–5070 (CLUB), 33–1/4806–1213 (RESTAURANT)** • gay-friendly • also restaurant • live music • events

Les What's Gouine On? 6 rue des Taillandiers (at Disquaires bar, M° Bastille) • monthly women's dance party

RESTAURANTS

Bistrot Guillaume 5 rue Guillaume Bertrand 33–1/4700-4350

Sans Gêne 122 rue Oberkampf 33–1/4700-7011 • 5pm-2am, Sun brunch, clsd Mon • also bar

Le Sofa 21 rue St-Sabin (M° Bastille) 33–1/4314-0746 • 6pm-midnight, till 2am Th-Sat, clsd Sun • also bar

Le Tabarin 3 rue Amelot 33–1/4807-1522 • lunch Sun-Fri, dinner Sun-Sat • lesbians/gay men • full bar • piano bar

ENTERTAINMENT & RECREATION

L' ArtiShow 3 cite Souzy 33–1/4002-1803 • cabaret • also lunch & dinner served

O Chateau, Wine Tasting in Paris 100 rue de la Folie Mericourt 33–1/4473-9780 • gay-friendly • transgender-friendly • English-speaking French connoisseur

BOOKSTORES

Violette & Co 102 rue de Charonne (at boulevard Voltaire) 33–1/4372-1607 • 11am-8pm, 2pm-7pm Sun, clsd Mon • lesbian-owned

EROTICA

Démonia 22 ave Jean Aicard (at rue Oberkampf, M° St-Maur) 33–1/4314-8270 • clsd Sun • BDSM shop • lingerie • videos • toys

Paris—12

SEX CLUBS

Atlantide 13 rue Parrot (M° Gare de Lyon) 33–1/4342-2243 • gay/straight sauna w/ sexual atmosphere • men, women, transgender-friendly • private cabins • also bar

Paris—14

ENTERTAINMENT & RECREATION

Catacombes 1 Ave du Colonel Henri Rol-Tanguy (M° Denfert-Rochereau) 33–1/4322-4763 • a ghoulish yet intriguing tourist destination, these burial tunnels were the headquarters of the Résistance during World War II

GYMS & HEALTH CLUBS

Amphibi 73 rue Hallé (at rue Bézout, M° Alesia) 33–1/4047-5090 • sauna where everyone is welcome: gay, straight, male, female, bisexual, transgendered

Paris—16

ACCOMMODATIONS

Keppler 10 rue Keppler 33–1/4720-6505 • gay-friendly • near major tourist stops • also bar • kids/pets ok • WiFi • €300-1,000

Paris—18

BARS

Karambole Cafe 10 rue Hegesippe (M° Place de Clichy or La Fourche) 33–1/4293-3068 • 11:30am-2am, from 6pm Sat • gay/straight • artsy cafe by day • DJs by night

Le Tagada Bar 40 rue Trois-Frères (M° Abesses) 33–1/4255-9556 • 6pm-2am, clsd Mon • mostly gay men • upscale food

ENTERTAINMENT & RECREATION

Madame Arthur 75 bis rue des Martyrs 33–1/4255-6388 • drag diva • dinner show

Michou 80 rue des Martyrs (at Blvd de Clichy, M° Pigalle) 33–1/4606-1604 • infamous drag cabaret • dinner show

Paris—19

ACCOMMODATIONS

Friendlyfrenchy's Gay B&B 38 ave Jean Jaures (rue Michelet) 33–1/4354-3764 • mostly men • WiFi • €795

CAFES

Cafe Cherie 44 Blvd de la Villette (M° Belleville) 33–1/4202-0205 • 8am-2am • gay/straight • live music & DJs starting at 10pm • WiFi

Paris—20

ACCOMMODATIONS

Mama Shelter 109 rue de Bagnolet 33–1/4348-4848 • gay/straight • great location on the Right Bank • kichenettes • also restaurant & cool local bars • WiFi • €79+

ENTERTAINMENT & RECREATION

Père Lachaise Cemetery bd de Ménilmontant (M° Père-Lachaise) • perhaps the world's most famous resting place, where lie such notables as Chopin, Gertrude Stein, Oscar Wilde, Sarah Bernhardt, Isadora Duncan, Edith Piaf & Jim Morrison

GERMANY

Berlin

Berlin is divided into 5 regions:
Berlin—Overview
Berlin—Kreuzberg
Berlin—Prenzlauer Berg–Mitte
Berlin—Schöneberg-Tiergarten
Berlin—Outer

Berlin—Overview

INFO LINES & SERVICES

Gay AA for English Speakers at M-O-M **49–30/787–5188** • 5pm Tue, also Gay AA 8pm Th

Lesbenberatung (Lesbian Advice) Kulmer Str 20a (in Kreuzberg) **49–30/215–2000** • switchboard & center • staffed 10am-5pm, till 7pm Tue & Th

Mann-O-Meter Bülowstr 106 (at Nollendorfplatz) **49–30/216–8008** • 5pm-10pm, from 4pm wknds • gay switchboard & center • also cafe • also B&B referral service

Sonntags Club Greifenhagener Str 28 (S/U-Schönhauser Allee) **49–30/449–7590, 49–30/442–3702 (TRANSGENDER LINE)** • info line 10am-6pm daily • LGBT info • counseling • meetings • also cafe-bar • 5pm-midnight • lesbians/gay men • women's night Fri 8pm • transgender-friendly • live shows • videos • regular parties

Spinnboden Lesbian Archive & Library U-Bahn 8, Bernauerstr (in 2nd courtyard, 2nd flr) **49–30/448–5848** • call for hours • also by appt

ACCOMMODATIONS

Enjoy B&B Bülowstr 106 (at M-O-M, gay center) **49–30/2362–3610** • lesbians/gay men • accommodations referral service • €18-30

NIGHTCLUBS

MegaDyke Productions **49–30/7870–3094** • popular parties & events for lesbians, including L-Tunes at SchwuZ & annual pride events for lesbians in other locations • see www.megadyke.de for more details

RESTAURANTS

Paris Bar Kantstrasse152 **49–30/313–8052** • bistro • also bar

ENTERTAINMENT & RECREATION

Fritz Music Tour **49–30/3087–5633** • visit the haunts of David Bowie, Nina Hagen, Iggy Pop & Rammstein, among other popular musical acts

The Jewish Museum Berlin Lindenstr 9-14 **49–30/2599–3300** • 10am-8pm, till 10pm Mon • German-Jewish history & culture

Schwules (Gay) Museum U6/U7 Mehringdamm 61 **49–30/6959–9050** • 2pm-6pm, till 7pm Sat, clsd Tue • guided tours 5pm Sat (in German) • exhibits, archives & library

PUBLICATIONS

L-MAG Jackwerth Verlag, L-MAG, Tempelhofer Ufer 11 **49–30/235–5390, 49–30/2355–3932** • bimonthly nat'l lesbian magazine (in German)

Siegessäule **49–30/235–5390, 49–30/2355–3932** • free monthly LGBT city magazine (in German) • awesome maps

Berlin—Kreuzberg

ACCOMMODATIONS

Hotel Transit Hagelberger Straße 53–54 **49–30/789–0470** • gay-friendly • loft-style hotel in 19th-c factory • also bar • €21-168

The Mövenpick Hotel Schöneberger Strasse 3 (at Stresemannstr) **49–30/230–060** • gay-friendly • convenient location • also space-agey bar • €100-300

BARS

Barbie Bar Mehringdamm 77 (at Kreuzbergstr) **49–30/6956–8610** • 3pm-close • lesbians/gay men • lounge • terrace

Barbie Deinhoffs Schlesische Str 16 **49–173/434–6363** • popular • 6pm-2am,till 6am Fri-Sat • lesbians/gay men • dancing/DJ • cabaret

Bierhimmel Oranienstr 183 (U-Kottbusser Tor) **49–30/615–3122** • 1pm-3am • gay/ straight • young crowd

Mobel Olfe Reichenbergerstrasse 177 (at Skalitzer) **49–30/2327–4690** • 6pm-close Tue-Sun • popular • lesbians/gay men

Rauschgold Mehringdamm 62 (U-Mehringdamm) **49–30/7895–2668** • 8pm-close • lesbians/gay men

Roses Oranienstr 187 (at Kottbusser Tor) **49–30/615–6570** • 10pm-close • popular • lesbians/gay men • transgender-friendly • young crowd

Sofia Wrangelstrasse 93 • open 9am, from 11am Sat and 8pm Sun • lesbians/gay men

NIGHTCLUBS

L-Tunes Mehringdamm 61 (at SchwuZ) **49–30/7870–3094** • 10pm last Fri only • mostly women • dancing/DJ • events

BARS
CLUBS
SAUNAS
HOTELS

Gay Guide Global Directory

www.gayguide.net

SchwuZ (SchwulenZentrum)
Mehringdamm 61 (enter through Café
Sundstroem) **49–30/629–0880** • from 11pm
Fri-Sat • mostly gay men • more women last
Fri • dancing/DJ • live/drag shows • young
crowd

Serene Bar Schwiebusser Str 2
49–30/6904–1580 • lesbians/ gay men •
popular Girls Bar Th • Girls Dance Sat

Berlin

LGBT Pride:
Christopher Street Day, 3rd or 4th
Saturday in June, web: www.csd-
berlin.de.

Annual Events:
February - Berlinale: Berlin Int'l Film
Festival w/ Queer Teddy Award
49-30/259-200, web: www.berli-
nale.de.
June - Lesbian & Gay City Festival/
Stadtfest, web: www.regenbo-
genfonds.de.
Sept- Folsom Europe, web:
www.folsomeurope.com.
October - Lesbian Film Festival
49–30/852-2305, web:
www.lesbenfilmfestival.de.
October - Wigstoeckel transgender/
drag festival, web:
www.wigstoeckel.com.
November - Jazz Fest Berlin,
www.berlinerfestspiele.de.
November/ December - Verzaubert
Int'l Queer Film Festival, web:
www.verzaubertfilmfest.com.

City Info:
Berlin-Tourism 49-30/250–025,
web: www.btm.de.
Europa Center 49–30/2649-7940,
web: www.europa-center-
berlin.de.

Weather:
Berlin is on the same parallel as
Newfoundland, so if you're visiting in the winter, prepare for
snow and bitter cold. Summer is
balmy while spring and fall are
beautiful, if sometimes rainy.

Transit:
Taxifunk Berlin 49–800/443–322,
web: www.taxifunkberlin.de.
Jet Express-Bus X9 from Tegel
Airport to central Berlin
49–30/19449.
U-Bahn (subway) and bus
49–30/19449, web: www.bvg.de.
S-Bahn (elevated train) 49-
30/2974-3333, web: www.s-
bahn-berlin.de.

Attractions:
Bauhaus Design Museum
49–30/254–0020, web:
www.bauhaus.de.
Brandenburg Gate.
Charlottenburg Palace 49–30/2655-
7656.
Egyptian Museum
49–30/2090–5544.
Gay Museum 49–30/6959-9050,
web: www.schwulesmuseum.de.
Homo Memorial (at Nollendorfplatz
station).
The Jewish Museum Berlin 49-
30/2599-3300, web:
www.juedisches-museum-
berlin.de.
Kaiser Wilhelm Memorial Church.
Käthe-Kollwitz Museum
49–30/882–5210, web:
www.kaethe-kollwitz.de.
Museuminsel (Museum Island)
49–30/266–424-242, web:
www.smb.spk-berlin.de.
New National Gallery
49–30/266–424-510, web:
www.neue-nationalgalerie.de.
Reichstag 49–30/2273–2152, web:
www.bundestag.de.

SO 36 Oranienstr 190 (at Kottbusser Tor) 49–30/6140–1306, 49–30/6140–1307 • popular • gay/ straight • dancing/DJ • transgender-friendly • live shows • videos • young crowd • wheelchair access • theme nights include Café Fatal (ballroom dancing) & Gayhane (Turkish night)

CAFES

Drama Mehringdamm 63 49–30/6746–9562 • opens 2pm, also bar & terrace

Ken Obentrautstr 19 (U-Mehringdamm) • new dance club Fri-Sat

Melitta Sundström Mehringdamm 61 (at Gneisenaustr, U-Mehringdamm) 49–30/692–4414 • 10am-8pm, till 4pm Sat, clsd Sun • lesbians/ gay men • terrace • wheelchair access • also LGBT bookstore

Muvuca Gneisenaustr 2a (at Mehringdamm) 49–30/6165–6310 • 4pm-close • radical/ political int'l cafe • Portuguese food

RESTAURANTS

Amrit Oranienstr 202 49–30/612–5550 • noon-1am • Indian

Kaiserstein Mehringdamm 80 49–30/7889–5887 • 9am-1am • int'l

Locus Marheinekeplatz 4 49–30/691–5637 • 10am-1:30am • popular • lesbians/ gay men • Mexican • full bar • lesbian-owned

Restaurant Z Friesenstr 12 49–30/692–2716 • 5pm-1am • Greek/ Mediterranean

SUMO Bergmanstr 89 49–30/6900–4963 • noon-midnight • trendy Japanese

EROTICA

Altelier Dos Santos Mehringdamm 119 (U Platz der Luftbrucke) 49–30/5059–9919 • noon-6pm, till 4pm Sat • lesbian-owned custom leather & fetish wear

Playstixx Waldemarstrasse 24 49–30/6165–9500 • makers & sellers of silicone toys for women & lovers

Sexclusivitäten Fürbringer Str 2 49–30/693–6666 • lesbian sex shop • toys • leather • videos • Open Salon sex party noon-8pm Fri • also escort service

Berlin—Prenzlauer Berg-Mitte

ACCOMMODATIONS

Andel's Hotel Landsberger Allee 106 49–30/453–053 • gay-friendly • WiFi • also restaurant • wheelchair access

Arte Luise Kunsthotel Luisenstr 19 (Mitte) 49–30/284–480 • gay-friendly • former palace w/ rooms re-imagined by local artists • near River Spree • €49-240

Intermezzo Hotel for Women Gertrud-Kolmar Str 5 (at Brandenburger Tor) 49–30/2248–9096 • women only • wheelchair access • €49-120

Schall & Rauch Pension Gleimstr 23 (at Schönhauser Allee) 49–30/443–3970, 49–30/448–0770 • lesbians/ gay men • €45-70 • also bar & restaurant

BARS

Besenkammer Bar Rathausstr 1 (at Alexanderplatz, under the S-Bahn bridge) 49–30/242–4083 • 24hrs • lesbians/ gay men • tiny "beer bar"

Betty F*** Mulackstrasse 13 (at Gormannstrasse) • lesbians/ gay men • tiny neighborhood bar

Cafe Amsterdam Gleimstr 24 (at Schönhauser Allee) 49–30/448–0792, 49–30/231–6796 • 9am-3am, till 5am Fri-Sat • cafe-bar • gay/ straight • transgender-friendly • young crowd • terrace • wheelchair access • also pension

Marietta Stargarder Str 13 49–30/4372–0646 • 10am-2am, till 4am Sat-Sun • lesbians/ gay men

Perle Sredzkistrasse 64 • 8pm-close • lesbians/ gay men • innovative lighting & electronica

Reingold Novalisstr 11 (U-Oranienburger Str) 49–30/2838–7676 • gay/ straight • more gay Th • food served • lesbian-owned cocktail lounge

Sanatorium 23 Frankfurter Allee 23 49–30/4202–1193 • gay/straight • trendy cafe/bar, also guesthouse

Sharon Stonewall Kleinen Präsidentenstr 3 (at Hackeschen Market) 49–30/2408–5502 • opens 7pm, clsd Mon

Zum Schmutzigen Hobby/ Nina's Bar Rykestrasse 45 • 6pm-close • lesbians/ gay men • dancing/DJ • drag shows • transgender-friendly

NIGHTCLUBS

Berghain Am Wrietzener Bahnhof (off Strasse der Pariser Kommune, near Ostbahnhof station) 49–30/2936–0210 • lesbians/ gay men • converted power station is now popular dance club

Chantals House of Shame Schönhauser Allee 176A (Club Bassy) • 11pm Th & Bad Girls club monthly parties

Dice Club Voltairestr 5 (nr Alexa shopping center) 49–30/2021–5857 • 24hrs Fri-Sat • gay//straight • dancing/DJ

Girls Town Karl-Marx-Allee 33 (at Kino International, U-Schillingstr) 49–30/2475–6011 • 2nd Sat every other month • mostly women • dancing/DJ • huge, popular lesbian club

GMF Alexanderstrasse 7 (, at Week End, U-Alexanderplatz) 49–30/2809–5396 • mostly gay men • Sun only 11pm-close

Irrenhouse Am Friedrichshain 33 (at Geburtstagsklub) • 3rd Sat • lesbians/ gay men • dancing/DJ • drag shows • transgender-friendly • Nina Queer's monthly drag party

KitKat Club Kopenickerstrasse 76 (enter on Bruckenstrasse) 49–30/2173–6841 • 8pm-close Th, 11pm-8am Fri-Sat • gay/ straight • theme nights • also S/M club • cabaret

Klub International Karl-Marx-Allee 33 (at Kino International, U-Schillingstr) 49–30/6904–0780 • 11pm-close 1st Sat • mostly gay men • dancing/DJ • largest gay club in Berlin • cover charge

Loreley Karl-Liebknecht-Strasse 11 • mostly gay men • popular Fri • dancing/DJ

Milkshake Am Wrietzener Bahnhof (off Strasse der Pariser Kommune, near Ostbahnhof station, at Berghain) • 3rd Sat, every other month • mostly women • dancing/DJ • transgender-friendly

NBI Schönhauser Allee 36 49–30/6730–4457 • gay/straight • former brewery now open-air shopping & entertainment space • young crowd

Sage Club Köpenicker Str 76 (at Brückenstr) 49–30/278–9830 • 11pm-7am Th-Sun • gay/ straight • more gay wknds • live music venue • dancing/DJ • transgender-friendly

Spy Club Friedrichstr/ Unter den Linden (at Cookies) 49–30/2809–5396 • last Sat only • lesbians/ gay men • dancing/DJ

CAFES

Ackerkeller Bergstrasse 68 49–30/280–8876 • non-profit LGBT club & cafe from 6pm Sun, 10pm Tue & Fri • dancing/DJ

Cafe Seidenfaden Dircksenstr 47 (U-Alexanderplatz) 49–30/283–2783 • noon-8pm, clsd Sun • women only • drug- & alcohol-free cafe • info board • nonsmoking

November Husemannstr 15 (at Sredzkistr) 49–30/442–8425 • 9am-2am • lesbians/ gay men • cafe-bar • terrace • brkfst buffet wknds

RESTAURANTS

Anda Lucia Savignyplatz 2 49–30/5471–0271 • 5pm-1am • tapas bar

Rice Queen Danziger Str 13 (U-Eberswalder Str) 49–30/4404–5800 • Asian

Schall & Rauch Wirtshaus Gleimstr 23 (at Schönhauser Allee) 49–30/443–3970, 49–30/448–0770 • 10am-close • lesbians/ gay men • beer/ wine

Thüringer Stuben Stargarder Str 28 (at Dunckerstr, S/U-Schönhauser Allee) 49–30/4463–3339 • 4pm-1am, from noon wknds • full Asian

BOOKSTORES

Ana Koluth Schönhauser Allee 124 49–30/8733–6980 • 10am-8pm, till 6pm Sat, clsd Sun • lesbian-owned

EROTICA

Blackstyle Seelower Str 5 (S/U-Schönhauser Allee) 49–30/4468–8595 • clsd Sun • latex & rubber wear • also mail order

Berlin—Schöneberg-Tiergarten

ACCOMMODATIONS

Arco Hotel Geisbergstr 30 (at Ansbacherstr, U-Wittenbergplatz) 49–30/235–1480 • gay/ straight • B&B inn • centrally located • kids/ pets ok • wheelchair access • gay-owned • €57-117

Berlin B&B 49–30/2648–4756 • lesbians/ gay men • full brkfst • WiFi • gay-owned • €30-40

Hotel California Kurfürstendamm 35 (at Knesebeckstr, U-Uhlandstr) 49–30/880–120 • gay-friendly • cafe/bar• nonsmoking flr • kids ok • €74-89

Hotel Hansablick Flotowstr 6 (at Bachstr, off Str des 17 Juni) 49–30/390–4800 • gay-friendly • full brkfst • kids/ pets ok • WiFi • €60-145

BARS

Die Kleine Philarmonie Schaperstr 14 (Wilmersdorf, U-Kurfürstendamm) 49–30/8872–7483

Eldorado Motzstr 20 (U-Nollendorfplatz) 49–30/8431–6901 • 24hrs • mostly gay men • food served • music bar • terrace

HarDie's Kneipe Ansbacherstr 29 (in Wittenbergplatz) 49–30/2363–9842 • noon-midnight, till 2am wknds • gay/straight • cafe/pub • older crowd

Kumpelnest 3000 Lützowstr 23 (at Potsdamer Str, U-Kurfürstenstr) 49–30/261–6918 • 5pm-5am, till 8am Fri-Sat • popular wknds • gay-friendly • cocktail bar • dancing/DJ • transgender-friendly • young crowd

Nah-Bar Kalkreuthstr 16 49–30/3150–3062 • opens 2pm, from 5pm Sat • mostly women

Neues Ufer Haupstrasse 157 (U-Bahn Kleistpark) 49–30/784–1578 • 9am-2am, clsd wknds • lesbians/gay men • older crowd

Pussy-Cat Kalckreuthstr 7 (U-Nollendorfplatz) 49–30/213–3586 • 6pm-6am • lesbians/gay men • food served

Spot Eisenacher Str 2 (at Nollendorfplatz) 49–30/213–2267 • 4pm-4am, open later wknds, from 6pm in winter • mostly gay men • neighborhood bar • food served

Together/Margie's Fraunerbar Hohenstauffenstr 53 (off Luther Str, U-Viktoria Luise Platz) 49–30/2191–6300 • 6pm-1am, till 3am Fri, 9pm-4am Sat • lesbians/gay men

Vielharmonie Motzstr 8 (at Nollendorfplatz) 49–30/3064–7302 • 6pm-close • mostly gay men • food served

NIGHTCLUBS

Propaganda Nollendorfplatz 5 (at Goya Theater) • 2nd Sat only • mostly gay men • dancing/DJ • drag shows

CAFES

Cafe Berio Maaßenstr 7 (at Winterfeldtstr, U-Nollendorfplatz) 49–30/216–1946 • 8am-1am, from noon wknds • popular • int'l • brkfst all day • also bar • seasonal terrace • wheelchair access

Cafe Savigny Grolmanstr 53–54 (at Savignyplatz) 49–30/4470–8386 • 9am-1am • artsy crowd • full bar • terrace

Men & Media Nollendorfstr 23 49–30/2191–7524 • noon-midnight • gay cybercafe

PositHiv Cafe Bülowstr 6 49–30/216–8654 • 3pm-11pm, from 6pm Sat, clsd Mon • PWA's and their friends • wheelchair access

Windows Martin-Luther-Str 22 (at Motzstr, U-Wittenbergplatz) 49–30/214–2384 • 8am-1am • lesbians/gay men • full bar • terrace

RESTAURANTS

Diodata Goltzstrasse 51 49–30/2191–7884 • 11am-11pm, 10am-3pm Sun • Viennese

Fritz & Co Wittenbergplatz • organic snack bar • look for the rainbow flags

Gnadenbrot Martin-Luther-Str 20a 49–30/2196–1786 • 3pm-1am • cheap & good

Ma Vie Motzstrasse 28 49–30/2363–1200 • 8am-close • French bistro

More Motzstrasse 28 (at Martin-Luthersrrasse) 49–30/2363–5702 • 9am-midnight • popular

Sissi Motzstr 34 49–17/8236–15 74 • great Austrian food, terrace and location

ENTERTAINMENT & RECREATION

Xenon Kino Kolonnenstr 5-6 49–30/7800–1530 • gay & lesbian cinema

Berlin—Outer

ACCOMMODATIONS

Artemisia Women's Hotel Brandenburgischestr 18 (at Konstanzerstr) 49–30/873–8905, 49–30/869–9320 • the only hotel for women in Berlin • a real bargain • quiet rooms • bar • sundeck w/ an impressive view • some shared baths • nonsmoking rooms available • €49-104

Charlottenburger Hof Stuttgarter Platz 14 (at Wilmersdorfer Str) 49–30/329–070 • gay-friendly • centrally located • also Cafe Voltaire • open 24hrs • also bar • €56-140

BARS

Himmelreich Simon Dach Str 36 (off Warschauer Str, in Friedrichshain, U-Frankfurter Tor) 49–30/2936–9292 • from 6pm Mon-Fri, 2pm-close wknds • lesbians/gay men • women's night Tue

NIGHTCLUBS

Haus B Warschauer Platz 18 49–30/296–0800 • 10pm-5am, till 7am Fri-Sat, clsd Tue & Th • popular • lesbians/gay men • dancing/DJ • live shows • terrace • cover charge

Mermaids Falckensteinstr 47 (at Cornet Club) • 10pm 3rd Sat, May-Sept only • mostly women • dancing/DJ • party by the water

CAFES

Schrader's Malplaquetstr 16b (at Utrechter Str, Wedding) 49–30/4508–2663 • also bar • gay-owned

RESTAURANTS

Cafe Rix Karl-Marx-Str 141 (in Neükolln) 49–30/686–9020 • 10am-midnight • Mediterranean • plenty veggie • also bar

Kurhaus Korsakow Grunbergerstrasse 81 (in Friedrichshain) 49–30/5473–7786 • 5pm-close, from 9am wknds

IRELAND

Dublin

INFO LINES & SERVICES

AA 105 Capel St (at Outhouse) 353–1/842–0700 • call for meeting times

Dublin Lesbian Line 353–1/872–9911 • 7pm-9pm Mon & Th

Gay Switchboard Dublin 353–1/872–1055 • 7:30pm-9:30pm Mon-Fri

Outhouse 105 Capel St 353–1/873–4999 • LGBT community center, cafe, library, meetings

ACCOMMODATIONS

The Clarence 6-8 Wellington Quay 353–1/407–0800 • gay-friendly • owned by Bono & The Edge of U2 • kids ok • WiFi • wheelchair access

The Dylan Eastmoreland Place 353–1/660–3000 • gay/ straight • €59-99

Hotel Capri 58–59 Middle Abbey St 353–1/872–0361 • gay-friendly • centrally located

The Merchant House 8 Eustace St (Temple Bar Area) 353–1/633–4477

Nua Haven Gay Guesthouse 41 Priory Rd 353–87/686–7062, 087 /686–7062 • lesbians/gay men • nonsmoking • €100

Dublin

LGBT PRIDE:
June. web: www.dublinpride.org.

ANNUAL EVENTS:
March - St. Patrick's Day 353–1/676–3205, web: www.stpatricksday.ie.

May - Dublin Gay Theatre Festival, web: www.gaytheatre.ie.

CITY INFO:
Dublin Tourism 353–1/605–7700, 353–1/437–0969, web: www.visit-dublin.com.

BEST VIEW:
Crossing the River Liffey on the Ha'Penny Bridge, or on the ferry to Holyhead.

WEATHER:
Wet and mild, with summers averaging in the 60°s and winters in the 40°s. Frequent rain keeps the Emerald Isle green.

TRANSIT:
Dublin Bus 353–1/873–4222, web: www.dublinbus.ie.

DART (Dublin Area Rapid Transport) 353–1/703–3504, web: www.irishrail.ie.

ATTRACTIONS:
Book of Kells 353–1/896-1661, web: www.bookofkells.ie.

Guinness Storehouse 353–1/408–4800, web: www.guinness-storehouse.com.

The Hugh Lane Gallery 353–1/222–5550, web: www.hughlane.ie.

James Joyce Centre 353-1/878-8547, web: www.jamesjoyce.ie.

Kilmainham Gaol 353–1/453–5984, web: www.heritageireland.ie.

Malahide Castle 353–1/846–2184, web: www.malahidecastle.com.

National Botanic Gardens 353–1/804-0300, web: www.botanicgardens.ie.

Phoenix Park.

St. Michan's Church (mummies!) 353–1/872–4154.

Waterloo House 8-10 Waterloo Rd **353–1/660–1888** • 5 star hotel • gay/ straight • resraurant & bar • €199-599

BARS

The Dragon 64-45 S Great Georges St **353–1/478–1590** • 5pm-11:30pm, till 2:30am Th-Sat, till 11pm Sun • lesbians/ gay men • dancing/DJ

Front Lounge 33 Parliament St **353–1/670–4112** • noon-11:30pm, till 2am Fri-Sat, till 1am Sun • popular • lesbians/ gay men • dancing/DJ • transgender-friendly • karaoke

The George 87 S Great George St **353–1/671 3298, 353–1/671 3819** • open 7 days till late • popular • lesbians/ gay men • dancing/DJ • drag shows • Sun bingo

Panti Bar 7-8 Capel St **353–1/874–0710** • 5pm-close • lesbians/ gay men • dancing/DJ • food • drag shows • wheelchair access

NIGHTCLUBS

Glitz St. Stephen's Green Centre (Dandelion Nightclub) **353–1/478–0300 (BREAK FOR THE BORDER), 353–85/727–3874** • 11pm-close Tue only • lesbians/ gay men • dancing/DJ

KAMP/ Partie Monster 8 Lower Leeson St (at Sugar Club) • lesbians/ gay men • debauched dance parties • drag shows • transgender-friendly

Mother Exchange St (at Copper Alley, Arlington Hotel) • 10:30pm Sat only • lesbians/ gay men • dancing/DJ

Nimhneach 39-40 Arran Quay (at Voodoo Lounge) **353–1/873–6013** • gay/ straight • fetish & BDSM party • strict dress code • call or see www.nimhneach.ie for dates

Pod Harcourt St (at Hatch St, at the Old Railway Station) **353–1/476–3374** • 11pm-close, clsd Sun-Tue • popular Fri • gay/ straight • dancing/DJ

Prhomo 6-8 Wicklow St (at Grafton, at Base Bar) • 10:30pm Th only • lesbians/ gay men • dancing/DJ

Q & A **353–1/670–9202 (TEMPLE BAR MUSIC CENTRE)** • "queer & alternative" dance party • check www.queerandalternative.com for dates & location • dancing/DJ • cover charge

Spy Powerscourt Townhouse, S William St **353–1/677–0014** • gay/ straight • dancing/DJ • 4 floors

CAFES

Irish Film Institute Bar & Restaurant 6 Eustace St (in Temple Bar) **353–1/679–5744** • lunch & dinner • next to independent cinema • light meals • plenty veggie

Lovinspoon Cafe 13 N Frederick St **353–1/804–7604** • 7am-6pm, clsd Sun (except summers)

RESTAURANTS

Brasserie Sixty6 66 S Great Georges St **353–1/400–5878** • brkfst, lunch, dinner, wknd brunch • meat & seafood • WiFi

La Cave 28 S Anne St **353–1/679–4409** • 12:30pm-close, from 6pm Sun • French

The Chameleon 1 Lower Fownes St **353–1/671–0362** • 5pm-11pm, from 4pm Sun, clsd Mon • Indonesian

Cornucopia 19 Wicklow **353–1/677–7583** • 8:30am-9pm, till 8pm Sat, noon-7pm Sun • affordable vegetarian

L' Ecrivain 109A Lower Baggot St **353–1/661–1919** • lunch Mon-Fri, dinner Mon-Sat, clsd Sun • also piano bar • reservations recommended

Eden Meeting House Square (entrance on Sycamore) **353–1/670–5372** • lunch & dinner, wknd brunch • patio dining

Fire Restaurant Mansion House, Dawson St **353–1/676–7200** • 5:30pm-close, noon-3pm jazz lunch Sat, clsd Sun

FXB Crow St **353–1/671–1248** • 5:30pm-close • steak & seafood

Gruel 68A Dame St **353–1/670–7119** • lunch & dinner

Halo Ormond Quay (in the Morrison Hotel) **353–1/878–2400** • Fri & Sat dinner • creative fusion food • upscale • vegetarian dishes • reservations recommended

Juice 73-83 S Great Georges St (across from the Globe) **353–1/475–7856** • lunch & dinner, wknd brunch • vegetarian

Just Off Francis 78 Thomas St **353–1/473–8807** • 11am-11pm, till 9pm Sat-Sun

Mermaid Cafe 69-70 Dame St **353–1/670–8236** • lunch & dinner, Sun brunch • gay/ straight

Odessa 14 Dame Court **353–1/670–7634** • lunch & dinner, wknd brunch • local hot spot • gay/ straight

Shack 24 E Essex St **353–1/679–0043** • lunch & dinner

Town Bar & Grill 21 Kildare St **353–1/662–4724** • lunch & dinner, Sun brunch • Italian

Trocadero 4 Saint Andrew St **353–1/677–5545** • 5pm-midnight, clsd Sun

The Winding Stair Restaurant 40 Lower Ormond Quay 353–1/872–7320 • lunch & dinner • Irish • young crowd • also bookshop

ENTERTAINMENT & RECREATION

Gloria 353–87/750–0062 (DEBORAH) • lesbian & gay choir

Irish Queer Archive 2 Kildare St (National Library of Ireland) 353–87/01–603–0207, 087/255–4043 •

BOOKSTORES

Books Upstairs 36 College Green 353–1/679–6687 • 10am-7pm, till 6pm Sat, 2pm-6pm Sun (summers only)

Chapters Bookstore Ivy House, Parnell St 353–1/872–3297 • LGBT section

The Winding Stair Bookshop 40 Lower Ormond Quay 353–1/872–7320 • 10am-7pm-5pm, til 8pm Th-Sat, from noon Sun • also restaurant • young crowd

PUBLICATIONS

GCN (Gay Community News) Unit 2 Scarlet Row, Essex St W, Temple Bar, 8 353–1/671–0939, 353–1/671–9076 • monthly LGBT newspaper • many resources

ITALY

Rome

Note: M°=Metro station

INFO LINES & SERVICES

Circolo di Cultura Omosessual Mario Mieli Via Efeso 2a (M° San Paolo) 39–06/541–3985 (HELP LINE) • 4pm-7pm Mon-Fri • switchboard, meetings & discussion groups

Gay Help Line 800/713–713 • 4pm-8pm, clsd Sun

ACCOMMODATIONS

58 Le Real de Luxe Via Cavour 58, 4th flr (near Colosseum) 39–06/482–3566, 39–399/805–2485 (CELL) • gay/ straight • B&B inn • kids ok • nonsmoking • WiFi • wheelchair access • €65–150

Albergo Del Sole al Pantheon Piazza della Rotonda 63 39–06/678–0441 • gay-friendly • 4-star hotel • jacuzzi • kids ok •€130-500

Ares Rooms Via Domenichino 7 39–06/474–4525, 39–340/278–1248 (CELL) • gay-friendly • some shared baths • €30-160

B&B Inandout Rome Via Arco del Monte (at Viale Trastevere) 39–339/784–0653 • gay/ straight • in 18th-c palace • kids/ pets ok • nonsmoking • WiFi • wheelchair access • lesbian-owned • €65-130

Best Place Via Turati 13 39–329/213–2320 • lesbians/ gay men • reservations required • €50-110

Bologna B&B 6 Piazza Bologna (at Via Sambucuccio D'Alando) 39–06/4424–0244, 39/34781–0481 (CELL) • gay/ straight • central location • some shared baths • kids/ pets ok • €50-118

Claridge Hotel Via Liegi 62 39–06/845–441 • gay-friendly • near Borghese park • gym w/ sauna & Turkish bath

Daphne Veneto Via di San Basilio 55 39–06/8745–0086 • gay-friendly • small, cozy inn in heart of historical Rome • kids ok • nonsmoking • €90-550 • also Daphne Trevi atvia Degli Avignonesi 20

Discover Roma Via Castelfidardo 50 39–06/4938-2080 • lesbians/ gay men • woman-owned • €70-160

Domus International 39–06/6889–2918 • gay/ straight • short-term apt rentals in the heart of Rome • kids/ pets ok • weekly rates

Franklin Via Rodi 29 39–06/3903-0165 • gay-friendly • music-themed hotel w/ CD library • €100-470

Gaspare B&B Via Balilla 16 39–06/328–833–3486 • lesbians/ gay men • WiFi • €40-120

Gayopen B&B Via dello Statuto 44, Apt 18 (at Via Merulana, Piazza Vittorio) 39–06/482–0013 • gay/ straight • B&B • full brkfst • kids/ pets ok • lesbian & gay-owned • €60-90

Hotel Altavilla Via Principe Amedeo 9 39–06/474–1186 • gay-friendly • pets ok • also bar • €55-200

Hotel Derby Via Vigna Pozzi 7 (Largo delle Sette Chiese) 39–06/513-4955, 39–06/513–6978 • gay-friendly • small hotel in heart of Rome • kids/ pets ok • wheelchair access • €95-195

Hotel Edera Via A Poliziano 75 39–06/7045-3888 • gay-friendly • €103-196

Hotel Labelle Via Cavour 310 39–06/679–4750 • lesbians/ gay men • near the Roman Forum • €60-244

Hotel Scott House Via Gioberti 30 39–06/446-5379 • gay-friendly • €35-88

Hotel Welcome Piram Via Amendola 7 **39–06/4890–1248** • lesbians/ gay men • hot tubs • €90-380

Italy-Accom Via Dei Greci 26 (at Spanish Steps) **39–06/3600–1394** • reservation service for Venice, Rome, Florence, Positano, Sicily, Calabria, & Tuscany • also tours • see www.italy-accom.com for more info

Nicolas Inn Via Cavour 295 (at Via dei Serpenti) **39–06/9761–8483, 39–338/937–8387** • gay-friendly • elegant rooms located near the Colosseum & Roman Forum • nonsmoking • WiFi • owned/ operated by native English speaker • €90-180

Orsa Maggiore for Women Via San Francesco de Sales 1/a (at Via della Lungara) **39–06/689–3753** • women-only • inside 16th-c former convent • nonsmoking • €26-138

Pensione Ottaviano Via Ottaviano 6 **39–06/3973–8138** • gay-friendly • in quiet area near St Peter's Square • hostel • €23-50

The Rainbow B&B Viale Giulio Cesare 151 **39–347/507–0344 (CELL)** • lesbians/ gay men • WiFi • €80-185

Relais le Clarisse Via Cardinale Merry del Val 20 (at Viale Trastevere) **39–06/5833–4437** • gay/ straight • nonsmoking • WiFi • jacuzzis • Mediterranean garden • on historic site in central Rome • lesbian-owned • €140-300

Rentflatsinitaly.com Via Principe Umberto (at Piazza Vittorio Emanuelle) **39–069/784–3916** • gay-friendly • some shared baths • €80-120

Roman Reference Via dei Capocci 94 **39–06/4890–3612** • gay-friendly • apts • kids ok

Rome

WHERE THE GIRLS ARE:
Discussing politics at a cafe, or dancing at one of the one-nighters that make up lesbian nightlife in Rome. Visit the bulletin board at the Libreria Babele or the Circolo Mario Mieli center for the latest events.

LGBT PRIDE:
June/July. web: www.romapride.it.

ANNUAL EVENTS:
June-September - Gay Village, web: www.gayvillage.it.

CITY INFO:
Comune di Rome 39-06/060-606, web: www.comune.roma.it.
Enjoy Rome 39–6/445–1843, web: www.enjoyrome.com. Via Marghera 8a.

WEATHER:
Late summer is hot and humid. Winter is mild but rainy. The best times to visit Rome are late spring and early fall.

ATTRACTIONS:
Baths of Caracalla 39–06/3996-7700 or 39-06/574-5748.
Campo dei Fiori.
Capitoline Museums 39–06/8205–9127, web: www.museicapitolini.org.
Colosseum 39–06/3996-7700.
Galleria Borghese 39–06/328–10, web: www.galleriaborghese.it.
Pantheon 39–06/6830–0230.
Roman Forum 39–06/3996–7700.
Spanish Steps.
St. Peter's.
Trevi Fountain.
The Vatican and Vatican Museums (includes National Etruscan Museum, Sistine Chapel, and Raphael Rooms) 39–06/6988–4341, web: www.vatican.va

TRANSIT:
Taxi stands are located in several popular piazzas. Only hire official yellow or white taxis. You can also call 3570 for pick-up service.
ATAC general info: 800/431–784 (in Rome), tourist lines: 39-06/4695–2284, web: www.atac.roma.it.

Sandy Hostel Via Cavour 136 **39-06/4884-4585** • gay-friendly • great location near Colosseum, Roman Forum & Spanish Steps • €25-53

Scalinata di Spagna Piazza Trinità dei Monti 17 (M° Piazza di Spagna) **39-06/6994-0896, 39-06/679-3006 (BOOKING #)** • gay-friendly • roof garden • kids/ pets ok • nonsmoking • WiFi • €130-700

www.romecityapartments.com Via Quintino Sella 23 (at Via Boncompagni) **39-06/4201-6891** • gay-friendly • wide range of central apts in Rome from budget to luxury for tourist & business stays • nonsmoking • €80-400

BARS

Coming Out Via San Giovanni in Laterano 8 (near Colosseum) **39-06/700-9871** • 5pm-2am • popular • lesbians/ gay men • transgender-friendly • food served • live music Th • karaoke • lesbian-owned

Garbo Vicolo di Santa Margherita 1a (in Trastevere, Tram 8) **39-06/5832-0782, 39-06/581-6700** • 10pm-3am, clsd Mon • lesbians/ gay men • cocktail bar • food served • gay-owned

Il Giardino dei Ciliegi Via dei Fienaroli 4 **39-06/580-3423** • 5pm-2am, from 1pm Sun • lesbians/ gay men • tea salon

NIGHTCLUBS

L' Alibi Via di Monte Testaccio 40–44 (M° Piramide) **39-06/574-3448** • 11pm-4am, clsd Mon-Tue • popular • lesbians/ gay men • dancing/DJ • live shows • rooftop garden in summer • hosts Gloss & Tommy • young crowd

Amigdala Via delle Conce 14 (at Rising Love) • 2nd & 4th Sat only • lesbians/ gay men • dancing/DJ • electronica & queer culture

Gorgeous Via del Commercio 36 (at Alpheus) **39-06/574-7826** • 10pm-4am Sat • lesbians/ gay men • dancing/DJ

Muccassassina **39-06/541-3985** • 10:30pm-5am Fri only (Sept-June) • popular • lesbians/ gay men • dancing/DJ • karaoke • live shows • young crowd • cover charge • location changes so call ahead

Venus Rising Via Libetta 13 **39-06/574-8277** • last Sun only • special events for women • check www.venusrising.it for upcoming parties

CAFES

Oppio Caffè Via delle Terme di Tìti 72 **39-06/474-5262, 39-347/510-8594 (CELL)** • brkfst, lunch & dinner • open 24hrs in Aug • popular • lesbians/ gay men • full bar • live shows • terrace w/ great view

RESTAURANTS

Asino Cotto Ristorante Via dei Vascellari 38 (in Travestere, Tram 8) **39-06/589-8985** • lunch & dinner, clsd Mon • creative gourmet Mediterranean • reservations required • gay-owned

La Carbonara Via Panisperna 214 **39-06/482-5176** • lunch & dinner, clsd Sun • classic Roman cuisine since 1906

Città in Fiore Via Cavour 269 **39-06/482-4874** • lunch Th-Mon, dinner nightly • lesbians/ gay men • Chinese

Ditirambo Piazza della Cancelleria 74-75 (near Campo dei Fiori) **39-06/687-1626**

La Focaccia Via della Pace 11 **39-06/6880-3312** • 11am-2am • pizza

Gelateria San Crispino Via Panetteria 42 (near Trevi Fountain) **39-06/679-3924** • noon-12:30am, till 1:30am Fri-Sat, clsd Tue • gelato!

Mater Matuta Via Milano 47 (basement) **39-06/4782-5746** • lunch Mon-Fri, dinner nightly • also wine bar

Osteria del Pegno Vicolo Montevecchio 8 (Plaza Navona) **39-06/6880-7025** • lunch & dinner, clsd Wed winter • Italian • large pizza selection • wheelchair access

Ristorante da Dino Via dei Mille 10 (at Piazza Indipendenza) **39-06/491-425** • clsd Wed • family run Roman food at reasonable prices near Termini Station

La Taverna di Edoardo II Vicolo Margana 14 **39-06/6994-2419** • 7:30pm-midnight, clsd Tue • lesbians/ gay men • full bar • wheelchair access

ENTERTAINMENT & RECREATION

Gay Village **39-06/753-8396** • gay summer festival

Through Eternity Via Astura 2/B **39-06/700-9336** • walking tours of Rome • gay-owned

RETAIL SHOPS

Hydra II Via Urbana 139 **39-06/489-7773** • leather, vinyl, clubwear, western, vintage & more

NETHERLANDS

Amsterdam

Amsterdam is divided into 5 regions:
Amsterdam—Overview
Amsterdam—Centrum
Amsterdam—Jordaan
Amsterdam—Rembrandtplein
Amsterdam—Outer

Amsterdam—Overview

INFO LINES & SERVICES

COC-Amsterdam Rozenstraat 14 (in the Jordaan) **31–20/626–3087** • info line 10am-5pm, also cafe 8pm-11:30pm Wed-Fri • also sponsors women's parties at clubs around town • www.cocamsterdam.nl for info

Gay/ Lesbian Switchboard
31–20/623-6565 • noon-10pm, 4pm-8pm wknds • English spoken

Pink Point Westermarkt (Raadhuisstraat & Keizersgracht, in the Jordaan by Homomonument) **31–20/428–1070** • 10am-6pm • info on Homomonument & general LGBT info • friendly volunteers • queer souvenirs & gifts

Wild Side • women's S/M support group • meetings, events & play parties • meets at COC

ACCOMMODATIONS

Simply Amsterdam Apartments
31–20/620–6608 • gay-friendly • apts, studios, canal houses & houseboat • kids/ pets ok • gay-owned • €120-280

NIGHTCLUBS

Fuckin' Pop Queers/ Ultrasexi/ Multisexi • lesbians/ gay men • monthly queer dance parties at different clubs around the city • check ultrasexi.com for details

Girlesque • mostly women (cool gay guys welcome) • huge quarterly dance parties • check www.girlesque.hyves.nl for info

Venus Freaks • "men-friendly women's dance parties" • check www.venusfreaks.nl for info

ENTERTAINMENT & RECREATION

The Anne Frank House Prinsengracht 263-267 (in the Jordaan) **31–20/556–7100, 31–20/556–7105 (INFO TAPE)** • the final hiding place of Amsterdam's most famous resident

Boom Chicago Leidseplein 12 (Leidseplein Theater) **31–20/423–0101 (TICKETS)** • English-language improv comedy • also dinner & drinks • also distributes free Boom! magazine to Amsterdam • €18-20 not including food/ drink

Homomonument Westermarkt (in the Jordaan) • moving sculptural tribute to lesbians & gays killed by Nazis

MacBike Stationsplein 12 (next to Centraal Station) **31–20/620-0985** • rental bikes & map for self-guided tour of Amsterdam's gay points of interest

De Pijp near Albert Cuypmarkt • gay-friendly neighborhood teeming w/ lots of interesting shops & restaurants

The van Gogh Museum Paulus Potterstr 7 (on the Museumplein) **31–20/570–5200** • 10am-6pm, till 10pm Fri • a must-see museum dedicated to this Dutch master painter • wheelchair access

PUBLICATIONS

COC Update 31–20/623–4596 • news & events calendar for COC

Expreszo 31–20/359–0713 • for LGBT youth (in Dutch)

Gay News Amsterdam 31–20/679–1556 • bilingual paper • extensive listings

Gay & Night 31–20/788–1360 • free monthly bilingual entertainment paper w/ club listings

GK Magazine 31–499/39–10–00 • nat'l LGBT newspaper in Dutch w/ English summaries

Amsterdam—Centrum

ACCOMMODATIONS

Amsterdam B&B Barangay
31–6/2504–5432 • gay/ straight • 1777 town house • near tourist attractions • full brkfst • nonsmoking • WiFi • gay-owned • €68-138

Amsterdam Central B&B Oudebrugsteeg 6-II (at Warmoesstraat) **31–62/445–7593** • lesbians/ gay men • cozy B&B apts near main gay area & train station • in 16th-c guesthouse • also apartments • WiFi • full brkfst • gay-owned • €95-250

Avenue Hotel NZ Voorburgwal 33 (at St Jacobstraat) **31–20/530-9530** • gay/ straight • WiFi • €150-350

Bulldog Oudezijds Voorburgwal 220 (at St Jansstraat) **31–20/620-3822** • gay-friendly • hostel in Red Light District • dorms & private rooms • brkfst included • coffeeshop & lounge/ bar • WiFi • wheelchair access

Cosmos Hostel Nieuwe nieuwstraat 17-1 (at NZ Voorburgwal) **31–20/625-2438** • gay-friendly • hostel in 17th-c bldg formerly a hotel • WiFi • no curfew • ages 18-35 only • nonsmoking • €20-40 (dorm) & €75 (rooms)

Crowne Plaza Amsterdam City Centre NZ Voorburgwal 5 **31–20/620-0500, 877/227-6963 (US#)** • gay-friendly • pool • restaurant & bar • wheelchair access • €305-335

Friendzz Oudezijds Achterburgwal 34 **31-6/4140-4820** • lesbians/ gay men • full brkfst • €85-95 • gay-owned

Mauro Mansion Geldersekade 16 (at OZ Kolk) **31-0/620-710_332**

NH City Centre Hotel Spuistraat 288–292 **31–20/420-4545** • gay-friendly • kids/ pets ok • WiFi • wheelchair access • €83-229

Amsterdam

LGBT Pride:

1st wknd in August, web: www.amsterdampride.nl.

Annual Events:

April 30 - Queen's Birthday/ Roze Wester Festival, web: www.gala-amsterdam.nl.

May - Memorial Day & Liberation Day.

May/ June - Holland Festival, web: www.hollandfestival.nl.

August - Heart's Day. Drag festival in the Red Light District, web: www.hartjesdagen.nl.

October - Leather Pride, web: www.leatherpride.nl.

City Info:

Amsterdam Tourism & Convention Board 31-20/201-8800, web: www.amsterdamtourist.nl. Visit their office directly opposite Centraal Station. Netherlands Board of Tourism, web: www.holland.com.

Transit:

31–20/677-7777.
Can also be found at taxi stands on the main squares.
KLM Bus 31–20/653–4975.
GVB 0900-8011 (€.50 per minute), web: www.gvb.nl, or visit their office across from the Centraal Station (Stationsplein 10). Trams, buses & subway.

Attractions:

Anne Frank House 31–20/556-7105, web: www.annefrank.org.

Hermitage Amsterdam 31-20/530-8751, web: www.hermitage.nl.

Homomonument, web: www.homomonument.nl.

Jewish Historical Museum 31–20/531-0310, web: www.jhm.nl.

Rembrandt House 31–20/520-0400, web: www.rembrandthuis.nl.

Rijksmuseum 31–20/674-7000, web: www.rijksmuseum.nl.

Stedelijk Museum of Modern Art 31–20/573-2911, web: www.stedelijk.nl.

Vincent van Gogh Museum 31–20/570-5200, web: www.vangoghmuseum.nl.

Weather:

Temperatures hover around freezing in the winter and rise to the mid-60°s in the summer. Rain is possible year-round.

NH Grand Hotel Krasnapolsky Dam 9 (at Warmoesstraat) **31–20/554–9111** • gay-friendly • full-service hotel • in the city center opposite Royal Palace • WiFi • wheelchair access • € 157-324

Old Harbour Apartments Prins Hendrikkade 125-1 **31–20/428–5758** • gay/ straight • private entrances & patio • nonsmoking • gay-owned € 90-160

Palace B&B Spuistraat 224 **31–6/4260–8847** • gay/ straight • 1794 bldg w/ indoor garden • nonsmoking • WiFi • gay-owned € 99-149

Victoria Hotel Amsterdam Damrak 1-5 (opposite Centraal Station) **31–20/623–4255, 800/791–9161** • gay-friendly • 4-star hotel • pool • gym • restaurants & bar • WiFi • wheelchair access • € 265-505

Winston Hotel Warmoesstraat 129 **31–20/623–1380** • gay-friendly • hipster hotel • rockers & artists • popular bar • live DJs • gallery • some shared baths • € 60-90

BARS

De Barderij Zeedijk 14 (at OZ Kolk) **31–20/420–5132** • noon-1am, till 3am Fri-Sat • mostly gay men • large neighborhood bar/ brown café • older crowd

Cafe Mandje Zeedijk 63 (at Stormsteeg) **31–20/622–5375** • gay/ straight • originally opened in 1927 as Amsterdam's first gay bar by dyke-on-bike Bet van Beeren

De Engel van Amsterdam Zeedijk 21 (at OZ Kolk) **31–20/427–6381** • 1pm-1am, till 3am Fri-Sat • mostly gay men • patio

Getto Warmoesstraat 51 (at Niezel) **31–20/421–5151** • 4pm-1am, till 2am Fri-Sat, till midnight Sun, clsd Mon • popular • lesbians/ gay men • live DJs • also restaurant till 11pm • Sun brunch

Prik Spuistraat 109 **31–20/320–0002** • 4pm-1am, till 3am Fri-Sat • lesbians/ gay men • food served • patio

NIGHTCLUBS

Club NL Nieuwezijds Voorburgwal 169 (at KeizerRijk) **31–20/622–7510** • 10pm-3am, till 4am Fri-Sat • gay/ straight • lounge w/ DJs

Club Stereo Jonge Roelensteeg 4 (at Kalvertstraat) **31–20/770–4037** • 7pm-1am, till 3am Fri-Sat • gay/ straight • dancing/DJ • live shows

CAFES

Dampkring Haarlemmerstraat 24 **31–20/638–0705** • smoking coffeeshop • great fresh OJ

Gary's Late Night TT Vasumweg 260 **31–20/637–3643** • noon-3am, till 4am Fri-Sat • popular • fresh muffins & bagels • organic fair-trade coffee

Puccini Bomboni Staalstraat 17 **31–(0)20/626–5474** • If you love chocolate, do we have a cafe for you!

RESTAURANTS

Cafe de Jaren Nieuwe Doelenstraat 20-22 **31–20/625–5771** • 10am-1am, till 2am Fri-Sat • some veggie • full bar • terrace • young crowd

Cafe de Schutter Voetboogstraat 13-15 (upstairs) **31–20/622–4608** • noon-1am, till 3am Fri-Sat • popular local hangout • plenty veggie • full bar • terrace

Cafe Latei Zeedijk 143 (in Red Light District) **31–20/625–7485** • 8am-6pm, from 9am Sat, from 11am Sun • Indian food • great coffee hangout • everything you see you can buy, too • WiFi

Greenwoods Singel 103 (near Dam Square) **31–20/623–7071** • English-style brkfst & tea snacks

Hemelse Modder Oude Waal 11 **31–20/624–3203** • 6pm-10pm • popular • lesbians/ gay men • French/ int'l • also full bar • wheelchair access • gay-owned

Kitsch Utrechtsestraat 42 **31–20/625–9251** • 6pm-close, clsd Sun • kitsch & disco

Krua Thai Staalstraat 22 **31–20/622–9533** • 5pm-10:30pm • terrace • wheelchair access • also at Spuistraat 90a, 620-0623 • full bar

La Strada NZ Voorburgwal 93-95 **31–20/625–0276** • 4pm-1am, till 3am wknds • popular • food served till 10pm • Mediterranean • plenty veggie • full bar • terrace • lesbian-owned

Het Land van Walem Keizersgracht 449 **31–20/625–3544** • lunch & dinner • int'l • inexpensive • local crowd • canalside terrace • wheelchair access • lesbian-owned

Maoz Muntplein 1 **31–20/420–7435** • 11am-1am, till 3am wknds • vegetarian/ falafel

Old Highlander Sint Jacobsstraat 8 **31–20/420–8321** • noon-1am, till 2am wknds • Scottish food • brkfst all day

't Sluisje Torensteeg 1 **31–20/624–0813** • 6pm-close, clsd Mon-Wed • popular steak house • lesbians/ gay men • transgender-friendly • full bar (open later) • drag shows nightly

Song Kwae Kloveniersburgwal 14 (near Nieuwmarkt & Chinatown) 31–20/624–2568 • 1pm-10:30pm • Thai • full bar • terrace

BOOKSTORES

The American Book Center Spui 12 31–20/625–5537 • 10am-8pm, till 9pm Th, 11am-6:30pm Sun • large LGBT section • wheelchair access

Boekhandel Vrolijk Gay & Lesbian Bookshop Paleisstraat 135 (at Spuistraat, near Dam Square) 31–20/623–5142 • 10am-6pm, 11am-6pm Mon, 10am-5pm Sat, from 1pm Sun • LGBT books, videos & gadgets • also mail order

RETAIL SHOPS

Conscious Dreams Kokopelli Warmoesstr 12 31–20/421–7000 • 11am-10pm • popular • "smart warehouse" • WiFi

Gays & Gadgets Spuistraat 44 31–20/330–1461 • cards, gifts & art gallery

Magic Mushroom Spuistraat 249 31–20/427–5765 • 11am-7pm, till 8pm Fri-Sat • "smartshop": magic mushrooms & more • also Singel 524, 31-20/422-7845

GYMS & HEALTH CLUBS

The Fitness & Health Garden Jodenbreestraat 158 31–20/320–0233 • gay/ straight

Splash Looiersgracht 26-30 31–20/624–8404 • gym & wellness center

EROTICA

Absolute Danny Oudezijds Achterburgwal 78 (in the Red Light District) 31–20/421–0915 • 11am-9pm • upscale erotica • woman-owned

DeMask Zeedijk 64 31–20/423–3090 • 11am-7pm, clsd Sun • rubber & leather clothing

Female & Partners Spuistraat 100 31–20/620–9152 • 11am-6:30pm, 1pm-6pm Sun • fashions & toys for women • also mail order

Amsterdam—Jordaan

ACCOMMODATIONS

Budget Hotel Clemens Amsterdam Raadhuisstraat 39 (at Herengracht) 31–20/624–6089 • gay-friendly • small hotel in Amsterdam's center • some shared baths • WiFi • woman-owned • €60-155

Chic and Basic Amsterdam Herengracht 13-19 (at Brouwersgr) 31–20/522–2345 • gay-friendly • "the quiet hotel" • €85-140+

The Dylan Keizersgracht 384 (at Runstraat) 31–20/530–2010 • gay-friendly • sleep in high style • also restaurant • €285-1,650

Hotel Acacia Lindengracht 251 (at Lijnbaansgr) 31–20/622–1460 • gay-friendly • "homey hotel in heart of Jordaan" • also self-catering studios & houseboat • WiFi

Hotel Brian Singel 69 (at Lijnbaanssteeg) 31–20/624–4661 • gay-friendly • cheap & no frills but friendly • shared baths • €25-35/ person

Hotel Pulitzer Prinsengracht 315–331 (at Reestraat) 31–20/523–5235 • gay-friendly • occupies 24 17th-c buildings on 2 of Amsterdam's most picturesque canals • €215-1,000

Hotel Rembrandt Centrum Herengracht 255 (at Hartenstraat) 31–20/622–1727, 31–20/623–6638 • gay/ straight • canalside hotel near Dam Square • nonsmoking rooms available • €65-225

Maes B&B Herenstraat 26 (at Keizersgr) 31–20/427–5165 • gay/ straight • nonsmoking • WiFi • gay-owned • €85-285

Marnixkade Canalview Apartments 31–6/1012–1296 • popular • lesbians/ gay men • fully furnished apts in 19th-c canal house on a quiet canal in heart of Jordaan • nonsmoking • WiFi • gay-owned • €150-175

Sunhead of 1617 Herengracht 152 (at Leliegracht & Raadshuisstraat) 31–20/626–1809 • gay/ straight • B&B • full brkfst • kids/ pets ok • nonsmoking • also several canal apts • WiFi • gay-owned • €89-159 (B&B), €441-5040/ week (apts)

BARS

Cafe de Gijs Lindengracht 249 (at Lijnbaansgr) 31–20/638–0740, 31–6/2537–3674 • 4pm-1am • 1st Wed of month hosts T&T, social gathering for transvestites & transsexuals, from 10pm

Saarein 2 Elandsstraat 119 (at Hazenstraat) 31–20/623–4901 • 4pm-1am, till 2am Fri-Sat, clsd Mon • mostly women • food served • brown cafe

NIGHTCLUBS

de Trut Bilderdijkstraat 165 (at Kinkerstraat) 31–20/612–3524 • 11pm-4am Sun only • lesbians/ gay men • hip underground dance party in legalized squat • alternative • young crowd

CAFES

Cafe 't Smalle Egelantiersgracht 12
31–20/623–9617 • 10am-1am, till 2am wknds
• brown cafe • full bar • outdoor seating

Rokerij Singel 8 **31–20/422–6643** • smoking
coffeeshop • 3 other locations

RESTAURANTS

Bojo Lange Leidsedwarsstraat 49–51 (near
Leidseplein) **31–20/622–7434** • 11am-9pm,
from 4:30pm wknds • popular • Indonesian

De Bolhoed Prinsengracht 60 (at Tuinstr)
31–20/626–1803 • noon-10pm, from 11am
Sat • vegetarian/ vegan

Burger's Patio 2e Tuindwarsstr 12
31–20/623–6854 • 6pm-1am • Italian • plenty
veggie

Foodism Oude Leliestraat 8 **31–20/627–6464**
• noon-10pm, till 6pm wknds • great soups &
sandwiches • funky & fun

Granada Leidsekruisstraat 13
31–20/625–1073 • 5pm-close • Spanish •
tapas • also bar • live music wknds

De Vliegende Schotel Nieuwe Leliestraat
162 **31–20/625–2041** • 4pm-11:30pm, kitchen
till 10:45pm, so come early • vegetarian & fish
• some vegan • nonsmoking section

ENTERTAINMENT & RECREATION

De Looier Art & Antiques Market
Elandsgracht 109 **31–20/624–9038,
31–20/427–4990** • 11am-5pm, clsd Fri

BOOKSTORES

Xantippe Unlimited Prinsengracht 290
31–20/623–5854 • 1pm-6pm, from 10am Sat,
noon-5pm Sun • women's bookstore • lesbian
section • English titles • lesbian-owned

RETAIL SHOPS

Dare to Wear Buiten Oranjestraat 15
31–20/686–8679 • piercing, jewelry &
accessories

House of Tattoos Haarlemmerdijk 130c
31–20/330–9046 • 11am-6pm, from 1pm Sun
• great tattoos, great people

Lust for Leather Lindengracht 220
31-6/5573–4047 • 2pm-6pm 1st Sat or by
appointment • hip showroom • day & fetish
wear

SEX CLUBS

Sameplace Nassaukade 120
31–20/475–1981 • gay/ straight • men only
Mon • transgender-friendly • dancing/DJ •
theme nights • darkroom

EROTICA

Black Body Lijnbaansgracht 292 (across
from Rijksmuseum) **31–20/626–2553** • clsd
Sun • rubber clothing specialists • leather •
toys • DVDs • wheelchair access

Amsterdam—Rembrandtplein

ACCOMMODATIONS

Amsterdam House 's Gravelandseveer 7 (at
Kloveniersburgwal) **31–20/626–2577 &
624–6607 (HOTEL), 800/618-1008 (US#)** • gay-
friendly • 16-room hotel, 16 comfortably
furnished apts & 10 lovely houseboats • €85
(hotel), €135-325(apt), €165-325 (houseboat)

Dikker & Thijs Fenice Hotel Prinsengracht
444 (at Leidsestraat) **31–20/620–1212** • gay-
friendly • 4-star hotel on canal • nonsmoking
rooms • bar & restaurant

Eden Hotel Amstel 144 **31–20/530–7878** •
gay-friendly • 3-star hotel • nonsmoking
rooms • brasserie overlooking River Amstel •
WiFi • wheelchair access

Hotel de l'Europe Nieuwe Doelenstraat 2-8
31–20/531–1777 • gay-friendly • grand hotel
on the River Amstel • fitness center • pool •
€345-2,150

Hotel Monopole Amstel 60 (at
Kloveniersburgwal) **31–20/624–6271** • gay-
friendly • centrally located • nonsmoking
rooms available • kids ok • €65-165 • also
Cafe Rouge

Hotel Orlando Prinsengracht 1099 (at
Amstel River) **31–20/638–6915** • gay-friendly
• beautifully restored 17th-c canal house •
gay-owned • €90-160

Hotel The Golden Bear Kerkstraat 37 (at
Leidsestraat) **31–20/624–4785** • lesbians/ gay
men • the oldest gay hotel in Amsterdam,
since 1948 • WiFi • gay-owned • €70-132

Hotel Waterfront Singel 458 (at
Koningsplein) **31–20/421–6621** • gay-friendly
• rooms & studios • brkfst • located in city's
center • €120-190

ITC Hotel Prinsengracht 1051 (at
Utrechtsestraat) **31–20/623–0230,
31–20/623–1711** • lesbians/ gay men • 18th-c
canal house • great location • also bar &
lounge • WiFi • lesbian- & gay-owned • €55-
130

Seven Bridges Reguliersgracht 31 (at
KeizersGracht) **31–20/623–1329** • gay-friendly
• small & so elegant • canalside w/ view of 7
bridges (surprise!) • brkfst brought to you •
€85-250

Bars

April Reguliersdwarsstraat 37 (at St Jorisstraat, enter rear) 31–20/625–9572 • 8pm-1am, till 3am Fri-Sat • popular happy hour • mostly gay men • 3 bars • videos

ARC Reguliersdwarsstraat 44 (at Geelvinckssteeg) 31–20/689–7070 • 4pm-1am, till 3am Fri-Sat • gay/ straight • dancing/DJ • hip 20-something crowd • also restaurant

Cafe Rouge Amstel 60 (at Kloveniersburgwal) 31–20/420–9881 • 4pm-1am, till 3am wknds • mostly gay men • neighborhood bar

Chez Rene Amstel 50 (at Kloveniersburgwal) 31–20/420–3388 • 8pm-3am, till 4am Fri-Sat • lesbians/ gay men • lesbian-owned

Entre Nous Halvemaansteeg 14 (at Reguliersbreestr) 31–20/623–1700 • 9pm-3am, till 4am Fri-Sat • lesbians/ gay men • neighborhood bar

Hot Spot Cafe Amstel 102 (at Bakkersstr) 31–20/622–8335 • 9pm-3am, from 8pm Fri-Sun • mostly gay men • neighborhood bar

Mankind Weteringstraat 60 (at Weteringschans) 31–20/638–4755 • noon-11pm, clsd Sun • mostly gay men • canalside terrace • food served till 8pm • Dutch/ English • WiFi

Reality Girlz Reguliersdwarsstraat 125 31–20/639–3012 • 8pm-1am, till 3am Fri-Sat, clsd Mon-Tue • mostly women • neighborhood bar • mixed crowd

Soho Reguliersdwarsstraat 36 (at St Jorisstraat) 31–20/422–3312 • 6pm-1am, till 4am Fri-Sat • popular • lesbians/ gay men • young crowd • British pub 1st flr • lounge upstairs • happy hour 10pm-11pm

Vivelavie Amstelstraat 7 (at Rembrandtplein) 31–20/624–0114 • 3pm-3am, till 4am Fri-Sat • mostly women

Nightclubs

Club Roque Amstel 178 (at Wagenstraat) 31–20/421–0900 • 11pm-5am clsd Sun-Tue • lesbians/ gay men • dancing/DJ

Studio 80 Rembrandtplein 17 (at Amstelstraat) 31–20/521–8333 • 9pm-5am Th-Sat • gay/ straight • dancing/DJ

Cafes

Betty, Too Reguliersdwarsstraat 29 (at Leidsestraat) • 10am-1am • occasional gay events

Downtown Coffeeshop Reguliersdwarsstr 31 (at Koningsplein) 31–20/622–9958 • 10am-8pm, till 10pm Fri-Sat • popular • mostly gay men • terrace open in summer

Happy Feelings Kerkstr 51 31–20/423–1936 • 11am-midnight, till 1am Fri-Sat • smoking coffeeshop • publisher's choice

The Other Side Reguliersdwarsstraat 6 (at Koningsplein) 31–72/625–5141 • 11am-1am • mostly gay men • smoking coffeeshop • gay-owned

Restaurants

Garlic Queen Reguliersdwarsstr 27 31–20/422–6426 • 6pm-close, clsd Mon-Tue • even the desserts are made w/ garlic!

Golden Temple Utrechtsestr 126 31–20/626–8560 • brkfst, lunch & dinner • mix of Indian, Mexican & Mediterranean • oldest vegetarian & vegan restaurant in city • nonsmoking

De Huyschkaemer Utrechtsestraat 137 31–20/627–0575 • noon-1am, till 3am wknds

Le Monde Rembrandtplein 6 31–20/626–9922 • 8am-11pm, brkfst till 4pm (open 4pm-10pm Mon-Fri in winter) • lesbians/ gay men • Dutch/ Brazilian • plenty veggie • terrace dining • gay-owned

Rose's Cantina Reguliersdwarsstraat 38–40 (near Rembrandtplein) 31–20/625–9797 • 5pm-11pm • popular • Tex-Mex • full bar

Saturnino Reguliersdwarsstraat 5 31–20/639–0102 • noon-midnight • lesbians/ gay men • Italian • full bar

Erotica

Xarina Singel 416 31–20/624–6383 • latex clothing & accessories

Amsterdam—Outer

Accommodations

Abba Budget Hotel Overtoom 122 (1st Constantijn Huygenstraat) 31–20/618–3058 • gay-friendly • brkfst buffet • free safety deposit boxes • "smoker"-friendly • € 25-55

Amsterdam B&B Roeterstraat 18 (at Nieuwe Achtergracht) 31–20/624–0174 • gay friendly • full brkfst • powered by green energy • kids ok • nonsmoking • WiFi • gay-owned • € 90-250

Between Art & Kitsch Ruysdaelkade 75-2 (at Daniel Stalpertstraat) 31–20/679–0485, 31–6/4744–2072 (CELL) • gay-friendly • near museums • WiFi • € 70-90

Blue Moon B&B Weteringschans 123A (at Weteringstraat) **31–20/428-8800** • gay/ straight • WiFi • gay-owned • €105-165

Chico's Guesthouse Sint Willibrordusstraat 77 (at Van Woustraat & Ceintuurbaan, near Sarphatipark) **31-20/675-4241** • gay-friendly • in De Pijp • €50-90

The Collector B&B De Lairessestr 46 hs (in museum area) **31–6/1101-0105 (CELL)**, **31-20/673-6779** • gay-friendly • B&B • full brkfst • WiFi • kids ok • gay-owned • €90-120+

Freeland Hotel Marnixstraat 386 (at Leidsegracht) **31-20/622-7511** • gay-friendly • 2-star hotel • full brkfst • WiFi • gay-owned • €60-156

Hemp Hotel Frederiksplein 15 (at Achtergracht) **31-20/625-4425** • only in Amsterdam: sleep on a hemp mattress, eat a hemp roll (THC-free) for brkfst or drink hemp beer in the downstairs Hemp Temple bar • €60-75

Hotel Aadam Wilhelmina Koninginneweg 169 (at Emmalaan) **31-20/662-5467** • gay-friendly • charming • full brkfst buffet • some shared baths • €65-225

Hotel Arena Gravesandestraat 51 (at Mauritskade) **31-20/850-2400** • gay-friendly • huge hotel in former orphanage • popular nightclub in former chapel • WiFi • also restaurant & cafe-bar • €80-275

Hotel Fita Jan Luijkenstraat 37 (at Van Baerlestraat) **31-20/679-0976** • small family-owned hotel • WiFi • nonsmoking • €105-165

Hotel Kap Den Texstraat 5 **31-20/624-5908** • gay/ straight • bikes available to rent • also self-catering apt • gay-owned • €48-152

Hotel Rembrandt Plantage Middenlaan 17 (at Plantage Parklaan) **31-20/627-2714** • gay-friendly • beautiful brkfst room w/ 17th-c art • near Rembrandtplein • nonsmoking • €75-175

Hotel Sander Jacob Obrechtstraat 69 (at N Maesstraat) **31-20/662-7574** • gay-friendly • also 24hr bar & coffee lounge • €80-165+

Kerstin's B&B Kwakerstraat 2h (at Bilderdijkkade) **31-20/612-6969** • gay-friendly • B&B & self-catering apt • overlooking new canal • nonsmoking • kids ok • €85 (B&B); €115 (apt)

Lilianne's Home Sarphatistraat 119 (at Roeterstraat, at Weesperplein Station) **31-20/627-4006** • women only • brkfst • shared bath • nonsmoking • also apt • €100

Lloyd Hotel Oostelijke Handelskade 34 **31-20/561-3636, 31-20/561-3604** • gay-friendly • hip hotel for all budgets in cool Eastern Harbor area • WiFi • €95-450

NL Hotel Nassaukade 368 (at B Toussaintstraat) **31-20/689-0030** • gay/ straight • WiFi • gay-owned • €85-200

Prinsen Hotel Vondelstraat 36-38 (near Leidseplein) **31-20/616-2323** • gay-friendly • also bar • €100-210

Stayokay Amsterdam Vondelpark Zandpad 5 (at Stadhouderskade) **31-20/589-8996** • gay-friendly • inside Vondelpark • bar & restaurant • WiFi • wheelchair access • €23-45

BARS

Garbo Amsteldijk 223 (at Miranda Paviljoen & Brasseriede Lakey) • 4pm-midnight 1st Sat only • women only • dancing/DJ • dinner also served

NIGHTCLUBS

Flirtation Oostelijke Handelskade 4 (at Piet Heinkade, at Club Panama) • bi-monthly women's dance party • check local listings for next event

Melkweg Lijnbaansgracht 234 (at Leidseplein) **31-20/531-8181** • gay/ straight • popular live-music venue • restaurant • theater • cinema • gallery

ToNight @ Arena Gravesandestraat 51 (at Hotel Arena) **31-20/850-2400** • theme nights • come to see the club itself—a restored chapel from an orphanage

RESTAURANTS

An Weteringschans 76 (in Museum Quarter) **31-20/624-4672** • dinner only, clsd Sun-Mon • Japanese • patio • cash only

De Peper Overtoom 301 **31-20/412-2954** • 7pm-close Sun, Tue & Fri • sliding scale, volunteer-run vegan cafe • also monthly queer & women's parties

De Waaghals Frans Halsstraat 29 **31-20/679-9609** • 5pm-9:30pm, clsd Mon • int'l vegetarian

SCOTLAND

Edinburgh

INFO LINES & SERVICES

LGBT Centre for Health & Wellbeing 9 Howe St **44–0131/523–1100**

ACCOMMODATIONS

94DR 94 Dalkeith Rd **44–131/662–9286** • gay/ straight • guesthouse central location • full brkfst • WiFi • gay-owned • £60-140

Ardmor House 74 Pilrig St (at Leith Walk) **44–0131/554–4944** • lesbians/ gay men • Victorian • kids/ pets ok • nonsmoking • wheelchair access • gay-owned • £50-110

Averon Guest House 44 Gilmore Pl **44–0131/229–9932** • gay-friendly • comfortable guesthouse in city center • full brkfst • nonsmoking • £24-42

Ayden Guest House 70 Pilrig St **44–0131/554–2187** • gay/ straight • guesthouse in quiet, central location • in-house chef cooks fabulous brkfst • WiFi • lesbian-owned • £25-50/ person

Edinburgh

LGBT PRIDE:

June. Alternates between Edinburgh and Glasgow (odd years in Edinburgh), web: www.gay-pride.org.uk/events/ edinburgh.php.

ANNUAL EVENTS:

August - Edinburgh Fringe Festival 44-0131/226-0026, web: www.edfringe.com.
October - Glasgay! annual celebration of queer culture (in Glasgow) 44-141/552-7575, web: www.glasgay.co.uk.

CITY INFO:

44-0131/625-8625, web: www.edin-burgh.org.

WEATHER:

60°s-70°s in summer, with nice, long days. Winter brings temps in the 40°s. Be prepared for rain year-round.

BEST VIEW:

Hike from the Dunsapie Loch parking lot to the top of Arthur's Seat (an extinct volcano). Or take the steps from Waterloo Place, at the E end of Princes St, to Calton Hill. If you're feeling ambitious, continue up the spiral stairs to the top of Nelson Monument.

ATTRACTIONS:

Camera Obscura, web: www.camera-obscura.co.uk.
Edinburgh Castle, web: www.edin-burghcastle.gov.uk.
Mansfield Traquair Centre murals, web: www.mansfieldtraquair.org.uk.
Nat'l Galleries, web: www.national-galleries.org.
Nat'l Museum of Scotland, web: www.nms.ac.uk.
Nelson Monument.
Palace of Holyroodhouse, web: www.royalcollection.org.uk.
Princes St Gardens.
Scotch Whisky Experience, web: www.whisky-heritage.co.uk.

TRANSIT:

Central Taxis 44-0131/229-2468, web: www.taxis-edinburgh.co.uk.
Airlink 44-0131/555-6363, web: www.flybybus.com.
Lothian Buses 44-0131/555-6363, web: www.lothianbuses.com.

Garlands 48 Pilrig St (off Leith Walk) **44-0131/554-4205** • gay/ straight • Georgian town house • full brkfst • nonsmoking • WiFi • gay-owned • £30-65/ person

Six Mary's Place Guest House Raeburn Pl (Stockbridge) **44-0131/332-8965** • gay-friendly • B&B • vegetarian brkfst • nonsmoking

The Witchery by the Castle Castlehill (The Royal Mile) **44-0131/225.5613** • gay-friendly • B&B • full brkfst • theatrical suites at the gates of Edinburgh castle • also restaurant • £195

BARS

The Auld Hoose 23-25 St Leonards St **44-0131/668-2934** • 11:30am-1am, from 12:30pm Sun • gay/ straight • neighborhood bar • food served

Cafe Habana 22 Greenside Pl **44-0131/558-1270** • 1pm-1am • lesbians/gay men • theme nights • popular pre-clubbing • WiFi

Cafe Nom de Plume 60 Broughton St **44-0131/478-1372** • 11am-11pm, till 1am Fri-Sat • food served

CC Bloom's 23 Greenside Pl (at Leith Walk) **44-0131/556-9331** • 6pm-3am, from 7pm Sun • mostly gay men • dancing/DJ • live shows • theme nights

Deep Blue 1 Barony St (below Blue Moon) **44-0131/556-2788** • 4pm-1am • popular • lesbians/gay men • food served • gay-owned

Frenchies Bar 89 Rose Street Ln N **44-0131/225-7651** • 2pm-1am • lesbians/gay men • neighborhood bar

Fur Burger Picardy Pl (at GHQ) • 11pm 2nd Fri only • mostly women • dancing/DJ

Newtown Bar 26-B Dublin St **44-0131/538-7775** • noon-1am, till 2am Fri-Sat • lesbians/gay men • dancing/DJ • food served • WiFi

Planet 6 Baxter's Pl (at Leith Walk) **44-0131/556-5551** • 4pm-1am • lesbians/gay men • popular • food served

Priscilla's 17 Albert Pl (Leith Walk) **44-0798/659-1695** • noon-1am, from 5pm Sat • mostly gay men • karaoke • cabaret • drag shows

The Regent 2 Montrose Terrace **44-0131/661-8198** • 11am-1am, from 12:30pm Sun • mostly gay men • food served • WiFi

The Street 2 Picardy Pl **44-0131/556-4272** • 4pm-1am, from noon wknds • gay/ straight • dancing/DJ • food served • patio

Theatre Royal Bar 25-27 Greenside Pl **44-0131/557-2142** • noon-midnight, clsd Sun • gay-friendly • good ale

NIGHTCLUBS

DV8 Fetish Club 258 Morrison St (in Spiders Web basement) **44-0131/228-1949** • gay/ straight • monthly fetish party • private club

GHQ 4 Picardy Pl **44-0131/550-1780** • 9pm-3am • lesbians/ gay men • dancing/DJ • theme nights

Luvely Faith Nighclub, 207 Cowgate **44-0131/557-4656** • 10:30pm-5am 1st Sat only • gay/ straight • dancing/DJ

Velvet 6 Blair St (at The Speakeasy) **44-0131/558-3758** • 10:30pm-3am 3rd Sat • mostly women • dancing/DJ

CAFES

Blue Moon 1 Barony St **44-0131/556-2788** • 11am-midnight, from 10am wknds • popular • lesbians/ gay men • food served • gay-owned

Cafe Lucia 13–29 Nicolson St (next to Edinburgh Festival Theatre) **44-0131/662-1112** • 10am-10pm

Filmhouse Cafe 88 Lothian Rd **44-0131/229-5932, 44-0131/228-2688** **(CINEMA)** • 10am-11:30pm, till 12:30am • beer/wine • also cinema

RESTAURANTS

Black Bo's Vegetarian Restaurant 57/61 Blackfriars St **44-(0)131/557.6136** • 6pm-10pm, also bar till 1am • full bar • vegetarian

Henderson's 94 Hanover St **44-0131/225.2131** • organic vegetarian • also deli & cafe • beer/ wine

Tower Restaurant & Terrace National Museum of Scotland, Chambers St (at George IV Brigde) **44-(0)131/225.3003** • lunch & dinner • panoramic views of Edinburgh's castle & historic skyline • wheelchair access

Valvona & Crolla 19 Elm Row **44-0131/556-6066** • clsd Sun • oldest Italian deli in Scotland

ENTERTAINMENT & RECREATION

The Luvvies • LGBT community theatre company

BOOKSTORES

Bobbie's Bookshop 220 Morrison St **44-0131/538-7069** • 10am-5pm, clsd Sun

Word Power 43-45 W Nicolson St **44-0131/662-9112** • 10am-6pm, noon-5pm Sun • independent

RETAIL SHOPS

Q Store 5 Barony St **44-0131/477-4756** • 11am-5pm Sat-Wed, till 6pm Sat, 1pm-5pm Sun • pride store

NATIONAL PUBLICATIONS

ScotsGay **44-0131/539-0666** • Scotland's premier magazine for lesbians, gays, bisexuals & friends, published monthly

EROTICA

Leather and Lace 8 Drummond St **44-0131/557-9413** • 10am-9pm, from noon Sun, toys, clothing & videos

SPAIN

Barcelona

Note: M°=Metro station

INFO LINES & SERVICES

Casal Lambda Verdaguer y Callís 10 (M° Drassanes) **34/93-319-5550** • 5pm-9pm • community center • cafe • archives • library • also publish magazine

Col-Lectiu Gai de Barcelona (CGB) **34/609-922-789** • staffed 7pm-9pm Mon-Sat • also publishes Info Gai

Coordinadora Gai Lesbiana Vicant d'Hongria 156, E-08014 **34/900-601-601** • 7pm-9pm Mon-Fri, 6pm-8pm Sat • nat'l gay group

ACCOMMODATIONS

Barcelona City Centre **34/653-900-039** • mostly gay men • in Eixample District • kids/ pets ok • WiFi • gay-owned • €55-70

Beauty & the Beach B&B **34/93-266-0562** • exclusively gay, lesbians welcome • full brkfst • right across from gay nude beach • nonsmoking rooms (allowed on terrace) • WiFi • wheelchair access • gay-owned • €85-115

California Hotel Rauric 14 (at Ferran, M° Liceu) **34/93-317-7766** • gay/ straight • includes brkfst

Casa de Billy Barcelona Rambla Catalunya 85, Piso 5, Puerta 1 (at Mallorca) **34/93-426-3048** • gay/ straight • shared baths • full brkfst • nonsmoking • WiFi • €75-110

Catalonia Albéniz Aragó 591-593 **34/93-265-2626** • gay-friendly • food served • wheelchair access • €90-144

Catalonia Duques de Bergara Bergara 11 **34/93-301-5151** • gay-friendly • 4-star hotel in the heart of old Barcelona • WiFi • €147-249

Éos Gran Via de los Corts Catalanes 575 (M° Universitat) **34/93-451-8772, 34/617-931-439** • lesbians/ gay men • B&B in gay district • gay-owned • €30-100

Fashion House Bruc 13 Principal **34/63-790-4044** • lesbians/ gay men • shared baths • €55-115

GayStay BCN C / Piquer 15, Pral 3 (at Carrer de Mata) **34/676-145-909** • mostly men • WiFi • gay-owned

Gran Hotel Catalonia Balmes 142-146 **34/93-415-9090** • gay-friendly • 4-star hotel • kids ok • food served • wheelchair access • €124-249

HCC St Moritz Diputació 264 **34/93-412-1500, 34/93-412-1236** • gay-friendly • in historic-artistic bldg built in 1883 • also restaurant & bar • WiFi • wheelchair access

Hostal Absolut Centro Casanova 72 (at Balmes) **34/649-550-238** • mostly gay men • hostel • some shared baths • gay-owned • €50-85

Hostal Que Tal Mallorca 290 (at Bruch) **34/93-459-2366** • mostly gay men • hotel • €45-84

Hotel Axel Aribau 33 (at Consell de Cent) **34/93-323-9393** • lesbians/ gay men • full brkfst • pool • WiFi • also restaurant • also Skybar • wheelchair access • €89-321

Hotel Colon Avenida Catedral 7 **34/93-301-1404** • gay-friendly • €144-256

Hotel Majestic Barcelona Paseo de Gracia 68 (in city center) **34/93-488-1717** • gay-friendly • 5-star hotel • rooftop pool • wheelchair access • €189-400

Room Mate Emma Carrer Rosselló 205 **34/932-385-606** • gay-friendly • nighclub vibe • WiFi • €100+

Suite Gaudi Barcelona B&B Rambla de Cataluña, 103, 1°-A (at Provença) **34/93-215-0658** • gay-friendly • kids/ pets ok • lesbian-owned • €45-135

BARS

Aire/ Sala Diana Valencia 236 (btwn Enriq. Granados & c/ Balmes) **34/93-451-8462** • 11pm-3am, clsd Sun-Wed • seasonal • mostly women • dancing/DJ • cafe-bar • women only Sun • young crowd

Al Maximo Assaonadora 25 • lesbians/ gay men • neighborhood bar

El Balcon des Aquiles Lleo 9 • 7pm-3am • mostly gay men • neighborhood bar • theme nights

Bar Plata Consejo de Ciento 233 (at Urgell) • 5pm-2am • mostly gay men

BimBamBum Casanova 48 • 11pm-3am, clsd Mon-Tue • mostly gay men • dancing/DJ

El Cangrejo Villarroel 86 • 10:30pm-3am Th-Sat • popular • lesbians/ gay men • dancing/DJ

La Chapelle Muntaner 65 • mostly gay men • cafe by day

El Chapulín Muntaner 92 (at Valencia) 34/93-452-5593 • 1pm-late, clsd Sun • lesbians/ gay men • food served • Mexican

Chiringuito Gay Lorenzo El dulce deseo de Lorenzo, Playa Mar Bella • mostly gay men • beach bar • open during summer

Dacksy Consell de Cent 247 • 5pm-3am • lesbians/ gay men • trendy cocktail lounge

Kodigo G Muntaner 24 (M° Universitat) 34/93-451-6536 • 6pm-2am, till 3am wknds • funky decor • lesbians/ gay men

Lust Casanova 75 (at Consell de Cent) • 9pm-2:30am, clsd Mon, pre-clubbing bar • lesbians/ gay men

La Madame Ronda Sant Pere 19-21 (M° Urquinaona) 34/93-426-8444 • from midnight Sun only • gay/ straight • dancing/DJ

Mandarina Diputació 157 (M° Urgell) 34/93-323-3393 • 6pm-3am • lesbians/ gay men • food served • terrace

Barcelona

LGBT Pride:
July.

Annual Events:
February - Carnival.
July - Gay/Lesbian Film Festival, 34/93-319-5550, web: www.cinemalambda.com.
July - Grec Summer Festival 34/93-316-1000, web: www.barcelon-afestival.com.
August - Festa Major de Gràcia (huge street party) 34/93-459-3080, web: www.festamajorde-gracia.cat.

City Info:
34/93-368-9700, web: www.barcelonaturisme.com.

Best View:
Torre de Collserola, 34/93-406-9354, web: www.torre-decollserola.com.
Giant glass elevator takes you 944 ft into the air to a platform

Weather:
Barcelona boasts a mild Mediterranean climate, with summer temperatures in the 70°s-80°s, and 40°s-50°s in winter. Rain is possible year-round, with July being the driest month.

Attractions:
Barcelona Museum of Contemporary Art 34/93-412-0810, web: www.macba.es.
Barrì Gotic.
Boqueria Market 34/93-318-2017, web: www.boqueria.info.
Catedral de Barcelona 34/93-310-7195 or 34/93-310-4935, web:catedralbcn.org
Fundació Joan Miró 34/93-443-9470, web: www.bcn.fjmiro.es.
Museu Picasso 34/93-256-3000, web: www.museupicasso.bcn.es.
National Museum of Catalan Art 34/93-622-0376, web: www.mnac.es.
Parc Güell.
La Sagrada Familia 34/93-207-3031, web: www.sagradafamilia.org.

Transit:
Radio Taxi 34/93-303-3033, web: www.radiotaxi033.com.
Aerobus to Plaza de Cataluña 34/93-415-6020 , web: www.emt-amb.com.
Transports Metropolitans de Barcelona 34/93-318-7074, web: www.tmb.net.

Museum Cafe & Club Sepulveda 178 (at Urgell) • 6:30pm-3am • mostly gay men

Padam Padam Rauric 9 34/93–302–5062 • 7pm-3am, clsd Sun • lesbians/ gay men • also cafe • classical music

People Lounge Villaroel 71 (at Diputacion) • 8pm-3am • mostly gay men • older crowd • WiFi

Punto BCN Muntaner 63–65 (enter on Consejo de Ciento Yragón, M° Universitat) 34/93–453–6123 • 6pm-2:30am, till 3am wknds • popular • mostly gay men • upscale cafe-bar • wheelchair access

La Rosa Brusi 39 (btwn Augusta & San Elias, M° Plaza Molina) 34/93–414–6166 • 10pm-3am Th-Sun • mostly women • dancing/DJ • live shows • neighborhood bar • first lesbian bar in Barcelona

Z:eltas Casanova 75 (M° Gran Vía/ Urgell) 34/93–454–1902 • 10:30pm-3am • mostly gay men • dancing/DJ • lounge • live shows • videos

Zelig Carme 116 (M° San Antonio) 34/93–441–5622 • 7pm-2am, till 3am wknds, clsd Mon • gay/ straight • dancing/DJ • food served

NIGHTCLUBS

Arena Classic Diputació 233 (at Balmes, M° Universitat) 34/93–487–8342 • 12:30am-5am Fri-Sat only • popular • mostly gay men • dancing/DJ • Spanish music • live shows • videos • theme nights • young crowd • cover charge

Arena Sala Madre Balmes 32 (at Diputació, M° Universitat) 34/93–487–8342 • 12:30am-5am, clsd Mon (except in Aug) • popular • mostly gay men • dancing/DJ • food served • live shows Wed • videos • young crowd • cover charge

Les Fatales • mostly women • dancing/DJ • parties around Barcelona • check lesfatales.org for details

Kiut Consell de Cent 280 (M° Universitat) • midnight-5:30am, clsd Mon-Wed • lesbians/ gay men • dancing/DJ

Metro Sepúlveda 185 (M° Universitat) 34/93–323–5227 • midnight-5am, from 1am Mon • popular • mostly gay men • dancing/DJ • leather • drag shows • videos • young crowd • cover charge

Souvenir Barcelona Noi del Sucre 75 (Viladecans) • afterhours club 6am-1pm Sat-Sun & holidays

CAFES

People Lounge Villarroel 71 (M° Urgell) 34/93–451–5986 • 7pm-3am • mostly gay men • dancing/DJ • full bar • young crowd

RESTAURANTS

7 Portes Passeig d'Isabel II, 14 34/93–319–3033, 34/93–319–2950 • 1pm-1am • Catalan • upscale • over 150 years old!

El Berro Diputació 180 34/933–236–956 • 7am-3am, from 9am wknds • inexpensive diner-style restaurant • also bar

Botafumeiro El Gran de Gràcia 81 34/93–218–4230, 34/93–217–9642 • 1pm-1am • Galician seafood • full bar • reservations recommended

Castro Casanova 85 (M° Urgell) 34/93–323–6784 • 1pm-4pm & 9pm-midnight, clsd Sun • Catalan • full bar • live shows

dDivine Balmes 24 (M° Universitat) 34/93–317–2248 • 9:30pm-1am, clsd Sun-Tue • dinner show hosted by "Divine" • lesbians/ gay men • reservations recommended

Eterna Consell de Cent 127-129 (at Villarroel) 34/93–424–2526 • 1pm-4pm Mon-Fri, 9:30pm-midnight Th-Sat, clsd Sun • lesbians/ gay men • drag shows

La Flauta Magica c/ de Banys Vells 18 (M° Jaume I) 34/93–268–4694 • dinner nightly • vegetarian/ organic • wheelchair access

Iurantia Casanova 42 (M° Urgell) 34/93–454–7887 • lunch Mon-Fri, dinner Mon-Sat, clsd Sun • pizzeria • reservations recommended

Little Italy Carrer del Rec 30 (near Passeig del Born) 34/93–319–7973 • 1pm-4pm & 9pm-midnight • live jazz

Madrid-Barcelona Carrer d'Arago 282 (M° Passeig de Gracia) 34/93–215–7027 • lunch & dinner, clsd Sun • located on old railway line • Catalan

Marquette Diputació 172 (M° Universitat) 34/93–454–6398 • 1pm-4pm & 9:30pm-midnight, dinner only Sat-Sun • popular • lesbians/ gay men • transgender-friendly • Italian food • fabulous drag cabaret • reservations recommended

Sazzerak Consejo de Ciento 211 34/93–451–1138 • full bar

Tafino Consejo de Ciento 193 • 1pm-4pm Mon-Fri, 8:30pm-midnight Tue-Sat

Tu Sabes C Marc Aureli 38-40 34/615–999–282 • 9am-11pm Fri-Sat

La Veronica Rambla de Raval 2-4 **34/93-329-3303** • 1pm-1am, clsd Mon • popular pizzeria • terrace

ENTERTAINMENT & RECREATION

Mar Bella • popular gay beach

Museu Picasso Montcada 15-23 **34/93-256-3000** • early Picasso works

Parc Guell Mount Tibidado • mosiacs & sculpture by Gaudi

BOOKSTORES

Antinous Josep Anselm Clavé 6 (btwn Las Ramblas & Ample, M° Drassanes) **34/93-301-9070** • clsd Sun • LGBT • books • gifts • also cafe • wheelchair access

Cómplices Cervantes 2 (at Avinyó, M° Liceu) **34/93-412-7283** • 10:30am-8:30pm, from noon Sat, clsd Sun • LGBT • Spanish & English titles

Nosotr@s Casanova 56 (M° Urgell) **34/93-451-5134** • LGBT books • magazines • gifts • videos • DVDs

PUBLICATIONS

Gay Barcelona Av Roma 152 **34/93-454-9100** • monthly gay magazine

Info Gai 34/93-453-4125 • free bi-monthly newspaper in Catalan

Nois 34/93-454-3805 • free gay monthly

EROTICA

Erotic Museum of Barcelona Ramblas 96 34/93-318-9865 • 10am-midnight (seasonal hours)

Madrid

Note: M°=Metro station

INFO LINES & SERVICES

COGAM (Colectivo de Lesbianas, Gays, Transexuales, y Bisexuales de Madrid) Puelda 9 (Bajo) **34/91-522-4517** • LGBT center • groups • library • also cafe-bar

Gai Inform 34/91-523-0070 • 5pm-9pm Mon-Fri, in English Th 7pm-9pm • helpline

ACCOMMODATIONS

Camino de Soto Puente de la Reine 18, Soto del Real **34-66/744-1351** • gay/straight • located 40 minutes from Madrid • full brkfst • pool • WiFi • gay-owned

Chueca Pension Gravina 4 (at Calle Hortaleza) **34/91-523-1473** • mostly gay men • hostel • kids ok • WiFi • €40-85

Hostal CasaChueca Calle San Bartolomé 4 (at San Marcos) **34/91-523-8127** • mostly gay men • gay-owned • €45-80

Hostal Hispano Hortaleza 38, 2nd flr (at Perez Galdos, M° Chueca) **34/91-531-4871, 34/91-531-2898** • gay-friendly • €39-70

Hostal La Fontana Valverde 6, 1° (M° Gran Vía) **34/91-521-8449, 34/91-523-1561** • lesbians/gay men • €28-70

Hostal la Zona Calle Valverde 7, 1 & 2 (at Gran Vía) **34/91-521-9904** • mostly gay men • full brkfst • all rooms w/ private baths & balconies • WiFi • gay-owned • €50-85

Hostal Oporto Calle Zorilla 9 (M° Sol) **34/91-429-7856** • gay-friendly • 10-minute walk to gay scene • WiFi • €45-95

Hostal Puerta del Sol Plaza Puerta del Sol 14, 4° (at Calle de Alcalá, M° Sol) **34/91-522-5126** • mostly gay men • centrally located • WiFi • wheelchair access • gay-owned • €60-100

Hostal Sonsoles Calle Fuencarral 18 (M° Chueca) **34/91-532-7523** • mostly gay men • €20-40

Hotel Catalonia Gaudí Gran Vía 7-9 (at Alcalá) **34/91-531-2222** • gay-friendly • WiFi • kids ok • wheelchair access • €126-204

Hotel Urban Madrid Carrera de San Jerónimo 34 **34/91-787-7770** • gay-friendly • upscale hotel w/ 3 restaurants & rooftop pool • WiFi

Hotel Villa Real Plaza de Las Cortes, 10 **34/91-420-3767** • gay/ straight • restaurant & bar • full brkfst • WiFi

BARS

El 51 Hortaleza 51 (in Chueca) **34/91-521-2564** • 6pm-3am, from 4pm wknds • popular • mostly gay gay men • upscale cocktail lounge

Ambienta2 22 San Bartolome (at Figueroa) **34/606-939592** • 6pm-2am, till 2:30am wknds, from noon Sun • lesbians/gay men • dancing/DJ • drag shows • live entertainment • theme nights

Bar Lio Pelayo 58 • 7pm-2am, till 2:30am wknds • lesbians/gay men • neighborhood bar • drag shows • transgender-friendly

Bar Nike Augusto Figueroa 22 (at Barbieri) **34/915-210-751** • mostly gay men • neighborhood bar • food served • younger crowd • cafeteria-style • popular early evenings

La Bohemia Plaza de Chueca 10 (M° Chueca) • 8pm-close • mostly women • neighborhood cafe-bar

Enfrente Infantas 12 (M° Gran Vía) **34/68–779–1462** • 8pm-3am • mostly gay men • leather • DJs Th & Sun

Fulanita de Tal Calle del Conde de Xiquena 2 (at Prim) • mostly women • stylish & hip • dancing/DJ

LL Pelayo 11 (M° Chueca) **34/91–523–3121** • 6pm-close • popular • gay/ straight • neighborhood bar • dancing • strippers • drag shows • videos • darkroom • cruisy

La Lupe de Lavapies Torrecilla del Leal 12 (M° Antón Martín) **34/91–527–5019** • 5pm-2:30am • lesbians/ gay men • cabaret • flea market Sun

El Mojito Olmo 6 (M° Antón Martín) **34/91–531–1141** • 9pm-3am, till 3:30am Fri-Sat • lesbians/ gay men • cocktail bar • great music

Museo Chicote Calle Gran Via 12 **34/915–326–737** • 9pm-3am • gay/ straight • 50s style lounge • food served • live shows

Rick's Calle del Clavel 8 (at Infantas, M° Gran Vía, ring to enter) **34/91–531–9186** • 11pm-6am, open later Fri-Sat, 9pm-2am Sun • popular • mostly gay men • dancing/DJ • young crowd • "see-and-be-scene"

Soho Plaza de Chueca 6 • lesbians/ gay men • patio

Studio 54 Madrid Barbieri 7 (btwn San Marcos & Infantas, M° Chueca) • midnight-close, clsd Sun-Wed • lesbians/ gay men • dancing/DJ • live shows

Truco Calle de Gravina 10 (at Plaza de Chueca) **34/91–532–8921** • 8pm-close, clsd Mon-Tue • popular • mostly women • dance bar • great parties • seasonal terrace

Why Not San Bartolomé 6 (M° Gran Vía) • 9pm-3am, till 5am Fri-Sat • gay/ straight

NIGHTCLUBS

Boite Calle Tetuan 27 (Plaza del Carmen) **34/91–522–9620** • gay/ straight • dancing/DJ • check listings for gay club nights

Cool Isabel la Católica 6 (M° Santo Domingo) **34/91–542–3439** • sleek 2-flr ballroom • more gay Sat for "Bunker Bears Club"

DLRO Live Pelayo 35 (at Almirante) • 11pm-5:30am • mostly gay men • British pop music/DJ • go-go boys

Escape Gravina 13 (at Plaza de Chueca) **34/91–532–5206** • 10pm-5am Wed-Sun • mostly women • dancing/DJ • live shows

Griffin's Marqués de Valdeiglesias 6 (M° Banco de España) **34/91–522–2079** • 11pm-late Fri-Sat • mostly gay men • dancing/DJ • drag shows • entertainment

Madrid

LGBT PRIDE:
June, web: orgullolgtb.org.

ANNUAL EVENTS:
October/November - International Gay & Lesbian Film Festival, web: www.lesgaicinemad.com.

CITY INFO:
Oficina Municipale de Turismo 34/91-308-0400, web: www.esmadrid.com.

BEST VIEW:
From the funicular in the Parque des Atracciones.

WEATHER:
Winter temps average in the 40°s (and maybe even a little snow!). Summer days in Madrid are hot, with highs well into the 80°s.

TRANSIT:
Metro 34/90–244-4403, web: www.metromadrid.es.

ATTRACTIONS:
Chueca.
El Rastro (flea market).
Museo del Prado 34/91–330–2800, web: museoprado.mcu.es.
Museo Thyssen-Bornemisza 34/91–369–0151, web: www.museothyssen.org.
Museo de Reina Sofia (home of Picasso's 'Guernica') 34/91–774–1000, web: museor-einasofia.mcu.es.
El Retiro (park).
Royal Palace 34/91–454–8700, web: patrimonionacional.es.

Joy Eslava Arenal 11 (M° Sol)
34/91-366-3733 • 11:30pm-6pm • popular •
fabulous crowd • converted theater

Long Play Plaza de Vázquez de Mella 2 •
midnight-6am wknds only • lesbians/gay men
• dancing/DJ

Medea Cabeza 33 (M° Antón Martín)
34/91-369-3302 • 11pm-7am, till 10am Sun,
clsd Mon • popular wknds • women only •
men welcome as guests • dancing/DJ • cabaret
• young crowd • cover charge

Mito Augusto Figueroa 3 (M° Chueca)
34/65-532-8851 • 11pm-6:30pm • lesbians/
gay men • neighborhood bar • karaoke •
dancing/DJ • drag shows

Polana Barbieri 10 (M° Chueca)
34/91-532-3305 • 10pm-5am • trendy •
lesbians/gay men • dancing/DJ

Sachas Plaza de Chueca 1 (M° Chueca)
8pm-5am Th-Sun, bar open 8pm-3am nightly
• lesbians/gay men • dancing/DJ • drag shows
• terrace

Space of Sound Sala Macumba (at
Estación de Chamartín) **34/90-249-9994** •
midnight-close • lesbians/gay men • Sun only
• dancing/DJ

Tábata Vergara 12 (next to Teatro Real, M°
Opera) **34/91-547-9735** • 11:30pm-late Wed-
Sat • lesbians/gay men • dancing/DJ • young
crowd • cover charge

Trip Family • gay theme dance parties •
check tripfamily.com for events & details

Cafes

BAires Cafe Gravina 4 (M° Chueca)
34/91-532-9879 • 4pm-2am • lesbians/gay
men • also bar • hip crowd

Cafe Acuarela Gravina 10 (M° Chueca)
34/91-522-2143, 34/91-570-6907 • 3pm-
3am, from 11am Sat-Sun • lesbians/gay men
• bohemian cafe-bar • cocktails

Cafe Figueroa Augusto Figueroa 17 (at
Hortaleza, M° Chueca) **34/91-521-1673** •
4pm-midnight, till 2:30am wknds • lesbians/
gay men • also bar

Cafe la Troje Pelayo 26 (at Figueroa, M°
Chueca) **34/91-531-0535** • 5pm-2am •
popular • lesbians/gay men • full bar

D'Mystic Gravina 5 (M° Pelayo)
34/91-308-2460 • 9:30am-close • gay/
straight • popular • hot food served • hip cafe-
bar in Chueca area

El Jardin Infantas 9 (M° Gran Via)
34/91-521-9045, 34/91-523-1218 • noon-
2am, till 3am wknds • lesbians/gay men

Mama Inés Hortaleza 22 (M° Chueca)
34/91-523-2333 • gay/straight • 10am-2am •
sandwiches • pies

La Sastrería Hortaleza 74 (at Gravina, M°
Chueca) **34/91-532-0771** • 10am-2am, till
3am Fri-Sat, from 11am wknds • lesbians/gay
men • trendy cafe-bar • internet access

Star's Marqués de Valdeiglesias 5 (at
Infantas, M° Banco) **34/91-522-2712** • 8pm-
close, clsd Sun • mostly gay men • cafe-bar •
dancing/DJ Th-Sat

XXX Cafe Clavel 2 (M° Gran Vía)
34/91-532-8415 • noon-close • mostly gay
men • food served • cabaret wknds

Restaurants

A Brasileira Pelayo 49 (M° Chueca)
34/91-308-3625 • lunch & dinner • Brazilian

Al Natural Zorrilla 11 (M° Sevilla)
34/91-369-4709 • lunch & dinner •
vegetarian

El Armario San Bartolomé 7 (btwn Figueroa
& San Marcos, M° Chueca) **34/91-532-8377** •
lunch & dinner • lesbians/gay men •
Mediterranean

Artemisa Ventura de la Vega 4 (at Zorrilla)
34/91-429-5092 • lesbians/gay men •
vegetarian • also Tres Cruces 4 location, 34/91-
521-8721

Botin Cuchilleros 17 **34/91-366-4217** • one
of the oldest restaurants in the world (open
since 1725) & an old Hemingway haunt

Chez Pomme Pelayo 4 (M° Chueca)
34/91-532-1646 • lunch & dinner, clsd Sun •
int'l/vegetarian

Colby Fuencarral 52 (M° Chueca)
34/91-521-2554 • 9:30am-close, from
11:30am Sun

La Coqueta Libertad 3 **34/91-523-0647** •
clsd Sun • lunch & dinner • lesbians/gay men
• Mediterranean

Divina La Cocina Colmenares 13 (at San
Marcos, M° Chueca) **34/91-531-3765** • lunch
& dinner • lesbians/gay men • elegant &
trendy

Ecocentro Esquilache 2, 4, y 6 (at Pablo
Iglesias, M° Rios Rosas) **34/91-553-5502** •
open till midnight • vegetarian • natural foods
• also shop • herbalist school

El Chambao Manuel Malasana 16 (at Calle
de Monteleon) • tapas restaurant, also bar

Gula Gula Gran Via 1 (M° Gran Via)
34/91-522-8764 • lunch & dinner • popular
• lesbians/gay men • buffet/salad bar • full
bar • drag shows • reservations required

Juntos Libertad 9 • Italian

Lombok Augusto Figueroa 32 (M° Chueca) **34/91–531–3566** • lunch & dinner, clsd Sun • int'l

Momo Calle de la Libertad 8 **34/91–532–7162** • lunch & dinner • nonsmoking • charming staff • gay-owned

Moskada Francisco Silvela 71 (at General Oraa) **34/91–563–0630** • lunch Mon-Fri, dinner Mon-Sat, clsd Sun

Nina Manuel Malasana 10 (M° Bilbao) **34/91–591–0046** • open daily • contemporary Spanish food

Restaurante Miau Plaza de Santa Ana 6 **34/91–429–2272** • Madrileño cuisine & tapas

El Rincón de Pelayo Pelayo 19 (M° Chueca) **34/91–521–8407** • lunch & dinner • lesbians/ gay men

Sama-Sama San Bartolomé 23 (M° Chueca) **34/91–521–5547** • lunch & dinner, clsd Sun • Balinese decor • also Infante 5 location, 34/91-389-6890

Vegaviana Pelayo 35 **34/913–080–381** • lunch & dinner, clsd Sun-Mon • vegetarian

Bookstores

A Different Life Pelayo 30 (M° Chueca) **34/91–532–9652** • 11am-10pm • LGBT • books • magazines • music • videos • sex shop downstairs

Berkana Bookstore Hortaleza 64 **34/91–522–5599** • 10:30am-9pm, from 11:30am Sat, from noon Sun • LGBT • Spanish & English titles • ask for free gay map of Madrid • wheelchair access

Retail Shops

AKM Pelayo 14 (M° Chueca) **34/91–531–1388** • clsd Sun • military-style fashion & fetish store

Publications

Odisea Espiritu Santo 33 **34/91–523–2154** • free monthly magazine (en español)

Shangay Express **34/91–445–1741** • free bi-weekly gay paper • also publishes Shanguide

Gyms & Health Clubs

Energy Gym Hortaleza 19 (M° Gran Vía, Chueca) **34/91–531–1029, 34/91–522–3073**

Gimnasio V35 Valverde 35 (M° Gran Via) **34/91–523–9352** • mostly gay men

Holiday Gym Serrano Jover 3 (M° Argüelles) **34/91–547–4033** • gay-friendly • central location

Erotica

La Jugueteria Travesia de San Mateo 12 **34/91/308–7269**

Los Placeres de Lola Doctor Fourquet, 34 **34/91–468–6178** • noon-10pm, clsd Sun • women & their companions only • toys, leather, books & videos • also cafe

SR Pelayo 7 (M° Chueca) **34/91–523–1964** • clsd Sun • fetish, military, leather • gay-owned

Sitges

Accommodations

B My Guest B&B Ctra Sant Pere de Ribes **34/639–534–979** • women only penthouse apt • WiFi • lesbian-owned • €65-85

Los Globos Avda Ntra Sra de Montserrat 43 **34/93–894–9374** • lesbians/ gay men • kids/ pets ok • also bar • brkfst buffet • WiFi • wheelchair access • gay-owned • €59-125

Hotel Antemare Verge de Montserrat 48-50 **34/93–894–7000** • gay-friendly • pool • 1 block from beach • €120-250

Hotel Liberty Isla de Cuba 45 (at Artur Carbonell) **34/93–811–0872** • lesbians/ gay-men • seasonal • some women-only wknds • nonsmoking • WiFi • wheelchair access • gay-owned • €76-160

Hotel Renaixença Illa de Cuba 13 , 08070 **34/93–894–8375** • lesbians/ gay men • some shared baths • hotel bar • €93-119

Hotel Romàntic Sant Isidre 33 **34/93–894–8375** • popular • gay/ straight • 19th-c villa • full brkfst • some shared baths • seasonal • kids/ pets ok • also full bar • €52-119

Hotel Santa Maria Paseo de la Ribera 52 **34/93–894–0999** • gay/straight • clean & modest • great restaurant • €71-115

Parrot's Hotel Joan Tarrida 16 **34/93–894–1350** • lesbians/ gay men • WiFi • also bar & restaurant

San Sebastian Playa Port Alegre 53 **305/538–9697 (US#), 866/376–7831 (IN US)** • gay-friendly • jacuzzi • pool • also bar/ restaurant • no smoking • wheelchair access • €172-276

Sitges Royal Rooms C/ Sant Bonaventura 14 bajos (at Sant Francesc), Catalunya Spain **34/64–998–1148** • mosty gay men • WiFi • gay-owned • €75-120

El Xalet Isla de Cuba 21 **34/93–811–0872** • gay-friendly • brkfst included • pool • €60-150

BARS

Azul Sant Bonaventura 10 **34/93-894-7634** • 9pm-3am • mostly gay men • neighborhood bar

Blondies Port Alegre 10 (at San Sebastian Beach) • 5pm-3am, till 3:30am Fri-Sat, seasonal • gay/ straight • food served • terrace

Casablanca Pau Barrabeitg 5 **34/93-894-7082** • 8pm-close (clsd Mon off-season) • gay/ straight • bears • neighborhood bar • food served • darkroom • more lez Sun

Dark/ DSB Bonaire 14 • 5pm-3am • mostly men • sleek lounge

Marypili Joan Tarrida Ferratges 14 • 4pm-3am • mostly women • dancing/DJ • terrace

Mojito & Co Plaza Industrial 1 • mostly men • breezy lounge w/ outdoor seating

Parrot's Pub Plaza Industria 2 (at Primero de Mayo) **34/93-894-7881** • 5pm-close, seasonal • popular • lesbians/ gay men • leather • live shows • patio • also restaurant

XXL Joan Tarrida Ferratges 7 • 11pm-3:30am (wknds only off-season) • popular • mostly gay men • dancing/DJ

NIGHTCLUBS

Bourbon's Sant Bonaventura 13 **34/93-894-3347** • 10:30pm-3:30am (Sat only off-season) • popular • mostly gay men • dancing/DJ • videos • young crowd

Mediterraneo Sant Bonaventura 6 **34/93-894-3347** • 10pm-3:30am • popular • mostly gay men • dance bar • patio

New Port Taco 1-3 **34/93-452-0356** • 10pm-3am, clsd Mon • lesbians/ gay men • dancing/DJ • drag shows • strippers

Organic Bonaire 15 **34/93-894-2230** • opens 2:30am (wknds only off-season) • mostly gay men • transgender-friendly • dancing/DJ • singles party Th • darkroom • cover charge

El Piano Bonaventura 37 **34/93-814-6245** • 10pm-3am • lesbians/ gay men • piano bar • cabaret

Queenz Bonaire 17 • 10pm-3:30am, seasonal • mostly men • DJs • drag shows • cabaret

Trailer Angel Vidal 36 • 1am-6am, seasonal • popular • mostly gay men • dancing/DJ

CAFES

Cafe Al Fresco Carrer Major 33 **34/93-811-3307** • 9am-midnight

Cafe Sitges Sant Pau 32 • 11am-3pm, also 6pm-late Wed-Sun, clsd Tue • food served

Cine Cafe Jesus 55 **34/662-560-050** • 10am-midnight, clsd Tue • mostly gay men • Anglo-American • gay-owned

Mont Roig Cafe Marques de Montroig 11-13 **34/93-894-8439** • 9am-3am • patio • WiFi • also full bar

Sitges

ENTERTAINMENT:
Platjes del Mort ("Beach of the Dead") is the gay beach.

ANNUAL EVENTS:
February - Carnival, web: www.sitges.com/carnaval.
July - International Tango Festival, web: www.tangositges.com.
August - Festa Major, web: www.sitges.com/festamajor.
October - International Film Festival, web: www.cinemasitges.com.

CITY INFO:
34/93-894-4251, web: www.sitges-tour.com.

ATTRACTIONS:
Museu Cau Ferrat 34/93-894-0364, web: www.diba.es/museus/sitges.asp.
Museu Maricel 34/93-894-0364, web: www.diba.es/museus/sitges.asp.

TRANSIT:
Taxi Sitgest 34/93-894-1329, web: www.taxisitges.com.
MONBUS 34/93-893-7060, www.monbus.cat.

RESTAURANTS

Air Bahia Paseo Maritim 2 **34/93-894-2445** • popular • patio seating • water views • reservations recommended

Alma Tacó 16 **34/93-894-6387** • 8pm-close (clsd Tue-Wed off-season) • lesbians/ gay men • French • terrace

Beach House Sant Pau 34 **34/93-894-9029** • brkfst & dinner • full bar • patio • gay-owned

El Celler Vell Bonaventura 21 **34/93-811-1961** • dinner nightly, lunch Fri-Sun, clsd Wed • traditional Catalan

Kento Calle Bonaire 25 **34/938-948-011** • sushi

Ma Maison Bonaire 28 **34/93-894-6054** • lunch & dinner • popular • lesbians/ gay men • French • full bar • terrace

Mezzanine Espalter 8 **34/93-894-9940** • dinner only • French

Pic Nic Paseo de la Ribera **34/93-811-0040** • in front of gay beach • also internet cafe

So Ca/ Southern California Sant Gaudenci 9 **34/93-894-3046** • 1pm-close • also bar

Sucré-Salé Sant Pau 39 **34/93-894-2302** • lunch & dinner, clsd Tue off-season • crêpes • terrace

El Trull Mossèn Felix Clará 3 (off Major) **34/93-894-4705** • dinner only, clsd Wed • popular • lesbians/ gay men • French/ int'l

ENTERTAINMENT & RECREATION

Gay Beach (Platja de la Bassa Rodona) • in front of Calipolis Hotel & Picnic cafe

RETAIL SHOPS

Oscar Marqués de Montroig 2 (at Plaza Industria) **34/93-894-1976** • designer clothing for men & women

EROTICA

The Mask Bonaire 22 **34/93-811-2214** • 24hr wknds

JAPAN

Tokyo

INFO LINES & SERVICES

Akta Daini Nakae Bldg #301 (Shinjuku 2-15-13) **81–3/3226-8998** • 4pm-10pm • community center & HIV/ AIDS resource

ACCOMMODATIONS

Capitol Tokyu 10-3 Nagata-cho 2-chome (Chiyoda-ku) **81–3/3581-4511** • gay-friendly • near the Diet

Four Seasons Hotel 10-8 Sekiguchi 2-chome (Bunkyo-ku) **81–3/3943-2222** • gay-friendly • pool • surrounded by historic Japanese garden • wheelchair access • ¥50,000+

Hotel Century Southern Tower 2-2-1 Yoyogi (Shibuya-ku) **81–3/5354-0111** • gay-friendly • near gay district • ¥16,000-63,525

Keio Plaza Hotel 2-2-1 Nishi Shinjuku **81–3/3344-0111** • gay-friendly • swimming • restaurants & bars

Park Hyatt 3-7-1-2 Nishi Shinjuku **81–3/5322-1234** • gay-friendly • kids ok • restaurant & lounge • luxury hotel featured in *Lost in Translation* • pool • spa

Shinjuku Prince Hotel 30-1 Kabuki-cho 1-chome (Shinjuku-ku) **81–3/3205-1111, 800/542-8686 (US)** • gay-friendly • WiFi

Shinjuku Washington Hotel 3-2-9 Nishi-Shinjuku (Shinjuku-ku) **81–3/3343-3111** • gay-friendly • ¥10,400-24,000+

Tokyo International Hostel 18F Central Plaza (1-1 Kagurakashi, Shinjuku-ku) **81–3/3235-1107** • gay-friendly • 11pm curfew

BARS

Advocates 1-F, Dai-7 Tenka Bldg (Shinjuku 2-18-1) **81–3/3358-3988** • 6pm-4am • café-bar • lesbians/ gay men • young crowd

Alamas Cafe 1/F Garnet Bldg, Shinjuku 2-12-1 **81–3/3358-3988** • 6pm-2am, till 5am Fri-Sat, 3pm-midnight Sun • lesbians/ gay men • dancie club at night

Arty Farty 2F, #33 Kyutei Bldg (Shinjuku 2-11-7), Shinjuku-ku **81–3/5362-9720** • 6pm-5am, from 7pm Fri, from 5pm wknds, till 3am Sun, clsd Mon • mostly gay men • food served • young crowd

Chestnut & Squirrel Liam Oishi Bldg 3 (at Minx, Shibuya) **81–90/9834-4842** • 7pm-2am Wed only • mostly women

DNA 1/F Musashino Bldg, Shinjuku 2-13-10 **81-3/3341-4445** • 3pm-5am • gay/straight • neighborhood bar

GB B1, Shinjuku Plaza Bldg (Shinjuku 2-12-3), Shinjuku-ku **81-3/3352-8972** • 8pm-2am, till 3am Wed • mostly gay men

Hatch 3/F Tozaki Bldg, 2-7-4 Dougen-zaka Shibuya

Keivi 4F Yoshino Bldg, 17-10 Sakuragaoka **81-3/3496-0006** • 6pm-midnight • mostly gay men • neighborhood bar

Kinsmen 2F Shinjuku 2-12-16 (near Shinjuku Sanchome Station) **81-3/3354-4949** • 7pm-1am, till 3am Fri-Sat, clsd Mon • lesbians/ gay men

Kinswomyn 3F, Dai-Ichi Tenka Bldg (Shinjuku 2-15-10) **81-3/3354-8720** • 8pm-4am, clsd Tue • popular • women only

Tokyo

LGBT PRIDE:
August

ANNUAL EVENTS:
July - Tokyo International Lesbian & Gay Film Festival, web: www.tokyo-lgff.org.

CITY INFO:
Japan National Tourist Organization 81-3/3201-3331 or 212/757-5640 (US), web: www.jnto.go.jp.
Tokyo Convention & Visitors Bureau, web: www.tcvb.or.jp.

ATTRACTIONS:
Edo-Tokyo Museum 81-3/3626-9974, web: www.edo-tokyo-museum.or.jp.
Grand Sumo Tournaments, web: www.sumo.or.jp.
Imperial Palace, web: sankan.kunai-cho.go.jp.
Kabuki-za Theater 81-3/3541-3131, web: www.shochiku.co.jp/play/kabuk-iza/theater.
Meiji Jingu Shrine 81-3/3379-5511, web: www.meijijingu.or.jp.
Roppongi Kingyo 81-3/3478-3000, web: www.kingyo.co.jp.
Sensoji Temple 81-3/3842-0181.
Shinjuku Gyoen National Garden
Tokyo National Museum 81-3/3822-1111, web: www.tnm.jp.
Tsukiji Market, web: www.tsukiji-market.or.jp.
Ueno Park.

BEST VIEW:
From any of 3 major observation decks: Tokyo Metropolis Observatories, Bunkyo Civic Center of Edogawa City Office.

WEATHER:
Hot & rainy in the summer, cool (though rarely freezing) in the winter. Spring & fall are clear, mild & gorgeous.

TRANSIT:
Nihon Kotsu 81-3/5755-2151 (English), web: www.nihon-kotsu.co.jp.
Toei, web: www.kotsu.metro.tokyo.jp.
Tokyo Metro, web: www.toky-ometro.jp.

Lamppost 201 Yamahara Heights (Shinjuku 2-12-15) 81–3/3354–0436 • 7pm-3am • mostly men • piano bar

Madame Mar 204 Sunny Kopo (Sinjuku 2-7-2) 81–3/3354–7515 • 6pm-midnightt, till 2am Fri-Sat • popular • women only

Mars Bar 3F Hosono Bldg (2-15-13 Shinjuku-ku) 81–3/3354–7923 • 8pm-3am, till 5am Fri-Sun • mostly women • karaoke

Peach 1F (Shinjuku 2-15-8) 81–3/3351–7034 • 11pm-7am, clsd Sun-Mon • women only • in a brick building next to 'Hug' and across from 'Agit' • look for the peach mark on the door.

Sunny 2F Nakabayashi Tenpo (Shinjuku 2-15-8) 81–3/3356–0368 • 8pm-5am • one of the oldest lesbian bars in Tokyo • karaoke • neighborhood bar • piano bar

Tac's Knot 2F, Rm 202 (Shinjuku 3-11-12) 81–3/3341–9404 • 8pm-2am • lesbians/ gay men • also art exhibitions

Tamago 1F Yamahara Heights Bldg (Shinjuku 2-12-15) 81–3/3351–4838 • 9pm-5am • women only • drag king shows

Usagi on lock U facing block V, 5th Fl (up the narrow stairs) • mostly gay men • great balcony

Wordup Bar 2-10-7 2F TOM Bld Shinjuku 81–3/3353–2466 • mostly gay men • dancing/DJ

NIGHTCLUBS

Agit 1/F Matsui Bldg, Shinjuku 2-15-9 81–3/3350–8083 • lesbians/gay men • karaoke • lesbian owned

Arch B1F Hayakawa Bldg (Shinjuku 2-14-6) 81–3/3352–6297 • lesbians/ gay men • dancing/DJ • check www.clubarch.net for info on men-only & women-only nights

Diamond Cutter B1F Hayakawa Bldg (Shinjuku 2-14-6, at Arch) 81–3/3352–6297 (ARCH) • 9pm-5am 1st Fri only • women only • dancing/DJ • cabaret

Motel #203 2/F Sunny Co-op Bldg, Shinjuku 2-15-9 81–3/6383–4649 • 8pm-5am, till 2am Sun, clsd Tue, popular happy hour 8pm-9pm • women only • dancing/DJ

Rehab Lounge 2/F Sensho Bldg, Shinjuku 2-13-16 81–3/3355–7833 • 7pm-2am, till 3am Fri-Sat, popular happy hour 7pm-9pm • mostly gay men • dancing/DJ

Shangri-La Yume no Shima, Koto ward (at Ageha, Studio Coast) • bi-monthly • mostly men • dancing/DJ

RESTAURANTS

Angkor Wat 1-38-13 Yoyogi (Shibuya-ku) 81–3/3370–3019 • lunch & dinner • Cambodian

Ban Thai 1-23-14 Kabuki-cho, 3rd flr (Shinjuku) 81–3/3207–0068 • lunch & dinner

Chin-ya 1-3-4 Asukusa 81–3/3841–0010 • lunch & dinner • serving shabu-shabu & sukiyaki since 1880

Edogin 4-5-1 Tsukiji (Chuo-ku) 81–3/3543–4401 • 11am-9:30pm, clsd Sun • popular • sushi

Gonpachi 1-13-11 Nishi Azabu, 1F, 2F (Minato-ku) 81–3/5771–0170 • 11:30am-5am • izakaya

Kakiden 3-37-11 Shinjuku, 8th flr 81–3/3352–5121 • lunch & dinner • upscale Japanese

Kitchen Five 4-2-15 Nishi-Azabu (Minato-ku) 81–3/3409–8835 • 6pm-9:45pm • Mediterranean • woman chef

Las Chicas Jingumae 5-47-6 (off Shibuya), Shibuya-ku 81–3/3407–6865 • 11:30am-11pm • English spoken

Maisen 4-8-5 Jingu-mae (Shibuya-ku) 81–3/3470–0071 • specializes in tonkatsu

Moti 3F Roppongi Hama Bldg (6-2-35 Roppongi) 81–3/3479–1939 • noon-10pm • Indian

New York Grill 3-7-1-2 Nishi Shinjuku (at Park Hyatt Hotel, 52nd flr) 81–3/5323–3458 • lunch & dinner • American • reservations recommended

Sasa-no-yuki 2-15-10 Negishi (Taito-ku) 81–3/3873–1145 • 11am-9pm, clsd Mon • serving homemade tofu for 300 years

Tenmatsu 1-6-1 Dogen-zaka (Shibuya-ku) 81–3/3462–2815 • tempura

THAILAND

Bangkok

ACCOMMODATIONS

Baan Saladaeng 69/2 Soi Saladaeng 3, Saladaeng Rd (Silom, Bangrak) **66–2/2636–3038** • gay-friendly • upscale • near gay scene

Bangkok Rama Place, City Resort & Hotel 1546 Pattanakarn Rd (in Suan-Luang District) **66–2/722–6602–10** • gay-friendly • full brkfst • pool • kids ok • also restaurant • wheelchair access • lesbian-owned • 1,800-4,400 Baht

D&D Inn 68-70 Khaosan Rd (Phranakorn) **66–2/629–0525–8** • gay-friendly • "life's little luxuries at a price you can afford" • central location • pool • 550-1,350Baht

Elephantstay Royal Elephant Kraal & Village (74/1 M3 Tumbol Suanpik), Phra Nakhon Si Ayutthaya **66–81/668–7727, 66–87/116–3307** • gay/ straight • live w/, care for & learn about elephants • Thai-style bungalows • near Lopburi River • 1 hour to Bangkok • lesbian-owned • 4,000Baht

Hotel de Moc 78 Prajatipatai Rd, Pra-Nakorn **66–2/282–2831–3, 66–2/629–2100–5** • gay-friendly • pool • WiFi • wheelchair access

Lub d 4 Decho Rd (Silom, Bangrak) **66–2/634–7999** • gay-friendly • hostal with some private rooms • WiFi • 385-980Baht

Luxx 6/11 Decho Rd **66–2/635–8800** • gay-friendly • style-conscious, minimalist design hotel • full brkfst • 2,800-5,000Baht • WiFi

Old Bangkok Inn 607 Pra Sumen Rd (at Rajdamnern Ave, in Pra Nakhon) **66–2/629–1787** • environmentally-friendly • full brkfst • kids/ pets ok • nonsmoking • $97-236

Omyim Lodge 72-74 Naratiwat Rd Silom **66–2/635–0169** • gay/ straight • full brkfst • nonsmoking • kids ok • WiFi • lesbian- & gay-owned • 800-1,100Baht

Pinnacle Hotel 17 Soi Ngam Duphli, Rama 4 Rd, Sathorn **66–2/287–0111** • gay/ straight • sauna • fitness center • hot tub • 700-2,100Baht

Bangkok

WHERE THE GIRLS ARE:

Everywhere. Though there are few specifically lesbian establishments in Bangkok, nearly all are welcoming to Toms and Dees (the butch/ femme designations most Thais prefer to the l-word).

LGBT PRIDE:

Oct-Nov, web: www.bangkokpride.org.

ANNUAL EVENTS:

Jan - Chinese New Year Festival.
April - Songkran (Thai New Year or Water Festival).
May - Royal Ploughing Ceremony.
Aug 12 - Queen Sirikit's birthday.

CITY INFO:

Tourism Authority of Thailand 1672, web: www.tourismthailand.org.

BEST VIEW:

Baiyoke Sky Hotel observation deck.

ATTRACTIONS:

The Grand Palace 66–2/224–3328, web: palaces.thai.net.
The Jim Thompson House 66–2/216–7368, web: www.jimthompsonhouse.com.
Lumphini Park.
National Museum 66–2/224–1333.
Wat Arun 66–2/891–1149, web: www.watarun.org.
Wat Benchamabophit 66–2/282–7413.
Wat Pho 66–2/222–5910.
Wat Phra Kaeo 66–2/222–8181.

WEATHER:

Tropical, with heavy rains throughout the summer & drier weather Jan-Feb. Temperatures can dip as low as the 60°s Nov-Dec, and rise as high as the 90°s March-May.

TRANSIT:

SkyTrain 66–2/617-6000, web: www.bts.co.th.

Plaza Hotel Bangkok 178 Surawong Rd **66-2/677-6240** • gay-friendly • kids ok • pool • extra "joiner" charge for guests • 1,299-1,999Baht

Regency Park Hotel 12/3 Sukhumvit 22, Soi Sainamthip **66-2/259-7420** • gay-friendly • located in heart of Bangkok • full brkfst • pool • 1,900-4,250Baht

Sheraton Grande Sukhumvit 250 Sukhumvit Rd **66-2/649-8888** • gay-friendly • tropical garden • hot tub • spa • WiFi • wheelchair access • also Thai & Italian restaurant

Tarntawan Place Hotel 119/ 5-10 Surawong Rd **66-2/238-2620** • centrally located • kids ok • discount for gays • newly refurbished • WiFi • wheelchair access • 2,500-7,000Baht

The Unico Grande Silom 533 Silom Rd (Bang Rak) **66-2/237-8300, 66-2/635-0378** • gay-friendly • pool • sauna • gym • restaurant • bar • 2,500-3,700Baht

White Orchid 409 - 421, Yaowaraj Road **66-2/226-0026** • gay-friendly • also cafe

BARS

70's Bar 231/16 Sarasin (Chitlom) **66-2/253-4433** • lesbians/ gay men • dancing/DJ • retro lounge

The Balcony Pub & Restaurant 86-88 Silom Soi 4 (off Silom Rd) **66-2/235-5891** • 5:30pm-close • popular • mostly gay men • karaoke • terrace

Bed Supperclub 26 Soi Sukhumvit 11, Sukhumvit Rd, Klongtoey-nua, Wattana **66-2/651-3537** • 7:30pm-close • gay/ straight • dancing/DJ

Club Love Remix Ramkhamhaeng Soi 89/2 **66-2/378-4345, 66-1/987-4946** • gay/ straight • dancing/DJ • also restaurant

Expresso 8/10-11 Silom Rd, Soi 2 (Bang Rak) • mostly gay men • relaxed café-bar

Golden Dome 252/5 Ratchadapisek Rd Soi 18 (Huay Khwang) **66-2/692-8202** • lesbians/ gay men • cabaret • shows nightly at 5pm, 7pm & 9pm

Hamilton's Hideaway Soi Silom 2/1 (Saladeang BTS Station, Silom) **66-866/143-644** • 6pm-1am • mostly gay men • food served • live jazz • nonsmoking

JJ Park 8/3 Silom Rd, Soi 2 (Bang Rak) **66-2/233-3247** • 9pm-3am • gay/ straight • food • live music

Maxi's Bar 38/1-2 Duangthawee Plaza, Soi Pratoochai, Suriwong Rd **66-2/2266-4225** • 10am-2am • mostly gay men

MTV Remix Ramkhamhaeng Soi 24 **66-2/319-8340** • gay/ straight • dancing/DJ

@Richard's Pub & Restaurant 10/17 Silom Soi 2/1 **66-2/234-0459** • 6pm-2am • mostly men • neighborhood bar • food served

Telephone Pub & Restaurant 114/ 11 Silom Rd, Soi 4 **66-2/234-3279** • 6pm-1am • lesbians/ gay men • numbered telephones on all the tables • food served

Vega Sukhumvit 39 **66-2/258-8273, 66-2/662-6471** • 11am-2am • food served • karaoke • lesbian-owned

NIGHTCLUBS

9 Nightclub 90-96 Silom Rd, Soi 4 **66-2/266-3682** • mostly men • dancing/DJ • cabaret • drag shows

DJ Station 8/6-8 Silom Rd, Soi 2 (Bang Rak) • 11pm-2am • lesbians/ gay men • dancing/DJ

E-FUN (Extreme Fun for ladies) 29/67-69 Soi Soonvijai (aka Royal City Ave, or RCA) (Block D, Rama 9, 2 blocks left of Zeta, other side of St) • 3 story bar popular w/ more mature lesbians • live shows • patio

Pharaoh's Music Bar 104 Silom Soi 4 (above Sphinx) **66-2/234-7249** • 7pm-2am • gay/ straight • food • karaoke

Zeta 29/67-69 Soi Soonvijai (aka Royal City Ave, or RCA) (Block C, Rama 9) **66-2/203-0994, 66-2/203-1044** • 10pm-2am • women only • live music

CAFES

Bug & Bee 18 Silom Rd, Suriyawong (Bang Rak) **66-2/233-8118**

Coffee Society 12/3 Silom Rd (Suriyawong, Bang Rak) **66-2/235-9784** • 24hrs • coffee & light meals • WiFi • also art gallery

Dick's Cafe Bangkok 894/7-8 Soi Pratoochai (Duangthawee Plaza, off Surawong Rd) **66-2/637-0078** • 11am-1am • European-style cafe in the heart of the action • Thai & Western

RESTAURANTS

Cabbages & Condoms 6 Soi 12 Sukhumvit Rd (at Birds & Bees Resort) **66-2/229-4611** • 11am-10pm • Thai food w/ safe-sex education

Coyote on Convent Sivadon Building, 1/2 Convent Rd, Silom Bangrak **66-2/631-2325** • Mexican • ladies night 6pm-8pm Wed & 10pm-midnight Sat

Crêpes & Co 18/1 Sukhumvit Soi 12 (Klongtoey) **66-2/653-3990** • terrace • lounge • full bar

Eat Me Soi Pipat 2 (off Soi Convent) **66–2/238–0931, 66–2/233–1767** • 3pm-1am • upscale • also gallery • live music

Food Loft 1027 Ploenchit Rd, Lumpini, Pathumwan (Central Chisholm, 7th flr) **66–2/655–7777** • upscale int'l food

Full Moon 144/2 Silom Soi 10 **66–2/634–0766** • Thai food • gay-owned

Hemlock 56 Phra Arthit Rd, Chanasongkram **66–2/282–7507** • 6pm-2am • traditional Thai food • more lesbian wknds

Indigo 6 Convent Rd (off Silom Rd) **66–2/235–3268** • noon-1am, clsd Sun • gay/straight • patio • full bar • French

Loy Nava Dinner Cruises 37 Charoen Nakorn Rd, Klongsan **66–2/437–4932** • traditional Thai cuisine on rice barge on Chao Phraya River • reservations required

Mali 43 Sathorn Soi 1 **66–2/679–8693** • 8am-11pm • Thai & int'l

Mango Tree 37 Soi Tantawan (off Suriwong Rd) **66–2/236–2820** • popular • reservations recommended • traditional Thai food • live music nightly

May Kaidee 11-1 Racha Damnuem Rd, Banglampoo **66–9/137–3173, 66–2/281–7137** • 9am-11pm • innovative vegetarian restaurant • also 33 Samen Rd (Soi 1) • also guesthouse & massage

O...Ho... 2/8 Soi Sri Bumphen **66–2/286–5292** • 9am-midnight • Thai & Western menu • gay-owned

Omyim Restaurant 106 Soi Sribumpen Rama 4 Rd (Sathorn District) **66–8/1300–1778** • Thai & western menu • garden • also internet cafe next door • gay-owned

Once Upon a Time 32 Soi Petchaburi 17, Pratunam **66–2/252–8629** • 11am-11pm • Thai

Sweet Basil 1 Soi Sriwiang (off Silom Soi Pramuan) **66–2/234–1889, 66–2/238–3088** • popular • Vietnamese food

ENTERTAINMENT & RECREATION

Calypso Cabaret 296 Phaya Thai Rd, Pathumwan (at Asia Hotel) **66–2/261–6355** • lesbians/ gay men • cabaret • drag shows nightly at 8:30pm & 10pm

Mambo 496 Sukhumvit Soi 22 (at Washington Theatre) **66–2/259–5128** • lesbians/ gay men • cabaret • shows nightly at 8:30pm & 10pm

PUBLICATIONS

Spice **66–3/983–0256, 66–81/941–6769** • monthly gay magazine

AUSTRALIA

Sydney

INFO LINES & SERVICES

The Gender Centre **61–2/9569–2366** • free services for transgender/ transsexual people & their partners/ friends/ families • also publishes magazine *Polare*

Lesbian & Gay Counselling Service **61–2/8594–9596, 1–800/18–4527(OUTSIDE SYDNEY)** • 5:30pm-10:30pm, info & support

ACCOMMODATIONS

Apartment Hotel East Sydney 150 Liverpool St, E Sydney (at Oxford St) **61/404–793–159** • gay/ straight • 2-bdrm apts • nonsmoking • kids ok terrace & gourmet kitchen • A$254-759

Brickfield Hill B&B Inn 403 Riley St (at Foveaux), Surry Hills **61–2/9211–4886** • gay/straight • beautifully & carefully restored Victorian terrace-house in the gay Oxford St District • near beaches & downtown • WiFi • gay-owned • A$95-145

Chelsea Guest House 49 Womerah Ave (at Oswald Ln), Darlinghurst **61–2/9380–5994** • gay/ straight • Victorian w/ Italianate courtyard • nonsmoking • gay-owned • A$94-195

Hotel Stellar 4 Wentworth Ave (at Oxford St) **61–2/9264–9754** • lesbians/ gay men • kitchenette in each room • WiFi

Kirketon Boutique Hotel 229 Darlinghurst Rd (at Farrell Ave) **61–2/9332–2011, 800/332–920 (AUSTRALIA ONLY)** • gay-friendly • also restaurant & bars • kids ok • WiFi • $135-185

Medusa 267 Darlinghurst Rd (at Liverpool), Darlinghurst **61–2/9331–1000** • gay-friendly • modern boutique hotel • WiFi • A$310-420

Nomads Westend 412 Pitt St (at Goulburn St) **61–2/9211–4588, 1800/013–186** • gay-friendly • budget/ backpacker's accommodations • cafe • wheelchair access • A$24-85

Pensione Hotel 631-635 George St (at Goulburn St) **61–2/9265–8888, 800/885–886** • gay-friendly • also restaurant & bar • A$99-250

Victoria Court Hotel Sydney 122 Victoria St (at Orwell) **61–2/9357–3200, 1800/630–505 (IN AUSTRALIA)** • gay-friendly • historic B&B-inn in elegant Victorian • full brkfst • $37-130

Bars

Bar Cleveland/ Hershey Bar 443 Cleveland St (at Bourke), Surry Hills **61–2/9698–1908** • 11am-4am • noon-midnight Sun • gay/ straight • alternative • cocktail lounge • DJ • young crowd

The Beauchamp 265 Oxford St (at S Dowling), Darlinghurst **61–2/9331–2575** • noon-2am popular • gay/ straight • neighborhood bar • pronounced "Bee-chum" • gay-owned

Sydney

WHERE THE GIRLS ARE:
In Leichhardt (aka "Dykeheart") and Newtown.

LGBT PRIDE:
June - Sydney Gay & Lesbian Pride. 61–2/9550-6197

ANNUAL EVENTS:
January - Sydney Festival, web: www.sydneyfestival.org.au.
February/March - Sydney Gay & Lesbian Mardi Gras Festival. Nearly a month of events and parties. 61–2/9383–0900, web: www.mardigras.org.au.
May - Sydney Leather Pride Week 61–4/0414-691-123, web: www.sydneyleatherpride.org
September - Manly Jazz Festival 61–2/9976–1749, web: www.manly.nsw.gov.au/ manlyjazz.
October - Sleaze Ball 61–2/9383–0900, web: www.mardigras.org.au.

CITY INFO:
Sydney Tourist Information, web: www.discoversydney.com.au
Sydney Visitors Centre, 61–2/9240–8788, web: www.sydneyvisitorcentre.com.

BEST VIEW:
From the AMP Centrepoint Tower or Mrs Macquarie's Chair.

WEATHER:
Temperate—in the 50°s-70°s year-round. The summer months (January-March) can get hot and humid. Spring (September-December) sees the least rain. It's sunny most of the year. Bring a hat and lots of sunscreen!

TRANSIT:
Airport Express 61–2/131–500.
State Transit Authority 61–2/131–500, web: www.sta.nsw.gov.au.
Monorail 61–2/8584-5288, web: www.metrolightrail.com.au.

ATTRACTIONS:
Art Gallery of New South Wales 61–2/9225–1700, web: www.artgallery.nsw.gov.au.
Australian Museum 61–2/9320–6000, web: www.austmus.gov.au.
Bondi Beach.
Chinatown.
Darling Harbour.
Featherdale Wildlife Park 61–2/9622–1644, web: www.featherdale.com.au.
Manly beaches 61-2/9976-1430, web: www.manlyaustralia.com.au.
Museum of Contemporary Art 61–2/9245–2400, web: www.mca.com.au.
Queen Victoria Building, web: www.qvb.com.au.
The Rocks.
Royal Botanical Gardens 61–2/9231–8111, web: www.rbgsyd.nsw.gov.au.
Sydney Harbour Bridge.
Sydney Jewish Museum 61–2/9360–7999, web: sydney-jewishmuseum.com.au.
Sydney Opera House 61–2/9250–7111, web: www.sydneyoperahouse.com.
The Women's Library 61-2/9557-7060, web: www.thewomenslibrary.org.au.

Beresford Sundays 354 Bourke St (at Albion St), Surry Hills **61–2/9357–1111** • from noon Sun • lesbians/ gay men • fun in the sun

Clarence Hotel Bar & Bistro 450 Parramatta Rd (at Crystal St), Petersham **61–2/9560–0400** • 4pm-late, from noon Fri-Sun, clsd Mon • mostly gay men • karaoke

The Colombian 117-123 Oxford St (at Crown St), Darlinghurst **61–2/9360–2151** • 9am-6am • dancing/DJ

Flinders 63–65 Flinders St (at Hill St), Darlinghurst **61–2/9356–3622** • 24 hrs, popular late • gay/ straight • dancing/DJ • young crowd • more women 2nd & 3rd Sat for L Lounge

Green Park Hotel 360 Victoria St (at Liverpool), Darlinghurst **61–2/9380–5311** • 10am-2am, noon-midnight Sun • more gay Sun • stylish bar

Lava Bar 2 Oxford St (top flr of Burdekin Hotel), Darlinghurst **61–2/9331–3066** • 11am-1am, 4pm-4am Sat • gay/ straight • popular w/ lesbians Fri till 4am • live shows

Mr Mary's 106-110 George St (Redfern) **61–2/9690–0610** • 10am-4am • lesbians/ gay men • food served

The Oxford 134 Oxford St (at Bourke St, Taylor Square), Darlinghurst **61–2/9331–3467** • 24hrs • popular • lesbians/ gay men • 3 bars include the Polo Lounge, Supper club & Gilligans

The Palms On Oxford 124 Oxford St (at Bourke St, Taylor Square), Darlinghurst **61–2/9357–4166** • 8pm-late, clsd Mon-Tue • dancing/DJ

Phoenix Bar 34 Oxford St (at Exchange Hotel), Darlinghurst **61–2/9331–2956** • 10am-5am, till 7am Fri-Sun, clsd Mon-Tue • gay/ straight • sweaty downstairs dance den • 5 other bars in complex

The Stonewall 175 Oxford St (at Bourke), Darlinghurst **61–2/9360–1963** • 11am-6am • popular • mostly gay men • danciing/DJ • drag shows

ZanziBar 323 King St (at Phillips St), Newtown **62-2/9519–1511** • gay-friendly • food served • more gay Sun midday

NIGHTCLUBS

ARQ 16 Flinders St (at Taylor Square), Darlinghurst **61–2/9380–8700** • 9pm-late Th-Sun, clsd Mon-Wed • popular • mostly gay men • dancing/DJ • restaurant • drag shows Th • cover charge

Bitch • hot weekly women's parties • also big events on long wknds • www.bitchnews.com.au

The Black Boater 16 Wentworth Ave (at Lyons Ln) **61–2/9267–6440** • check www.theblackboater.com for events • more gay Sun afternoon for Bloody Mary Sunday

Chicks With Picks 20 Broadway Rd (at Kensington St, at Clare Hotel), Ultimo • 2nd Sun only • women's open mic

Gurlesque • for women & trans of all sexualities • check website for next event myspace.com/gurlesque_au

Hellfire 16-18 Oxford Square (on corner of Riley, at Rogues), Darlinghurst **61–2/9380–9244** • 9:30pm-late 3rd Fri • gay/ straight women-oriented fetish party • dancing/DJ • alternative • leather • burlesque • live shows • cover charge

Home Tenancy 101, Cockle Bay Wharf (at Wheat Rd, Darling Harbour) **61–2/9266–0600** • open Fri-Sun • popular • gay-friendly • hosts Homesexual (www.homesexual.com.au)

The Midnight Shift 85 Oxford St (at Riley), Darlinghurst **61–2/9360–4319** • 10pm-late Fri-Sat, also Saddle Bar • popular • mostly gay men

Moist 16 Flinders St (at Taylor Square, at ARQ), Darlinghurst **61–2/9380–8700** • last Fri only • popular • mostly women • dancing/DJ • drag king shows • cover charge

Nevermind 163 Oxford St, Darlinghurst • Fri-Sun only • gay/ straight • theme nights • cutting edge electronic music

Pussycat Club 134 Oxford St (at Bourke), Darlinghurst **61–2/9331–3467** • 3rd Sat only, mostly women • trans-friendly • dancing/DJ • cabaret & burlesque shows • all queers welcome

Queer Central 199 Enmore Rd (at Sly Fox Hotel), Enmore **61–2/9557–1016** • 9pm Wed only • mostly women • dancing/DJ • live performances

Rising Day Club 34 Oxford St (at Pelican), Darlinghurst • recovery club starts at 5:30am Sun • mostly gay men • dancing/DJ

Slide 41 Oxford St (at Pelican) **61–2/8915–1899** • 6pm-3am, 5pm-4am Fri, 7pm-4am Sat-Sun, clsd Mon-Tue • lesbians/ gay men • dancing/DJ • also restaurant • live music • cabaret

Tank 3 Bridge St (behind Establishment Hotel) **61–2/9251–9933** • 10pm-6am Fri-Sat, check locally for next DTPM gay party at this multi-award wining dance club on Sun nights

Velvet Wednesdays 324 King St (at the Bank Hotel), Newtown • 8pm Wed only • mostly women • dancing/DJ

CAFES

Cafe Sopra 7 Danks St **61–2/9699–3174** • 10am-3pm, from 8am Sat, clsd Mon • Italian vegetarian

Coffee, Tea or Me? 536 Crown St **61–2/9331–3452**

Victoire 285 Darling St **61–2/9818–5529** • great bread

Vinyl Lounge Cafe 17 Elizabeth Bay Rd, Elizabeth Bay **61–2/9326–9224** • 7am-4pm, from 8am wknds, clsd Mon • lesbians/gay men • light menu • plenty veggie • cash only

RESTAURANTS

Bentley Restaurant & Bar 320 Crown St **61–2/9332–2344** • noon-late, clsd Sun- Mon • tapas & small plates • excellent wine

Bertoni Casalinga 281 Darling St **61–2/9818–5845** • 6am-6pm, clsd Sat & Sun • Italian

Betty's Soup Kitchen 84 Oxford St, Darlinghurst **61–2/9360–9698** • noon-10pm, till midnight Fri-Sat • lesbians/gay men • healthy homecooking • plenty veggie

Bills Surry Hills 359 Crown St **61–2/9360–4762** • 7am-10pm • great ricotta pancakes

Billy Kwong 3/355 Crown St **61–2/9332–3300** • sustainable local and organic Chinese from 6pm daily • reservations recommended • wheelchair access

Bird Cow Fish 500 Crown St **61–2/9380–4090** • 9am-10pm, till 5pm Sun • bistro & espresso bar

The Boathouse on Blackwattle Bay End of Ferry Road (Glebe) **61–2/9518–9011** • lunch & dinner Tue-Sun • gourmet seafood • some veggie • great view • reservations required

Bright N Up 77 Oxford St, Darlinghurst **61–2/9361–3379** • 4:30pm-midnight

Chu Bay 312a Bourke St, Darlinghurst **61–2/9331–3386** • 5:30pm-11pm • Vietnamese • some veggie

Danks Street Depot 2 Danks St **61–2/9698–2201** • great brkfst

Fu Manchu 249 Victoria St, Darlinghurst **61–2/9360–9424** • lunch & dinner • chic noodle bar • plenty veggie • nonsmoking • cash only

Iku Wholefood Kitchen 25a Glebe Point Rd, Glebe **61–2/9692–8720, 800/732–962** • lunch & dinner • creative vegan/ macrobiotic fare • nonsmoking • outdoor seating • cash only

Last Drop Cafe 538 Marrickville Rd (Dulwich Hill) **61–2/9572–9800** • 7:30am-5:30pm, till 4pm Sat, clsd Sun • Greek food • also art gallery

Pink Peppercorn 122 Oxford St (near Taylor Square, Darlinghurst) **61–2/9360–9922** • 6pm-10:30pm • Laotian & Thai • gay-owned

Sean's Panorama 270 Campbell Parade, Bondi Beach **61–2/9365–4924** • lunch Sat-Sun, dinner Wed-Sat, clsd Mon-Tue

Thai Kanteen 541 Military Rd, Mosman **61–2/9960–3282** • lunch Th-Fri, dinner Tue-Sun, clsd Mon • modern Thai • gay-owned

Thai Pothong 294 King St (Newtown) **61–2/9550–6277** • lunch Tue-Sun, dinner nightly • wheelchair access

ENTERTAINMENT & RECREATION

Bondi Beach Bondi Beach • Sydney's most popular beach • more gay at north end

Lady Jane Beach/ Lady Bay Beach Watsons Bay • crowded nude beach • mostly men

McIver Baths/ Coogee Pool Beach St, Grant Reserve, Coogee • pool for women and children only

Obelisk Beach Middle Head Rd (at Chowder Bay Rd) • mostly men • gay beach • nudity permitted

Sydney by Diva departs from Oxford Hotel (in Taylor Square, Darlinghurst) **61–0/401–429–025, 61–4/0142–9025** • tour Sydney w/ drag queen host

Sydney Gay/ Lesbian Mardi Gras 94 Oxford St, Darlinghurst 2010 **61–2/9383–0900** • the wildest party under the rainbow on this planet (see www.mardigras.org.au)

The Women's Library 8-10 Brown St **61–2/9557–7060** • "books, journals, ephemera, & art by, for, & about women"

BOOKSTORES

The Bookshop Darlinghurst 207 Oxford St (near Darlinghurst Rd), Darlinghurst **61–2/9331–1103** • 10am-10pm • Australia's oldest LGBT bookstore • staff happy to help w/ tourist info

The Feminist Bookshop Orange Grove Plaza, Balmain Rd, Shop 9, Lilyfield **61–2/9810–2666** • 10:30am-6pm, till 4pm Sat, clsd Sun

Gertrude & Alice 46 Hall St (Bondi Beach) **61–2/9130–5155** • second-hand books • also coffee shop

PUBLICATIONS

▶**LOTL Magazine** **61–2/9332–2725** • Lesbians on the Loose • monthly magazine

SX Weekly **61–2/9360–8934** • free gay/ lesbian weekly

Sydney Star Observer **61–2/8263–0500** • weekly newspaper w/ club & event listings

GYMS & HEALTH CLUBS

City Gym 107–113 Crown St **61–2/9360–6247** • day passes available

Gold's Gym Sydney 58 Kippax St (level 1), Surry Hills **61–2/9211–2799** • 5:30am-9pm , 8am-8pm Sat, till 6pm Sun

SEX CLUBS

Aarows 17 Bridge St (at Pitt St), Rydalmere **61–2/9638–0553, /1300–062–541** • 24hrs • lesbians/ gay men • transgender-friendly • 18+

Camping & RV Spots

2011 Tours & Tour Operators

2011 Calendar

USA

ALABAMA

Geneva

Spring Creek Campground & Resort 163 Campground Rd (at Hwy 52 & Country Rd 4) **334/684–3891** • mostly gay men • cabins • also tent & RV sites • BYOB • pool • nudity ok • some theme wknds w/ DJ • WiFi • gay-owned • $17-85

ALASKA

Fairbanks

Billie's Backpackers Hostel 2895 Mack Rd **907/479–2034** • gay-friendly • kids ok • food served • women-owned • $30-80

ARIZONA

Apache Junction

Susa's Serendipity Ranch 4375 E Superstition Blvd **480/288–9333** • women only • guesthouses on 15-acre ranch • 2 RV hookups • great views! • hot tub • nonsmoking • pets ok • lesbian-owned • $75-90/ night, $1,500/ month

Bisbee

David's Oasis Camping Resort 5311 W Double Adobe Rd, McNeal **520/979–6650** • lesbians/ gay men • 21+ • pool • also bar & internet cafe • WiFi • gay-owned • $12-20

Copper Rainbow Bistro 5311 W Double Adobe Rd, McNeal **520/979–6650** • 5pm-10pm Fri-Sat, 2pm-7pm Sun • lesbian/ gay men • beer/ wine only

White Mountains

Arizona High Country Campground 5064 Sawmill Rd (1 mile off Hwy 260), Clay Springs **928/739–4383** • lesbians/ gay men • 10 campsites & RV hookups • WiFi • lesbian-owned • $30/ night, $2000/ season

CALIFORNIA

Clearlake

Edgewater Resort 6420 Soda Bay Rd (at Hohape Rd), Kelseyville **707/279–0208, 800/396–6224** • "gay-owned, straight-friendly" • cabin • camping & RV hookups • lake access & pool • theme wknds • boat facilities • WiFi • kids/ pets ok • lesbian-owned • $35-450

Joshua Tree Nat'l Park

Starland Retreat Yucca Valley **760/364–2069** • mostly gay men & radical faeries, but women very welcome • membership-only rustic rural camp • hot tub • nudity permitted

Mendocino

Orr Hot Springs 13201 Orr Springs Rd, Ukiah **707/462–6277** • gay-friendly • hostel-style cabins, private cottages & campsites • clothing-optional • kids ok • mineral hot springs • pool • guests must bring all own food • reservations required • $40 (camping), $185 (cottage)

Placerville

Rancho Cicada Retreat 10001 Bell Rd, Plymouth **209/245–4841, 877/553–9481** • mostly gay men • secluded riverside retreat in the Sierra foothills w/ 2-person tents & cabin • swimming • nudity • gay-owned • $42-160

Russian River

Guerneville Lodge 15905 River Rd (at Hwy 116), Guerneville **707/869–0102** • gay/straight • WiFi • nonsmoking • gay-owned • $35 (camping), $99-189 (inn)

▶ **Highlands Resort** 14000 Woodland Dr, Guerneville **707/869–0333** • lesbians/ gay men • country retreat on 4 wooded acres • hot tub • swimming • clothing-optional pool • $65-195; $20-25 rustic camping

Yosemite Nat'l Park

Rivendale Ranch **209/962–7425** • women only • nonsmoking • also RV hookups • women-owned • $110-150 ($25 RV)

The Yosemite Bug Rustic Mountain Resort 6979 Hwy 140, Midpines **209/966–6666, 866/826–7108** • gay-friendly • hostel w/ dorms, cabins, private rooms & tents • some shared baths • kids ok • nonsmoking • WiFi • wheelchair access • $22-150

COLORADO

Durango

Mesa Verde Far View Lodge 1 Navajo Hill, Mesa Verde National Park **602/331-5210, 800/449-2288** • gay-friendly • hotel • camping • RV hookups • inside nat'l park at 8250' elevation • views of 4 states • full brkfst • nonsmoking • WiFi • $120-160

FLORIDA

Fort Myers

The Resort on Carefree Blvd 3000 Carefree Blvd (at Cleveland Ave) **239/731-6366** • mostly women • 1- & 2-bdrm homes & RV lots • pool • nature trails • tennis • gym • kids/ pets ok • older crowd • nonsmoking • woman-owned • $650-800/ week

Miami

Something Special, A Lesbian Venture **305/696-8826** • women only • 1-bdrm apt on beach • also backyard camping & dining • $130

Tampa

Sawmill Camping Resort 21710 US Hwy 98, Dade City **352/583-0664** • popular • lesbians/ gay men • theme wknds w/ entertainment • RV hookups • cabins • tent spots • dancing • karaoke • pool • nudity • gay-owned • $17-120

GEORGIA

Dahlonega

Swiftwaters Womanspace **706/864-3229, 706/429-6802** • women only • on scenic river • full brkfst • hot tub • seasonal • nonsmoking • deck • dogs ok • women-owned • $50-75 (indoors), $15 (camping)

Dewy Rose

The River's Edge 2311 Pulliam Mill Rd **706/213-8081** • mostly gay men • cabins • camping • RV • live shows • pool • nudity • nonsmoking • wheelchair access • $16-100

Unadilla

Lumberjack's Camping Resort 50 Hwy 230 (at Hwy 41) **478/783-2267, 877/888-1688** • mostly gay men • campsites & RV hookups • on 150 acres • pool • live shows • WiFi • pets ok • gay-owned • also restaurant • $39+

HAWAI

Hawaii (Big Island)

Margo's Corner near South Point **808/929-9614** • cottage & 4 campsites • full brkfst & dinner • kids ok • sauna • WiFi • lesbian-owned • $90-130

Kalani Oceanside Retreat **808/965-7828, 800/800-6886** • gay/ straight • coastal wellness retreat & spa • pool • nudity • nonsmoking • WiFi • food served • wheelchair access • $40 (camping), $110-265 (retreat)

Kulana: The Affordable Artists Sanctuary 808/985-9055 • mostly women • artist retreat • camping, cabin & guest rooms available • no smoking, drugs or alcohol • kids ok • women-owned • $15 (camping), $18-40 (cabin); see website (www.discoverkulana.com) for visitor-to-resident-transition guidelines

ILLINOI

Du Quoin

The Pit 7403 Persimmon Rd **618/542-9470** • lesbians/ gay men • primitive camping • 18+ • nudity ok • swimming • gay-owned • free except $5 on holiday wknds

MAIN

Augusta

Maple Hill Farm B&B Inn Hallowell **207/622-2708, 800/622-2708** • gay/ straight • Victorian farmhouse on 130 acres • full brkfst • whirlpools • clothing optional swimming pond • nonsmoking • WiFi • wheelchair access • gay-owned • $90-205

Ogunquit

Beaver Dam Campground 551 School St, Rte 9, Berwick **207/698-2267** • gay friendly • campground on 20-acre spring fed pond • pool • kids/ pets ok • women owned • $29-85

MICHIGAN

Owendale

Windover Resort 3596 Blakely Rd **989/375-2586** • women only • seasonal private resort • campsites & RV hookups • pool • $25/ year membership fee • $21-76 camping fee

Saugatuck

The Bunkhouse B&B at Campit **269/543-4335, 877/226-7481** • lesbians/ gay men • cabins • private baths • access to Campit Resort amenities (see listing below) • pool • nonsmoking • WiFi $85-125

Campit Outdoor Resort 6635 118th Ave, Fennville **269/543-4335, 877/226-7481** • lesbians/ gay men • campsites • RV hookups • separate women's area • pool • seasonal • pets ok • WiFi • membership required • lesbian & gay-owned • $20-65

MINNESOTA

Kenyon

Dancing Winds Farmstay Retreat 6863 County 12 Blvd **507/789-6606** • gay/ straight • farmstay on 20-acre working farm • work exchange available • nonsmoking • kids ok • lesbian-owned • $105-125

MISSISSIPPI

Bay Saint Louis

Nella's Park 16145 Hwy 603 (near I-10), Kiln **228/581-0631** • gay/ straight • camping • kids/ pets ok • friendly & clean w/ fishing dock • casino nearby • close to New Orleans

MISSOURI

Branson

Branson Stagecoach RV Park 5751 State Hwy 165 **417/335-8185, 800/446-7110** • gay-friendly • pull-thru & back-in RV sites • cabins • pool • WiFi • gay-owned • $90

NEVADA

Gerlach

F Ranch 775/557-2804 • women only • B&B on remote NW Nevada working horse/ cattle ranch • April-Sept • bird-watching • kids ok • nonsmoking • $2,500-3,500 (per couple per week)

NEW MEXICO

Ramah

El Morro RV Park, Cabins & Cafe 4018 Hwy 53 **505/783-4612** • gay/ straight • in Zuni Mtns • full brkfst • nonsmoking • WiFi • also cafe • lesbian-owned • $10-94

NEW YORK

Adirondack Mtns

Falls Brook Yurts in Adirondacks John Brannon Rd, Minerva **518/761-6187** • gay-friendly • access to hiking, fishing & boating • kids/ pets ok • $95

Binghamton

Serenity Farms 386 Pollard Rd, Greene **607/656-4659** • gay/ straight • B&B • full brkfst • camping on 100 secluded acres • pool • pets ok • gay-owned • $65-119

Syracuse

Yellow Lantern Kampground 1770 Rte 13 N, Cortland **607/756-2959** • gay-friendly • kids/ pets ok • pool • short drive from Syracuse or Ithaca • 205 campsites & RV hookups • $23-28

NORTH CAROLINA

Asheville

Compassionate Expressions Mtn Inn & Healing Sanctuary 828/683-6633 • mostly women • cabins & rooms w/ a view of Blue Ridge Mtns • spa services • hot tub • on 40 acres • nonsmoking • wheelchair access • lesbian-owned • $90-120

Lofty Notions Campsite 828/287-0069 • lesbians/ gay men • 1 campsite overlooking waterfall • SE of Asheville • pool • kids ok • lesbian-owned • $200/ week

Brevard

Ash Grove Resort Cabins & Camping
749 E Fork Rd **828/885–7216** • gay/
straight • camping & cabins • on 14
wooded acres in Blue Ridge Mtns • hot
tub • nonsmoking • WiFi • gay-owned •
$100-145 (cabins), $22-45 (camping)

Raleigh/Durham/Chapel Hill

Fickle Creek Farm B&B 919/304–6287
• gay/ straight • passive solar B&B on
61-acre working farm • full brkfst • some
shared baths • kids ok • nonsmoking •
gay-owned • $90+

Ohio

Athens

**SuBAMUH (Susan B Anthony Memorial
UnRest Home) Womyn's Land Trust** PO
Box 5853, 45701 **740/448–6424,
740/448–7285** • women only • cabins &
camping • summer workshops • swimming • hot tub • nonsmoking • lesbian-
owned • $7 (tent), $12 (cabin) sliding
scale • rates per person

Oklahoma

Grand Lake

Southern Oaks Resort & Spa 2 miles S
of Hwy 28/ 82 Junction, Langley
918/782–9346, 866/452–5307 • gay-
friendly • 19 cabins on 30 acres • pool •
hot tub • nonsmoking • gay-owned •
$49-289

Oregon

Grants Pass

Rainbow Flyfishers at Copperland 840
Copper Dr (at Gray's Creek Rd) Murphy
541/862–2086 • women's land on 40
acres • cabin, campsites, RV hookups •
also guided flyfishing • nonsmoking •
WiFi • lesbian-owned • $45-400

WomanShare 541/862–2807 • women
only • cabins • shared kitchen • bathhouse • hot tub • girls/ pets ok • nonsmoking • lesbian-owned • $25-40

Pennsylvania

New Milford

Oneida Campground & Lodge
570/465–7011 • mostly gay men • seasonal • dedicated to the gay community
• RV hookups • 1 guest cottage • pool •
nudity • WiFi • gay-owned • $30-85

Pittsburgh

Camp Davis 311 Red Brush Rd, Boyers
724/637–2402 • April-Oct • lesbians/
gay men • cabins, trailer, & campsites •
pool • adults 21+ only • 1 hour from
Pittsburgh • $17 (tent sites), $25 (cabins), $30 (trailer) • rates per person

Poconos

The Woods Campground 845 Vaughn
Acres Ln, Lehighton **610/377–9577** •
lesbians/ gay men • 84 campsites • RV
spots • also cabins • swimming • 18+ •
WiFi • $22-63

South Dakota

Salem

Camp America 25495 US 81
605/425–9085 • gay-friendly • 35 miles
west of Sioux Falls • camping • RV
hookups • pool • kids/ pets ok • nonsmoking • WiFi • lesbian-owned • $18-

Tennessee

Gatlinburg

**Big Creek Stables & Big Creek
Outpost** 5019 Rag Mtn Rd, Hartford
423/487–5742, 423/487–3490 • gay/
straight • cabins • camping • horsebac
riding • kids ok • wheelchair access •
$25-150

Texas

Groesbeck

Rainbow Ranch Campground 1662 LC
800 **254/729–8484, 888/875–7596** • le
bians/ gay men • open all year • on La
Limestone • pool • campsites • cabins
house rental • nonsmoking • gay-owne
• $20-200

Lockhart

Lazy J Paradise Campground & Park 270 Hidden Path (CR 303 and FM 2001) **210/863-9314** • campground with RV area catering to the GLBT community • pool • WiFi • $7-35

Marfa

El Cosmico Hwy 67 **432/729-1950, 877/822-1950** • gay/straight • vintage trailer, yurt and teepee hotel and campground • WiFi • lesbian owned • $20-128

UTAH

Moab

Los Vados Canyon House **801/532-2651** • gay/ straight • retreat house in a red rock canyon • pool • kids 10 & over ok • nonsmoking • $250 • also tent cabin $25/ night when cabin is rented

VERMONT

Craftsbury Common

Greenhope Farm 2478 Wylie Hill Rd **802/586-7577** • gay/ straight • nonsmoking • kids ok • WiFi • lesbian-owned • $75-150

Townshend

Townshend State Park 2755 State Forest Rd **802/365-7500, 888/409-7579** • gay-friendly • campground • great hiking • open Memorial Day wknd to Labor Day wknd

VIRGINIA

Charlottesville

CampOut 804/301-3553, 888/357-6697 • women only • 100-acre rustic campground w/ 50 campsites • nonsmoking • wheelchair access • women-owned • $20-60 membership fee

Windsor

Blackwater Campground 7651 Whispering Pines Trail 757/357-7211 • gay-friendly • RV hookups & primitive camping • pool • pagan, medieval & gay events on wknds • kids/ pets ok • $25+

WASHINGTON

Bender Creek

Triangle Recreation Camp PO Box 1226, Granite Falls 98252 • lesbians/ gay men • members-only camping on 80-acre nature conservancy • (see www.camptrc.org) • $15/ night or $150/ year

Long Beach Peninsula

Anthony's Home Court 1310 Pacific Hwy N, Long Beach **360/642-2802, 888/787-2754** • gay/ straight • cabins & RV hookups • nonsmoking • WiFi • gay-owned • $100-175

The Historic Sou'wester Lodge, Cabins & RV Park Beach Access Rd (38th Pl), Seaview **360/642-2542** • gay-friendly • inexpensive suites • cabins w/ kitchens • vintage trailers • RV hookups • pets ok in cabins & trailers • nonsmoking

San Juan Islands

Lopez Farm Cottages & Tent Camping 555 Fisherman Bay Rd, Lopez Island **360/468-3555, 800/440-3556** • gay/ straight • on 30-acre farm • hot tub • nonsmoking • $40 (camping), $170-205 (cottages)

Seattle

Wild Lily Cabins B&B 25 miles W of Stevens Pass, Index **360/793-2103** • gay/ straight • cabins on Skykomish River • 1 hour from Seattle • cedar sauna • hot tub • camping available • nonsmoking • gay-owned • $118-175

WISCONSIN

Norwalk

Daughters of the Earth 18134 Index Ave **608/269-5301** • women only • women's land • camping • retreat space • lesbian-owned • $9 (camping), $15 (guest rooms)

CANADA

ALBERTA

Westrose

Pine Trails Getaway RR1 780/586-0002
• gay campground

BRITISH COLUMBIA

Birken

Birken Lakeside Resort 9179 Portage
Rd 604/452-3255 • gay-friendly • cabins
• campsites • hot tub • swimming • pets
ok • lesbian-owned • Can$80-212

NEW BRUNSWICK

Fredericton

River's Edge Campground 19 Cottage
Ln, Durham Bridge 506/458-1049,
800/370-1644 • lesbians/ gay men •
pool • outdoor activities • gay-owned •
camping/ RV hookups • WiFi • Can$25-
32

NOVA SCOTIA

Scotsburn

The Mermaid & the Cow West Branch
902/351-2714 • lesbians/ gay men •
cabin & 20 campsites • dogs ok on leash
• pool • lesbian-owned • $150 (cabin) &
$25 (camping)

ONTARIC

Grand Valley

Rainbow Ridge Resort Country Rd 109
(at Hwy 25 S) 519/928-3262 • lesbians/
gay men • trailers & tents • located on
72 acres on Grand River • pool • restau
rant • dance hall • day visitors welcome
• seasonal • pets ok • gay-owned •
Can$15+/ person

Hamilton

Cedars Campground 1039 5th
Concession W Rd, Millgrove
905/659-3655, 905/659-7342 • les-
bians/ gay men • private campground •
pool • also bar • dancing/DJ • restaurar
wknds • some veggie • Can$65-95 (cab-
ins), Can$16 (camping)

Turkey Point

The Point Tent & Trailer Resort 918
Charlotteville Rd #2, RR 1, Vittoria
519/426-7275 • mostly gay men • nud
ty ok • pool on 50 acres • gay-owned •
Can$18-65

PROVINCE OF QUÉBE

Joliette

L' Oasis des Pins 381 boul Brassard, St
Paul-de-Joliette 450/754-3819 • les-
bians/ gay men • pool • camping May-
Sept • restaurant open year-round

CRUISES

Women Only

Olivia Travel 415/962–5700, 800/631–6277 434 Brannan St, San Francisco, CA 94107 • exclusive cruise, resort & escape vacations for lesbians • *www.olivia.com*

➤ **Sweet 877/793–3830** PO Box 18888, 94619 Oakland • "Sweet is a lesbian travel company that visits amazing places, produces off-the-hook events, and creates fun and easy opportunities for women to make a difference. Now, that's Sweet" • see ad in front color section • *www.discoversweet.com*

Gay/Lesbian

Aquafest 800/592–9058 4801 Woodway #400-W, Houston, TX 77056 • LGBT groups mingle w/ mixed clientele on major cruise lines • *www.aquafestcruises.com*

Gayribbean Cruises 214/331–2264, 877/560–8318 Dallas, TX • gay & lesbian group cruise organizer • fabulous destinations • annual Halloween cruise from Galveston, TX • *www.gayribbeancruises.com*

Ocean Voyager 321/454–2083 4098 Judith Ave, Merritt Island, FL 32953 • hosted gay groups on mainstream upscale cruise ships • *www.oceanvoyager.com*

Port Yacht Charters 516/883–0998, 877/DO-A-BOAT 9 Belleview Ave, Port Washington, NY 11050 • custom charters worldwide, specializing in the Caribbean • commitment ceremonies • gourmet cuisine • *www.portyachtcharters.com*

R Family 866/732–6822 5 Washington Ave, Nyack, NY 10960 • family-friendly vacations designed especially for the LGBT community • *www.rfamilyvacations.com*

Rainbow Charters 808/347–0235 939 Kawaiki Pl, Honolulu, HI 96825 • gay & lesbian weddings • custom sailing cruises • whale-watching • snorkeling • sunset cruises • *www.RainbowChartersHawaii.com*

RSVP Vacations 800/328–7787 gay & lesbian cruise vacations • *www.rsvpvacations.com*

Sailing Affairs 917/453–6425 58 E 1st St #6-B, New York City, NY 10003 • gay sailboat charters, day trips, sunset sails & sailing vacations on 47-foot Beneteau • East Coast, Caribbean, Europe & Mediterranean • *www.sailingaffairs.com*

LUXURY TOURS

DavidTravel 949/723–0699 310 Dahlia Pl, Ste A, Corona del Mar, CA 92625-2821 • full service travel agency & tour operator • small luxury group departures & customized travel for individuals & groups • milestone events • *www.DavidTravel.com*

Out Traveller 27–074/171–8924 45 Amarja, Johannesburg, Gauteng 2188, South Africa • guided safaris to South Africa & East Africa • also Thailand, Bali & New Zealand • destination weddings • lesbian-owned • *www.out-traveller.com*

Steele Luxury Travel 646/688–2274 New York City, NY 10011 • unique travel experiences to exotic destinations worldwide • *www.steeletravel.com*

GREAT OUTDOORS ADVENTURES

Women Only

Abroad For Adventure 215/568–3322 2206 Brandywine St, Philadelphia, PA 19130 • fun, small groups for unique adventures w/a touch of luxury • Italy, Greece, Belize, Costa Rica, Isla Mujeres, Machu Picchu • travel with just the girls! • *www.abroadforadventure.com*

Adventure Associates of WA 206/932–8352, 888/532–8352 PO Box 16304, Seattle, WA 98116 • worldwide eco-adventures for women • cruises, cultural immersion, history & ruins, treks, safaris, hiking, kayaking & biking • *www.adventureassociates.net*

Adventures in Good Company 410/435–1965, 877/439–4042 5913 Brackenridge Ave, Baltimore, MD 21212 • outdoor & adventure travel for women of all ages & abilities • *www.adventuresingoodcompany.com*

Bushwise Women /61 266840178 PO Box 34, Mullumbimby, NSW 2482, Australia • international escapes & adventures for women • wilderness & cultural trips in New Zealand, Australia, Egypt & Europe • also hosts The Women's Accomodation Network • *www.bushwise.co.nz*

Call of the Wild Adventure Travel 650/265–1662, 888/378–1978 (OUTSIDE CA) PO Box 1412, Mountain View, CA 94042 • hiking, camping & cultural trips for all levels in Western US, Alaska, Mexico, New Zealand & Peru • longest-running adventure travel company for women • *www.callwild.com*

Chicks with Picks & Chicks Rock 970/626–4424 PO Box 486, Ridgway, CO 81432 • ice climbing & rock climbing for women • all levels welcome • *www.chickswithpicks.net*

Equinox Wilderness Expeditions 206/462–5246 2440 E Tudor Rd, Anchorage, AK 99507 • wilderness trips in Alaska, British Columbia & the Southwest US by raft, canoe, sea kayak & backpack • also ski tours near Whistler, BC • *www.equinoxexpeditions.com*

Grand Canyon Field Institute 928/638–2485, 866/471–4435 PO Box 399, Grand Canyon, AZ 86023 • women's educational backpacking classes in the Grand Canyon • also co-ed trips • *www.grandcanyon.org/fieldinstitute*

Herizen™ Life Adventures Int'l Inc 250/753–4253, 866/399–4253 1-5765 Turner Rd #176, Nanaimo, BC V9T 6M4, Canada • women-only retreats • sailing, yoga, riding & more in Baja, Mexico, Belize, British Columbia & British Virgin Islands • *www.herizenlifeadventures.com*

Mariah Wilderness Expeditions 530/626–6049, 800/462–7424 PO Box 1160, Lotus, CA 95651 • unique vacations for women on roads less traveled • multi-sport adventures • unique cultural & eco-explorations • *www.mariahwe.com*

National Women's Sailing Association 401/682–2064 26 Beach Rd, Hingham, MA 02043 • sailing seminars & workshops • *www.womensailing.org*

Nurture Through Nature 207/452–2929 77 Warren Rd, Denmark, ME 04022 • holistic personal retreats • solar-powered eco-cabin rentals • yoga • custom canoe & kayak tours • hiking & camping • *www.ntnretreats.com*

Octopus Reef Dive Training & Tours 808/875–8759 Maui, HI • experienced instructors teaching & guiding SCUBA divers in Maui • *www.OctopusReef.com*

Sea Sense: The Women's Sailing & Powerboating School 727/289–6917, 800/332–1404 PO Box 1961, St Petersburg, FL 33731 • US & worldwide sailing & powerboating courses • custom courses • also private, "on your own boat" courses • *www.seasenseboating.com*

Skigrlz 206/462–5246 2906 W Broadway #115, Vancouver, BC V6K 2G8, Canada • wilderness hiking & paddling trips in BC • *www.skigrlz.com*

Tethys Offshore Sailing for Women 206/789–5118 2442 NW Market St #498, Seattle, WA 98107 • join Capt Nancy Erley as learning crew for a week in the Pacific Northwest aboard the 38' Tethys • *www.tethysoffshore.com*

WalkingWomen 44 0/1757 249481 York, United Kingdom • women's walking vacations for all levels • England, Scotland, Ireland, Wales, Europe, & as far as Nepal & South Africa! • *www.walkingwomen.com/lesbians.htm*

Wild Women Expeditions 705/866–1260, 888/993–1222 PO Box 145, Stn B, Sudbury, C P3E 4N5, Canada • Canada's outdoor adventure company for women • adventure trips across Canada • decidedly dykey! • *www.wildwomenexp.com*

Wildlotus Adventures 00844/715–2440 43 Nghi Tam Rd, Tay Ho, Hanoi, Vietnam • tailor made tours & off the beaten path experiences for women in Vietman, Laos, Cambodia & Thailand • *www.wildlotusadventures.com*

Winter Moon Summer Sun 218/848–2442 3388 Petrell, Brimson, MN 55602 • dogsledding trips in winter • kayaking Lake Superior in summer • rustic accommodations w/ meals provided • www.wintermoonsummersun.com

Womanship 410/267–6661, 800/342–9295 137 Conduit St, Annapolis, MD 21401 • daily or live-aboard learning cruises for women • sail & "see" adventures in the Greek Isles, Turkey, Florida Keys & more • www.womanship.com

WomanTours 585/256–9807, 800/247–1444 2340 Elmwood Ave, Rochester, NY 14618 • fully-supported bicycle tours for women • call for a free catalog • www.womantours.com

Women On A Roll 310/578–8888 PO Box 5112, Santa Monica, CA 90409-5112 • travel, sporting, cultural & social club for women • wide range of events & trips • largest lesbian organization in Southern California • www.womenonaroll.com

Women's Flyfishing® 907/274–7113 PO Box 243963, Anchorage, AK 99524 • women-only fly-fishing schools & guided trips for women & couples in Alaska, Argentina & Mexico • we provide all gear & equipment • beginners welcome! • www.womensflyfishing.net

Mostly Women

▶ **Venus Charters 305/304–1181** Garrison Bight Marina, Key West, FL 33040 • snorkeling & dolphin-watching • light-tackle fishing • commitment ceremonies • see ad in Fort Lauderdale section • www.venuscharters.com

Gay/Lesbian

Alyson Adventures, Inc 305/296–9935, 800/825–9766 923 White St, Key West, FL 33040 • award-winning adventure travel & active vacations • hiking, biking & multi-sport activities • www.AlysonAdventures.com

Journeyweavers 607/277–1416 313 Washington St, Ithaca, NY 14850 • group & individual outdoor adventure & birding trips in Costa Rica & beyond • www.journeyweavers.com

Out in Alaska 877/374–9958 PO Box 82096, Fairbanks, AK 99708 • adventure travel throughout Alaska for LGBT travelers • your best bet for a fun & authentic Alaska vacation! • www.outinalaska.com

OutWest Global Adventures 406/446–1533, 800/743–0458 PO Box 2050, Red Lodge, MT 59068 • specializing in gay/ lesbian active & adventure travel • worldwide • www.outwestadventures.com

South American Journeys, LLC 51–84/22–3865 Tujunga, CA 91042 • yoga, writing workshops, hiking, camping, out-reach programs & more in Peru & South America • women-only & men-only trips available • www.southamericanjourneys.com

Undersea Expeditions 858/270–2900, 800/669–0310 PO Box 9455, Pacific Beach, CA 92169 • gay & lesbian scuba adventures worldwide • www.UnderseaX.com

Gay/Straight

Atlantis Yacht Charters 415/332–0800 Schoonmaker Pt Marina, 85 Liberty Ship Way #110-A, Sausalito, CA 94965 • group charters • www.yachtcharter.com

Come 2 Africa 27 72/394–7625 75 Impala St, Hazyview 1242, South Africa • custom tours, including Kruger Nat'l Park • www.come2africa.com

GoNorth Alaska Adventure Travel Center 907/479–7272, 866/236–7272 3500 Davis Rd, Fairbanks, AK 99709 • guided tours throughout Alaska & the Arctic • air taxis & transportation • camper, canoe & bike rentals • hostel accommodations • RV & SUV rental • www.GoNorth-Alaska.com

Himalayan High Treks 415/551–1005, 800/455–8735 241 Dolores St, San Francisco, CA 94103 • experience indigenous Buddhist & Hindu cultures • www.hightreks.com

Natural Habitat Adventures 303/449–3711, 800/543–8917 PO Box 3065, Boulder, CO 80307 • up-close encounters w/ the world's most amazing wildlife in its natural habitat • www.nathab.com

Open Eye Tours 808/572–3483, 808/280–5299 (CELL) PO Box 324, Makawao, HI 96768 • customized private land tours of Maui & other islands • visit popular spots or places seldom seen, walking or not • sharing Maui's best-kept secrets since 1983 • www.openeyetours.com

Pacific Yachting & Sailing 831/423–7245, 800/374–2626 790 Mariner Park Way, Santa Cruz, CA 95062 • international & local yachting vacations for gays, lesbians & mixed groups • also sailing instruction • www.pacificsail.com

Paddling South & Saddling South 707/942–4550, 800/398–6200 PO Box 827, Calistoga, CA 94515 • horseback, mountain-biking & sea-kayak trips in Baja • also women-only trips • call for complete calendar • www.tourbaja.com

Puffin Fishing Charters 907/224–4653, 800/978–3346 PO Box 606, Seward, AK 99664 • guided charter fishing • almost 30 years of experience • halibut, salmon & rockfish on vessels custom-built for Alaskan waters • www.puffincharters.com

Voyageur North Outfitters 218/365–3251, 800/848–5530 1829 E Sheridan, Ely, MN 55731 • canoe outfitting & trips • www.vnorth.com

Whitewater Connection 530/622–6446, 800/336–7238 PO Box 270, Coloma, CA 95613 • whitewater rafting adventures • www.whitewaterconnection.com

SPIRITUAL/HEALTH VACATIONS

Women Only

Phoenix Adventures in Wellness 610/966–9668 4840 Beck Rd, Emmaus, PA 18049 • adventures w/ like-minded women, creating connections w/ self, others & the Universe • gay-friendly • www.phoenixadventure.com

Sounds & Furies 604/253–7189 PO Box 21510, 1424 Commercial Dr, Vancouver, BC V5L 5G2, Canada • economical goddess tours for women • concerts featuring lesbian performers • www.soundsandfuries.com

Gay/Lesbian

Spirit Journeys 201/483–3111, 800/754–1875 134 River Rd, New Milford, NJ 97646 • spiritual retreats, workshops & adventure trips throughout the US & abroad • www.spiritjouneys.com

THEMATIC TOURS

Women Only

Canyon Calling 928/282–0916 200 Carol Canyon Dr, Sedona, AZ 86336 • worldwide multi-activity adventure trips for moderately fit women, including the premiere trip to New Zealand w/ Kiwi company founder • www.canyoncalling.com

Driftwood Dreamers 64–7/315–6627 93 Armstrong Rd, Opotiki, Bay of Plenty 3198, New Zealand • women's adventures in New Zealand • rugged landscapes, gorgeous beaches, fascinating Maori culture • www.driftwooddreamers.com

Ela Brasil Tours 203/840–9010 14 Burlington Dr, Norwalk, CT 06851 • custom trips to Brazil • promoting responsible travel & cultural diversity • EcoVolunteer programs • www.elabrasil.com

International Women's Studies Institute 650/654–6346 PO Box 1067, Palo Alto, CA 94300 • travel-study programs • cross-cultural • school credit available • www.iwsi.org

Mouriscastours 351/963–857–776 Faro, Portugal • private tours in Portugal • www.mouriscastours.com

Robin Tyler International Tours for Women 818/893–4075 15842 Chase St, North Hills, CA 91343 • upscale int'l five-star lesbian travel founded in 1990 • exotic locations include tours &private cruises in Egypt, Africa, the Amazon, the Galapagos, Machu Picchu, Greece, Turkey, Asia & beyond • *www.robintylertours.com*

Sights and Soul Travels 240/350–5643, 866/737–9602 13610 Chrisbar Ct, Germantown, MD 20874 • small group, upscale, women-only trips to Greece, England, Italy, France, Spain, the Amazon, South Africa & other top destinations • *www.sightsandsoul.com*

Tours of Exploration 604/886–7300, 800/690–7887 PO Box 1503, Gibsons, BC V0N 1V0, Canada • eco-cultural journeys to Ecuador & Bolivia for women • *www.toursexplore.com*

Towanda Women Motorcycle Tours 64–3/314–9097 PO Box 4437, Christchurch, New Zealand • motorcycle tours for women by women in Alaska, Europe, New Zealand & Australia • ride the best motorcycling roads in the world w/ like-minded women • *www.towanda.org*

Women's Motorcyclist Foundation 585/768–6054 7 Lent Ave, LeRoy, NY 14482 • works to improve the sport of motorcycling • also raises money for breast cancer • *www.womensmotorcyclistfoundation.org*

Mostly Women

French Escapade 510/483–5713, 866/483–5713 discover France, Belgium & more in small groups • themes include cooking, painting, wellness, writing & more • some women-only trips • lesbian owned/run • *www.frenchescapade.com*

Gay/Lesbian

Africa Outing 27–21/671–4028 3 Alcyone Rd, Claremont, Capetown 7708, South Africa • gay/lesbian safaris & more • tours customized to your needs • *www.afouting.com*

Brazil Fiesta Tours & Visa Service 415/986–1134, 800/200–0582 268 Bush St #3531, San Francisco, CA 94104 • tours to Brazil • Brazilian visa service • *www.brazilianvisas.com*

CM by Carlos Melia 347/944–0026 (US#), 54 9 11/5760–6959 (Argentina #) New York City • boutique gay travel to Argentina, Uruguay & New York City • all services tested by me • "Been There Done That" • *www.carlosmelia.com*

Gay Bali Tours 62–361/722 483 Griya Anyar 76A, Br. Kajeng-Suwung, 80361 Bali, Indonesia • professional tour operator for GLBT & their friends • travel to Bali & beyond • *www.bali-gay.net*

Gay Travel Brasil 55–21/3415–3126 Rua Sergipe 57 C 201, 20271- 310 Rio de Janeiro, Brazil • gay & lesbian travel in Brazil & South America • *www.gaytravelbrasil.com*

Go Pink China 86/1366–124–6689 Beijing, China • adding queer elements to city tours & national trips in China • *www.gopinkchina.com*

Going Your Way Tours 860/447–9180 123 Ledgewood Rd #509, Groton, CT 06340 • upscale customized group & individual itineraries worldwide • *www.goingyourwaytours.com*

Kuyay Travel 56–65/438–990 Puerto Rosales 46, 5550000 Puerto Varas, Los Lagos, Chile • gay-owned/run travel planner & tour host in Patagonia • *www.gaypatagonia.com*

MexGay Vacations 213/383–9491, 866/639–4299 333 S Grand Ave, Floor 25, Los Angeles, CA 90071 • specializing in gay travel to Mexico • *www.mexgay.com*

National Gay Pilots Association 214/336–0873 PO Box 7271, Dallas, TX 75209 • several annual gatherings • call for more info • *www.ngpa.org*

Pacific Ocean Holidays 808/545–5252, 800/735–6600 Honolulu, HI • Hawaii vacation packages • *www.gayhawaiivacations.com*

Planetdwellers 61–2/9294–5656 Shop 47 Elizabeth Bay Rd, Elizabeth Bay, NSW 2011, Australia • LGBT tours of Australia • come to OZ! • *www.planetdwellers.com.au*

Venture Out 415/626–5678, 888/431–6789 575 Pierce St #604, San Francisco, CA 94117 • high-end escorted tours for gay & lesbian travelers to countries around the world • *www.venture-out.com*

Winelovertours.com 860/861–2301 123 Ledgewood Rd #509, Groton, CT 06340 • upscale group tours & individual itineraries for foodies & winelovers • *www.winelovertours.com*

Gay/Straight

Alaska Railroad 907/265–2494, 800/544–0552 (RESERVATIONS) 431 W 1st Ave, Anchorage, AK 99501 • rail & tour packages • *www.alaskarailroad.com*

Asian Pacific Adventures 818/881–2745, 800/825–1680 18900 Hatteras St, Tarzana, CA 91356 • custom tours to Asia, including India, Thailand, China, Tibet, Vietnam, Japan & more • festivals, tribes, safaris & art • hiking & biking • *www.asianpacificadventures.com*

Brazil Ecojourneys 55–48/3389–5619 Estrada Rozalia Paulina Ferreira 1132, 88063-555 Armação, Florianopolis, SC, Brazil • incoming tour operator • South Brazil specialists • *www.brazilecojourneys.com*

Ecotour Expeditions, Inc 401/423–3377, 800/688–1822 PO Box 128, Jamestown, RI 02835 • small group boat tours of the Amazon & more • call for color catalog • *www.naturetours.com*

Heritage Tours Private Travel 212/206–8400, 800/378–4555 121 W 27th St #1201, New York, NY 10001 • custom private trips to Morocco, Spain, Portugal, Turkey & Southern Africa • *www.HTprivatetravel.com*

Holbrook Travel 352/377–7111, 800/451–7111 3540 NW 13th St, Gainesville, FL 32609 • natural history tours in Central America, South America & Africa • small groups • *www.holbrooktravel.com*

Inside/ Out 303/517–3400 humanitourism adventures • custom trips for 6 or more • *www.theinsideandout.com*

Lima Tours 51-1/619–6900 Jr De la Union 1040, Lima, Peru • personalized, gay-friendly tours to Peru • *www.limatours.com.pe*

New England Vacation Tours 802/464–2076, 800/742–7669 PO Box 560, West Dover, VT 05356 • gay/ lesbian tours (including fall foliage) conducted by a mainstream tour operator • www.newenglandvacationtours.com

Pacha Tours 800/722–4288 295 Madison Ave, 43rd flr, New York City, NY 10017 • trips to Turkey & Greece • www.pachatours.com

Shop Around Tours 212/684–3763 305 E 24th St #2-N, New York City, NY 10010 • for people who live to shop & love to travel • www.shoparoundtours.com

Wild Rainbow African Safaris 707/467–9676 308 Jones St, Ukiah, CA 95482 • unique excursions to Tanzania, South Africa, Zambia, Botswana & more • www.wildrainbowsafaris.com

CUSTOM TOURS

Costa Rica Experts 773/935–1009, 800/827–9046 3166 N Lincoln Ave #424, Chicago, IL 60657 • www.costaricaexperts.com

Travel & Culture 92-321/242–4778 702 Panorama Center Office Plaza, 75530 Karachi, Pakistan • tours, safaris & hotel reservations in Pakistan • www.travel-culture.com

VARIOUS TOURS

Women Only

See Jayne Play 813/263–4003 7321 Canal Blvd, Tampa, FL 33615 • European & Caribbean tours for women • lesbian-owned • www.seejayneplay.com

Thanks Babs, the Day Tripper 702/370–6961 Las Vegas, NV • outdoor tours, shows & attractions • Grand Canyon getaways • full service concierge for Las Vegas, state of NV, and the Southwest • it's like having a lesbian aunt in Las Vegas! • www.thanksbabs.com

Gay/Lesbian

Footprints 416/962–8111, 888/962–6211 19 Madison Ave #300, Toronto, ON M5R 2S2, Canada • custom-designed, private tours arranged to worldwide destinations • www.footprintstravel.com

Friends of Dorothy Travel® 415/864–1600, 800/640–4918 1177 California St #B, San Francisco, CA 94108 • unique gay & lesbian adventures • individual & group arrangements • www.fodtravel.com

Out & About Travel 800/842–4753 161 Federal St, Providence, RI 02903 • full-service travel agency specializing in gay & lesbian tours, cruises, adventure travel, ski trips, honeymoons, customized packages & more • serving the GLBT community since 1999! • www.gaytravelpros.com

Postcard Destinations 814/539–4999, 800/484–3250 x2621 188 Crystal St, Johnstown, PA 15906 • purveyors of gay travel worldwide since 1985 • tours, cruises, groups, customized trips, air, hotel • Italy/Germany/Spain specialists • gay-owned • www.postcarddestinations.com

Zoom Vacations 773/772–9666, 866/966–6822 2338 N Monticello Ave, Chicago, IL 60647 • takes gay group travel to the next level • experience the best of a destination w/ surprises, insider events & a sense of magic • www.zoomvacations.com

Events

January 2011

ongoing throughout the year: **Tranny Roadshow**   *TBA, USA*
on-going, touring, performance art extravaganza • check website for shows near you
☎617/666–1782 ✉ 56A Flint St, Somerville, MA 02145 Email:
trannyroadshow@yahoo.com Web: www.trannyroadshow.com

5-9: **Utah Gay & Lesbian Ski Week**   *Salt Lake City, UT*
ski at Alta, Snowbird, Solitude, Brighton, Snow Basin & The Canyons ☎877/429–6368
Email: wehojohn@aol.com Web: www.gayskiing.org

16-23: **Aspen Gay Ski Week**   *Aspen, CO*
LGBT • 3000+ attendees ☎970/925–4123, 866/564–8398 ✉ c/o Roaring Fork Gay &
Lesbian Community Fund, PO Box 3143, Aspen, CO 81612 Email: info@gayskiweek.com
Web: www.gayskiweek.com

16-Feb 6: **Midsumma Festival**   *Melbourne, Australia*
arts, culture & community • LGBT ☎61–3/9415–9819 ✉ Room C1.17 The Convent
1 St Heliers St, Abbotsford, VIC, Australia 3067 Email: admin@midsumma.org.au Web:
www.midsumma.org.au

19-23: **Winter Rendezvous**   *Stowe, VT*
annual week of gay skiing, winter sports & entertainment ☎587/445–7198 ✉ c/o
www.MJWAdventures.com, 50 Victory Rd, Boston, MA 02122 Email: info@winterren-
dezvous.com Web: www.winterrendezvous.com

30-Feb 6: **WinterPRIDE: Whistler Gay Ski Week**   *Whistler, BC, Canada*
annual gay/ lesbian ski week • parties for boys & girls! • top-notch DJs & venues • popular destination 75 miles N of Vancouver • LGBT • 3000+ attendees ☎604/288–7218,
866/787–1966 ✉ c/o GayWhistler, 1025, 106-4368 Main St, Whistler, BC, Canada V0N
1B4 Email: dean@gaywhistler.com Web: www.gaywhistler.com

March 2011

5: **Chicago Takes Off**   *Chicago, IL*
burlesque show to fight HIV/AIDS in the Chicagoland area • LGBT • 1400 attendees
☎773/989–9400 ✉ c/o TPAN, 5537 N Broadway, Chicago, IL 60640 Email:
r.lindsay@tpan.com Web: www.chicagotakesoff.org

8: **Mardi Gras**   *New Orleans, LA*
mixed gay/ straight ☎800/672–6124 ✉ c/o New Orleans Convention & Visitors
Bureau, 2020 St Charles, New Orleans, LA 70130 Web: www.neworleanscvb.com

9-14: **Winter Party for Women**   *Miami/ South Beach, FL*
mostly women ☎305/495–6969 (tickets) ✉ c/o Pandora Events, 1070 NE 83rd St,
Miami, FL 33138 Email: yesi@pandoraevents.com Web: www.pandoraevents.com

28-April 3: **Kraft Nabisco Golf Championship**   *Palm Springs, CA*
previously known as the Dinah Shore Golf Championship • mostly women
☎760/324–4546 Web: www.nabiscochampionship.com

29-April 3: **OutBoard**   *Breckenridge, CO*
annual lesbian/ gay snowboarding festival • 300+ attendees ☎877/38–BOARD ✉ 3724
Walnut St, Denver, CO 80205 Email: events@outboard.org Web: www.outboard.org

TBA: **Tempted To Touch**   *Las Vegas, NV*
weekend party in Vegas • hot DJs • day & night events • tour Las Vegas • multiracial
crowd • LGBT ☎678/362–6487 Web: www.tempted2touch4u.com

April 2011

3: **AIDS Walk Miami**   *Miami, FL*
5K walk-a-thon fundraiser benefiting Care Resource • LGBT ☎305/751–9255 ✉ c/o
CARE Resource, 3510 Biscayne Blvd #300, Miami, FL 33137 Email:
SBeko@careresource.org Web: www.aidswalkmiami.com

16: **Boybutante Ball** *Athens, GA*
LGBT • 1000+ attendees ☎706/227–3530 ✉ c/o Boybutante AIDS Foundation, Inc, PO Box 6013, Athens, GA 30604–6013 EMAIL: missthing@boybutante.org WEB: www.boybutante.org

24-May 1: **Philadelphia Black Gay Pride** *Philadelphia, PA*
a weekend of social & cultural activities • films, BBQ, spoken word, parties & more • LGBT ☎877/497–7247 ✉ c/o Philadelphia Black Pride, Inc, PO Box 40926, Philadelphia, PA 19107 EMAIL: phillyblackpride@gmail.com WEB: www.phillyblackpride.org

25-May 1: **Equality Forum** *Philadelphia, PA*
largest nat'l & int'l LGBT civil rights forum w/ panels, parties & special events ☎215/732–3378 x116 ✉ 1420 Locust St #300, Philadelphia, PA 19102 EMAIL: info@equalityforum.com WEB: www.equalityforum.com

30: **Queensday** *Amsterdam, Netherlands*
huge street festival to celebrate what was originally the birthday of the Queen Mother • LGBT WEB: www.queensdayamsterdam.eu

May 2011

2-15: **Int'l Dublin Gay Theatre Festival** *Dublin, Ireland*
☎353–87/657–3732 ✉ 179 S Circular Rd, Dublin, Ireland 8 EMAIL: info@gaytheatre.ie WEB: www.gaytheatre.ie

11-15: **Aqua Girl** *Miami Beach, FL*
a weekend of hot women's parties in Miami • mostly women ☎305/576–AQUA ✉ c/o Aqua Foundation for Women, 4500 Biscayne Blvd #340, Miami Beach, FL 33137 EMAIL: alisonburgos@mac.com WEB: www.aquagirl.org

13-15: **Gaylaxicon** *Atlanta, GA*
LGBT science fiction, fantasy, horror & gaming convention WEB: www.gaylacticnetwork.org

15: **Minnesota AIDS Walk** *Minneapolis, MN*
enjoy a 10K walk from Minnehaha Park & raise money for MN AIDS Project • mixed gay/ straight • 10,000 attendees ☎612/341–2060 ✉ c/o Minnesota AIDS Project, 1400 Park Ave S, Minneapolis, MN 55404 EMAIL: events@mnaidsproject.org WEB: www.mnaidsproject.org

25-30: **Annual Gay Bowling Tournament** *Toronto, ON, Canada*
check site for local tournaments throughout the year ✉ c/o IGBO, PO Box 30722, Charlotte, NC 28230 EMAIL: president@igbo.org WEB: www.igbo.org

26-30: **Mondo Homo Dirty South** *Atlanta, GA*
queer-centric festival featuring music, dance, crafts, performance & more ☎404/243–3476 ✉ 251 Tye St SE, Atlanta, GA 30316 EMAIL: homosouth@yahoo.com WEB: www.mondohomo.com

26-30: **Pensacola Memorial Day Weekend** *Pensacola, FL*
many parties on beaches & in bars • LGBT • 35,000+ attendees ☎850/438–0333 EMAIL: info@memorialweekendpensacola.com WEB: www.memorialweekendpensacola.com

27-June 12: **Spoleto Festival USA** *Charleston, SC*
one of the continent's premier avant-garde cultural arts festivals • 140+ performances of dance, theater & music from around the world • mixed gay/ straight ☎843/579–3100 ✉ c/o Spoleto Festival USA, PO Box 157, Charleston, SC 29402–0157 EMAIL: info@spoletousa.org WEB: www.spoletousa.org

31-June 6: **Gay Days Orlando** *Orlando, FL*
including Gay Day at Disney • 7 days of parties & fun for boys & girls alike! • LGBT ☎407/896-8431 ✉ c/o GayDays, Inc, PO Box 796, Gotha, FL 34734 EMAIL: chris@gaydays.com WEB: www.gaydays.com

TBA: **AIDS Walk New York** *New York City, NY*
AIDS benefit • mixed gay/ straight ☎212/807–9255 ✉ c/o Gay Men's Health Crisis, PO Box 10, Old Chelsea Stn, New York, NY 10113–0010 EMAIL: awnyinfo@aidswalk.net WEB: www.aidswalk.net

TBA: **DC Black Pride** *Washington, DC*
LGBT ✉ PO Box 77071, Washington, DC 20013 EMAIL: info@dcblackpride.org WEB:
www.dcblackpride.org

TBA: **Int'l Association of Country Western Dance Clubs Annual Convention** *TBA, USA*
also semi-annual conventions in March (Fort Lauderdale, FL) & October (San Francisco,
CA) • LGBT • 400-600 attendees ✉ c/o IAGLCWDC, 5534 Edmondson Pike, PMB 107,
Nashville, TN 37211 EMAIL: information@iaglcwdc.org WEB: www.outcountrydance.com

TBA: **Queer Up North** *Manchester, England*
queer culture & arts festival in Manchester, England ☎161/234–2942 ✉ Greenfish
Resource Centre
46-50 Oldham St, Manchester, England M4 1LE EMAIL: contact@queerupnorth.com WEB:
www.queerupnorth.com

TBA: **Splash: Houston Black Gay Pride** *Houston, TX*
LGBT ☎832/443–1016 ✉ c/o Houston Splash, PO Box 667248, Houston, TX 77266
WEB: www.houstonsplash.com

TBA: **We're Funny That Way** *Toronto, ON, Canada*
comedians from around the world perform at Canada's International Gay/Lesbian
Comedy Festival • LGBT ☎416/975–8555 ✉ c/o WFTW Productions, 2060 Queen St E
#45, Toronto, ON, Canada M4E 1C9 WEB: www.werefunnythatway.com

June 2011

ongoing: **LGBT Pride** *Cross-country, USA*
celebrate yourself & attend one – or many – of the hundreds of Gay Pride parades & fes-
tivities happening in cities around the world EMAIL: info@interpride.org WEB: www.inter-
pride.org

ongoing: **Music in the Mountains** *Grass Valley, CA*
summer music festival • mixed gay/ straight ☎530/265–6173 ✉ c/o Music in the
Mountains, 530 Searls Ave #A, Nevada City, CA 95959 WEB: www.musicinthemountains.org

ongoing: **National Queer Arts Festival** *San Francisco, CA*
performances & exhibitions in the San Francisco Bay Area highlighting artists from
around the country • LGBT ☎415/251–9935 ✉ c/o Queer Cultural Center, 934
Brannan St, San Francisco, CA 94103 EMAIL: director@QueerCulturalCenter.org WEB:
www.QueerCulturalCenter.org

1-5: **Girls in Wonderland** *Orlando, FL*
official women's parties of Gay Days Orlando • 4 days of fun! • tickets available thru
www.girlsinwonderland.com • mostly women ☎305/495–6969 (TICKETS) ✉ c/o
Pandora Events & Alison Burgos, 1213 NE 12th Ave, Fort Lauderdale, FL 33304 EMAIL:
yesi@pandoraevents.com WEB: www.girlsinwonderland.com

5-11: **AIDS LifeCycle** *San Francisco to Los Angeles, CA*
bike from San Francisco to Los Angeles to raise money for HIV/AIDS services
☎415/581–7077 ✉ c/o LA Gay/Lesbian Center & SF AIDS Foundation, 995 Market St
#200, San Francisco, CA 94103 EMAIL: info@aidslifecycle.org WEB: www.aidslifecycle.org

5: **AIDS Walk Boston & 5K Run** *Boston, MA*
mixed gay/ straight • 12,000 attendees ☎617/424–9255 ✉ c/o AIDS Action
Committee, 75 Amory St, Boston, MA 02119 EMAIL: walkinfo@aac.org WEB: www.aidswalk-
boston.org

10-12: **PrideFest** *Milwaukee, WI*
celebrate LGBT pride at Henry W Maier Festival Park ☎414/272–3378 ✉ c/o PrideFest,
PO Box 511763, Milwaukee, WI 53203–0301 WEB: www.pridefest.com

19: **Unofficial Gay Day at Cedar Point** *Sandusky, OH*
wear red to show your support on the unofficial Gay Day at this popular amusement
park • mixed gay/ straight WEB: www.cpgaydays.com

3-26: **Black Pride** *Columbia, SC*
☎803/799–9190 ✉ c/o SC Black Pride, PO Box 8191, Columbia, NC 29202 EMAIL:
info@southcarolinablackpride.org WEB: www.southcarolinablackpride.com

25-26: San Francisco LGBT Pride Parade/ Celebration *San Francisco, CA*
LGBT ☎415/864-0831 ✉ c/o SFLGBTPCC, 1800 Market St PMB 5, San Francisco, CA 94102 EMAIL: info@sfpride.org WEB: www.sfpride.org

TBA: **Black Gay Pride** *Memphis, TN*
LGBT ☎901/522-8459 WEB: www.brothersunited.com

TBA: **Black Gay Pride Boston** *Boston, MA*
celebrate Black pride in Boston EMAIL: info@bostonspyce.com WEB: www.bostonspyce.com

TBA: **Idapalooza Fruit Jam** *Dowelltown, TN*
queer music festival in backwoods TN • camping • vegetarian feasts ☎615/597-4409 ✉ 904 Vickers Hollow Rd, Dowelltown, TN 37059 EMAIL: idapalooza@gmail.com WEB: www.planetida.com

TBA: **Juneteenth Jamboree of New Plays** *New York City, NY*
annual theater festival • new works about the African American experience & its legacy • mixed gay/ straight ☎212/964-1904 ✉ c/o Juneteenth Legacy Theatre, 605 Water St, New York City, NY 10002 EMAIL: juneteenthlegacy@aol.com WEB: www.juneteenthlegacytheatre.com

TBA: **PDX Black Pride** *Portland, OR*
films, workshops, parties & more • LGBT EMAIL: staff@pridenw.org WEB: pridenw.org

TBA: **Windy City Black Pride** *Chicago, IL*
a weekend of parties, seminars & more • LGBT ☎888/922-7244 ✉ PO Box 803425, Chicago, IL 60680 WEB: www.windycityblackpride.org

July 2011

1-4: Int'l Gay Square Dance Clubs Convention *Atlanta, GA*
☎303/722-5276 ✉ c/o IAGSDC, PO BOX 9176, Denver, CO 80209 WEB: www.iagsdc.org

1-5: At the Beach/ LA Black Pride Weekend *Los Angeles, CA*
celebrate a weekend of Black gay pride across Los Angeles • LGBT ☎323/285-4225 ✉ c/o At The Beach Shorey, Inc, 6005 Ladera Ave, Los Angeles, CA 90056 EMAIL: atbla@atbla.com WEB: www.atbla.com

9-10: Ride for AIDS Chicago *Chicago, IL*
2-day bike ride to fight HIV/ AIDS in the Chicagoland area • LGBT • 200 attendees ☎773/989-9400 ✉ c/o TPAN, 5537 N Broadway, Chicago, IL 60640 EMAIL: r.lindsay@tpan.com WEB: www.rideforaids.com

17: AIDS Walk San Francisco *San Francisco, CA*
mixed gay/ straight • 27,000+ attendees ☎415/615-9255 ✉ c/o Miller Zeichik & Assoc PO Box 193920, San Francisco, CA 94119–3920 EMAIL: sfinfo@aidswalk.net WEB: www.aidswalk.net

25-31: North American Outgames *Vancouver, BC, Canada*
sports & cultural events • human rights conference • all leading up to Vancouver's pride parade on Sunday • LGBT ☎604/681-2153 EMAIL: outgames-registration@icsevents.com WEB: www.vancouver2011outgames.com

31: Crape Myrtle Festival *Raleigh-Durham, Chapel Hill, NC*
weeklong festival to raise money for AIDS & LGBT concerns • gala Saturday • also supporting events throughout the year • mixed gay/ straight • 500+ attendees ☎919/616-0615 ✉ c/o Crape Myrtle Festival, Inc, PO Box 12201, Raleigh, NC 27605 EMAIL: info@crapemyrtlefest.org WEB: www.crapemyrtlefest.org

TBA: **Blackout LGBTQ Pride** *Oakland, CA*
celebrate w/ a weekend of conferences, awards ceremonies & parties ☎510/621-3553 EMAIL: Tammymtaylor@yahoo.com WEB: www.oaklandblackout.com

TBA: **Charlotte Black Gay Pride** *Charlotte, NC*
art & performances, community forums, dance parties & more ☎704/953-8813

TBA: **EuroPride 2011** *Rome, Italy*
parties, politics, performance & more • there is something for everyone at this massive celebration of gay pride ✉ c/o European Pride Organisers Assoc, Buelowstrasse 106, Berlin, Germany D-10783 WEB: www.europride.info

SAN FRANCISCO
PRIDE

Celebration & Parade
June 25-26 2011

sfpride.org

TBA: **Hotter Than July Weekend**   *Detroit, MI*
the Midwest's oldest black same-gender-loving pride celebration • LGBT
☎888/755–9165 ✉ c/o Black Pride Society, PO Box 7378, Detroit, MI 48207 WEB: black-pridesociety.org

TBA: **IGLFA World Championship**   *Cologne, Germany*
Int'l Gay & Lesbian Football Association's annual soccer tournament EMAIL:
info@iglfa.org WEB: www.iglfa.org

TBA: **Tampa Black Pride**   *Tampa, FL*
celebrate African American gay pride in sunny Tampa • LGBT ☎813/775–5444 WEB:
www.tampablackpride.com

TBA: **Triangle Black Pride**   *Raleigh-Durham, Chapel Hill,*
celebrate & honor the diversity of the African American LGBTQ community in the
Triangle EMAIL: info@TriangleBlackPride.org WEB: triangleblackpride.org

August 2011

3-7: **Rendezvous 2011**   *Medicine Bow Nat'l Forest, WY*
5-day camping festival to celebrate LGBT pride • 400+ attendees ☎307/778–7645 ✉
c/o Wyoming Equality, PO Box 2531, Cheyenne, WY 82003 EMAIL:
info@wyomingequality.org WEB: www.wyomingequality.org

5-29: **Edinburgh Fringe Festival**   *Edinburgh, Scotland*
the largest arts festival in the world • dance, theater, music, comedy, events & more •
mixed gay/ straight ☎44-131/226–0026 ✉ 180 High St, Edinburgh, Scotland EH1 1QS
EMAIL: admin@edfringe.com WEB: www.edfringe.com

6-8: **Black Pride NYC**   *New York City, NY*
multicultural LGBT festival w/ a wide array of entertainment, forums, workshops &
events • LGBT EMAIL: soulja-promo@comcast.net WEB: www.nycblackpride.com

12-14: **Fire Island Black Out (FIBO)**   *Fire Island, NY*
3-day beach event for the LGBT community of color & friends • all are invited to attend
& enjoy, regardless of race, gender or orientation • LGBT ☎215/751–0808 ✉ c/o FIBO,
LLC, 2201 Race St, 2nd flr, Philadelphia, PA 19103 EMAIL: info@fireislandblackout.com
WEB: www.fireislandblackout.com

21-28: **"Camp" Camp**   *Porter, ME*
summer camp for LGBT adults • sports, pottery, theater, yoga & more • LGBT
☎888/924–8380 ✉ c/o Camp Camp, 545 Prospect Pl #2J, Brooklyn, NY 11238 EMAIL:
info@campcamp.com WEB: www.campcamp.com

31-Sept 5: **Atlanta Black Pride Weekend**   *Atlanta, GA*
celebrate Black Pride over Labor Day weekend in Atlanta • LGBT ☎678/799–8526 ✉
c/o In The Life Atlanta, 346 Auburn Ave NE, Atlanta, GA 30312 EMAIL:
c/o inthelifeatl.com WEB: www.inthelifeatl.com

TBA: **Gay Ski Week NZ**   *Queenstown, New Zealand*
☎64 21/83–4640 EMAIL: info@livewiregroup.co.nz WEB: www.gayskiweeknz.com

TBA: **Homo A Go Go**   *San Francisco, CA*
queer music, film, art, performance & activism festival • LGBT ☎415/347-5802 EMAIL:
info@homoagogo.com WEB: www.homoagogo.com

TBA: **Minnesota AIDS Trek**   *Twin Cities, MN*
annual 175-mile bike ride to fight AIDS • mixed gay/ straight ☎763/522–8067 ✉ 3017
York Ave N, Robbinsdale, MN 55422 EMAIL: admin@aids-trek.org WEB: www.aids-trek.org

TBA: **National Gay Softball World Series**   *TBA, US*
LGBT ☎412/362–1247 ✉ c/o NAGAAA, 1014 King Ave, Pittsburgh, PA 15206 WEB:
www.gaysoftballworldseries.com

TBA: **Northalsted Market Days**   *Chicago, IL*
a good ol' summer block party on Main St of Boys' Town, USA • LGBT ☎773/883–0500
✉ 3656 N Halsted St, Chicago, IL 61613 WEB: www.northalsted.com

TBA: **St Louis Black Pride**   *St Louis, MO*
✉ PO Box 4854, St Louis, MO 63108 EMAIL: info@st-louisblackpride.org WEB: www.st-louisblackpride.org

TBA: **UK Black Pride** *London, England*
☎44 020/8257 5358 ✉ PO Box 48500, London, England SE15 3LY WEB: www.ukblack-pride.org.uk

September 2011

18: **Out in the Park** *Springfield, MA*
unofficial gay day at Six Flags New England • wear red to show your support • LGBT • 1000+ attendees WEB: www.outinthepark.com

23: **Out On The Mountain** *Valencia, CA*
gay day at Six Flags Magic Mountain • LGBT EMAIL: outonthemountain@gmail.com WEB: www.outonthemountain.com

24-26: **Braking the Cycle** *Boston, MA to New York City, NY*
3-day AIDS charity fully-supported bike ride from Boston to New York • mixed gay/straight ☎212/989–1111 ✉ c/o Global Impact Productions, 127 W 26th St #402, New York City, NY 10001 EMAIL: sbratton@globalimpactpro.com WEB: www.brakingthecycle.org

30-Oct 2: **Gay Days Anaheim** *Anaheim, CA*
celebrate gay days at Disneyland • wear red to show your support EMAIL: gaydaysinfo@gaydaysanaheim.com WEB: www.GayDaysAnaheim.com

TBA: **AIDS Walk Colorado** *Denver, CO*
☎303/861–9255 ✉ c/o Colorado AIDS Project, 2490 W 26th Ave #A300, Denver, CO 80211 EMAIL: info@aidswalkcolorado.org WEB: www.aidswalkcolorado.org

TBA: **Black Gay Pride** *Dallas, TX*
LGBT ☎214/540–4494 ✉ 3100 Main St #208, Dallas, TX 75226 WEB: dfwpridemovement.org

TBA: **Howl Festival** *New York City, NY*
a cabaret from the underworld • outdoor murals • hip hop howl • all in Tompkins Square Park • mixed gay/ straight ☎212/243–3413 ✉ 335 E 10th St, New York City, NY 10011 EMAIL: info@howlnyc.org WEB: www.howlfestival.com

TBA: **Inferno Dominican Republic** *Punta Cana, Dominican Republic*
the premier Labor Day pride celebration • deluxe, all-inclusive accommodations • LGBT ☎305/891–7536 ✉ c/o Worldwide Travel Partners, 10800 Biscayne Blvd #201, Miami, FL 33161 EMAIL: info@infernodr.com WEB: www.infernodr.com

TBA: **Seattle AIDS Walk** *Seattle, WA*
mixed gay/ straight • 4000+ attendees ☎206/328–8979 ✉ c/o Lifelong AIDS Alliance, 1002 E Seneca, Seattle, WA 98122 EMAIL: events@llaa.org WEB: www.SeattleAIDSWalk.org

October 2011

ongoing: **October is Breast Cancer Awareness Month** *Cross-country, USA*
check local listings for fund-raising events in your area to fight breast cancer

2: **Castro Street Fair** *San Francisco, CA*
performance, arts & community groups street fair • co-founded by Harvey Milk ☎415/841–1824 ✉ PO Box 14405, San Francisco, CA 94114 EMAIL: info@castrostreetfair.org WEB: www.castrostreetfair.org

7-16: **Provincetown Women's Week** *Provincetown, MA*
very popular – make your reservations early! • also Single Women's Weekend in May • mostly women • 5000+ attendees ✉ c/o Women Innkeepers of Provincetown, PO Box 573, Provincetown, MA 02657 EMAIL: info@womeninnkeepers.com WEB: www.womeninnkeepers.com

11-16: **IAGLBC Annual Bridge Tournament** *Palm Springs, CA*
Int'l Association of Gay & Lesbian Bridge Clubs EMAIL: wehojohn@aol.com WEB: www.GayBridge.org

11: **National Coming Out Day** *Cross-country, USA*
check local listings for events in your area or visit www.hrc.com/ncop ☎202/628–4160, 800/777–4723 ✉ c/o Human Rights Campaign, 1640 Rhode Island Ave, Washington, DC 20036 EMAIL: hrc@hrc.org WEB: www.hrc.org/issues/coming_out.asp

13-16: **Sundance Stompede** *San Francisco, CA*
San Francisco's annual country/ western dance weekend • LGBT ☎415/820–1403 ✉ c/o Sundance Assoc, 2261 Market St PMB 225, San Francisco, CA 94114 EMAIL: info@stompede.com WEB: www.stompede.com

13-Nov 13: **Glasgay!** *Glasgow, Scotland*
UK's largest lesbian & gay multi-arts festival ☎44-141/552–7575 ✉ c/o Q Gallery & Studio, 87-91 Saltmarket, Glasgow, Scotland G1 5LE EMAIL: info@glasgay.co.uk WEB: www.glasgay.co.uk

16: **AIDS Walk Atlanta** *Atlanta, GA*
mixed gay/ straight • 10,000+ attendees ☎404/876–9255 ✉ PO Box 78187, Atlanta, GA 30357 EMAIL: walkinfo@aidatlanta.org WEB: aidswalkatlanta.com

16: **AIDS Walk LA** *Los Angeles, CA*
annual AIDS fundraiser in West Hollywood • mixed gay/ straight ☎213/201–9255 ✉ c/o MZA Events, Inc, 3550 Wilshire Blvd #890, Los Angeles, CA 90010 EMAIL: awlainfo@aidswalk.net WEB: www.aidswalk.net

TBA: **Black Pride** *Nashville, TN*
gay/ lesbian ☎615/974–2832, 800/845–4266x269 ✉ c/o Brothers United, PO Box 68335, Nashville, TN 37206 EMAIL: nashblackpride@aol.com WEB: www.brothersunited.org

TBA: **Get Wet Weekend** *Curaçao, Netherlands Antilles, Caribbean*
discover the Caribbean Dutch Paradise of Curaçao! • gay/ lesbian EMAIL: curacaogay-plasa@hotmail.com WEB: www.gaycuracao.com

TBA: **Int'l Drag King Extravaganza** *TBA, USA*
workshops, performances & more EMAIL: idkesteeringcommittee@yahoo.com WEB: www.idke.info

November 2011

5-6: **Greater Palm Springs Pride** *Palm Springs, CA*
free entertainment, dance parties, lots of people & a parade on Sunday ☎760/416–8711 ✉ 777 N Palm Canyon Dr #102, Palm Springs, CA 92262 EMAIL: info@PSPride.org WEB: www.PSPride.org

TBA: **Tranny Fest** *San Francisco, CA*
transgender multi-arts festival ✉ c/o Fresh Meat Productions, PO Box 460670, San Francisco, CA 94146 EMAIL: info@trannyfest.com WEB: www.trannyfest.com

December 2011

31: **Mummer's Strut** *Philadelphia, PA*
big New Year's Eve party • followed by New Year's Day Parade • mixed gay/ straight • $40-50 ☎215/336–3050 ✉ c/o Mummers Museum, 1100 S 2nd St, Philadelphia, PA 19147 EMAIL: parade@mummers.com WEB: www.mummers.com

TBA: **Holly Folly** *Provincetown, MA*
lesbian/ gay holiday celebration • fabulous parties • holiday concert • open houses • 1st wknd in December WEB: www.ptown.org

WOMEN'S FESTIVALS, PARTIES & GATHERINGS

January 2011

13-17: **Silver Threads Celebration** *St Petersburg Beach, FL*
4 day celebration for lesbians over 50 & their younger friends • women only ✉ PO Box 5081, Gulfport, FL 33737 EMAIL: silvertreds@aol.com WEB: www.silverthreadscelebration.com

TBA: **Girlfest** *Sunshine Coast, Queensland, Australia*
Australia's answer to Dinah Shore • pool parties, comedy, films, dancing, plus girls girls girls! • women only ☎61-07/3283–4933 ✉ PO Box 90, Woody Point, QLD, Australia 4019 EMAIL: enquiries@girlfest.org WEB: www.girlfest.org

March 2011

30-April 4: Girl Bar Dinah Shore Weekend   *Palm Springs, CA*
huge gathering of lesbians for mega dance parties, huge pool parties, comedy, national recording artists & yes, some golf watching • 5,000-8,000 attend • see website for ticket info • also www.girlbar.com • dinahshorevip@aol.com • women only ☎310/659–4551 Web: www.dinahshoreweekend.com

30-April 3: Club Skirts Dinah Shore Weekend   *Palm Springs, CA*
women only ☎415/596–8730 ✉ c/o Club Skirts, 2029 Paseo De Gracias, Palm Springs, CA 92262 Email: info@clubskirts.com Web: www.thedinah.com

April 2011

TBA: Women's Fun Weekend   *County Cork, Ireland*
entertainment, sports, dance parties & more! • women only Email: corkswomensfunweekend@gmail.com Web: www.corkwomensfunweekend.ie

May 2011

19-22: Lucy & Gail Dinah Does Vegas   *Las Vegas, NV*
the premiere vacation destination for lesbians of color, their partners & friends • women only ☎760/416–3545 ✉ c/o Chris Laben Co, 611 S Palm Canyon Dr #7-223, Palm Springs, CA 92264 Email: Lucyandgail@aol.com Web: www.dinahincolor.com

27-30: Women Outdoors National Gathering   *Hancock, NH*
camping • hiking • workshops • women only • 110+ attendees • $120-220 ✉ c/o Women Outdoors, Inc, PO Box 158, Northampton, MA 01061 Email: info@women-outdoors.org Web: www.women-outdoors.org

TBA: Herland Bi-Annual Retreats   *Oklahoma City, OK*
music, workshops, campfire events & potluck • girls of all ages & boys under 10 welcome • also in October • women only ☎405/521–9696 ✉ c/o Herland Sister Resources, 2312 NW 39th, Oklahoma City, OK 73112 Email: herland@herlandsisters.org Web: www.herlandsisters.org

TBA: Russian River Women's Wknd   *Guerneville, CA*
this village is packed w/ dykes for a weekend of pool parties, bumpin' night life, comedy, sports, outdoor activities & more • 75 miles north of San Francisco • mostly women ✉ c/o Tomcat Productions, PO Box 744, Guerneville, CA 95446 Email: rrwomensweekend@yahoo.com Web: www.russianriverwomensweekend.org

June 2011

22-26: Deaf Lesbian Festival   *Dublin, Ireland*
a celebration & global gathering of culturally identified deaf & lesbian women Email: deaflesbianfestival@gmail.com Web: www.deaflesbianfestival.org

25: San Francisco Dyke March   *San Francisco, CA*
join thousands of dykes of all shapes, colors & sizes for music, marching & more through the streets of the Mission & the Castro • women only ☎510/533–5489 Email: info@thedykemarch.org Web: www.thedykemarch.org

TBA: Southern Ontario Womyn's Drum Camp   *near Sarnia, ON and Port Huron, MI*
all levels welcome • on Lake Huron near Sarnia, ON & Port Huron, MI • Eastern Ontario Women's Drum Camp in Ottawa, also in June • women only • 120 attendees • $Can200-325 ☎613/599–4274 ✉ c/o JT Productions, 1090 Kipps Ln #116, London, ON, Canada N5Y 4S7 Email: info@drumcamps.ca Web: www.drumcamps.ca

July 2011

15-17: Fabulosa Fest   *Marin, CA*
women-centered music wknd • healing arts, film & crafts • mostly women Email: info@fabulosafest.com Web: www.fabulosafest.com

20-24: **Girl Splash** *Provincetown, MA*
4 days of comedy, music, dance parties & more • mostly women ✉ c/o Women Innkeepers of Provincetown, PO Box 573, Provincetown, MA 02657 Email: info@womeninnkeepers.com Web: www.womeninnkeepers.com

29-31: **OLOC (Old Lesbians Organizing for Change) Nat'l Gathering** *Tacoma, WA*
lesbians 60+ gather for workshops, guest speakers & entertainment to promote old lesbian pride & fight ageism • women only ☎888/706-7506 ✉ c/o OLOC, PO Box 5853, Athens, GA 45701 Email: info@oloc.org Web: www.oloc.org

TBA: **National Women's Music Festival** *Middleton, WI*
check website for details • mostly women ☎317/713-1144 ✉ c/o Women in the Arts, PO Box 1427, Indianapolis, IN 46206 Email: wia@wiaonline.org Web: www.wiaonline.org

August 2011

2-7: **Michigan Womyn's Music Festival** *near Hart, MI*
theater, music & dance performances • workshops, film festival & craft fair • ASL interpreting & differently-abled resources • child care • camping • women only • 5000-8000 attendees ☎231/757-4766 ✉ c/o WWTMC, PO Box 22, Walhalla, MI 49458 Web: www.michfest.com

TBA: **Women in the Woods** *Portland, OR*
rustic cabins • natural hot springs • all meals included • women only • 300-400 attendees ☎503/284-0722 ✉ c/o WIW, 7501 NE Glisan, Portland, OR 97213 Email: swat@womeninthewoods.com Web: www.womeninthewoods.com

TBA: **Womyn's Gathering** *Louisa, VA*
last wknd in Aug • camping, music & workshops • mixed gay/ straight • $40-140 ☎540/894-5126 ✉ c/o Twin Oaks Community, 138 Twin Oaks Rd, Luisa, VA 23093 Email: gathering@twinoaks.org Web: www.twinoaks.org/community/women

September 2011

2-5: **Festival of Babes** *TBA, USA*
fun, frivolous & flirtatious soccer tournament • Int'l Babes play hard & party harder • rotates btwn Vancouver, Seattle, Portland & San Francisco • women only Web: www.festivalofthebabes.com

6-11: **WomenFest** *Key West, FL*
live music • film festival • pool parties • comedy show • dance parties • golf tournament • women only ☎800/535-7797 ✉ c/o Key West Business Guild, 513 Truman Ave Key West, FL 33040 Email: moreinfo@womenfest.com Web: www.womenfest.com

9-11: **Ohio Lesbian Festival** *Kirkersville (E of Columbus), OH*
women only • 2000-3000 attendees ☎614/578-1764 ✉ c/o Ohio LBA, PO Box 82086, Columbus, OH 43202 Web: www.ohiolba.org

9-11: **Sisterspace Wknd** *Darlington, MD*
sliding scale • women only ☎215/546-4890 ✉ c/o Sisterspace of the Delaware Valley PO Box 22476, Philadelphia, PA 19110 Email: sweekend@sisterspace.org Web: www.sisterspace.org

15-18: **BOLD Fest** *Vancouver, BC, Canada*
Bold Old(er) Lesbians & Dykes meet up for the annual West Coast gathering ☎604/253-7189 ✉ c/o Sounds & Furies, PO Box 21510 1424 Commercial Dr, Vancouver, BC, Canada V5L 5G2 Email: soundsfuries@shaw.ca Web: www.soundsandfuries.com/BOLD.html

TBA: **Cambria Women's Weekend** *Cambria, CA*
where the forest meets the ocean and the women come OUT to play! ☎310/578-8888 ✉ c/o Women on a Roll, PO Box 5112, Santa Monica, CA 90409 Email: info@womenonaroll.com Web: www.cambriawomensweekend.com

TBA: **Iowa Women's Music Festival** *Iowa City, IA*
mostly women ☎319/335-1486 ✉ c/o Prairie Voices Productions, PO Box 3411, Iowa City, IA 52244 Email: festival@prairievoices.net Web: www.prairievoices.net

TBA: **Womynfest At Sea**   *sail from Miami, FL to the Caribbean*
womyn's festival on a cruise ship • music • comedy • workshops & more
☎813/404–5818 ✉ c/o Off Key Productions, LLC, 4532 W Kennedy Blvd #204, Tampa,
FL 33609 EMAIL: mele@mele.cc WEB: www.womynfestatsea.com

October 2011

TBA: **Decibelle**   *Chicago, IL*
workshops, panels, cinema & rockin' concerts featuring groundbreaking, fearless women
artists ☎303/946–9227 ✉ c/o Estrojam, 1125 Collyer St, Longmont, CO 80501 EMAIL:
info@decibelle.org WEB: www.decibelle.org

TBA: **Houston Women's Festival**   *Houston, TX*
women from Texas & beyond gather to enjoy music, art, culture & community • pro-
duced by the Athena Art Project • mostly women • 1,500 attendees ☎713/995–5251 ✉
c/o Athena Art Project, PO Box 70102, Houston, TX 77270 EMAIL: producer@hwfestival.org
WEB: www.hwfestival.org

TBA: **WomynSpirit Festival**   *Orangeville, ON, Canada*
celebrate Samhain at this queer-friendly womyn's pagan weekend • women only
☎416/481–7634 ✉ 107 Redpath Ave, Toronto, ON, Canada M4S 2J9 EMAIL: womynspir-
it.info@gmail.com WEB: sites.google.com/site/womynspirit/Home

TBA: **Wyld Womyn's Weekend**   *Maui, HI*
concerts • games • workshops • massage • gourmet food • dancing! • women only
☎808/264–4177 EMAIL: CindiCatering@hotmail.com WEB: www.womynswyldlife.com

November 2011

18-20: **Nia Gathering**   *Petaluma, CA*
lesbians of African descent gather to reflect on the past & build a postive future •
women only ☎510/306–6052 ✉ c/o NIA Collective, PO Box 10863, Oakland, CA 94610
EMAIL: nia@niacollective.org WEB: www.niacollective.org

24-27: **Women's White Party**   *Miami, FL*
mostly women ☎305/495–6969 **(TICKETS)** ✉ c/o Pandora Events, 1070 NE 83rd St,
Miami, FL 33138 EMAIL: yesi@pandoraevents.com WEB: www.womenswhiteparty.com

FILM FESTIVALS

January 2011

22-30: **Zinegoak**   *Bilbao, Spain*
LGBT film festival ☎34–94/415–6258 ✉ c/o HEGOAK, C/Dos de mayo 7, bajo, Bilbao,
Spain 48003 EMAIL: info@zinegoak.com WEB: www.zinegoak.com

28-Feb 5: **Reel Out Queer Film & Video Festival**   *Kingston, ON, Canada*
celebrating the best of queer independent film & video ☎613/549–7335 ✉ c/o Reelout
Arts Project Inc, 336A Barrie St, Kingston, ON, Canada K7K 3T1 EMAIL:
director@reelout.com WEB: www.reelout.com

February 2011

TBA: **Mardi Gras Film Festival**   *Sydney, Australia*
Sydney film festival corresponds with massive Mardi Gras event ☎61-2/9332–4938 ✉
c/o Queer Screen LTD, PO Box 1081, Darlinghurst, NSW, Australia 1300 WEB: www.queer-
screen.com.au

TBA: **Out at the Movies**   *Canton, NY*
LGBT film festival for Northern New York WEB: www.outatthemovies.org

March 2011

17-27: **Melbourne Queer Film Festival**   *Melbourne, Australia*
☎613/9662–4147 ✉ c/o MQFF, PO Box 21244
Little Lonsdale St, Victoria, Australia 8011 EMAIL: info@mqff.com.au WEB:
www.mqff.com.au

TBA: **Fusion**   *Los Angeles, CA*
Los Angeles' LGBT people of color film festival ☎213/480–7088 ✉ c/o Outfest, 3470
Wilshire Blvd #1022, Los Angeles, CA 90010 EMAIL: outfest@outfest.org WEB: www.out-
fest.org/fusion.html

TBA: **London Lesbian & Gay Film Festival**   *London, England*
grab your tickets for the largest LGBT film fest in Europe ☎44 (0)20/7928–3232 WEB:
www.llgff.org.uk

TBA: **QFest**   *St Louis, MO*
☎314/289–4152 EMAIL: mailroom@cinemastlouis.org WEB: www.stlqfest.org

TBA: **Verzaubert Int'l Queer Film Festival**   *Berlin, Germany*
screening in Berlin, Cologne, Frankfurt & Munich • also fall screening in November •
LGBT ☎49-30/861–4532 ✉ c/o Rosebud Entertainment, Oranienburger Str 39, Berlin,
Germany D-10117 EMAIL: info@verzaubertfilmfest.de WEB: www.verzaubertfilmfest.com

April 2011

21-May 1: **Miami Gay & Lesbian Film Festival**   *Miami, FL*
☎305/534–9924 ✉ PO Box 530280, Miami Beach, FL 33153 EMAIL: info@mglff.com
WEB: www.MGLFF.com

29-May 1: **London Lesbian Film Festival**   *London, ON, Canada*
women only Fri-Sat, open to all on Sunday ☎519/432–2303 ✉ c/o LLFF, PO Box
24087, London, ON, Canada N6H 5C4 EMAIL: shout@liff.ca WEB: www.llff.ca

TBA: **Birmingham Shout**   *Birmingham, AL*
LGBT film festival ☎205/324–0888 ✉ c/o Alabama Moving Images, 2312 1st Ave N,
Birmingham, AL 35203 EMAIL: info@bhamshout.com WEB: www.bhamshout.com

TBA: **Brisbane Queer Film Festival**   *Brisbane, Australia*
☎61 7/3358 8600 EMAIL: info@brisbanepowerhouse.org WEB: www.bqff.com.au

May 2011

5-15: **Boston LGBT Film Festival**   *Boston, MA*
☎617/369–3300 ✉ c/o Museum of Fine Arts, 465 Huntington Ave, Boston, MA 02115
WEB: www.bostonlgbtfilmfest.org

26-June 3: **Fairy Tales Int'l LGBT Film Festival**   *Calgary, AB, Canada*
☎403/244–1956 ✉ #2B 1230A 17th Avenue SW, Calgary, AB, Canada T2T 0B8 EMAIL:
info@fairytalesfilmfest.com WEB: www.fairytalesfilmfest.com

TBA: **Honolulu Rainbow Film Festival**   *Honolulu, HI*
☎808/675–8428 ✉ c/o Honolulu Gay & Lesbian Cultural Foundation, 758 Kapahulu
Ave #168, Honolulu, HI 96816 EMAIL: info@hglcf.org WEB: www.hglcf.org

TBA: **Inside Out: Toronto LGBT Film & Video Festival**   *Toronto, ON, Canada*
☎416/977–6847 ✉ c/o Inside Out, 401 Richmond St W #219, Toronto, ON, Canada
M5V 3A8 EMAIL: festival@insideout.ca WEB: www.insideout.ca

TBA: **Out Film CT**   *Hartford, CT*
gay & lesbian film festival at Cinestudio ☎860/586–1136 ✉ PO Box 231191, Hartford,
CT 06123 EMAIL: info@outfilmct.org WEB: www.outfilmct.org

TBA: **Out Takes LGBT Film Festival**   *Wellington, New Zealand*
festival also travels to Auckland & Christchurch, NZ ☎64-4/972–6775 ✉ c/o Reel
Queer Inc, PO Box 27070, Wellington, New Zealand 6141 EMAIL: info@outtakes.org.nz
WEB: www.outtakes.org.nz

TBA: **Translations: Transgender Film Festival** *Seattle, WA*
☎206/323–4274 ✉ c/o Three Dollar Bill Cinema, 1122 E Pike St #1313, Seattle, WA
98122 EMAIL: info@threedollarbillcinema.org WEB: www.threedollarbillcinema.org

June 2011

2-5: **Q Cinema** *Fort Worth, TX*
annual celebration of LGBT-themed movies ☎817/723–4358 ✉ c/o Q Cinema Inc, 9
Chase Ct, Fort Worth, TX 76110 EMAIL: todd@qcinema.org WEB: www.qcinema.org

10-12: **Queer Women of Color Film Festival** *San Francisco, CA*
films screened at Brava Theater • part of the Nat'l Queer Arts Festival ☎415/752–0868
✉ c/o QWOCMAP, 59 Cook St, San Francisco, CA 94118 EMAIL: festival@qwocmap.org
WEB: www.qwocmap.org

15-19: **Provincetown Int'l Film Festival** *Provincetown, MA*
mixed gay/ straight ☎508/487–3456 ✉ PO Box 605, Provincetown, MA 02657 EMAIL:
info@ptownfilmfest.org WEB: www.ptownfilmfest.org

16-26: **Frameline: San Francisco Int'l LGBT Film Festival** *San Francisco, CA*
get your tickets early for a slew of films about us • LGBT • 65,000+ attendees
☎415/703–8650 ✉ c/o Frameline, 145 9th St #300, San Francisco, CA 94103 EMAIL:
info@frameline.org WEB: www.frameline.org

TBA: **Identities Queer Film Festival** *Vienna, Austria*
☎43-1/524–6274 ✉ c/o DV8 Film, PO Box 282, Vienna, Austria A1070 EMAIL:
office@identities.at WEB: www.identities.at/index/en/

TBA: **Mix Milano Int'l LGBT Film Festival** *Milan, Italy*
EMAIL: festivalmix@libero.it WEB: www.cinemagaylesbico.com

TBA: **NewFest: New York LGBT Film Festival** *New York City, NY*
☎646/290–8136 ✉ c/o The New Festival, 68 Jay St #218, Brooklyn, NY 11201 EMAIL:
info@newfest.org WEB: www.newfest.org

TBA: **TLVFest: Israel Int'l LGBT Film Festival** *Tel Aviv, Israel*
films will also show in Jerusalem & Haifa ✉ c/o TLVFEST, Yair Hochner
2 Sprinzak St, Tel Aviv, Israel 64738 EMAIL: tlvfest@gmail.com WEB: www.tlvfest.com

July 2011

7-17: **Outfest** *Los Angeles, CA*
Los Angeles' lesbian/ gay film & video festival in mid-July ☎213/480–7088 ✉ c/o
Outfest, 3470 Wilshire Blvd #1022, Los Angeles, CA 90010 EMAIL: outfest@outfest.org
WEB: www.outfest.org

TBA: **Gaze: Dublin Int'l Lesbian & Gay Film Festival** *Dublin, Ireland*
✉ The Priory
John West St, Dublin, Ireland 8 EMAIL: info@gaze.ie WEB: www.gaze.ie

TBA: **Mostra Lambda Barcelona** *Barcelona, Spain*
LGBT film festival ✉ c/o Casal Lambda, Verdaguer i Callis 10, Barcelona, Spain 08003
EMAIL: mostra@lambdaweb.org WEB: www.cinemalambda.com

TBA: **Philadelphia QFest** *Philadelphia, PA*
☎267/765–9800 WEB: www.phillycinema.org

TBA: **Tokyo Int'l Lesbian & Gay Film Festival** *Tokyo, Japan*
✉ 3-10-18-401, Takada, Toshima-ku, Tokyo, Japan 171-0033 WEB: www.tokyo-lgff.org

August 2011

9-14: **Flickers: Rhode Island Int'l Film Festival** *Providence, RI*
don't miss the Gay & Lesbian Film Fest • mixed gay/ straight ☎401/861–4445 ✉ c/o
RIIFF, PO Box 162 , Newport, RI 02840 EMAIL: info@film-festival.org WEB: www.film-festival.org

frameline35
San Francisco International LGBT Film Festival
June 16-26, 2011   www.frameline.org

three
dollar bill
cinema

There's more to see in Seattle than the sights.

Keeping audiences entertained since 1996, Three Dollar Bill Cinema promotes and produces LGBT film events throughout the year, including free outdoor movies every summer, our Spring Film Series of vintage queer classics, the Seattle Lesbian & Gay Film Festival in October, and other unique events every month!

Check out our website or find us on Facebook to see what's happening on your next visit to Seattle.

three
dollar bill
cinema

www.threedollarbillcinema.org

19-29: **FilmOut San Diego**   *San Diego, CA*
LGBT film festival ✉ 1010 University Ave #1869, San Diego, CA 92103 EMAIL:
michael@filmoutsandiego.com WEB: www.filmoutsandiego.com

TBA: **North Carolina Gay & Lesbian Film Festival**   *Durham, NC*
☎919/560–3040 ✉ c/o Carolina Theatre, 309 W Morgan St, Durham, NC 27701 WEB:
festivals.carolinatheatre.org/ncglff

TBA: **Vancouver Queer Film & Video Festival**   *Vancouver, BC, Canada*
LGBT ☎604/844–1615 ✉ c/o Out on Screen, 405-207 West Hastings St, Vancouver, BC,
Canada V6B 1H7 WEB: www.queerfilmfestival.ca

September 2011

30-Oct 6: **Out on Film**   *Atlanta, GA*
LGBT ☎678/237–7206 ✉ c/o IMAGE Film & Video Center, 456 Kensington Parc Dr,
Atlanta, GA 30318 EMAIL: jim.farmer@outonfilm.org WEB: www.outonfilm.org

TBA: **Austin Gay & Lesbian International Film Festival**   *Austin, TX*
☎512/302–9889 ✉ c/o AGLIFF, 1216 E 51st St, Austin, TX 78723 EMAIL: info@agliff.org
WEB: www.agliff.org

TBA: **Fresno Reel Pride**   *Fresno, CA*
annual lesbian & gay film festival in central California ☎559/999–7971 ✉ PO Box
4647, Fresno, CA 93744 EMAIL: info@reelpride.com WEB: www.reelpride.com

TBA: **Milwaukee LGBT Film/ Video Festival**   *Milwaukee, W*
☎414/229–4758 ✉ Film Dept/ UWM
Mitchell Hall B70, Milwaukee, WI 53211 EMAIL: lgbtfilm@uwm.edu WEB:
www4.uwm.edu/psoa/programs/film/lgbtfilm

TBA: **Pikes Peak Lavender Film Festival**   *Colorado Springs, CO*
☎719/633–5600 ✉ PO Box 1987, Colorado Springs, CO 80901 EMAIL: info@pplff.org
WEB: www.pplff.org

TBA: **Queer Lisbon**   *Lisbon,, Portuga*
Portugal's only LGBT film festival ☎351 91/402 28 86 EMAIL: info@queerlisboa.pt WEB:
www.queerlisboa.pt

October 2011

7-11: **Southwest Gay & Lesbian Film Festival**   *Albuquerque, N*
also in Santa Fe, NM ☎505/243–1870 ✉ c/o Closet Cinema, 1209 7th St NW #A,
Albuquerque, NM 87102 EMAIL: info@closetcinema.org WEB: www.closetcinema.org

14-23: **Barcelona Int'l Gay & Lesbian Film Festival**   *Barcelona, Spai*
gay/ lesbian ☎973/664–421 ✉ c/o FICGLB, Sant Pere 44, Barcelona, Spain 25656
EMAIL: info@barcelonafilmfestival.org WEB: www.barcelonafilmfestival.org

14-23: **Pittsburgh Int'l Lesbian & Gay Film Festival**   *Pittsburgh, P.*
☎412/422–6776 ✉ c/o PLGFS, PO Box 81237, Pittsburgh, PA 15217 EMAIL:
info@plgfs.org WEB: www.plgfs.org

TBA: **Berlin Lesbian Film Festival**   *Berlin, German*
☎49–172/381–2883 ✉ c/o LesbenFilmFestival Berlin, Dudenstrasse 22, Berlin,
Germany 10965 EMAIL: filmfestivalberlin@yahoo.com WEB: www.lesbenfilmfestival.de

TBA: **Cineffable: Paris Int'l Lesbian & Feminist Film Festival**   *Paris, Franc*
✉ c/o Cineffable, 37 Ave Pasteur, Montreuil, France 93100 EMAIL: contact@cineffable.f
WEB: www.cineffable.fr

TBA: **Copenhagen Gay & Lesbian Film Festival**   *Copenhagen, Denma*
☎45/2843–4217 ✉ Oster Farimagsgade 16B, Copenhagen, Denmark DK-2100 EMAIL
kontakt@cglff.dk WEB: www.cglff.dk

TBA: **Hamburg Int'l Lesbian & Gay Film Festival**   *Hamburg, German*
☎49–40/348–0670 ✉ c/o Querbild e.V., Schanzenstr 45, Hamburg, Germany D-2035
EMAIL: mail@lsf-hamburg.de WEB: www.lsf-hamburg.de

TBA: **image+nation: Montréal Int'l LGBT Film Festival** *Montréal, QC, Canada*
LGBT ☎514/285–4467 ✉ c/o Image + Nation, 4067 boul St Laurent #404, Montréal, QC H2W 1Y7 EMAIL: info@image-nation.org WEB: www.image-nation.org

TBA: **Madrid LGBT Film Festival** *Madrid, Spain*
☎34–91/593–0540 ✉ c/o Fundación Triángulo, Meléndez Valdés, 52 1ro D, Madrid, Spain 28015 EMAIL: info@lesgaicinemad.com WEB: www.lesgaicinemad.com

TBA: **Out in Africa** *Cape Town, South Africa*
the only film festival of its kind on the African continent • also in Johannesburg ☎27 21/461 40 27 ✉ PO Box 15707, 8000 Vlaeberg, South Africa EMAIL: info@oia.co.za WEB: www.oia.co.za

TBA: **Out OK** *Tulsa, OK*
Oklahoma's int'l LGBT film festival ☎918/682–4654 x3 ✉ PO Box 2757, Muskogee, OK 74402 EMAIL: pau@out-ok.com WEB: www.out-ok.com

TBA: **Portland Lesbian & Gay Film Festival** *Portland, OR*
✉ c/o Film Action Oregon, 4144 NE Sandy Blvd, Portland, OR 97212 EMAIL: info@plgff.org WEB: www.plgff.org

TBA: **Q Film Festival** *Long Beach, CA*
showcasing films of interest to the queer community ☎562/434–4455 ✉ c/o The Center Long Beach, 2017 E 4th St, Long Beach, CA 90814 EMAIL: info@centerlb.org WEB: www.centerlb.org

TBA: **Reel Affirmations: The Nation's LGBT Film Festival** *Washington, DC*
lesbian/ gay films ☎202/315–1319 ✉ c/o One In Ten, PO Box 73587, Washington, DC 20056 EMAIL: info@oneinten.org WEB: www.reelaffirmations.org

TBA: **Reel Pride** *Winnipeg, MB, Canada*
LGBT film festival ☎204/997–3841 ✉ c/o Winnipeg G&L Film Society, 393 Portage Ave #Y300, Winnipeg, MB, Canada R3B 3H6 EMAIL: reelpride@hotmail.com WEB: www.reel-pride.org

TBA: **Sacramento Int'l Gay & Lesbian Film Festival** *Sacramento, CA*
☎916/689–3284 ✉ 1017 L St #379, Sacrmento, CA 95814 EMAIL: general@siglff.org WEB: www.siglff.org

TBA: **Seattle Lesbian & Gay Film Festival** *Seattle, WA*
☎206/323–4274 ✉ c/o Three Dollar Bill Cinema, 1122 E Pike St #1313, Seattle, WA 98122 EMAIL: info@threedollarbillcinema.org WEB: www.threedollarbillcinema.org

TBA: **St John's International Women's Film Festival** *St John's, NL, Canada*
mixed gay/ straight • 4500 attendees ☎709/754–3141 ✉ PO Box 984, St John's, NL, Canada A1C 5M3 EMAIL: info@womensfilmfestival.com WEB: www.womensfilmfestival.com

TBA: **Tampa Bay Int'l Gay & Lesbian Film Festival** *Tampa Bay, FL*
☎813/879–4220 ✉ c/o Friends of the Festival, PO Box 18445, Tampa, FL 33679 WEB: www.tiglff.com

November 2011

-12: **Reeling: Chicago Lesbian & Gay Int'l Film Fest** *Chicago, IL*
☎773/293–1447 ✉ c/o Chicago Filmmakers, 5243 N Clark St, 2nd flr, Chicago, IL 60640 EMAIL: reeling@chicagofilmmakers.org WEB: www.reelingfilmfestival.org

BA: **Florence Queer Festival** *Florence, Italy*
LGBT film festival EMAIL: info@florencequeerfestival.it WEB: www.florencequeerfestival.it

BA: **Long Island Gay & Lesbian Film Festival** *Huntington, NY*
✉ PO Box 360, E Northport, NY 11731 EMAIL: info@liglff.org WEB: www.liglff.org

BA: **Mezipatra** *Prague, Czech Republic*
Czech LGBT film festival ✉ c/o STUD Brno, Smejkalova 75, Brno, Czech Republic 61600 EMAIL: info@mezipatra.cz WEB: www.mezipatra.cz

TBA: **Mix: New York Lesbian & Gay Experimental Film Fest** *New York City, NY*
film, videos, installations & media performances • write for info ☎212/742–8880 ✉ c/o MIX NYC, 79 Pine St PMB 132, New York, NY 10005 EMAIL: info@mixnyc.org WEB: www.mixnyc.org

TBA: **OUT TAKES Dallas** *Dallas, TX*
LGBT film festival ☎972/988–6333 ✉ c/o The OUT TAKES Foundation, 3818 Cedar Springs #405, Dallas, TX 75219 EMAIL: info@outtakesdallas.org WEB: www.outtakesdallas.org

TBA: **Paris Gay & Lesbian Film Festival** *Paris, France*
✉ 8 rue du Repos, Paris, France 75020 EMAIL: info@ffglp.net WEB: www.ffglp.net

LEATHER & FETISH

January 2011

14-17: **Mid-Atlantic Leather Weekend** *Washington, DC*
LGBT ☎202/588–2562 ✉ c/o Centaur MC, PO Box 34061, Washington, DC 20043 EMAIL: registration@leatherweekend.com WEB: www.leatherweekend.com

21-23: **Southwest Leather Conference** *Phoenix, AZ*
workshops, vendors & fetish ball • MASTER/slave, Bootblack & Daddy/boy contests • LGBT ✉ c/o SWLC, 4757 E Greenway Rd #107B PMB 225, Phoenix, AZ 85032 EMAIL: registration@southwestleather.org WEB: www.south-westleather.org

April 2011

8-10: **Leather Leadership Conference** *Los Angeles, CA*
join us to develop & strengthen problem-solving & camaraderie in the leather community • LGBT ✉ c/o LLC c/o Larry Manion, PO Box 190482, St Louis, MO 63119 EMAIL: info@leatherleadership.org WEB: www.leatherleadership.org

8-10: **Rubbout** *Vancouver, BC, Canada*
don't miss this annual gay rubber weekend • men only ☎604/683–8000 ✉ 320-1255 Seymour St, Vancouver, BC, Canada V6B 0H1 EMAIL: mitchkenyon@shaw.ca WEB: www.rubbout.com

14-17: **International Ms Bootblack Contest** *San Francisco, CA*
workshops • parties • vending • contest takes place the weekend of International Ms Leather weekend • mixed gay/ straight EMAIL: Rhonda@IMsL.org WEB: www.IMsL.org

14-17: **International Ms Leather Contest** *San Francisco, CA*
contest • workshops • parties • vending • mixed gay/ straight EMAIL: Rhonda@IMsL.org WEB: www.IMsL.org

29-May 1: **Northwest Leather Celebration** *San Jose, CA*
host of the NW regional Master/slave contest • LGBT ✉ c/o smOdyssey, 840 S 6th St, San Jose, CA 95112 EMAIL: info@northwestleathercelebration.com WEB: www.northwest-leathercelebration.com

June 2011

9-12: **Southeast Leatherfest** *Atlanta, GA*
LGBT ✉ c/o Southeast Leatherfest, PO Box 487, Hiram, GA 30141 WEB: www.seleatherfest.com

10-13: **Desire: Leather Women Unleashed** *Palm Springs, CA*
weekend retreat for leather- & kinky women ☎206/963–5844 ✉ PO Box 4124, Costa Mesa, CA 92628 EMAIL: info@desireleatherwomen.com WEB: www.desireleatherwomen.com

19: Folsom Street East   *New York City, NY*
New York City's answer to the famous San Francisco fetish street fair • LGBT
☎212/727–9878 ✉ c/o GMSMA, 332 Bleecker St #D-23, New York, NY 10014
EMAIL: info@folsomstreeteast.org WEB: www.folsomstreeteast.org

July 2011

4-18: CampOUT   *Walton, WV*
games, auctions, a fully equipped outdoor dungeon & swimming • presented by La
Garou Leather Club • very trans friendly • everyone welcome to attend regardless of
sexual orientation, or gender identity • LGBT ☎419/376–6724 ✉ PO Box 140713,
Toledo, OH 43614 EMAIL: campout.staff@gmail.com WEB: lagarou.org/campout.htm

TBA: International Deaf Leather   *TBA, USA*
weekend of events, including Mr & Ms Deaf Leather Contest ✉ c/o Int'l Deaf Leather,
1128 Carlton Ave, Stockton, CA 95203 EMAIL: president@@internationaldeafleather.org WEB:
www.internationaldeafleather.org

TBA: Thunder in the Mountains   *Denver, CO*
weekend of pansexual leather events & seminars • kinky comedy revue • talent show •
LGBT • 800+ attendees ☎303/698–1207 ✉ c/o Thunder in the Mountains, LLC, 258
Acoma St, Denver 80223–1339 EMAIL: MrLthrCO@aol.com WEB: www.thunderinthemoun-
tains.com

August 2011

-7: Pantheon of Leather   *Los Angeles, CA*
annual leather/ SM/ fetish community service awards & int'l Mr & Ms Olympus Leather •
mixed gay/ straight ✉ PO Box 381239, Los Angeles, CA 90038 EMAIL: tljandcuir@aol.com
WEB: www.internationalolympusleather.com

September 2011

Folsom Europe   *Berlin, Germany*
✉ c/o Folsom Europe e.v., Nollendorfplatz 8/9, 10777 Berlin, Germany EMAIL:
info@folsomeurope.com WEB: www.folsomeurope.com

5: Folsom Street Fair   *San Francisco, CA*
huge SM/ leather street fair, topping a week of kinky events • LGBT • thousands of local
& visiting kinky men & women attendees ☎415/861–3247 ✉ c/o Folsom Street
Events, 965 Mission St #200, San Francisco, CA 94114 EMAIL: info@folsomstreetevents.org
WEB: www.folsomstreetevents.org

November 2011

7: Santa Clara County Leather Weekend   *San Jose, CA*
3 days of leather celebration in the San Jose area • LGBT ✉ c/o Santa Clara County
Leather Assoc, c/o Billy deFrank LGBT Ctr
938 The Alameda, San Jose, CA 95126 EMAIL: info@sccleather.org WEB: www.SCCLeather.org

CONFERENCES & RETREATS

February 2011

6: Creating Change Conference   *Minneapolis, MN*
for lesbians, gays, bisexuals, transgendered people & queers into social activism •
2500+ attendees ☎202/393–5177 ✉ c/o National Gay & Lesbian Task Force, 1325
Mass Ave NW #600, Washington, DC 20005 EMAIL: thetaskforce@thetaskforce.org WEB:
www.creatingchange.org

March 2011

TBA: **Transgender Leadership Summit**   *TBA, USA*
join transgender activists to help create a unified voice to advance the movement for transgender equality • 200+ attendees ☎415/865–0176 ✉ c/o Transgender Law Center, 870 Market St #823, San Francisco, CA 94102 EMAIL: info@transgenderlawcenter.org WEB: www.transgenderlawcenter.org

May 2011

12-15: **Saints & Sinners**   *New Orleans, LA*
LGBT writers & readers from around the country gather for a hot weekend of readings, panels & performance • 300 attendees • $100 ☎504/581–1144 ✉ 938 Lafayette St #514, New Orleans, LA 70113 EMAIL: saintsinnola@aol.com WEB: www.sasfest.com

TBA: **Lambda Literary Awards**   *New York City, N*
the Lammies are the Oscars of LGBT writing & publishing • LGBT ☎213/458–3570 ✉ c/o Lambda Literary Foundation, 5482 Wilshire Blvd #1595, Los Angeles, CA 90036 EMAIL: info@Lambdaliterary.org WEB: www.lambdaliterary.org

July 2011

9-12: **GCLS Literary Convention**   *Orlando, F*
Golden Crown Literary Society's annual gathering to share & explore the many facets of lesbian literature ☎321/722–3704 ✉ c/o GCLS, PO Box 120849, Gainesville, FL 3265: EMAIL: nat.burns@goldencrown.org WEB: www.gclscon.com

13-17: **RAD Conference: Rainbow Alliance of the Deaf**   *Denver, C*
workshops • conferences • keynote speakers • social events • come celebrate deaf culture & identity EMAIL: secretary@rad.org WEB: www.rad.org

21-24: **Gender Odyssey**   *Seattle, W*
3 days of panels, workshops & meetings • entertainment, art exhibit & vendors • focus on transmen, transwomen & other gender variant people • open to all ☎206/306–8383 ✉ c/o Transgender Center, 3962 Hoff Rd, Bellingham, WA 98225 EMAIL: info@genderodyssey.org WEB: www.genderodyssey.org

September 2011

TBA: **Nat'l Lesbian & Gay Journalists Assoc Convention**   *TBA, US*
workshops • keynote speakers • entertainment ☎202/588–9888 x10 ✉ c/o NLGJA, 1420 K St NW #910, Washington, DC 20005 EMAIL: info@nlgja.org WEB: www.nlgja.org

TBA: **Southern Comfort Conference**   *Atlanta, C*
entertainers & leaders from the entire spectrum of the transgender community offering 5 days of learning, networking & fun ☎702/336–1202 ✉ 2107 N Decatur Rd #207, Decatur, GA 30033 EMAIL: alexis@sccatl.org WEB: www.sccatl.org

October 2011

13-16: **National LGBT MBA Conference**   *TBA, U*
career fair & discussions of sexual orientation, gender & leadership in the workplace b MBA students & out Fortune 500 company leaders • LGBT • 800+ attendees EMAIL: info@reachingoutmba.org WEB: www.reachingoutmba.org

SPIRITUAL GATHERINGS

February 2011

18-21: PantheaCon   *San Jose, CA*
pagan convention • mixed gay/ straight ☎510/653–3244 ✉ c/o Ancient Ways, 4075 Telegraph Ave, Oakland, CA 94609 EMAIL: store@ancientways.com WEB: www.ancientways.com

May 2011

20-22: A Gathering of Priestesses & Goddess Women   *Wisconsin Dells, Southwestern WI*
women's spirituality conference • also Hallows Gathering in October • women only ☎608/226–9998 ✉ c/o Re-formed Congregation of the Goddess, PO Box 6677, Madison, WI 53716 EMAIL: rcgi@rcgi.org WEB: www.rcgi.org

TBA: Ancient Ways Festival   *Stone City Pagan Sanctuary, CA*
annual 4-day mixed gender/orientation spring festival • pan-pagan rituals, workshops & music w/ lesbian/gay campsite • mixed gay/ straight ☎510/653–3244 ✉ c/o Ancient Ways, 4075 Telegraph Ave, Oakland, CA 94609 EMAIL: store@ancientways.com WEB: www.ancientways.com

June 2011

19-26: Pagan Spirit Gathering   *near Salem, MO*
summer solstice celebration • primitive camping • workshops • rituals • advance registration required • mixed gay/ straight ☎608/924–2216 ✉ c/o Circle Sanctuary, PO Box 9, Barneveld, WI 53507 EMAIL: circle@circlesanctuary.org WEB: www.circlesanctuary.org/psg

August 2011

1-14: Elderflower Womenspirit Festival   *Mendocino, CA*
earth-based spirituality retreat • honoring the feminine through the Goddess • women & girls only ☎510/848–1460 ✉ PO Box 410236, San Francisco, CA 94141 EMAIL: info@elderflower.org WEB: elderflower.org

BA: BC Witchcamp   *near Vancouver, BC, Canada*
weeklong Wiccan intensive at Evans Lake • mixed gay/ straight ☎250/598–9229 ✉ c/o Wtich Camp of BC Society, 1266 Gladstone Ave, Victoria, BC, Canada V8T 1G6 EMAIL: witchcampbcinfo@gmail.com WEB: www.bcwitchcamp.ca

BREAST CANCER BENEFITS

January 2011

going throughout the year: **Susan G Komen Race for the Cure Series**   *Cross-country, USA*
5K & 1-mile run/fitness walks in cities around the country to fight breast cancer • call for local city dates • organized by local affiliate offices ☎877/GO–KOMEN ✉ c/o Susan G Komen for the Cure, 5005 LBJ Fwy #250, Dallas, TX 75244 WEB: www.komen.org

March 2011

TBA: Boarding for Breast Cancer Board-a-thon   *TBA, USA*
help raise money & awareness for breast cancer • live music & pro exihibitions at ski resorts around the country • mixed gay/ straight ☎323/467–2663 ✉ 6230 Wilshire Blvd #179, Los Angeles, CA 90048 EMAIL: email@b4bc.org WEB: www.b4bc.org

July 2011

22-24: **Susan G Komen 3 Day for the Cure**   Boston, MA
walk 60 miles in 3 days to raise money for the Susan G Komen Breast Cancer
Foundation • mixed gay/ straight ☎800/**996–3329** EMAIL: coaches@the3day.org WEB:
www.the3day.org

August 2011

5-7: **Susan G Komen 3 Day for the Cure**   Chicago, IL
walk 60 miles in 3 days to raise money for the Susan G Komen Breast Cancer
Foundation • mixed gay/ straight ☎800/**996–3329** EMAIL: coaches@the3day.org WEB:
www.the3day.org

12-14: **Susan G Komen 3 Day for the Cure**   Detroit, MI
walk 60 miles in 3 days to raise money for the Susan G Komen Breast Cancer
Foundation • mixed gay/ straight ☎800/**996–3329** EMAIL: coaches@the3day.org WEB:
www.the3day.org

19-21: **Susan G Komen 3 Day for the Cure**   Minneapolis/St Paul, MN
walk 60 miles in 3 days to raise money for the Susan G Komen Breast Cancer
Foundation • mixed gay/ straight ☎800/**996–3329** EMAIL: coaches@the3day.org WEB:
www.the3day.org

September 2011

16-18: **Susan G Komen 3 Day for the Cure**   Seattle, WA
walk 60 miles in 3 days to raise money for the Susan G Komen Breast Cancer
Foundation • mixed gay/ straight ☎800/**996–3329** EMAIL: coaches@the3day.org WEB:
www.the3day.org

October 2011

ongoing: **October is Breast Cancer Awareness Month**   Cross-country, US
check local listings for fund-raising events in your area to fight breast cancer

14-16: **Susan G Komen 3 Day for the Cure**   Philadelphia, PA
walk 60 miles in 3 days to raise money for the Susan G Komen Breast Cancer
Foundation • mixed gay/ straight ☎800/**996–3329** EMAIL: coaches@the3day.org WEB:
www.the3day.org

21-23: **Susan G Komen 3 Day for the Cure**   Atlanta, GA
walk 60 miles in 3 days to raise money for the Susan G Komen Breast Cancer
Foundation • mixed gay/ straight ☎800/**996–3329** EMAIL: coaches@the3day.org WEB:
www.the3day.org

28-30: **Susan G Komen 3 Day for the Cure**   Tampa Bay,
walk 60 miles in 3 days to raise money for the Susan G Komen Breast Cancer
Foundation • mixed gay/ straight ☎800/**996–3329** EMAIL: coaches@the3day.org WEB:
www.the3day.org

November 2011

4-6: **Susan G Komen 3 Day for the Cure**   Dallas,
walk 60 miles in 3 days to raise money for the Susan G Komen Breast Cancer
Foundation • mixed gay/ straight ☎800/**996–3329** EMAIL: coaches@the3day.org WEB:
www.the3day.org

11-13: **Susan G Komen 3 Day for the Cure**   TBA,
walk 60 miles in 3 days to raise money for the Susan G Komen Breast Cancer
Foundation • mixed gay/ straight ☎800/**996–3329** EMAIL: coaches@the3day.org WEB:
www.the3day.org

18-20: **Susan G Komen 3 Day for the Cure**   *San Diego, CA*
walk 60 miles in 3 days to raise money for the Susan G Komen Breast Cancer
Foundation • mixed gay/ straight ☎800/996–3329 EMAIL: coaches@the3day.org WEB:
www.the3day.org

KIDS' STUFF

June 2011

TBA: **Keshet Camp: Jewish Family Camp**   *Yosemite, CA*
a rainbow camp for LGBT families & their friends • sports, music, arts & crafts & more •
different sessions for different ages • usually Labor Day wknd ☎415/543–2267 ✉ c/o
Camp Tawonga, 131 Steuart St, San Francisco, CA 94105 EMAIL: info@tawonga.org WEB:
www.tawonga.org

July 2011

TBA: **Camp Ten Oaks**   *Ottawa, ON, Canada*
summer camp for LGBTQ kids & kids from LGBTQ families • ages 8-17 • also Project
Acorn leadership retreat for ages 16-24 ☎613/321–2824 ✉ 255 Montreal Rd #205,
Ottawa, ON, Canada K1L 6C4 EMAIL: info@tenoaksproject.org WEB: www.camptenoaks.org

August 2011

TBA: **Camp It Up! LGBT Family Camp**   *Quincy, CA*
week-long program at Feather River Camp • swimming • horseback riding • arts & crafts
• music, dance & theater • family spa & salon! • since 1990 • 250+ attendees WEB:
www.campitup.org

TBA: **Camp Ten Trees**   *Western WA*
residential summer camp • one week for LGBTQA youth ages 13-17 • one week for kids
ages 8-17 of LGBTQA/ non-traditional families ☎206/288–9568 ✉ c/o Camp Ten
Trees, 1122 E Pike St, #1488, Seattle, WA 98122 EMAIL: info@camptentrees.org WEB:
www.camptentrees.org

TBA: **Family Week**   *Provincetown, MA*
join hundreds of LGBT parents, kids & allies for a week of workshops, boat rides, camp-
fires, sandcastle competitions & more • LGBT ☎617/502–8700 ✉ c/o Family Equality
Council, PO Box 206, Boston, MA 02108 EMAIL: info@familyequality.org WEB: www.family-
equality.org

BA: **Mountain Meadow Summer Camp**   *Southern New Jersey*
camp for kids w/ LGBTQ parents & their allies • sliding scale fee • youth age 9-17
☎215/772–1107 ✉ c/o Mountain Meadow Country Experience, 1315 Spruce St #411,
Philadelphia, PA 19107 EMAIL: inquiries@mountainmeadow.org WEB: www.mountainmead-
ow.org

sweet

september 24 - october 1, 2011

Isla Mujeres
RESORT

fun on the isle of women

Sweet
DISCOVER SWEET.COM
CALL 877 793 3830
CST# 2091755-40